Collins
COBUILD

Phrasal Verbs
Dictionary

HarperCollins Publishers
Westerhill Road
Bishopbriggs
Glasgow
G64 2QT
Great Britain

Second Edition 2002; reissued 2011

© HarperCollins Publishers 1989, 2002, 2011

ISBN 978-0-00-742376-7

Collins®, COBUILD® and Bank of English®
are registered trademarks of
HarperCollins Publishers Limited

www.collinslanguage.com

A catalogue record for this book is available
from the British Library

Typeset by Morton Word Processing,
Scarborough, England
and Rosetta Publishing, Peebles

Printed and bound in Italy by Rotolito

Acknowledgements
We would like to thank those authors and
publishers who kindly gave permission for
copyright material to be used in the Collins
Word Web. We would also like to thank
Times Newspapers Ltd for providing
valuable data.

CONTENTS

Second Edition

Founding Editor-in-Chief
John Sinclair

Publishing Director
Lorna Sinclair Knight

Editorial Director
Michela Clari

Managing Editor
Maree Airlie

Project Manager
Carol McCann

Editors
Alison Macaulay
Maggie Seaton
Phyllis Gautier

Lexicographers
Elizabeth Potter
Bob Grossmith
Duncan Marshall

Computing Staff
Mark Taylor

From the First Edition

Editor-in-Chief
John Sinclair

Editorial Director
Patrick Hanks

Senior Editor
Rosamund Moon

Editors
Stephen Bullon
Ramesh Krishnamurthy

Assistant Editors
Elaine Pollard
Deborah Yuill

Computer Officer
Tim Lane

HarperCollins Publishers
Annette Capel
Lorna Heaslip
Douglas Williamson

Secretarial Staff
Sue Smith
Joanne Brown

The original project design was done by Helen Liebeck, and we would like to thank her for her exceptional contribution. We would also like to thank Sheila Dignen for work on the Particles Index and editorial assistance; Alex Collier for work on the Particles Index and computational and editorial assistance; Katy Shaw and Janet Whitcut for their detailed reading of the text; Jeremy Clear for his formative comments at the planning stage; Ela Bullon for her work on the synonyms and antonyms; Malcolm Goodale for revisions to the Particles Index; Henri Béjoint and Ken Church for comments and advice.

Introduction

The **Collins COBUILD Dictionary of Phrasal Verbs** concentrates on one particular aspect of the grammar and vocabulary of English: combinations of verbs with adverbial or prepositional particles.

These combinations are generally called *phrasal verbs*. They are extremely common in English and are often a particular problem for learners of English. There are several reasons for this. One reason is that in many cases, even though students may be familiar with both the verb in the phrasal verb and with the particle, they may not understand the meaning of the combination, since it can differ greatly from the meanings of the two words used independently. For example, *give, put, up,* and *off* are all very common words which students will encounter in their first weeks of learning English, and yet the combinations *give up* and *put off* are not transparent. The meanings are unrelated to the meanings of the individual words in the combinations. The fact that phrasal verbs often have a number of different meanings adds to their complexity.

There are some particular grammatical problems associated with phrasal verbs. For example, there are restrictions on the positions in which an adverb can be placed in relation to the object of a verb. Some particles, such as *about, over, round,* and *through* can be used as both adverbs and prepositions in particular phrasal verb combinations, although in other combinations they are restricted to one word class only, either adverb or preposition but not both. Some phrasal verbs are not normally used with pronouns as objects, others are normally only used with pronouns as objects. The Extra Column of this dictionary gives detailed information about grammatical behaviour of phrasal verbs: see pages xiii-xx for an explanation of all grammatical labels.

There are other difficulties, such as the fact that there are frequently strong collocational associations between phrasal verbs and other words. Thus, in some cases a particular word or small set of words is the only one normally found as the subject or object of a particular verb. We show on page x how the explanations in the dictionary give guidance on this.

It is often said that phrasal verbs tend to be rather 'colloquial' or 'informal' and more appropriate to spoken English than written, and even that it is better to avoid them and choose single-word equivalents or synonyms instead. Yet in many cases phrasal verbs and their synonyms have different ranges of use, meaning, or collocation. Single-word synonyms are often much more formal in style than phrasal verbs, so that they seem out of place in many contexts. We include notes throughout the text on synonyms and antonyms to help with this.

The set of English phrasal verbs is constantly growing and changing. New combinations appear and spread. Yet these new combinations are rarely made on a random basis, but form patterns which can to some extent be anticipated. Particles often have particular meanings which they contribute to a variety of combinations and which are productive: that is, these fixed meanings are used in order to create new combinations. At the back of this dictionary there is an index of the particles, showing the different meanings and listing the phrasal verbs containing those meanings. In this way, you can understand the patterns underlying the combinations, and you can see the relationship in meaning between, for example, *cool off, ease off,* and *wear off,* or between *hook up, join up,* and *link up.*

The **Collins COBUILD Dictionary of Phrasal Verbs** lists over three thousand combinations of verbs with adverbs or prepositions, explaining over five and a half thousand different meanings. These are combinations which are in common use in everyday modern English. Furthermore, the key phrasal verbs in the dictionary have also been labelled using the symbol ★. We have based this information on the *Bank of English*, Collins' vast database of contemporary language which has been taken from a wide range of sources and styles, and now totals over *450 million words*.

What sort of item can you expect to find in this dictionary? Different people have different definitions of 'phrasal verb', and different ideas about which particles can be used to form phrasal verbs. The following table contains all the particles which we use in this dictionary.

aback	around	between	of	through
about	as	beyond	off	to
above	aside	by	on	together
across	at	down	onto	towards
after	away	for	out	under
against	back	forth	over	up
ahead	before	forward	overboard	upon
along	behind	from	past	with
among	below	in	round	without
apart	beneath	into		

In addition, there are cases of combinations with two particles, such as *out of* and *in with*.

Although there are many different combinations of verbs with particles, it is possible to point to four main types of combination:

1. combinations where the meaning of the whole cannot be understood by knowing the meanings of the individual verbs and particles. Examples are *go off* (= explode), *put off* (= postpone), and *turn down* (= reject).

2. combinations where the verb is always used with a particular preposition or adverb, and is not normally found without it. Examples are *refer to* and *rely on*. We also include similar cases where a verb is always used with a particular preposition or adverb in a particular meaning, such as *lead to* and *want for*.

3. combinations where the particle does not change the meaning of the verb, but is used to suggest that the action described by the verb is performed thoroughly, completely, or continuously. For example, in *slave away* and *slog away*, the particle *away* adds an idea of continuousness to the idea of hard work. These combinations are sometimes called 'completive-intensives'.

4. combinations where the verb and particle both have meanings which may be found in other combinations and uses, but where there is overwhelming evidence in our data that they occur together. For example, in the combination *fight back*, the verb *fight* has the same meaning that it normally does in isolation, and *back* is used in a similar way in other combinations such as *phone back* and *strike back*. Yet *fight* and *back* frequently occur together in our data, and we have decided to treat this as a unit in the dictionary. Such combinations are sometimes called 'literal phrasal verbs'. In addition, we mention as the first meaning of *come out*, 'leave a place' and *go up*, 'move to a higher position'. These meanings can of course be easily understood. However, *come out* has nineteen meanings altogether in this dictionary and *go up* has thirteen: most of these are not transparent and cannot be understood so easily. We have decided not to give literal meanings and combinations for all verbs in the dictionary. We have, however, widened the scope of our coverage in the cases of thirty-eight common verbs which occur in a large number of combinations with different particles, and which have many non-transparent meanings. These verbs are especially problematic for students of English.

The thirty-eight verbs are:

break	fall	kick	make	put	stay
bring	get	knock	move	run	stick
call	give	lay	pass	send	take
cast	go	lie	play	set	talk
come	hang	live	pull	sit	throw
cut	hold	look	push	stand	turn
do	keep				

We include in this dictionary fixed expressions with verbs and particles, together with the word *it*: for example, *go for it* and *step on it*. We do not include other fixed expressions with verbs and particles: for example, *keep up with the Joneses*, *push up the daises*, and *skate on thin ice*. These are idioms, rather than phrasal verbs, and they are included in a companion volume, the **Collins COBUILD Dictionary of Idioms**, which has been updated and revised for the second edition.

The following table summarizes the combinations which we include and those which we do not.

Example	Phrasal Verb Type	Included?	Category No.	Reason
We really went to town.	idiom	no		*town* is part of the idiom
The town went up.	non-literal	yes	**go up 10**	new meaning = explode
The number refers to the day.	fixed particle	yes	**refer to 3**	*refer* always occurs with *to*
It's going along fine.	completive	yes	**go along 4**	particle reinforces verb
Thomas hit him back.	semi-literal	yes	**hit back 1**	frequent occurrence
We went up the hill.	literal	yes	**go up 1**	common verb and particle
Don't walk on the grass.	literal	no		meaning is clear

The new second edition of the **Collins COBUILD Dictionary of Phrasal Verbs** gives extensive information about thousands of phrasal verbs in English. The information is presented in a very simple way, with thousands of examples of real English taken from the *Bank of English*. We hope that you will find this new edition useful, easy to use, and above all interesting and informative. Since we published our first COBUILD dictionary, many people have written to us with comments and advice. This has proved invaluable, and we have benefited greatly from it.

You can e-mail us at cobuild@ref.collins.co.uk or write to us at the address below. We look forward to hearing from you with your comments and suggestions.

Professor John Sinclair
Founding Editor-in-Chief

Dr Rosamund Moon
(Editor, first edition)
University of Birmingham

COBUILD
HarperCollins Publishers
Westerhill Road
Bishopbriggs
Glasgow G64 2QT
U.K.

Using the Dictionary

Finding phrasal verbs and meanings

The order of entries is alphabetical, according to the verb in the phrasal verb headword. Phrasal verbs which contain the same verb but different particles are arranged in alphabetical order of the particle, for example **nose about** is followed by **nose around**. Note also, for example, that all the phrasal verbs containing the verb *go* are explained before phrasal verbs containing other verbs beginning with the letters *go–*, such as *goad* and *gouge*.

Some phrasal verb combinations contain two particles. In the dictionary, combinations like this, where the second particle is compulsory, are listed as phrasal verb headwords, in their correct alphabetical place in the sequence, for example **get out, get out of, get over** etc.

Other phrasal verbs are typically, but not always, used with a second particle. In these cases, the second particle is mentioned in the definition and shown as an optional structure in the Extra Column, but it does not appear in the phrasal verb headword. For a full explanation of all grammatical labels and syntactic structures, see pages xiii-xx.

Onto is a special problem as it can be spelled both as one word and as two. We show both spellings if it is a phrasal verb headword in its own right, for example **get on to**, **get onto**. In other cases where *–to* is optional, we mention it in the explanation, and in the Extra Column as *+to*, but not in the actual headword. Phrasal verbs with *into* are treated separately from ones with *in*, even though there may be little difference in meaning.

Many phrasal verbs have more than one meaning. The different meanings are numbered and are usually arranged in order of frequency, so that the commonest ones come first.

Guide to the Dictionary Entries

INFLECTED FORMS

HEADWORD

boom /buːm/ (booms, booming, boomed)

boom out When someone **booms out** something or when their voice **booms out**, they speak in a very loud, deep voice. □ *He boomed out: 'Good evening ladies and gentlemen!'... A great voice boomed out the words which announced their arrival.*

V+ADV+QUOTE, V+ADV+N: NO PASSIVE

boot /buːt/ (boots, booting, booted)

PHRASAL VERBS

boot out If someone **is booted out** of a job or a place, they are forced to leave it. [INFORMAL] □ *No wonder Gertrude booted me out... The member who made that speech was booted out by Conservative Party leaders.*

NOTE **Kick out** means almost the same as **boot out**, and **expel** is a more formal word.

V+PRON+ADV, V+N+ADV, V+ADV+N: ALSO+of

GRAMMATICAL LABELS

boot up When you **boot up** a computer, you make it ready to use by putting in the instructions which it needs in order to start working. □ *I can boot up from a floppy disk, but that's all... Go over to your PC and boot it up.*

V+ADV+N, V+N+ADV, V+PRON+ADV, V+ADV

KEY VOCABULARY

border /bɔːʳdəʳ/ (borders, bordering, bordered)

*★border on

MEANING SPLITS

1 A country that **borders on** another country is next to that country and shares a border with it. □ *The Soviet republic of Moldavia borders on Romania.*

V+PREP

EXAMPLES FROM THE BANK OF ENGLISH

2 When you say that something **borders on** a particular state or condition, you mean that it is almost in that state or condition. □ *I was in a state of excitement bordering on insanity... Their rough treatment of each other bordered on brutality.*

V+PREP

NOTE **Verge on** means almost the same as **border on**.

STRESS PATTERNS

bore /bɔːʳ/ (bores, boring, bored)

bore into If someone's eyes **bore into** you, they are staring intensely at you. □ *Vorster's eyes bored into me. He said 'We are at war. You cannot afford to refuse.'*

V+PREP

REGIONAL INFORMATION

CROSS-REFERENCE

boss /bɒs/ (bosses, bossing, bossed)

☑ **About** is used mainly in British English.

boss about → See **boss around**

boss around If you say that someone **bosses** you **around** or **bosses** you **about**, you mean that they keep telling you what to do in a way that is irritating. □ *He was never one to boss people about... He started bossing people around.*

V+N+ADV, V+PRON+ADV

SYNONYM NOTE

NOTE **Order around** means almost the same as **boss around**.

PRONUNCIATION

botch /bɒtʃ/ (botches, botching, botched)

DERIVED WORD

botch up If you **botch up** a piece of work, you do it very badly or clumsily. [INFORMAL] □ *He really botched up the last job he did for us.*

♦ If you make a **botch-up** of something that you are doing, you do it very badly or clumsily [INFORMAL] □ *Tourists were victims of a computer botch-up.*

V+ADV+N, V+PRON+ADV, V+N+ADV
N-COUNT

STYLE LABELS

Regional and Style Labels

AMERICAN — used mainly in the USA
AUSTRALIAN — used mainly in Australia
BRITISH — used mainly in Britain

FORMAL — used mainly in official situations
INFORMAL — used mainly in informal situations, conversations, and personal letters
JOURNALISM — used mainly in newspapers, television, and radio
LEGAL — used mainly in legal documents, and by the police in official situations
LITERARY — used mainly in novels, poetry, and other literature
OFFENSIVE — likely to offend people
OLD-FASHIONED — no longer in general common use
RUDE — used mainly to describe words which some people consider taboo
SPOKEN — used mainly in speech
TECHNICAL — used mainly about a specialist subject, such as business or science
VERY RUDE — used mainly to describe words which most people consider taboo
WRITTEN — used mainly in writing

Guide to the Dictionary Entries

Verb forms

All the forms or inflections of a verb are given in bold letters and in brackets at the beginning of each sequence of phrasal verbs containing that verb. They are listed in the order: base form, third person form of the present tense (*–s* form), present participle (*–ing* form), past tense (*–ed* form), and past participle (*–n* form) if this is different from the past tense form. If there are alternative spellings for a form, both spellings are given. Any other irregularities are explained in a note after the forms.

leap /liːp/ **(leaps, leaping, leaped/leapt)**

bid /bɪd/ **(bids, bidding)**
> ☑ The form **bid** is used in the present tense and is the past tense and past participle of the verb.

Spelling

If a verb has two spellings, for example if it is spelled differently in British English and American English, this is mentioned in a note after the forms.

plough /plaʊ/ **(ploughs, ploughing, ploughed)**
> ☑ **Plough** is also spelled **plow** in American English.

Pronunciation and stress

The pronunciation of every verb is shown in full after the headword. Variations in pronunciation are also shown where relevant.

duke /djuːk, AM duːk/ **(dukes, duking, duked)**

The stress pattern for each phrasal verb headword has also been clearly indicated by underlining, to show where the stress falls. A note has been given in the text to point out any variations.

★come by
> ☑ In meaning 2 the stress is on **come**.

1 When someone **comes by**, they come to see you for a short time, on a casual or informal basis. ❑ *Tom had said he would come by at five... They came by his office.*   V+ADV, V+PREP

2 If you **come by** something, you obtain it by chance or without much thought or planning. ❑ *He had not come by these things through his own labour... Good jobs were hard to come by.*   V+PREP

As a general rule, in V+ADV combinations, the stress usually falls on the particle, and in V+PREP combinations, the stress usually falls on the verb. In phrasal verbs with two particles, such as **get on with**, the stress usually falls on the first particle.

Explanations

The explanations of phrasal verbs in the **Collins COBUILD Dictionary of Phrasal Verbs** are written in simple English. They do not just tell you about the meaning of the phrasal verb, but also show you how it is typically used: what kinds of word collocate with it, what kind of thing is usually mentioned as the subject or object of the verb, and what sort of sentence structure it is used in. For example, the explanation for **map out** says:

> If you **map out** a plan or task, you work out in detail how you will do it.

This tells you that a person is usually mentioned as the subject of the verb, whereas the object is usually a word which is similar in meaning to plan or task. In the same way, the explanation for the first meaning of **keep on** says:

> If you **keep on** doing something, you continue to do it and do not stop.

This tells you that you usually use the phrasal verb with the *-ing* form of a verb. This kind of grammatical information is also given in the Extra Column.

Examples

The **Collins COBUILD Dictionary of Phrasal Verbs** contains a large number of examples taken from the *Bank of English*. They show how speakers and writers of English actually use phrasal verbs. These examples are chosen to illustrate typical uses of phrasal verbs and to show the grammatical patterns associated with the phrasal verbs. They are generally arranged in the same order as the patterns appear in the Extra Column.

Style and usage

Phrasal verbs are generally more common in spoken or informal English than in written or formal English. When phrasal verbs are only found in very informal contexts, we state this in the explanation. Similarly, we tell you when a particular phrasal verb is found mainly in either British English or American English, or when it is used only in certain contexts, such as in journalism or formal language. This information is shown at the end of the explanation in small capital letters and in square brackets. These labels are listed on page ix.

Synonyms and antonyms

Synonyms are words which mean almost the same as each other, and antonyms are words which mean the opposite. In this dictionary, we give notes on synonyms and antonyms after the explanation and examples. They are introduced by the symbol NOTE . There are very few cases where two words or expressions mean exactly the same as each other, but you should be able to substitute the synonyms which we give in most contexts, without greatly changing the meaning. We often give another phrasal verb as a synonym, and in most cases you can look up the other word to find out about any differences between them: there may be differences in grammar as well as slight differences in meaning. Many phrasal verbs have synonyms which are single words, but these words are often more formal. The synonym notes give information about this, and about other differences in usage. The antonyms which we give are usually other phrasal verbs, and in most cases these pairs of antonyms describe opposite processes, such as *put on* and *take off*, or *come in* and *go out*.

Derived words

It is quite common in English for nouns and adjectives to be formed by combining verbs and particles, and they are often very closely related to phrasal verbs. For example, if someone makes a *getaway*, they *get away* from a place in a hurry, perhaps after committing a crime. Sometimes the order of verb and particle is reversed: an *off-putting* person is someone who *puts* you *off* or causes you to dislike them. Sometimes both orders are found: *break-out* and *outbreak* are both linked to the phrasal verb **break out**. In the **Collins COBUILD Dictionary of Phrasal Verbs**, we give such nouns and adjectives in the entries for the phrasal verb combinations, so that *getaway* is explained in the entry for **get away**. If they are closely linked with a meaning of the phrasal verb, they appear in the same paragraph, after the examples and any synonym notes, and they are introduced by the symbol ◆. If there is not such a clear link to a meaning of the phrasal verb, they appear in a paragraph on their own.

Cross-references

Sometimes, verbs can be used with different particles, but the phrasal verb combinations may mean exactly the same as each other. For example, you can often substitute *about* or *around* for *round* without changing the meaning at all, although there is a difference between British and American usage in this case. In such cases, we treat the identical meanings together at one form, and put a cross-reference at the other ones. There may be a difference in formality between the variations: *upon* is generally more formal than *on*, and we mention this in the explanation.

The Particles Index

At the end of the **Collins COBUILD Dictionary of Phrasal Verbs** is an index to the particles which occur in the phrasal verbs we have included. This index explains the common meanings that particles contribute to phrasal verb combinations, and lists the phrasal verbs in which those meanings appear. New phrasal verbs are continually being created, and you may hear or read a combination which we have not included. By using the index, you should be able to understand the meaning of many such new combinations.

Grammatical Labels and Syntactic Patterns

In the **Collins COBUILD Dictionary of Phrasal Verbs**, grammatical information is given in the Extra Column, to the right of the main text. The Extra Column shows all the ways in which phrasal verbs are normally used, setting out each pattern on a separate line, generally showing the most frequent patterns first. The following pages explain the meanings of the abbreviations and words in the Extra Column, and show how to use the information.

Grammatical information about phrasal verbs is given as a series of patterns. In each pattern, we state the word classes of the words in order, linking them together with +. We use / to indicate alternatives.

Grammatical labels

The following abbreviations are used in the patterns. They are given in alphabetical order. **ADV, N, PREP, PRON, REFL,** and **V** are the most important abbreviations as they are used in the basic patterns to give information about verb transitivity and the particles. We explain the meaning of structures with prepositions such as +to or +with after the other abbreviations. Pages xvii-xx give further information about phrasal verb syntactic patterns.

A means adjunct. An adjunct consists of an adverb or prepositional phrase, and usually expresses time, place, manner, or condition. **A** is used in **WITH A** or **+A** to indicate that you use the phrasal verb with an adjunct in addition to the particle in the phrasal verb itself. An example is **go down 4** which is labelled **V+ADV: USUALLY+A**.
EG *I have to go down to Brighton.*

ADJ means adjective and it is used in **WITH ADJ** or **+ADJ** to indicate that you use an adjective after the phrasal verb. An example is **turn out 2** which is labelled *it*+**V+ADV: WITH ADJ**.
EG *It's turned out nice again.*

ADJECTIVE is used in the Extra Column to indicate that a derived word is used as an adjective.

ADV means adverb or adverbial particle. It usually refers to the adverb in the phrasal verb headword, but we also sometimes use it when mentioning following structures. **ADV/PREP** means that the particle can be used as an adverb or preposition, but that it is more often used as an adverb. We usually use this notation when we need to simplify a long list of patterns. An example is **take around** which is labelled **V+N+ADV/PREP, V+PRON+ADV/PREP**.
EG *I took my godson around my laboratory.*

C means complement. A complement consists of an adjective or noun group, and adds information about the subject of the verb, or sometimes its object. **C** is used in **WITH C** or **+C** to indicate that you use the phrasal verb with a complement. An example is **come up 17** which is labelled **V+ADV: WITH C/A**.
EG *Dorothy always came up smiling.*

ERGATIVE is used to refer to a group of verbs which can be either transitive or intransitive. If the verb is transitive, it links a subject and an object, describing how the subject affects or causes a change in the object. If the verb is intransitive, the subject is the thing that is affected or changed, and there may be no mention of what causes the

change. The subject of the verb when it is intransitive refers to the same person or thing as the object of the verb when it is transitive. An example is **open up 5.**
EG *Supermarkets, drugstores, and service stations will open up ... Anyone can open up a café tomorrow provided they've got permission.*

if is used in +*if* to indicate that you use the phrasal verb with a clause beginning with the conjunction *if*. An example is **make out 2** which includes the pattern **V+ADV+***if***.**
EG *I can't make out if Nell likes him or not.*

IMPERATIVE is used in patterns such as **IMPERATIVE: V+ADV** to indicate that the phrasal verb is always used in the imperative or in reported imperatives, for example after the verb *tell*. It is used in **ALSO IMPERATIVE** to indicate that the phrasal verb is often used in the imperative. The imperative form of a verb is its base form, and there is no subject. You use imperatives when you are giving orders, making invitations, reacting to someone else's actions or words, and so on. Examples are **roll on 2** which is labelled **IMPERATIVE: V+ADV** and **roll up 4** which is labelled **V+ADV: ALSO IMPERATIVE.**
EG *Roll on four o' clock!*
EG *Roll up! Roll up! Come and see the Elephant Man.*

-ING is used in **WITH -ING** or **+-ING** to indicate that you use the phrasal verb in a structure with the present participle, or -ing form, of another verb. An example is **end up 2** which includes the pattern **V+ADV: WITH -ING.**
EG *We ended up taking a taxi there.*

it is used in **V+***it***+ADV** or **V+***it***+PREP** to indicate that the object of the verb must be the pronoun *it*. Note that you cannot use these structures in the passive. An example is **sweat out 1** which includes the pattern **V+***it***+ADV.**
EG *He sweated it out to the end.*

We give the pattern **V+PREP+***it* when the preposition must be followed by *it*. In these cases, *it* does not have a specific meaning, but is often used to refer vaguely to the general situation. Such expressions are often regarded as idioms, but we include them here for the sake of completeness. An example is **ask for 3** which is labelled **V+PREP, V+PREP+***it***.**
EG *When I reported the attack they said 'Are you sure you didn't ask for it?'*

N means noun group: that is, a phrase consisting of a noun and perhaps a determiner such as *a* or *the* and an adjective. The noun group may also consist of an indefinite pronoun such as *someone, everybody,* or *nothing,* but not a personal pronoun or reflexive pronoun, as these are referred to as **PRON** or **REFL**: see below.

N refers to the object of the verb, so we use **N** in order to show that a verb is transitive, and to show where you put the adverb in the headword in relation to the object of the verb. Very often, two possible positions are indicated with two patterns, **V+ADV+N** and **V+N+ADV**. You usually follow the pattern **V+ADV+N** when you want to give a special focus or emphasis to the noun group, for example because the noun group contains new information. You usually follow the pattern **V+N+ADV** when you do not want to give special focus to the noun group, for example because the noun group contains information that has already been given. It is often the case that you follow the pattern **V+ADV+N** when the object or **N** is a long noun group or has a relative clause dependent on it, and you follow the pattern **V+N+ADV** when the object or **N** is fairly short, perhaps consisting of only one or two words. This is because we tend to use short noun groups when we are referring to something which has already been mentioned or whose identity is clear in the situation.

If the particle in the headword is a preposition, you almost always put the object of the verb between the verb and the prepositional phrase, and this is coded as **V+N+PREP**. An example is **ask into** which is labelled **V+N+PREP, V+PRON+PREP**.
EG *Mr Coles asked me into his office.*

Transitive phrasal verbs can be used in the passive unless the Extra Column says NO PASSIVE, for example **show off 2**:
EG *He was eager to show off the new car.*

N-COUNT is used in the Extra Column to indicate that a derived word is used as a count or countable noun. This means that you can use it in the plural and that if you use it in the singular, you must use a determiner such as *a* or *the* in front of it. We do not give the plural form unless it is considered irregular.

NEGATIVE is used in **WITH NEGATIVE** to indicate that you use the phrasal verb in a negative structure. This can mean that the verb is used in the negative, or that the clause contains a negative structure using words such as *hardly, scarcely*, or *never*. An example is **dream of 1** which is labelled **V+PREP: WITH NEGATIVE**.
EG *I wouldn't dream of asking my mother to look after her.*

N-PLURAL is used in the Extra Column to indicate that a derived word is only used in the plural. It does not have a singular form, and you use it with a plural verb.

N-SING is used in the Extra Column to indicate that a derived word does not have a plural form, and that you must use a determiner such as *a* or *the* in front of it. You use it with a singular verb.

NUMBER is used in **WITH NUMBER** to indicate that you use a number after the phrasal verb, for example **talk down 4**:
EG *When he makes you an offer, you send me in and I'll talk him down another thousand.*

N-UNCOUNT is used in the Extra Column to indicate that a derived word is used as an uncount or uncountable noun. This means that it does not have a plural form, and that you cannot use it after *a* or *one*. You use it with a singular verb.

PASSIVE is used in **USUALLY PASSIVE** to indicate that the phrasal verb is usually used in the passive, for example **throw back 8**:
EG *Ethnic groups were thrown back on their own resources.*

It is also used in **NO PASSIVE** to indicate that the phrasal verb is never used in the passive, although it contains a transitive verb, for example **tide over**:
EG *I only want to borrow enough to tide me over till Monday.*

It is used in **HAS PASSIVE** after a notation such as **V+PREP** or **V+ADV+PREP** in order to indicate that although the verb is intransitive, you can use it in the passive, with the object of the preposition becoming the subject of the verb. An example is **look after** which is labelled **V+PREP: HAS PASSIVE**.
EG *Look after my garden.*
    She wasn't being well looked after at all.

If a phrasal verb is always passive, its pattern is given as **PASSIVE: V+ADV**, and so on. We do not mention any object because a verb does not have an object when it is passive. An example is **tog up** which is labelled **PASSIVE: V+ADV**.
EG *Sheila was all togged up like a camper.*

PREP means preposition or prepositional particle. You need to put a noun group after

the preposition. **PREP/ADV** means that the particle can be used as a preposition or adverb, but that it is more often used as a preposition. We usually use this notation when we need to simplify a long list of patterns. An example is **sink in 4** which includes the pattern **V+N+PREP/ADV**.
EG *The cat suddenly leapt off a roof and sank her claws in his neck.*

PRON means personal pronoun. As the personal pronoun is the object of the verb, you use the object form. The object forms are *me, you, him, her, it, one, us,* and *them.* If you use a personal pronoun as the object of the verb, you always put it between the verb and its particle.

QUOTE is used in **+QUOTE** to indicate that you use the phrasal verb as a reporting verb, with direct speech or a quote. An example is **point out 2** which includes the pattern **V+ADV+QUOTE**.
EG *'It's a golden opportunity, really,' Johnson pointed out.*

RECIPROCAL is used about a group of verbs which refer to a relationship or connection between two people or two groups as part of their meaning. If only one person or group is mentioned as the subject of the verb, then you mention the other one after the preposition *with.* You can also mention both people or groups as the subject of the verb. In this case, you do not use the preposition *with,* although you sometimes use the adverb *together.* An example is **join up 1**:
EG *We joined up with two young men and went along to a road-house... The two families joined up for the rest of the holiday.*

REFL means reflexive pronoun. The reflexive pronouns are *myself, yourself, himself, herself, itself, oneself, ourselves, yourselves,* and *themselves.* You use a reflexive pronoun when the object of the verb refers to the same person or thing as the subject of the verb, and you usually put it between the verb and its particle. We give the pattern **V+PREP+REFL** when the preposition must be followed by a reflexive pronoun, for example **get above**.
EG *She was restrained from getting above herself by a natural modesty.*

REPORT is used in **+REPORT** to indicate that you use the phrasal verb as a reporting verb, with indirect speech or a reported clause, usually beginning with the conjunction *that.* An example is **find out 1** which includes the pattern **V+ADV+REPORT**.
EG *I've just found out that I won't have to start until Wednesday.*

to–**INF** is used in **+*to*–INF** or **WITH *to*–INF** to indicate that you use the phrasal verb in a structure with *to* and the infinitive, or base form, of another verb. An example is **set out 2** which has the pattern **V+ADV+*to*–INF**.
EG *This chapter sets out to explain some of the relevant terms and principles.*

V means verb. It refers to the verb in the phrasal verb headword. You normally need to use a subject with the verb, unless the verb is imperative.

VERB is used in some patterns to indicate that you use another verb after the phrasal verb. An example is **sit back 2** which is labelled **V+ADV: USUALLY WITH *and*+VERB**.
EG *All they have to do is sit back and enjoy the fun.*

WH is used in **+WH** to indicate that you use the phrasal verb with a clause beginning with a **WH**-word: *who, what, when, where, whom, whose, how, why, which,* or *whether.* An example is **make out 2** which includes the pattern **V+ADV+WH**.
EG *Sylvia could not make out how it had happened.*

to, with, from, on, etc The patterns sometimes mention a particular preposition. In these cases, the phrasal verb is often used with the preposition in the structures mentioned. For example, the Extra Column notes may say **USUALLY+to** or **ALSO+of** to indicate that a phrasal verb is usually followed by *to*, or often followed by *of*. Examples are **square up 2** which is labelled **V+ADV: USUALLY+to** and **slave away** which is labelled **V+ADV: ALSO+at**.

EG *You've got to square up to failure and try to carry on.*
EG *Joseph slaved away at cutting the grass.*

Syntactic Patterns

You can find out how to use phrasal verbs grammatically by looking at the patterns in the Extra Column. Most phrasal verbs have two or more patterns. The Extra Column shows all the possible patterns, with each pattern appearing on a separate line. They are mainly given in frequency order: that is, the commonest pattern appears first. However, we group transitive patterns separately from intransitive ones. The patterns are usually separated by a comma (,) or sometimes with OR.

> **⋆sweep up**
>
> 1 If you **sweep up** things from a place, you collect them with a broom in order to get rid of them. ❑ *Kathy was in the middle of the crossing, sweeping up the glass from my broken headlights... The gardening girls were sweeping up leaves and cutting the grass... They can sweep up afterwards.*
>
> V+ADV+N,
> V+N+ADV,
> V+PRON+ADV,
> V+ADV

The patterns give information on the following points:

1 Verb transitivity

Verbs can be transitive or intransitive: that is, some verbs have objects and others do not.

If the verb is transitive, the pattern will include **N**, **PRON**, or **REFL**, and you need to use an object with the verb.

V+N+ADV means that the verb has an object (**N**), and that the object must come in front of the adverb (**ADV**).
EG *I took Andrea out to dinner one evening.*

V+ADV+N means that the verb has an object (**N**), and that the object comes after the adverb (**ADV**).
EG *First, add up all your regular payments.*

V+PRON+ADV means that the verb must have an object which can be a personal pronoun (**PRON**), and that the object comes in front of the adverb (**ADV**).
EG *They called me in for questioning.*

V+REFL+ADV means that the verb has an object which must be a reflexive pronoun (**REFL**), and that the object must come in front of the adverb (**ADV**).
EG *I shut myself away in the library that night and wrote a letter.*

You can use transitive phrasal verbs in the passive unless the Extra Column includes the note **NO PASSIVE**.

If the verb is intransitive, the pattern will not include **N**, **PRON**, or **REFL**. For example, one of the patterns given at **shut up 1** is **V+ADV**, so you know that the verb does not have an object.
EG *Everybody shuts up as soon as you mention it.*

If the verb is sometimes transitive and sometimes intransitive, both transitive and intransitive patterns will be given in the Extra Column. For example, **sweep up 1** which is labelled **V+ADV+N, V+N+ADV, V+PRON+ADV, V+ADV**.

EG *The gardening girls were sweeping up leaves and cutting the grass.*
EG *They can sweep up afterwards.*

A few phrasal verbs are ditransitive. That is, they are used with two objects: a direct object and an indirect object. The patterns for ditransitive verbs include both objects. The first object mentioned is the indirect one and the second is the direct object. For example, **hand back 1** includes the pattern **V+PRON+ADV+N**. This means that the adverb comes between the indirect object, which must be a pronoun, and the direct object, which must be a full noun group.

EG *The girl handed him back his card.*

2 Word classes of particles

The particles in phrasal verbs are sometimes adverbial and sometimes prepositional. If the particle is a preposition, you need a noun group after it. This noun group is called a prepositional object: do not confuse it with the object of the verb.

If the particle is an adverb, the pattern will include **ADV**. If the particle is a preposition, the pattern will include **PREP**. Examples are: **move off** which is labelled **V+ADV**:
EG *The fleet of cars prepared to move off.*
and **rely on 1** which is labelled **V+PREP**:
EG *She is forced to rely on her mother's money.*

If the particle can be used either as an adverb or a preposition, then this is shown as two separate patterns. An example is **come in 1** which is labelled **V+ADV, V+PREP**. This means that the particle *in* can be used as an adverb:
EG *Jeremy came in looking worried.*
or as a preposition:
EG *'Come in the house,' she said.*

For phrasal verbs with a large number of patterns, we sometimes combine the patterns and say: **ADV/PREP** or **PREP/ADV**. This means that the particle can be either an adverb or a preposition. The order of the two particles reflects their frequency: the more frequent of the two is placed first. An example is **put on 4** which includes the pattern **V+N+ADV/PREP**.
EG *She put lipstick on before every class... They must have put ointment on my burns.*

If there are two particles in the phrasal verb, the Extra Column will give a pattern containing **ADV+PREP** or **ADV+ADV** in the same order as the two particles. Examples are: **catch up with**, where *up* is an adverb and *with* is a preposition,
EG *When Birmingham authorities finally caught up with her, she had spent all the money.*
and **put back on**, where both *back* and *on* are adverbs.
EG *Put your clothes back on, Sara.*

3 Positioning of particles

If the verb is transitive, you need to know where to put the particle in relation to the object. Does the particle come between the verb and the object of the verb, or does it follow the object? You can see where to put the particle by looking at the order of elements in the patterns. Each possible position for the particle is shown. For example, if the Extra Column has **V+ADV+N**, you put the particle between the verb and its object.

An example is **clean out 1**:
EG *I was cleaning out my desk at the office on my last day there.*
If it has **V+N+ADV**, you put the particle after the object. **Clean out 1** also has this pattern:
EG *I spent three days cleaning our flat out.*

If several patterns are given for a phrasal verb, you can follow any of them. In most cases, an adverb can come in front of or after the object, as in **clean out 1**. You choose where to put the object and adverb in relation to one another according to whether the object contains new information or whether it refers to something that is already known. The explanation of the abbreviation **N** on page xiv gives guidance on this.

Some phrasal verbs are only found in one pattern; if only one pattern is given, you should follow that pattern. An example is **put up 6**, which is labelled simply **V+ADV+N**.
EG *We had put up a fierce struggle.*

If the object is a pronoun, then you always put the adverb after the object. This is shown as **V+PRON+ADV**. An example is **set down 1**:
EG *The Colonel lifted his cup, glared at it, set it down again.*

4 Additional structures

In many cases, there are particular structures which you have to use with the phrasal verb. The Extra Column shows this information after listing the patterns. Usually this information is introduced by a colon (:). An example is **come up to 2** which is labelled **V+ADV+PREP: WITH NEGATIVE**. This means that the verb is intransitive, has a preposition, and is usually used in the negative or with a negative word somewhere near it.
EG *It must be said that it never really came up to expectations.*

If a structure is not compulsory, we indicate this with **USUALLY** or **ALSO**. **USUALLY** means that the phrasal verb is usually used in this structure. **ALSO** means that this structure often occurs, but is optional. Examples are **head back** which is labelled **V+ADV: USUALLY+A**, and **lock out 2** which is labelled **V+REFL+ADV: ALSO+of**. **Head back** is usually, though not always, followed by an adjunct of some kind:
EG *We wanted him to turn around and head back to L.A.*
and **lock out** is often followed by a prepositional phrase beginning with *of*:
EG *I've locked myself out of the car again!*

5 Sequences of Patterns

The following sequences of patterns are the commonest ones which occur in the **Collins Cobuild Dictionary of Phrasal Verbs**. Sequences of patterns have been counted as a single type if the only difference between them is the order in which they are listed, or the particular compulsory structure which is mentioned. The patterns have been listed in order of how frequently they occur in the dictionary, with the most common given first. All these patterns occur twenty or more times, with the most frequent pattern occurring over 1250 times. This means that a very few basic patterns account for most cases.

In each case, the notation is shown as it might appear in the Extra Column, followed by an explanation and an example of the notation.

V+ADV+N, V+N+ADV, V+PRON+ADV	transitive verb with adverb: the adverb may follow or precede the object, eg. **lock out 1**
V+ADV	intransitive verb with adverb, eg. **log out**

V+PREP	intransitive verb with preposition, eg. **head for 1**
V+PREP: HAS PASSIVE	intransitive verb with preposition: the verb can have a passive, with the object of the preposition becoming the subject of the passive verb, eg. **hear from 1**
V+N+PREP, V+PRON+PREP	transitive verb with preposition, eg. **see in**
V+N+ADV, V+PRON+ADV	transitive verb with adverb: the adverb must follow the object, eg. **see out 1**
V+ADV+PREP	intransitive verb with adverb and preposition, eg. **hold on to 1**
V+ADV, V+PREP	intransitive verb with particle which can function as an adverb or a preposition, eg. **shine through**
V+ADV+N, V+PRON+ADV	transitive verb with adverb: the adverb must precede the object when the object is a full noun group, and follow it if it is a personal pronoun, eg. **slough off 1**
V+ADV, V+N/PRON+ADV, V+ADV+N: ERGATIVE	ergative verb with adverb: the adverb may precede or follow the object when present (see notes on page xiii on ERGATIVE), eg. **line up 1**
V+ADV+N	transitive verb with adverb and full noun group as object: the adverb must precede the object, eg. **line up 5**
PASSIVE: V+ADV	passive verb with adverb: the verb is always passive and the particle is an adverb, eg. **snow in**
V+ADV: WITH A etc	intransitive verb with adverb and a compulsory following structure such as an adjunct, eg. **spill over 3**
PASSIVE: V+PREP	passive verb with a preposition: the verb is always passive, and the particle is a preposition, eg. **starve for**
V+ADV, V+N+ADV, V+PRON+ADV: ERGATIVE	ergative verb with adverb: the adverb can come only after the object when present (see notes on page xiii on ERGATIVE), eg. **loosen up 2**
V+N+ADV+PREP, V+PRON+ADV+PREP	transitive verb with adverb followed by preposition: the object can be a noun group or pronoun and must come in front of the adverb, eg. **let in on**
V+ADV+N, V+N+ADV	transitive verb with adverb and full noun group as object: the adverb may precede or follow the object, eg. **see out 3**
V+N+PREP	transitive verb with preposition and full noun group as object of the verb, eg. **have against**
V+N+PREP, V+PRON+PREP, V+REFL+PREP	transitive verb with preposition: the object can be a noun group, pronoun, or reflexive pronoun and must come in front of the preposition, eg. **let into 1**

Aa

abide /əbaɪd/ (abides, abiding, abided)

abide by If you **abide by** a law, an agreement, or a decision, you accept it and behave in accordance with it. ❑ *Germany and Russia agreed informally to abide by the agreement... Both parties must agree to abide by the court's decision.*

V+PREP:
HAS PASSIVE

NOTE **Observe** and **respect** mean almost the same as **abide by**, and **flout** means the opposite.

accede /ækˈsiːd/ (accedes, acceding, acceded)

accede to If you **accede to** someone's request or opinion, you allow it or agree with it, usually rather unwillingly. [FORMAL] ❑ *He was upset by my refusal to accede to his request... To accede to such a contention would set a dangerous precedent.*

V+PREP:
HAS PASSIVE

account /əkaʊnt/ (accounts, accounting, accounted)

★account for

1 If you **account for** something that has happened or that you have done, you explain how it happened or why you did it. ❑ *He was always prepared to account for his actions... This cannot be accounted for in such a straightforward way.*

V+PREP:
HAS PASSIVE

2 If something **accounts for** a particular fact or situation, it causes or explains it. ❑ *Now, the gene they discovered today doesn't account for all those cases.*

V+PREP:
HAS PASSIVE

NOTE **Explain** means almost the same as **account for**.

3 If someone or something can **be accounted for**, people know where they are or what has happened to them. ❑ *There was no means of ensuring that all of them were accounted for... A sizeable sum of money could not be accounted for... Mrs White is accounted for. Dr and Mrs Gill aren't... 'Everyone here?'—'All accounted for.'—'All right, pay attention.'*

V+PREP:
HAS PASSIVE,
USUALLY PASSIVE

4 If something **accounts for** a particular part or proportion of something, it forms that part or proportion of the whole. ❑ *Children's needs account for a good part of the family budget... Tea accounted for three fifths of Sri Lanka's exports... 50 percent of 1974 manufacturing sales were accounted for by foreign-owned enterprises.*

V+PREP:
HAS PASSIVE

5 If a sum of money **is accounted for**, it has been included in a budget. ❑ *Grants for each student must be accounted for by the issuing authority... Indeed, the B-bomber is barely accounted for in existing defence budgets.*

V+PREP:
HAS PASSIVE,
USUALLY PASSIVE

NOTE **Budget for** means almost the same as **account for**.

6 To **account for** someone or something also means to defeat or destroy them. [OLD-FASHIONED] ❑ *...an identical shot to the identical ball which accounted for him on Friday... We were helped immeasurably by a run-out which accounted for Salim.*

V+PREP:
HAS PASSIVE

acquaint /əkweɪnt/ (acquaints, acquainting, acquainted)

acquaint with

1 If you **are acquainted with** something, you know about it and are familiar with it. [FORMAL] ❑ *Students became acquainted with all aspects of biology before choosing the course... He was well acquainted with sorrow, disappointment, and loneliness... She had acquainted herself with our technology... I will acquaint you with the facts.*

V+N+PREP,
V+PRON+PREP,
V+REFL+PREP:
USUALLY PASSIVE

2 If you **are acquainted with** someone, you know them slightly but they are not a close friend. [FORMAL] ❑ *I hear you're acquainted with Jerry Pierce... Mrs Grunblatt used to be acquainted with a painter.*

PASSIVE:
V+PREP

act /ækt/ (acts, acting, acted)

★act on If you **act on** or **act upon** advice or information, you do what has been advised or suggested. **Act upon** is more formal. ❑ *Why didn't you act on my warning?... They were content to provide information on which others could act... The recommendations could not, for reasons of finance, be fully acted on. ...acting upon his advice... We must use these powers and act upon them.*

V+PREP:
HAS PASSIVE

The symbol ★ shows key phrasal verbs

act out

1 When you **act out** your feelings or ideas, you express them in your behaviour, especially as a means of relieving nervous tension or emotion. ❑ *Children act out their frustration in temper tantrums.*

V+ADV+N,
V+PRON+ADV

2 If you **act out** an event which has happened, you copy the actions which took place and make them into a play. ❑ *The teacher gets the students to act out some historic event.*

V+ADV+N,
V+PRON+ADV

3 If someone **is acting out**, they are behaving aggressively because they are upset or unhappy. [AMERICAN] ❑ *One way of helping kids is to provide a significant male role model to boys who are showing signs of acting out.*

V+ADV

act up

1 If something **is acting up**, it is not working properly. [FORMAL] ❑ *Her washing machine was acting up again.*

V+ADV

NOTE **Play up** means almost the same as **act up**.

2 If a child **is acting up**, they are behaving badly. [INFORMAL] ❑ *I'm sorry he had to act up like this.*

V+ADV

NOTE **Play up** means almost the same as **act up**.

act upon → See act on

add /æd/ (adds, adding, added)

★**add in** If you **add** something **in**, you include it as a part of something else. ❑ *We had to add in a couple of extra scenes... If you add in his gains of last year he'd made no less than £20,000.*

V+ADV+N,
V+PRON+ADV,
V+N+ADV

★**add on** If you **add** something **on**, you attach it to something else or include it as part of something else. ❑ *If the tip hasn't been added on, you will see the words 'service not included'... They add on about nine per cent for service.*

V+ADV+N,
V+PRON+ADV,
V+N+ADV

add together

1 If you **add together** several numbers, you calculate their total. ❑ *If you add these two numbers together what do you get?... These amounts are added together to produce the total earnings... To work out the number of units, add together all your contributions.*

V+N+ADV,
V+PRON+ADV,
V+ADV+N

NOTE **Add up** means almost the same as **add together**.

2 If you **add** several things **together**, you put them all in one place so that they are combined. ❑ *...adding the eggs and butter together in a bowl... She got one pail of boiling water and one of cold water and added them together in a tub.*

V+N+ADV,
V+PRON+ADV,
V+ADV+N

NOTE **Mix** means almost the same as **add together**.

★add up

1 If you **add up** several numbers, you calculate their total. ❑ *We add all the marks up... First, add up all your regular payments.*

V+N+ADV,
V+ADV+N,
V+PRON+ADV

NOTE **Add together** means almost the same as **add up**.

2 If you say that facts or events **add up**, you mean that you can understand their significance. ❑ *It all added up. I became aware that Halliday was the thief.*

V+ADV

3 If small amounts of something **add up**, they gradually increase. ❑ *Even small savings, 5 pence here or 10 pence there, can add up... It's the little minor problems that add up.*

V+ADV

★add up to

1 If numbers or amounts **add up to** a particular total, they result in that total. ❑ *This adds up to 75,000 miles of new streets.*

V+ADV+PREP

NOTE **Amount to** means almost the same as **add up to**.

2 You talk about things **adding up to** something when they result in it or suggest it. ❑ *This adds up to a formidable list of qualifications... Most of the evidence adds up to the clear conclusion that human beings are able to control their feelings. ...the shapes, the glowing colours; they all seem to add up to a work of art.*

V+ADV+PREP

adhere /ædhɪəʳ/ (adheres, adhering, adhered)

adhere to

1 If you **adhere to** a rule or agreement, you act in the way that it says you should. ❑ *...their failure to adhere to the warder's instructions... The fire regulations have been adhered to.*

V+PREP:
HAS PASSIVE

2 If you **adhere to** an opinion or belief, you support or hold it. ❑ *Many people adhered to this view. ...idealists who adhered to the principles expounded by Professor Read.*

V+PREP

admit /ædmɪt/ (admits, admitting, admitted)

admit of If an event or situation **admits of** something, it makes it possible for 　V+PREP
that thing to happen. [FORMAL] ❑ *The relevant statute admitted of one interpretation only.*
NOTE　Allow means almost the same as **admit of**.

agree /əgriː/ (agrees, agreeing, agreed)

★**agree with**

1 If you **agree with** an action or suggestion, you approve of it. ❑ *You didn't want* 　V+PREP
to ask anybody whether they agreed with what you were doing... In his heart he knew they'd
agree with his stand.

2 If a particular food or drink **does** not **agree with** you, it gives you indigestion. 　V+PREP:
My milk didn't seem to agree with the baby. 　WITH NEGATIVE
NOTE　Upset means almost the same as **not agree with**.

3 If something **agrees with** you, it makes you feel healthy and contented. [OLD- 　V+PREP
FASHIONED] ❑ *The sea air really agrees with her.*
NOTE　Suit means almost the same as **agree with**.

aim /eɪm/ (aims, aiming, aimed)

★**aim at**

1 If you **aim at** something, you plan or hope to achieve it. ❑ *We should aim at two-* 　V+PREP:
thirds of the average wage. ...aiming at a higher production level... All Fair Rent Associations 　HAS PASSIVE
aim at helping people with real housing needs. ...a fresh package of public spending cuts
aimed at bringing down the government borrowing requirements.

2 If an action or activity **is aimed at** someone, it is intended to help them or af- 　V+N+PREP,
fect them in some way. ❑ *I knew that all this publicity was not really aimed at me as an* 　V+PRON+PREP:
individual... Many of the devices are aimed at people with lumbago. 　USUALLY PASSIVE
NOTE　Be directed at means almost the same as **be aimed at**.

allow /əlaʊ/ (allows, allowing, allowed)

★**allow for**

1 When you **allow for** something such as a problem, delay, or expense in your 　V+PREP:
planning, you make sure that you have enough time, money, or resources in order to 　HAS PASSIVE
deal with it if it occurs. ❑ *If you are self-employed, allow for tax and national insurance.*
...long-term fixed-price contracts which did not allow for the escalation of costs.

2 If you **allow for** something that does not yet exist, you take action or make 　V+PREP
plans so that it will be possible. ❑ *Pasta can be frozen, but should be undercooked to al-*
low for the reheating... His original plans allowed for meadows and a lake for recreation.

allude /əluːd/ (alludes, alluding, alluded)

allude to If you **allude to** something, you mention it in an indirect way. [FOR- 　V+PREP:
MAL] ❑ *They very soon learned not to allude to the subject. ...a controversial question to* 　HAS PASSIVE
which we may briefly allude... This is only rarely alluded to in even indirect terms.
NOTE　Refer to means almost the same as **allude to**.

amount /əmaʊnt/ (amounts, amounting, amounted)

★**amount to**

1 If you say that something **amounts to** a particular sum or number, you mean 　V+PREP
that its total is that quantity. ❑ *...very high fees which amount to £2,000. ...her entire*
fortune, which amounted by then to a considerable sum of money. ...a huge infantry force
which with reserves amounted to 200,000 men.
NOTE　Add up to and **total** mean almost the same as **amount to**.

2 If you say that an idea, feeling, statement, or action **amounts to** something, you 　V+PREP
mean that it seems like that to you. ❑ *His attitude towards her amounted to loathing...*
The proposals amounted to a new charter for the mentally ill... The message amounted to little
more than personal regards.

3 If you say that something **amounts to** little, you mean that it is unimportant, 　V+PREP
and if you say that it **amounts to** a great deal, you mean that it is important. ❑ *The*
trouble had amounted to hardly anything... It had never amounted to much.

angle /æŋgəl/ (angles, angling, angled)

angle for If you **are angling for** something, you try to make someone offer it 　V+PREP
to you without asking for it directly. ❑ *He got the invitation to Washington he had been*

angling for... I am quite sure she was not angling for some sort of reconciliation.
NOTE **Fish for** means almost the same as **angle for**.

answer /ˈɑːnsər, ˈæn-/ (answers, answering, answered)

answer back If someone, especially a child, **answers** you **back** or **answers back**, they speak rudely to you when you have spoken to them. ❑ *What do you do with a child who answers back?... He answered back vehemently... At first I couldn't resist the temptation to answer teachers back.*
V+ADV,
V+N+ADV,
V+PRON+ADV

answer for

1 If you say that someone has something to **answer for**, you mean that they have done something bad and should be held responsible for it. ❑ *The cosmetic industry has much to answer for... If they start terror tactics the entire army will have to answer for his actions... I think the motorist has a lot to answer for. He expects too much.*
V+PREP

2 If you can **answer for** someone or for a quality of theirs, you mean that you are sure they are reliable and trustworthy, or have that quality. ❑ *I can answer for his loyalty.*
V+PREP

NOTE **Vouch for** means almost the same as **answer for**.

answer to

1 If someone or something **answers to** a particular description, they have the characteristics described. ❑ *He knew of several boys who might answer to that description.*
V+PREP

NOTE **Fit** means almost the same as **answer to**.

2 If something **answers to** your needs or requirements, it will fill your needs. ❑ *The Militia must have had something that answered to our national military needs.*
V+PREP

NOTE **Satisfy** means almost the same as **answer to**.

3 When someone **answers to** a person who has authority over them, they give them the information that is officially required. [FORMAL] ❑ *The young couple line up to enter the wedding tent after answering to the official scribe.*
V+PREP

ante /ˈænti/ (antes, anted)

ante up If you **ante up** an amount of money, you pay your share, sometimes unwillingly. [AMERICAN, INFORMAL] ❑ *Paul Reichmann offered to ante up $2 million.*
V+PREP

apprise /əˈpraɪz/ (apprises, apprising, apprised)

apprise of When you **apprise** someone **of** something, you inform them about it. [FORMAL] ❑ *I apprised him of the political situation in Washington.*
V+PRON+PREP,
V+N+PREP

NOTE **Tell** is a more general word for **apprise**.

approve /əˈpruːv/ (approves, approving, approved)

★**approve of**

1 If you **approve of** an action, event, or suggestion, you are pleased about it. ❑ *My grandfather did not approve of my father's marriage... His return to the office was widely approved of.*
V+PREP:
HAS PASSIVE

2 If you **approve of** someone or something, you like and admire them. ❑ *He did not approve of my pictures. ...the desire to be loved and approved of.*
V+PREP:
HAS PASSIVE

argue /ˈɑːrgjuː/ (argues, arguing, argued)

argue down If you **argue** someone **down**, you succeed in getting them to accept your point of view during an argument. [AMERICAN] ❑ *When we're discussing politics, I can always argue him down.*
V+N+ADV,
V+PRON+ADV,
V+ADV+N

argue out When you **argue out** an idea or plan, you discuss in detail all the aspects and possible consequences of it in order to reach a decision. ❑ *Our proposals were argued out in meetings that seemed never to end... We would discuss it and argue it out in the church.*
V+ADV+N,
V+PRON+ADV,
V+N+ADV

NOTE **Thrash out** is a more informal expression for **argue out**.

argue out of If you **argue** someone **out of** doing something, you persuade them not to do it. ❑ *He argued a homosexual clergyman out of suicide... Bill tried to argue him out of it for a while.*
V+N+ADV+PREP,
V+PRON+ADV+PREP

NOTE **Talk out of** is a less formal expression for **argue out of**.

arse /ˈɑːrs/ (arses, arsing, arsed)

☑ **Arse** is a rude, offensive word used in spoken British English.

arse ab<u>ou</u>t You say that someone **is arsing about** or **arsing around** when V+ADV
they are behaving in a silly and irritating way instead of getting on with what they
are supposed to be doing.

NOTE **Muck about** is an informal but less rude expression for **arse about**.

arse ar<u>ou</u>nd → See **arse about**

ask /ɑːsk, æsk/ (**asks, asking, asked**)

ask after If you **ask after** someone, you ask for information about them, for ex- V+PREP
ample how they are and if they are well, or what they are doing at the present time.
❑ *She asked after my father... She asked after his health... If anyone should ask after me, say
I'm at the Thunderbird hotel.*

NOTE **Inquire after** means almost the same as **ask after**.

ask ar<u>ou</u>nd If you **ask around** when you need help with something, you ask V+ADV,
several people, usually people you do not know, to help you. ❑ *She asked around but* V+PREP
*no-one seemed to know where the little boy had gone... I asked around the village to see if
any of the old men would like to come with me.*

★**ask for**

1 If you **ask for** something, you say that you would like to have it. ❑ *She asked for* V+PREP:
a drink of water... The publisher asked for time to think it over... Send it by recorded delivery HAS PASSIVE
and ask for a receipt.

NOTE **Request** is a more formal word for **ask for**.

2 If you **ask for** someone when you are making a phone call, you say that you V+PREP
would like to speak to them. ❑ *Call the town hall and ask for the pest controller... He rang
the office and asked for Cynthia.*

3 If you say that someone **is asking for** something unpleasant such as punish- V+PREP,
ment, trouble, or other problems, or if you say that they **are asking for** it, you V+PREP+*it*
mean that they behave in a way that makes it more likely or possible for those
things to occur. ❑ *To plan a route all in one go was asking for trouble. It was obviously a
better idea to do it in bits... He had no business crawling out of the dark. He was batty. He
asked for it... When I reported the attack they said 'Are you sure you didn't ask for it?'*

ask in If you **ask** someone **in**, you invite them to come into the room or building V+N+ADV,
that you are in. ❑ *The vicar went across the hall to ask Mrs. Daniels in... Gerald had gone* V+PRON+ADV
*out for a while. Mr Sutton asked me in. ...neighbours that ask you in for coffee every now and
again.*

ask <u>in</u>to If you **ask** someone **into** a place, you invite them to come in. ❑ *It gave* V+N+PREP,
me an excuse to ask him into the cabin... They asked me into their classrooms to watch them V+PRON+PREP
teach... Mr Coles asked me into his office.

★**ask <u>ou</u>t** If you **ask** someone **out**, you invite them to go somewhere with you. V+N+ADV,
❑ *Every few weeks he and his wife would ask Brody and Ellen out to dinner... It had to be a* V+PRON+ADV,
cheap restaurant, since he was asking her out... I kept being asked out by men. V+ADV+N

ask <u>o</u>ver If you **ask** someone **over**, you invite them to come and visit you. V+PRON+ADV,
❑ *One evening he asked me over to inspect the house... He asked us over to his flat... What if* V+N+ADV:
he asks you over for the evening? ALSO+*to*

ask r<u>ou</u>nd If you **ask** someone **round**, you invite them to come and visit you. V+PRON+ADV,
[BRITISH, INFORMAL] ❑ *I hoped he'd ask me round to his pad... 'She's asked me round on Fri-* V+N+ADV:
day,' said the Count... I'll ask Sylvia Wicks round for a drink. ALSO+*to*

aspire /əspaɪər/ (**aspires, aspiring, aspired**)

aspire to If you **aspire to** something, you have a strong ambition to achieve it. V+PREP:
❑ *Edward Heath has always aspired to leadership... She had achieved none of the height she* HAS PASSIVE
had aspired to.

attend /ətend/ (**attends, attending, attended**)

attend to

1 If you **attend to** something such as a problem, you deal with it. ❑ *I had two* V+PREP:
items of business to attend to before I could relax... Everyone has his own affairs to attend HAS PASSIVE
to... If we do not attend to the problem, it will certainly grow.

NOTE **See to** means almost the same as **attend to**.

2 If you **attend to** someone who needs something, you help them or look after V+PREP:
them. ❑ *I see now that I should have attended to her myself... Henry was attended to in a* HAS PASSIVE

competent manner... It can, too easily, be assumed that one is attending to them when one is merely fussing.

auction /ˈɔːkʃən/ (auctions, auctioning, auctioned)

auction off If furniture or property **is auctioned off**, you get rid of it by selling it at an auction. ❏ *The furniture was auctioned off... We auctioned off all my grandad's war memorabilia.*

V+N+ADV,
V+ADV+N,
V+PRON+ADV

average /ˈævərɪdʒ/ (averages, averaging, averaged)

average out When you **average out** a set of numbers, you work out the average or approximate figure. ❏ *We find that, averaging it out, only 8,000 chairs could have been purchased... We sort of averaged out the estimates.*

V+N+ADV,
V+PRON+ADV,
V+ADV+N

average out at If a set of numbers **averages out at** a particular figure, that figure is the average for the set of numbers. ❏ *'How many hours do you work?' 'I suppose it averages out at about 40 a week.'*

V+ADV+PREP

Bb

back /bæk/ **(backs, backing, backed)**

★back away

1 If you **back away** from someone or something, you move slowly backwards away from them, usually because you are nervous or frightened. ❑ *The waitress, having put the tray down, rose and backed away... They moved towards each other, then they backed away... He was vaguely aware of the fur-coated woman backing away from him.*

NOTE **Retreat** is a more formal word for **back away**.

2 If you **back away** from an idea or suggestion, you avoid supporting it or commenting on it, and try to dissociate yourself from it. ❑ *The administration appeared to back away from official criticism of the Prime Minister.*

V+ADV:
ALSO+*from*

V+ADV:
ALSO+*from*

★back down

If you **back down** on something, you accept someone else's point of view or agree to do what they want you to do, even though you do not really want to. ❑ *Eventually he backed down on the question of seating. ...but the men refused to back down. ...asserting his authority and making them back down.*

NOTE **Give in** means almost the same as **back down**.

V+ADV:
ALSO+*on*

★back off

1 If you **back off**, you try to avoid a fight or difficult situation by moving away or not becoming involved in it. If you tell someone to **back off**, you are telling them not to interfere with something you are doing. ❑ *Brody was ready for a fight, but he backed off... They backed off, handing him what money they had... A part of him was always backing off from these events... Back off, or I shoot!*

NOTE **Withdraw** is a more formal word for **back off**.

2 If you **back off** from a claim, demand, or commitment that you made earlier, or if you **back off** it, you withdraw it. ❑ *A spokesman says the president has backed off from his threat to boycott the conference... The union has publicly backed off that demand.*

V+ADV:
ALSO IMPERATIVE,
ALSO+*from*

V+PREP,
V+ADV:
USUALLY+*from*

back onto

If a building **backs onto** something, the back of it faces in that direction. ❑ *...the Gardens and the houses backing onto them.*

V+PREP

★back out

1 If you **back out** of an arrangement, you decide not to do something you had previously agreed to do. ❑ *You can't back out now. A deal's a deal... They openly express the worry that the Japanese will back out of the agreements.*

NOTE **Pull out** means almost the same as **back out**.

2 If you **back out** or **back** your car **out**, you move your car backwards out of a confined space, such as a garage or a parking place. ❑ *Joe threw the car into gear and backed out... Harold backed out of the parking lot.*

V+ADV:
ALSO+*of*

V+ADV,
V+N+ADV,
V+PRON+ADV:
ALSO+*of*

★back up

1 If you **back up** a statement, you supply evidence to prove that it is true or reasonable. ❑ *The more bills you can include to back up your claim, the happier the finance department will be... He backed this up with a few horrifying anecdotes... Their demands for independence were backed up with quotes from western political writers.*

NOTE **Support** means almost the same as **back up**.

2 If you **back** someone **up**, you give them help or support them. ❑ *They asked local administrators to back them up. ...troops backed up by police and paramilitary rangers... He had loyally backed one of their number up in his false statement... Baker said later that he would back up Goldwater in whatever he decided to do.*

NOTE **Support** means almost the same as **back up**.

◆ **Back-up** is extra help or support from people or machines, which you need in order to be able to achieve what you want. ❑ *...the tremendous computer back-up which*

V+ADV+N,
V+PRON+ADV,
V+N+ADV

V+PRON+ADV,
V+N+ADV,
V+ADV+N

N-UNCOUNT

each mission required... We don't really need any back-up, do we? We solve our own problems.

♦ If you have something such as a second piece of equipment or set of plans as **back-up**, you have arranged for it to be available for use in case the first one does not work. ❑ *Use a conventional heating system as back-up. ...the sheer strength of the back-up crew of 25 actors.* — N-UNCOUNT

NOTE **Stand-by** means almost the same as **back-up**.

3 If an idea or intention **is backed up** by action, action is taken to support or confirm it. ❑ *The Secretary General says the declaration must now be backed up by concrete and effective actions... It is time the Government backed up its advert campaigns with tougher measures.* — V+ADV+N, V+PRON+ADV, V+N+ADV

4 If you **back up** when you are driving, you move your car backwards a little way. ❑ *I backed up three hundred yards to the entrance... You back up the car and I'll get the suitcases... I can't back it up. I can't get it into reverse gear.* — V+ADV, V+ADV+N, V+N+ADV, V+PRON+ADV

NOTE **Reverse** means almost the same as **back up**.

5 If you **back up**, you walk backwards a little way. ❑ *She backed up a few steps, then ran at the water.* — V+ADV

NOTE **Retreat** is a more formal word for **back up**.

6 If vehicles **back up**, they form a line of traffic which has to wait before it can move on. ❑ *Traffic into London on the M11 was backed up for several miles.* — V+ADV

bag /bæg/ **(bags, bagging, bagged)**

bag up If you **bag up** something, you put it into bags. ❑ *Bag up as many of the leaves as you can... We'll bag them up tonight and they can be delivered tomorrow.* — V+ADV+N, V+PRON+ADV, V+N+ADV

bail /beɪl/ **(bails, bailing, bailed)**

☑ **Bail** is also spelled **bale** in paragraphs 2, 3 and 4.

★bail out

1 If you **bail out** someone who is in custody, you pay bail on their behalf so that they can be released. ❑ *I went down to the Hall of Justice to bail my friend out... Look, can you come down here and bail me out?* — V+N+ADV, V+PRON+ADV, V+ADV+N

2 If you **bail** someone **out**, you help them out of a difficult situation. ❑ *We need government assistance to bail us out should things go wrong... Their sole mission in Vietnam was to bail out Marines in trouble. ...a financial package designed to bail out the Missile Development Corporation.* — V+PRON+ADV, V+ADV+N, V+N+ADV

NOTE **Rescue** means almost the same as **bail out**.

3 If you **bail out** of an aircraft, you jump out of it with a parachute because it is damaged and likely to crash. ❑ *One pilot was seen to bail out... Were they bomber crews that had bailed out?* — V+ADV: ALSO+of

4 If you **bail out** a small boat, or if you **bail** water **out** of it, you remove water from the inside of it using a container, often because the boat is leaking or sinking. ❑ *...bailing out the rain water from the bottom of the boat... Quickly! You bail the water out and I'll paddle... We couldn't bail out fast enough and were forced to abandon it.* — V+ADV+N, V+N+ADV, V+PRON+ADV, V+ADV

balance /bæləns/ **(balances, balancing, balanced)**

balance against When you **balance** one thing **against** another, you assess the importance of the first thing in relation to the second. ❑ *...balancing the assumptions of Marxist theory against the values and needs of a government... Conflicting claims and interests had to be balanced one against the other.* — V+N+PREP, V+PRON+PREP

NOTE **Set against** means almost the same as **balance against**.

balance out If two or more things **balance out**, they are equal in amount or value. ❑ *If I am overdrawn one month, it should theoretically balance out in the following months.* — V+ADV

NOTE **Even out** means almost the same as **balance out**.

balance up When things **balance up** or when you **balance** them **up**, they become equal in amount or value, or you make them equal. ❑ *How the forces balance up is really a matter of opinion... The Clearing House is where the major banks daily balance up their claims on each other.* — V+ADV, V+ADV+N, V+N+ADV, V+PRON+ADV

bale /beɪl/ **(bales, baling, baled)** → See **bail**

balk /bɔːlk, AM bɔːk/ **(balks, balking, balked)**

☑ Balk is also spelled **baulk**.

balk at If you **balk at** something, you are very reluctant to do it or to let it happen. ❑ *I balked at cleaning the lavatory... The administration does not baulk at such a prospect.*   V+PREP

NOTE **Jib at** means almost the same as **balk at**.

ball /bɔːl/ **(balls, balling, balled)**

ball up When you **ball** something **up**, it becomes round. ❑ *She balled the handkerchief up and threw it at his feet... Brian's face balled up like a fist.*   V+N+ADV, V+PRON+ADV, V+ADV

balls /bɔːlz/ **(ballses, ballsing, ballsed)**

☑ Balls is a rude, offensive word used in spoken British English.

balls up If you **balls** something **up**, you spoil it by making a lot of mistakes. ❑ *You've ballsed it all up... Don't balls up the next one! ...the way you balls things up.*   V+PRON+ADV, V+ADV+N, V+N+ADV

NOTE **Cock up, mess up**, and **botch** mean almost the same as **balls up**.

♦ A **balls-up** is something that is done very badly because of mistakes or carelessness. ❑ *Our union, in a classic balls-up, voted both ways. ...the man who could sort out other people's balls-ups.*   N-COUNT

NOTE **Cock-up** means almost the same as **balls-up**.

band /bænd/ **(bands, banding, banded)**

band together If people **band together**, they meet and act together as a group in order to try and achieve something. ❑ *Everywhere, small groups of women banded together to talk about liberation... More and more people are banding themselves together to get things done... Producing countries have been successful recently in banding their interests together.*   V+ADV, V+REFL+ADV, V+N+ADV, V+PRON+ADV, V+ADV+N: NO PASSIVE

NOTE **Unite** means almost the same as **band together**.

bandage /bændɪdʒ/ **(bandages, bandaging, bandaged)**

bandage up If you **bandage up** a wound or part of someone's body, you wrap it up completely in a bandage. ❑ *...to bandage up a patient's leg... I bandaged him up with a rag.*   V+ADV+N, V+PRON+ADV, V+N+ADV

NOTE **Bind up** means almost the same as **bandage up**.

bandy /bændi/ **(bandies, bandying, bandied)**

☑ About is used mainly in British English.

bandy about → See **bandy around**

bandy around

1 When people **bandy** words **around** or **bandy** them **about**, they use them a lot without paying much attention to their meanings. ❑ *We bandy about such phrases as 'the moral fabric' of a society. ...just another label for journalists to bandy about... Abstruse terms and jargon are bandied by experts.*   V+ADV+N, V+N+ADV, V+PRON+ADV

2 If ideas **are bandied around** or **bandied about**, a lot of people hear and talk about them. ❑ *The idea was bandied about that legislation might help to curb the militants... Various suggestions were bandied around by the younger members.*   PASSIVE: V+ADV

bang /bæŋ/ **(bangs, banging, banged)**

☑ About is used mainly in British English.

bang about

1 If you **bang** something **about** or **bang** it **around**, you treat it very roughly and risk damaging it. [INFORMAL] ❑ *Don't bang your vacuum cleaner about – it's a sensitive machine... If you have a tendency to bang things around, take more time.*   V+N+ADV, V+PRON+ADV

NOTE **Bash about** means almost the same as **bang about**.

2 If you **bang about** in a place, you move around doing things noisily. [INFORMAL] ❑ *We listened to her singing while she banged about in the kitchen... I heard her banging about and beating the walls.*   V+ADV, V+PREP

NOTE **Clatter about** means almost the same as **bang about**.

3 If something **bangs about**, it moves around rapidly and knocks into things that are nearby. ❑ *The contents of the case were prevented from banging about... I heard a tennis ball banging about.*   V+ADV

4 If a person **has been banged about** or **banged around**, someone has attacked them and hit them several times. ❑ *She had been terrorized and banged around badly.*

NOTE **Bash about** means almost the same as **bang about**.

V+N+ADV,
V+PRON+ADV,
V+ADV+N:
USUALLY PASSIVE

bang ar<u>ou</u>nd

1 If you **bang around** from one place to another, you move from one to the other without staying anywhere for very long. [INFORMAL] ❑ *After the divorce, Mark moved East and began banging around from job to job.*

V+ADV:
WITH A

2 → See **bang about**

bang aw<u>ay</u> If you **bang away** when you hit something, you continue hitting it noisily and with a lot of energy. ❑ *He used the knocker vigorously. Nothing happened. He banged away even harder... He keeps banging away at the guy.*

V+ADV:
USUALLY+A

bang d<u>ow</u>n If you **bang** something **down**, you put it down violently so that it makes a loud noise. ❑ *He banged the window down... 'Pride be hanged' said the old woman, banging his supper plate down in front of him... He banged down the phone angrily.*

V+N+ADV,
V+ADV+N,
V+PRON+ADV

NOTE **Slam down** means almost the same as **bang down**.

bang <u>i</u>nto If you **bang into** someone, you bump against them accidentally. ❑ *You couldn't turn round without banging into her. ...the cars banging into each other.*

V+PREP

bang <u>o</u>n If you **bang on** about something, you talk or write about it repeatedly for a long time in an uninteresting or boring way. [BRITISH, INFORMAL] ❑ *...an unusual treat to read a contemporary American authoress who is not banging on interminably about some freaky minority fancy.*

V+ADV:
ALSO+*about*

bang <u>ou</u>t

1 If you **bang out** a tune on a piano, you play it noisily and rather badly. [INFORMAL] ❑ *He was banging out 'Au Clair de la Lune' for all he was worth.*

V+ADV+N,
V+N+ADV,
V+PRON+ADV

2 If you **bang out** something that you have written on a typewriter, or on a computer keyboard, you type it very quickly and noisily. [INFORMAL] ❑ *...bent over my typewriter in the press tent, banging out a couple of thousand words... I managed to bang a few pages out last night.*

V+ADV+N,
V+N+ADV,
V+PRON+ADV

bang <u>u</u>p If someone **is banged up**, they are in prison. [BRITISH, INFORMAL] ❑ *He was banged up for fifteen years.*

PASSIVE:
V+ADV

NOTE **Be imprisoned** is a more formal expression for **be banged up**.

bank /bæŋk/ (banks, banking, banked)

★bank <u>o</u>n If you **bank on** a situation, you rely on it and expect to get some advantage out of it. ❑ *Green Cross is clearly banking on these advantages to outweigh the drawbacks... Don't bank on it.*

V+PREP

NOTE **Count on** and **bet on** mean almost the same as **bank on**, and **rely on** is a more formal expression.

bank <u>u</u>p

1 To **bank up** something solid such as earth or sand means to pile it into a mound or against a wall. ❑ *The storm had banked up the snow against the front door.*

V+ADV+N,
V+N+ADV,
V+PRON+ADV

NOTE **Build up** means almost the same as **bank up**.

♦ Something solid which is **banked-up** is piled up into a mound. ❑ *...threatening, banked-up clouds on the horizon.*

ADJECTIVE

2 If you **bank up** a fire, you put a large quantity of coal onto it so that it will keep burning for a long time. ❑ *Mother nursed the fire with skill, banking it up every night and blowing hard on the coals.*

V+PRON+ADV,
V+N+ADV,
V+ADV+N

bargain /bɑːrgɪn/ (bargains, bargaining, bargained)

bargain f<u>o</u>r If something happens that you **had** not **bargained for** or **bargained on**, you did not expect it to happen. If it happens more than you **bargained for**, it happens to a greater extent than you expected. ❑ *This was one complication he had not bargained for... They went more slowly than Ralph had bargained for... Some of them might get more than they bargained for... I hadn't bargained on taking the kids as well.*

V+PREP:
HAS PASSIVE

NOTE **Reckon on** means almost the same as **bargain for**, and **anticipate** is a more formal word.

bargain <u>o</u>n → See **bargain for**

barge /bɑːʳdʒ/ (barges, barging, barged)

barge in If you **barge in**, you rudely interrupt what someone else is doing or saying. ❑ *I'm sorry, I won't barge in again... If anyone barged in, it was you, not her... They went barging in late at night.*   V+ADV

barge into

1 If you **barge into** a place, you rush or push into it in a rough and rude way. ❑ *Most women would have come barging into the kitchen with ironic or unhelpful suggestions... You don't barge into the garage as you did in the old mechanic's institute.*   V+PREP

2 If you **barge into** a conversation, you rudely interrupt the person who is speaking. ❑ *Renate spoke stiffly to her when she barged into these conversations.*   V+PREP

NOTE **Butt in** means almost the same as **barge into**.

3 If you **barge into** someone, you bump against them rather roughly and rudely while you are walking. ❑ *I hate shopping in town – people are always barging into you.*   V+PREP

NOTE **Jostle** means almost the same as **barge into**.

barge through If you **barge through** a crowd of people, you push past them rudely. ❑ *I got up from my seat, my drink half finished, and barged through the ladies with their lagers. ...barging through the yelling crowd.*   V+PREP

NOTE **Push through** means almost the same as **barge through**.

bark /bɑːʳk/ (barks, barking, barked)

bark out If you **bark out** an order, you shout it out loudly and suddenly. ❑ *Bill Fry stood on the bridge, barking out orders through a megaphone... 'Company, halt,' he barked out.*   V+ADV+N, V+ADV+QUOTE, V+PRON+ADV

base /beɪs/ (bases, basing, based)

★**base on** If something **is based on** or **based upon** another thing, it takes its general form, subject, or nature from that other thing. **Base upon** is more formal. ❑ *The new agreement is based on the original United Nations proposal. ...movies based on Britain and British life... I base all my characters on someone. ...the images upon which we base our behaviour.*   V+N+PREP, V+PRON+PREP: USUALLY PASSIVE

base upon → See base on

bash /bæʃ/ (bashes, bashing, bashed)

bash about If you **bash** something **about**, you treat it very roughly and risk damaging it. [BRITISH, INFORMAL] ❑ *It's rather bashed about. ...keeping it in running order and not bashing it about.*   V+N+ADV, V+PRON+ADV

NOTE **Bang about** means almost the same as **bash about**.

bash in

1 If you **bash** something **in**, you break it or damage it by hitting it very hard. [INFORMAL] ❑ *The doors had to be broken down, or the windows bashed in... I'll bash your silly head in.*   V+N+ADV, V+PRON+ADV, V+ADV+N

2 → See bash up

bash on If you **bash on** with a task, you carry on doing it, often in a rather unenthusiastic way. [INFORMAL] ❑ *I'd better bash on with this report.*   V+ADV: ALSO+with

NOTE **Get on** means almost the same as **bash on**.

bash out If you say that someone **bashes** something **out**, you mean that they produce it quickly or in large quantities, but without much care or thought. [INFORMAL] ❑ *Up to then, they'd merrily bashed out albums in between tours... Their ambitions are to bash out good grub with minimal fuss.*   V+ADV+N, V+N+ADV, V+PRON+ADV

bash up If someone **bashes up** a person or thing, or **bashes** them **in**, they attack them violently and hurt or damage them. [BRITISH, INFORMAL] ❑ *Her son seemed to feel the need to bash up things and wreck things... Kill the pig! Bash him in!*   V+ADV+N, V+PRON+ADV, V+N+ADV

batten /bætən/ (battens, battening, battened)

batten down If you **batten** something **down**, you make it secure by fixing pieces of wood across it or by closing it firmly. ❑ *...a ship battened down for a storm.*   V+N+ADV, V+ADV+N, V+PRON+ADV

batten on If you say that someone **battens on** a particular person or thing, you disapprove of the fact that they become successful by forming a close connection with that person or thing. ❑ *He got round my mother and battened on her. ...the growth of extremist parties, battening on fears about mass immigration and unemployment.*   V+PREP

The symbol ★ shows key phrasal verbs

batter /bǽtər/ (batters, battering, battered)

batter down To **batter down** something such as a door means to hit it repeatedly and hard so that it breaks and falls down. ❏ *...mud walls that the rains have battered down.*

V+ADV+N,
V+N+ADV,
V+PRON+ADV

NOTE **Break down** means almost the same as **batter down**.

baulk /bɔːlk/, AM bɔːk/ (baulks, baulking, baulked) → See balk

bawl /bɔːl/ (bawls, bawling, bawled)

bawl out

1 If someone **bawls** you **out**, they tell you off angrily. [INFORMAL] ❏ *I was used to being bawled out at school for not doing homework... Schultzy wasn't there to bawl him out... Just for my benefit he bawled out a junior clerk.*

V+N+ADV,
V+ADV+N,
V+PRON+ADV

2 If you **bawl** something **out**, you shout or sing it very loudly and rather harshly. ❏ *...hecklers bawling out, 'What about pensions?'... They bawl out the lusty old favourites.*

V+ADV+N,
V+N+ADV,
V+PRON+ADV,
V+ADV+QUOTE

bear /beər/ (bears, bearing, bore, borne)

bear down on

1 If something large **bears down on** or **bears down upon** someone or something, it moves quickly towards them in a threatening way. **Bear down upon** is more formal. ❏ *We struggled to turn the boat as the wave bore down on us.*

V+ADV+PREP

2 To **bear down on** something means to push or press downwards with steady pressure. ❏ *The roof support structure had collapsed and the entire weight was bearing down on the ceiling.*

V+ADV+PREP

bear down upon → See bear down on

bear on If a fact or situation **bears on** or **bears upon** something, it is relevant to it or affects it. [FORMAL] ❏ *Certain facts bearing on the choice of time should be carefully considered... Government was only one of the forces bearing on the lives of the inhabitants... The group would require an analysis of existing activities which bear upon the problems.*

V+PREP

bear out If someone or something **bears out** what you are saying, they support what you are saying. ❏ *She provided a strong counter-argument, with some witnesses to bear her out... The machine did not in fact bear out the claims made for it... Harris's assertion is hardly borne out by the facts.*

V+PRON+ADV,
V+ADV+N,
V+N+ADV

bear up

1 If you **bear up** when experiencing difficulties or problems, you remain cheerful and show courage in spite of them. ❏ *You have to bear up under the strain.*

V+ADV

2 If something **does** not **bear up**, it is not good enough or accurate enough when you examine it carefully. ❏ *The results just don't bear up at all.*

V+ADV

NOTE **Stand up** means almost the same as **bear up**.

bear upon → See bear on

bear with If you ask someone to **bear with** you, you are asking them to be patient. ❏ *If you'll bear with me, Frank, just let me try to explain.*

V+PREP

beat /biːt/ (beats, beating, beaten)

beat back If you **are beaten back**, you are forced to move backwards by someone or something that is stronger than you. ❏ *Firemen battled to save the man but they were beaten back by flames and thick smoke... Soldiers used heavy truncheons to beat the protestors back.*

V+N+ADV,
V+PRON+ADV,
V+ADV+N

beat down

1 When the sun **beats down**, it is very hot and bright. ❏ *The sun was beating down on the fields.*

V+ADV

2 When the rain **beats down**, it rains very hard. ❏ *...torrential rains that beat down on her like hailstones.*

V+ADV

NOTE **Pour down** means almost the same as **beat down**.

3 When you **beat** someone **down**, you force them to accept a lower price for something that they are selling you. ❏ *I beat him down from £500 to £400.*

V+PRON+ADV,
V+ADV+N,
V+N+ADV

NOTE **Knock down** means almost the same as **beat down**.

beat off If you **beat off** someone who is opposing or attacking you, you prevent them from winning or overcoming you. ❏ *...beating off the opposition.*

V+ADV+N,
V+PRON+ADV

beat on If someone **beats on** you, they hit or kick you many times so that you   V+PREP
are badly hurt. [AMERICAN] ❑ *...beating on Lamin... They were dragged and beaten on.*

beat out

1 If you **beat out** sounds on a drum, you make the sounds by hitting the drum.   V+ADV+N,
❑ *The drummers walked among them, beating out a rhythm to match their movements...*   V+N+ADV,
The lookout drummer beat out the news.   V+PRON+ADV

2 If you **beat out** a fire, you stop it burning by hitting it with a blanket, brush, or   V+N+ADV,
other object.   V+ADV+N,
    V+PRON+ADV
NOTE **Extinguish** is a more formal word for **beat out**.

3 If you **beat out** someone in a competition, you defeat them. [AMERICAN] ❑ *Indi-*   V+ADV+N,
anapolis has beat out nearly 100 other cities as the site for the huge United Airlines mainte-   V+N+ADV,
nance center... If we are certain a rival will beat us out, we are wide open to jealousy.   V+PRON+ADV

beat out of If someone **beats** another person **out of** something, they get that   V+N+ADV+PREP,
thing by deceiving the other person or behaving dishonestly. ❑ *If he could beat his un-*   V+PRON+ADV+PREP
cle out of a dollar he'd do it.

★beat up

1 If someone **beats** you **up**, they hit or kick you many times so that you are badly   V+PRON+ADV,
hurt. ❑ *They beat her up in the street... I'd beat up anybody who made a pass at you... He*   V+ADV+N,
told us that he had been beaten up by the police.   V+N+ADV
NOTE **Bash up** means almost the same as **beat up**.

♦ If someone gives you a **beating up**, they hit or kick you many times so that you   N-SING
are badly hurt. ❑ *I can honestly tell you that I've never seen any beating-up or torture.*

2 Something that is **beat-up** or **beaten-up** is old and in bad condition. [INFOR-   ADJECTIVE
MAL] ❑ *...a beat-up old armchair. ...a beaten-up yellow mini.*

3 If you **beat** yourself **up** about something, you feel guilty about it, even though it   V+REFL+ADV
may not be your fault. [AMERICAN] ❑ *I let the fans down with that miss and I'm beating*
myself up for it.

beat up on

1 If someone **beats up on** you, they hit or kick you many times so that you are   V+ADV+PREP
badly hurt. [AMERICAN] ❑ *You couldn't beat up on a guy who looked that sick... You can't*
beat up on a little kid like that.

2 If someone **beats up on** another person, they threaten them or treat them un-   V+ADV+PREP
kindly. [AMERICAN, INFORMAL] ❑ *She had to beat up on every customer just to get the bills*
paid.

beaver /biːvər/ **(beavers, beavering, beavered)**

beaver away If someone is **beavering away**, they are working very hard at a   V+ADV
job. ❑ *He beavers away, putting up one house after another.*
NOTE **Slog away** means almost the same as **beaver away**.

become /bɪkʌm/ **(becomes, becoming, became)**

✓ The form **become** is used in the present tense and is the past participle of the
verb.

★become of If you wonder what **has become of** someone or something, you   V+PREP
wonder where they are and what has happened to them. If you wonder what will
become of them, you wonder about their future. ❑ *What a terrific cheek he had, that*
chap Boon. I wonder what became of him... Whatever became of that gold watch you used to
have?

bed /bed/ **(beds, bedding, bedded)**

bed down

1 If you **bed** someone **down**, you put them to bed. ❑ *...after the kids were bedded*   V+N+ADV,
down.   V+ADV+N,
    V+PRON+ADV

2 If you **bed down** in a place where you do not normally sleep, you sleep there,   V+ADV
for example because you are travelling or are in an unusual situation. ❑ *Servants no*
longer bedded down in the drawing room.
NOTE **Doss down** is a more informal expression for **bed down**.

3 When soil or another substance **beds down**, it becomes firm, so that further   V+ADV
movement or use will not shake it loose. ❑ *...to allow the loose fibres to bed down.*

NOTE Settle means almost the same as **bed down**.

bed out If you **bed out** young plants, you take them from the pot or seed tray where they have been growing and plant them in the ground. ❑ *Britons bed out plants by the tens of millions every spring.*

V+ADV+N,
V+PRON+ADV,
V+N+ADV

NOTE **Plant out** means almost the same as **bed out**.

beef /biːf/ (beefs, beefing, beefed)

beef up If you **beef** something **up**, you strengthen it or make it more interesting, significant, or important. [INFORMAL] ❑ *They had beefed up the early evening news programme.*

V+ADV+N,
V+N+ADV,
V+PRON+ADV

beg /beg/ (begs, begging, begged)

beg off If someone **begs off**, they say apologetically that they are unable to do something that they had agreed to do. ❑ *They arranged another meeting but I begged off.*

V+ADV,
V+PREP

NOTE **Cry off** means almost the same as **beg off**.

begin /bɪgɪn/ (begins, beginning, began, begun)

begin by → See begin with

★begin with

1 If you **begin with** something, or **begin by** doing it, you deal with it or do it first. ❑ *The broadcast began with close-up film of babies crying... We decided that we would begin with something familiar... We should begin by looking at this question.*

V+PREP

2 If something that is printed or written **begins with** a particular letter, word, or sentence, this letter, word, or sentence is its first part. ❑ *Think of all the names beginning with D.*

V+PREP

belch /beltʃ/ (belches, belching, belched)

belch out If a machine or chimney **belches out** something such as smoke or fire, large amounts of smoke or fire come from it. ❑ *The power-generation plant belched out five tonnes of ash an hour. ...the vast quantities of smoke belching out from the volcano.*

V+ADV+N,
V+PRON+ADV,
V+N+ADV,
V+ADV:
ERGATIVE,
ALSO+from

believe /bɪliːv/ (believes, believing, believed)

★believe in

1 If you **believe in** God or things such as fairies or miracles, you feel sure that they exist. ❑ *I don't believe in ghosts... I believe in reincarnation.*

V+PREP

2 If you **believe in** an idea or policy, you are in favour of it because you think it is right. ❑ *...all those who believe in democracy... Do you believe in public expenditure cuts?... You believed in giving everybody access to all the information.*

V+PREP

NOTE **Support** means almost the same as **believe in**, and **oppose** means the opposite.

3 If you **believe in** someone or in something that they are doing, you have confidence in them and think that they will be successful. ❑ *No one would believe in us or what we were doing.*

V+PREP

NOTE **Have confidence in** means almost the same as **believe in**.

belly /beli/ (bellies, bellying, bellied)

belly out When a large piece of fabric such as the sail of a ship **bellies out**, it becomes rounded because the wind is filling it. ❑ *The child pulled on a rope and the canvas bellied out.*

V+ADV

NOTE **Billow** means almost the same as **belly out**.

belong /bɪlɒŋ, AM -lɔːŋ/ (belongs, belonging, belonged)

★belong to

1 If something **belongs to** someone, it is owned by them or associated with them. ❑ *This land does not belong to the university... He had taken some valuables belonging to another person. ...a myth belonging to some tribe in Western Australia... He recognized the voice as belonging to a senior foreman.*

V+PREP

2 If you say that something **belongs to** a person or thing, you mean that they have it, do it, or control it. ❑ *The last word belonged to the chairwoman... The future belonged to automation.*

V+PREP

3 If someone **belongs to** a club, an organization, or a group, they are a member of

V+PREP

bind up

it. ❑ *The majority of the nation did not belong to trade unions... She belongs to the Labour Party.*

4 If someone or something **belongs to** a particular type or category, they are of that type or in that category. ❑ *...several million bats, belonging to eight different species... Henry and I belong to very different generations.* V+PREP

5 If someone or something **belongs to** a particular place or time, they come from that place or time. ❑ *His wife belongs to the village... They have a strong sense of belonging to a farm... Today's children belong to an age of films.* V+PREP

belt /belt/ (belts, belting, belted)

belt out If you **belt out** a song, you sing or play it very loudly. [INFORMAL] ❑ *She was belting out 'My Way' at the top of her voice.* V+ADV+N, V+PRON+ADV, V+N+ADV

belt up

1 If you tell someone to **belt up**, you tell them in a very impolite way to stop talking. [BRITISH, INFORMAL] V+ADV: ALSO IMPERATIVE

NOTE **Shut up** means almost the same as **belt up**.

2 When you **belt up** while travelling in a car or a plane, you fasten yourself into the seat with a safety belt. V+ADV

bend /bend/ (bends, bending, bent)

★bend down If you **bend down** when you are standing up, you move the top part of your body downwards. ❑ *He asked me to bend down so that he could stand on my shoulders.* V+ADV

★bend over If you **bend over**, you move the top part of your body downwards and forwards. ❑ *She had to bend over sharply because the roof was so low... He watched them bend over the documents to sign them.* V+ADV, V+PREP

bet /bet/ (bets, betting)

☑ The form **bet** is used in the present tense and is the past tense and past participle of the verb.

★bet on

1 If you **bet on** something happening, you expect it to happen. ❑ *Just don't bet on old Arnold gaining a lot of ground with her... That is something which few people would have been prepared to bet on ten years ago.* V+PREP

NOTE **Bank on** and **count on** mean almost the same as **bet on**.

2 If you **bet on** something, you rely on it and expect it to help you. ❑ *Wall Street is betting on Britain's Grand Metropolitan, which has long wanted to expand its U.S.holdings.* V+PREP

NOTE **Bank on** and **count on** mean almost the same as **bet on**.

bid /bɪd/ (bids, bidding)

☑ The form **bid** is used in the present tense and is the past tense and past participle of the verb.

bid up If someone **bids up** the value of something, they try to increase it, for example by offering to buy it at a higher price than usual. ❑ *...the British passion for bidding up the price of each other's houses... They agreed to bid the picture up to 4,500 francs.* V+ADV+N, V+N+ADV, V+PRON+ADV

big /bɪg/ (bigs, bigging, bigged)

big up

1 If you **big** something **up**, you tell people that it is very good. [INFORMAL] ❑ *They organised free workshops in schools with actors aged five and upwards bigging up drug prevention.* V+N+ADV, V+PRON+ADV, V+ADV+N

2 If you **big** it **up**, you enjoy yourself a lot in a social situation, especially in a way that other people notice. [INFORMAL] ❑ *You bigged it up, and were proved wrong in thinking you were hard enough.* V+it+ADV

bind /baɪnd/ (binds, binding, bound)

bind over If someone **is bound over** by a court or a judge, they are given an order and are legally obliged to do as the order says for a particular period of time. ❑ *The magistrate bound him over to keep the peace.* V+PRON+ADV, V+N+ADV

bind up If you **bind up** a wound, you wrap a bandage around it to stop it bleeding or to protect it. [OLD-FASHIONED] ❑ *...bathing it, dressing it, feeding it, binding up its* V+ADV+N, V+PRON+ADV, V+N+ADV wounds... 'Bind that up, nurse' said the doctor when he arrived.

NOTE Bandage up means almost the same as bind up.

bind up with If something **is bound up with** a particular problem, situation, or activity, it is closely connected with the problem, situation, or activity. ❑ *All this was bound up with what was happening in Egypt... Wanting her was bound up with the notion of changing her.*

PASSIVE:
V+ADV+PREP

bitch /bɪtʃ/ (bitches, bitching, bitched)

bitch up If you **bitch** something **up**, you ruin or spoil it. [INFORMAL, RUDE] ❑ *I was bitching up my marriage and your daughter's life... She couldn't bitch up the relationship of two people she liked.*

V+ADV+N,
V+N+ADV,
V+PRON+ADV

bite /baɪt/ (bites, biting, bit, bitten)

bite back

1 If you **bite back** a remark or feeling, you stop yourself from saying it or showing it. ❑ *The word 'Sorry' rises to Morris's lips, but he bites it back... He poured some more soda into his glass, biting back his anger.*

V+PRON+ADV,
V+ADV+N,
V+N+ADV:
NO PASSIVE

NOTE **Suppress** is a more formal word for **bite back**, and **choke back** means almost the same.

2 If a person or a group of people who have been defeated, criticized, or insulted **bite back**, they respond strongly or angrily. ❑ *He is quickly on the attack, biting back at the questioner until the original question is lost.*

V+ADV

bite into If an object **bites into** something firm, it cuts or presses into its surface. ❑ *His collar was biting into his neck.*

V+PREP:
HAS PASSIVE

black /blæk/ (blacks, blacking, blacked)

★black out

1 If you **black out**, you lose consciousness for a short time. ❑ *Marianne told me you blacked out... I was able, before blacking out, to note that he had a gun.*

V+ADV

NOTE **Pass out** means almost the same as **black out**.

♦ A **blackout** is a temporary loss of consciousness or memory. ❑ *I started having these memory lapses, blackouts they're called. ...an element of danger for someone prone to blackouts.*

N-COUNT

2 If a room or a building **is blacked out**, it is made completely dark by someone switching off all the lights and covering the windows. ❑ *The room had been blacked out.*

V+ADV+N,
V+N+ADV,
V+PRON+ADV

♦ A **blackout** is a period of time when the electricity supply to a place stops completely. ❑ *The blackout was caused by the failure of the Northeast power station. ...a fifteen-hour power blackout.*

N-COUNT

NOTE **Power cut** means almost the same as a **blackout**.

♦ The **blackout** is a period of time during a war when buildings and streets are kept as dark as possible at night, so that enemy aircraft cannot see them and bomb them. ❑ *They used to get very cross if I prevented them from getting home before the blackout.*

N-SING

3 If people **black out** a television or radio programme, they prevent it being broadcast, usually in protest against something. ❑ *...blacking out tonight's episode of 'Dallas'.*

V+ADV+N,
V+N+ADV,
V+PRON+ADV

♦ A **blackout** is the prevention of the broadcasting of a radio or television programme. ❑ *The radio blackout would last only an hour.*

N-COUNT

♦ A news **blackout** is the prevention of the reporting of news about a particular event. ❑ *Talks had been held under a news blackout.*

N-COUNT

4 If you **black out** a piece of writing, you colour over it in black so that it cannot be seen. ❑ *U.S. government specialists went through each page, blacking out any information a foreign intelligence expert could use... Some Welsh activists have started blacking out English language road signs.*

V+ADV+N,
V+PRON+ADV,
V+N+ADV

5 If you **black out** a feeling or an emotion, you hide it and refuse to think about it. ❑ *He was not only living in the past, but he blacked out all subsequent reality. ...blacking out the sense of danger.*

V+ADV+N,
V+PRON+ADV

NOTE **Block out** means almost the same as **black out**.

blare /ble͟ər/ (blares, blaring, blared)

blare out When a device such as a radio or record player **is blaring out** noise or music, it produces loud noise or music. You can also say that loud noise or music **blares out**. ❑ *A radio was blaring out the news... Loud hailers blared out 'Keep in line! Keep in line!'... Indian music had been blaring out all evening... The first movement of the Emperor Concerto blared out.*

V+ADV+N, V+ADV+QUOTE, V+ADV: ERGATIVE

blast /blɑːst, blæst/ (blasts, blasting, blasted)

blast away

1 If someone **blasts away** with a gun or if a gun **blasts away**, they fire the gun continuously for a period of time. ❑ *...riding up and down Wall Street, blasting away with a six-shooter in each hand... The big ships blasted away five to six miles offshore.*

V+ADV: ALSO+with

2 When something such as a radio or music band **is blasting away**, it plays music very loudly for a period of time. ❑ *The marching bands were still blasting away.*

V+ADV

NOTE **Blare out** means almost the same as **blast away**.

blast off When a space rocket **blasts off**, it leaves the ground at the start of a journey into space. ❑ *...blasting off to commence its two-year mission.*

V+ADV: USUALLY+A

♦ **Blast-off** is the moment when a rocket leaves the ground and rises into the air. ❑ *A Saturn V blast-off is the most magnificent spectacle.*

N-UNCOUNT

NOTE **Lift-off** means almost the same as **blast-off**.

blast out When something such as a radio or a music band **blasts out** music or noise, or when music or noise **is blasting out**, very loud music or noise is produced. ❑ *The band blasts out its version of the school song. ...four more of the shrieks blasted out.*

V+ADV+N, V+ADV: ERGATIVE

NOTE **Blare out** and **blast away** mean almost the same as **blast out**.

blaze /ble͟ɪz/ (blazes, blazing, blazed)

blaze away

1 If a fire or flame **is blazing away**, it is burning very strongly and brightly. ❑ *It's terribly unhealthy in here with the stoves blazing away like that.*

V+ADV

2 If a light **blazes away**, it shines very brightly. ❑ *The signs outside the motels, hotels, and night clubs blaze away.*

V+ADV

3 If someone **blazes away** with a gun, they fire the gun rapidly and continuously for a period of time. ❑ *The Captain continued to blaze away with his machine gun... The police burst into the building blazing away with their guns... He was amazed to see one man calmly standing up, blazing away with a Sten gun... He came out, blazing away.*

V+ADV: ALSO+with

NOTE **Blast away** means almost the same as **blaze away**.

4 If someone **blazes away**, they talk very loudly for a period of time and do not allow anyone else to interrupt them. [AMERICAN] ❑ *The ante-room was empty, except for Miss Saunders blazing away... This American senator will blaze away the whole evening.*

V+ADV

NOTE **Sound off** means almost the same as **blaze away**.

blaze up If a fire **blazes up**, it suddenly begins to burn strongly and brightly. ❑ *...pouring great jugs of oil over it, to make it blaze up as rapidly as possible when lit.*

V+ADV

bleat /bliːt/ (bleats, bleating, bleated)

bleat on about If you say that someone **is bleating on about** something, you mean that they are talking about it a great deal in a way which makes them sound weak and irritating; used showing disapproval. [BRITISH] ❑ *It's no good bleating on about it, you ought to do something about it.*

V+ADV+PREP

blend /blend/ (blends, blending, blended)

★**blend in** If something **blends in** with its surroundings, it is so similar to the surroundings in appearance that it becomes difficult to see it separately. ❑ *I could not see them – they blended in so well with the landscape... A submarine is often not picked up by radar, as it will often blend in with the ocean floor... Their coloration allows them to blend in.*

V+ADV: ALSO+with

blend into If something **blends into** something in the background, it is so similar to the background in appearance or sound that it is difficult to see or hear it separately. ❑ *The clothes are deliberately chosen to blend into their surroundings... Tree snakes are bright green, but they blend so well into foliage... The words of the driver blending into the roar of the engine.*

V+PREP

NOTE **Merge into** means almost the same as **blend into**.

bliss /blɪs/ **(blisses, blissing, blissed)**

bliss out If something **blisses** you **out**, it makes you extremely happy. [AMERICAN, INFORMAL] ❑ *It was my chosen profession. I was good at it. It blissed me out, as Eddie used to say.*

♦ Someone who is **blissed-out** is extremely happy. [AMERICAN, INFORMAL] ❑ *...blissed-out babies and mothers.*

V+PRON+ADV, V+N+ADV, V+ADV+N

ADJECTIVE

block /blɒk/ **(blocks, blocking, blocked)**

block in

1 If you **block** someone **in**, you park your car so close to their car that they cannot drive away. ❑ *Eric was late because I blocked him in by mistake.*

2 If you **block in** a figure that is drawn only with an outline, you fill it in by covering the area inside the figure with paint, ink, or pencil. ❑ *Let me have another look at it after you've blocked in the buildings.*

NOTE **Shade in** and **colour in** mean almost the same as **block in**.

V+PRON+ADV, V+N+ADV, V+ADV+N
V+ADV+N, V+PRON+ADV, V+N+ADV

block off When you **block off** a road or the entrance to a building, you put some- thing across it and cover it completely so that nothing can pass through it. ❑ *The soldiers blocking off the jail were in position... I got off the bus and the road was blocked off.*

NOTE **Close off** and **seal off** mean almost the same as **block off**, and **obstruct** is a more formal word.

V+ADV+N, V+N+ADV, V+PRON+ADV

★block out

1 Something that **blocks out** light from a place prevents it from entering. ❑ *...satellites that would block out sunlight.*

NOTE **Shut out** means almost the same as **block out**, and **exclude** is a more formal word.

V+ADV+N, V+N+ADV, V+PRON+ADV

2 If something **blocks out** something else, it is in front of it so that you cannot see it. ❑ *The trees almost successfully block out the brick houses... The woman wore her bonnet well forward, blocking out her view of the world on both sides.*

NOTE **Obscure** is a more formal word for **block out**.

V+ADV+N, V+PRON+ADV

3 If someone **blocks out** something such as news or information, they prevent other people from hearing about it. ❑ *Governments can try to block out unwelcome ideas from abroad.*

NOTE **Suppress** is a more formal word for **block out**.

V+ADV+N, V+PRON+ADV

4 If you **block out** a feeling or an idea, you try not to think about it. ❑ *...dissatisfaction blurring, even blocking out that appreciation... They attempt to withdraw from it, to block it out.*

NOTE **Shut out** means almost the same as **block out**, and **suppress** is a more formal word.

V+ADV+N, V+PRON+ADV

block up

1 If you **block up** something, you close it up completely so that nothing can get through it. ❑ *Never block up ventilators... Drains must be left clear, so don't let leaves block them up.*

NOTE **Obstruct** is a more formal word for **block up**.

V+ADV+N, V+PRON+ADV, V+N+ADV

2 If something **blocks up**, it becomes covered or filled and nothing can pass through it. ❑ *The sink keeps blocking up.*

V+ADV

blot /blɒt/ **(blots, blotting, blotted)**

blot out

1 If one thing **blots out** another thing, it hides it or stops it from being seen or heard. ❑ *The resulting dust cloud could have blotted out the sun. ...a dry rustling that blotted out all other sounds... One side of his face was blotted out by a large birthmark.*

V+ADV+N, V+PRON+ADV, V+N+ADV

2 If a particular idea, experience, or feeling that you have **blots out** all other ones, it is the only one that you can think about. ❑ *The money had blotted out everything else... Panic wells up and blots out your real abilities.*

NOTE **Obscure** is a more formal word for **blot out**.

V+ADV+N, V+PRON+ADV

3 If you try to **blot out** a memory or thought, you try not to think of it. ❑ *...casting around for something that will blot out his failures as President... 'The way to blot him out,' I said, 'is not to think about him'.*

NOTE **Block out** means almost the same as **blot out**.

V+ADV+N, V+PRON+ADV, V+N+ADV

For a full explanation of all grammatical labels, see pages xiii-xx

blot up If you **blot up** a small amount of liquid, you remove it by pressing something absorbent onto it. ❑ *She blotted up the juice from the beans with her bread.*
NOTE **Mop up** means almost the same as **blot up**.

V+ADV+N,
V+PRON+ADV,
V+N+ADV

blow /bl<u>ou</u>/ (**blows, blowing, blew, blown**)

☑ **About** is used mainly in British English.

blow ab<u>ou</u>t → See **blow around**

blow ar<u>ou</u>nd If things **blow around** or **blow about** in the wind, or if they **are blown around** or **blown about**, the wind moves them around in different directions. ❑ *She got terribly blown about... My papers had been blown about, and some were missing. ...all that dust blowing around.*

V+N+ADV,
V+PRON+ADV,
V+ADV:
ERGATIVE,
USUALLY PASSIVE

★blow aw<u>ay</u>

1 If something **blows away** or if the wind **blows** it **away**, the wind moves it away from the place where it was. ❑ *It turned into dust and blew away when he turned his back... The wind blew his papers away... Use near an open window to blow away fumes.*

V+ADV,
V+N/PRON+ADV,
V+ADV+N:
ERGATIVE

2 If you **blow** something **away**, you blow on it so that it moves away from the place where it was. ❑ *Shake them in your hand and blow the husks away.*

V+N/PRON+ADV,
V+ADV+N:
NO PASSIVE

3 If a bomb or explosion **blows away** part of your body, it removes it or destroys it. ❑ *...a marine whose face had been blown away.*

V+N+ADV,
V+PRON+ADV,
V+ADV+N

4 If you say that you **are blown away** by something, you mean that you are very impressed by it. [INFORMAL] ❑ *I was blown away by the tone and the quality of the story... She just totally blew me away with her singing.*

V+N+ADV,
V+PRON+ADV:
USUALLY PASSIVE

5 If someone **blows** another person **away**, they kill them by shooting them. [INFORMAL] ❑ *He'd like to get hold of a gun and blow them all away.*

V+N+ADV,
V+PRON+ADV

blow b<u>a</u>ck If something **blows back** or **is blown back**, the wind moves it back in the direction it was coming from. ❑ *The tear-gas that we'd fired was blowing back over our positions... The ashes blew back into Ralph's face from the dying fire... The wind blew all the smoke back down the chimney.*

V+ADV,
V+N+ADV,
V+PRON+ADV,
V+ADV+N:
ERGATIVE,
USUALLY+A

blow d<u>ow</u>n If something **blows down** or **is blown down**, the wind makes it fall to the ground. ❑ *...deckchairs and tents which had blown down in the storm... Several trees had been blown down... The tent was blown down during the gale.*

V+ADV,
V+ADV+N,
V+N+ADV,
V+PRON+ADV:
ERGATIVE

NOTE **Blow over** means almost the same as **blow down**.

★blow off

1 If something **blows off** or **is blown off**, it is removed from a place by the wind. ❑ *Your hat won't blow off... Several roofs were blown off... He was blown off his horse.*

V+ADV/PREP,
V+N+ADV/PREP,
V+PRON+ADV/PREP:
ERGATIVE

2 If a bomb or explosion **blows off** a part of your body, it removes it. ❑ *I didn't want my head blown off... He probably would have blown his hand off if he'd fired it.*

V+N+ADV,
V+PRON+ADV,
V+ADV+N

3 If someone you are having a romantic relationship with **blows** you **off**, they end the relationship. [AMERICAN, INFORMAL] ❑ *I was in love with her and she blew me off.*

V+N+ADV,
V+PRON+ADV

NOTE **Dump** means almost the same as **blow off**.

4 If you **blow** something **off**, you act as if it is not important. [AMERICAN, INFORMAL] ❑ *I've never seen him get down about anything. I've seen him angry, but he sort of blows it off.*

V+N+ADV,
V+PRON+ADV

NOTE **Shrug off** means almost the same as **blow off**.

5 If you **blow off** something that you have planned to do, you do not do it. [AMERICAN, INFORMAL] ❑ *A true diva would have blown off the interview. Instead, Lopez apologises for the delay.*

V+N+ADV,
V+ADV+N,
V+PRON+ADV

NOTE **Cancel** means almost the same as **blow off**.

★blow <u>ou</u>t

1 When a person or the wind **blows out** a flame or fire, they stop it burning. ❑ *Rudolph blew out the candles... The wind almost blew out the flame.*

V+ADV+N,
V+N+ADV,
V+PRON+ADV

NOTE **Extinguish** is a more formal word for **blow out**, and **put out** means almost the same.

2 If a storm **blows** itself **out**, it comes to an end. ❑ *This little dust storm will blow itself out soon enough... Eventually the storm blew itself out.*

V+REFL+ADV

3 A **blow-out** is a meal that is larger than you normally have. [INFORMAL] ❑ *Have a*

N-COUNT

blow-out on your birthday.

NOTE **Binge** means almost the same as **blow-out**.

4 If the wind or an explosion **blows out** windows, or if they **blow out**, they break violently and fall down. ❑ *The blasts blew out windows in about 40 buildings and scattered debris over hundreds of metres.*   V+N/PRON+ADV, V+ADV+N, V+ADV; ERGATIVE

5 If a tyre **blows out**, it bursts. ❑ *Phil was hurt recently in a car accident when a tyre blew out.*   V+ADV

♦ A **blow-out** is a sudden loss of air from a tyre because the tyre has burst. ❑ *My car had a blow-out... A lorry travelling south had a tyre blow-out and crashed through the central reservation.*   N-COUNT

NOTE **Puncture** means almost the same as **blow-out**.

6 If you **blow** someone **out**, you end a relationship with them. [INFORMAL] ❑ *We had a shouting match because she'd blown me out for a new boyfriend whom I didn't like.*   V+N+ADV, V+PRON+ADV

7 If something **blows** you **out**, it impresses you very much. [INFORMAL] ❑ *When I first saw the body of work from which this picture comes, it really blew me out.*   V+N+ADV, V+PRON+ADV

NOTE **Blow away** means almost the same as **blow out**.

8 A **blow-out** is a sudden uncontrolled rush of oil or gas from a well.   N-COUNT

★blow over

1 If something such as an argument or some trouble **blows over**, it comes to an end and is forgotten about. ❑ *The row has blown over... Gary told me that it would blow over and that I shouldn't worry so much.*   V+ADV

2 When a storm **blows over**, it becomes less fierce and ends.   V+ADV

NOTE **Die down** means almost the same as **blow over**.

3 If something **is blown over**, the wind makes it fall to the ground. ❑ *All light-weight structures were blown over.*   V+N+ADV, V+PRON+ADV, V+ADV+N

NOTE **Blow down** means almost the same as **blow over**.

★blow up

1 If you **blow** something **up** or if it **blows up**, it is destroyed by an explosion. ❑ *He was going to blow the place up... They now have enough nuclear weapons to blow themselves up many times over... The battleship Maine has been blown up in Havana Harbour... One of the submarines blew up and sank.*   V+N+ADV, V+REFL+ADV, V+ADV+N, V+PRON+ADV, V+ADV; ERGATIVE

2 If you **blow up**, you lose your temper and become very angry. [INFORMAL] ❑ *It takes considerable character not to blow up.*   V+ADV

NOTE **Explode** is a more formal word for **blow up**.

3 If a difficult or dangerous situation **blows up**, it begins suddenly and unexpectedly. ❑ *Then this murder case blew up, and we had to drop it... Occasionally trouble blew up; challenges were exchanged... The situation blew up in Miller's face when a demonstration turned into a riot.*   V+ADV

4 If you **blow up** something such as a balloon or a tyre, you fill it with air. ❑ *We spent the afternoon blowing up balloons for the party.*   V+ADV+N, V+N+ADV, V+PRON+ADV

NOTE **Inflate** is a more formal word for **blow up**.

5 If you **blow up** a photograph or picture, you print a larger copy of it. ❑ *Once the photos had been blown up, the gun in his hand was clearly visible.*   V+ADV+N, V+PRON+ADV, V+ADV+N

NOTE **Enlarge** is a more formal word for **blow up**.

♦ A **blow-up** is an enlargement of a photograph or picture.   N-COUNT

6 If a storm **blows up**, the weather becomes stormy. ❑ *We were warned of a storm blowing up off the East coast.*   V+ADV

NOTE **Get up** means almost the same as **blow up**, and **die down** means the opposite.

bluff /blʌf/ (bluffs, bluffing, bluffed)

bluff into If you **bluff** someone **into** doing something, you persuade them to do it by telling them something that is not true. ❑ *He wanted to try to bluff them into thinking that he was being stern.*   V+PRON+PREP, V+N+PREP

blunder /blʌndəʳ/ (blunders, blundering, blundered)

☑ **About** is used mainly in British English.

blunder about → See blunder around

blunder around If you blunder around or blunder about, you move about in a clumsy or uncertain way, for example because you cannot see properly. ❑ *I can't blunder about without specs... They screamed and blundered about... She was blundering around the kitchen.*

V+ADV, V+PREP

blunder through If you blunder through an exam or other activity, you manage to finish it although you are not all sure whether what you are doing is right. ❑ *He blundered through the exercises somehow.*

V+PREP, V+ADV

NOTE **Muddle through** means almost the same as **blunder through**.

blurt /blɜːʳt/ **(blurts, blurting, blurted)**

blurt out If you blurt something out, you say it suddenly, without thinking about it. ❑ *The astounded Reichert could only blurt out 'Where have you come from?'... I blurted out that I had got a job... Frank blurted out the news of Sir James's arrival... I hadn't intended to blurt it out.*

V+ADV+QUOTE, V+ADV+REPORT, V+ADV+N, V+PRON+ADV, V+N+ADV

board /bɔːʳd/ **(boards, boarding, boarded)**

board out If you board out someone who is in your care, you send them to stay with someone else for a period of time. [BRITISH] ❑ *Almost half of all children in care were boarded out with foster parents.*

V+N+ADV, V+PRON+ADV, V+ADV+N

board up If you board up a door or window, you fasten boards over it so that it is covered up. ❑ *Shopkeepers were boarding up their windows... Some of the old shops were boarded up.*

V+ADV+N, V+N+ADV, V+PRON+ADV

bob /bɒb/ **(bobs, bobbing, bobbed)**

☑ About is used mainly in British English.

bob about → See bob around

bob around If something bobs around or bobs about, it moves gently up and down, like something floating on water. ❑ *John's head was bobbing about among the fishing boats... They bobbed around like corks.*

V+ADV

bob up

1 If something bobs up, it suddenly floats to the surface after it has been under water. ❑ *Suddenly an object bobbed up from below the surface.*

V+ADV

2 If someone bobs up, they appear or reappear suddenly. ❑ *Here and there at the cliff top soldiers bobbed up.*

V+ADV

NOTE **Pop up** means almost the same as **bob up**.

bog /bɒg/ **(bogs, bogging, bogged)**

★**bog down** If you are bogged down in a task, you are not progressing quickly because you are being too careful or spending too much time on minor problems. ❑ *The outsider is not bogged down by a particular way of doing things... Don't get bogged down in details.*

PASSIVE: V+ADV

bog off If you tell someone to bog off, you are telling them rudely to go away. [BRITISH, INFORMAL]

V+ADV: ALSO IMPERATIVE

boil /bɔɪl/ **(boils, boiling, boiled)**

boil away When a liquid that is being heated boils away, it changes into steam or vapour. ❑ *...causing the engine to overheat and the water to boil away... They cooked it until the water was boiled away.*

V+ADV

NOTE **Evaporate** is a more formal word for **boil away**.

boil down

1 When you boil down a liquid, you boil it until it decreases in amount, because some of it has changed into steam or vapour. ❑ *Boil the sauce down until it is really thick... A panful of spinach boils down to virtually nothing.*

V+N/PRON+ADV, V+ADV+N, V+ADV: ERGATIVE

2 If you boil down an amount of information, you keep only the most important parts and details. ❑ *...sorting through data and boiling it down.*

V+PRON+ADV, V+N+ADV, V+ADV+N

NOTE **Condense** means almost the same as **boil down**, and **pad out** means the opposite.

★**boil down to** If you say that a situation, issue, or question boils down to a particular thing, you mean that this is the most important aspect of it. ❑ *What it all seemed to boil down to was money... The question boils down to one of social priorities.*

V+ADV+PREP

The symbol ★ shows key phrasal verbs

★boil over

1 When a liquid that is being heated **boils over**, it rises and flows over the edge of its container. ❑ *The milk's boiling over... The kettle had boiled over.*   V+ADV

2 If a situation in which people are very angry **boils over**, they become so angry that the situation gets out of control. ❑ *The simmering quarrel between the opposing parties boiled over... Sleepy as he was, his temper promptly boiled over again.*   V+ADV

boil up

1 When you **boil up** a liquid, you heat it until it boils. ❑ *If the insides of aluminium pans discolour, boil up some water in them with a squeezed lemon... I kept a stockpot last winter and boiled it up every day... When the juice is boiled up with sugar it forms jelly.*   V+ADV+N, V+N+ADV, V+PRON+ADV

2 If you say that anger **boils up** in you, you mean that you suddenly feel very angry. ❑ *The feeling of fury boils up in them.*   V+ADV

bolster /ˈbəʊlstər/ (bolsters, bolstering, bolstered)

bolster up To **bolster up** someone or something means to support them or help them. ❑ *...a strike fund to bolster up employees fighting their employers... To bolster up their case, they quoted a speech by Ray Gun.*   V+ADV+N, V+PRON+ADV

bolt /bəʊlt/ (bolts, bolting, bolted)

bolt down If you **bolt down** your food, you eat it very quickly. [INFORMAL] ❑ *...bolting down his lunch and rushing off to the airport.*   V+ADV+N, V+N+ADV, V+PRON+ADV

bomb /bɒm/ (bombs, bombing, bombed)

bomb along If you **bomb along**, you move or travel very quickly. [INFORMAL] ❑ *We went bombing along the motorway at 90 mph.*   V+PREP, V+ADV

bomb out If a building **is bombed out** or if people in a building **are bombed out**, the building is completely destroyed by a bomb. ❑ *Their factories were bombed out. ...people bombed out in the war.*   PASSIVE: V+ADV

bone /bəʊn/ (bones, boning, boned)

bone up on If you **bone up on** a subject, you revise it. [INFORMAL] ❑ *He had been boning up on French history.*   V+ADV+PREP

NOTE **Swot up on** means almost the same as **bone up on**.

book /bʊk/ (books, booking, booked)

★book in

1 When you **book in**, you announce that you have arrived at a hotel and sign your name in a register. [BRITISH] ❑ *It was too late to go shopping, so he booked in at the Ritz Hotel.*   V+ADV

NOTE **Check in** means almost the same as **book in**, and **check out** means the opposite.

2 When you **book** someone **in**, you arrange for them to stay somewhere such as a hotel. You can also say that you **book** someone **in** when you arrange for them to register for something such as a course, event, or appointment. [BRITISH] ❑ *I had booked us in at a hotel in Torquay... The theatre company had already booked them in for another show long before we arrived on the scene... She booked Mr Bashton in to see the doctor on Tuesday.*   V+PRON+ADV, V+N+ADV

★book into

1 When you **book into** a hotel, you inform the receptionist that you have arrived and sign your name in a register. [BRITISH] ❑ *He had booked into the Warsaw Hotel.*   V+PREP

NOTE **Check into** means almost the same as **book into**, and **check out of** means the opposite.

2 When you **book** someone **into** a hotel, you arrange for a room to be reserved for them there. [BRITISH] ❑ *He had been booked into this hotel by the travel agent.*   V+N+PREP, V+PRON+PREP

★book up

1 If you **book up** for something such as a course, event, or other organized activity, you arrange to take part in it. ❑ *'Can I help you?'—'Yes, I want to book up for what you have on the window.'... We've still got time to book up for the French course.*   V+ADV: ALSO+for

2 If something such as a hotel, concert, plane, or course **is booked up**, it has no rooms, seats, or tickets left. ❑ *Ski resorts have been booked up for weeks... Are they fully booked up?... There are no more flights available to East London tonight. They're booked up.*   PASSIVE: V+ADV

boom /buːm/ **(booms, booming, boomed)**

> **boom out** When someone **booms out** something or when their voice **booms out**, they speak in a very loud, deep voice. ❑ *He boomed out: 'Good evening ladies and gentlemen!'... A great voice boomed out the words which announced their arrival.*

V+ADV+QUOTE,
V+ADV+N:
NO PASSIVE

boot /buːt/ **(boots, booting, booted)**

> **boot out** If someone **is booted out** of a job or a place, they are forced to leave it. [INFORMAL] ❑ *No wonder Gertrude booted me out... The member who made that speech was booted out by Conservative Party leaders.*

V+PRON+ADV,
V+N+ADV,
V+ADV+N:
ALSO+of

> NOTE **Kick out** means almost the same as **boot out**, and **expel** is a more formal word.

> **boot up** When you **boot up** a computer, you make it ready to use by putting in the instructions which it needs in order to start working. ❑ *I can boot up from a floppy disk, but that's all... Go over to your PC and boot it up.*

V+ADV+N,
V+N+ADV,
V+PRON+ADV,
V+ADV

border /bɔːʳdəʳ/ **(borders, bordering, bordered)**

★**border on**

> **1** A country that **borders on** another country is next to that country and shares a border with it. ❑ *The Soviet republic of Moldavia borders on Romania.*

V+PREP

> **2** When you say that something **borders on** a particular state or condition, you mean that it is almost in that state or condition. ❑ *I was in a state of excitement bordering on insanity... Their rough treatment of each other bordered on brutality.*

V+PREP

> NOTE **Verge on** means almost the same as **border on**.

bore /bɔːʳ/ **(bores, boring, bored)**

> **bore into** If someone's eyes **bore into** you, they are staring intensely at you. ❑ *Vorster's eyes bored into me. He said 'We are at war. You cannot afford to refuse.'*

V+PREP

boss /bɒs/ **(bosses, bossing, bossed)**

> ☑ **About** is used mainly in British English.

> **boss about** → See boss around

> **boss around** If you say that someone **bosses** you **around** or **bosses** you **about**, you mean that they keep telling you what to do in a way that is irritating. ❑ *He was never one to boss people about... He started bossing people around.*

V+N+ADV,
V+PRON+ADV

> NOTE **Order around** means almost the same as **boss around**.

botch /bɒtʃ/ **(botches, botching, botched)**

> **botch up** If you **botch up** a piece of work, you do it very badly or clumsily. [INFORMAL] ❑ *He really botched up the last job he did for us.*

V+ADV+N,
V+PRON+ADV,
V+N+ADV

> ♦ If you make a **botch-up** of something that you are doing, you do it very badly or clumsily [INFORMAL] ❑ *Tourists were victims of a computer botch-up.*

N-COUNT

bottle /bɒtəl/ **(bottles, bottling, bottled)**

> **bottle out** If you **bottle out** just before doing something difficult or frightening, you lose your courage at the last moment, and do not do it. [BRITISH, INFORMAL] ❑ *She'll bottle out when she sees the other competitors.*

V+ADV:
ALSO+of

> NOTE **Chicken out** means almost the same as **bottle out**.

bottle up

> **1** If you **bottle up** a strong feeling, you deliberately do not express it for a long time, although you find this very difficult. ❑ *All the rage that had been bottled up in him for so long flooded out in a torrent of abuse.*

V+ADV+N,
V+PRON+ADV,
V+N+ADV

> **2** If you **bottle up** a liquid, you transfer it from a large container into several smaller bottles. ❑ *Bottle up that Benylin and put it on the shelves... She's in the cellar, bottling the home-made wine up... All the ginger beer was bottled up and ready for the party.*

V+ADV+N,
V+N+ADV,
V+PRON+ADV

bottom /bɒtəm/ **(bottoms, bottoming, bottomed)**

> **bottom out** When something that was getting worse or decreasing **bottoms out**, it stops doing so and remains steady. ❑ *Even if the recession has bottomed out, it will not help the unemployed... Death rates have not bottomed out by any means. ...bottoming out of the downward spiral.*

V+ADV

> NOTE **Level out** means almost the same as **bottom out**.

bounce /baʊns/ **(bounces, bouncing, bounced)**

★**bounce back** If you **bounce back** after a disappointing or unpleasant experi-

V+ADV

ence, you return quickly to your normal activities or to your previous level of enthusiasm or success. ❑ *You'll bounce back, don't worry... My bet is he'll bounce right back.*

NOTE **Recover** is a more general word for **bounce back**.

bow /baʊ/ (bows, bowing, bowed)

bow down

1 If you **bow down**, you bow very low in order to show great respect. ❑ *The servants were commanded to bow down.*

V+ADV:
ALSO+to

2 If you refuse to **bow down** to another person, you refuse to show them respect or to behave in a way which you think would make you seem weaker or less important than them. ❑ *We should not have to bow down to anyone.*

V+ADV:
USUALLY+to

NOTE **Kow-tow** means almost the same as **bow down**.

3 If you **are bowed down** by something, you are made unhappy and anxious by it, and lose hope. ❑ *I am bowed down by my sins.*

PASSIVE:
V+ADV

bow out If you **bow out** of something, you stop doing it or taking part in it, often in order to allow someone else to take your place. ❑ *We may do one more performance before we bow out.*

V+ADV:
ALSO+of

NOTE **Step down** means almost the same as **bow out**.

bow to If you **bow to** someone's wishes, or **bow to** pressure from someone, you change your plans and do what they want you to do. ❑ *They are inclined to bow to all her wishes... The Minister seems to be bowing to pressure from industry to ignore the recommendations.*

V+PREP

NOTE **Yield to** means almost the same as **bow to**.

bowl /boʊl/ (bowls, bowling, bowled)

bowl out To **bowl out** a team in cricket means to get all their players out and end their innings. ❑ *We were bowled out for 220 runs.*

V+N+ADV,
V+PRON+ADV,
V+ADV+N

NOTE **Dismiss** is a more formal word for **bowl out**.

bowl over

1 If you **bowl** someone **over**, you knock them down by colliding with them when you are moving very quickly. ❑ *They leapt aside to avoid being bowled over by three boys.*

V+N+ADV,
V+PRON+ADV,
V+ADV+N

NOTE **Knock over** means almost the same as **bowl over**.

2 If you **are bowled over** by someone or something, you are very impressed or deeply affected by them because they are so surprising, different, or exciting. ❑ *I was bowled over by the beauty of Malawi... The sight of her just bowled him over.*

V+N+ADV,
V+PRON+ADV

NOTE **Overwhelm** is a more formal word for **bowl over**.

box /bɒks/ (boxes, boxing, boxed)

box in

1 If you **are boxed in** somewhere, you are unable to move because you are surrounded by people, by parked cars, or by other obstructions. ❑ *Unless you go ahead early on in the race there's a danger you'll get boxed in... Some fool parked his car too close to mine and boxed me in.*

V+N+ADV,
V+PRON+ADV,
V+ADV+N

NOTE **Hem in** means almost the same as **box in**.

2 If something **boxes** you **in**, it puts you in a situation where you have very little choice about what you can do. ❑ *Part of winning a mandate is having clear goals and not boxing yourself in... We are not trying to box anybody in, we are trying to find a satisfactory way forward.*

V+PRON+ADV,
V+N+ADV,
V+REFL+ADV

♦ Someone who is **boxed in** has very little choice about what they can do. ❑ *The Chancellor is boxed in by inflation targets and sterling.*

ADJECTIVE

box off To **box off** an area means to make a small enclosed area within a larger area by building walls around it. ❑ *You could box off the area under the stairs to make a cupboard.*

V+N+ADV,
V+PRON+ADV,
V+ADV+N

box up If you **box** something **up**, you put it into boxes. ❑ *...boxing up medical supplies... I boxed all those books up, so I think it's your turn to do something now.*

V+ADV+N,
V+N+ADV,
V+PRON+ADV

branch /brɑːntʃ, bræntʃ/ (branches, branching, branched)

branch off

1 A road or path that **branches off** from another, larger one starts from it and goes in a slightly different direction. ❑ *The road to Oxford branches off here... A dirt path branched off the main road.*

V+ADV,
V+PREP

2 If you **branch off** when you are speaking, you start talking about something slightly different. ❑ *Do you not think then, to branch off that subject a little, that their up-bringing is important too?*

V+ADV,
V+PREP

branch <u>out</u> If you **branch out**, you do something different from your normal activities or work, especially something unusual or risky. ❑ *I can't think why we didn't move years ago when we felt the urge to branch out... She decided to branch out alone and launch a concerted campaign.*

V+ADV

brave /breɪv/ **(braves, braving, braved)**

brave <u>out</u> If you **brave out** a dangerous or upsetting situation, you face it and deal with it in a brave way. ❑ *We'll just have to brave out the return journey on our own.*

V+ADV+N,
V+N+ADV,
V+PRON+ADV

brazen /breɪzᵊn/ **(brazens, brazening, brazened)**

brazen <u>out</u> If you have done something wrong and you **brazen** it **out**, you behave confidently and show no shame or regret. ❑ *Of course he'll brazen it out; he's got no scruples at all.*

V+*it*+ADV

break /breɪk/ **(breaks, breaking, broke, broken)**

★break aw<u>ay</u>

1 When you **break away** from a group, you stop being part of it, for example because of a disagreement. ❑ *Two United Party senators broke away to form the Federal Party... Another sect had broken away from the long-established Plymouth Brethren.*
NOTE **Split off** means almost the same as **break away**.

V+ADV:
USUALLY+*from*

♦ A **breakaway** group is one that has separated from a larger group. ❑ *How well is Britain's new breakaway party likely to do in the General Election?*

ADJECTIVE

♦ A **breakaway** is the act of breaking away from a group. ❑ *The move towards a final breakaway began on 10 February.*

N-COUNT

2 If you **break away** from someone who is holding you, you move away from them suddenly. ❑ *She made a half-hearted attempt to break away... Florrie broke away and rushed upstairs.*

V+ADV:
ALSO+*from*

3 If a part of something **breaks away**, it separates and moves away. ❑ *Australia had broken away from Antarctica and continued to drift.*

V+ADV:
USUALLY+*from*

4 If you **break away** from a belief or a habit, you reject it. ❑ *...the tendency to break away from tradition.*

V+ADV:
USUALLY+*from*

★break d<u>own</u>

1 When an arrangement, plan, or discussion **breaks down**, it fails because of a problem or disagreement. ❑ *The talks broke down over differences on doctrine... An unhappy marriage which eventually breaks down often results in disturbed children.*
NOTE **Founder** is a formal word for **break down**.

V+ADV

♦ The **breakdown** of an arrangement, plan, or discussion is the failure or collapse of it. ❑ *There was a serious breakdown of communications... Politicians blame the police for the breakdown in community relations.*

N-COUNT

2 When a machine or a vehicle **breaks down**, it stops working. ❑ *The telephone communication system had broken down... Mum's TV has broken down.*
NOTE **Pack up** and **conk out** are more informal expressions for **break down**.

V+ADV

♦ If you have a **breakdown** when you are travelling in a car, the car stops working. ❑ *Spark plugs in bad condition make you very prone to breakdowns... We had a breakdown on the motorway.*

N-COUNT

♦ A **broken-down** vehicle or a machine no longer works because it has something wrong with it. ❑ *...pushing a broken-down car.*

ADJECTIVE

3 To **break down** an idea, a statement, or information means to separate it into smaller parts in order to understand it or deal with it more easily. ❑ *Learn to break down large tasks into manageable units. ...trying to break it down into concepts that they could cope with... With a computer you can break the data down to suit particular requirements.*

V+ADV+N,
V+PRON+ADV,
V+N+ADV

♦ A **breakdown** of a set of figures is a simpler version of it arranged in separate sections. ❑ *Can you give me the breakdown for London?*

N-COUNT

4 When a substance **breaks down** or when something **breaks** it **down**, it changes as a result of a chemical or biological process. ❑ *The residue breaks down before reaching the sewer... Enzymes break down proteins by chemical action.*

V+ADV,
V+ADV+N,
V+N+ADV,
V+PRON+ADV:
ERGATIVE

5 If you **break down** a problem or obstacle, you weaken or remove it so that it no longer prevents you from doing something. ❑ *This would help break down the barriers between young and old. ...women who play the 'little girl role' to break down a man's resistance.* V+ADV+N,
V+N+ADV,
V+PRON+ADV

NOTE **Overcome** means almost the same as **break down**.

♦ The **breakdown** of an idea or a tradition is the ending of it. ❑ *There had been a breakdown of class in England.* N-COUNT

6 If someone **breaks down**, they start crying uncontrollably. ❑ *He was afraid he was going to break down and cry.* V+ADV

7 If someone **breaks down**, they become very depressed and ill because they cannot cope with their problems. ❑ *She broke down completely and had to go into hospital... I was under enormous pressure for about 2 years before I broke down.* V+ADV

NOTE **Crack up** means almost the same as **break down**.

♦ A **breakdown** is an illness involving severe mental depression which needs psychiatric treatment. ❑ *You'll give yourself a nervous breakdown... I shall have another breakdown if I stay in this house.* N-COUNT

8 To **break down** something such as a door or wall means to hit it hard so that it breaks and falls to the ground. ❑ *...breaking down the gates... The water floods their homes or breaks down the walls.* V+ADV+N,
V+N+ADV,
V+PRON+ADV

NOTE **Smash down** means almost the same as **break down**, and **demolish** is a more formal word.

♦ A **broken-down** building is in very bad condition. ❑ *...a narrow street of broken-down shops.* ADJECTIVE

★break in

1 If someone **breaks in**, they get into a building illegally or by force. ❑ *The police broke in and arrested all the brothers... They had broken in through a gardener's gate.* V+ADV

♦ A **break-in** is the act of getting into a building illegally or by force. ❑ *The break-in and robbery had taken them only twenty minutes.* N-COUNT

2 If you **break in** when someone is talking or doing something, you interrupt them. ❑ *'Don't look at me,' Etta broke in brusquely... 'Crow...' began Spear excitedly, but his wife broke in.* V+ADV:
ALSO+QUOTE

NOTE **Butt in** and **cut in** mean almost the same as **break in**.

3 If you **break** someone **in**, you get them used to a new job or situation. ❑ *Chief Brody liked to break in his young men slowly.* V+ADV+N,
V+PRON+ADV,
V+N+ADV

4 When you **break in** a new pair of shoes, you wear them for short periods of time until they become comfortable enough for normal use. ❑ *...good weather recently for breaking in new boots.* V+ADV+N,
V+PRON+ADV

5 If you **break in** a wild or young horse, you train it to be obedient and unafraid of humans. ❑ *...her first chance to break in a pony.* V+ADV+N,
V+PRON+ADV,
V+N+ADV

break in on If you **break in on** a person or a conversation, you interrupt them. ❑ *Sorry to break in on you like this, Dr Marlowe... Could we just break in on that question?* V+ADV+PREP

★break into

1 If someone **breaks into** a room or a building, they enter it illegally or by force. ❑ *He broke into a shop one night and killed the proprietor... Offices were broken into and files removed.* V+PREP:
HAS PASSIVE

2 If you **break into** an action or activity, you suddenly start doing it. ❑ *When Rudolph saw her, he broke into a run... Piggy broke into noisy laughter... The boys broke into applause.* V+PREP

NOTE **Burst into** means almost the same as **break into**.

3 If you **break into** an activity or process that is going on, you interrupt it. ❑ *He became so pensive that she did not like to break into his thought.* V+PREP

NOTE **Disturb** means almost the same as **break into**.

4 If you **break into** a new activity or business, you start becoming involved in it. ❑ *...women wanting to break into the labour market.* V+PREP

NOTE **Get into** and **move into** mean almost the same as **break into**.

5 If you **break into** a sum of money that you have been saving, you start to spend V+PREP it. ❑ *She was so desperate that she broke into her holiday money.*

NOTE **Dip into** means almost the same as **break into**.

6 If you **break into** a container of food or drink, you open it and start to eat or drink the contents. ❑ *Let's break into a bottle of champagne to celebrate.* V+PREP

7 When you **break** something **into** smaller parts, you divide it into smaller parts. ❑ *...breaking words into syllables... You can break each feeding period into several parts.* V+N+PREP, V+PRON+PREP

break in upon If one thing **breaks in upon** another, it affects it suddenly and strongly. [FORMAL] ❑ *The Revolution broke in upon a culture which had petrified.* V+ADV+PREP

★break off

1 If a part of something **breaks off** or if you **break** it **off**, it separates or is removed by force. ❑ *A little bit has broken off... I broke a branch off and stabbed at the ground with it... Garroway broke off another piece of bread.* V+ADV, V+N/PRON+ADV, V+ADV+N: ERGATIVE

2 If you **break off** when speaking, you suddenly stop. ❑ *He broke off, only to resume almost immediately... 'I thought...' he broke off, then smiled. 'Sorry, not my business.'* V+ADV

3 If you **break off** something that you are doing, you stop doing it. ❑ *He would break off the rehearsal. ...breaking off their game reluctantly to say goodbye.* V+ADV+N, V+PRON+ADV

4 If you **break off** a relationship or agreement, you end it. ❑ *Men seem to be more skilled at breaking off relationships than women.* V+ADV+N, V+PRON+ADV, V+N+ADV

NOTE **Terminate** is a more formal word for **break off**.

★break out

1 If something unpleasant **breaks out**, it begins suddenly. ❑ *War broke out in Europe on 4 August... This row broke out on the eve of the Congress... A fire broke out on the third floor.* V+ADV: USUALLY+A

◆ An **outbreak** of something unpleasant is a sudden occurrence of it. ❑ *...a severe outbreak of food poisoning... Outbreaks of looting were reported.* N-COUNT

2 If a noise **breaks out**, it begins suddenly. ❑ *The clamour broke out at once... The smiles broaden, laughter breaks out.* V+ADV

3 If someone **breaks out** of a place where they are a prisoner, they escape from it. ❑ *He broke out one spring night in 1946 and hitched south.* V+ADV: ALSO+from/of

◆ A **break-out** is the act of escaping from a place. ❑ *We debated whether to make our break-out on Christmas Eve.* N-COUNT

4 If you **break out** of a routine, a habit, or a restricting situation, you manage to change it and do something different. ❑ *We've got to break out of this vicious circle... She has managed to break out of the mould and achieve something.* V+ADV: ALSO+of

5 If you **break out** in a rash or a sweat, or if it **breaks out** on your body, it suddenly appears on your skin. ❑ *She broke out in a rash... She felt the sweat break out on her forehead.* V+ADV: USUALLY+A

★break through

1 If you **break through** a barrier, you force your way through it. ❑ *I struggled up the side and broke through the elder bushes... Some of the crowd attempted to break through police cordons... A horse broke through the fence.* V+PREP

2 If you **break through** a problem that prevents you from doing something, you find a way to deal with it or remove it. ❑ *She could not break through such a barrier of indifference... They gradually broke through my reserve.* V+PREP

NOTE **Overcome** is a more formal word for **break through**.

◆ A **breakthrough** is an important development or achievement. ❑ *Scientists are hovering on the brink of a major breakthrough. ...a breakthrough in government-industry relations.* N-COUNT

3 If a quality or aspect of something **breaks through**, it begins to appear or to be noticed. [LITERARY] ❑ *Sometimes the artistic impulses break through in your work. ...a young person, whose spirit is just breaking through.* V+ADV

4 If the sun **breaks through** the clouds, it becomes visible after being hidden by them. ❑ *The pitch will dry up quickly if the sun breaks through.* V+PREP, V+ADV

★break up

1 When something **breaks up** or when you **break** it **up**, it becomes divided into smaller parts. ❑ *The great southern land-mass eventually began to break up... Most birds still have a need to break up their food... Here the paddy land is broken up like a jigsaw puzzle.* V+ADV, V+ADV+N, V+N+ADV, V+PRON+ADV: ERGATIVE

The symbol ★ shows key phrasal verbs

♦ If the **break-up** of a ship, spacecraft, or other vehicle occurs, it suddenly breaks into two or more pieces, usually after a collision. ❏ ...*the dramatic break-up of oil tankers.*
N-COUNT

2 If a group or organization **breaks up**, or if something **breaks** it **up**, the people in it separate from each other. ❏ *His committee broke up into rival groups... There is nothing like sudden wealth for breaking up an ordinary family.*
V+ADV,
V+ADV+N,
V+N+ADV,
V+PRON+ADV:
ERGATIVE

NOTE **Split up** means almost the same as **break up**.

♦ When the **break-up** of a group, organization, or system occurs, it comes to an end. ❏ *We are on the brink of a break-up of the two-party system.*
N-SING

3 If you **break up** with your wife, husband, boyfriend, or girlfriend, your relationship with that person ends. ❏ *Tim and I broke up... Their marriage is breaking up... Had you already broken up with your boyfriend?*
V+ADV,
V+ADV+with:
RECIPROCAL

NOTE **Split up** and **finish** mean almost the same as **break up**.

♦ If the **break-up** of a marriage or a relationship occurs, it comes to an end. ❏ *...all marriage break-ups are traumatic.*
N-COUNT

4 If a gathering of people **breaks up** or if you **break** it **up**, it is brought to an end. ❏ *The long drunken party had just broken up... The crowd broke up in panic... The rest of us were trying to break the skirmish up. ...disruptive tactics of breaking up meetings.*
V+ADV,
V+N/PRON+ADV,
V+ADV+N:
ERGATIVE

5 If an event or activity **breaks up** your day, it helps to make your day less boring, because it is different from what you do the rest of the time. ❏ *Meals and drinks break up the hospital day... These games could be used to break up the monotony.*
V+ADV+N,
V+N+ADV,
V+PRON+ADV

6 If you **break up** something that is all one colour or pattern, you add new colours or patterns to make it more interesting. ❏ *...a modern logo at the top, breaking up what used to be slabs of grey type. ...a portrait which has been broken up into rectangles of different colours.*
V+ADV+N,
V+PRON+ADV,
V+N+ADV

7 When schools or schoolchildren **break up**, the school term ends and the children start their holidays. [BRITISH] ❏ *We're lucky, we break up quite early.*
V+ADV

8 If you say that someone **is breaking up** when you are speaking to them on a mobile telephone, you mean that you can only hear parts of what they are saying because the signal is interrupted. ❏ *The line's gone; I think you're breaking up.*
V+ADV

9 If something **breaks** someone **up**, it causes them to lose control and begin to laugh or cry. ❏ *Kindness breaks me up; it makes me cry.*
V+N+ADV,
V+PRON+ADV

break with

1 If you **break with** a friend, or a group you belong to, you disagree with them and end your association with them. [FORMAL] ❏ *In 1929 he broke with the Liberal Party over Lloyd George's policies.*
V+PREP

2 If you **break with** a custom or tradition, you reject it and do something different. [FORMAL] ❏ *We have broken irretrievably with the past... He broke with precedent by making his maiden speech on a controversial subject.*
V+PREP:
HAS PASSIVE

breathe /briːð/ (breathes, breathing, breathed)

★breathe in When you **breathe in**, you take air into your lungs through your nose or mouth. ❏ *Breathe in slowly... We lifted our heads to breathe in the fresh air... If you use a spray, don't breathe it in.*
V+ADV,
V+ADV+N,
V+PRON+ADV,
V+N+ADV

NOTE **Inhale** is a more formal word for **breathe in**.

★breathe out When you **breathe out**, you make the air in your lungs come out through your nose or mouth. ❏ *She breathed out through parted lips... She breathed it out slowly and spoke reasonably calmly... They breathed out smoke.*
V+ADV,
V+PRON+ADV,
V+N+ADV,
V+ADV+N

NOTE **Exhale** is a more formal word for **breathe out**.

breeze /briːz/ (breezes, breezing, breezed)

breeze in If someone **breezes in**, they enter a place in a carefree and relaxed way. ❏ *She just breezed in, as if nothing had happened.*
V+ADV

breeze out If someone **breezes out**, they leave a place in a carefree and relaxed way. ❏ *She breezed out of the bathroom, whistling loudly.*
V+ADV:
ALSO+of

brew /bruː/ (brews, brewing, brewed)

brew up

1 If you **brew up**, you make a pot of tea. [BRITISH, INFORMAL] ❏ *I'll be brewing up about ten. ...brewing up their morning cuppa.*
V+ADV,
V+ADV+N

2 When a difficult or unpleasant situation **is brewing up**, it starts to develop. ❑ *It was obvious that a big storm was brewing up.*   V+ADV

brick /brɪk/ **(bricks, bricking, bricked)**

brick in If you **brick** something **in**, you build a wall of bricks to enclose it or to fill it. ❑ *They decided to brick the old fireplace in.*   V+N+ADV, V+PRON+ADV

brick off If you **brick off** an area, you build a wall of bricks that separates this area from another. ❑ *The lift was long dead, and the shaft bricked off.*   V+ADV+N, V+N+ADV, V+PRON+ADV

brick up If you **brick up** a hole or space, you build a wall of bricks to enclose it or to fill it. ❑ *To stop burglars you'd have to board or brick the windows up... Two workmen bricked up the window.*   V+N+ADV, V+ADV+N, V+PRON+ADV

brighten /braɪtᵊn/ **(brightens, brightening, brightened)**
★**brighten up**

1 If someone **brightens up**, they suddenly look or feel much happier. ❑ *She seemed to brighten up a bit at this.*   V+ADV

NOTE **Perk up** is a more informal expression for **brighten up**.

2 If you **brighten** a place **up**, you make it more colourful and attractive. ❑ *These flowers will brighten up your garden.*   V+ADV+N, V+N+ADV, V+PRON+ADV

3 Someone or something that **brightens up** a situation makes it more pleasant and enjoyable. ❑ *The music brightened things up a little... She brightened up the rather gloomy masculine atmosphere.*   V+N+ADV, V+PRON+ADV, V+ADV+N

NOTE **Liven up** means almost the same as **brighten up**.

4 If the weather **brightens up**, it becomes clearer and sunnier. ❑ *It should brighten up in the afternoon.*   V+ADV

brim /brɪm/ **(brims, brimming, brimmed)**
brim over

1 When a container or the liquid in it **brims over**, the liquid spills out. ❑ *He splashed wine into Daniel's glass until it brimmed over onto the tablecloth.*   V+ADV

NOTE **Overflow** means almost the same as **brim over**.

2 Someone or something that **brims over** with something else is full of it. ❑ *...parents brimming over with joy and pride... I was brimming over with questions.*   V+ADV: ALSO+with

bring /brɪŋ/ **(brings, bringing, brought)**

★**bring about** To **bring** something **about** means to cause it to happen. ❑ *The Administration helped bring about a peaceful settlement. ...the smog brought about by car exhausts... But why was all this happening? What had brought it about?... Naturally, one wonders what may have taken place to bring the separation about.*   V+ADV+N, V+PRON+ADV, V+N+ADV

★**bring along** If you **bring** someone or something **along**, you bring them with you when you come to a place. ❑ *Bring your friends along... He brought along several examples of his work.*   V+N+ADV, V+ADV+N, V+PRON+ADV

★**bring back**

1 If something **brings back** an event or memory from your past, it makes you think about it. ❑ *Losing a lover can bring back memories of childhood loss... It brings it all back... Seeing the place again would bring all the horrors back to me.*   V+ADV+N, V+PRON+ADV, V+N+ADV

2 When people **bring back** something that existed in an earlier time, they introduce it again. ❑ *He was all for bringing back the cane as a punishment in schools. ...bringing back old crafts.*   V+ADV+N, V+PRON+ADV

NOTE **Revive** is a more formal word for **bring back**.

★**bring down**

1 If people or events **bring down** a government or ruler, they cause them to lose their power. ❑ *A national strike would bring the government down... Unofficial strikes had brought down the regime.*   V+N+ADV, V+ADV+N, V+PRON+ADV

NOTE **Topple** means almost the same as **bring down**.

2 To **bring down** the level of something means to reduce it. ❑ *The promised measures included steps to bring down prices. ...to bring population growth down further.*   V+ADV+N, V+N+ADV, V+PRON+ADV

3 To **bring down** someone or something with a gun means to shoot them so that they fall to the ground. ❑ *A rifleman actually managed to bring down an enemy airplane... He was going to open fire from the ground and bring him down.*   V+ADV+N, V+PRON+ADV, V+N+ADV

4 If someone **brings** a person **down**, they make them fall, or pull them to the   V+ADV+N, ground. ❏ *Clough scored a penalty when Sealy brought down Hodge... He brought the girl down rather heavily with a kind of rugger tackle.*

5 If someone or something **brings** you **down**, they make you feel unhappy, depressed, or disappointed. ❏ *It brings you down with a thump... Whatever he said seemed to bring Sally down.*

NOTE **Get down** means almost the same as **bring down**.

V+N+ADV,
V+PRON+ADV

V+PRON+ADV,
V+N+ADV

bring forth To **bring forth** something means to produce it or cause it to happen. [FORMAL] ❏ *This brought forth a shudder of revulsion... In time, this policy will bring forth new results.*

NOTE **Result in** means almost the same as **bring forth**.

V+ADV+N,
V+PRON+ADV

★bring forward

1 If you **bring forward** a meeting or an event, you arrange for it to be at an earlier time or date than was planned. ❏ *Ask him to bring the meeting forward to eight o'clock... The match would have to be brought forward.*

NOTE **Put back** means the opposite of **bring forward**.

V+ADV+N,
V+N+ADV,
V+PRON+ADV

2 If you **bring forward** an argument or proposal, you state it so that people can consider it and discuss it. ❏ *He brought forward some very cogent arguments... The Government had invited us to bring forward proposals for the expansion of Stansted airport.*

NOTE **Put forward** means almost the same as **bring forward**.

V+ADV+N,
V+N+ADV,
V+PRON+ADV

3 When the total at the bottom of a page or column of figures **is brought forward**, it is written at the top of the next page or column and added to the amounts on that page or in that column. [TECHNICAL] ❏ *...reductions in public expenditure of 200m pounds brought forward.*

NOTE **Carry over** means almost the same as **bring forward**.

PASSIVE:
V+ADV

★bring in

1 When a government or other organization **brings in** a new law, rule, or system, they introduce it. ❏ *We intend to bring in legislation to control their activities... The firm has just brought in a three-shift system.*

V+ADV+N,
V+PRON+ADV,
V+N+ADV

2 Someone or something that **brings in** money makes or earns it. ❏ *Tourism is a big industry, bringing in £7 billion a year.*

V+ADV+N,
V+N+ADV,
V+PRON+ADV

3 If you **bring** someone **in**, you ask them to take part in an activity. ❏ *Why did they wait so long before bringing Patton in to command the corps?... Police had to be brought in to protect him... It would be fatal to bring in an outsider.*

NOTE **Call in** means almost the same as **bring in**.

V+N+ADV,
V+PRON+ADV,
V+ADV+N

4 If you **bring in** a particular point or subject, you include it or mention it. ❏ *Try to bring in the moral points as well... Oh, the English always start bringing in Shakespeare!*

V+ADV+N,
V+N+ADV,
V+PRON+ADV

5 When a jury **bring in** a particular verdict, they officially give it as their verdict. [LEGAL] ❏ *A verdict was brought in of accidental death.*

V+ADV+N

★bring into

1 If you **bring** someone **into** an event or group, you ask them to take part in it or be part of it. ❏ *Jordan has got to be brought into this... He planned to bring Northcliffe into the government.*

V+N+PREP,
V+PRON+PREP

2 If you **bring** a subject **into** a discussion or situation, you talk about it or introduce it in order to arouse people's interest. ❏ *A second major function of election campaigns is to bring issues into the political arena... Advertisers always bring sex into it.*

V+N+PREP,
V+PRON+PREP

bring off If someone **brings off** something difficult, they do it successfully. [INFORMAL] ❏ *The most brilliant manoeuvre was brought off by Japan... The Ghost is the hardest thing to bring off in 'Hamlet'.*

NOTE **Pull off** means almost the same as **bring off**.

V+N+ADV,
V+ADV+N,
V+PRON+ADV

bring on

1 Something that **brings on** an illness or pain causes it to occur. ❏ *It'll bring on his cough again... The journey had already brought on a severe attack of angina... Convulsions are brought on by irritation of the brain.*

V+ADV+N,
V+N+ADV,
V+PRON+ADV

2 To **bring** someone **on** means to improve their ability to do something. ❏ *I want to learn to be a coach so that I can help to bring on young cricketers.*

V+ADV+N,
V+PRON+ADV,
V+N+ADV

3 If you **bring** shame or trouble **on** someone, you cause them to experience it. ❏ *He brought it all on himself... Don't bring shame on the family.*

V+PRON+PREP,
V+N+PREP

bring up

★bring out

1 When a person or company **brings out** a new product, they produce it and sell it. ❑ *I've just brought out a little book on Dostoevski... Colin Bradbury has now brought out a second album.*

V+ADV+N,
V+PRON+ADV,
V+N+ADV

2 Something that **brings out** a particular kind of behaviour or feeling in someone causes them to reveal it although they do not normally have it or show it. ❑ *These dreadful circumstances bring out the worst in absolutely everybody... He brings out the animal in me.*

V+ADV+N:
USUALLY+*in*

3 If an actor or musician **brings out** a particular quality or feature in a work that they are performing, they make people aware of that quality or feature. ❑ *The effect is to bring out all sorts of things in the poetry... In both works, Giulini brings out a sort of serenity.*

V+ADV+N

4 To **bring** someone **out** means to encourage them to be less shy or quiet. ❑ *He talks to them and brings them out... It's really brought him out, and it's done him the world of good.*

V+PRON+ADV,
V+N+ADV

5 If someone **brings out** some words, they say them with difficulty or with an effort. ❑ *They even brought out a few English words... 'It's so typical,' Etta at last brought out.*

V+ADV+N,
V+ADV+QUOTE

bring out in If something **brings** you **out in** a rash or in spots, it causes you to have them on your skin. ❑ *...if some food or other disagrees with them and brings them out in a rash... The cold was bringing her out in goose-pimples.*

V+PRON+ADV+PREP,
V+N+ADV+PREP

★bring over If you **bring** someone or something **over**, you take them with you from one place, house, or country to another. ❑ *...a big white china mug which she brought over to us very carefully... I brought over a nut cake. ...aircraft bringing over US military personnel.*

V+ADV+N,
V+PRON+ADV,
V+N+ADV

bring round

1 If someone is unconscious and you **bring** them **round**, you make them conscious again. ❑ *Nobody was making any attempt to bring her round.*

V+PRON+ADV,
V+N+ADV

NOTE **Bring to** means almost the same as **bring round**.

2 If someone disagrees with you and you **bring** them **round**, you cause them to change their opinion and agree with you. ❑ *We suggested a fox hunt; nothing was so sure to bring Alethea round... We tried to bring him round to our point of view. ...lessons to do with bringing people round.*

V+PRON+ADV,
V+N+ADV:
USUALLY+*to*

NOTE **Win over** means almost the same as **bring round**.

bring to If you **bring** someone **to**, you revive them and make them conscious again after they have been unconscious. ❑ *She was eventually brought to after several minutes of unconsciousness.*

V+N+ADV,
V+PRON+ADV

NOTE **Bring round** means almost the same as **bring to**.

bring together If you **bring together** people who have never met, you introduce them to each other. If you **bring together** people who have quarrelled or parted, you cause them to live or work together again. ❑ *It's also brought together artists from diverse parts of the country... This was only just sufficient to bring them together again.*

V+ADV+N,
V+PRON+ADV,
V+N+ADV

★bring up

1 When you **bring up** a child, you look after it until it is grown up and you try to give it particular beliefs and attitudes. ❑ *I brought up two children alone... Tony was brought up strictly.*

V+ADV+N,
V+N+ADV,
V+PRON+ADV

NOTE **Raise** means almost the same as **bring up**.

♦ Your **upbringing** is the way your parents treat you and the things that they teach you to care about and believe in. ❑ *Tony never rebelled against his upbringing. ...a strict upbringing.*

N-SING

2 When you **bring up** a particular subject, you mention it or introduce it into a discussion or conversation. ❑ *I advised her to bring the matter up at the next meeting... I am sorry to bring up the subject of politics yet again.*

V+N+ADV,
V+ADV+N,
V+PRON+ADV

NOTE **Raise** means almost the same as **bring up**.

3 When you **bring up** food, you vomit. [INFORMAL] ❑ *That child is bringing up his breakfast!... I had some toast, but brought it up again soon after.*

V+ADV+N,
V+PRON+ADV,
V+N+ADV:
NO PASSIVE

NOTE **Throw up** is a more informal expression for **bring up**.

4 If someone **brings up** wind, air is forced up from their stomach through their mouth. ❑ *It's hard for the baby to bring up wind.*

V+ADV+N,
V+N/PRON+ADV:
NO PASSIVE

bring up on

1 If you **are brought up on** something, you have or experience a lot of it when you are a child. ❑ *My wife was brought up on junk foods... My brother John was a trumpet player and brought me up on trad jazz.*
V+N+ADV+PREP,
V+PRON+ADV+PREP:
HAS PASSIVE

2 If you **bring** a child **up on** a certain amount of money, you only have that amount of money to feed, clothe, and care for them. ❑ *We were poor and Mom had to bring us up on nothing.*
V+N+ADV+PREP,
V+PRON+ADV+PREP:
HAS PASSIVE

3 If you **bring** something **up on** a computer screen, you make it appear there. ❑ *When a customer comes in we can bring their account up on screen and deal with any queries.*
V+N+ADV+PREP,
V+PRON+ADV+PREP:
HAS PASSIVE

bristle /brɪsəl/ (bristles, bristling, bristled)
bristle with

1 Something that **bristles with** sharp, spiky things has a large number of them sticking out of it. ❑ *...a creature with a long nose, bristling with whiskers. ...five command ships bristling with radar and radio antennae.*
V+PREP

2 When a place or situation **bristles with** things, it seems to be full of them. ❑ *The hotel was bristling with policemen at every entrance... The porcelain and pottery section fairly bristled with exciting things.*
V+PREP

3 If you **bristle with** an emotion, you feel uncomfortable because of it and show this in your expression or behaviour. ❑ *He bristled with a kind of subdued panic... She smiled and bristled with embarrassment.*
V+PREP

broaden /brɔːdən/ (broadens, broadening, broadened)
broaden out

1 When a road or river **broadens out**, it becomes wider. ❑ *Aldgate High Street broadens out east to Whitechapel High Street.*
V+ADV

2 When something **broadens out** or when you **broaden** it **out**, it includes a larger number of things or people, or becomes more general. ❑ *The definition of antiques broadens out until it becomes things your grandmother owned... We were broadening out these struggles to attack the capitalists.*
V+ADV,
V+ADV+N,
V+PRON+ADV,
V+N+ADV:
ERGATIVE

brood /bruːd/ (broods, brooding, brooded)

brood on If you **brood on** or **brood upon** something, you think about it seriously for a period of time. **Brood upon** is more formal. ❑ *He brooded on this for a while, and then spoke. ...brooding on the events of the past. ...brooding upon the antiquity of the church.*
V+PREP

NOTE **Dwell on** means almost the same as **brood on**.

brood over If you **brood over** something unpleasant or difficult, you think about it a lot, seriously, and often unhappily. ❑ *The more you sit and brood over your problems, the bigger they get. ...questions to brood over.*
V+PREP

brood upon → See **brood on**

brown /braʊn/ (browns, browning, browned)

brown off If you **are browned off** with something, you no longer feel any enthusiasm for it, and may even be annoyed about it. [BRITISH, INFORMAL, OLD-FASHIONED] ❑ *He was a bit browned off with the job.*
V+PRON+ADV,
V+N+ADV:
USUALLY PASSIVE

brush /brʌʃ/ (brushes, brushing, brushed)

brush aside If you **brush aside** a remark or some information, you refuse to take any notice of it because it seems unimportant. ❑ *Miss Crabbe continued, brushing aside this interruption... She brushed his protests aside, politely.*
V+ADV+N,
V+N+ADV,
V+PRON+ADV

NOTE **Ignore** and **dismiss** mean almost the same as **brush aside**.

brush away If you **brush** an idea or thought **away**, you ignore it because you do not want to think about it. ❑ *She hurriedly brushed the thought away.*
V+N+ADV,
V+PRON+ADV,
V+ADV+N

NOTE **Dismiss** is a more formal word for **brush away**.

brush by If you **brush by** someone, you walk quickly past them, almost touching them and without stopping, usually in order to avoid talking to them. ❑ *I brushed by him, opened the door and stopped.*
V+PREP

brush down If you **brush down** something you are wearing, or if you **brush** yourself **down**, you remove dirt from your clothes with quick, light strokes of your hands. ❏ *She crawled out and brushed down her skirt... He was brushing himself down.*

V+ADV+N,
V+REFL+ADV,
V+N+ADV,
V+PRON+ADV

brush off

1 If you **brush** someone **off**, you avoid them or avoid speaking to them, because you want to end your relationship with them. ❏ *...buying her an expensive present, and then brushing her off in the nicest way possible... By brushing me off like this, she had probably done me a favour.*

V+PRON+ADV,
V+N+ADV

♦ If you give someone the **brushoff**, you brush them off. [INFORMAL] ❏ *She gave me the brushoff once too often.*

N-SING

2 If you **brush** someone **off** when they are talking to you, you refuse to listen to them. ❏ *He was not the sort of reporter to be brushed off like that.*

V+N+ADV,
V+PRON+ADV,
V+ADV+N

NOTE **Rebuff** is a more formal word for **brush off.**

3 If you **brush off** a remark or some information, you refuse to consider or discuss it because you think it is not important. ❏ *President Carter brushed the story off at a press conference.*

V+N+ADV,
V+PRON+ADV,
V+ADV+N

NOTE **Brush aside** means almost the same as **brush off,** and **dismiss** is a more formal word.

brush off on If a quality or characteristic **brushes off on** you, it influences the way that you behave. ❏ *...in the hope of having some of their poise brush off on them... Something he called 'basic emotions' should inevitably brush off on him.*

V+ADV+PREP

brush out If you **brush out** your hair, or if you **brush out** the tangles or knots, you brush your hair very thoroughly to get rid of the tangles. ❏ *She was brushing out my tangled hair with sharp brush strokes. ...brushing it out, washing it, drying it.*

V+ADV+N,
V+PRON+ADV,
V+N+ADV

brush past If you **brush past** someone or something, you walk quickly past them, often nearly touching them. ❏ *She laughed, and brushed past me out of the room... A marine brushed past us.*

V+PREP

brush up If you **brush up** a subject you know but have not used for a while, you revise or improve your knowledge of it. ❏ *I would like to brush up my zoology. ...helped them to brush up their French.*

V+ADV+N,
V+PRON+ADV,
V+N+ADV:
NO PASSIVE

brush up on If you **brush up on** something, you improve it, or revise your knowledge of it. ❏ *He was in New York, brushing up on his image as an expert in foreign affairs.*

V+ADV+PREP

bubble /bʌbəl/ **(bubbles, bubbling, bubbled)**

bubble over with If you **are bubbling over with** feelings or ideas, you are very excited and show it in your behaviour. ❏ *He was bubbling over with excitement... Mrs Finch was most enthusiastic and bubbled over with suggestions.*

V+ADV+PREP

bubble under If something **is bubbling under**, it is continuing, but in quiet way that not many people notice. ❏ *The confrontation has been bubbling under for nearly a year... Having bubbled under for years, jungle music is about to go mainstream.*

V+ADV

bubble up If a liquid **bubbles up**, it rises up in the form of bubbles. ❏ *Champagne bubbled up over the edge of the glass. ...thermal springs, bubbling up from the core of the earth.*

V+ADV

buck /bʌk/ **(bucks, bucking, bucked)**

buck for If you **are bucking for** something, you are working very hard to get it. [AMERICAN] ❏ *She is bucking for a promotion.*

V+PREP

buck up

1 If you **buck up** a person or their spirits, you make them feel more cheerful. [BRITISH, INFORMAL] ❏ *J.B.Priestley bucked us all up in the war... I need something to buck my spirits up today. ...as hopeless as the attempt to buck up Mrs. Halverston.*

V+PRON+ADV,
V+N+ADV,
V+ADV+N

2 If you **buck up**, you become more cheerful. [BRITISH, INFORMAL] ❏ *She bucked up a bit once she started going out with Phillip... Come on, Charlie, buck up! It's not the end of the world, is it?*

V+ADV:
ALSO IMPERATIVE

3 If you tell someone to **buck up** or to **buck up** their ideas, you are telling them to start behaving in a more positive and efficient manner. [INFORMAL] ❏ *People are saying if we don't buck up we'll be in trouble... Buck up your ideas or you'll get more of the*

V+ADV,
V+ADV+N,
V+N+ADV,
V+PRON+ADV:
ALSO IMPERATIVE

same treatment.

NOTE **Pull one's socks up** means almost the same as **buck up**.

4 You say **'buck up'** to someone when you want them to hurry up. [INFORMAL, OLD-FASHIONED] ❑ *Buck up, we haven't got all day!*   IMPERATIVE, V+ADV

bucket /bʌkɪt/ (buckets, bucketing, bucketed)

bucket down If rain **buckets down**, it falls very heavily. [BRITISH, INFORMAL] ❑ *It really started bucketing down this afternoon.*   V+ADV

NOTE **Pelt down** means almost the same as **bucket down**.

buckle /bʌkəl/ (buckles, buckling, buckled)

buckle down If you **buckle down** to something, you start working seriously at it. ❑ *I'm going to buckle down to the training course... We buckled down and got on with our work.*   V+ADV: ALSO+to

NOTE **Knuckle down** means almost the same as **buckle down**.

buckle in If you **buckle** someone **in**, you fasten them into a seat with a buckle. ❑ *You need a strap to buckle the baby in... Help me buckle him in.*   V+N/PRON+ADV, V+ADV+N, V+REFL+ADV

buckle into If you **buckle** someone **into** a seat, you fasten them there with a buckle. ❑ *She was buckling her son into his harness... He was buckling himself into the seat of the plane.*   V+N+PREP, V+REFL+PREP, V+PRON+PREP

NOTE **Strap into** means almost the same as **buckle into**.

buckle on If you **buckle** something **on**, you attach it by means of buckles. ❑ *He buckled his stylish belt on... He buckled on his revolver.*   V+N+ADV, V+PRON+ADV, V+ADV+N

NOTE **Put on** means almost the same as **buckle on**.

buckle under If you **buckle under** to a person or situation, you do what they require you to do, even though you do not want to. ❑ *...their unwillingness to buckle under blindly to authority... No, damn it! She wouldn't buckle under to the verdict of Wilbur Birdsall.*   V+ADV: ALSO+to

buckle up When you **buckle up** in a car or a plane, you fasten your seat belt. [INFORMAL] ❑ *A sign just ahead of me said, Buckle Up. It's the Law.*   V+ADV

budge /bʌdʒ/ (budges, budging, budged)

budge up If you **budge up**, you move along a seat in order to make space for someone else to sit down. [INFORMAL] ❑ *Budge up, will you.*   V+ADV: ALSO IMPERATIVE

budget /bʌdʒɪt/ (budgets, budgeting, budgeted)

budget for If you **budget for** something, you take account of it in your calculations. ❑ *The Chancellor budgeted for an unemployment rate of 8.5 per cent... These expenses can all be budgeted for.*   V+PREP: HAS PASSIVE

bug /bʌg/ (bugs, bugging, bugged)

bug off If you tell someone to **bug off**, you are telling them to go away [AMERICAN, INFORMAL] ❑ *'Bug off, grandpa,' the boy said, as the light turned green.*   IMPERATIVE, V+ADV

bug out

1 If someone or something **bugs** you **out**, they annoy you. [INFORMAL] ❑ *Three people think the song is about them - that's really bugged me out.*   V+N+ADV, V+PRON+ADV

2 If someone **bugs out** of a place, they leave it quickly. [AMERICAN, INFORMAL] ❑ *It appears we're going to bug out of here and not leave anything here.*   V+ADV: ALSO+of

♦ A **bug-out** is when someone leaves a place quickly. [AMERICAN, INFORMAL] ❑ *The purpose of the demonstration was to force a unilateral bug-out of American troops.*   N-SING

3 If someone's eyes **bug out**, they suddenly open very wide, for example because the person is surprised, hurt, or interested. [INFORMAL] ❑ *The trucker's gray eyes bugged out and he staggered backward.*   V+ADV

bugger /bʌgər/ (buggers, buggering, buggered)

☑ **Bugger** is a rude, offensive word used in spoken British English.

bugger about

1 If you **bugger about** or **bugger around**, you waste time doing unnecessary things. ❑ *What the hell do you mean by buggering about like this?*   V+ADV

2 If you **bugger** someone **about** or **bugger** them **around**, you treat them badly by not being honest with them, or by continually changing plans which affect them.   V+PRON+ADV, V+N+ADV

❏ *Those Nationalists have been buggering you around for years.*

NOTE Mess around means almost the same as **bugger about**.

bugger around → See **bugger about**

bugger off

1 If someone **buggers off**, they go away quickly or suddenly. ❏ *His wife just bug-gered off.* · V+ADV

2 If you say '**bugger off**' to someone, you are telling them rudely to go away. ❏ *Oh, bugger off and leave me in peace.* · IMPERATIVE, V+ADV

bugger up If you **bugger** something **up**, you ruin it or spoil it. ❏ *If you bugger things up at this stage, I'll kill you.* · V+N+ADV, V+PRON+ADV, V+ADV+N

build /bɪld/ (builds, building, built)

★build in

1 If you **build in** an idea or some information, you include it as part of a larger plan. ❏ *This will enable the designers to build in a further piece of information. ...the advan-tages of not having all the traditional prejudices built in.* · V+ADV+N, V+PRON+ADV

NOTE **Incorporate** is a formal word for **build in**.

♦ A quality that is **inbuilt** in a person or thing is one that they have from the time they were born or produced. ❏ *The child has got an inbuilt feeling of inferiority... This kind of thinking has inbuilt limitations.* · ADJECTIVE

2 If furniture **is built in**, it is made in such a way that it is in the wall, or is part of it. ❏ *All the kitchen cupboards have been built in, of course.* · V+ADV+N, V+N+ADV, V+PRON+ADV

♦ **Built-in** furniture is made in such a way that it is part of a wall and cannot be moved around. ❏ *...a built-in wardrobe.* · ADJECTIVE

NOTE **Fitted** means almost the same as **built-in**.

♦ **Built-in** devices or features are included in something as an essential part of it. ❏ *...missiles equipped with built-in homing devices.* · ADJECTIVE

build into

1 If something **is built into** a wall or space, it is made to be part of it or to fit in to it. ❏ *There was a cupboard built into the whitewashed wall. ...a bar which he had built into a corner of his living room.* · V+N+PREP, V+PRON+PREP

2 If you **build** something **into** a policy, system, or product, you make it a part of it. ❏ *They tried to build authoritarian principles into the draft manifesto. ...the inequalities built into our system of financing... Existing political groupings could be built into the new structure of colonial rule.* · V+N+PREP, V+PRON+PREP: HAS PASSIVE

★build on

1 If an organization, system, or product **is built on** or **built upon** something, it is developed from that thing. **Build upon** is more formal. ❏ *How could peace be built on a foundation of reckless science and violence? ...an outlook built on illusion rather than real-ity.* · V+N+PREP, V+PRON+PREP

NOTE **Base on** means almost the same as **build on**.

2 If you **build on** or **build upon** the success of something, you take advantage of it to make further progress. **Build upon** is more formal. ❏ *We must try to build on the success of these growth industries. ...building on existing skills and traditions.* · V+PREP: HAS PASSIVE

★build up

1 If something **builds up** or if you **build** it **up**, it gradually increases in amount, size, or intensity. ❏ *Mud builds up in the lake... We helped to build up the wealth of this country... We're trying to build up a collection of herbs and spices.* · V+ADV, V+ADV+N, V+N+ADV, V+PRON+ADV: ERGATIVE

NOTE **Accumulate** is a more formal word for **build up**.

♦ A **build-up** is a gradual increase in something. ❏ *Over the island the build-up of clouds continued. ...a massive build-up of nuclear weapons.* · N-COUNT

♦ **Built-up** shoes are shoes with very thick soles and heels that people wear in order to appear taller than they really are. ❏ *I noticed that he was wearing built-up boots.* · ADJECTIVE

2 If people **build up** an organization, society, or system, they gradually develop it or improve it. ❏ *Japan successfully built up a modern capitalist economy... His organization-al knowledge and personal reputation has built the business up.* · V+ADV+N, V+N+ADV, V+PRON+ADV

3 If you **build up** someone's trust or confidence, you gradually make them more trusting or more confident. ❏ *Being a cop means building up trust with the people on the streets.* · V+ADV+N, V+N+ADV, V+PRON+ADV

The symbol ★ shows key phrasal verbs

4 If you **build up** someone or something, you tell people that they are very special or important. ❑ *I've built up Mr Reston's credentials... He does not need to build me up.*

V+ADV+N,
V+PRON+ADV,
V+N+ADV

♦ A **build-up** is a description of a person or thing in which you tell people that the person or thing is very special or important. ❑ *She was getting a fair amount of publicity build-up.*

N-COUNT,
N-UNCOUNT

5 If you **build** someone **up** after they have been ill, you help them to get better and stronger. ❑ *The patient needs building up... We must build him up before he can go home.*

V+N+ADV,
V+PRON+ADV,
V+ADV+N:
NO PASSIVE

6 When an area near a city or town **is built up**, a lot of houses are built there. ❑ *It has been like this since the area was built up several years ago... The park and riverside are all now built up.*

PASSIVE:
V+ADV

♦ A **built-up** area is a part of a city or town where there are many buildings. ❑ *...the built-up area on the fringes of Kilmarnock.*

ADJECTIVE

build upon → See build on

build up to If you **build up to** something you want to do or say, you try to prepare people for it by starting to do it or introducing the subject gradually. ❑ *Other actions we need to take may be more difficult, and we may have to build up to them gradually... Carl was building up to something.*

V+ADV+PREP

bulk /bʌlk/ **(bulks, bulking, bulked)**

bulk out If someone or something **bulks out** or **bulks up**, they become bigger or heavier. ❑ *He bulked up for the part so he'd look convincing as a prison guard... I was on a weights programme to bulk out.*

V+ADV

bulk up → See bulk out

bum /bʌm/ **(bums, bumming, bummed)**

☑ **About** is used mainly in British English. In American English, **around** is much more common than **round**.

bum about → See bum around

bum around If you **bum around**, **bum about**, or **bum round**, you travel casually for pleasure and with very little money. [INFORMAL] ❑ *I just bummed around northern Europe for a few months.*

V+ADV,
V+PREP

2 If you **bum around**, **bum about**, or **bum round**, you live in a very lazy way, doing very little. [INFORMAL] ❑ *They've just bummed around, all of them... Are you going to bum around all summer?*

V+ADV

bum out If something **bums** you **out**, it makes you feel sad or angry. [AMERICAN, INFORMAL] ❑ *He got a job in LA and broke up with me over the phone, and it totally bummed me out.*

V+N+ADV,
V+PRON+ADV

♦ If you are **bummed-out**, you feel sad or angry. [AMERICAN, INFORMAL] ❑ *He was probably pretty bummed-out by getting fired and all; but he was calm.*

ADJECTIVE

bum round → See bum around

bumble /bʌmbəl/ **(bumbles, bumbling, bumbled)**

☑ **About** is used mainly in British English.

bumble about → See bumble around

bumble around When someone **bumbles around** or **bumbles about**, they behave in a confused, disorganized way, making mistakes and usually not achieving anything. ❑ *...armies of tourists bumbling around... Most of us are novices on the computer. We bumble about on them and have great fun.*

V+ADV

bump /bʌmp/ **(bumps, bumping, bumped)**

★**bump into** If you **bump into** someone you know, you meet them by chance. ❑ *I bumped into Mary an hour ago... I probably won't see him any more unless I bump into him on the street.*

V+PREP

NOTE **Run into** means almost the same as **bump into**.

bump off To **bump** someone **off** means to kill them. [INFORMAL] ❑ *In his imagination, he bumps off his wife half a dozen times.*

V+ADV+N,
V+PRON+ADV,
V+N+ADV

NOTE **Murder** is a more formal word for **bump off**.

bump up To **bump** something **up** means to increase it suddenly by a large amount. [INFORMAL] ❑ *She was going to charge £140, but the extra work bumped up the price to £200... This will bump up the workforce yet again.*

V+ADV+N,
V+PRON+ADV,
V+N+ADV

bump up against If you **bump up against** someone, you meet them and get to know them by chance. ❑ *He rarely bumped up against anyone who approved of what he was doing... You bumped up against some miners in a pub.*

V+ADV+PREP

bunch /bʌntʃ/ (bunches, bunching, bunched)

bunch together → See bunch up

bunch up

1 If you **bunch up** a piece of material, you squash it up to make a tight bundle. ❑ *She was holding her skirts bunched up over one arm... His suit was bunched up over his shoulders.*

V+N+ADV,
V+PRON+ADV,
V+ADV+N

2 If people or things **bunch up** or **bunch together**, or if you **bunch** them **up** or **bunch** them **together**, they move close to each other so that they form a small tight group. ❑ *They were bunching up, almost treading upon each other's heels... People were bunched up at all the exits... If they need to bunch aircraft more closely together to bring in one that is short of fuel, they will do so.*

V+ADV,
V+PRON+ADV,
V+N+ADV

bundle /bʌndəl/ (bundles, bundling, bundled)

bundle off If you **bundle** someone **off** somewhere, you send them there in a hurry. ❑ *My father bundled me off to school. ...making sure she is not bundled off too roughly.*

V+PRON+ADV,
V+N+ADV,
V+ADV+N

NOTE **Pack off** means almost the same as **bundle off**.

bundle up

1 If you **bundle up** a mass of things, you make a bundle by gathering or tying them together. ❑ *My mother bundled up all my comics and threw them out... She bundled up her knitting and put it away... The rest of my things were bundled up in a pillowcase.*

V+ADV+N,
V+PRON+ADV,
V+N+ADV

2 If you **bundle up**, you dress in a lot of warm clothes because the weather is very cold. ❑ *We bundled up warmly against the cold... She bundled them up and walked them down to the railway station... They were bundled up in tweeds and flannels.*

V+ADV,
V+N+ADV,
V+PRON+ADV:
ERGATIVE

NOTE **Wrap up** means almost the same as **bundle up**.

bung /bʌŋ/ (bungs, bunging, bunged)

bung up If you **bung up** a hole, you put something in it so that the hole is filled or blocked. [INFORMAL] ❑ *Don't put tea leaves down the sink, they bung it up.*

V+PRON+ADV,
V+N+ADV,
V+ADV+N

NOTE **Block up** is a more formal expression for **bung up**.

bunk /bʌŋk/ (bunks, bunking, bunked)

bunk off If you **bunk off** from school or work, you leave without permission and do something else. [BRITISH, INFORMAL] ❑ *We thought nothing of bunking off school and travelling 100 miles to find this or that record.*

V+ADV,
V+PREP

NOTE **Play truant** is a more formal expression for **bunk off**.

buoy /bɔɪ, AM buːi/ (buoys, buoying, buoyed)

buoy up

1 If you **buoy** someone **up**, you keep them cheerful in a situation in which they might feel depressed. ❑ *He did his best to buoy her up.*

V+PRON+ADV,
V+N+ADV

2 To **buoy** something **up** means to keep it afloat and stop it from sinking. ❑ *The float needs to be fairly big so that it buoys up the 1/2 oz of lead necessary to sink the bait.*

V+ADV+N,
V+N+ADV,
V+PRON+ADV

3 To **buoy** something **up** also means to support it and help it to survive. ❑ *...newspapers buoyed up with advertising... This may help to buoy up the family's motive for saving.*

V+ADV+N,
V+N+ADV,
V+PRON+ADV

burn /bɜːrn/ (burns, burning, burned/burnt)

burn away If something **burns away**, or if it **is burned away**, it burns or catches fire until it disappears completely. ❑ *...an ashtray, where a cigarette has burned away, while they have been busy... The cardboard was burned away from the metal binding wire... We were trying to burn away the net.*

V+ADV,
V+ADV+N,
V+PRON+ADV,
V+N+ADV:
ERGATIVE

★burn down If a building **burns down** or if someone **burns** it **down**, it is completely destroyed by fire. ❑ *The mansion burned down four years ago. ...peasants burning down the huts of chiefs... He could have burned the place down... His school had been burned down in the riots.*

V+ADV,
V+ADV+N,
V+N+ADV,
V+PRON+ADV:
ERGATIVE

The symbol ★ shows key phrasal verbs

burn off

1 If someone **burns off** energy, they use it. ❑ *This will improve your performance and help you burn off calories.*
`V+ADV+N, V+PRON+ADV`

2 If you **burn** something **off**, you remove it by burning or heating it. ❑ *...burning the flaking paint off beforehand.*
`V+ADV+N, V+N+ADV, V+PRON+ADV`

★burn out

1 If a fire **burns out** or **burns** itself **out**, it stops burning because there is nothing left to burn. ❑ *We let the fire burn out... All the fires had now burned themselves out.*
`V+ADV, V+REFL+ADV`

♦ A **burnt-out** or **burned-out** vehicle or building has been very badly damaged by fire. ❑ *They barricaded the streets with burnt-out cars.*
`ADJECTIVE`

NOTE **Gutted** means almost the same as **burnt-out**.

2 If a piece of machinery **burns out** or if you **burn** it **out**, it stops working because it has been used too much or too roughly. ❑ *If his points or plugs burn out, he's done for... The exhaust valve on my car has burnt out three times in 46,000 miles... He's gonna burn out the pistons for sure.*
`V+ADV, V+ADV+N, V+PRON+ADV, V+N+ADV: ERGATIVE`

3 If you **burn** yourself **out** or **burn out**, you become exhausted or ill by working too hard. [INFORMAL] ❑ *I don't want you to burn yourself out.*
`V+REFL+ADV, V+ADV`

♦ Someone who is **burnt-out** or **burned-out** is unable to do things because they are too tired, weak, or ill. [INFORMAL] ❑ *...an old burnt-out actor... I was burnt-out emotionally.*
`ADJECTIVE`

burn up

1 If something **burns up**, it is completely destroyed by fire or strong heat. ❑ *The satellite had burned up on re-entering the atmosphere... Most of it is burned up or falls as dust.*
`V+ADV: ALSO PASSIVE: V+ADV`

2 If you say that an engine **burns up** fuel, you mean that it uses a lot of fuel.
`V+ADV+N`

3 If you say that something **burns** you **up**, you mean that it makes you feel angry and upset. [INFORMAL] ❑ *His attitude just burns me up... The girls seemed to be burned up about something.*
`V+PRON+ADV, V+N+ADV, V+ADV+N`

burst /bɜːʳst/ (bursts, bursting, burst)

burst in on If you **burst in on** someone, you suddenly and quickly enter the room that they are in. ❑ *He suddenly burst in on me.*
`V+ADV+PREP`

★burst into

1 If you **burst into** tears, laughter, or song, you suddenly begin to cry, laugh, or sing. ❑ *I keep bursting into tears... Uncle Tony burst into song... The delegates burst into loud applause.*
`V+PREP`

2 If something **bursts into** flames, it suddenly starts to burn. ❑ *The newspapers burst into flames.*
`V+PREP`

3 If you say that something **bursts into** a particular situation or state, you mean that it suddenly changes into that situation or state. ❑ *This weekend's fighting is threatening to burst into full-scale war... The engine burst into life.*
`V+PREP`

NOTE **Erupt** means almost the same as **burst into**.

4 When plants **burst into** leaf, blossom, or flower, their leaves or flowers open.
`V+PREP`

★burst out

1 If you **burst out** laughing or crying, you suddenly begin laughing or crying, usually loudly. ❑ *Mrs Oliver felt a sudden desire to burst out crying... To my amazement, he burst out laughing.*
`V+ADV+-ING`

♦ An **outburst** is a sudden and strong expression of emotion, or a sudden period of activity. ❑ *I apologize for my outburst just now. ...degrading outbursts of drunken violence.*
`N-COUNT`

2 You use **burst out** when you are reporting what someone said, to indicate that they said it suddenly and loudly. ❑ *Then he burst out, 'Get into the car, Phil, can't you?'*
`V+ADV+QUOTE`

3 If a situation or problem **bursts out**, it suddenly appears. ❑ *Malaria is bursting out again all over the world... Then war burst out.*
`V+ADV`

NOTE **Break out** means almost the same as **burst out**.

bury /beri/ (buries, burying, buried)

bury away If something **is buried away** somewhere, it is put in a place where it is difficult to find or reach it. ❑ *Buried away inside the paper, in a tiny paragraph, was an account of his visit.*
`PASSIVE: V+ADV`

buy off

bury in If you **bury** yourself or your head **in** something that you are reading, you concentrate hard on it. ❑ *He buried himself deep in the wine list... Their faces were buried in their evening newspapers.*

NOTE **Immerse** is a more formal word for **bury in**.

V+REFL+PREP,
V+N+PREP

bust /bʌst/ (busts, busting, busted)

☑ The form **bust** is used in the present tense and can also be used as the past tense and past participle of the verb.

bust out of If you **bust out of** a place, you escape from it using force. [INFORMAL] ❑ *He bust out of jail.*

V+ADV+PREP

bust up

1 If you **bust up** an event or meeting, you stop it from continuing by causing a disturbance or fight. [INFORMAL] ❑ *They busted up the Miss America competition last November... They could come and bust up the meeting like they did yesterday.*

V+ADV+N,
V+PRON+ADV

NOTE **Break up** is a less informal expression for **bust up**.

2 If you **bust** something **up**, you break it. [INFORMAL] ❑ *They bought a new chair to replace the one they'd busted up.*

V+ADV+N,
V+PRON+ADV,
V+N+ADV

3 If you **bust up** with your boyfriend or girlfriend, you have a quarrel with them and end your relationship. [INFORMAL] ❑ *She's been staying here since she bust up with Toby... They bust up last year.*

V+ADV,
V+ADV+with:
RECIPROCAL

♦ A **bust-up** is a serious quarrel or a fight. [INFORMAL] ❑ *There was a bust-up down at the pub last night.*

N-COUNT

bustle /bʌsəl/ (bustles, bustling, bustled)

☑ About is used mainly in British English.

bustle about → See bustle around

bustle around If you **bustle around** or **bustle about**, you do things or move about in a busy and determined way. ❑ *She bustled about, humming to herself... He bustles about with all sorts of plans to occupy him... She was bustling around preparing a snack... She bustled around the kitchen.*

V+ADV,
V+PREP

butt /bʌt/ (butts, butting, butted)

butt in If you **butt in**, you rudely interrupt a conversation or activity. ❑ *You can't just butt in on someone else's discussion... I was always butting in and saying the wrong thing.*

V+ADV:
ALSO+on

butt out If you say 'Butt out' to someone, you are telling them angrily and rudely to go away or to stop interfering. [AMERICAN, INFORMAL] ❑ *Butt out before I throw you out.*

IMPERATIVE,
V+ADV

butter /bʌtər/ (butters, buttering, buttered)

butter up If you **butter** someone **up**, you praise or try to please them, because you want to ask them a favour. [BRITISH, INFORMAL] ❑ *I'm buttering him up for a pay rise.*

V+PRON+ADV,
V+N+ADV,
V+ADV+N

button /bʌtən/ (buttons, buttoning, buttoned)

button up If you **button up** a shirt, coat, or other piece of clothing, you fasten it by pushing its buttons through buttonholes. ❑ *He began to gather his papers and button up his coat... She put her blouse on and buttoned it up.*

V+ADV+N,
V+PRON+ADV,
V+N+ADV

NOTE **Do up** means almost the same as **button up**.

buy /baɪ/ (buys, buying, bought)

buy in If you **buy in** something such as food, you buy large amounts of it for a future occasion, or for a time when it might not be available. ❑ *We bought in a few loaves of bread.*

V+ADV+N,
V+N+ADV,
V+PRON+ADV

buy into When someone **buys into** a business or organization, they buy part of it, for example in order to gain some control over it. ❑ *He's been trying for years to buy into the printing industry... He was chief executive of a tiny discount clothing chain which he had bought into a year before.*

V+PREP

buy off If you **buy** someone **off**, you pay them money so that they do not act against you. ❑ *The workers were bought off by their employers... They have no money to buy off the police... He thought he could buy them off.*

V+ADV+N,
V+PRON+ADV,
V+N+ADV

buy out

1 If you **buy** someone **out**, you buy their share of a property or business that you previously owned together. ❑ *He sold off the shops to buy out his partner... We bought him out.* — V+N+ADV, V+PRON+ADV, V+ADV+N

♦ A **buyout** occurs when a group of people join together to buy the company that they previously worked for. ❑ *Nobody has talked to us about a management buyout.* — N-COUNT

2 If you **buy** yourself **out** of the armed forces, you pay a sum of money so that you can leave before the end of the period you had agreed to stay for. ❑ *He managed to buy himself out of the navy.* — V+REFL+ADV: ALSO+of

buy over

If you **buy** someone **over**, you win their support by giving them money. ❑ *She was not able to buy him over.* — V+PRON+ADV, V+N+ADV, V+ADV+N

★buy up

If someone **buys up** land or property, they buy large quantities of it, or all that is available. ❑ *They were trying to buy up every acre in sight.* — V+ADV+N, V+PRON+ADV, V+N+ADV

buzz /bʌz/ (buzzes, buzzing, buzzed)

☑ **About** is used mainly in British English. In American English, **around** is much more common than **round**.

buzz about → See buzz around

buzz around

1 If something **buzzes around**, **buzzes round**, or **buzzes about**, it moves along making a buzzing sound. ❑ *...those light planes I had seen buzzing around all day. ...a fly buzzing round her head... There was a wasp buzzing about her ear and she wanted to kill it.* — V+ADV, V+PREP

2 If someone **buzzes around**, **buzzes round**, or **buzzes about**, they move around a place very quickly and busily. ❑ *The rickshaw drivers buzz around... He is always buzzing about the office.* — V+ADV, V+PREP

buzz off

If someone **buzzes off**, they go away. People sometimes say **buzz off** as a rude way of telling someone to go away. [BRITISH, INFORMAL] ❑ *'Now buzz off,' shouted Mrs Coggs... We'll buzz off at midday.* — V+ADV: ALSO IMPERATIVE

buzz round → See buzz around

Cc

call /kɔːl/ (calls, calling, called)

call after If you **call** someone or something **after** a person or thing, you give them the same name as that other person or thing. [BRITISH] ❏ *She was called after Caddy, a character in a William Faulkner novel.*
 `V+PRON+PREP, V+N+PREP`
 [NOTE] **Name after** means almost the same as **call after**.

call away If you **are called away**, you are asked to stop doing something in order to go somewhere else. ❏ *They were called away to another case... He's been called away on business.*
 `V+N+PREP, V+PRON+PREP: USUALLY PASSIVE`

★call back

1 If you **call back**, you contact someone who has contacted you previously, often by telephone, or at the place where you last saw them. ❏ *Pitts called back on Thursday, saying he hadn't been able to make the arrangements... You can call back and collect your shoes tomorrow.*
 `V+ADV`

2 If you **call** someone **back**, you telephone them again in return for a telephone call they have made to you. ❏ *I told him I would call him back when I had some news... I shall make some enquiries and call you back.*
 `V+PRON+ADV, V+N+ADV: NO PASSIVE`
 [NOTE] **Ring back** means almost the same as **call back**.

3 If you **call** someone **back** when they are walking away from you, you ask them to return. ❏ *He moved away as inconspicuously as he could, but Binta called him back, probably to reprimand him... She walked away heavily and slowly, as if waiting to be called back.*
 `V+PRON+ADV, V+N+ADV`

call by If you **call by**, you visit a place for a short time, especially when you are going somewhere else afterwards. ❏ *I'll call by with your tape recorder this afternoon.*
 `V+ADV`

call down on If you **call** curses or vengeance **down on** someone, you pray that something unpleasant will happen to them. [FORMAL] ❏ *She called God's vengeance down on her husband.*
 `V+N+ADV+PREP, V+ADV+N+PREP: NO PASSIVE`

★call for

1 If you **call for** someone or something, you go to the building where they are to collect them. ❏ *I'll call for you about eight... The parcel was kept at the Post Office until someone called for it.*
 `V+PREP: HAS PASSIVE`

2 If you **call for** an action, you demand that it should be done. ❏ *The declaration called for an immediate cease-fire... Democrats are calling for a two-year tax cut... New automatic gates and assurances on safety have been called for.*
 `V+PREP: HAS PASSIVE`

3 If something **calls for** a particular action or quality, it needs it in order to be successful. ❏ *Controlling a class calls for all your skill as a teacher... The script called for the whole story to be shot in darkness... Mountaineering ability was not called for.*
 `V+PREP: HAS PASSIVE`
 [NOTE] **Require** means almost the same as **call for**.

4 You describe a remark or criticism as **uncalled-for** when you think that it should not have been made, because it was unkind or unfair. ❏ *That last remark was uncalled-for. ...an uncalled-for outburst.*
 `ADJECTIVE`

5 If you **call** someone or something **for** a person or thing, you give them the same name as that other person or thing. [AMERICAN] ❏ *They're going to call it the Bentley Mulsanne for the name of that stretch of the track at Le Mans.*
 `V+N+PREP, V+PRON+PREP`
 [NOTE] **Name for** means almost the same as **call for**.

call forth If you **call** something **forth**, you make it exist. [FORMAL] ❏ *He is not capable of calling forth much emotion in his readers... Excitement is hardly likely to be called forth by a series of scales and arpeggios.*
 `V+ADV+N, V+PRON+ADV`
 [NOTE] **Inspire** means almost the same as **call forth**.

★call in

1 If you **call** someone **in**, you ask them to come and help you or do something for you. ❑ *Before you call in the water board, check that the pipes are not frozen... They called me in for questioning... The Army was called in to quell the rioting.*

V+ADV+N,
V+PRON+ADV,
V+N+ADV

NOTE **Send for** means almost the same as **call in**.

2 If you **call in**, you contact someone you know by visiting them, or by telephoning them. ❑ *He hadn't called in to see the Duke after he had left us... He called in to say he was feeling ill.*

V+ADV

3 If someone **calls** something **in**, they ask for it to be returned, for example because it might be dangerous or because it is needed. ❑ *Ford are calling some of their Escorts in to check their brakes... The university called in all library books for stocktaking.*

V+ADV+N,
V+N+ADV,
V+PRON+ADV

NOTE **Recall** is a more formal word for **call in**.

★call off

1 If you **call off** an event or an arrangement that has been planned, you cancel it. ❑ *I can't call off the ceremony now... If you can't behave yourself, we might as well call the whole thing off... Classes will be called off on Thursday and Friday.*

V+ADV+N,
V+N+ADV,
V+PRON+ADV

2 If you **call** a dog or a person **off**, you order them to stop attacking something or someone else. ❑ *He called his dog off when he saw that mine was frightened of it.*

V+N+ADV,
V+PRON+ADV,
V+ADV+N

★call on

1 If you **call on** someone, you pay them a short visit. ❑ *Don't bother to call on me or ring me... Mrs Knight seldom seemed to call on Charlotte... The four of us called on him in his room.*

V+PREP:
HAS PASSIVE

2 If you **call on** someone to do something, you appeal to them to do it. ❑ *The Opposition called on the Prime Minister to stop the arms deal... She was called on to testify.*

V+PREP:
WITH *to*-INF,
HAS PASSIVE

3 If you **call on** or **call upon** something, you use it in order to achieve something. [FORMAL] ❑ *The woman has to call on her willpower. ...calling on the assistance of my parents... You will have plenty of reserves to call upon.*

V+PREP

★call out

1 If you **call** something **out**, you shout it. ❑ *'Don't jump,' she called out... She turned into the yard, calling out to the porter that she'd arrived... Karen called out and told us to be quiet... One boy rushed forward, calling out his father's name.*

V+ADV+QUOTE,
V+ADV+REPORT,
V+ADV,
V+ADV+N,
V+N/PRON+ADV

2 If you **call** someone **out**, you ask them to come to help, especially in an emergency. ❑ *I called the coastguard out... The National Guard has been called out by Governor Duck... The ambulance had been called out.*

V+N+ADV,
V+PRON+ADV,
V+ADV+N

3 If you **call out** a group of workers, you order them to go on strike. ❑ *They were called out for half a day.*

V+ADV+N,
V+N+ADV,
V+PRON+ADV

call out for If a situation **calls out for** a particular action, there is a very strong need for that action. ❑ *Even the smallest act of oppression calls out for universal condemnation.*

V+ADV+PREP

call over

1 If you **call** someone **over**, you ask them to come to you, usually in order to speak with them or to give them something. ❑ *I called the waitress over and said, 'Bring us a bottle of red wine'... He called over the producer to speak to her.*

V+N+ADV,
V+PRON+ADV,
V+ADV+N

2 If you **call over**, you visit someone for a short time. ❑ *It's OK, we'll be calling over shortly anyway.*

V+ADV

NOTE **Call round** means almost the same as **call over**.

call round If you **call round** to a place, you visit it for a short time. ❑ *I called round to a dozen places to get the proper size of bulb.*

V+ADV:
ALSO+*to*

★call up

1 If you **call** someone **up**, you telephone them. ❑ *People call me up to talk about what's on their minds... About ten minutes after I had checked in, I called her up... The radio station had an open line on which listeners could call up to discuss various issues.*

V+PRON+ADV,
V+N+ADV,
V+ADV:
NO PASSIVE

NOTE **Phone up** and **ring up** mean almost the same as **call up**.

2 If someone **is called up**, they are ordered to join the army, navy, or air force. ❑ *I was extremely lucky not to be called up at the time... The reserves began to be called up.*

V+N+ADV,
V+PRON+ADV,
V+ADV+N:
USUALLY PASSIVE

NOTE **Draft** means almost the same as **call up**.

♦ If a person gets their **call-up** papers, they receive an official order to join the army, navy, or air force.

ADJECTIVE

♦ A **call-up** is the number of people who are ordered to report for service in the
armed forces.   N-COUNT

3 If someone in authority in an activity or event **calls up** someone, they ask them   V+ADV+N,
to take part, or choose them to do a particular task. ❑ *He has ample time to call up re-*   V+N+ADV,
placements... The captain called up Geffin to take the next kick... Jack Charlton called him up   V+PRON+ADV
for the World Cup qualifier in Spain.

NOTE **Call in** and **send for** mean almost the same as **call up**.

4 If something **calls up** a memory or an idea of something, it makes you think   V+ADV+N
about them. ❑ *The museum called up memories of my childhood... The city called up images*
of the emperors of China.

NOTE **Conjure up** means almost the same as **call up**, and **evoke** is a more formal
word.

5 If you **call up** information from a computer, you obtain it. ❑ *He was able to call*   V+ADV+N,
up the information he needed. ...data lodged in the computer which can be called up at the   V+N+ADV,
press of a button.   V+PRON+ADV

call upon

1 If you **are called upon** to do something, you are asked to do it. [FORMAL] ❑ *Lord*   V+PREP:
Shawcross was called upon to declare the hotel open... The chairman will call upon me for my   HAS PASSIVE,
appraisal of the domestic and international situation.   USUALLY PASSIVE

2 → See **call on**

call /kɑːm/ (calms, calming, calmed)

★calm down

1 If you **calm down** or if someone **calms** you **down**, you become less upset, ex-   V+ADV,
cited, or lively. ❑ *'Please, Mrs Kinter,' said Brody. 'Calm down. Let me explain'... An officer*   V+PRON+ADV,
tried to calm them down but had no success... When she had calmed herself down, she start-   V+REFL+ADV,
ed the engine.   V+N+ADV:
                                                                                                ERGATIVE

2 If a situation **calms down** or if you **calm** it **down**, it becomes quieter and less   V+ADV,
tense. ❑ *He told me that things appeared to be calming down a bit... Dad managed to calm*   V+N+ADV,
things down.   V+PRON+ADV,
                                                                                                V+ADV+N:
                                                                                                ERGATIVE

NOTE **Settle down** means almost the same as **calm down**.

camp /kæmp/ (camps, camping, camped)

camp out If you **camp out**, you sleep outdoors in a tent. ❑ *All right, tonight we'll*   V+ADV
camp out.

camp up If you **camp** it **up**, you deliberately act in an exaggerated or affected   V+*it*+ADV
way. [INFORMAL] ❑ *They were really camping it up.*

cancel /kænsəl/ (cancels, cancelling, cancelled)

☑ American English uses the spellings **canceling** and **canceled**.

cancel out If one thing **cancels** another thing **out** or if two things **cancel**   V+ADV+N,
each other **out**, they have opposite effects, so that when they are combined no real   V+N+ADV,
effect is produced. ❑ *The drug produces side effects, tending to cancel out the benefits... In-*   V+PRON+ADV
creased productivity and generous staffing could be said to cancel each other out... Noise
would be reduced but this would be cancelled out by extra traffic at Luton airport.

care /keər/ (cares, caring, cared)

★care for

1 If you **care for** someone or something, you look after them and keep them in a   V+PREP:
good state or condition. ❑ *Only £65 million was given to help care for the mentally re-*   HAS PASSIVE
tarded... Who would care for the farm when they were away?... Pets must be properly cared
for.

♦ **Uncared-for** people or animals have not been looked after properly and as a re-   ADJECTIVE
sult are hungry, dirty, or ill. ❑ *Thousands of children were left uncared-for. ...uncared-for*
cats.

2 If you do not **care for** something, you do not like it. [OLD-FASHIONED] ❑ *He didn't*   V+PREP:
drink, he didn't care for the taste of it... I did not care for the play.   WITH NEGATIVE

3 If you **care for** someone, you love them. ❑ *Here is a young man whom I care for*   V+PREP
and who cares for me.

carry /kæri/ (carries, carrying, carried)

carry away If you get **carried away**, you are so enthusiastic about something that you behave in a silly or hasty way. ❑ *They can't be allowed to be carried away by their feelings... She can get so carried away making the design that she forgets to put the dinner on.*

PASSIVE:
V+ADV

carry back If something **carries** you **back**, it reminds you of something that happened in the past. ❑ *That marvellous smile carried me back nearly twenty-four years.*

V+N+ADV,
V+PRON+ADV

NOTE **Take back** means almost the same as **carry back**.

carry forward When the sum of the figures on a page or in a column **is carried forward**, it is written at the top of the next page or column so that it can be added to the figures on that page or in that column. ❑ *The total is then carried forward for next month's accounts.*

V+N+ADV,
V+PRON+ADV:
USUALLY PASSIVE

NOTE **Bring forward** means almost the same as **carry forward**.

carry off

1 If you **carry off** something that is difficult to do, you succeed in doing it. ❑ *She would have carried everything off beautifully... He looked at her to see how she was carrying off the lie.*

V+N+ADV,
V+PRON+ADV,
V+ADV+N:
NO PASSIVE

NOTE **Bring off** means almost the same as **carry off**.

2 If you **carry off** a prize or an award, you win it. ❑ *Vita carried off all the prizes... Liane Aukin carried off the Best Play Adaptation.*

V+ADV+N,
V+N+ADV,
V+PRON+ADV

★carry on

1 If you **carry on** with an activity, you continue doing it. ❑ *Are you telling me to carry on with my investigation?... The guest speaker was not in the least disturbed, but carried on reading from his script... It was the worst possible place to carry on his research.*

V+ADV+with,
V+ADV+N/-ING

2 If you **carry on** when you are in a difficult or unpleasant situation, you manage to continue with your normal, everyday activities. ❑ *A few carry on as if nothing had happened... I could never have carried on without their support.*

V+ADV

NOTE **Go on** means almost the same as **carry on**.

3 If you **carry on** a particular kind of work, activity, or a conversation, you take part in it. ❑ *Our work is carried on in an informal atmosphere... She could not carry on a normal conversation.*

V+ADV+N

NOTE **Conduct** is a more formal word for **carry on**.

4 If you **carry on** about something, you make a fuss about it. [INFORMAL] ❑ *The child was screaming and carrying on.*

V+ADV

♦ A **carry-on** is behaviour that you think is annoying and unnecessary; used showing disapproval. [BRITISH, INFORMAL] ❑ *Well, what a carry-on.*

N-SING

5 If you **carry on** with someone, you have a love affair with them; used showing disapproval. [INFORMAL] ❑ *Helen was carrying on with Hogan.*

V+ADV+with,
V+ADV:
RECIPROCAL

★carry out

1 If you **carry out** a task, you do it. ❑ *They have to carry out many administrative duties... 'Woman' magazine has just carried a survey out... The first experiments were carried out by Dr Preston McLendon.*

V+ADV+N,
V+N+ADV,
V+PRON+ADV

2 If you **carry out** an idea, suggestion, or instruction, you put it into practice. ❑ *He explained that he was simply carrying out instructions... Men at the top make the decisions, men at the bottom carry them out... He gave guarantees that such a policy will be carried out if his Party achieves office.*

V+ADV+N,
V+PRON+ADV,
V+N+ADV

carry over

1 If you **carry** something **over** from one situation to another, you allow it continue to exist in the new situation. ❑ *Small children live a life of fantasy and they carry this fantasy over into action. ...large deficits customarily carried over to next year's budget.*

V+N+ADV,
V+PRON+ADV,
V+ADV+N

2 If a set of figures on a page **is carried over**, it is written at the top of the next page. ❑ *The sum total to be carried over amounts to £76.*

PASSIVE:
V+ADV

NOTE **Be brought forward** means almost the same as **be carried over**.

carry through

1 If you **carry through** a plan, you succeed in putting it into practice. ❑ *...the task of carrying through the necessary reforms... We are united on these policies and determined to carry them through.*

V+ADV+N,
V+PRON+ADV,
V+N+ADV

2 If something **carries** you **through** a period of time, it makes it possible for you

V+PRON+PREP,

to survive or endure something unpleasant during that time. ❑ *They stole some grain – not much – but enough to carry them through a few weeks... A rich season meant prosperity enough to carry the town through a lean winter.*

V+N+PREP:
NO PASSIVE

cart /kɑːrt/ (carts, carting, carted)

cart off If you **cart** someone **off**, you take them somewhere without asking them whether they want to go there or not. [INFORMAL] ❑ *His father was carted off to jail... I was terrified they'd get me carted off to a police hospital.*

V+N+ADV,
V+PRON+ADV,
V+ADV+N

NOTE Pack off means almost the same as **cart off**.

carve /kɑːrv/ (carves, carving, carved)
carve out

1 If something or someone **carves out** something such as a particular area, they create it in a large area, often with difficulty. ❑ *It has taken the Colorado River a century to carve a canyon out of the red clay soil... The river sliced through sediments, carving out the gorge... A small airport had been carved out of the forest.*

V+N+ADV,
V+ADV+N,
V+PRON+ADV:
USUALLY+of

2 If you **carve out** something for yourself, you create or obtain it, often with difficulty. ❑ *The company is carving out a huge slice of the electronics market... He stayed to carve out a kingdom for himself and his followers. ...the role that green politics is carving out for itself.*

V+ADV+N,
V+N+ADV,
V+PRON+ADV:
NO PASSIVE

carve up

1 If you **carve up** an area, you divide it into smaller areas. ❑ *The junta would carve up that vast region into a number of slave-holdings... They prepared to carve up the British Empire.*

V+ADV+N,
V+N+ADV,
V+PRON+ADV

2 If you **carve** someone **up**, you wound them badly with a knife. [INFORMAL] ❑ *He'd probably carve the victim up in the end.*

V+N+ADV,
V+PRON+ADV

NOTE Cut up means almost the same as **carve up**.

cash /kæʃ/ (cashes, cashing, cashed)
★cash in

1 If you **cash in** an investment such as shares or premium bonds, you exchange them for money. ❑ *She had to cash in her premium bonds to raise a bit of money... I used to have a few shares, but I cashed them in last year.*

V+ADV+N,
V+PRON+ADV,
V+N+ADV

2 If you **cash in** on a situation, you take advantage of it, especially by doing something slightly unfair or dishonest. ❑ *...cashing in on other's people's inequality... I don't blame businessmen for cashing in.*

V+ADV:
ALSO+on

cast /kɑːst, kæst/ (casts, casting)

☑ The form **cast** is used in the present tense and is the past tense and past participle of the verb. **About** is used mainly in British English. In American English, **around** is much more common than **round**.

cast about → See cast around

cast around If you **cast around**, **cast about**, or **cast round** for something, you look for it. [FORMAL] ❑ *Jack cast about on the bare rock and looked anxious... I cast around for a place to live.*

V+ADV:
ALSO+for

cast aside If you **cast** someone or something **aside**, you get rid of them because you no longer like them or approve of them. [FORMAL] ❑ *The figure who is an honour to his country is cast aside and disgraced... Her son cast aside his Christian forbearance.*

V+ADV+N,
V+N+ADV,
V+PRON+ADV

cast away

1 If you **cast** something **away**, you get rid of it completely. [LITERARY] ❑ *He says he finds his life of little account and is proud to cast it away.*

V+PRON+ADV,
V+N+ADV,
V+ADV+N

2 A **castaway** is a person who has managed to swim or float to a lonely island or shore after their ship has been wrecked. ❑ *...castaways marooned on a desert island.*

N-COUNT

cast back If you **cast** your mind **back** to something that happened in the past, you think about it again and try to remember it. ❑ *He cast his mind back over the day.*

V+N+ADV:
NO PASSIVE

cast down

1 If someone **is cast down**, they lose their social status. [FORMAL] ❑ *Men of high status were cast down... Why were we cast down so far?*

PASSIVE:
V+ADV

NOTE Raise means the opposite of **cast down**.

The symbol ★ shows key phrasal verbs

2 If someone **is cast down** by something, they are sad or worried because of it. ❑ *I am not cast down by it because I believe in the fundamental strength of the business... Ever since I saw the diary excerpts I've been cast down.*

PASSIVE:
V+ADV

NOTE **Depressed** means almost the same as **cast down**.

3 If you **cast** your eyes **down**, you look downwards. [FORMAL] ❑ *Her eyes were cast down.*

V+N+ADV,
V+ADV+N

NOTE **Lower** is a less formal word for **cast down**.

4 If you are **downcast** you are feeling sad and pessimistic. ❑ *Cameron seemed unusually downcast and taciturn.*

ADJECTIVE

cast off

1 If you **cast** something **off**, you get rid of it because you no longer want it or because it is preventing you from making progress. ❑ *Organizations must cast off those bureaucratic practices.*

V+ADV+N,
V+N+ADV,
V+PRON+ADV

NOTE **Discard** is a more formal word for **cast off**.

♦ **Cast-off** clothes or **cast-offs** are clothes which you give to someone else, because they do not fit you or you do not like them. ❑ *...the embarrassing position of wearing cast-off shoes or sports jackets... They had dressed up in Winifred's cast-offs.*

ADJECTIVE,
N-PLURAL

♦ **Cast-off** is also used to describe something which people have got rid of because it is no longer wanted or it has become a nuisance. ❑ *...cast-off ideas.*

ADJECTIVE

2 When you **cast off**, you remove or untie the rope fastening a boat to a harbour wall so that the boat can move away. ❑ *Hendricks cast off the bow line and walked to the stern... She gave the order to cast off.*

V+ADV+N,
V+ADV:
NO PASSIVE

3 In knitting, when you **cast off** stitches, you remove them from the needle after doing a special stitch, especially in order to finish a piece of knitting.

V+ADV+N,
V+ADV

cast on In knitting, when you **cast on** stitches, you make them on a needle in order to begin a piece of knitting. ❑ *Using 4mm needles cast on 53 stitches... I'm just casting on.*

V+ADV+N,
V+ADV

cast out To **cast out** something or someone means to get rid of them or make them leave a place. [FORMAL] ❑ *She had abandoned him, she had cast him out... What will such vulnerable creatures do when they are cast out into the open?*

V+PRON+ADV,
V+N+ADV,
V+ADV+N

♦ An **outcast** is someone who is rejected and ignored by other people. ❑ *...a social outcast who has spent some time in jail.*

N-COUNT

cast round → See cast around

cast up If something **is cast up** on the shore or on a beach, it is left there by the sea at high tide. ❑ *His body was cast up onto the shore.*

V+N+ADV,
V+PRON+ADV,
V+ADV+N

NOTE **Wash up** means almost the same as **cast up**.

catch /kætʃ/ (catches, catching, caught)

⋆catch on

1 If someone **catches on** to something, they understand and learn it. ❑ *He'll catch on eventually... They finally caught on to our game.*

V+ADV:
ALSO+to

NOTE **Cotton on** means almost the same as **catch on**.

2 If something **catches on**, it becomes popular. ❑ *The idea is catching on... Ballroom dancing caught on.*

V+ADV

catch out

1 If you **catch** someone **out**, you make them make a mistake, often by an unfair trick. [BRITISH] ❑ *Fancy trying to catch me out!*

V+N+ADV,
V+PRON+ADV

2 If you **are caught out** by something that happens unexpectedly, you find yourself in an unfortunate situation or weak position. [BRITISH] ❑ *He had also been caught out by the nationalization of Britain's oil industry... I am not going to be caught out by a new war.*

PASSIVE:
V+ADV

⋆catch up

1 If you **catch up** with someone who is in front of you, you reach them by walking faster than they are walking. ❑ *He is dawdling behind, not wanting to catch up... Simon tried to catch up with the others... She stood still, allowing him to catch her up.*

V+ADV:
USUALLY+with:
V+PRON+ADV,
V+N+ADV

2 If you **catch up** with someone, you reach the same standard or level as they are. ❑ *Most leaders were obsessed with catching up with the West.*

V+ADV:
ALSO+with

3 If you **catch up** on friends who you have not seen for some time or on their

V+ADV:

lives, you talk to them and find out what has happened in their lives since you last talked together. ❏ *The ladies spent some time catching up on each other's health and families... She plans to return to Dublin to catch up with the relatives she has not seen since she married.*

USUALLY+*on*/*with*

★catch **up in**
1 If you **are caught up in** something, you are involved in it, usually unwillingly. ❏ *...a society caught up in complex, high-speed change... You are bound to be caught up in events.*

PASSIVE: V+ADV+PREP

2 You can also say that you **are caught up in** something when it prevents you from moving. ❏ *I got caught up in the traffic... A bird had got caught up in the net.*

PASSIVE: V+ADV+PREP

catch up on When you **catch up on** something, you spend time doing something that you have not had time to do properly until now. ❏ *I was just catching up on my sleep... They would be going to the office to catch up on some correspondence.*

V+ADV+PREP

★catch **up with**
1 If the police or the authorities **catch up with** someone who has done something wrong, they succeed in finding them, especially in order to arrest or punish them. ❏ *When Birmingham authorities finally caught up with her, she had spent all the money.*

V+ADV+PREP

2 If something **catches up with** you, you find yourself in an unpleasant situation which you have been able to avoid but which you are now forced to deal with. ❏ *I am sure that the truth will catch up with him... Poverty may catch up with the apparently most secure.*

V+ADV+PREP

cater /keɪtər/ (caters, catering, catered)
★cater for To **cater for** a person or group means to provide all the things that they need or want in a particular situation. [BRITISH] ❏ *We can cater for all age groups in our summer schools... Newspapers cater for a variety of tastes... In a consumer society no effort is made to cater for the needs of the elderly... Hotels like this are not geared to cater for parties like ours.*
NOTE In American English, **cater to** means almost the same as **cater for**.

V+PREP: HAS PASSIVE

cater to To **cater to** a need or taste means to provide things which satisfy it. ❏ *Terry catered to the public taste for new plays.*

V+PREP

cave /keɪv/ (caves, caving, caved)
cave **in**
1 When something such as a roof or a ceiling **caves in** or when something **caves** it **in**, it collapses inwards. ❏ *In order to prevent the sides caving in, it is usually lined with bricks... The blow caved in his skull.*

V+ADV, V+ADV+N, V+PRON+ADV: ERGATIVE

♦ A **cave-in** is the sudden collapse of a roof or ceiling into a building or room below it.

N-COUNT

2 If you **cave in**, you give in or surrender to someone or something, especially when you are under pressure. ❏ *I more or less caved in, though I still defended my explanation... The spies had given the invaders a few days to cave in.*
NOTE **Capitulate** is a more formal word for **cave in**.

V+ADV

centre /sentər/ (centres, centring, centred)
> ☑ In American English, the spellings **center, centers, centering** and **centered** are used; **around** is also much more common than **round**.

centre around If something **centres around** or **centres round** a person or thing, they are the main feature or subject of attention; usually used when you are generalizing rather than describing the specific details of a subject. ❏ *The workers' demands centred around pay and conditions... Our holidays centred very much round horse-racing.*

V+PREP, V+N+PREP, V+PRON+PREP: ERGATIVE

★centre on If something **centres on** or **centres upon** a person or thing, it concentrates on them; usually used when you are describing specific details rather than generalizing. ❏ *Attention was for the moment centred on Michael Striker... The struggle was now centred upon Pennsylvania.*

V+PREP, V+N+PREP, V+PRON+PREP: ERGATIVE

centre round → See centre around

centre upon → See centre on

chain /tʃeɪn/ **(chains, chaining, chained)**

chain up If you **chain up** someone or something, you fasten them to something using a chain. ❑ *The rowing boats were chained up.*

V+N+ADV,
V+PRON+ADV,
V+ADV+N

chalk /tʃɔːk/ **(chalks, chalking, chalked)**

chalk up If you **chalk up** a victory, a success, or a number of points in a game, you achieve it. ❑ *They chalked up several victories... She's chalked up four wins already this season.*

V+ADV+N

NOTE **Notch up** means almost the same as **chalk up**.

chance /tʃɑːns, tʃæns/ **(chances, chancing, chanced)**

chance on If you **chance on** or **chance upon** something or someone, you meet or discover them unexpectedly. **Chance upon** is more formal. ❑ *I chanced on an old friend in the street... He'd chanced upon an old book.*

V+PREP:
HAS PASSIVE

chance upon → See **chance on**

change /tʃeɪndʒ/ **(changes, changing, changed)**

change down When you **change down**, you move the gear lever on a car or bicycle in order to use a lower gear. [BRITISH] ❑ *You'll have to change down into second to get round the corner.*

V+ADV

★**change over**

1 To **change over** from one thing to another means to stop doing, using, or having one thing and start doing, using, or having something else. ❑ *The school changed over from having a system of streaming to having mixed ability classes... They had been Liberal till several years ago, then they changed over to Conservative.*

V+ADV:
USUALLY WITH *from/to*

♦ A **changeover** is a change from one activity, system, or way of working to another one. ❑ *The changeover took place at Easter.*

N-COUNT

2 You say that two people **change over** when each of them does what the other person was previously doing or when each of them goes to where the other person was. ❑ *Let's change over – you paint the wall and I'll paint the door.*

V+ADV

change up When you **change up**, you move the gear lever on a car or bicycle in order to use a higher gear. [BRITISH] ❑ *She changed up into fourth.*

V+ADV

charge /tʃɑːrdʒ/ **(charges, charging, charged)**

charge up To **charge up** a battery means to pass an electrical current through it in order to make it more powerful or to make it last longer. ❑ *There was nothing in the brochure about having to drive it every day to charge up the battery.*

V+ADV+N,
V+N+ADV,
V+PRON+ADV

chase /tʃeɪs/ **(chases, chasing, chased)**

chase after

1 If you **chase after** someone, you run after them or follow them quickly in order to catch them. ❑ *...hundreds of warriors chasing after a fugitive... I couldn't chase after them; they were too quick for me.*

V+PREP

2 If you **chase after** something you want or need, such as work, money, or the solution to a problem, you try very hard to obtain it. ❑ *His work involves a hunt for ideas – he chases after solutions... I had chased after easy alternatives.*

V+PREP

chase away If someone or something **chases away** worries, fears, or other bad feelings, they cause those feelings to change and become happier. ❑ *Ellery's return will help to chase away some of the gloom... The rise in industrial production helped chase away lingering fears that the economy is slipping into a new recession.*

V+ADV+N,
V+N+ADV,
V+PRON+ADV

NOTE **Get rid of** means almost the same as **chase away**.

chase down

1 If you **chase** someone **down**, you run after them or follow them quickly and catch them. [AMERICAN] ❑ *Ness chased the thief down and held him until police arrived... For thousands of years, chasing down game was the main activity in which humans were involved.*

V+N+ADV,
V+PRON+ADV,
V+ADV+N

2 If you **chase** someone or something **down**, you manage to find them after searching for them. ❑ *That's when I chased her down to be the singer in my band... Bank officials argued that it is not their job to chase down every asset of every bank debtor.*

V+N+ADV,
V+PRON+ADV,
V+ADV+N

NOTE **Track down** means almost the same as **chase down**.

chase off If you **chase** someone **off**, you run after them in order to frighten them or force them to go away. ❑ *Male birds use harsh, rattling cries to chase off other thrushes... There was another snake. The dog chased it off.*

V+ADV+N,
V+PRON+ADV,
V+N+ADV

chase up

1 If you **chase** someone **up**, you contact them to remind them to do something for you, or to ask them something. ❑ *I'll chase her up for those reports... I've been trying to find you, chasing up people you'd worked with.*

V+PRON+ADV,
V+ADV+N,
V+N+ADV

2 If you **chase** something **up**, you try to find it because it is needed. ❑ *You'd better chase those addresses up tomorrow... Someone else is in charge of chasing up the missing books.*

V+N+ADV,
V+PRON+ADV,
V+ADV+N

NOTE **Track down** means almost the same as **chase up**.

chat /tʃæt/ (**chats, chatting, chatted**)

★**chat up** If you **chat** someone **up**, you talk to them in a friendly way because you are sexually attracted to them. [BRITISH, INFORMAL] ❑ *He would rather be chatting the stewardess up... How could Sheila be so stupid, chatting up two louts like that?... The last I saw of her she was being chatted up by this bloke.*

V+N+ADV,
V+PRON+ADV,
V+ADV+N

cheat /tʃiːt/ (**cheats, cheating, cheated**)

cheat on

1 If you **cheat on** your sexual partner, you behave dishonestly towards them by secretly having a relationship with someone else. ❑ *A private detective has been assigned to find out whether she's cheating on her husband.*

V+PREP

NOTE **Be unfaithful to** means almost the same as **cheat on**.

2 To **cheat on** someone also means to lie to them or behave dishonestly towards them. ❑ *He can cheat on us, but he's smart enough to say somebody else did it.*

V+PREP:
HAS PASSIVE

3 If someone **cheats on** something such as an agreement or their taxes, they do not do what they should do under a set of rules. [AMERICAN] ❑ *Their job is to check that none of the signatory countries is cheating on the agreement.*

V+PREP

check /tʃek/ (**checks, checking, checked**)

★**check in**

1 When you **check in** or when someone **checks** you **in** at a hotel, you arrive at the hotel, collect the key to your room, and fill in any forms which are necessary. ❑ *I checked in at the Gordon Hotel... He worked at the front desk checking in the guests when they arrived.*

V+ADV,
V+ADV+N,
V+N+ADV,
V+PRON+ADV:
ERGATIVE

2 When you **check in** at an airport or when someone **checks** you **in**, you show your ticket before getting on the plane. ❑ *He checked in without baggage for a flight to Rome... The remaining passengers were still being checked in.*

V+ADV,
V+N/PRON+ADV,
V+ADV+N:
ERGATIVE

♦ A **check-in** is the place in an airport where you check in. ❑ *We were supposed to notice damaged bags at the check-in but seldom did. ...a check-in counter.*

N-COUNT

check into When you **check into** a hotel or if someone **checks** you **into** it, you arrive at the hotel, collect the key to your room, and fill in any forms which are necessary. ❑ *With no money, we could hardly think about checking into a motel.*

V+PREP,
V+N+PREP,
V+PRON+PREP:
ERGATIVE

check off When you **check off** a list of things, you count them to make sure everything is right. ❑ *We waited while Mr Wilde checked off the things on the list... I store the details in a file to check off when I am ready to go.*

V+ADV+N,
V+N+ADV,
V+PRON+ADV

★**check out**

1 When you **check out** of a hotel where you have been staying, you pay the bill and leave. ❑ *The following morning he checked out... She checked out of the hotel and took the train to Paris.*

V+ADV:
ALSO+of

2 If you **check** something **out**, you find out about it or examine it because you want to make sure that everything is correct or safe. ❑ *An officer would be checking out the statement Mrs. Mossman just made... Frank was going to check out the restaurant floor to see whether anything unusual was going on... It might be difficult to transfer your money, so check it out with the manager.*

V+ADV+N,
V+PRON+ADV,
V+N+ADV

3 If something **checks out**, it is correct or satisfactory. ❑ *She was in San Diego the weekend Jensen got killed. It checked out... Everything checks out.*

V+ADV

4 If you **check** someone **out**, you obtain information about them secretly to find out if they are telling the truth. ❑ *They knew his habits, Luca thought, they must have*

V+PRON+ADV,
V+ADV+N,
V+N+ADV

been checking him out... Jenny was reserving judgement until she could check out the two men who had called her.

5 In a shop, if you **check out** the things you want to buy, you pay for them at a special counter. [AMERICAN] ❑ *Wait before you check those cards out, and I'll get some too.*　　V+N+ADV, V+PRON+ADV, V+ADV+N

♦ In a supermarket, a **checkout** is a counter where you pay for the things you have bought. ❑ *Only two checkouts were operating... The checkout queues are short in this small-town supermarket.*　　N-COUNT

★check up If you **check up** on someone or something, you obtain information about them, often secretly. ❑ *The council had checked up on her and decided that she was unsuitable for employment... He had been aware that they would be checking up on him... They think there is a security leak and are trying to check up.*　　V+ADV: USUALLY+on

♦ A **check-up** is an examination by a doctor to see that your health is all right. ❑ *See the doctor for a blood test and check-up.*　　N-COUNT

cheer /tʃɪəʳ/ (cheers, cheering, cheered)

cheer on If you **cheer** someone **on**, you cheer loudly in order to encourage them. ❑ *Some students stood on the roof, cheering the rioters on... There was no one there to cheer him on or applaud.*　　V+N+ADV, V+PRON+ADV, V+ADV+N

★cheer up When you **cheer up** or when someone or something **cheers** you **up**, you stop feeling depressed and become more cheerful. ❑ *She cheered up a little as Miss Livingstone went out... Her friends tried to cheer her up, telling her she wasn't missing much... She bought strawberries to cheer herself up.*　　V+ADV, V+PRON+ADV, V+REFL+ADV, V+N+ADV, V+ADV+N: ERGATIVE

NOTE **Buck up** means almost the same as **cheer up**.

cheese /tʃiːz/ (cheeses, cheesing, cheesed)

cheese off If you **are cheesed off** with something, you are annoyed, bored, or disappointed with it. [BRITISH, INFORMAL] ❑ *I was really cheesed off when he didn't turn up.*　　V+PRON+ADV, V+N+ADV: USUALLY PASSIVE

chew /tʃuː/ (chews, chewing, chewed)

chew on If you **chew on** an idea or a problem, you think about it carefully for a long time. ❑ *He chewed on the idea that his brother had suggested... You've given me a lot to chew on.*　　V+PREP

NOTE **Consider** is a more formal word for **chew on**.

chew out If you **chew** someone **out**, you tell them off in a very angry way. [INFORMAL] ❑ *He chewed out the player, who apologized the next time I saw him... When Tom got back to Dallas, Perot called him over and chewed him out.*　　V+N+ADV, V+ADV+N, V+PRON+ADV

chew over If you **chew** something **over**, you think carefully about it. ❑ *In discussion we chew over problems and work out possible solutions. ...chewing over the happenings of the day.*　　V+ADV+N, V+N+ADV, V+PRON+ADV

NOTE **Mull over** means almost the same as **chew over**.

chew up

1 If you **chew** food **up**, you chew it until it is completely crushed or softened. ❑ *Lally put it into her mouth and chewed it up happily... Peas and beans are too tough to be chewed up.*　　V+PRON+ADV, V+N+ADV, V+ADV+N

2 If something **is chewed up**, it has been destroyed or damaged in some way. [INFORMAL] ❑ *Every spring the ozone is chewed up, and the hole appears. ...rebels who are now chewing up Government-held territory... This town is notorious for chewing people up and spitting them out.*　　V+ADV+N, V+N+ADV, V+PRON+ADV

chicken /tʃɪkɪn/ (chickens, chickening, chickened)

chicken out If you **chicken out** of something, you decide not to do it because you are afraid; used showing disapproval. [INFORMAL] ❑ *He didn't want to look as if he was chickening out. ...trying to chicken out of going to the dentist.*　　V+ADV: ALSO+of

chill /tʃɪl/ (chills, chilling, chilled)

chill out To **chill out** means to relax after you have done something tiring or stressful. [INFORMAL] ❑ *After raves, we used to chill out in each others' bedrooms.*　　V+ADV

chime /tʃaɪm/ (chimes, chiming, chimed)

chime in If someone **chimes in**, they say something just after someone else has spoken. ❑ *Bill Henderson chimed in with 'This is an emergency situation...' 'Yes,' he chimed in, 'there's where the future of this wretched country lies.'*

V+ADV:
ALSO+with,
USUALLY+QUOTE

chime in with If one thing **chimes in with** another thing, the two things are consistent with each other and seem to belong together. ❑ *These influences could only chime in with the growing feeling of despair.*

V+ADV+PREP

chip /tʃɪp/ (chips, chipping, chipped)

chip away at

1 If you **chip away at** something such as an idea, a feeling, or a system, you gradually make it weaker or less likely to succeed by repeated efforts. ❑ *Instead of an outright coup attempt, the rebels want to chip away at her authority.*

V+ADV+PREP

NOTE **Erode** means almost the same as **chip away at.**

2 If you **chip away at** a debt or an amount of money, you gradually reduce it. ❑ *The group had hoped to chip away at its debts by selling assets.*

V+ADV+PREP

chip in

1 If you **chip in** to pay for something, you contribute part of the cost so that you and several other people pay for it together. [INFORMAL] ❑ *If anyone was ill, they all chipped in to pay the doctor's bill... They all ought to chip in and buy a present.*

V+ADV

NOTE **Club together** means almost the same as **chip in.**

2 If someone **chips in** during a conversation, they interrupt it by saying something. ❑ *'Do you know,' said Mrs Oliver, chipping in again, 'whether Celia was there or not?'... 'Come on, back to work' chipped in the older man.*

V+ADV:
ALSO+QUOTE

chip off If a coating **chips off** a surface, or if you **chip** it **off**, it gradually becomes detached from the surface. ❑ *With extreme care, she began chipping off the white paint... The car was only two years old, and already the paint had started to chip off.*

V+N+PREP/ADV,
V+PRON+PREP/ADV,
V+ADV+N,
V+ADV:
ERGATIVE

choke /tʃəʊk/ (chokes, choking, choked)

choke back

1 If you **choke back** a strong emotion, you force yourself not to show it. ❑ *I choked back the sobs... She spoke with difficulty, choking back the tears.*

V+ADV+N:
NO PASSIVE

NOTE **Suppress** means almost the same as **choke back.**

2 If you **choke back** something you are saying, you stop yourself from saying it. ❑ *'I'm –' she choked back the word... He turned to yell for Helen, but choked it back.*

V+ADV+N,
V+N+ADV,
V+PRON+ADV

choke off To **choke off** financial growth means to restrict or control the rate at which a country's economy can grow. ❑ *They warned the Chancellor that raising taxes in the Budget could choke off the recovery.*

V+ADV+N,
V+PRON+ADV

chop /tʃɒp/ (chops, chopping, chopped)

chop down If you **chop down** a tree, you cut through its trunk with an axe so that it falls to the ground. ❑ *...trying to chop down the stump of a small holly tree... I chopped the saplings down every year, but they always grew back.*

V+ADV+N,
V+N+ADV,
V+PRON+ADV

chop off If you **chop** something **off**, you cut it off with a sudden or decisive stroke, using something such as a knife. ❑ *Keep your foot still, or I'll chop it off at the knee. ...women in the fields, chopping off the long golden stalks of corn.*

V+PRON+ADV,
V+ADV+N,
V+N+ADV

chop up If you **chop** something **up**, you cut it into small pieces. ❑ *Soak the plants, then chop them up as small as you can... Fruit tastes delicious when chopped up and sprinkled with wine.*

V+PRON+ADV,
V+N+ADV,
V+ADV+N

chow /tʃaʊ/ (chows, chowing, chowed)

chow down If you **chow down** you eat, especially in a restaurant. [INFORMAL] ❑ *We sent Marina Hyde to find out how and where you chose to chow down... The only available indulgence is to chow down on some homemade quiche and scones.*

V+ADV:
ALSO+on

chuck /tʃʌk/ (chucks, chucking, chucked)

chuck away If you **chuck** something **away**, you throw it away, because you do not want it or cannot use it any longer. [INFORMAL] ❑ *'What are you going to do with all those old clothes?'—'Oh, just chuck them away I think'... This heater had to be chucked away because it didn't work.*

V+PRON+ADV,
V+N+ADV,
V+ADV+N

NOTE **Chuck out** means almost the same as **chuck away.**

chuck in If you **chuck in** your job or other activity, you stop doing it. [BRITISH, INFORMAL] ❑ *He got a new job, but when he found out that he paid as much tax as Paddy earned, he chucked it in.*
`V+PRON+ADV, V+N+ADV, V+ADV+N; NO PASSIVE`

NOTE **Jack in** and **pack in** mean almost the same as **chuck in**.

chuck out

1 If you **chuck** someone **out** of a place, you force them to leave. [INFORMAL] ❑ *I could never forgive them for chucking me out... Why did you leave? Were you chucked out?*
`V+PRON+ADV, V+N+ADV, V+ADV+N`

NOTE **Throw out** means almost the same as **chuck out**.

♦ **Chucking-out** time is the time when public houses close. [BRITISH, INFORMAL] ❑ *Is it chucking-out time already?*
`ADJECTIVE`

2 If you **chuck** something **out**, you throw it away because you do not want it any longer. [INFORMAL] ❑ *Chuck those old boots out, for goodness sake... She chucked out loads of books that could have been given to Oxfam.*
`V+N+ADV, V+PRON+ADV, V+ADV+N`

NOTE **Chuck away** means almost the same as **chuck out**.

chuck up

1 If you **chuck up** a job or other activity, you stop doing it. [BRITISH, INFORMAL] ❑ *He was just one of the lads who had chucked his job up.*
`V+N+ADV, V+PRON+ADV, V+ADV+N`

NOTE **Chuck in** means almost the same as **chuck up**.

2 If someone **chucks up**, they vomit. [INFORMAL] ❑ *They get drunk and then they chuck up everywhere.*
`V+ADV, V+N+ADV, V+ADV+N, V+PRON+ADV`

NOTE **Throw up** means almost the same as **chuck up**.

churn /tʃɜːrn/ (churns, churning, churned)

churn out To **churn** things **out** means to produce them in large numbers very quickly. ❑ *His campaign organization began churning out tracts and posters... My brain was churning out objections at an incredible rate... The routine calculations that had to be churned out grew and grew.*
`V+ADV+N, V+N+ADV, V+PRON+ADV`

NOTE **Pump out** means almost the same as **churn out**.

churn up

1 If something **churns up** mud or water, it moves it about violently. ❑ *The wind churned up the water into a swirling foam... The silt in the lakes has been churned up by motorboats.*
`V+ADV+N, V+N+ADV, V+PRON+ADV`

2 If something **churns** you **up**, it makes you feel worried or frightened. ❑ *Something seemed to be churning her up inside... I would be churned up and destroyed inside by irrepressible desires.*
`V+PRON+ADV, V+N+ADV`

clam /klæm/ (clams, clamming, clammed)

clam up If someone **clams up**, they refuse to say anything about a subject. [INFORMAL] ❑ *Lonnie just clammed up as if he had already said too much... We had a row, and I clammed up and said nothing for a complete half-hour.*
`V+ADV`

clamp /klæmp/ (clamps, clamping, clamped)

clamp down To **clamp down** on people or activities means to take strong official action to stop or control them. ❑ *The authorities have got to clamp down on these trouble-makers... The Federal Reserve clamped down on bank lending.*
`V+ADV; USUALLY+on`

NOTE **Crack down** means almost the same as **clamp down**.

♦ A **clampdown** is a sudden restriction on an activity by a government or other authority. ❑ *...a clampdown on wasteful spending.*
`N-COUNT`

clap /klæp/ (claps, clapping, clapped)

clap out

1 If you **clap out** a tune, you produce it by hitting your hands together in a way which matches the rhythm of the tune. ❑ *A leader is selected, and he or she begins to clap out a rhythm which the others quickly duplicate... The actor claps out a beat, which fits into the collective rhythm... You clap it out, and I'll join in when I get the hang of it.*
`V+ADV+N, V+N+ADV, V+PRON+ADV`

2 Something such as a machine that is **clapped-out** is old and no longer working properly. [BRITISH, INFORMAL] ❑ *The last car was a clapped-out old Ford.*
`ADJECTIVE`

NOTE **Beat-up** means almost the same as **clapped-out**.

class /klɑːs, klæs/ (classes, classing, classed)

class among If you **class** someone or something **among** a particular group, you consider them to be a member of that group. ❑ *At one time the arts of reading and*
`V+N+PREP, V+PRON+PREP`

writing were classed among the great mysteries of life for the majority of people... Would you class young Paddy Martyn among the best?

claw /klɔː/ (claws, clawing, clawed)

claw at When people or animals **claw at** something, they try to get hold of it or damage it by using their nails or claws. ❑ *...shaking her head and clawing at my trousers. ...scrabbling with my hands, clawing at the rock as I fell.*　　V+PREP

claw back

1 If someone **claws back** some of the power they have lost, they get some of it back again. [BRITISH] ❑ *In the meantime his generals will want to claw back some of their old influence.*　　V+ADV+N, V+N+ADV, V+PRON+ADV

2 If an organization **claws back** money, it finds a way of getting money back which it has spent earlier. [BRITISH] ❑ *The Government was determined to claw back the extra supplementary benefit... They will eventually be able to claw back all or most of the debt.*　　V+ADV+N, V+N+ADV, V+PRON+ADV

♦ A **clawback** is a method of getting money back which was spent earlier. [BRITISH] ❑ *Extending the cover for 12 months could trigger a further clawback of state support.*　　N-COUNT

clean /kliːn/ (cleans, cleaning, cleaned)

clean down If you **clean down** a building or part of a building, you clean or wash it thoroughly. ❑ *First, clean down the walls... Nicola cleaned the windows down, while Alan made a cup of tea.*　　V+ADV+N, V+N+ADV, V+PRON+ADV

★clean out

1 If you **clean** something **out**, you clean it very thoroughly and remove anything that is not wanted or needed. ❑ *I spent three days cleaning our flat out... I was to massage the wound and clean it out every day... I was cleaning out my desk at the office on my last day there.*　　V+N+ADV, V+PRON+ADV, V+ADV+N

♦ A **clean-out** is the activity of cleaning a place very thoroughly and throwing away things you do not want or need. ❑ *I was just having a little clean-out in the kitchen.*　　N-COUNT

2 If you **clean out** a person, you take all the money they have. If you **clean out** a place, you take everything of value that is in it. [INFORMAL] ❑ *I've got no more money—they cleaned me out... Thomas thought idly of cleaning out the cash register.*　　V+ADV+N, V+N+ADV, V+PRON+ADV

★clean up

1 If you **clean up** someone or something, you clean them fairly thoroughly. ❑ *Clean up food spills at once... He winced as I cleaned up his face. ...the costs of cleaning up rivers and beaches.*　　V+ADV+N, V+N+ADV, V+PRON+ADV

2 If you **clean up** a place, you clean it thoroughly and make it tidy. ❑ *It must be very depressing to spend your life cleaning up after people you never see... They would stay behind to help me clean up the classroom... He cleaned the room up before leaving.*　　V+ADV, V+ADV+N, V+N+ADV, V+PRON+ADV

NOTE **Clear up** means almost the same as **clean up**.

♦ A **clean-up** is a thorough clean. ❑ *This room could do with a good clean-up.*　　N-COUNT

3 If the police or the authorities **clean up** a place, they make it free from crime. ❑ *Then they can begin to clean up the cities... City authorities have long wanted to clean up Times Square.*　　V+ADV+N, V+N+ADV, V+PRON+ADV

4 If people **clean up**, they make a large profit from a business deal. [INFORMAL] ❑ *People who buy shares now will clean up when the price rises.*　　V+ADV

clean up after If you **clean up after** someone, you clean or tidy a place that they have made dirty or untidy. ❑ *At the end, he nursed Lilly and cleaned up after her without minding.*　　V+ADV+PREP: NO PASSIVE

clear /klɪər/ (clears, clearing, cleared)

clear away When you **clear away**, you put away the things that you have been using. ❑ *After dinner, when we had cleared away and washed up, we went for a walk... Brody stood up and began to clear away the soup bowls... Clear the cutlery away.*　　V+ADV, V+ADV+N, V+N+ADV, V+PRON+ADV

NOTE **Tidy away** means almost the same as **clear away**.

clear off If you say '**clear off**' to someone, you are telling them in a rude way to go away. [BRITISH, INFORMAL] ❑ *Now you clear off and leave me alone... He was told to clear off by the publican.*　　IMPERATIVE, V+ADV

NOTE **Buzz off** means almost the same as **clear off**.

The symbol ★ shows key phrasal verbs

★**clear out**

1 If you **clear out** of a place, you leave it. [INFORMAL] ❏ *I've got to clear out of my place by next week... I woke one night around midnight and decided to clear out... Just clear out and leave me in peace!*

NOTE **Get out** means almost the same as **clear out**.

2 If you **clear out** a cupboard, a room, or a house, or if you **clear** things **out** of it, you tidy it and throw away the things you no longer need. ❏ *It's about time I cleared out the kitchen cupboards... These cards had to be cleared out at fairly short intervals.*

♦ A **clear-out** is the activity of collecting together all the things that you do not want and throwing them away. [BRITISH, INFORMAL] ❏ *...a general clear-out of our archives.*

> V+ADV:
> ALSO+of,
> ALSO IMPERATIVE

> V+ADV+N,
> V+N+ADV,
> V+PRON+ADV

> N-COUNT

★**clear up**

1 When you **clear up** or **clear** something **up**, you tidy things and put them away. ❏ *I was too tired to clear up... I wonder who clears all this up... Go and clear up your room.*

2 If you **clear up** a problem, disagreement, or misunderstanding, you settle it or give a satisfactory explanation for it. ❏ *Inspector Standish was trying to clear up a tiresome problem... I went to clear the matter up with him.*

NOTE **Sort out** means almost the same as **clear up**.

3 If someone's illness **clears up**, they recover from it. ❏ *I was very lucky, it was only a minor infection and it all cleared up in a week... The neck pains could clear up on their own.*

4 When bad weather **clears up**, it stops raining or being cloudy. ❏ *I'm going back till this weather clears up.*

NOTE **Brighten up** means almost the same as **clear up**.

> V+ADV,
> V+N+ADV,
> V+PRON+ADV,
> V+ADV+N

> V+ADV+N,
> V+N+ADV,
> V+PRON+ADV

> V+ADV

> V+ADV

climb /klaɪm/ (climbs, climbing, climbed)

climb down If you **climb down** in an argument or dispute, you admit that you are wrong. ❏ *Even after these facts were published, he was unwilling to climb down.*

NOTE **Back down** means almost the same as **climb down**.

♦ A **climb-down** is the act of admitting that you are wrong and agreeing to accept what someone else wants. ❏ *Many strikes end in a climb-down on the part of the management.*

> V+ADV

> N-COUNT

clock /klɒk/ (clocks, clocking, clocked)

clock in

1 When workers **clock in** or **clock on** at a factory or office, they record the time that they arrive by putting a special card into a device. ❏ *If they are late clocking in, they lose pay.*

2 If someone or something **clocks in** at a particular weight, they register that amount after being weighed. ❏ *The van clocked in at 2,000 pounds... Now she clocks in at 9st 7lbs after going on the diet.*

NOTE **Weigh in** means almost the same as **clock in**.

3 If something such as a record or film **clocks in** at a particular amount of time, it lasts for that amount of time. ❏ *There are four more songs, each clocking in at around 12 minutes.*

> V+ADV

> V+ADV:
> USUALLY+at

> V+ADV:
> USUALLY+at

clock off → See **clock out**

clock on → See **clock in**

clock out When workers **clock out** or **clock off** at a factory or office, they record the time that they leave by putting a special card into a device. ❏ *It's time to clock out.*

> V+ADV

clock up To **clock up** a large number or total means to reach that total. ❏ *He has clocked up more than 171,750 miles in a lifetime of running... Manufactured exports clocked up an average 5% increase in volume.*

NOTE **Notch up** means almost the same as **clock up**.

> V+ADV+N

clog /klɒg/ (clogs, clogging, clogged)

clog up If something **clogs up** or **is clogged up**, it becomes blocked and no longer works properly. ❏ *We have to call a mechanic every time the waste disposal unit clogs up... If the cooling unit is clogged up it can't do its job efficiently.*

> V+ADV:
> OR PASSIVE:
> V+ADV:
> ERGATIVE

close /kləuz/ **(closes, closing, closed)**

★**close down**

1 If someone **closes down** a factory or an organization, or if it **closes down**, all work or activity stops there, usually for ever. ❏ *They're closing down my old school... The mines had been closed down following a geological survey... If the firms failed to make enough money, they would close down.*

V+ADV+N,
V+N+ADV,
V+PRON+ADV,
V+ADV:
ERGATIVE

NOTE **Shut down** means almost the same as **close down**.

2 When a television or radio channel **closes down**, it stops broadcasting for the day. [BRITISH] ❏ *Channel 4 closes down at midnight.*

V+ADV

◆ **Closedown** is the end of broadcasting for the day on the television or radio. [BRITISH]

N-UNCOUNT

close in

1 If a group of people **close in** on a person or a place, they come nearer and nearer to them and gradually surround them. ❏ *They closed in on the struggling pig... Several of the onlookers closed in upon the group... Now the police were closing in.*

V+ADV:
ALSO+on/upon

2 If something **closes in** on a person or a place, it approaches or is present in a threatening way. ❏ *I can feel the danger closing in... As night closed in, the invasion force continued to wait... The heat was closing in on the island.*

V+ADV:
ALSO+on/upon

3 When the days **close in**, there are gradually fewer hours of daylight as winter gets nearer.

V+ADV

close off If an area **is closed off**, a barrier is put round it or a door is shut, so that nobody can get into it. ❏ *They lived in a castle in which most of the rooms were permanently closed off... He hadn't been down that road since they closed it off... The iron door closing off our section slid open.*

V+N+ADV,
V+PRON+ADV,
V+ADV+N:
USUALLY PASSIVE

NOTE **Seal off** means almost the same as **close off**.

close on If you **close on** something or someone, you gradually get nearer and nearer to them, often in a threatening way. ❏ *The fish closed on the woman and hurtled past. ...Soviet T-34s closing on the camp so suddenly... Snodin brought down Olsen as he closed on the Everton goal.*

V+PREP

NOTE **Close in on** means almost the same as **close on**.

close out If you **close out** light or sound, you prevent it from reaching a place, for example by using a screen of some kind. ❏ *Then the canvas flap dropped shut, closing out the light from the middle ground between their trenches and ours... She shut the window, closing out the sound of the midday traffic.*

V+ADV+N

★**close up**

1 When you **close up** a building or a business, you close it completely and securely. ❏ *The big house was closed up for the holidays... The officials had closed up for the day.*

V+ADV+N,
V+N/PRON+ADV,
V+ADV

2 If something **closes up** or if you **close** it **up**, it closes completely. ❏ *One of his eyes seemed to be closing up... She closed up the atlas and put it back on the shelf... He closed the luggage up and stored it by the door.*

V+ADV,
V+ADV+N,
V+N/PRON+ADV:
ERGATIVE

3 If people **close up**, they move nearer to each other. ❏ *She told the children to close up to allow everyone into the hall... The two motor cycle riders closed up.*

V+ADV

cloud /klaud/ **(clouds, clouding, clouded)**

cloud over

1 If it **clouds over** or if the sky **clouds over**, the sky becomes covered with clouds. ❏ *The sky had clouded over completely... It was clouding over and we thought it was going to rain.*

V+ADV

2 If your face **clouds over**, you suddenly look sad or angry. ❏ *I saw Hamish's face cloud over... His face clouded over with anguish.*

V+ADV

3 If your eyes **cloud over**, they become dull and blank. ❏ *As we watched, his eyes clouded over; he twitched and then lay still.*

V+ADV

NOTE **Mist over** means almost the same as **cloud over**.

club /klʌb/ **(clubs, clubbing, clubbed)**

club together If people **club together** to do or buy something, they all give money in order to share the cost of it. [BRITISH] ❏ *We all clubbed together to buy her a present when she retired.*

V+ADV:
ALSO+to-INF

NOTE **Chip in** means almost the same as **club together**.

clue /kluː/ (clues, clueing, clued)

clue up If you **are clued up** about something, you know about it and understand it. [BRITISH, INFORMAL] ❑ *You need to have good leaders who are all clued up.*

V+PRON+ADV,
V+N+ADV:
USUALLY PASSIVE

cluster /klʌstər/ (clusters, clustering, clustered)

> ✓ In American English, **around** is much more common than **round**.

cluster around If people **cluster around** or **cluster round** a place, they
stand around it in a tight group. ❑ *He watched the happy parents cluster around their
darling sons... Sometimes they stop and cluster round a patch of ground.*

V+PREP,
V+ADV

NOTE **Gather around** means almost the same as **cluster around**.

cluster round → See cluster around

clutter /klʌtər/ (clutters, cluttering, cluttered)

clutter up If you **clutter up** a place, you fill it untidily with a lot of unnecessary things. ❑ *The room was cluttered up with all kinds of things.*

V+ADV+N,
V+N+ADV,
V+PRON+ADV

coax /kouks/ (coaxes, coaxing, coaxed)

coax into If you **coax** someone **into** doing something, you persuade them to
do it by speaking in a gentle and pleasant way to them. ❑ *You just coax them into doing it... Even Dr Cox was coaxed into having some mutton.*

V+N+PREP,
V+PRON+PREP

cobble /kɒbəl/ (cobbles, cobbling, cobbled)

cobble together If you **cobble** something **together**, you make or produce it
roughly or quickly, by using things that are available to you. ❑ *Its author has cobbled
together a guide to the islands.*

V+ADV+N,
V+N+ADV,
V+PRON+ADV

cock /kɒk/ (cocks, cocking, cocked)

cock up If you **cock** something **up**, you do it so badly that you completely ruin
or spoil it. [BRITISH, INFORMAL, RUDE] ❑ *We don't want to cock the whole thing up.*
♦ A **cock-up** is something that is done very badly. [BRITISH, INFORMAL, RUDE] ❑ *There
has been a series of cock-ups.*

V+N+ADV,
V+PRON+ADV,
V+ADV+N
N-COUNT

coil /kɔɪl/ (coils, coiling, coiled)

coil up If you **coil** something **up**, you wind it into a continuous series of loops.
❑ *He coiled up the garden hose.*

V+ADV+N,
V+N+ADV,
V+PRON+ADV

collect /kəlekt/ (collects, collecting, collected)

collect up If you **collect** things **up**, you collect them all together. ❑ *They collected up their gear... She was asked to collect up the briefcases and the books.*

V+ADV+N,
V+N+ADV,
V+PRON+ADV

colour /kʌlər/ (colours, colouring, coloured)

> ✓ American English uses the spellings **color, colors, coloring,** and **colored**.

colour in If you **colour in** a shape or outline that is drawn on paper, you give it
different colours using paints or crayons. ❑ *She was busy colouring in her picture.*

V+ADV+N,
V+N+ADV,
V+PRON+ADV

colour up When someone **colours up**, their face becomes red because they are
angry or embarrassed.

V+ADV

NOTE **Blush** means almost the same as **colour up**.

comb /koum/ (combs, combing, combed)

comb out If you **comb out** your hair, or if you **comb** something **out** of it,
you comb it very thoroughly in order to remove anything that should not be there,
such as tangles or knots. ❑ *Head lice attach their eggs to the base of your hair, and you
can't comb them out.*

V+PRON+ADV,
V+N+ADV,
V+ADV+N

come /kʌm/ (comes, coming, came)

> ✓ The form **come** is used in the present tense and is the past participle of the
> verb. In American English, **around** is much more common than **round**.

★**come about** When you say how something **comes about**, you explain how it
happens. ❑ *The discovery of adrenalin came about through a mistake... How did the invitation come about?*

V+ADV

★**come across**

1 When someone **comes across**, they cross a room, water, or other area towards
the place where you are. ❑ *At that point he came across the room and took her firmly by
the shoulder... Some people have been coming across in aeroplanes.*

V+PREP,
V+ADV

2 If you **come across** someone or something, you find or meet them by chance, without having expected to or without having thought about it. ❏ *Everyone has come across the sort of problem which seems impossible to solve... I came across a man hoeing a field... I've never come across anything like this.* — V+PREP

3 If someone or something **comes across** as having a particular characteristic, they give you the impression of having that characteristic. ❏ *He wasn't coming across as the idiot I had expected him to be... This was the image that was coming across.* — V+ADV: USUALLY+*as*

4 When an idea or meaning **comes across**, you understand exactly what was meant. ❏ *Do you think this idea comes across in the play?... Did you think that this came across well?* — V+ADV

NOTE **Come over** means almost the same as **come across**.

★come after

1 When something **comes after** a particular event or point in time, it happens later than that event or time. ❏ *Learning should come after play... It was not looked on, by the generations that came after, as the high point of their civilization.* — V+PREP, V+ADV

NOTE **Follow** means almost the same as **come after**.

2 If someone **comes after** you, they chase you or hunt you. ❏ *The faster I retreated, the faster they came after me.* — V+PREP

★come along

1 When someone **comes along** a road or other area of ground, they move along it towards you. ❏ *The children came along the beach... Ralph was coming along, holding his spear.* — V+PREP, V+ADV

2 If someone **comes along**, they go somewhere with you or go to the same place as you. ❏ *Thank you for coming along at this somewhat inconvenient time... But why don't you come along with us?* — V+ADV: ALSO+*with*

3 When something or someone **comes along**, they happen or arrive, without your having thought much about it beforehand. ❏ *When the harvest came along, the boy who was doing the milking fell ill... A new generation of planners came along who were much more scientifically based.* — V+ADV

4 If something or someone **is coming along**, they are making progress or developing in the way you want. ❏ *There are even cookers which tell you how the meat is coming along.* — V+ADV

NOTE **Come on** means almost the same as **come along**.

5 You say '**come along**' to someone when you want them to hurry up. ❏ *Come along now, little ones, off to bed.* — IMPERATIVE, V+ADV

NOTE **Come on** and **hurry up** mean almost the same as **come along**.

6 You say '**come along**' to someone when you want to encourage them to do something. ❏ *He took out a flask of brandy and poured a measure. 'Come along now, old chap. Put this down.'* — IMPERATIVE, V+ADV

7 You say '**come along**' to someone when you think that they are saying something untrue or unreasonable. ❏ *Come along now, Marsha, the personal sphere is political as well.* — IMPERATIVE, V+ADV

come apart If something **comes apart**, it breaks or collapses. ❏ *He pulled both ends of the stick, and it came apart in two pieces.* — V+ADV

★come around

1 When someone **comes around** or **comes round**, they call at your house to see you for a short time. ❏ *I could come round this evening if you like... Don't call. Come round. About eleven... He abruptly stopped calling or coming round to visit.* — V+ADV

NOTE **Come over** means almost the same as **come around**.

2 When someone **comes around** or **comes round**, they visit or attend to you as part of a series of visits or as part of a routine. ❏ *The driver came around to collect fares... The stewardess came round with the local paper.* — V+ADV

3 When letters or other things **come around** or **come round**, they are circulated or sent to a group of people. ❏ *A departmental memo just came round to say that Mangel's coming here.* — V+ADV

4 If you **come around** or **come round** to an idea, belief, or suggestion, you change your mind and start to like it or agree with it. ❏ *He knew I would have to come* — V+ADV: USUALLY+*to*

round to his way of thinking in the end... You two used to be such friends. You'll come around to his side in the end... But you'll find she'll come round. Parents always do.

5 If something **comes around** or **comes round**, it happens as a regular or pre-   V+ADV dictable event. ❑ *Don't wait for April to come round before planning your vegetable garden... She'll be a jolly tough candidate to beat when the election comes round. ...when the new academic year came around in the autumn.*

come at

1 If someone **comes at** you, they move towards you in order to attack you. ❑ *The*   V+PREP *bear came at me.*

2 If things such as questions, ideas, or events **come at** you, they are all presented   V+PREP to you at the same time in a way that you find threatening, confusing, or exciting. ❑ *A new question was coming at him. ...particularly encouraged by all of this information coming at them at once.*

★come away

1 If you **come away** from a place, you leave it. ❑ *He came away with the uncomfort-*   V+ADV; *able feeling that he had been brainwashed... Come away. There's going to be trouble.*   ALSO IMPERATIVE

2 When something **comes away** from something else, it becomes separated or de-   V+ADV; tached from it very easily and without needing force. ❑ *She picked up the book. The*   ALSO+from *cover had come away from the spine... They dissect it, everything comes away very neatly.*

★come back

1 When someone or something **comes back**, they return to the place where you   V+ADV are. ❑ *He came back from the war... Are you ever coming back home?*

2 When something **comes back** after a period of inactivity, it starts to happen   V+ADV again. ❑ *That shelter might fall down if the rain comes back.*

3 When something **comes back** after being unfashionable for a time, it becomes   V+ADV fashionable again. ❑ *Ostrich feathers never really came back... At last reliability and efficiency seem to be coming back into fashion.*

NOTE **Go out** means the opposite of **come back**.

♦ If something makes a **comeback**, it becomes fashionable again. ❑ *Body painting*   N-COUNT *made a brief comeback in the 1960s.*

♦ If someone makes or stages a **comeback**, they become successful again at some-   N-COUNT thing that they were successful at before. ❑ *I tried to make a comeback.*

4 When a person, answer, or message **comes back**, you get a response to some-   V+ADV thing you have said or done. ❑ *Lally's voice came back from the dark... The message which came back was that I could order books from the library.*

5 If something that you had forgotten **comes back** to you, you remember it, often   V+ADV; quite suddenly. ❑ *Then the scene of their encounter came back to him with a sense of em-*   USUALLY+to *barrassment... Against his will, it all came back to him.*

★**come back to** If you **come back to** a particular topic or idea, you mention or   V+ADV+PREP start to discuss it again. ❑ *He always came back to this point... We'll come back to that question a little later. ...to come back to what Brian was saying.*

come before If people, problems, or cases **come before** a judge, court of law,   V+PREP or other authority, they are brought or discussed there as part of an official process, so that a decision can be made about them. ❑ *His case came before a tribunal... The major came before the Armed Services Committee.*

come between If something **comes between** two people, it causes trouble   V+PREP between them and so spoils their friendship. ❑ *I had come between him and his girlfriend... Nothing like that came between me and the people I met.*

★come by

☑ In meaning 2, the stress is on **come**.

1 When someone **comes by**, they come to see you for a short time, on a casual or   V+ADV, informal basis. ❑ *Tom had said he would come by at five... They came by his office.*   V+PREP

2 If you **come by** something, you obtain it by chance or without much thought or   V+PREP planning. ❑ *He had not come by these things through his own labour... Good jobs were hard to come by.*

★come down

1 When someone or something **comes down**, they move from a higher position   V+PREP,

to a lower one, or move towards the place where you are. ❑ *We came down the aircraft* `V+ADV`
steps... A taxi came down the street... After supper, she came down to the pump with me...
They came down from the bridge.

2 When someone in a building **comes down**, they move downstairs towards you. `V+ADV,`
❑ *I showered, dressed and came down for breakfast... I heard you come down the stairs with* `V+PREP`
him.

NOTE **Descend** is a more formal word for **come down**.

3 If someone **comes down** to a place near you, they visit it or move there; used `V+ADV:`
when the place is farther south or is in the country. ❑ *He said he wanted his mother to* `USUALLY+A`
come down to New York... This is Mr Stuart. He's come down from London to talk to me.

4 When something **comes down**, it collapses or falls to the ground, or someone `V+ADV`
dismantles it or moves it to a lower position. ❑ *In the storm a tree came down... Bricks*
flew in all directions as walls came down... Then, when they reached a deep creek, the
big, red-ochred sails came down... Her cheeks were flushed, and her top-knot had come
down.

5 If a plane **comes down**, it lands or crashes. ❑ *Almost all the division's gliders came* `V+ADV`
down on or close to the field... The plane circled and came down in flames.

6 If the cost, level, or amount of something **comes down**, it becomes cheaper or `V+ADV`
less than it was before. ❑ *Prices could come down only if wages came down... Local govern-*
ment expenditure has come down by 20% since 1975.

NOTE **Decrease** is a more formal word for **come down**, and **go up** means the opposite.

7 If you **come down** when you are making an offer or suggesting an amount, you `V+ADV,`
decrease the original offer or amount. ❑ *Get on the phone at once, please, and offer to* `V+ADV+N`
come down a couple of hundred dollars.

8 Something that **comes down** to a particular point extends downwards as far as `V+ADV:`
that point. ❑ *The window came down almost to the ground... His eyebrows came down over* `WITH A`
his nose.

9 If something such as a tradition, belief, or land **comes down** to a group of peo- `V+ADV:`
ple, it is passed to that generation of people from a previous one. ❑ *...the religious doc-* `ALSO+to`
trines which have come down to us. ...one of the most moving objects that has come down
to us from the distant past.

NOTE **Be handed down** means almost the same as **come down**.

10 If a sign, message, or noise **comes down** to you, you receive it or hear it. `V+ADV:`
❑ *Now word had come down that a large mass of activists was in the vicinity... An instruc-* `USUALLY+A`
tion came down from Paris to investigate him... A cry came down from above.

11 If rain or snow or fog **comes down**, it falls heavily. ❑ *...when the monsoon* `V+ADV`
breaks, and the rain comes down... Five inches of snow had fallen and more was coming
down... But then the fog came down.

12 When university students **come down**, they leave university, especially at the `V+ADV`
end of their degree course, or at the end of term. [BRITISH] ❑ *He came down from Ox-*
ford in 1958.

NOTE **Go up** means the opposite of **come down**.

13 If you **come down** in favour of something or on the side of something, you `V+ADV:`
decide that that is the right or appropriate thing to do. ❑ *The subcommittees both* `WITH A`
came down in favour of the conservation programme... They came down strongly on the side
of Pigott.

14 You say that something is a **come-down** if you think that it is not as good as `N-SING`
something else that you have just done or had. ❑ *Professionally it is considered a come-*
down to work in portrait classes... What a comedown!

come down on If you **come down on** someone, you blame them for some- `V+ADV+PREP`
thing, and criticize them severely for allowing it to happen. ❑ *Social workers like me*
come down harder on parents than on their children... Don't come down on me before you
understand.

★come down to If a problem or question **comes down to** a particular thing, `V+ADV+PREP`
that is the most important or relevant factor to be considered. ❑ *Your final choice of*
kitchen may well come down to cost... It all comes down to the mathematics taught in
schools... When it comes down to it, that's what I hired him for.

The symbol ★ shows key phrasal verbs

come down with If you **come down with** an illness or disease, you catch it or develop it. ❑ *She came down with pneumonia... He came down with appendicitis.* · V+ADV+PREP

NOTE **Contract** is a more formal word for **come down with**.

★**come for**

1 When someone **comes for** a person or thing, they come to where you are in order to get them and take them away. ❑ *I said I would come for Dolly in the afternoon... The police came for Humboldt... I'll come for the sandwiches later.* · V+PREP

2 If someone **is coming for** you, they move towards you in a threatening way, as if they might attack you. ❑ *Jake was coming for me with a knife.* · V+PREP

come forth

1 If you **come forth** with a suggestion or with information, you make that suggestion or give the information. [LITERARY] ❑ *The British came forth with a second proposal... A witness came forth to testify that the young man had been present.* · V+ADV: ALSO+with

NOTE **Come forward** means almost the same as **come forth**.

◆ Someone who is **forthcoming** willingly gives information when you ask them about something. ❑ *He was disinclined to talk about that: nor was he forthcoming on the way in which he had risen to power.* · ADJECTIVE

◆ If something is **forthcoming**, it is given or made available. [FORMAL] ❑ *No evidence of this was forthcoming.* · ADJECTIVE

2 If something **comes forth**, it appears and moves towards you. [LITERARY] ❑ *Great rockets of flame came forth. ...casting spells before the hunt to make the animals come forth.* · V+ADV

3 A **forthcoming** event is planned to happen soon. ❑ *I wrote to the Minister asking his advice on the forthcoming presidential election.* · ADJECTIVE

★**come forward** If someone **comes forward** to do something, they offer to do it. ❑ *When we first came here people came forward to help us... Many people came forward to accuse her of various misdemeanours.* · V+ADV

come forward with If you **come forward with** a suggestion, proposal, or idea, you make that suggestion or proposal, or state your idea. ❑ *They came forward with ambitious plans for the centre.* · V+ADV+PREP

★**come from**

1 If you **come from** a particular place, you were born there or grew up there. You can also say that someone **comes from** a particular type of family or a particular social class when they have experienced the type of life that is usually associated with that type of family or social class. ❑ *'Where do you come from?'—'India'... They all came from well-off families... Julie does not come from a very theatrical background.* · V+PREP

2 If one thing **comes from** another thing, the second thing is its source or origin. ❑ *Did you know the word 'idea' comes from Greek?... Where is the money to come from?... There was a smell of something cooking coming from the oven.* · V+PREP

3 If you say that you know where someone **is coming from**, you mean that you understand their situation, attitude, or emotional state. [INFORMAL] ❑ *I just don't get where he's coming from, that guy.* · V+PREP

★**come in**

1 When someone **comes in**, they enter the room or building where you are. ❑ *There was a knock on the door. 'Come in'... Jeremy came in looking worried... 'Come in the house,' she said.* · V+ADV, V+PREP

2 When someone **comes in** somewhere such as a place of work or business or hospital, they arrive there in order to work, carry out business, receive treatment, and so on. ❑ *I came in early today... I was asked to come in for a few days to help out... He came in with a broken leg.* · V+ADV

3 When someone such as a builder or cleaner **comes in**, they come to your house in order to carry out work there. ❑ *I can't get anybody to come in and do anything in my house... I've also telephoned the local builder to come in tomorrow morning.* · V+ADV

4 When someone or something **comes in** from another place, they arrive at or approach the place where you are. ❑ *...the businessman who came in from the capital by air. ...the vast import of processed fish, coming in through the commercial docks.* · V+ADV

5 When a plane, ship, train, or bus **comes in**, it arrives at its destination or a station or bus stop. ❑ *Father and son could see the planes coming in over the fields... A ship had just come in from Turkey... She waited near the bus terminus until the last bus came in.* · V+ADV

♦An **incoming** plane or passenger is travelling towards a place and about to arrive. ADJECTIVE
❑ ...*the incoming passengers at London Airport.*
NOTE **Outward** means the opposite of **incoming**.

6 When light, sound, air, or rain **comes in**, it penetrates a barrier or hole and V+ADV
reaches the place where you are. ❑ *It was dark inside the wood. No sunlight came*
in at all... The wind was strong, rain was coming in, she thought it wiser to close the shut-
ters.

7 If something such as information, a report, or a letter **comes in**, you receive it. V+ADV
❑ ...*in the reports that are coming in from Thailand... I'm waiting for some new orders com-*
ing in any time... A call had come in telling us that arrests had been made.
NOTE **Arrive** means almost the same as **come in**, and **go out** means the opposite.
♦ An **incoming** message, letter, or phone call has been sent to you or is received by ADJECTIVE
you. ❑ *I throw incoming mail in a wicker basket.*
NOTE **Outgoing** means the opposite of **incoming**.

8 If you have money **coming in**, you earn it or receive it as your normal income. V+ADV
❑ *The taxman is entitled to details of the money you have coming in... There is practically no*
money coming in to buy food, furniture or clothing.
♦ Your **income** is the amount of money that you earn from your work or business, N-COUNT
or from other sources such as pension or investments. ❑ *My monthly income was over*
two hundred pounds.

9 When something such as a fashion **comes in**, it becomes fashionable. ❑ *Thicker* V+ADV
fabrics and darker colors came in.
NOTE **Go out** means the opposite of **come in**.

10 When something new such as an invention or law **comes in**, it is introduced V+ADV
and begins to have an effect. ❑ *We used coal gas before natural gas came in. ...with the*
Health and Safety at Work Act coming in last year.

11 When something in a shop **comes in**, a supply of it reaches the shop and it be- V+ADV
comes available. ❑ ...*when copies of George Jackson's 'Soledad Brother' came in... We're*
waiting for the new brochures to come in.

12 If someone **comes in** on a discussion, they join in, sometimes interrupting V+ADV:
someone who is already speaking. ❑ *Let me just come in on this, because Clive is not giv-* ALSO+on
ing the whole story... Could I come in here?

13 If someone **comes in** on an arrangement, they join a group of other people V+ADV:
and take part in what they are planning to do. ❑ *He should come in on the deal... He* ALSO+on/with
was sorry that he had asked Fred Caldwell to come in with him.

14 When a government **comes in**, it wins an election and starts governing the V+ADV
country. ❑ *Labour governments come in promising to expand public expenditure... Mrs*
Thatcher's government came in pledging to arrest and reverse this trend.
♦ An **incoming** official or administration is one that has just been newly appointed ADJECTIVE
or elected. ❑ *They gave their loyalty to the incoming Government... The outgoing and in-*
coming Administrations will not agree.
NOTE **Outgoing** means the opposite of **incoming**.

15 You ask or mention where something or someone **comes in** when you are talk- V+ADV
ing about how they are involved in a situation. ❑ *I still don't see where you come in...*
'It's highly illogical.'—'Well logic doesn't come in anyway does it?'

16 When the tide **comes in**, it rises, so that the water reaches higher up the shore. V+ADV
❑ *The tide was coming in and all the muddy banks were being covered.*
NOTE **Go out** means the opposite of **come in**.
♦ An **incoming** tide or wave is coming towards you. ADJECTIVE

17 When a season, month, or period of weather **comes in**, it begins. ❑ *Winter came* V+ADV
in with a dark, hungry sadness... We have some improved weather coming in here soon.

18 If something **comes in** useful or handy, it is a useful thing to have. ❑ *Savings* V+ADV+ADJ
may come in useful for holidays... A toothbrush would come in handy.

19 When someone or something **comes in** a particular position or rank, they are V+ADV+C
in that position or rank in a sequence or at the end of a competition. ❑ *David had be-*
gun the day well by coming in third in the junior riding class.

20 When cricketers, baseball players, and so on **come in**, they begin to bat. ❑ *He* V+ADV
made a Test century only a week ago, coming in at number nine.

The symbol ★ shows key phrasal verbs

come in for If someone or something **comes in for** criticism, blame, or abuse, they are criticized, blamed, or insulted. ❑ *British industry does come in for a great deal of criticism... The officers often came in for abuse... The Unions come in for a lot of knocking.*   V+ADV+PREP

★**come into**

1 If someone **comes into** a room, house, or other place, they enter it. ❑ *Boylan came silently into the room.... They came into the bookstore.*   V+PREP

NOTE **Enter** is a more formal word for **come into**, and **leave** means the opposite.

2 If someone or something **comes into** being, sight, use, force, and so on, they be-   V+PREP gin to exist, be noticed or used, have an effect, and so on. ❑ *Christianity came into being in a hostile environment... Some people stared at me when I came into sight... This technique is rapidly coming into use today... New legislation came into force in 1981.*

3 If you say that something **comes into** it or **comes into** a situation or subject,   V+PREP+*it*, you mean that it is relevant to the situation or subject that you are talking about. ❑ *I*   V+PREP *don't quite see how the wigs come into it... Where does money come into it? ...psychological factors that come into it... The judge decided that it was not discrimination, since sex did not come into the overt reason given for the action.*

4 When a government **comes into** office or power, it wins an election and starts   V+PREP governing the country. ❑ *...before the Conservative Government came into office... The Labour Government came into power in March 1974.*

5 If someone **comes into** money, property, or a title, they inherit it. ❑ *She came*   V+PREP *into some money on her mother's death.*

come of

1 You talk about something **coming of** a situation when you are mentioning its   V+PREP result or consequences. ❑ *I'll let you know what comes of the meeting... I'm relieved to learn no great harm came of it.*

2 If a person **comes of** a particular family or group of ancestors, he or she is de-   V+PREP scended from them. [LITERARY] ❑ *She came of a family that had lived there for many years... The boys came of a sea-faring line.*

★**come off**

1 If someone or something **comes off** an area, place, or vehicle, they leave it.   V+PREP, ❑ *She saw him come off the plane... The umpires came off after just one ball.*   V+ADV

2 When something **comes off**, it becomes unfastened or unstuck, or it is removed.   V+ADV, ❑ *All the wallpaper's coming off... He tugged at the metal handle and it came off in his*   V+PREP *hand.*

3 If an event or action **comes off**, it is successful or effective. ❑ *Gary tried to smile*   V+ADV *but it didn't come off, his heart wasn't in it... I hope this business comes off all right.*

4 If you **come off** well or badly at the end of a process, you are in a good or bad   V+ADV: position as a result of it. ❑ *As usual, he came off second best... Families in the wealthier*   WITH A/C *classes come off comparatively better.*

NOTE **End up** means almost the same as **come off**.

5 When a play or film **comes off**, it stops being performed or shown in a particu-   V+ADV lar theatre or cinema. ❑ *The production had to come off because the theatre was already booked for a pantomime.*

6 If something such as mist, wind, or a smell **comes off** a particular place or   V+PREP thing, it originates or radiates from that place or thing. ❑ *There was a mist coming off the water... It was a warm day, and even with the wind that came off the river his father was sweating.*

7 If someone **comes off** something such as a drug, medicine, or alcohol, they stop   V+PREP taking it. ❑ *...the therapeutic community where she finally came off drugs... It's about time you came off the booze.*

8 If you say **'Come off** it!' to someone, you are indicating that you do not believe   IMPERATIVE, what they have just said, or think it is unreasonable. [INFORMAL] ❑ *Come off it, Mr*   V+PREP+*it* *Davis. The oil was ordered three months ago... 'Oh, come off it,' Freya said. 'Nazir hated him'... Come off it, Jim, that's not a letter.*

★**come on**

☑ In meanings 5 and 6, the stress is on **come**.

1 You say **'come on'** to someone when you want to encourage them or comfort   IMPERATIVE, them. ❑ *Come on, I'll help you back to the hotel... Come on, Mike, say you'll do it.*   V+ADV

2 You say **'come on'** to someone when you want them to hurry up. ❑ *There's something I want you to see. Come on, child, come on!* | IMPERATIVE, V+ADV

NOTE **Come along** means almost the same as **come on**.

3 When you **come on** somewhere, you go there. ❑ *'Hello, there,' said Brody. 'Come on in.'... Gertrude had come on to Rome instead of staying in France... Come on over – quick as you can.* | V+ADV: WITH A

♦ **Oncoming** means moving towards you. ❑ *...oncoming traffic.* | ADJECTIVE

4 When an actor or actress **comes on**, he or she appears on a stage or in a scene of a film. ❑ *...shuffling in the wings, waiting to come on... Olivier dominated the play from the moment he came on the stage.* | V+ADV, V+PREP

5 If someone **comes on** the phone, they begin speaking to you. ❑ *One of the most powerful men in France came on the line... There was this silence and then my mother came on.* | V+PREP, V+ADV

6 If you **come on** something, you find it unexpectedly or by chance. ❑ *I came on the idea by pure chance... It was half an hour before he came on the note in his tray.* | V+PREP

NOTE **Chance on** means almost the same as **come on**.

7 When a power supply or device **comes on**, it starts functioning. ❑ *At nine the street lights came on... The loudspeaker came on with a soft popping noise.* | V+ADV

NOTE **Go off** means the opposite of **come on**.

8 When a programme or film **comes on**, it starts to be broadcast or screened. ❑ *At seven the Swiss news came on.* | V+ADV

9 When a season or period of time or weather **comes on**, it approaches or begins. ❑ *...on a fall evening, as the twilight came on... Christmas came on. ...as though a terrible heat was coming on.* | V+ADV

10 If a cold, headache, or some other medical condition **is coming on**, it is just starting. ❑ *I felt a cold coming on... At lunch a bad headache came on, and he went home.* | V+ADV

11 If something **is coming on**, it is making progress or developing. ❑ *My new book is coming on quite well now... He must've come on a bit in eight hours!* | V+ADV

NOTE **Come along** means almost the same as **come on**.

12 If someone **comes on** in a particular way, they behave in that way. [INFORMAL] ❑ *...really coming on hard, solid and uncompromising... Williams doesn't come on too strong.* | V+ADV: WITH ADJ

13 When someone **comes on** to someone else, they behave in an openly sexual way towards them. [INFORMAL] ❑ *She comes on like a cheap hooker, hips swaying... I get scared when men come on to me.* | V+ADV: ALSO+to

♦ A **come-on** is an openly sexual remark or action which is intended to attract someone. [INFORMAL] ❑ *Remarks like this are a tease, a come-on.* | N-COUNT

★come on to, come onto

1 When someone **comes on to** a stage, court, or other area, they enter it. ❑ *She has something. Whenever she came on to the stage everybody held their breath... Fifteen minutes later Sinclair came onto the court and beat his opponent hollow.* | V+ADV+PREP

2 If you **come on to** a particular topic or idea, you start discussing it. ❑ *I want to come on to the question of disease in a minute... Now here we come onto another contentious subject.* | V+ADV+PREP

NOTE **Turn to** means almost the same as **come on to**.

3 If something **comes onto** the market, it becomes available. ❑ *Very little top grade land came onto the market.* | V+PREP

★come out

1 When someone **comes out** of their house or room, or a place where they were hidden, they leave it or appear from it. ❑ *After an hour or so he comes out into a small clearing... We came out of the tunnel.* | V+ADV: ALSO+of

2 If someone **comes out** with you, you go somewhere together socially. ❑ *Let's ring him up and see if he'll come out for a pint... Would you like to come out with me?* | V+ADV: USUALLY+with

3 If someone **comes out** to the country where you are, they visit you there. ❑ *Maybe one day soon, I'll come out and visit you. ...when she came out to Egypt, or Malaya or wherever it was.* | V+ADV: ALSO+to

4 If someone **comes out** of an organization or institution, they leave it. ❑ *She had* | V+ADV:

deteriorated after coming out of hospital... He came out of the army with a lump sum.   ALSO+of

NOTE **Go in** means the opposite of **come out**.

5 If something **comes out** of a particular place or source, it originates there or is   V+ADV:
produced there. ❑ *Dance music started coming out of the radiogram... She opened her*   USUALLY+of
mouth to scream, but no sounds came out. She was pale with rage... There were flames com-
ing out of the engine... Information coming out of the country was unreliable.

6 If something **comes out** of a container, you remove it from there. ❑ *I pulled the*   V+ADV:
trigger as the gun came out of the case... He was frightened. One hand came out of his pock-   USUALLY+of
et.

7 When something **comes out** from or onto a particular point, it joins something   V+ADV
else at that point. ❑ *...the four big arteries and the two veins coming out from the base of*
the heart... The road comes out onto a broad paved drive.

8 If something **is coming out**, it is becoming separated from the thing that it was   V+ADV:
attached to. ❑ *My shirt had come out of the top of my shorts... I had noticed then that her*   ALSO+of
hair was coming out in patches.

9 When information **comes out**, it is revealed or made public. ❑ *All the facts came*   V+ADV
out after Seery's death... It came out that the more money you make the less tax you are like-
ly to pay... Tess burst into tears, and the story came out.

10 When a gay person **comes out**, they let people know that they are gay. [INFOR-   V+ADV
MAL] ❑ *...the few gay men there who dare to come out... I came out as a lesbian when I*
was still in my teens.

11 If you **come out** for or against something, you declare that you do or do not   V+ADV:
support it. ❑ *He came out in support of the claim... Most Trade Union Group members came*   WITH A
out against the document.

12 When something such as a book **comes out**, it is published or becomes avail-   V+ADV
able to the public. ❑ *Over the summer his book had come out... He asked me to send him*
any new stamps which might come out.

NOTE **Appear** means almost the same as **come out**.

13 If something **comes out** in a particular position or in a particular way, it is in   V+ADV:
that position or condition at the end of a competition, process, or period of time.   WITH A/C
❑ *Who do you think will come out on top?... The press was coming out of the affair very bad-*
ly... The numbers came out exactly right.

♦ The **outcome** of something such as an action or process is its result. ❑ *There were*   N-COUNT
not many people who dared predict the outcome of the general election... It was a complicat-
ed sequence of events that led to this most extraordinary outcome.

14 If what you say **comes out** in a particular way, it is said in that way. ❑ *The*   V+ADV:
words came out more harshly than she had intended... 'I'm sorry,' said Tim. It came out in a   WITH A
whisper.

15 If workers **come out**, they go on strike. [BRITISH] ❑ *The work force promptly came*   V+ADV
out... The whole of London Transport came out in protest when a conductor got the sack.

16 When the sun, moon, or a star **comes out**, it appears in the sky. ❑ *It was cold*   V+ADV
and the sun never came out once.

17 If colours, stains, or marks **come out**, they disappear or fade. ❑ *Be careful when*   V+ADV
you're washing that towel or the colour will come out... The stains just would not come out. It
was blood.

18 If a photograph or something that has been photographed **comes out**, it is suc-   V+ADV:
cessful. ❑ *He is an excellent photographer. All his pictures come out very well. Every detail*   USUALLY+A
shows... Annabel did not come out well.

19 When flowers, leaves, or plants **come out**, the flowers or leaves develop and   V+ADV
open. ❑ *As soon as the leaves came out, the blossoms appeared.*

★**come out in** If you **come out in** spots, you become covered with them.   V+ADV+PREP
[BRITISH]

NOTE **Break out in** means almost the same as **come out in**.

★**come out of** If one thing **comes out of** something else, the first thing results   V+ADV+PREP
from the second. ❑ *Expert systems have come out of artificial intelligence research.*

come out with If someone **comes out with** something, they say it, often un-   V+ADV+PREP
expectedly. ❑ *Occasionally they come out with fascinating snippets of gossip... John came*
out with an unusual proposal.

★come **over**

1 When someone **comes over**, they move across a room or other place towards you. ❑ *He came over and stood beside me... Come over here, George, and I'll tell you... The bartender came over and put her drink down in front of her.* — V+ADV

2 When someone **comes over**, they come to the country which you are talking about from a country overseas. ❑ *He'd come over on leave from Northern Ireland... He'd met her on the plane coming over... Do you fancy coming over for 2 weeks?* — V+ADV

3 When someone **comes over**, they call at your house to see you for a short time. ❑ *You can come over tomorrow at four... He wanted me to come over for lunch... I've got some friends coming over.* — V+ADV

NOTE **Come around** means almost the same as **come over**.

4 If someone **comes over** to a grouping or organization, they leave their old grouping or organization and join a rival one. ❑ *They all came over to the new party. ...the five who came over from Labour.* — V+ADV

NOTE **Defect** is a more formal word for **come over**.

5 If a voice, sound, or message **comes over** a phone, radio, or loudspeaker, it is transmitted or broadcast and you hear it. ❑ *The voice that came over the phone was unrecognizable... The news came over the radio... Captain Walker's voice came over at full strength.* — V+PREP, V+ADV

6 If a change or feeling **comes over** you, it affects you or happens to you, perhaps making you behave in an uncharacteristic way. ❑ *A great change had come over me since the previous night... A look of contentment came over her face.* — V+PREP

7 If you **come over** dizzy, shy, funny, and so on, you start feeling that way. [INFORMAL] ❑ *She comes over all shy when she has to meet new people.* — V+ADV: WITH ADJ

8 When an idea or meaning **comes over**, you understand exactly what was meant. ❑ *I don't think that the larger symbolic purpose really comes over in this particular painting... The message of the opera came over with unmistakeable power.* — V+ADV

NOTE **Come across** means almost the same as **come over**.

9 If someone or something **comes over** as having a particular characteristic, they give you the impression of having that characteristic. ❑ *It came over as a clear US victory... He actually does come over as someone who really would like to do this.* — V+ADV: USUALLY+as

NOTE **Come across** means almost the same as **come over**.

★come **round**

1 → See **come around**

2 When someone **comes round**, they recover consciousness. ❑ *She was bending over him as he came round.* — V+ADV

NOTE **Come to** means almost the same as **come round**, and **pass out** means the opposite.

★come **through**

1 When someone **comes through** the room where you are, they enter the room and cross it. ❑ *He came through from an inner office... She's poorly. Would you come through, Doctor... I came through the hall and heard him talking.* — V+PREP, V+ADV

2 When someone **comes through** the town or place where you are, they travel through it, perhaps stopping there briefly. ❑ *Bob had recently come through Frankfurt, and stayed awhile... I told him so quite frankly when he came through town last year.* — V+PREP, V+ADV

3 When something such as a phone call, message, document, or authorization **comes through**, you receive it, often after some procedure has been carried out. ❑ *A call came through asking for assistance... Has my visa come through yet?... She intended to look for a car as soon as the money came through.* — V+ADV

4 If you **come through** with something, you produce or do something that is expected of you. ❑ *He finally came through with the documents... The state legislature, for its part, came through with $9.4 million.* — V+ADV: USUALLY+with

5 If a quality, impression, or idea **comes through**, you perceive it in what has been said or done. ❑ *I think the teacher's own personality has got to come through... What came through most forcibly was a sense of excitement... He was an intellectual charmer. His charm comes through in his letters.* — V+ADV: ALSO+as

NOTE **Come across** means almost the same as **come through**.

6 If you **come through** a dangerous or difficult situation, you survive it and re- — V+PREP, cover from it. ❑ *Most of the troops came through the fighting unharmed... They are going to come through all right.*   V+ADV

7 When the sun or moon **comes through**, you begin to see it through the clouds. ❑ *The sun was struggling to come through... There was a wisp of sun coming through the mist.*   V+ADV, V+PREP

NOTE **Break through** means almost the same as **come through**.

come to

☑ In meaning 2, the stress is on **come**.

1 If someone **comes to**, they recover consciousness. ❑ *That's about all I remember, until I came to in a lifeboat.*   V+ADV

NOTE **Come round** means almost the same as **come to**, and **pass out** means the opposite.

2 If something **comes to** a particular number or amount, its total is that number or amount. ❑ *My income now comes to £165 a week.*   V+PREP

*come under

1 If you **come under** criticism, attack, pressure, and so on, you are criticized or attacked, or put under pressure. ❑ *The premier came under severe criticism... The housing strategy is almost certain to come under increasing attack... British produce came under pressure from foreign competition.*   V+PREP

2 If something **comes under** a particular authority or control, it is managed, controlled, or owned by it. ❑ *Day Nurseries come under the Department of Health and Social Security. ...popular demand that health care should come under public ownership.*   V+PREP

3 If one thing **comes under** a particular heading or category, it is in that class or category. ❑ *Records and tapes come under published material... The loss sustained by the statue came under the heading of fair wear and tear.*   V+PREP

*come up

1 When someone or something **comes up**, they move from a lower position to a higher one, or move towards the place where you are. ❑ *Daintry came up the great staircase towards them... I came up the garden... His head went down then, but his heels came up.*   V+PREP, V+ADV

2 When someone in a building **comes up**, they move upstairs towards you. ❑ *I was about to come up and wake you... You'd better come up to my room afterwards.*   V+ADV

3 If someone **comes up** to you, they approach you until they are standing next to you. ❑ *An man came up and spoke to him... Bill came up to Ralph... She came up to him and threw her arms around him.*   V+ADV: ALSO+to

4 If someone **comes up** to a place near you, they visit it or move there; used when the place is farther north or is in a city. ❑ *I will come up to see you one of these days... A couple of months ago we sold the farm and came up north here.*   V+ADV: WITH A

5 If someone **comes up** when they are underwater, they rise to the surface of the water. ❑ *I came up, and swam across a few yards... An instant later he came up spluttering.*   V+ADV

6 If something **comes up** in a conversation or meeting, it is mentioned or discussed. ❑ *His name came up at a buffet lunch... Egyptian art came up as a topic... An interesting point came up here.*   V+ADV

7 If a job **comes up**, it becomes available. ❑ *When I applied here, I didn't know this post in Oxford would come up... He was willing to take any job that came up.*   V+ADV

8 If something **is coming up**, it is about to happen or take place. ❑ *There's a royal wedding coming up... The SDP are fighting any election that comes up anywhere... It was just coming up to ten o'clock in the morning.*   V+ADV

9 When a problem, situation, or event **comes up**, it happens, perhaps unexpectedly. ❑ *I can't see you tonight. Something's come up... If anything urgent comes up you can always get me on the phone... A rather delicate assignment has come up.*   V+ADV

NOTE **Crop up** means almost the same as **come up**.

10 In a court of law, if a case **comes up**, it is presented to the magistrates or judge. ❑ *A case on Corporate fraud came up in the Chancery Courts recently.*   V+ADV

11 If something **comes up** to or as far as a particular point or level, it reaches that point or level. ❑ *Measure how far the water comes up... Few of them come up to its quality.*   V+ADV: USUALLY+to

12 When the sun or moon or a star **comes up**, it rises. When the dawn **comes up**, it begins to grow light. ❑ *The sun comes up in the East... Slowly a full moon comes up*   V+ADV *from the horizon. ...as dawn came up over the New Jersey skyline.*

NOTE **Go down** means almost the opposite of **come up**.

13 If a wind, sound, or light, and so on **comes up**, it appears and grows stronger, V+ADV
louder, or brighter. ❑ *By ten o'clock a breeze had come up – not strong, but fresh... A roar
of applause came up as the spotlight hit me... The film had ended and the lights came up.*

14 When a seed, plant, or bulb **comes up**, it grows and pushes through the soil. V+ADV
❑ *The grass was high and had come up with a rush.*

15 You talk about information **coming up** when it appears, for example on a V+ADV
computer screen, or on announcement boards in stations and airports. ❑ *It didn't
come up on their computer.*

16 If someone **comes up** in society or their profession, they achieve a higher sta- V+ADV:
tus in it. ❑ *Boulton was a Birmingham craftsman who came up the hard way... Evie and her* USUALLY+A
mother had come up in the world.

NOTE **Go down** means the opposite of **come up**.

♦ Someone or something that is **up-and-coming** is likely to be very successful in ADJECTIVE
the future. ❑ *He was one of the up-and-coming young businessmen in town.*

17 If you say that someone or something **comes up** a particular thing, you mean V+ADV:
that they appear that way at the end of a process or period of time or activity. WITH C/A
❑ *Dorothy always came up smiling... He went to Harvard a shy young boy and came up a
mature man. ...especially rabbit skins, which come up beautifully.*

★**come up against** If you **come up against** a problem or difficulty, you are V+ADV+PREP
faced with it and have to deal with it. ❑ *Everyone comes up against discrimination sooner
or later... The first time I did this I came up against an unforeseen problem.*

★**come up for**

1 When someone or something **comes up for** consideration or action of some V+ADV+PREP
kind, the time arrives when they have to be considered or dealt with. ❑ *The TV rights
contract came up for renegotiation in 1988... These three clubs could come under close scruti-
ny when their licenses come up for renewal... An adjacent twenty-seven-acre field came up for
sale.*

2 If someone **comes up for** election, they are put forward as a candidate in an V+ADV+PREP
election. ❑ *A third of my colleagues will come up for election next May.*

★**come upon**

1 If you **come upon** someone or something, you meet or find them unexpectedly. V+PREP
❑ *They rounded a turn and came upon a family of lions... She had been thrown into confusion by suddenly coming upon a photo of Terry.*

NOTE **Come across** means almost the same as **come upon**.

2 If an idea or feeling **comes upon** you, it develops without your really being V+PREP
aware of it. ❑ *His new outlook on life had come upon him gradually... Embarrassment came
upon me... Suddenly there came upon me once again the memory of that afternoon.*

★**come up to**

1 To **be coming up to** a time or state means to be getting near to it. ❑ *Some of* V+ADV+PREP
them are coming up to retirement... It was just coming up to ten o'clock.

NOTE **Approach** means almost the same as **come up to**.

2 If something **does** not **come up to** expectations or a particular standard, it is V+ADV+PREP:
not as good as people expected it to be. ❑ *It must be said that it never really came up to* WITH NEGATIVE
expectations... I think perhaps Christine wasn't coming up to scratch.

★**come up with**

1 If you **come up with** a plan, idea, or solution, you think of it and suggest it. ❑ *I* V+ADV+PREP
*hope to come up with some of the answers... It didn't take her long to come up with a very
convincing example... The commission came up with a compromise.*

2 If you **come up with** a sum of money, you provide it when it is needed. ❑ *You* V+ADV+PREP
*have no choice but to come up with the £120,000... Revlon came up with $750,000 to fund
a research program.*

cone /koʊn/ **(cones, coning, coned)**

cone off To **cone off** a road or an area of ground means to place a line of large V+ADV+N,
plastic cones there to prevent people driving on part of it. [BRITISH] ❑ *The police were* V+N+ADV,
busy coning off the road where the accident had taken place.* V+PRON+ADV

confide /kənfaɪd/ (confides, confiding, confided)

★confide in If you **confide in** someone, you tell them about a private problem or some other secret matter. ❑ *His father probably doesn't confide in him a great deal... May I confide in you? ...men friends in whom he can confide... People don't confide much in a security officer.*

V+PREP

conjure /kʌndʒəʳ, AM kuːn-/ (conjures, conjuring, conjured)

conjure up If you **conjure up** a particular picture or idea of something, or if your words **conjure** it **up**, you make other people imagine that idea or picture. ❑ *They listened in astonishment while James conjured up pictures of fantastic machines... The word 'unemployment' still conjures up an image of men in cloth caps.*

V+ADV+N,
V+N+ADV,
V+PRON+ADV

NOTE **Evoke** is a more formal word for **conjure up**.

conk /kɒŋk/ (conks, conking, conked)

conk out If something, such as a machine or vehicle, **conks out**, it stops working or breaks down. [BRITISH, INFORMAL] ❑ *The washing machine has finally conked out.*

V+ADV

connect /kənekt/ (connects, connecting, connected)

connect up If a piece of equipment or a place **is connected up** to a source of power or water, it is joined to that source so that it has power or water. ❑ *The shower is easy to install – it needs only to be connected up to the hot and cold water supply... They turned the barricade into a potential death trap by connecting it up to the mains.*

V+N+ADV,
V+PRON+ADV,
V+ADV+N:
ALSO+to

contract /kəntrækt/ (contracts, contracting, contracted)

contract in If you **contract in** to a scheme or arrangement, you formally say that you want to take part in it. [BRITISH, FORMAL] ❑ *You have to contract in if you want to participate in the scheme.*

V+ADV:
ALSO+to

contract out

1 If you **contract out** of a scheme or arrangement, you formally say that you do not want to take part in it. [BRITISH, FORMAL] ❑ *You can apply to the Pensions Board to contract out... She wants to contract out of the private health scheme.*

V+ADV:
ALSO+of

2 If you **contract out** of something that you are expected to do or take part in, you withdraw from it or fail to do it. ❑ *Generally, the unions have contracted out of their responsibilities. ...contracting out of defence arrangements.*

V+ADV:
USUALLY+of

3 If a company **contracts out** work to another company, it employs that company to do it, rather than doing it itself. ❑ *...a move towards contracting out more work to private firms... We've now started contracting out some of these services.*

V+ADV+N,
V+N+ADV

cook /kʊk/ (cooks, cooking, cooked)

cook up

1 If someone **cooks up** a dishonest scheme, they plan it; used showing disapproval. [INFORMAL] ❑ *They tend to cook up all sorts of little deals... The Ministry cooked up a meaningless mission to Canada.*

V+ADV+N,
V+N+ADV,
V+PRON+ADV

NOTE **Concoct** is a more formal word for **cook up**.

2 If someone **cooks up** an explanation or a story, they make it up. [INFORMAL] ❑ *She'll cook up a convincing explanation.*

V+ADV+N,
V+N+ADV,
V+PRON+ADV

3 If you **cook up** a meal, you make it, often quickly. ❑ *She could really cook up a good meal... He cooked up a very good mushroom omelette.*

V+ADV+N,
V+N+ADV,
V+PRON+ADV

NOTE **Rustle up** means almost the same as **cook up**.

cool /kuːl/ (cools, cooling, cooled)

★cool down

1 If something **cools down** or if you **cool** it **down**, it becomes cooler until it reaches the temperature that you want it to be at. ❑ *The engine will take half an hour to cool down... Rinse the bowl in cold water to cool it down.*

V+ADV,
V+N/PRON+ADV,
V+ADV+N:
ERGATIVE

2 If someone **cools down** or if you **cool** them **down**, they become less angry. ❑ *Tom had cooled down considerably... I had changed, and was cooling down slightly... I had the greatest difficulty in cooling him down.*

V+ADV,
V+PRON+ADV,
V+N+ADV:
ERGATIVE

NOTE **Calm down** means almost the same as **cool down**.

cool off

1 If someone or something that is too hot **cools off**, they become cooler. ❑ *We cooled off from the heat with a refreshing swim... These metal attachments normally take*

V+ADV

longer than that to cool off... As the weather cooled off he exchanged the robe for a thick blanket.

2 If you **cool off**, you become less excited or enthusiastic about something. ❑ *He seems to have cooled off on the negotiation idea... Vita's love for him was cooling off.*   V+ADV

♦ A **cooling-off** period is an agreed period of time during which unions and management will try to resolve a dispute before taking any serious action. ❑ *Our union is opposed to any cooling-off period.*   ADJECTIVE

coop /kuːp/ (coops, cooping, cooped)

coop up If someone **is cooped up** in a place, they are kept in a place which is too small or which does not give them much freedom. ❑ *...a prisoner cooped up in a cell... She had been cooped up in her aunt's house for ten days... After being cooped up for so long, it was pleasant to be out driving.*   PASSIVE: V+ADV

cop /kɒp/ (cops, copping, copped)

cop off with If you **cop off with** someone, you meet them and start a sexual or romantic relationship with them. [BRITISH, INFORMAL] ❑ *Did the thought that you might just possibly cop off with her ever cross your mind?*   V+ADV+PREP

NOTE **Get off with** means almost the same as **cop off with**.

cop out If you **cop out** of doing something, you avoid doing it because you are afraid or embarrassed about it; used showing disapproval. [INFORMAL] ❑ *My friend and I simply copped out of the plan altogether... You're the one that's copping out, not me.*   V+ADV: ALSO+of

NOTE **Duck out** means almost the same as **cop out**.

♦ If you say that something is a **cop-out**, you think that someone is not doing what they should do; used showing disapproval. [INFORMAL] ❑ *Such international co-operation is often merely a cop-out.*   N-COUNT

copy /kɒpi/ (copies, copying, copied)

copy down If you **copy down** what someone has said or written, you write it on a piece of paper. ❑ *Can you copy down his address for me?*   V+ADV+N, V+N+ADV, V+PRON+ADV

copy in If you **copy** someone **in**, you make sure that they receive a letter, memo, or other piece of written information that you are sending to several people. ❑ *We've copied in all interested parties... Make sure you're copied in.*   V+ADV+N, V+N+ADV, V+PRON+ADV

copy out If you **copy out** a piece of writing, you write it down exactly as it was written before. ❑ *I remember copying out the whole play... He jotted down each entry then copied it out with abbreviations. ...the words of a pop song, copied out and stuck above the bed.*   V+ADV+N, V+PRON+ADV, V+N+ADV

cordon /kɔːrdən/ (cordons, cordoning, cordoned)

cordon off If someone in authority **cordons off** an area, they prevent people from entering or leaving it by putting up a barrier. ❑ *I remember the officials having to cordon off an area in Whitehall... The city was split into areas, cordoned off by barbed wire.*   V+ADV+N, V+N+ADV, V+PRON+ADV

NOTE **Close off** means almost the same as **cordon off**.

cork /kɔːrk/ (corks, corking, corked)

cork up If you **cork up** a bottle, you close it by putting a cork in it. ❑ *Let Miss Drew have what she wants; then cork up the bottle.*   V+ADV+N, V+N+ADV, V+PRON+ADV

cost /kɒst, AM kɔːst/ (costs, costing, costed)

cost out When something that you plan to do or make **is costed out**, the amount of money you need is calculated in advance. ❑ *...training days for charity staff on how to draw up contracts and cost out proposals... It is always worth having a loft conversion costed out.*   V+N+ADV, V+PRON+ADV, V+ADV+N

cotton /kɒtən/ (cottons, cottoning, cottoned)

cotton on If you **cotton on** to something, you understand it or realize it. [BRITISH, INFORMAL] ❑ *At long last he has cottoned on to the fact that I'm not interested in him!... The other man cottoned on and came running.*   V+ADV: ALSO+to

NOTE **Catch on** means almost the same as **cotton on**.

cotton to If you **cotton to** someone or something, you start to like them. [AMERICAN, INFORMAL] ❑ *His style of humor was very human, and that's why people cotton to him... It seemed to me that I was being shut out of the dialogue and that's something I just don't cotton to.*   V+PREP: NO PASSIVE

The symbol ★ shows key phrasal verbs

couch /kaʊtʃ/ (couches, couching, couched)

couch in If something **is couched in** a particular type of language, it is expressed in that type of language. ❑ *Here was a resolution couched in forthright terms... It was all couched in legal jargon.*

PASSIVE:
V+PREP

cough /kɒf, AM kɔːf/ (coughs, coughing, coughed)
cough up

1 If you **cough up** or if you **cough up** an amount of money, you give someone money that they need or that you owe them. [INFORMAL] ❑ *They'll cough up the hundred million... Come on, cough up.*

V+ADV,
V+ADV+N

NOTE **Pay up** means almost the same as **cough up**.

2 If you **cough up** something such as blood or phlegm, you get rid of it from inside your throat by forcing it out of your mouth with a sudden, harsh noise. ❑ *She coughed up phlegm... He sounded as if he was coughing his insides up.*

V+ADV+N,
V+N+ADV,
V+PRON+ADV

count /kaʊnt/ (counts, counting, counted)

count against If an action or characteristic **counts against** you, it is a disadvantage to you and may help to cause you to be punished, rejected, or defeated. ❑ *It would count heavily against me if I got the Director into trouble.*

V+PREP

count among If you **count** someone or something **among** a particular group, you consider them to be a member of that group. ❑ *Gradually, these youngsters became decent, honest citizens, many of whom I used to count among my friends... My mother had admitted that people who had counted themselves among her friends had broken down under the pressure.*

V+N+PREP,
V+REFL+PREP,
V+PRON+PREP

count down If you **count down**, you count numbers aloud in reverse order until you reach zero, especially before something happens, such as a spacecraft being launched. ❑ *We have begun counting down to lift-off.*

V+ADV

♦ A **countdown** is the counting aloud of numbers in reverse order before something happens, especially before a spacecraft is launched. ❑ *Millions stand transfixed as the countdown begins.*

N-COUNT

★count for If you say that a particular thing **counts for** something, you mean that it is valuable or important. ❑ *I felt that all my years there counted for nothing... They feel they don't count for anything.*

V+PREP

count in If you **count** someone **in**, you include them in a particular activity. ❑ *You can count me in for the next outing.*

V+PRON+ADV,
V+N+ADV

NOTE **Count out** means the opposite of **count in**.

★count on

1 If you **count on** or **count upon** something, you expect it to happen and include it in your plans. **Count upon** is more formal. ❑ *Doctors could now count on a regular salary... The campaign can count on the public support of a few Labour MPs... I didn't count on meeting you here... At least it could be counted upon to stay in one place.*

V+PREP,
V+PREP+-ING:
HAS PASSIVE

NOTE **Rely on** means almost the same as **count on**.

2 If you **count on** or **count upon** someone, you rely on them to support you or help you. **Count upon** is more formal. ❑ *You can count on me... They count upon their parents for leadership and love... He cannot always be counted on.*

V+PREP:
HAS PASSIVE

NOTE **Depend on** means almost the same as **count on**.

★count out

1 If you **count out** coins or banknotes, you count them as you move them one by one from one pile to another or as you give them to someone else. ❑ *She counted out the money... He counted out five wads of twenty notes each.*

V+ADV+N,
V+N+ADV,
V+PRON+ADV

2 If someone **counts** you **out**, they exclude you from a particular activity. ❑ *If you're going to gossip, you can count me out.*

V+PRON+ADV

3 When a referee **counts out** a boxer who has been knocked down, he or she counts to ten before the boxer can get up, and the boxer loses the match.

V+N+ADV,
V+ADV+N,
V+PRON+ADV

count towards If something **counts towards** something that you want, it adds to the things that give you the right to have it. ❑ *Any contributions you have paid will count towards your pension.*

V+PREP

★count up If you **count up** all the things in a group, you count them in order to find how many there are. ❑ *I counted up my years of teaching experience.*

NOTE **Add up** means almost the same as **count up**.

V+ADV+N,
V+N+ADV,
V+PRON+ADV

count upon → See count on

cover /k_ʌvəʳ/ **(covers, covering, covered)**

cover over To **cover** something **over** means to cover it completely with something else. ❑ *The sky was covered over with cloud.*

NOTE **Obscure** is a more formal word for **cover over**.

V+N+ADV,
V+ADV+N,
V+PRON+ADV

★cover up

1 If you **cover** something **up**, you place or spread something else over it in order to protect it or hide it. ❑ *Cover yourself up with this sheet... She took a blanket out of the car and covered up the windows.*

V+REFL+ADV,
V+ADV+N,
V+N+ADV,
V+PRON+ADV

2 If you **cover up** something that you do not want people to know about, you hide it from them. ❑ *She tried to cover up for Willie... She hoped to cover up anything unpleasant that might be said... He alleged that the President knew about Watergate and tried to cover it up.*

V+ADV,
V+ADV+N,
V+PRON+ADV,
V+N+ADV

NOTE **Conceal** is a more formal word for **cover up**.

♦ A **cover-up** is an attempt to hide the truth so that people do not realize that there has been a crime or mistake. ❑ *He denied that he took any part in the cover-up.*

N-COUNT

crack /kræk/ **(cracks, cracking, cracked)**

★crack down To **crack down** on a group of people means to become stricter in making them obey rules or laws and in punishing those who do not obey the rules. ❑ *The police cracked down on vandals and drug offenders... Her first reaction to the riots was to crack down hard.*

V+ADV:
USUALLY+on

NOTE **Clamp down** means almost the same as **crack down**.

♦ A **crackdown** is strong official action taken to punish people who break laws or rules in order to make sure that the laws or rules are obeyed in future. ❑ *...a crackdown on criminals.*

N-COUNT

crack on If you **crack on** with a job or task, you continue doing it quickly and energetically. [BRITISH, INFORMAL] ❑ *And then there is the white sauce to get ready. So let's crack on... Now the aim was to crack on with a survey of the lands beyond the mountains.*

V+ADV:
USUALLY+with

NOTE **Get on** means almost the same as **crack on**.

crack up

1 If someone **cracks up**, they lose control of themselves and become mentally ill. ❑ *I'd crack up if there wasn't someone I could talk to.*

V+ADV

NOTE **Break down** means almost the same as **crack up**.

♦ If someone has a **crack-up**, they lose control of themselves and become mentally ill. [INFORMAL] ❑ *People gossiped about his crack-up.*

N-COUNT

NOTE **Breakdown** means almost the same as **crack-up**.

2 If you **crack up** or if someone or something **cracks** you **up**, you laugh a lot. [INFORMAL] ❑ *She told stories that cracked me up and I swore to write them down so you could enjoy them too... We all just cracked up laughing.*

V+ADV,
V+N+ADV,
V+PRON+ADV

NOTE **Crease up** means almost the same as **crack up**.

crank /kræŋk/ **(cranks, cranking, cranked)**

crank out If you say that a company or person **cranks out** a quantity of similar things, you mean they produce them quickly, and without much imagination or effort; used showing disapproval. [INFORMAL] ❑ *In 1933 the studio cranked out fifty-five feature films... The writer must have cranked it out in his lunch-hour.*

V+ADV+N,
V+PRON+ADV

NOTE **Turn out** means almost the same as **crank out**.

crank up

1 If you **crank up** a machine or a device, you make it function at a greater level. [BRITISH] ❑ *Just crank up your hearing aid a peg or two.*

V+ADV+N,
V+N+ADV,
V+PRON+ADV

2 If you **crank up** a machine or device, you start it. [AMERICAN] ❑ *...May's warm weather, which caused Americans to crank up their air conditioners.*

V+ADV+N,
V+N+ADV,
V+PRON+ADV

NOTE **Start up** means almost the same as **crank up**.

3 If you **crank up** the volume of something, you turn it up until it is very loud. ❑ *Someone cranked up the volume of the public address system... By about six, they're crank-*

V+ADV+N,
V+N+ADV,
V+PRON+ADV

ing the music up loud again.

NOTE **Turn up** means almost the same as **crank up**.

4 To **crank** something **up** means to increase it or make it more intense. [BRITISH] ❑ *The incident that cranked up the fear was the murder of Brian Smith.*

V+N+ADV,
V+ADV+N,
V+PRON+ADV

crash /kræʃ/ **(crashes, crashing, crashed)**

☑ **About** is used mainly in British English.

crash about → See **crash around**

crash around To **crash around** or **crash about** means to move about and make a lot of loud noises. [INFORMAL] ❑ *We heard thundering booms as the boilers started crashing about... What on earth is she doing, crashing around upstairs like that?*

V+ADV

crash out

1 If a noise **crashes out**, it starts and is very loud. ❑ *The applause crashed out... The opening chords crashed out.*

V+ADV

NOTE **Ring out** means almost the same as **crash out**.

2 If you **crash out**, you fall asleep. [INFORMAL] ❑ *She had crashed out on the floor.*

V+ADV

NOTE **Flake out** means almost the same as **crash out**.

crate /kreɪt/ **(crates, crating, crated)**

crate up To **crate** something **up** means to put it into a crate so that it can be stored or taken somewhere. ❑ *We decided to keep the painting, rather than crate it up with everything else... They can't carry that machine unless it's properly crated up.*

V+PRON+ADV,
V+N+ADV,
V+ADV+N

cream /kriːm/ **(creams, creaming, creamed)**

cream off

1 To **cream off** people from a group means to take them away and treat them in a special way, because you think that they are better than the rest of the group. ❑ *The best pupils would be creamed off and given a superior training... They decided to cream part of the staff off for more complicated tasks.*

V+N+ADV,
V+ADV+N,
V+PRON+ADV

2 If a person or organization **creams off** a large amount of money, they take it and use it for themselves; used showing disapproval. [INFORMAL] ❑ *This means smaller banks can cream off big profits during lending booms... Funds raised through selling these magazines are creamed off to support armed violence.*

V+N+ADV,
V+ADV+N,
V+PRON+ADV

crease /kriːs/ **(creases, creasing, creased)**

crease up If someone or something **creases** you **up**, they make you laugh a lot. [BRITISH, INFORMAL] ❑ *She creased me up with her tall stories!... We were all creased up with laughter.*

V+PRON+ADV

creep /kriːp/ **(creeps, creeping, crept)**

creep in If something such as a word or custom **creeps in**, it gradually becomes used by people. ❑ *New gestures do occasionally manage to creep in and establish themselves... The word 'intelligence' is beginning to creep back in... Elements of military uniform creep in.*

V+ADV

NOTE **Slip in** means almost the same as **creep in**.

creep into If an attitude or a feeling **creeps into** something, it begins to be expressed or felt gradually. ❑ *A certain lassitude is creeping into our meetings... A note of impatience creeps into her voice... The shadow of doubt began to creep into her mind.*

V+PREP

creep up on

1 If you **creep up on** someone, you move slowly closer to them without being seen by them. ❑ *One child stands facing a wall while all the others creep up on him... He was aware of something dangerous creeping up on them under cover of the bush.*

V+ADV+PREP

2 If a feeling or state **creeps up on** you, you begin to experience it very slowly. ❑ *She paused, fighting the dizziness that was creeping up on her... A sense of unreality was beginning to creep up on me.*

V+ADV+PREP

NOTE **Come over** means almost the same as **creep up on**.

crop /krɒp/ **(crops, cropping, cropped)**

crop up If something **crops up**, it happens or appears suddenly and unexpectedly. ❑ *There was one word that cropped up in each of the reports... I can come now, unless any other problems crop up.*

V+ADV

NOTE **Come up** means almost the same as **crop up**.

cross /krɒs, AM krɔːs/ **(crosses, crossing, crossed)**

★**cross off** If you **cross off** one or more words on a list, you draw a line through them to indicate that they are no longer on the list. ❏ *I crossed my name off the list... You should cross it off.*

V+N+PREP/ADV,
V+PRON+PREP/ADV,
V+ADV+N

NOTE **Delete** means almost the same as **cross off**.

★**cross out** If you **cross out** one or more words on a page, you draw a line through them, usually because they are wrong or because you do not want people to read them. ❏ *Now and then he frowned, crossed something out and rewrote it... I crossed out 'Unpublished' and made it 'Works in preparation'... I would promptly write it down and then cross it out again.*

V+N+ADV,
V+ADV+N,
V+PRON+ADV

NOTE **Delete** means almost the same as **cross out**.

★**cross over**

1 When you **cross over**, you go across to the other side of something such as a road, room, or border. ❏ *We crossed over into Tennessee... I crossed over to a grocery store... The car had crossed over the river.*

V+ADV,
V+PREP

2 If you **cross over** to a different side in a disagreement, you change to that side. ❏ *If we ever crossed over to their side, war would be declared.*

V+ADV:
ALSO+to

NOTE **Go over** means almost the same as **cross over**.

crouch /kraʊtʃ/ **(crouches, crouching, crouched)**

crouch down If you **crouch down**, you move to a position in which your legs are bent under you so that you are close to the ground and slightly leaning forward. ❏ *Two of them crouched down behind the car... She passed quite close to him, but he crouched down, and did not see her face.*

V+ADV

crowd /kraʊd/ **(crowds, crowding, crowded)**

☑ In American English, **around** is much more common than **round**.

crowd around If a group of people **crowd around** or **crowd round** someone or something, they gather closely together around that person or thing. ❏ *Children were always crowded around the ticket booth... The boys crowded round him... We crowded round eagerly, then felt disappointed.*

V+PREP,
V+ADV

NOTE **Surround** is a more formal word for **crowd around**.

crowd in If a group of people or things **crowd in**, a lot of them try to get into a place at the same time. ❏ *The TV men crowded in, examining our equipment.*

V+ADV

NOTE **Pile in** means almost the same as **crowd in**.

crowd in on If a lot of things **crowd in on** you, you have to think about them all at once and they upset you or worry you. ❏ *Other worries were crowding in on Gavin... All the things and places that I loved so well keep crowding in on me now in this gloomy bedroom.*

V+ADV+PREP

crowd into If a group of people or things **crowd into** a place, or if you **crowd** them **into** it, they are all pushed or squeezed into a place that is too small for them. ❏ *Outside, shiny cars crowded into the courtyard... He helped his dad and brother crowd the animals into a truck... Reporters and photographers were crowded into the lobby.*

V+PREP,
V+N+PREP,
V+PRON+PREP

crowd out To **crowd** someone or something **out** means to deliberately take up so much space that they are forced to leave or move away. ❏ *I tried to keep my place in the queue, but they crowded me out.*

V+N+ADV,
V+PRON+ADV,
V+ADV+N

NOTE **Push out** and **squeeze out** mean almost the same as **crowd out**.

crumble /krʌmbəl/ **(crumbles, crumbling, crumbled)**

crumble away

1 If an old building or piece of land **is crumbling away**, parts of it keep breaking off. ❏ *Britain's coastline stretches 4000 kilometres and much of it is crumbling away.*

V+ADV

NOTE **Disintegrate** means almost the same as **crumble away**.

2 If something such as a system, relationship, or hope **crumbles away**, it comes to an end. ❏ *Opposition more or less crumbled away.*

V+ADV

crumple /krʌmpəl/ **(crumples, crumpling, crumpled)**

crumple up If you **crumple up** a piece of paper, you squash it into a ball. ❏ *She looked at the scrap of paper, crumpled it up, and threw it into the wastebasket.*

V+PRON+ADV,
V+N+ADV,
V+ADV+N

NOTE **Screw up** means almost the same as **crumple up**.

The symbol ★ shows key phrasal verbs

cry /kraɪ/ **(cries, crying, cried)**

cry off If you **cry off**, you change your mind and decide not to do something that you had arranged or agreed to do. [INFORMAL] ❑ *She cried off at the last moment... He was engaged once, but he cried off.* · V+ADV

★cry out If you **cry out**, you suddenly shout or cry loudly because you are surprised or in pain. ❑ *She cried out in terror... Ralph cried out: 'Oh God, Oh God!'... They cried out their greetings.* · V+ADV, V+ADV+QUOTE, V+ADV+N: NO PASSIVE

cry out against If you **cry out against** something, you complain about it because you do not approve of it. ❑ *People are crying out against the new laws.* · V+ADV+PREP

♦ An **outcry** is a reaction of strong disapproval and anger shown by the public or media about an action or decision. ❑ *There was a public outcry about selling arms to the rebels.* · N-COUNT

cry out for If one thing is **crying out for** another, it needs it very much. ❑ *There is a vast surplus of workers crying out for employment... Its controls were crying out for adjustment.* · V+ADV+PREP

cuddle /kʌdəl/ **(cuddles, cuddling, cuddled)**

cuddle up When you **cuddle up** to someone, you sit or lie as near to them as possible and you cuddle them. ❑ *They tried to cuddle up and get warm under the bed-clothes... There was a woman cuddled up close to him.* · V+ADV: USUALLY+A

NOTE **Snuggle up** means almost the same as **cuddle up**.

cue /kjuː/ **(cues, cueing, cued)**

cue up If you **cue up** a tape, record, or CD, you put it at the place where you want it to start playing, so that you can start it there immediately. ❑ *Their skill in cueing up records to blend seamlessly into one long piece of dance music is what puts the superstar DJs in a class of their own.* · V+ADV+N, V+N+ADV, V+PRON+ADV

curl /kɜːrl/ **(curls, curling, curled)**

★curl up

[1] If you **curl up**, you lie down bringing your arms, legs, and head in towards your stomach, for example because you sleep in that position. ❑ *He curled up in the chair... She could see the cat curled up asleep on the sofa.* · V+ADV

[2] When something flat, such as a leaf or a piece of paper, **curls up**, its edges bend towards its centre. ❑ *As the tree bark dries it curls up into sticks.* · V+ADV

curtain /kɜːrtən/ **(curtains, curtaining, curtained)**

curtain off If part of a room is **curtained off**, it is separated from the rest of the room by a curtain. ❑ *The rear of the passenger cabin was curtained off... We need to curtain off a section of the altar.* · V+ADV+N, V+N+ADV, V+PRON+ADV

cut /kʌt/ **(cuts, cutting)**

☑ The form **cut** is used in the present tense and is the past tense and past participle of the verb.

cut across

[1] If you **cut across** a place, you go across it because it is the shortest route to another place. ❑ *I wanted to cut across country for the next hundred miles.* · V+PREP

[2] If an issue or problem **cuts across** divisions or differences between people, the people agree about it although they disagree about most other things. ❑ *Issues, however, tended to cut across party lines. ...the development of institutional arrangements cutting across ethnic barriers.* · V+PREP

[3] If something **cuts across** a rule or law, it contradicts or breaks it. ❑ *...a religion that does not cut across scientific laws.* · V+PREP

cut away If you **cut away** a part of something, you remove it by cutting it, using a knife, saw, scissors, and so on. ❑ *All the rotten wood must be cut away and burned... Cut it away with a sharp knife.* · V+N+ADV, V+PRON+ADV, V+ADV+N

★cut back If you **cut back** something such as expenditure, you reduce it. ❑ *Congress cut back the funds for NASA's space programme... The factory has cut back its work force by 50%... We are all having to cut back.* · V+ADV+N, V+N+ADV, V+PRON+ADV, V+ADV

♦ A **cutback** is a reduction in something, especially in the number of people that a firm or organization employs. ❑ *...the cutback in public services.* · N-COUNT

★cut back on If you **cut back on** something such as expenditure, you try to re-   V+ADV+PREP
duce it, often because you can no longer afford it. ❑ *The government has had to cut*
back on public expenditure... They had to cut back on their charitable donations.

★cut down

1 If you **cut** something **down**, you reduce it or do it less often. ❑ *...the need to cut*   V+ADV+N,
down pollution... Save time for yourself by cutting your shopping down to twice a week... The   V+N+ADV,
text was too long so we cut it down... 'I wouldn't drink that whisky if I were you,' he said.   V+PRON+ADV,
'Cut down.'   V+ADV

2 If you **cut down** a tree, you cut through its trunk so that it falls to the ground.   V+N+ADV,
❑ *A quarter of forestry reserves had been cut down by 1974... How much is it going to cost*   V+PRON+ADV,
us to cut all these trees down?   V+ADV+N

NOTE **Chop down** means almost the same as **cut down**.

★cut down on If you **cut down on** something, you try to reduce it or do it less   V+ADV+PREP
often. ❑ *She had cut down on smoking. ...how to cut down on housework.*

cut in

1 If you **cut in**, you interrupt someone when they are speaking. ❑ *'You have to em-*   V+ADV:
ploy a professional,' cut in the Englishman quietly... Mrs Travers began a reply, but Mrs Patel   ALSO+QUOTE
cut in again.

NOTE **Break in** means almost the same as **cut in**.

2 If you **cut** someone **in**, you give them a share of the profits you have made on a   V+N+ADV,
business deal or sale. ❑ *We haven't got to cut Sam in have we? He didn't help much... I*   V+PRON+ADV,
think we should cut in all those who helped us organize the auction in the first place.   V+ADV+N

cut into If you **cut into** something, you push a knife or similar tool into it in or-   V+PREP
der to mark it, damage it, or remove something from it. ❑ *I cut into the meat and felt a*
sudden twinge of nausea.

★cut off

1 If you **cut** a part of something **off**, you remove it completely by cutting it, using   V+ADV+N,
a knife, saw, scissors, and so on. ❑ *They held a gun to his head and threatened to cut off*   V+N+ADV,
his ears.   V+PRON+ADV

♦ An **off-cut** is a piece of something that has been removed by cutting. ❑ *You can*   N-COUNT
make your own frames from Perspex off-cuts. ...burning the off-cuts and chippings.

♦ **Cut-off** jeans or trousers have been shortened by cutting off a large part of the   ADJECTIVE
legs. ❑ *...wearing cut-off jeans and a t-shirt.*

2 If someone **is cut off**, they are separated and isolated from other people. ❑ *The*   V+N+ADV,
battalions found themselves pinned down and cut off... Many mothers feel cut off during the   V+ADV+N,
day... The town was cut off by the floods... We have cut ourselves off from the old ways of   V+REFL+ADV,
thinking.   V+PRON+ADV:
    ALSO+from,
    USUALLY PASSIVE

3 To **cut off** the supply of something means to stop it. ❑ *People have been suggest-*   V+ADV+N,
ing that we should cut off economic aid... Gas supplies had now been cut off.   V+N+ADV,
    V+PRON+ADV

♦ A **cut-off** or a **cut-off** point is the level or limit at which you decide that some-   N-COUNT,
thing should stop happening. ❑ *Forty-five pounds is our cut-off, and we'll only go that*   ADJECTIVE
high if we really have to... We thought it was already past the cut-off point.*

4 If you **cut** someone **off** or **cut off** what they are saying, you stop them saying it.   V+PRON+ADV,
❑ *I waved my hand to cut him off... 'Jenny, I'm sorry.'—'Stop.' She cut off my apology.*   V+ADV+N,
    V+N+ADV

NOTE **Silence** is a more formal word for **cut off**.

5 To **cut** someone **off** also means to disconnect them when they are having a tele-   V+PRON+ADV,
phone conversation. ❑ *Don't complain when they cut you off by mistake.*   V+N+ADV

★cut out

1 If you **cut out** part of something, you remove it by cutting it. ❑ *Badly decayed*   V+N+ADV,
timber should be cut out and replaced... There were pictures of animals cut out of magazines   V+ADV+N,
and tacked to the wall.   V+PRON+ADV:
    ALSO+of

♦ A **cut-out** is a shape that has been cut from card or cardboard. ❑ *...a cut-out of a*   N-COUNT
girl. ...two cardboard cut-outs.

2 If you **cut out** part of something that someone has written, you remove it from   V+ADV+N,
the text and do not print or broadcast it. ❑ *He cut out all references to the Baron being*   V+N+ADV,
ugly... Her publishers insisted on cutting several stories out of her memoirs.   V+PRON+ADV:
    ALSO+of

3 If you **cut out** something that you are doing or saying, you stop doing or saying   V+ADV+N,
it. If you tell someone to **cut** it **out**, you are telling them angrily to stop misbehav-   V+N+ADV,
    V+PRON+ADV:

ing, joking, or being unreasonable. ❑ *He ought to cut out the drinking... 'Look,' he said, 'let's cut out all this encounter-group rubbish'... She said in a shrill brief whine: 'Cut it out!'*

ALSO IMPERATIVE:
V+*it*+ADV

NOTE **Stop** means almost the same as **cut out**.

4 To **cut out** something unnecessary or unwanted means to remove it completely from a situation. For example, if you **cut out** a particular type of food, you stop eating it. ❑ *I've simply cut egg yolks out entirely... We will be pressing ahead with our policies on privatisation, deregulation and cutting out waste... A guilty plea cuts out the need for a long trial.*

V+ADV+N,
V+N+ADV,
V+PRON+ADV

NOTE **Eliminate** means almost the same as **cut out**.

5 If you **cut** someone **out** of an activity or job, you do not allow them to do it. ❑ *He'll cut you out of the operation completely... I don't think I should be cut out of the trip.*

V+PRON+ADV,
V+N+ADV:
USUALLY+*of*

6 If an object **cuts out** the light, it is between you and the light, so that you are in the dark or shade. ❑ *Great trees soar above to cut out most of the light.*

V+ADV+N,
V+N+ADV,
V+PRON+ADV

7 If an engine **cuts out**, it suddenly stops working. ❑ *The engine's cut out again.*

V+ADV

♦ A **cut-out** is an automatic device that turns off a motor or engine, for example because there is something wrong with it. ❑ *...a cut-out to prevent the battery from overcharging.*

N-COUNT

cut through

1 To **cut through** something such as water means to move or pass through it easily and smoothly. ❑ *The big canoe was cutting through the water.*

V+PREP

2 If a path **cuts through** a forest or jungle, it goes through it. ❑ *We were making our way down a path that cut through the pine forest.*

V+PREP

3 If you **cut through** a place, you go through it because it is the shortest route to another place. ❑ *We cut through a field of cows.*

V+PREP

★cut up

1 If you **cut** something **up**, you cut it into several pieces. ❑ *You start the lesson by cutting up a worm... He has to have his food cut up for him.*

V+ADV+N,
V+N+ADV,
V+PRON+ADV

NOTE **Slice up** means almost the same as **cut up**.

2 If you **are cut up** about something, you are upset or angry about it. [BRITISH, INFORMAL] ❑ *She's really cut up about getting a D in Maths.*

PASSIVE:
V+ADV

3 If one driver **cuts** another driver **up**, the first driver pulls in too close in front of the second one, for example after overtaking. ❑ *They were crossing from lane to lane, cutting everyone up.*

V+N+ADV,
V+PRON+ADV

Dd

dab /dæb/ (dabs, dabbing, dabbed)

dab at If you **dab at** something, you touch it several times with quick, stabbing movements. ❑ *She dabbed at her mouth with the lace handkerchief... 'You're horrid!' Sarah said, shaking her finger at them and dabbing at her eyes.*

V+PREP

dab on If you **dab** a substance **on** a surface, you put it on with quick, light strokes. ❑ *She dabbed some powder on her nose... Dab some antiseptic on the wound... The liquid has to be dabbed on three times a day.*

V+N+PREP,
V+PRON+PREP,
V+N+ADV,
V+PRON+ADV

dabble /dæbəl/ (dabbles, dabbling, dabbled)

dabble in If you **dabble in** an activity or subject, you take part in it or study it occasionally, but not seriously. ❑ *They wear heavy boots and dabble in right-wing politics... He had dabbled in composition, but now devoted himself wholly to his piano playing... Despite my having dabbled in psychiatry and social work, I really know very little about people.*

V+PREP

dally /dæli/ (dallies, dallying, dallied)

dally with If you **dally with** an idea or plan, you think about it but not in a serious way. [OLD-FASHIONED] ❑ *I'm dallying with the idea of giving up my job... She dallies with mischievous half-truths.*

V+PREP

NOTE **Toy with** means almost the same as **dally with**.

dam /dæm/ (dams, damming, dammed)

dam up

1 To **dam up** a river means to put something across it to hold back the water. ❑ *The boards dammed up the creek enough to form a huge bath tub... The old channels are dammed up in the hope that the water will seek out a new course.*

V+ADV+N,
V+N+ADV,
V+PRON+ADV

2 If you **dam up** your feelings and emotions, you prevent yourself from expressing them. ❑ *...passions too long dammed up by society and its laws.*

V+N+ADV,
V+PRON+ADV,
V+ADV+N

NOTE **Bottle up** means almost the same as **dam up**.

damp /dæmp/ (damps, damping, damped)

damp down

1 To **damp down** a situation that involves a great deal of emotion, growth, or change means to reduce the amount of effort and intensity in it. ❑ *Neighbouring countries had been of little or no help in damping down the crisis. ...increasing strength abroad at the cost, if necessary, of damping down progress at home... Missiles were fired at stand-off ranges by the Tornados to damp things down a little.*

V+ADV+N,
V+N+ADV,
V+PRON+ADV

NOTE **Dampen down** means almost the same as **damp down**.

2 If you **damp down** a fire, you make it burn more slowly by reducing the flow of air.

V+ADV+N,
V+PRON+ADV,
V+N+ADV

3 If you **damp down** a surface, you spray it with a small amount of water. ❑ *The surface had been smoothed over, levelled out and damped down with water... His hair was damped down as if it had been wet.*

V+ADV+N,
V+N+ADV,
V+PRON+ADV

NOTE **Dampen down** means almost the same as **damp down**.

dampen /dæmpən/ (dampens, dampening, dampened)

dampen down

1 To **dampen down** a situation that involves a great deal of emotion, growth, or change means to reduce the amount of effort and intensity in it. ❑ *A policy of high interest rates has the effect of further dampening down the economy.*

V+ADV+N,
V+N+ADV,
V+PRON+ADV

NOTE **Damp down** means almost the same as **dampen down**.

2 If you **dampen down** a surface, you spray a small amount of water over it.

V+ADV+N,
V+N+ADV,
V+PRON+ADV

NOTE **Damp down** means almost the same as **dampen down**.

The symbol ★ shows key phrasal verbs

dash /dæʃ/ (dashes, dashing, dashed)

dash off

1 If you **dash off** to a place, you go there very quickly. ❑ *He dashed off to lunch at the Hard Rock Cafe... They dashed off to Paris for a couple of days.*   V+ADV: USUALLY+*to*

2 If you **dash off** a short piece of writing, you write it quickly and without careful thought. ❑ *She bombarded the market with letters, dashing off several each week... She dashed off a note to the ASA. ...others seemed to have been dashed off in seconds.*   V+ADV+N

NOTE **Scribble** means almost the same as **dash off**.

date /deɪt/ (dates, dating, dated)

date back

If something **dates back** to a particular time, it has existed since that time. ❑ *...a Jewish burial ground dating back to the New Testament period... The current idea for defending western Europe dates back to 1967. ...cultures that date back much further than the era of colonization... Much of this debt dated back many years.*   V+ADV: WITH A

date from

If something **dates from** a particular time, it started or was made at that time. ❑ *All the cupboards and appliances dated from the 1950s... The present controversy dates from 1986.*   V+PREP

dawn /dɔːn/ (dawns, dawning, dawned)

dawn on

If a fact or idea **dawns on** or **dawns upon** you, you suddenly begin to realize what is happening or what the real nature of your situation is. **Dawn upon** is more formal. ❑ *It never dawned on her that her life was in danger... It slowly dawned on me that something unusual was happening... The awful truth dawned upon him.*   V+PREP

NOTE **Strike** means almost the same as **dawn on**.

dawn upon → See dawn on

deal /diːl/ (deals, dealing, dealt)

★deal in

1 If a company or shop **deals in** a particular type of goods, it buys and sells those goods. ❑ *...the shop that deals only in trousers... Julie's father owned a business that dealt in bulk orders of paper.*   V+PREP

2 Someone who **deals in** a particular activity or subject is involved with it or knowledgeable about it. ❑ *Go to the legal adviser who deals in road accidents.*   V+PREP

NOTE **Deal with** means almost the same as **deal in**.

deal out

1 If you **deal out** punishment to someone, you inflict it on them. ❑ *Beatings and other cruelties were dealt out to those who had been captured... And the same punishment would be dealt out to any boy who was ever late for his class.*   V+ADV+N: ALSO+*to*

NOTE **Mete out** and **administer** are more formal ways of saying **deal out**.

2 When you **deal out** playing cards, you give each player a number of cards. ❑ *He drank the last of his whisky, then swiftly dealt out the next hand.*   V+ADV+N, V+N+ADV, V+PRON+ADV

★deal with

1 When you **deal with** something that needs attention, you do what is necessary in order to achieve the result that is wanted. ❑ *They learned to deal with any sort of emergency... The Finance Officer deals with all the finances of the university... The work is dealt with by a Stipendiary Magistrate.*   V+PREP: HAS PASSIVE

NOTE **Handle** means almost the same as **deal with**.

2 If a book, speech, film or theory **deals with** a particular topic or idea, this is one of the subjects that is discussed or expressed in it. ❑ *There are some issues you just can't deal with in a popular magazine. ...a motion dealing with the educational training of the nation... These questions will be dealt with in chapter 7.*   V+PREP: HAS PASSIVE

NOTE **Cover** means almost the same as **deal with**.

3 If you **deal with** a person or organization, you do business with them. ❑ *I planned to deal with this bank for many years. ...if you're dealing with a US company, you are not protected.*   V+PREP

4 If you **deal with** an unpleasant emotion or an emotionally difficult situation, you recognize it, and remain calm in spite of it. ❑ *She saw a psychiatrist who used hypnotism to help her deal with her fear... He was able to deal with his captivity by maintaining a high degree of anger about the unfairness of his capture.*   V+PREP

NOTE **Cope with** means almost the same as **deal with**.

debar /dɪbɑːr, diː-/ **(debars, debarring, debarred)**

debar from If you **are debarred from** doing something, you are prevented from doing it by a regulation or law. [FORMAL] ❑ *She saw no reason why public industries alone should be debarred from the normal commercial right to expand... This state of affairs effectively debars us from full and equal participation.*
V+N+PREP,
V+PRON+PREP

decide /dɪsaɪd/ **(decides, deciding, decided)**

★**decide on** If you **decide on** or **decide upon** something, you choose it or make up your mind about it after careful thought. **Decide upon** is slightly more formal. ❑ *He decided on a career in the army... They are due to meet on 22 August to decide on further action... The men would be selected according to criteria which had to be decided upon.*
V+PREP:
HAS PASSIVE

decide upon → See decide on

deck /dek/ **(decks, decking, decked)**

deck out If you **are decked out** in something, you put on very grand clothes for a special occasion. ❑ *He enjoyed being at his father's side, decked out in embroidered coats stiff with gold... I decked myself out in a suit and tie, and set off.*
V+REFL+ADV,
V+PRON+ADV:
ALSO+in/with

NOTE Dress up means almost the same as **deck out**.

declare /dɪkleər/ **(declares, declaring, declared)**

declare for If you **declare for** something or someone, you say that you are in favour of them. ❑ *The Catalans declared for Charles and a civil war erupted in Valencia and Aragon... Only a month earlier, Mr. Stenholm had declared for the tax cut.*
V+PREP

defer /dɪfɜːr/ **(defers, deferring, deferred)**

defer to If you **defer to** someone, you accept their opinion or do what they want you to do, even though you do not agree with it. ❑ *No longer did MPs defer to the Speaker... He's a medical man and we'd be fools not to defer to him in medical matters... Despite being one of the most powerful industrialists in the world, he was in no way deferred to by his Swiss guests.*
V+PREP:
HAS PASSIVE

delight /dɪlaɪt/ **(delights, delighting, delighted)**

delight in If you **delight in** something, you get a lot of pleasure from it. ❑ *Morris delighted in hard manual work... Be prepared for friends who delight in breaking bad news. ...someone who delights in controversy... He has his favourite sources and delights in their academic approach.*
V+PREP

deliver /dɪlɪvər/ **(delivers, delivering, delivered)**
deliver of

1 If you **deliver** yourself **of** an opinion, you express it in a confident way. [FORMAL] ❑ *He delivered himself of a judgment lifting the ban... She delivered herself of her view of that morning's events... Having arrived at a measured opinion, he delivered himself of it.*
V+REFL+PREP

2 If a woman **is delivered of** a baby, she gives birth to it. [OLD-FASHIONED] ❑ *After twelve hours of labour she was delivered of a son.*
PASSIVE:
V+PREP

deliver up If you **deliver** something **up**, you surrender it or give it to someone because you have been ordered to do so. ❑ *The Court ordered three weeks ago that he must deliver up the evidence.*
V+ADV+N,
V+N+ADV,
V+PRON+ADV

delve /delv/ **(delves, delving, delved)**
delve in → See delve into
delve into

1 If you **delve into** or **delve in** something, you search vigorously deep inside it. ❑ *They delved into their desks for their pens... She walked to a cavity in the wall and delved about in it... I held the basket while she delved in the boxes.*
V+PREP

2 If you **delve into** something, you try in a determined way to discover more information about it. ❑ *...a good source for anyone interested in delving into the history of London... To find out, one needs to delve into the past. ...delving into the secrets of nature.*
V+PREP

depart /dɪpɑːt/ **(departs, departing, departed)**

depart from If you **depart from** an accepted belief, method, or type of behaviour, you do or believe something different. ❑ *Children born in this country are British and we ought not to depart from that principle... Lenin departed from Marx on the role of the*
V+PREP:
HAS PASSIVE

peasantry... In the next couple of hours, we departed from the script to produce a completely unorthodox finish.

depend /dɪpend/ (depends, depending, depended)
*depend on

1 If you **depend on** or **depend upon** someone or something, you need them in order to be able to exist, survive or continue. ❑ *Our lives and those of all other animals depend on oxygen... These factories depend upon natural resources.... They do benefit from adult attention which can always be depended on.*

NOTE **Rely on** means almost the same as **depend on**.

V+PREP:
HAS PASSIVE

2 If you can **depend on** or **depend upon** someone or something, you know that you can trust them to provide help or do something reliably. ❑ *I knew I could depend on you... This country is an ally you can depend on... Can he be depended upon to provide regular deliveries?*

NOTE **Rely on** and **trust** mean almost the same as **depend on**.

V+PREP:
HAS PASSIVE

3 If a result or situation **depends on** or **depends upon** particular circumstances, it will be affected or changed according to what those circumstances are. ❑ *The success of the meeting depends largely on whether the chairman is efficient... What you saw depended on where you were... The amount of money you make depends on the amount of sweat you put in... The screens on which the text is displayed will vary in size depending upon what one wants to do with it.*

V+PREP:
USUALLY+WH

depend upon → See depend on

deprive /dɪpraɪv/ (deprives, depriving, deprived)
*deprive of If you **deprive** someone **of** something, you take it away from them or prevent them from having it. ❑ *Imprisonment deprives the offender of his liberty... When the heart stops, the brain is deprived of fresh blood and oxygen... 'I'm not trying to deprive you of the necessities of life,' I explained.*

V+N+PREP,
V+PRON+PREP

derive /dɪraɪv/ (derives, deriving, derived)
derive from

1 If you **derive** pleasure or benefit **from** something, it gives you pleasure or some advantage. ❑ *They derive enormous pleasure from their grand-children... They nest near the house where they derive some protection from the harsh weather.*

V+N+PREP,
V+PRON+PREP

2 If something **derives from** or **is derived from** something else, it develops or comes from that thing. ❑ *This argument derives from a belief in the importance of education... We may expect that economics must derive its aims and objectives from a study of man... The word 'detergent' is derived from the Latin word for 'cleaner'.*

V+PREP,
V+N+PREP,
V+PRON+PREP:
ERGATIVE

descend /dɪsend/ (descends, descending, descended)
descend on If you **descend on** or **descend upon** a place or person, you arrive suddenly without being invited. **Descend upon** is more formal. ❑ *I gather that I'm the second uninvited guest to descend upon your house today!... Were FBI agents really lurking around waiting to descend on him?... The Vikings descended on the Saxon coast.*

V+PREP

descend to If you **descend to** something, you behave in a way that is considered unacceptable or unworthy of you. ❑ *All too soon they will descend to spreading scandal and gossip... Gareth was vexed that he should descend to such a fatuous remark.*

V+PREP

descend upon → See descend on

despair /dɪspeər/ (despairs, despairing, despaired)
despair of If you **despair of** something, you feel that there is no hope that it will happen, improve, or survive. ❑ *He despaired of ever having the courage to ask her. ...people who despair of American society... At many times, both during and after the birth, her life was despaired of.*

V+PREP:
HAS PASSIVE

deter /dɪtɜːr/ (deters, deterring, deterred)
deter from If someone or something **deters** you **from** doing something, they persuade you not to do it by showing that it is difficult or unpleasant. ❑ *Such discrimination may deter more women from seeking work... The punishment did not deter you from committing further offences?... He stole my gold watch, but this did not deter him from telephoning a few weeks later to chat about old times.*

V+N+PREP,
V+PRON+PREP:
WITH -ING

NOTE **Put off** is a more informal expression for **deter from**.

detract /dɪtrækt/ **(detracts, detracting, detracted)**

detract from If something **detracts from** something else, it makes that thing V+PREP
seem less good or reduces its effect. ❑ *Although these may not be harmful to health, they
certainly detract from the quality of life.*
[NOTE] **Diminish** means almost the same as **detract from**.

deviate /diːvieɪt/ **(deviates, deviating, deviated)**

deviate from If someone or something **deviates from** normal or expected be- V+PREP
haviour or ways of doing something, they behave or act differently. ❑ *...people who
deviate from society's ideas of what is normal... I do not see any reason to deviate from the
classical view.*
[NOTE] **Depart from** means almost the same as **deviate from**.

devolve /dɪvɒlv/ **(devolves, devolving, devolved)**

devolve on → See devolve to

devolve to If someone in authority **devolves** a job, duty, or privilege **to, on,** V+N+PREP,
or **upon** another person or group, they transfer it to that person or group. ❑ *...the* V+PRON+PREP,
methods by which authority can be devolved to local and regional communities... It is facing V+PREP:
growing pressures to devolve authority on sub-sections within the organization... From now ERGATIVE
on the task must devolve upon us all.

devolve upon → See devolve to

dictate /dɪkteɪt/ **(dictates, dictating, dictated)**

dictate to If you **dictate to** someone, you tell them what they should do. V+PREP:
❑ *They are hardly in a position to dictate to the Labour party... They found themselves domi-* HAS PASSIVE
nated and dictated to by nations smaller than themselves.

die /daɪ/ **(dies, dying, died)**

die away If a sound or emotion **dies away**, it gradually becomes weaker or V+ADV
fainter and finally disappears. ❑ *Now that the cheers and excitement had died away, it
seemed oddly quiet.*
[NOTE] **Fade** means almost the same as **die away**.

die back If a plant **dies back**, its leaves die but its roots remain alive. ❑ *Cut the* V+ADV
leaves when the plant starts to die back after flowering.

★**die down** If something **dies down**, it becomes much quieter or less intense. V+ADV
❑ *She waited until the laughter had died down... The wind has died down now.*
[NOTE] **Subside** is a more formal word for **die down**.

die off If a group of people or animals **dies off**, all the people or animals in that V+ADV
group die, often over a short period of time. ❑ *Even the wild animals were dying off...
Their children are dying off like flies.*

★**die out** If something **dies out**, it becomes less common and eventually disap- V+ADV
pears. ❑ *Traditional grocers' shops are fast dying out... Use of the abacus has only recently
died out in Japan.... Many species died out.*

dig /dɪg/ **(digs, digging, dug)**

dig around

1 If you **dig around** in a place or container, you search for something in every V+ADV:
part of it. ❑ *I went home to dig around in my closets for some old tapes.* USUALLY+in
[NOTE] **Rummage around** means almost the same as **dig around**.

2 If you **dig around**, you try to find information about someone or something. V+ADV
❑ *They said, after digging around, the photo was a fake.*

dig in

1 When you are gardening, if you **dig** a substance **in**, you mix it deep into the V+N+ADV,
soil. ❑ *Dig the compost in thoroughly and make sure you give it plenty of water in the eve-* V+PRON+ADV,
ning. V+ADV+N

2 If soldiers **dig in** or **dig** themselves **in**, they dig trenches for protection and pre- V+ADV,
pare for an attack by the enemy. ❑ *...the 2nd Battalion which was dug in along the north-* V+REFL+ADV
ern perimeter.

3 If you say that someone **is digging in**, you mean that they are not changing V+ADV
their mind or weakening their efforts, although they may be losing a contest or fac-

ing difficult problems. ❑ *A yawning North-South gulf has opened up with both sides digging in.*

NOTE **Entrench** means almost the same as **dig in**.

4 If you tell someone to **dig in**, you are telling them to start eating. [INFORMAL]

V+ADV:
USUALLY IMPERATIVE

NOTE **Tuck in** means almost the same as **dig in**.

dig into If you **dig into** something, you put your hand in it to search for something. ❑ *He dug into his pocket for his money.*

V+PREP

NOTE **Delve into** means almost the same as **dig into**.

dig out

1 If you **dig** someone or something **out** of a place, you get them out by digging or by forcing them from the things surrounding them. ❑ *...digging minerals out of the Earth... Rescue crews have been digging people out of collapsed buildings. ...trying to dig out a trombone from under four saxophones.*

V+N+ADV,
V+ADV+N,
V+PRON+ADV:
ALSO+of/from

NOTE **Extract** means almost the same as **dig out**.

2 If you **dig** something **out**, you find it and get it out after it has been hidden, covered with things or stored for a long time. ❑ *I've had it for years; I just dig it out because it goes with this suit... We had dug out our tour books and maps ready for the holiday... Could you dig out the infant mortality figures for 1957? ...an old monograph which was dug out for me from a dusty storage room.*

V+PRON+ADV,
V+N+ADV,
V+ADV+N:
ALSO+from/of

NOTE **Fish out** means almost the same as **dig out**.

dig over If you **dig over** the earth, you break it up with a fork or spade so that plants can grow there. ❑ *Dad spent most of the afternoon digging over the old vegetable patch.*

V+ADV+N,
V+PRON+ADV,
V+N+ADV

★dig up

1 If you **dig up** something that has been buried or that is growing, you remove it from the ground. ❑ *...digging up potatoes in the vegetable garden.*

V+ADV+N,
V+N+ADV,
V+PRON+ADV

2 If you **dig up** an area of land, you dig holes in it. ❑ *Yesterday they continued the search, digging up the back yard of a police station.*

V+ADV+N,
V+N+ADV,
V+PRON+ADV

3 If you **dig up** information that is not widely known, you discover it after a determined search. ❑ *Journalists had dug up some hair-raising facts about the company.*

V+ADV+N,
V+N+ADV,
V+PRON+ADV

NOTE **Unearth** means almost the same as **dig up**.

4 If you **dig up** something or someone, you find them and use or employ them. [INFORMAL] ❑ *When something happens anywhere in the world, NPR digs up an expert from someplace or other... If you dug up an old medical book from the sixties, it would tell you that childhood leukemia is incurable.*

V+N+ADV,
V+ADV+N,
V+PRON+ADV

NOTE **Unearth** means almost the same as **dig up**.

din /dɪn/ (dins, dinning, dinned)

din into If someone **dins** something **into** you, they repeat it in a forceful way to make you remember it. ❑ *It was dinned into us that we mustn't talk to strangers.*

V+N+PREP,
V+PRON+PREP

NOTE **Drum into** means almost the same as **din into**.

dine /daɪn/ (dines, dining, dined)

dine off → See dine on

dine on If you **dine on** or **dine off** a particular sort of food, you eat it for dinner. [FORMAL] ❑ *I stayed in the compartment and dined on a chocolate bar. ...creatures that are only too glad to dine off a prairie dog if given a chance.*

V+PREP

dine out If you **dine out**, you have dinner at a restaurant or at someone else's home. ❑ *By seven he was showering in his own flat before dining out in the West End.*

V+ADV

NOTE **Eat out** means almost the same as **dine out**.

dip /dɪp/ (dips, dipping, dipped)

dip in If you tell someone to **dip in**, you are inviting them to take their share of something, especially food. ❑ *Dip in, everybody! – The food's on the table.*

V+ADV

NOTE **Dig in** and **tuck in** mean almost the same as **dip in**.

dip into

1 If you **dip into** a book or subject, you look at it occasionally and briefly without reading or studying it seriously. ❑ *If you want to know more, I suggest you dip into 'The English Legal System' by K.T. Eddey.*

V+PREP

2 If you **dip into** your savings or your pocket, you spend some money which you

V+PREP

dispose of

had intended to keep. ❏ *He would be compelled to dip into capital to maintain his standard of living... This could be secured by restoring the grant and dipping into reserves.*

disabuse /dɪsəbjuːz/ **(disabuses, disabusing, disabused)**

disabuse of If you **disabuse** someone **of** something, you persuade them that what they believe is untrue. [FORMAL] ❏ *'Well, I think I can disabuse you of that notion,' he said solemnly.*   V+N+PREP, V+PRON+PREP

disagree /dɪsəgriː/ **(disagrees, disagreeing, disagreed)**

★**disagree with**

1 If you **disagree with** a particular action or proposal, you disapprove of it and believe that it is wrong. ❏ *He said he was resigning because he disagreed with the company's labour policies... If the farmer disagreed with the decision, he could take the case to court.*   V+PREP

2 If a particular food or drink **disagrees with** you, it makes you feel unwell. ❏ *They'd both eaten something that disagreed with them... Oranges and chocolate disagree with me, they give me migraines.*   V+PREP

disapprove /dɪsəpruːv/ **(disapproves, disapproving, disapproved)**

★**disapprove of** If you **disapprove of** something or someone, you feel or show that you do not like them or do not approve of them. ❏ *The other directors disapproved of his methods... Gluttonous drinking was especially disapproved of.*   V+PREP: HAS PASSIVE

discourse /dɪskɔːrs/ **(discourses, discoursing, discoursed)**

discourse on If someone **discourses on** something, they talk about it for a long time in a confident way. [FORMAL] ❏ *Politicians discourse learnedly on the greenhouse effect.*   V+PREP

dish /dɪʃ/ **(dishes, dishing, dished)**

★**dish out**

1 If you **dish out** something, you give an amount of it to each person in a group. [INFORMAL] ❏ *...dishing out presents in the Christmas bazaar... He was burdened with endless paperwork dished out by bureaucrats, and he hated it.*
NOTE **Dole out** means almost the same as **dish out**.   V+ADV+N, V+N+ADV, V+PRON+ADV

2 To **dish out** punishment or criticism means to punish or criticize someone. [INFORMAL] ❏ *I had to be able to withstand anything the warder could dish out... See, you can dish it out, but you can't take it!*   V+ADV+N, V+PRON+ADV, V+N+ADV

3 When you **dish out** food, you serve it to people. [INFORMAL] ❏ *We could not wash the saucepans until the food was dished out... The amount of food dished out to each person varied according to his rank.*   V+ADV+N, V+N+ADV, V+PRON+ADV: ALSO+to
NOTE **Dish up** means almost the same as **dish out**.

4 If someone **dishes** it **out** to you, they strongly criticize or punish you. [INFORMAL] ❏ *He's a big man and he's prepared to dish it out if he has to.*   V+it+ADV: USUALLY+to

dish up When you **dish up** food, you put it into serving dishes or onto plates so that it is ready to eat. [INFORMAL] ❏ *We tried dishing up earlier, but people complained... Collect these plates while I go and dish up the main course... Until I've dished it up and we've eaten it, I won't be able to relax... I dare say she will dish you up something nice for dinner.*   V+ADV, V+ADV+N, V+PRON+ADV, V+N+ADV, V+PRON+ADV+N
NOTE **Serve** is a more formal word for **dish up**.

dispense /dɪspens/ **(dispenses, dispensing, dispensed)**

dispense with If you **dispense with** something, you stop using it or get rid of it because you no longer need it. [FORMAL] ❏ *Should we not dispense with the services of Mrs. Baggot?... The weather had turned warm enough for her to dispense with her fur coat... His knowledge of foreign affairs is too precious to be dispensed with.*   V+PREP: HAS PASSIVE

dispose /dɪspouz/ **(disposes, disposing, disposed)**

★**dispose of**

1 If you **dispose of** something, you get rid of it, for example, by throwing it away or selling it. ❏ *They had no authority to dispose of the land... It may cost industry more to dispose of its waste in a safer manner... I've got a houseful of things in Chicago to dispose of... Miles of telex tape had to be disposed of.*   V+PREP: HAS PASSIVE

2 If you **dispose of** a problem, task, or question, you deal with it. ❏ *That, then, is*   V+PREP:

the first point disposed of... Medical evidence would be enough to dispose of any suggestion that I was guilty... They soon got down to business, once the formalities were disposed of. **HAS PASSIVE**

3 To **dispose of** a person or an animal means to kill them. [FORMAL] ❏ *I disposed of one of the rats that came nosing round the hut... Stein will have to be disposed of; you realize that, don't you?* **V+PREP: HAS PASSIVE**

NOTE **Destroy** means almost the same as **dispose of**.

dissociate /dɪsˈoʊʃieɪt/ **(dissociates, dissociating, dissociated)**

dissociate from If you **dissociate** yourself **from** something or someone, you show that you are not connected with them in order to avoid trouble or blame. [FORMAL] ❏ *Bailey dissociated himself from this group... As a member of the Community, it is impossible to dissociate ourselves from this problem.* **V+REFL+PREP**

dissolve /dɪzˈɒlv/ **(dissolves, dissolving, dissolved)**

dissolve into If you **dissolve into** or **dissolve in** tears or laughter, you begin to cry or laugh, because you cannot control yourself. ❏ *She dissolved into tears at the mention of Munya's name.* **V+PREP**

dive /daɪv/ **(dives, diving, dived)**

☑ American English uses the form **dove** as the past tense and past participle of the verb.

dive in If you **dive in** when you start something new, you start doing it enthusiastically and without any preparation. ❏ *He just dived in before I could get there and caused absolute havoc.* **V+ADV**

NOTE **Rush in** means almost the same as **dive in**.

dive into

1 If you **dive into** something such as a bag, you put your hand into it quickly in order to get something out. ❏ *He suddenly dived into the chest and produced a wig.* **V+PREP**

2 If you **dive into** an activity, you start doing it enthusiastically and without any preparation. ❏ *Don't dive headlong into a task which you know you can't complete.* **V+PREP**

NOTE **Rush into** means almost the same as **dive into**.

divest /daɪˈvest, AM dɪ-/ **(divests, divesting, divested)**

divest of

1 If you **divest** yourself **of** a belief or attitude, you realize that you were wrong. [FORMAL] ❏ *They will have to divest themselves of the notion that they have that power.* **V+REFL+PREP**

NOTE **Rid of** means almost the same as **divest of**.

2 If you **divest** yourself **of** something that you are carrying or wearing, you take it off or put it down. [FORMAL] ❏ *She divested herself of her bag... He began thankfully to divest himself of his suit.* **V+REFL+PREP**

3 If you **divest** someone or something **of** a role, function, or quality, you cause them to lose it. [FORMAL] ❏ *...divesting public housing of its welfare role... If they were honourable, they would resign and divest themselves of their status as Christian ministers.* **V+N+PREP, V+PRON+PREP, V+REFL+PREP**

NOTE **Strip of** means almost the same as **divest of**.

divide /dɪvˈaɪd/ **(divides, dividing, divided)**

★divide by If you **divide** a larger number **by** a smaller number, you calculate how many times the smaller number can fit into the larger number. ❏ *Divide 35 by 7... 35 divided by 7 is 5... Add 7 and 5, divide by 3 and add 2... This total is then divided by 52 to arrive at your weekly payment.* **V+N+PREP, V+PRON+PREP, V+PREP**

★divide into If you **divide** a smaller number **into** a larger number, you calculate how many times the smaller number can fit into the larger number. ❏ *Divide 7 into 35.* **V+N+PREP, V+PRON+PREP**

divide off If something **divides** things **off**, it forms a barrier that keeps them separate. ❏ *Huge iron gates divide off the east end of the church.* **V+ADV+N, V+N+ADV, V+PRON+ADV**

NOTE **Separate off** means almost the same as **divide off**.

★divide up

1 If you **divide** something **up**, you separate it into completely separate groups or parts. ❏ *Film divides motion up into a series of static images... We're dividing our group up... The imagination can divide up the stick into a number of different sections... The house has* **V+N+ADV, V+PRON+ADV, V+ADV+N**

been divided up and used as flats.

NOTE **Split up** means almost the same as **divide up**.

2 If you **divide up** a quantity of something, you share it out among a number of people or groups. □ *The Spanish and Portuguese divided up Latin America between them... We divided the meat up amongst you so it could all be eaten before it went bad... The proceeds had to be divided up among about four hundred people.*

V+ADV+N,
V+N+ADV,
V+PRON+ADV

NOTE **Parcel out** means almost the same as **divide up**.

divvy /dɪvi/ (**divvies, divvying, divvied**)

divvy up If you **divvy up**, or if you **divvy** something **up**, you share out the profits from what you have been doing with other people. [INFORMAL] □ *We'll divvy up as soon as we get back to the club... Johnson was free to divvy up his share of the money as he chose.*

V+ADV,
V+N+ADV,
V+ADV+N,
V+PRON+ADV

do /duː/ (**does, doing, did, done**)

do as → See do for

★**do away with**

1 To **do away with** something means to get rid of it. □ *Our medicines have not done away with disease... You cannot do away with violence by using violence... At the sight of all the food, thoughts of diets were done away with.*

V+ADV+PREP:
HAS PASSIVE

NOTE **Eliminate** is a more formal word for **do away with**.

2 To **do away with** someone means to kill them. [INFORMAL] □ *Who on earth would want to do away with a harmless boy like Antonio?... They were prepared to do away with Denton, and anyone else who stood in the way... I was afraid of being done away with.*

V+ADV+PREP:
HAS PASSIVE

NOTE **Do in** means almost the same as **do away with**.

do down If you **do** someone **down**, you make them appear stupid, unpleasant or unsuccessful by criticizing them. [BRITISH] □ *Jeanette remained determined to do Armand down one way or another... You enjoy trying to do each other down... She argued out of sheer spite and desire to do him down... Don't do yourself down.*

V+N+ADV,
V+PRON+ADV,
V+REFL+ADV

do for

1 If you **are done for** or if something **does for** you, your life or chance of success has been ruined. [INFORMAL] □ *If his battery fails, he's done for... She tried with her right hand, but she couldn't work it. She was done for.*

V+PREP:
HAS PASSIVE,
USUALLY PASSIVE

2 If you say that something will **do for** or **do as** another thing, you mean that you can use it instead of the other thing. [INFORMAL] □ *A few lamps did for the lighting... They could buy nothing, and sacks had to do for raincoats.*

V+PREP

NOTE **Serve for** means almost the same as **do for**.

3 If someone **does for** another person, they are employed by that person to clean their house or flat. [INFORMAL, OLD-FASHIONED] □ *Agnes did for us for thirteen years.*

V+PREP

do in

1 To **do** someone **in** means to kill them. [INFORMAL] □ *They might do you in while you're sleeping... They had decided to do their victim in... Be careful!—He'll do himself in!*

V+PRON+ADV,
V+N+ADV,
V+REFL+ADV

NOTE **Bump off** means almost the same as **do in**.

2 If you say that you **are done in**, you mean that you are completely exhausted. [INFORMAL] □ *Not to put too fine a point on in, you seem done in... 'We need a rest. I feel done in,' he said untruthfully... Walking up that hill just about did me in, I can tell you.*

V+N+ADV,
V+PRON+ADV

do out If you **do out** a cupboard or room, you clean and tidy it thoroughly. [INFORMAL] □ *She offered to do out the cell for me... I must do these cupboards out tomorrow... It still isn't right—I'll have to do it out again.*

V+ADV+N,
V+N+ADV,
V+PRON+ADV

do out in If a room or building **is done out in** a particular colour or style, it is decorated or furnished in that way. [BRITISH] □ *The bedroom was done out in pale pink... I'm thinking of having it done out in yellow and blue. ...a modernistic place done out in oiled pinewood.*

V+N+ADV,
V+PRON+ADV,
V+ADV+N:
USUALLY PASSIVE

do out of If you **do** someone **out of** something, you unfairly prevent them from having or getting it. [INFORMAL] □ *They asked if I was trying to do Miss Claybon out of a job. ...assurances that the worker is not being done out of wage increases. ...an investment which they tried to do me out of.*

V+N+ADV+PREP,
V+PRON+ADV+PREP

do over

1 If you **do** something **over**, you do it again from the beginning. [AMERICAN] □ *'Do*

V+N+ADV,

we have to do this over?' I said... That essay was no good, I'll have to do it over. V+PRON+ADV

NOTE **Do again** means almost the same as **do over**, and **redo** is a more formal word.

2 If you **do over** a house, you clean or decorate it and change its furnishings. V+ADV+N
[AMERICAN, INFORMAL] ❏ *Mrs Kennedy did over the White House... The hall looked as if it had been done over for a school prom.*

NOTE **Do up** means almost the same as **do over**.

3 If someone's house **has been done over**, burglars have broken in and stolen V+N+ADV,
things from it. [BRITISH, INFORMAL] ❏ *That place has been done over a few times.* V+PRON+ADV:
USUALLY PASSIVE

4 To **do** someone **over** means to hit and kick them in order to hurt and injure V+PRON+ADV,
them. [BRITISH, INFORMAL] ❏ *He was done over by a gang of youths... But they did me over* V+N+ADV
only the other day.

NOTE **Beat up** and **duff up** mean almost the same as **do over**.

★do up

1 If you **do** something **up**, you fasten it. ❏ *I can't do my top button up... He started to* V+N+ADV,
do up his boots, pulling fiercely at the laces... 'Don't talk to me like that,' she said, doing up V+ADV+N,
her suitcase... He would undo a window cord, do it up again and walk back. V+PRON+ADV

2 If a woman **does** her hair **up**, she arranges it so that it is tied or fastened close to V+N+ADV,
her head rather than hanging loosely. ❏ *She did her hair up in a knot on top of her* V+PRON+ADV,
head... Her hair was done up in a neat bun at the back of her head. V+ADV+N

3 If you **do up** an old building, you repair and decorate it and put in modern facil- V+ADV+N,
ities. [BRITISH] ❏ *...huge old houses in the south east that people are doing up... The thea-* V+N+ADV,
tre was horrible, done up as cheaply as possible... They wanted payment in cash for doing up V+PRON+ADV
the kitchen of one of his cottages.

NOTE **Renovate** is a more formal word for **do up**.

4 If something **is done up** in a parcel or bundle, it is wrapped in material or paper V+N+ADV,
or tied together. ❏ *I gave her a box, nicely done up in flowered paper. ...a big bunch of* V+PRON+ADV,
flowers done up in white tissue and tied with a blue ribbon. V+ADV+N:
USUALLY PASSIVE

5 If you say that a person or room **is done up** in a particular way, you mean they V+ADV+N:
are dressed or decorated in that way, often a way that is rather ridiculous or extreme. USUALLY PASSIVE
❏ *...Beatrice, usually done up like the fairy on the Christmas tree... She's had her blond hair*
done up exactly like Jackie's.

★do with

1 If you explain that one thing **has** something **to do with** or is **to do with** an- V+PREP:
other thing, you mean that the two things are related or connected in some way. ONLY AS *to*-INF
❏ *My interest in MPs had nothing to do with Parliament at all... Lateral thinking is to do with*
new ideas... What's his job? He's something to do with the Foreign Office... Mind your own
business; it's got nothing to do with you.

2 If you say you could **do with** something, you mean that you need it or would V+PREP
like it. ❏ *I think we could all do with a good night's sleep... The staff could probably do with*
some more money.

★do without

1 If you **do without** something, you manage or survive in spite of not having it. V+PREP,
❏ *Many Victorian households did without a bathroom altogether... If you don't have ciga-* V+ADV
rettes, you must simply do without.

NOTE **Go without** means almost the same as **do without**.

2 If you say that you could **do without** something, you mean that you would pre- V+PREP
fer not to have it or it is of no benefit to you. [INFORMAL] ❏ *He could do without her*
rhetorical questions at five o'clock in the morning. ...those who love France but can do with-
out the natives... Like all teenagers there's one thing she'd rather do without – spots.

dob /dɒb/ (dobs, dobbing, dobbed)

dob in When someone has done something wrong, if you **dob** them **in**, you get V+PRON+ADV,
them into trouble by telling a person in authority what they did. [INFORMAL] ❏ *If you* V+N+ADV
dob me in, I'll get you. That's a promise.

dole /dəʊl/ (doles, doling, doled)

dole out If you **dole** something **out**, you give an amount of it to each person or V+ADV+N,
animal in a group. ❏ *From the bridge, children dole out their sandwich crusts to the ducks...* V+N+ADV,
Gus was doling out crumbled cookies from a large tin box... The problem had something to V+PRON+ADV

do with how the money was doled out; only three of the six had actually received anything.
NOTE **Dish out** and **hand out** mean almost the same as **dole out**.

doll /dɒl/ (dolls, dolling, dolled)

   doll up If you **doll** yourself **up**, you put on smart or fashionable clothes. [INFORMAL] ❑ *He was all dolled up in the latest gear... She started dolling herself up to go out.*
   NOTE **Dress up** means almost the same as **doll up**.
V+REFL+ADV:
USUALLY PASSIVE

dope /doʊp/ (dopes, doping, doped)

   dope up If someone **is doped up**, they are in a state where they cannot think clearly because they are under the influence of drugs. [INFORMAL] ❑ *Irene gave evidence that Mackie and Bell were doped up... They were all so doped up they wouldn't even know the war had started until it was too late... That's right, dope them up, keep them quiet.*
   NOTE **Drugged** means almost the same as **doped up**.
V+N+ADV,
V+PRON+ADV:
USUALLY PASSIVE

dose /doʊs/ (doses, dosing, dosed)

   dose up If you **dose** someone **up**, you give them the full amount of a medicine or a drug that can be given at one time. ❑ *We'll dose her up with it and see how she responds.*
V+PRON+ADV,
V+N+ADV,
V+REFL+ADV

doss /dɒs/ (dosses, dossing, dossed)

   doss down If you **doss down** in a temporary bed or unusual place, you sleep there for a short time. [BRITISH, INFORMAL] ❑ *...a rusty stretcher where he had dossed down once or twice... He'll be dossing down in the living room for a couple of weeks.*
   NOTE **Kip down** means almost the same as **doss down**.
V+ADV

dote /doʊt/ (dotes, doting, doted)

   dote on If you **dote on** or **dote upon** someone, you love them so much that you cannot see their faults. ❑ *This guy she's just married, he dotes on her.*
   NOTE **Adore** means almost the same as **dote on**.
V+PREP:
HAS PASSIVE

   dote upon → See dote on

double /dʌbəl/ (doubles, doubling, doubled)

   double back
   1 If you **double back**, you turn and go back in the direction that you came from. ❑ *When nobody was watching, they doubled back.*
   NOTE **Turn back** means almost the same as **double back**.
V+ADV

   2 When a line **doubles back** on itself, it bends in the middle, so that the second part is parallel to the first part. ❑ *The queue doubled back on itself.*
V+ADV:
USUALLY WITH on+REFL

   double over → See double up
   double up
   1 If two people **double up**, they both use the same thing because there is not enough for them to have one each. ❑ *There weren't enough offices for everyone, so we had to double up... Families who had previously doubled up in the same accommodation were housed in the new units.*
V+ADV

   2 If you **double up** or **double over**, you bend your body quickly, for example because you are laughing a lot or because you are in pain. ❑ *His companion doubled up with laughter, holding his stomach... She was doubled over, her whole face distorted with pain... The pain caught me and doubled me over in agony.*
V+ADV,
V+N+ADV,
V+PRON+ADV:
ERGATIVE

doze /doʊz/ (dozes, dozing, dozed)

   doze off If you **doze off**, you fall into a light sleep. ❑ *I leant back against the sunny wall and dozed off... It was about midnight and she'd just dozed off.*
   NOTE **Nod off** means almost the same as **doze off**.
V+ADV

drag /dræg/ (drags, dragging, dragged)

   drag along → See drag on
   drag down
   1 Someone who **drags** someone else **down**, reduces them to an inferior social status or to lower standards of behaviour. ❑ *His mother hates me. She thinks I drag him down.*
V+N+ADV,
V+PRON+ADV

   2 Something that **drags** you **down** makes you feel weak or depressed. ❑ *That bout of flu really dragged me down... I felt dragged down by the obligations of making the film.*
V+N+ADV,
V+PRON+ADV

The symbol ★ shows key phrasal verbs

drag in When you are talking, if you **drag in** a particular subject, you mention something that is not relevant and that other people do not want to discuss. ❏ *They disapproved of my dragging in his wealth.*

V+ADV+N,
V+PRON+ADV,
V+N+ADV

drag into To **drag** something or someone **into** an event or situation means to involve them in it when it is not necessary or not desirable. ❏ *It was the politicians who were dragging politics into sport, not the sportsmen... That's no reason for dragging you into it.*

V+N+PREP,
V+PRON+PREP

drag on If an event or process **drags on** or **drags along**, it progresses very slowly and takes longer than seems necessary. ❏ *Some legal cases have dragged on for eight years... The civil war dragged on... His divorce was dragging along.*

V+ADV

drag out

1 If you **drag** something **out**, you make it last for longer than is necessary. ❏ *We did not know how to prevent them from dragging out the talks.*

V+ADV+N,
V+N+ADV,
V+PRON+ADV

NOTE **Spin out** means almost the same as **drag out**, and **prolong** is a more formal word.

2 If you **drag** something **out** of someone, you persuade them to tell you something that they do not want to tell you. ❏ *The truth had to be dragged out of him... It was hard to drag this sort of stuff out of him.*

V+N+ADV,
V+PRON+ADV:
USUALLY+of

drag up If someone **drags up** an unpleasant event or an old story from the past, they mention it when people do not want to be reminded of it. ❏ *There's no need to drag that up again.*

V+PRON+ADV,
V+N+ADV,
V+ADV+N

NOTE **Bring up** is a more general expression for **drag up**.

draw /drɔː/ **(draws, drawing, drew, drawn)**

draw back If you **draw back**, you move away from something because you are surprised or because you do not like it. ❏ *A little blood dribbled down the stick. Instinctively the boys drew back.*

V+ADV

NOTE **Recoil** is a more formal word for **draw back**.

♦ A **drawback** is a disadvantage caused by an unpleasant or unhelpful characteristic that someone or something has. ❏ *Her only drawback is that she's so stupid... This machine has a major drawback from the technological point of view.*

N-COUNT

draw down If you **draw down** an unpleasant reaction, you do something which makes other people criticize you. ❏ *In doing so, he drew down the anger of the senior members of the party.*

V+ADV+N

★draw in

1 When the days or evenings **are drawing in**, it is getting dark at an earlier time each evening because autumn or winter is approaching. [BRITISH]

V+ADV

2 When a train **draws in** at a station, it arrives there and stops.

V+ADV

NOTE **Pull in** and **come in** mean almost the same as **draw in**.

3 If you **draw in** breath, you breathe deeply. ❏ *He moved closer to her and drew in a deep breath.*

V+ADV+N

NOTE **Take in** means almost the same as **draw in**.

4 If you **draw** someone **in**, you cause them to become involved with something you are involved with. ❏ *It won't be easy for you to draw him in... You gradually fall under the spell and get drawn in deeper and deeper.*

V+N+ADV,
V+PRON+ADV

draw into If you **draw** someone **into** an activity or situation, you cause them to become involved in it. ❏ *Quite by chance I got drawn into a kind of party downstairs... Peter drew her into the discussion.*

V+PRON+PREP,
V+N+PREP

draw off If you **draw off** a quantity of liquid from a larger amount, you remove that quantity, usually through a pipe or tube. ❏ *She drew off some of the beer, to see if it was ready to drink.*

V+ADV+N,
V+N+ADV,
V+PRON+ADV

draw on

☑ In meanings 2 and 3, the stress is on dr<u>a</u>w.

1 As a period of time **draws on**, it gets nearer or passes gradually. ❏ *As the winter months draw on, the leaves fall and the days get shorter... The evening drew on, and Andrew and I got drunk.*

V+ADV

NOTE **Wear on** means almost the same as **draw on**.

2 If you **draw on** or **draw upon** something, you make use of it in order to do

V+PREP:

something. ❑ *He was able to draw on vast reserves of talent. ...the subconscious informa-* HAS PASSIVE
tion the expert draws on without even realizing that he has it... They draw upon a variety of
sources in developing their theory.

3 When someone **draws on** a cigarette, they breathe in through it and inhale the V+PREP
smoke deeply.

★draw out

1 When a train **draws out**, it moves out of the station. V+ADV

NOTE **Pull out** means almost the same as **draw out**.

2 If you **draw out** a sound, you make it longer. ❑ *'Ah,' she said, smiling, drawing out* V+ADV+N,
the 'ah'. V+PRON+ADV,
V+N+ADV

3 If something **is drawn out** it takes much longer than is normal or necessary. ❑ *I* V+ADV+N,
wonder whether this debate is going to be short and decisive, or drawn out by a reluctance to V+N+ADV,
use nuclear weapons. V+PRON+ADV:
USUALLY PASSIVE

4 If someone or something **draws out** information or an emotion from you, they V+ADV+N,
make you say or express it. ❑ *...the way in which its forms and colours draw out certain* V+N+ADV,
emotions in the viewer... It was impossible to draw the truth out of him. V+PRON+ADV:
ALSO+*of*

NOTE **Elicit** means almost the same as **draw out**.

5 If you **draw** someone **out**, you make them feel less nervous and more willing to V+N+ADV,
talk. ❑ *Why not make conversation with them, draw them out, make them laugh and feel at* V+PRON+ADV
ease?

6 When the days or evenings **are drawing out**, it is getting dark later each even- V+ADV
ing because spring or summer is approaching.

★draw up

1 When you **draw up** a document, list, or plan, you prepare it and write it out. V+ADV+N,
❑ *A charter was drawn up, setting out their policies... The committee drew up a five-point* V+N+ADV,
plan to revive the economy. V+PRON+ADV

NOTE **Formulate** is a formal word for **draw up**.

2 When a vehicle **draws up**, it comes to a particular place and stops. ❑ *Just before* V+ADV
eleven a bus drew up... The taxi drew up before the house on Sixty-second Street.

NOTE **Pull up** means almost the same as **draw up**.

3 If you **draw up** a chair, you bring it nearer to a person or place, so that you can V+ADV+N,
sit close to them. ❑ *Draw up a chair, and we'll go through these notes of yours... He drew* V+N+ADV,
his stool up to the table. V+PRON+ADV

NOTE **Pull up** means almost the same as **draw up**.

4 If you **draw** yourself **up**, you make your back very straight so that you look as V+REFL+ADV
tall as possible. ❑ *He drew himself up. 'I apologise,' he said... Its whiskers began to twitch.*
Slowly, it drew itself up to an extreme height.

draw upon → See draw on

dream /driːm/ (dreams, dreaming, dreamed/dreamt)

★dream of

1 If you say you would not **dream of** doing something, you are emphasizing that V+PREP:
you would never do it in any circumstances. ❑ *I wouldn't dream of asking my mother to* WITH NEGATIVE,
look after her. HAS PASSIVE

2 Something that is **undreamed of** is much better, worse, or more unusual than ADJECTIVE
you ever imagined or thought was possible. ❑ *People now have achieved a physical mo-*
bility previously undreamed of.

dream on If you tell someone to **dream on**, you are telling them that their IMPERATIVE,
hopes or wishes are not realistic. [BRITISH, INFORMAL] ❑ *If you get lucky on the lottery to-* V+ADV
night, think you might snap up a mansion? Dream on.

★dream up If you **dream up** a plan or idea, you work it out or create it in your V+ADV+N,
mind. ❑ *He would never dream up a desperate scheme like that on his own... The jamboree* V+PRON+ADV
had been dreamed up by the Duke.

dredge /dredʒ/ (dredges, dredging, dredged)

dredge up If you **dredge up** something from the past, you remember it with V+ADV+N,
some difficulty and perhaps without much enthusiasm. ❑ *...all these old verses that we* V+N+ADV,
seem to dredge up from early memories. V+PRON+ADV

NOTE **Dig up** means almost the same as **dredge up**.

The symbol ★ shows key phrasal verbs

dress /drɛs/ (dresses, dressing, dressed)
dress down

[1] If you **dress down**, you wear clothes that are less smart than usual. ❑ *She dresses* V+ADV
down in dark glasses and baggy clothes to avoid hordes of admirers.

♦ **Dress-down day** is a day of the week, usually Friday, when employees are al- N-SING
lowed to dress more casually than usual. ❑ *There is a theory that a 'dress-down day' ac-*
tually makes people more productive.

[2] To **dress** someone **down** means to punish them by telling them angrily that V+N+ADV,
they have done something wrong. ❑ *The Foreign Minister was dressed down in public.* V+PRON+ADV

NOTE **Reprimand** means almost the same as **dress down**, and **tell off** is a more
informal expression.

♦ If someone gives you a **dressing-down**, they punish you by telling you angrily N-SING
that you have behaved badly. ❑ *The Duke gave him a severe dressing-down for his drunk-*
enness.

NOTE **Reprimand** and **telling-off** mean almost the same as **dressing-down**.

★**dress up**

[1] If you **dress up** or **dress** yourself **up**, you put on clothes that are smarter than V+ADV,
the ones you usually wear because you are going somewhere special. ❑ *Rather than sit* V+REFL+ADV
at home, they all get dressed up and go out... She was glad that she was all dressed up and
had done her hair that morning.

[2] When people or children **dress up** or when they **are dressed up**, they wear V+ADV:
old fashioned clothes or costumes to disguise themselves, to play a game, or to go to ALSO PASSIVE:
a fancy-dress party. ❑ *You could get someone to dress up as a pig. ...an actor dressed up* V+ADV
like a U.S. GI.

♦ **Dressing-up** is a game in which children put on old or unusual clothes and pre- N-UNCOUNT
tend to be different people.

[3] If you **dress** something **up**, you make it seem more attractive, interesting, or ac- V+N+ADV,
ceptable than it really is. ❑ *The offer was simply an old one dressed up for gullible Euro-* V+PRON+ADV,
pean socialists. V+ADV+N

NOTE **Tart up** is a more informal expression for **dress up**.

drift /drɪft/ (drifts, drifting, drifted)

☑ **About** is used mainly in British English.

drift about → See drift around
drift along → See drift around

drift apart If people who have had a close relationship **drift apart**, they be- V+ADV
come less close and the relationship gradually comes to an end. ❑ *Back home again,*
we more or less drifted apart. ...the feeling that they had drifted apart during those previous
months... European and American politics seem to be drifting apart.

drift around Someone who **drifts around**, **drifts about**, or **drifts along** V+ADV
does not have a settled way of life and has no definite plans or aims. ❑ *He drifted*
about from job to job for over a year... She sort of drifts around and doesn't do anything
much... They feel they may as well drift along through adolescence.

drift off If you **drift off**, you gradually fall asleep. ❑ *Finally, he gave up worrying* V+ADV:
and drifted off to sleep... I slept again, drifting off to the sound of the bells... Occasionally he ALSO+*to/into*
would drift off into fitful, moaning sleep.

NOTE **Doze off** means almost the same as **drift off**.

drill /drɪl/ (drills, drilling, drilled)

drill into If you **drill** something **into** someone, you teach it to them by making V+N+PREP,
them repeat it many times. ❑ *...the rigid training rules that had been drilled into him at* V+PRON+PREP
the academy... It was drilled into them that no matter what happens they must never drop
the paddle.

NOTE **Drum into** means almost the same as **drill into**.

drink /drɪŋk/ (drinks, drinking, drank, drunk)

drink down If you **drink down** a liquid in a glass, cup, or other container, you V+ADV+N,
drink it all quickly, often without stopping. ❑ *I drank down my double Scotch eagerly...* V+N+ADV,
He drank the bourbon down in two long draughts... Come on, you'd better drink that down. V+PRON+ADV

drop in

drink in If you **drink in** something that you see or hear, you concentrate all your attention on it and experience the strong effect that it has on you. ❏ *He stood still, drinking in the beauty of the countryside... She sat listening attentively to the speaker, drinking it all in.*

V+ADV+N,
V+N+ADV,
V+PRON+ADV

NOTE **Take in** means almost the same as **drink in**.

drink to When you **drink to** someone or something, you raise your glass and say their name before drinking, to show that you hope they will be happy or successful. ❏ *The barman set their glasses in front of them and they drank to Mary Jane... They agreed on their plan and drank to it.*

V+PREP

drink up When you **drink up**, you finish what you are drinking completely. ❏ *Drink up. Here comes another bottle of wine... Drink your milk up and then you can go out to play.*

V+ADV,
V+N+ADV,
V+PRON+ADV,
V+ADV+N

drive /draɪv/ **(drives, driving, drove, driven)**

drive at If you ask what someone **is driving at**, you are asking what they are trying to say. ❏ *What are you driving at?... She knew at once what I was driving at... I can see what you're driving at, but I'm still not convinced.*

V+PREP

NOTE **Get at** means almost the same as **drive at**.

drive away To **drive** someone or something **away** means to behave in a way that forces them to leave. ❏ *'Flies!' Etta cried and attempted to drive them away by waving her hand. ...spectators whose habits and foul language drive others away... The scenes and the outbursts drove away most of her old friends.*

V+PRON+ADV,
V+N+ADV,
V+ADV+N

drive down To **drive down** prices or costs means to force them to become lower. ❏ *Airlines play one manufacturer off against the other to drive down prices.*

V+ADV+N,
V+N+ADV,
V+PRON+ADV

drive off If you **drive off** someone or something that you see as a threat, you force them to go away. ❏ *The crowd pelted the spies, driving them off before they'd seen anything... They claimed they had driven off a major force.*

V+PRON+ADV,
V+ADV+N,
V+N+ADV

★**drive out** To **drive** someone or something **out** means to force them to leave or disappear. ❏ *Some people want to drive others out of the party... The magic man came to Juffure to drive out evil spirits... The system seemed to drive out all love and liberty.*

V+N+ADV,
V+ADV+N,
V+PRON+ADV:
ALSO+of

NOTE **Expel** is a more formal word for **drive out**.

drone /drəʊn/ **(drones, droning, droned)**

drone on If someone **drones on**, they talk in a boring way for a long time in a low, monotonous voice. ❏ *I remember him droning on about how important it was to study literature... The President droned on, not daring to look at the camera.*

V+ADV:
ALSO+about

drool /druːl/ **(drools, drooling, drooled)**

drool over If you **drool over** someone or something, you look at them with desire because you find them very attractive. ❏ *You go round in that bikini and he's drooling over you all the time. ...youths drooling over pornographic pictures.*

V+PREP

drop /drɒp/ **(drops, dropping, dropped)**

drop away

1 If support or interest **drops away**, it becomes less strong. ❏ *Public interest in the royal marriage has dropped away... Trade Union support dropped away.*

V+ADV

NOTE **Drop off** means almost the same as **drop away**.

2 If land or ground **drops away**, it slopes down so that it is at a lower level to where you are or from a particular point that has been mentioned. ❏ *To the south the hills dropped away to farmland... From the house, the garden drops away, surrounded by a rural scene of woodland.*

V+ADV

★**drop back** If someone who is moving along **drops back**, they go slower to allow other people to pass them. ❏ *The two motor-cycles dropped back to take up position at the rear of the convoy.*

V+ADV

NOTE **Fall back** means almost the same as **drop back**.

★**drop by** To **drop by** means to visit someone informally without having arranged the visit. ❏ *If there's anything you want to see, just drop by.*

V+ADV

NOTE **Drop in** and **drop round** mean almost the same as **drop by**.

★**drop in** If you **drop in** on someone, you visit them without making any formal arrangement to do so. ❏ *I thought I'd just drop in and see how you were... I dropped in on*

V+ADV:
ALSO+on

her during the afternoon.

NOTE **Drop by, drop round,** and **pop in** mean almost the same as **drop in**.

♦ A **drop-in** centre is a building provided by a local authority where people can go during the day or evening and use the facilities or get help with welfare problems. ❑ *I've been working at the drop-in centre for the last three months.*

ADJECTIVE

★drop off

1 When you are driving, if you **drop** one of your passengers **off**, you take them to where they want to go and leave them there. ❑ *I can drop Daisy off on my way home.*

V+N+ADV, V+PRON+ADV, V+ADV+N

2 If you **drop off** to sleep, you go to sleep. ❑ *I come to see him, and what does he do? He drops off to sleep!... I couldn't get to sleep, and when I did eventually drop off, I was assaulted by dreams.*

V+ADV: ALSO+to

NOTE **Doze off** means almost the same as **drop off**.

3 If support or interest **drops off**, it becomes less strong. ❑ *Three days later interest had dropped off, and we could walk the streets without being recognised.*

V+ADV

NOTE **Drop away** means almost the same as **drop off**.

★drop out

1 If you **drop out** of a group, you stop belonging to it. If you **drop out** of school or college, you leave before finishing your course. ❑ *Four of the original thirty five dropped out of the group because they decided they couldn't afford the fare... Some are thrown out and some drop out voluntarily... He had dropped out of college in the first term.*

V+ADV: ALSO+of

♦ A **drop-out** is someone who leaves school or college before finishing their course; sometimes used showing disapproval. [OLD-FASHIONED] ❑ *This part of town is full of hippies and drop-outs.*

N-COUNT

2 If someone **drops out**, they reject the accepted ways of society and live outside the usual system; used showing disapproval. ❑ *She encourages people to keep their jobs rather than dropping out to live in a commune.*

V+ADV

3 If a word or expression **drops out** of the language, it is no longer used. ❑ *Today the word 'teeny-bopper' has virtually dropped out of usage.*

V+ADV: USUALLY+of

drop round

1 To **drop round** means to visit someone without making any formal arrangement to do so. ❑ *I'll drop round when I've finished the shopping.*

V+ADV

NOTE **Drop in** and **drop by** mean almost the same as **drop round**.

2 If you **drop** something **round**, you take it to a person's home for them. ❑ *Bill can drop your books round on his way home.*

V+N+ADV, V+PRON+ADV

drown /draʊn/ (drowns, drowning, drowned)

drown out If something **drowns out** a sound, it makes so much noise that it is impossible to hear that sound properly. ❑ *The noise from the plane drowned out the noise of the guns... The music had been blaring all evening, drowning out the speakers in the tent.*

V+ADV+N, V+N+ADV, V+PRON+ADV

drum /drʌm/ (drums, drumming, drummed)

drum into If you **drum** something **into** someone, you make them remember it by repeating it to them regularly. ❑ *I have had the art of tidiness drummed into me... Such expectations are drummed into every growing child.*

V+N+PREP, V+PRON+PREP

NOTE **Din into** means almost the same as **drum into**.

drum out To **drum** someone **out** of an organization means to force them to leave it. [OLD-FASHIONED] ❑ *He had been drummed out of the club for indecent behaviour.*

V+N+ADV, V+PRON+ADV: USUALLY+of

NOTE **Kick out** means almost the same as **drum out**, and **expel** is a more formal word.

drum up If you **drum up** support for a cause or campaign, you do things to get people's support for it. ❑ *We were busy canvassing and drumming up support... They attempted to drum up support from students... His bandwagon rolled from state to state, drumming up radical delegates to support him.*

V+ADV+N

NOTE **Gather** means almost the same as **drum up**.

dry /draɪ/ (dries, drying, dried)

dry off When something wet **dries off**, the moisture that was on its surface disappears. ❑ *I'll walk the dog for a while till she dries off... As soon as the sweat dries off, you get hot... She took one of the big towels and dried him off.*

V+ADV, V+N+ADV, V+PRON+ADV: ERGATIVE

★**dry out**

1 If something that contains moisture **dries out**, it loses all the moisture that was
in it and becomes hard and completely dry. ❑ *The soil gets as hard as brick when it dries
out... How could the eggs be prevented from drying out? ...drying out wet boards before laying a floor.*

V+ADV,
V+ADV+N,
V+N+ADV,
V+PRON+ADV:
ERGATIVE

2 If someone who has been an alcoholic **dries out**, they are cured of alcoholism.
[INFORMAL] ❑ *Every two months Erika disappeared to a health farm where she dried out and
ate lettuce.*

V+ADV

★**dry up**

1 If something **dries up** or if something **dries** it **up**, it loses all the moisture that
was in it. ❑ *My mouth always dries up under stress... She tried drying her hair in front of the
gas fire, but the gas dried it up and frizzled the ends... It dried up the ends.*

V+ADV,
V+N/PRON+ADV,
V+ADV+N:
ERGATIVE

2 If a river, lake, or well **dries up**, it becomes empty of water, usually because of
hot weather or lack of rain. ❑ *In the dry season these wells dry up and water has to be
bought from vendors... On Wednesday, his goldfish pond dried up in mysterious circumstances.*

V+ADV

◆ A **dried-up** river or lake is completely empty of water. ❑ *...dried-up river-beds.*

ADJECTIVE

3 When you **dry up** or **dry up** the dishes after they have been washed, you wipe
the water off them with a cloth. ❑ *I started to dry up a cup rather slowly... If you use two
washing up racks, you rarely need to dry up.*

V+ADV+N,
V+N+ADV,
V+PRON+ADV,
V+ADV

◆ **Drying-up** or the **drying-up** is the job of drying dishes and cutlery after they
have been washed; also used to refer to the things that need to be dried. ❑ *We helped
with the drying-up in a thoughtful silence... I can't come yet, I've got all this drying-up to do.*

N-UNCOUNT,
N-SING

4 If you **dry up** when you are speaking, you stop in the middle of what you were
saying because you cannot think what to say next. ❑ *Halfway through the speech she
dried up completely... We did a new play every week and we all used to dry up and make
mistakes.*

V+ADV

5 If something **dries up**, it stops being productive. ❑ *They had not contemplated the
possibility of supplies drying up... They found their business drying up and were finally forced
to close... The market for luxury goods dried up during the recession.*

V+ADV

6 If you say '**dry up**' to someone, you are telling them in a rather rude way to stop
talking and be quiet. [BRITISH, INFORMAL, OLD-FASHIONED]

IMPERATIVE,
V+ADV

NOTE **Shut up** and **belt up** mean almost the same as **dry up**.

7 Someone who is **dried-up** looks old, small, wrinkled, and perhaps bad-tempered.
❑ *...a sour, dried-up man with gold-rimmed spectacles.*

ADJECTIVE

NOTE **Wizened** and **withered** are more formal words for **dried-up**.

dub /dʌb/ (**dubs, dubbing, dubbed**)

dub in When film-makers **dub in** a voice, they use the recorded voice of one actor in place of the voice of the actor who appears on the film. ❑ *Later on, probably, a
different voice will be dubbed in.*

V+N+ADV,
V+PRON+ADV,
V+ADV+N

dub into If a film **is dubbed into** another language, the sound is replaced by a
different recording so that the actors appear to be speaking in a different language.
❑ *Hawaii-five-O sells in forty-seven countries and is dubbed into seven languages.*

V+N+PREP,
V+PRON+PREP:
USUALLY PASSIVE

dub over When a sound **is dubbed over** a film, a different recording is used so
that the sound is not the original one. ❑ *Many sequences showed wounded prisoners
pleading, whether genuinely or with false voices dubbed over, for peace.*

PASSIVE:
V+ADV,
V+PREP

duck /dʌk/ (**ducks, ducking, ducked**)

duck out If you **duck out** of something that you are supposed to do, you avoid
doing it. [INFORMAL] ❑ *He ducked out of an appointment as aide to a General... They are
used by adults to duck out of their responsibilities... He got her into this mess in the first place
and is now ducking out without providing her with essential support.*

V+ADV:
USUALLY+of

NOTE **Back out** and **cop out** mean almost the same as **duck out**.

duff /dʌf/ (**duffs, duffing, duffed**)

duff up To **duff** someone **up** means to hit and kick them in order to injure
them. [BRITISH, INFORMAL] ❑ *Well, I put the boot in and duffed him up... He would have
liked to have duffed up half the people in the club.*

V+PRON+ADV,
V+ADV+N,
V+N+ADV

NOTE **Beat up** and **do over** mean almost the same as **duff up**.

duke /djuːk, AM duːk/ **(dukes, duking, duked)**

duke out If two people or groups **duke** it **out**, they fight or compete with one   V+*it*+ADV
another. [AMERICAN] ❏ *It's time for the authorities to give companies more freedom to duke
it out until the best wins.*

NOTE **Fight out** means almost the same as **duke out**.

dumb /dʌm/ **(dumbs, dumbing, dumbed)**

dumb down If you **dumb down** something, you make it easier for people to   V+ADV+N,
understand, especially when this spoils it; used showing disapproval. ❏ *This sounded*   V+N+ADV,
like a case for dumbing down the magazine, which no one favored.   V+PRON+ADV

dummy /dʌmi/ **(dummies, dummying, dummied)**

dummy up If someone **dummies up**, they keep a secret by pretending not to   V+ADV
know anything about it when they are asked. [INFORMAL] ❏ *I dummied up, and I believe
the police approved of this.*

dump /dʌmp/ **(dumps, dumping, dumped)**

dump on If you **dump on** someone or something, you treat them unfairly, for   V+PREP:
example by criticizing them too severely or giving them unpleasant tasks to do.   HAS PASSIVE
❏ *You let people dump on you... I could dump on my home town, but no outsider had better
try... Housework and child-rearing were being roundly dumped on... White House officials
thought it best not to dump on him gratuitously.*

dust /dʌst/ **(dusts, dusting, dusted)**

dust down

1 If you **dust** something **down**, you remove dust from it with a brush or dry   V+ADV+N,
cloth. ❏ *Dust down the walls and wipe paintwork thoroughly before starting. ...the distracted*   V+PRON+ADV,
mother, dusting down the frills and trimmings.   V+N+ADV

2 If you say that someone **dusts** something **down**, you mean they are using an   V+N+ADV,
old idea or method, rather than trying something new. [BRITISH] ❏ *Critics were busy*   V+ADV+N,
dusting down the same superlatives they had applied to their first three films.   V+PRON+ADV

NOTE **Dust off** means almost the same as **dust down**.

3 If you say that someone has **dusted** himself or herself **down**, you mean that   V+REFL+ADV
they have managed to recover from a severe problem which has affected their life.
[BRITISH] ❏ *Tina Turner dusted herself down, got rid of Ike and became the greatest show on
earth.*

dust off

1 If you **dust off** your clothes or your hands, you brush the dust from them.   V+ADV+N,
❏ *'What a mess!' she said dusting off her hands... He dusts off his trousers and gets in the*   V+N+ADV,
car.   V+PRON+ADV

2 If you say that someone **dusts** something **off**, you mean they are using an old   V+N+ADV,
idea or method, rather than trying something new. ❏ *I'll dust off an old expression I*   V+ADV+N,
used to employ... Long-mothballed projects like widening the Suez Canal are being dusted off.   V+PRON+ADV

NOTE **Dust down** means almost the same as **dust off**.

3 If you say that someone has **dusted** himself or herself **off**, you mean that they   V+REFL+ADV
have managed to recover from a severe problem which has affected their life. ❏ *When
we are rejected, although we have been hurt we can pick ourselves up, dust ourselves off and
start again.*

dwell /dwel/ **(dwells, dwelling, dwelled/dwelt)**

dwell on If you **dwell on** or **dwell upon** something, you think or speak about   V+PREP
it a great deal. **Dwell upon** is more formal. ❏ *Accept the pleasures of past experiences
without dwelling upon the miseries... People are reluctant to dwell on the subject of death.*

dwell upon → See **dwell on**

Ee

earmark /ˈɪəʳmɑːʳk/ **(earmarks, earmarking, earmarked)**

  earmark for If sums of money or other resources **are earmarked for** a purpose, people in authority have decided that they should be used for that purpose. ❑ *At least $100,000 in CRP's budget was earmarked for 'Convention Security'... Two sites have been earmarked for industrial use.*

V+N+PREP,
V+PRON+PREP:
USUALLY PASSIVE

earth /ɜːʳθ/ **(earths, earthing, earthed)**

  earth up If you **earth up** vegetables or plants, you pile more soil around them in order to protect their roots or to encourage the roots to grow. ❑ *I went and earthed up my celery. ...planted by dropping them straight onto muck, then earthing them up... We didn't earth the clumps up until later in the year.*

V+ADV+N,
V+PRON+ADV,
V+N+ADV

ease /iːz/ **(eases, easing, eased)**

  ease off

  1 If something **eases off**, it becomes slower or less intense. ❑ *The pace of our activity gradually eased off... The headaches eased off and mum decided she had better continue her treatment... The rain had eased off.*

V+ADV

  2 If you **ease off** clothes that you are wearing, you take them off carefully and gently. ❑ *She bent down and eased off her shoes... We got him onto a couch and I eased off his right boot... She took hold of the bandage and eased it off.*

V+ADV+N,
V+PRON+ADV,
V+N+ADV:
NO PASSIVE

  ease up

  1 If something **eases up** it is reduced in degree, speed, or intensity. ❑ *The rain had eased up... New figures indicate the recession may be easing up.*

V+ADV

  2 If you **ease up**, you stop putting so much energy or effort into what you are doing. ❑ *You're working too hard and need to ease up... We aren't going to ease up – we are going to increase the pressure.*

V+ADV

  NOTE **Slow down** means almost the same as **ease up**.

  ease up on If you **ease up** on someone or something, your behaviour or attitude towards them becomes less severe or strict. [INFORMAL] ❑ *The manager does not intend to ease up on his players for some time... Officials have eased up on the press restrictions.*

V+ADV+on

eat /iːt/ **(eats, eating, ate, eaten)**

  eat away

  1 If an animal **eats** something **away**, it eats it gradually and partially destroys it. ❑ *...who let cockroaches and rats eat away his walls without lifting a hand to preserve his property... I feel as if worms are eating away my brain.*

V+ADV+N,
V+N+ADV,
V+PRON+ADV

  2 If something **is eaten away** by water or chemicals, it is gradually destroyed by the physical force of the water or the action of the chemicals. ❑ *...a sandbank that was already eaten away by the advancing water. ...such chrome as had not yet been eaten away by rust... As the rain fell, water rushed down every gully, eating away the road... He watches the crumbling walls while the waves eat them away.*

V+ADV+N,
V+N+ADV,
V+PRON+ADV:
USUALLY PASSIVE

  3 If a disease or a feeling **eats** someone **away**, it causes them physical or mental harm. ❑ *You have this cancer inside you eating you away.*

V+PRON+ADV,
V+N+ADV

  eat away at

  1 If water or chemicals **eat away at** something solid, they gradually destroy it. ❑ *...rivulets eating away at the foundations.*

V+ADV+PREP

  2 To **eat away at** someone's hopes, aims, or feelings means to gradually destroy or weaken them. ❑ *Inflation eats away at any advantage which might have been gained by lower-paid workers... She eats away at their resolve... Corruption eats away at the founda-*

V+ADV+PREP

tions of trust between people.

NOTE Undermine means almost the same as **eat away at**.

eat in When you **eat in**, you have a meal at home rather than going out to a res-   V+ADV
taurant. ❑ *'We won't be eating in tonight,'* Shoshana said. ...*the full kitchen gave them the
option of eating in or dining out.*

NOTE **Eat out** means the opposite of **eat in**.

eat into

1 If something **eats into** a part of your body, it presses or pokes hard into it and   V+PREP
may cause you pain. ❑ *He could see where the stockings ended and the garters ate into the
flesh... There was a nail eating into his toe.*

2 If a chemical or a chemical process **eats into** a physical object, it affects the ob-   V+PREP
ject and gradually destroys it. ❑ *Iron pans are not suitable as vinegar eats into them.*

3 If something **eats into** resources such as money or land, it gradually uses more   V+PREP
of them than was expected. ❑ *Repayment of past loans has been eating increasingly into
aid transfers.*

NOTE **Encroach on** means almost the same as **eat into**.

4 If a feeling or an event **eats into** you, it upsets you deeply and you cannot for-   V+PREP
get about it. ❑ *That laughter constantly rang in his ears and ate into him... The problems
ate into all their affections.*

★eat out When you **eat out**, you have a meal at a restaurant instead of at home.   V+ADV
❑ *Do you eat out a lot in London?... Willie liked to eat out in restaurants and stay up late in
bars.*

NOTE **Eat in** means the opposite of **eat out**.

♦ **Eating out** is the activity of having a meal in a restaurant. ❑ *Eating out was be-   N-UNCOUNT
yond their means... I really enjoy eating out or cooking for friends at home.*

★eat up

1 If people or animals **eat up** food, they eat all the food that they have been given   V+ADV+N,
or all that is available. ❑ *If you eat up all your cereal, I'll give you a piece of chocolate.* ...*if*   V+PRON+ADV,
your animals stray away and eat up the crops growing in another man's field... She sat on   V+N+ADV
my bed and made me eat it all up.

NOTE **Polish off** is a more informal expression for **eat up**.

2 If you say **'Eat up'** to someone, you are encouraging them to eat as much as   IMPERATIVE,
they can and to enjoy their food. ❑ *He also took a strange pleasure in watching me eat.*   V+ADV
'Eat up, girl, that's it,' he would say.

3 If water or chemicals **eat up** something, they destroy it gradually, by physical   V+ADV+N,
force or by a chemical process. ❑ *Nothing at all would be left to stop the wind and the*   V+PRON+ADV,
rain eating up the land... The beautiful islands were eaten up by sand and erosion.   V+N+ADV

4 If you **are eaten up** by a negative feeling, you feel it very deeply and you can-   V+ADV+N,
not stop yourself from feeling it. ❑ *Many of the older country folk are eaten up with jeal-*   V+N+ADV,
ousy of the young... It's what we all do, shamelessly, when we're eaten up by suspicion...   V+PRON+ADV:
Cynicism was his stock in trade, but now it seemed to be eating him up.   USUALLY PASSIVE

NOTE **Consume** is a more formal word for **eat up**.

5 If something **eats up** money, time, or other resources, it gradually uses the entire   V+ADV+N,
amount that is available. ❑ *Gambling had eaten up his fortune... Housing estates were eat-*   V+PRON+ADV,
ing up good agricultural land.   V+N+ADV

ebb /eb/ (ebbs, ebbing, ebbed)

ebb away If a feeling or your strength **ebbs away**, it gradually becomes weaker   V+ADV
until it disappears completely. ❑ *Their rage ebbed away, to be replaced by fear... Their
confidence in him seems to be ebbing away.*

edge /edʒ/ (edges, edging, edged)

edge out If someone **edges out** someone else, they just manage to beat them   V+ADV+N,
or get in front of them in a game, race, or contest. ❑ *In the second race, Germany and*   V+N+ADV,
France edged out the British team by less than a second... McGregor's effort was enough to   V+PRON+ADV:
edge Johnson out of the top spot.   ALSO+of

edit /edɪt/ (edits, editing, edited)

edit out If you **edit out** parts of a film or a piece of writing, you remove them   V+N+ADV, because they are not necessary or because they might offend some people. ❏ *They'll have to edit all the names out... 'Don't worry, Irv,' said Middleton. 'We can edit that out.'*

V+PRON+ADV, V+ADV+N

egg /eg/ (eggs, egging, egged)

egg on If you **egg** someone **on**, you encourage them to do something foolish or daring. ❏ *Some egged him on, while the more sober did their best to lead him away... Egged on by Iago, Othello makes up his mind to kill Desdemona.*

V+PRON+ADV, V+N+ADV, V+ADV+N

eke /iːk/ (ekes, eking, eked)

eke out

[1] If you **eke** something **out**, you make it last as long as possible, by using it carefully. ❏ *Migrants send home cash that helps eke out low village incomes. ...eking out rations and fuel and quietly waiting to die. ...a whole packet and not just the halves we've been using to eke it out.*

V+ADV+N, V+PRON+ADV, V+N+ADV: NO PASSIVE

[2] If you **eke out** a living or an existence, you obtain with difficulty the food or money that you need in order to live. ❏ *...people trying to eke out a living in forest areas... She eked out a poor existence by boiling and selling toffee.*

V+ADV+N: NO PASSIVE

elaborate /ɪlæbəreɪt/ (elaborates, elaborating, elaborated)

elaborate on If you **elaborate on** or **elaborate upon** something already mentioned, you give more details about it or explain it more clearly. **Elaborate upon** is more formal. ❏ *Cook confirmed what Mr Cowie had said, and elaborated on it. ...a myth which was gleefully elaborated upon by several generations of science-fiction writers.*

V+PREP: HAS PASSIVE

elaborate upon → See elaborate on

emanate /emaneɪt/ (emanates, emanating, emanated)

emanate from If something **emanates from** a particular person or thing, they started it or caused it. [FORMAL] ❏ *These ideas are said to emanate from Henry Kissinger... A dim glow of light still emanated from the room.*

V+PREP

embark /ɪmbɑːʳk/ (embarks, embarking, embarked)

embark on

[1] If you **embark on** or **embark upon** something new, difficult, or exciting, you start doing it. **Embark upon** is more formal. ❏ *Peru embarked on a massive programme of reform. ...to embark upon a new translation of the Bible.*

V+PREP: HAS PASSIVE

[2] If you **are embarked on** or **embarked upon** a course of action, you have already started doing it. **Embark upon** is more formal. ❏ *We are already embarked on a course which might have quite sweeping consequences... We knew that you were embarked upon some more special undertaking.*

PASSIVE: V+PREP

embark upon → See embark on

embroider /ɪmbrɔɪdəʳ/ (embroiders, embroidering, embroidered)

embroider on If you **embroider on** a story or account, you add details to it from your imagination in order to try and make it more interesting. ❏ *Other ancient writers have embroidered on these early reports.*

V+PREP: HAS PASSIVE

NOTE Embellish is a more formal word for **embroider on**.

empty /empti/ (empties, emptying, emptied)

empty out If you **empty out** a container, or **empty** something **out** of it, you remove the contents from it. ❏ *They emptied out their sacks... We'd take his pipe and empty out the tobacco... You ought to empty the water out of those boots... I took the bag and emptied it out on the bed.*

V+ADV+N, V+N+ADV, V+PRON+ADV

encroach /ɪnkroʊtʃ/ (encroaches, encroaching, encroached)

encroach on

[1] To **encroach on** or **encroach upon** something means to change it gradually by taking away parts of it, or by taking more and more of it; used showing disapproval. [FORMAL] ❏ *This new law doesn't encroach on the rights of the citizen... The Populists saw the village as a natural society upon which capitalism was encroaching.*

V+PREP: HAS PASSIVE

[2] If someone or something **encroaches on** or **encroaches upon** an area of land, they gradually occupy more and more of it. [FORMAL] ❏ *The invading army were encroaching on national territory. ...tropical countries where the forest is being encroached upon.*

V+PREP: HAS PASSIVE

encroach upon → See encroach on

end /end/ (ends, ending, ended)

*end up

[1] If you **end up** in a particular place or situation, you are in that place or situation
after a series of events, even though you did not originally intend to be. ❑ *Two of my*
friends ended up in prison for armed robbery... Sylvia ended up with no money, no husband
and no house and a two-year-old child... If we go on in this way, we shall end up with mil-
lions and millions of unemployed.

V+ADV:
WITH A

NOTE **Wind up** and **finish up** mean almost the same as **end up**.

[2] If you **end up** doing something after a period of time, you do it even though
you did not originally intend to. ❑ *We ended up taking a taxi there... We always end up*
arguing.

V+ADV:
WITH -ING

NOTE **Finish up** means almost the same as **end up**.

endow /ɪndaʊ/ (endows, endowing, endowed)

endow with If someone or something **is endowed with** a particular quality
or talent, they have it or are given it. [FORMAL] ❑ *Nature has endowed the Cobra Lily*
with the means of catching its own food. ...a man endowed with great leadership talents.

V+N+PREP,
V+PRON+PREP:
USUALLY PASSIVE

engage /ɪngeɪdʒ/ (engages, engaging, engaged)

*engage in If you **engage in** an activity, you take part in it. If you **are en-**
gaged in an activity, you are involved in it. ❑ *It was considered inappropriate for a former Presi-*
dent to engage in commerce... Often he would engage in conversation with complete stran-
gers.

V+PREP

engage on If you **are engaged on** or **engaged upon** an activity, you are
doing it. **Engage upon** is more formal. ❑ *Accountants engaged on this kind of work*
rarely have expense accounts... We would just like to know what you're engaged on at the
moment... The artist engaged upon a quest for the 'essence' of painting.

PASSIVE:
V+PREP

engage upon → See **engage on**

enlarge /ɪnlɑːʳdʒ/ (enlarges, enlarging, enlarged)

enlarge on If you **enlarge on** or **enlarge upon** a subject, you give more details about it. [FORMAL] ❑ *This thought has only just occurred to me – I can't enlarge on it!...*
I went on to enlarge upon the difficulties of naming a cat.

V+PREP:
HAS PASSIVE

NOTE **Expand on** means almost the same as **enlarge on**.

enlarge upon → See **enlarge on**

enquire /ɪnkwaɪəʳ/ (enquires, enquiring, enquired) → See **inquire**

enter /entəʳ/ (enters, entering, entered)

enter for If you **enter for** a competition, race, or examination, or if someone
enters you **for** it, you take part in it. ❑ *She fully intends to enter for it... At least four*
Republicans are officially entered for the race.

V+PREP,
V+N+PREP,
V+PRON+PREP:
ERGATIVE

*enter into

[1] If you **enter into** an agreement or arrangement, you take part in it. ❑ *The com-*
pany had entered into unprofitable contracts. ...a suicide pact entered into by the mother's
sister and her husband. ...young people who enter into a trial marriage.

V+PREP:
HAS PASSIVE

[2] If you **enter into** a discussion with someone, you start it or become involved in
it. ❑ *The Labour Government refused to enter into negotiations... Airlines found it cheaper to*
pay up rather than enter into a prolonged dispute... No correspondence will be entered into.

V+PREP:
HAS PASSIVE

[3] If something **enters into** something else, it affects it and is an important factor
in it. ❑ *All sorts of emotional factors enter into the relationship... Repression enters into every*
aspect of human life.

V+PREP

enter on → See **enter upon**

enter upon When you **enter upon** or **enter on** something, you start to do it.
[FORMAL] ❑ *Brandt entered upon this new policy in the 1960s... She knew she had entered*
upon her sentence of life imprisonment.

V+PREP:
HAS PASSIVE

NOTE **Embark on** means almost the same as **enter upon**.

enthuse /ɪnθjuːz, AM -θuːz/ (enthuses, enthusing, enthused)

enthuse over If you **enthuse over** something, you talk about it in a way that
shows that you are excited and pleased about it. ❑ *She was enthusing over something*

V+PREP:
HAS PASSIVE

that had caught her eye. ...enthusing over a weekend spent in the Lake District. ...a piece of good fortune that could not be enthused over enough.

erode /ɪrˈəʊd/ (erodes, eroding, eroded)

erode away

1 If rock or soil **is eroded away** or if it **erodes away**, wind, water, or the weather causes it to crumble and break, and eventually disappear. ❑ *The central tower there has eroded away to little more than a circular wall... The deposits that had accumulated on the mountainside were eroded away.*

V+ADV:
OR PASSIVE:
V+ADV:
ERGATIVE

NOTE **Wear away** means almost the same as **erode away**.

2 If someone's power, authority, or freedom **erodes away** or **is eroded away**, it gradually becomes weaker until it is no longer significant. ❑ *You would think colonialism of this kind would have eroded away... Our sovereign right to legislate has been eroded away.*

V+ADV:
OR PASSIVE:
V+ADV:
ERGATIVE

even /ˈiːvən/ (evens, evening, evened)

even out

If you **even** something **out** or if it **evens out**, its distribution becomes more equal because some of it moves from one place to another. ❑ *In Asia, irrigation systems help to even out the supply of water over the growing season... No amount of 'social engineering' will even out the world's unfairness.*

V+ADV+N,
V+N+ADV,
V+PRON+ADV,
V+ADV:
ERGATIVE

NOTE **Balance out** means almost the same as **even out**.

even up

To **even up** a game or competition means to make it more equally balanced than it was, by making the weaker side stronger than it was, or by making the stronger side weaker than it was. ❑ *Frank and I will change sides. That should even things up a bit... The straight answer to unequal competition is to even up access to capital and government services for all levels of producer.*

V+N+ADV,
V+PRON+ADV,
V+ADV+N

NOTE **Balance** means almost the same as **even up**.

expand /ɪkspˈænd/ (expands, expanding, expanded)

expand on

If you **expand on** or **expand upon** a topic you have already mentioned, you give more information or details about it. **Expand upon** is more formal. ❑ *I went on to expand upon this theme... This highly relevant observation is expanded on by Dr. White.*

V+PREP:
HAS PASSIVE

NOTE **Enlarge on** means almost the same as **expand on**.

expand upon → See expand on

explain /ɪkspleˈɪn/ (explains, explaining, explained)

explain away

If you **explain away** a mistake or unpleasant situation, you give reasons to show that it is not as bad or important as people think. ❑ *Mr Stewart tried to explain away the police interest in Waddell... There is a difference, but I cannot really explain it away... All this can, of course, be explained away for other reasons.*

V+ADV+N,
V+PRON+ADV,
V+N+ADV

NOTE **Excuse** means almost the same as **explain away**.

eye /aɪ/ (eyes, eyeing, eyed)

eye up

If someone **eyes** you **up**, they look at you carefully because they find you sexually attractive. [BRITISH, INFORMAL] ❑ *I made tea while she sat there eyeing me up. ...eyeing up the girl in the corner.*

V+PRON+ADV,
V+N+ADV,
V+ADV+N

NOTE **Ogle** means almost the same as **eye up**.

Ff

face /feɪs/ (faces, facing, faced)

face about If you **face about**, you turn so that you are looking in the opposite direction. ❑ *She walked backwards a couple of steps, and then faced about, and walked toward me.*

V+ADV

face down In a situation of conflict or disagreement, if you **face** someone **down**, you gain the advantage by acting confidently and looking at them boldly. ❑ *She was intent on facing down her opponents.*

V+ADV+N,
V+PRON+ADV,
V+N+ADV

face out If you **face out** a difficult situation, you deal with it by behaving firmly or defiantly. [BRITISH] ❑ *We'll just have to face this crisis out.*
NOTE See through means almost the same as **face out**.

V+ADV+N,
V+N+ADV,
V+PRON+ADV

★face up to If you **face up to** a difficult situation, you accept it and deal with it. ❑ *We may as well face up to the fact that it isn't going to work... His situation was desperate, but he faced up to it... Issues like these simply cannot be ignored; the problems have to be faced up to.*

V+ADV+PREP:
HAS PASSIVE

factor /fæktər/ (factors, factoring, factored)

factor in If you **factor in** a particular cost or element, you include it in a calculation you are making. ❑ *Using a computer model they factored in the costs of transplants for those women who die... Some employers not only know this, but factor it in.*

V+ADV+N,
V+N+ADV,
V+PRON+ADV

factor into If you **factor** a particular cost or element **into** a calculation you are making, you include it. ❑ *You'd better consider this and factor this into your decision making.*

V+N+PREP,
V+PRON+PREP

fade /feɪd/ (fades, fading, faded)

★fade away

1 If something **fades away**, it slowly becomes less intense, frequent or common until it ends or disappears completely. ❑ *The sun's warmth began to fade away... Your new-found enthusiasm for running will soon fade away. ...a vague rumour which would fade away and be forgotten.*

V+ADV

2 If a sound or sight **fades away**, it gradually becomes quieter or less easy to see and eventually disappears. ❑ *On the right were the hills fading away into the misty morning... The music gradually faded away as the procession moved off down the street.*
NOTE Recede is a more formal word for **fade away**.

V+ADV

3 If someone **fades away**, they become weaker and die. ❑ *He was fading quietly away day by day... She'd fade away and die.*

V+ADV

fade in To **fade in** or **fade up** a picture or sound on television, film, CD, or radio means to introduce it gradually and make it brighter or louder until people can see it or hear it properly. [TECHNICAL]

V+ADV+N,
V+PRON+ADV,
V+N+ADV

fade out

1 If something **fades out**, it slowly becomes less intense, frequent or common until it ends or disappears completely. ❑ *This sort of protest tends to fade out... Childhood diseases tend to fade out as the child reaches adolescence.*
NOTE Fizzle out means almost the same as **fade out**.

V+ADV

2 When a sound or radio signal **fades out**, it slowly becomes less loud or strong until you can no longer hear it or receive it. ❑ *The sound of the chopper had faded out.*

V+ADV

3 To **fade out** a picture or sound on television, film, CD, or radio means to make it disappear gradually. [TECHNICAL]

V+ADV+N,
V+PRON+ADV,
V+N+ADV

fade up → See fade in

faff /fæf/ (faffs, faffing, faffed)

faff about If someone **is faffing about** or **faffing around**, they are doing un-

V+ADV

necessary things in a fussy or disorganized way and not really achieving very much.
[BRITISH, INFORMAL]

faff ar<u>ou</u>nd → See faff about

fag /fæg/ (fags, fagging, fagged)

   fag <u>out</u> If something **fags** you **out**, it makes you feel tired and exhausted.   V+PRON+ADV,
[BRITISH, INFORMAL] ❏ *That last game really fagged me out!*   V+REFL+ADV, V+N+ADV

   [NOTE] **Wear out** is a less informal expression for **fag out**.

   ♦ If you are **fagged out**, you feel tired and exhausted. [BRITISH, INFORMAL] ❏ *Certain-*   ADJECTIVE
ly you look quite fagged out.

fall /fɔ:l/ (falls, falling, fell, fallen)

   fall ab<u>ou</u>t If you say that people **are falling about**, you mean that they are   V+ADV
laughing uncontrollably. [BRITISH, INFORMAL] ❏ *When we complained, they fell about*
laughing.

★fall ap<u>ar</u>t

   1 If something **falls apart**, it breaks into pieces, usually because it is weak, old, or   V+ADV
badly made. ❏ *...clothing which lasts a little while and then falls apart. ...a flimsy shack*
that was falling apart.

   [NOTE] **Disintegrate** is a more formal word for **fall apart**.

   2 If an organization, system or relationship **falls apart**, it no longer works effec-   V+ADV
tively and eventually fails or ends completely. ❏ *The conference was to have taken place*
in 1932, but it fell apart when France and Italy refused to participate... Their marriage began
to fall apart.

   [NOTE] **Collapse** means almost the same as **fall apart**.

   3 If someone **is falling apart**, they are unable to think or behave normally and   V+ADV
calmly because they are in such a difficult or unpleasant situation. [INFORMAL] ❏ *It*
was something to do, it kept you from falling apart.

   [NOTE] **Crack up** means almost the same as **fall apart**.

★fall aw<u>ay</u>

   1 If something **falls away**, it breaks off from the surface that it was attached to.   V+ADV:
❏ *Patches of plaster had fallen away between the windows... The bark was curling and falling*   USUALLY+PREP
away... The rock fell away and exposed the skeletons.

   [NOTE] **Fall off** means almost the same as **fall away**.

   2 Where land **falls away**, it slopes gently downwards. ❏ *I got to the ridge expecting*   V+ADV:
to see a gentle slope falling away in front of me. ...a long field that fell away from the house   USUALLY+PREP
towards thick woods.

   3 If an unpleasant quality or a difficulty **falls away**, it disappears and no longer af-   V+ADV
fects you. [LITERARY] ❏ *His film star affectations had fallen away... All practical difficulties*
fell away.

   4 If the degree, amount, or strength of something **falls away**, it becomes less or   V+ADV
smaller. ❏ *During the general strike, the party's membership fell away... Student support fell*
away.

   [NOTE] **Fall off** means almost the same as **fall away**.

   5 If a sound **falls away**, it gradually becomes quieter until you can no longer hear   V+ADV
it. ❏ *The drone of the engine falls away again... His voice fell away and I couldn't catch his*
next few words.

   [NOTE] **Die away** and **fade away** mean almost the same as **fall away**.

fall b<u>a</u>ck

   1 If an army **falls back** during a battle or war, it retreats. ❏ *They fell back in confu-*   V+ADV
sion, surprised by the direction of attack.

   2 If you **fall back**, you suddenly move backwards away from someone or some-   V+ADV:
thing because they have upset or frightened you. ❏ *I watched him fall back in horror...*   ALSO+in
He fell back with a scream.

   [NOTE] **Recoil** is a more formal word for **fall back**.

   ★fall b<u>a</u>ck on If you **fall back on** or **fall back upon** something that you know   V+ADV+PREP
you can rely on, you use it or do it when other things have failed. ❏ *We have a writ-*
ten script to fall back on if we run out of things to discuss... He invariably falls back on senti-
mental clichés about peace and love... Teachers fall back upon authority.

NOTE **Resort to** means almost the same as **fall back on**.

♦ A **fall-back** method, plan, or system, is one which you have in case the first method, plan, or system you use is unsatisfactory or fails to work. ❑ *...the fall-back proposals of his opponents.*   ADJECTIVE

NOTE **Back-up** means almost the same as **fall-back**.

fall back upon → See fall back on

★fall behind

1 If you **fall behind** when moving with a group of people, you move more slowly than them, so they get ahead of you. ❑ *He began to limp and fell so far behind that I decided to let him rest... Don't fall behind the leaders or you'll never catch up.*   V+ADV, V+PREP

NOTE **Lag behind** means almost the same as **fall behind**.

2 If someone or something **falls behind**, they do not achieve the standard that is expected of them or that is achieved by similar people or things. ❑ *...children who fall behind with their reading... Vicars' salaries have fallen behind those of many of the laity.*   V+ADV, V+PREP

3 If you **fall behind** with something that you have to do by a certain time, you fail to do it and gradually get later and later with it. ❑ *The programme had fallen so far behind that there was little chance of meeting the deadline... Unfortunately, we have fallen behind with the payments.*   V+ADV: ALSO+with

★fall down

1 If someone or something **falls down** when they have been in an upright or standing position, they become unbalanced and drop to the ground. ❑ *He tripped and fell down... The pile of hymn books fell down and scattered all over the floor... I remember him falling down the cellar steps.*   V+ADV, V+PREP

2 If something such as a building or bridge **falls down**, it collapses and breaks into pieces because it is old, weak, or damaged. ❑ *That shelter might fall down if the rain comes back. ...a one room wooden shack, part of which fell down while I was there.*   V+ADV

3 If a building **is falling down**, it is in very bad condition and may collapse. ❑ *The house was cheap because it was falling down.*   V+ADV

4 If something such as an argument, idea, or method **falls down**, it has a weakness in it which is likely to make it fail. ❑ *In one area only did the comparison fall down... This is where a lot of teachers fall down.*   V+ADV

5 The **downfall** of a successful or powerful institution or person is their failure or ruin. ❑ *...the downfall of a dictator.*   N-COUNT

♦ Something that is the **downfall** of a particular person or thing is the thing that causes the person or thing to be ruined or to fail. ❑ *Bad publicity was our downfall.*   N-COUNT

★fall for

1 If you **fall for** someone or something, you are attracted towards them and like them very much. ❑ *He fell for her the moment he set eyes on her... I bought it yesterday, falling for it because it was extremely simple.*   V+PREP

2 If you **fall for** something that is not true, you are tricked into believing it. ❑ *It was a stupid trick and I fell for it... The working class were not going to fall for this one.*   V+PREP

fall in

1 If a roof or ceiling **falls in**, it collapses and falls to the ground.   V+ADV

NOTE **Cave in** means almost the same as **fall in**.

2 If soldiers, scouts, or other people in a procession **fall in**, they get into a line one behind the other. ❑ *Pick up your gear and fall in... As he began to march around the lawn, people fell in behind him.*   V+ADV: ALSO+behind

NOTE **Fall out** means the opposite of **fall in**.

★fall into

1 If something or someone **falls into** a particular state, they begin to be in that state. ❑ *The practice had fallen into disuse and been forgotten... He fell into disfavour with his superiors... She fell into debt.*   V+PREP

2 If you **fall into** an activity or way of behaving, you start to do it, often without intending to. ❑ *His colleagues refused to support him and fell into disagreements with the union leadership... We fell into fits of hysteria at each other's antics.*   V+PREP

3 If something **falls into** a particular group or category, it is classified as belonging to that group or category. ❑ *The main thesis of the book was that human beings fall into two opposing types... My work really falls into three parts.*   V+PREP

4 If you **fall into** conversation or a discussion with someone, usually someone you have just met, you start having a conversation or discussion with them. ❑ *Over breakfast at my motel, I fell into conversation with the owner of a hardware shop.*

V+PREP

fall in with

1 If you **fall in with** an existing idea, plan or system, you accept it and do not try to change it. ❑ *I didn't know whether to fall in with this arrangement... Instead of challenging the lie she falls in with it.*

V+ADV+PREP

NOTE **Go along with** means almost the same as **fall in with**.

2 If you **fall in with** someone, you meet them by chance and often become friends with them. ❑ *He had the luck to fall in with the American humorist, Tom Lehrer.*

V+ADV+PREP

★fall off

1 If something **falls off**, it separates from the thing to which it was attached. ❑ *Their scales fall off and the fish die... Some rotten apples fall off the bough.*

V+ADV,
V+PREP

NOTE **Drop off** means almost the same as **fall off**.

2 If the degree, amount, or standard of something **falls off**, it becomes less or lower. ❑ *The flow of western capital is falling off just when it is most needed... We knew that the numbers of overseas students would fall off drastically... Economic growth will fall off only slightly.*

V+ADV

NOTE **Drop** means almost the same as **fall off**.

♦ If there is a **falling-off** of something, there is a decrease in the degree or intensity of it. ❑ *There was a definite falling-off of active interest... A falling-off in business was expected.*

N-SING

fall on

1 If a responsibility or duty **falls on** or **falls upon** someone, it becomes their responsibility or duty. **Fall upon** is more formal. ❑ *It would fall on her to make the final decision... Without a producer, the weight of responsibility fell upon me.*

V+PREP

NOTE **Fall to** means almost the same as **fall on**.

2 If something unpleasant **falls on** or **falls upon** someone, it happens to them. **Fall upon** is more formal. [LITERARY] ❑ *All of these ills have fallen upon us.*

V+PREP

NOTE **Befall** means almost the same as **fall on**.

3 If someone **falls on** you, they hug you eagerly because they are very happy or excited. ❑ *People were falling on each other in delight and tears.*

V+PREP

4 If you **fall on** something when it arrives or appears, you eagerly seize it or welcome it. ❑ *They fell on the sandwiches with alacrity.*

V+PREP

5 If someone **falls on** or **falls upon** you, they attack you suddenly and violently. **Fall upon** is more formal. ❑ *They fell on one another like wolves.*

V+PREP

NOTE **Set upon** means almost the same as **fall on**.

6 If your eyes **fall on** or **fall upon** someone or something, you see or notice them. **Fall upon** is more formal. ❑ *His gaze fell on a small white bundle... His eyes fell on Laing, who was hunched in a corner.*

V+PREP

7 If a date **falls on** a certain day of the week, it occurs on that day. ❑ *My birthday falls on a Thursday this year.*

V+PREP

★fall out

1 If something **falls out** of a container, it leaves the container and drops towards the ground. ❑ *...tobacco cans falling out of the cupboard... He had to cling to Melanie to avoid falling out.*

V+ADV:
ALSO+of

2 If something such as hair or a tooth **falls out**, it becomes loose and separates from your body. ❑ *After about two weeks, your hair starts to fall out. ...baby teeth which get loose and then fall out.*

V+ADV

3 If you **fall out** with someone, you have an argument and are no longer friendly with them. ❑ *I've fallen out with certain members of the band... Everybody stands to lose if the partners fall out... Fancy falling out over something as trivial as that!*

V+ADV,
V+ADV+with:
RECIPROCAL

4 When soldiers or people in a parade or formation **fall out**, they leave their positions and the formation is broken up.

V+ADV

NOTE **Fall in** means the opposite of **fall out**.

5 **Fallout** is the radiation that affects a particular place or area after a nuclear explosion has taken place. ❑ *Exposure to radioactive fallout would be much worse than previously anticipated.*

N-UNCOUNT

★fall over

1 If someone or something that is standing **falls over**, they become unbalanced and end up lying on the ground. ❑ *He pushed back his chair so hard that it fell over... 'Look at me!' He pretended to fall over... He nearly fell over an old lady in a wheelchair.*

V+ADV, V+PREP

NOTE **Topple over** means almost the same as **fall over**.

2 If people **are falling over** themselves to do something, they are very eager to do it. [INFORMAL] ❑ *Of course, they were all falling over to serve us... Governments were falling over each other to win these valuable contracts.*

V+ADV, V+PREP+REFL, V+PREP

★fall through

If an arrangement or plan **falls through**, something goes wrong before it can be completed and it has to be abandoned. ❑ *We arranged to book a villa and it fell through... Any number of things could lead to a sale falling through.*

V+ADV

fall to

1 If a responsibility or duty **falls to** someone, it becomes their responsibility or duty. ❑ *That task fell to Mrs Isabel Travers... It fell to Philip Crow to act the part of host.*

V+PREP

NOTE **Fall on** means almost the same as **fall to**.

2 If someone **falls to** doing something, they start doing it. [LITERARY] ❑ *The party fell instead to blaming the voters... I fell to musing on the revolution.*

V+PREP: USUALLY+-ING

fall under

If something **falls under** a particular category, it belongs in that category. ❑ *'Portrait of an Artist' falls under autobiography, not fiction.*

V+PREP

fall upon → See fall on

fan /fæn/ (fans, fanning, fanned)

fan out

1 If a group of people or things **fan out**, they move forwards together from the same point and gradually spread farther away from each other. ❑ *The five of us fanned out at intervals of not more than fifteen feet.*

V+ADV

2 If something **fans out**, or if it **is fanned out**, it has or forms a shape which is narrow at one end and wide at the other. ❑ *They were already waiting where the little valley fanned out into the savannah... The birds lay with their wings fanned out and their beaks open.*

V+ADV, V+ADV+N, V+N+ADV, V+PRON+ADV: ERGATIVE

farm /fɑːrm/ (farms, farming, farmed)

farm out

If you **farm out** something that is your responsibility, you send it to other people for them to deal with or look after. ❑ *Many European businesses found it satisfactory to farm out big clerical jobs to London agencies... She may have farmed the child out in order to remarry.*

V+ADV+N, V+N+ADV, V+PRON+ADV

fart /fɑːrt/ (farts, farting, farted)

☑ **Fart** is a rude word used mainly in very informal British English.

fart about

If someone **is farting about** or **farting around**, they are wasting time doing silly things instead of doing what needs to be done. ❑ *There'd be none of this farting about in the supermarket.*

V+ADV

NOTE **Mess around** is a less rude expression for **fart about**.

fart around → See fart about

fasten /fɑːsən, fæs-/ (fastens, fastening, fastened)

fasten on

1 If you **fasten on** to something or **fasten** your attention **on** or **upon** it, you concentrate all your attention or efforts on it. ❑ *Once she had fastened on to a scheme she did not let go... Your attention is fastened on that... They cannot fasten on profit as the only object of their work... Such goods are fastened on as symbols of high status... His mind fastened upon it now: escape.*

V+ADV+to, V+N+PREP, ALSO V+PREP: HAS PASSIVE

NOTE **Latch on to** means almost the same as **fasten on**.

2 If someone **fastens on** to you, they keep following you or wanting to be with you when you want them to go away. ❑ *The doctor had fastened on to an official of the Russian embassy.*

V+ADV+to

fasten up

If you **fasten** something **up**, you close it using buttons, straps, and so on. ❑ *Fasten your coat up.*

V+N+ADV, V+PRON+ADV, V+ADV+N

NOTE **Do up** means almost the same as **fasten up**.

fasten upon → See fasten on

fend off

fathom /fˈæðəm/ **(fathoms, fathoming, fathomed)**

fathom out If you **fathom** something **out**, you eventually understand it as a result of thinking carefully about it. ❑ *What I can't fathom out is why he did it.*

NOTE **Work out** means almost the same as **fathom out.**

V+ADV+N,
V+N+ADV,
V+PRON+ADV

fatten /fˈætən/ **(fattens, fattening, fattened)**

fatten up If you **fatten up** an animal, you give it a lot of food so that it reaches the weight that you want it to be. ❑ *They take twice as long to fatten up as European cattle.*

V+ADV+N,
V+N+ADV,
V+PRON+ADV

fear /fˈɪər/ **(fears, fearing, feared)**

fear for If you **fear for** someone or something, you are very worried that they might be in danger. ❑ *Morris began to fear for the life of Mrs Reilly... She feared for her daughters.*

V+PREP

feed /fˈiːd/ **(feeds, feeding, fed)**

feed off → See **feed on**

feed on If an idea, feeling, system or process **feeds on** or **feeds off** something, it continues to exist or grow because of that thing. ❑ *Creativity and curiosity are part of the same thing, they feed on each other... Art feeds off life.*

V+PREP

feed up If you **feed up** an animal, child, or invalid, you give them plenty of nourishing food to eat in order to make them strong and healthy. [BRITISH] ❑ *Farmers feed up their sheep prior to mating... 'She can have her baby here. Harriet'll feed her up, won't you Harriet?'*

V+ADV+N,
V+N+ADV,
V+PRON+ADV

NOTE **Build up** means almost the same as **feed up.**

feel /fˈiːl/ **(feels, feeling, felt)**

feel for If you **feel for** someone who has a problem or is upset, you have sympathy for them. ❑ *Boy, I feel for you guys.*

V+PREP

NOTE **Sympathize with** means almost the same as **feel for.**

feel out If you **feel** someone **out**, you carefully try to discover their opinions, attitudes, or ideas, without asking them directly. [INFORMAL] ❑ *We felt him out, he wasn't willing.*

V+PRON+ADV,
V+N+ADV

NOTE **Sound out** means almost the same as **feel out.**

feel up To **feel up** someone means to touch their body in order to gain sexual excitement.

V+PRON+ADV,
V+N+ADV,
V+ADV+N

NOTE **Touch up** means almost the same as **feel up.**

feel up to If you **feel up to** doing something, you feel physically and mentally able to do it. ❑ *'I just hope I feel up to eating,' said Dr Cox... I require an assistant. Feeling up to it now?... We set out for a climb that I don't think any of us felt up to.*

V+ADV+PREP

fence /fˈens/ **(fences, fencing, fenced)**

fence in

1 If something **is fenced in**, it is surrounded by a fence. ❑ *...a sloping area which is fenced in by iron railings... My little vegetable garden was fenced in with wire mesh.*

V+N+ADV,
V+PRON+ADV:
USUALLY PASSIVE

2 If you **are fenced in** by someone or something, they are so close to you that you are unable to move or leave. ❑ *He put his hand on the post behind her so that he had her fenced in and could look down on her.*

V+N+ADV,
V+PRON+ADV,
V+ADV+N:
USUALLY PASSIVE

fence off If an area **is fenced off**, it is separated from other areas by a fence. ❑ *By the nineteenth century, almost all land had been fenced off and made private... They had found a plot of land and fenced it off.*

V+ADV+N,
V+N+ADV,
V+PRON+ADV

fend /fˈend/ **(fends, fending, fended)**

fend off

1 If you **fend off** someone who is attacking you, you try to prevent them from hurting you by putting your arms or an object in front of you. ❑ *He fended him off with his shovel... He raised his arms to fend off the blows.*

V+PRON+ADV,
V+ADV+N,
V+N+ADV

NOTE **Ward off** means almost the same as **fend off.**

2 If you **fend off** questions, problems or things that you do not want, you avoid dealing with them or refuse to accept them. ❑ *It was the first time Daniel had spoken, except to fend off questions... He was continually fending off unwanted meals.*

V+ADV+N,
V+PRON+ADV

The symbol ★ shows key phrasal verbs

ferret /ˈfɛrɪt/ **(ferrets, ferreting, ferreted)**

ferret out If you **ferret out** information or the location of someone, you dis- | V+ADV+N,
cover it by searching thoroughly in a determined way. [INFORMAL] ❑ ...*ferreting out the* | V+N+ADV,
details of private lives... He demonstrated his competence at ferreting out errors... We had | V+PRON+ADV
taken the decision to try and ferret him out.
NOTE **Unearth** means almost the same as **ferret out**.

fess /fɛs/ **(fesses, fessing, fessed)**

fess up If you **fess up**, you admit that you have done something wrong. | V+ADV
[AMERICAN, INFORMAL] ❑ *As a retired homicide detective in New York said, 'When you get a*
guy to fess up as to why he did it, you get very shoddy answers.'
NOTE **Confess** means almost the same as **fess up**.

fetch /fɛtʃ/ **(fetches, fetching, fetched)**

fetch up If you **fetch up** somewhere, you arrive there, usually without intend- | V+ADV
ing to. [INFORMAL]
NOTE **Land up** means almost the same as **fetch up**.

fiddle /ˈfɪdəl/ **(fiddles, fiddling, fiddled)**

☑ **About** is used mainly in British English.

fiddle about → See **fiddle around**
fiddle about with → See **fiddle around with**

fiddle around If you **fiddle around** or **fiddle about**, you do small tasks | V+ADV:
without effort or interest and do not achieve very much. ❑ *Eddie and I were fiddling* | USUALLY+A
around making last-minute adjustments... He was fiddling about in the parlour... I spent two
hours fiddling about with this table.
NOTE **Mess around** means almost the same as **fiddle around**.

fiddle around with
1 If you **fiddle around with** or **fiddle about with** a machine, you do things to | V+ADV+PREP
it to try and make it work. ❑ *Two of them got out to fiddle around with the engine.*
NOTE **Tinker** means almost the same as **fiddle around**.
2 If you say that someone **is fiddling around with** or **fiddling about with** | V+ADV+PREP
something, you mean that they are changing it in a way that you disapprove of.
❑ *Right now in Congress, they're fiddling around with the budget and so on... One always*
wonders when a man starts fiddling about with his Will.

fight /faɪt/ **(fights, fighting, fought)**

★fight back
1 If you **fight back** when someone attacks you or causes you problems, you de- | V+ADV
fend yourself and try to beat them or stop them. ❑ *Our forces were fighting back desper-*
ately... If we did that, the importing countries could fight back with laws of their own.
NOTE **Retaliate** and **resist** are more formal words for **fight back**.
2 If you **fight back** an emotion, you try very hard not to let it affect you. ❑ *I wait-* | V+ADV+N,
ed, fighting back my fear. ...standing in the early morning silence, fighting back my unease... | V+PRON+ADV
She fought back the tears.

fight down If you **fight down** a desire or temptation, you try very hard to re- | V+ADV+N,
sist it. ❑ *He had to fight down the impulse to sneak out.* | V+PRON+ADV

★fight off
1 If you **fight off** something unpleasant or unwanted, you succeed in getting rid | V+ADV+N,
of it or overcoming it. ❑ *...the ailments we can fight off if we are enjoying ourselves...* | V+PRON+ADV
...grieving over his sons and fighting off despair... You shouldn't have to fight off too much
competition for the job.
2 If you **fight off** someone who has attacked you, you fight with them, and suc- | V+ADV+N,
ceed in making them go away or stop attacking you. ❑ *The woman fought off the at-* | V+PRON+ADV
tacker.

fight out When two people or groups **fight** something **out** or **fight** it **out**, | V+N+ADV,
they fight or argue until one of them wins. ❑ *The European nations were fighting it out* | V+it+ADV,
on the battlefields... These decisions were fought out between contending groups. | V+ADV+N

figure /ˈfɪɡər, AM -ɡjər/ **(figures, figuring, figured)**

figure on If you **figure on** something, you assume or plan that it will happen. | V+PREP

[INFORMAL] ❏ *How soon are you figuring on getting married?... I figured on going out to-night.*

NOTE **Reckon on** and **count on** mean almost the same as **figure on**.

★**figure out** If you **figure out** the solution to a problem, the answer to a question, or the reason for something, you work it out and understand it. [INFORMAL] ❏ *I've figured out what the trouble is... We tried to figure out a way to get to Wimbledon... You've got everything figured out, haven't you?... I just can't figure him out.*

V+ADV+N,
V+N+ADV,
V+PRON+ADV

figure up If you **figure up** a cost or amount, you add numbers together to get the total. [AMERICAN] ❏ *He figured up the balance in their checking account.*

V+PREP

NOTE **Calculate** means almost the same as **figure up**.

file /faɪl/ (files, filing, filed)

file away If you **file away** a fact or idea, you make an effort to remember it because you think it might be useful. ❏ *Dan carefully filed away this added reason for hating Joe Parker.*

V+N+ADV,
V+PRON+ADV,
V+ADV+N

fill /fɪl/ (fills, filling, filled)

★**fill in**

1 If you **fill in** a crack or a hole, you put a substance into it so that the surface becomes level. ❏ *She bought a packet of cement mix and began, herself, to fill in some holes.*

V+ADV+N,
V+N+ADV,
V+PRON+ADV

2 If you **fill in** a form or the details on a form, you write all the information that is requested in the appropriate spaces. [BRITISH] ❏ *We filled in all the customs forms... Ask for a claim form, fill it in and send it to the social security office... Fill in your name here.*

V+ADV+N,
V+PRON+ADV,
V+N+ADV

NOTE **Fill out** and **fill up** mean almost the same as **fill in**.

3 If you **fill in** a shape, you paint or draw all over the space inside the lines so that it becomes covered with colour. ❏ *You could get the kids to fill in the various pieces in different colours... She drew a circle and filled it in.*

V+ADV+N,
V+PRON+ADV,
V+N+ADV

NOTE **Colour in** means almost the same as **fill in**.

4 If you **fill** someone **in** on a situation or event, you give them more information about it so that they have all the details. ❏ *I'll fill you in on the details now... Come back to the office and I'll fill you in.*

V+PRON+ADV,
V+N+ADV:
ALSO+on

5 If you **fill in** a period of time in which you are inactive or bored, you find things to do during it. ❏ *They then drove to Girvan to fill in time... There were ten long days to fill in... He obviously said it to fill in an awkward pause.*

V+ADV+N,
V+PRON+ADV,
V+N+ADV

6 If you **fill in** for someone, you do the work that they normally do because they are temporarily unable to do it. ❏ *One of the other girls is sick and I said I'd fill in.*

V+ADV:
ALSO+for

NOTE **Stand in** means almost the same as **fill in**.

★**fill out**

1 If you **fill out** a form, you write all the information that is requested in the spaces on the form. ❏ *Brody was filling out forms about the accident... I found the death certificate forms and filled them out.*

V+ADV+N,
V+PRON+ADV,
V+N+ADV

NOTE **Fill in** and **fill up** mean almost the same as **fill out**.

2 If a thin person **fills out**, they become fatter. ❏ *He'd filled out a lot since I'd last seen him.*

V+ADV

★**fill up**

1 If you **fill up** a container, you put a large amount of something into it, so that it becomes full. ❏ *Fill the tank up, please... I filled up a test tube with potassium permanganate. ...when you filled it up to the brim.*

V+N+ADV,
V+ADV+N,
V+PRON+ADV:
ALSO+with

2 If something **fills up** a space or area, it is so big or is present in such large numbers that the whole space seems to be occupied. ❏ *The computer was massive, filling up a whole room.*

V+ADV+N,
V+N+ADV,
V+PRON+ADV

3 If a place, area or container **fills up**, it becomes crowded or full. ❏ *His office began to fill up with people... Belfast hotels filled up with journalists from around the world.*

V+ADV:
ALSO+with

4 If you **fill up** a period of time with a particular activity, you spend the time in this way. ❏ *The point was to fill up the day with meaningless activities.*

V+ADV+N,
V+N+ADV,
V+PRON+ADV:
USUALLY+with

NOTE **Take up** means almost the same as **fill up**.

5 If you **fill** yourself **up**, you eat as much as you can. ❏ *No filling yourselves up with sandwiches, beer, and chips!... You would see the boys and girls filling themselves up before they left.*

V+REFL+ADV,
V+PRON+ADV,
V+N+ADV:
ALSO+with

6 A type of food that **fills** you **up** makes you feel that you have eaten a lot, even though you have only eaten a small amount. ❑ *Potatoes fill us up without overloading us with calories.*

V+PRON+ADV,
V+N+ADV

7 If you **fill up** a form, you complete it, giving all the information that is requested. ❑ *Sorry to interrupt, but I've some forms to fill up.*

V+ADV+N,
V+N+ADV,
V+PRON+ADV

NOTE **Fill in** and **fill out** mean almost the same as **fill up**.

film /fɪlm/ (films, filming, filmed)

film over If your eyes **film over**, they become covered with a very thin layer of tears.

V+ADV

filter /fɪltər/ (filters, filtering, filtered)

filter out To **filter out** something from a substance means to remove it by passing the substance through an obstacle such as a net, or through another substance such as sand. ❑ *The problem would involve filtering out some of the tar... Any excess is filtered out of the blood stream by the kidneys... This forms a protective screen around the planet, filtering out damaging ultra-violet radiation.*

V+ADV+N,
V+PRON+ADV,
V+N+ADV:
ALSO+of

find /faɪnd/ (finds, finding, found)

find against When a judge **finds against** one of the people contesting a court case, he or she comes to a judgment in favour of the other person. [LEGAL]

V+PREP:
HAS PASSIVE

find for When a judge **finds for** one of the people contesting a court case, he or she comes to a judgement in favour of this person. [LEGAL] ❑ *The judge had found for the husband, describing him as a caring and responsible father.*

V+PREP:
HAS PASSIVE

★find out

1 If you **find out** something, you learn something that you did not already know. ❑ *I found out the train times... I'm only interested in finding out what the facts are... I've just found out that I won't have to start until Wednesday... I've been trying to find this out for weeks.*

V+ADV+N,
V+N+REPORT,
V+N+ADV,
V+PRON+ADV

NOTE **Discover** means almost the same as **find out**.

2 If someone **is found out**, another person discovers that they have been dishonest or have done something wrong. ❑ *The manager had found him out and was going to sack him... I'm the sort of man who's always found out... Our lies are found out but remain unchallenged.*

V+PRON+ADV,
V+N+ADV:
USUALLY PASSIVE

NOTE **Rumble** is an informal word for **find out**.

finish /fɪnɪʃ/ (finishes, finishing, finished)
★finish off

1 When you **finish off** something that you are doing, you complete it by doing the last part. ❑ *He had finished off his thesis... The herdsmen were just finishing off the milking... We had to work until midnight to finish them off.*

V+ADV+N,
V+PRON+ADV,
V+N+ADV

2 When you **finish off** by doing a particular thing, you do it as the last part of an event or series of actions. ❑ *He used to play the piano on Saturday nights and always finished off with 'Spread A Little Happiness'... Can I finish off by asking you one question?*

V+ADV:
USUALLY+A

NOTE **Conclude** is a more formal word for **finish off**.

3 When you **finish off** food or drink, you eat or drink the last bit of it, so that there is none left. ❑ *We decided to go back and finish off the wine... He had cooked a chicken and they'd finished it off together in one afternoon.*

V+ADV+N,
V+PRON+ADV,
V+N+ADV

NOTE **Polish off** is an informal expression for **finish off**.

4 If something **is finished off** in a particular way, it is decorated in that way or made to look neat and attractive by this method. ❑ *The shirt had a silver cross on the left breast and the neck was finished off with a frill.*

V+N+ADV,
V+PRON+ADV,
V+ADV+N:
USUALLY PASSIVE

5 To **finish off** a person or animal means to kill them. ❑ *Now was the time to go ahead and finish the intruders off... I'll never go there again as long as I live. It nearly finished me off.*

V+PRON+ADV,
V+N+ADV,
V+ADV+N

★finish up

1 If you **finish up** in a particular place or situation, you are in it at the end of an event or process. ❑ *She'll be going on tour, starting in Southampton and finishing up in London... They all finished up stranded on the beaches... They finished up serving in a shop... Maybe you too will finish up as Prime Minister.*

V+ADV:
USUALLY+A

NOTE **End up** and **wind up** mean almost the same as **finish up**.

2 When you **finish up** something that you have been eating or drinking, you eat or drink the last part of it. ❑ *They were just finishing up their lunch... They never finish up their puddings.*
V+ADV+N, V+PRON+ADV, V+N+ADV

3 When you **finish up** something that you are doing, you complete it by doing the last part of it. [AMERICAN] ❑ *Hendricks was finishing up his paper work when Brady walked in... I was just finishing up work on some Schubert manuscripts.*
V+ADV+N

NOTE **Finish off** means almost the same as **finish up**.

finish up with If you **finish up with** something, this is the result of your activity or efforts. ❑ *Whichever way you do it, you must finish up with the same voltage drop... If you deleted that, you would finish up with a two sentence paragraph.*
V+ADV+PREP

★**finish with** If you **finish with** someone or something, or **are finished with** them, you stop dealing with them or end your involvement or connection with them. ❑ *I haven't finished with you yet... I thought I had finished with the play for ever... He had decided several years before that he was finished with marriage.*
V+PREP: HAS PASSIVE, ALSO PASSIVE: V+PREP

fire /ˈfaɪər/ (fires, firing, fired)

fire away You say to someone '**Fire away**' to indicate that you are ready for them to begin speaking. [INFORMAL]
IMPERATIVE, V+ADV

NOTE **Shoot** means almost the same as **fire away**.

fire off

1 If you **fire off** a shot, you press the mechanism which causes a bullet or other missile to be released from a gun. ❑ *The sniper popped up and fired off a single round... He pointed the pistol and fired off a shot.*
V+ADV+N

2 If you **fire off** questions or suggestions, you say a lot of them quickly, one after the other. ❑ *Tony used to fire off his own suggestions faster than I could write them down.*
V+ADV+N, V+N+ADV, V+PRON+ADV

fire up If you **fire** someone **up**, you make them feel very enthusiastic or angry about something. ❑ *I knew that Sam was trying to fire Costantino up. He kept saying 'You beat him, you beat him'... The whole idea was to fire up his enthusiasm and let him enjoy himself... Returning to the Moon, I contend, is the only tangible way to get the public all fired up about space again.*
V+N+ADV, V+PRON+ADV, V+ADV+N: ALSO+about

firm /fɜːrm/ (firms, firming, firmed)

firm up

1 If you **firm up** part of your body, you exercise to improve the condition of the muscles and reduce the amount of fat. ❑ *This exercise will help to firm up those flabby thighs.*
V+ADV+N, V+N+ADV, V+PRON+ADV

NOTE **Tone up** means almost the same as **firm up**.

2 If you **firm up** an idea or plan, you make decisions about all the details that have not yet been arranged. ❑ *I think we're all agreed on the basic approach; we can firm up the details at next week's meeting.*
V+ADV+N, V+N+ADV, V+PRON+ADV

3 If a financial institution **firms up** the price or value of something, they take action to protect and maintain its price or value. ❑ *OPEC has agreed to freeze its global oil production slightly in order to firm up crude prices.*
V+PREP

fish /fɪʃ/ (fishes, fishing, fished)

fish for If you **fish for** information or praise, you try and get it from someone in an indirect way. ❑ *I think he was just fishing for compliments... I was never invited, and I never fished for an invitation. ...questions that fished for some indication as to how they were doing.*
V+PREP

NOTE **Angle for** means almost the same as **fish for**.

fish out

1 If you **fish** something **out** of a liquid, substance, or container, you pull it out or take it out. ❑ *Patterson had brought his briefcase, and he fished out a package which he gave to Amsburg... One of her earrings dropped into her scrambled egg, and she fished it out and screwed it back on. ...corpses being fished out of the water.*
V+ADV+N, V+PRON+ADV, V+N+ADV: ALSO+of

2 If an area of water **is fished out**, most of the fish living in it have been caught. ❑ *It is becoming clear that parts of the Pacific are in danger of being fished out.*
V+N+ADV, V+PRON+ADV: USUALLY PASSIVE

fit /fɪt/ (fits, fitting, fitted)

✓ **Fit** is sometimes used in American English as the past tense and past participle.

★fit in

1 If you manage to **fit in** a person or task, you manage to find time to deal with them. ❑ *You seem to fit in an enormous amount every day... They can't do it today, so they will fit it in when they have a van in that area... I'm on holiday next week, but I can fit you in on the 9th.*
NOTE **Squeeze in** means almost the same as **fit in**.

V+ADV+N,
V+PRON+ADV,
V+N+ADV

2 If you **fit in** as part of a group, you seem to belong there because you are similar to the other people in it. ❑ *You can't bring outsiders into a place like this; they wouldn't fit in; they would upset the whole atmosphere... You would have to try to adapt yourself to fit in.*

V+ADV

3 If you say that something or someone **fits in**, you understand how they form part of a particular situation or system. ❑ *It's difficult to know where these books fit in.*

V+ADV

★fit into

1 If you **fit into** a particular group, you seem to belong there because you are similar to the other people in it. ❑ *These children are unable to fit into ordinary society... I would have to exercise great effort to fit into a predominantly white world.*

V+PREP

2 If something or someone **fits into** a category, classification, or explanation, you can see that they belong to it or are part of it and understand why. ❑ *...odd things that don't fit into any category... Where does David fit into all this?*

V+PREP

★fit in with

If something **fits in with** a system, method, idea, or situation, it is suitable and works successfully as part of it. ❑ *The old sort of love no longer fits in with our changing needs... They manufacture mild steel to fit in with modern methods of production... I'm willing to fit in with your way of doing things.*

V+ADV+PREP,
V+N+ADV+PREP,
V+PRON+ADV+PREP:
ERGATIVE

fit out

If you **fit** someone or something **out**, you provide them with equipment and other things that they need. ❑ *He started to fit out a ship in secret till the British Ambassador found out about it... When the men arrive, they fit them out in combat uniforms and jungle boots.*
NOTE **Kit out** means almost the same as **fit out**.

V+ADV+N,
V+PRON+ADV,
V+N+ADV,
V+REFL+ADV:
ALSO+in/with

fit up

1 If you **fit** someone or something **up**, you provide them with equipment or other things that they need. ❑ *Dr Bell was wanting to fit you up with a contraceptive... He could fit himself up at modest cost.*

V+PRON+ADV,
V+REFL+ADV,
V+N+ADV,
V+ADV+N

2 If someone **fits** you **up**, they provide false evidence and convince other people that you are guilty of a crime or other serious offence, although you are innocent. [BRITISH, INFORMAL]
NOTE **Frame** is a more formal word for **fit up**.

V+PRON+ADV,
V+N+ADV,
V+ADV+N

fix /fɪks/ (fixes, fixing, fixed)

fix on If you **fix on** a particular thing, you decide that this is what you will have or do. ❑ *Have you fixed on a date for the party yet?... We seem to have fixed on the same day for supermarket shopping.*
NOTE **Set** means almost the same as **fix on**.

V+PREP:
HAS PASSIVE

★fix up

1 If you **fix** someone **up** with something they need, you provide it for them. ❑ *They told me that they could fix me up with tickets for the opera... 'Can I stay at your place for a short time,' she said appealingly, 'till I get fixed up?'*

V+N/PRON+ADV,
V+ADV+N,
V+REFL+ADV:
ALSO+with

2 If you **fix** something **up**, you make the arrangements that are necessary to achieve it. ❑ *Have you done anything about fixing up a meeting place?... We'll fix up a nice meal for the three of us... I'll talk to Sonny about fixing things up.*
NOTE **Arrange** is a more formal word for **fix up**.

V+ADV+N,
V+N+ADV,
V+PRON+ADV

3 If you **fix up** something, you build it quickly and roughly because you need it immediately. ❑ *We tried to fix up a shelter from the wind... I've fixed up this sort of wire barricade.*
NOTE **Rig up** is a more informal expression for **fix up**.

V+ADV+N,
V+PRON+ADV,
V+N+ADV

4 If you **fix up** something that needs repair or attention, you do the work that is necessary to improve it or make it suitable. ❑ *He was fixing up the flat, ready to move in... You promised us money to fix up the streets and alleys.*
NOTE **Do up** means almost the same as **fix up**.

V+ADV+N,
V+N+ADV,
V+PRON+ADV

fizzle /fɪzəl/ (fizzles, fizzling, fizzled)

fizzle out If something **fizzles out**, it ends in a weak or disappointing way, of-   V+ADV
ten after starting strongly. ❑ *The strike fizzled out after three days... It wasn't long before
interest in it fizzled out... The discussion fizzled out after a few minutes.*
NOTE **Peter out** means almost the same as **fizzle out**.

flag /flæg/ (flags, flagging, flagged)

flag down If you **flag down** a vehicle, you wave at it as a signal for the driver   V+ADV+N,
to stop. ❑ *We flagged down the tractor and clambered aboard.*   V+N+ADV,
                                                                                           V+PRON+ADV

flail /fleɪl/ (flails, flailing, flailed)

☑ **About** is used mainly in British English.

flail about → See **flail around**

flail around If your arms or legs **flail around** or **flail about**, or if you **flail**   V+ADV,
them **around** or **flail** them **about**, they wave around in an energetic but uncon-   V+N+ADV,
trolled way. ❑ *He starting flailing around and hitting Vincent in the chest... Ennis began to*   V+PRON+ADV
flail his arms around and struggle.

flake /fleɪk/ (flakes, flaking, flaked)

flake off If something **flakes off**, it separates from the surface it was attached   V+ADV
to. ❑ *The paint was flaking off the walls of the shop.*

flake out If you **flake out**, you collapse or fall asleep, usually because you are   V+ADV
exhausted. [INFORMAL] ❑ *When I got to the top I just flaked out... I flaked out on my bed.*

flake out on If you **flake out on** someone, you do not do something that you   V+ADV+PREP
should do, or that you have said you will do. [AMERICAN] ❑ *'How long have you been
deputy project director?' 'Eleven months, ever since Miriel flaked out on us.'*

flare /fleər/ (flares, flaring, flared)

flare out Something that **flares out** spreads outwards at one end to form a wide   V+ADV
shape. ❑ *She pirouetted, making the skirt flare out... The long feathered tail flared out behind it.*
NOTE **Fan out** means almost the same as **flare out**.

flare up

1 If fire or a flame **flares up**, it suddenly burns very fiercely and brightly. ❑ *The fire*   V+ADV
*flared up high and showed up their little group clearly... He set fire to it, then stood watching
it flare up.*
NOTE **Blaze** means almost the same as **flare up**.

2 If something such as violence, conflict, or an emotion **flares up**, it suddenly be-   V+ADV
comes very intense or serious. ❑ *The argument between the two groups flared up at the
meeting... The conflict flared up into civil war... Panic flared up in her.*
NOTE **Erupt** is a more formal word for **flare up**.

♦ If there is a **flare-up** of a previous situation, condition, or emotion, it suddenly   N-COUNT
occurs again. ❑ *...the incident which produced this new flare-up of anxiety... The disease
had shown occasional flare-ups, particularly in the South West.*

3 If someone **flares up** at you, they suddenly get very angry with you, often with-   V+ADV:
out good reason. ❑ *He was being thoroughly objectionable, flaring up at her over quite rea-*   ALSO+at
sonable requests... She would sometimes flare up at me as a way of relieving her own panic.

♦ A **flare-up** is a sudden argument or situation of conflict. ❑ *Ian found himself in an-*   N-COUNT
other flare-up over umpiring.

flash /flæʃ/ (flashes, flashing, flashed)

flash back If your mind **flashes back** to an event in your past, you suddenly   V+ADV
remember it very forcefully. ❑ *My mind flashed back to past demonstrations... His mind
flashed back to what the sisters had said... Soshnick's mind flashed back to the notorious lipstick murders in Chicago.*

♦ A **flashback** is an occasion, especially in a film or a play, when someone sudden-   N-COUNT
ly remembers an event in their past. ❑ *... a brief flashback to the four earlier murders.*

flatten /flætən/ (flattens, flattening, flattened)

flatten out

1 If you **flatten** something **out** or if it **flattens out**, it becomes flat or flatter.   V+ADV+N,
❑ *...a bulldozer flattening out the ruts in the road. ...where the foothills flattened out to*   V+N+ADV,
                                                                                               V+PRON+ADV,

meet the Bay shore... To the north of the ridge, the country flattened out into a blue expanse.

V+ADV:
ERGATIVE

2 If something **flattens out** differences or variations in things, it reduces the differences or variations and the things become more like each other. ❑ *Comprehensive schools assisted in flattening out all regional accents.*

V+ADV+N,
V+N+ADV,
V+PRON+ADV

flesh /flɛʃ/ (fleshes, fleshing, fleshed)

flesh out If you **flesh** something **out**, you give more information about it or add details to make it complete. ❑ *Those are the main points I'll be talking about. Now I'll flesh them out for you... We had several ideas for the initial concept of the scene and we are now seeing them fleshed out for the first time.*

V+PRON+ADV,
V+N+ADV,
V+ADV+N

flick /flɪk/ (flicks, flicking, flicked)

flick over If you **flick over** the pages of a magazine or book, you turn the pages quickly. ❑ *He put his head down at once, flicking over the pages with a practised hand.*

V+ADV+N,
V+N/PRON+ADV:
NO PASSIVE

flick through If you **flick through** a magazine, book, or pile of papers or cards, you turn over pages or individual items quickly to get a brief idea of what they contain. ❑ *He flicked through the passport, not understanding a word... The interviewer started flicking through job cards... She got out a book and began to flick through.*

V+PREP,
V+ADJ

NOTE **Leaf through** means almost the same as **flick through**.

fling /flɪŋ/ (flings, flinging, flung)

fling into If you **fling** yourself **into** an activity, you begin to do it with a lot of enthusiasm, energy and effort. ❑ *...before we fling ourselves into the mad world of pleasure... She flung herself into her work.*

V+REFL+PREP

NOTE **Throw into** means almost the same as **fling into**.

fling off If you **fling off** your clothes, you take them off very quickly and carelessly. ❑ *She ran into the bedroom, where she flung off her dress and took out a clean one.*

V+N+ADV,
V+PRON+ADV

NOTE **Throw off** means almost the same as **fling off**.

fling out If you **fling out** a remark, you say it quickly in a rather aggressive way. ❑ *...lurking in an office somewhere, ready to fling out their routine insults in response to any enquiry... 'I told you,' she flung out, 'I won't hear anything more about Mr Edwards.'*

V+ADV+N,
V+ADV+QUOTE,
V+PRON+ADV,
V+N+ADV

flip /flɪp/ (flips, flipping, flipped)

flip through If you **flip through** a magazine, book, or pile of papers or cards, you turn over pages or individual items quickly to get a brief idea of what they contain. ❑ *Renshaw flipped through the book... She flipped through a card-index... 'Read it yourself,' he said, flipping through until he found the page.*

V+PREP,
V+ADV

NOTE **Flick through** means almost the same as **flip through**.

flirt /flɜːt/ (flirts, flirting, flirted)

★flirt with

1 If you **flirt with** someone, you behave towards them in a teasing way that suggests you are sexually attracted to them. ❑ *Now Belinda was flirting shamelessly with another man.*

V+PREP

2 If you **flirt with** the idea of doing or having something, you consider the idea without making any definite plans. ❑ *Burlington has flirted with the idea of a wood-burning electrical generator... Channon flirted with the idea of running for the Presidency.*

V+PREP:
HAS PASSIVE

NOTE **Toy with** and **dally with** mean almost the same as **flirt with**.

float /floʊt/ (floats, floating, floated)

float around

1 If a rumour or idea **is floating around**, it is being discussed or thought about in a general, rather vague way. ❑ *There are a lot of weird ideas floating around... I have a lot of ideas floating around between books that don't come to anything.*

V+ADV

2 If you say that something **is floating around**, you mean that you have seen it recently somewhere nearby, but you do not know exactly where. [INFORMAL] ❑ *There's a bag of sweets floating around somewhere. Would you like one?*

V+ADV

flood /flʌd/ (floods, flooding, flooded)

★flood in If people or things **flood in** somewhere, they arrive there in large numbers. ❑ *Cheap sandals began to flood in from Korea... US reinforcements were now flooding in... Letters flooded in to MPs.*

V+ADV:
ALSO+to

flood into If people or things **flood into** a place, large numbers of them arrive in a short space of time. ❑ *Nine million people a year were flooding into the Third World cities... By now, messages were flooding into command posts all over Normandy.*
NOTE Pour into means almost the same as **flood into**.

V+PREP

flood out If people **are flooded out**, they have to leave their homes because river or sea water has risen to an unusually high level and come into the buildings. ❑ *If the rain continued, we'd be flooded out.*

V+N+ADV, V+PRON+ADV, V+ADV+N: USUALLY PASSIVE

flop /flɒp/ **(flops, flopping, flopped)**

flop down If you **flop down**, you let your body fall quickly downwards, usually because you are exhausted. ❑ *They flop down, yelling, and pound with their hands and feet... Jimmie flopped down in the chair... He flopped down next to her.*

V+ADV: USUALLY+A

flounder /flaʊndər/ **(flounders, floundering, floundered)**

☑ **About** is used mainly in British English.

flounder about → See flounder around
flounder around

1 If someone or something **flounders around** or **flounders about** in a place, they move very unsteadily, and perhaps keep falling over. ❑ *They had flown aboard and floundered about in vain trying to escape.*

V+ADV

2 If someone **flounders around** or **flounders about** in a situation, they are confused and cannot think or express themselves clearly. ❑ *He was floundering about, patently trying to organize some kind of argument.*

V+ADV

flow /floʊ/ **(flows, flowing, flowed)**

flow from If a situation, product, or quality **flows from** something, it occurs as a natural result of it. ❑ *The consequences that flow from this view are endless... Films and television programmes would flow from this collaboration.*
NOTE Stem from means almost the same as flow from.

V+PREP

flow over If a feeling **flows over** you, you suddenly feel it very strongly. ❑ *He couldn't suppress the contempt that flowed over him.*

V+PREP

fluff /flʌf/ **(fluffs, fluffing, fluffed)**

fluff out If you **fluff** something **out** or **fluff** it **up**, you make it softer, looser, or lighter, for example by shaking or brushing it. ❑ *She fluffed her hair out in big waves... Put the mashed potato in the oven for 20 minutes, fluff it up with a fork and serve.*

V+N+ADV, V+PRON+ADV, V+ADV+N

fluff up → See fluff out

flunk /flʌŋk/ **(flunks, flunking, flunked)**

flunk out If you **flunk out**, you are dismissed from a school or college because your work is not good enough. [AMERICAN, INFORMAL] ❑ *You're gonna flunk out if you just sit there watching me study!*

V+ADV

flush /flʌʃ/ **(flushes, flushing, flushed)**

flush out If you **flush out** someone or something, you find them and force them to come out or be revealed. ❑ *They went into the area to flush out guerrillas who were sheltering there. ...secrets which Cobb will painstakingly flush out.*

V+ADV+N, V+N+ADV, V+PRON+ADV

flutter /flʌtər/ **(flutters, fluttering, fluttered)**

☑ **About** is used mainly in British English.

flutter about → See flutter around
flutter around If someone **flutters around** or **flutters about**, they move about quickly and nervously without seeming to have any definite purpose. ❑ *Unable to sit down, she would flutter about from room to room... They wasted half their time fluttering around the invalid.*

V+ADV, V+PREP

flutter down If something light **flutters down**, it moves slowly and gently through the air towards the ground. ❑ *The pieces of paper flutter down like large butterflies in the darkness... The first flakes of snow began to flutter down early in the afternoon.*

V+ADV

fly /flaɪ/ **(flies, flying, flew, flown)**

fly at If you **fly at** someone, you suddenly get very angry with them and express this, either in words or by attacking them. ❑ *One day the man flew at me in a temper...*

V+PREP

The symbol ★ shows key phrasal verbs

She looked at him as though she were about to fly at his face.

NOTE **Go for** means almost the same as **fly at**.

fly in If someone **flies in**, or people or things **are flown in**, they arrive in a place by aeroplane. ❑ *Howard had flown in from Atlanta at my request... Portable units had been flown in.*

> V+ADV,
> V+ADV+N:
> ERGATIVE

fly into If you **fly into** a rage or a panic, you suddenly become very angry or start to panic. ❑ *She flies into a temper if I make a mistake... Something dropped onto his back and he flew into a flat panic.*

> V+PREP

fly out If someone **flies out**, or people or things **are flown out**, they go or are sent somewhere by aeroplane. ❑ *I decided to fly out to Bombay in order to help... The RAF had flown out the vital equipment.*

> V+ADV,
> V+ADV+N:
> ERGATIVE

fob /fɒb/ (fobs, fobbing, fobbed)

fob off If you **fob** someone **off** with something, you persuade them to accept it, although it is not what they wanted or asked for. ❑ *He may try to fob you off with a prescription for pills... She felt she was being fobbed off.*

> V+PRON+ADV,
> V+N+ADV,
> V+ADV+N:
> USUALLY+with

fog /fɒg/ (fogs, fogging, fogged)

fog up If something made of glass **fogs up**, it becomes difficult to see through because it is covered with tiny drops of water that make it cloudy.

> V+ADV

NOTE **Steam up** means almost the same as **fog up**.

foist /fɔɪst/ (foists, foisting, foisted)

foist on If you **foist** something **on** someone, or **foist** it **upon** them, you force them to have it or experience it. **Foist upon** is more formal. ❑ *They were not out to lead, to foist their ideas and views on the people... We do not want to foist answers on anyone. ...the kinds of ideas foisted upon us all our lives.*

> V+N+PREP,
> V+PRON+PREP

foist upon → See foist on

fold /fould/ (folds, folding, folded)

fold in In cooking, if you **fold** something **in**, you mix it gently and carefully into a mixture, keeping as much air in the mixture as possible. ❑ *When the batter is ready, fold in the egg white with a metal spoon.*

> V+ADV+N,
> V+N+ADV,
> V+PRON+ADV

fold into In cooking, if you **fold** one substance **into** another, you mix them gently and carefully, keeping as much air in the mixture as possible. ❑ *Beat the egg whites until stiff and then fold them carefully into the sauce... Using a metal spoon, fold the dry ingredients into the cream.*

> V+PREP

fold up

1 If you **fold** something **up**, you make it into a smaller, neat shape by folding it several times. ❑ *She began to fold up the blanket... He was just folding the map up when he spotted it.*

> V+ADV+N,
> V+N+ADV,
> V+PRON+ADV

NOTE **Unfold** means the opposite of **fold up**.

2 If the petals of a flower **fold up**, they close and come together in the centre of the flower. ❑ *The buds had folded up against the light.*

> V+ADV,
> V+REFL+ADV

NOTE **Close up** means almost the same as **fold up**.

3 If a business or organization **folds up**, it closes or comes to an end because it has been unsuccessful. ❑ *She had known too many businesses fold up through bad management... They had no choice but to fold up their offshore operations.*

> V+ADV,
> V+ADV+N,
> V+N+ADV,
> V+PRON+ADV:
> ERGATIVE

NOTE **Pack up** means almost the same as **fold up**.

follow /fɒloʊ/ (follows, following, followed)

follow out If you **follow out** instructions you do exactly what you have been told to do. ❑ *She knew she could trust him to follow out her instructions. ...following out the teachings of their religious leaders.*

> V+ADV+N,
> V+PRON+ADV

NOTE **Carry out** means almost the same as **follow out**.

follow through

1 If you **follow** an idea **through** and carefully consider how it would work and what its effects would be. ❑ *Tempting though it may be to follow this point through, it is not really relevant.*

> V+N+ADV,
> V+PRON+ADV,
> V+ADV+N

2 If you **follow through** a series of actions, you complete all the stages to achieve something or to get to the end. ❑ *She was the only journalist to follow the story through...*

> V+N+ADV,
> V+ADV+N,
> V+PRON+ADV

For a full explanation of all grammatical labels, see pages xiii-xx

The offensive action was swiftly followed through to the early attainment of victory.

♦ An action that completes something or is a natural continuation of it is called the **follow-through**. ❑ *This wouldn't halt the attack but it would at least blunt the follow-through.*   N-SING

3 In a sport such as golf, tennis, or football, to **follow through** means to complete the movement after hitting the ball by continuing to move your arm or leg in the same curve. ❑ *You're not following through after playing the stroke.*   V+ADV

♦ In sport, the **follow-through** is the completion of a movement after hitting the ball. ❑ *The follow-through is part of the kick.*   N-SING

★**follow up**

1 If you **follow** something **up**, you try to find out more about it and perhaps do something about it. ❑ *It's an idea which has been followed up by the local council... I followed up an advertisement for a second-hand Volkswagen. ...according to the fisherman who followed up the reports.*   V+N+ADV, V+ADV+N, V+PRON+ADV

NOTE **Investigate** is a more formal word for **follow up**.

2 If you **follow up** one action with another, you do the second action soon after the first. ❑ *The President followed up the first round of voting by challenging his opponent to a public debate... They must attend the course, and this is followed up by personal visits... He murmured the word quietly and with great venom, following up with a string of oaths.*   V+ADV+N, V+N+ADV, V+PRON+ADV, V+ADV: USUALLY+with/by

♦ A **follow-up** or a **follow-up** activity is done as a continuation or second part of something done previously. ❑ *This conference is a follow-up to an earlier one in Gabon... He needed follow-up treatment from a specialist doctor.*   N-COUNT, ADJECTIVE

fool /fuːl/ (fools, fooling, fooled)

✓ **About** is used mainly in British English.

fool about → See **fool around**

fool around

1 If you **fool around** or **fool about**, you behave in a playful or childish way. ❑ *The boys passed them, laughing and fooling around and talking loudly... He was always fooling about.*   V+ADV

2 If you **fool around** or **fool about** with something dangerous, you behave in a careless or irresponsible way. ❑ *Chemicals are very dangerous things to fool around with... I don't want to have to fool around trying to dock two boats in the dark.*   V+ADV: ALSO+with

NOTE **Mess around** means almost the same as **fool around**.

3 If someone **fools around** with another person, especially when one of them is married, they have a casual sexual relationship with them. ❑ *I'll bet you were fooling around with Miss Roach. ...that fellow who's fooling around with your wife.*   V+ADV: ALSO+with

force /fɔːrs/ (forces, forcing, forced)

force back If you **force back** an emotion or desire, you manage, with an effort, to prevent it from affecting you. ❑ *He forced back the strong urge to stroke her.*   V+ADV+N, V+PRON+ADV

NOTE **Suppress** and **fight back** mean almost the same as **force back**.

★**force into** If you **force** someone **into** doing something, you make them do it, although they do not want to. ❑ *...to force landlords into increasing their wages. ...forcing him into the role of confidant... 'No one's forcing you into it,' Joyce said.*   V+N+PREP, V+PRON+PREP

force on If you **force** something **on** someone, or **force** it **upon** them, you make them accept, use, or deal with it when they would prefer not to. **Force upon** is more formal. ❑ *...the missiles which the Americans are forcing, he believes, upon Britain... I forced some more of the salt and water on him.*   V+N+PREP, V+PRON+PREP

force upon → See **force on**

forge /fɔːrdʒ/ (forges, forging, forged)

forge ahead If you **forge ahead**, you make a lot of progress, or more progress than someone else. ❑ *The company has made use of the absence of competition to forge ahead... They could see the army forging ahead along the road.*   V+ADV

fork /fɔːrk/ (forks, forking, forked)

fork out If you **fork out** for something, you pay money for it. [INFORMAL] ❑ *It's likely that she will be prepared to fork out extra cash to install a tape player... His old man's*   V+ADV, V+ADV+N: USUALLY+A *forked out at last. ...the fortune I had already had to fork out on her education.*

NOTE Cough up means almost the same as **fork out**.

form /fɔːᵊm/ (forms, forming, formed)

form up When a group of people or things **form up**, they move into position in lines. ❏ *The yachts formed up in Hampton Roads... The police arrived as the procession was forming up... Form yourselves up into two columns and follow me!*

V+ADV,
V+REFL+ADV,
V+N+ADV,
V+PRON+ADV:
ERGATIVE

foul /faʊl/ (fouls, fouling, fouled)

foul up If someone **fouls up** a plan, situation, or relationship, they spoil it by doing something wrong or stupid. [INFORMAL] ❏ *So many good projects have been fouled up by elementary mistakes in planning... He does seem to have fouled up negotiating practice in the docks.*

V+ADV+N,
V+N+ADV,
V+PRON+ADV

NOTE Mess up means almost the same as **foul up**.

♦ A **foul-up** is a state of disorder or trouble which is the result of mistakes or carelessness. [INFORMAL] ❏ *The Centre hates that kind of foul-up.*

N-COUNT

freak /friːk/ (freaks, freaking, freaked)

freak out If someone **freaks out**, they suddenly behave in a very strange and uncontrolled way, for example because of a sudden shock or the effect of drugs. [INFORMAL] ❏ *When I gave him an application form, he just freaked out completely... He was freaking the colonel out a little bit... Well, I'm freaked out by what we're seeing... It freaks him out every time.*

V+ADV,
V+N+ADV,
V+PRON+ADV:
ERGATIVE

free /friː/ (frees, freeing, freed)
free up

1 To **free up** someone or something means to make them available for a task or function that they were previously not available for. ❏ *It can handle even the most complex graphic jobs, freeing up your computer for other tasks.*

V+ADV+N,
V+N+ADV,
V+PRON+ADV

2 To **free up** a market, economy, or system means to make it operate with fewer restrictions and controls. ❏ *...policies for freeing up markets and extending competition.*

V+ADV+N,
V+N+ADV,
V+PRON+ADV

freeze /friːz/ (freezes, freezing, froze, frozen)

freeze out If you **freeze** someone **out** of an activity or situation, you prevent them from being involved in it by creating difficulties or being unfriendly. ❏ *Producers try to freeze out parasitic middle men.*

V+ADV+N,
V+N+ADV,
V+PRON+ADV:
ALSO+of

NOTE Squeeze out means almost the same as **freeze out**.

freeze over If a pond, lake or river **freezes over** or **is frozen over**, it becomes covered with a layer of ice. ❏ *In really hard winters, the Thames has been known to freeze over. ...when the Lakes were frozen over.*

V+ADV:
ALSO PASSIVE:
V+ADV

NOTE Ice over and ice up mean almost the same as **freeze over**.

freeze up If an area of water or a pipe or machine **freezes up** or **is frozen up**, it becomes completely blocked or covered with ice. ❏ *It was so cold last winter that even the river froze up... The lock has frozen up.*

V+ADV:
ALSO PASSIVE:
V+ADV

NOTE Ice up means almost the same as **freeze up**.

♦ If there is a **freeze-up**, it is so cold that pipes and areas of water become blocked with ice. ❏ *If we get a freeze-up, let him have a bit more hay and make sure unfrozen water is available.*

N-COUNT

freshen /freʃ°n/ (freshens, freshening, freshened)
freshen up

1 If you **freshen up** or **freshen** yourself **up**, you wash and make yourself look neat and tidy. ❏ *Sarah and Barry returned to their hotel to freshen up... I shall just have time to change and freshen up.*

V+ADV,
V+REFL+ADV

2 If you **freshen** something **up**, you make it look cleaner, brighter and more attractive. ❏ *New wallpaper and curtains will freshen up the place.*

V+N+ADV,
V+PRON+ADV,
V+ADV+N

frig /frɪg/ (frigs, frigging, frigged)

frig about If someone says that you **are frigging about** or **frigging around**, they mean that you are wasting time when you should be doing something. [BRITISH, INFORMAL]

V+ADV

NOTE Mess around is a less informal expression for **frig about**.

frig around → See frig about

frighten /fraɪtᵊn/ (frightens, frightening, frightened)
frighten away

[1] If you **frighten away** a person or animal or **frighten** them **off**, you make them afraid so that they run away and do not harm you. ❑ *He waved his torch to frighten away some animal, probably a hyena... It flaps its wings and flashes a huge pair of eye spots which frighten the killer away... We were waving our arms to frighten them off.*

V+ADV+N,
V+N+ADV,
V+PRON+ADV

NOTE **Scare off** means almost the same as **frighten away**.

[2] To **frighten away** or **frighten off** someone who is expressing an interest in a person or activity means to make them doubtful or nervous so that they decide to withdraw their interest or support. ❑ *He managed to woo the Communists on his left without frightening off the middle-of-the-road voters. ...so as not to frighten away the potential middle-class allies.*

V+N+ADV,
V+ADV+N,
V+PRON+ADV

NOTE **Scare off** means almost the same as **frighten away**.

frighten into If you **frighten** someone **into** something, you make them so frightened that they do something which they might not otherwise have done. ❑ *'Don't you dare,' he said, frightening her into silence.*

V+N+PREP,
V+PRON+PREP

frighten off → See **frighten away**

frighten out of If you **frighten** someone **out of** something, you make them so afraid that they do not do something that they had intended to do. ❑ *She refused to be frightened out of going.*

V+N+ADV+PREP,
V+PRON+ADV+PREP

fritter /frɪtər/ (fritters, frittering, frittered)

fritter away If you **fritter away** time or money, you waste it by spending it in a foolish way, a little bit at a time. ❑ *It is all too easy to fritter away the best hours of the day shopping... She was determined she would not fritter away her vacation... The money just goes though, doesn't it; you just fritter it away.*

V+ADV+N,
V+PRON+ADV,
V+N+ADV

NOTE **Squander** is a more formal word for **fritter away**.

frost /frɒst, AM frɔːst/ (frosts, frosting, frosted)

frost over When something made of glass **frosts over** or **frosts up**, or **is frosted over** or **frosted up**, it becomes covered with frost. ❑ *It must have been cold last night, my windscreen's frosted over.*

V+ADV:
ALSO PASSIVE:
V+ADV

frost up → See **frost over**

frown /fraʊn/ (frowns, frowning, frowned)

frown on → See **frown upon**

frown upon If something **is frowned upon** or **is frowned on**, people disapprove of it. ❑ *Broadway's licentious plays were frowned upon... Society frowns upon such behaviour.*

V+PREP:
HAS PASSIVE,
USUALLY PASSIVE

fry /fraɪ/ (fries, frying, fried)

fry up If you **fry up** food, you fry it to make a quick, casual meal. [BRITISH] ❑ *Make yourself useful and fry up some bacon.*

V+ADV+N,
V+PRON+ADV

♦ A **fry-up** is a quick, casual meal consisting of fried food. [BRITISH, INFORMAL]

N-COUNT

fuck /fʌk/ (fucks, fucking, fucked)

✓ **Fuck** is an extremely rude word, which most people find very offensive. **About** is used mainly in British English.

fuck about → See **fuck around**

fuck around To **fuck around** or **fuck about** means to behave in a way that is silly, stupid, or unnecessary and annoys other people.

V+ADV,
V+N+ADV,
V+PRON+ADV

NOTE **Mess around** is a more polite, informal expression for **fuck around**.

fuck off 'Fuck off' is a very insulting way of telling someone to go away or to stop interfering.

IMPERATIVE,
V+ADV

NOTE **Get lost** is a less offensive expression for **fuck off**.

fuck over If someone **fucks** you **over**, they cheat you or behave very badly towards you. ❑ *Frustrated, Bason complained to Goldstone. 'They're just fucking us over!' he snapped.*

V+N+ADV,
V+PRON+ADV

fuck up If someone **fucks** something **up**, they make a mess of it.

V+N+ADV,
V+PRON+ADV,
V+ADV+N

NOTE **Mess up** is a more polite, informal expression for **fuck up**.

The symbol ★ shows key phrasal verbs

♦ A **fuck-up** occurs when someone does something completely wrong.   N-COUNT

fur /fɜːr/ **(furs, furring, furred)**

fur up

1 If a kettle or water pipe **furs up**, the inside of it becomes covered with a hard   V+ADV
grey layer of calcium carbonate and other chemicals in the water. [BRITISH]

2 If your veins or arteries **fur up** or **are furred up**, they become blocked, so that   V+ADV,
your blood cannot flow properly. [BRITISH] □ *Three of my veins had furred up and I need-*   V+ADV+N,
ed a triple bypass... Oxidized cholesterol may be responsible for furring up the arteries.   V+N+ADV,
V+PRON+ADV:
ERGATIVE

fuss /fʌs/ **(fusses, fussing, fussed)**

fuss over If you **fuss over** someone or something, you pay a lot of attention to   V+PREP:
them, showing too much concern or affection. □ *He was fed the best pieces and fussed*   HAS PASSIVE
over by his admiring brothers... His mother fussed over him a bit too much, I think... Matty
was inclined to fuss over her health.

Gg

gad /gæd/ (gads, gadding, gadded)

> ☑ **About** is used mainly in British English.

gad about If you **gad about** or **gad around**, you go to a lot of different places looking for amusement and entertainment. [INFORMAL, OLD-FASHIONED] ❑ *I begrudged them gadding about while I did all the work... This is hardly the time to be gadding around.*

V+ADV

> [NOTE] **Gallivant** means almost the same as **gad about**.

♦ If you describe someone as a **gadabout**, you mean that they do not take things seriously, and spend their time looking for amusement and entertainment. [INFORMAL, OLD-FASHIONED] ❑ *Henry's been very good. He may be quiet and not very pushing, but no one could call him a gadabout.*

N-COUNT

gad around → See **gad about**

gain /geɪn/ (gains, gaining, gained)

gain on If you **gain on** someone or something that you are chasing, you gradually get nearer to them. ❑ *You'll have to drive faster – they're gaining on us... We were gaining on him towards the end of the race.*

V+PREP

gamble /gæmbᵊl/ (gambles, gambling, gambled)

gamble away If you **gamble** money **away**, you lose it by betting on the result of a game or a competition. ❑ *Fred gambled his profits away... He's only just received the money, but now Tim will gamble all of it away.*

V+N+ADV,
V+PRON+ADV,
V+ADV+N

gamble on

1 If you **gamble on** the result of a game or a competition, you bet money on that result. ❑ *He gambled heavily on the horses... He still gambled modestly on the football pools.*

V+PREP

2 If you **gamble on** something, you take a risky action or decision in the hope of gaining money, success, or an advantage. ❑ *...gambling on the assumption that the file had been lost... I gambled on immunity from the law and lost.*

V+PREP:
HAS PASSIVE

gang /gæŋ/ (gangs, ganging, ganged)

gang up If people **gang up** on someone else, they unite against them in a fight or argument. [INFORMAL] ❑ *Telling dirty jokes is a way that men gang up on women... They are ganging up against you... National groups are ganging up to claim their rights.*

V+ADV:
USUALLY WITH *on/against*

gather /gæðəʳ/ (gathers, gathering, gathered)

> ☑ In American English, **around** is much more common than **round**.

gather around If people **gather around** or **gather round** someone or something, they come together in a group and surround them. ❑ *The boys gathered around the old man to hear his stories... Little crowds would gather around them to clap and listen... The boys gathered round the fire.*

V+PREP,
V+ADV

> [NOTE] **Cluster around** means almost the same as **gather around**.

gather in If you **gather in** a group of people or things, you bring them safely together into one place. [OLD-FASHIONED] ❑ *The men have three weeks to gather their harvest in... Emergency teams were organized to gather in all the unattended casualties... The main crops have to be gathered in and stored for the winter.*

V+N+ADV,
V+ADV+N,
V+PRON+ADV

gather round → See **gather around**

gather up If you **gather up** a number of things, you bring them together into a group. ❑ *She watched Willie gather up the papers and stuff them carelessly in his pocket... Gather up all the tools and put them away... I saw her gathering her bits and pieces up for the move to the new flat.*

V+ADV+N,
V+N+ADV,
V+PRON+ADV

NOTE Get together means almost the same as **gather up**, and **assemble** is a more formal word.

gear /gɪəʳ/ (gears, gearing, geared)

gear to If something **is geared to** or **geared towards** a particular purpose, it is organized or designed to be suitable for that purpose. ❑ ...*a system of values geared to man's needs.* ...*gearing our efforts to what the market really wants... Higher education is increasingly geared towards careers.*

V+N+PREP,
V+PRON+PREP

gear towards → See **gear to**

gear up If someone or something **is geared up** to do something, or if they **gear** themselves **up** to do it, they are prepared and able to do it. ❑ *Many football teams are not geared up to attack... Science is not geared up to cope with the problems of human development... Martin and Liz were gearing themselves up to a full-time job.*

V+PRON+ADV,
V+N+ADV,
V+REFL+ADV:
USUALLY PASSIVE WITH
to/to-INF

gee /dʒiː/ (gees, geeing, geed)

gee up To **gee** someone **up** means to encourage them to perform well. [BRITISH, INFORMAL] ❑ *Crawley needed no one to gee him up. He sounded positive before the game even started... In the last 36 months he has travelled 38 times round the world, geeing up sales forces and motivating marketing men.*

V+N+ADV,
V+PRON+ADV,
V+ADV+N

NOTE **Encourage** is a more formal word for **gee up**.

gen /dʒen/ (gens, genning, genned)

gen up If you **gen up** on something, you find out as much information about it as you can. ❑ *He's genning up on the legal position before he signs the contract... She genned up on the character before taking on the role.*

V+ADV:
USUALLY+on

NOTE **Swot up** means almost the same as **gen up**.

♦ If you are **genned up** on a subject, you know a lot about it. ❑ *She's really genned up on all these old customs and traditions.*

ADJECTIVE

NOTE **Well-informed** is a more formal word for **genned up**.

get /get/ (gets, getting, got)

✅ **Gotten** is used in American English as the past participle. **About** is used mainly in British English. In American English, **around** is much more common than **round**.

get about

1 If you can **get about** after you have been ill or when you are old, you are able to move around without much difficulty. ❑ *I can't get about as much as I used to... She gets Stuart to help her, otherwise she just couldn't get about, she'd just be stuck there... I can get about with a stick.*

V+ADV

2 → See **get around**

get above If you say that someone **is getting above** themselves, you mean that they are behaving as if they are better than everyone else. ❑ *She was restrained from getting above herself by a natural modesty.*

V+PREP+REFL

★get across If an idea or argument **gets across**, or if you **get** it **across**, you succeed in making other people understand it. ❑ *The speaker needs to know that his words are getting across... We managed to get our message across... It was difficult to get across the basic idea.*

V+ADV,
V+N+ADV,
V+ADV+N,
V+PRON+ADV:
ERGATIVE

NOTE **Get over** and **put across** mean almost the same as **get across**.

get after If you **get after** someone, you try to catch them, especially after they have committed a crime. ❑ *It is their job to get after the villains as fast as possible.*

V+PREP

NOTE **Pursue** is a more formal word for **get after**.

get ahead If you **get ahead**, you are successful in your career. ❑ *The bright young man can get ahead quickly in industry... You've got to be sharp to get ahead.*

V+ADV

NOTE **Get on** means almost the same as **get ahead**.

★get along

1 If you **get along** with someone, you have a friendly relationship with them. ❑ *He worked hard and was easy to get along with... They just can't get along together... The two men do get along well.*

V+ADV+with,
V+ADV+together,
V+ADV:
RECIPROCAL

NOTE **Get on** means almost the same as **get along**.

2 If you **are getting along** in a situation, you are coping with it or making pro-

V+ADV:

gress in it, although it may be difficult. ❑ *Some parents never ask how their children are* *getting along... With his ninety dollars a week and her sixty they got along well enough...* *How are you getting along with the German course?... You can get along fine without a* *washing machine.*

ALSO+*with*

NOTE **Get on** means almost the same as **get along**, and **manage** is a more formal word.

3 If you say that you must **get along**, you mean that you must leave, because you have to go somewhere else. ❑ *Well, I'd better be getting along, the train's due.*

V+ADV

★**get around**

1 If you **get around**, you go to a lot of different places as part of your way of life. ❑ *Getting around will help to increase your experience.*

V+ADV

2 If news **gets around**, **gets about**, or **gets round**, a lot of people hear about it and it becomes well-known. ❑ *The news got around, and there were always plenty of visitors to the exhibition... Startling rumours began to get about... The word got round that Morris was going to England... Gossip gets round the film industry much faster than in other places.*

V+ADV,
V+ADV+REPORT,
V+PREP

3 To **get around** a problem or difficulty means to overcome it. ❑ *None of these countries has found a way yet to get around the problem of the polarization of wealth.*

V+PREP

NOTE **Get over** means almost the same as **get around**.

4 If you **get around** or **get round** a difficulty or restriction, you find a way of avoiding it or of escaping its effects. ❑ *Irving got round the problem in a novel way... To get round the law their plays were staged in private houses... An impasse has developed and I don't know how to get round it.*

V+PREP:
HAS PASSIVE

NOTE **Bypass** is a more formal word for **get around**.

5 If you say that someone **gets around**, you mean that they have many casual sexual relationships. [INFORMAL] ❑ *She's that kind of person; she gets around.*

V+ADV

get around to If you **get around to** or **get round to** doing something, you do it after a long delay because you were previously too busy or reluctant to do it. ❑ *I didn't get round to taking the examination... It took her two years to get around to buying a car.*

V+ADV+PREP

★**get at**

1 If you **get at** something, you manage to reach or obtain it. ❑ *Keep your tool box where you can get at it... The bull was trying to smash the fence so that he could get at me... You can't get at the public records until one hundred years has elapsed.*

V+PREP:
HAS PASSIVE

2 If you **get at** something that is secret, you succeed in discovering the truth about it. ❑ *He does attempt to get at the underlying truth of the situation... He wanted to get at the heart of this puzzling episode. ...a determination to get at the facts.*

V+PREP

NOTE **Find out** means almost the same as **get at**.

3 If you ask someone what they **are getting at**, you are asking them to explain what they mean. ❑ *I don't know what you are getting at... The audience had no idea what we were getting at... I know what you're getting at, and you're right.*

V+PREP

NOTE **Drive at** means almost the same as **get at**.

4 If you say that someone **is getting at** you, you mean that they keep criticizing you in an unkind way. [BRITISH, INFORMAL] ❑ *You're always getting at me... His attitude only strengthened my resolve not to let him get at me.*

V+PREP:
HAS PASSIVE

NOTE **Pick on** means almost the same as **get at**.

5 If someone **has been got at**, they have been persuaded by threats or bribes to say something untrue or to act in an unfair way. ❑ *He allowed the Foreign Office to be got at by the Prime Minister... I should have won; I'm sure the judges had been got at.*

V+PREP:
HAS PASSIVE,
USUALLY PASSIVE

★**get away**

1 If you **get away** from a place or a person's company, you succeed in leaving them. ❑ *You've got to get away from home... I wish you could get away from all those people... She wanted to get away, but didn't want to appear rude.*

V+ADV:
USUALLY+*from*

2 If you **get away**, you go away to have a holiday. ❑ *Is there any chance of you getting away this summer?... I might crack up if I don't get away for a while... It's nice to get away in the autumn.*

V+ADV

3 When someone or something **gets away** from a place, or when you **get** them **away**, they escape. ❑ *They got away through Mrs Barnett's garden... I was determined not*

V+ADV,
V+PRON+ADV,
V+N+ADV:

to let him get away... I prayed for a helicopter to come and get me away from there.
ERGATIVE

♦ If someone makes a **getaway**, they leave a place in a hurry, often after committing a crime. ❑ *Duffield had already made his getaway down the stairs... They leapt aboard the getaway cars.*
N-COUNT, ADJECTIVE

4 People sometimes say **'Get away'** to show that they do not believe what has just been said. [INFORMAL] ❑ *Get away! We can't have that... 'I've been arrested,' I said—'Get away with you!' he laughed.*
IMPERATIVE, V+ADV

NOTE **Go on** means almost the same as **get away**.

★get away from If you **get away from** a common or existing way of behaving or doing something, you start behaving or doing things in a different way. ❑ *We need to get away from the idea that technology is essential... They wanted to get away from the rigid timetables of the past... I thought he'd got away from that film star image.*
V+ADV+PREP

NOTE **Break away from** means almost the same as **get away from**.

★get away with If you **get away with** something that you should not have done, you are not criticized or punished for doing it. ❑ *I'm not going to allow Anne to get away with an offensive remark like that... He might have bribed her–and got away with it.*
V+ADV+PREP

★get back

1 If you **get back** to a place or position, you return there after you have been somewhere else. ❑ *I've got to get back to London... What time have you got to get back?... You're shivering. Get back to bed.*
V+ADV: USUALLY+A

2 If you **get** someone or something **back** to a place, you take them there after they have been away from it. ❑ *We're going to get you right back home where we can look after you properly... Did you get your books back to the library in time?*
V+PRON+ADV, V+N+ADV: USUALLY+A, NO PASSIVE

3 If you **get** something **back** after you have lost it, you have it once again. ❑ *All he wants to do is get his girlfriend back... She had all her antique jewellery stolen, and I don't think she'll get it back now... He would get back his old job.*
V+N+ADV, V+PRON+ADV, V+ADV+N: NO PASSIVE

4 When you **get** your breath **back**, you pause and relax after a very tiring or exciting activity, until you start feeling normal again. ❑ *...trying to get her breath back after a spell of coughs... I got my breath back and tried to work it out.*
V+N+ADV

5 If you tell someone to **get back**, you are telling them to move away from someone or something. ❑ *If you come near, I'll scream. Get back!*
IMPERATIVE, V+ADV

NOTE **Stand back** and **back off** mean almost the same as **get back**.

6 If you **get** someone **back**, you punish or hurt them in return for something unpleasant that they have done to you. [INFORMAL] ❑ *I'll get him back for all the nasty things he said.*
V+PRON+ADV, V+N+ADV

NOTE **Pay back** means almost the same as **get back**.

get back at If you **get back at** someone, you criticize or punish them in return for something unpleasant that they have done or said to you. [INFORMAL] ❑ *He hated meanness, and seemed to consider it his duty to get back at those guilty of this.*
V+ADV+PREP

get back into If you **get back into** an activity that you were doing before, you start being involved in it again. ❑ *Maybe you could get back into journalism... Japanese investors are getting back into the market... Now her kids are grown up, she'd like to get back into research.*
V+ADV+PREP

★get back to

1 If you **get back to** what you were doing or talking about before, you start doing it or talking about it again. ❑ *Eddie wanted to get back to sleep... Now I really must get back to work... Let's just get back to the argument.*
V+ADV+PREP

NOTE **Go back to** means almost the same as **get back to**.

2 If you **get back to** someone, you contact them again after a short period of time, often by telephone. ❑ *Leave a message and I'll get back to you... I couldn't get back to you in time to tell you the new arrangements.*
V+ADV+PREP

get behind

1 If you **get behind** with some work that you are doing, you are slow and do not make as much progress as other people who are doing the same sort of work. ❑ *I'm not surprised Sarah gets behind at school–her parents just aren't interested... If you get behind with your reading in your final year, you'll never catch up.*
V+ADV: ALSO+with

NOTE **Fall behind** means almost the same as **get behind**.

For a full explanation of all grammatical labels, see pages xiii-xx

2 If you **get behind** someone or something, you support them and try to help them to succeed. [AMERICAN] ❏ *'It's a pity they don't get behind us,' Fleck said... They will support reform if it sticks, but will not get behind it until it does.*

V+PREP

get beyond If you **get beyond** a particular thing, you make progress so that you are no longer concerned with that thing. ❏ *In some schools, you never get beyond counting coloured pips... She had got beyond the stage of prizing what was rare or expensive... As a musician, he has not got beyond playing Le Sacre du Printemps.*

V+PREP

NOTE **Go beyond** means almost the same as **get beyond**.

get by

1 If you **get by**, you just manage to survive and have a fairly satisfactory life. ❏ *He had managed to get by without much reading or writing... They slide through life, getting by as best they can... Khan's father had just enough land to get by.*

V+ADV

2 If you **get by** in a difficult situation, you manage to cope with it. ❏ *You can get by in any English conversation with a very limited vocabulary... It's possible to get by in a job interview by just talking about your interests.*

V+ADV: ALSO+*in*

3 If someone or something that is moving **gets by**, they manage to get past an obstacle. ❏ *The truck began hooting to get by... I moved away from the doorway to let her get by.*

V+ADV

NOTE **Pass** means almost the same as **get by**.

★get down

1 When someone or something **gets down** they move from a higher position or level to a lower one. To **get** someone or something **down** means to move them from a higher position or level to a lower one. ❏ *When we eventually got down the mountain, he was rushed to hospital... Wait until the temperature gets down to zero!... You'll never get the piano down the stairs.*

V+ADV/PREP, V+N+ADV/PREP, V+PRON+ADV/PREP: ERGATIVE

2 If you **get down** from an object that you are sitting, standing, or lying on, you move off it and on to the ground. ❏ *He got down from the step ladder... George has climbed up that tree, and now he can't get down.*

V+ADV: USUALLY+*from*

3 If children ask to **get down** when they have been sitting at a table and eating a meal, they are asking permission to get down from their chair and leave the table, because they have finished eating.

V+ADV

4 If you are standing somewhere and **get down**, you bend down and sit, kneel or lie on the ground. ❏ *The soldiers shouted to us to get down... The woman got down on her knees and peered at the baby... They got down on the ground.*

V+ADV: ALSO+*on*

5 If you **get down** to a place, you go there. [INFORMAL] ❏ *Get down there and find out what they're planning. ...people who can't get down to the seaside as often as they want... I rushed my lunch to get down to the garage by half past one.*

V+ADV: ALSO+*to*

6 If you **get** food **down**, you swallow it, especially with difficulty. [INFORMAL] ❏ *I felt better yesterday, but I'm finding it hard to get food down... He spat it out because he couldn't get it down.*

V+N+ADV, V+PRON+ADV: NO PASSIVE

7 If you **get down** what someone is saying, you write it down. ❏ *They'd have to get all the conversation down... Have you got the details down?... I keep repeating myself so that you can get it down.*

V+N+ADV, V+PRON+ADV, V+ADV+N: NO PASSIVE

NOTE **Take down** means almost the same as **get down**.

8 If something **gets** you **down**, it makes you unhappy. ❏ *It isn't just the work that gets her down... He said I shouldn't let my circumstances get me down... The loneliness really started to get my mother down after a few months.*

V+PRON+ADV, V+N+ADV: NO PASSIVE

NOTE **Depress** is a slightly more formal word for **get down**.

get down to When you **get down to** something, you start doing it seriously and with a lot of attention. ❏ *I got down to work... Let's get down to business... These problems that we have never got down to tackling.*

V+ADV+PREP

★get in

1 If you **get in** a place such as a car, house, or room, you go inside it. ❏ *Never get in a stranger's car... He nearly knocked me over in his eagerness to get in the house... I walked to the van, got in and drove away.*

V+PREP, V+ADV

2 When someone or something **gets in**, they arrive at a place where people are expecting them to be. ❏ *He asked if you'd ring back when you got in... What time does the coach get in, do you know?... He's got an obsession about staff getting in on time.*

V+ADV

3 If you **get in** a building, you succeed in gaining admission to it. ❑ *Nobody could get in or out without a pass... 'We went to the late show.'—'Oh, you managed to get in, did you?'... It cost three pounds to get in.*

V+ADV,
V+PREP

4 If you **get** something **in** from outside, you bring it inside to protect it from the weather. ❑ *You might at least have got the washing in.*

V+N+ADV,
V+ADV+N,
V+PRON+ADV

5 To **get** crops or the harvest **in** means to gather them from the land and take them to a particular place. ❑ *We didn't get the harvest in until Christmas, there was so much snow.*

V+N+ADV,
V+ADV+N,
V+PRON+ADV

6 If you **get in** some provisions or supplies, you buy them when you go shopping, because you have no more left. ❑ *We must remember to get some more coffee in.*

V+N+ADV,
V+ADV+N

7 If you **get** someone **in**, you ask them to come and help you or to do something for you. ❑ *Get an expert in to deal with faulty wiring... I'll get in the police if they keep up this racket much longer.*

V+N+ADV,
V+ADV+N,
V+PRON+ADV

NOTE **Call in** means almost the same as **get in**.

8 When a political party or a politician **gets in**, they are elected. ❑ *What would Labour do if they got in ?... She got in by more than 5,000 votes.*

V+ADV

9 If you **get in** something such as work, practice, or exercise, you arrange your time so that you are able to do it, even though you are very busy doing other things. ❑ *The idea was to get in a little golf... They get in all the work they can... I really need to get some practice in before the performance.*

V+ADV+N,
V+N+ADV,
V+PRON+ADV:
NO PASSIVE

NOTE **Fit in** means almost the same as **get in**.

10 If you **get** something **in** when lots of people are talking at the same time, you eventually succeed in saying something. ❑ *Phillip got a question in about the rates... Tinker had to get in the last word... 'What I wanted to say,' I finally got in, 'is that I've a set of instructions at home.'*

V+N+ADV,
V+ADV+N,
V+ADV+QUOTE,
V+PRON+ADV

get in on If you **get in on** an activity that is already taking place, you start taking part in it, often without being asked or invited to. [INFORMAL] ❑ *'He even gets in on the photography shows,' she said indignantly. ...studio assistants who got in on the act. ...getting in on the satellite system.*

V+ADV+PREP

★get into

1 If you **get into** a place, you enter it or reach it. ❑ *They got into the hut through a hole in the wall... I turned off the lights and got into bed... We got into the village at about one o'clock.*

V+PREP

2 If you **get into** an activity, you start being involved in it. ❑ *I always get into arguments with people... He was determined to get into politics... He had got into the campaign right at the end.*

V+PREP

3 If you **get into** a difficult situation, or if someone **gets** you **into** it, you are involved in it, often without intending to be. ❑ *Make sure you don't overspend and get into debt... There was no telling what sort of trouble she'd get into... 'I'm in trouble,' said Carmen, 'and you got me into it.'... He got himself into a frightful muddle recently.*

V+PREP,
V+PRON+PREP,
V+REFL+PREP,
V+N+PREP:
ERGATIVE,
NO PASSIVE

4 If you **get into** a particular habit or way of behaving, you start to have that habit or behave in that way. ❑ *She'd got into the habit of sulking... We tend to get into a certain way of thinking... I really need to get into a routine.*

V+PREP

5 If you **get into** a subject, you start getting interested in it. [INFORMAL] ❑ *She got into health foods and astrology... I just can't get into those sort of books.*

V+PREP

6 If you **get into** an organization such as a school, team, or club, you are accepted as a member of that organization. ❑ *There was no chance of her getting into University... Darwin failed to get into medical school at Cambridge... If I don't get into the first team this year, I'm not playing at all.*

V+PREP

7 If you **get into** your clothes, you put them on rather awkwardly or with difficulty. ❑ *I became so fat I couldn't get into any of my clothes. ...hopping on one foot to get into her shorts.*

V+PREP

8 You ask what **has got into** someone when you mean that they are behaving in a strange or unexpected way. [INFORMAL] ❑ *What's got into her these days?... I don't know what's got into you, Laing.*

V+PREP

get in with If you **get in with** someone, you flatter them and become friendly with them, often because you think that they can help you; used showing disapprov-

V+ADV+PREP

al. ❑ *She takes good care to get in with the people who matter... She had been married and divorced, and this chap got in with her.*

★get off

1 If you **get off** something that you have been standing, sitting, or lying on, you move your body from it, usually onto the ground. ❑ *She started to get off the table... He got off his bicycle... She was getting off the bed.* — V+PREP

2 If you **get off** a bus, train, or plane, you leave it. ❑ *When the train stopped, he got off... Get off at Mayfield Church... I had no reason for getting off the bus near the Palais.* — V+ADV, V+PREP

NOTE **Get out** means almost the same as **get off**.

3 When you **get off**, you leave a place. ❑ *I can't get off for another hour and a half... I have to be getting off now... Did Myra get off all right?* — V+ADV

NOTE **Get away** means almost the same as **get off**.

4 If you **get** someone **off** to a place, you send them there, or take them part of the way there. ❑ *I can't stay, I've got to get the children off to school... We'll get these two young men off first, then we can sort things out... Some of the mothers wanted to get their kids off to bed.* — V+N+ADV, V+PRON+ADV: ALSO+to

5 If you **get** a letter, parcel, or message **off**, you send it. ❑ *He eventually got his letter off... Get this message off to the addressee.* — V+N+ADV, V+PRON+ADV, V+ADV+N

6 If you tell someone to **get off** a piece of land, you are telling them to leave a place where they should not be. ❑ *I told them to get off the university playing fields... A cop would tell the noisy kids to get off the street.* — V+PREP

7 If you tell someone to **get off** the phone, you are telling them to stop using it. ❑ *I told him to get off the phone... Will you kindly get off the phone – you've been on for hours.* — V+PREP

8 You say '**Get off**' to someone when you are telling them not to touch you, or not to touch something. ❑ *Colin kept trying to kiss me, so I told him to get off... Get off that cake, it's for tomorrow!* — IMPERATIVE, V+ADV, V+PREP

9 If you **get** something **off**, you remove it. ❑ *Get your shirt off... The top's stuck and I can't get it off. ...stains you can't get off your skin.* — V+N+ADV/PREP, V+PRON+ADV/PREP

10 If you **get** something **off** someone, you succeed in persuading them to give it to you. [INFORMAL] ❑ *They're more concerned with getting a meal off us... I'll get some money off my dad.* — V+N+PREP, V+PRON+PREP

11 If you **get** time **off**, you do not have to go to work during that period. ❑ *Years ago, a nanny was lucky to get an afternoon off a week... I wouldn't get next Monday off... She can't get time off to go to the clinic.* — V+N+ADV, V+PRON+ADV: NO PASSIVE

12 If you **get off** when you have done something wrong, or if someone **gets** you **off**, you receive only a small punishment for what you have done. ❑ *He got off with a £50 fine... She had her suspicions that she would not get off so easily... 'Do you think you'll get her off?'—'I'm not a lawyer!'* — V+ADV, V+PRON+ADV, V+N+ADV: ERGATIVE

13 If you **get off** the subject that you are talking about, you change it and start to talk about something else instead. If you **get off** the point in a discussion or argument, you start talking about things that are not relevant to it. ❑ *I think we'd better get off this subject... Let's get off politics and get onto the real issues here... Michael, you're getting off the point.* — V+PREP

14 If you **get off** or **get off** to sleep, you succeed in falling asleep in spite of something that makes it difficult for you to sleep. [BRITISH] ❑ *I just couldn't get off last night.* — V+ADV: USUALLY+to

get off on
If you **get off on** something, you become very excited by it. [INFORMAL] ❑ *I saw you watching the fight and getting off on it... Rock-climbing is such a high – I really get off on it.* — V+ADV+PREP

get off with
If you **get off with** someone, you begin a romantic or sexual relationship with them. [BRITISH, INFORMAL] ❑ *Mike thinks I'm trying to get off with his girlfriend... If a man's getting off with a girl, people notice it.* — V+ADV+PREP

★get on

1 If you **get on** an object, you move your body so that you are sitting, standing, or lying on it. ❑ *I'd get on my horse and go out to her place... He tried to get on the wall but it was too high.* — V+PREP

2 If you **get on** a bus, train, or plane, you get into it. ❑ *She got on the bus every* — V+PREP, *morning... Some new passengers were getting on.* V+ADV

NOTE **Board** is a more formal word for **get on**.

3 If you **get on** the telephone to someone, or if you **get** them **on** it, you talk to V+PREP,
them on the telephone. ❑ *He got on the phone to President Thompson... Mrs. Callahan* V+N+PREP,
spent days trying to get Lieutenant Donovan on the phone... Get him on the phone at once! V+PRON+PREP:
NO PASSIVE

4 If you **get** a piece of clothing **on**, you dress yourself in it. ❑ *Get your coat on... I* V+N+ADV,
left the pyjamas on the bed and told him to get them on... Amy told Paul to get on his san- V+PRON+ADV,
dals. V+ADV+N

NOTE **Put on** means almost the same as **get on**.

5 If you **get on** with an activity, you start doing it or continue doing it. ❑ *Let me* V+ADV:
get on with my dinner... Perhaps we can get on with the meeting... He suggested to his col- USUALLY+with
league that perhaps they should get on.

6 If you ask how someone **is getting on** with an activity, you are asking about V+ADV:
their progress. ❑ *Sylvia asked politely how Paul was getting on at school... How are you get-* ALSO+with
ting on?... It's all to do with how he's getting on with his painting.

NOTE **Get along** means almost the same as **get on**.

7 If you **get on** in your career, you are successful. [BRITISH] ❑ *She's got to study to* V+ADV:
get on... I must get on in my job because of the children... You have to push yourself to get ALSO+in
on in the academic world.

NOTE **Get ahead** means almost the same as **get on**.

8 To **get on** without someone or something means to manage to continue or suc- V+ADV:
ceed without them. ❑ *The party will get on better without him... If they cannot get on* ALSO+without
without help, what's the point of employing them?... We'll just have to get on as best we
can.

9 If you **get on** with someone, you like them and have a friendly relationship with V+ADV,
them. ❑ *It's funny how they don't get on, Mark and Cyril... You seem to be getting on well* V+ADV+with,
with the Chairman... The two communities are not prepared to get on together. V+ADV+together:
RECIPROCAL

NOTE **Get along** means almost the same as **get on**.

10 If someone **gets on** a committee or a television or radio programme, or **gets** V+PREP,
themselves **on** it, they are successful in being accepted to take part in it. ❑ *Ford is* V+REFL+PREP
likely to get on the board of the new financial company... Perhaps they would even get on the
Ed Sullivan show... She's hoping to get herself on the panel for 'Any Questions'.

11 If you say that someone **is getting on**, you mean that they are old. [INFORMAL] V+ADV
❑ *Now I'm getting on, these stairs are a little difficult for me... They were getting on in years*
now.

12 If you say that time **is getting on**, you mean that there is not much time left V+ADV
before something is expected to happen, or before something must be done.

get on at If you **get on at** someone, you continually criticize them in an un- V+ADV+PREP
kind way. ❑ *I didn't want him getting on at you.*

NOTE **Keep on at** means almost the same as **get on at**.

get on for If something **is getting on for** an amount, it is nearly that amount. V+ADV+PREP
❑ *This building must be getting on for four hundred years old... I am getting on for twenty*
and have become engaged... It was getting on for four o' clock.

get on to, get onto

1 If you **get on to** a particular topic, you start talking about it in a lecture or con- V+ADV+PREP
versation after you have been talking about something else. ❑ *That's something we'll*
get on to in the future... Bobby and Denise got on to talking about old movies... I don't know
how we got on to this.

2 If you **get on to** someone, you contact them. [BRITISH] ❑ *I'll get on to her right* V+ADV+PREP
away... Get straight on to the department chief about it... John, I want you to get on to Cen-
tral Records.

3 If someone in authority **gets onto** you, they find out about something that you V+ADV+PREP
have been trying to keep secret. ❑ *The police got on to the infiltrators... I don't imagine*
they will get on to this if we keep quiet... It wasn't long before the Ministry of Information got
on to him.

★get out

1 If you **get out** of a place, you leave it. ❑ *We got out of the car... Brody got out of* V+ADV:
bed... I'm going to get out of New York... She got out and slammed the door. USUALLY+of

2 If you **get** someone **out** of a place, you help or order them to leave it. ❑ *The safest way to save his life was to get him out of the country... It would take hours for the Marines to get their wounded out... Get me out of here!*

V+N+ADV,
V+PRON+ADV:
USUALLY+of

3 If you **get** someone **out** of a difficult or dangerous situation, you help them to escape from it. ❑ *Who got you out of that mess in Omaha?... I got you into this and now I must get you out.*

V+PRON+ADV,
V+N+ADV:
USUALLY+of

♦ A **getout** is something which helps you to avoid or prevent an unwanted situation. ❑ *What we need is a safe getout... Insurance companies always have a getout clause of some kind.*

N-COUNT,
ADJECTIVE

4 If you **get out**, you go to places and meet people, because you want to have an enjoyable and interesting life. ❑ *Get out and enjoy yourself... You've got to get out and make friends.*

V+ADV

NOTE **Go out** means almost the same as **get out**.

5 If you **get** something **out**, you take it out of the place or container that it is in. ❑ *I got my little wireless out of the rucksack... 'Where's my mug?'—'I thought you just got it out.'... He got out his book and started to read.*

V+N+ADV,
V+PRON+ADV,
V+ADV+N:
ALSO+of

6 If you **get** dirt or other unwanted substances **out** of something, you remove them from it. ❑ *I couldn't get the stain out of your green dress.*

V+N+ADV,
V+PRON+ADV:
ALSO+of

7 If you **get out** a product or a piece of work, you manufacture it or produce it so that it is available to people. ❑ *The American Cancer Society got out its first report in 1954... They can't get the book out before Christmas.*

V+ADV+N,
V+N+ADV,
V+PRON+ADV

NOTE **Bring out** means almost the same as **get out**.

8 If you **get** something **out** that you are trying to say, you manage to say it. ❑ *She couldn't get a word out for the moment... He was sobbing so hard he couldn't get anything out.*

V+N+ADV,
V+PRON+ADV

9 If news or information **gets out**, it becomes known. ❑ *The news got out in the end... The word got out that he would go ahead.*

V+ADV,
V+ADV+REPORT

NOTE **Leak out** and **come out** mean almost the same as **get out**.

10 If you **get out** of something such as an organization or club, you leave it and stop being a member of it. ❑ *The EU? The sooner we get out the better.*

V+ADV:
USUALLY+of

NOTE **Pull out** means almost the same as **get out**.

11 In cricket, if you **get** a batsman **out**, you end their innings, for example by bowling the ball and hitting the wicket, or catching the ball after they have hit it.

V+N+ADV,
V+PRON+ADV

★get out of

1 If you **get** pleasure or satisfaction **out of** something that you do or experience, you enjoy it and think that it is worthwhile. ❑ *We all got a great deal of pleasure out of our school days... She got a lot of fun out of sweeping the front porch of the restaurant... I think she got more out of the course than I did.*

V+N+ADV+PREP

2 If you **get out of** doing something, you avoid doing it. ❑ *She always got out of washing up... We'll do anything to get out of work... I had to go to school, and if I could have got out of it, I would.*

V+ADV+PREP

NOTE **Wriggle out of** means almost the same as **get out of**.

3 If you **get** something **out of** someone, you persuade them to give it you, even though they do not really want to. ❑ *Next time Jim turns up we can get a few pounds out of him. ...trying to get some kind of confession out of me.*

V+N+ADV+PREP,
V+PRON+ADV+PREP

4 If you **get out of** a habit or an activity that you do regularly, you stop doing it. ❑ *If I get out of my routine, I'm finished!*

V+ADV+PREP

★get over

1 If you **get over** an illness or other unpleasant experience, you recover from it. ❑ *Have you got over the shock?... George did not get over his homesickness for some time... I'm glad to hear you have got over your cold.*

V+PREP

2 If you **get over** a problem or difficulty, you find a way of dealing with it. ❑ *One mother got over this problem by leaving her baby with someone else... The unhappy situation in the Labour Party could be got over if we changed to the American system.*

V+PREP

3 If you say that you cannot **get over** an unexpected event or a surprising fact, you mean that you find it difficult to believe that it happened or is true. ❑ *Sergeant Brown couldn't get over it as Evans solemnly handed over the money he had stolen... She could not get over the fact that someone so handsome could be so unlikeable.*

V+PREP:
WITH NEGATIVE

4 If you **get** an idea, argument, or suggestion **over**, you succeed in making other people understand it. ❑ *This is the only way I know of getting my message over to you clearly... One must first get over the idea that this method is completely new... How do I get it over to you?*

NOTE **Get across** means almost the same as **get over**.

V+N+ADV,
V+ADV+N,
V+PRON+ADV:
USUALLY+to

5 If you **get over** to a place, you go there or arrive there. If you **get** someone **over** to it, you arrange for them to come and visit you. ❑ *We could get over to your house by about six o'clock... I thought I might get him over to dinner one evening. ...the bureaucratic obstacles to getting her son over from Jamaica.*

V+ADV,
V+PRON+ADV,
V+N+ADV:
ERGATIVE,
NO PASSIVE

get over with If you **get** something **over with**, you do and complete something unpleasant that must be done. ❑ *Can we just get this questioning over with?... He wanted to get this miserable business over with as quickly as possible... Give Woods his final warning now and get it over with.*

V+N+ADV+with,
V+PRON+ADV+with

★get round

1 → See **get around**

2 If you **get round** someone, you persuade them to let you do or have something, by flattering them. ❑ *She could always get round him in the end... Bryan failed to get round Joan.*

V+PREP:
HAS PASSIVE

NOTE **Win over** means almost the same as **get round**.

3 If you **get round** when you are in a race, you manage to finish it. ❑ *I felt really tired, but I did get round the course... Schumacher got round in just over two hours and twenty minutes.*

V+ADV,
V+PREP

get round to → See get around to

★get through

1 If you **get through** a task, you succeed in finishing it. ❑ *It is difficult to get through this amount of work in such a short time... We managed to get through our meeting early... Exercises are not a chore to be got through, but a means of training your body... As soon as I get through with this washing, I'll help you.*

V+PREP:
HAS PASSIVE,
ALSO+with

2 If you **get through** a difficult or unpleasant experience, or someone or something **gets** you **through** it, you survive it. ❑ *He was going to get through the war and go home... She needs her coffee to get through the day... My wits got me through. ...the pain of adolescence that she got me through.*

V+ADV/PREP,
V+PRON+ADV/PREP,
V+N+ADV/PREP:
ERGATIVE,
NO PASSIVE

3 If a person or an idea **gets through** to you, you understand what they say or mean. ❑ *Howard, how do I get through to you?... The actor really got through to the audience that night... As the idea got through, she smiled. ...words which somehow will get through to the child.*

V+ADV:
USUALLY+to

4 If you **get through** to someone on the telephone, you succeed in contacting them. ❑ *I telephoned Juliet in hospital and got through without difficulty... Sorry you couldn't get through on the phone last week... I've been trying for a whole hour to get through to you.*

V+ADV:
ALSO+to

5 If something **gets through** to a place, it finally succeeds in reaching that place. ❑ *...information that got through to Russia... I expect the letters just aren't getting through... The real emergencies were not getting through to the hospital.*

V+ADV:
ALSO+to

6 If you **get through** an examination, or if someone or something **gets** you **through** it, you pass it. [BRITISH] ❑ *They haven't got a chance of getting through... He qualifies if he gets through his two subjects this year... It's hard work and nothing else that gets you through.*

V+ADV/PREP,
V+PRON+ADV/PREP,
V+N+ADV/PREP:
ERGATIVE,
NO PASSIVE

7 If you **get through** to a particular stage in a competition, or if someone or something **gets** you **through** to it, you succeed in reaching that stage. ❑ *Steve Davis has got through to the final again... It was only luck that got us through to the next round. ...if United get through the 6th Round of the cup.*

V+ADV,
V+PRON+ADV,
V+N+ADV:
ERGATIVE,
NO PASSIVE

8 If you **get through** an amount of something, you use it completely. [BRITISH] ❑ *When he got through all his money he went back to Canada... I got through about twelve pounds' worth of drink.*

V+PREP

NOTE **Run through** means almost the same as **get through**.

9 If a law or proposal **gets through**, it is officially approved by something such as a parliament or committee. ❑ *If this new White Paper gets through, there will be no subsidized meals... The proposals might not have been able to get through Congress... The Bill got*

V+ADV/PREP,
V+N+ADV/PREP,
V+PRON+ADV/PREP:
ERGATIVE

get up

through all its stages and became law... The opposition got the amendment through with a majority of 117.

★**get to**

1 When you **get to** a place, you arrive there. ❑ *It was midnight before we got to the village.*   V+PREP

2 If you **get to** doing something, you gradually begin to do it without intending to. [INFORMAL] ❑ *I got to thinking how lonely she must be.*   V+PREP

NOTE **Fall to** is a literary expression for **get to**.

3 If an experience or emotion **gets to** you, it affects you strongly, although you try not to let it. [INFORMAL] ❑ *Don't let it get to you... The horror of war was beginning to get to me.*   V+PREP

★**get together**

1 When people **get together**, they meet in order to discuss something or to spend time together. ❑ *Workers and supervisors get together to discuss their grievances... Do you think we could get together at Christmas? ...getting childminders together in local self-help groups... He got together a band of thieves.*   V+ADV, V+N+ADV, V+ADV+N, V+PRON+ADV: ERGATIVE

♦ A **get-together** is an informal meeting or party. ❑ *We're having a little get-together to celebrate Helen's promotion.*   N-COUNT

2 If you **get** several things **together**, you collect them and put them all in one place. ❑ *I got my letters and papers together... Well, as long as you've got all your own stuff together, too... I got together the rest of the notes and fastened them with rubber bands.*   V+N+ADV, V+ADV+N, V+PRON+ADV

NOTE **Gather up** means almost the same as **get together**, and **assemble** is a more formal word.

3 If you **get together** a plan or a meeting of some kind, you organize it or arrange for other people to take part in it. ❑ *The Defense Front got together a sizeable demonstration of support... Have you got that syllabus together yet?... I don't know whether he's got the time to get anything together yet.*   V+ADV+N, V+N+ADV, V+PRON+ADV

4 If you **get** money **together**, you succeed in getting all the money that you need in order to pay for something. ❑ *Almost all of the children had got the money together themselves... Somehow we have to get the fees together.*   V+N+ADV, V+PRON+ADV, V+ADV+N

NOTE **Scrape up** means almost the same as **get together**, and **raise** is a more formal word.

5 If you **get** yourself **together**, you succeed in controlling your feelings so that you behave calmly and reasonably. ❑ *Gladys got herself together enough to see a lawyer.*   V+REFL+ADV

NOTE **Pull together** means almost the same as **get together**.

★**get up**

1 When someone or something **gets up**, they move from a lower position or level to a higher one. To **get** someone or something **up** means to move them from a lower position or level to a higher one. ❑ *I knew they'd have difficulty getting up that mountain... You'll never get him up those stairs.*   V+ADV/PREP, V+N+ADV, V+PRON+ADV/PREP: ERGATIVE

2 If you **get up**, you rise to a standing position after you have been sitting or lying down. ❑ *I had to get up from my stool... He got up off the floor... She got up and strode across the room.*   V+ADV

3 When you **get up**, or when someone **gets** you **up**, you get out of bed. ❑ *Morris decided it was time to get up... Don't get me up in the morning... We had until 7.15 to get ourselves up... Then we had to get the children up and dressed.*   V+ADV, V+N/PRON+ADV, V+REFL+ADV: ERGATIVE

4 If you **get up** to a place, you visit it or travel there, especially when the place is farther north than you or is in a city. ❑ *He'll have to get up to London for the day... I want to get up there again this summer... You'd better get up to his flat and sort things out.*   V+ADV: WITH A

5 If you **get up** something such as a public event or meeting, you arrange it or organize it, especially with very little preparation. [OLD-FASHIONED] ❑ *The women got up a march and picket to move them out of the school... An impromptu dance was got up in his honour.*   V+ADV+N, V+N+ADV, V+PRON+ADV

NOTE **Fix up** means almost the same as **get up**.

6 If someone **has got** themselves **up** in unusual or strange clothes, or if they **are got up** in them, they are dressed in unusual or strange clothes. ❑ *...the days when band leaders got themselves up in braided jackets... Several people were got up as frontiersmen. ...children got up in spaceman outfits.*   V+REFL+ADV: OR PASSIVE: V+ADV: USUALLY+A

The symbol ★ shows key phrasal verbs

NOTE **Rig out** means almost the same as **get up**.

♦ A **get-up** is an unusual or strange set of clothes. ❑ *Who does she think she is, in that get-up?* — N-COUNT

7 If the wind or a storm **gets up**, it starts to blow very strongly. — V+ADV

★**get up to** When you talk about what someone **gets up to**, you are referring to what they do, especially when it is something you do not approve of. [BRITISH, INFORMAL] ❑ *What did you get up to while I was away?... When I found out what they used to get up to I was absolutely horrified... I don't really think he'd get up to anything behind my back.* — V+ADV+PREP

get with If you **get with** it, you become aware of the latest events, developments, or ideas. [INFORMAL] ❑ *Get with it. Go and see Tess, take your partner.* — V+PREP+*it*

ginger /dʒɪndʒəʳ/ (gingers, gingering, gingered)

ginger up If you **ginger** something **up**, you make it more interesting and exciting. [INFORMAL] ❑ *...sharply gingering up what was left.* — V+ADV+N, V+PRON+ADV, V+N+ADV

NOTE **Spice up** means almost the same as **ginger up**.

give /gɪv/ (gives, giving, gave, given)

★give away

1 If you **give** something **away**, you give it to someone without taking money in return. ❑ *She has given away jewellery worth millions of pounds... I could not decide whether to keep the money he left me or give it away... Her little boy had cried so when they had given the dog away.* — V+ADV+N, V+PRON+ADV, V+N+ADV

♦ A **give-away** is something which you are given free, for example a free gift that you get when you buy something else. ❑ *There was a give-away calendar on the wall.* — N-COUNT, ADJECTIVE

2 If you **give away** information that is meant to be secret, you let other people know about it, sometimes by mistake. ❑ *I didn't feel like giving away more information than I had to... Don't give the story away, silly!... He often wondered what the twins thought of him, but they gave nothing away.* — V+ADV+N, V+N+ADV, V+PRON+ADV

NOTE **Reveal** is a more formal word for **give away**.

♦ A **give-away** is an action or remark by someone which reveals something that they were trying to keep secret. — N-SING

3 If someone **gives away** an advantage, they accidentally cause their opponent or enemy to have that advantage. ❑ *We gave away a silly goal... Military advantages should not be given away.* — V+ADV+N, V+PRON+ADV, V+N+ADV

NOTE **Concede** means almost the same as **give away**.

4 If you **give** yourself **away**, your actions or words accidentally reveal something about you which you wanted to keep hidden. If you **give** someone else **away**, you reveal something about them. ❑ *I was too afraid that I might give myself away by saying or doing something incomprehensible... His hands were beginning to give him away.* — V+REFL+ADV, V+PRON+ADV, V+N+ADV

NOTE **Betray** is a formal or literary word for **give away**.

5 When people get married in a church, the person who officially presents the bride to her husband during the ceremony **gives** her **away**. ❑ *She asked her uncle to give her away... He was going to give his daughter away.* — V+PRON+ADV, V+N+ADV, V+ADV+N

★give back

1 If you **give** something **back**, you return it to the person who gave it to you or who it belongs to. ❑ *I gave the trowel back... You've got to give them back... He gave them back to her... I gave the book back to Indhar... I gave back his ring and his jacket... I gave her back her newspaper... He gave the driver back his license... Did you give me the keys back?* — V+N+ADV, V+PRON+ADV: ALSO+*to*: OR V+ADV+N, V+PRON+ADV+N, V+N+ADV+N, V+PRON+N+ADV

2 If something **gives back** a quality, characteristic, or freedom that someone has lost, it restores to them that quality, characteristic, or freedom. ❑ *The new Parliament at last gave back a voice to those who had been silent for a generation. ...so that we can give hope back to young people... He brought before them all the warriors he had defeated and gave them back their freedom.* — V+ADV+N, V+N+ADV: USUALLY+*to*: ALSO V+PRON+ADV+N, V+N+ADV+N

★give in

1 If you **give in**, you admit that you will have to do something you have been trying not to do, or that you will not be able to do something you wanted to do. ❑ *I resolved not to give in... We mustn't give in to threats... They will argue and fight against it,* — V+ADV: ALSO+*to*

but they will give in if they see that you are sure it's the right thing to do.

NOTE **Surrender** means almost the same as **give in**.

2 If you **give in** a piece of work, you hand it to a teacher or to someone who will assess it. ❏ *...students giving in dissertations... You have to give in any project-based work by the end of next week.*   V+ADV+N, V+N+ADV, V+PRON+ADV

NOTE **Hand in** means almost the same as **give in**.

give off

1 When objects or processes **give off** heat, light, smoke, or sound, they release it into the air. ❏ *...the tremendous heat given off by the fire... This gas, in the presence of oxygen, gives off an intensely hot flame... The brake-pads started to melt, giving off a smell like burnt toast.*   V+ADV+N

NOTE **Produce** means almost the same as **give off**.

2 If a person **gives off** a particular quality, you notice it very easily in their appearance or actions. ❏ *Politicians always give off an air of importance... He gave off a tremendous intellectual aura.*   V+ADV+N

NOTE **Radiate** means almost the same as **give off**.

3 If you **give off** doing something, you completely stop doing it. [BRITISH, INFORMAL] ❏ *Chaplin never gave off doing bits of business for the amusement of friends or guests.*   V+ADV+N/-ING: NO PASSIVE

NOTE **Give over** means almost the same as **give off**.

give onto If a door or window **gives onto** a particular place, it leads straight there, or has a view over it. ❏ *The narrow steps give onto St. James's Park... The door gave onto a path which skirted the house.*   V+PREP

NOTE **Open onto** means almost the same as **give onto**.

★give out

1 If you **give out** a number of things, you distribute them among a number of different people. ❏ *They also give out information about courses for teachers of English... We made the tea and I gave it out, watched by her mother... Large sheets of paper were given out.*   V+ADV+N, V+PRON+ADV, V+N+ADV

NOTE **Hand out** means almost the same as **give out**.

2 If something **gives out**, it stops working, because it is old, damaged, or tired. ❏ *The fuse in a plug will give out occasionally... Both tyres had finally given out... My voice was about to give out.*   V+ADV

NOTE **Pack up** is a more informal expression for **give out**.

3 When a supply of something **gives out**, there is no more left. ❏ *Turn all the taps on until the water gives out... The oxygen gave out.*   V+ADV

NOTE **Run out** means almost the same as **give out**.

4 When news or information **is given out**, it is announced, sometimes unofficially. ❏ *On the same day it was given out that fresh documents had been discovered... Uncle Nick stopped going to church, and gave it out that he was writing a book.*   PASSIVE: V+ADV+REPORT, ALSO V+*it*+ADV

5 When someone or something **gives out** light, heat, or a sound, they produce light, heat, or sound in a noticeable way. [LITERARY] ❏ *Tail lights give out red reflections onto the wet road... The stove still gave out a dying heat... She hugged her knees closer and gave out a loud girlish laugh.*   V+ADV+N

6 If you **give out** something such as a scream or a sigh, you sigh, scream, or make some other sound. ❏ *He gave out a scream of pain.*   V+PREP: NO PASSIVE

NOTE **Let out** means almost the same as **give out**.

give over

1 If you **give over** an activity, you suddenly stop doing it. [INFORMAL] ❏ *I gave over my restless re-arranging and sat by the windows.*   V+ADV+N: NO PASSIVE

NOTE **Give off** means almost the same as **give over**.

2 If you tell someone to **give over**, you want them to stop doing something that is annoying you. [INFORMAL] ❏ *If you don't give over, I'll smack you... She asked me to give over humming.*   V+ADV: ALSO+-ING

NOTE **Leave off** means almost the same as **give over**.

give over to

1 If something **is given over to** a particular activity or purpose, it is used only for that activity or purpose. ❏ *The response was so great that a whole page had to be given*   V+ADV+N+PREP, V+N+ADV+PREP, V+PRON+ADV+PREP:

The symbol ★ shows key phrasal verbs

over to readers' letters... The hills of the north and west are given over mainly to sheep farm-   USUALLY PASSIVE
ing... They gave over the remaining lodgings to her senior courtiers.

2 If you **give** yourself **over to** an activity, you spend all your time and effort do-   V+REFL+ADV+PREP
ing it. ❑ *During this period Tim gave himself over to an orgy of pleasure... I gave myself over*
to dreams for a few minutes.

NOTE **Give up to** means almost the same as **give over to**.

3 If you **give** something **over to** someone, you let them have it, so that they can   V+N+ADV+PREP,
look after it or have responsibility for it. ❑ *I'm quite thankful to give the business over to*   V+PRON+ADV+PREP
the girls now... We had it formally given over to us about three weeks ago.

★give up

1 If you **give up** an activity or belief, you stop doing it or believing in it. ❑ *She*   V+ADV+N,
never completely gave up hope... I'll never be able to give up smoking... 'Sugar?'—'No, I gave   V+ADV+-ING,
it up during the war.'   V+PRON+ADV,
   V+N+ADV

2 If you **give up** a task, you stop doing it because it is too difficult, or because you   V+ADV+N,
are no longer interested in it. ❑ *Even Ruskin gave up the attempt in despair... Gaskell con-*   V+PRON+ADV,
sidered ways of making a kite and gave it up... You couldn't keep it clean, although they nev-   V+ADV+-ING,
er gave up trying. ...but the main thing is not to give up.   V+ADV

3 If you **give** something **up**, you allow someone else to have it, because you no   V+N+ADV,
longer need it or they need it more than you do. ❑ *They expect men to give their seats*   V+ADV+N,
up to them in buses... He even gave up his bed, while he and Eddie slept outside.   V+PRON+ADV:
   ALSO+*to*

NOTE **Relinquish** is a formal word for **give up**.

4 If police or enemy troops are looking for you and you **give** yourself **up**, you al-   V+REFL+ADV
low yourself to be arrested or captured. ❑ *Griffiths replied that he could not give himself*
up... Goodall again urged him to give himself up.

NOTE **Surrender** means almost the same as **give up**.

5 To **give** someone **up** who is wanted by the police means to tell the police where   V+PRON+ADV,
that person is so that they can be arrested. ❑ *They interrogated her forcefully, but still she*   V+N+ADV
wouldn't give me up.

NOTE **Betray** means almost the same as **give up**.

6 If you **give** someone **up** that you are having a relationship with, you decide to   V+PRON+ADV,
end the relationship. ❑ *You haven't tried to make her give him up?... Really, Daisy and I*   V+N+ADV
gave each other up years ago.

NOTE **Throw over** is a more informal expression for **give up**.

7 If you **give up** your time to do something for someone else, you spend a lot of   V+ADV+N
your own time doing it. ❑ *...a very elderly man known as George who gave up his Satur-*
day mornings to play for the team... She got advice from the more established runners who
gave up their time to help the newcomers like herself.

8 If you **give up** your job, you resign from it. ❑ *She'd had to give up her job... I see*   V+ADV+N,
that you gave up teaching to nurse your mother... He had to work so hard for £30 a week   V+PRON+ADV,
that he gave it up, and looked for another job.   V+N+ADV

NOTE **Quit** means almost the same as **give up**.

9 You say **give** it **up** for someone when you are asking an audience to applaud   V+*it*+ADV+PREP
someone. [INFORMAL] ❑ *Ladies and gentlemen, our number one winner tonight, please, give*
it up for Miss Tara.

give up on If you **give up on** someone or something, you stop trying to do   V+ADV+PREP
something that involves them, because you think you will never succeed or understand them. ❑ *Ever hopeful, McKellen never gave up on the cinema... So many women give*
up on men after pursuing them. ...a kind of mystery that one gives up on.

NOTE **Abandon** means almost the same as **give up on**.

give up to If you **give** yourself or your life **up to** a particular thing, you devote   V+REFL+ADV+PREP,
all your time, thought, and energy to it. ❑ *She gave herself up to an inner vision of hap-*   V+N+ADV+PREP
piness... For months after this happened I gave myself up to dreams of revenge. ...a life given
up to sexual excess.

NOTE **Give over to** means almost the same as **give up to**.

glance /glɑːns, glæns/ **(glances, glancing, glanced)**

glance off If something **glances off** an object, it hits the object at an angle   V+PREP,
and bounces away in another direction. ❑ *The ball glanced off his foot into the net... The*   V+ADV
light glanced off her teeth and her thick glasses.

For a full explanation of all grammatical labels, see pages xiii-xx

glaze /gleɪz/ (glazes, glazing, glazed)

glaze over If your eyes **glaze over**, they become dull in appearance and your   V+ADV
expression shows that you are not paying attention. ❏ *I can see people's eyes start to
glaze over at this point... It is obvious that their eyes glaze over at long lists of technical
terms.*

glory /glɔːri/ (glories, glorying, gloried)

glory in If you **glory in** a situation or activity, you behave in a way which shows   V+PREP
that you enjoy it very much. ❏ *The women were glorying in this new-found freedom. ...a
beard of the brightest carrot-orange, a beard that any pirate could have gloried in.*
[NOTE] **Revel in** means almost the same as **glory in**.

gloss /glɒs, AM glɔːs/ (glosses, glossing, glossed)

gloss over If you **gloss over** a problem, a mistake, or an embarrassing mo-   V+PREP:
ment, you ignore it or deal with it quickly in order to try and make it seem unim-   HAS PASSIVE
portant. ❏ *'I was leaving anyway,' I said, to gloss over the tense moment... Truffaut glosses
over such contradictions... In an election campaign much of this could be glossed over.*

go /goʊ/ (goes, going, went, gone)

> ☑ In American English, **around** is much more common than **round**.

★go about

1 The way you **go about** a task or problem is the way you deal with it. ❏ *I'd been*   V+PREP
*wondering how to go about it... Clearly we've gone about this the wrong way. ...a guide on
how to go about setting up a committee.*
[NOTE] **Tackle** means almost the same as **go about**.

2 When you **go about** a job or regular activity, you continue doing it in your   V+PREP
usual way. ❏ *He wanted to be left alone to go about his business... All along the coast, people went about their usual daily chores.*

3 When you **go about** a place, you move wherever you want to in it. ❏ *I could go*   V+PREP,
about the house as freely as I liked... I learned with difficulty to go about the streets amid   V+ADV
*cat-calls... He'd have liked to keep me at home, to stop me going about, but he couldn't do
anything about it.*

4 If you **go about** doing something, you do it regularly. [BRITISH] ❏ *...learning that*   V+ADV+-ING
one cannot go about hurting others.
[NOTE] **Go around** means almost the same as **go about**.

5 If you **go about** in a particular way, you usually dress or behave in that way.   V+ADV:
[BRITISH] ❏ *Why couldn't he be like other men and go about in his shirt sleeves?... Traders*   WITH A
like our grandfathers went about on foot.
[NOTE] **Go around** means almost the same as **go about**.

6 If you **go about** with someone, or if you **go about** together, you regularly   V+ADV+with,
meet them and go to different places with them. ❏ *You used to go about with him very*   V+ADV+together:
frequently... They seldom went about together.   RECIPROCAL

7 If a story or piece of news **is going about**, a lot of people hear it or talk about   V+ADV
it. [BRITISH] ❏ *Blood-curdling stories were going about concerning what they intended to
do... The rumour went about that he had had some hand in getting her the sack.*
[NOTE] **Go around** means almost the same as **go about**, and **circulate** is a more
formal word.

go after

1 If you **go after** someone, you follow them or chase them, sometimes in order to   V+PREP
attack them. ❏ *Don't you think you should go after Frederica? She seemed quite upset...
Luca Brasi went after them and the story is that he killed six men.*

2 If you **go after** something, you try to get it. ❏ *My husband had gone after a job...*   V+PREP
Go after a better deal. ...a goal, something he can go after.

go against

1 If something **goes against** an idea, principle, or rule, it conflicts with it or   V+PREP
contradicts it. ❏ *The teaching of the Bible clearly goes against it... She'll just say something
that goes against everything I've been trying to say.*

2 If you **go against** someone or their advice or wishes, you do something differ-   V+PREP
ent from what they have advised you or want you to do. ❏ *One thing must be under-*

stood. *I will never go against you... They want to assert themselves, even if it means going against their parents' wishes at times.*

3 If a decision or judgement **goes against** someone, for example in a court of law, it is unfavourable to them, and they lose the case. ❑ *The verdict went against his brother... We would have abided by the Inspector's decision if it had gone against us.*   V+PREP

NOTE **Favour** means the opposite of **go against**.

4 If something **goes against** you, it happens in a way that is bad or unfortunate for you. ❑ *We have got one more chance. One more. But if it goes against us next time... He indicated that the war was going against them and would soon be brought to a close.*   V+PREP

5 If one group of soldiers **goes against** another, they attack them or prepare to attack. ❑ *We have picked three hundred to go against the British... Crazy Horse told the young men not to go against those other Indians far away.*   V+PREP

★go ahead

1 When someone **goes ahead** with something which they planned, promised, or asked permission to do, they begin to do it. If a plan or project **goes ahead**, the work involved starts to be done. ❑ *They are going ahead with the missile... The case will be discussed and he will be told whether or not he can go ahead... The unloading had gone ahead very briskly... The ballot will go ahead immediately.*   V+ADV: ALSO+*with*

NOTE **Proceed** is a more formal word for **go ahead**.

♦ If you give the **go-ahead** for a plan or project, or give someone the **go-ahead**, you give permission or approval to someone to start doing something. ❑ *You have the go-ahead from the Prime Minister.*   N-SING

2 You tell someone to **go ahead** when you are suggesting that they do something, or are permitting or challenging them to do it. ❑ *He said to go ahead if we arrived before him... 'Would you like to hear it?'—'Go ahead.'... He threatened to prosecute us, and I told him to go ahead.*   V+ADV: ALSO IMPERATIVE

3 If someone **goes ahead**, they go in front of someone else who is going in the same direction or to the same place. ❑ *You go ahead this time, we'll stay behind... The minibus went ahead of us.*   V+ADV: ALSO+*of*

4 A **go-ahead** person or organization is ambitious and tries hard to succeed, often by using new methods. ❑ *...its go-ahead young secretary. ...promising a 'dynamic and go-ahead Britain'.*   ADJECTIVE

NOTE **Enterprising** means almost the same as **go-ahead**.

★go along

1 If you **go along** in a particular direction or manner, you move in that direction or manner. ❑ *I went along to the recording room... I went along the corridor until I found a door open... We were going along fast on this dirt road when my car had a blow-out.*   V+ADV, V+PREP

2 When you **go along** to an event or to do something, you go there, often in a fairly casual way. ❑ *Go along and talk to a solicitor... It's a sort of party, that's all, and I said I might go along.*   V+ADV

3 If you do something as you **go along**, you do it while you are doing something else and often without any planning, rather than doing it as a separate task. ❑ *Record your answers as you go along... You have to add everything up as you go along... I recited poems that I made up as I went along.*   V+ADV

4 If you describe how something **is going along**, you describe how it is progressing. ❑ *It was going along nicely, as it had every night so far.*   V+ADV: WITH A

★go along with

1 If you **go along with** a person or idea, you agree with the person or idea, and accept that what they are saying is true. ❑ *I am willing to go along with Celli... I go along with the view that languages are essentially communication systems.*   V+ADV+PREP

NOTE **Support** means almost the same as **go along with**.

2 If you **go along with** a rule, decision, or policy, you accept it and obey it. ❑ *You agreed to go along with the decision... He is convinced that Rogers will go along with the deal voluntarily.*   V+ADV+PREP

NOTE **Abide by** is a more formal expression for **go along with**.

★go around

1 If you **go around** or **go round** a group of people or places, you visit them, or you attend to each of them in turn. ❑ *Michelle, will you quickly go round and collect the*   V+ADV, V+PREP *exercise books up?... If you're in London you can go around the art galleries and things like that.*

2 If you **go around** or **go round** a country or other place, you travel in that place and visit a lot of different things. ❏ *I'd like to go round Africa myself... One of them went around the world as a ship's steward... Interlaken was a very good centre for going round and seeing things.*   V+PREP, V+ADV

3 If you **go around** or **go round** a room, building, or other area, you walk through every part of it or make a circuit of it. ❏ *Bond went round the room and examined the windows... She went around the house making sure that all doors were locked... Let's go around the block before we go in... He took four hours to go round the golf course.*   V+PREP, V+ADV

4 If you **go around** or **go round** a bend, you move in a curving direction. ❏ *The car goes around a curve, and vanishes behind the trees. ...a nasty curve where the train track went round a bend.*   V+PREP

5 If you **go around** or **go round** an object or obstacle, you move in a circular direction so that you can get past it or get to the other side. ❏ *He went round the table... When the rifle was assembled he laid it on the bonnet of the car and went round to the boot again.*   V+PREP, V+ADV

6 If you **go around** or **go round** in a particular way, you dress or behave in that way very often or regularly. ❏ *The kids go around barefoot... They go round in stockinged feet to see who is in and who is out... Ann says Auntie Jo goes around the house with no clothes on in the mornings.*   V+ADV, V+PREP: WITH A

NOTE **Go about** means almost the same as **go around**.

7 If you **go around** or **go round** doing something, often something that other people disapprove of, you are in the habit of doing it or do it repeatedly. ❏ *I don't go around deliberately hurting people's feelings... They're always going round sticking posters on walls... You mustn't go around telling people things that aren't true.*   V+ADV+-ING

NOTE **Go about** means almost the same as **go around**.

8 If you **go around** or **go round** with someone, or if you **go around** or **go round** together, you regularly meet them and go to different places with them. ❏ *Don't go around with them... They go round with their fellow countrymen... Do you think it's wise for us to go round together like this?*   V+ADV+with, V+ADV+together: RECIPROCAL

NOTE **Go about** means almost the same as **go around**.

9 If a story or piece of news **is going around** or **going round**, a lot of people hear it or talk about it. ❏ *A rumour went round that he had after all survived... A lot of spooky stories began going around... But these days there are fewer jokes than usual going around this grim, grey city.*   V+ADV, V+PREP

NOTE **Go about** means almost the same as **go around**.

10 If an illness **is going around** or **going round** a group of people, a lot of them catch it. ❏ *'There's a virus going around,' he said. 'My wife had it last week.'*   V+ADV, V+PREP

11 If there is enough of something to **go around** or **go round**, there is enough of it to be shared among a group of people, or to do all the things for which it is needed. ❏ *There were never enough textbooks to go around... The money just won't go round... But the fact remains that there is plenty of food to go around.*   V+ADV, V+PREP

go at If you **go at** a task or activity, you start doing it in an energetic or enthusiastic way. ❏ *The breakfast arrived and he went at it like a starving refugee... He handed me the cables and I went at them for the customary hour... I went at it flat-out today.*   V+PREP

★go away

1 If you **go away**, you leave a place or a person's company. If you **go away** from home, you leave it and spend time somewhere else, especially as a holiday. ❏ *She went away to think about it... I want to be alone now. Just go away... She had gone away for a few days... What did you do over the summer? Did you go away?... Daddy is to go away on a business trip.*   V+ADV

♦ A bride's **going-away** outfit is the set of clothes which she puts on after the wedding before leaving on honeymoon. ❏ *I changed into my going-away outfit.*   ADJECTIVE

2 If something, especially a problem, **goes away**, it disappears. ❏ *Sometimes the fever lasts for a day or two and then goes away... The sounds seemed to be going away. ...those thoughts which came at night and would not go away.*   V+ADV

NOTE **Come back** means the opposite of **go away**.

*go back

1 If you **go back**, you return to a place where you were before. ❑ *In six weeks we've got to go back to West Africa... I went back to the kitchen and poured my coffee... It started to rain but I had not the strength to go back for an umbrella.*

V+ADV:
ALSO+to

2 If something **goes back** to a particular time in the past, it was made, built, or started at that time. ❑ *The shop goes back to 1707. ...French national leaders, going back at least as far as Joan of Arc... The countryman's recollections go back a long way.*

V+ADV:
WITH A

NOTE **Date back** means almost the same as **go back**.

3 If you are discussing something and **go back** to a time in the past, you begin to consider things that happened at that time. ❑ *To trace its origins, we have to go back some thirty million years... To understand how this state of affairs came about, we have to go back to colonial days.*

V+ADV:
ALSO+to

4 If you say that someone cannot **go back**, you mean that they can never again be in a situation that they were in before, because too many things have changed. ❑ *However much he wished it, he couldn't go back. He had shed the past... He had left home and there was no going back.*

V+ADV:
WITH NEGATIVE

5 If someone **goes back** to a partner that they had previously left, they start living with them again or having a relationship with them again. ❑ *Her lover went back to his wife.*

V+ADV:
USUALLY+to

6 When schools or schoolchildren **go back**, they start a new term after the holidays.

V+ADV

NOTE **Break up** means the opposite of **go back**.

7 When people on strike **go back**, they end the strike and start working again. ❑ *I say to those men, if you give in and go back now, many of you will lose your jobs.*

V+ADV

NOTE **Come out** means the opposite of **go back**.

8 When something which you have bought or borrowed **goes back**, you take it to the place where you got it, sometimes in order to change it. ❑ *These shoes will have to go back... The glasses have gone back to the wineshop.*

V+ADV:
ALSO+to

9 When the clocks **go back** in Britain in the autumn, everyone sets their clocks one hour earlier, to Greenwich Mean Time.

V+ADV

NOTE **Go forward** means the opposite of **go back**.

go back on If you **go back on** a promise, agreement, or statement, you do not do what you promised or agreed, or you deny what you said. ❑ *It wouldn't be fair, wouldn't be right, to go back on those promises... I can't go back on my word... Now you're going back on what you told me earlier.*

V+ADV+PREP

go back over If you **go back over** something, you consider it again. ❑ *He went back over the accounts of the inquest... There was no point in going back over it.*

V+ADV+PREP

*go back to

1 If you **go back to** something which you stopped doing or using, you start doing or using it again. ❑ *She had gone back to staring out of the window... No, I'm all right, go back to sleep... Now go back to your work!*

V+ADV+PREP

2 If you **go back to** a point in a discussion or conversation, you start talking about it again. ❑ *I think that goes back to what we were talking about earlier on... Going back to this point, there is a limited amount of government aid available.*

V+ADV+PREP

3 If things **go back to** normal or **go back to** a state, they return to the state they were in before something else happened. ❑ *Despite such feelings things soon went back to normal... The temperature went back to normal... Things will merely go back to being as bad as they were a month ago.*

V+ADV+PREP

NOTE **Revert to** is a more formal expression for **go back to**.

go before

☑ In meaning 2, the stress is on **go**.

1 You refer to what **has gone before** when you are referring to previous events, for example when you are comparing a situation with one in the past. ❑ *The meeting was different from any that had gone before. ...a topic which had nothing to do with what had gone before... Each stage depends on what has gone before.*

V+ADV

2 If people, problems, or cases **go before** a judge, court of law, or other authority, they are officially considered or investigated so that a decision or judgement can be

V+PREP

made. ❑ *The matter has gone before a grand jury.*

go below On a boat, if you go down the stairs into the living or   V+ADV,
sleeping area. ❑ *Quint went below and returned with two coils of rope... When the other*   V+PREP
three had gone below decks, Mandria turned to Ari.

★**go beyond** To **go beyond** a particular thing means to do something more ex-   V+PREP
treme, more serious, greater, or better. ❑ *They wanted to go beyond one-day strikes... In*
this series I have tried to go beyond the narrower meaning of the word civilised.... His inter-
ests went beyond political economy.

★**go by**

☑ In meaning 4, the stress is on **go**.

1 If you say that a period of time **has gone by**, you mean that it has passed.   V+ADV
❑ *Eight years went by... As time goes by more devices come on to the market... Sometimes*
hours go by without him saying a word... In years gone by, many problems came my way.

♦ **Bygone** means happening or existing a very long time ago. ❑ *...a home built to the*   ADJECTIVE
standards of a bygone age. ...empires established in bygone centuries.

2 If someone or something **goes by**, they pass you without stopping. ❑ *I saw a car*   V+ADV,
come along the street and I paused to let it go by... It was like watching a parade go by...   V+PREP
The small blue car goes by the opening between the shed and the end of the wall.

3 If someone **goes by** a place, they go there for a short time in order to do or get   V+PREP,
something. ❑ *Let's go by the store for a minute... I can go by and ask her.*   V+ADV

NOTE **Drop by** means almost the same as **go by**.

4 If you **go by** a particular thing, you use the information or guidance that it gives   V+PREP
you in order to do or understand something. ❑ *I try to go by reason as far as possible...*
'It's not much to go by.'—'All the same I'm pretty sure of it.'

NOTE **Go on** means almost the same as **go by**.

5 If you let someone's remarks or actions **go by**, you do not let them affect you.   V+ADV,
❑ *He was able to let these go by without feeling any anxiety... I let this comment on my*   V+PREP
meanness go by me.

★**go down**

1 When someone or something **goes down**, they move from a higher position to   V+PREP,
a lower one. ❑ *Frank quickly turned to go down the hill as fast as he could... She had heard*   V+ADV
the song break out as she was going down the stairs... At a colliery in Leicestershire the min-
ers refused to go down the pit. ...like a diver going down to the bottom of the ocean.

2 When someone or something **goes down**, they collapse or fall over. ❑ *He heard*   V+ADV
a mine explode and saw Jefferson go down... He let out a howl and went down in a heap.

NOTE **Fall down** means almost the same as **go down**.

3 If you **go down** in a building, you move downstairs. ❑ *I must go down and put on*   V+ADV
my necklace... Together they went down to breakfast.

4 If you **go down** to a place, you visit it or travel there, especially when the place   V+ADV:
is farther south than you or is in the country. ❑ *I have to go down to Brighton... I didn't*   USUALLY+A
go down to see Mother during this time... I think you ought to go down there tomorrow
morning.

5 If you **go down** the shop, bank, pub, and so on, you go there for a short while.   V+PREP,
[INFORMAL, SPOKEN] ❑ *Let's go down the bank then. ...decide to go down to the rope shop*   V+ADV
and look at samples.

6 Something that **goes down** to a particular point or in a particular direction ex-   V+ADV:
tends as far as that point or in that direction. ❑ *One road goes north, the other one goes*   WITH A
down to Ullapool... The steps go down in the direction of the river. ...a steep slope that went
down towards open meadows.

7 If you **go down** on your knees or on all fours, you lower your body until it is   V+ADV:
supported by your knees, or by your hands and knees. ❑ *Ferdinand began to go down*   WITH on
on one knee... He turned sharply to the right, went down on his hands and knees and
crawled forward slowly.

NOTE **Get down** means almost the same as **go down**.

8 If the cost, level, standard, or amount of something **goes down**, it becomes   V+ADV
cheaper, lower, or less than it was before. ❑ *We expect the price of food in real terms to*
go down, not up... The Conservative vote actually went down by 1.6 per cent... He knew that
the water level had gone down.

NOTE **Decrease** is a more formal word for **go down**, and **go up** means the opposite.

9 If you say that something **has gone down**, you mean that its quality or standard has become worse. ❑ *It's gone down a lot, the food... The neighbourhood has gone down since we came.*   V+ADV

NOTE **Deteriorate** is a more formal word for **go down**.

10 If a tyre, balloon, or something else which has been inflated **goes down**, air is lost from it, and it becomes flatter or smaller.   V+ADV

NOTE **Deflate** is a more formal word for **go down**.

11 To **go down** means to happen. [INFORMAL] ❑ *'What's going down? Any ideas?'*   V+ADV

NOTE **Happen** means almost the same as **go down**.

12 If a swelling on your body or skin **goes down**, it becomes less swollen or disappears completely. ❑ *She discovered that the inflammation had gone down.*   V+ADV

13 When something **goes down** in a particular way, it gets a particular kind of reaction from a person or group of people. ❑ *He gave a humorous account, which went down quite well, of how he had done it... This ruling would go down badly in Britain and Germany.*   V+ADV: WITH A

14 If you talk about food or drink **going down** well, you mean that it is eaten or drunk with enjoyment. [INFORMAL] ❑ *A cup of tea would go down nicely.*   V+ADV: WITH A

15 When the sun or moon **goes down**, it sets. ❑ *We ought to be moving. The sun's going down... After the moon went down the noise grew louder.*   V+ADV

NOTE **Come up** means the opposite of **go down**.

16 If a ship **goes down**, it sinks. If a plane **goes down**, it crashes. ❑ *He came to the surface yards away from where his boat had gone down.*   V+ADV

17 You say that you will **go down** in a particular way when you expect the consequences of your actions to be serious, but you still intend to do what you have planned. ❑ *I thought I might as well go down truculently, so I replied: 'I'm not prepared to discuss this'... She was determined to go down fighting.*   V+ADV: WITH A/C/-ING

18 In sport, if a person or team **goes down**, they are defeated in a match or contest. ❑ *Rafter went down by three sets to one.*   V+ADV

NOTE **Lose** means almost the same as **go down**.

19 In sport, if a person or team **goes down**, they move to a lower position in an official list, or to a lower division in a league. [BRITISH]   V+ADV

NOTE **Go up** means the opposite of **go down**.

20 If something **goes down** in writing, it is written down. ❑ *They were interested in whatever we had to say, and I have no doubt it went down in their notes afterwards.*   V+ADV: WITH A

21 If a computer **goes down**, it stops functioning temporarily.   V+ADV

22 When university students **go down**, they leave university, especially at the end of their degree course, or at the end of term. [BRITISH]   V+ADV

NOTE **Go up** means the opposite of **go down**.

23 When someone having sex **goes down**, they start kissing or sucking their partner's genitals. [INFORMAL]   V+ADV

go down as If someone or something **goes down as** a particular thing, they are regarded, remembered, or recorded as that thing. ❑ *Helping your neighbour can go down in the teacher's view as cheating... Although this will go down as my day, he and Neil Foster were the real heroes... You, Freneau, would go down in history as his assassin.*   V+ADV+PREP

go down with If you **go down with** an illness, you catch it or develop it. ❑ *I was feeling tired and ill and finally went down with gastric flu.*   V+ADV+PREP

NOTE **Contract** is a more formal word for **go down with**.

★go for

1 If you **go for** a particular thing, you choose it or aim to achieve it. If you say **'Go for** it' to someone, you are encouraging them to choose a particular thing or to attempt to do something difficult. ❑ *They urged the Chancellor to go for the first option. ...a tendency to go for even grander projects... We'd better just hope for the best, and hope they don't go for our route.*   V+PREP: ALSO IMPERATIVE: V+PREP+it

2 If you **go for** someone or something, you like them very much. [INFORMAL] ❑ *I don't go for talk like that... His eyes were too fixed and pale, I never really went for them.*   V+PREP

3 If you **go for** someone or something, you attack them. ❑ *He went for me with the*   V+PREP

bread-knife... I have been twice attacked by owls. They go for the eyes, you know, and flap
their wings in your face.

4 If you say that a statement you have made about one person or thing **goes for**   V+PREP
another person or thing, you mean that the statement is also true of the second person or thing. ❏ *The same goes for Bardolph... The Alliance was the most important thing
there was, and that went for America as well as Europe.*

5 If something **goes for** a particular price, it is sold for that amount. ❏ *Some old*   V+PREP
machines go for as much as 35,000 pounds.

NOTE **Fetch** means almost the same as **go for.**

6 If you have a particular thing **going for** you, it gives you an advantage in a   V+PREP
situation. [INFORMAL] ❏ *He's got a lot more going for him than just his store. The store's
just a beginning... Davey, our captain, had this incredible streak going for him: seven years
and he'd never played on a losing side.*

go forth When someone **goes forth**, they leave the place where they were,   V+ADV
usually in order to carry out some task or plan. [LITERARY] ❏ *...going forth in triumph
from slavery into freedom.*

go forward

1 If something **goes forward**, it makes progress and begins to happen. ❏ *If our*   V+ADV
*present plans go forward we shall bring in an assistant for you... Preparations were going for-
ward for the annual Caxley Musical Festival.*

2 If someone's name **goes forward** as a candidate for a job or in a election, they   V+ADV
are proposed as a candidate. ❏ *He has allowed his name to go forward.*

3 When the clocks **go forward** in Britain in the spring, everyone sets their clocks   V+ADV
one hour later, to British Summer Time.

NOTE **Go back** means the opposite of **go forward.**

★go in

1 When you **go in** somewhere, especially your own house, you enter it. ❏ *Let's go*   V+ADV,
in and have some coffee... I pushed open the door of the office and went in... As you go in   V+PREP
the door, remember that coffee table I told you about.

2 When people, especially soldiers, **go in**, they enter a place or area of conflict, and   V+ADV
become involved in the situation there. ❏ *...an instruction to warriors to go in and kill...
The third American seaborne attack was going in.*

NOTE **Pull out** means the opposite of **go in.**

3 When you **go in** somewhere such as a place of work or business or hospital, you   V+ADV
go there in order to work, to carry out business, to receive treatment, and so on.
❏ *He'll still be in hospital then. He's going in for a minor operation... She hadn't the strength
to go in to work more than two or three mornings a week.*

4 When someone **goes in** an organization, they join it. [INFORMAL] ❏ *I'm not quali-*   V+PREP,
fied enough to go in on a high level, not young enough to start near the bottom... I thought   V+ADV
you were going in the Navy.

NOTE **Come out** means the opposite of **go in.**

5 If something **goes in** a container, object, or opening, it fits into it. ❏ *I think the*   V+PREP,
thing's too big to go in the car... All those things could easily go in the dining-room cup-   V+ADV
board... The key wouldn't go in.

6 You talk about structures or equipment **going in** when they are being built or   V+ADV
installed. ❏ *...after the new breakwater went in and the municipal pier... A new paved
street went in.*

7 If the sun **goes in**, it goes behind a cloud and can no longer be seen. [BRITISH]   V+ADV

NOTE **Come out** means the opposite of **go in.**

8 You talk about information or a fact **going in** when you mean that you have   V+ADV
understood it and remembered it. [INFORMAL] ❏ *Nothing seemed to go in.*

NOTE **Sink in** means almost the same as **go in.**

go in for

1 If you **go in for** a particular kind of thing, you like it and regularly do it, wear   V+ADV+PREP
it, use it, and so on. ❏ *I don't go in for that sort of fishing. ...the fruit-trees some previous
owner had gone in for... I've never gone in for jewellery.*

2 If you decide to **go in for** a particular kind of work, you decide to do it as your   V+ADV+PREP
job or career. ❏ *I thought of going in for teaching... She was better educated than I was;*

The symbol ★ shows key phrasal verbs

there was some talk of her going in for accountancy or law.

NOTE **Go into** and **take up** mean almost the same as **go in for**.

3 If you **go in for** a competition, you take part in it. ❏ *...the people who went in for*   V+ADV+PREP
the Olympic Games.

NOTE **Enter** is a more formal word for **go in for**.

★go into

1 When you **go into** a room, building, or other place, you enter it or go there.   V+PREP
❏ *She went into the bedroom and shut the door... He was unwilling to go into the garden...*
Clem had to go into town on business... We were going into China through Shumchun.

2 When people, especially soldiers, **go into** a place or area of conflict, they go   V+PREP
there and become involved in the situation there. ❏ *...the troops who were ready to go*
into Sicily... The police were not going into the barricaded areas.

3 When you **go into** work, hospital, school, and so on, you go there in order to   V+PREP
work, receive treatment, or study. ❏ *She was now far from well, and had to go into hospi-*
tal for blood transfusions.

4 If you **go into** a particular kind of work, you decide to do it as your job or ca-   V+PREP
reer. ❏ *Ever thought of going into journalism?... I didn't want to go into politics, but I felt I*
had to.

NOTE **Go in for** and **take up** mean almost the same as **go into**.

5 If you **go into** an organization, you join it. ❏ *There are so few coloured recruits go-*   V+PREP
ing into the police force... He went into the army and I never heard from him again.... There
was no serious dissent over Britain going into Europe.

6 If you **go into** a particular matter, you describe it fully or in detail. ❏ *I've gone*   V+PREP:
into this example in some detail... The problems involved are highly technical and I won't go   HAS PASSIVE
into them... There was no time to go into the question of the rights and wrongs of the strug-
gle.

NOTE **Discuss** means almost the same as **go into**.

7 If you **go into** a particular matter, you examine or investigate it in detail. ❏ *My*   V+PREP:
solicitors are going into the question of my jewellery. ...as one goes more deeply into a sub-   HAS PASSIVE
ject.

8 If someone **goes into** a long speech, outburst of laughter, piece of music, and so   V+PREP
on, they start speaking, laughing, or playing. ❏ *He went into a long monologue. ...the*
other boys, who at first went into screams of derisive laughter... He was deaf and had to be
nudged whenever the band went into the national anthem.

NOTE **Launch into** means almost the same as **go into**.

9 When someone or something **goes into** a particular state or situation, they be-   V+PREP
gin being in that state or situation. ❏ *Hours passed and he just went into a coma... The*
police were looking for Paddy and he had gone into hiding... New weapons were ready to go
into service... Don went into the lead.

10 If you **go into** an election, competition, or exam and so on, you start taking   V+PREP:
part in it. ❏ *The party will go into the next election with two serious handicaps... It would*   USUALLY+A
have been reckless to go into a Test with only six batsmen.

11 If time, effort, or money **goes into** something, it is spent or used to do it, get   V+PREP
it, or make it. If particular ingredients **go into** something, they are used to make it.
❏ *Three years of research went into the making of those films... Money and effort has gone*
into improving their performance. ...the information that goes into the reports of FBI opera-
tions.

12 If things **go into** a container, they fit in it or they are put there. ❏ *I put my main*   V+PREP
stuff into a rucksack, while my money and passport went into a small canvas shoulder-bag...
We are looking for a different box for these to go into.

13 If someone or something **goes into** a particular kind of movement, they   V+PREP
start moving in the way mentioned. ❏ *The plane went into a nose dive... I went into a*
skid.

14 If a vehicle or its driver **goes into** another vehicle, it hits the other vehicle.   V+PREP
❏ *Three cars went into me... I went into the mini in front.*

NOTE **Crash into** means almost the same as **go into**.

go in with

If you **go in with** someone, you form a business partnership or   V+ADV+PREP
working relationship with them. ❏ *As a matter of business I would go in with him... They*

must choose whether to accept British Aerospace's homegrown version, or to go in with the Americans.

★go off

1 If you **go off** somewhere, you leave the place where you were, usually in order to do something. ❏ *He had gone off to work... She went off to look at the flowers... Eileen decided to go off on a visit of her own... He went off to his room and had a cold shower.*
NOTE **Go away** means almost the same as **go off**.

V+ADV:
USUALLY+A

2 If a gun **goes off**, it is fired. If a bomb **goes off**, it explodes. ❏ *The gun went off as he was putting it away... I could hear the bombs going off... The probability of a nuclear weapon going off by accident is slight.*

V+ADV

3 If something such as an alarm, bell, or flashbulb **goes off**, it operates, making a sudden loud noise or flash. ❏ *Every Sunday morning Donald's alarm went off in time for him to go to early Mass... The hall-buzzer went off. ...smiling as flashbulbs go off on all sides.*

V+ADV

4 If a light, heating system, broadcasting station, or electric device **goes off**, it stops operating. ❏ *The light only goes off at night... The heating's gone off and I'm freezing in this draughty old place. ...until the music station went off the air.*
NOTE **Come on** means the opposite of **go off**.

V+ADV

5 If an event or arrangement **goes off** well, smoothly, or without problems, it is successful or happens without any problems. ❏ *The meeting went off well... They wanted all the arrangements to go off smoothly... The ceremony at the Arc de Triomphe went off exactly as planned.*

V+ADV:
WITH A

6 If something such as a road or line **goes off** from another, it separates from it and extends in a different direction. ❏ *There's a little road goes off to the right. ...a pencilled diary, the writing going off in all directions.*

V+ADV:
WITH A

7 You talk about people **going off** in a different direction or at a tangent, when they start discussing or doing something different, unexpected, or unuseful. ❏ *Without them a campaign can go off in the wrong direction... He suddenly went off at a tangent and came out with some fascinating stories about his life out East.*

V+ADV:
WITH A

8 If you **go off** someone or something, you stop liking them. [BRITISH, INFORMAL] ❏ *He's gone off the idea... I'm into home-made silver jewellery, none of your musty old filigree, I've gone off that... I think she's going off him a bit.*

V+PREP

9 If you **go off** a drug, you stop taking it. ❏ *There has been such bad publicity about the pill lately that a lot of us are going off it.*
NOTE **Come off** means almost the same as **go off**, and **go on** means the opposite.

V+PREP

10 If you **go off**, you fall asleep. [INFORMAL] ❏ *A moment later she said: 'Oh, I nearly went off again.'... They were all quiet, and went off to sleep at 10.00.*
NOTE **Drop off** means almost the same as **go off**.

V+ADV:
ALSO+to

11 If food or drink **goes off**, it becomes stale, sour, or rotten. [BRITISH] ❏ *You must drink it up within a fortnight or it will go off... Food that has 'gone off' has been infected with bacteria that cause illness.*
NOTE **Decay** is a more formal word for **go off**.

V+ADV

go off on If someone **goes off on** you, they show that they are very angry with you about something. [AMERICAN, INFORMAL] ❏ *She says that he then exploded. 'He went off on me'.*

V+ADV+PREP

go off with

1 If someone **goes off with** another person, they leave their husband, wife, or lover and have a relationship with that person. ❏ *My boyfriend went off with my best friend. ...going off with another man after being married eight years.*
NOTE **Run off with** means almost the same as **go off with**.

V+ADV+PREP

2 If someone **goes off with** something that belongs to someone else, they leave a place, taking that thing with them. ❏ *She had let him go off with her papers... He had gone off with a large sum belonging to Uncle Nick.*
NOTE **Make off with** means almost the same as **go off with**.

V+ADV+PREP

★go on

✓ In meanings 12, 15, 17, and 19, the stress is on **go**.

1 If you **go on** doing something, or **go on** with an activity, you continue to do it. ❏ *I went on writing... While she was pouring out their drinks, she went on talking... The BAA argues that air traffic is increasing and will go on doing so... They can't go on with their ex-*

V+ADV:
WITH -ING/with

aminations... I would have liked to have gone on with this method.

NOTE **Carry on** means almost the same as **go on**.

2 If something **goes on** throughout a period of time, it continues to happen or ex- V+ADV:
ist. ❑ *The fighting had gone on all through the night... The noise went on and on... How* USUALLY+A
long do you think the rain will go on?... He seems quite happy to let things go on as they
are... The strike went on for over a year before it was finally settled.

♦ An **ongoing** situation has been happening for quite a long time and is continu- ADJECTIVE
ing to happen. ❑ *...an ongoing economic crisis. ...an ongoing discussion.*

3 If you say that something **is going on**, you mean that it is taking place at the V+ADV
present time. ❑ *There's a big argument going on... When I asked what was going on, she*
refused to say anything... Something very odd was going on.

NOTE **Happen** means almost the same as **go on**.

♦ You use the word **goings-on** to refer to activities that you think are strange or N-PLURAL
amusing or that you do not approve of. ❑ *...an amusing story about goings-on at Harry's*
Bar.

4 If you **go on** to do something, you do it after you have finished something else. V+ADV:
❑ *He later went on to form a successful computer company... I finished by describing Jeremy* WITH to-INF/to
in some detail, and then going on to talk of his cousin Monty... Once you have given the cor-
rect answer to the problem in step one you can go on to step two.

5 If you **go on** in a particular direction, you continue to travel or move in that di- V+ADV:
rection. If you **go on** to a place, you go to it from the place that you have reached. USUALLY+A
❑ *I went on up the hill... You can't go on, there's a diversion... Are you sure you don't want*
to go on to Italy?... Go on home... Please go on ahead of me, and I will follow slowly.

6 You say that land, rock, or a road **goes on** when you are referring to the way V+ADV
which it extends or its direction. ❑ *...incredible canyons and vast, flat, moon valleys that*
seem to go on for ever... Below the subsoil lies rock, and rock goes on down to the centre of
the Earth.

7 You refer to a period of time **going on** when you mean that it passes and when V+ADV
you are describing events during that period. ❑ *I get more depressed, as time goes on...*
As the afternoon went on the strike became total in both cities.

NOTE **Wear on** means almost the same as **go on**.

8 If someone **goes on** in a conversation, they continue talking, perhaps after an V+ADV:
interruption. ❑ *'You know,' he went on, 'it's extraordinary.'... 'Sounds serious,' I said, 'go* ALSO+QUOTE
on.'... She knew he wasn't listening, but she went on all the same.... He went on for 35 min-
utes without a pause.

9 If someone **goes on** about something, or **goes on** at you, they continue talking V+ADV:
to you about the same thing, often in an annoying way. [INFORMAL] ❑ *I went on at my* ALSO+about/at
father to have safety belts fitted... Don't go on about it... Although his long book is funny,
most of it is familiar, and it does go on.

10 You say **'Go on'** to someone to persuade or encourage them to do something. IMPERATIVE,
[INFORMAL] ❑ *Go on, have a biscuit... Well, phone them up, go on! Go on, get on the phone.* V+ADV

NOTE **Come on** means almost the same as **go on**.

11 You say **'Go on'** to someone to indicate that you do not believe what they IMPERATIVE,
have said. [INFORMAL] ❑ *Go on – you're kidding.* V+ADV

NOTE **Get away** means almost the same as **go on**.

12 If you say, for example, that you have something to **go on**, you mean that you V+PREP
have some information on which you can base an opinion or judgement. ❑ *I'm only*
going on what I've seen at Mr Gladwell's... He had nothing to go on. There were no clues.

13 If a light, machine, or other device **goes on**, it begins operating. ❑ *The light goes* V+ADV
on automatically... The tape recorder went on and he started to talk.

NOTE **Go off** means the opposite of **go on**.

14 If one object **goes on** another, the first object fits or is put onto the second. V+ADV,
❑ *He went back to the rifle. The silencer went on easily, swivelling round the end of the bar-* V+PREP
rel... He sat down to put on his shoes and socks. The shoes would hardly go on.

NOTE **Come off** means the opposite of **go on**.

15 If an amount of money or a commodity **goes on** something, it is spent or used V+PREP
on that thing. ❑ *A fair amount of money goes on equipment and research expenditure...*

Nearly half of French aid went on technical cooperation... Over 40 per cent of fuel used in agriculture goes on heating greenhouses.

16 When an actor or actress **goes on**, they appear in a play or make an entrance onto the stage. ❏ *I'm going to be sick. I can't go on tonight. Get my understudy... I went on in one of the crowd scenes for five pounds a week... The second girl now showed no eagerness to go on stage.* `V+ADV, V+PREP`

17 If you **go on** a drug, you start taking it. ❏ *They went on the Pill and suffered side-effects.* `V+PREP`

NOTE **Come off** means the opposite of **go on**.

18 If you say that someone **is going on** a particular age, you mean that they are approaching that age. [INFORMAL] ❏ *Renata was going on thirty, divorced... I am thirty-four now, going on thirty-five.* `V+PREP: WITH NUMBER`

19 If you **are gone on** someone, you are infatuated with them. [INFORMAL, OLD-FASHIONED] ❏ *I was a bit flattered because he was so gone on me.* `PASSIVE: V+PREP`

go on with If you say that you have enough **to be going on with**, you mean that you have enough for the present time. [INFORMAL] ❏ *Don't bother, that's enough to be going on with... With her three children, it'll make a nice little family to be going on with.* `V+ADV+with`

★go out

1 When you **go out** of a room, building, or other place, you leave it. ❏ *He picks up his camera bag and goes out, locking the door... Why don't we go out into the garden?... She went out of the building and through the main gate.* `V+ADV: ALSO+of`

NOTE **Come in** means the opposite of **go out**.

2 When you **go out**, you leave your house and go somewhere else, for example in order to shop, visit friends, see a film, and so on. ❏ *I have to go out. I'll be back late tonight. ...all dressed up to go out to a party. ...an invitation to actually go out climbing.* `V+ADV`

NOTE **Stay in** means the opposite of **go out**.

3 If you **are going out** with someone, you spend time with them socially and have a romantic or sexual relationship with them. ❏ *My parents wouldn't let me go out with boys... David used to say that you were the best dancer he ever went out with... Your daughter and Michael Corleone have been going out together for over a year.* `V+ADV, V+ADV+with, V+ADV+together: RECIPROCAL`

NOTE **Date** means almost the same as **go out**.

4 If you **go out** to a place, especially somewhere abroad or far away, you travel there. ❏ *She had decided to get married and stay in England and not go out to Africa... They want me to go out West and do a movie... They might find you a seat on some flight going out tonight.* `V+ADV: USUALLY+A`

♦ **Outgoing** traffic or an **outgoing** plane or passenger is travelling away from the place where you are. ❏ *They searched all outgoing traffic. ...incoming and outgoing passengers.* `ADJECTIVE`

5 If you talk about people **going out** and doing something, you mean that they do it by making an effort and after planning to do it. [INFORMAL] ❏ *Saying that we need something is very different from going out and fighting for it... Violence on television actually incites people to go out and do violent acts... I told your father I'd go out and get a job.* `V+ADV: WITH and+VERB`

6 If news, a message, or a letter **goes out**, it is announced, published, or sent, often officially. ❏ *The news went out from Washington that he was dead... Word went out that he'd arrived... That is the instruction that's gone out to our members.* `V+ADV`

NOTE **Come in** means the opposite of **go out**.

♦ An **outgoing** message, letter, or phone call is one sent or made from the place where you are. ❏ *Wouldn't that cause less of a delay in outgoing mail?* `ADJECTIVE`

NOTE **Incoming** means the opposite of **outgoing**.

7 Money that **goes out** is spent on bills and regular expenses. ❏ *Even though you are earning a good salary you probably find the money going out virtually as fast as it comes in.* `V+ADV`

NOTE **Come in** means the opposite of **go out**.

♦ You use **outgoings** to refer to the money which you have to spend regularly, for example in order to pay your rent or bills. ❏ *...approving payment of the bills for her* `N-PLURAL` regular outgoings.

NOTE **Expenses** means almost the same as **outgoings**.

8 If a television or radio programme **goes out**, it is broadcast. [BRITISH] ❏ *The series* V+ADV
goes out on Tuesday evenings on BBC 2... We need to record it on video-tape the day before
it actually goes out on the air.

9 If a light **goes out**, it stops shining. ❏ *The lights went out in the big tent... Stay* V+ADV
there. The light's gone out and I won't be able to find you if you move around.

NOTE **Come on** means the opposite of **go out**.

10 If a fire or something that is burning **goes out**, it stops burning. ❏ *His room was* V+ADV
freezing. His fire had gone out, and I sat there shivering... I'm afraid my cigarette has gone
out again.

11 If a person or team **goes out** of a competition, they are defeated in a game and V+ADV:
therefore can no longer take part in the competition. ❏ *Newcastle went out of the com-* ALSO+of
petition, losing 2-1 on aggregate.

12 If something **goes out**, it stops being fashionable or used, and is replaced with V+ADV:
something else. ❏ *Steam went out and diesel was introduced... Shoes can sometimes go out* ALSO+of
of fashion overnight... I think it's rapidly going out of use.

NOTE **Come in** means the opposite of **go out**.

13 If something **goes out**, it is unwanted and someone gets rid of it. ❏ *All these* V+ADV
desks go out! This is an apartment house not an office building!

14 When the tide **goes out**, it falls, so that the water reaches lower up the shore. V+ADV
❏ *...just after the tide has gone out over the vast salt-marshes.*

NOTE **Come in** means the opposite of **go out**.

15 You use **outgoing** to describe a person who is very friendly and open in their ADJECTIVE
behaviour; used showing approval. ❏ *Adler was an outgoing, sociable kind of man... She*
became very outgoing and popular.

NOTE **Extrovert** means almost the same as **outgoing**.

16 You use **outgoing** to describe a person who has held an office or position and ADJECTIVE
who is just about to be replaced by someone else. ❏ *Congress opens with an address by*
the outgoing president. ...the outgoing government.

NOTE **Incoming** means the opposite of **outgoing**.

go out for To **go out for** something means to try to do it or be chosen for it. V+ADV+PREP
[AMERICAN] ❏ *In seventh grade Mark went out for three sports but was rather poor in two of*
them... You should go out for Supreme Court Justice.

go out of If you say that a quality, especially a positive quality, **has gone out** V+ADV+PREP
of someone or something, you mean that they no longer have it. ❏ *Some of the*
urgency has gone out of the market... All the heart seemed to have gone out of him... It is
still discussed in general terms, but the vigour has gone out of the debate.

★go over

1 When you **go over** to someone or something, you move towards them and V+ADV:
reach them. ❏ *'Mabel,' he said, going over to her... She got up and went over to her suit-* USUALLY+to/and
case, opened it, and took out an envelope... There was a phone on the desk. Eva went over
and lifted the receiver and dialled.

2 If you **go over** to someone's house, you visit them for a short time. ❏ *When I got* V+ADV:
home I found a phone message from Jeremy, asking me to go over the next evening... Can we USUALLY+to/and
go over to Ann's today?... Mr Steinberg had often invited me to go over and stay.

NOTE **Go round** means almost the same as **go over**.

3 If you **go over** to a place overseas, you travel there. ❏ *My editor asked me to go* V+ADV:
over to England to cover a British general election. ...just to save yourself the trouble of going USUALLY+to
over to Paris.

4 If you **go over** something, you examine, discuss, or think about it very carefully V+PREP:
and systematically. ❏ *We could go over the whole project and see if there are any prob-* HAS PASSIVE
lems... What's the point of going over all that?... He knew that every square inch had already
been gone over with microscopic care.

♦ If you give something a **going-over**, you examine it carefully. [INFORMAL] ❏ *They* N-SING
had been giving our report a careful going-over... His room had received a thorough going-
over.

5 If someone gives you a **going-over**, they attack you violently, usually as a pun- N-SING ishment or a warning. [INFORMAL] ❑ *Someone had given young Allen a very thorough going-over indeed. 'What happened this time?' I asked.*

6 If something **goes over** well or badly, people react favourably or unfavourably V+ADV to it. ❑ *I got him to sing 'Sonny Boy', but it did not go over very well... I wondered how such a session would go over in America.*

go overboard If someone **goes overboard**, they react more strongly or act V+ADV more extremely than you think they should have done. ❑ *You're going a little bit overboard... They went rather overboard and said that it was the best film they'd ever seen.*

go over to

1 In a conflict, if someone **goes over to** a group of people, they join them after V+ADV+PREP previously belonging to a rival group. ❑ *The traitor Jan went over to the side of the very people who had assassinated his brothers... Who was loyal and who had gone over to the other group?... They had gone over to the enemy.*

2 If someone or something **goes over to** a different way of doing things, they V+ADV+PREP change to it. ❑ *We went over to the American system... The school will go over to mixed ability teaching.*

★go round

1 → See **go around**

2 If you **go round** to someone's house, you visit them for a short time. ❑ *I'll go* V+ADV *round and see Nell later... Manfred rang up and asked me to go round to see him... It wasn't until Friday evening that I was able to go round to Clive's house.*

NOTE **Go over** means almost the same as **go round**.

3 If you **go round** in a circle, you move in a circular direction. ❑ *The speedboat* V+ADV *driver has to stop or go round in circles.*

4 If something **goes round**, it spins or turns continuously like a wheel. ❑ *The* V+ADV *wheels of the bicycle were going round so fast that the spokes blurred into one... The tape is still going round... The blue light is going round and round on top of the police car.*

NOTE **Revolve** is a more formal word for **go round**.

★go through

✔ In meaning 3, the stress is on **go**.

1 If you **go through** an event or period of time, especially an unpleasant one, you V+PREP experience it. ❑ *Not all girls go through this stage... I'm too old to go through that again... Doctors and teachers both have to go through a long period of expensive professional training.*

NOTE **Undergo** means almost the same as **go through**.

2 If someone or something **goes through** an official procedure, they are made to V+PREP: do all the things that are required. ❑ *She would have to go through all the legal formal-* HAS PASSIVE *ities... You did not have to go through a passport check in Mulhouse airport... If the set procedure is not gone through, then the machine cuts out.*

3 If you **go through** someone in order to do something, that person must deal V+PREP with the matter before you can continue or get approval for it. ❑ *You have to go through the Head of Department... Industrial matters go through the regional trade group machinery.*

4 If a law, agreement, or official decision **goes through**, it is approved by the peo- V+ADV ple who have the power or authority to do so. ❑ *The adoption went through... We believed the deal would not be allowed to go through.*

5 If you **go through** a room, you enter it and cross it. ❑ *She went through the kitch-* V+PREP, *en and out of the back door... We went through a large room into a smaller one... Eva went* V+ADV *through to the galley.*

6 If you **go through** a town or country, you cross it or stop there briefly on your V+ADV way to somewhere else. ❑ *You must be going through Frankfurt anyway... To go through Germany would be to risk suspicion.*

7 If you **go through** a lot of things such as papers or clothes, you examine them V+PREP: carefully, usually in order to sort them into groups or to search for something. HAS PASSIVE ❑ *They went through her things... I began going through my pockets. Nothing was missing... Her correspondence had been gone through. Why?*

NOTE **Look through** means almost the same as **go through**.

8 If you **go through** a list, story, or plan, you say, describe, or discuss it from be- V+PREP:

ginning to end. ❑ *You'd better go through the names... Could you go through roughly*   HAS PASSIVE
what's required?... Secretary Cox went through the treaty point by point.

NOTE **Run through** means almost the same as **go through**.

9 If someone **goes through** something such as a series of actions or movements,   V+PREP:
they perform it. ❑ *They watched Pat going through some of the movements she had*   HAS PASSIVE
learned.... The music started and we went through a series of warm-up exercises.

10 If you **go through** a supply of something, you use it all so that there is none   V+PREP
left. ❑ *Somehow, they had gone through the whole bottle of wine.*

NOTE **Get through** means almost the same as **go through**, and **consume** is a
more formal word.

11 If something such as a piece of clothing **has gone through**, there is a hole in   V+ADV
it, because you have worn or used it so much. ❑ *...an old suit whose jacket had gone*
through at the elbows.

NOTE **Wear through** means almost the same as **go through**.

12 In sport, if a person or team **goes through**, they win one stage of a competi-   V+ADV:
tion and go on to the next stage. ❑ *Spain beat South Korea 3-1 and look set to go*   ALSO+*to*
through... West Germany go through to Sunday's final in Rome against the defending cham-
pions, Argentina.

go through with If you **go through with** a decision or an action, you con-   V+ADV+PREP
tinue to do what is necessary in order to achieve it or complete it, although this may
be difficult or unpleasant. ❑ *Landy was already taking it for granted that I was going to*
go through with this business, and I resented his attitude... The government was determined
to go through with that legislation.

go together

1 If two things **go together**, they are often found in association with each other.   V+ADV
❑ *This had been the basis of both wealth and military power; the two went together... Fear*
and hatred seem to go together.

2 If two people **go together**, they spend time with each other and have a roman-   V+ADV
tic or sexual relationship. [AMERICAN] ❑ *We've been going together for two years.*

NOTE **Go out** means almost the same as **go together**.

go towards If one thing **goes towards** another, it contributes part of it. If an   V+PREP
amount of money **goes towards** something, it is used as part of its cost. ❑ *My bo-*
nus will go towards a deposit on the flat... Any money received from now on will go towards
aid for future victims... Most of the calories in our food go towards maintaining our body tem-
perature. ...the thinking that went towards the basic ideas.

go under

1 If someone or something, especially a business, **goes under**, they fail, lose pow-   V+ADV
er, become bankrupt, and so on. ❑ *Ten thousand small businesses have gone under... The*
high civilizations of the East went under one by one. ...but it was Ramsay Macdonald who
went under, while the party survived.

NOTE **Collapse** means almost the same as **go under**.

2 If someone or something in the water **goes under**, they sink below the surface   V+ADV
of the water. ❑ *He thrashed about for some time before he went under... The lifeboat will*
sink and we shall all go under.

NOTE **Come up** means the opposite of **go under**.

3 You talk about land **going under** the plough, the mower, and so on when you   V+PREP
mean that it is being ploughed or mown, and often when you want to suggest that it
is being completely changed or destroyed. You can also talk about trees **going un-**
der something such as the axe when you mean that they are being cut down. ❑ *The*
park had largely gone under the plough... The first fields of winter wheat were going under
the combine... Woods were going under the chain-saw right across the country.

★go up

1 When someone or something **goes up**, they move from a lower position to a   V+PREP,
higher one. ❑ *...a party of mountaineers going up the mountain... When I tried to go up*   V+ADV
the stairs he pushed me aside... Rockets went up to the moon.

2 If you **go up** in a building, you move upstairs. ❑ *She went up to her bedroom... We*   V+ADV
can go up in the elevator... If you'll excuse me a moment, I'll go up and change for dinner.

3 If you **go up** to someone or something, you move towards them until you are   V+ADV:

standing next to them. ❑ *I went up to Clem where he sat smoking... Go up and introduce yourself, after the meeting is over... They walked along a gravel drive and went up to the car.*

ALSO+to

4 If you **go up** to a place, you visit it or travel there, especially when the place is farther north than you or is in a city. ❑ *We all went up to the pub... Whatever do you want to go up there for, on a dreadful afternoon like this?... We'll go up to London early next week.*

V+ADV:
USUALLY+A

5 Something that **goes up** to a particular point or in a particular direction, extends as far as that point or in that direction. ❑ *...a dark mat of greenish-black pine trees going up to a high ridge... One road goes up north to Durness... These timetables only go up to the 30th of March.*

V+ADV:
WITH A

6 If the cost, level, standard, or amount of something **goes up**, it becomes more expensive, higher, or greater than it was before. ❑ *The price of petrol and oil related products will go up steadily... The expenditure on relief will go up to $400 million... That's why the crime rate is going up the way it is – seventeen per cent in Houston.*

V+ADV

NOTE **Rise** means almost the same as **go up**, and **come down** and **go down** mean the opposite.

7 If you **go up** when you are making an offer or suggesting an amount, you increase the original offer or amount. ❑ *I'm being rather reckless, I can't help it – I'll go up as high as fifteen pounds.*

V+ADV,
V+ADV+N:
NO PASSIVE

8 If a building, wall, or other structure **goes up**, it is built or fixed in place. ❑ *Small blocks of flats are going up... Steel crowd barriers go up several hours before each ceremony... Billboards went up all over town.*

V+ADV

NOTE **Come down** means the opposite of **go up**.

9 If something such as a curtain **goes up**, it is raised. ❑ *There was a burst of applause as the curtain went up... It had the effect of a blind going up too quickly.*

V+ADV

NOTE **Come down** means the opposite of **go up**.

10 If something **goes up**, it explodes or suddenly starts to burn. ❑ *In seconds it had gone up in flames... I'm surprised the whole place didn't go up... Another fuel-tank went up and the first fire-bells began sounding from the distance.*

V+ADV

11 If a cheer, shout, or other noise **goes up**, a lot of people cheer, shout, or make that sound at the same time. ❑ *A huge cheer went up. ...that afternoon when her sister had heard the shout of 'Fire!' go up at the Caxley cinema... A kind of gasp went up from the tables.*

V+ADV

12 When university students **go up**, they begin a degree course or return to university at the start of term. [BRITISH] ❑ *She said why didn't I do some exams and go up to University with her... Before going up to Oxford, I started a diary.*

V+ADV:
ALSO+to

NOTE **Go down** means the opposite of **go up**.

13 In sport, if a person or team **goes up**, they move to a higher position in a list, or to a higher division in a league. [BRITISH] ❑ *I think Stoke will go up this season.*

V+ADV

NOTE **Go down** means the opposite of **go up**.

★**go with**

1 If one thing **goes with** another, the two things are often found in association together. ❑ *...the sigh of satisfaction that goes with pleasant tiredness. ...wealth and the considerable potential power that goes with it. ...a girl with the temperament that goes with being a redhead.*

V+PREP

NOTE **Attend** is a formal word for **go with**.

2 If one thing **goes with** another, the two things officially or properly belong together, so that if you get one, you also get the other. ❑ *...the house which went with his old job. ...the two essays I wrote to go with Peter's photographs... I did not want the thirty acres of pasture that went with the place.*

V+PREP

3 If you **go with** a plan, idea, or the people who are proposing it, you decide to support them and try to make them succeed. [AMERICAN] ❑ *We have to go with the White House and Mr Muller on this one... North Carolina was not going with abortion to embarrass McGovern.*

V+PREP

4 If someone **is going with** another person, they are having a sexual or romantic relationship with that person. [INFORMAL] ❑ *He never went with other women. He never looked at another woman.*

V+PREP

go without If you **go without** something, you do not have it or do it. ❑ *The family went without food all day... How long could you go without sleep?... If they couldn't get coal, they had to go without.*

NOTE **Do without** means almost the same as **go without**.

V+PREP,
V+ADV

goad /goʊd/ (goads, goading, goaded)

goad into If you **goad** someone **into** doing something they did not want to do, you make them angry so that they do it. ❑ *Campaigners hope to goad parliament into reforming the electoral system... She was being goaded into denouncing and mocking her best friend.*

V+N+PREP,
V+PRON+PREP

goad on If you **are goaded on** by someone or something, they encourage you to do more than you intended to or to do it more energetically. ❑ *They could always be goaded on to one more patrol... Clement had played a prominent part in the suppression of the Templars, goaded on by the French king.*

V+N+ADV,
V+PRON+ADV,
V+ADV+N:
USUALLY PASSIVE

NOTE **Spur on** means almost the same as **goad on**.

gobble /ɡɒbəl/ (gobbles, gobbling, gobbled)

gobble down If you **gobble down** food or **gobble** it **up**, you very quickly eat all of it. [INFORMAL] ❑ *He gobbled down the two remaining eggs. ...truck drivers gobbling up hot dogs dripping with mustard... He had a huge sack of apples and he was gobbling them down.*

V+ADV+N,
V+PRON+ADV,
V+N+ADV

NOTE **Wolf down** means almost the same as **gobble down**.

gobble up

1 If an organization **gobbles up** a smaller organization, it takes control of it or destroys it. ❑ *Banc One of Ohio has built an empire in the mid-west by gobbling up smaller banks.*

V+ADV+N,
V+N+ADV,
V+PRON+ADV

2 If something **gobbles up** money, property, or resources, it uses or takes more of them than seems reasonable. ❑ *Research and development now gobble up a sizeable chunk of the military budget... British agriculture gobbled up more energy than it produced.*

V+ADV+N

3 → See **gobble down**

goof /ɡuːf/ (goofs, goofing, goofed)

goof around If someone **goofs around**, they spend their time doing silly things. [INFORMAL] ❑ *They just goof around, roll around on the floor and fight.*

V+ADV

NOTE **Mess around** means almost the same as **goof around**.

goof off If you **goof off**, you spend your time in a lazy or foolish way when you are supposed to be doing something more important. [AMERICAN, INFORMAL] ❑ *He never goofed off into restaurants when he was on patrol... He was always flirting with all the waitresses and letting them goof off on the job.*

V+ADV

NOTE In British English, **skive off** is an informal expression for **goof off**.

gouge /ɡaʊdʒ/ (gouges, gouging, gouged)

gouge out If you **gouge** something **out**, you force it violently from the place where it is, using your fingers, a tool, or a machine. ❑ *...bulldozers gouging out basements... Her eyes had been gouged out.*

V+ADV+N,
V+N+ADV,
V+PRON+ADV

grab /ɡræb/ (grabs, grabbing, grabbed)

grab at

1 If you **grab at** an object or person, you make a desperate attempt to hold on to them. ❑ *She fell on her knees to grab at the money... I grabbed at it with both hands... Marsha grabbed at her hair like a lifeline.*

V+PREP

2 If you **grab at** a chance or opportunity, you take advantage of it eagerly. ❑ *Why didn't you grab at the chance to go to New York?*

V+PREP

grapple /ɡræpəl/ (grapples, grappling, grappled)

grapple with If you **grapple with** a problem or difficult task, you try many different methods to solve it or do it. ❑ *I grappled with this moral dilemma... He was one of the few scientists who had seriously grappled with these problems.*

V+PREP:
HAS PASSIVE

NOTE **Wrestle with** means almost the same as **grapple with**.

grasp /ɡrɑːsp, ɡræsp/ (grasps, grasping, grasped)

grasp at

1 If you **grasp at** something, you take it with your hands and hold it very firmly.

V+PREP

❑ *He raised his hands above his head, grasping at the escape hatch.*
NOTE **Grab at** means almost the same as **grasp at**.

2 If you **grasp at** an opportunity, you try to take advantage of it, even though you are not very likely to succeed. ❑ *The specialists had given him some slight hope, but he was not grasping at it.*   V+PREP
NOTE **Clutch at** means almost the same as **grasp at**.

grass /grɑːs, græs/ (grasses, grassing, grassed)

grass on If someone **grasses on** you, they give information to people in authority that causes you to be punished or to have problems. [BRITISH, INFORMAL] ❑ *The rumour had started that I had grassed on the lesbians, and had been moved away.*   V+PREP
NOTE **Inform on** is a more formal expression for **grass on**.

grass over To **grass over** an area of ground means to plant grass all over it. ❑ *You've grassed over the back garden, I see... There had been a path to it but the farmer had let it grass over.*   V+ADV+N, V+ADV+PRON+ADV, V+ADV

grass up If one person **grasses up** another, the first person tells the police or other authorities about something criminal or wrong which the second person has done. [BRITISH, INFORMAL] ❑ *How many of them are going to grass up their own kids to the police?*   V+ADV+N, V+N+ADV, V+PRON+ADV

grind /graɪnd/ (grinds, grinding, ground)

grind away To **grind away** means to work very hard, but in an uninteresting way. [INFORMAL] ❑ *The old machinery is still grinding away... Millions of children today are forced to spend precious hours of their lives grinding away at pointless tasks.*   V+ADV: ALSO+at
NOTE **Plug away** means almost the same as **grind away**.

grind down

1 If someone **grinds** you **down**, they persistently attack you, annoy you, or treat you cruelly until you can no longer fight back or defend yourself. ❑ *The sheer weight of numbers and arms began to grind them down... Rich men are always grinding down poor men... See how the working people of Britain are ground down.*   V+PRON+ADV, V+ADV+N, V+N+ADV
NOTE **Wear down** means almost the same as **grind down**.

2 If you **grind** something **down**, you rub it against a hard surface or on a machine in order to make it smooth or sharp. ❑ *First, you must grind the components down fine... You put it on the grindstone and grind it down to shape... The hardest rock in the world will be ground down in time.*   V+N+ADV, V+PRON+ADV, V+ADV+N

grind on When something **grinds on**, it continues in a very boring way for a long time. ❑ *Slowly the meeting ground on... I wished I could stop his voice grinding on and on.*   V+ADV

grind out

1 If a person or machine **grinds out** information or work, they produce it in a boring or routine manner. [INFORMAL] ❑ *...a computer which grinds out decisions after computing the information. ...a printing press which ground out leaflets in several colours.*   V+ADV+N, V+N+ADV, V+PRON+ADV
NOTE **Churn out** means almost the same as **grind out**.

2 If you **grind out** a lighted cigarette, you press it down firmly with your hand or foot in order to stop it burning. ❑ *She ground out her cigarette too soon. ...cigarette ends ground out on the carpet.*   V+ADV+N, V+N+ADV, V+PRON+ADV
NOTE **Stub out** means almost the same as **grind out**.

grind up If you **grind** something **up**, you completely crush it until it becomes a fine powder. ❑ *The seeds are ground up for commercial mustards... They would smash the bottles with a hammer until they were ground up... It is not easy to grind it up in a coffee grinder.*   V+N+ADV, V+ADV+N, V+PRON+ADV

gross /grəʊs/ (grosses, grossing, grossed)

gross out If something **grosses** you **out**, it makes you feel disgusted. [INFORMAL] ❑ *Ordinarily, Anastasia was grossed out when her father spoke to total strangers in public... Your eating habits even grossed out my mother.*   V+N+ADV, V+ADV+N, V+PRON+ADV
NOTE **Disgust** is a more formal word for **gross out**.

♦ If something such as comedy or humour is **gross-out**, it makes you feel disgusted. [INFORMAL] ❑ *There's something about the Farrelly brothers' gross-out humour that is hilarious.*   ADJECTIVE

♦ A **gross-out** is something which makes you feel disgusted. [INFORMAL] ❑ *The film escalates to a series of gross-outs.* N-COUNT

grow /grəʊ/ **(grows, growing, grew, grown)**

grow apart If people who have a close relationship **grow apart**, they gradually start to have different interests and opinions from each other, and their relationship starts to fail. ❑ *As we travelled together, we started to grow apart... The brothers grew further and further apart.* V+ADV

NOTE **Drift apart** means almost the same as **grow apart**.

grow away from If you **grow away from** someone, you develop different views and opinions so that you gradually have less in common with them. ❑ *There have been times when I feared that you might grow away from us and be reluctant to return... In truth, also, she had grown away from her friends.* V+ADV+PREP

grow into

1 If you **grow into** a job or situation, you gradually learn how to do it or deal with it skilfully. ❑ *Mr Mzali has grown into the job.* V+PREP

2 If a child **grows into** an item of clothing, he or she becomes taller or bigger so that the clothing fits properly. ❑ *It's a bit big, but she'll soon grow into it.* V+PREP

grow on If someone or something **grows on** you, you start to like them, although you did not like them at first. ❑ *She was someone whose charm grew very slowly on you... I hated to give up my apartment. It had really grown on me over the last seven months... The hill has an enduring beauty which grows on you.* V+PREP

grow out If you **grow out** a hairstyle or let it **grow out**, you let your hair grow so that the style changes or so that you can cut off the part that you do not want. ❑ *I also let my hair go darker and grew out my fringe... The red rinse had grown out completely.* V+ADV+N, V+N+ADV, V+PRON+ADV, V+ADV: ERGATIVE

grow out of

1 When you **grow out of** childish behaviour or interests, you become more mature and stop behaving immaturely or having those interests. ❑ *I've rather grown out of my taste for ice cream... She had never grown out of the beliefs acquired in childhood.* V+ADV+PREP

NOTE **Outgrow** means almost the same as **grow out of**.

2 If a child **grows out of** an item of clothing, he or she becomes so tall or big that the clothing no longer fits them properly. ❑ *It cost a small fortune and she grew out of it in three months.* V+ADV+PREP

3 If one idea or plan **grows out of** another, it develops from it. ❑ *She'd had an idea for a story that grew out of a dream... Out of this would grow a broad socialist programme.* V+ADV+PREP

♦ An **outgrowth** of something is a natural development from it or result of it. ❑ *This theory was an outgrowth of Einstein's 'unified field theory'.* N-SING

★**grow up**

1 As you **grow up**, you gradually change from being a child to being an adult. ❑ *I had grown up in the district... They grew up in the early days of television... Children should grow up with a fond attitude towards all humanity.* V+ADV

♦ A **grown-up** is an adult. [INFORMAL] ❑ *We could see a grown-up coming. ...older couples, with grown-up children of their own.* N-COUNT, ADJECTIVE

♦ If you say that a child is being **grown-up**, you mean that he or she is behaving in a mature way. ❑ *Your brother's awfully grown-up for his age.* ADJECTIVE

2 If you tell someone to **grow up**, you want them to stop behaving in a silly or childish way. [INFORMAL] ❑ *'Grow up, Mother.' Jeannie's voice was harsh... Lally said that it was time we all grew up.* V+ADV: USUALLY IMPERATIVE

3 When a place, organization, or idea **grows up**, it starts to exist and becomes larger or more important. ❑ *Cities grew up as markets; centres of religion or trade... The idea has grown up that science cannot be wrong... Complaints and controversy grew up around the scene.* V+ADV

NOTE **Develop** means almost the same as **grow up**.

grow up on If you **grew up on** something, it was always present during your childhood and has had a strong influence on you. ❑ *Tony grew up on tales of London politics.* V+ADV+PREP

grub /grʌb/ (grubs, grubbing, grubbed)

> ☑ **About** is used mainly in British English.

grub about → See grub around

grub around If you **grub around** or **grub about** for something, you search   V+ADV
for it with effort, for example by moving things or by digging. ❑ *He was tired of grubbing about in the public library for material. ...hunched up and grubbing around in the mud.*
NOTE **Root about** means almost the same as **grub about**.

grub out If you **grub out** trees or plants, you dig them out of the ground,   V+ADV+N,
usually because they are no longer wanted. ❑ *I took down the saplings and grubbed out*   V+N+ADV,
the intervening bushes.   V+PRON+ADV

grub up If you **grub** something **up**, you dig it out of the ground. ❑ *...grubbing up*   V+ADV+N,
hedgerows... They grubbed up roots and gathered berries. ...birds grubbing up insects.   V+N+ADV,
    V+PRON+ADV

guard /gɑːrd/ (guards, guarding, guarded)

guard against If you **guard against** something, you do what is necessary to   V+PREP:
make sure that it does not happen or does not affect you. ❑ *They need to guard*   HAS PASSIVE
*against eating too much if they want to keep fit... It does suggest some ways in which we can
guard against the same mistakes in the future... Jealousy is something to be particularly
guarded against.*

guess /ges/ (guesses, guessing, guessed)

guess at If you **guess at** something, you try to give an answer or opinion when   V+PREP:
you do not really have enough information. ❑ *We can only guess at the number of*   HAS PASSIVE
*deaths it has caused... We'll have to guess at what went on there... Its shape and size were
not yet known or even guessed at.*

gulp /gʌlp/ (gulps, gulping, gulped)

gulp down If you **gulp down** food or drink, you eat or drink it all very quickly   V+ADV+N,
by swallowing large quantities of it at a time. ❑ *After gulping down his breakfast in the*   V+PRON+ADV,
morning, he hurried to the station... The old man gulped down his coffee... Obediently, Scylla   V+N+ADV
gulped it down.

gum /gʌm/ (gums, gumming, gummed)

gum up

1 If your eyes or nose **are gummed up**, they are blocked by mucus so that it is   V+N+ADV:
difficult to open your eyes or to breathe easily. ❑ *When he woke in the morning his eyes*   USUALLY PASSIVE
were all gummed up... Cliff, too, was gummed up.

2 To **gum** something **up** means to stop it working properly or efficiently. [INFOR-   V+N+ADV,
MAL] ❑ *Regulators may gum up an efficient system... The house price chain is gummed up.*   V+ADV+N,
    V+PRON+ADV

gun /gʌn/ (guns, gunning, gunned)

gun down To **gun** someone **down** means to shoot them when they are not in   V+ADV+N,
a position to defend themselves. ❑ *Nobody has ever gunned down a New York police cap-*   V+PRON+ADV,
tain and gotten away with it... They can gun him down without the police intervening...   V+N+ADV
Sonny's father was gunned down on the street.

gun for If someone **is gunning for** you, they are trying in a very determined   V+PREP
way to harm you or cause you trouble. [INFORMAL] ❑ *I do not wish to have half the
school gunning for me.*

gussy /gʌsi/ (gussies, gussying, gussied)

gussy up If someone **is gussied up**, they are dressed very smartly. If something   V+N+ADV,
is gussied up, it is made more interesting or attractive. [AMERICAN, INFORMAL]   V+ADV+N,
❑ *They all got gussied up. ...plans to gussy up the venues, offering better food and games ar-*   V+PRON+ADV:
cades.   USUALLY PASSIVE

gut /gʌt/ (guts, gutting, gutted)

gut out If you **gut** it **out**, you continue doing something even though it is diffi-   V+*it*+ADV
cult and you are not succeeding. ❑ *Sometimes you have got to gut it out when you're
playing bad.*

Hh

hack /hæk/ (hacks, hacking, hacked)

hack about If someone **hacks about** the wording of a text, they change it and cut parts out, without caring much about what was originally written. ❑ *My book's been hacked about terribly by the editor... Her prompt-books show how she used to hack about plays.*
V+N+ADV,
V+ADV+N,
V+PRON+ADV

hack at If you **hack at** something, you try to cut it using strong, rough strokes of an axe or knife. ❑ *They hacked at the jungle undergrowth with machetes.*
V+PREP

hack away at If you **hack away at** something, you cut it with strong, rough strokes using a sharp tool such as an axe or knife. ❑ *He started to hack away at the tree bark.*
V+ADV+PREP

hack down If you **hack down** something such as a tree, you cut it down roughly. ❑ *The thick brush was hacked down and burned. ...if a mad axe-man was hacking down the door.*
V+N+ADV,
V+ADV+N,
V+PRON+ADV

hack off

1 If you **hack** something **off**, you remove it by cutting it roughly or violently. ❑ *Someone had hacked his head off... He hacked off three of the branches in a rage.*
NOTE **Chop off** means almost the same as **hack off**.
V+N+ADV,
V+ADV+N,
V+PRON+ADV

2 If someone or something **hacks** you **off**, they make you feel angry. [INFORMAL] ❑ *I'm really hacked off with you people!*
NOTE **Piss off** is a more informal expression for **hack off**.
V+N+ADV,
V+PRON+ADV

hack through If you **hack through** a wood, jungle, scrub, and so on, you move through it by cutting down branches, bushes, and other things. ❑ *The undergrowth becomes so thick we have to hack through it.*
V+PREP

hail /heɪl/ (hails, hailing, hailed)

hail as If a person, event, or achievement **is hailed as** important or successful, they are praised publicly and said to be important or successful. ❑ *They were hailed as heroes by the entire Labour movement... The discovery was hailed as the scientific sensation of the century.*
V+N+PREP,
V+PRON+PREP:
USUALLY PASSIVE

hail from Someone who **hails from** a particular place was born there or lives there. [FORMAL] ❑ *I hail from America.*
V+PREP

ham /hæm/ (hams, hamming, hammed)

ham up If an actor, actress or other performer **hams** it **up**, they exaggerate every word and gesture as they perform, often deliberately in order to amuse the audience. ❑ *She was obviously hamming it up for the benefit of the watching tourists. ...like a bad actor, blustering, hamming it up.*
V+*it*+ADV

hammer /hæmər/ (hammers, hammering, hammered)

hammer away at If you **hammer away at** something, you work at it constantly and with great energy. ❑ *They were all hammering away at their work.*
V+ADV+PREP

hammer in If you **hammer in** an object such as a nail, you hit it with a hammer. ❑ *The workers kneel on the ground and hammer the small stones in.*
V+ADV+N,
V+N+ADV,
V+PRON+ADV

hammer out If you **hammer out** an agreement, you achieve it after a long or difficult discussion. ❑ *There will be trouble unless we actually sit down together and hammer out an agreement for the future. ...procedures hammered out over recent years.*
V+ADV+N,
V+N+ADV,
V+PRON+ADV

hand /hænd/ (hands, handing, handed)

hand around When you **hand around** or **hand round** something such as food, you pass it from one person to another in a group. ❑ *She handed round the*
V+ADV+N,
V+N+ADV,
V+PRON+ADV

cakes... He took the tray in and handed the glasses round. ..the free Jamaican cigars that were always handed around at official functions.

★**hand back**

1 If you **hand** something **back** to someone, you return it to them after you have borrowed or taken it from them. ❑ *He handed back his room key to the receptionist... I examined the lighter, then handed it back... The girl handed him back his card.*

V+ADV+N,
V+PRON+ADV,
V+N+ADV:
ALSO+to:
OR V+PRON+ADV+N

NOTE **Give back** means almost the same as **hand back**.

2 If someone presenting a television or radio programme **hands** the viewers or listeners **back**, they move the transmission to the place or studio where the broadcast began. ❑ *...handing you back now to Jeremy Stevens at the scene of the accident... I'm now going to hand our audience back to the newsroom for a bulletin.*

V+PRON+ADV,
V+N+ADV:
USUALLY+to

hand down

1 If possessions, skills, or knowledge **are handed down**, they are given or left to people who are younger or belong to a younger generation. ❑ *...a house, a plot of land or durable goods which can be handed down from generation to generation... Technical skills such as blacksmithing are usually handed down from father to son as a family tradition.*

V+N+ADV,
V+ADV+N,
V+PRON+ADV:
USUALLY PASSIVE

NOTE **Pass on** means almost the same as **hand down**.

♦ **Hand-me-downs** are things, especially clothing, which have been used by other people before you and which have been given to you for your use. ❑ *...my elder sister's hand-me-downs.*

N-PLURAL

2 If a decision or judgement **is handed down**, it is given publicly by a court or other official body. ❑ *Late the next day, September 15, the indictments were handed down by the grand jury.*

V+N+ADV,
V+ADV+N,
V+PRON+ADV:
USUALLY PASSIVE

★**hand in**

1 If you **hand in** a piece of work, you give it to someone so that they can read, correct, or deal with it. ❑ *In July he handed in the finished version of the novel to the publishers... At half-past eleven they finished, handed their papers in, and smiled with relief.*

V+ADV+N,
V+N+ADV,
V+PRON+ADV

2 If you **hand** something **in**, you give it to someone in authority because it belongs to them or because it is their responsibility to deal with it. ❑ *All the knives had to be handed in with the keys to the larder and the fridge... I had hidden my books and not handed them in... He took off his protective shoes and overalls, handed in his radiation film badge, and walked out.*

V+N+ADV,
V+PRON+ADV,
V+ADV+N

3 If you **hand in** your notice or your resignation, you resign from your job. ❑ *I was tempted to hand in my resignation at once... I handed in my notice and left.*

V+ADV+N,
V+N+ADV,
V+PRON+ADV

hand on If you **hand** something **on** to someone, you give it or leave it to them.
❑ *Property is something handed on from generation to generation... They handed on their knowledge to their children.*

V+N+ADV,
V+ADV+N,
V+PRON+ADV

NOTE **Pass on** means almost the same as **hand on**.

★**hand out**

1 If you **hand** something **out** to people, you give each person in a group one of a set of similar or identical things. ❑ *They handed out questionnaires to the participants... There were helpers outside and inside the Cathedral to guide visitors, hand out leaflets, and control queues... Make a list of names, see if they're all present, and hand the books out.*

V+ADV+N,
V+N+ADV,
V+PRON+ADV:
ALSO+to

♦ A **handout** is a gift of money, clothing, or food, which is given free to poor people by people who are richer than they are or by an organization or charity. ❑ *We said that we wouldn't be relying on handouts from anyone for our future.*

N-COUNT

♦ A **handout** is also a document which gives information about something and is given to people free. ❑ *The handout explains what that means. ...public relations handouts.*

N-COUNT

2 If you **hand out** advice to someone, you give them advice and expect them to follow it. ❑ *She answers the phone and hands out advice and help to overseas students.*

V+ADV+N,
V+N+ADV,
V+PRON+ADV

3 If a judge or person in authority **hands out** a sentence or penalty, they say that somebody should be punished in that way. ❑ *The penalties which he handed out last week were extremely unfair. ...the jail sentence handed out to the Czech dramatist.*

V+N+ADV,
V+ADV+N,
V+PRON+ADV:
ALSO+to

★**hand over**

1 If you **hand** something **over** to someone, you give it to them so that they own it. ❑ *Samuel was about to hand over large sums of money to his local hospital... If you don't do what I ask, I'll take the money and hand it over to him.*

V+N+ADV,
V+PRON+ADV,
V+ADV+N:
ALSO+to

2 When you **hand over** someone such as a prisoner to someone else, you give the

V+PRON+ADV,

control of and responsibility for them to that other person. ❑ *Britain was under no ob-ligation to hand him over to America... Children are often handed over to the child-minder at seven a.m.... I was handed over to two Police sergeants.*

V+N+ADV,
V+ADV+N:
ALSO+to

♦ A **handover** is the official transfer of responsibility for something from one or-ganization or person to another. ❑ *...a refusal to countenance a handover of power.*

N-SING

3 If you **hand over** to someone or **hand** something **over** to them, you give them the responsibility for dealing with a particular situation or problem. ❑ *Sir John handed over to his deputy and left... In 1977 the problem was handed over to a computer... I will willingly retire from this investigation and hand it over.*

V+ADV,
V+N+ADV,
V+ADV+N,
V+PRON+ADV:
ALSO+to

hand <u>o</u>ver to If you **hand over to** someone during a discussion or debate, you invite or allow them to start talking after you have finished saying something. ❑ *Now let's hand over to Kate in the newsroom.*

V+ADV+PREP

hand r<u>ou</u>nd → See **hand around**

hand to If you say that you have got to **hand** it **to** someone, you mean that you admire their skill or achievements, and that you think they deserve a lot of praise. [INFORMAL] ❑ *You have to hand it to them, they're wonderful entertainers.*

V+*it*+PREP

hang /hæŋ/ **(hangs, hanging, hung)**

☑ **About** is used mainly in British English. In American English, **around** is much more common than **round**.

★hang ab<u>ou</u>t

1 → See **hang around**

2 If you ask someone to **hang about**, you ask them to wait or stop for a moment what they are doing or saying. [INFORMAL] ❑ *Now hang about, I'm not going to let you get away with a statement like that.*

IMPERATIVE,
V+ADV

★hang ar<u>ou</u>nd

1 If you **hang around**, **hang about**, or **hang round**, you stay in the same place doing nothing, usually because you are waiting for something or someone. [INFOR-MAL] ❑ *We had to hang around for a while... When I got to school I hung round outside the classroom plucking up courage to go in... She was left to hang about the platform on her own.*

V+ADV,
V+PREP

2 If you **hang around**, **hang about**, or **hang round** a place, you spend a lot of time there, often doing very little. ❑ *They hang around street corners... They hang about the bus shelters, waiting for an unsuspecting victim. ...little flies that hang round rotting fruit.*

V+PREP

3 If you **hang around**, **hang about**, or **hang round** someone, or if you **hang around**, **hang about**, or **hang round** with them, you spend a lot of time with them. [INFORMAL] ❑ *He was always hanging around his bigger brother... You needn't think you can hang about with us... I was becoming more cynical, probably from hanging around with news-papermen.*

V+PREP,
ALSO V+ADV+with,
V+ADV+together:
RECIPROCAL

hang b<u>a</u>ck

1 If you **hang back** in a place such as a school or office, you stay there after everyone else has gone home. ❑ *Often I hung back after classes to ask more questions.*

V+ADV

NOTE **Stay behind** means almost the same as **hang back**.

2 If you **hang back** before doing something, you hesitate before doing it, for example because you are unwilling or afraid to do it. ❑ *The driver was hanging back, still flashing his lights... The rest of the children hung back, watching her.*

V+ADV

3 If a person or organization **hangs back**, they do not do something immediately. ❑ *They will then hang back on closing the deal... Even his closest advisers believe he should hang back no longer.*

V+ADV:
ALSO+on

★hang <u>o</u>n

☑ In meanings 2 and 4, the stress is on **hang**.

1 If you **hang on**, you wait for a short while. [INFORMAL] ❑ *Hang on a minute... I hung on a bit longer.*

V+ADV:
ALSO IMPERATIVE

NOTE **Hold on** means almost the same as **hang on**.

2 Something that **hangs on** something else depends on it in order to be successful. ❑ *Everything hangs on money at the moment... It was a tricky area and his own political future hung on it.*

V+PREP

NOTE **Hinge on** means almost the same as **hang on**.

3 If you **hang on**, you hold something very tightly in order to support yourself or

V+ADV:

protect yourself. ❑ *Hang on tight, folks!... Waves rolled over the little deck and he had to hang on to avoid being washed overboard.*   ALSO IMPERATIVE

NOTE Hold on means almost the same as hang on.

4 If you **hang on** someone's words or if you **hang onto** them, you listen very   V+PREP
carefully to everything they say, because you are very interested. ❑ *I have seen upwards of a thousand people hang on his words with breathless silence.*

5 If you **hang on**, you manage to survive, achieve success, or avoid failure in spite   V+ADV
of great difficulties or opposition. ❑ *Without the support of my parents I would have probably cracked up completely. But I managed to hang on... Manchester United hung on to take the Cup.*

hang onto, hang on to

1 If you **hang onto** something, you hold it very tightly in your hands. ❑ *We were*   V+ADV+PREP
both hanging onto the side of the boat... Claude moaned, and hung on to Tom's shoulder.

2 You can also say that you **hang onto** something when you keep it even though   V+ADV+PREP
it may not be useful or valuable. ❑ *We can hang onto the old jacket for another season.*

3 If you **hang onto** a position or condition that you have such as power or safety,   V+ADV+PREP
you try hard to keep it when something is threatening it. ❑ *...patients who managed to hang onto life for three to four months... He is desperately hanging on to his job.*

4 → See **hang on**

★hang out

1 If you **hang out** clothes that you have washed, you hang them on a clothes line   V+ADV+N,
to dry. ❑ *Mrs Poulter was hanging out her washing.*   V+N+ADV,
V+PRON+ADV

NOTE Peg out means almost the same as hang out.

2 If you **hang out** somewhere, you live there or spend a lot of time there. [INFOR-   V+ADV:
MAL] ❑ *I don't hang out at the factory... He spends a lot of time hanging out with friends.*   WITH A

♦ A **hangout** is a place where you like spending a lot of time because you can relax   N-COUNT
there and meet other people. [INFORMAL] ❑ *This bar became one of my favourite hangouts.*

hang over

1 If something such as a problem **hangs over** you, it worries you a lot. ❑ *I had the*   V+PREP
Open University examination hanging over me. ...the threat of deportation hanging over me.

2 A **hangover** is an idea, attitude, or state of mind which existed in the past but   N-COUNT
which is no longer important or relevant now. ❑ *You've still got this hangover of ideas... That sort of thinking is a hangover from the past.*

3 Someone who is **hungover** feels tired and ill because they have drunk too much   ADJECTIVE
alcohol. [INFORMAL] ❑ *I felt really hungover, although I only had two pints last night.*

4 If you have a **hangover**, you feel tired and ill because you have drunk too much   N-COUNT
alcohol.

hang round → See hang around

hang together

1 Two people or groups that **hang together** stay with each other and support   V+ADV
each other even though they may disagree on some things. ❑ *We have argued. But we have in the end hung together... Scientists within a specialty tend to hang together.*

2 Things such as ideas that **hang together** are properly organized and fit reason-   V+ADV
ably to form a whole or unit. ❑ *All aspects of the struggle hang together... The play doesn't hang together yet.*

★hang up

1 If you **hang** something **up** in a high place or position, you attach it there so   V+ADV+N,
that it does not touch the ground. ❑ *Howard hangs up his scarf on the hook behind the*   V+N+ADV,
door... In the rush to get the job done he didn't hang his notice up.   V+PRON+ADV

2 Something that **is hanging up** in a high place or position is attached there so   V+ADV
that it does not touch the ground. ❑ *There are some old tools hanging up in the shed.*

3 If you **hang up** or you **hang up** the phone, you end a phone call and put back   V+ADV,
the receiver. ❑ *'Thank you. Goodbye.' He hangs up... 'Good night.' He hung up the phone.*   V+ADV+N

4 If you **hang up** something that you use for a particular activity, you stop using   V+ADV+N:
it because you are giving up the activity. ❑ *If your one joy is playing squash, don't hang*   NO PASSIVE
up your racquet.

5 Someone who is **hung up** finds it difficult to deal with certain situations and   ADJECTIVE ideas and so becomes nervous or worried. [INFORMAL] ❏ *You're hung up about your father.*

♦ A **hang-up** is a feeling of fear or embarrassment about something that makes it very difficult for you to deal with certain situations and ideas. [INFORMAL] ❏ *He's got a hang-up about flying. ...adolescent hang-ups.* — N-COUNT

hang up on If you **hang up on** someone who you are speaking to on the phone, you end the phone call suddenly and unexpectedly by putting back the receiver. ❏ *He didn't answer. He just hung up on me.* — V+ADV+PREP

hang with If you **hang with** people, you spend a lot of time with them. [AMERICAN, INFORMAL] ❏ *There's this group of people, from a circle we used to hang with, who've been playing nasty pranks on us.* — V+PREP

NOTE **Hang out with** means almost the same as **hang with**.

hanker /hæŋkəʳ/ (hankers, hankering, hankered)

hanker after If you **hanker after** or **hanker for** something, you have a great desire or longing for it. ❏ *We always hankered after a bungalow of our own.* — V+PREP

NOTE **Crave** is a more formal word for **hanker after**.

hanker for → See **hanker after**

happen /hæpən/ (happens, happening, happened)

happen along If something or someone **happens along**, they arrive or appear unexpectedly and by chance. ❏ *I hadn't been very observant myself. But then, I hadn't been expecting a murder to happen along... She just happened along while we were waiting for the bus.* — V+ADV

happen on If you **happen on** someone or something, you find them or meet them by chance. [LITERARY, OLD-FASHIONED] ❏ *We happened on them in the street.* — V+PREP: HAS PASSIVE

NOTE **Come across** is a more common expression for **happen on**.

hare /heəʳ/ (hares, haring, hared)

hare off If you **hare off**, you run or move quickly away from a place. ❏ *Lebel was haring off down the street, yelling.* — V+ADV

hark /hɑːʳk/ (harks, harking, harked)

hark back to

1 If you **hark back to** something in the past, you remember it or remind someone of it. [LITERARY] ❏ *Increasingly she harked back to our 'dear little' mews... He consistently harked back to St. Thomas Aquinas.* — V+ADV+PREP

2 If something **harks back to** another thing in the past, it is similar to it. [LITERARY] ❏ *...the decorative use of brick harking back to the old farmhouse style.* — V+ADV+PREP

harp /hɑːʳp/ (harps, harping, harped)

harp on If you **harp on** a subject, you keep on talking about it although other people may not want you to. ❏ *But you were the one who kept harping on death, Mother... You do harp on so.* — V+PREP, V+ADV

hash /hæʃ/ (hashes, hashing, hashed)

hash over If people **hash over** a subject or problem, they discuss it in great detail. [AMERICAN] ❏ *Meetings of situational groups should not be devoted to hashing over the past.* — V+ADV+N, V+N+ADV, V+PRON+ADV

hatch /hætʃ/ (hatches, hatching, hatched)

hatch out When a baby bird, insect, or other animal **hatches out** or an egg **hatches out**, the baby animal comes out of the egg by breaking the shell. ❏ *The larva hatches out and lives in the soil... Each of these eggs hatches out into a tiny grub.* — V+ADV: ALSO+*into*

haul /hɔːl/ (hauls, hauling, hauled)

haul in If the police or authorities **haul** someone **in**, they arrest them. ❏ *...boys were regularly hauled in drunk... Wait and get your evidence before you go hauling him in.* — V+N+ADV, V+PRON+ADV, V+ADV+N

haul off If someone **is hauled off**, they are taken to a place against their will. ❏ *Youths are being dragged off buses and hauled off to jail... They tried to haul me off but I resisted.* — V+N+ADV, V+PRON+ADV, V+ADV+N

NOTE **Cart off** means almost the same as **haul off**.

haul up If you **are hauled up** in a court of law or before someone in authority, you are forced to appear in that court or before that person, because you are thought to have broken the law or disobeyed orders. ❑ *He got hauled up in court for assaulting a student... Galileo was hauled up before the Inquisition on charges of heresy.*

PASSIVE:
V+ADV:
WITH A

have /hæv, hæf/ (has, having, had)

✓ **Have got** is often used in informal English in some meanings to mean the same as **have**.

have against If you **have** something **against** someone or something, you disapprove of them because of something you think they did wrong in the past. ❑ *I asked what you had against him... I've never had anything personal against you.*

V+N+PREP

have away → See **have off**

have in If you **have in** workers or experts, you ask them to come to your home or workplace to do some work for you. ❑ *They are having a maid in to care for the house... It's not a normal routine to have Special Branch men in to search when one of us dies.*

V+N+ADV,
V+PRON+ADV

have off If someone **has** it **off** or **has** it **away** with another person, they have sex with them. [BRITISH, INFORMAL] ❑ *Mary had had it off with a waiter in a Greek restaurant. ...love orgies, teenagers having it off and all that.*

V+*it*+ADV,
V+*it*+ADV+*with*:
RECIPROCAL

★have on

1 If you **have on** a piece of clothing, you are wearing it. ❑ *She had on an old bathrobe... Perhaps it had been a nightdress after all, she had certainly had nothing on underneath it.*

V+ADV+N,
V+N+ADV,
V+PRON+ADV:
NO PASSIVE

2 If you **have** a radio, television, or hi-fi **on**, it is switched on and you are usually listening to it or watching it. ❑ *...having the radio on at full blast till all hours.*

V+N+ADV,
V+PRON+ADV:
NO PASSIVE

3 If you **have** someone **on**, you tease them by pretending that something is true when it is not true. ❑ *Or was he having me on? I didn't like to ask.*

V+PRON+ADV,
V+N+ADV,
V+ADV+N

4 If you **have** information **on** someone, you know something about them that you can use to influence them, blackmail them, or prove them guilty in a court. ❑ *'Are you sure Central Records have got nothing on him?' Inspector Flint shook his head.*

V+N+PREP:
NO PASSIVE

have out

1 If you **have** something **out** such as a tooth, your appendix, your tonsils, and so on, a dentist or doctor removes them from your body. ❑ *I had gone to hospital to have my tonsils out. ...having a tooth out on the National Health.*

V+N+ADV,
V+PRON+ADV:
NO PASSIVE

2 If you **have** something **out** with someone, you talk to them about something that has been causing disagreement or unpleasantness between you for some time. ❑ *He felt like picking up the telephone and having it out with him there and then.*

V+PRON+ADV,
V+N+ADV:
ALSO+*with*

hawk /hɔːk/ (hawks, hawking, hawked)

hawk about → See **hawk around**

hawk around If something **is hawked around**, **hawked about**, or **hawked round** a place or a group of people, it is offered for sale. [BRITISH] ❑ *It was hawked around the city streets... For years after her son's death, his mother hawked his manuscript around until she managed to persuade a publisher to accept it.*

V+N+PREP/ADV,
V+PRON+PREP/ADV,
V+ADV+N:
USUALLY PASSIVE

hawk round → See **hawk around**

head /hɛd/ (heads, heading, headed)

★head back If you **head back**, you stop travelling or moving forward and begin your return journey to the place that you came from. ❑ *I didn't head back at once but swam parallel with the shore towards the rocks... We wanted him to turn around and head back to L.A.*

V+ADV:
USUALLY+A

★head for

1 If you **head for** a place, you start moving or travelling towards it. ❑ *We had decided to head for Miami... I headed for the door.*

V+PREP

NOTE **Make for** means almost the same as **head for**.

2 If you **are heading for** or **are headed for** a situation, that situation is becoming more and more likely. ❑ *Mr Reagan was heading for a personal triumph.*

V+PREP:
ALSO PASSIVE:
V+PREP

head into If you **are heading into** a situation or a period of time, especially an unpleasant one, you are starting to experience it. ❑ *She was heading into another of her bad times by the looks of things.*

V+PREP

★head off

1 If you **head off** a person, animal, or vehicle, you try to stop them moving in a particular direction, for example by standing in their way. ❑ *The boys fanned out, trying to head off the goats... I leapt to my feet with the purpose of heading him off.*

V+ADV+N,
V+PRON+ADV,
V+N+ADV

2 If you **head off** something unpleasant, you prevent it from happening. ❑ *Governments may allow wages to rise faster than productivity in order to head off possible unrest... We do too little to head off disaster.*

V+ADV+N,
V+PRON+ADV

3 If you **head off** in a particular direction, you go in that direction. ❑ *She headed off towards the garage.*

V+ADV:
WITH A

★head towards If you **are heading towards** or **are headed towards** a situation or a period of time, the situation or period of time is slowly getting nearer or becoming more likely. ❑ *We were heading towards the General Election.*

V+PREP:
ALSO PASSIVE:
V+PREP

head up If you **head up** a group or team, you take charge of it and are responsible for it. ❑ *I headed up the basketball team at high school.*

V+ADV+N,
V+N+ADV,
V+PRON+ADV

heal /hi:l/ **(heals, healing, healed)**

heal over When a wound **heals over**, the wounded part of your body becomes healthy and normal again. ❑ *When the cord falls off it may leave a raw spot, which takes a number of days to heal over.*

V+ADV

heal up When a wound or other injury **heals up**, the injured part of your body becomes healthy and normal again. ❑ *After his hoof had healed up, Boxer worked harder than ever.*

V+ADV

heap /hi:p/ **(heaps, heaping, heaped)**

heap on If you **heap** praise or criticism **on** or **upon** a person or thing, you praise or criticize them a lot. **Heap upon** is more formal. ❑ *Film director Kenneth Loach heaped praise on the Young Socialists. ...his silent acceptance of the abuse that was being heaped upon him.*

V+N+PREP

heap up If you **heap** things **up**, you put them on top of each other in a large pile. ❑ *Swearing hoarsely, he heaped up the pillows... We saw garbage heaped up almost to the top.*

V+ADV+N,
V+N+ADV,
V+PRON+ADV

NOTE **Pile up** means almost the same as **heap up**.

♦ If you refer to **heaped-up** things, you mean that they are on top of each other in a large pile. ❑ *...heaped-up piles of rice.*

ADJECTIVE

heap upon → See **heap on**

hear /hɪəʳ/ **(hears, hearing, heard)**

★hear about If you **hear about** something or someone, you get news or information concerning them. ❑ *The more I hear about him, the less I like him... I heard about the bomb from Mr Zapp.*

V+PREP

★hear from

1 If you **hear from** someone, you receive a letter or telephone call from them. ❑ *Very occasionally I hear from her.*

V+PREP:
HAS PASSIVE

2 If you **hear from** someone in a meeting or debate, you listen to their opinions. ❑ *I would have liked to hear more from the patient.*

V+PREP

★hear of If you **hear of** someone or something, you get news or information about them for the first time. ❑ *I heard of his death as I was walking into the hospital... I have never heard of him.*

V+PREP:
HAS PASSIVE

♦ An event or situation which is **unheard of** rarely happens, and is therefore very surprising or shocking when it does happen. ❑ *Contracts and written agreements are quite unheard of... This is an unheard-of outrage.*

ADJECTIVE

♦ Someone who is **unheard-of** is not famous or well-known. ❑ *...an unheard-of author.*

ADJECTIVE

hear out If you **hear** someone **out**, you listen without interrupting until they have finished speaking. ❑ *This time you're going to hear me out... Do not be afraid to hear her out.*

V+PRON+ADV,
V+N+ADV

heat /hiːt/ (heats, heating, heated)

★**heat up**

[1] When something **heats up**, it gradually becomes hotter. ❑ *The air over the great land mass heats up in summer and rises... Leave a space for hot air to escape as the bottles heat up.*

V+ADV

[2] If you **heat up** cooked food after it has become cold, you make it hot again. ❑ *He debated heating up the pot roast... It should be delicious cold. Or shall we heat it up?*

V+ADV+N,
V+PRON+ADV,
V+N+ADV

NOTE **Warm up** means almost the same as **heat up**.

[3] If a situation **heats up**, it starts to change very quickly. ❑ *Things were heating up so fast in the US that I did not want to make any rash predictions.*

V+ADV

heave /hiːv/ (heaves, heaving, hove)

heave to In a boat or ship with sails, if the crew **heave to**, they stop the boat, using the sails instead of the anchor. ❑ *Couldn't we heave to, or whatever it is you do?*

V+ADV

heave up If you **heave up**, you vomit. ❑ *He had heaved up his dinner... He heaved up all over the carpet, lay back on the sofa, and fell fast asleep.*

V+ADV+N,
V+N+ADV,
V+PRON+ADV,
V+ADV:
NO PASSIVE

NOTE **Throw up** means almost the same as **heave up**.

hedge /hedʒ/ (hedges, hedging, hedged)

☑ **About** is used mainly in British English. In American English, **around** is much more common than **round**.

hedge about with → See hedge around with

hedge against If you **hedge against** something unpleasant, you do something to try and prevent it from affecting you. ❑ *This deposit provides a way of hedging against fluctuating interest rates.*

V+PREP

hedge around with If something **is hedged around with**, **hedged about with**, or **hedged round with** problems or restrictions, they cause it to be very difficult or complicated. ❑ *The concessions were hedged around with so many restrictions... Her freedom was hedged round with duties and restrictions.*

PASSIVE:
V+ADV+PREP

hedge in If someone or something **is hedged in** by problems or restrictions, the problems or restrictions prevent them from being effective or acting freely. ❑ *The proposals were hedged in with legal niceties... It still hedged the ballot in with a provision that two-thirds of the members had to vote.*

V+ADV+N,
V+N+ADV,
V+PRON+ADV:
USUALLY PASSIVE

hedge round with → See hedge around with

heel /hiːl/ (heels, heeling, heeled)

heel over When someone or something **heels over**, they lean very far to one side, as if they are about to fall. ❑ *At this point, they both heeled over sharply in the crowd... After a moment, he felt as if he were heeling over backwards.*

V+ADV:
USUALLY+A

help /help/ (helps, helping, helped)

help along To **help** a process **along** means to cause it to take place more quickly or more easily. ❑ *You may need to help the process along by pressing with a spoon... Respiratory diseases are often helped along by malnutrition.*

V+N+ADV,
V+PRON+ADV

help off with If you **help** someone **off with** a piece of clothing, you help them to remove it. ❑ *I went to help her off with her cloak... Help me off with my boots... Let me help you off with your coat.*

V+PRON+ADV+PREP,
V+N+ADV+PREP

help on with If you **help** someone **on with** a piece of clothing, you help them to dress. ❑ *Mrs Bixby followed her husband to the door and helped him on with his coat.*

V+PRON+ADV+PREP,
V+N+ADV+PREP

★**help out** If you **help out** or **help** someone **out**, you do them a favour, such as lending them money or doing some of their work. ❑ *Neighbourhood associations help out the poor with funeral expenses... I was asked to come in for a few days to help them out.*

V+ADV+N,
V+PRON+ADV,
V+ADV:
ALSO+with

help to If you **help** someone **to** food or drink, you serve it to them. ❑ *I helped him to some more scotch... She was in the kitchen, helping herself to my biscuits.*

V+PRON+PREP,
V+REFL+PREP,
V+N+PREP

help up If you **help** someone **up**, you help them to stand up again after they have been sitting down or after they have fallen. ❑ *Please help me up. Thank you... She had taken him by the hand, and was helping him up... Howard fastens the button, and helps Henry up from the bench.*

V+PRON+ADV,
V+N+ADV,
V+ADV+N

hem /hem/ (hems, hemming, hemmed)

hem in

1 If a place **is hemmed in** by things, it is enclosed by them. ❑ ...*these roads, being wide and not hemmed in by buildings.* ...*the fields in the valley, hemmed in by hedges.*

2 If people **are hemmed in** by something, they feel that it prevents them from doing what they want to do. ❑ ...*men and women whose lives are hemmed in by bureaucracy.* ...*in our case, hemmed in by so many illusions.* ...*other dimensions than those which seem to hem us in.*

V+ADV+N,
V+N/PRON+ADV:
USUALLY PASSIVE

V+N+ADV,
V+PRON+ADV,
V+ADV+N:
USUALLY PASSIVE

herd /hɜːrd/ (herds, herding, herded)

herd together
If you **herd** people or animals **together**, you gather them into a group. ❑ *The dogs rushed about trying to herd them together... Panic gripped me as they herded us together like sheep.*

V+PRON+ADV,
V+N+ADV,
V+ADV+N

herd up
If you **herd** people or animals **up**, you make them move together to form a group. ❑ *Their dogs helped to herd them up again before any damage was done... Kunta herded up his goats as quickly as he could.*

V+PRON+ADV,
V+ADV+N,
V+N+ADV

NOTE **Round up** means almost the same as **herd up**.

hew /hjuː/ (hews, hewing, hewed, hewn)

☑ The past participle is either **hewed** or **hewn**.

hew down
If you **hew down** something that is standing, such as a tree, you cut through it so that it falls down. [LITERARY] ❑ *They had to hew down several trees and make a raft.*

V+ADV+N,
V+N+ADV,
V+PRON+ADV

NOTE **Chop down** means almost the same as **hew down**.

hew out
If you **hew out** something, you make it by cutting it roughly from a large piece of stone, wood, or ground. [LITERARY] ❑ *Excavators have hewn out an underground car park for 1,000 cars.*

V+ADV+N,
V+N+ADV,
V+PRON+ADV

NOTE **Carve out** means almost the same as **hew out**.

hide /haɪd/ (hides, hiding, hid, hidden)

*hide away

1 If you **hide** something **away**, you put it in a place where nobody else can find it. ❑ *He looked at his drawings of the rocks and hid them away again... I've kept it, but hidden away in a secret place.*

V+PRON+ADV,
V+N+ADV,
V+ADV+N

NOTE **Stash away** means almost the same as **hide away**.

2 If you **hide away**, you go somewhere without telling people where you are going, because you do not want them to find you. ❑ *You see, I may need somewhere to hide away for a week or two.* ...*a small, inexpensive apartment where I could hide away during the hours I wanted to work.*

V+ADV

♦ A **hideaway** is a place where you go without telling other people, because you do not want them to find you. ❑ ...*a Hollywood producer's desert hideaway.*

N-COUNT

3 If someone or something **is hidden away**, they are very far from places where people live or often go. ❑ ...*Rhodes' impressive tomb, hidden away in the country.*

PASSIVE:
V+ADV

hide behind

1 If you **hide behind** something, you use it as an excuse to conceal your real ideas or feelings. ❑ *We can always hide behind the fact that he has no statistical evidence.*

V+PREP

2 If you **hide** a feeling or characteristic **behind** something, you try to hide the fact that you have it. ❑ *He hid his feelings behind a gruff abruptness... An astute and lively mind lay hidden behind his slow movements.*

V+N+PREP,
V+PRON+PREP

*hide from

1 If you **hide from** someone, you go somewhere where they cannot see you. ❑ *They hid from him among the trees.*

V+PREP:
HAS PASSIVE

2 If you **hide from** something, you try to pretend that you do not know it although you do. ❑ *All I could do was to hide from the truth.*

V+PREP

3 If you **hide** something **from** someone, you try to prevent them from seeing it or noticing it. ❑ *He hid the ignition key from her... After Jesus said this, he went off and hid himself from them... The truth was being hidden from the public.*

V+N+PREP,
V+REFL+PREP,
V+PRON+PREP

hide out
If you **hide out**, you go somewhere without telling people where you are going, because you do not want them to find you. ❑ *If the press were really after*

V+ADV:
USUALLY+A

me it would be better to hide out until it all blew over... He has been hiding out in a provincial village.

♦ A **hideout** is a place where you go without telling people where you are going, because you do not want them to find you. ❑ *Perhaps they used this house as a hideout?... Their leaders took to hideouts in the Pondoland hills.*

N-COUNT

hide up If you **hide up**, you go somewhere without telling people where you are going, because you do not want them to find you. ❑ *Kitty, we know that Dov Landau is safe. He is hiding up at Gera.*

V+ADV

hike /haɪk/ (hikes, hiking, hiked)
hike up

1 If you **hike up** a piece of clothing that you are wearing, you pull it up with a quick movement. ❑ *He hiked up his trouser leg... Mrs Halverston hiked up her skirt and sprang onto the tailgate.*
NOTE **Hitch up** means almost the same as **hike up**.

V+ADV+N,
V+N+ADV,
V+PRON+ADV

2 If someone **hikes up** a price or other sum of money, they increase it suddenly and by a large amount. ❑ *...buy up supplies while they are cheap and hence hike the price up... The newly installed government hiked the timber export royalty up.*
NOTE **Push up** means almost the same as **hike up**.

V+N+ADV,
V+ADV+N,
V+PRON+ADV

hinge /hɪndʒ/ (hinges, hinging, hinged)

hinge on If one thing **hinges on** or **hinges upon** another, its existence or qualities depend entirely on the existence or qualities of the other thing. ❑ *He said everything hinged on what happened to the United States economy... Their future well-being hinged upon victory.*
NOTE **Hang on** means almost the same as **hinge on**.

V+PREP

hinge upon → See hinge on

hint /hɪnt/ (hints, hinting, hinted)

hint at If you **hint at** something, you suggest in a very indirect way that it is true or likely. ❑ *It was the only time Natalie had hinted at the possibility of their marriage breaking up... The weather forecast has already hinted at snow showers in the north... Marriage had already been hinted at.*
NOTE **Imply** means almost the same as **hint at**.

V+PREP:
HAS PASSIVE

hire /haɪər/ (hires, hiring, hired)

hire out If you **hire out** something such as a car or a person's services, you allow them to be used in return for payment. ❑ *Holborn library hires out reproductions and original pictures. ...labourers whom they would be glad to hire out on moderate terms.*
NOTE **Rent out** means almost the same as **hire out**.

V+ADV+N,
V+N+ADV,
V+PRON+ADV

hit /hɪt/ (hits, hitting)

☑ **Hit** is used in the present tense and is the past tense and past participle of the verb.

hit at

1 If you **hit at** someone, you aim a blow at them. ❑ *When I refused he hit at my shoulders and arms with the strap.*

V+PREP

2 If you **hit at** something, you try to damage it. ❑ *To begin with, little effort was made to hit at the morale of the Russians themselves.*

V+PREP

★hit back

1 If you **hit back** or **hit** someone **back**, you hit them after they have hit you. ❑ *Thomas staggered and then hit back... I still refused, and felt ready to hit back if he hit me again... Then Marks will pretend to hit the child back.*

V+ADV,
V+N+ADV,
V+PRON+ADV

2 If you **hit back** at someone, you criticize or harm them after they have criticized or harmed you. ❑ *John was obsessed with hitting back at those who had wronged him... If someone infringes upon your personal freedom, you hit back.*

V+ADV:
ALSO+at

hit off If two people **hit** it **off**, they like each other and become friends as soon as they meet. ❑ *They had hit it off from the first evening... My mother-in-law and Tom did not hit it off.*

V+it+ADV:
ALSO+with,
RECIPROCAL

hit on

1 If you **hit on** or **hit upon** an idea, you think of it, especially when it is a solu-

V+PREP

tion to a problem. ❑ *Tired of letting the cat in and out, he hit on the idea of cutting a hole in the door... Many ideas were considered and rejected before he finally hit on the plan he decided to adopt... The architects independently hit upon the same idea for the chief feature.*

NOTE **Stumble on** means almost the same as **hit on**.

2 If someone **hits on** you, they speak or behave in a way that shows they want to have a sexual relationship with you. [INFORMAL] ❑ *She was hitting on me and I was surprised and flattered.*

V+PREP

*hit out

1 If you **hit out** in a fight, you aim punches in all directions around you, trying to hit the person or people who are fighting you or trying to capture you. [BRITISH] ❑ *Ralph hit out; then he and a dozen others were rolling over, hitting, biting, scratching... A sick fear and rage swept him. Fiercely he hit out at the filthy thing in front of him.*

V+ADV:
ALSO+at

NOTE **Lash out** means almost the same as **hit out**.

2 If you **hit out** at someone you disagree with, you attack or criticize them strongly. ❑ *The Prime Minister hit out at colleagues in Europe. ...hitting out with the full might of state apparatus.*

V+ADV:
ALSO+at

NOTE **Lash out** means almost the same as **hit out**.

hit upon → See hit on

hitch /hɪtʃ/ (hitches, hitching, hitched)

hitch up If you **hitch up** a piece of clothing, you pull it up to a higher position on your body. ❑ *Stein hitched up his trousers and tucked in his shirt... Hitching her dress up she lay back in the chair.*

V+ADV+N,
V+N+ADV,
V+PRON+ADV

hive /haɪv/ (hives, hiving, hived)

hive off If you **hive off** a business or a part of a business, you sell it or transfer it to someone, usually for a large profit. [BRITISH] ❑ *...included a provision to hive off London Transport to the LCC... In 1968 he tried an alternative approach, hiving off the nuclear research lab.*

V+ADV+N,
V+N+ADV,
V+PRON+ADV

NOTE **Sell off** means almost the same as **hive off**.

hoard /hɔːrd/ (hoards, hoarding, hoarded)

hoard away If you **hoard** something **away**, you hide it and keep it hidden until you want it. ❑ *All we could think about sometimes was chocolate: we used to hoard it away in our lockers.*

V+PRON+ADV,
V+N+ADV,
V+ADV+N

hoard up If you **hoard up** something, you try to keep a lot of it, so that you can use it later. ❑ *You always seem to hoard up stuff.*

V+ADV+N,
V+N+ADV,
V+PRON+ADV

hoke /hoʊk/ (hokes, hoking, hoked)

hoke up If you **hoke** something **up**, you pretend that it exists and make it seem to be more important than it really is. [AMERICAN, INFORMAL] ❑ *It suited Humboldt to hoke that up.*

V+N+ADV,
V+ADV+N,
V+PRON+ADV

hold /hoʊld/ (holds, holding, held)

hold against If you **hold** something **against** someone, you allow something that they did wrong in the past to influence you and cause you to deal harshly with them. ❑ *Nationalising for the wrong reasons will be held against him when the crunch comes... He's a good friend of mine. He won't hold it against us.*

V+N+PREP,
V+PRON+PREP

*hold back

1 If you **hold back**, or if something **holds** you **back**, you hesitate before you act or speak, because you are not sure what to do or say. ❑ *Police have held back from going into a holy place to arrest him... I have noticed that you do not hold back in our discussions... She couldn't quite say what it was that held her back.*

V+ADV,
V+PRON+ADV,
V+N+ADV,
V+REFL+ADV

2 If you **hold** someone **back**, you prevent them from leaving a place. ❑ *Judy held him back. 'Don't, Bal,' she said... They were doubtful as to how far they would be able to hold back all their units.*

V+PRON+ADV,
V+ADV+N,
V+N+ADV

3 If you **hold** a person or their career **back**, you prevent them from making progress. ❑ *If she is ambitious, don't try to hold her back. ...the prejudices which are holding you back in your career.*

V+PRON+ADV,
V+N+ADV,
V+ADV+N

4 If you **hold back** an event or development, you prevent it from taking place or cause it to happen more slowly. ❑ *The rise in living standards has been held back for so*

V+N+ADV,
V+ADV+N,
V+PRON+ADV:

long... Worry about the environment has been one of the key restraints in holding back economic development. ...holding back on the spread of consumer non-essentials. `ALSO+on`

5 If you **hold back** resources, you keep them in reserve to use later. ❑ *They need the money immediately and cannot hold back their goods to push the price up... 10 per cent of their funding will be held back until they start the new project.* `V+ADV+N, V+N+ADV, V+PRON+ADV`

6 If you **hold back** information, you do not reveal it. ❑ *'You knew Gareth quite well at one time, then?' He could hold it back no longer. 'Yes, at Oxford.'... I can see you are holding certain things back, things you haven't said.* `V+PRON+ADV, V+N+ADV, V+ADV+N`

NOTE **Suppress** is a more formal word for **hold back**.

7 If you **hold back** tears or laughter, you do not allow yourself to cry or laugh, because you do not want to show your emotions. ❑ *Most of us were either crying or doing our best to hold back the tears... He could no longer hold back convulsive laughter, and stopped speaking.* `V+ADV+N, V+N+ADV, V+PRON+ADV: NO PASSIVE`

NOTE **Keep back** means almost the same as **hold back**, and **contain** is a more formal word.

★hold down

1 If you **hold** someone or something **down**, you use force to keep them in a particular place and to stop them from moving. ❑ *Ash was barely eight years old, but it had taken four men to hold him down, for he was strong and wiry... I was trying all the time to hold down the lid of the box with one hand.* `V+PRON+ADV, V+ADV+N, V+N+ADV`

2 If someone **holds down** a group of people, they do not allow them to have freedom, power, or rights. ❑ *There would still not be enough forces to hold down the previously subject peoples... Levi put up a rather better show, holding the Romans down till November.* `V+ADV+N, V+N+ADV, V+PRON+ADV`

NOTE **Keep down** means almost the same as **hold down**.

3 If you **hold down** a job, you manage to keep it, although it may be difficult for you to do so. ❑ *There is nothing surprising about finding a woman holding down a successful job in high finance... You have to rely on reason, not authority, if you hold down a job.* `V+ADV+N, V+N+ADV, V+PRON+ADV`

4 If you **hold down** wages, prices, or costs, you prevent them from increasing very much. ❑ *Did they think that Sir Geoffrey's policy would hold down inflation?... Such fights are unavoidable if long-term costs are to be held down.* `V+ADV+N, V+N+ADV, V+PRON+ADV`

NOTE **Keep down** means almost the same as **hold down**.

5 If you **hold down** an emotion such as fear or hysteria, you do not allow yourself to show or express it. ❑ *I could hold my emotions down no longer... The figure fades and I hold panic down.* `V+N+ADV, V+ADV+N, V+PRON+ADV: NO PASSIVE`

6 If you cannot **hold down** food, you are unable to eat it without vomiting. ❑ *The patient loses his appetite and cannot hold down some kinds of food.* `V+ADV+N, V+N+ADV, V+PRON+ADV: NO PASSIVE`

NOTE **Keep down** means almost the same as **hold down**.

hold forth If you **hold forth** on a topic, you talk about it for a long time, often in a rather boring way. ❑ *He was busy holding forth on the pleasures of travel. ...holding forth about the duty of Christian missionaries... I was holding forth to the actors when I suddenly heard peals of laughter.* `V+ADV: USUALLY WITH on/about`

hold in If you **hold in** an emotion, you do not allow yourself to express it. ❑ *Women are expected to hold in their anger... She wanted to cry but held in the tears... 'Running about naked in a garden!' The old woman could hold it in no longer: such a mixture of impropriety and carelessness was unbearable.* `V+ADV+N, V+PRON+ADV, V+N+ADV`

★hold off

1 If you **hold off** an enemy, an opponent, or an attack, you prevent them from successfully attacking you or competing against you. ❑ *The warriors tried to hold the soldiers off until the women and children could escape. ...watching my teammates try to hold off Al Redding's determined efforts to score... The French and British wanted to hold off Portuguese textile competition.* `V+N+ADV, V+ADV+N, V+PRON+ADV`

NOTE **Fight off** means almost the same as **hold off**.

2 If you **hold off** doing something, you delay doing it or making a decision about it. ❑ *He might be so scared that he'll hold off our offer too... Everyone holds off buying as long as they can, if they think the price still has a way to drop.* `V+ADV+N, V+ADV+-ING, V+ADV: NO PASSIVE`

3 If the rain **holds off**, it does not rain, although you had expected it to. ❑ *That storm was really something. We were just blessed that it held off for the picnic.* `V+ADV`

hold on

★hold on

1 If you **hold on**, you grasp something firmly or lean against it, in order to pre-   `V+ADV:`
vent yourself from falling over. ❑ *I grabbed hold of the front and held on for dear life...*   `ALSO+to`
Someone was standing behind the ladder and holding on to it for support.

2 If you are in a difficult situation but **hold on**, you force yourself to continue do-   `V+ADV`
ing something or to stick to a decision you have made. ❑ *The thought depressed her*
violently. But she held on. It would pass. She had to breathe deeply... I would find myself
again if I could just hold on, be quiet, and lie down.
NOTE **Give up** means the opposite of **hold on**.

3 If you ask someone to **hold on**, you want them to wait for a short time. ❑ *Hold*   `V+ADV:`
on a moment, please... Do you mind holding on while I find out?... Hold on! One at a time!   `USUALLY+A`
NOTE **Hang on** means almost the same as **hold on**.

★hold on to, hold onto

1 If you **hold on to** something that is in your hand, you grip it tightly so that it   `V+ADV+PREP`
cannot fall or cannot be taken away from you. ❑ *Jordache took a step back, holding on*
to the drawing... They all held firmly on to their brief-cases.

2 If you **hold on to** someone, you keep your arms round them so that they can-   `V+ADV+PREP`
not move or go away. ❑ *I stayed where I was on the sofa and held on to Humboldt... Then*
suddenly they stopped, holding on to each other and laughing.

3 If you **hold on to** something that you have, you keep it for yourself and do not   `V+ADV+PREP`
let anyone else have it. ❑ *He permitted Rudolph to hold on to the money he earned. ...poli-*
ticians like himself who want to hold on to power at all costs... He could sell off blocks of
stock while holding on to the controlling interest in the corporation.

4 If you **hold on to** something that is old-fashioned, you continue to keep it or   `V+ADV+PREP`
use it. ❑ *...where people hold on to unmarketable skills. ...developing electric cars instead of*
holding on to the old-fashioned internal combustion engine.

5 If you **hold on to** something, you keep it for a longer time than would normally   `V+ADV+PREP`
be expected. ❑ *People hold onto letters for years and years.*

6 If you ask someone to **hold on to** something for you, you want them to look af-   `V+ADV+PREP`
ter it until you ask for it back. ❑ *Will you hold on to this for me for a couple of days?*

7 If you **hold on to** a belief, idea, or principle, you continue to believe in it and   `V+ADV+PREP`
do not change or abandon it. ❑ *If enough people can hold on to their dream, this will be-*
come possible... Helen spoke carefully, no longer holding on to the delusion that she was en-
gaged in a casual conversation.

★hold out

1 If you **hold out** your hand, you stretch it out in front of you, usually in order to   `V+ADV+N,`
take something from someone or to shake hands with them. ❑ *Daintry held out his*   `V+N+ADV,`
hand for the briefcase... She held out a hand and he shook it.   `V+PRON+ADV`

2 If you **hold** something **out**, you hold it in front of you, so that someone can   `V+ADV+N,`
take it or look at it. ❑ *He held out his plate for a second portion... He held out his arm.*   `V+PRON+ADV,`
'Look.'... He took off his glasses and held them out to Ralph.   `V+N+ADV:`
  `ALSO+to`

3 If you **hold out**, you manage to resist an enemy, an opponent, or an attack.   `V+ADV:`
❑ *They could either surrender or hold out, risking starvation or death at the hands of*   `ALSO+against`
Carson's soldiers... But even he began to despair of holding out indefinitely against the pres-
sures building up... It was just a matter of holding out one day at a time.
NOTE **Give in** means the opposite of **hold out**.

♦ A **holdout** is someone who resists an enemy, an opponent, or an attack. ❑ *The*   `N-COUNT`
only holdout at first was the old Afrikaner... Manuelito was the last of the holdouts.

4 If you **hold out** hope of something, you are hopeful that it will happen or suc-   `V+ADV+N:`
ceed. ❑ *Benn himself held out no hopes for victory... Science may hold out some prospect of*   `NO PASSIVE`
feeding the hungry multitudes. ...a programme which held out the possibility of a successful
attack on poverty and inequality.

5 If supplies of something **hold out**, there is enough for you to use for a certain   `V+ADV`
period of time. ❑ *I decided to stay in that place as long as the water held out... The room*
was expensive, but my cash was holding out better than I had expected.
NOTE **Last out** means almost the same as **hold out**.

hold out for If you **hold out for** something, you insist on having it and refuse   `V+ADV+PREP`
to accept anything less than you are asking for. ❑ *Jamaica was holding out for a higher*

sugar price. ...every Cheyenne and Arapaho chief who had held out for peace with the white men... Tanya offered thirty-five dollars; the passenger held out for forty-five.

hold out on If you **hold out on** someone, you refuse to tell them something that you know or give them something that you promised to give them. ❑ *I couldn't hold out on him any more.* V+ADV+PREP

hold over

1 If you **hold** something **over** someone, you use it in order to threaten them or make them do what you want. ❑ *He held the Will over her like a threat... 'Now I've got something to hold over you!' he said.* V+N+PREP, V+PRON+PREP

2 If you **hold** something **over**, you decide not to discuss it or deal with it until a future date. ❑ *Its proposals should be held over until everyone has had a good think... The prize may be held over until a subsequent year when two awards may be awarded.* V+N+ADV, V+PRON+ADV, V+ADV+N

NOTE **Defer** is a more formal word for **hold over**.

3 A **holdover** is something that exists after the time that it was intended for or when it was appropriate. ❑ *...a holdover from early infancy... The present curriculum is a holdover from the past.* N-SING

hold to

1 When you **hold** one thing **to** another, you take it in your hands, put it next to the other thing, and keep it there. ❑ *I struggled on, holding the cage tight to my chest.* V+N+PREP, V+PRON+PREP

2 If you **hold to** an opinion, belief, or habit, you will not or cannot change it. ❑ *The country must not hold to rigid concepts of international alignments... Later at a brief meeting, he would hold to his decision. ...if all the points which were raised were held to by the British government.* V+PREP: HAS PASSIVE

NOTE **Stick to** means almost the same as **hold to**.

hold together

1 When you **hold** people **together** or when they **hold together**, they manage to live or work together without arguing or disagreeing, although they have different ideas, interests, or opinions. ❑ *...if the parents hold the family together in spite of friction... Chiang's design was simply to hold together some sort of Nationalist Army... A group can hold together unless there's a general exodus.* V+N+ADV, V+ADV+N, V+ADV, V+PRON+ADV: ERGATIVE

2 If something **holds together**, it stays in good condition. ❑ *The problem now seemed to be whether the car would hold together. ...the original bag, which held together long enough.* V+ADV

★hold up

1 If you **hold up** your hand or something you have in your hand, you move it upwards into a particular position and keep it there. ❑ *Ralph held up his hand. 'Why shouldn't we get our own?'... The Englishman held up the rifle... The children were meant to hold up the President's book.* V+ADV+N, V+N+ADV, V+PRON+ADV

NOTE **Raise** is a more formal word for **hold up**.

2 If one thing **holds up** another, it is placed under the other thing in order to support it and prevent it from falling. ❑ *...steel girders to hold up skyscrapers... These books hold the bed up.* V+ADV+N, V+N+ADV, V+PRON+ADV

NOTE **Prop up** means almost the same as **hold up**.

3 If something or someone **holds up** an activity or arrangement, they delay it or make it late. ❑ *These slogans persuaded her to hold up the procession... The EC threatened to hold up the negotiations... The whole thing was held up about half an hour.* V+ADV+N, V+N+ADV, V+PRON+ADV

♦ A **hold-up** is a delay or something which causes a delay. ❑ *I nearly missed my flight owing to a traffic hold-up.* N-COUNT

4 If someone **holds** you **up**, they point a weapon at you in order to make you give them money or valuables. ❑ *He held me up at the point of a gun... Banks were held up with pistols and sawn-off shotguns.* V+N+ADV, V+PRON+ADV, V+ADV+N

NOTE **Rob** means almost the same as **hold up**.

♦ A **holdup** is a robbery in which weapons are used to force people to give their money or valuables to the robbers. ❑ *Seven people were wounded towards the end of July in different hold-ups.* N-COUNT

5 If you **hold up** someone or their behaviour or habits, you use them as an example to tell people your opinion about them and persuade them to agree with you. ❑ *What do you hold up to the children as being desirable goals?... He would hold them up to* V+N+ADV, V+PRON+ADV, V+REFL+ADV, V+ADV+N: USUALLY+A

The symbol ★ shows key phrasal verbs

contempt and ridicule... I don't hold myself up as a good churchgoer... I wasn't the sort of child anyone would ever hold up as an example to others.

6 If equipment or clothing **holds up**, it remains in good condition after rough use. ❏ *How did your boots hold up?*   V+ADV

7 If something such as a type of business **holds up** in difficult conditions, it stays in a reasonably good state. ❏ *Children's wear is one area that is holding up well in the recession.*   V+ADV

8 If ideas, systems, or plans **hold up**, they remain convincing or effective after examination or use. ❏ *Your argument, though appealing, doesn't hold up... None of his stories would hold up in public.*   V+ADV

NOTE **Stand up** means almost the same as **hold up**.

hold with If you do not **hold with** an activity or idea,, you do not approve of it. ❏ *You know I don't hold with letter-writing. ...a man who did not hold with the notion that it was necessary.*   V+PREP: WITH NEGATIVE

NOTE **Agree with** means almost the same as **hold with**.

hole /hoʊl/ (holes, holing, holed)

hole out In golf, if you **hole out** in a certain number of points, you finish one of the holes or the course with that number of points. ❏ *In the six rounds he played, he never holed out in less than 92.*   V+ADV: USUALLY+in

hole up If you **hole up** somewhere, you hide yourself there. [INFORMAL] ❏ *The men were holed up on the top floor of the hotel... San Francisco was where she holed up... I was ready to hole up there indefinitely.*   V+ADV: ALSO PASSIVE: V+ADV: USUALLY+A

hollow /hɒloʊ/ (hollows, hollowing, hollowed)

hollow out If you **hollow out** something that is solid, you make a space in it by removing the inside part of it. ❏ *Some kids had hollowed out tunnels in a maize field... Then we hollow it out a little... They spent the night in a small snow hole they had hollowed out under a rock.*   V+ADV+N, V+PRON+ADV, V+N+ADV

♦ Something that is **hollowed-out** has had the inside part of it removed. ❏ *...a hollowed-out tree-stump.*   ADJECTIVE

home /hoʊm/ (homes, homing, homed)
home in

1 If something which is travelling through the air or through water **homes in** on something else, it moves directly towards it very rapidly. ❏ *The missile can thus home in on the target with pinpoint accuracy... The shark turned, homing in on the stream of blood.*   V+ADV: USUALLY+on

2 If you **home in** on a particular subject or topic, you pay more attention to it and deal with it in detail. ❏ *She homed in on the things we were discussing.*   V+ADV: USUALLY+on

hook /hʊk/ (hooks, hooking, hooked)
★hook up

1 If a computer or other electronic machine **is hooked up**, it is connected to similar machines or a central power supply. ❏ *...receivers, hooked up to screens and displaying information immediately... The loud-speaker system was hooked up. ...hooking it up to an electronic typewriter.*   V+N+ADV, V+PRON+ADV, V+ADV+N: ALSO+to, USUALLY PASSIVE

NOTE **Link up** means almost the same as **hook up**.

♦ A **hook-up** is an electronic or radio connection between computers or other electronic machines. ❏ *...telephone and TV antenna hook-ups.*   N-COUNT

2 If you **hook** something **up**, you hang or fix it in a particular position, using a hook. ❏ *Hook up that hose, Lucius... We had to hook the log chains up to the axle.*   V+ADV+N, V+N+ADV, V+PRON+ADV

3 If one person, especially a musician, **hooks up** with another, the two people start working with each other. You can also say that two people **hook up**. ❏ *They moved to LA where they hooked up with drummer Ginger Baker... Seeing as how we got on so well together, it just seemed natural that we should hook up.*   V+ADV, V+ADV+with: RECIPROCAL

hoot /huːt/ (hoots, hooting, hooted)

hoot down If someone who is making a speech **is hooted down**, the people in the audience force them to stop talking by shouting at them. ❏ *Scientists who tried to speak at the recent meeting were hooted down... One of the Presidents of the Royal Society*   V+N+ADV, V+PRON+ADV, V+ADV+N: USUALLY PASSIVE

was hooted down when he gave a talk.
NOTE **Boo** and **shout down** mean almost the same as **hoot down**.

hoot off If someone who is performing on stage **is hooted off**, the people in the audience force them to stop performing and to leave the stage by shouting at them. ❑ *The comic was hooted off after ten minutes... He was hooted off the stage.*
NOTE **Boo** means almost the same as **hoot off**.

V+N+ADV,
V+PRON+ADV,
V+N+PREP,
V+PRON+PREP

hoover /ˈhuːvər/ **(hoovers, hoovering, hoovered)**

hoover up To **hoover** something **up** means to take large amounts of it for yourself, especially when this is unfair. ❑ *He wants the cash to hoover up recession-hit hotels and pubs while prices are low.*

V+N+ADV,
V+PRON+ADV,
V+ADV+N

hop /hɒp/ **(hops, hopping, hopped)**

hop off If you tell someone to **hop off**, you are telling them rather rudely to go away. [INFORMAL] ❑ *Hop off, I'm busy.*
NOTE **Buzz off** means almost the same as **hop off**.

IMPERATIVE,
V+ADV

hope /hoʊp/ **(hopes, hoping, hoped)**

★**hope for** If you **hope for** something, you want it and expect to have it. ❑ *They cannot hope for a rise bigger than two per cent... He paused, hoping for evidence of interest... It's already too late to hope for a good summer.*

V+PREP:
HAS PASSIVE

horn /hɔːrn/ **(horns, horning, horned)**

horn in If you **horn in** on an activity or situation, you force your way into it when you are not welcome. [AMERICAN] ❑ *...horning in on all the exciting bits.*

V+ADV:
USUALLY+on

horse /hɔːrs/ **(horses, horsing, horsed)**

✓ About is used mainly in British English.

horse about → See horse around

horse around If you **horse around** or **horse about**, you play roughly and rather carelessly. [INFORMAL] ❑ *He loved to horse around with them. ...having all the fun, horsing around.*
NOTE **Fool around** means almost the same as **horse around**.

V+ADV

hose /hoʊz/ **(hoses, hosing, hosed)**

hose down If you **hose** something **down**, you clean it using water from a hose. ❑ *Could you not get the sanitation department to hose the place down?... Joseph was hosing down the new tractor... He had to enter the chamber and hose it down.*
NOTE **Wash down** means almost the same as **hose down**.

V+N+ADV,
V+ADV+N,
V+PRON+ADV

hose out When you **hose** something **out**, you clean the inside of it using water from a hose. ❑ *Would you mind hosing the bins out this afternoon?... She hosed out the barn.*
NOTE **Wash out** means almost the same as **hose out**.

V+N+ADV,
V+ADV+N,
V+PRON+ADV

hot /hɒt/ **(hots, hotting, hotted)**

hot up When an event **hots up**, it becomes more active or exciting. [BRITISH] ❑ *Now the pace really began to hot up... The U.S. election campaign was hotting up.*

V+ADV,
V+N+ADV,
V+PRON+ADV,
V+ADV+N:
ERGATIVE

hound /haʊnd/ **(hounds, hounding, hounded)**

hound out If someone **is hounded out** of a place, they are forced to leave it. ❑ *They were hounded out of their small shack... The police had hounded the gypsies out mercilessly. ...hounding him out of house and home.*

V+N+ADV,
V+PRON+ADV,
V+ADV+N:
ALSO+of

howl /haʊl/ **(howls, howling, howled)**

howl down If someone **is howled down**, they are prevented from speaking by other people who shout at them. [BRITISH] ❑ *He was howled down by monarchists.*
NOTE **Shout down** means almost the same as **howl down**.

V+N+ADV,
V+PRON+ADV,
V+ADV+N:
USUALLY PASSIVE

huddle /ˈhʌdəl/ **(huddles, huddling, huddled)**

✓ About is used mainly in British English. In American English, **around** is much more common than **round**.

huddle about → See huddle around

huddle around If people **huddle around**, **huddle about** or **huddle round** something, they gather near it and stand or sit close to it. ❑ *They huddled about their*

V+PREP/ADV:
ALSO PASSIVE:
V+PREP/ADV

crackling fires... They huddled around to listen... The actors were all huddled round the direc-tor.

NOTE **Cluster around** means almost the same as **huddle around**.

huddle down If you **huddle down**, you move your body so that your legs are   V+ADV
bent under you and you are close to the ground. ❑ *Kunta then huddled down as well...
What a pair of idiots you must have looked, huddled down there.*

huddle round → See **huddle around**

huddle together

1 If people **huddle together**, they stand, sit, or lie close to each other because   V+ADV;
they are cold or frightened. ❑ *All we did was huddle together for warmth... We can huddle*   ALSO PASSIVE:
together while we wait. ...evacuees, huddled together on railways stations.   V+ADV

2 If a group of buildings **are huddled together**, they are very close to each other.   PASSIVE:
❑ *...a row of old houses huddled together... I passed a small group of caravans, huddled to-*   V+ADV
gether a hundred yards from the main road.

huddle up When people **huddle up**, they sit or stand very close to each other,   V+ADV
for example because they are frightened or cold. ❑ *When she left her seat it was to huddle up with her sister... There was a figure standing close to me, huddled up against the
wind.*

hunger /hʌŋgəʳ/ (hungers, hungering, hungered)

hunger after If you **hunger after** something, you want it very much and try   V+PREP
to get it. ❑ *What makes people hunger after power?*

NOTE **Hanker after** means almost the same as **hunger after**.

hunger for If you **hunger for** something, you want it very much, usually be-   V+PREP
cause you have not been able to have it for a long time. ❑ *...a meeting place for Span-
iards who hunger for Flamenco music. ...all that she had hungered for so fiercely.*

hunker /hʌŋkəʳ/ (hunkers, hunkering, hunkered)

hunker down

1 If you **hunker down**, you sit close to the ground so that you are balanced on   V+ADV
your feet with your legs bent. [AMERICAN] ❑ *He hunkered down by the open door... I
hunkered down for the long wait.*

NOTE **Crouch down** means almost the same as **hunker down**.

2 If you say that someone **hunkers down**, you mean that they are trying to avoid   V+ADV
doing things that will make them noticed or put them in danger. [AMERICAN] ❑ *Their
strategy for the moment is to hunker down and let the furor die.*

NOTE **Lie low** means almost the same as **hunker down**.

hunt /hʌnt/ (hunts, hunting, hunted)

hunt down If you **hunt** someone or something **down**, you succeed in finding   V+PRON+ADV,
them after you have been searching for them. ❑ *I hid, but they hunted me down in the*   V+ADV+N,
end... If there's a beast, we'll hunt it down!... It was obvious that the militia had hunted   V+N+ADV
down their victims.

NOTE **Track down** means almost the same as **hunt down**.

hunt out If you **hunt out** something, you succeed in finding it after you have   V+ADV+N,
been looking for it. ❑ *I hunted out our Christmas tree lights... The women set out to hunt*   V+N+ADV,
out feminist centres... Just let me hunt my bag out – it's here somewhere.   V+PRON+ADV

NOTE **Dig out** means almost the same as **hunt out**.

hunt up If you **hunt up** something that is needed, you manage to find it. ❑ *The*   V+ADV+N,
staff there aren't very good at hunting up information for you... I trusted he wasn't likely to   V+N+ADV,
hunt up that particular page again.   V+PRON+ADV;
   NO PASSIVE

NOTE **Chase up** means almost the same as **hunt up**.

hurl /hɜːʳl/ (hurls, hurling, hurled)

☑ **About** is used mainly in British English. In American English, **around** is much
more common than **round**.

hurl about → See **hurl around**

hurl around If you **hurl** things **around**, **hurl** them **about**, or **hurl** them   V+N+PREP/ADV,
round, you throw them forcefully in lots of different directions. ❑ *She overturned the*   V+PRON+PREP/ADV

chairs and hurled the cushions about. ...food she could hurl around the kitchen... It looked like someone had been hurling bottles of ink around.

hurl round → See **hurl around**

hurry /hʌri, AM hɜːri/ **(hurries, hurrying, hurried)**

hurry on

1 If you **hurry on**, you continue walking quickly or running without stopping. ❑ *Their staring eyes made me hurry on... The man hurried on with a preoccupied look on his face.*
V+ADV

2 If you **hurry on** to say something, you quickly continue speaking and do not allow anyone else to stop you. ❑ *Having admitted this, Robertson hurried on to say that it was not intentional... Before hurrying on to other aspects of Beaverbrook's career, he explained the background.*
V+ADV: USUALLY+to

★hurry up

1 If you tell someone to **hurry up**, you are telling them to do something more quickly. ❑ *Hurry up, Bill... She yelled down to Robin to hurry up... I can't hurry up! Not if you keep on shouting!*
V+ADV: ALSO IMPERATIVE

NOTE **Buck up** means almost the same as **hurry up**.

2 If you **hurry** someone **up**, you make them do something more quickly than they would have done. ❑ *The nurse stood outside the washrooms to hurry us up... The man burst in on the general, hurrying him up for their lunch date.*
V+PRON+ADV, V+N+ADV

3 If you **hurry** something **up**, you make it happen faster or sooner than it would have done. ❑ *Can't you hurry things up a bit?... If you want the ice in a fridge to melt more quickly, you can hurry it up by leaving the door open.*
V+N+ADV, V+PRON+ADV, V+ADV+N

NOTE **Speed up** means almost the same as **hurry up**.

hush /hʌʃ/ **(hushes, hushing, hushed)**

hush up

1 If people in authority **hush** something **up**, they prevent the public from knowing about it. ❑ *The police had hushed the matter up... My association with these men had been hushed up... The incident didn't remain altogether hushed up.*
V+N+ADV, V+PRON+ADV, V+ADV+N

NOTE **Cover up** means almost the same as **hush up**, and **suppress** is a more formal word.

2 If you **hush** someone **up**, you persuade them in a nice way to be quiet. ❑ *She hushed him up as only she could.*
V+PRON+ADV, V+N+ADV

3 If people in authority **hush** someone **up**, they try to stop that person from revealing information which they want to keep secret. ❑ *The government was only too quick to hush him up.*
V+PRON+ADV, V+N+ADV

hype /haɪp/ **(hypes, hyping, hyped)**

hype up

1 If you **hype** someone **up**, you make them excited and eager to do something. ❑ *I realized the job was not to hype up the team, but to calm them down.*
V+N+ADV, V+ADV+N, V+PRON+ADV

NOTE **Psych up** means almost the same as **hype up**.

2 If you **hype** something **up**, you make it seem more attractive or interesting. ❑ *The ad-men try to hype up even the silliest little media event... It's been hyped up out of all proportion.*
V+ADV+N, V+N+ADV, V+PRON+ADV

Ii

ice /aɪs/ (ices, icing, iced)

ice over When something **ices over** or **is iced over**, it becomes covered with a layer of ice. ❑ *The lake began to ice over... The road becomes treacherous when it is iced over.*

NOTE Freeze over means almost the same as **ice over**.

V+ADV:
ALSO PASSIVE:
V+ADV

ice up When something **ices up** or **is iced up**, it becomes so cold that ice forms around it or inside it so that it cannot function properly. ❑ *The lock, in these conditions, may ice up and become unusable. ...the fast-flowing streams that were totally iced up.*

NOTE Freeze up means almost the same as **ice up**.

V+ADV:
OR PASSIVE:
V+ADV

identify /aɪdentɪfaɪ/ (identifies, identifying, identified)
identify with

1 If you **are identified with** something, you are very closely involved or associated with it. ❑ *During the 1950's he was identified with certain radical causes... Of the 34 candidates nearly a third were identified with revolutionary groups.*

PASSIVE:
V+PREP

2 If you **identify with** someone, you feel that you have something in common with them and can understand them better because of this similarity. ❑ *They find it much harder to identify with the boss... He couldn't identify with other people's troubles.*

V+PREP

idle /aɪdəl/ (idles, idling, idled)

☑ About is used mainly in British English.

idle about → See idle around

idle around If you **idle around** or **idle about**, you spend your time relaxing or doing nothing. ❑ *I can't have you idling around the house all afternoon. ...so I had a spell of idling about at home, not knowing what to do.*

V+PREP,
V+ADV

idle away If you **idle away** a period of time, you relax by sitting or lying somewhere and doing nothing. ❑ *...three old men, idling away the summer afternoon under the trees.*

V+ADV+N

NOTE While away means almost the same as **idle away**.

impinge /ɪmpɪndʒ/ (impinges, impinging, impinged)

impinge on If something **impinges on** or **impinges upon** you, it forces you to change the way you normally behave. [FORMAL] ❑ *Your political opinions will necessarily impinge on your public life... Economic circumstances impinge on them. ...the quarrels and antagonisms whose development does not impinge upon the historical development of Africa.*

V+PREP:
HAS PASSIVE

NOTE Affect is a less formal word for **impinge on**.

impinge upon → See impinge on

impose /ɪmpoʊz/ (imposes, imposing, imposed)
*impose on

1 If you **impose** something **on** people, or **impose** it **upon** them, you use your authority to force them to accept it. ❑ *She was a harsh mother and imposed severe discipline on her children... The Government tried to impose a five per cent limit on public employees... Peace terms were imposed upon Germany.*

V+N+PREP,
V+PRON+PREP

2 If someone **imposes on** or **imposes upon** you, they unreasonably expect you to do something for them or to spend time with them when you do not really want to. ❑ *Clarissa was like that, she imposed on people... Relatives have imposed enormously upon you lately.*

V+PREP:
HAS PASSIVE

impose upon → See impose on

impress /ɪmprɛs/ (impresses, impressing, impressed)
impress on

1 If you **impress** something **on** someone, or **impress** it **upon** them, you talk about it emphatically in order to make them understand its importance. ❑ *The following day he impressed on the Government the danger of 45,000 redundancies... The authorities impressed on him the need for a psychiatric consultation... They are still trying to impress it upon us that we have not yet succeeded.*   V+N+PREP, ALSO V+PREP, V+it+PREP: WITH REPORT

2 If something **impresses** itself **on** or **impresses** itself **upon** a situation, it has a powerful effect on the situation. ❑ *...the enduring menace which clings to the place and impresses itself on strangers.*   V+REFL+PREP

3 If you **impress** something **on** or **impress** it **upon** something else, you cause the image or memory of it to remain on the other thing. ❑ *I repeated the last verse several times, hoping to impress it on my memory.*   V+PRON+PREP, V+N+PREP, V+PREP

impress upon → See **impress on**

improve /ɪmpruːv/ (improves, improving, improved)
★**improve on** To **improve on** or **improve upon** a previous achievement means to reach a better standard or achieve a better result than previously. ❑ *I found that the film improved on the book... For social justice, this system could hardly be improved upon.*   V+PREP: HAS PASSIVE

improve upon → See **improve on**

impute /ɪmpjuːt/ (imputes, imputing, imputed)
impute to If you **impute** blame or an unpleasant action **to** someone or something, you suggest that they were responsible for it or caused it. [FORMAL] ❑ *No blame can be imputed to him... They had been guilty not of the crimes imputed to them but of uttering falsehoods about their order... It is hard to impute a rise in output to any one factor.*   V+N+PREP, V+PRON+PREP

NOTE **Attribute** means almost the same as **impute to**.

include /ɪnkluːd/ (includes, including, included)
★**include in**

1 If you **include** someone **in** a particular plan or activity, you allow them to take part in it. ❑ *Governments found themselves forced to include employees in the dialogue... He sought to include them in what had happened.*   V+N+PREP, V+PRON+PREP

2 If you **include** one thing **in** with another thing, you make it a part of that other thing. ❑ *Most restaurants now include the tip in with the price of the meal... Nothing should be included in the curriculum unless it is relevant... Few novelists would have dared include it in a work of fiction.*   V+N+PREP, V+PRON+PREP: ALSO+with

NOTE **Incorporate** is a more formal word for **include in**.

include out If you say to someone '**include me out**', you are saying in a humorous way that you do not want to join them in a particular activity. [INFORMAL] ❑ *If you're going to carry on like this, you can include me out!*   V+PRON+ADV

indulge /ɪndʌldʒ/ (indulges, indulging, indulged)
indulge in If you **indulge in** a particular activity, you take great pleasure in doing it because it is something you really enjoy. [FORMAL] ❑ *He indulged heavily in conversation and drink... Could I still indulge in outdoor activities like sailing and fell walking?... A social pastime may be indulged in for its own sake.*   V+PREP: HAS PASSIVE

inform /ɪnfɔːʳm/ (informs, informing, informed)
inform on If you **inform on** someone, you give information about them to the police or other authority so that they are accused of having done something wrong because of what you said. ❑ *It can be difficult for a child to inform on someone he knows. ...to inform on an acquaintance who had allegedly engaged in treasonable activities.*   V+PREP: HAS PASSIVE

NOTE **Betray** means almost the same as **inform on**.

infringe /ɪnfrɪndʒ/ (infringes, infringing, infringed)
infringe on If something **infringes on** or **infringes upon** you, it affects your behaviour by making it difficult for you to do what you want. ❑ *No man was allowed to infringe on the livelihood of his neighbour... They infringe on our own children's right to freedom. ...citizens with legal rights which were being infringed upon.*   V+PREP: HAS PASSIVE

NOTE **Encroach on** and **restrict** mean almost the same as **infringe on**.

infringe upon → See **infringe on**

ink /ɪŋk/ (inks, inking, inked)
ink in
1 If you **ink** something **in**, you write it in ink to show that it is now your definite or final version, having previously written it in pencil. ❑ *The revisions can now be inked in... Then you go over it later and ink them in.*
NOTE **Pencil in** means the opposite of **ink in**.

V+N+ADV,
V+PRON+ADV,
V+ADV+N

2 If you **ink** someone or something **in**, you decide that they will definitely be used for a particular purpose after you have discussed various possibilities. [INFORMAL] ❑ *Gooch was the opener we had inked in after his tour of West Indies.*

V+N+ADV,
V+PRON+ADV,
V+ADV+N

inquire /ɪnkwaɪər/ (inquires, inquiring, inquired)

☑ **Inquire** is also spelled **enquire.**

inquire after If you **inquire after** someone, you ask how they are or what they are doing. ❑ *She inquired after Mrs Carstair's daughter... I inquired after Mrs. Merry's health.*
NOTE **Ask after** means almost the same as **inquire after.**

V+PREP

inquire into When a person or committee **inquires into** a matter, they make a thorough, formal investigation of the matter. ❑ *A Royal Commission was established in 1919 to inquire into all aspects of income tax... When he got back to Berlin he would inquire into the whole business again... It will not, one guesses, be much inquired into.*

V+PREP:
HAS PASSIVE

insist /ɪnsɪst/ (insists, insisting, insisted)
★**insist on** If you **insist on** or **insist upon** something, you ask for it firmly and refuse to accept any alternative. ❑ *Most universities insist on an interview before they accept a student... I insisted on a contract that gave me some sort of security... He insisted on paying for the meal... Crawford insisted upon carrying Billy's bag.*

V+PREP:
HAS PASSIVE

insist upon → See insist on

insure /ɪnʃʊər/ (insures, insuring, insured)
insure against
1 If you **insure against** something unpleasant, you take action to prevent it happening or affecting you. ❑ *During years of good rainfall they expand their stocks to insure against drought... Attempts were made to insure against that possibility.*

V+PREP

2 If you **are insured against** something happening, you have bought an insurance policy so that you will be paid compensation if it happens. ❑ *If you bring your bicycle you must have it insured against theft... I don't even know if I'm insured against this kind of thing... His neighbour's house is not insured against fire.*

PASSIVE:
V+PREP

interfere /ɪntərfɪər/ (interferes, interfering, interfered)
★**interfere in** If you **interfere in** something, you become involved in it and start changing it when it is not really your business. ❑ *Well next time, don't interfere in things that don't concern you... It makes him furious to have anyone interfere in one of his jobs.*
NOTE **Meddle in** means almost the same as **interfere in.**

V+PREP

interfere with
1 If something **interferes with** a process or situation, it prevents the process or situation from continuing efficiently or successfully. ❑ *Problems of obtaining spare parts for mines are likely to interfere with production... His father-in-law had interfered with his marriage right from the very beginning.*

V+PREP

2 When sound or radio waves **interfere with** each other, they interrupt each other so that they cannot be heard or received easily. ❑ *Why did their calls not interfere with one another, jamming the signals?... There was evidence of pirate radios interfering with shipping.*

V+PREP

3 Someone who **interferes with** a child touches the child's sexual organs or tries to have sex with the child; used showing disapproval. ❑ *They were interfered with by their babysitter.*
NOTE **Molest** means almost the same as **interfere with.**

V+PREP:
HAS PASSIVE

intrude /ɪntruːd/ (intrudes, intruding, intruded)
intrude on If something **intrudes on** or **intrudes upon** your mood or way of life, it has an unwelcome or unpleasant effect on it. ❑ *Nothing was allowed to intrude*

V+PREP:
HAS PASSIVE

itch for

on their evening ritual... A park would intrude on the region's way of life... Some women would feel intruded upon.

intrude upon → See **intrude on**

inure /ɪnjʊəʳ/ **(inures, inuring, inured)**

inure to If you **are inured to** something unpleasant, you are used to it and accept it as being unavoidable. [FORMAL] ❑ *...a child so inured to punishment that he no longer cares... To such a din I was already inured... They inure themselves to a lifetime of self-restraint.*
V+N+PREP,
V+REFL+PREP,
V+PRON+PREP:
USUALLY PASSIVE

inveigh /ɪnveɪ/ **(inveighs, inveighing, inveighed)**

inveigh against If you **inveigh against** something, you strongly criticize it. [FORMAL] ❑ *It is fashionable in some quarters to inveigh against a 'competitive ladder' society.*
V+PREP

NOTE **Rail against** is a less formal expression for **inveigh against**.

invite /ɪnvaɪt/ **(invites, inviting, invited)**

☑ In American English, **around** is much more common than **round**.

invite around If you **invite** someone **around** or **invite** them **round**, you ask them to come and visit you in your home. ❑ *He hoped the Count would invite him round, but he didn't... She invited a few friends around for drinks.*
V+PRON+PREP,
V+N+PREP

★**invite in** If you **invite** someone **in**, you ask them politely to come into your house, usually when they have knocked on the door or rung the bell. ❑ *Aren't you even going to invite me in? ...inviting her friends in to play poker.*
V+PRON+ADV,
V+N+ADV

invite out If you **invite** someone **out**, you ask them to go with you to a play, show, party, and so on. ❑ *To cheer her up, Morris invited her out for a meal... Once he had invited Frederica out for a ride on his motorbike.*
V+PRON+ADV,
V+N+ADV

NOTE **Ask out** is a more informal expression for **invite out**.

invite over If you **invite** someone **over**, you ask them to come and visit you in your home. ❑ *The neighbours felt free to invite one of them over for a party... I've invited them over on Thursday for the barbecue.*
V+N+ADV,
V+PRON+ADV

invite round → See **invite around**

iron /aɪəʳn/ **(irons, ironing, ironed)**

iron out If you **iron out** small problems or difficulties, you find a way to solve them or overcome them. ❑ *The point of practice is, of course, to iron out such problems... I thought most of our problems were ironed out.*
V+ADV+N,
V+N+ADV,
V+PRON+ADV

itch /ɪtʃ/ **(itches, itching, itched)**

itch for If you **itch for** something, you want it very much. ❑ *...Democrats itching for more vigorous opposition. ...itching for a fight.*
V+PREP

Jj

jab /dʒæb/ (jabs, jabbing, jabbed)

jab at If you **jab at** something, you make repeated, short, stabbing movements at it with something long and thin. ❑ *She could hear him jabbing viciously at the keys of the typewriter... He grabbed Eric's spear and jabbed at Robert with it... He raised his voice and jabbed his finger at me.*

> V+PREP,
> V+N+PREP,
> V+PRON+PREP:
> NO PASSIVE

NOTE **Poke at** means almost the same as **jab at**.

jabber /dʒæbəʳ/ (jabbers, jabbering, jabbered)

jabber away If someone **jabbers away**, they talk so quickly that it is difficult to understand what they say. ❑ *My German's pretty rusty, but it acted like magic – he started jabbering away.*

> V+ADV

jack /dʒæk/ (jacks, jacking, jacked)

jack in If you **jack in** a job, course, or other regular activity, you stop doing it altogether. [BRITISH, INFORMAL] ❑ *One of these days I'm going to jack this job in and sail round the world... There is simply no answer. You might as well jack it in then and there.*

> V+N+ADV,
> V+PRON+ADV,
> V+ADV+N:
> NO PASSIVE

NOTE **Pack in** means almost the same as **jack in**.

jack off If someone **jacks off**, they masturbate. [AMERICAN, RUDE]

> V+ADV

NOTE **Jerk off** and **toss off** mean almost the same as **jack off**.

jack up

1 If you **jack up** a car or heavy object, you raise it off the ground using a jack or other lifting device. ❑ *Make sure you've got the tools ready before you jack up the car.*

> V+N+ADV,
> V+PRON+ADV,
> V+ADV+N

2 If prices **are jacked up**, they are higher than you expect them to be or think they ought to be. ❑ *The price of the part is jacked up way beyond its old price... In 1973 the oil producing countries jacked up oil prices by 400%.*

> V+ADV+N,
> V+N+ADV

NOTE **Inflate** is a more formal word for **jack up**.

3 If someone **jacks up**, they take a drug such as heroin or cocaine by injecting it. [INFORMAL]

> V+ADV

jam /dʒæm/ (jams, jamming, jammed)

jam on If you **jam on** the brakes while you are driving, you stop suddenly and with a lot of force. [INFORMAL] ❑ *Suddenly she jammed on the jeep brakes.*

> V+ADV+N,
> V+N+ADV

jam up

1 If people or things **are jammed up** against an object, they are placed very close to the object so that they cannot move easily. ❑ *Gareth's bed now sat jammed up against the French windows.*

> PASSIVE:
> V+ADV:
> ALSO+against

2 If people or traffic **jam up** a place or if it **jams up**, they block it so that it is difficult to move. ❑ *Of course the queues jam up walkways and staircases, because nobody has thought about designing any space to put them... The French annual holiday fortnight can jam things up.*

> V+N+ADV,
> V+ADV+N,
> V+PRON+ADV,
> V+ADV:
> ERGATIVE

♦ If there is a **jam-up**, traffic blocks the road so that it is difficult to move. ❑ *...a total jam-up of every lane of every motorway in Britain.*

> N-SING

jazz /dʒæz/ (jazzes, jazzing, jazzed)

jazz up If you **jazz** something **up**, you make it more interesting or exciting. [INFORMAL] ❑ *They've certainly jazzed this place up since the last time I was here.*

> V+N+ADV,
> V+PRON+ADV,
> V+ADV+N

NOTE **Liven up** means almost the same as **jazz up**.

♦ Music that is **jazzed-up** has been changed or re-arranged in order to sound more like popular music or jazz. [INFORMAL] ❑ *...a jazzed-up version of one of the Brandenburg Concertos.*

> ADJECTIVE

jerk /dʒɜːrk/ (jerks, jerking, jerked)

jerk around If you say that someone is **jerking** you **around**, you mean that they are not being honest with you about something. [INFORMAL] ❑ *Don't jerk me around, Mr Crook... We're being jerked around, and I don't like it.*

V+N+ADV,
V+PRON+ADV

jerk off If someone **jerks off**, they masturbate. [INFORMAL, RUDE]
[NOTE] **Jack off** and **toss off** mean almost the same as **jerk off**.

V+ADV,
V+N/PRON+ADV,
V+ADV+N

jerk out If you **jerk out** a remark, you say it very abruptly after first hesitating. ❑ *'I can't argue...with you...' he jerked out... 'Dead flowers?' jerked out Mr. Roberts with extreme surprise... 'Enough to drive you mad!' His words jerked out as he darted breathlessly about.*

V+ADV+QUOTE,
V+ADV+N,
V+ADV:
NO PASSIVE

jib /dʒɪb/ (jibs, jibbing, jibbed)

jib at If you **jib at** doing something, you are reluctant to do it. [OLD-FASHIONED] ❑ *He had begun to jib at carrying out the orders of his masters... 'I hope I may be struck blind'. He jibbed at using the word 'dead'.*

V+PREP

jockey /dʒɒki/ (jockeys, jockeying, jockeyed)

jockey for If someone **jockeys for** position or status, they compete against other people to improve their own position or status. ❑ *Rival trade unions continuously jockey for position... People jockeyed for status, in the social vacuum created by independence.*

V+PREP

jog /dʒɒg/ (jogs, jogging, jogged)

jog along If you **jog along** in a situation, you continue in it and accept what happens to you, without trying to change it. ❑ *They assume that any job carries with it daily stretches of boredom, so they jog along for thirty, forty years without complaint... The human animal jogs happily along in this way.*

V+ADV

join /dʒɔɪn/ (joins, joining, joined)

★join in If you **join in** an activity with other people, you become involved in what they are doing. ❑ *He took his coat off and joined in the work... Several people joined in the applause... Is this a private fight or can anyone join in?... Then they began to sing and in a moment all the voices joined in.*

V+PREP,
V+ADV

★join up

1 If one person **joins up** with another or if two people **join up**, they decide to go somewhere together. ❑ *We joined up with two young men and went along to a roadhouse... The French division joined up with the rest of the Southern Army Group... The two families joined up for the rest of the holiday.*
[NOTE] **Get together** means almost the same as **join up**.

V+ADV+with,
V+ADV:
RECIPROCAL

2 If someone **joins up**, they become a member of the army, the navy, or the air force. ❑ *I didn't join up until 1940 in the end... Just before joining up and going abroad I met Elizabeth.*
[NOTE] **Enlist** means almost the same as **join up**.

V+ADV

3 If you **join up** two things or if they **join up**, they become fastened together. ❑ *I used to join up all his paper clips in a long chain. ...busy trying to join them up... This takes place when two cells join up and exchange genes.*
[NOTE] **Link up** means almost the same as **join up**.

V+ADV+N,
V+PRON+ADV,
V+N+ADV,
V+ADV:
ERGATIVE

jolly /dʒɒli/ (jollies, jollying, jollied)

jolly along If you **jolly** someone **along**, you keep them in a good mood, often so that they will continue to do something for you, such as work. ❑ *It's no good jollying her along, telling her to take it easy... Harold, you've been jollying me along for quite long enough.*

V+PRON+ADV,
V+N+ADV

jot /dʒɒt/ (jots, jotting, jotted)

jot down If you **jot** something **down**, you write it down briefly in the form of a short informal note. ❑ *Renshaw jotted down a few particulars in his notebook... He jotted some notes down... She noted the exact time of the call and jotted it down on the tablecloth.*
[NOTE] **Note down** means almost the same as **jot down**.

V+ADV+N,
V+N+ADV,
V+PRON+ADV

juggle /dʒʌgəl/ (juggles, juggling, juggled)

juggle with

1 If you **juggle with** things such as numbers or ideas, you keep adjusting them

V+PREP:

slightly until they fit together in the best possible way. ❑ *Still juggling with figures and*   HAS PASSIVE
possibilities, she remained alert... He was juggling with formulae and documents.

2 If you **are juggling with** several objects, you are having difficulty holding onto   V+PREP
all of them. ❑ *He juggled with the controls... The basket is far safer than juggling with large*
pans of boiling water and a colander.

jumble /dʒˈʌmbᵊl/ **(jumbles, jumbling, jumbled)**

jumble up If things **are jumbled up**, they are mixed together or confused, so   PASSIVE:
that it is difficult to tell them apart. ❑ *The bits and pieces were jumbled up with a lot of*   V+ADV
stuff that would never be needed again... They range from grade 5 to grade 1, and they're all
jumbled up.

NOTE **Mix up** means almost the same as **jumble up**.

jump /dʒˈʌmp/ **(jumps, jumping, jumped)**

★**jump at** If you **jump at** an opportunity or offer, you accept it immediately.   V+PREP:
❑ *Any one of them would jump at the chance of being with Dolly Clare... Private companies*   HAS PASSIVE
have not exactly jumped at the opportunity... They have to persuade their own members not
to jump at superficially attractive offers.

NOTE **Leap at** means almost the same as **jump at**.

jump in

1 If you **jump in**, you act quickly, often without thinking much about what you   V+ADV
are doing. ❑ *The Government had to jump in and purchase millions of dollars worth of sup-*
plies.

2 During a conversation or discussion with someone, if you **jump in**, you interrupt   V+ADV
them or say something that they do not want you to say. ❑ *Before Brian jumps in I*
would like to say something... Goldsmith jumped in with a public rebuke for Beckett's 'irre-
sponsibility'.

NOTE **Butt in** means almost the same as **jump in**.

jump on If you **jump on** someone, you criticize them as soon as you notice that   V+PREP:
they have said or done something wrong. ❑ *You don't need to jump on a child for mak-*   HAS PASSIVE
ing up stories occasionally... He felt no matter how I qualified the term, I would be jumped
on.

jump out at If something **jumps out at** you, it is so obvious that you notice it   V+ADV+PREP
immediately. ❑ *The quality of the prose jumps out at you from the start of chapter one.*

jump up

1 If someone who is sitting down **jumps up**, they suddenly stand up. ❑ *He slumped*   V+ADV
back into his chair and then jumped up again... 'Mabel!' he cried, jumping up from his chair.

2 **Jumped-up** people consider themselves to be more important than they really   ADJECTIVE
are; used showing disapproval. [BRITISH, INFORMAL] ❑ *...a jumped-up office boy.*

jut /dʒˈʌt/ **(juts, jutting, jutted)**

jut out

1 If an area of land or an object **juts out**, it sticks out so that it is more obvious   V+ADV
than the surrounding parts. ❑ *The pillar leaned into a steady overhang, jutting out at least*
twenty feet from the wave-washed base... The road climbs to a high point that apparently
juts out into the ocean.

NOTE **Protrude** is a more formal word for **jut out**.

2 If you **jut out** your chin, you thrust it forwards, often to show your determina-   V+ADV+N,
tion to do something. ❑ *She jutted out her chin and went out into the street with a little*   V+ADV:
flouncing movement of disdain... Bond's jaw was jutting out dangerously.   ERGATIVE

NOTE **Stick out** means almost the same as **jut out**.

Kk

keel /kiːl/ (keels, keeling, keeled)

keel over If someone **keels over**, they fall over sideways. ❏ *One of the middle-aged athletes keeled over and was rushed to hospital... He suddenly keeled over with a heavily-loaded tray... The others had either keeled over or were laughing hysterically.* `V+ADV`

keep /kiːp/ (keeps, keeping, kept)

keep at If you **keep at** it, or **keep** someone **at** it, you continue, or make them continue, working at a job or task or trying hard, even if it is very difficult or unpleasant. ❏ *It is hard, but you've just got to keep at it... I kept at it for another hour... Necessity had kept her at it... Ron told me to keep her at it till Monday.* `V+PREP+it,` `V+PRON+PREP+it,` `V+N+PREP+it:` `ERGATIVE`

NOTE **Persevere** is a more formal word for **keep at**, and **stick at** and **stick to** mean almost the same.

★keep away

1 If you **keep away** from somewhere, you avoid going there. ❏ *They kept away from the forest... It would be better to keep away and not attempt to enter the city until she knew what was happening there... The more you keep away from the shops the less money you'll spend.* `V+ADV:` `ALSO+from`

NOTE **Stay away** means almost the same as **keep away**.

2 If you **keep** someone **away** from somewhere, you prevent them from going near there. ❏ *Keep your kids away from those bulls... The male takes extreme measures to keep raiders away from the eggs... If you don't keep them away, they'll take over.* `V+N+ADV,` `V+PRON+ADV,` `V+ADV+N:` `ALSO+from`

3 If you **keep** something unpleasant or unwanted **away**, you prevent it from affecting and harming you. ❏ *...a dog shampoo that kept away lice and ticks.* `V+ADV+N,` `V+N+ADV,` `V+PRON+ADV`

★keep back

1 If you **keep** part of something **back**, you make sure that you do not use or give away all of it, so that you still have some to use at a later time. ❏ *Remember to keep back enough cream to make the topping... She did keep some things back for when Pam came.* `V+ADV+N,` `V+N+ADV,` `V+PRON+ADV`

NOTE **Reserve** is a more formal word for **keep back**.

2 If you **keep** some information **back**, you do not tell all that you know about something. ❏ *You can't write an autobiography without keeping something back. ...keeping back the existence of the documents.* `V+N+ADV,` `V+ADV+N,` `V+PRON+ADV`

NOTE **Withhold** is a more formal word for **keep back**.

3 If you **keep back** your emotions, feelings, or ideas, you try not to let other people know about them. ❏ *When I looked at Charlene, Kendra, Franklin, Margaret, Howard – I couldn't keep back the tears. ...keeping back our innermost thoughts and plans.* `V+ADV+N`

NOTE **Hold back** means almost the same as **keep back**.

★keep down

1 If you **keep** the number, size, or amount of something **down**, you stop it increasing and try to keep it at a low level. ❏ *The French too are very concerned to try and keep costs down... This keeps prices down... Can you keep the noise down. ...the need to keep down public borrowing.* `V+N+ADV,` `V+ADV+N,` `V+PRON+ADV`

2 If you **keep down** or if you **keep** your head **down**, you stay in a lying or low position in order to avoid being seen or attacked. ❏ *Keep down!... They kept their heads down.* `V+ADV,` `V+N+ADV:` `NO PASSIVE`

3 If someone **keeps** a group of people or a nation **down**, they keep them in a state of powerlessness, and prevent them from being completely free. ❏ *For centuries men have been trying to keep women down.* `V+N+ADV,` `V+PRON+ADV,` `V+ADV+N`

NOTE **Oppress** is a more formal word for **keep down**.

4 If you can't **keep** food or drink **down**, you are unwell, and vomit if you try to `V+N+ADV,` eat or drink. ❏ *I can't keep anything down, not even water... He took a drink and kept it down.*

NOTE **Hold down** means almost the same as **keep down**.

V+ADV+N,
V+PRON+ADV:
NO PASSIVE

★**keep from**

1 If you **keep** someone **from** doing something, you stop them doing it. ❏ *The sergeant tried to keep me from going... We tied rope round the bundles to keep them from falling off... These long discussions kept me from my studies.*

V+PRON+PREP,
V+N+PREP

2 If you **keep from** doing something, you manage with difficulty to stop yourself doing it. ❏ *I have managed to keep from revealing it... I could not keep from stepping in.*

V+PREP+-ING

NOTE **Resist** is a more formal word for **keep from**.

3 If you **keep** information **from** someone, you do not tell them about it. ❏ *There was something so simple and innocent about James then that keeping anything from him seemed utterly wrong.*

V+N+PREP,
V+PRON+PREP

keep in

1 If a parent or teacher **keeps** children **in**, they make them stay indoors or they make them stay late at school, usually as a punishment. ❏ *John was kept in at school one day last week... We'll all be kept in after school.*

V+N+ADV,
V+PRON+ADV,
V+ADV+N

2 If you **keep in** when you are walking, cycling, or driving along a road or path, you stay near the edge of the road or path, instead of being in the middle of it. ❏ *Keep in! You'll be run over if you don't watch it!*

V+ADV

keep in with If you **keep in with** someone, you stay friendly with them, often in order to gain some advantage for yourself. [BRITISH] ❏ *If I wanted to stay with the firm I ought to try to keep in with him... They kept in with each other and had secrets.*

V+ADV+PREP

★**keep off**

1 If you **keep** someone or something **off** a particular area, you prevent them from going onto it. If you **keep off** an area, you do not go there yourself. ❏ *In Scotland you have no right to keep people off your land unless they are doing damage... Having a job helps keep them off the streets... If you don't keep off the street with your bicycle, I'll take it away... He kept off the fell... Christopher was warned to keep off.*

V+N+PREP/ADV,
V+PRON+PREP/ADV,
V+ADV+N,
V+PREP/ADV

2 If you **keep** something **off** someone, you prevent it from touching, harming, or attacking them. ❏ *Keep those dogs off her! ...a bamboo shelter to keep the rain off... She had a veil pulled down all round her hat to keep off the flies.*

V+N+PREP/ADV,
V+ADV+N,
V+PRON+PREP/ADV

3 If you **keep off** a particular food or drink, you avoid eating or drinking it, usually because you know that it will make you ill. ❏ *She can drink skimmed milk, but she has to keep off butter... Keep him off the booze, that's all.*

V+PREP,
V+PRON+PREP,
V+N+PREP

4 If you **keep off** a particular subject, you deliberately do not talk about it. ❏ *He kept off the question of whose fault it was.*

V+PREP

NOTE **Avoid** means almost the same as **keep off**.

5 If rain or snow **keeps off**, it does not begin. ❏ *Luckily the rain kept off.*

V+ADV

NOTE **Hold off** means almost the same as **keep off**.

★**keep on**

1 If you **keep on** doing something, you continue to do it and do not stop. ❏ *Mike reckoned he could keep on talking for one and a half hours... Keep on rinsing until the water is clear... He kept on staring at me... We just keep on collecting the stuff for ever.*

V+ADV+-ING

NOTE **Carry on** means almost the same as **keep on**.

2 If you **keep** someone **on** at work or school, you continue to employ them although their contract has ended or they are old enough to retire, or you continue to educate them although they are old enough to leave. ❏ *I think Bessie likes to keep Isabel on for the sake of her family... Only half the workforce will be kept on after this order has been completed... She had to start work while her brothers were kept on at expensive private schools.*

V+N+ADV,
V+PRON+ADV,
V+ADV+N

3 If you **keep on** about something, you continue to talk about it in a boring or repetitive way. [BRITISH, INFORMAL] ❏ *She kept on about the stupid car... 'Say yes,' Betty said, 'or he'll just keep on and on.'*

V+ADV:
ALSO+*about*

NOTE **Go on** and **harp on** mean almost the same as **keep on**.

keep on at If you **keep on at** someone, you repeatedly ask them something or tell them something in a way that annoys them. [BRITISH, INFORMAL] ❏ *I made no reply, but he kept on at me... They will not ask, so we have to keep on and on at them.*

V+ADV+PREP

For a full explanation of all grammatical labels, see pages xiii-xx

★**keep out**

1 To **keep** someone or something **out** of a place means to prevent them from entering it or being there. ❑ *...a guard dog to keep out intruders... This should keep them out.*

V+ADV+N,
V+PRON+ADV,
V+N+ADV

2 If a sign says '**Keep Out**', it is warning you not to go onto that piece of land. ❑ *'Private property. Keep out.'*

IMPERATIVE,
V+ADV

★**keep out of**

1 If you **keep** someone **out of** an unpleasant situation, you avoid involving them in it. ❑ *You should try and keep him out of it, or it will only complicate things further... We should bend over backwards to keep young people out of prison... Keep Piggy out of danger.*

V+PRON+ADV+PREP,
V+N+ADV+PREP

2 If you **keep out of** an unpleasant situation, you avoid becoming involved in it. ❑ *You keep out of this. It's got nothing to do with you... I kept out of trouble as best I could... We kept out of her way and never spoke to her again.*

V+ADV+PREP

NOTE **Stay out of** means almost the same as **keep out of**.

★**keep to**

1 If you **keep to** a regulation or agreement, you do exactly what you are expected or supposed to do. ❑ *We must keep to the deadlines... Keep to the letter of the law... Try to keep to a routine.*

V+PREP:
HAS PASSIVE

NOTE **Stick to** means almost the same as **keep to**.

2 If you **keep to** a particular subject, you talk only about that subject, and do not talk about anything else. ❑ *I wish you'd keep to the point.*

V+PREP:
HAS PASSIVE

NOTE **Stick to** means almost the same as **keep to**, and **get off** means the opposite.

3 If you **keep** something **to** a particular number or amount, you limit it to that number or amount. ❑ *Keep it to a minimum... It has been kept to an extremely tempting price. ...the kind of play whose casts you keep to a minimum... We can easily keep to single figures.*

V+PRON+PREP,
V+N+PREP,
V+PREP

4 If you **keep to** something such as a path or river, you do not move away from it as you go somewhere. ❑ *Please keep to the paths.*

V+PREP

NOTE **Stick to** means almost the same as **keep to**.

5 If you **keep to** a place such as your bed or a room in your home, you stay there for a period of time, for example if you are ill or if the weather is bad. ❑ *He kept to his bed when he had flu. ...a shy boy who keeps to his bedroom practising magic tricks.*

V+PREP

NOTE **Stay in** means almost the same as **keep to**.

6 If you **keep** something **to** yourself, you do not tell anyone about it. ❑ *If I tell her, she won't keep it to herself... People may get embarrassed, so keep it to yourself.*

V+PRON+PREP,
V+N+PREP:
WITH REFL

keep under If someone **keeps** you **under**, they keep you in a state of unconsciousness by giving you drugs. ❑ *She was kept under with a mixture of morphine and chloroform.*

V+PRON+ADV,
V+N+ADV

★**keep up**

1 If you **keep up** an activity, you continue to do it and do not let it stop or end. ❑ *I tried to keep up the conversation... He was unable to keep up the payments... The tanks kept up a steady fire... A wildebeest can run at the same speed and keep it up for longer.*

V+ADV+N,
V+PRON+ADV,
V+N+ADV

NOTE **Maintain** is a more formal word for **keep up**.

2 If you **keep up** with a situation in which things are changing quickly or greatly, you manage to deal with it. ❑ *...the struggle to keep up with inflation... It has increased so much that our imagination can't keep up... The flow of decisions could be accelerated to keep up with the faster pace of life.*

V+ADV:
USUALLY+with

3 If you **keep up**, you work at the necessary speed so that you do as well as other people or so that you get all your work done in the required time. ❑ *They appear to be able to keep up with the class... I shall be taking work home every night, you know, to keep up... I never quite manage to keep up with the rest.*

V+ADV:
ALSO+with

NOTE **Fall behind** means the opposite of **keep up**.

4 If you **keep** it **up**, you continue working hard, trying hard, or achieving the standard that you have in the past. ❑ *Being human, he can only keep it up for eight hours a day... He kept it up until they had gone... It's no good. I can't keep it up, you see... This is good. Keep it up!*

V+it+ADV

5 If you **keep up** with someone else, you move at the same speed as them. ❑ *I*

V+ADV:

The symbol ★ shows key phrasal verbs

started to run a bit so that she had to hurry to keep up with me... They will have to get off the highway because they can't keep up. — ALSO+with

6 If you **keep** something **up**, you prevent it from growing less in amount or size, or worse in quality. ❑ I can't see how we can keep this pace up for more than a day or two... Morris could keep up the pace no longer... It's important to keep up the standard. — V+N+ADV, V+PRON+ADV, V+ADV+N

7 If you **keep up** a subject or skill that you learned a long time ago, you continue to study, practise, or use it. ❑ I do try and keep up my physics... He's managed to keep his Spanish up quite well. — V+ADV+N, V+N+ADV, V+PRON+ADV

8 If one process **keeps up** with another, it increases at the same speed and in the same way as the other is increasing. ❑ Supply could never have kept up with consumption... Pensions were increased to keep up with the rise in prices. — V+ADV: USUALLY+with

9 If you **keep up** with a situation, you learn all the most recent facts about it. ❑ They kept up with what was happening in their work... Even friends have trouble keeping up with each other's whereabouts. — V+ADV: USUALLY+with

10 If you **keep** someone **up**, you delay them going to bed. ❑ I ought never to have kept you up so late... I am sorry. I won't keep you up a minute longer. — V+PRON+ADV, V+N+ADV

11 If you **keep up** a building, you look after it and make sure that it remains in good condition. ❑ I'd never get any of the estate people to live in it now. If you'll keep it up you're welcome to it. — V+PRON+ADV, V+N+ADV, V+ADV+N

NOTE Maintain means almost the same as **keep up**.

♦ The **upkeep** of a building is the continual process of keeping it in good condition. ❑ We have to pay for the upkeep of the chapel. — N-UNCOUNT

NOTE Maintenance means almost the same as **upkeep**.

keep up with If you **keep up with** a friend, you stay in contact with them by writing, telephoning, or seeing them regularly. ❑ We've kept up with each other ever since we left school. — V+ADV+PREP

key /kiː/ (keys, keying, keyed)

key in When you are using a computer and you **key** something **in**, you give the computer instructions by typing something on the keyboard. ❑ To extract information you key in the word you require... Key in the appropriate words. — V+ADV+N, V+N+ADV, V+PRON+ADV

NOTE Enter and type in mean almost the same as **key in**, and input is a more technical word.

key up If you **are keyed up**, you are very excited or nervous because something important or dangerous is about to happen. ❑ His anger surprised him: he was more keyed up than he had anticipated. ...consciously look for signs of being keyed up too much. — PASSIVE: V+ADV

NOTE Tense means almost the same as **keyed up**.

kick /kɪk/ (kicks, kicking, kicked)

☑ **About** is used mainly in British English. In American English, **around** is much more common than **round**.

kick about → See kick around

kick against If you **kick against** a situation you cannot control, you show your dislike and impatience by reacting against it. [BRITISH] ❑ He's always kicking against the system. — V+PREP

NOTE Kick out against means almost the same as **kick against**.

kick around

1 You say that something **is kicking around**, **kicking about**, or **kicking round** somewhere when you mean that it is lying there and does not seem wanted or important. ❑ His old bike has been kicking about among the bushes for days... There's a lot of difference between a fresh herring and one which may have been kicking around in a deep freeze for months. — V+ADV

NOTE Lie around means almost the same as **kick around**.

2 When people **kick around** ideas or suggestions, they discuss them informally. ❑ The first step was to call in some writers and kick around ideas. — V+ADV+N, V+N+ADV

3 If someone **kicks** you **around**, they treat you very badly, roughly, or unfairly. [INFORMAL] ❑ She shouldn't let her brother kick her around like that... I don't feel that anyone can kick me around any more. — V+PRON+ADV, V+N+ADV

NOTE Push around means almost the same as **kick around**.

For a full explanation of all grammatical labels, see pages xiii-xx

kick back

1 If someone **kicks back** an amount of money, they illegally return some money to a person who is buying something as a bribe in order to encourage them to buy it. ❑ *The doctors kicked back a percentage of the fee.*   V+ADV+N

◆ A **kickback** is a bribe paid to a representative of a government or firm to encourage them to place an order. ❑ *He's systematically taken kickbacks from the hiring agencies he works through.*   N-COUNT

2 If someone **kicks back**, they relax. [AMERICAN, INFORMAL] ❑ *As soon as they've finished up, they do a little bit of lunch and kind of kick back and wait for the next show.*   V+ADV

NOTE **Relax** is a more formal word for **kick back**.

kick down

If you **kick down** a door or other structure, you kick it violently with your foot so that it falls or collapses. ❑ *They tried to kick down the front door... I nearly kicked the door down in my fury.*   V+ADV+N, V+N+ADV, V+PRON+ADV

NOTE **Break down** and **smash down** mean almost the same as **kick down**.

★kick in

1 If you **kick in** something such as a door or window, you kick it violently with your foot so that it breaks into pieces. ❑ *The fireman kicked in one of the windows... Doors and windows were smashed with sledge-hammers, television sets kicked in, and clothes slashed to ribbons.*   V+ADV+N, V+N+ADV, V+PRON+ADV

NOTE **Smash in** means almost the same as **kick in**.

2 If something **kicks in**, it begins to take effect. ❑ *An energy saving mode automatically kicks in after a designated time to dim the screen and reduce power consumption... When you're confronted with the problem, emotions kick in, fear kicks in, and you don't always do the rational and thought-out approach.*   V+ADV

3 If someone **kicks in** a particular amount of money, they provide that amount of money to help pay for something. [AMERICAN] ❑ *Kansas City area churches kicked in $35,000 to support the event... To keep it going, Lenoire kicked in her own earnings from acting.*   V+ADV+N, V+PRON+ADV

NOTE **Contribute** means almost the same as **kick in**.

★kick off

1 When you **kick off** your shoes, you shake your feet so that your shoes come off. ❑ *He became conscious of the weight of his clothes and kicked his shoes off fiercely... Mark kicked off his shoes and climbed down into the stream.*   V+ADV+N, V+N+ADV, V+PRON+ADV

2 When you **kick off** an event or discussion, you start it. ❑ *At 10 p.m. Prince Charles kicks off 45 minutes of fireworks... They kicked off a two-month tour of the U.S. with a party in Washington... Are we ready for the debate? Right. Who kicks off?*   V+ADV+N, V+ADV

3 When football players **kick off**, they start the game by kicking the ball from the centre of the pitch. ❑ *The first goal was scored within twenty seconds of kicking off.*   V+ADV

◆ The **kick-off** is the kick that officially starts a game of football, or the time that the game starts. ❑ *The kick-off's at 3 o'clock.*   N-SING

4 To **kick** someone **off** an area of land means to force them to leave it. [INFORMAL] ❑ *We can't kick them off the island.*   V+N+ADV, V+PRON+ADV

★kick out

If you **kick** someone **out** of a place or an organization, you force them to leave it. ❑ *I'm afraid I'm going to have to kick you out into the rain... They kicked her out of her house... Franklin had been unilaterally kicked out of the organization... He started off at university but he got kicked out.*   V+PRON+ADV, V+N+ADV, V+ADV+N: ALSO+of

NOTE **Throw out** means almost the same as **kick out**.

kick out against

If you **kick out against** a situation that you cannot control, you show your dislike and impatience by reacting against it in a violent or extreme way. ❑ *...a lorry-driver who suddenly kicked out against the daily grind of his life.*   V+ADV+PREP

NOTE **Kick against** means almost the same as **kick out against**.

kick over

If someone **kicks** something **over**, they kick it so that it falls to the ground. ❑ *John, beside himself with rage, had kicked over the table and grabbed at her... Roger led the way through the sand castles, kicking them over.*   V+ADV+N, V+PRON+ADV, V+N+ADV

NOTE **Knock over** means almost the same as **kick over**.

kick round → See kick around

kick up

1 If someone **kicks up** a fuss or a row, they get very annoyed or upset about some-   V+ADV+N

The symbol ★ shows key phrasal verbs

thing, especially when this seems unnecessary to you. ❑ *He kicked up a great fuss and swore our friendship was at an end... Why are you kicking up all this fuss?*

2 If you **kick up** dust or dirt with your feet, you create a cloud of dust or dirt as you move along a dusty road. ❑ *They struggled amid the dust clouds that their feet kicked up. ...turf kicked up by flying hoofs.*
V+ADV+N,
V+N+ADV

NOTE **Raise** means almost the same as **kick up**.

kill /kɪl/ (kills, killing, killed)

★kill off If you **kill** something **off**, you completely destroy it. ❑ *This discovery killed off one of the last surviving romances about the place... The bacteria had been killed off.*
V+ADV+N,
V+N+ADV,
V+PRON+ADV

NOTE **Wipe out** means almost the same as **kill off**, and **eradicate** is a more formal word.

kip /kɪp/ (kips, kipping, kipped)

kip down If you **kip down** at someone's house, you sleep there for the night instead of going home. [BRITISH, INFORMAL] ❑ *Why don't you take one of these mattresses and kip down here?*
V+ADV

NOTE **Doss down** means almost the same as **kip down**.

kiss /kɪs/ (kisses, kissing, kissed)

kiss away If you **kiss** something unpleasant **away**, you try to sympathize with someone by kissing them. [INFORMAL] ❑ *I would have kissed the fever away if I had been closer to you.*
V+N+ADV,
V+PRON+ADV

kiss off

1 If someone tells you to **kiss off**, they are telling you rudely to go away. [AMERICAN, INFORMAL] ❑ *I can remember her telling Derek to kiss off and Malcolm standing on the other side of the room, laughing.*
V+ADV

2 If you **kiss** someone or something **off**, you get rid of them quickly. ❑ *Buchanan kissed off the issue with two short sentences.*
V+N+ADV,
V+ADV+N,
V+PRON+ADV

kiss up to If you **kiss up to** someone, especially someone powerful or important, you are nice to them. [INFORMAL] ❑ *Some people seem to absorb success and advancement by kissing up to the boss.*
V+ADV+PREP

NOTE **Suck up to** means almost the same as **kiss up to**.

kit /kɪt/ (kits, kitting, kitted)

kit out If someone or something **is kitted out** or **kitted up**, they are provided with everything they need for a particular situation, for example with clothing, equipment, or furniture. [BRITISH, INFORMAL] ❑ *Beginners can be kitted out for less than a hundred pounds... The range of electronic equipment with which they will be kitted out will be phenomenal.*
PASSIVE:
V+ADV

NOTE **Fit out** means almost the same as **kit out**.

kit up → See kit out

kneel /niːl/ (kneels, kneeling, kneeled/knelt)

kneel down When you **kneel down**, you sit with your legs bent underneath you and your weight on your knees. ❑ *He knelt down beside the unconscious girl... He kneeled down and prayed to Allah... My sister was kneeling down, peering over the floor.*
V+ADV

knit /nɪt/ (knits, knitting, knitted)

> ☑ The form **knit** is used in the present tense, and can also be used as the past tense and past participle of the verb.

knit together When two things **knit together**, or **are knit** or **knitted together**, they join together to form a whole. ❑ *After a lot of practice the side begins to knit together... Knit together the parts of each speech... Telephone reservation systems have not been knitted together... The Slav world has become unified and knit together.*
V+ADV,
V+ADV+N,
V+N+ADV,
V+PRON+ADV:
ERGATIVE

NOTE **Fuse** means almost the same as **knit together**.

knit up If you **knit up** something such as a jumper, you knit the whole of it. ❑ *I knitted up the front of a cardigan this evening.*
V+ADV+N,
V+N+ADV,
V+PRON+ADV

knock /nɒk/ (knocks, knocking, knocked)

knock about → See knock around

knock about with → See knock around with

knock around

1 If a person **is knocked around** or **knocked about**, someone hits or kicks them several times. [BRITISH, INFORMAL] ❑ *He was only a little kid, and he knocked him around... One of them was knocked about and wounded... This fellow has been knocking a policeman about in the gutter.*
V+N+ADV,
V+PRON+ADV:
USUALLY PASSIVE

2 If you **knock** an idea **around** or **knock** it **about**, you discuss it with other people so that they can suggest ways of improving it. [BRITISH, INFORMAL] ❑ *We'll get together tonight and knock some ideas around... The document was knocked about and redrafted by a dozen hands.*
V+N+ADV,
V+ADV+N

3 If someone **knocks around** or **knocks about**, they get experience in a lot of different situations, especially by travelling to different places and meeting people. ❑ *I knocked around for a few years after university... I'm a bachelor, I've knocked about the world a bit, known a few women.*
V+ADV,
V+PREP

4 If someone or something **is knocking around** or **knocking about** somewhere, they are present there, usually not doing anything in particular. [BRITISH] ❑ *My brothers should be knocking around somewhere... There's the odd Scotsman knocking about here who's looking for someone to play golf.*
V+ADV

NOTE **Hang around** means almost the same as **knock around**.

knock around with If you **knock around with** someone or **knock about with** them, you spend your spare time with them, either because you are one of their friends or because you are their special boyfriend or girlfriend. [BRITISH] ❑ *Who's she knocking around with now?... He's knocking about with a gang from the next village.*
V+ADV:
USUALLY+*with*

NOTE **Consort with** is a more formal expression for **knock around with**.

★knock back

1 If you **knock back** an alcoholic drink, you drink it fairly quickly. ❑ *He won't be too happy when he comes up here and finds me knocking back his favourite whisky... Davis knocked the drinks back with a fine abandon... She had poured Eva another Tequila, and insisted she take a bite of lemon before knocking it back.*
V+ADV+N,
V+N+ADV,
V+PRON+ADV

NOTE **Swig** means almost the same as **knock back**.

2 If something **knocks** you **back** a particular amount of money, it costs you that amount of money. [INFORMAL] ❑ *How much did that car knock you back? A few thousand?*
V+PRON+ADV+N

NOTE **Set back** means almost the same as **knock back**.

3 If someone **knocks back** an offer or suggestion, they reject it. [BRITISH, INFORMAL] ❑ *Most clubs aren't in the position to knock back the offer of a few hundred pounds.*
V+ADV+N,
V+N+ADV,
V+PRON+ADV

NOTE **Reject** is a more formal word for **knock back**.

4 If a person or process **is knocked back**, they fail to make progress. [BRITISH] ❑ *Marie persisted in her attempts to seek out Mirena and was knocked back several more times... 'They have not knocked us back and we have asked them to get back to us,' said a spokesman.*
V+N+ADV,
V+PRON+ADV,
V+ADV+N:
USUALLY PASSIVE

♦ If someone or something suffers a **knockback**, they fail to make progress. ❑ *The schedule has suffered a knockback.*
N-COUNT

★knock down

1 If you **knock** someone **down**, you hit them or push them, deliberately or accidentally, so that they fall to the ground. ❑ *I bumped into and nearly knocked down a person at the bus stop... I was nearly knocked down by a hefty slap on the back.*
V+N+ADV,
V+PRON+ADV,
V+ADV+N

NOTE **Knock over** means almost the same as **knock down**.

2 If a car or other vehicle **knocks** someone **down**, it hits them so that they fall to the ground and may be injured or killed. ❑ *A bus came screeching to a stop, practically knocking him down. ...knocked down by cars as they dash among the traffic.*
V+PRON+ADV,
V+N+ADV,
V+ADV+N

NOTE **Knock over** means almost the same as **knock down**.

3 To **knock down** a building or part of a building means to demolish it. ❑ *...their plan to knock down once and for all the hated Berlin Wall... I'd knock the wall down between the front room and dining room.*
V+ADV+N,
V+N+ADV,
V+PRON+ADV

NOTE **Pull down** means almost the same as **knock down**.

4 If you **knock down** an idea or opinion, you argue successfully against it, so that it is no longer considered valid. ❑ *Jane has systematically knocked down every one of her friend's suggestions...* ♦ *The argument is in a form in which you can easily knock it down.*
V+ADV+N,
V+PRON+ADV,
V+N+ADV

The symbol ★ shows key phrasal verbs

NOTE **Demolish** means almost the same as **knock down**.

A **knockdown** argument or piece of reasoning is very powerful and difficult to argue against. ❑ *Opponents of expansion believe they have a knockdown argument.*

ADJECTIVE

5 If you **knock** someone **down** when they are selling you something, or if you get a price **knocked down**, you persuade the seller to reduce the price. ❑ *I tried to knock him down a few pounds but he wouldn't have it... We managed to knock the price down quite a lot because it was torn... The bust had been knocked down for £5 to the antique dealer.*

V+PRON+ADV+N,
V+N+ADV,
V+PRON+ADV,
V+N+ADV+N

♦ A **knockdown** price is one that is a lot lower than it would be normally. ❑ *I got it for a knockdown price.*

ADJECTIVE

NOTE **Reduced** is a less informal word for **knockdown**.

★knock off

1 If you **knock** something **off** a shelf or other surface, you hit it so that it falls to the ground. ❑ *A stone was placed on a brick and had to be knocked off by another stone when it was aimed at.*

V+N+ADV/PREP,
V+PRON+ADV/PREP,
V+ADV+N

2 If a seller **knocks off** an amount from the price or cost of something, he or she reduces the price or cost by that amount. ❑ *He said he'd knock £50 off the price... They offered to pay back about a million pounds of it by knocking it off the price of future work.*

V+N+PREP/ADV,
V+PRON+PREP/ADV,
V+ADV+N

3 When you **knock off**, you finish work at the end of the day or before a break. [INFORMAL] ❑ *We knock off at 5... About half past six we knocked off.*

V+ADV

4 If you **knock** something **off** a list or document, you remove it. ❑ *Tighter rules for benefit entitlement have knocked many people off the unemployment register.*

V+N+ADV/PREP,
V+PRON+ADV/PREP,
V+ADV+N

5 To **knock** someone **off** means to murder them. [INFORMAL] ❑ *I think he had one of his elderly relatives knocked off so that he could inherit the fortune.*

V+N+ADV,
V+PRON+ADV,
V+ADV+N

NOTE **Bump off** means almost the same as **knock off**.

6 If you **knock off** a piece of work, you finish it very quickly and easily. [INFORMAL] ❑ *I thought I could knock off a couple of essays in no time.*

V+ADV+N,
V+N+ADV,
V+PRON+ADV

7 If someone **knocks** something **off**, they steal it. [BRITISH, INFORMAL] ❑ *He was planning to knock off a few videos, but the boss found out and got there just in time to stop him.*

V+ADV+N,
V+N+ADV,
V+PRON+ADV

NOTE **Nick** means almost the same as **knock off**.

8 If someone **knocks off** a bank or a shop, they carry out a robbery there. [BRITISH, INFORMAL] ❑ *He'd knocked off three banks before they caught up with him.*

V+ADV+N

9 To **knock** someone **off** means to have sex with them. [BRITISH, INFORMAL, RUDE]

V+N/PRON+ADV,
V+ADV+N

10 If you say '**Knock it off!**' to someone, you are telling them to stop doing something which is annoying you. [INFORMAL] ❑ *'Knock it off, Pyle,' said the boy... Knock it off. Anyhow, who the hell do you think you're laughing at?*

IMPERATIVE,
V+it+ADV

★knock out

1 To **knock** someone **out** means to cause them to become unconscious or to fall asleep. ❑ *The old man hit him so hard that he knocked him out... The tablet had knocked her out for four solid hours... The explosion hurt no one, except that it knocked out Colonel Lacour.*

V+PRON+ADV,
V+N+ADV,
V+ADV+N

NOTE **Bring round** means the opposite of **knock out**.

♦ A **knock-out** dose of medicine or injection makes you become unconscious or fall asleep. ❑ *...knock-out drops.*

ADJECTIVE

♦ In boxing or wrestling, a **knockout** is a blow that makes your opponent fall to the ground and unable to stand up before the referee has counted to ten. ❑ *Davies won by a knockout.*

N-COUNT

2 If a person or team **is knocked out** of a competition, they are defeated, so that they take no more part in the competition. ❑ *Connors just avoided being knocked out in the second round... Their aim is for the Social Democrats to knock out the Labour Party.*

V+ADV+N,
V+N+ADV,
V+PRON+ADV;
ALSO+of

NOTE **Eliminate** is a more formal word for **knock out**.

♦ A **knockout** competition is one in which several competitors or teams take part, and the winner of each match goes on to the next round while the loser drops out, until one competitor or team is the winner. ❑ *... the world's greatest knockout competition.*

ADJECTIVE

3 In war, if something **is knocked out** by enemy action, it is destroyed or dama-

PASSIVE:

ged enough to prevent it from working properly. ❏ *Radars were knocked out, aircraft* V+ADV
were shot down... Almost 2000 tanks had been knocked out of action by missiles.

♦ A **knockout** blow or victory is one that completely destroys an opponent. ❏ *In* ADJECTIVE
*fact, the time was not right for the sort of knockout blow which he intended... Rahman scored
a shock knockout victory over Lewis in Johannesburg in April.*

4 If you **knock out** a piece of work, you do it very quickly without paying much V+ADV+N,
attention to detail. ❏ *He can knock out a short story in less than a day.* V+N+ADV,
V+PRON+ADV

5 If an event or piece of news **knocks** you **out**, it shocks you so much that you V+PRON+ADV,
cannot think clearly or react immediately. ❏ *I didn't mean to be rude. I was sort of* V+N+ADV
knocked out... The news absolutely knocked me out.

NOTE **Stun** means almost the same as **knock out**.

6 If something **knocks** you **out**, it impresses you greatly and is much better than V+PRON+ADV,
you had expected. ❏ *Her performance completely knocked me out.* V+N+ADV

NOTE **Astound** and **stun** are more formal words for **knock out**.

♦ If you say that someone is a **knockout**, you mean that they are extremely attrac- N-SING,
tive or clever. ❏ *Sandra looked a knockout in her new dress... He lives in the cutest little* ADJECTIVE
house you ever saw, with a knockout wife and two daughters.

7 If a characteristic **is knocked out** of someone, they are influenced very strongly PASSIVE:
so that they lose the characteristic. ❏ *His natural flair was in danger of being knocked out* V+ADV:
of him... He had all the fight knocked out of him. ALSO+of

★**knock over** To **knock** someone or something **over** means to push them or hit V+N+ADV,
them so that they fall or turn on their side. ❏ *I got knocked over by a car when I was* V+PRON+ADV,
six... Careful you don't knock the paint over... He managed to knock over a box. V+ADV+N

knock together → See **knock up**

knock up

1 If you **knock** something **up** or **knock** it **together**, you make it or build it very V+ADV+N,
quickly, using whatever materials are available. [BRITISH, INFORMAL] ❏ *They do not ask* V+N+ADV,
official permission to knock up a ramshackle home to live in... Do you want me to knock up V+PRON+ADV
*a meal for you?... The residents here pay rents to the landlords who knocked the shacks to-
gether.*

2 If you **knock** someone **up**, you knock on the door of their bedroom or of their V+PRON+ADV,
house during the night in order to wake them. [BRITISH, INFORMAL] ❏ *He knocked me* V+N+ADV
up at 4 to ring for an ambulance.

NOTE **Rouse** is a formal word for **knock up**.

3 If a man **knocks** a woman **up**, he makes her pregnant. [AMERICAN, INFORMAL] V+N/PRON+ADV,
❏ *He was rumored to have knocked up the 1955 head cheerleader.* V+ADV+N

4 In a game such as tennis, squash, or badminton, when the players **knock up**, V+ADV
they practise hitting the ball or shuttlecock to each other before they begin a game.
❏ *At tennis I prefer to knock up endlessly rather than play a match.*

♦ A **knock-up** is a period of time in which the players practise hitting the ball or N-COUNT
shuttlecock to each other before beginning a game of tennis, squash, or badminton.
❏ *Let's have a knock-up before we start.*

know /nəʊ/ (**knows, knowing, knew, known**)

★**know about** If you **know about** a subject, you have studied it and understand V+PREP
part or all of it. ❏ *What do you know about the film industry?... She knew a bit about*
acoustics.

know as If someone or something **is known as** a particular name, they are V+PRON+PREP,
called by that name. ❏ *...Lev Davidovitch Bronstein, otherwise known as Leon Trotsky.* V+N+PREP:
...William Kent, known to his friends and family as Will... In South America they are known USUALLY PASSIVE
as army ants, in Africa as drivers.

know of If you **know of** something, you have heard of it but you do not neces- V+PREP
sarily have a lot of information about it. ❏ *I know of one girl who moved into a flat with*
two others... Many people did not even know of their existence.

knuckle /nʌkəl/ (**knuckles, knuckling, knuckled**)

knuckle down If someone **knuckles down**, they begin to work or study very V+ADV:
hard, especially after a period when they have done very little. ❏ *It's high time you* ALSO+to
knuckled down to some hard study... Don't you think you ought to knuckle down a bit?... The

The symbol ★ shows key phrasal verbs

thought of knuckling down to a mundane routine was quite frightening.

NOTE **Buckle down** means almost the same as **knuckle down**.

knuckle under If you **knuckle under**, you do what someone else tells you to V+ADV
do or what a situation forces you to do, because you realize that you have no choice.
❑ *He refused to knuckle under and was asked to leave.*

NOTE **Buckle under** means almost the same as **knuckle under**.

LI

lace /leɪs/ **(laces, lacing, laced)**

lace up If you **lace up** something with laces attached to it, you fasten it by pulling the ends of the laces tight and tying them together. ❑ *He bent and laced up his
shoes.*

NOTE **Do up** is a more informal, general expression for **lace up**.

♦ **Lace-ups** are shoes which fasten with laces. ❑ *Maria's lace-ups had got holes in the
toes.*

V+ADV+N,
V+N+ADV,
V+PRON+ADV

N-PLURAL

ladle /leɪdəl/ **(ladles, ladling, ladled)**

ladle out

1 To **ladle out** something such as money, information or advice means to give it
freely and in large quantities. [INFORMAL] ❑ *...the knowledge that is ladled out daily in
high schools.*

NOTE **Dish out** and **dole out** mean almost the same as **ladle out**.

2 If you **ladle out** soup, stew, and so on, you serve it into dishes, using a large
spoon or ladle. ❑ *Ladle it out into jars lined with coarse cheesecloth... She was just ladling
out the spaghetti which was liberally covered with olive oil, tomato sauce and basil.*

V+ADV+N,
V+N+ADV,
V+PRON+ADV

V+PRON+ADV,
V+ADV+N,
V+N+ADV

lag /læg/ **(lags, lagging, lagged)**

lag behind

1 When two or more people are moving along, if someone **lags behind**, that person moves more slowly than the others and so fails to keep with them. ❑ *He set off at
a brisk walk, Kate lagging behind. ...not to lag behind the others, but to keep in close, compact formation.*

NOTE **Fall behind** means almost the same as **lag behind**.

2 If someone or something **lags behind** another person or thing, they fail to
achieve as much. ❑ *Britain's economic development must lag behind that of almost every
other industrial nation... In recent months increases in earnings have lagged behind the tax
and price index.*

NOTE **Fall behind** means almost the same as **lag behind**.

V+ADV,
V+PREP

V+PREP,
V+ADV

lam /læm/ **(lams, lamming, lammed)**

lam into To **lam into** someone means to attack them violently. ❑ *The men
lammed into him brutally, kicking and punching.*

NOTE **Lay into** means almost the same as **lam into**.

V+PREP

land /lænd/ **(lands, landing, landed)**

land in If someone or something **lands** you **in** trouble or a difficult situation,
you find yourself in a difficult situation because of them. ❑ *How do we get out of the
terrible situation this Government has landed us in?... You know, I wouldn't be surprised if
he'd landed himself in prison... They said I had better give them the information they wanted
or I would land in 'a lot of trouble'.*

NOTE **Get into** means almost the same as **land in**.

V+PRON+PREP,
V+REFL+PREP,
V+N+PREP,
V+PREP

land up If you **land up** in a place or situation, you arrive at that place or are in
that situation, often without having intended to. [BRITISH, INFORMAL] ❑ *He landed up
in the special hospital in Leningrad. ...a bunch of social misfits who have landed up teaching
English.*

NOTE **End up** and **wind up** mean almost the same as **land up**.

V+ADV:
USUALLY+A

land with If you **are landed with** a difficult or unpleasant situation, you have
to deal with it or accept it because you cannot avoid it. [BRITISH, INFORMAL] ❑ *...a
clergyman landed with a rectory the size of a mansion... You landed us with that awful*

V+N+PREP,
V+PRON+PREP:
USUALLY PASSIVE

Hector whom I'd never seen in my life.

NOTE Saddle with and lumber with mean almost the same as land with.

lap /læp/ (laps, lapping, lapped)

lap up

1 When an animal **laps up** a drink, it drinks it. ❏ *The cat lapped up the milk as if it had not been fed for days.*

V+ADV+N, V+N+ADV, V+PRON+ADV

2 If someone **laps up** praise, attention or information, they accept it eagerly and with great enjoyment. ❏ *He continued looking round, smiling, lapping up the attention... Jago sparkled with charm and Dolly lapped it up... The feud was instantly lapped up by the press.*

V+ADV+N, V+PRON+ADV, V+N+ADV

lapse /læps/ (lapses, lapsing, lapsed)

lapse into If you **lapse into** a more relaxed or less acceptable kind of behaviour, you start behaving in that way because you have relaxed your self control. ❏ *He sat down and lapsed into an unhappy silence... She seemed to lapse into a troubled sleep. ...fearing my voice might go out of control and lapse into croaks of broken English.*

V+PREP

NOTE Sink into means almost the same as lapse into.

large /lɑːrdʒ/ (larges, larging, larged)

large up If someone **larges** it **up**, they enjoy themselves in a noisy way. [INFORMAL] ❏ *Chaweng is the capital of holiday island Ko Samui, and you can watch pasty Europeans large it up 24 hours a day.*

V+it+ADV

NOTE Live it up means almost the same as large it up.

lark /lɑːrk/ (larks, larking, larked)

lark about If you **lark about**, you enjoy yourself by doing silly things. [BRITISH, INFORMAL] ❏ *We had a lovely holiday, sunbathing and larking about. ...their favourite spare-time activity, larking about at the Club.*

V+ADV

NOTE Fool around and mess around mean almost the same as lark about.

lash /læʃ/ (lashes, lashing, lashed)

lash down

1 If you **lash** someone or something **down**, you fasten them firmly in a particular position, using ropes. ❏ *It was lashed down by at least a dozen steel cables... It doesn't weigh much, and I can lash it down out of the way.*

V+N+ADV, V+PRON+ADV, V+ADV+N

2 If rain **lashes down**, it falls very heavily. ❏ *The rain lashed down so fiercely that we could hardly see.*

V+ADV

lash into If you **lash into** someone, you criticize or scold that person very angrily and severely. ❏ *They listened to Jimmie lashing into the extremists... I opened my mouth to lash into him.*

V+PREP: HAS PASSIVE

NOTE Lay into means almost the same as lash into.

lash out

1 If you **lash out**, you attempt to hit someone with sudden violent movements of your arms or legs or with a weapon. ❏ *When cornered, they lash out with savage kicks... He tried to pin Kitty to the wall, but she lashed out and tore from his grasp.*

V+ADV: ALSO+with

NOTE Hit out means almost the same as lash out.

2 If you **lash out** at someone, you speak to them very angrily or cruelly, criticizing or scolding them. ❏ *I lashed out at Kurt, calling him every name under the sun... Harris used the opportunity to lash out against the Committee.*

V+ADV: USUALLY WITH at/against

3 If you **lash out** on something, you spend a lot of money to buy it. ❏ *I should have to consider carefully before lashing out on something much dearer.*

V+ADV: ALSO+on

NOTE Splash out means almost the same as lash out.

last /lɑːst, læst/ (lasts, lasting, lasted)

last out

1 To **last out** a period of time, means to manage to stay alive, to continue functioning or to reach the end of a difficult experience. ❏ *I'm afraid she might not last out the winter... I don't think I can last out without any cigarettes... Do you think the car will last out until the end of the year?*

V+ADV: USUALLY+A

2 If a supply of something **lasts out** a period of time, there is enough of it for as long as it is needed or for that period of time. ❏ *The heater in the village hall needed*

V+ADV+N, V+N+ADV, V+ADV:

two bottles of fuel to last out a full meeting... How long will our coal reserves last out? NO PASSIVE
NOTE Hold out means almost the same as **last out**.

latch /lætʃ/ (latches, latching, latched)
latch on to, latch onto
1 If someone **latches on to** you, they demand your attention and expect you to spend a lot of time with them. ❑ *These kids know what they like and latch on to adults who can provide surprises and suggest new games... Just as he was about to leave, he was latched on to by a girl he'd met that morning.* | V+ADV+PREP: HAS PASSIVE

2 If someone **latches onto** something, they realize it or learn about it. ❑ *They never once latched onto the fact that he was using his own code... Once the landlords latched on to what was happening, out they went.* | V+ADV+PREP: HAS PASSIVE

3 If something **latches onto** something else, it attaches itself firmly to that thing. ❑ *The grubs hatch and make their way underground where they latch onto plant stems and hack them open.* | V+ADV+PREP

laugh /lɑːf, læf/ (laughs, laughing, laughed)
★laugh at
If you **laugh at** someone or something, you make jokes about them. ❑ *I don't think it's nice to laugh at people's disabilities... Not even a saint enjoys being laughed at in this kind of misfortune... The noise of the bells is said to fracture the towers but architects laugh at this and say it is rubbish.* | V+PREP: HAS PASSIVE

NOTE Ridicule is a more formal word for **laugh at**.

laugh off
If you **laugh off** a difficult or serious situation, you try to suggest that it is amusing and unimportant. ❑ *Despite being in serious trouble with the Government, Northcliffe attempted to laugh the matter off... Smith laughed off the insult by telling reporters that he was flattered that someone had taken notice of his work.* | V+N+ADV, V+ADV+N, V+PRON+ADV

launch /lɔːntʃ/ (launches, launching, launched)
launch into
If you **launch into** something such as a speech, task, or fight, you start it with enthusiasm. ❑ *She launched into a long speech about duty and patriotism... It was ironic that the movement should have launched itself into battle at this time... Then the chorus launches into an ecstatic song.* | V+PREP, V+REFL+PREP

lavish /lævɪʃ/ (lavishes, lavishing, lavished)
lavish on
If you **lavish** money, time or affection **on** someone or **lavish** it **upon** them, you spend a lot of money or time on them or give them a lot of affection. ❑ *Everything was lavished on her one and only child... Why do the media lavish so much attention on people like Hinckley?... I'm not about to lavish money on you; I have little enough myself.* | V+N+PREP

NOTE Heap on means almost the same as **lavish on**.

lavish upon → See lavish on

lay /leɪ/ (lays, laying, laid)
☑ Lay is also the past tense of the verb **lie**.

lay about
1 If someone **lays about** with a weapon, they use it to hit anyone who is nearby in a violent, uncontrolled way. You can also say that someone **lays about** themselves with a weapon when they attack other people in this way. ❑ *His two assistants sprang forwards and began to lay about the boys with sticks... He rushed out of his house, armed with a sword and a hatchet, and laid about himself fiercely, killing two of the animals.* | V+PREP, V+ADV+REFL: USUALLY+with

2 If someone is described as a **layabout**, that person is very lazy and never does any work. ❑ *'Perhaps your assistant could do it?'—'Charlie? That bone idle layabout. Not him.'* | N-COUNT

lay aside
1 If you **lay aside** something that you have been using or dealing with, you leave it for a while to do something else. ❑ *He laid the newspaper aside and turned his attention to breakfast... I've been reading this instead of doing my work; I can't seem to lay it aside... She was more restless than Anne and laid aside her books sooner.* | V+N+ADV, V+PRON+ADV, V+ADV+N

NOTE Put aside means almost the same as **lay aside**.

2 If you **lay aside** a feeling, belief or attitude that you have experienced, you stop or reject it so that it no longer affects you. ❑ *They tried to lay aside their usual inhibitions and say whatever came into their heads... People found the performances gave them a* | V+ADV+N, V+N+ADV, V+PRON+ADV

great deal of pleasure once prejudices against this kind of music were laid aside.
NOTE **Set aside** means almost the same as **lay aside**.

lay before If you **lay** an idea or a problem **before** someone, you present it to them in detail for them to consider and give their advice, opinion, or judgement. ❑ *If you have any proof of that allegation, I advise you to lay it before the police... The Wildlife and Countryside Bill had been laid before Parliament in October 1979.*
NOTE **Put before** means almost the same as **lay before**.

V+PRON+PREP,
V+N+PREP

lay by

1 If you **lay** a store of something **by**, you save it for future use. ❑ *I've got some savings laid by for my old age.*
NOTE **Put by** means almost the same as **lay by**.

V+N+ADV,
V+PRON+ADV,
V+ADV+N

2 A **lay-by** is a short strip of road by the side of a main road, where cars can stop for a while. ❑ *Pull into the next lay-by.*

N-COUNT

★lay down

1 If you **lay** something **down**, you put it down on a surface. If you **lay** yourself **down**, you move your body so that you are lying flat on a surface. ❑ *Albert laid his pipe down carefully on the table beside him... She took the key out of his pocket and said, 'Here. You keep it. I might lay it down somewhere and mislay it.'... She laid herself down on a long seat... Uncle Nick laid down his pencil and pushed the sheet of paper away from him.*

V+N+ADV,
V+PRON+ADV,
V+REFL+ADV,
V+ADV+N

2 If laws, rules, or people in authority **lay down** what people should do, they state that this is what must be done. ❑ *...laws which lay down what employers and employees must and must not do... As institutions they lay down no formal entry requirements... A government should lay down national policy for various sectors of education.*
NOTE **Stipulate** is a more formal word for **lay down**.

V+ADV+N,
V+PRON+ADV

3 If something such as food **is laid down**, it is stored for future use. ❑ *Wine that is too young to drink now should be laid down for a few years to allow it to mature... Carbohydrate not used up in work during the day will get laid down by the body as fat.*

V+N+ADV,
V+PRON+ADV,
V+ADV+N:
USUALLY PASSIVE

4 To **lay down** something new means to establish or create it. ❑ *Adolescence is important because the habits that are laid down then seem to last for a lifetime... After injury the haematoma is invaded by repair cells which lay down scar tissue.*

V+ADV+N,
V+PRON+ADV,
V+N+ADV

5 If something such as an area of grass or a path or airstrip **is laid down**, it is constructed covering an area of ground. ❑ *A new golf course has been laid down over a swamp... The Seabees laid down a 600-metre tarmac airstrip and built a beer hall.*

V+ADV+N,
V+N+ADV,
V+PRON+ADV:
USUALLY PASSIVE

6 When layers of sediment, sand, or rock **are laid down**, the layers settle and form into a solid mass over a long period of time. ❑ *Most sedimentary stone has been laid down in layers under water and therefore splits easily.*

V+ADV+N,
V+PRON+ADV:
USUALLY PASSIVE

7 If you **lay down** something such as an attitude, belief, or position that you have held, you give it up or reject it. [FORMAL] ❑ *It had been a great relief to be able to lay down the mantle of authority which I had borne for so long... The Law Lords concluded that a peer could not lay down his title.*
NOTE **Lay aside** means almost the same as **lay down**.

V+ADV+N,
V+N+ADV,
V+PRON+ADV

8 If people who have been at war **lay down** their arms or weapons, they stop fighting and make peace. [LITERARY] ❑ *There was no guarantee that the members of these units would lay down their arms.*

V+ADV+N

9 If someone **lays down** their life for a cause, they are killed because they are involved in it or support it. [LITERARY] ❑ *Not so many people today are willing to lay down their lives for their country any more.*
NOTE **Give** means almost the same as **lay down**.

V+ADV+N

lay in If you **lay in** an amount of something, you buy it and store it to be used later. ❑ *The Governor has laid in a plentiful supply of champagne and Havana cigars. ...people responsible for laying in food stocks for a city full of children.*
NOTE **Buy in** means almost the same as **lay in**.

V+ADV+N,
V+N+ADV,
V+PRON+ADV

lay into

1 If someone **lays into** another person, they start to hit and kick that person violently. ❑ *The special patrol group laid into them, forcing them to run into the near-by park... I was going to lay into her but the other two girls grabbed my arms.*

V+PREP:
HAS PASSIVE

2 If someone **lays into** you, they start to criticize you severely. ❑ *Before we went out*

V+PREP:

Bob really laid into us: 'You're not even trying! For heaven's sake put some effort into it.'... I HAS PASSIVE
was wearing one brown shoe and one black. He loved that, seeing the chance to lay into me:
'Been getting up in the dark again, eh?'

NOTE **Lash into** means almost the same as **lay into**.

3 If you **lay into** food or drink, you eat or drink it very eagerly and in large quan- V+PREP
tities. [INFORMAL]

NOTE **Tuck into** means almost the same as **lay into**.

★lay off

1 If workers **are laid off**, they are told by their employer that they have to leave V+N+ADV,
their jobs, either for a period of time or permanently, because there is no more work V+ADV+N,
V+PRON+ADV:
for them to do. ❑ *So if demand falls, the company lays men off... City workers are being* USUALLY PASSIVE
laid off at the rate of 100 a week.

♦ If there is a **layoff**, workers are told by their employer to leave their jobs. ❑ *Textile* N-COUNT
companies announced 2,000 fresh layoffs last week.

♦ A **layoff** is also a period of time in which people do not work or take part in their N-COUNT
normal activities, often because they are resting or are injured. ❑ *He was bowling badly*
after his long layoff.

2 If you tell someone to **lay off**, you are telling them to leave you alone, to stop V+ADV,
criticizing you, or to stop doing something which is annoying you. [INFORMAL] V+PREP:
ALSO IMPERATIVE
❑ *They had warned him to lay off, but he'd kept cutting in just the same... Anyway, I don't*
do it indiscriminately. You know that, but lay off me, or I might.

3 If you **lay off** something or **lay off** doing something, you give it up or stop do- V+ADV+N,
ing it. [INFORMAL] ❑ *Cut down on the starches, lay off the fudge sundaes and milk shakes...* V+ADV:
NO PASSIVE
Tom, lay off that sherry – it's terrible... 'Why not lay off till Monday?'—'I can't.'

lay on

✔ In meanings 2 and 3, the stress is on **lay**.

1 If you **lay on** something such as food, entertainment, or a service, you provide or V+ADV+N,
supply it. [BRITISH] ❑ *The organisers had laid on buses to transport people from the city...* V+N+ADV,
V+PRON+ADV
Early this evening, the press laid on an informal drinks party for us... Every kind of facility was
laid on for their amusement.

2 To **lay** blame or responsibility **on** or **lay** it **upon** someone means to state offi- V+N+PREP,
cially that they are responsible for something. **Lay upon** is a more formal expres- V+PRON+PREP
sion. ❑ *So far, women have been able to lay most of the blame on men. ...administrative*
duties laid upon them by Acts of Parliament... Responsibility for these people was therefore
laid on the Assistance Committees.

3 To **lay** stress or emphasis **on** or **lay** it **upon** something means to stress or em- V+N+PREP
phasize it. **Lay upon** is a more formal expression. ❑ *Less emphasis is laid on rivalry and*
competition, and more on co-operation... The Government has laid great stress on harnessing
private enterprise and voluntary help.

NOTE **Put on** means almost the same as **lay on**.

4 If you **lay** it **on**, you deliberately exaggerate a statement, gesture, or emotion in V+*it*+ADV
order to try to impress people or draw their attention to it. [INFORMAL] ❑ *He moved his*
chair all the while to make sure we didn't exchange eye-signals. He laid it on so thick that we
were bound to try to outwit him... I used grander expressions and laid it on much more thick-
ly than I should have done.

★lay out

1 If you **lay** something **out**, you put it in a particular place, spread out and neatly V+ADV+N,
arranged. ❑ *Lally was setting the table, laying out the plates and cups... I watched him start* V+N+ADV,
V+PRON+ADV
to lay the papers out on the table in the conference room... Handle the paper very carefully,
then lay it out on racks to dry.

NOTE **Put out** means almost the same as **lay out**.

2 If you **lay out** an idea or information, you express or present it clearly and thor- V+ADV+N,
oughly. ❑ *The situation is laid out very clearly in a briefing paper from the Ramblers Associa-* V+PRON+ADV
tion. ...laying out the relationship between racism today and the problems experienced in the
past.

NOTE **Set out** means almost the same as **lay out**.

3 If a garden, building, town, and so on **is laid out** in a particular way, it is de- PASSIVE:
signed or arranged in that way. ❑ *The homestead, shop and outbuildings were spaciously* V+ADV:
USUALLY+A

lay up

laid out. ...a garden laid out with terraces, fountains and shady walks.

♦ The **layout** of something such as a garden, building, or piece of writing is the way in which the parts of it are arranged. ❑ *...the general layout of the farm. ...the poor lay-out and organization of the report.*   N-COUNT

4 To **lay out** a dead person means to clean their body and dress them for the funeral. ❑ *After her death, no one could be found to lay her out.*   V+PRON+ADV, V+N+ADV, V+ADV+N

5 If someone **lays** a person **out**, they knock that person unconscious by hitting them violently. [INFORMAL] ❑ *Someone crept up behind Allen and laid him out with some heavy and solid object... Mother leapt out of bed. 'No one's going to lay out our Laurie!'*   V+PRON+ADV, V+ADV+N, V+N+ADV

NOTE **Knock out** means almost the same as **lay out**.

6 If you **lay out** money on something, you spend a large amount of money on it. [INFORMAL] ❑ *Some people might be too hard up midweek to lay out large sums. ...a note-book in which he kept a record of petty expenses he laid out on errands.*   V+ADV+N, V+N+ADV

NOTE **Shell out** and **fork out** mean almost the same as **lay out**.

lay up

1 If an illness **lays** you **up**, or if you **are laid up** with it, it causes you to stay in bed. [INFORMAL] ❑ *The baby was just beginning to walk when an illness laid her up... The gentleman had been laid up for five days with a bad cold.*   V+PRON+ADV, V+N+ADV: OR PASSIVE: V+ADV+with

2 If a car, boat, or piece of equipment **is laid up**, it is not in use, usually because it is being repaired. ❑ *The boats which took crews to Arctic waters had been laid up... The car had been laid up after Guy's death, but it was quite easy to get back on the road again.*   V+N+ADV, V+ADV+N, V+PRON+PREP: USUALLY PASSIVE

3 If you **lay up** something, you gradually save quantities of it for future use. [OLD-FASHIONED] ❑ *Hunter-gatherers simply do not lay up stocks against future shortages... This is one of those golden days to lay up as treasure for the future.*   V+ADV+N

4 If a person or animal **lays up** somewhere, they go there to hide or do nothing for a while. [INFORMAL] ❑ *If the fox does lay up, you can dig him out... There are ways and means of recapturing a ferret if he lays up... For two pins I'd lay up today, but I don't like to let Miss Read down.*   V+ADV

lay upon → See lay on

laze /leɪz/ (lazes, lazing, lazed)

☑ **About** is used mainly in British English.

laze about → See laze around

laze around If you **laze around** or **laze about**, you relax and enjoy yourself, not doing any work or anything that requires effort. ❑ *...cleaning and washing up while the other women laze about... He likes to laze around listening to music.*   V+ADV

NOTE **Lounge around** means almost the same as **laze around**.

lead /liːd/ (leads, leading, led)

lead in If you **lead in**, you start a formal discussion or meeting by making a short speech. ❑ *She led in with a few introductory remarks, then handed over to the main speaker.*   V+ADV

♦ A **lead-in** is a short introductory speech at the beginning of a formal discussion or meeting. ❑ *Six people missed the lead-in.*   N-COUNT

lead off

1 If a road, path, corridor, or room **leads off** a place, it connects directly with that place. ❑ *From the lift shaft four straight corridors lead off at right angles... There is a lane leading off right beside the Restaurant du Canal... Two tiny rooms led off the living-room. ...two doors leading off the hallway.*   V+ADV+A, V+PREP

2 If someone **leads off** in a meeting, performance, or event, they start it. ❑ *The chairman led off with a financial statement... He said, 'Join in with me, if you will, in singing ...' And then he led off in a different key from the one in which the organist was playing.*   V+ADV

3 In baseball, the player who **leads off** is the first player to bat for their team in a game or inning. ❑ *Terry Puhl leads off for the Houston Astros.*   V+ADV: ALSO+for

♦ The **lead-off** player is the first to play for their team in a game or inning. ❑ *...lead-off batter Otis Nixon.*   ADJECTIVE

lead on If someone **leads** you **on**, they deceive you by giving you false information or by behaving in a misleading way. ❑ *A girl doesn't indulge in antics like that unless she's been led on artfully by a man. ...cunningly leading them on; never letting them see that you know.*   V+N+ADV, V+PRON+ADV, V+ADV+N

lead on to

1 If one event or action **leads on to** another, it causes it or makes it possible. [BRITISH] ❑ *It is often the case that early interests lead on to a career... This discovery led on to studies of the immune system.* V+ADV+PREP

2 If a door, gate, or bridge **leads on to** a place, the place is on the other side of it. ❑ *There were glass doors leading on to this balcony.* V+ADV+PREP

★lead to

If something **leads to** a situation or event, usually an unpleasant one, it begins a process which causes that situation or event to happen. ❑ *The trend could lead to a decrease in standards... He warned yesterday that a pay rise for teachers would lead to job cuts.* V+PREP

★lead up to

1 The events and periods of time that **lead up to** a final situation happen one after the other until that situation is reached. ❑ *Witnesses gave their testimony of events leading up to and following Gregory's death. ...the riots of the early 1830s that led up to the reform bill. ...during the days leading up to the special conference.* V+ADV+PREP

2 If someone **leads up to** a particular subject in a conversation, they gradually guide the conversation to a point where they can introduce the subject. ❑ *Ever since you came in you've been leading up to this one question... What was he leading up to, in his deliberate, Scottish way?* V+ADV+PREP

leaf /liːf/ (leafs, leafing, leafed)

leaf through

If you **leaf through** a book or magazine, you turn the pages quickly without reading or looking at them carefully. ❑ *While he is waiting he leafs through a magazine... She took another volume out of the bookcase and began leafing through the pages.* V+PREP

NOTE **Thumb through** means almost the same as **leaf through**.

leak /liːk/ (leaks, leaking, leaked)

leak out

If information or news that should have been kept secret **leaks out**, it becomes known to other people. ❑ *News of their engagement leaked out just before Christmas... Terrible stories were leaking out about the cruelties.* V+ADV

NOTE **Get out** means almost the same as **leak out**.

lean /liːn/ (leans, leaning, leaned/leant)

lean on

1 If someone **leans on** you, they try to influence you by putting pressure on you or threatening you. ❑ *They can lean on the administration by threatening to withhold their subscriptions... Film production is an enormously competitive business, so the producers lean on the writers and the writers have a straight choice.* V+PREP: HAS PASSIVE

NOTE **Pressurize** is a more formal word for **lean on**.

2 If you **lean on** a particular person or thing, you depend on them for support and encouragement. ❑ *He leant on the calm and steadfast Kathy... They lean heavily upon each other for support... During this transition period, the world is likely to lean increasingly on the solid fossil fuels (coal and shale).* V+PREP

NOTE **Rely on** means almost the same as **lean on**.

lean out

If you **lean out** of an open window or other opening, you put your head and shoulders through the gap so that you are looking outside. ❑ *She leaned out and waved at him... A large number of people seemed to be leaning out of the window.* V+ADV: ALSO+of

lean over

If someone or something **leans over**, they bend in a particular direction. ❑ *You'll have to lean over to see it... He was leaning over me.* V+ADV, V+PREP

lean towards

If you **lean towards** or **lean toward** a particular idea, belief, or type of behaviour, you have a tendency to think or act in a particular way. ❑ *Politically, I lean towards the right... Most scientists would probably lean toward this viewpoint.* V+PREP

leap /liːp/ (leaps, leaping, leaped/leapt)

leap at

If you **leap at** a chance or opportunity, you accept it quickly and eagerly. ❑ *I can't understand why you didn't want to go; I would have leaped at the chance.* V+PREP

NOTE **Jump at** means almost the same as **leap at**.

leap on

1 If someone **leaps on** or **leaps upon** you, they suddenly move towards you and V+PREP:

take hold of you roughly or violently. ❑ *And then, before I could leap on Derek, I saw a little blind kid... He had been leapt upon by a wolf while out hunting.*

HAS PASSIVE

2 If you **leap on** or **leap upon** an idea or suggestion, you suddenly become interested in it or enthusiastic about it. ❑ *They leap on the suggestion with artificial enthusiasm... This is something you should leap upon and become involved with.*

V+PREP:
HAS PASSIVE

NOTE **Seize on** means almost the same as **leap on**.

leap out If someone or something **leaps out**, they suddenly appear from a place where they have been hiding. ❑ *They opened the gate, and I leapt out. ...when a rapist leaps out on a victim.*

V+ADV

leap out at If something such as an idea or something that is written down **leaps out at** you, it suddenly becomes very obvious or striking. ❑ *Her name leapt out at me from the list of applicants.*

V+ADV+PREP

leap upon → See **leap on**

leave /liːv/ **(leaves, leaving, left)**

leave aside If you **leave aside** an idea or suggestion, you do not think or talk about it straight away, although you intend to think about it or discuss it later. ❑ *Let's leave generalities aside and get back to Mr. Bashton. ...leaving aside the question of Meehan's guilt or innocence, the general view was that the Crown's evidence was not strong enough to convict.*

V+N+ADV,
V+ADV+N,
V+PRON+ADV

★leave behind

1 If you **leave** someone or something **behind**, you do not take them with you when you go somewhere. ❑ *'I can't carry this,' I said. 'We'll have to leave some behind.'... I couldn't leave Hilary behind to cope on her own. Not for six months... He sat there, glancing at the newspaper that had been left behind.*

V+N+ADV,
V+PRON+ADV,
V+ADV+N

2 To **leave behind** an object or situation means to cause or allow it to remain after leaving a place. ❑ *The police departed, leaving behind an unsolved mystery... The truck chugged away leaving a trail of debris behind it... When the water retreated the silt that it had left behind had coated the surface of the road... I worried a good deal about the debts I would leave behind if I were killed.*

V+ADV+N,
V+N+ADV/PREP,
V+PRON+ADV/PREP

3 If you **leave** a particular idea, attitude or state **behind**, you reject or abandon it in order to develop or progress. ❑ *We must leave adolescence behind and grow up... To escape from the vicious circle in which he finds himself trapped he will have to leave behind a whole complex of thoughts and prejudices.*

V+N+ADV,
V+ADV+N,
V+PRON+ADV

4 If someone **is left behind**, for example in their work or studies, they do not progress or develop as successfully as other people. ❑ *You had to follow closely if you wanted to avoid being left behind... If you don't know your technical jargon, you're going to be left behind.*

V+N+ADV,
V+PRON+ADV:
USUALLY PASSIVE

★leave off

1 If you **leave** someone or something **off** a list, you do not include them in that list. ❑ *Hopper was too important to be left off the guest list.*

V+N+PREP,
V+PRON+PREP

2 If you **leave off** a piece of clothing, you do not wear it on a particular occasion. ❑ *It's so hot I feel like leaving this helmet off... She had, in the excitement of the moment, left off some crucial garment.*

V+N+ADV,
V+ADV+N,
V+PRON+ADV

3 If you **leave off** doing something, you stop doing it. ❑ *Waddell left off hitting Mrs Ross and came over and struck Mr Ross... He sat down at the piano again and started playing from where he left off... She will take over where the midwife leaves off.*

V+ADV:
ALSO+-ING

4 If something **leaves off** at a particular point, it stops or ends there. ❑ *It picks up where the earlier story leaves off.*

V+ADV

5 If you tell someone to **leave off**, you are telling them to stop annoying you. [INFORMAL] ❑ *Just leave off, will you!*

IMPERATIVE,
V+ADV

NOTE **Lay off** means almost the same as **leave off**.

★leave out

1 If you **leave** someone or something **out**, you do not include them in an activity or group. ❑ *One or two scenes in the play were left out of the performance... I'm aware that we've had to leave out much interesting and important work... 'I shan't be available' said our host, 'so you will have to leave me out.'*

V+N+ADV,
V+ADV+N,
V+PRON+ADV:
ALSO+of

2 If you tell someone to **leave** it **out**, you are telling them that you do not believe what they are saying. [BRITISH, INFORMAL]

V+it+ADV

leave over If something such as money or food **is left over**, it remains when the rest has been taken away or used. ❏ *'What's left over then Tony?'—'About forty-five pence.'... Mothers and children usually get what is left over.*

PASSIVE:
V+ADV

♦ A **leftover** is something that belongs to a past period of time and surprisingly still exists, although most other things of that period no longer do. ❏ *...a leftover from our hunting past.*

N-COUNT

♦ **Leftovers** are the food that remains uneaten after a meal. ❏ *The leftovers were thrown to the village dogs.*

N-PLURAL

♦ **Leftover** is used to describe an amount of something that remains after you have finished using it. ❏ *...a bottle of leftover perfume.*

ADJECTIVE

lend /lɛnd/ **(lends, lending, lent)**

lend out If you **lend** something **out**, you allow someone to borrow it for a particular period of time. ❏ *She had lent out her camera and never got it back... Sorry, that book's been lent out.*

V+ADV+N,
V+N+ADV,
V+PRON+ADV

let /lɛt/ **(lets, letting)**

✓ The form **let** is used in the present tense and is the past tense and past participle of the verb.

★let down

1 If someone or something **lets** you **down**, they fail to do something that you have been relying on them to do. ❏ *He would never let a mate down... Charlie's never let me down yet.... You're so silly. You regularly let yourself down, don't you?... It would be best to run away now but she could not let down Jimmie: he needed help.*

V+N+ADV,
V+PRON+ADV,
V+REFL+ADV,
V+ADV+N

♦ If you say that something is a **letdown**, you mean that it is disappointing. ❏ *For the visitor expecting something special, it is a bit of a letdown.*

N-COUNT

2 If something **lets** you **down**, it is the reason you are not as successful as you could have been. ❏ *Many believe it was his shyness and insecurity which let him down... Sadly, the film is let down by an excessively simple plot.*

V+N+ADV,
V+PRON+ADV,
V+N+ADV

3 If you **let down** something that is filled with air, such as a tyre, you allow air to escape from it. [BRITISH] ❏ *June said, 'I dare you to go in and let down the tyres.'*

V+ADV+N,
V+N+ADV,
V+PRON+ADV

NOTE **Deflate** is a more formal word for **let down**.

4 If you **let down** a garment such as a dress, skirt, or pair of trousers, you undo the hem at the bottom and sew it up again in a different place to make the garment longer.

V+ADV+N,
V+N+ADV,
V+PRON+ADV

NOTE **Lengthen** means almost the same as **let down**.

★let in

1 If you **let** someone **in**, you allow them to come into a place, usually by opening the door for them. ❏ *Go and let them in, Howard... Lock the door and don't let anyone in... Evidently she had let herself in with a front-door key.*

V+PRON+ADV,
V+N+ADV,
V+REFL+ADV,
V+ADV+N

NOTE **Admit** is a more formal word for **let in**.

2 If something **lets in** water, mud, air, or light, it has a hole or crack which allows the water, mud, air, or light to get into it. ❏ *My old boots had been letting in water... I jump out of bed and pull up the shade and let all that sunlight in... Punch two holes, one to let the milk out, the other to let air in.*

V+ADV+N,
V+N+ADV,
V+PRON+ADV:
NO PASSIVE

3 An **inlet** is a narrow strip of water which goes from a sea or lake into the land or between two islands. ❏ *The inlet was a cleft in the gorge, open on both sides.*

N-COUNT

let in for If you **let** someone **in for** something, you involve them in something that causes them difficulty, unpleasantness, or unnecessary expense. [INFORMAL] ❏ *You don't realize, darling, what you've let me in for... We stood in front of that awful hotel and thought, what have we let ourselves in for?*

V+PRON+ADV+PREP,
V+REFL+ADV+PREP,
V+N+ADV+PREP

let in on If you **let** someone **in on** something that is secret or not generally known, you tell them about it or allow them to become involved. ❏ *He didn't let Uncle Harold in on the news... They are going to let all of us in on their little secret.*

V+N+ADV+PREP,
V+PRON+ADV+PREP

★let into

1 If you **let** someone **into** a building or room, you allow them to go into it, especially by opening the door for them. ❏ *Mr Thomas had let him into the church with the spare key... Irene Cameron let herself into Griffiths's flat at about mid-day... You let a boy like that into your house!... Then I was let into the inner office.*

V+PRON+PREP,
V+REFL+PREP,
V+N+PREP

2 If you **let** someone **into** a secret or your confidence, you allow them to know something that you have not told anyone else. ❑ *They agreed to let him into their secret... No one else can be let into this plan.*

V+PRON+PREP,
V+N+PREP

NOTE **Let in on** means almost the same as **let into**.

3 If something **has been let into** a surface, it has been fixed into a hollow or hole in the surface so that it does not stick out. ❑ *...around the places where the hot water radiators were let into the floor... She adjusted the lace front let into her dress.*

V+N+PREP,
V+PRON+PREP:
USUALLY PASSIVE

NOTE **Set into** means almost the same as **let into**.

★let off

1 If you **let** someone **off** a job or task that they should be doing, you say that they need not do it. [BRITISH] ❑ *They tried to get the teacher to let them off homework... He believes that if he works all day he should be let off domestic chores.*

V+PRON+PREP,
V+N+PREP,
V+N+ADV,
V+PRON+ADV

2 If you **let** someone **off**, you give them a lighter punishment than was expected or no punishment at all. ❑ *He let me off with a reprimand... They'll tell you to be more careful next time and let you off... It never occurred to me to ask to be let off.*

V+PRON+ADV,
V+N+ADV,
V+ADV+N:
ALSO+with

3 If you **let off** a gun, a bomb, or a firework, you fire it or cause it to explode. ❑ *His hearing is so poor that you could let off a gun within inches of him and he wouldn't flinch... I paid for those rockets and I'm going to let them off.*

V+ADV+N,
V+PRON+ADV,
V+N+ADV

4 If something or someone **lets off** a sound or energy, they suddenly make the sound or release the energy. ❑ *Just then my kettle let off a shrill whistle... Malcolm's cot squeaked as he jumped spiritedly up and down, letting off the final ounce or two of energy.*

V+ADV+N

5 If someone **lets off**, they release air from their anus. [INFORMAL]

V+ADV

6 If the driver of a vehicle **lets** someone **off**, he or she stops to allow that person to get out of the vehicle. ❑ *We drove home slowly. He stopped in front of the porch to let me off.*

V+PRON+ADV,
V+N+ADV,
V+ADV+N

let on If you **let on** about something, you tell someone about something that was intended to be kept secret, or express an emotion that you wanted to hide. [INFORMAL] ❑ *Don't let on we went to that dance... 'Oh,' Jules said. He didn't let on that he knew the whole story... Mary was shaken by the news, I could tell, although she didn't let on in the tone of her response.*

V+ADV,
V+ADV+REPORT

★let out

1 If you **let** someone **out**, you allow them to leave a place, especially by opening or unlocking a door. ❑ *The other prisoners were locked into their cells before I was let out of mine... I began to long to be released. 'Please let me out,' I kept pleading with the doctors... If I'm still asleep in the morning, just let yourself out.*

V+N+ADV,
V+PRON+ADV,
V+REFL+ADV,
V+ADV+N

2 To **let out** something such as water, air, or breath means to allow it to flow out freely. ❑ *He let the water out and refilled the bath with cold water... Piggy let out his breath with a gasp.*

V+N+ADV,
V+ADV+N,
V+PRON+ADV

♦ An **outlet** is a hole or pipe through which water or air can flow out. ❑ *Clean the sink outlet.*

N-COUNT

3 If you **let out** a particular sound, you make that sound. [LITERARY] ❑ *He had slipped and fallen on the uneven ground and was letting out loud uncontrolled shrieks and wails... The dogs picked up a scent and broke into a fast run, letting out excited yelps... Montclair let out a low whistle.*

V+ADV+N:
NO PASSIVE

NOTE **Emit** is a more formal word for **let out**.

4 If you **let** something **out**, you say something that you should have kept secret. ❑ *'She's gone to buy a paper.' As soon as I said this I cursed myself for letting it out.*

V+PRON+ADV,
V+N+ADV,
V+ADV+N

♦ An **outlet** is a means of expressing and releasing emotions, feelings, or ideas which you have inside you. ❑ *...outlets for political expression.*

N-COUNT

5 If you **let out** a house, room, or flat, you make it available for people to rent. ❑ *My father owned two houses which he let out as rooms to his friends... Rents received from letting out your home are liable to tax.*

V+ADV+N,
V+N+ADV,
V+PRON+ADV

NOTE **Rent out** means almost the same as **let out**.

6 If you **let out** a garment such as a dress or pair of trousers, you make it larger by undoing the seams and sewing closer to the edge of the material. ❑ *I'll have to let this dress out a bit before the wedding next week.*

V+ADV+N,
V+N+ADV,
V+PRON+ADV

NOTE **Take in** means almost the same as **let out**.

7 If something **lets** you **out**, it frees you from getting involved in a difficult or un-

V+PRON+ADV,

pleasant situation. [INFORMAL] ❏ *'What now?'—'Recorders, I think.'—'Well, that lets me* | V+N+ADV:
out, anyway. I can't play them.'... Mark Rutland's suggestion had let me out nicely. | NO PASSIVE

♦ A **let-out** is something that allows you to avoid an unpleasant or difficult situa- | N-COUNT
tion. ❏ *There are a few let-outs from this impossible situation.*

8 An **outlet** is a shop or organization which sells the goods made by a particular | N-COUNT
manufacturer. ❏ *Several commercial outlets had already expressed an interest.*

let through To **let** someone or something **through** means to allow them to | V+PRON+ADV,
pass a control point or move through something that is blocking the way. ❏ *To my* | V+ADV+N,
astonishment, the group opened up politely and let us through... Police at the entrance re- | V+N+ADV:
fused to let me through... It was raining heavily and I guessed that the skylight would be let- | NO PASSIVE
ting through a regular steady trickle into my classroom.

let up If something **lets up**, it stops or becomes less in degree or intensity. ❏ *Day* | V+ADV
followed day and still the heat did not let up... We thought that the rain would probably let
up after a while.

[NOTE] **Ease off** means almost the same as **let up**.

♦ If there is a **let-up**, the degree or intensity of something becomes less. ❏ *There was* | N-COUNT
a noticeable let-up of police violence in the community.

let up on If you **let up on** someone or something, you stop being so harsh or | V+ADV+PREP
strict with them. ❏ *Though Sybbis complained bitterly, Mama would not let up on her...*
There were some moves to let up on this curfew a little bit.

level /levəl/ (levels, levelling, levelled)

✓ American English uses the spellings **leveling** and **leveled**.

level against → See **level at**

level at If you **level** a criticism or accusation **at** someone, or **level** it **against** | V+N+PREP,
them, you criticize or accuse them. ❏ *...accusations which he could have levelled against* | V+PRON+PREP
Christopher... This criticism has been levelled at the government... A number of unfriendly
glances were levelled at him.

level off

1 If something that is increasing, decreasing, or developing **levels off** or **levels** | V+ADV
out, it stops changing or developing and stays at the point it has reached. ❏ *Econom-*
ic growth has almost certainly started to level off... This growth in demand for fossil fuels lev-
elled off after 1973... The population will probably reach 320 millions before levelling out.

[NOTE] **Stabilize** means almost the same as **level off**.

2 If you **level** a surface **off** or **level** it **out**, you make it flat by smoothing or cut- | V+PRON+ADV,
ting off any lumps or bumps. ❏ *Fill the scoop with the powder and level it off with a* | V+ADV+N,
knife... Using a smooth stone, he levelled off the mound into a plate-sized disk... A scraper | V+N+ADV
can be used for levelling out small humps of earth.

3 If an aircraft or boat **levels off** or **levels out**, it travels horizontally after travel- | V+ADV
ling upwards or downwards. ❏ *The planes levelled off at 20,000 feet and headed north...*
The boat angled slightly upwards and levelled off.

level out → See **level off**

level up To **level** things **up** means to make them more equal by adjusting the | V+N+ADV,
position or standard of one or more of them. ❏ *Their lead was lost in the next match* | V+PRON+ADV,
when New Zealand's historic win levelled things up. | V+ADV+N

[NOTE] **Even up** means almost the same as **level up**.

level with If you **level with** someone, you tell them the truth and do not keep | V+PREP
anything secret. [INFORMAL] ❏ *You're not levelling with me... I've always levelled with you,*
haven't I, Sam?

lick /lɪk/ (licks, licking, licked)

lick up If you **lick** something **up**, you remove it from a surface, using your | V+ADV+N,
tongue. ❏ *I could lick up the sauce while no-one was watching... It licks up the insects with* | V+N+ADV,
its long tongue. | V+PRON+ADV

lie /laɪ/ (lies, lying, lay, lain)

✓ **About** is used mainly in British English. In American English, **around** is much
more common than **round**.

lie about → See **lie around**

lie ahead If an event or situation **lies ahead**, it is likely to happen in the future.   V+PREP
❑ *...my romantic visions of what lay ahead... Harder decisions lie ahead... The task that lies ahead looks positively frightening.*

★lie around

1 If someone **lies around**, **lies about**, or **lies round**, they spend their time relax-   V+ADV,
ing and being lazy. [INFORMAL] ❑ *They were lying about in the doorways... Afterward sev-   V+PREP
en of us lay around on the living room floor, smoking... People lay around in the sun, mostly
undressed, playing instruments.*

NOTE **Lounge around** means almost the same as **lie around**.

2 If things are left **lying around**, **lying about**, or **lying round**, they are left   V+ADV,
somewhere, especially in an untidy way. ❑ *...an old boot which some fool had carelessly   V+PREP
left lying about... Do you have any money you don't want to leave lying around the
house?... A sheet of paper could lie around for centuries without being burnt.*

NOTE **Kick around** means almost the same as **lie around**.

lie back If you **lie back**, you move from a sitting position into a horizontal posi-   V+ADV
tion by lowering your head and shoulders backwards until you are lying on your
back. ❑ *Now lie back and relax.*

lie before If something **lies before** you, you will have to do it or experience it   V+PREP
in the future. [FORMAL] ❑ *...the only choice that lies before him... Endless hours of pleasure
lie before you... She is aware that a most formidable task lies before her.*

lie behind The thing that **lies behind** a situation or event is the reason or ex-   V+PREP
planation for it. ❑ *It's this kind of irresponsibility that lay behind the crisis. ...the real cause
that lay behind the rise in divorce.*

NOTE **Underlie** means almost the same as **lie behind**.

★lie down

When you **lie down**, you move into a horizontal position, usually in   V+ADV
order to rest or sleep. ❑ *I helped her to lie down again... We lay down side by side... Go
and lie down on your bed.*

♦ If you have a **lie-down**, you lie down on a bed and have a short rest. [INFORMAL]   N-SING
❑ *I think I'll go and have a lie-down for a while.*

lie in If you **lie in**, you intentionally stay in bed later than usual in the morning.   V+ADV
[BRITISH, INFORMAL] ❑ *I think I'll lie in tomorrow... Late evenings were no problem for him,
as he could lie in till late morning.*

♦ If you have a **lie-in**, you stay in bed later than usual in the morning to have a rest   N-SING
or because you are feeling lazy. [BRITISH, INFORMAL] ❑ *The meeting's not until ten o'clock,
so I can have a lie-in.*

lie round → See **lie around**

lie up If you **lie up** somewhere, you go there to hide or rest for a while. ❑ *The best*   V+ADV
*thing to do would be to make for the cave. He could lie up there safely... Small infantry de-
tachments were still lying up in hilly country, waiting for the weather to change.*

lie with

1 If a duty, fault, or choice **lies with** someone, it is their responsibility or choice.   V+PREP
[FORMAL] ❑ *Are you saying that the fault generally lies with the management?... Responsibil-
ity, they implied, lay with the owners... So, in many cases, the decision lies with the doctor...
The burden of proof lies with the accuser.*

2 If one person **lies with** another person, they have sex with each other. [OLD-   V+PREP
FASHIONED]

lift /lɪft/ (lifts, lifting, lifted)

lift off When an aircraft or rocket **lifts off**, it leaves the ground and rises into the   V+ADV
air. ❑ *The plane lifted off just as the ground seemed to open to swallow it... The fish broke
water a few yards from the boat, like a rocket lifting off.*

NOTE **Take off** means almost the same as **lift off**.

♦ **Lift-off** is the launching of a rocket into space, when it leaves the ground and   N-COUNT,
rises into the air. ❑ *...lift-off from a floating launch pad.*   N-UNCOUNT

★lift up

1 If you **lift** something **up**, you hold it in your hands or arms and move it   V+ADV+N,
upwards. ❑ *Stephen was attempting to lift up the two pint tankards from the bar... He was   V+PRON+ADV,
only 5 feet 8 inches tall, but he would lift me up as if I was a featherweight... Hooper lifted*   V+N+ADV

the bucket up on to the table.

NOTE **Lift** means almost the same as **lift up**.

2 If you **lift up** part of your body, you move it to a higher position. ❑ *She lifted up her head to smile at him... I had to lift my tongue up so she could see whether I had swallowed anything.*

V+ADV+N,
V+N+ADV,
V+PRON+ADV

NOTE **Raise** means almost the same as **lift up**.

3 If you **lift up** your voice, you speak or sing more loudly. [FORMAL, LITERARY] ❑ *It was John who lifted up his voice in answer.*

V+ADV+N

4 **Uplift** is something which helps people to have a better life, for example by improving their social conditions. ❑ *He devoted his life to their uplift.*

N-UNCOUNT

5 **Uplift** is an increase in the rate or amount of something. ❑ *...the profit uplift.*

N-UNCOUNT

light /laɪt/ (lights, lighting, lighted/lit)

light on → See light upon

light out If you **light out**, you leave a place in a hurry. [AMERICAN, INFORMAL] ❑ *The cats lit out and found safety on the roof.*

V+ADV

★light up

1 If a source of brightness **lights up** something, it shines light on the whole of it, making it easy to see. ❑ *Above the town the fire was still blazing, lighting up the sky... The match lit up her face... Someone turned his car around so that the headlights lit us up.*

V+ADV+N,
V+PRON+ADV,
V+N+ADV

NOTE **Illuminate** is a more formal word for **light up**.

2 If something **lights up**, a bulb inside it is turned on, making the thing shine brightly. ❑ *A yellow arrow lights up to tell the driver when the indicators are on... It's like a typewriter, but the letters light up instead of going onto paper.*

V+ADV

♦ **Lighting-up** time is the time when car drivers are required by law to switch their car lights on.

ADJECTIVE

3 If your face or your eyes **light up**, you suddenly look very happy or excited. ❑ *His face lit up at the sight of Cynthia... He looked glum for a minute; then I saw his face light up.*

V+ADV

4 If you **light up**, you put a match to a cigarette, cigar, or pipe and you start smoking it. [INFORMAL] ❑ *George lit up and puffed away for a while... He paused to light up his pipe.*

V+ADV,
V+ADV+N,
V+N+ADV

light upon If you **light upon** or **light on** something, you suddenly notice or find it, or it suddenly comes into your thoughts. ❑ *Her eyes then lit upon the piece of paper in the corner... The latter point was the kind of thing that philosophers lighted upon.*

V+PREP:
HAS PASSIVE

NOTE **Hit upon** means almost the same as **light upon**.

lighten /laɪtən/ (lightens, lightening, lightened)

lighten up If someone tells you to **lighten up**, they think you should be less serious and make an effort to be more relaxed and happy. ❑ *Come on, this is a party. Lighten up.*

V+ADV

liken /laɪkən/ (likens, likening, likened)

liken to If you **liken** one thing or person **to** another, you show or suggest something about the nature and qualities of the first by comparing them to the second. ❑ *The pursuit of females has often been likened to a hunt... The botanist John Ray likened their taste to parsnip. ...likening her to a tuning fork.*

V+N+PREP,
V+PRON+PREP

limber /lɪmbər/ (limbers, limbering, limbered)

limber up If you **limber up** just before taking part in an activity or sport, you prepare your body by doing a few exercises to make your muscles more flexible. ❑ *I had no time to limber up on the practice range... They were just limbering up.*

V+ADV

NOTE **Loosen up** means almost the same as **limber up**.

line /laɪn/ (lines, lining, lined)

★line up

1 If people or things **line up** or if you **line** them **up**, they stand in a row or form a queue. ❑ *The children line up under the shade of a thatched roof... They lined us up and marched us off... He lined the three cartridges up on the edge of the table.*

V+ADV,
V+N/PRON+ADV,
V+ADV+N:
ERGATIVE

2 A **line-up** is a row or queue of people who are waiting for something. [AMERICAN] ❑ *He was clearly unhappy about the length of the line-up ahead of him.*

N-COUNT

3 A **line-up** is a row of people who have been assembled in a police station. One of

N-COUNT

the people is a suspected criminal, and victims or witnesses of the crime try to identify that person. [BRITISH]

4 If you **line** something **up**, you move it so that it is straight or in its correct position in relation to something else. ❏ *Adjust them so that the two are exactly lined up...
The little plane's nose dipped and we lined up, poised above the landing strip... The exposure
is automatic; he lines up the scene in the viewfinder and rotates the focus ring.*

V+N+ADV,
V+ADV,
V+ADV+N,
V+PRON+ADV:
ERGATIVE

5 If you **line up** something or someone in preparation for an event, you arrange
for them to be ready and available for that event. ❏ *I had lined up a wonderful cast... A
formal greeting party was lined up... It was weak stuff compared to what the Tories had lined
up in their policy statement.*

V+ADV+N

NOTE **Fix up** means almost the same as **line up**.

◆ A **line-up** is a series of things or group of people that are assembled for a particular activity or event. ❏ *The England line-up for the match against Poland was announced
this morning.*

N-COUNT

6 If you **line up** with, behind, or alongside someone, you support them. If you
line up against them, you oppose them. ❏ *This gave the Revolutionary Socialists the perfect excuse to line up behind Arosemena... We can already see that the company will line up
against Toyota and Nissan... Most of the others will line up with the Tattaglias.*

V+ADV:
WITH A

linger /lɪŋgəʳ/ (lingers, lingering, lingered)

linger on If something or someone **lingers on**, they remain or continue to exist
for a long time, especially longer than was expected. ❏ *Many of the old ways were
dropped, but some of the habits lingered on... Tom lingered on after she had died.*

V+ADV

link /lɪŋk/ (links, linking, linked)

★link up

1 If you **link up** with someone, you meet them somewhere, usually before travelling on to another place with them. ❏ *We drove on from Florence and linked up with
them in Rome.*

V+ADV,
V+ADV+with:
RECIPROCAL

NOTE **Meet up** means almost the same as **link up**.

2 If you **link up** two items or places, you connect them to each other in some way.
❏ *This computer can be linked up to other computers... Should we be linking up with other
movements in the UK?*

V+N+ADV,
V+PRON+ADV,
V+ADV+N,
V+ADV

NOTE **Join up** means almost the same as **link up**.

◆ A **link-up** is a connection or meeting between two systems or machines. ❏ *...the
link-up of the US Apollo and Soviet Soyuz spacecraft.*

N-COUNT

liquor /lɪkəʳ/ (liquors, liquoring, liquored)

liquor up If someone **is liquored up**, they have drunk too much alcohol.
[AMERICAN] ❏ *I'm sure plenty of them go out and get liquored up, but I've never yet seen
one bit of unpleasantness on the streets.*

PASSIVE:
V+ADV

listen /lɪsən/ (listens, listening, listened)

listen in If you **listen in** to a conversation, radio programme, or other source of
communication, you listen to it. ❏ *Do you really think they bother to listen in to us?... I
was listening in last night. The television was rubbish so I turned on your radio programme.*

V+ADV:
USUALLY+A

listen out for If you **listen out for** something that you are expecting to hear,
you keep alert and make an effort to be ready to hear it when it occurs. ❏ *Will you listen out for the car arriving? They should be here soon... Listen out for the signal to start.*

V+ADV+PREP

★**listen to** When you **listen to** someone who is talking, or **listen to** a sound, you
give your attention to them or to the sound. ❏ *He never listened to anyone. ...listening
to Benny Goodman playing 'Paper Doll'... Our ideas were listened to sympathetically.*

V+PREP:
HAS PASSIVE

live /lɪv/ (lives, living, lived)

live by If you **live by** a particular rule, belief, or ideal, you always behave in the
way in which it says you should behave. ❏ *I know a man who really tries to live by the
Ten Commandments... He refuses to live by rules set up by others... How far would a Social
Democratic Government actually live by its principles and surrender much of its power?*

V+PREP

NOTE **Abide by** means almost the same as **live by**.

live down If you are unable to **live down** a mistake, failure, or foolish action,
you are unable to make people forget that you did it. ❏ *'You'd be the laughing stock of*

V+PRON+ADV,
V+ADV+N,
V+N+ADV

the neighbourhood,' she said, 'you'd never live it down.' ...the story of a young girl who finds it impossible to live down her past.

live for If you **live for** a particular thing, it is the most important thing in your life and you consider it as your reason for living. ❑ *...a man who lived for pleasure... She really lives for her work. ...people fighting off despair, with really nothing to live for.*   V+PREP

live in

1 If someone such as a servant or student **lives in**, they sleep and eat in the place where they work or study. ❑ *Would you be prepared to live in?... Members of staff and some senior postgraduates live in as tutors to keep an eye on the welfare of students.*   V+ADV

♦ **Live-in** servants or workers sleep and eat in the place where they work. ❑ *Martha was the live-in maid who kept house and cooked.*   ADJECTIVE

♦ A **live-in** boyfriend or girlfriend lives in the same house as the person they are having a sexual relationship with. ❑ *She has a demanding job and a live-in boyfriend.*   ADJECTIVE

2 If a building or room looks **lived-in**, it looks comfortable and welcoming but perhaps rather untidy because it is used often. ❑ *His bedroom had a lived-in look.*   ADJECTIVE

★live off

1 If you **live off** another person or a particular source of money, that is where you get the money that you need. ❑ *They continued to live off the rents of their farms, as they always had done... Roland had not worked for two months when I met him, and had been living off savings accumulated in the previous season.*   V+PREP

2 If you **live off** a particular kind of food, it is the only kind of food you eat, usually because this is all that is available. ❑ *He'd been living off pork pies since Monday... Dadda would catch fish and we used to live off fish and scones and sweet potatoes.*   V+PREP

NOTE **Live on** means almost the same as **live off**.

★live on

☑ In meaning 3, the stress is on **on**.

1 If you **live on** a particular amount of money, you have that amount of money to buy things. ❑ *How do you expect me to live on £150 a year?... I don't have enough to live on... Up to now John and I had both been living on what was left of his money.*   V+PREP

2 If you **live on** a particular kind of food, it is the only kind of food you eat, usually because this is all that is available. ❑ *She lived on berries and wild herbs. ...the growing army of young workers who were living on peanut butter sandwiches.*   V+PREP

NOTE **Live off** means almost the same as **live on**.

3 If someone or something **lives on**, they continue to exist or live. ❑ *She lives on, crippled as before, but happy now... The Marilyn Monroe legend lives on in Hollywood... The tradition lives on, handed down from generation to generation... In Brazil and Guiana, African culture lived on, though not unchanged.*   V+ADV

live out

1 If you **live out** a particular set of things that you are fated or intended to do, you actually do them. [FORMAL] ❑ *Each of us lives out our destiny. ...allowing children to live out their natural interests.*   V+ADV+N: NO PASSIVE

NOTE **Fulfil** is a more formal word for **live out**.

2 If you **live out** your life in a particular place or in particular circumstances, you remain in that place or in those circumstances until the end of your life. ❑ *He lived out the remaining 56 years of his life in London.*   V+ADV+N: USUALLY+A

live through If you **live through** a difficult or dramatic event or change, you experience it and survive it. ❑ *You've got to have courage to live through something like that. ...providing sufficient help to enable the children to live through the family breakup... This was essentially a period to be lived through.*   V+PREP: HAS PASSIVE

NOTE **Endure** is a more formal word for **live through**.

★live together

1 If two people **live together**, they share the same house and have a sexual relationship but are not married to one another. ❑ *Increasing numbers of young people choose to live together rather than to marry.*   V+ADV

NOTE **Cohabit** is a formal word for **live together**.

2 You can also say that people **live together** when they live in the same house. ❑ *...groups of students living together.*   V+ADV

live up If you **live** it **up**, you have a very enjoyable and exciting time, usually spending a lot of money and doing all the things that you want to do. ❑ *Next week we report to camp. We're going to live it up meanwhile... We spent a week living it up in the luxury of the Intercontinental Hotel... We had little chance of living it up on our meagre expense accounts.*

V+*it*+ADV

★live up to If someone or something **lives up to** people's expectations, they are as good as they were expected to be. ❑ *The film didn't live up to my expectations... She succeeded, to my mind, in living up to her extraordinary reputation.*

V+ADV+PREP:
HAS PASSIVE

NOTE **Match up to** means almost the same as **live up to**.

★live with

1 If you **live with** someone, you live in the same house as them. ❑ *He lived with his mother until he was thirty-seven.*

V+PREP

2 You can also say that you **live with** someone when you share a house with them and have a sexual relationship with them but are not married to them. ❑ *The social security found she was living with a man... She's living with somebody now.*

V+PREP

3 If you have to **live with** an unpleasant or unwelcome situation, you have to accept it and carry on with your life or work. ❑ *They have to live with the consequences of their decision... The job involved a lot of stress and pressure, but you learnt to live with it... The fear of death is something that has to be lived with.*

V+PREP:
HAS PASSIVE

NOTE **Put up with** is a more informal expression for **live with**.

liven /ˈlaɪvən/ **(livens, livening, livened)**

liven up

1 If something **livens up** a place or event, or if it **livens up**, it becomes more interesting and exciting. ❑ *...arranging events that help to liven up the community... There are lots of new shops and things. The place is really livening up.*

V+ADV+N,
V+N/PRON+ADV,
V+ADV:
ERGATIVE

2 If something **livens** you **up**, or if you **liven up**, you become more cheerful and energetic. ❑ *At least the incident had livened her up... Jane livened up then.*

V+PRON+ADV,
V+N+ADV,
V+ADV:
ERGATIVE

NOTE **Perk up** means almost the same as **liven up**.

load /loʊd/ **(loads, loading, loaded)**

load down

1 If you **load** someone **down** with things, you give them a large number of things to carry or hold. ❑ *She loaded her daughter down with packages. ...loaded down with two reels of cable and several field phones.*

V+N+ADV,
V+PRON+ADV,
V+ADV+N:
USUALLY+*with*

2 If you **are loaded down** with work or responsibilities, you have more than you can reasonably manage. ❑ *I'm loaded down with work at the moment.*

PASSIVE:
V+ADV:
USUALLY+*with*

NOTE **Be snowed under** means almost the same as **be loaded down**.

load up If you **load up** a vehicle or animal with things, or if you **load** things **up**, you put them into the vehicle or onto the animal, so that they can be taken somewhere. ❑ *They helped us load up the mule wagons with fresh meat and vegetables... Load up the dirty dishes first of all... I usually took off my coat while I was loading up.*

V+ADV+N,
V+N+ADV,
V+PRON+ADV,
V+ADV

loaf /loʊf/ **(loafs, loafing, loafed)**

✔ **About** is used mainly in British English. In American English, **around** is much more common than **round**.

loaf about → See **loaf around**

loaf around If you **loaf around**, **loaf about**, or **loaf round**, you spend your time being lazy and doing nothing that requires effort or hard work. ❑ *She just loafed about for three years... We loafed around all morning.*

V+ADV,
V+PREP

NOTE **Laze around** means almost the same as **loaf around**.

loaf round → See **loaf around**

loan /loʊn/ **(loans, loaning, loaned)**

loan out If you **loan** something **out**, you allow someone to borrow it for a particular period of time. ❑ *It serves you right for loaning your car out... The team were unable to loan out a replacement.*

V+N+ADV,
V+ADV+N,
V+PRON+ADV

lock /lɒk/ **(locks, locking, locked)**

★lock away

1 If you **lock** something **away**, you put it in something such as a safe, cupboard,

V+ADV+N,

or drawer, which you lock so that no-one else can get it. ❑ *He switched off the heating and locked away the food whenever he left the house... We should be able to function as a group without having to lock stuff away... Everything of value must be locked away.* | V+N+ADV, V+PRON+ADV

NOTE **Shut away** means almost the same as **lock away**.

2 To **lock** someone **away** means to put them into prison or a special psychiatric hospital. ❑ *Her political activities had got her dismissed, then locked away.* | V+N+ADV, V+PRON+ADV, V+ADV+N

NOTE **Lock up** means almost the same as **lock away**.

3 If you **are locked away** or you **lock** yourself **away** somewhere, you go there to be away from other people because you do not want to be disturbed. ❑ *She locked herself away in her room and wouldn't come out... When I was finishing my thesis I was locked away in my office for weeks.* | V+REFL+ADV: ALSO PASSIVE: V+ADV

NOTE **Shut away** means almost the same as **lock away**.

4 If someone **locks** information **away**, they prevent it from becoming generally known. ❑ *...a report which the government preferred to keep locked away: but the union felt the public were entitled to know the truth.* | V+N+ADV, V+PRON+ADV, V+ADV+N

NOTE **Suppress** is a more formal word for **lock away**.

★lock in If you **lock** someone **in**, you put them in a room or a building and lock the door so that they cannot get out. ❑ *After they had locked me in, the officer in charge came to see me... Tusker had dragged Bloxsaw into the garage and locked him in... The prisoners were not locked in.* | V+PRON+ADV, V+N+ADV, V+ADV+N

★lock out

1 If you **lock** someone **out** of a place, you prevent them from entering it by locking the doors. ❑ *One November night he locked her out of the house... One member of the delegation locked another out of the room they shared... I went to Renata's apartment for dinner one night and found myself locked out.* | V+PRON+ADV, V+N+ADV, V+ADV+N

2 If you **lock** yourself **out** of a place, you go out of a door which locks automatically, forgetting to take the keys, with the result that you cannot get inside again. ❑ *I went to empty the bins and found that I'd locked myself out... I've locked myself out of the car again!* | V+REFL+ADV: ALSO+of

3 In an industrial dispute, if the management of a place of work **locks out** the workers, it closes the factory or office and prevents the workers from coming in, because the workers refuse to accept the management's proposals. ❑ *The miners refused; the owners then locked them out... Cigar workers were locked out in industrial disputes.* | V+PRON+ADV, V+N+ADV, V+ADV+N

♦ A **lockout** is a situation in which the management of a place of work closes it and prevents the workers from coming in until they accept the management's proposals. ❑ *The Court can now grant an injunction to stop a strike or lockout.* | N-COUNT

★lock up

1 To **lock** someone **up** means to put them in prison or a special psychiatric hospital. ❑ *They locked him up as a madman... The idea of being locked up in jail filled her with horror.* | V+PRON+ADV, V+N+ADV, V+ADV+N

NOTE **Lock away** means almost the same as **lock up**.

♦ A **lockup** is a jail or a cell in a police station. [AMERICAN, INFORMAL] ❑ *They hustled him off and put him in the lockup.* | N-COUNT

2 When you **lock up** or **lock** a house or building **up**, you make sure that all the doors and windows are properly closed or locked so that burglars cannot get in. ❑ *I was waiting for him to leave so that I could lock up... He locked the house up and went away.* | V+ADV, V+PRON+ADV, V+N+ADV, V+ADV+N

♦ A **lock-up** shop or garage is one that is available for rent. [BRITISH] ❑ *The lease was for a lock-up shop on Kingsbury Road. ...a row of lock-up garages.* | ADJECTIVE

3 If something **is locked up** in a particular place or state, it is in that place or state and cannot easily be taken out, used, or changed. ❑ *So much water locked up in the ice caps caused a lowering of the sea level... The majority of the money required is locked up in the costs of raw materials.* | V+N+ADV, V+PRON+ADV, V+ADV+N: USUALLY PASSIVE

log /lɒg, AM lɔːg/ **(logs, logging, logged)**

★log in When someone who is using a computer **logs in** or **logs on**, they gain access to the system, usually by keying a special word. | V+ADV

NOTE **Log out** means the opposite of **log in**.

log into When someone **logs into** a computer system, they gain access to the   V+PREP
system, usually by keying a special word.

log off → See log out

★log on → See log in

log out When someone **logs out** or **logs off**, they finish using a computer sys-   V+ADV
tem.

NOTE **Log in** means the opposite of **log out**.

loll /lɒl/ (lolls, lolling, lolled)

☑ **About** is used mainly in British English. In American English, **around** is much
more common than **round**.

loll about → See loll around

loll around If you **loll around**, **loll about**, or **loll round** somewhere, you lie   V+ADV,
or stay there in a lazy way, doing nothing in particular. ❑ *He kept saying he should be*   V+PREP
at home and not lolling about in the summer sun. ...walking up hills, taking photographs,
and generally lolling around... They lolled about the place.

NOTE **Loaf around** means almost the same as **loll around**.

loll round → See loll around

long /lɒŋ, AM lɔːŋ/ (longs, longing, longed)

★long for If you **long for** something, you want it very much. ❑ *I longed for a*   V+PREP:
change of scenery. ...refugees longing for their homeland.   HAS PASSIVE

♦ A **longed-for** thing or event is one that someone wants very much. ❑ *At last the*   ADJECTIVE
longed-for refreshment arrived.

look /lʊk/ (looks, looking, looked)

☑ In American English, **around** is much more common than **round**.

★look after

1 If you **look after** someone or something, you take care of them and do what is   V+PREP:
necessary for them to stay in good condition. ❑ *Does your husband accept that he*   HAS PASSIVE
ought to be looking after the baby?... Look after my garden... She wasn't being well looked
after at all.

2 If you **look after** something, you are responsible for it and deal with it. ❑ *Do you*   V+PREP:
think Walker should stay there all the time to look after things?... The duty of the local   HAS PASSIVE
authority is to look after the interests of local people... Ventilation and drainage problems are
often looked after by semi-qualified staff.

NOTE **Attend to** is a more formal expression for **look after**.

3 If you **look after** something that belongs to someone else, you take charge of it   V+PREP:
for them so that you can prevent it from being lost or damaged. ❑ *Will you look after*   HAS PASSIVE
my money for me while I go swimming?

4 If you say that you can **look after** yourself, you mean that you are able to avoid   V+PREP+REFL
being harmed or cheated by other people.

look ahead If you **look ahead**, you think about what is going to happen in   V+ADV
the future and perhaps make plans. ❑ *We're trying to look ahead. ...if we look ahead and*
project existing trends ten years forward... You'll need to look ahead four or five years.

look around

1 If you **look around** or **look round**, you turn to look at something behind you.   V+ADV
❑ *He stopped suddenly and looked round.*

2 If you **look around** or **look round**, you look in various directions to find some-   V+ADV,
thing, or to see what is there. ❑ *He looked around for a chair and, since there*   V+PREP
wasn't one, sat on the floor... 'What's the general feeling?' He looked round at the company.

★look at

1 If you **look at** something, you turn your eyes towards it so that you can see it.   V+PREP:
❑ *She looks at him and smiles faintly. ...looking at a picture.*   HAS PASSIVE

2 If you **look at** a book, newspaper, or piece of writing, you read it, or parts of it,   V+PREP:
fairly quickly and not very thoroughly. ❑ *I've looked at your essay and I think it's very*   HAS PASSIVE
good.

NOTE **Look through** means almost the same as **look at**.

3 If an expert **looks at** something, they examine it and decide how it should be   V+PREP:

dealt with. ❏ *That leg's a bit swollen. I'd like Doctor Wells to look at it... Their mouths are forced open for their teeth and their throats to be looked at.*   HAS PASSIVE

4 If you **look at** a subject, problem, or situation, you think carefully about it or study it. ❏ *Bowlby looked at children in institutions and claimed that they suffered no deprivation at all... However, there is one further category of evidence to be looked at.*   V+PREP; HAS PASSIVE

5 If you **look at** a situation in a particular way, you judge it or consider it in that way. ❏ *If you're a Democrat, you look at things one way, and if you're a Republican you look at them in a very different way... Look at it my way... If life had to be looked at in terms of high moments, or peaks, then nothing had happened.*   V+PREP; HAS PASSIVE

NOTE **See** means almost the same as **look at**.

look away If you **look away** from something, you turn your eyes away from it so that you can no longer see it. ❏ *Their eyes met and Ida blushed and looked away... It looked up at Mrs Bixby with bright yellow eyes, then looked away again and carried on eating.*   V+ADV

★**look back**

1 If you **look back**, you turn to see what is behind you. ❏ *Jack turned and looked back at Ralph... I looked back and saw my car moving slowly down the hill.*   V+ADV

2 If you **look back** on something, you think about something that happened in the past. ❏ *It all seems very pathetic when I look back, but it was painful enough at the time... The past always seems better when you look back on it. ...when I look back upon my life.*   V+ADV; ALSO+on/upon

★**look down** If you **look down**, you lower your eyes to see what is below. ❏ *The man looked down at his shaking legs... He paused on the narrow ledge and looked down.*   V+ADV

look down on If you **look down on** someone or something, you think they are inferior or unimportant. ❏ *The farm labourer used to be looked down on... They are arrogant and aggressive people. They look down on us... Why do the English look down on everything foreign?*   V+ADV+PREP; HAS PASSIVE

NOTE **Despise** means almost the same as **look down on**.

★**look for**

1 If you **are looking for** something, you are trying to find it. ❏ *I went to look for him there and at first could not find him... The priest had found the book he was looking for and was checking a reference... We started to look for a house with a garden.*   V+PREP

2 If you **are looking for** something such as the solution to a problem, you are trying to achieve it or think of it. ❏ *Britain is looking for a peaceful, diplomatic solution... What we are looking for is a firm commitment on the part of the government.*   V+PREP; HAS PASSIVE

NOTE **Seek** is a more formal word for **look for**.

♦ **Unlooked-for** is used to describe something which you did not expect or want to happen. ❏ *...an unlooked-for change in the weather.*   ADJECTIVE

★**look forward to**

1 If you **look forward to** something that is going to happen, you want it to happen because you expect to enjoy it. ❏ *I'm quite looking forward to seeing Rick again... I looked forward to leaving school... I did not look forward with any confidence to my meeting with the manager.*   V+ADV+PREP; HAS PASSIVE

2 If you say that someone **is looking forward to** something useful or positive, you mean they expect it to happen. ❏ *Motor traders are looking forward to a further increase in vehicle sales.*   V+ADV+PREP

look in

1 If you **look in** on a person or **look in** at a place, you visit that person or place for a short time, especially when your visit was not planned in advance. ❏ *Could I look in on Sam?... I think I'll look in on my parents on the way home from work... I'll look in at the newsagent's and pick up a paper.*   V+ADV; USUALLY+A

NOTE **Drop in** and **call in** mean almost the same as **look in**.

2 If you are trying to take part in an activity and you do not get a **look-in**, you are unable to take part because other people are more successful or forceful than you. ❏ *James talks so much that all the others barely get a look-in.*   N-SING

★**look into** If you **look into** a particular problem, subject or situation, you find out and examine the facts relating to it. ❏ *In 1959 a working party was set up to look into the problem... They wanted an independent financial controller to look into the city's ac-*   V+PREP; HAS PASSIVE counts... *The causes of these misunderstandings and anxieties should be looked into.*

NOTE **Investigate** is a more formal word for **look into**.

*look on

✅ In meaning 2, the stress is on **look**.

1 If you **look on** while something happens, you watch it without taking part your-   V+ADV
self. ❑ *His parents looked on with a triumphant smile as he collected his prize... Police boats
sped down the river while families picnicking on the banks looked on in amazement.*

♦ **Onlookers** are the people watching an event take place, without taking part in it.   N-COUNT
❑ *Reporters and onlookers lined the fence beside the airfield. ...an accompanying ragged
cheer from the crowd of onlookers.*

2 If you **look on** or **look upon** something in a particular way, you think of it in   V+PREP:
that way. **Look upon** is slightly more formal. ❑ *If she went out with Mark after turning*   WITH A,
                                                                                                HAS PASSIVE
*down an invitation from John, he'd look on it as the deadliest insult... Houses are looked upon
as investments... The nuclear powers would not look kindly upon such a development.*

*look out

1 You say or shout **'look out'** to warn someone that they are in danger. ❑ *'Look*   IMPERATIVE,
out,' I said. 'There's someone coming.'   V+ADV

NOTE **Watch out** means almost the same as **look out**.

♦ A **lookout** is a place that is quite high up, from which someone can watch the   N-COUNT
area around them to see what is happening and to watch for any danger.

♦ A **lookout** is also someone who is watching for danger. ❑ *Two of the burglars were*   N-COUNT
tipped off by a lookout and escaped.

2 If you **look out** something that is stored away, you search for it, find it and take   V+ADV+N,
it out. ❑ *I had looked out my register and red and blue pens for marking it... Let me have a*   V+PRON+ADV,
                                                                                                 V+N+ADV:
note saying what you want, and we'll look it out.   NO PASSIVE

NOTE **Dig out** means almost the same as **look out**.

*look out for

1 If you **look out for** something that you want or expect, you pay attention to   V+ADV+PREP:
things around you so that you notice it and can take action when it occurs or is   HAS PASSIVE
there. ❑ *It's a film we shall look out for in the next couple of months... 'It's worth a visit if
you're interested.'—'Thank you. I'll look out for it.'... They have little or no idea of what hazards to look out for.*

NOTE **Watch out for** means almost the same as **look out for**.

2 If you **look out for** yourself or **look out for** your own interests, you make sure   V+ADV+PREP
that you have all the advantages possible and that you protect yourself from danger.
❑ *As for the girl, she had to start looking out for herself one day... No! It means we all look
out for each other in the family.*

look over If you **look** something or someone **over**, you examine or inspect   V+ADV+N,
them in order to get a general idea of what they are like. ❑ *Sometimes he'd look over*   V+PRON+ADV,
                                                                                          V+N+ADV
the article I'd written, shrug, and tear it up... If you're worried, get the vet to look it over.

*look round

1 → See **look around**

2 If you **look round** a building or place, you walk round it and look at the differ-   V+PREP,
ent parts of it to see what it is like. ❑ *Shall we look round the Cathedral this afternoon?...*   V+ADV
We began to look round the schoolroom with nostalgia.

NOTE **Go round** means almost the same as **look round**.

3 If you **are looking round** for something, you try to find it by making general   V+ADV:
enquiries or trying various different things, usually over a period of time. ❑ *Tell me*   USUALLY+for
*when you decide to give up. Then I can look round for somebody who'd like the job!... Their
group split up, and those that were left looked round for other amusement.*

*look through

1 If you **look through** something such as a window or a doorway, you turn your   V+PREP,
eyes in that direction to see what is on the other side of it. ❑ *Michael looked through*   V+ADV
*the window down into the street... The skipper looked through his binoculars at the long col-
umn of ships... She looked through to the garden.*

2 If you **look through** a group of things or you **look through** a place such as a   V+PREP:
cupboard, box, or room, you examine all the things there, usually because you are   HAS PASSIVE

trying to find something. ❑ *He looked through the clothing on the bed... They'll look through the applications and pick out the ones that seem promising... Did you look through all your drawers, darling, and cupboards?... Finally, having nothing else to do, I looked through the bookshelves.*

NOTE **Go through** means almost the same as **look through**.

3 If you **look through** something that has been written or printed, you read it, usually fairly quickly and briefly. ❑ *If you have revision notes you may find it helpful to look through them on the morning of the examination... He looked through the timetable. Yes, the Lima flight left at 10.00h.*

V+PREP:
HAS PASSIVE

4 If someone **looks through** another person, they look at that person without showing that they have seen them or recognized them, for example because they are angry or deep in thought. ❑ *They looked straight through him.*

V+PREP

look to

1 If you **look to** someone or something for something such as help or advice, you rely on them to provide it. ❑ *We should look to the economists for advice on how to overcome inflation... They look to others to structure time for them... People look to education to bring this about.*

V+PREP:
HAS PASSIVE,
WITH *for* OR *to* -INF

NOTE **Turn to** means almost the same as **look to**.

2 If you **look to** something, you make sure that you maintain it in good condition and that it is not neglected. [FORMAL] ❑ *They must look to their defences... Look to your health.*

V+PREP

NOTE **Attend to** means almost the same as **look to**.

3 If you **look to** something that will happen in the future, you think about it, often with a particular emotion. ❑ *Some New Englanders look to the future with a certain anxiety.*

V+PREP:
USUALLY+A

★look up

1 If you **look up**, you raise your eyes to see what is above. ❑ *As he heard the one-word message that followed, he looked up in disbelief... I suddenly looked up and saw Mark Rutland watching me... She only grunted, not even looking up from her work.*

V+ADV

2 If you **look up** a piece of information in a book, or on a timetable or map, you look there to find the information. ❑ *He consulted his dictionary to look up the meaning of the word 'apotheosis'... Look up the address of the nearest children's clinic... Lally said it would help me with my geography if I went and looked it up on a map.*

V+ADV+N,
V+PRON+ADV,
V+N+ADV:
USUALLY+A

3 If you **look** someone **up** or **look up** a place where you used to go, you visit the person or place after not having seen them for a long time. ❑ *Look me up when you're next in the area... She did not look me up even when her husband lost all his money and deserted her... We walked to the South Strand district to look up old haunts.*

V+PRON+ADV,
V+ADV+N,
V+N+ADV

4 If a situation **is looking up**, it is improving. [INFORMAL] ❑ *That summer of 1962, things were at last looking up in Boston.*

V+ADV

look upon → See **look on**

★look up to
If you **look up to** someone, you respect and admire them. ❑ *She looks up to her father... The students look up to you and admire you.*

V+ADV+PREP:
HAS PASSIVE

loom /luːm/ (looms, looming, loomed)

loom ahead If a dangerous or unpleasant situation **looms ahead**, it is approaching and is likely to happen quite soon. ❑ *If car production continues at its present rate, bottlenecks and virtual exhaustion loom ahead... She saw her great choice looming ahead.*

V+ADV

loom up If something **looms up**, it appears as a large, unclear shape, often in a way that seems frightening or threatening. ❑ *...a huge Victorian edifice that loomed up against the skyline... Cape Perpetua loomed up out of the fog.*

V+ADV:
USUALLY+A

loose /luːs/ (looses, loosing, loosed)

loose off If you **loose off** an explosive device, you make it explode by setting light to it or firing it. [BRITISH] ❑ *Adam loosed off a magnesium flare... The enemy loosed a few grenades off.*

V+ADV+N,
V+N+ADV,
V+PRON+ADV

loose upon If something unpleasant **is loosed upon** a place or person, it is allowed to affect them. [FORMAL] ❑ *...anarchy is loosed upon the world. ...the nature of the aggression being loosed upon her.*

PASSIVE:
V+PREP

The symbol ★ shows key phrasal verbs

loosen /lu:sᵊn/ (loosens, loosening, loosened)

loosen up

1 When you **loosen up** or **loosen up** part of your body, you make your muscles more flexible and relaxed by doing exercises. ❏ *Swing a couple of clubs to loosen up, or do one of these exercises... If the muscles are painful, I do exercises for a few minutes to loosen them up... There is too much tension around the joints, they need loosening up.*

V+ADV,
V+PRON+ADV,
V+N+ADV,
V+ADV+N:
ERGATIVE

2 If someone who has been tense and anxious **loosens up**, they become more relaxed and more comfortable with other people. ❏ *Her second drink loosened her up... At first, every word had to be wrung from him; but as the day wore on, he loosened up and became more and more talkative.*

V+PRON+ADV,
V+N+ADV,
V+ADV:
ERGATIVE

lop /lɒp/ (lops, lopping, lopped)

lop off

1 If you **lop** something **off**, you cut it away from what it was attached to, usually with a quick, strong stroke. ❏ *He swung the sword, and lopped my arm off... If the tree gets too big, you could always lop off a few branches.*

V+N+ADV,
V+ADV+N,
V+PRON+ADV

NOTE **Chop off** means almost the same as **lop off**.

2 If someone **lops** an amount **off** a larger quantity, they reduce the larger quantity by that amount. [INFORMAL] ❏ *Moorcroft lopped six seconds off the Rono record... To get their estimate, they took the current figure and lopped off a little to allow for energy conservation.*

V+N+PREP/ADV,
V+ADV+N,
V+PRON+PREP/ADV

NOTE **Knock off** means almost the same as **lop off**.

lord /lɔːrd/ (lords, lording, lorded)

lord over If someone **lords** it **over** you, they act in a way that shows that they think they are better than you, for example by telling you what to do. ❏ *...to be able to lord it over the boy at the bottom of the class... Isn't it enough that you have brought us here? Do you also have to lord it over us?*

V+*it*+PREP

NOTE **Queen over** means almost the same as **lord over**.

lose /lu:z/ (loses, losing, lost)

★lose out If you **lose out**, you suffer a loss or disadvantage. ❏ *Children who fail at school lose out in the employment race and remain in poverty. ...to ensure that the small farmer and the part-timer do not lose out.*

V+ADV:
USUALLY+A

NOTE **Miss out** means almost the same as **lose out**.

lose out to If you **lose out to** someone else, this person is more successful than you and puts you at a disadvantage or causes you to fail. ❏ *Both companies are losing out to overseas competition.*

V+ADV+PREP

lounge /laʊndʒ/ (lounges, lounging, lounged)

✓ **About** is used mainly in British English. In American English, **around** is much more common than **round**.

lounge about → See lounge around

lounge around If you **lounge around**, **lounge about**, or **lounge round**, you spend your time in a relaxed and lazy way, doing nothing that requires any effort. ❏ *...people who were lounging about, apparently with nothing to do... She had seen a couple of other men lounging around the house... We lounge round the pool and just always have a really good time.*

V+ADV,
V+PREP

NOTE **Loaf around** means almost the same as **lounge around**.

lounge round → See lounge around

louse /laʊs/ (louses, lousing, loused)

louse up To **louse** something **up**, means to spoil it or ruin it completely. [INFORMAL] ❏ *There isn't a mechanic alive who doesn't louse up a job once in a while... It could louse up your divorce petition.*

V+ADV+N,
V+N+ADV,
V+PRON+ADV

NOTE **Foul up** means almost the same as **louse up**.

luck /lʌk/ (lucks, lucking, lucked)

luck out If you **luck out**, you are fortunate or lucky in something. [AMERICAN, INFORMAL] ❏ *We lucked out on our connections – we had a chopper that carried us back to base.*

V+ADV:
ALSO+*on*

lumber /lˈʌmbəʳ/ (lumbers, lumbering, lumbered)

lumber with If you **are lumbered with** something difficult, unpleasant, or unwanted, you have to deal with it or accept it, even though you do not want to. [BRITISH, INFORMAL] ❑ *I can see I'm going to get lumbered with it if I'm not careful... New families were unwilling to lumber themselves with too much land.*

V+N+PREP,
V+REFL+PREP:
USUALLY PASSIVE

NOTE Saddle with means almost the same as **lumber with**.

lump /lˈʌmp/ (lumps, lumping, lumped)

lump together If you **lump together** different things or people, you consider them in the same way or combine them into one large group. ❑ *She believes it is a mistake to lump all these issues together. ...pensioners, treated as children and lumped together regardless of their right to dignity or respect.*

V+N+ADV,
V+PRON+ADV,
V+ADV+N

lust /lˈʌst/ (lusts, lusting, lusted)

lust after

1 If you **lust after** or **lust for** something, you have a very strong desire to possess it. ❑ *They lusted after the gold of El Dorado... She is like a child lusting for toys.*

V+PREP:
HAS PASSIVE

NOTE Crave means almost the same as **lust after**.

2 If you **lust after** or **lust for** someone, you feel a strong sexual desire for them. ❑ *She had lusted after other men... How I lusted for that girl!*

V+PREP:
HAS PASSIVE

lust for → See lust after

luxuriate /lʌgzˈʊərieɪt/ (luxuriates, luxuriating, luxuriated)

luxuriate in If you **luxuriate in** something, you experience great pleasure from it. ❑ *I luxuriated in my retirement. ...Kontarsky, luxuriating in the congratulations of his superiors.*

V+PREP

Mm

magic /mǽdʒɪk/ (magics, magicking, magicked)

magic away If you **magic** something **away**, you make it disappear very quickly or unexpectedly. ❑ *He can magic a child's tears away in no time at all... The problem was large in his life; he could not magic it away.*

V+N+ADV,
V+PRON+ADV,
V+ADV+N

mail /meɪl/ (mails, mailing, mailed)

mail out If someone **mails out** things such as letters, leaflets, or bills, they send them to a large number of people at the same time. [AMERICAN] ❑ *This week, the company mailed out its annual report.*
NOTE **Send out** means almost the same as **mail out**.

V+N+ADV,
V+PRON+ADV,
V+ADV+N

major /méɪdʒər/ (majors, majoring, majored)

major in If you **major in** a particular subject, you study it as your main subject at university. ❑ *I decided to major in French... White had majored in Chinese history at Harvard.*

V+PREP

make /meɪk/ (makes, making, made)

make after If you **make after** someone or something, you chase them. ❑ *They made after him in the car.*

V+PREP

make away with

1 If you **make away with** something, you steal it and take it away with you. [INFORMAL] ❑ *He's afraid someone might make away with the takings.*
NOTE **Make off with** means almost the same as **make away with**.

V+ADV+PREP

2 If you **make away with** someone, you kill them. If you **make away with** yourself, you kill yourself.
NOTE **Do away with** means almost the same as **make away with**.

V+ADV+PREP:
WITH REFL

★make for

1 If you **make for** a place, you move towards it, usually rather hurriedly. ❑ *The best thing now would be to make for the top of Brill Hill... I made for my corner seat and sat down gratefully.*
NOTE **Head for** means almost the same as **make for**.

V+PREP

2 If something **makes for** a particular situation, that situation is likely to result from it. ❑ *I don't know if unilateral disarmament would make for peace or would make for war... What are the values that make for happy family life?*
NOTE **Produce** is a more formal word for **make for**.

V+PREP

★make into

1 If you **make** one thing **into** something else, you change it in some way so that it becomes that other thing. ❑ *...a knitwear jersey which Mary wanted to make into a short dress... They're having two houses made into one... They tore down nearly half that forest to make it into farmland.*
NOTE **Turn into** means almost the same as **make into**.

V+N+PREP,
V+PRON+PREP

2 If someone or something **makes** you **into** a particular type of person, they influence or affect you so that you become that type of person. ❑ *I kept trying to make Benedick into more of a soldier... The pressures we have to live with will make us into freaks.*
NOTE **Turn into** means almost the same as **make into**.

V+N+PREP,
V+PRON+PREP

★make of

If you ask a person what they **make of** someone or something, you want to know what their impression, understanding, or opinion of that person or thing is. ❑ *I wondered what they made of it all... What are we to make of what they're telling us?... He perplexed people – they didn't know quite what to make of him.*

V+PREP

make off If you **make off**, you leave somewhere as quickly as possible, often in order to escape. ❏ *The vehicle made off at once... She released the child suddenly and he made off.*

V+ADV

make off with If you **make off with** something, you steal it and take it away with you. ❏ *Otto made off with the last of the brandy... The dog ran down there and tried to make off with one of his sausages.*

V+ADV+PREP

NOTE **Make away with** means almost the same as **make off with**.

★make out

1 If you can **make** something **out**, you manage to see or hear it. ❏ *He could just make out the number plate of the car. ...mumbling something she couldn't quite make out... I looked in the water, and at first I could not make her out anywhere.*

V+ADV+N,
V+N+ADV,
V+PRON+ADV:
USUALLY+MODAL

2 If you **make out** something that is difficult to understand, you manage to understand it. ❏ *I can't make out if Nell likes him or not... Sylvia could not make out how it had happened... What I couldn't make out was your motive... This idea perplexed me so much that I stopped for a few seconds to try to make it out.*

V+ADV+if,
V+ADV+WH,
V+N+ADV,
V+PRON+ADV,
V+ADV+N:
NO PASSIVE

NOTE **Work out** means almost the same as **make out**.

3 If you **make out** that something is the case, you try to cause people to believe it. ❏ *It really is not as easy as some of them make out... People tried to make out that the play was about Britain... The other professors make out he hasn't published enough.*

V+ADV:
USUALLY WITH REPORT

NOTE **Imply** means almost the same as **make out**.

4 If you **make** someone **out** to be something, you give the impression that they are that sort of person. ❏ *I'm not the monster you'd like to make me out to be... Men aren't as sensible as they make themselves out to be... They made a minor poet out to be a major literary figure.*

V+PRON+ADV,
V+REFL+ADV,
V+N+ADV:
WITH to-INF

5 If you **make out** a case for something, you try to establish or prove that it is the best thing to do. ❏ *You could certainly make out a case for this point of view... Alice continued making out her case.*

V+ADV+N,
V+N+ADV,
V+PRON+ADV:
USUALLY+for/against

6 If you **make out** to do something, you pretend to do it. [INFORMAL] ❏ *He opened a drawer and made out to be looking for something in it.*

V+ADV+to-INF

7 When you **make out** a form or cheque, you write on it all the necessary information. ❏ *Did you make out a receipt?... I made a cheque out for £1200... 'Who do I make it out to?'—'Hourmont Travel Limited please.'*

V+ADV+N,
V+N+ADV,
V+PRON+ADV

NOTE **Write out** means almost the same as **make out**.

8 If you **make out**, you manage to survive or live reasonably well. [INFORMAL] ❏ *'How am I going to make out alone?'... They are tough youngsters. They'll make out.*

V+ADV

NOTE **Cope** and **get by** mean almost the same as **make out**.

9 If two people **are making out**, they are engaged in sexual activity. [AMERICAN, INFORMAL] ❏ *...pictures of the couple making out in their underwear on the beach.*

V+ADV:
RECIPROCAL

make out with If you **make out with** another person, you succeed in persuading them to have sex with you. [INFORMAL]

V+ADV+PREP

NOTE **Score** means almost the same as **make out with**.

make over If you **make** something **over**, you legally transfer the ownership of it from one person to another. ❏ *You should make the business over to me—with enough money to carry on... I was willing to make over every acre I had.*

V+N+ADV,
V+PRON+ADV,
V+ADV+N:
USUALLY+to

★make up

1 The people or things that **make up** something form that thing. ❏ *Women now make up two-fifths of the British labour force... All substances are made up of molecules... Nearly half the Congress is made up of lawyers.*

V+ADV+N,
V+PRON+ADV:
ALSO PASSIVE:
V+ADV+of

NOTE **Comprise** is a more formal word for **make up**.

◆ The **make-up** of something is the different parts that it consists of and the way that these are arranged. ❏ *...the physical make-up of computers.*

N-UNCOUNT

◆ Someone's **make-up** is their character. ❏ *There are things in my make-up which do not bear close examination.*

N-UNCOUNT

2 If you **make up** something such as a story, you invent it, sometimes in order to deceive people. ❏ *He was a good storyteller, and used to make up tales about animals... A person wouldn't make up a story that was so easy to check... She told herself, 'Don't be stupid, you're making things up.'... He couldn't remember the full titles but I knew he wouldn't make them up.*

V+ADV+N,
V+N+ADV,
V+PRON+ADV

The symbol ★ shows key phrasal verbs

♦ A **made-up** story, excuse, or reason is one which has been invented and is not actually true. ❑ *It's all a made-up story and you know it. ...made-up reasons.* ADJECTIVE

3 When you **make up** your mind, you decide which of a number of possible things you will have or will do. ❑ *He has a hard time making up his mind... I can't decide; help me make my mind up... If you don't make your mind up soon, I'll make it up for you.* V+ADV+N, V+N+ADV, V+PRON+ADV

4 If you **make up** an amount, you add something to it so that it is as large as it should be. ❑ *Put one hundred into the firm's account out of my personal account to make up the balance... It's going to be fifteen cents short, but Mr Hogganbeck will make it up... Make this liquid up to 250 ml.* V+ADV+N, V+PRON+ADV, V+N+ADV; ALSO+to

5 If you **make up** time or hours, you work some extra hours because you have previously taken some time off work. ❑ *They'll have to make up time lost during the strike.* V+ADV+N, V+N+ADV, V+PRON+ADV

6 If you **make** something **up**, you prepare it so that it is ready for someone to use or have. ❑ *When making up meals, select a well-balanced diet... We'll wait in the parlour while you make it up.* V+N+ADV, V+ADV+N, V+PRON+ADV

♦ Something that is **made-up** has already been prepared so that you do not have to make it yourself. ❑ *Add 1 teaspoonful white vinegar to 1 pint made-up carpet shampoo.* ADJECTIVE

7 If you **make up** a bed, you put sheets and blankets on it so that someone can sleep there. ❑ *Her mother made up a bed in her old room.* V+ADV+N, V+N+ADV, V+PRON+ADV

8 If you **make up**, or if you **make** yourself **up**, you put substances such as lipstick, powder, and eye-shadow on your face. ❑ *It was time to start making up for the evening performance... You need to wash, change that dress, and make up... She spent two hours making herself up.* V+ADV, V+REFL+ADV

♦ If you or your face, lips, or eyes are **made-up**, you are wearing make-up. ❑ *...freshly made-up lips... She had magnificent eyes, heavily made-up.* ADJECTIVE

♦ **Make-up** is substances such as lipstick, powder, and eye-shadow, which women use to make themselves look more attractive, or which actors use when they are acting. ❑ *...eye make-up. ...a mirror to check their make-up in.* N-UNCOUNT

NOTE **Cosmetics** is a more formal word for **make-up**.

9 If two people **make up** with each other, or **make** it **up**, they become friends again after they have had a quarrel. ❑ *They'd kissed and made up... They had a quarrel but later Marsha wanted to make it up... I want you to make up with her.* V+ADV, V+it+ADV, V+ADV+with: RECIPROCAL

10 If you **make** it **up** to someone, you do something to repay a favour they have done for you, or to show that you are sorry for disappointing them in some way. ❑ *They can make it up to the baby in other ways... Somehow, some day, he'd make it up to his father.* V+it+ADV: USUALLY+to

★**make up for** To **make up for** something that is damaged, lost, or missing means to replace it or compensate for it. ❑ *Massive reductions in other areas would be required to make up for the expected shortfall in revenues... She asked me questions about my interest in mathematics, as if to make up for excluding me from the conversation... She hurried on to make up for the minutes she had lost.* V+ADV+PREP

make up to If you **make up to** someone, you try to get them to like you by being friendly towards them, usually because you want them to give you something. ❑ *...politicians making up to rich businessmen... 'Do you really think I was trying to make up to him?'—'Well, it looked very much like it.'* V+ADV+PREP

make with If you tell someone to **make with** something, you mean that you want them to do what is necessary or appropriate at the time. [AMERICAN, INFORMAL] ❑ *They'll make with the jokes and forget the time.* V+PREP: ALSO IMPERATIVE

map /mæp/ (maps, mapping, mapped)

map out If you **map out** a plan or a task, you work out in detail how you will do it. ❑ *We began to map out plans for our counter-offensive. ...the course that they have mapped out for him... I have it all mapped out, you need not worry.* V+ADV+N, V+N+ADV, V+PRON+ADV

mark /mɑːʳk/ (marks, marking, marked)

mark as Someone or something that **marks** someone **as** a particular type of person indicates that they are that type of person. ❑ *They put me in jail and marked me as an enemy of society. ...a degree of self-esteem which marks them as special.* V+PRON+PREP, V+N+PREP

NOTE **Label** and **mark down as** mean almost the same as **mark as**.

★mark down

1 If you **mark** something **down**, you write it down. ❑ *I marked the number down on a scrap of paper... If you witness an accident, mark down the licence number of the car.*
NOTE **Jot down** means almost the same as **mark down**.

V+N+ADV,
V+ADV+N,
V+PRON+ADV

2 To **mark down** the price of something means to reduce its price. ❑ *The prices of beer, cigarettes, and whiskey have been marked down... Trousers are marked down from £39.95 to £20.00.*
NOTE **Reduce** means almost the same as **mark down**, and **mark up** means the opposite.

V+N+ADV,
V+ADV+N,
V+PRON+ADV

♦ A **mark-down** is a reduction in the price of something.

N-COUNT

3 If a teacher **marks** a student **down**, they put a lower grade on the student's work. ❑ *If you miss out a comma, they mark you down on it... He got marked down because the examiner could not read his handwriting... Wrong spellings get you marked down in exams.*
NOTE **Mark up** means the opposite of **mark down**.

V+PRON+ADV,
V+N+ADV,
V+ADV+N

mark down as

If you **mark** someone **down as** a particular type of person, you consider that they have qualities which make them that type of person. ❑ *I would have marked him down as a genius... None of the suspects had been marked down as businessmen.*
NOTE **Mark as** means almost the same as **mark down as**.

V+PRON+ADV+PREP,
V+N+ADV+PREP

mark off

1 If you **mark off** a piece of something such as ground, you separate it from everything around it, usually by making a fence or some other barrier. ❑ *He has marked off the area with lengths of string... We now mark off certain forests to protect them.*

V+ADV+N,
V+N+ADV,
V+PRON+ADV

2 If something **marks** one thing **off** from another, it makes the two things very different from one another. ❑ *...the personality differences that mark her off from her brother. ...physical characteristics which marked him off clearly from other men. ...someone who is not marked off by a wholly different accent or style of life.*
NOTE **Distinguish** is a more formal word for **mark off**.

V+PRON+ADV,
V+N+ADV,
V+ADV+N:
USUALLY+*from*

3 If you **mark off** an item on a list, you draw a line through it or next to it, to show that it has been dealt with. ❑ *He bought a street map of Paris, and in a small notebook marked off the places he most wanted to see... Each day was marked off with a neat X.*
NOTE **Cross off** and **tick off** mean almost the same as **mark off**.

V+ADV+N,
V+N+ADV,
V+PRON+ADV

★mark out

1 When someone **marks out** a area of land which is to be used for a particular purpose, they indicate that area by drawing special lines to show where it begins and ends. ❑ *He marked out a football pitch on the playing field... When planting seedlings I prefer to mark out the rows in advance... The landing strip at Lukla was marked out for the pilots of incoming aircraft.*

V+ADV+N,
V+N+ADV,
V+PRON+ADV

2 If a particular quality or feature **marks** a person **out**, it makes them seem noticeably different from other people. ❑ *There was a stillness about Ralph that marked him out... It is this latter role which marks out management in capitalist society.*
NOTE **Distinguish** means almost the same as **mark out**.

V+PRON+ADV,
V+ADV+N,
V+N+ADV

3 If you say that someone **is marked out** to achieve a particular thing, you mean that they will probably eventually achieve it. ❑ *Ian was always marked out to become a musician... He thought of himself as a great man, marked out by destiny for his task.*
NOTE **Be destined** means almost the same as **be marked out**.

PASSIVE:
V+ADV

mark up

1 To **mark up** the price of something means to increase its price. ❑ *Corporations mark up prices 1,000 per cent in order, they say, to pay for research... These have been marked up since last week.*
NOTE **Put up** means almost the same as **mark up**, and **mark down** means the opposite.

V+ADV+N,
V+N+ADV,
V+PRON+ADV

♦ A **mark-up** is an increase in the price of something, for example the difference between its cost and the price that you sell it for. ❑ *The percentage mark up is calculated by the market trader's association.*

N-COUNT

2 If a teacher **marks** a student **up**, they put a higher grade on the student's work.

V+N+ADV,

❏ ...*the less able child who you might mark up.* V+ADV+N,
V+PRON+ADV

NOTE **Mark down** means the opposite of **mark up**.

3 If you **mark up** a number or score, you count it or record it by writing it on a surface such as a wall or board so that other people can see it. ❏ *Mark the score up on the whiteboard... Every time a plane flew overhead, he marked it up.* V+N+ADV,
V+ADV+N,
V+PRON+ADV

marry /mæri/ (marries, marrying, married)

marry above If you say that someone **has married above** themselves, you mean that they have married someone who is higher than them in social rank. [FORMAL] ❏ *She married above herself. We all thought so at the time.* V+PREP+REFL

marry beneath If you say that someone **has married beneath** themselves, you mean that they have married someone who is below them in social rank. [FORMAL] ❏ *It is the opinion of every Greek citizen that the Duke married beneath himself.* V+PREP+REFL

marry into If you **marry into** a family, especially a wealthy family, you marry someone in that family and so become a part of it. ❏ *He had visions of marrying into the family and starting an empire.* V+PREP

marry off If you **marry** someone **off**, you find a suitable person for them to marry. ❏ *He had ideas about marrying off his daughter to Fouad... They wanted to marry her off to this Prince.* V+ADV+N,
V+PRON+ADV,
V+N+ADV

marry out If someone **marries out**, they marry someone who is not of the same religion as they are. [OLD-FASHIONED] ❏ *Her father disowned her when she told him she was marrying out.* V+ADV

marry up If things **marry up** or if you **marry** them **up**, they are brought together. ❏ *A line of hairs was inserted around the hairline, and then a part-wig was made to marry up with it... A system by which parts would be flown in from the United States to marry up with equipment pre-stocked in the Federal Republic.* V+ADV,
V+N+ADV,
V+PRON+ADV:
ALSO+with,
ERGATIVE,
RECIPROCAL

marvel /mɑːᵛrvəl/ (marvels, marvelling, marvelled)

☑ American English uses the spellings **marveling** and **marveled**.

marvel at If you **marvel at** something, you are filled with surprise and admiration by it. ❏ *Early travellers marvelled at the riches of Mali.* V+PREP

mash /mæʃ/ (mashes, mashing, mashed)

mash up If you **mash up** food, you crush it until it is soft and smooth in texture. ❏ *Mash up the strawberries and strain the pips out... When you first serve chopped vegetables to a baby, mash them up pretty fine with a fork.* V+ADV+N,
V+PRON+ADV,
V+N+ADV

mask /mɑːsk, mæsk/ (masks, masking, masked)

mask out If part of a photograph **is masked out**, it is covered so that it does not appear when the photograph is printed. [TECHNICAL] ❏ *Two people had been masked out.* V+ADV+N,
V+N+ADV,
V+PRON+ADV

masquerade /mæskəreɪd/ (masquerades, masquerading, masqueraded)

masquerade as To **masquerade as** something means to pretend to be that thing. ❏ *He might try to masquerade as a policeman... There were many heated little speeches from the floor masquerading as questions.* V+PREP

match /mætʃ/ (matches, matching, matched)
match against

1 If you **match** one thing **against** another, you make the two things compete against one another to see which one is better. ❏ *Many amateurs were matching themselves against the professionals... The horse had consistently beaten every horse matched against him for fifteen or twenty miles around.* V+N+PREP,
V+PRON+PREP

2 You can also say that you **match** one thing **against** another when you compare the two things to see whether they are similar. ❏ *...adding up the money from the canvas sack and matching it against the list of bills... The book invites you to match your own experience against the examples we describe.* V+PRON+PREP,
V+N+PREP

★match up If two things **match up**, or if you **match** them **up**, they are similar or compatible with each other in some way. ❏ *...examining the fingerprints on those documents and checking that they match up... Somehow we manage to match up our gestures with those of our companions... It is not always easy to match up individuals with counselors... You might have trouble matching them up.* V+ADV,
V+ADV+N,
V+PRON+ADV,
V+N+ADV:
ALSO+with,
ERGATIVE,
RECIPROCAL

match up to If something **matches up to** something else, it is good enough for it. ❏ ...*setting themselves a challenge and then matching up to it... You do not exactly match up to the requirements here.*
NOTE Measure up to means almost the same as **match up to**.

maul /mɔːl/ (mauls, mauling, mauled)

maul around If you **maul** something **around**, you handle it or pull it roughly. [INFORMAL] ❏ *She stared at her reflection while mauling her face around.*

V+N+ADV,
V+PRON+ADV

max /mæ!ks/ (maxes, maxing, maxed)

max out If you **max out** something, especially money or credit, you use all of it. [INFORMAL] ❏ *The thieves maxed out my Visa card and withdrew absolutely everything from my savings account... I'm just about maxed out on all three of my credit cards.*

V+ADV+N,
V+N+ADV,
V+PRON+ADV

measure /mɛʒər/ (measures, measuring, measured)

measure against If you **measure** someone or something **against** another person or thing, you judge their value using that other person or thing as a standard. ❏ *They realised how little their mistakes really mattered when you measured them against the crimes of the people in power... It now sounds quite sophisticated when you measure it against other programmes.*

V+PRON+PREP,
V+N+PREP

measure out If you **measure out** a certain amount of something, you measure that amount and take it or mark it because it is the amount that you want. ❏ *She carefully measured out a double whisky... He watched her measure out the black leaves into the pot... He dug into the can and measured out a small spoonful of the powder... The material had been measured out and bought.*

V+ADV+N,
V+N+ADV,
V+PRON+ADV

★**measure up**

1 When you **measure up**, you measure something such as a room or house, for example because you are going to decorate it or buy carpets or curtains for it. [INFORMAL] ❏ *...interior decorators waiting to start measuring up for new carpets... Hopefully we can get carpets down in the house so that we can have somebody over to measure it up and things like that.*

V+ADV,
V+PRON+ADV,
V+ADV+N

2 If you say that someone **measures up**, you mean that they are of a good enough standard. ❏ *When we don't measure up, we must find out why.*

V+ADV

measure up to If you **measure up to** a standard or to someone's expectations, you are good enough to achieve the standard or fulfil the person's expectations. ❏ *...ensuring that people in jobs are capable of measuring up to their responsibilities... He had an uncomfortable feeling of not being able to measure up to his father's expectations.*
NOTE Live up to means almost the same as **measure up to**.

V+ADV+PREP

meddle /mɛdəl/ (meddles, meddling, meddled)

meddle in If you **meddle in** something, you interfere in it. ❏ *He's never wanted me to meddle in his affairs... He refused to meddle in such matters.*

V+PREP

meddle with If you **meddle with** something, you interfere with it or try to change it when people do not want you to. ❏ *What business was it of mine to meddle with Hilary Jackson's affairs?... I don't let anyone else meddle with my stoves... The press barons were not unusual in meddling with the editorial policies of their papers.*

V+PREP:
HAS PASSIVE

meet /miːt/ (meets, meeting, met)

★**meet up**

1 If you **meet up** with someone, you meet them, either by chance or because you have arranged to. ❏ *We planned to meet up with them later in Florence... We can all meet up again at about 10.30... She and Smithy should meet up, they'd get on famously.*

V+ADV,
V+ADV+with:
RECIPROCAL

2 If two or more things **meet up**, they join or come together at a particular place. ❏ *The two wires will meet up here... This track should meet up with the main road.*

V+ADV,
V+ADV+with:
RECIPROCAL

★**meet with**

1 If you **meet with** a particular experience or event, you experience it or it happens to you. ❏ *...an inquest on a child who met with an accident... Enemy troops could still expect to meet with armed resistance... Strikes met with little success... Almost everything else in the report meets with my approval.*

V+PREP

2 If you **meet** something **with** a particular reaction, you react to it in this way.

V+N+PREP,

❑ *The men had met this refusal with indifference. ...their determination to meet any attack with retaliation.*   V+PRON+PREP

3 To **meet with** someone means to meet them after arranging to do so. [AMERICAN] ❑ *We can meet with the professor Monday night... A few months later, Sir Lew came to America to meet with my agent and make a deal.*   V+PREP

mellow /mɛloʊ/ (mellows, mellowing, mellowed)

mellow out If someone **mellows out**, or if someone or something **mellows** them **out**, they become calm and relaxed. ❑ *Chris has really mellowed out... Has marriage mellowed you out?*   V+ADV, V+PRON+ADV, V+N+ADV

melt /mɛlt/ (melts, melting, melted)

melt away

1 When something **melts away**, it gradually disappears. ❑ *A great empire has melted away. ...watching his fortune melt away... My fears have long since melted away.*   V+ADV

NOTE **Fade away** means almost the same as **melt away**.

2 If people **melt away**, they move so that you can no longer see them. [FORMAL] ❑ *Most people melted away as if I had leprosy... After that, we just melted away through the wood... Others got up and melted away into the dark shadow of the front door.*   V+ADV

3 If something **melts away** or if heat **melts** it **away**, it melts completely until it has disappeared. ❑ *...until it melted away and she could swallow... The temperatures dissolved dog collars and melted away jackets. ...melting it away entirely.*   V+ADV, V+ADV+N, V+PRON+ADV, V+N+ADV: ERGATIVE

melt down If you **melt down** an object, you heat it until it melts, so that you can use the material to make something else. ❑ *Railings were melted down for cannon... It is now economically viable to melt down old glass. ...all this talk about melting the stuff down.*   V+N+ADV, V+N+ADV, V+PRON+ADV

♦ When there is a **meltdown** in a nuclear reactor, the fuel rods melt and radioactivity is released into the atmosphere because of a fault in the cooling system. ❑ *A wrong command nearly led to a meltdown of one of the ship's two nuclear reactors.*   N-COUNT, N-UNCOUNT

melt into

1 If a feeling such as anger **melts into** a more gentle feeling, it changes into it. ❑ *...feeling his strength and aggression melt into tender care. ...a sternness which slowly melted into a sort of maternal affection.*   V+PREP

2 If you **melt into** something such as a crowd of people, you hide among them so that people do not notice you. ❑ *They often wanted to melt into the teeming millions.*   V+PREP

merge /mɜːrdʒ/ (merges, merging, merged)

merge in If something **merges in** with its surroundings, it is difficult to see or distinguish it clearly because it is similar in colour or appearance to the other thing. ❑ *The furniture and carpets merge in with the wallpaper to give an overpowering impression.*   V+ADV: ALSO+with

NOTE **Blend in** means almost the same as **merge in**.

★merge into If one thing **merges into** another, it becomes difficult to see or distinguish it clearly because it is similar in colour or appearance to the other thing. ❑ *They were painted so that they would appear to merge into the landscape... Creepers came from farther above where the rock merged into leaves and shadows.*   V+PREP

NOTE **Blend into** means almost the same as **merge into**.

mess /mɛs/ (messes, messing, messed)

☑ **About** is used mainly in British English.

★mess about → See mess around

mess about with → See mess around with

★mess around

1 If you **mess around** or **mess about**, you spend time doing unimportant or silly things rather than concentrating on your work. [INFORMAL] ❑ *...talking, playing, messing about together... Some of the lads had been messing around when they should have been working.*   V+ADV

NOTE **Muck about** means almost the same as **mess around**.

2 If you **mess** someone **around** or **mess** them **about**, you treat them badly, for example by not being honest with them, or by continually changing plans which af-   V+N+ADV, V+PRON+ADV fect them. [BRITISH, INFORMAL] ❑ *He had been messing Helen around... I think it would be awful to have a man messing you about.*

mess ar<u>ou</u>nd with If you **mess around with** or **mess about with** something, you touch it or interfere with it when you are not supposed to. ❑ *She didn't want you coming and messing about with things.*

V+ADV+PREP: HAS PASSIVE

[NOTE] **Tamper with** means almost the same as **mess around with**.

★mess <u>up</u>

1 If you **mess up** something that has been carefully made or done, you spoil it. [INFORMAL] ❑ *That will mess up the whole analysis... If she got caught with me now it would mess up the rest of her life... I don't think I messed it up too badly.*

V+ADV+N, V+PRON+ADV, V+N+ADV

♦ A **mess-up** is a situation in which something has been done very badly or wrongly. [INFORMAL] ❑ *There was some mess-up over the availability of dates.*

N-COUNT

2 If you **mess** something **up**, you make it untidy or dirty. [INFORMAL] ❑ *Most of the evening was spent in messing up the kitchen. ...children messing things up while she is busy cooking the dinner... You could wear a hat so that your hair doesn't get messed up.*

V+ADV+N, V+N+ADV, V+PRON+ADV

3 If something **messes** someone **up**, it causes them to be very confused or worried, or to have psychological problems. [INFORMAL] ❑ *That really messed them up, especially the boys.*

V+N+ADV, V+PRON+ADV

4 If you **mess up**, you do something very badly. [INFORMAL]

V+ADV

mess with If you **mess with** something or someone dangerous, you become involved with them. [INFORMAL] ❑ *We don't mess with grass or heroin or any of that stuff... That was a silly thing to do. You can't mess with those lads.*

V+PREP: HAS PASSIVE

mete /miːt/ **(metes, meting, meted)**

mete <u>out</u> If a punishment **is meted out** to someone, it is given to them. [FORMAL] ❑ *This punishment was meted out to me because of my political beliefs... Magistrates meted out fines of as much as £1,000.*

V+ADV+N: ALSO+to

[NOTE] **Deal out** means almost the same as **mete out**.

militate /mɪlɪteɪt/ **(militates, militating, militated)**

militate ag<u>ai</u>nst If something **militates against** something else, it makes it less likely to happen or succeed. [FORMAL] ❑ *Family tensions can militate against learning... Large comprehensive schools militate against individuality by their very size.*

V+PREP

[NOTE] **Discourage** means almost the same as **militate against**.

mill /mɪl/ **(mills, milling, milled)**

☑ **About** is used mainly in British English. In American English, **around** is much more common than **round**.

mill ab<u>ou</u>t → See **mill around**

mill ar<u>ou</u>nd When a crowd of people **mill around**, **mill about**, or **mill round**, they all move around within a particular place or area. ❑ *There were hundreds of boys and girls milling around on the lawn... Students and staff were milling about. ...the throng which milled about the streets of Hampstead.*

V+ADV, V+PREP

mill r<u>ou</u>nd → See **mill around**

mind /maɪnd/ **(minds, minding, minded)**

mind <u>out</u> If you tell someone to **mind out**, you are telling them to be careful. ❑ *He shouted out as Jack snatched the glasses off his face. 'Mind out! Give 'em back! I can hardly see!'*

IMPERATIVE, V+ADV

[NOTE] **Look out** and **watch out** mean almost the same as **mind out**.

minister /mɪnɪstər/ **(ministers, ministering, ministered)**

minister to If you **minister to** people or their needs, you make sure that they have everything they need or want. [FORMAL] ❑ *He needed a skilled and energetic servant to minister to his comforts. ...like those cartoon explorers being ministered to by grateful Polynesians.*

V+PREP: HAS PASSIVE

miss /mɪs/ **(misses, missing, missed)**

★miss <u>out</u>

1 If you **miss out** something or someone, you fail to include them in something. [BRITISH] ❑ *You can miss out a comma because you're writing too quickly... We missed out*

V+ADV+N, V+PRON+ADV, V+N+ADV

all the interesting bits... You could put it at the beginning rather than miss it out.

NOTE **Leave out** means almost the same as **miss out**.

2 If you **miss out**, you have not been involved in something which you feel would have been of interest or benefit to you. ❑ *This is an area where I think men miss out... People who have never read in this way continue to feel they have missed out somewhere... They can't help fearing they will miss out on promotion.*

V+ADV;
ALSO+*on*

mist /mɪst/ (mists, misting, misted)

mist over

1 If a piece of glass **mists over** or **is misted over**, it becomes covered with tiny drops of moisture, so that you cannot see through it easily. ❑ *His spectacles were misting over with the exertion... The window of my cubicle was misted over with heat.*

V+ADV;
OR PASSIVE:
V+ADV

NOTE **Steam up** and **mist up** mean almost the same as **mist over**.

2 If your eyes **mist over**, you cannot see easily because there are tears in your eyes. ❑ *Grandpa Hindley's eyes still misted over when he told the tale... I saw his eyes mist over when he thought no one was looking.*

V+ADV

mist up

If a piece of glass **mists up** or **is misted up**, it becomes covered with tiny drops of moisture, so that you cannot see through it easily. ❑ *Could you pass that cloth, the windscreen has misted up again... The windows were all misted up.*

V+ADV;
OR PASSIVE:
V+ADV

NOTE **Mist over** and **steam up** mean almost the same as **mist up**.

mix /mɪks/ (mixes, mixing, mixed)

★mix in

1 If you **mix** a substance **in**, you put it with another substance and stir it so that the two substances are blended together. ❑ *Stir the mixture gradually, mixing in the flour... I think he must have mixed in a little more sand than usual.*

V+ADV+N,
V+N+ADV,
V+PRON+ADV

NOTE **Add in** means almost the same as **mix in**.

2 If you **mix in**, you join in an activity and talk in a friendly way to the other people there. ❑ *He didn't feel like mixing in.*

V+ADV

mix into

If you **mix** one substance **into** another, you put it with the other substance and stir it so that the two substances are blended together. ❑ *Mix a tiny pinch of it into a big jar of face cream.*

V+N+PREP,
V+PRON+PREP

★mix up

1 If you **mix up** two things or people, you confuse them, so that you think that one of them is the other one. ❑ *I have somehow mixed up two events... People even mix us up and greet us by each other's names.*

V+ADV+N,
V+PRON+ADV,
V+N+ADV

NOTE **Muddle up** means almost the same as **mix up**.

♦ If you are **mixed up**, or if your mind is **mixed up**, you are confused, often because of emotional or social problems. ❑ *I got mixed up and forgot which one I'd gone to first. ...your mixed-up students... Tim was in a strange mixed-up frame of mind.*

ADJECTIVE

♦ A **mix-up** is a mistake which causes confusion or misunderstanding. ❑ *Due to some administrative mix-up the letters had not been sent out.*

N-COUNT

NOTE **Muddle** means almost the same as **mix-up**.

2 If you **mix up** a number of things, you put them all together in a random way so that they are not in any particular order. ❑ *I'd cut a big bunch of flowers – all different kinds mixed up... He mixes up all the chromosomes and shakes them around.*

V+N+ADV,
V+ADV+N,
V+PRON+ADV

3 If you **mix up** a solution or a mixture, you make it by mixing different things together. ❑ *Ira mixed up a solution in a jar... Have you been mixing up paste again?*

V+ADV+N,
V+N+ADV,
V+PRON+ADV

mix up in

If you are **mixed up in** something such as a crime or a scandal, you are involved in it. ❑ *Are you going to get mixed up in this gang war the papers are talking about?... He would rather not have to get mixed up in it.*

PASSIVE:
V+ADV+PREP

mix up with

If you are **mixed up with** a group of people, you are spending a lot of time with them; used showing disapproval. ❑ *She had got mixed up with the son of a big Mafia chief... He felt that it had been a mistake to get mixed up with the French radicals.*

PASSIVE:
V+ADV+PREP

mix with

If someone **mixes** it **with** someone else, they fight them. [INFORMAL] ❑ *Don't try mixing it with him, Ted. He'll murder you.*

V+*it*+PREP

model /mɒdəl/ (models, modelling, modelled)

☑ American English uses the spellings **modeling** and **modeled**.

model on If you **model** yourself **on** someone or if you **model** your behaviour **on** their behaviour, you copy them, because you admire them and want to be like them. ❑ *The children have their parents on which to model themselves... Mary had modelled her handwriting on Sister Catherine's.*

V+N+PREP, V+REFL+PREP, V+PRON+PREP

NOTE **Base on** means almost the same as **model on**.

molder /mˈoʊldər/ **(molders, moldering, moldered)** → See **moulder**

monkey /mˈʌŋki/ **(monkeys, monkeying, monkeyed)**

☑ **About** is used mainly in British English.

monkey about → See **monkey around**

monkey about with → See **monkey around with**

monkey around If someone **is monkeying around** or **monkeying about**, they are behaving in a silly and playful way. [INFORMAL] ❑ *The twins have been monkeying about in the attic again. ...coming and monkeying around in my affairs.*

V+ADV

monkey around with If someone **monkeys around with** or **monkeys about with** something, they touch it or interfere with it when they are not supposed to. [INFORMAL] ❑ *Have you been monkeying about with my typewriter again?*

V+ADV+PREP

mooch /mˈuːtʃ/ **(mooches, mooching, mooched)**

☑ **About** is used mainly in British English.

mooch about → See **mooch around**

mooch around When you **mooch around** or **mooch about**, you wander around a place with no particular purpose or aim. ❑ *There was absolutely nothing to do but mooch about... He mooched about the house in his pyjamas... He was mooching around in his studio.*

V+ADV, V+PREP

moon /mˈuːn/ **(moons, mooning, mooned)**

☑ **About** is used mainly in British English.

moon about → See **moon around**

moon around If you **moon around** or **moon about**, you spend time doing nothing because you are feeling unhappy. ❑ *He was mooning about by himself... Most of that afternoon he mooned around.*

V+ADV

moon over If you **moon over** someone, you spend your time just thinking about them because you are in love.

V+PREP

mop /mˈɒp/ **(mops, mopping, mopped)**

★**mop up**

1 If you **mop up**, or if you **mop up** a liquid that has been spilt, you wipe it with a cloth so that the liquid is absorbed. ❑ *Mother started mopping up the oil... First mop it up, then try to remove the stain with cold water... I've mopped up with a bit of old cloth.*

V+ADV+N, V+PRON+ADV, V+ADV, V+N+ADV

2 To **mop up** the last members of a group means to use them or deal with them in some way. ❑ *School leavers will be mopped up by youth opportunity schemes... We have new factories all along Deeside and still we can't mop up the pool of unemployed.*

V+ADV+N, V+PRON+ADV

3 When an army **mops up** resistance, it deals with any people who are still fighting against it. ❑ *All resistance will be mopped up within two hours.*

V+ADV+N

NOTE **Eliminate** means almost the same as **mop up**.

♦ In a **mop-up** operation, soldiers go into an area and deal with any people still there who are fighting against them. ❑ *Some flew back to the Dak To area and the mop-up operations there.*

ADJECTIVE

mope /mˈoʊp/ **(mopes, moping, moped)**

☑ **About** is used mainly in British English.

mope about → See **mope around**

mope around If you **mope around** or **mope about** a place, or if you **mope around** or **mope about**, you wander around aimlessly, looking and feeling unhappy. ❑ *I moped around the house for a few days... He was moping about the hallway.*

V+PREP, V+ADV

moulder /mˈoʊldər/ **(moulders, mouldering, mouldered)**

☑ **Moulder** is spelled **molder** in American English.

moulder away Something that **is mouldering away** is decaying slowly in the place where it has been left. ❑ *In twenty years you might be down-and-out or mouldering away in some old folks' home.* V+ADV

NOTE **Rot away** means almost the same as **moulder away**.

mount /maʊnt/ (mounts, mounting, mounted)

mount up If something **mounts up**, it increases, because more and more is being added to it all the time. ❑ *The soil becomes more and more acidic as pollution mounts up... You put a little money by each week and you'll be surprised how it mounts up.* V+ADV

NOTE **Build up** means almost the same as **mount up**.

mourn /mɔːrn/ (mourns, mourning, mourned)

mourn for If you **mourn for** someone, you are very sad because they have died, and you show how sad you are in the way that you behave. ❑ *He continued to mourn for his son Joseph.* V+PREP: HAS PASSIVE

mouth /maʊð/ (mouths, mouthing, mouthed)

mouth off If you say that someone **is mouthing off**, you mean that they are talking loudly and saying something which nobody wants to hear. [INFORMAL] ❑ *...mouthing off opinions about everything under the sun... I just get fed up with him mouthing off all the time.* V+ADV+N, V+ADV

move /muːv/ (moves, moving, moved)

☑ **About** is used mainly in British English. In American English, **around** is much more common than **round**.

★**move about** → See move around

★**move along**

1 When someone or something **moves along** a road or other place, or when you **move** them **along** there, they go forwards along it. ❑ *He caught at a short section of ladder and began to move along it... She was obliged to hold herself upright as she moved along... We had to move the pump along the bank of the stream... When they got their appliances out, they were quite unable to move them along the roads.* V+PREP/ADV, V+N+PREP/ADV, V+PRON+PREP/ADV: ERGATIVE

2 If someone, especially a police officer, tells you to **move along**, they mean that you should leave and not stand or wait in a particular place. ❑ *Just move along, please. Move along... He said, 'I'm afraid you girls had better move along.'* V+ADV: USUALLY IMPERATIVE

3 If a task that you are doing **is moving along**, you are continuing with it and making good progress. ❑ *Things were moving along... The work moved along smoothly.* V+ADV

★**move around**

1 When you **move around**, **move about**, or **move round** a place, you keep going from one part of it to another part. ❑ *She moved about the office, her sari rustling... Don't you try to move around for a bit... We move round the country doing contract work.* V+PREP, V+ADV

2 If you **move around**, **move about**, or **move round**, you keep changing your job or keep changing the place where you live. ❑ *The men should move about freely, getting the best wages they can... The managers will not be required to move around from place to place. ...agitators that moved round from one meeting to the next.* V+ADV

3 When you **move** something **around**, **move** it **about**, or **move** it **round**, you move it from one position or place to another. ❑ *A poltergeist is a noisy and tiresome 'spirit' which moves furniture about... Don't move the injured limb around... She could not keep her body still but had to keep moving it about... Oil had to be moved about in ships.* V+N+ADV, V+PRON+ADV

4 If employees **are moved around**, **moved about**, or **moved round**, their employer moves them to a different job or department. ❑ *Promising young executives are being moved around from one branch to another... I get moved about because I'm good... It means you can move people round and promote those who are ready.* V+N+ADV, V+PRON+ADV

5 When you **move around** or **move round** an obstacle, you move so that you can get past it. ❑ *I moved round the desk... He was lying on the sidewalk, people moving around him as if he were not there... She moved round the car and disappeared.* V+PREP

★**move away**

1 If you **move away**, you go and live in a different town or area of a country. ❑ *They had decided to retire from farming and move away... We had some very dear friends many years ago that moved away from this area.* V+ADV: ALSO+from

2 When someone or something **moves away** from a place or position, or when you **move** them **away**, they leave it. ❑ *If he tried to move away now, everybody would notice... The boat moved away from the bobbing barrels... He moved the hand away but didn't release it... He demanded that I should move her away.*

V+ADV,
V+N+ADV,
V+PRON+ADV:
ERGATIVE,
ALSO+*from*

move away from If you **move away from** a particular idea, method, or habit, you stop having it. ❑ *The Government had moved away from a simple concern with teacher training... From then on he began to move slowly away from the Labour Party.*

V+ADV+PREP:
HAS PASSIVE

★move down

1 When someone or something **moves down**, or when you **move** them **down**, they go from a higher position to a lower one. ❑ *We moved down the side of the mountain. ...families that move up or down the social scale... His pen moved down to the next question on a list... Rodrigo tried to move her head down.*

V+ADV/PREP,
V+N+ADV/PREP,
V+PRON+ADV/PREP:
ERGATIVE

NOTE **Move up** means almost the same as **move down**.

2 If you **move down** to an area of a country, you go to live there, especially when the place is farther south. ❑ *They're moving down from New Jersey... I moved down here on security work.*

V+ADV:
USUALLY+A

3 At school or work, if you **move down**, or if someone **moves** you **down**, you go to a lower level, grade, or class. ❑ *If they fail their mathematics exams they move down a year, and take them again... There's a chance I might be moving you down a group.*

V+ADV,
V+N+ADV,
V+PRON+ADV:
ERGATIVE

4 If the rate, level, or amount of something **moves down**, it decreases. ❑ *Do you really think the unemployment figures are moving down?*

V+ADV

NOTE **Go down** and **fall** mean almost the same as **move down**, and **move up** means the opposite.

★move in

1 When you **move in**, you begin to live in a different house or place. ❑ *I couldn't move in until the first of July... We had moved in at the height of the summer.*

V+ADV

NOTE **Move out** means the opposite of **move in**.

2 If someone **moves in** with you, they come to live with you. ❑ *He moved in with Mrs Camish... We had already decided that I would move in with Margaret... Are your parents going to move in?*

V+ADV:
USUALLY+*with*

NOTE **Move out** means the opposite of **move in**.

3 If a group of people **move in** on a place or person, they go towards them in order to attack them. ❑ *He began to move in on Tom... Five men with rifles came out of the bushes and moved in for the kill.*

V+ADV:
USUALLY+*on*

NOTE **Close in** means almost the same as **move in**.

4 If someone **moves in** on a particular activity, they start to be involved in it and take over from someone else, often in an unfair way; used showing disapproval. ❑ *Professional drug pushers moved in and organized the trade... Those with the most advanced technology will soon move in to exploit the sea's resources.*

V+ADV:
ALSO+*on*

★move into

1 When you **move into** a house or particular area of a town, you start to live there. ❑ *She moved into lodgings... We were the first black family to move into that area... She'd just moved into the neighbourhood from Connecticut.*

V+PREP

2 When you **move** something or someone **into** a place, you take them to that place and leave them there. ❑ *I could move my things into that room... West wants to move them into the invasion areas immediately... The furniture was moved back into my cell.*

V+N+PREP,
V+PRON+PREP

3 If a group of people **move into** a particular activity or area of business, they start to be involved in it. ❑ *About 30 companies have moved into the 'personal stereo' business... They tried to move into a market where sales are counted in hundreds rather than thousands. ...moving into the field of continuing education.*

V+PREP

4 If the army, the police, or some other group **move into** an area, they go there in order to carry out a particular task. ❑ *...fire brigades and rescue squads moving into the area... The army had moved into Czechoslovakia on the 20th.*

V+PREP

★move off
When vehicles or people **move off**, they start to leave a place. ❑ *The fleet of cars prepared to move off... We move off on the cycles as fast as possible. ...cars blowing their horns at him to move off.*

V+ADV

NOTE **Set off** means almost the same as **move off**.

The symbol ★ shows key phrasal verbs

★move on

1 When someone on a journey **moves on**, they leave a place where they had stopped briefly and continue the journey. ❑ *They moved on as soon as the cloud lifted... The next night we had to move on to the third line of trenches... After three weeks in Hong Kong, we moved on to Japan.*

NOTE **Carry on** means almost the same as **move on**.

V+ADV:
ALSO+to

2 If you **move on**, you finish one thing and turn your attention to something else. ❑ *Let's leave it there, thank you very much, and move on... The men moved on to talk about something else... Get the actors to move on to the next scene.*

NOTE **Go on** and **carry on** mean almost the same as **move on**.

V+ADV:
ALSO+to/to-INF

3 If you **move on** from your present job, you leave it and start another one which will be better for you. ❑ *John wanted to move on from the Post to a bigger paper... This training will work to your advantage when you want to move on.*

NOTE **Progress** is a more formal word for **move on**.

V+ADV:
ALSO+from

4 If someone such as a policeman **moves** you **on**, they order you to leave a particular place. ❑ *...waiting on a park bench in the winter weather for a cop to come and move him on... An angry motorist was moved on by police.*

V+PRON+ADV,
V+N+ADV,
V+ADV+N

5 If people's ideas, knowledge, or beliefs **move on**, they change and become more modern. ❑ *The world is about to move on from the era where knowledge comes in books... Public opinion had moved on... Computers moved on an evolutionary step.*

V+ADV

6 If time **moves on**, it passes. ❑ *As the months moved on, I realized how inadequate these measures were... As time moved on, the hunters clearly had in their heads an organized plan.*

NOTE **Wear on** means almost the same as **move on**.

V+ADV

★move on to, move onto

If you **move on to** a particular topic, you bring that topic into a conversation or lecture after you have been talking about something else. ❑ *If we now move on to voting behaviour the pattern becomes more complicated... The conference was able to move on to other matters of a wider interest... We moved on to the topic of careers... Let me move onto quite a different area.*

NOTE **Turn to** and **come on to** mean almost the same as **move on to**.

V+ADV+PREP

★move out

1 When you **move out**, you stop living in a particular house or place and go to live somewhere else. ❑ *The fellow that lived there moved out without a trace... I want to move out of Birmingham... People began moving out of the neighbourhood.*

NOTE **Move in** means almost the same as **move out**.

V+ADV:
ALSO+of

2 If you **move** someone **out** of a place, you arrange for them to leave that place. ❑ *Mohammed Kassi had moved most of his men out of Fort Esther... The council agreed to move out families with three children... It was time to move her out of her apartment and into a home.*

V+N+ADV,
V+ADV+N,
V+PRON+ADV:
ALSO+of

3 If an organization or group of people **move out** of a particular activity or area of business, they stop being involved in it. ❑ *People are moving out of manufacture into the service industries... Well, the big companies are all moving out.*

V+ADV:
USUALLY+of

★move over

1 If you **move over**, you change the system or method you are using and do things in a different way. ❑ *There have been suggestions that we ought to move over towards a more monetarist economy. ...moving over to solar powered energy.*

V+ADV:
USUALLY+A

2 If you ask someone to **move over**, you are asking them to change their position so that there is room for you. ❑ *Move over a bit, will you?... Aurelia moved over and the maid sat down on the footstool.*

V+ADV

3 At work, if you **move over**, you start to do a different job in the same company in order to let someone else do the job that you originally had. ❑ *She decided to move over and make way for one of the younger women... They will have to move over and make room for new management.*

NOTE **Step aside** means almost the same as **move over**.

V+ADV

4 When something **moves over** a surface such as land or water, it goes forward slowly across it. [LITERARY] ❑ *The ship entered Port Phillip Bay and moved over the quiet water towards Melbourne... Pockets of cloud moved over the fields... The train moved southward over the icy countryside.*

V+PREP

For a full explanation of all grammatical labels, see pages xiii-xx

★move round

1 → See **move around**

2 If you **move round**, you change your position so that you can get closer to something. ❏ *Will you three sitting at the back please move round... Mrs Thorne moved round and sat down next to them.* | V+ADV

move towards If you **move towards** a different way of organizing something, you make preparations to introduce new methods. ❏ *Crosland's move towards 'mass' higher education was still to be for a minority... Lawson put forward proposals for moving towards a more permanent system of managed exchange rates.* | V+PREP

★move up

1 When someone or something **moves up**, or when you **move** them **up**, they go from a lower position to a higher one. ❏ *The tribe moved up the hill a few feet... He moved up quickly and easily... She moved her feet up and down... Move it up a bit.* | V+ADV/PREP, V+N+ADV/PREP, V+PRON+ADV/PREP: ERGATIVE

NOTE **Move down** means the opposite of **move up**.

2 At school or work, if you **move up**, or if someone **moves** you **up**, you go to a higher level, grade, or class. ❏ *This means the executive can move up quickly... Apprentices move up to become engineers and managers.* | V+ADV, V+N+ADV, V+PRON+ADV: ERGATIVE

3 If you ask someone to **move up**, you are asking them to change their position so that there is more room. ❏ *Move up, John, let the lady sit down... She moved up so close to my chair.* | V+ADV

NOTE **Move over** means almost the same as **move up**.

4 When soldiers or policemen **move up** or when they **are moved up**, they are ordered to go to a particular position and be ready to act. ❏ *It would be some time before their tanks could move up... If we're expecting an invasion the squadrons should be moved up, not back!... Two army groups had been moved up.* | V+ADV, V+N+ADV, V+PRON+ADV, V+ADV+N: ERGATIVE

5 If the rate, level, or amount of something **moves up**, it increases. ❏ *Rates for one to 12 months have moved up ... He mentioned that our salaries weren't in fact moving up.* | V+ADV

NOTE **Go up** and **rise** mean almost the same as **move up**, and **go down** means the opposite.

mow /moʊ/ (mows, mowing, mowed, mown)

☑ The past participle is either **mowed** or **mown**.

mow down If a large number of people **are mowed down** or **are mown down**, they are all killed violently at one time. ❏ *Several children had strayed onto an airport runway and been mown down by a jet... Six prisoners tried to bolt. Kilver's men promptly mowed them down... Someone has purchased a machine gun and mown down a whole neighbourhood.* | V+N+ADV, V+PRON+ADV, V+ADV+N

muck /mʌk/ (mucks, mucking, mucked)

☑ **Muck** is an informal word used mainly in British English.

muck about

1 If you **muck about** or **muck around**, you behave in a stupid way and waste time. ❏ *She was mucking about with a jug of flowers on the table... You mustn't start mucking around... You! What were you mucking about in the dark for?* | V+ADV

NOTE **Mess around** means almost the same as **muck about**.

2 If you **muck** someone **about**, you annoy or upset them, especially by changing your mind about a plan or arrangement you have made. ❏ *The people at the housing association muck the customers about... I've got no time for people who muck you about.* | V+N+ADV, V+PRON+ADV

NOTE **Mess around** means almost the same as **muck about**.

muck about with If you **muck about with** or **muck around with** something, you alter it, often making it worse than it was. ❏ *The president's wife doesn't muck around with policy or sit in on Cabinet meetings.* | V+ADV+PREP

muck around → See **muck about**

muck around with → See **muck about with**

muck in If you **muck in**, you join in with an activity or you help other people with a job. ❏ *Management kept the same hours as the men and mucked in whenever it was necessary... Couldn't she muck in with David for the time being? ...supervisors who mucked in with the workers. ...pulling our weight, mucking in together.* | V+ADV, ALSO V+ADV+with, V+ADV+together: RECIPROCAL

muck out If you **muck out** a place where animals are kept, or you **muck** the animals **out**, you clean the place where they live. ❑ *...a small boy helping to muck out the pigsty at the bottom of his garden... The stables have to be mucked out and all the routine jobs done... Don't forget to muck the horses out.*

V+ADV+N,
V+N+ADV,
V+PRON+ADV

muck up

1 If you **muck** something **up**, you do it so badly that you do not achieve what you wanted to. ❑ *That clever boy from Oxford mucked the interview up... I've taken my driving test twice, and both times I've mucked it up... I muck up even some of the simplest scales when I'm playing the piano.*

V+N+ADV,
V+PRON+ADV,
V+ADV+N

2 If you **muck** your clothes **up**, you make them dirty. ❑ *Don't you go mucking up that clean dress now.*

V+ADV+N,
V+N+ADV,
V+PRON+ADV

muddle /mˈʌdəl/ (**muddles, muddling, muddled**)

muddle along If you **muddle along**, you live or exist without a proper plan or purpose in your life. ❑ *The church has lost its way, muddling along from Sunday to Sunday.*

V+ADV

muddle through If you **muddle through**, you manage to do something even though you do not really know how to do it properly. ❑ *The children are left to muddle through on their own... Even top managers have to muddle through as best they can.*

V+ADV

NOTE **Get by** means almost the same as **muddle through**.

muddle up

1 If you **muddle** things **up**, you cause them to become mixed up or in the wrong order. ❑ *I'm afraid I've muddled your directions up... Later they may muddle up your names with those of your cousins... Put them so that you can reach them easily, and they will not get muddled up with the other things... You've got it all muddled up.*

V+N+ADV,
V+ADV+N,
V+PRON+ADV:
ALSO+with

NOTE **Mix up** means almost the same as **muddle up**.

2 If you **muddle** someone **up**, you confuse them by what you are saying or doing. ❑ *Don't keep interfering, you'll muddle me up.*

V+N+ADV,
V+PRON+ADV

muffle /mˈʌfəl/ (**muffles, muffling, muffled**)

muffle up If you **are muffled up** or if you **muffle** yourself **up**, you are wearing a lot of heavy clothes. ❑ *A boy muffled up in a blue scarf was busy scribbling something in a book... Fancy muffling yourself up like that on a day like today.*

PASSIVE:
V+ADV,
ALSO V+REFL+ADV

NOTE **Wrap up** means almost the same as **muffle up**.

mug /mˈʌg/ (**mugs, mugging, mugged**)

mug up If you **mug up** a subject, you study it over a short period of time so that you can remember the main facts about it. [BRITISH, INFORMAL] ❑ *She's upstairs mugging up history or geography or something... I must mug up my French before the exam.*

V+ADV+N,
V+N+ADV,
V+PRON+ADV

NOTE **Swot up** means almost the same as **mug up**.

mull /mˈʌl/ (**mulls, mulling, mulled**)

mull over If you **mull** something **over**, you think about it seriously and for a long time, often before deciding what to do. ❑ *I mulled that question over for a while... I sat there and tried to mull things over in my mind... Nell began to mull over the injustices of her new role... He returned to his office to mull over these coincidences.*

V+N+ADV,
V+PRON+ADV,
V+ADV+N

NOTE **Chew over** means almost the same as **mull over**.

multiply /mˈʌltɪplaɪ/ (**multiplies, multiplying, multiplied**)

multiply out If you **multiply out** two numbers, you multiply them. ❑ *...to multiply out the two terms. ...multiply it out.*

V+ADV+N,
V+PRON+ADV,
V+N+ADV

muscle /mˈʌsəl/ (**muscles, muscling, muscled**)

muscle in If you **muscle in** on something, you force your way into a situation where you have no right to be and where you are not welcome. ❑ *They are jealous of your success and resent the way you are muscling in on their territory.*

V+ADV:
USUALLY+on

NOTE **Push in** means almost the same as **muscle in**.

muscle out If someone is **muscled out**, they are forced out of a situation or position where they want to be by someone who uses force or unfair methods. ❑ *He had a café by the station until he was muscled out by the Council.*

PASSIVE:
V+ADV:
ALSO+of

muss /mʌs/ (musses, mussing, mussed)

   muss up If your hair **is mussed up**, it looks untidy, as if it has not been
combed. [AMERICAN] ❑ *You can't drag her through there without mussing up her hair in
the process.*

   V+ADV+N,
   V+N+ADV,
   V+PRON+ADV

muster /mʌstəʳ/ (musters, mustering, mustered)

   muster up If you **muster up** your strength, energy, or courage, you make a
great effort in order to do something. ❑ *I mustered up enough courage to put in a request for a pay rise... Stanitsyn couldn't muster up the necessary forcefulness the role demanded... I mustered up all my strength.*

   V+ADV+N,
   V+N+ADV:
   ALSO+to-INF

   NOTE **Summon up** means almost the same as **muster up**.

Nn

naff /næf/ (naffs, naffing, naffed)

naff off If you tell someone to **naff off**, you are telling them rudely or angrily to go away. [BRITISH, INFORMAL]

IMPERATIVE, V+ADV

nail /neɪl/ (nails, nailing, nailed)

nail down

1 If something **is nailed down**, it is fastened securely by means of nails. ❑ *The lid of the box was nailed down... If it won't stay there we'll have to nail it down.*

V+N/PRON+ADV, V+ADV+N: USUALLY PASSIVE

2 If you **nail** someone **down**, you force them to state clearly their opinions or intentions. ❑ *We can go over to see them tomorrow and nail them down to some kind of commitment.*

V+PRON+ADV, V+N+ADV

NOTE **Pin down** means almost the same as **nail down**.

3 If you **nail down** something uncertain or unknown, you manage to describe it more accurately. ❑ *If you stay here the next few hours, we can nail it down, whether it's malignant or nonmalignant. ...an ambiguity which can never be satisfactorily nailed down.*

V+PRON+ADV, V+N+ADV, V+ADV+N

NOTE **Pin down** means almost the same as **nail down**.

nail up

1 If you **nail** something **up**, you fix it to a wall or other vertical surface so that it can be seen. ❑ *She passed a house with a brass plate nailed up outside. ...the warning notice that he had nailed up on the pole.*

V+ADV+N, V+N+ADV, V+PRON+ADV

2 If someone or something **is nailed up** in a room or other space, they are confined there, often because the entrance has been sealed using nails. ❑ *She was not burnt but nailed up in a barrel and thrown into the sea.*

PASSIVE: V+ADV

name /neɪm/ (names, naming, named)

★name after If you **name** someone or something **after** a person or thing, you give them the same name as the other person or thing. [BRITISH] ❑ *Then Cain built a city and named it after his son... She is named after her great-grandmother.*

V+PRON+PREP, V+N+PREP

name for If you **name** someone or something **for** a person or thing, you give them the same name as the other person or thing. [AMERICAN] ❑ *Hayman Creek was named for Charles Hayman. ...Cape Perpetua, sighted by Captain Cook in 1778 and named by him for Saint Perpetua.*

V+N+PREP, V+PRON+PREP

narrow /nærəʊ/ (narrows, narrowing, narrowed)

★narrow down If you **narrow down** something such as a choice or subject, you consider only the most suitable or important parts, and ignore the rest. ❑ *They narrowed the choice down to about a dozen sites... We finally narrowed down the list of candidates to three... Can we narrow it down a bit, David?*

V+N+ADV, V+ADV+N, V+PRON+ADV

nestle /nesəl/ (nestles, nestling, nestled)

nestle up

If you **nestle up** to someone, you move close to them so that you are pressing against them, usually because you are cold or frightened. ❑ *Then Marsha began to nestle up to Lynn, whimpering like a dog.*

V+ADV: USUALLY+to

nibble /nɪbəl/ (nibbles, nibbling, nibbled)

nibble at

1 When a mouse or other small animal **nibbles at** something, it takes small bites out of it quickly and repeatedly. ❑ *I saw squirrels in the yew trees nibbling at the moist red berries.*

V+PREP

2 If you **nibble at** your food, you eat it slowly, taking small bites, because you are not very hungry. ❑ *The two Belgian tourists nibble quietly at their food... Frank's father had only nibbled at the dish.*

V+PREP

For a full explanation of all grammatical labels, see pages xiii-xx

nod /nɒd/ **(nods, nodding, nodded)**

nod off If you **nod off**, you fall asleep, usually unintentionally, while you are sit-   V+ADV
ting down. [INFORMAL] ❑ *They just sit and chat to each other, or nod off... I nodded off
with Diggity snoring in my arms as usual.*
NOTE **Doze off** means almost the same as **nod off**.

nose /nəʊz/ **(noses, nosing, nosed)**

> ✓ **About** is used mainly in British English. In American English, **around** is much
> common than **round**.

nose about → See nose around

nose around If you **nose around**, **nose about** or **nose round**, you look for   V+ADV
interesting things or information in a place which belongs to someone else.
[INFORMAL] ❑ *They had nosed around for someone with a grudge against Curry but hadn't
found anyone... Coal-dust covered his feet as he nosed about among the boilers.*
NOTE **Poke around** means almost the same as **nose around**.

nose out

1 If you **nose out** information, you discover it by searching something thorough-   V+ADV+N,
ly. [INFORMAL] ❑ *I am not interested in nosing out the details of someone else's agony... He*   V+N+ADV,
noses the truth out eventually.   V+PRON+ADV
NOTE **Uncover** is a more formal word for **nose out**.

2 If you **nose out** other people in a competition or race, you gradually improve   V+N+ADV,
your position in relation to them so that you win. ❑ *Lendl was nosed out by the young-*   V+PRON+ADV,
er man this year.   V+ADV+N

nose round → See nose around

notch /nɒtʃ/ **(notches, notching, notched)**

notch up If you **notch up** something such as a score, total, or prize, you   V+ADV+N
achieve it. ❑ *The Tory candidate had notched up eleven hundred more votes than Mr
Jones... The firm has notched up the Queen's Award for export six times.*
NOTE **Chalk up** means almost the same as **notch up**.

note /nəʊt/ **(notes, noting, noted)**

★**note down** If you **note down** something, you make short notes about it, so   V+ADV+N,
that you can refer to them later. ❑ *...noting down his observations as he made them...*   V+PRON+ADV,
The teacher will demonstrate an experiment to the students who will then note it down and   V+N+ADV
write it up.

number /nʌmbəʳ/ **(numbers, numbering, numbered)**

number among If someone or something **is numbered among** a particular   V+N+PREP,
group, they are a member of that group. ❑ *They can each be numbered among the truly*   V+PRON+PREP
*great Open champions... Trade unions number among their members a substantial proportion
of the total electorate.*

Oo

object /əbdʒekt/ **(objects, objecting, objected)**

★**object to** If you **object to** something, you do not like it or approve of it. ❑ *The other tenants objected to Jeremy's habit of playing the piano at three in the morning... The plan has been objected to by the local residents' association.*

V+PREP:
HAS PASSIVE

occur /əkɜːr/ **(occurs, occurring, occurred)**

★**occur to** If a thought or idea **occurs to** you, you suddenly think of it or realize it. ❑ *As soon as that thought occurred to him, he felt worse... It never occurred to me to ask... It had never occurred to her that he might insist on paying.*

V+PREP:
ALSO+REPORT

offend /əfend/ **(offends, offending, offended)**

offend against If something **offends against** a law, rule, or principle, it breaks it. [FORMAL] ❑ *This would offend against the principle of fairness... To behave like that would offend against her conventions.*

V+PREP:
HAS PASSIVE

offer /ɒfər, AM ɔːfər/ **(offers, offering, offered)**

offer up To **offer up** prayers, praise, or a sacrifice means to pray to God or praise Him, or to make a sacrifice. ❑ *I went through the motions of offering up the prayer. ...the five daily prayers that are offered up to Allah... They are preparing to offer me up as a sacrifice, Jordache.*

V+ADV+N,
V+N+ADV,
V+PRON+ADV

ooze /uːz/ **(oozes, oozing, oozed)**

ooze out If a gas or liquid **oozes out** from somewhere, it slowly appears or leaks there. ❑ *It caused dense yellow smoke to ooze out through the tiles. ...horrible to see blood oozing out... Tears oozed slowly out from between her eyelids.*

V+ADV:
USUALLY+A

open /oupən/ **(opens, opening, opened)**

open off If a place or area **opens off** a road, path, or corridor, it connects directly with it. ❑ *Squares and little streets open off the main road. ...the turret-room that opens off the corridor on the left.*

V+PREP

open onto If a building or room **opens onto** another place, you can go straight from one to the other, for example through a door. ❑ *There are small back-to-back houses, whose doors open directly onto the street... All three doors opened onto a small private courtyard. ...the white arch that opens onto the sea terrace.*

V+PREP

NOTE **Give onto** means almost the same as **open onto**.

★**open out**

[1] If something that is in one piece or is packed closely together **opens out**, or if you **open** it **out**, it gradually separates. ❑ *The flower only opens out in full sun. ...bending the toes and opening them out... The fibres were opened out with the aid of a needle.*

V+ADV,
V+N/PRON+ADV,
V+ADV+N:
ERGATIVE

[2] If you **open out** something that is folded, you unfold it so that you can see or use it. ❑ *She opened out the board and began to set out the chessmen... He opened out the paper and began to read... He picked the letter up and opened it out.*

V+ADV+N,
V+PRON+ADV,
V+N+ADV

[3] If a place **opens out** into another place, it gradually becomes wider until you reach the second place. ❑ *Giltspur Street opens out into West Smithfield... The mountains finally opened out into the plain... As the road opened out, Francis glanced at his watch.*

V+ADV:
USUALLY+into

[4] If someone **opens out**, they become relaxed and start to talk more freely. ❑ *She found it difficult to open out to people... He opened out quite dramatically... In the lounge, over his coffee, Crike opened out.*

V+ADV

NOTE **Open up** means almost the same as **open out**.

[5] If something such as a discussion, topic, or subject **opens out**, or if you **open** it **out**, it starts to involve more people or things than it did before. ❑ *Obviously, this question could open out into the justification of such action... It would certainly be desirable to open out this debate... The books and exhibitions opened it out still further.*

V+ADV,
V+ADV+N,
V+PRON+ADV,
V+N+ADV:
ERGATIVE

For a full explanation of all grammatical labels, see pages xiii-xx

★open up

1 When a place or area **is opened up**, it becomes easier to get to, and there are more opportunities for development or trade. ❑ *The government was determined to open up the Sioux reservation for settlement. ...a fishing policy which will increase quotas and open up trawling grounds.*

V+ADV+N,
V+N+ADV,
V+PRON+ADV

2 When an opportunity **opens up**, or when a situation **opens** it **up**, that opportunity is given to you. ❑ *All sorts of possibilities began to open up... Fast transport and instantaneous communications open up a new dimension of freedom... A whole new world had been opened up for him by his rich American wife.*

V+ADV,
V+ADV+N:
ERGATIVE

3 If someone **opens up**, they start to relax and to say exactly what they know or think about something or someone. ❑ *After five or six beers Doring had opened up about Klara and Springer... We notice how new volunteers react, join in, begin to open up.*

V+ADV

NOTE **Open out** means almost the same as **open up**.

4 When you **open up** a building, you unlock and open the door so that people can get in. ❑ *Open up! It's snowing out here... The police opened up for them... Paul opened up his tiny store and café as usual.*

V+ADV,
V+ADV+N,
V+PRON+ADV,
V+N+ADV

5 If a new shop or business **opens up** or if someone **opens** it **up**, it starts to trade. ❑ *Supermarkets, drugstores, and service stations will open up... Anyone can open up a café tomorrow provided they've got permission... I was wondering whether to open up a new factory.*

V+ADV,
V+ADV+N,
V+PRON+ADV:
ERGATIVE

6 If a surgeon **opens up** a patient, or **opens up** a part of their body, they operate on them. [INFORMAL] ❑ *The doctor wants to open up the Eustachian tube... She had to open me up soon or it'd be too late.*

V+ADV+N,
V+PRON+ADV,
V+N+ADV

7 If someone with a gun **opens up**, they start shooting. ❑ *They opened up as the convoy came abreast of them... Suddenly they heard a nearby flak battery open up.*

V+ADV

8 If you **open up** when you are driving a car, you suddenly begin to go much faster. [INFORMAL] ❑ *After twenty miles he opened up... I throw my hand ahead in a 'Speed up!' gesture. He nods and opens up.*

V+ADV

NOTE **Accelerate** is a more formal word for **open up**.

9 If you **open up** a lead in a race or competition, you get yourself into a position where you are leading, usually by quite a long way. ❑ *The Chinese quartet had opened up a lead of more than two minutes.*

V+ADV+N,
V+N+ADV,
V+PRON+ADV

10 In a game, competition, or sporting activity, if the players **open up**, they begin to play in a more exciting and determined way. ❑ *Real Madrid suddenly opened up and, surprisingly, led by two goals to nil... It was a good hour or more before the game opened up.*

V+ADV

operate /ɒpəreɪt/ (operates, operating, operated)

★operate on When doctors **operate on** a patient, they cut open their body in order to remove, repair, or replace a damaged part of it. ❑ *We can't operate on the vein until the ulcer is healed... I hope to operate on her on Sunday... His knees have been operated on three times.*

V+PREP:
HAS PASSIVE

oppose /əpəʊz/ (opposes, opposing, opposed)

★oppose to

1 If you **are opposed to** something, you disagree with it or disapprove of it. ❑ *I am opposed to capital punishment... It was the principles that the TUC were opposed to.*

PASSIVE:
V+PREP

2 If one thing **is opposed to** another, they are contrasted in order to show how different they are from each other. ❑ *Art, when it is opposed to Science, is often romantic. ...politics, here opposed to good works... You can oppose realism to idealism.*

V+N+PREP,
V+PRON+PREP:
USUALLY PASSIVE

opt /ɒpt/ (opts, opting, opted)

★opt for If you **opt for** a particular thing, you decide to do or have that thing. ❑ *A woman who opts for a career and stays single may have greater commitment to the work than the single man who has not made the same sacrifices... Many Poles appeared to have opted for the poll boycott.*

V+PREP

opt in If you **opt in** to a particular arrangement or activity, you take part in it. ❑ *The independent schools, although not yet able to opt in to grant-maintained status, can play their part... The stakes for playing the game will be increased, and some players will no longer be able to opt in.*

V+ADV:
ALSO+to

The symbol ★ shows key phrasal verbs

***opt out** If you **opt out** of something, you choose to be no longer involved in it. ❑ *Today there is a growing tendency for people to opt out. ...hospitals are opting out of health authority control. ...people who had opted out of the rat race.*

V+ADV:
USUALLY+*of*

order /ˈɔːrdər/ (orders, ordering, ordered)

> ☑ **About** is used mainly in British English.

order about → See **order around**

order around If you **order** someone **around** or **order** them **about**, you tell them what to do in an unpleasant and unsympathetic way; used showing disapproval. ❑ *He went on behaving as if he were a soldier, ordering everyone about... It was intolerable that those two fat slobs could order Carolyn around... They think because they've got money they can order you about.*

V+N+ADV,
V+PRON+ADV

NOTE **Push around** means almost the same as **order around**.

own /oʊn/ (owns, owning, owned)

***own up** If you **own up** to something wrong that you have done, you admit that you did it. ❑ *Come on, own up! Who did it?... No-one owned up to taking the money.*

V+ADV:
ALSO+*to*

NOTE **Confess** is a more formal word for **own up**.

Pp

pace /peɪs/ **(paces, pacing, paced)**

pace off → See pace out

pace out If you **pace out** or **pace off** a distance, you measure that distance by counting the number of steps you have to take. ❑ *Placing the gun beside a tree he paced out a hundred and fifty paces... Laverne paced off the sections and tied pieces of yarn to twigs to mark the spot for each post.*

V+ADV+N,
V+PRON+ADV:
NO PASSIVE

pack /pæk/ **(packs, packing, packed)**

pack away If you **pack** something **away**, you put it in a bag or suitcase. ❑ *He and Flecker pack everything away into the canvas bag... I packed away the shorts and vest that I had worn the previous day... The food was packed away.*

V+N+ADV,
V+ADV+N,
V+PRON+ADV

★pack in

1 If someone **packs in** things or people, they fit a lot of them into a limited space or time. ❑ *Prison authorities concentrate too much on packing in as many inmates as possible... It's kind of a referendum, though a lot of issues are packed in.*

V+ADV+N,
V+N+ADV,
V+PRON+ADV

NOTE **Cram in** means almost the same as **pack in**.

2 If you **pack in** a job or activity, you stop doing it because you have had enough of it. [BRITISH, INFORMAL] ❑ *It's a good job. I don't think he'd pack it in... They may decide that enough is enough and just pack it all in... If you suddenly decide that pleasure is more important than business, well, pack in the business and go after the pleasure.*

V+PRON+ADV,
V+ADV+N,
V+N+ADV

NOTE **Jack in** means almost the same as **pack in**.

3 If you **pack** someone **in**, you stop having a romantic or sexual relationship with them. [INFORMAL] ❑ *She's just packed her boyfriend in.*

V+N+ADV,
V+PRON+ADV

4 If something such as a film, play, or other form of entertainment **packs** people **in**, it attracts them in large numbers. [INFORMAL] ❑ *...music that packs them in at South Kensington.*

V+PRON+ADV,
V+N+ADV

NOTE **Pull in** means almost the same as **pack in**.

pack into

1 If someone **packs** a lot of something **into** a limited space or time, they fit a lot into it. ❑ *...packing more events or tasks into less time... I have tried to pack a good deal into a few words.*

V+N+PREP,
V+PRON+PREP

NOTE **Cram into** means almost the same as **pack into**.

2 If people or things **are packed into** a place, so many of them are put in there that the place becomes very full. ❑ *Some 700 people were packed into a hotel room.*

V+N+PREP,
V+PRON+PREP:
USUALLY PASSIVE

NOTE **Be crammed into** means almost the same as **be packed into**.

pack off If you **pack** someone **off** somewhere, you send them there to stay for a period of time, even though they may not want to go there. [INFORMAL] ❑ *They pack their sons off to boarding school... I packed her off to bed with a hot water bottle... Years ago he had been packed off to one of the colonies... The unfortunate sufferer might even be packed off to hospital.*

V+N+ADV,
V+PRON+ADV,
V+ADV+N:
USUALLY+to

pack out When a place **is packed out** with people, it is extremely crowded. ❑ *The course was run by Eleanor Macdonald, whose seminar last year was packed out.*

PASSIVE:
V+ADV

★pack up

1 If you **pack up** your belongings, you put all your belongings in a case or bag, often because you are leaving one place and going to another. ❑ *It was a sad day indeed when we had to pack up our things and board the bus... All right, pack the files up. Take them back to registry.*

V+ADV+N,
V+N+ADV,
V+PRON+ADV

2 If you **pack up** a job or activity, you stop what you are doing and go somewhere else or do something else. [INFORMAL] ❑ *Everyone packed up and went home... She*

V+ADV,
V+ADV+N,
V+PRON+ADV:

The symbol ★ shows key phrasal verbs

packed up and left next day... I started playing cricket when I was eleven and only packed up five years ago... She says she's packing up work.   NO PASSIVE

3 If a machine **packs up**, it stops working because it has broken. [BRITISH, INFORMAL] ❑ *Our car packed up.... The heating in the hall packed up.*   V+ADV

NOTE **Break down** means almost the same as **pack up**.

4 If a part of the body **packs up**, it stops working. [BRITISH, INFORMAL] ❑ *In the end, it was his stomach and lungs that packed up.*   V+ADV

pad /pæd/ (pads, padding, padded)

pad out If you **pad out** a piece of writing or a speech with unnecessary words or pieces of information, you include them in order to make it longer and hide the fact that you have not got much to say. ❑ *He had to pad out his 300 pages with comments on his hero's digestive problems... She has a habit of padding out her essays with a lot of long quotes.*   V+ADV+N, V+N+ADV, V+PRON+ADV: USUALLY+with

paint /peɪnt/ (paints, painting, painted)

paint out If you **paint** something **out**, you cover or hide it with paint. ❑ *Branwell later painted his own figure out of the portrait of his sisters... The sign had been painted out, and could no longer be read.*   V+N+ADV, V+ADV+N, V+PRON+ADV

paint over If you **paint over** something that has already been painted or drawn, you cover it with paint so that it is hidden. ❑ *When it was discovered, the guards painted over it in grey... You saw off the bolt and paint the door over.*   V+PREP, V+N+ADV, V+PRON+ADV, V+ADV+N

paint up If you **paint** something **up**, you decorate it with paint, usually in a rather showy way. ❑ *The house has been painted up... His face was all painted up.*   V+N+ADV, V+PRON+ADV, V+ADV+N

pair /peəʳ/ (pairs, pairing, paired)

pair off When two people **pair off** or when someone **pairs** them **off**, they come together for a particular purpose or activity, for example at the beginning of a romantic relationship. ❑ *They'll probably pair off for company... They show no inclination to pair off with each other... One of the girls feels the need to pair people off... People are paired off according to their level of competence.*   V+ADV, V+N+ADV, V+PRON+ADV, V+ADV+N: ERGATIVE, ALSO+with, RECIPROCAL

pair up If you **pair up** with someone, you agree to do something together. ❑ *Statistics show that disabled women have a greater chance of pairing up with able-bodied men... His enthusiasm was infectious to anyone he was paired up with.*   V+ADV+with, V+ADV: RECIPROCAL

NOTE **Team up** means almost the same as **pair up**.

palm /pɑːm/ (palms, palming, palmed)

palm off

1 If someone **palms** something **off** on you, they give or sell it to you in order to get rid of it. ❑ *See what kind of cement those bloody crooks palmed off on me!... I said he was an expert at palming things off... They spend their lives having children, and then palming them off on somebody else.*   V+N+ADV, V+PRON+ADV: USUALLY+on

2 If someone asks you something and you **palm** them **off** with an excuse or a lie, you tell them something which is not necessarily true or relevant, but which you hope will satisfy them and stop them bothering you. [BRITISH] ❑ *There's no point in asking her where she's been, because she'll only palm you off with excuses... Don't let them palm you off.*   V+PRON+ADV, V+N+ADV: USUALLY+with

pan /pæn/ (pans, panning, panned)

pan out When you talk about the way that things **pan out**, you are saying that this is the way that things develop from a particular situation. [INFORMAL] ❑ *Things didn't pan out too well.*   V+ADV

NOTE **Work out** means almost the same as **pan out**.

pander /pændəʳ/ (panders, pandering, pandered)

pander to If you **pander to** someone or to their wishes, you do everything that they want, often in order to get some advantage for yourself. ❑ *Big business firms pander to the teenagers because they've got the money and the time to spend it... The older children are encouraged to pander to their slightest whim... His firm was pandering to what he called the 'swinish luxury of the rich'.*   V+PREP: HAS PASSIVE

paper /peɪpəʳ/ (papers, papering, papered)

paper over If someone **papers over** a difficulty or mistake, they deliberately   V+PREP:

give the impression that things are going well and try to hide the difficulty or mistake. ❑ *...trying to paper over the crisis... There is no papering over the fact that basic disputes exist... After the General Election of 1964 the differences were papered over.* `HAS PASSIVE`

parcel /ˈpɑːrsəl/ **(parcels, parcelling, parcelled)**

☑ American English uses the spellings **parceling** and **parceled.**

parcel out When you **parcel** something **out**, you divide it into several parts or amounts and give them to different people. ❑ *The responsibility for it had been parcelled out among them. ...the parcelling out of the land among the delighted neighbours.* `V+N+ADV, V+ADV+N, V+PRON+ADV`

parcel up

1 When you **parcel** something **up**, you wrap it as a parcel, with paper, string, tape, and so on. ❑ *We spent all of last night parcelling up the Christmas presents for the children.* `V+ADV+N, V+N+ADV, V+PRON+ADV`

NOTE **Wrap up** means almost the same as **parcel up.**

2 When something **is parcelled up**, it is divided into separate sections. ❑ *The Arab Near East after World War 1 was parcelled up into a number of new states.* `PASSIVE: V+ADV: USUALLY+A`

pare /peər/ **(pares, paring, pared)**

pare down When you **pare** something **down**, you reduce it and make it smaller or less extensive. ❑ *I want to pare down my political involvements to a minimum... The translator had done Dostoevsky a disservice in paring down 'The Brothers Karamazov' to essentials... I had pared my possessions down to almost nothing.* `V+ADV+N, V+N+ADV, V+PRON+ADV: USUALLY+to`

pare off When you **pare off** the skin or outer layer of something, you cut it off using a knife or other sharp tool. ❑ *The remains of the brown outer layer should be pared off with a knife.* `V+ADV+N, V+N+ADV, V+PRON+ADV`

part /pɑːrt/ **(parts, parting, parted)**

part from

1 When two people **part from** each other, they leave each other, often when they are separating at the end of a relationship. [FORMAL] ❑ *I know that I should have parted from you long ago, except that I could not endure to... He had parted from Gertrude in some kind of dreadful moral muddle... I very nearly parted from her in Copenhagen.* `V+PREP`

2 If you **are parted from** someone or something, you cannot be with them, even though you want to be. ❑ *He had never been parted from her before... It's perfectly natural that a mother should not wish to be parted from her children. ...one who has been too long parted from dear friends.* `PASSIVE: V+PREP`

★**part with** If you **part with** something that is valuable or that you would prefer to keep, you give it or sell it to someone else. ❑ *I took the book, thanked her, and told her I would never part with it... She didn't want to part with the money... I might just be persuaded to part with it.* `V+PREP: HAS PASSIVE`

NOTE **Hold on to** means the opposite of **part with.**

partake /pɑːrˈteɪk/ **(partakes, partaking, partook, partaken)**

partake in If you **partake in** an activity, you become involved in it and take part. [FORMAL, OLD-FASHIONED] ❑ *Young people deprived of the right to partake in social decision-making will grow more and more unstable... I was made to partake in a good deal of menial work.* `V+PREP`

partake of

1 If you **partake of** food or drink, you eat or drink it. [FORMAL, OLD-FASHIONED] ❑ *He did not partake of either meal, preferring to sit at the table sipping whisky while we ate... He was invited to partake of refreshment in the Senior Common Room.* `V+PREP`

2 If something **partakes of** a particular quality, it has that quality. [FORMAL, OLD-FASHIONED] ❑ *Education is most vital when it partakes of the nature of discovery.* `V+PREP`

partition /pɑːrˈtɪʃən/ **(partitions, partitioning, partitioned)**

partition off If you **partition off** part of something, you separate that part from the rest by placing a partition between the two parts. ❑ *They were partitioned off from the chauffeur by the thick glass. ...in the kitchenette that Miss Gilderthorp had partitioned off from her father's original stone kitchen.* `V+N+PREP, V+PRON+PREP`

pass /pɑːs, pæs/ **(passes, passing, passed)**

☑ In American English, **around** is much more common than **round.**

pass along

1 If something **passes along** or **passes down** a path or place, it moves along   V+PREP
there. ❑ *Footsteps passed along the corridor above... He nodded hello as he passed along the
row of people at the bar... Thousands of people must have passed down Whitehall without
seeing it.*

2 If you **pass** something **along**, you send it or give it to someone else. ❑ *I'll pass it*   V+N+ADV,
along to the management.   V+PRON+ADV

★pass around If you **pass** things **around** or **pass** them **round**, you give them   V+ADV+N,
from one person to another in a group. ❑ *Her mother passed round plates of jelly and*   V+N+ADV,
custard... Go on Ron, just take a light and pass the matches round... She opened the moun-   V+PRON+ADV
*tain of gifts and passed them around... I've got a couple of pictures you might like to pass
around.*

pass as To **pass as** or **pass for** something means to appear to be that thing.   V+PREP
❑ *You may pass as a remarkably witty man. ...that brief period that passes for summer in
those high latitudes.*

pass away

1 When something **passes away**, it slowly disappears. ❑ *A hurt look appeared in*   V+ADV
Jack's eyes and passed away... All hopes of compromise had now passed away.

2 You can say that someone **passed away** to mean that they died, especially if   V+ADV
you want to avoid saying the word 'die'. ❑ *Your husband sent the letter to us shortly before he passed away... She passed away within three weeks of her sister.*

NOTE **Pass on** means almost the same as **pass away**.

3 If you **pass** time **away** in a particular place, you are there for that time. ❑ *He*   V+ADV+N,
condescended to pass away a few days in my company... Children in inner city areas are   V+N+ADV
doomed to pass away their days with illegal child-minders.

pass between

1 You say that remarks, letters, looks, and so on **pass between** two people when   V+PREP
those people say things, or write to each other, or look at each other. ❑ *...the usual
greetings that passed between them... No words passed between us. ...the letters that
passed between them in the final years.*

2 When something **passes between** two people or places, it moves past or   V+PREP,
through them so that they are on either side of it. ❑ *She passed between the two of*   V+N+PREP,
them... The nail has passed between the bones at the base of the foot... They then pass it be-   V+PRON+PREP
tween two millstones.

★pass by

1 If you **pass by** something or if you **pass** it **by**, you go past it without stopping.   V+PREP,
❑ *We pass by another marker... A tall bearded silhouette passed by... I was just passing by*   V+ADV,
and I saw your car... Helen flinched as the younger woman passed her by.   V+PRON+ADV

♦ **passer-by, passers-by.** A **passer-by** is a person who is walking past something   N-COUNT
or someone. ❑ *One of the boys had stopped a passer-by and asked him to phone an ambulance... Passers-by dived in to rescue them.*

♦ A **bypass** is a main road which is built to take traffic round the edge of a town ra-   N-COUNT
ther than through the middle. ❑ *...the construction of a new by-pass around the ancient
town of Sandwich. ...the Oxford bypass.*

2 If something **passes** you **by**, it happens and finishes before you notice it or can   V+PRON+ADV
take advantage of it. ❑ *...an old friend whose works up to now have passed me by... The
great drama and passion of the world had already passed him by... Life was passing her by.*

★pass down

1 If things such as stories, traditions, or characteristics **are passed down**, they are   V+N+ADV,
told, taught, or given to someone who belongs to a younger generation. ❑ *Reading lit-*   V+PRON+ADV,
tle, they remembered the tales passed down from father to son... Our sense of the past is de-   V+ADV+N:
veloped by our knowledge of history, by the accumulated heritage of art, music, literature,   USUALLY PASSIVE WITH
and science passed down to us through the years. ...stories his own father had passed down   to/from
to him.

NOTE **Hand down** means almost the same as **pass down**.

2 If you **pass** something **down**, you give it to someone who is standing or sitting   V+N+ADV,
below you. ❑ *Can you pass the receipts down, Pat?... Simon passed them down to the out-*   V+PRON+ADV,
stretched hands.   V+ADV+N

3 → See **pass along**

pass for → See **pass as**

★**pass off**

1 If an event **passes off** in a particular way, especially in a satisfactory way, it happens and ends in that way. ❑ *Most of these situations pass off without mishap... It had passed off amicably enough.*   V+ADV: WITH A

2 If you **pass** something unpleasant **off** lightly, you say or pretend that it was not really very important or serious. ❑ *I had thought he would pass this off lightly... She passed off his criticisms contemptuously, considering his opinion of little value.*   V+N+ADV, V+ADV+N, V+PRON+ADV: WITH A

NOTE **Shrug off** means almost the same as **pass off**.

3 If something such as a feeling or condition **passes off**, it gradually disappears. ❑ *Fortunately the effects of the gas passed off relatively quickly... The attack, or whatever it was, had passed off just as asthma does.*   V+ADV

NOTE **Wear off** means almost the same as **pass off**.

pass off as If you **pass** something **off as** a particular thing, you convince people that it is that thing, when in fact it is not so valuable or important, or does not have the right characteristics. ❑ *The painting had been passed off as early Flemish, or Dutch... The man who made the cabinet passed it off as an antique... He passed himself off as a Frenchman.*   V+N+ADV+PREP, V+PRON+ADV+PREP, V+REFL+ADV+PREP

★**pass on**

1 If you **pass** something **on** to someone, you give it to them, for example after you have used it or after someone else has given it to you. ❑ *He handed a typewritten sheet to King to pass on to Smith... He only had shoes which other folk passed on to him... The union head office may be able to pass on useful information... I once made an appeal to mothers of twins to tell me what solutions they had found for their problems, so that I could pass them on.*   V+N+ADV, V+ADV+N, V+PRON+ADV: ALSO+to

2 If things such as stories, traditions, or money **are passed on**, they are taught or given to someone who belongs to a younger generation. ❑ *Skills such as this should be passed on... The original Harris Company was founded in 1732, and father passed the business on to son for eight generations... Perhaps their own mothers do not have the time or skills to pass on these hobbies... She assumed that her mother would wish to pass on to her the bulk of her fortune... I have nothing that I can pass on to you.*   V+N+ADV, V+ADV+N, V+PRON+ADV: USUALLY PASSIVE, ALSO+to

NOTE **Hand down** means almost the same as **pass on**.

3 When parents **pass on** something such as a physical characteristic to their children, the children develop it or have it because of the genes that they inherit from their parents. ❑ *How do parents pass genes on to their offspring?... These different abilities may be passed on through several generations.*   V+N+ADV, V+ADV+N, V+PRON+ADV: ALSO+to

NOTE **Transmit** is a more formal word for **pass on**.

4 If you **pass** someone **on** to someone else, you put them in contact with the second person because you think they might be able to help. ❑ *If you want confirmation of my authority in this case I'll pass you right on to the Director-General... We passed him on to a fashion-designer friend... I was passed on to another doctor.*   V+PRON+ADV, V+N+ADV: ALSO+to

5 If a company **passes on** costs or savings to their customers, they alter their prices and charge either more or less than usual to take account of changes in production costs. ❑ *Governments have tried to prevent firms from passing on cost increases... Any such saving will automatically be passed on to all clients.*   V+ADV+N, V+PRON+ADV: ALSO+to

6 If you **pass on** to a new subject while you are writing or speaking, you begin to talk about it. ❑ *They passed on to other matters... They passed on to the matter of entertainment.*   V+ADV: ALSO+to

NOTE **Move on** means almost the same as **pass on**.

7 If you **pass on** to a different place in a journey or to a different stage in a process, you continue the journey or process. ❑ *We passed on to a small pantry and entered the dining room... They stay until they are eleven, when they pass on to a secondary school... The man lowered his eyes and quickly passed on.*   V+ADV

8 You can say that someone **passed on** to mean that they died, especially if you want to avoid using the word 'die'. ❑ *They say poor Miss Parr's passed on... A pity Sir Edmund's passed on... It's five years to the day since she passed on.*   V+ADV

NOTE **Pass away** means almost the same as **pass on**.

★**pass out**

1 If you **pass out**, you lose consciousness for a short time. ❑ *I thought I was going to pass out... He passed out while I was in the room... My head thumped solidly on a rock and I passed out.* `V+ADV`

NOTE **Black out** means almost the same as **pass out**.

2 If you **pass** something **out**, you distribute it among a number of people. ❑ *We all sat cross-legged on the grass, and I passed out the lemonade... They passed out enormous bribes to port officials.* `V+ADV+N, V+N+ADV, V+PRON+ADV`

NOTE **Hand out** means almost the same as **pass out**.

3 When a police, army, navy, or air force cadet **passes out**, he or she satisfactorily finishes his or her course of training. [BRITISH] ❑ *He was killed in Belfast only two weeks after passing out from Sandhurst.* `V+ADV`

★**pass over**

1 If you **are passed over** for a job or position that you are trying to get, it is given to someone who is less well-qualified or experienced than you. ❑ *He got it into his head he was being passed over for promotion... Neither of us got the job. We were both passed over.* `PASSIVE: V+ADV`

NOTE **Be rejected** means almost the same as **be passed over**.

2 If you **pass over** a particular topic in a conversation, you deliberately do not discuss it. ❑ *He didn't give a reason and Robertson passed it over in silence... He passed over the events of that week.* `V+PRON+ADV, V+ADV+N, V+N+ADV`

NOTE **Ignore** means almost the same as **pass over**.

3 When something **passes over**, it moves overhead without stopping. ❑ *The glacial winds pass over the waters... A helicopter had passed over a few moments before.* `V+PREP, V+ADV`

♦ An **overpass** is a main road which is built like a bridge so that it is above another road. ❑ *They're building a new overpass.* `N-COUNT`

NOTE **Flyover** means almost the same as **overpass**.

4 **Passover** is a Jewish festival that begins in late March or early April and that lasts for eight days. ❑ *...the story of the Passover... Passover is a family occasion.* `N-UNCOUNT`

★**pass round** → See pass around

pass through To **pass through** a period of time or series of stages means to exist before, during, and after that period or those stages and to develop during them. ❑ *Mrs Yule had to pass through a few years of much bitterness... Humanity was believed to pass through four great ages... The revolutionary movement has passed through a succession of distinctive phases.* `V+PREP`

pass to When something **passes to** someone, it becomes their property or responsibility. ❑ *Her property passes to her next of kin... Responsibility for security there would now pass to Westminster.* `V+PREP`

pass under When someone or something **passes under** another thing, they move underneath it without stopping. ❑ *We pass under the trees along the road... After four miles the stream passes under the road.* `V+PREP`

♦ An **underpass is** a road or footpath that goes underneath something, for example under another road or a railway. ❑ *...the Knightsbridge Underpass... The underpass is closed because of fire.* `N-COUNT`

pass up If you **pass up** something such as an opportunity, you do not take advantage of it. ❑ *Certainly, Mr Gerran would willingly pass up any potential profit if the need arose... She never passed up a chance to eat in a restaurant.* `V+ADV+N, V+PRON+ADV`

paste /peɪst/ (pastes, pasting, pasted)

paste up If you **paste** something **up**, you attach it to a wall or other vertical surface, using glue or paste. ❑ *Soldiers had pasted up leaflets condemning the petrol bombings... A broad sheet of paper was pasted up on the door of the church.* `V+ADV+N, V+N+ADV, V+PRON+ADV`

pat /pæt/ (pats, patting, patted)

pat down If someone **is patted down**, an official searches them to see if they are carrying a weapon or illegal items. [AMERICAN, INFORMAL] ❑ *Leona was patted down and her luggage searched.* `V+N+ADV, V+PRON+ADV, V+ADV+N: USUALLY PASSIVE`

NOTE **Frisk** means almost the same as **pat down**.

pay for

patch /pætʃ/ (patches, patching, patched)

patch together If something **is patched together**, it is made from a number of parts in a hurried or careless way. ❏ *A new government was patched together with the help of the military... She couldn't, as some writers do, just patch together old material.*

NOTE Cobble together means almost the same as **patch together**.

V+N+ADV,
V+ADV+N,
V+PRON+ADV:
USUALLY PASSIVE

★patch up

1 If you **patch up** something which is damaged or broken, you mend it rather roughly so that it can be used. ❏ *They have to patch up the mud walls that the rains have battered. ...to do a reasonable job patching things up.*

NOTE Fix up means almost the same as **patch up**.

V+ADV+N,
V+N+ADV,
V+PRON+ADV

2 If a doctor or surgeon **patches** you **up**, they temporarily bandage you or perform a small operation after you have been injured. [INFORMAL] ❏ *I have spent a good deal of my time patching up the children who have been wounded. ...the little injury that cannot be patched up simply for lack of money.*

NOTE Treat means almost the same as **patch up**.

V+ADV+N,
V+PRON+ADV

3 If you **patch up** a quarrel or relationship with someone, you try to be friends again and not to quarrel any more. ❏ *Many a village quarrel was patched up that morning... He finally decided to overlook his mates' unkindness and try to patch things up... The Labour party patched up its quarrels after the right won the battle over disarmament.*

V+N+ADV,
V+ADV+N,
V+PRON+ADV

4 If people or countries **patch up** a deal, they manage to agree on it after difficult discussions. ❏ *Trade ministers patched up a compromise.*

V+ADV+N,
V+PRON+ADV

pattern /pætərn/ (patterns, patterning, patterned)

pattern on If something new **is patterned on** something else that already exists, it uses the original thing as a model and is designed and made to be similar to it. ❏ *The 'Daily Dispatch' was patterned on the British press... He always used a Hoffritz safety razor patterned on the old-fashioned heavy-toothed Gillette type.*

PASSIVE:
V+PREP

pave /peɪv/ (paves, paving, paved)

pave over When a road or an area of ground **is paved over**, it is covered with blocks of stone, bricks, or concrete so that it is suitable for walking or travelling on. ❏ *The carriage paths were paved over only ten years ago... The next court, paved over with white marble slabs, had a central fountain.*

PASSIVE:
V+ADV

paw /pɔː/ (paws, pawing, pawed)

paw at When an animal **paws at** something, it tries to touch it with its paw or hoof. ❏ *Back in the yard Boxer was pawing with his hoof at the stable-lad... The dog pawed at the doorknob again and again.*

V+PREP

pay /peɪ/ (pays, paying, paid)

★pay back

1 If you **pay** money **back** to someone or **pay** them **back**, you give them money that you previously borrowed from them. ❏ *She thanked him for the cheque, saying that when the estate was finally settled she would pay back all the money he had sent her... I'm going to pay every penny of it back to him... With the salary you mentioned you ought to be able to pay it back in one month... Loan me a hundred dollars, I'll pay you back on Monday when I go to the bank.*

NOTE Repay means almost the same as **pay back**.

V+ADV+N,
V+N+ADV,
V+PRON+ADV:
ALSO+to

2 If you **pay** someone **back** for doing something unpleasant to you, you do something unpleasant to them as a punishment. ❏ *I felt that I would like to wake her up to pay her back for keeping me awake... I was now prepared to pay him back for his treacheries.*

V+PRON+ADV,
V+N+ADV:
USUALLY+for

★pay for

1 If you **pay for** something, you give someone money for it. ❏ *They will still need an estimated $2 billion to pay for food and other imports... He allowed Rudolph to pay for the drinks... The ticket was reserved but not paid for.*

V+PREP:
HAS PASSIVE

2 If something that you buy eventually **pays for** itself, it saves you more money than it originally cost because it is so efficient that you do not need to spend as much money as you used to. ❏ *In Sri Lanka hiring rates are so high that a tractor can pay for itself in less than two years... All these things are possible and would pay for themselves by saving on energy brought in from outside... Fix up a hand shower. It soon pays for itself by halving your bathwater bills.*

V+PREP+REFL

3 If you say that someone will have to **pay for** something bad that they have done, you mean that they will be punished or forced to do something else which they do not want to do. ☐ *The obvious implication was that Kruger would have to pay for his mistake in banning me... Maybe uniformity is one of the prices we have to pay for sociability in a more mobile society.*

V+PREP

★pay in When you **pay** money **in**, you put it or transfer it into a bank account. ☐ *They wanted the number of his bank account so that they might pay it in... Reginald called in at the bank to pay his first cheque in.*

V+PRON+ADV,
V+N+ADV,
V+ADV+N

★pay into When you **pay** money **into** a bank account, you put it or transfer it into the account. ☐ *...a girocheque, which you can cash at the post office, or pay into a bank account... Then I began to draw the money out in cash and pay it into my account under my own name at the Midland Bank.*

V+N+PREP,
V+PRON+PREP

NOTE **Deposit** means almost the same as **pay into**.

★pay off

1 If you **pay off** a debt or bill, you give someone the total amount of money that you owe them so that you are no longer in debt. ☐ *He had used the firm's money to pay off gambling debts... The most common reason for borrowing is to pay off existing loans... So she fell into debt and had to pay it off by selling her house.*

V+ADV+N,
V+PRON+ADV,
V+N+ADV

NOTE **Repay** means almost the same as **pay off**.

2 If you **pay** someone **off**, you try to stop them threatening you or causing you trouble by giving them money. ☐ *Mr. Hagen, I can't afford to look ridiculous. I have to pay Johnny off... His lawyer raised money to pay off the convicted defendants in the Watergate case.*

V+N+ADV,
V+PRON+ADV,
V+ADV+N

NOTE **Buy off** means almost the same as **pay off**.

♦ A **payoff** is a payment that you make to someone so that they do not cause trouble for you. ☐ *It was usually possible to make a payoff to a high police official to keep quiet.*

N-COUNT

3 If you **pay off** workers, you pay them what you owe them for work that they have done for you and then dismiss them. ☐ *Mrs Foster persuaded the driver to carry her two large cases to the top of the steps. Then she paid him off and rang the bell... I paid the taxi off at the end of the street and walked down to my flat... All troops were immediately paid off and discharged.*

V+PRON+ADV,
V+N+ADV,
V+ADV+N

4 If an action **pays off**, it is successful. ☐ *It was a risk and it paid off... Their anti-aircraft precautions had paid off well.*

V+ADV

♦ A **payoff** is the useful result of an action. ☐ *Some carry out research without daring to hope that there could be a practical pay-off... There's a risk and payoff for both sides.*

N-COUNT

★pay out

1 If you **pay out** a large amount of money, you spend it on a particular item or activity. ☐ *They pay out half of their income in rent... She had paid out good money to send Julie to school... Every Friday twelve or thirteen thousand pounds was paid out in wages.*

V+ADV+N,
V+N+ADV,
V+PRON+ADV

2 When an insurance policy **pays out**, the person who has the policy receives the money that they are entitled to receive. ☐ *Many policies pay out only after a period of weeks or months.*

V+ADV

3 When you **pay out** a rope or cable, you unwind it in a controlled way. ☐ *Ned paid out the rope and carried the block to the tree... Then the boat is dropped back, downtide, paying out the steel anchor cable as we go.*

V+ADV+N,
V+PRON+ADV

★pay up When you **pay up**, you give someone the money that you owe them, even though you would prefer not to. ☐ *Come on, pay up... Things might not go too well if he didn't pay up... Even when suspecting fraud, airlines found it cheaper to pay up quickly than enter into a prolonged dispute... When I was ill they paid up £500 immediately.*

V+ADV,
V+ADV+N

peal /piːl/ (peals, pealing, pealed)

peal out When sounds **peal out**, they can be heard clearly over a long distance. ☐ *And the bells would peal out across the town and countryside. ...so many hammered tones pealing out in oppressive arpeggios.*

V+ADV

NOTE **Resound** means almost the same as **peal out**.

peck /pɛk/ (pecks, pecking, pecked)

peck at If you **peck at** your food, you eat only small amounts of it, because you are ill or not hungry, or because you do not like the food. [INFORMAL] ❑ *Throughout the meal, I could do no more than peck at my food, constantly watching the clock.*

V+PREP

peel /piːl/ (peels, peeling, peeled)

peel off

1 If you **peel** the outer layer **off** something or if it **peels off**, you remove it or it separates easily. ❑ *I peeled some moss off the wood... She peeled the wrapping paper off. ...gleaming sheets of metal that had been partly peeled off like the skin of an orange... On the statues, the gold leaf was beginning to peel off.*

V+N+PREP/ADV,
V+PRON+PREP/ADV,
V+ADV+N,
V+ADV:
ERGATIVE

2 If you **peel off** some money from a pile of banknotes, you take some of the notes from the top of the pile one at a time. ❑ *He took a wad of bills out of his side pocket and peeled off five tens... I was paid in small bills peeled off a thick wad of larger ones.*

V+ADV+N

3 If you **peel off** a tight piece of clothing, you remove it by pulling it slowly. ❑ *She peeled off her sweater... Once in the hotel, Mick and I peeled off our boots... Chris began to peel off her dress.*

V+ADV+N,
V+N+ADV,
V+PRON+ADV

NOTE **Strip off** means almost the same as **peel off**.

4 If some of a group of moving vehicles or people **peel off**, they leave the group and follow a course that curves away to one side. ❑ *As the cars arrived, the police motorcycle escorts had to peel off and circle round the courtyard... Even as he saw this, one of the bodyguards peeled off to come ahead and see what was wrong.*

V+ADV

peg /pɛg/ (pegs, pegging, pegged)

peg away If you **peg away** at something, you continue doing it in a very determined way, even though it is difficult or unpleasant. [INFORMAL] ❑ *He would rather keep on pegging away at a beginner's book... We found that it didn't help much to peg away at the same passage.*

V+ADV:
USUALLY+at

NOTE **Plug away** means almost the same as **peg away**.

peg out

1 If someone **pegs out**, they die. [BRITISH, INFORMAL] ❑ *If he leaves me he has to give me half the house money but if I peg out all she has to do is move in... If I don't warm up first, I'll just peg out halfway round the course.*

V+ADV

2 If someone **pegs out**, they are too exhausted to carry on with what they have been doing. [BRITISH, INFORMAL] ❑ *I nipped round the corner for a quick beer and nearly pegged out on the spot.*

V+ADV

NOTE **Flake out** means almost the same as **peg out**.

3 If you **peg out** clothes or sheets that you have just washed, you fasten them to a washing line with pegs. ❑ *She trudged up the garden and began to peg out the clothes on the line... Mrs Poulter began to peg out a bit of her washing... As soon as she had pegged it out, it began to rain.*

V+ADV+N,
V+PRON+ADV,
V+N+ADV

NOTE **Hang out** means almost the same as **peg out**.

4 If you **peg** something **out**, you spread it on the ground and fasten it there with pegs. ❑ *...a sheepskin pegged out on the grass... We pegged the tent out with considerable difficulty.*

V+N+ADV,
V+PRON+ADV,
V+ADV+N

pelt /pɛlt/ (pelts, pelting, pelted)

pelt down If it is pelting down with rain, it is raining very hard. [INFORMAL] ❑ *He guessed that it must be rain pelting down. ...the rain pelted down outside.*

V+ADV

NOTE **Pour down** means almost the same as **pelt down**.

pen /pɛn/ (pens, penning, penned)

pen in

1 If you **pen in** animals, you make them move into an enclosed area such as a pen. ❑ *...like a collie dog trying to pen in some reluctant sheep... They were penned in like cattle.*

V+ADV+N,
V+N+ADV,
V+PRON+ADV

2 If a person or their abilities **are penned in**, they are restricted by the situation that they are in. ❑ *Clergymen can feel penned in too.*

V+N+ADV,
V+PRON+ADV,
V+ADV+N

pen up If people or animals **are penned up**, they are kept together in an enclosed area. ❑ *A thousand were penned up in a small building. ...the boredom of endless hours penned up in a hot and dusty railway carriage.*

V+N+ADV,
V+PRON+ADV,
V+ADV+N

pencil /pɛnsəl/ (pencils, pencilling, pencilled)

☑ American English uses the spellings **penciled** and **penciling**.

pencil in If something **is pencilled in**, it is written in pencil rather than ink on a piece of paper because you are not sure whether it is correct or because you want to see if it looks all right. ❑ *She had pencilled in a tentative title, 'The Song of the Salesman'... Two other dates were proposed, with something just pencilled in for both of those evenings as well.*

V+ADV+N, V+N+ADV, V+PRON+ADV

pension /pɛnʃən/ (pensions, pensioning, pensioned)
pension off

1 If someone **is pensioned off**, they are made to retire from work and given money by their employers or the government. ❑ *Many people go on working as useful citizens at an age when we would pension them off... In 1958, Kleiber was pensioned off and allowed to buy the security company at a bargain price.*

V+PRON+ADV, V+N+ADV, V+ADV+N

2 If you **pension off** something that you use regularly, you stop using it completely. [INFORMAL] ❑ *So I settled for an orange hunting hat, pensioning off the blue denim one I had started with.*

V+ADV+N, V+N+ADV, V+PRON+ADV

pep /pɛp/ (peps, pepping, pepped)
pep up

1 If you **pep** something **up**, you make it more lively or interesting. ❑ *Undoubtedly, he realised that the conference needed pepping up... Kellogg has good reason to try to pep up its product line.*

V+N+ADV, V+PRON+ADV, V+ADV+N

NOTE **Liven up** means almost the same as **pep up**.

2 If something **peps** you **up**, it gives you more energy. ❑ *Morell gave him an extra dose of glucose to pep him up.*

V+PRON+ADV, V+N+ADV, V+ADV+N

NOTE **Perk up** means almost the same as **pep up**.

pepper /pɛpər/ (peppers, peppering, peppered)
pepper with

1 To **pepper** something **with** small things means to throw lots of the things at it or to sprinkle them onto its surface. ❑ *...peppered them with a hail of bullets from his pocket pistol... 'There,' he insisted, his abrupt English peppering the air with faint showers of spittle.*

V+PRON+PREP, V+N+PREP

2 If something **is peppered with** things, there are a lot of the things on it or in it. ❑ *...a monotonous plateau of rust red and ochre peppered with the pastel green of acacia. ...an elderly black face, its cheeks peppered with several days' growth of grey whiskers... The satellite was peppered with glittering particles.*

PASSIVE: V+PREP

3 If you **pepper** your speech or writing **with** a particular type of language, you use a lot of that type of language when you speak or write. ❑ *Sir Derek peppered his speech with learned references. ...whose French is heavily peppered with such Americanisms.*

V+N+PREP, V+PRON+PREP

perk /pɜːrk/ (perks, perking, perked)
perk up

1 If someone **perks up**, or if someone or something **perks** them **up**, they suddenly become more cheerful, interested, active, or exciting. ❑ *He was being a bore, that's why. A proper misery. He perked up when we got there, though... Peter perked up. He rose from his chair... There are more agreeable ways to perk up your appetite.*

V+ADV, V+ADV+N, V+N+ADV, V+PRON+ADV: ERGATIVE

NOTE **Liven up** means almost the same as **perk up**.

2 If you **perk** something **up**, you make it more interesting. ❑ *To make th bland taste more interesting, the locals began perking it up with local produce... Psychologial twists perk up an otherwise predictable story line.*

V+ADV+N, V+N+ADV, V+PRON+ADV

3 If sales, prices, or economies **perk up**, or if something **perks** them **up**, they begin to increase or improve. [JOURNALISM] ❑ *House prices could perk up during the autumn... Anything that could save the company money and perk up its cash flow was examined.*

V+ADV+N, V+N/PRON+ADV, V+ADV: ERGATIVE

4 If you **perk up** coffee, you make some coffee to drink, using a percolator. [AMERICAN] ❑ *Aw, let me treat you—I was going to perk some up for Muscle Mar anyway.*

V+N+ADV, V+ADV+N, V+PRON+ADV

permit /pərmɪt/ (permits, permitting, permitted)

permit of If something **permits of** a particular thing, it makes it possible. [FORMAL] ❑ *An institution like the concentration camp permits of no really succesful defence.*

V+PREP

pertain /pər<u>teɪ</u>n/ **(pertains, pertaining, pertained)**

> **pertain to** If one thing **pertains to** another thing, it relates to that other thing, affects it, or is only valid for it. [FORMAL] ❏ *The rules pertaining to one set of circumstances do not necessarily pertain to another. ...to write about things that don't directly pertain to him... I was given free access to all official documents pertaining to the Revolution.*

V+PREP

peter /p<u>iː</u>tər/ **(peters, petering, petered)**

> **peter out** If something **peters out**, it gets smaller, less intense, or less important and gradually stops completely. ❏ *The tracks petered out a mile or two later... The attack petered out after two hours... His rage petered out.*

V+ADV

phase /f<u>eɪ</u>z/ **(phases, phasing, phased)**

> **phase in** If you **phase in** a new product, method, or idea, you introduce it gradually. ❏ *Beveridge's original plan was to phase in adequate old-age pensions in the period up to 1956... There is probably more than enough time to phase in this enormous resource well before fossil fuels become exhausted.*

V+ADV+N,
V+N+ADV,
V+PRON+ADV

> ♦ The **phasing in** of a new product, method, or idea is its gradual introduction into a system. ❏ *...the phasing in of long-term alternatives. ...the phasing-in of 'market rents.'*

N-SING

> **phase into** If you **phase** a new product, method, or idea **into** a system, you introduce it gradually into the system. ❏ *It is now under development but may require a decade or two to be phased into mass production... Vacuum tube collectors are being phased into an oil-fired district heating scheme at Uppsala.*

V+N+PREP,
V+PRON+PREP

> ★**phase out** If you **phase out** a product, method, or idea, you gradually stop using it. ❏ *The Thatcher government is planning to phase out earnings-related supplements... Gold has been phased out of the monetary system. ...would be willing to phase out nuclear weapons.*

V+ADV+N,
V+N+ADV,
V+PRON+ADV

> ♦ The **phasing out** of a product, method, or idea is the process of gradually ceasing to use it. ❏ *1977 saw the phasing out of child tax allowances.*

N-SING

phone /f<u>oʊ</u>n/ **(phones, phoning, phoned)**

> ★**phone back** If you **phone back** or **phone** someone **back**, you phone them for a second time or after they have phoned you. ❏ *The leader of the team phoned back... She phoned back to say that it was only an eleven-day trip... I said I'd phone them back this morning... We will know when I've phoned my agent back.*

V+ADV,
V+PRON+ADV,
V+N+ADV:
NO PASSIVE

> NOTE **Call back** and **ring back** mean almost the same as **phone back**.

> **phone down** If you are in a building and you **phone down** to a person or a place, you phone someone on one of the floors below you, usually to ask them to do something for you. ❏ *I'll phone down to the restaurant and arrange it now... She phoned down to the desk to say she'd be keeping the suite... He phoned down an order, more or less at random, for Haydn's Third Symphony.*

V+ADV,
V+ADV+N,
V+PRON+ADV:
ALSO+to

> **phone for** If you **phone for** something, you phone someone to ask them to provide it for you. ❏ *When we've had breakfast you can phone for a taxi... The other boy must have phoned for the ambulance.*

V+PREP:
HAS PASSIVE

> ★**phone in**

> [1] If you **phone in** to a radio or television station, you phone them because you want to talk on a programme that is being broadcast at the time. ❏ *It's called Fan Fare – people can phone in and actually speak to local football managers... She phoned in to the Charles Boon show.*

V+ADV:
ALSO+to

> ♦ A **phone-in** or **phone-in** programme is a radio or TV programme in which members of the public can phone and give their opinions or ask questions while the programme is being broadcast. ❏ *There's a phone-in about it. ...a late-night phone-in programme. ...the independent TV phone-in. ...the new phone-in version.*

N-COUNT,
ADJECTIVE

> [2] If you **phone in** to an organization that provides special help for people who are in trouble, such as drug addicts, alcoholics, and people contemplating suicide, you phone them because you need their help. ❏ *There is a 24-hour religious service; you can phone in and be saved anytime.*

V+ADV:
ALSO+to

> [3] If you work for an organization such as a newspaper, the armed forces, or the police and **phone in** information, you phone them to tell them where you are or what you are doing, or to tell them the information. ❏ *Within minutes, they phoned in*

V+ADV+N,
V+N+ADV,
V+PRON+ADV,
V+ADV

another bulletin... Lewis phoned the details in to a rewrite man. ...a news story which a reporter had just phoned in... She phoned in to say that the situation was now improving.

4 If you have a job and **phone in**, you phone your employers, usually to tell them that you are ill and cannot work that day. ❑ *Judy phones in to say she has food poisoning... She had phoned in and said she was sick.*   V+ADV

phone round If you **phone round**, you phone several people or organizations, for example to invite them to an event or to ask them for help or information. [BRITISH] ❑ *...while we were phoning round for our survey... I think the best idea is to phone round and see if anyone runs a bus there on Sundays.*   V+ADV

phone through If you **phone through**, you make a phone call, usually to get or give information or make some arrangements. ❑ *At the end of the week he phoned through with the news of a possible job... I'll be phoning through later this afternoon for the result.*   V+ADV

★phone up When you **phone** someone **up**, you dial their phone number and speak to them on the phone. ❑ *I've got to phone her up tonight... So I phoned the place up and they said they had about 6... I said to my father, 'Phone up the police.'... The landlord is phoning up tomorrow to see if he's got it.*   V+PRON+ADV, V+N+ADV, V+ADV+N, V+ADV

NOTE **Ring up** and **call up** mean almost the same as **phone up**.

pick /pɪk/ (picks, picking, picked)

pick at

1 If you **pick at** the food that you are eating, you eat very small amounts of it because you are not hungry. ❑ *'When the war is over,' he said, picking at his plate, 'I'm going to go down there and settle.'... She picked at her food, without appetite. ...like a hen picking at grain.*   V+PREP: HAS PASSIVE

NOTE **Nibble at** means almost the same as **pick at**.

2 If you **pick at** something, you keep pulling it or scratching it with your fingers. ❑ *Monkeys and apes pick at one another's fur as a social ritual... Tortyev was content to pick at his fingernails.*   V+PREP

3 If you **pick at** a person or their work, you criticize small details in their actions, ideas, or work. ❑ *A work on such a scale is bound to have some small weak spots to pick at.*   V+PREP

pick off

1 If someone **picks off** animals or enemy soldiers, aircraft, or weapons, they shoot at them one at a time and kill or destroy them. ❑ *A single hunter attempting to pick off animals in groups usually has little luck... He circled the soldiers guarding the horses, and began picking them off one by one.*   V+ADV+N, V+PRON+ADV, V+N+ADV

2 If you **pick off** something, you remove it by pulling it or scratching it with your fingers or a tool. ❑ *They probe around the base of their quills to pick off fleas... Try picking it off with a comb or your finger.*   V+ADV+N, V+PRON+ADV, V+N+ADV

★pick on

1 If you **pick on** someone, you treat them badly or in an unfair way, often repeatedly. ❑ *'Why pick on Johan?' I said. 'John also deserted us.'... The older men pick on the boys and are always looking for faults... They'll be protected by the union from being picked on by the boss if they do complain.*   V+PREP: HAS PASSIVE

NOTE **Get at** means almost the same as **pick on**.

2 If you **pick on** one particular person or thing, you choose that one. [BRITISH] ❑ *Of all the girls in town, he picked on Mr Zapp's daughter... Why did we pick on Verice, for God's sake?*   V+PREP

★pick out

1 If you **pick out** someone or something when they are difficult to see or recognize, you manage to see or recognize them. ❑ *We could just barely pick it out when the light was right... Irene Burns picked out Meehan as one of the two men who gave her a lift... One could just pick out the letters AGR.*   V+PRON+ADV, V+ADV+N, V+N+ADV

NOTE **Make out** means almost the same as **pick out**, and **discern** is a more formal word.

2 If you **pick out** one person or thing from a group, you choose them. ❑ *He picks out a flat spot without any rocks on it... They'll look through the applications, they'll pick out the ones they like, and invite you in for interview.*   V+ADV+N, V+N+ADV, V+PRON+ADV

NOTE **Select** means almost the same as **pick out**.

pick up

3 If part of a painting or design **is picked out**, it is in a different material or colour so that it is very noticeable. ❑ *...his coronet, picked out in gloss paint. ...my name, the letters picked out in silver.*

PASSIVE:
V+ADV:
USUALLY+*in*

4 If someone or something **is picked out** by a light, the light shines only on them, so they are seen very clearly. ❑ *I saw teeth in the dimness – gleaming teeth picked out by our street light... Elizabeth was picked out by a tiny spotlight... The indirect glow from the light picked out their silhouettes.*

V+N+ADV,
V+ADV+N,
V+PRON+ADV:
USUALLY PASSIVE

5 If you **pick out** a tune on a musical instrument, you play it slowly and awkwardly because you do not know it very well or cannot play the instrument very well. ❑ *He picked out a tune on the piano and after a while tried singing along to it.*

V+ADV+N,
V+N+ADV,
V+PRON+ADV

pick over If you **pick over** a group of things, you examine them carefully and choose only the things you want and throw away or reject anything you do not want. ❑ *Never use soft or damaged fruit. Pick it over carefully and remove the stalks and hulls... I saw one old lady picking over a pile of old coats in a corner.*

V+PRON+ADV,
V+ADV+N,
V+N+ADV

pick through If you **pick through** things, you examine them carefully. ❑ *Pick through the pieces and see if you can find one you like. ...some rather old hymn books that Angelica picked through but didn't seem to take any notice of.*

V+PREP:
HAS PASSIVE

★pick up

1 If you **pick** something **up**, you lift it up from a particular place. ❑ *He stooped down to pick up the two pebbles... The telephone rang and Judy picked it up... The air was full of flying objects, picked up by the tearing winds.*

V+ADV+N,
V+PRON+ADV,
V+N+ADV

NOTE **Lift up** means almost the same as **pick up**.

2 When you **pick** yourself **up** after you have fallen or been knocked down, you stand up again, often with difficulty. ❑ *Then he jumped off the horse, stumbled and fell, picked himself up and ran for cover.*

V+REFL+ADV

3 When you **pick up** someone or something that is waiting to be collected, you go to the place where they are and take them away, often in a car. ❑ *We drove to the airport the next morning to pick up Susan... She was going over to her parents' house to pick up some clean clothes for Owen... I picked her up at Covent Garden to take her to lunch with my mother.*

V+ADV+N,
V+N+ADV,
V+PRON+ADV

♦ **Pick-up** places or things are available for people to collect and take away. ❑ *Well-organized teams of agents see the shipments through from the pick-up point to their destinations.*

ADJECTIVE

4 If someone **is picked up** by the police or another group, they are arrested or taken somewhere to be asked questions. ❑ *He was picked up by government agents for questioning... I don't want you to be picked up for vagrancy... I could fix it so that the highway patrol pick him up for drunk driving and put him in jail all night.*

V+ADV+N,
V+N+ADV,
V+PRON+ADV:
USUALLY PASSIVE

NOTE **Take in** means almost the same as **pick up**.

5 If you **pick up** a skill, habit, or attitude, you learn it or start having it without making any effort. ❑ *Did you pick up any Swedish?... The kids pick it up really fast but lose it just as quickly... He'll soon start to pick the job up.*

V+ADV+N,
V+PRON+ADV,
V+N+ADV

6 If you **pick** something **up**, you find or get it by chance, often when you were not looking for it or expecting to get it. ❑ *I may pick up a couple of useful ideas for my book... Her mother had liked to pick up bargains in basement sales. ...the fragments of information they picked up on their night-time visits.*

V+ADV+N,
V+N+ADV,
V+PRON+ADV

7 If you **pick up** an illness, you get it from somewhere or something. ❑ *They've picked up a really nasty infection from something they've eaten.*

V+ADV+N,
V+N+ADV,
V+PRON+ADV

NOTE **Catch** means almost the same as **pick up**.

8 If you **pick up** a prize, a reputation, or something else that improves your situation, you gain it or win it. ❑ *It picked up the Best Musical Award... He was picking up a lot of support because the public admired his policies.*

V+ADV+N,
V+PRON+ADV

9 If you say that someone **picks up** the tab, the bill, or the cheque, you mean that they pay for something. ❑ *Who's picking up the tab for the research?... The company lays men off and the national government picks up the bill in unemployment pay... I'm delighted, but you must really let me pick up the check.*

V+ADV+N,
V+PRON+ADV

10 If someone **picks up** a particular amount of money for the work they do, they earn that amount of money. [INFORMAL] ❑ *A welding overseer picks up 400 pounds a week.*

V+ADV+N:
NO PASSIVE

The symbol ★ shows key phrasal verbs

11 If you **pick up** someone you do not know, you start talking to them and being friendly towards them, usually because you want to have a sexual relationship with them. [INFORMAL] ❑ *I doubt whether Tony ever picked up a woman in his life... Then she went into the bar and nobody tried to pick her up.*

V+ADV+N,
V+PRON+ADV,
V+N+ADV

♦ A **pick-up** is a situation in which someone is trying to start a sexual relationship with someone they have just met. [INFORMAL] ❑ *But the girl clearly knows a pick-up when she sees one. ...from sexual suggestions to attempted pick-ups.*

N-COUNT

12 If a person or animal **picks up** a faint smell or a quiet sound, they become aware of it. ❑ *He sniffed the air, trying to pick up their scent... Kunta's ears picked up a strange, muted sound.*

V+ADV+N,
V+N+ADV,
V+PRON+ADV

NOTE **Detect** is a more formal word for **pick up**.

13 If a piece of equipment such as a radio or microphone **picks up** a signal or sound, it receives or detects it. ❑ *It was easier to pick up Radio Luxembourg than Radio One. ...bugging devices that were capable of picking up both telephone and room conversations... Signals from the Command Post's radio must have been picked up by Soviet direction finders.*

V+ADV+N,
V+N+ADV,
V+PRON+ADV

14 If you **pick up** a mistake or other feature in something, you notice it. ❑ *...so that if there is a mistake you'll pick it up... She should be picking up inconsistencies as they occur.*

V+PRON+ADV,
V+ADV+N,
V+N+ADV

15 If you **pick up** a point or topic that someone has mentioned, you go back to it and say something relating to it. ❑ *I'd like to pick up the point David made... The President picked up the theme.*

V+ADV+N,
V+PRON+ADV

16 If you **pick up** something that you had stopped doing, you start doing it again, usually from the point where you had stopped. ❑ *I really do feel I'm picking up where I left off about twelve years ago... He'd love to pick up their conversation where they'd left off.*

V+ADV,
V+ADV+N,
V+N+ADV,
V+PRON+ADV

NOTE **Resume** is a more formal word for **pick up**.

17 If trade, business, or the economy of a country **picks up**, it gradually increases or improves after a period of inactivity or decline. ❑ *The economy is picking up... Retail demand for diamonds has picked up in recent weeks... People like her are waiting for trade to pick up.*

V+ADV

♦ A **pick-up** in trade, business, or the economy of a country is an increase or improvement in it. ❑ *Small traders are now reporting a significant pick-up in business. ...a sales pick-up.*

N-SING

18 If someone **picks up**, or their health **picks up**, they get better. ❑ *A good dose of tonic will help you to pick up.*

V+ADV

19 A **pick-me-up** is a drink that you have in order to make you feel healthier and more energetic. [INFORMAL]

N-COUNT

NOTE **Tonic** means almost the same as **pick up**.

20 When a vehicle **picks up** speed, or its speed **picks up**, it begins to move more quickly. ❑ *Brian started the engine and pulled away slowly, but picked up speed once he entered Oakwood Drive.*

V+ADV+N,
V+ADV:
ERGATIVE

21 When you **pick up** the pieces after a disaster, you do what you can to get the situation back to normal again. ❑ *Do we try and prevent problems or do we try and pick up the pieces afterwards?... She died, and somehow I never picked up the pieces and started again.*

V+PREP

pick up on

1 If you **pick up on** something, you notice it and it affects your attitude or behaviour. ❑ *A girl picks up on her mother's fear or dislike of sex. ...picking up on the woman's embarrassment.*

V+ADV+PREP

2 If you **pick** someone **up on** something that they have said or done, you tell them that you think that it is wrong. [BRITISH] ❑ *May I just pick him up on what he said about women?*

V+PRON+ADV+PREP,
V+N+ADV+PREP

NOTE **Take up on** means almost the same as **pick up on**.

pick up with

If you **pick up with** someone, you start meeting then regularly and doing things together. ❑ *Mother used to be wild with me the way I'd pick up with just anyone.*

V+ADV+PREP

piece /piːs/ (pieces, piecing, pieced)

piece out If you **piece out** the truth or facts about something, you gradually manage to discover them. ❏ *Her partner can piece out what is being said.*
V+ADV+N,
V+N+ADV,
V+PRON+ADV

NOTE **Work out** and **suss out** mean almost the same as **piece out**.

★piece together

1 If you **piece together** the truth about something, you gradually discover it. ❏ *From hints and whispers we pieced together the explanation... As the questioning continued he began to piece it together... She had not yet been able to piece together exactly what had happened... Using manuscript sources, it has been possible to piece the whole story together.*
V+ADV+N,
V+PRON+ADV,
V+ADV+WH,
V+N+ADV

NOTE **Work out** means almost the same as **piece together**, and **deduce** is a more formal word.

2 If you **piece** something **together**, you gradually make or form it by joining several things or elements together. ❏ *...a nation struggling to piece together a new identity... He would fish out torn love letters from waste baskets and piece them together carefully.*
V+ADV+N,
V+PRON+ADV,
V+N+ADV

pig /pɪɡ/ (pigs, pigging, pigged)

pig out If you say that people **are pigging out**, you are criticizing them for eating a very large amount at one meal; used showing disapproval. [INFORMAL] ❏ *He had probably pigged out in a fast-food place beforehand.*
V+ADV

NOTE **Gorge** means almost the same as **pig out**.

pile /paɪl/ (piles, piling, piled)

pile in If a group of people **pile in**, they all get into a place or vehicle at once in rather a disorganized way. ❏ *There was room for all four of us, and we piled in.*
V+ADV

NOTE **Crowd in** means almost the same as **pile in**.

pile into If a group of people **pile into** a place or vehicle, they all get into it at once in rather a disorganized way. ❏ *Hurriedly we packed up and piled into the bus... Businessmen pile into London in enormous numbers.*
V+PREP

NOTE **Crowd into** means almost the same as **pile into**.

pile on

1 If people **pile on** to something such as a vehicle or platform, they all try to get on it at once in a disorganized way. ❏ *There was a crowd of schoolkids, all piling on to the train and trying to grab the best seats.*
V+ADV:
ALSO+to

2 If you **pile on** something such as suggestions, instructions, or work, you give a lot of them to other people to deal with. ❏ *They really pile the work on, don't they?... Responsibility is also piled on by all that is written about the effects of bad parenting... She would not want even more suggestions to pile on to the list of do's and don'ts.*
V+N+ADV,
V+ADV+N,
V+PRON+ADV:
ALSO+to

pile out If a group of people **pile out** of a place, they all get out of it at once in rather a disorganized way. ❏ *The crowd of children piled out of the house... Everyone but me piled out of the car... They all piled out with their cameras.*
V+ADV:
ALSO+of

★pile up

1 If things **pile up** or if you **pile** them **up**, they collect somewhere or you put them somewhere, forming a pile. ❏ *Masses of cloud piled up in the sky over the distant hills... When magazines pile up on the floor, don't complain... He piled up the teacups... He told his men to gather some rocks and pile them up... Her hair had been piled up on top of her head.*
V+ADV,
V+ADV+N,
V+PRON+ADV,
V+N+ADV:
ERGATIVE

NOTE **Heap up** means almost the same as **pile up**.

2 A **pile-up** is a road accident in which several vehicles crash into each other. ❏ *There had been a twenty-car pile-up on the M1.*
N-COUNT

3 If you **pile up** work, problems or losses, or if they **pile up**, you get more and more of them. ❏ *All these disasters piled up on the unfortunate Bangladeshis... As the bills piled up, she had not known where to turn... Problems were piling up at work... Last year alone, the company piled up losses totalling £4 billion.*
V+ADV,
V+ADV+N,
V+PRON+ADV,
V+N+ADV:
ERGATIVE

NOTE **Mount up** means almost the same as **pile up**.

pin /pɪn/ (pins, pinning, pinned)

pin down

1 If you try to **pin down** something which is hard to define or describe, you try to say exactly what it is or what it is like. ❏ *He was afraid he might never be able to pin down his own insights, let alone convey them to others... Police forces are continuing inquiries*
V+ADV+N,
V+N+ADV,
V+PRON+ADV

to try and pin the whereabouts of the suspect down.

NOTE **Nail down** means almost the same as **pin down**, and **specify** is a more formal word.

2 If you **pin** someone **down**, you force them to make an exact statement about something, which they have tried to avoid doing. ❑ *He was worried and anxious to pin Kishan Kumar down to some definite commitment... The more he had tried to pin them down on what they were talking about the vaguer they got... Try to pin him down to a date.*

NOTE **Nail down** means almost the same as **pin down**.

V+N+ADV,
V+PRON+ADV:
ALSO+to

3 If someone or something **pins** you **down**, they force you into a particular position so that you cannot move. ❑ *The strong arms were around me, pinning me down so that I couldn't move... Whole battalions found themselves pinned down by German fire... They pinned down the guards.*

NOTE **Hold down** means almost the same as **pin down**.

V+PRON+ADV,
V+ADV+N,
V+N+ADV

pin on

1 If you **pin** the blame or responsibility for something **on** someone, or **pin** it **upon** them, you say that they did it or caused it. ❑ *It amused Wilf to watch him trying to pin a crime on him he hadn't committed... The Court was unable to pin responsibility upon any person... You can't pin that on me.*

V+N+PREP,
V+PRON+PREP

2 If you **pin** your faith or hopes **on** or **pin** them **upon** something or someone, you hope very much that they will help you to produce the result you want. ❑ *He increasingly pinned his hopes on the prospect of a split in the opposition party... I pin my faith on public opinion.*

V+N+PREP

pin up

1 If you **pin up** a poster or a notice, you fix it to a wall so that it can be seen easily. ❑ *I did not bother to pin either of them up on my wall. ...pinning up the letters the women send to each other... The map was pinned up and became the centre of attention... The chart for sight testing was pinned up on the partition.*

V+N+ADV,
V+ADV+N,
V+PRON+ADV:
ALSO+on

NOTE **Put up** means almost the same as **pin up**.

♦ A **pin-up** is a picture of an attractive woman or man, often a model wearing very few clothes, or of a famous person. ❑ *The bathroom wall was plastered with pin-ups of film stars.*

N-COUNT,
ADJECTIVE

2 If you **pin up** part of a piece of clothing or material, you use pins to fasten the bottom of it to a part of it that is higher up. ❑ *She was bending down, pinning up the hem of her sister's dress.*

V+ADV+N,
V+N+ADV,
V+PRON+ADV

3 If a woman **pins** her hair **up**, she makes it into a bun or a similar hairstyle and fixes it in place with hairpins. ❑ *Mrs Waites was pinning up her freshly-washed hair... Her hair was pinned up, but wisps escaped here and there.*

V+ADV+N,
V+N+ADV,
V+PRON+ADV

pin upon → See pin on

pine /paɪn/ (pines, pining, pined)

pine away If someone **pines away**, they gradually become weaker and die because they are very unhappy. ❑ *I believe she actually pined away – lost her will to live... A young lady found her lover was unfaithful, and pined away.*

V+ADV

NOTE **Waste away** means almost the same as **pine away**.

pipe /paɪp/ (pipes, piping, piped)

pipe down If you tell someone to **pipe down**, you are telling them to talk more quietly or to stop talking altogether. [INFORMAL] ❑ *Pipe down at the back there.*

IMPERATIVE,
V+ADV

pipe up If someone who has been silent for a while **pipes up**, they start speaking. ❑ *'It's all very well for you, Elizabeth,' he piped up... They heard Patsy's youngest pipe up: 'What about the girls?*

V+ADV,
V+ADV+QUOTE

piss /pɪs/ (pisses, pissing, pissed)

☑ **Piss** is a very rude, informal word.

piss about If someone **pisses about** or **pisses around**, they waste a lot of time and annoy other people by behaving in a silly or childish way. [BRITISH]

V+ADV

piss around → See piss about

piss away If you **piss** something **away**, you waste it in a silly way. ❑ *'I'm seeth-* V+N+ADV,
V+ADV+N,
V+PRON+ADV
ing because we pissed away the points,' the coach said.

NOTE Squander is a more formal word for **piss away**.

piss down If it **is pissing down**, it is raining very hard. [BRITISH] ❑ *It was really* V+ADV
pissing down out there.

★**piss off**

1 If a person tells someone else to **piss off**, that person is telling them in a rude IMPERATIVE,
V+ADV
way to go away, usually because they have done something annoying. [BRITISH]

2 If someone **is pissed off** with something, or if someone or something **pisses** V+PRON+ADV,
V+N+ADV
them **off**, they feel bored and irritated by them. ❑ *This guy was beginning to piss me*
off... I'm thoroughly pissed off with all of them.

pit /pɪt/ (pits, pitting, pitted)

pit against If one thing **is pitted against** another thing, it is put in competi- V+N+PREP,
V+PRON+PREP:
HAS PASSIVE
tion with it. ❑ *He was pitted against a really first-class player. ...heretical beliefs pitted*
against a moral philosophy. ...pitting his judgement against theirs.

pitch /pɪtʃ/ (pitches, pitching, pitched)

pitch for If someone is **pitching for** something, they are trying to persuade V+PREP
other people to give it to them. ❑ *...laws prohibiting the state's accountants from pitching*
for business... It was middle-class votes they were pitching for.

pitch in If you **pitch in**, you help other people to do a task, using a lot of energy V+ADV:
ALSO+with
or enthusiasm. ❑ *They will be expected to pitch in and make their own beds... During the*
cane season everyone pitched in.

NOTE Muck in means almost the same as **pitch in**.

pitch into

1 If you **pitch into** a job that you have to do, you start doing it with a lot of ener- V+PREP
gy. ❑ *Brisk rubbing of hands here, as though we are about to pitch into some job of work like*
washing a window... Be careful not to pitch into your exercises before warming up.

NOTE Dive into means almost the same as **pitch into**.

2 If someone **pitches into** you, they attack you, either by hitting you, or by in- V+PREP:
HAS PASSIVE
sulting and criticizing you. [INFORMAL] ❑ *The boss really pitched into me and told me I*
wasn't working hard enough.

NOTE Lay into means almost the same as **pitch into**.

pivot /pɪvət/ (pivots, pivoting, pivoted)

pivot on If something **pivots on** or **pivots upon** something else, it depends on V+PREP
this thing which is very important to its success or progress. ❑ *Success or failure pivot-*
ed on a single exam.

NOTE Hang on means almost the same as **pivot on**.

pivot upon → See pivot on

plague /pleɪɡ/ (plagues, plaguing, plagued)

plague with

1 If you **are plagued with** unpleasant things, they keep happening and cause PASSIVE:
V+PREP
you a lot of trouble or suffering. ❑ *Simon Keswick was plagued with kidney trouble while*
in the colony... The inner-city school is plagued with problems... His summer cold was one of
the worst he had ever been plagued with.

2 If you **plague** someone **with** something such as questions or requests, you keep V+N+PREP,
V+PRON+PREP
bothering them by asking them for things. ❑ *Readers were urged to plague their*
Congressmen with letters of protest... He plagues her with questions.

plan /plæn/ (plans, planning, planned)

plan ahead If you **plan ahead**, you make arrangements in advance for some- V+ADV
thing. ❑ *They advised him to plan ahead for an election... I admire people who plan ahead...*
Few individuals or families plan ahead systematically... They soon discover they cannot cheat
by planning ahead.

★**plan for** If you **plan for** a particular thing or event, you consider it when you are V+PREP:
HAS PASSIVE
making your arrangements. ❑ *A commission was established in Tokyo to plan for the needs*
of the city... You should also plan for the effect of Capital Transfer Tax... The number of these
was never quantified and thus never specifically planned for.

★plan on

1 If you **plan on** doing something, you intend to do it. ❑ *I plan on staying in London for the foreseeable future... The troops were planning on attacking Poland exactly one week later.*

V+PREP:
HAS PASSIVE

2 If you **have not planned on** a particular thing, you have not realized that it might happen and so have not considered it when making your arrangements. ❑ *I hadn't planned on the bad weather... I didn't plan on so many people coming.*

V+PREP:
HAS PASSIVE

NOTE **Expect** is a more general word for **plan on**.

plan out If you **plan out** a particular task or course of events, you decide in detail what you are going to do. ❑ *She planned out how she would phrase the lyrics... Sit down earlier in the week to plan everything out... The work of the coming week was planned out.*

V+ADV+N,
V+N+ADV,
V+PRON+ADV

plan up If a meeting or an arrangement **is planned up**, it is prepared and people are ready to take part in it. ❑ *We've got all the interviews planned up now.*

PASSIVE:
V+ADV

plane /pleɪn/ (planes, planing, planed)

plane down If you **plane down** a piece of wood, you make it smaller or smoother using a plane. ❑ *The piece was reduced in size by planing down the four corners.*

V+ADV+N,
V+N+ADV,
V+PRON+ADV

plant /plɑːnt, plænt/ (plants, planting, planted)

plant out When you **plant out** seedlings or young plants, you plant them in the ground in the place where they are to be left to grow. ❑ *I trimmed the hornbeam hedge and planted out a bed of asters... We had to rear it in a nursery and plant it out.*

V+ADV+N,
V+PRON+ADV,
V+N+ADV

play /pleɪ/ (plays, playing, played)

✔ **About** is used mainly in British English.

★play about → See play around
play about with → See play around with
play along

1 If you **play along** with someone, you pretend to agree with them or accept what they say even though you do not really believe it. ❑ *With an acutely disturbed patient it may be necessary to play along during the initial phase of the treatment... He had realized I wouldn't play along with his plan to drop the union agreement.*

V+ADV:
USUALLY+with

2 If you **play** someone **along**, you deliberately keep them waiting for a decision. ❑ *You've been playing her along, haven't you?... Why had she been such a fool as to think she could play him along?*

V+PRON+ADV,
V+N+ADV

★play around

1 When children **play around** or **play about** somewhere, they play there. ❑ *Mumma would be ironing while the kids played around. ...a little boy playing about in a sand heap... Don't play around public toilets... Didn't I tell you to play around the yard?*

V+ADV,
V+PREP

2 If you **play around**, you have sex with people other than your husband, wife, or partner. ❑ *You don't think he's playing around, do you?*

V+ADV

play around with

1 If you **play around with** or **play about with** something, you keep moving it from one place or position to another. ❑ *We spent the whole afternoon playing around with bits of string... I put the shells on a screen and played around with them until I got something attractive.*

V+ADV+PREP

2 You can also say that someone **plays around with** or **plays about with** something when they change it or interfere with it in a way which you disapprove of. ❑ *I think it's frightening that people are going to play around with the hormone content of plants.*

V+ADV+PREP:
HAS PASSIVE

NOTE **Mess around with** and **tamper with** mean almost the same as **play around with**.

3 If someone **plays around with** another person, they have a sexual relationship with them although they have have no serious feelings for them. ❑ *You've just been playing around with me.*

V+ADV+PREP

play at

1 If you say that someone is **playing at** something, you disapprove of the fact that they are doing it casually and not very seriously; used showing disapproval. ❑ *We were still playing at war – dropping leaflets instead of bombs.*

V+PREP:
NO PASSIVE

For a full explanation of all grammatical labels, see pages xiii-xx

2 If someone, especially a child, **plays at** being a particular kind of person or being in a particular kind of situation, they pretend to be that person or be in that situation. ❑ *The children play at being French children... From time to time I have wandered into Sotheby's, playing at being a connoisseur. ...playing at soldiers.* `V+PREP`

3 If you do not know what someone **is playing at**, you do not understand what they are doing or what they are trying to achieve. [INFORMAL] ❑ *She began to wonder what he was playing at... 'What do you think you're playing at?' he said. 'I can't sell this.'* `V+ADV`

★**play back** When you **play back** a tape or film on which you have recorded sound or pictures, you operate the machine it is in so that you can listen to it or watch it. ❑ *I played back a taped interview with Dr. Sanger... Let's play the tape back and hear the conversation again... There would be months in which they could play it back at leisure.* `V+ADV+N, V+N+ADV, V+PRON+ADV`

◆ The **playback** of a tape is the operation of the machine it is in so that you can listen to it or watch it. ❑ *The conversation had been recorded for playback... Then all you have to do is press the playback button.* `N-UNCOUNT`

★**play down** If you **play** something **down**, you try to make people think that it is unimportant, or less important than it really is. ❑ *He played down his enhanced authority... The Minister tried to play down the seriousness of the problem... Because it was important, he wished to play it down.* `V+ADV+N, V+PRON+ADV, V+N+ADV`

NOTE **Exaggerate** and **play up** mean the opposite of **play down**.

play off When two people or teams who have the same number of points in a sports competition **play off**, they play a match to decide which one is the winner. ❑ *Liverpool and Everton will play off for third place.* `V+ADV`

◆ A **play-off** is a match between two people or teams who have the same number of points, to decide which one is the winner. ❑ *...a play-off for third place.* `N-COUNT`

play off against If you **play** people **off against** each other, you cause them to compete or argue so that you gain an advantage. ❑ *It is easy for a child to play one parent off against the other... The multinational companies can play individual markets off against each other... Here was an example of one section being played off against another.* `V+N+ADV+PREP, V+PRON+ADV+PREP`

★**play on**

✓ In meanings 3 and 4, the stress is on **on**.

1 If you **play on** or **play upon** people's feelings, attitudes, or weaknesses, you deliberately use them in order to achieve what you want. **Play upon** is more formal. ❑ *He used to play on their prejudices and their fears... Try to find your opponent's weaknesses and play on them relentlessly... She was forced to play upon the fears of others.* `V+PREP`

NOTE **Exploit** means almost the same as **play on**.

2 If a writer or speaker **plays on** or **plays upon** a particular idea or word, he or she cleverly makes use of different aspects of it, often for a humorous effect. **Play upon** is more formal. ❑ *Shatrov plays on a historical theme in his latest work.* `V+PREP`

3 If you **play on**, you continue playing a musical instrument. ❑ *She forced herself to play on.* `V+ADV`

4 If the referee tells players to **play on** during a game of football or rugby, he or she is telling them to continue playing even though someone has broken the rules of the game. ❑ *The referee told them to play on.* `V+ADV`

play out

1 If you talk about people **playing out** a scene, drama, or series of events, you mean that they take part in events which seem fated to happen and over which they have no control. ❑ *One day this scene would have to be played out between them... Mother and father play out the roles assigned to them... The final drama was played out on June 17th.* `V+ADV+N`

NOTE **Enact** means almost the same as **play out**.

2 When actors **play out** a scene, they act it. ❑ *The actors are asked to now play out the scene using only the three lines they've chosen.* `V+ADV+N`

3 You can say that people **play out** their feelings or fantasies when they express them in their actions. ❑ *Often unconscious anxieties get played out in our attitudes towards other people... We're just playing out fantasies.* `V+ADV+N`

4 If you feel **played out**, you feel exhausted and unable to do anything else. ❑ *I* `ADJECTIVE` *was very tired and feeling very played out.*

NOTE **Worn out** means almost the same as **played out**.

play through If you **play** a piece of music **through**, you play it from beginning to end. ❑ *Eddie Neils played all the songs through... She opened a book of Bach prel-
udes and played one through.*
V+N+ADV,
V+PRON+ADV

★play up

1 If you **play up** a fact or feature, you emphasize it and try to make people think
that it is more important than it really is. ❑ *The temptation is to play up the sensational
aspects of the story... Newspaper reports play up the few accidents and injuries which do occur.*
V+ADV+N

NOTE **Exaggerate** means almost the same as **play up**, and **play down** means the
opposite.

2 If a machine or a part of your body **is playing up** or **is playing** you **up**, it is
not working properly or is hurting. [BRITISH, INFORMAL] ❑ *Our phone is playing up... Is
your arm playing up?... My leg's playing me up again.*
V+ADV,
V+PRON+ADV,
V+N+ADV

3 If children **are playing up** or **are playing** you **up**, they are being naughty and
are difficult to control. [BRITISH, INFORMAL] ❑ *The kids are playing up again... Ian played
him up a lot and nearly wore him out.*
V+ADV,
V+PRON+ADV,
V+N+ADV

play upon → See play on

play up to If you **play up to** someone, you behave in a way which will please
or amuse them, for example by flattering them. ❑ *I think he feels that when he's got an
audience he's got to play up to it and impress everyone... I played up to his vanity.*
V+ADV+PREP

★play with

1 When children **play with** a toy, they handle it or use it to amuse themselves, often in an imaginative way. ❑ *He was hoping that I would come back and bring him some
new toys to play with. ...dolls that are not played with.*
V+PREP:
HAS PASSIVE

2 If you **play with** something, you keep moving it from one position or place to
another without thinking about what you are doing, for example because you are
bored or nervous. ❑ *I sat there playing with a bottle of suntan lotion... Don't play with your
napkin ring, Sam... She would sprinkle granulated sugar onto her porridge and then start idly
playing with it.*
V+PREP

3 If you **play with** the idea of doing something, you consider doing it, although
you will probably not do it. ❑ *Thomas played with the idea of letting Coyne make all the
arrangements... He had played with the idea of moving her to an apartment of her own.*
V+PREP

NOTE **Toy with** means almost the same as **play with**.

4 If a writer or speaker **plays with** words or ideas, he or she uses them in a clever
and unusual way for a special effect. ❑ *He had been playing with themes of rebirth and
renaissance... Novelists have often played with these ambiguities... I spend many hours playing with words.*
V+PREP

5 When a child **plays with** another child, the two children play together. ❑ *You'll
enjoy having other boys to play with... Go upstairs and play with your friends... Every baby
needs to be smiled at, talked to, and played with.*
V+PREP:
HAS PASSIVE

6 If you say that someone **is playing with** someone else, you mean that they are
behaving towards them in an insincere way. ❑ *'Albert,' she said, 'Stop playing with me
like this.'*
V+PREP

7 If someone **plays with** himself or herself, he or she masturbates. [INFORMAL]
V+PREP+REFL

plead /pliːd/ (pleads, pleading, pleaded)

★plead for

1 If you **plead for** something, you ask for it very strongly and in an emotional
way. ❑ *Mrs Hogan had phoned to plead for Philip's assistance... She would come and plead
for help and comfort... The more he pleaded for mercy, the more they beat him.*
V+PREP

2 When a lawyer **pleads for** someone, they speak for them and try to defend them in court. ❑ *...the difficult task of pleading for a defendant who was obviously
guilty.*
V+PREP

★plead with If you **plead with** someone, you ask them for something in an intense and emotional way. ❑ *I pleaded with him to tell me... They pleaded with us to pull
them out of the water... I pleaded with her, but Joan didn't want to go.*
V+PREP

plod /plɒd/ (plods, plodding, plodded)

plod away If you **plod away** at a particular job or task, you continue doing it without much enthusiasm. ❑ *Oh, keep plodding away, it'll get done!*
V+ADV:
ALSO+at

plod on If you **plod on**, you continue walking or doing something at the same slow pace as before. ❑ *She plodded on with her work, feeling tired and jaded.*
V+ADV

plonk /plɒŋk/ (plonks, plonking, plonked)
plonk down
1 If you **plonk** something **down**, you put it down roughly or carelessly. [BRITISH, INFORMAL] ❑ *...plonking down tea in front of me... They just plonk their feet down.*
V+ADV+N,
V+N+ADV,
V+PRON+ADV

2 If you **plonk down** or **plonk** yourself **down**, you sit down heavily and clumsily. [BRITISH, INFORMAL] ❑ *She plonked down in an armchair and lit a cigarette.*
V+ADV,
V+REFL+ADV

plop /plɒp/ (plops, plopping, plopped)
plop down If you **plop down** or **plop** yourself **down** somewhere, you sit down quickly but gently. [INFORMAL] ❑ *I plopped down on one of the dark red sofas... He plopped himself down on the grass.*
V+ADV,
V+REFL+ADV

[NOTE] **Sit down** means almost the same as **plop down**.

plot /plɒt/ (plots, plotting, plotted)

plot against If people **plot against** someone, they plan secretly to kill them or remove them from power. ❑ *Anyone convicted for suspicion of plotting against the king will be executed. ...people who think they're being plotted against.*
V+PREP:
HAS PASSIVE

plot out If you **plot out** a plan or course of events, you decide in advance what you will do. ❑ *We had plotted out a first rough plan... I had already plotted out the scenario in my mind.*
V+ADV+N,
V+N+ADV,
V+PRON+ADV

[NOTE] **Plan out** means almost the same as **plot out**.

plough /plaʊ/ (ploughs, ploughing, ploughed)

☑ **Plough** is also spelled **plow** in American English.

plough ahead If something or someone **ploughs ahead**, they increase or move ahead steadily. ❑ *Output continued to plough ahead.*
V+ADV

[NOTE] **Forge ahead** means almost the same as **plough ahead**.

plough back If you **plough** profits **back** into a business, you spend them on improving the business so that you can make more money. ❑ *He was happy to plough the first profits back into the business. ...a private rental system in which the profits are ploughed back into expanding the housing stock.*
V+N+ADV,
V+ADV+N,
V+PRON+ADV:
USUALLY+into

plough in If someone **ploughs in** a crop, they dig the plants into the ground to make the soil more fertile. ❑ *The stalks are left to be ploughed in for the next planting. ...grow the crop and then plough it in.*
V+N+ADV,
V+ADV+N,
V+PRON+ADV

★**plough into**
1 If something **ploughs into** something else, it crashes into it with a lot of force. ❑ *The car skidded before ploughing into the bank... Four tank regiments ploughed into the two brigades on the left.*
V+PREP:
HAS PASSIVE

2 If money **is ploughed into** something, it is spent on it or invested in it in large amounts. ❑ *...huge sums of money which could be ploughed into computing... Ford has ploughed more than 400 million pounds into its Halewood operation since 1982... The days when local authorities could protect schools by ploughing more money into them are over.*
V+N+PREP,
V+PRON+PREP:
USUALLY PASSIVE

3 If a crop **is ploughed into** the land, someone digs the plants into the ground to make the soil more fertile. ❑ *The crop can be grown as green manure to be ploughed into the land... The process is helped by ploughing the muck into the garden during the autumn.*
V+N+PREP,
V+PRON+PREP:
USUALLY PASSIVE

plough on If you **plough on**, you continue walking or doing something even though it is difficult for you. ❑ *...as they ploughed on to their destination... Jimmie hesitated for a moment and then ploughed on... Does faith mean ploughing blindly on without learning any lessons from our experiences?*
V+ADV

plough through
1 If you **plough through** a meal or piece of work, you eat it all or do it all, although it is difficult because there is a lot of it. ❑ *They must be given time to plough through their meals. ...gloomily ploughing through a plate of spaghetti... It would cost a fortune to pay someone to plough through all these.*
V+PREP

2 To **plough through** something also means to move through it, sometimes with difficulty. ❑ *The barrels kept coming, ploughing through the water... They ploughed slowly through the deluge.* — V+PREP

3 If a vehicle or a missile **ploughs through** something, it goes violently or carelessly through it as though it is out of control. ❑ *The car ploughed through three gardens and flattened a tree.* — V+PREP: NO PASSIVE

plough up If an area of land **is ploughed up**, the soil is turned over using a plough, especially on land which is being changed from grassland to land which will be used for growing crops. ❑ *They told him to plough up his meadows... They spent part of the time ploughing up the area... Nearly half of Wiltshire's chalk grassland was ploughed up to grow corn.* — V+ADV+N, V+N+ADV, V+PRON+ADV

plow /plaʊ/ **(plows, plowing, plowed)** → See plough

pluck /plʌk/ **(plucks, plucking, plucked)**

pluck at If you **pluck at** something, you take hold of it and pull it towards you with a sharp movement. ❑ *Lucas plucked at my blazer and asked if he could come too... He was sweating, and plucked now and then nervously at his shirt.* — V+PREP

NOTE **Pull at** means almost the same as **pluck at**.

plug /plʌg/ **(plugs, plugging, plugged)**

plug away If you **plug away** at something, you keep trying very hard to do something which you consider difficult or uninteresting. ❑ *He told them that they must keep plugging away... She plugged away at her maths.* — V+ADV: ALSO+at

★plug in If you **plug in** a piece of electrical equipment, you connect it to an electricity supply by pushing its plug into an electric socket. ❑ *I plugged in the kettle... He put on a record and plugged in the earphones... The lady across the aisle showed him how to plug his headphones in... A television set is a fire risk if left plugged in overnight.* — V+ADV+N, V+N+ADV, V+PRON+ADV

NOTE **Unplug** means the opposite of **plug in**.

★plug into

1 If you **plug** a piece of electrical equipment **into** something, you connect it to the thing, for example by means of a plug. ❑ *She plugged an electric razor into a wall-socket... He has a flash gun plugged into his camera... Portable computers can be plugged into TV sets... Plug it into the mains.* — V+N+PREP, V+PRON+PREP

2 If a piece of electrical equipment **plugs into** a source of electricity or another piece of equipment, it is designed to be powered by electricity or to be connected to the other piece of equipment. ❑ *The one we have at home plugs into the mains... The telephone plugs into ordinary telephone sockets.* — V+PREP

3 If you **plug** something **into** a hole or slot, you fit it into the hole or slot. ❑ *...balls of wax which you plug into your ear... He has a hearing device plugged into his ear.* — V+N+PREP, V+PRON+PREP

4 If you **plug into** a computer system, you are able to use it or see the information stored on it. ❑ *It is possible to plug into remote databases to pick up information.* — V+PREP

5 If you **plug into** a group of people or their ideas, you find out about them and try to understand them. [INFORMAL] ❑ *What I'm really trying to do is to plug into people's fantasies... This gave us a chance to plug into a new network of friends.* — V+PREP

plug up If you **plug up** a hole, you put something in it so that it is blocked. ❑ *The other opening was plugged up... She suggested plugging up the hole. ...plugging them up as the holes appeared.* — V+N+ADV, V+ADV+N, V+PRON+ADV

NOTE **Block up** and **bung up** mean almost the same as **plug up**.

plumb /plʌm/ **(plumbs, plumbing, plumbed)**

plumb in If you **plumb in** a bath, toilet, or washing machine, you connect it to the water and drainage pipes in a building. [BRITISH] ❑ *We've bought the washing machine, but it needs to be plumbed in... If there's a leak, it may not have been plumbed in properly.* — V+N+ADV, V+PRON+ADV

plumb into If you **plumb** something **into** the heating, water, or drainage system in a building, you connect it to that system. [BRITISH] ❑ *The shower can be plumbed into the existing central heating system.* — V+N+PREP, V+PRON+PREP

plump /plʌmp/ **(plumps, plumping, plumped)**

plump down

1 If you **plump down** or **plump** yourself **down**, you sit down suddenly or clum- — V+ADV,

point to

sily. [INFORMAL] ❏ *She plumped down with such force in one of the chairs... Clara plumped herself down on the bed.*
V+REFL+ADV

NOTE **Plonk down** means almost the same as **plump down**.

2 If you **plump** something **down**, you put it down suddenly and carelessly. [INFORMAL] ❏ *I plumped down my heavy paper bag and stood staring at the bar.*
V+ADV+N, V+N+ADV, V+PRON+ADV

NOTE **Plonk down** means almost the same as **plump down**.

plump for If you **plump for** someone or something, you choose them, often after a lot of hesitation or careful thought. ❏ *In the event, they plumped for a three-stage conference... The oil industry had plumped for unmanned underwater robots instead... Few gentlemen would now care to plump for an army career.*
V+PREP

NOTE **Opt for** means almost the same as **plump for**.

plump out If someone **plumps out**, they become fatter. [OLD-FASHIONED] ❏ *Zelly was plumping out in all the right places... Her face had plumped out.*
V+ADV

NOTE **Fill out** means almost the same as **plump out**.

plump up If you **plump up** something soft, you squeeze and shake it back into its proper shape. ❏ *'Serves him right,' said Mrs Waites, plumping up her pillow, 'Cathy and me took a week.'... The other woman plumped up the cushions and switched on the table lamps.*
V+ADV+N, V+N+ADV, V+PRON+ADV

plunge /plʌndʒ/ (plunges, plunging, plunged)

plunge in If you **plunge in**, you begin doing something suddenly, without thinking carefully or preparing for it. ❏ *...simply plunging in and hoping for the best... I plunged in hastily with another question... Tom hesitated, then plunged in. 'I'll start with my father.'*
V+ADV

plunge into If you **plunge into** an activity or particular subject, you start doing it suddenly or become deeply involved in it, often without thinking carefully or preparing for it first. ❏ *Marx plunged immediately into political work... My father abandoned common sense and plunged into a financial gamble... The men did not plunge deeply into any subject.*
V+PREP

NOTE **Dive into** means almost the same as **plunge into**.

ply /plaɪ/ (plies, plying, plied)

ply with

1 If you **ply** someone **with** food or drink, you keep on giving them more of it. ❏ *Dolly plied me with marshmallows and potato chips... They had plied him with too much drink... We sat and talked, plied with sugary tea prepared by Mum.*
V+PRON+PREP, V+N+PREP

2 If you **ply** someone **with** questions, you keep asking them questions. ❏ *I plied him with questions about his novel... Walking alongside, Lamin would ply Kunta with a steady stream of questions.*
V+PRON+PREP, V+N+PREP

point /pɔɪnt/ (points, pointing, pointed)

★point out

1 If you **point** an object or person **out**, you cause people to notice them or look at them, perhaps by indicating with your hand or head. ❏ *I'll point Lundberg out to you... I try to point it out to Chris, but by the time he looks it's gone... They go together up the stone stairway to the street, and she points out the café.*
V+N+ADV, V+PRON+ADV, V+ADV+N: ALSO+to

2 If you **point** something **out**, you give people an important piece of information or correct their mistaken ideas. ❏ *She pointed out that he was wrong... 'It's a golden opportunity, really,' Johnson pointed out. ...as I pointed out to you in a letter published last week... Mr Merritt pointed this problem out to you the other day... Critics were quick to point out the weaknesses in these arguments... He points out to Patrick that the garage also sells cigarettes.*
V+ADV+REPORT, V+ADV+QUOTE, V+N+ADV, V+ADV+N, V+PRON+ADV: ALSO+to

★point to

1 If you **point to** a fact or event, you use it as proof or evidence in an argument or discussion. ❏ *They point proudly to the administration's success... Optimistic Democrats can point to signs of change... She pointed to new opportunities in the area.*
V+PREP: HAS PASSIVE

2 If one fact or event **points to** another, it indicates that the other one is likely to be true or to happen. ❏ *There are many ways of defining poverty, but all point to the same*
V+PREP: HAS PASSIVE

conclusion. ...*if the baby has any of the symptoms that point to a severe infection... Does slow talking point to slow mental development?*

point up If you **point up** a fact or opinion, you emphasize it. [FORMAL] ❏ *Haig's speech pointed up the gap that still exists between U.S. and Europe... A series of coups also points up an unsuspected radical current... But this merely points up the differences again... The discussions seem to point up the mystical nature of the writing.*

V+ADV+N,
V+PRON+ADV

poke /pəʊk/ **(pokes, poking, poked)**

☑ **About** is used mainly in British English. In American English, **around** is much more common than **round**.

poke about → See **poke around**

poke around If you **poke around**, **poke about**, or **poke round** in a place, you look casually at the things there, often picking them up or moving them, because you want to find something but you are not sure what you want or what it looks like. ❏ *I found him poking about among your cupboards... Barbara poked around in the radical bookshops... 'Poke round for the matches, dear boy,' said Mother.*

V+ADV:
USUALLY+A

♦ If you have a **poke around**, a **poke about**, or a **poke round**, you search for something casually. ❏ *I went once myself to have a poke around.*

N-SING

poke at If you **poke at** something or someone, you push something sharp towards them and touch them with it, often repeatedly. ❏ *The chef poked at his little charcoal pile... Gretchen poked at his cheek with two fingers. 'Don't look so glum,' she said.*

V+PREP:
HAS PASSIVE

NOTE **Prod at** means almost the same as **poke at**.

poke out

1 If something **pokes out**, you only see part of it because the rest is hidden or covered. ❏ *A bottle of wine poked out of a silver ice bucket... We were warm under the cover, but our heads poked out and got very cold.*

V+ADV:
ALSO+of

NOTE **Stick out** means almost the same as **poke out**, and **protrude** is a more formal word.

2 If you **poke** something **out**, you move it so that it suddenly appears from a place where it was hidden or covered. ❏ *I poke my head out of the tent... She poked her tongue out at me.*

V+N+ADV,
V+PRON+ADV,
V+ADV+N:
ALSO+of

NOTE **Stick out** means almost the same as **poke out**.

poke round → See **poke around**

poke through If something **pokes through**, it is visible or becomes visible, after having pierced a surface or come through a hole. ❏ *His face is ruddy; white stubble is poking through. ...a wet armchair with a rusty spring poking through the fabric... He wore his tie poked through a ring... His secretary poked her head through an adjoining door.*

V+ADV/PREP,
V+N+ADV/PREP,
V+PRON+ADV/PREP:
ERGATIVE

poke up

1 If something **pokes up**, it is visible over the top of something else, or it becomes visible after being hidden under something. ❏ *Tufts of coarse grass were beginning to poke up among the gravel... Right in the middle there pokes up the Norman tower.*

V+ADV:
USUALLY+A

2 If you **poke up** a fire, you use a poker or other sharp tool to remove ash and make the fire burn more strongly. [OLD-FASHIONED] ❏ *I tucked him up, poked up the fire and went out into the hall... Leland had poked the fire up and thrown on another log.*

V+ADV+N,
V+N+ADV,
V+PRON+ADV

polish /ˈpɒlɪʃ/ **(polishes, polishing, polished)**

polish off

1 If you **polish off** food, you eat all of it. [INFORMAL] ❏ *She can polish off her favourite dish in 10 minutes... He'd just polished off the ham and eggs... The guests were probably deciding what they would polish off next.*

V+ADV+N,
V+PRON+ADV,
V+N+ADV

NOTE **Eat up** means almost the same as **polish off**.

2 If you **polish off** a task, you finish it completely and quickly. ❏ *I get all my office work ready in time for that day and it gets polished off in one go.*

V+ADV+N,
V+PRON+ADV,
V+N+ADV

3 If you **polish off** an opponent, especially in sports, you beat them. [JOURNALISM] ❏ *He polished off his opponents 21-2, 21-8 and 21-8... South Africa resume this morning on 278 for seven and England could well polish them off first thing.*

V+ADV+N,
V+PRON+ADV,
V+N+ADV
V+ADV+N,
V+N+ADV,
V+PRON+ADV

polish up

1 If you **polish up** a skill, a quality you have, or a piece of work you have done, you improve it by spending more time or effort on it. ❏ *Anne was polishing up her clas-*

V+ADV+N,
V+PRON+ADV

sical Greek. ...to polish up a fading memory before it is too late.

NOTE **Brush up** means almost the same as **polish up**.

2 If you **polish up** an object, you rub it with a cloth to make it shine. ❏ *My sister had the spoons and was polishing them up with a yellow duster... I polished up the handle of the big front door.* V+PRON+ADV,
V+ADV+N,
V+N+ADV

ponce /pɒns/ (ponces, poncing, ponced)

ponce about If you say that someone **is poncing about** or **poncing around**, you mean that they are not doing what they are supposed to be doing or not doing it properly or seriously; used showing disapproval. [BRITISH, INFORMAL] ❏ *Stop poncing around and help me with this box.* V+ADV

NOTE **Muck about** and **lark about** mean almost the same as **ponce about**.

ponce around → See **ponce about**

pony /pəʊni/ (ponies, ponying, ponied)

pony up If you **pony up** a sum of money, you pay the money that is needed for something, often unwillingly. [AMERICAN, INFORMAL] ❏ *The IMF is not prepared to pony up the second half of the $4 billion... People can't even afford to pony up for movie tickets.* V+ADV+N,
V+ADV:
ALSO+for

NOTE **Stump up** means almost the same as **pony up**.

pop /pɒp/ (pops, popping, popped)

★**pop in** If you **pop in**, you go to a friend's house or a shop casually. [BRITISH, INFORMAL] ❏ *They pop in for a coffee and a chat... I can pop in tomorrow perhaps and let you know.* V+ADV

pop off

1 If you **pop off** somewhere, you leave the place that you are in. [BRITISH, INFORMAL] ❏ *'I've got to pop off just now,' Elizabeth said... Well, you'd better pop off for lunch now, Deirdre. I'll carry on.* V+ADV

2 If you say that someone **has popped off**, you mean that they have died. [BRITISH, INFORMAL] ❏ *I'll come to your funeral when you pop off.* V+ADV

3 If someone **pops off**, they say or write something very angrily or in a very emotional way. [AMERICAN, INFORMAL] ❏ *The others are meeting to see what they can do to shut him up. He's been popping off to the press.* V+ADV

pop on If you **pop on** an item of clothing, you put it on quickly. [BRITISH, INFORMAL] ❏ *Pop on your party frock and come down to the Yandina Club.* V+ADV+N,
V+PRON+ADV,
V+N+ADV

★**pop out**

1 If someone or something that you could not see **pops out**, they suddenly appear. ❏ *A station wagon popped out of the leafy shade of the avenue... Suddenly she popped out from behind a bush.* V+ADV:
USUALLY+A

2 If you are in a building and **pop out**, you go out of the building. [BRITISH, INFORMAL] ❏ *I popped out for a drink. ...leaving her to pop out and ring you... I popped out to the car park to cool off.* V+ADV:
USUALLY+A

pop up

1 If someone or something **pops up**, they appear in a place or situation unexpectedly. ❏ *Glazunov had popped up out of nowhere. ...one of those military rebels who pops up every so often... Problems kept popping up.* V+ADV

NOTE **Surface** is a more formal word for **pop up**.

2 If the pictures in a children's book **pop up**, they stand up from the pages as you open it. ❏ *...such as folded pictures that pop up from a book.* V+ADV

◆ **Pop-up** describes pictures that stand up from the pages of a book or the books that contain such pictures. ❏ *Some books are toys in disguise, like those with pop-up pictures.* ADJECTIVE

pore /pɔːr/ (pores, poring, pored)

pore over If you **pore over** writing, a map, or a chart, you look at it and examine it very carefully. ❏ *Monks pored over ancient texts... He got out the chart and pored over it in a vain attempt to discover where they were. ...like a boy poring over a stamp album.* V+PREP:
HAS PASSIVE

portion /pɔːrʃən/ (portions, portioning, portioned)

portion out If you **portion** something **out**, you give a part of it to each person in a group. ❏ *...the pie that Tim was carefully portioning out... The presents were then fur-* V+ADV+N,
V+N+ADV,
V+PRON+ADV *ther portioned out.*

NOTE **Share out** means almost the same as **portion out**.

post /poʊst/ (posts, posting, posted)

post up If you **post up** a notice or sign, you fix it to a wall or noticeboard so that people can see it. ❑ *The same week a holiday list was posted up in the main office... The price was posted up plain to see. Thirty New Francs... She used to post it up for all to see.*

V+N+ADV,
V+ADV+N,
V+PRON+ADV:
USUALLY+A

potter /pɒtər/ (potters, pottering, pottered)

potter about If you **potter about** or **potter around**, you pass the time in a gentle, unhurried way, doing small and unimportant tasks. [BRITISH] ❑ *The house was refreshingly peaceful, and I pottered about enjoying my leisure and solitude... He loved to potter around in the garden... We pottered around several antique shops.*

V+ADV,
V+PREP

potter around → See **potter about**

pounce /paʊns/ (pounces, pouncing, pounced)

pounce on

1 If someone **pounces on** or **pounces upon** you, they suddenly come up to you and take hold of you roughly or violently. ❑ *Three men wearing masks pounced on Mr Culshaw... He was pounced upon by a gang of youths.*

V+PREP:
HAS PASSIVE

2 If you **pounce on** or **pounce upon** something that someone says or does, you eagerly draw attention to it. ❑ *His colleagues were watching his every step, ready to pounce upon any slip he made... Pouncing on an idea as soon as it appears kills the idea... Any coincidence was pounced upon and discussed avidly.*

V+PREP:
HAS PASSIVE

NOTE **Seize on** means almost the same as **pounce on**.

pounce upon → See **pounce on**

pour /pɔːr/ (pours, pouring, poured)

pour away If you **pour** a liquid **away**, you pour it out of a container because you no longer need it or cannot use it any more. ❑ *Instead of pouring the digested liquid food away, we absorb the food ingredients into our bloodstream... Three days' milk has been poured away so far... The dregs of powder paint had been poured away and gleaming jam jars awaited.*

V+N+ADV,
V+PRON+ADV,
V+ADV+N

NOTE **Throw away** is a more general expression for **pour away**.

pour down When rain **pours down**, it falls very heavily. ❑ *The rain poured down, the rivers overflowed, and the wind blew hard against the cabin door... The rain still poured down.*

V+ADV

NOTE **Pelt down** means almost the same as **pour down**.

♦ A **downpour** is a very heavy shower of rain. ❑ *...sheltering from a downpour.*

N-COUNT

pour forth When things **pour forth**, they emerge from somewhere suddenly and in large quantities. ❑ *The primus poured forth a hissing cloud of noxious paraffin vapour... They poured forth from their homes, shouting and clapping.*

V+ADV,
V+ADV+N:
ERGATIVE

★pour in When people or things **pour in**, they arrive somewhere very quickly and in large numbers. ❑ *At first the British did not quite know what to do with these people pouring in over their border... Messages of encouragement poured in... Food donations have poured in from all over the country.*

V+ADV

NOTE **Flood in** means almost the same as **pour in**.

★pour into

1 When people or things **pour into** a place, they arrive there very quickly and in large numbers. ❑ *There were hundreds in our ranks as we poured into the building... In a matter of hours telegrams and telephone calls began to pour into the sheriff's office... When this drain blocked up the floods poured into our kitchen.*

V+PREP

NOTE **Flood into** means almost the same as **pour into**.

2 If you **pour** money or supplies **into** an activity or organization, a lot of money or supplies are given in order to do the activity or help the organization. ❑ *The Government continues to pour billions of pounds into its massive road-building programme.*

V+N+PREP,
V+PRON+PREP

pour off When you **pour off** some liquid from a container, you pour some of the liquid out and leave the rest in the container. ❑ *If you use this rich milk, you should pour off a little of the cream... Pour off half the quantity and add an equal amount of boiled water.*

V+ADV+N,
V+N+ADV,
V+PRON+ADV

pour on To pour scorn **on** someone or **pour** it **upon** them means to talk about them or their ideas with contempt and show that you have a very low opinion of them. ❑ *He wasn't content merely to pour scorn on my arguments... But when it comes to the control of the police, he poured contempt upon elected people.*

V+N+PREP

★**pour out**

1 If you **pour out** a drink, you fill a cup or glass with the drink. ❑ *Castle poured out two glasses of whisky... Tim poured out some more wine. ...hostesses pouring tea out from silver tea pots.*

V+ADV+N,
V+N+ADV,
V+PRON+ADV

NOTE Serve means almost the same as **pour out**.

2 If you **pour out** your thoughts, feelings, or experiences, you suddenly tell someone all about them, quickly and without being able to stop yourself. ❑ *I was on the verge of pouring out all my feelings... He poured out a horrifying story... I poured it all out to him – the arguments, fights, the hatred... My accumulated resentments poured out in response to this unwarranted attack.*

V+ADV+N,
V+N+ADV,
V+PRON+ADV,
V+ADV:
ERGATIVE

♦ **Outpourings** are things that you say or write which seem uncontrolled and irrational and indicate that you are very angry or upset about something. ❑ *...the hysterical outpourings of fanatics.*

N-COUNT

3 When things or people **pour out**, they come out of somewhere suddenly and in large amounts or numbers. ❑ *Black smoke was pouring out of the slanted chimney... Energy and enthusiasm seemed to be pouring out of people... Water was pouring out of the tap... I saw them pour out by the thousands and scurry frantically to get away... Factories poured out new plastics, cheap, sturdy and reliable.*

V+ADV,
V+ADV+N,
V+PRON+ADV:
ERGATIVE,
ALSO+of

♦ An **outpouring** is a large quantity of things emerging from somewhere very quickly. ❑ *The explosion of the volcano set free a red-hot catastrophic outpouring. ...the almost inexhaustible outpouring of heat from the interior of the earth.*

N-COUNT

pour upon → See pour on

power /paʊəʳ/ (powers, powering, powered)

power up When an engine or computer **powers up** or **is powered up**, it is switched on and starts working. ❑ *Discovery's navigation system is being powered up today... The engines began to power up with a loud vibrating hum.*

V+ADV,
V+N+ADV,
V+PRON+ADV,
V+ADV+N

preclude /prɪkluːd/ (precludes, precluding, precluded)

preclude from If a set of circumstances **precludes** you **from** doing something, they make it impossible for you to do it. ❑ *Its methodology would preclude critics from explaining why one book is better than another... It sets limits on the powers of the Government, and precludes it from acting unconstitutionally.*

V+N+PREP,
V+PRON+PREP

predispose /priːdɪspoʊz/ (predisposes, predisposing, predisposed)

predispose to If something **predisposes** you **to** or **presidposes** you **towards** a particular action, belief, or state, it has a great influence on you, and causes you to do that action, have that belief, or be in that state. [FORMAL] ❑ *His education and his history as a Government official predispose him to bureaucratic modes of thinking and acting... It is now known that too much alcohol from any source predisposes one to a heart attack... She is predisposed towards action because she is confused by events beyond her control.*

V+PRON+PREP,
V+N+PREP

predispose towards → See predispose to

preside /prɪzaɪd/ (presides, presiding, presided)

preside over

1 If you **preside over** an official occasion or event, you are in charge of it and are considered by other people to be in control of it or responsible for it. [FORMAL] ❑ *He had presided over a seminar for theoretical physicists... I did not become His Majesty's Prime Minister in order to preside over the dissolution of the British Empire. ...the men presiding over this quiet revolution... On 31 January the two bodies held a joint rally, presided over by Lord George-Brown.*

V+PREP:
HAS PASSIVE

2 If an object **presides over** a place, it is much larger or taller than anything else there, and therefore dominates the area. [FORMAL] ❑ *A large figure in stone presides massively over the approach to the museum. ...an arid landscape, presided over by looming mountains.*

V+PREP:
HAS PASSIVE

press /pres/ (presses, pressing, pressed)

press ahead If you **press ahead** with an activity or task, you begin or con-

V+ADV:

tinue doing it in a determined way, knowing that it may take a long time or be very difficult. ❑ *He has pressed ahead with talks... They have pressed ahead with bigger and more profitable schemes... Mrs Castle, whose pride is at stake, is determined to press ahead.* NOTE **Go ahead** means almost the same as **press ahead**.

USUALLY+*with*

press for

1 If you **press for** something, you try hard to achieve it or obtain it by working to persuade people that it is important and necessary. ❑ *He continued to press for a peaceful solution... The landless labourers formed a union to press for higher wages... He pressed for full public ownership... When I pressed him for an explanation his voice turned cold.*

V+PREP,
V+PRON+PREP,
V+N+PREP

2 If you **are pressed for** time or money, you do not have enough of it. ❑ *He was always pressed for money and usually in poor health... I told him I was a little pressed for time.*

PASSIVE:
V+PREP

press into If you **press** someone **into** an activity, you force them to become involved in it or to take it up. ❑ *The expedition to capture the Brighton fishermen and press them into naval service had been a total failure... She found herself pressed into the role of assistant astronomer... I was pressed into rugby under compulsion.*

V+PRON+PREP,
V+N+PREP

★press on

1 If you **press on** with an activity or task, you continue doing it, despite the fact that it is difficult and might not succeed. ❑ *They courageously pressed on with their vital repair work... Babbage pressed on alone, achieving little... We are just pressing on regardless.* NOTE **Carry on** means almost the same as **press on**, and **give up** means the opposite.

V+ADV:
ALSO+*with*

2 If you **press on** with a journey, you continue it, even though it is becoming more difficult or dangerous. ❑ *Otto would press on with all speed for Bear Island... The rest of us said a prayer and pressed on... I wanted to press on, in spite of the weather.* NOTE **Carry on** means almost the same as **press on**, and **turn back** means the opposite.

V+ADV

3 → See **press upon**

press upon If you **press** something **upon** someone, or **press** it **on** them, you give it to them in a very forceful way so that they cannot avoid taking it, even if they do not really want it. ❑ *I pressed biscuits and lemonade upon them... They were flattered enough by the gifts that were pressed upon them... I refused the five shillings that she tried to press on me.* NOTE **Thrust upon** means almost the same as **press upon**.

V+N+PREP,
V+PRON+PREP

pretty /prɪti/ (pretties, prettying, prettied)

pretty up If you **pretty** something **up**, you try to make it appear more attractive or acceptable. ❑ *...men starting to pretty themselves up a bit with state-of-the-art ties and socks... There was so much of it he didn't have time for prettying it up. ...robots called after film stars and all prettied up with ribbons.*

V+REFL+ADV,
V+PRON+ADV,
V+N+ADV,
V+ADV+N

prevail /prɪveɪl/ (prevails, prevailing, prevailed)

prevail on If you **prevail on** or **prevail upon** someone to do something which they are reluctant to do, you succeed in persuading them to do it. [FORMAL] ❑ *He prevailed on the head reception clerk to book him a single room... Finally she prevailed upon George Clinton to allow his name to go on the ballot paper... Ted had been prevailed upon to bring his flute.*

V+PREP:
HAS PASSIVE

prevail upon → See **prevail on**

prey /preɪ/ (preys, preying, preyed)

prey on

1 An animal or bird that **preys on** or **preys upon** other creatures lives by catching and eating them. ❑ *Short-eared owls prey on voles as well as small birds... It is itself preyed upon by the cod shoals.*

V+PREP:
HAS PASSIVE

2 Someone who **preys on** or **preys upon** other people exploits them or gets satisfaction from treating them badly or violently, and is constantly looking for new victims. ❑ *...successful producers, writers, directors, actors, who preyed on beautiful women with lustful hatred... His favourite victims are innocent young women in nightdresses; he also preys upon young men.*

V+PREP:
HAS PASSIVE

For a full explanation of all grammatical labels, see pages xiii-xx

prod at

3 If something **preys on** or **preys upon** your mind, it worries you a lot and you cannot stop thinking about it. ❑ *Barton reluctantly agreed, but the decision preyed on his mind... When you're not punished for it it preys on your conscience... It's intolerable only if you let it prey upon your mind.*   V+PREP

prey upon → See **prey on**

prick /prɪk/ (pricks, pricking, pricked)

prick out If you **prick out** young plants, especially seedlings, you plant them in small holes which you make in the soil using a thin stick. ❑ *...pricking out an inch-high seedling in fine soil... Prick the young plants out and continue feeding them each week.*   V+ADV+N, V+N+ADV, V+PRON+ADV

prick up If someone **pricks up** their ears or if their ears **prick up**, they suddenly start to listen eagerly after hearing an interesting sound or an important piece of information. ❑ *She stopped talking to prick up her ears... Ears which prick up at the mention of royalty are sure to be disappointed.*   V+ADV+N, V+N+ADV, V+ADV: ERGATIVE

print /prɪnt/ (prints, printing, printed)

print off If you **print off** a certain number of copies of something, you print as many as you need at that time. ❑ *Any items needed for permanent reference could be printed off as soon as located on a copying machine.*   V+ADV+N, V+N+ADV, V+PRON+ADV

♦ An **offprint** is a separately printed copy of an article or chapter from a book. ❑ *He gave me some offprints of papers in which he expressed doubts about the Copenhagen interpretation.*   N-COUNT

★**print out** When a computer, or a machine attached to a computer, **prints out** information, it reproduces it on paper. ❑ *He had determined that it should not only calculate tables, but also print them out on paper at the end. ...TV transmitters that would actually display or print out the material in his own living room... The projects are printed out, ready to use.*   V+PRON+ADV, V+ADV+N, V+N+ADV

♦ **Printout** is paper on which information from a computer has been printed, either by the computer itself or by a printing machine attached to the computer. ❑ *The computer printouts are on Howie's desk every morning.*   N-COUNT, N-UNCOUNT

print up If someone **prints up** something such as a book or newspaper, they produce it in large quantities using a machine. [AMERICAN] ❑ *Community workers here are printing up pamphlets for peace demonstrations... Hey, I know what, I'll get a bumper sticker printed up.*   V+ADV+N, V+N+ADV, V+PRON+ADV

prise /praɪz/ (prises, prising, prised)

✓ **Prise** is sometimes spelled **prize**.

prise out If you **prise** something **out** of someone, you succeed in getting it from them only with difficulty because they are very unwilling to give it to you. [BRITISH] ❑ *They hope that the growing publicity will prise more money out of the California State Legislature to create more training programmes... Christopher had prized out of her in an unguarded moment some recollection about her early schooldays.*   V+N+ADV, V+ADV+N, V+PRON+ADV: ALSO+of

[NOTE] In American English, **pry out** means almost the same as **prise out**.

prize /praɪz/ (prizes, prizing, prized) → See **prise**

proceed /prəsiːd/ (proceeds, proceeding, proceeded)

proceed against To **proceed against** a person or organization means to begin a legal action against them. [FORMAL] ❑ *Card reaffirmed that he would give evidence if the State proceeded against me... The Inquisition proceeded against all those whose allegiance was in question... The publishers sought to take action so that the offenders might be proceeded against with all speed and dignity.*   V+PREP: HAS PASSIVE

[NOTE] **Prosecute** means almost the same as **proceed against**.

proceed from If something **proceeds from** a particular idea, it starts there and seems to be a logical conclusion. ❑ *...a conviction which proceeds from the belief that they possess absolute truth... Optimism was proceeding from the sort of results that were coming through.*   V+PREP

prod /prɒd/ (prods, prodding, prodded)

prod at If you **prod at** something, you hit it with your fingertip or with a long instrument such as a stick or spoon. ❑ *She prodded at the contents of the pan... They*   V+PREP *would prod at the cows with sticks to get them moving.*

NOTE **Poke at** means almost the same as **prod at.**

pronounce /prənaʊns/ **(pronounces, pronouncing, pronounced)**

pronounce on If you **pronounce on** or **pronounce upon** something, you   V+PREP
give an expert opinion or judgment about it. [FORMAL] ❑ *She was asked to pronounce
on the merits of an eighteenth century table. ...an official body set up to pronounce upon
questions of national economic planning.*

pronounce upon → See **pronounce on**

prop /prɒp/ **(props, propping, propped)**

★**prop up**

  1 If you **prop** something **up**, you support it in a particular position by putting   V+PRON+ADV,
  something underneath it or resting it against something. ❑ *So we left off the door in*   V+N+ADV,
  the summer and just propped it up in the winter. ...like the timbers that are sometimes used   V+REFL+ADV,
  to prop a building up during alterations... He propped himself up on an elbow and watched   V+ADV+N
  her... Anne lay in bed, propped up with pillows.

  2 If a government or group of people **props up** an organization or country which   V+ADV+N,
  is unlikely to survive on its own, they give it support and help it to survive. ❑ *The*   V+PRON+ADV
  *Government does not intend to prop up declining industries... Between 1975-79 Labour
  propped up the old order and papered over the cracks with the TUC by means of a compromise... We should prop up countries run on more or less liberal lines.*

protect /prətɛkt/ **(protects, protecting, protected)**

★**protect against**

  1 To **protect** someone or something **against** an unpleasant event or situation   V+PREP,
  means to prevent the unpleasant event or situation from happening, or from having   V+N+PREP,
  a harmful effect. ❑ *Mr. Reagan said his plan would stimulate the economy and protect*   V+PRON+PREP
  *against inflation... Babies are protected against diseases like measles by their mothers' milk...
  Tanning lotions may help a little, but they can't protect you against a large amount of sunshine.*

  NOTE **Protect from** means almost the same as **protect against.**

  2 If an insurance policy **protects** you **against** events such as death, injury, or   V+N+PREP,
  theft, it promises to give money to you or your family if that event happens. ❑ *Lloyds*   V+PRON+PREP,
  Bank travellers cheques protect your money against loss and theft... Part of the deal would   V+PREP
  protect the consumer against serious injury.

  NOTE **Insure against** means almost the same as **protect against.**

★**protect from** To **protect** someone or something **from** an unpleasant event or   V+PRON+PREP,
situation means to prevent that event or situation from having a harmful effect.   V+REFL+PREP,
❑ *His hat was pulled down over his face to protect it from the sun... Any animal will struggle*   V+N+PREP
*to protect itself from a threat of death... He's probably a nice old gentleman who simply
wants to be protected from the irritations of everyday existence.*

  NOTE **Protect against** means almost the same as **protect from.**

provide /prəvaɪd/ **(provides, providing, provided)**

provide against To **provide against** a particular event, situation, or circum-   V+PREP:
stance means to prevent it from happening. [FORMAL] ❑ *The landlord insisted on a cov-*   HAS PASSIVE
*enant to provide against the client's insolvency... It is not always possible to ensure that all
risks are provided against.*

★**provide for**

  1 If you **provide for** someone, you give them money, clothes, and the other   V+PREP:
  things they need. ❑ *Parents are expected to provide for their children... Our nursery pro-*   HAS PASSIVE
  vides for all the needs of very young children... Is he provided for financially?

  2 If you **provide for** a possible future event, you make arrangements to deal with   V+PREP:
  it. [FORMAL] ❑ *The original estimates did provide for 3 per cent per annum inflation... In eco-*   HAS PASSIVE
  *nomics, the solution offered may provide for freedom... The original agreement had indeed
  provided for the possibility of a review.*

  NOTE **Allow for** means almost the same as **provide for.**

  3 If a law or decision **provides for** a course of action, it makes that course of ac-   V+PREP:
  tion possible. [FORMAL] ❑ *The Act provided for financial penalties to be imposed on all of-*   HAS PASSIVE
  fenders.

For a full explanation of all grammatical labels, see pages xiii-xx

★provide with If you **provide** someone **with** something, you give it to them or lend it to them so that they have it when they need it. ❑ *Your brother Rudolph was good enough to provide me with your address in New York... I provided him with money and a basket... The first aim is to provide readers with a comprehensive text.*

V+PRON+PREP, V+N+PREP

prune /pruːn/ (**prunes, pruning, pruned**)

prune back

1 When you **prune back** a tree or bush, you cut off some of the branches so that it will grow better the next year. ❑ *Apples, pears and cherries can be pruned back when they've lost their leaves.*

V+ADV+N, V+N+ADV, V+PRON+ADV

2 If you **prune back** something, you get rid of all the parts that you do not need. ❑ *The company has pruned back its workforce by 20,000 since 1989.*

V+ADV+N, V+N+ADV, V+PRON+ADV

pry /praɪ/ (**pries, prying, pried**)

pry out If you **pry** something such as information **out** of someone, you persuade them to tell you although they may be very unwilling to. [AMERICAN] ❑ *...their attempts to pry the names out of the Bureau of Alcohol, Tobacco and Firearms.*

V+N+ADV, V+PRON+ADV, V+ADV+N: ALSO+of

NOTE In British English, **prise out** means almost the same as **pry out**.

psych /saɪk/ (**psychs, psyching, psyched**)

✔ Psych and psychs are also spelled **psyche** and **psyches**.

psych out If you **psych out** your opponent in a contest, you try to make them feel less confident by behaving in a very confident or aggressive way. [INFORMAL] ❑ *'What's psyching you out?' What could I tell her that she didn't already know?*

V+PRON+ADV, V+N+ADV, V+ADV+N

psych up If you **psych** yourself **up** before a contest or a difficult task, you prepare yourself for it mentally by telling yourself that you can win or succeed. [INFORMAL] ❑ *As usual, they spent an hour before the kick-off psyching themselves up.*

V+REFL+ADV

psyche /saɪki/ (**psyches, psyching, psyched**) → See psych

puff /pʌf/ (**puffs, puffing, puffed**)

puff away If someone **puffs away** when they are smoking a cigarette or a pipe, they keep sucking smoke into their mouth and blowing it out again. ❑ *George would light up and puff away for a while... Richie nodded and puffed away on his pipe.*

V+ADV

puff out

1 When part of your body **puffs out**, or when you **puff** it **out**, it becomes larger and rounder as if it is filled with air. ❑ *A swelling that puffs out quickly on a child's skull after a fall doesn't mean anything serious in itself if there are no other symptoms... He sat back and puffed out his cheeks... Mr Willet puffed out his moustache with disgust.*

V+ADV, V+ADV+N, V+N+ADV, V+PRON+ADV: ERGATIVE

2 If you are **puffed out**, you are tired and short of breath because you have just done some hard physical exercise. ❑ *I had a couple of jogs and was very puffed out... By the time we had climbed up to the top of Long Burgh Hill I was pretty well puffed out.*

ADJECTIVE

puff up

1 If part of your body **puffs up** as a result of an injury or allergy, it becomes swollen. ❑ *Her whole body was puffing up like a balloon from the steroids.... He could feel the side of his head puff up.*

V+ADV

NOTE **Swell up** means almost the same as **puff up**.

2 Someone who is **puffed up** is very proud of themselves because they think that they are very important; used showing disapproval. ❑ *I was expecting that he would return all puffed up with himself.*

ADJECTIVE

pull /pʊl/ (**pulls, pulling, pulled**)

✔ About is used mainly in British English. In American English, **around** is much more common than **round**.

pull about → See pull around

pull ahead

1 If you **pull ahead**, you gradually increase the amount by which you are ahead of someone or something behind you. ❑ *The cars climbed to higher and higher speeds, each straining to pull ahead... I spurted towards the foot of the hill and pulled ahead of Robin.*

V+ADV: ALSO+of

NOTE **Fall behind** means the opposite of **pull ahead**.

2 If you **pull ahead** of other people, you gradually become more skilful or success-

V+ADV:

ful than they are. ❑ *Fiona seemed clever and would probably pull ahead of him.*

USUALLY+*of*

NOTE **Get ahead** means almost the same as **pull ahead**, and **fall behind** means the opposite.

pull apart

1 When you **pull** something **apart** or when it **pulls apart**, it separates into two or more pieces. ❑ *Cameron pulled the soft dough apart... She joined her thumb and index finger, and then pulled them gently apart. ...if you pull apart one of those calculators... The flesh pulled apart, and bloody entrails spilled out.*

V+N+ADV,
V+PRON+ADV,
V+ADV+N,
V+ADV:
ERGATIVE

2 If you **pull** people or animals **apart** when they are fighting, you separate them using force. ❑ *I rushed in and tried to pull the dogs apart... William got hurt trying to pull them apart.*

V+N+ADV,
V+PRON+ADV

3 If someone **pulls apart** something that you have written or said, they criticize it severely. ❑ *The critics just pulled his last novel apart... She just pulled my argument apart in about five minutes.*

V+N+ADV,
V+PRON+ADV

NOTE **Take apart** means almost the same as **pull apart**.

4 To **pull** someone **apart** means to cause them great mental suffering. ❑ *Their rows are enough to pull that child apart... She was pulled apart by his thoughtlessness.*

V+N+ADV,
V+PRON+ADV

NOTE **Tear apart** means almost the same as **pull apart**.

pull around

1 If you **pull** someone or something **around** or **pull** them **about**, you move or handle them in a rough, violent way. ❑ *A novice rider often pulls the horse about to hurry it out of its stride... Wrestlers push and pull one another around the ring... Stop pulling me about. Who do you think you are?*

V+N+ADV,
V+PRON+ADV

2 When you **pull** someone or something **around** or **pull** them **round**, you turn them so that they are facing in the opposite direction. ❑ *I pulled her round to face me... The helicopter pulled round in a tight circle... She pulled her car around to the side of the station.*

V+N+ADV,
V+PRON+ADV

pull aside If you **pull** someone **aside**, you take them away to a different part of a room in order to have a private conversation with them. ❑ *Willie would pull him aside by the elbow and whisper to him... The Major pulled me aside and said, 'Listen.'*

V+N+ADV,
V+PRON+ADV

NOTE **Take aside** means almost the same as **pull aside**.

pull at

1 If you **pull at** something, you hold it and move it towards you and then let it go again. ❑ *They walked along the path in silence, pulling at the tall summer grasses... 'Come home now, Jim,' she said, pulling at his sleeve.*

V+PREP

2 If you **pull at** a cigarette or pipe, you take a long, deep breath of smoke from it when it is in your mouth. ❑ *'Oh, I'm not complaining,' Arnold said, pulling at his cigarette.*

V+PREP

★pull away

1 When a vehicle **pulls away**, it starts moving forward. ❑ *The bus pulled away... He shoved the truck into gear and pulled away from the scene of the accident.*

V+ADV:
ALSO+*from*

NOTE **Pull off** means almost the same as **pull away**.

2 If you **pull away** from someone who is holding you, you suddenly move away from them. ❑ *She bent and kissed the top of his head, but he pulled away... He burst into tears and pulled away from me.*

V+ADV:
ALSO+*from*

NOTE **Pull back** means almost the same as **pull away**.

3 If you **pull** someone or something **away**, you take hold of them and remove them using force. ❑ *Hendricks bent down to pull some of the weed away... I pulled away her hands which covered her face... I was impressed by his bookshelves, but he pulled me away before I could examine them too closely.*

V+N+ADV,
V+ADV+N,
V+PRON+ADV

4 If something **pulls away** from something else, it becomes separated or detached from it. ❑ *The sole had pulled away from the shoe.*

V+ADV:
ALSO+*from*

NOTE **Come away** means almost the same as **pull away**.

5 If you **pull away** from someone that you have had close links with, you deliberately become less close to them. ❑ *Other daughters, faced with their mother's emotional hunger, pull away... He'd pulled away from her as if she had leprosy.*

V+ADV:
ALSO+*from*

★pull back

1 If you **pull back**, you suddenly move away from someone or something. ❑ *He*

V+ADV:

tried to kiss her but she pulled back... She pulled back from the window. ALSO+from

NOTE Draw back means almost the same as **pull back**.

2 When you **pull** someone or something **back**, you hold them and move them V+N+ADV,
backwards. ❑ He pulled his chair back... The women pulled their children back in fear... He V+PRON+ADV, V+ADV+N:
unexpectedly laid his hand on my arm and pulled me back... He walked over to the bed and ALSO+from
pulled back the covers.

3 When an army **pulls back** or **is pulled back**, it leaves its position and retreats. V+ADV,
❑ The troops were being hard pressed as they pulled back... The enemy is not willing to pull V+N+ADV, V+PRON+ADV,
back from any of its present positions. ...a Marine who'd just pulled his whole squad back. V+ADV+N: ERGATIVE

NOTE Withdraw means almost the same as **pull back**.

4 If you **pull back** from something, you decide not to proceed with it, because you V+ADV:
are afraid of what might happen. ❑ It is hard to believe they will pull back from this deal... ALSO+from
He knows when to pull back. It has always been one of his great virtues.

NOTE Back out and draw back mean almost the same as **pull back**.

★**pull down**

1 If you **pull** something **down**, you move it from a higher position to a lower one. V+N+ADV,
❑ She pulled his head down to kiss him... They pulled down the window shades... She pulled V+ADV+N, V+PRON+ADV
up a sleeve to show him; then she pulled it down again... He wore a brown cloth cap with
the peak pulled down over his eyes.

NOTE Pull up means the opposite of **pull down**.

2 If a building or other structure **is pulled down**, it is deliberately destroyed, so V+N+ADV,
that the land that it is on can be used. ❑ Why did they pull all those houses down?... It V+ADV+N, V+PRON+ADV
was proposed to pull down Chartres Cathedral... The council said it would close the flats and
pull them down.

NOTE Demolish is a more formal word for **pull down**, and put up means the opposite.

3 If someone or something **pulls** you **down**, they make you feel depressed and V+PRON+ADV,
cause you to fail or do badly at something. [INFORMAL] ❑ Those snobs are going to pull V+N+ADV
me down if they can... I'm not being pulled down by anybody.

NOTE Drag down means almost the same as **pull down**.

4 The amount of money someone **pulls down** is the amount of money they earn V+ADV+N
regularly from their job. [AMERICAN, INFORMAL] ❑ Daniel was pulling down a weekly income of fifty dollars.

pull for If you **are pulling for** someone, you help or support them when they V+PREP
are having problems. [INFORMAL] ❑ A lot of officers here have been pulling for you... We
were really pulling for the kid.

NOTE Root for means almost the same as **pull for**.

★**pull in**

1 When a car, lorry, or bus **pulls in**, it is driven to the side of the road or to a V+ADV:
place where it can stop. ❑ He pulls in behind a Citroen... They decided to pull in at the first USUALLY+A
small taverna in the next village... They saw a filling station and pulled in.

NOTE Pull up means almost the same as **pull in**.

♦ A **pull-in** is a cafe on a main road where you can get cheap meals. [BRITISH, N-COUNT
INFORMAL] ❑ We stopped at a pull-in on the way.

2 When a train **pulls in**, it arrives at a station and stops. ❑ As the 4.30 to Newcastle V+ADV
pulled in, there was a mad scramble to get on.

NOTE Pull out means the opposite of **pull in**.

3 To **pull** people **in** means to attract them in large numbers. ❑ Higher wages in the V+ADV+N,
cities pull in the rural poor... The football matches pulled in big crowds... Let's face it, it's not V+PRON+ADV, V+N+ADV
the low prices that's pulling them in, is it?

4 When the police **pull** someone **in**, they go to find them and arrest them. V+N+ADV,
[INFORMAL] ❑ The police decided to pull the suspects in. ...asking about the identity of that V+ADV+N, V+PRON+ADV
man we pulled in... Police pulled in the elusive Jonathan Logan.

5 If you **pull in** a particular amount of money, especially a large amount, you earn V+ADV+N,
it. [INFORMAL] ❑ I got greedy. I was pulling in money hand over fist. V+N+ADV, V+PRON+ADV: NO PASSIVE

NOTE Rake in means almost the same as **pull in**.

★**pull into**

1 When a car, train, or other vehicle **pulls into** a place, it arrives there and stops. V+PREP

The symbol ★ shows key phrasal verbs

❏ *He pulled into the small parking lot... The car had pulled into the side... The London train pulled into the branch line station... At Barog, the train pulled into a siding.*

2 If someone or something **pulls** you **into** a particular situation, activity, or arrangement, they involve you in it. ❏ *Harbouring refugees can pull a neutral country into a conflict. ...pulling Britain into the mainstream of digital telephones... We have been pulled into an arrangement against our will.*

V+N+PREP,
V+PRON+PREP

★pull off

1 When you **pull** your clothes **off**, you take them off quickly. ❏ *I managed to pull my boots off... Anne had already kicked off her shoes and was pulling off her socks... Thomas unlaced the gloves and pulled them off Dominic's hands... Waddell noticed the watch on her wrist, and pulled it forcibly off her.*

V+N+ADV/PREP,
V+N+ADV,
V+PRON+ADV/PREP

2 If you **pull** something **off**, you succeed in doing something which is very difficult to achieve. ❏ *She had succeeded, triumphantly: she had pulled it off... You have just pulled off one of the biggest arms deals in the twentieth century... Bradlee was one of the few persons who could pull that kind of thing off.*

V+PRON+ADV,
V+ADV+N,
V+N+ADV

NOTE **Carry off** means almost the same as **pull off**.

3 When a vehicle **pulls off** the road, it is driven a little way off the road so that it can stop. ❏ *We pull off the road and stop. ...looking for a restful place to pull off... I pulled off the road and stopped to see what was wrong.*

V+PREP,
V+ADV

4 When a stationary vehicle **pulls off**, it starts moving forward. ❏ *The car pulled off. 'Where are we going?' I asked brightly... I left the house, just as the man had pulled off to circle the block once again.*

V+ADV

NOTE **Pull away** means almost the same as **pull off**.

5 If you **pull off** a person or animal that is attacking someone, you take hold of them and move them away, using force. ❏ *I hit her about the head and my dad had to pull me off... My fingers itched to pull her off, but they were pretty evenly matched.*

V+PRON+ADV,
V+N+ADV,
V+ADV+N

★pull on

☑ In meanings 2 and 3, the stress is on **pull**.

1 When you **pull on** your clothes, you put them on quickly. ❏ *He started to pull on his shorts... He pulled his shirt and trousers on... I dragged my dress out and pulled it on.*

V+ADV+N,
V+N+ADV,
V+PRON+ADV

2 If you **pull on** something, you take hold of it firmly and move it towards you. ❏ *He began to pull on the rope... He noticed an electrical cord, and pulled on it... Push the fishhook clean through instead of pulling on it.*

V+PREP

3 If you **pull on** a cigarette or pipe, you draw smoke into your mouth by breathing in when the pipe or cigarette is between your lips. ❏ *The vicar pulled on his pipe and resumed the story.*

V+PREP

★pull out

1 When a vehicle **pulls out**, it is driven out of a place and into the road. You also say that the vehicle **pulls out** when it is driven out of one traffic lane into another. ❏ *Ellen waited at the door until the last of the cars had pulled out of the driveway... I saw a bus pull out in front of us... Ginny revved up the Jeep again and pulled out.*

V+ADV

2 When a train **pulls out** of a station, it leaves the station. ❏ *He turned in his seat as the train pulled out... Her parents were beaming approval as the train pulled out of the station.*

V+ADV:
ALSO+of

NOTE **Draw out** means almost the same as **pull out**.

3 If you **pull out** of an activity or agreement, you decide not to continue it. ❏ *We've invested too much money and manpower to pull out now... Gary Player once had to pull out of an important championship because he hurt his neck... The Swedish conglomerate have pulled out of the bidding... He pulled his party out of the coalition.*

V+ADV,
V+N+ADV,
V+PRON+ADV:
ERGATIVE,
USUALLY+of

NOTE **Back out** means almost the same as **pull out**.

4 If an army **pulls out** of a place or region or if it **is pulled out**, it leaves the place or region and no longer operates there. ❏ *Troops had begun to pull out of the area... They ordered me to pull my men out of Fort Esther immediately... The Prime Minister has reaffirmed his intention of pulling all 10,000 of them out by the end of June.*

V+ADV,
V+N+ADV,
V+PRON+ADV:
ERGATIVE,
ALSO+of

NOTE **Withdraw** means almost the same as **pull out**.

♦ When there is a **pull-out**, soldiers leave a place which they have occupied or where they have been fighting. ❏ *United Nations officers supervising the pull-out said they expected 3,000 to be out by the weekend. ...an impending pull-out.*

N-SING

5 When you **pull** something **out** of a place, you remove it from that place. ❑ *Pull the baby's arms out of the sleeves first... She almost pulled him out of his chair... I watched her pull herself out of the sand... He would pull out his notebook and begin writing.*

V+N/PRON+ADV,
V+REFL+ADV,
V+ADV+N:
ALSO+of

♦ A **pull-out** section in a magazine is a separate part in the middle that you can remove easily.

ADJECTIVE

6 If you **pull out** information or ideas from a lot of other things, you separate them from those things so that you can use them on their own. ❑ *The computer does a search through its file and pulls out all information relevant to that word.*

V+ADV+N,
V+N+ADV,
V+PRON+ADV

NOTE **Take out** means almost the same as **pull out**, and **extract** is a more formal word.

★pull out of If you **pull out of** a difficult or unhappy situation or if someone **pulls** you **out of** it, you succeed in getting out of it. ❑ *I know I've got to pull out of this relationship somehow, but I can't... We must pull the country out of this 'economic calamity'.*

V+ADV+PREP,
V+N+ADV+PREP,
V+PRON+ADV+PREP:
ERGATIVE

★pull over

1 When a vehicle **pulls over**, it moves closer to the side of the road. ❑ *The patrolmen put their spotlight on the car, and told me to pull over... A green VW pulled over next to me.*

V+ADV

2 If the police **pull** a car **over**, they signal to the driver to drive the car to the side of the road and stop. ❑ *He had been pulled over for going through a red light. ...a police car pulling over a lorry.*

V+N+ADV,
V+ADV+N,
V+PRON+ADV

3 A **pullover** is a woollen piece of clothing that covers the upper part of your body and your arms. ❑ *...a very smart black pullover.*

N-COUNT

NOTE **Sweater** and **jumper** mean almost the same as **pullover**.

pull round

1 If you **pull round** after you have been ill or unconscious, you start to recover. ❑ *He'll pull round, don't worry... She's beginning to pull round.*

V+ADV

2 → See **pull around**

pull through

1 When someone who is very ill **pulls through** or when a doctor **pulls** them **through**, they recover. ❑ *The doctors said he'll pull through... I can't thank the nurses enough for pulling him through.*

V+ADV,
V+N+ADV,
V+PRON+ADV:
ERGATIVE

2 If you **pull through** a difficult situation or if something **pulls** you **through** it, you manage to survive it. ❑ *I had a rough old time from then on, I can tell you! But I pulled through... This was Vanessa's plan for pulling me through... He got a loan to pull him through a bad patch.*

V+ADV/PREP,
V+PRON+ADV/PREP,
V+N+ADV/PREP:
ERGATIVE

pull to

pull to When you **pull** a door **to**, you move it so that it is closed or very nearly closed. ❑ *Pull the door to, will you. I want to talk to you... She pulled the blinds to when I came in.*

V+N+ADV,
V+PRON+ADV

NOTE **Shut** means almost the same as **pull to**.

pull together

1 When you **pull** yourself **together**, you control your feelings and behave calmly after you have been upset or angry. ❑ *That's quite enough of that. Pull yourself together now and stop this at once... He had taken some minutes alone in his room to pull himself together.*

V+REFL+ADV

2 If people **pull together**, they co-operate with each other because they share the same aims, and ignore the things which they disagree about. ❑ *We all pulled together during the war... This is one thing we must all pull together on.*

V+ADV

NOTE **Band together** means almost the same as **pull together**.

3 If you **pull together** several different topics or ideas, you bring them into a lecture or article in an orderly or interesting way. ❑ *I want to pull together the threads of earlier programmes... To understand this syndrome, we must pull facts together from such fields as psychology and neurology... Write a series of articles on the events and try to pull them together.*

V+ADV+N,
V+N+ADV,
V+PRON+ADV

4 If you **pull** an event or meeting **together**, you organize it for other people. ❑ *I helped to pull a committee together down there... In the meantime, a campus-wide rally was being pulled together. ...the art auction we pulled together. ...pulling together a challenge to*

V+N+ADV,
V+ADV+N,
V+PRON+ADV

this repression.

NOTE **Set up** means almost the same as **pull together**.

pull under If someone or something **pulls** you **under** when you are in water, they pull you down so that the water completely covers you. ❑ *As the rope came tight it pulled him under... One of our girl pupils delighted in pulling other pupils under the water.*

V+PRON+ADV,
V+N+ADV,
V+N+PREP,
V+PRON+PREP

★**pull up**

1 When a vehicle **pulls up**, it slows down and stops. ❑ *The rain stopped as we pulled up to the hotel... The ambulance was just pulling up... Braun shifted forward and told the driver to pull up.*

V+ADV

2 If you **pull up** a chair, you move it so that you can sit close to something. ❑ *I pulled up a chair and sat back to watch the news... She looked at me indifferently as I pulled up a stool... Gertrude took another chair and pulled it up near Tim's.*

V+ADV+N,
V+N+ADV,
V+PRON+ADV

NOTE **Draw up** means almost the same as **pull up**.

3 When you **pull** something **up**, you raise it from a lower position to a higher one. ❑ *She pulled the sheet up... He had to pull up his pants which had started slipping... He laid hold of the branch to pull himself up. ...buckets that were pulled up from the well.*

V+N+ADV,
V+ADV+N,
V+PRON+ADV

4 If you **pull up** something which is fixed to the ground or the floor, you remove it with force. ❑ *They started pulling up the floorboards... They lowered the tent pole and pulled up the stakes... Don't pull the plants up... Either dig the weeds out, or pull them up.*

V+ADV+N,
V+N+ADV,
V+PRON+ADV

5 If someone **pulls** you **up** on something, they scold or criticize you severely for something that you have done. [INFORMAL] ❑ *If they don't like what you're doing they'll soon pull you up on it... When I asked about the photographs, the young man pulled me up quite sharply.*

V+PRON+ADV,
V+N+ADV:
ALSO+on

6 If someone or something **pulls** you **up**, they do or say something that suddenly makes you stop moving or talking. ❑ *Mr Wright pulled me up as soon as I left the classroom... Kate pulled herself up short and shouted: 'Don't start that again.'*

V+PRON+ADV,
V+REFL+ADV

7 If you tell someone to **pull up**, you are telling them to rest more. [INFORMAL] ❑ *He said if I didn't pull up a bit I was in danger of a complete breakdown.*

V+ADV

NOTE **Ease up** means almost the same as **pull up**.

8 If you **pull up** in something that you are doing, you improve at it and reach the same standard as other people. ❑ *These marks seem to be satisfactory so that means you've pulled up quite a bit... It's taken ten years of investment to pull up to present U.S. standards.*

V+ADV

NOTE **Catch up** means almost the same as **pull up**.

pump /pʌmp/ (pumps, pumping, pumped)

pump away

1 To **pump away** means to move vigorously and continuously in and out or up and down. ❑ *His heart was pumping away... This machine is pumping away all the time... John pumped away on the starter.*

V+ADV

2 To **pump** a liquid or gas **away** means to remove it by forcing it to flow in a particular direction, using a pump. ❑ *We had pumped most of the water away by the afternoon... The oil spillage was pumped away, but most of the damage had already been done. ...pumping sewage away.*

V+N+ADV,
V+ADV+N,
V+PRON+ADV

pump in If you **pump** money or resources **in**, you contribute a lot of money or resources towards a particular organization, plan, or project. [INFORMAL] ❑ *We had to pump a lot of money in to get the scheme to work... They needed to pump more supplies in... The Government could pump in funds to help improve technology.*

V+N+ADV,
V+ADV+N

NOTE **Inject** is a more formal word for **pump in**.

pump into If you **pump** money or resources **into** a particular organization, plan, or project, you put a lot of money or resources into it. [INFORMAL] ❑ *Commercial organizations will have to pump colossal funds into new technology... Investors pumped £5 billion into the Stock Exchange last year.*

V+N+PREP,
V+PRON+PREP

pump out

1 To **pump** a liquid or gas **out** means to remove it from a place by forcing it to flow in a particular direction, using a pump. ❑ *...steam engines, developed originally to pump water out of the mines... This machine pumps unwanted salt water out and then replaces it with fresh... We seal one of the tubes and pump out all the air.*

V+N+ADV,
V+ADV+N,
V+PRON+ADV:
ALSO+of

2 To **pump out** someone's stomach means to remove the contents of their stom-

V+N+ADV,

ach using a pump, because they have swallowed poison or taken an overdose of drugs. ❏ *I became conscious again as they pumped out my stomach.*

V+ADV+N,
V+PRON+ADV

3 To **pump** things **out** means to produce or supply them continually in large amounts. [INFORMAL] ❏ *...a radio station pumping out pop music... He automatically pumps three articles out each week... They fired continuously, each gun pumping out four or five rounds a minute.*

V+ADV+N,
V+N+ADV,
V+PRON+ADV

NOTE **Churn out** means almost the same as **pump out**.

4 If pop music **pumps out**, it plays very loudly. ❏ *Teenage disco music pumped out at every station.*

V+ADV

pump out of If you **pump** information **out of** someone, you force them to tell you something that they want to keep secret. ❏ *I tried to pump it out of him, but he wouldn't say a word.*

V+PRON+ADV+PREP,
V+N+ADV+PREP

★pump up

1 If you **pump up** something such as a tyre, you fill it with air, using a pump. ❏ *Do your tyres need pumping up?... I don't know how long it took to pump up the dinghy... Not having pumped up his tyres, the effort was too much for him.*

V+ADV+N,
V+N+ADV,
V+PRON+ADV

NOTE **Blow up** means almost the same as **pump up**, and **inflate** is a more formal word.

2 To **pump** liquid **up** from a place underground means to force it out of that place to the surface, using a pump. ❏ *Oil has to be pumped up from deep boreholes... You could use a windmill to pump up water from the well.*

V+N+ADV,
V+ADV+N,
V+PRON+ADV:
USUALLY+*from*

3 If you **pump** yourself **up** for something, you prepare yourself for it mentally, especially by telling yourself that you can succeed. [INFORMAL] ❏ *They find it difficult to pump themselves up for the games.*

V+REFL+ADV:
ALSO+*for*

NOTE **Psych up** means almost the same as **pump up**.

punch /pʌntʃ/ **(punches, punching, punched)**

punch in

1 If you **punch in** a number on a machine, you push the machine's buttons or keys in order to give it a command to do something. ❏ *You can bank by phone in the USA, punching in account numbers on the phone.*

V+ADV+N,
V+N+ADV,
V+PRON+ADV

2 When workers **punch in** at a factory or office, they record the time that they arrive by putting a special card into a machine. [AMERICAN]

V+ADV

NOTE **Clock in** means almost the same as **punch in**, and **punch out** means the opposite.

punch into If you **punch** numbers **into** a machine, you push the machine's buttons or keys in order to give it a command to do something. ❏ *...a code which allows them into the hotel once they punch the number into a special keyboard.*

V+N+PREP,
V+PRON+PREP

punch out

1 When you **punch** something **out** of a substance such as wood, metal, or paper, you make it out of that substance by making a hole or other shape in it using a special machine or tool. ❏ *...an old-fashioned machine that punches out coins... We had a copy punched out on the telex tape ready for transmission.*

V+N+ADV,
V+ADV+N,
V+PRON+ADV

2 When workers **punch out** at a factory or office, they record the time that they leave by putting a special card into a machine. [AMERICAN]

V+ADV

NOTE **Clock out** means almost the same as **punch out**, and **punch in** means the opposite.

3 To **punch** someone **out** means to hit them so hard that they fall over. ❏ *They're bullies and I feel like punching them out.*

V+N+ADV,
V+ADV+N,
V+PRON+ADV

4 If someone threatens to **punch** your lights **out**, they are threatening to hit you hard on the face. [INFORMAL] ❏ *He said, 'You are lucky I didn't punch your lights out.'*

V+N+ADV

punch up

1 In a shop, when someone **punches** an amount of money **up** on the cash register, they press the keys of the cash register in order to add up the figures. ❏ *It was only after he'd punched it up that I realized I'd lost my purse.*

V+PRON+ADV,
V+N+ADV,
V+ADV+N

2 A **punch-up** is a fight. [BRITISH, INFORMAL] ❏ *'Looks as though you've been in a real punch-up,' says the barmaid... An employee said it was 'a very big punch-up.'*

N-COUNT

push /pʊʃ/ (pushes, pushing, pushed)

> ✅ **About** is used mainly in British English. In American English, **around** is much more common than **round**.

push about → See push around

push ahead

1 When you **push ahead**, you continue doing something, using a lot of energy or enthusiasm. ❏ *Now was the time to push ahead and finish the enemy off... By the time dinner was finished, he was clearly in a mood to push ahead.*

NOTE **Push on** and **press on** mean almost the same as **push ahead**.

V+ADV

2 If you **push ahead** with a plan, arrangement, or event, you continue with it, often when there are problems, or when other people want you to stop. ❏ *The Government was anxious to push ahead with a fresh round of negotiations... Michael Ward is pushing ahead with loans and help for projects... Djibouti has pushed ahead with an optimistic development strategy.*

V+ADV:
USUALLY+*with*

push along If you say that you must **push along**, you mean that you must leave a place. [INFORMAL] ❏ *I must be pushing along now, it's getting late.*

NOTE **Push off** means almost the same as **push along**.

V+ADV

push around

1 When you **push** something **around**, push it **about**, or **push** it **round**, you move it from one position to another without lifting it away from the surface that it is on. ❏ *The boy pushed bits of lamb chop and lettuce around his plate... Tony was playing with cotton reels, pushing them slowly round the table... She stared at the china pieces and pushed them about.*

V+N+PREP/ADV,
V+PRON+PREP/ADV

2 If someone **pushes** you **around** or **pushes** you **about**, they tell you what to do in a rude and insulting way. ❏ *If we let them push us around on the little things they'll want to take over everything... He began to push people around intellectually... I'm sick and tired of being pushed around.*

V+PRON+ADV,
V+N+ADV

push aside

1 When you **push** something or someone **aside**, you move them to a position where they are not in your way. ❏ *As soon as we had finished our tea, we pushed all the crockery aside... Stuart pushed him aside and climbed behind the wheel... He leaned forward and pushed aside his notes.*

V+N+ADV,
V+PRON+ADV,
V+ADV+N

2 If you **push** something **aside**, you treat it as unimportant and pay attention to something else instead. ❏ *He quickly pushed all thought of it aside... These issues tend to get pushed aside and forgotten... Teaching is pushed aside as a non-starter.*

NOTE **Brush aside** means almost the same as **push aside**.

V+N+ADV,
V+PRON+ADV,
V+ADV+N

⋆push back

1 When a group of people such as a crowd or an army **is pushed back**, they are forced to move backwards. ❏ *The Allied forces were pushed back... People protested but the police pushed them back.*

V+N+ADV,
V+PRON+ADV,
V+ADV+N

2 When you **push** something or someone **back**, you move them backwards. ❏ *She had pushed her sunglasses back, so they rested on her hair... His hair was over his eyebrows and he pushed it back... He had pushed back his chair so hard that it fell over.*

V+N+ADV,
V+PRON+ADV,
V+ADV+N

push by If someone **pushes by**, they press roughly and rudely into other people as they go past them. ❏ *...ignorant old men who just push by to get on the bus... She just pushed by us without so much as an 'excuse me'.*

NOTE **Push past** means almost the same as **push by**.

V+ADV,
V+PREP

⋆push for If you **push for** something, you constantly encourage other people to help you achieve it. ❏ *Winston Churchill had pushed for the creation of an Arab state... He is pushing for secret balloting in Communist Party elections.*

NOTE **Press for** means almost the same as **push for**.

V+PREP

push forward

1 If you **push forward** your ideas, opinions, or beliefs, you try very hard to get other people to pay attention to them. ❏ *...the most effective means of pushing forward the interests of workers... He pushed forward his own and the Party's principles.*

NOTE **Promote** is a more formal word for **push forward**.

V+ADV+N,
V+PRON+ADV

2 If someone **pushes** themselves **forward**, they try rather unpleasantly to make

V+REFL+ADV

other people pay attention to them. ❑ *We didn't like to push ourselves forward. ...that new woman pushing herself forward! ...pushing himself forward in an unseemly manner.*

push in

1 When someone **pushes in**, they unfairly come into a queue in front of other people who have been waiting longer; used showing disapproval. ❑ *Felicity pushed in next to Howard... If she pushed in again, I would say something to her... No-one was allowed to push in.*   V+ADV

2 When someone **pushes in**, they force their way into a group, situation, or activity where they are not welcome. ❑ *Arthur Coggs isn't the sort that pushes in where he's not wanted!'... The wife can push in and take over the man's place.*   V+ADV

★push into

1 If you **push** someone **into** doing something, you use your influence to persuade or force them to do it. ❑ *...trying to push the government into giving money for scientific research. ...determination not to be pushed into acceptance of nuclear missiles.*   V+N+PREP, V+PRON+PREP

2 If you **are pushed into** a difficult or unpleasant situation, you are forced into it by other people or by your circumstances. ❑ *You may well find yourself being pushed into this role... Children at this age are easily alarmed by being pushed into an unfamiliar situation.*   V+N+PREP, V+PRON+PREP: USUALLY PASSIVE

push off

1 When you **push off**, you leave the person or place that you are visiting. [INFORMAL] ❑ *I gave him a good talking-to. Then I pushed off... He must have pushed off when he heard us.*   V+ADV

2 If someone tells you to **push off**, they are telling you in a rude way to go away. ❑ *'I've got something to show you.'—'You push off,' I said... 'What do you want me to do?' she said. 'Nothing. You can push off now.'*   IMPERATIVE, V+ADV

3 When something such as a boat or a sledge **pushes off** from its starting point, or when you **push** it **off**, it starts to go forwards. ❑ *As the launch pushed off, the sea turned from smooth to choppy... The boats were pushed off and drifted down the river.*   V+ADV, V+N+ADV, V+PRON+ADV: ERGATIVE

push on

1 When you **push on**, you continue travelling somewhere. ❑ *I felt restless and wanted to push on... If we want to get in before dark we must push on.*   V+ADV

2 When you **push on** with something that you are doing, you continue doing it with a lot of energy or enthusiasm. ❑ *...as we push on with our explanations... I must push on with these enquiries as fast as I can... He must push on through the timetable.*   V+ADV: USUALLY+with

NOTE **Carry on** means almost the same as **push on**.

3 If someone **pushes** something **on** you, **pushes** it **onto** you, or **pushes** it **upon** you, they insist on giving or selling it to you even though you do not really want it. ❑ *...an insurance salesman persistently trying to push an unwanted policy on him... Several boxes will be sold, and many more can be pushed upon the public.*   V+N+PREP, V+PRON+PREP

push onto → See push on

★push out

1 When you **push** someone or something **out** of a place, you use force to remove them from there. ❑ *He pushed Minnie out and slammed the door... The blue car has been pushed out of the garage... I was pushed out of the door before I could put on my shoes.*   V+N+ADV, V+PRON+ADV, V+ADV+N: ALSO+of

2 If people **push** you **out** of an organization or an activity, they force you to leave it by being very unpleasant to you. ❑ *You're having a bad time and now you push me out... She was practically pushed out of the society for political reasons.*   V+PRON+ADV, V+N+ADV: ALSO+of

3 To **push out** something means to produce a lot of it and send it out somewhere. [INFORMAL] ❑ *Computers can push out information to the external world in a variety of ways. ...the shoddy culture pushed out by TV films and magazines.*   V+ADV+N, V+N+ADV, V+PRON+ADV

NOTE **Churn out** means almost the same as **push out**.

★push over

1 If you **push** someone or something **over**, you push them so that they fall onto the ground. ❑ *The children were pushing each other over on the sand... No one knew who pushed the guard over the wall... They knocked all the books off the shelves, pushed over the table and left.*   V+N+ADV/PREP, V+ADV+N, V+PRON+ADV/PREP

NOTE **Knock over** means almost the same as **push over**.

The symbol ★ shows key phrasal verbs

2 You say that something is a **pushover** when it is easy to do or easy to get. ❑ *'I'm supposed to give my views on Europe.'—'Sounds like a pushover.'*   N-SING

3 You say that someone is a **pushover** when they are easy to persuade or influence. ❑ *You won't have much trouble with her–she's a pushover.*   N-SING

push past If someone **pushes past** you, they press into you rather roughly or   V+PREP,
push you out of the way as they go past you. ❑ *People entering or leaving had to push*   V+ADV
past them... She began to push past him to the door but Arthur stopped her... He began to push past after Margaret.

NOTE **Push by** means almost the same as **push past**.

push round → See push around

★push through

1 If you **push** something **through**, you succeed in getting it accepted, often with   V+N+ADV/PREP,
difficulty. ❑ *The Government were determined to push the legislation through... The admin-*   V+ADV+N,
istration pushed four measures through Congress. ...the confidence to push through a long-   V+PRON+ADV/PREP
term project.

2 If you **push through** things that are blocking your path, you use force in order   V+PREP,
to be able to move past them. ❑ *She was certainly not going to push through any of those*   V+ADV
people... I pushed through the turnstile... Everyone turned silent as they saw Ari approach. He pushed through and stared at the ground.

3 If you **push** someone **through** an examination or course, you help them to pass   V+N+PREP,
or finish it. ❑ *...constant pressure to push everyone through the exam... His mother had*   V+PRON+PREP,
pushed him through Junior and Grammar School to Oxford... It takes determination and guts   V+REFL+PREP
to push yourself through a hard running schedule.

NOTE **Get through** means almost the same as **push through**.

push to When you **push** a door or window **to**, you close it or partially close it   V+N+ADV,
by pushing it away from you. ❑ *Push that gate to before the dog gets out... No, don't*   V+PRON+ADV
shut it, just push it to a bit.

push towards If you **push towards** a particular aim, you try very hard to   V+PREP
achieve something or to get other people to accept it. ❑ *The forces pushing towards standardization will probably be contained... In early pieces, he seemed to be pushing to-wards a new form of expression.*

push up

1 To **push up** the price, rate, or amount of something means to increase it.   V+ADV+N,
❑ *...shortages that have helped push up inflation... That might push the price up astronomi-*   V+N+ADV,
cally... The party had pushed up its share of the vote.   V+PRON+ADV

2 If you do **push-ups**, you exercise by lying flat on your stomach, then pushing   N-COUNT
your body up using your arms and keeping your back and legs straight. ❑ *George got out of bed and did fifty push-ups.*

push upon → See push on

put /pʊt/ (puts, putting)

✓ The form **put** is used in the present tense and is the past tense and past participle of the verb. In American English, **around** is much more common than
round.

put about

1 If you **put about** something that is untrue or uncertain, you tell it to people   V+PRON+ADV,
and cause it to become well-known. [BRITISH] ❑ *A rumour was put about to the effect*   V+ADV+N:
that he had been drunk... They had an even harder struggle to counteract the lies put about   USUALLY PASSIVE:
by Mr. Jones... His mother put it about that he had robbed her of everything.   ALSO V+it+ADV:
WITH REPORT

2 If you **put** one thing **about** another, you place it so that it surrounds or encloses   V+N+PREP,
the other thing. [BRITISH] ❑ *She knelt beside him and put her arms about him and soothed*   V+PRON+PREP
away the boy's tears... He sat her down in the chair and put a blanket about her shoulders.

3 When a ship **puts about** or when it **is put about**, it changes its path and be-   V+ADV,
gins to sail in the opposite direction. ❑ *Three hours out of Southampton we had to put*   V+N+ADV,
about and go back.   V+PRON+ADV:
ERGATIVE

put above If you **put** one thing **above** another, you consider it to be more im-   V+N+ADV
portant than the other thing. ❑ *...a tradition which put freedom of conscience above the*

law and authority.

NOTE Put **before** means almost the same as **put above**.

★put acr**o**ss

1 If you **put across** information, ideas, or opinions, you succeed in telling them or explaining them to someone. ❏ *I was grateful that I had been given the chance to put across my point of view. ...an attempt to put a message across to the public... I try to put that across every time I write.*
V+ADV+N,
V+N+ADV,
V+PRON+ADV

NOTE **Convey** is a more formal word for **put across**.

2 If you **put** one thing **across** another, you place it on top of the other thing or against it, so that it reaches from one side to the other. ❏ *Somebody put some boards across the stream. ...putting my fingers across her lips.*
V+N+PREP

put ar**ou**nd

1 If you **put** something **around** or **put** it **round** another thing, you place it so that it surrounds the other thing. **Put around** is slightly more formal. ❏ *He was in his garden putting the compost round his roses... He had to put it round my waist and tie it... She put her arms around me... I knelt on the floor beside her and put an arm round her shoulders.*
V+N+PREP,
V+PRON+PREP

2 If information or a story **is put around** or **put round**, it becomes known by many people. ❏ *The report had been put round by the Left to cause trouble... It's just a rumour put round by students... Somebody put around a rumour that I was getting divorced.*
V+N+ADV,
V+PRON+ADV,
V+ADV+N:
USUALLY PASSIVE

★put as**i**de

1 If you **put aside** an activity, a problem, or an attitude, you stop doing it, thinking about it, or showing it. ❏ *Brigit Stott puts aside her own work and dedicates herself to Albert. ...putting aside for the moment the fact that you may not get the job... I put the idea aside, and for a year thought no more of it.*
V+ADV+N,
V+N+ADV,
V+PRON+ADV

NOTE **Set aside** means almost the same as **put aside**.

2 If you **put aside** an object you were using or looking at, you place it somewhere next to you because you do not need it for the moment. ❏ *Jimmie put aside his pipe... The old man put his books aside and spoke to us... He put it aside along with the envelope.*
V+ADV+N,
V+N+ADV,
V+PRON+ADV

NOTE **Lay aside** means almost the same as **put aside**.

3 If you **put aside** money or other resources, you save it for a particular purpose or until you need it. ❏ *Perhaps you want to put money aside towards the cost of a house or a car... Whatever is left should be put aside and kept for tomorrow... Many women find it hard to put aside this time for themselves.*
V+N+ADV,
V+ADV+N,
V+PRON+ADV

NOTE **Put by** means almost the same as **put aside**.

put at If the cost, age, or value of something **is put at** a particular amount, it is estimated to be that amount. ❏ *The pipeline's cost is now put at 2.7 billion pounds... The consensus of opinion put the date at 1900.*
V+N+PREP,
V+PRON+PREP:
USUALLY PASSIVE

★put aw**ay**

1 If you **put** something **away**, you place it tidily somewhere, for example in a cupboard, drawer, or pocket. ❏ *She put her shopping away in the kitchen... The girl, bent over her notebook, closed it and put away her pen... Albert folded the newspaper neatly and put it away on the side table.*
V+N+ADV,
V+ADV+N,
V+PRON+ADV

2 If you **put away** food or drink, you eat or drink a lot of it. [INFORMAL] ❏ *I've put away more white wine than is good for my digestion... I had put away half a bottle of tequila during the evening... He put away sandwiches and coffee and was still hungry.*
V+ADV+N,
V+PRON+ADV

3 If you **put** money **away**, you save it. ❏ *...the regular sums that you put away for holidays... You may just want to put something away for a rainy day. ...a child putting away some pocket money each week.*
V+ADV+N,
V+N+ADV,
V+PRON+ADV

NOTE **Put by** means almost the same as **put away**.

4 If someone **is put away** by people in authority, they are sent to prison or a mental hospital. [INFORMAL] ❏ *They were put away in prisons and labour camps... They had to put him away again. The poor man is crazy.*
V+N+ADV,
V+PRON+ADV,
V+ADV+N:
USUALLY PASSIVE

NOTE **Lock away** means almost the same as **put away**.

5 If someone **is put away**, they are killed. [INFORMAL] ❏ *...the story of one Marine putting a wounded friend away with a pistol shot... He probably deserved being put away by a bullet.*
V+N+ADV,
V+PRON+ADV,
V+ADV+N

*put back

1 If you **put** something **back** somewhere, you place it in the position it was in before it was moved. ❑ *She put the telephone back and stood absolutely still... I put it back as soon as I ate... Shall I put it in the box for you?... I was put back into the cell.*

V+N+ADV,
V+PRON+ADV,
V+ADV+N:
USUALLY+A

NOTE **Replace** is a more formal word for **put back**.

2 If you **put** your head **back**, you move it so that your face is pointing upwards. ❑ *He put his head back and closed his eyes... He put his head back and smiled up into the rain... Sponge put his head back and roared with laughter... I was lost. I put back my head and howled.*

V+N+ADV,
V+ADV+N

3 If you **put** someone or something **back** in their previous state, you change them so that they are in that state again. ❑ *He puts the car back in gear and drives on... This is enough to put them back to sleep... 'Programme for Action' must be put back on the agenda.*

V+N+ADV,
V+PRON+ADV:
USUALLY+A

4 To **put back** an event, appointment, or task means to postpone it. [BRITISH] ❑ *The effect is to put back the date of opening of the third airport... These bills have to be put back to a day when there will be time.*

V+ADV+N,
V+N+ADV,
V+PRON+ADV:
USUALLY+A

NOTE **Defer** is a more formal word for **put back**, and **bring forward** means the opposite.

5 To **put back** the progress or development of something means to slow it down. ❑ *It is easy to risk the progress you have made and put your training back a week or two.*

V+N+ADV,
V+PRON+ADV,
V+ADV+N:
USUALLY+A

NOTE **Set back** means almost the same as **put back**.

6 If you **put** a clock or watch **back**, you adjust it so that it shows an earlier time, for example when you travel from one time zone to another. ❑ *I put my watch back an hour before we landed at Kennedy Airport.*

V+N+ADV,
V+PRON+ADV,
V+ADV+N

NOTE **Put forward** means the opposite of **put back**.

7 If you **put back** alcoholic drink, you drink a large amount of it in a short time. [INFORMAL] ❑ *I'd put back a fair amount of gin the night before.*

V+ADV+N,
V+N+ADV,
V+PRON+ADV

NOTE **Knock back** means almost the same as **put back**.

put back into If you **put** money **back into** a business or a country's economy, you use some of the profits or taxes to pay for new development. ❑ *The Government didn't put any money back into the economy... Only a small percentage of this revenue is being put back into maintaining roads... We were all looking for a hopeful budget to put some money back into our operations.*

V+N+ADV+PREP,
V+PRON+ADV+PREP,
V+ADV+N+PREP

*put back on

If you **put** clothes **back on**, you dress in them and wear them again after taking them off. ❑ *She has put her shirt back on but not her jeans... Put your clothes back on, Sara... Ben took off his glasses, wiped them, and put them back on.*

V+N+ADV+ADV,
V+PRON+ADV+ADV

put before

1 If you **put** food **before** someone, you place it in front of them so that they can eat it. ❑ *Put the food before the child, say nothing... I eat what's put before me... Billy looked at the supper tray she had put before him ... The waiter put cherry cake before Klaus.*

V+N+PREP,
V+PRON+PREP

2 If you **put** facts or ideas **before** someone in authority, you officially present them to them. ❑ *Grant did not put any of this evidence before the jury. ...the plan he wished to put before them... Have you put the consequences before her?*

V+N+PREP,
V+PRON+PREP

3 If you **put** one thing **before** another, you give it more importance than the other thing. ❑ *Industry was put before agriculture... He is generally expected to put his work before his family. ...a disciplined man who will put duty before pleasure.*

V+N+PREP,
V+PRON+PREP

*put behind

1 If you **put** an unhappy event **behind** you, you try to forget it and not allow it to affect you now or in the future. ❑ *I thought when I went to England I would put all that behind me... She spoke of him as part of a life she had put behind her... Some people seem to be able to put it behind them, but I cannot help remembering.*

V+N+PREP,
V+PRON+PREP

2 If you **put** effort or resources **behind** a person or project, you use them to support that person or project. ❑ *Be sure to investigate thoroughly any such schemes before putting your money behind them... We're putting our professional expertise behind it... How many women trade unionists put their weight behind women's struggles in the community?*

V+N+PREP,
V+PRON+PREP

put by If you **put by** a sum of money or a supply of something, you save it so that you can use it later. [BRITISH] ❑ *I put by a few shillings in order to buy that... Arthur Coggs had prudently put it by for future use.*

V+ADV+N,
V+PRON+ADV,
V+N+ADV

NOTE **Put aside** means almost the same as **put by**.

For a full explanation of all grammatical labels, see pages xiii-xx

★put down

1 If you **put down** something that you are holding or carrying, you place it somewhere. □ *Greene put his drink down on the table... Put it down there, Mrs Meynard, that's lovely... She puts down her case, and kisses him.*

V+N+ADV/PREP,
V+PRON+ADV/PREP,
V+ADV+N

NOTE **Set down** means almost the same as **put down**, and **pick up** means the opposite.

2 You can say that you **put down** the phone or the receiver when you replace it after you have finished speaking to someone. □ *'Oh God,' she muttered and put the phone down hurriedly... She put down the receiver and went to find Mrs Castle.*

V+N+ADV,
V+PRON+ADV,
V+ADV+N

3 If you **put down** a lawn, a carpet, or other covering, you place it so that it covers the ground or a flat surface. □ *Before we move in we want to put carpets down... We put down a bed of chippings... Large plantations of beech were put down in the eighteenth and nineteenth centuries.*

V+N+ADV,
V+ADV+N,
V+PRON+ADV

4 If someone **puts down** poison, they spread it on the ground to kill pests. □ *Badgers may be the innocent victims of poison put down to kill foxes... How do they get rid of these rats and mice? Do they put down poison?*

V+ADV+N,
V+N+ADV,
V+PRON+ADV

5 If you **put down** a part of your body, you move it to a lower position. □ *He put his face down and sniffed the rose... She puts down her head, and starts reading... Then she put one hand down into the box. ...yet you can put your foot down and touch it any time.*

V+ADV+N,
V+PRON+ADV,
V+PRON+ADV:
NO PASSIVE

NOTE **Lower** is a more formal word for **put down**.

6 If you **put down** money when you are buying something, you pay some of the money when you take it, and pay the rest of the money in regular amounts after that. □ *You will often be required to put down a deposit on a car or a house. ...before putting down the first month's rent.*

V+ADV+N,
V+N+ADV,
V+PRON+ADV

7 When you **put down** words or numbers, you write or type them somewhere. □ *All you have to do is put down exactly what we've just said... You haven't put Professor Mangel's name down on the list... They're very difficult to put down on paper.*

V+ADV+N,
V+N+ADV,
V+PRON+ADV

8 If someone in a meeting **puts down** a question, motion, or amendment, they officially ask for it to be discussed and voted on. [TECHNICAL] □ *The Tribune Group had put down a motion condemning the Government's policy... We could therefore expect hundreds of amendments to be put down by the Tories.*

V+ADV+N,
V+N+ADV

NOTE **Table** is a more formal word for **put down**.

9 If people in authority **put down** opposition, they oppose it and stop it by using force. □ *The rebellion was put down by European troops... He urged his princely patrons to put it down with the utmost ferocity. ...successfully putting down a series of revolts.*

V+N+ADV,
V+PRON+ADV,
V+ADV+N

NOTE **Suppress** is a more formal word for **put down**.

10 If you **put down** a person or their ideas, you criticize them and make them appear foolish or unimportant. □ *We've been encouraged all our life to put down women's talk. ...her infuriating habit of putting people down in small ways. ...if someone puts you down and is really mean and rotten to you... It is very hard not to feel put down and ugly and undesirable.*

V+ADV+N,
V+N+ADV,
V+PRON+ADV

NOTE **Slag off** is a very informal expression for **put down**.

♦ A **put-down** is a statement or action that is intended to criticize a person or their ideas and make them appear foolish or unimportant. □ *...all the put-downs you have to contend with. ...a dismissive put-down.*

N-COUNT

11 When someone **puts** a baby **down**, they put it to sleep in a bed or cot. □ *After Ira had left, I fed Wendy and put her down for her nap. ...a woman who has just put the baby down for a rest.*

V+PRON+ADV,
V+N+ADV

12 If you **put** someone **down** for something or to do something, you make an official choice, application, or decision so that they can have it or do it. □ *He ended up putting his name down for architecture instead... Morris had recommended putting Philip down to teach English. ...having a father rich enough to put you down for Eton the moment you're born.*

V+N+ADV,
V+PRON+ADV:
USUALLY+for OR to-INF

13 If you **put down** or **put** yourself **down** for something, you formally apply to have it or do it. □ *There were morning sessions for women. My wife put down for Tuesdays and Thursdays... I've put myself down to teach Russian.*

V+ADV,
V+REFL+ADV:
USUALLY+for OR to-INF

14 If a vet **puts down** an animal, he or she kills it, for example because it is old, ill, or dangerous. [BRITISH] □ *The Canine Defence League will not put down healthy ani-*

V+ADV+N,
V+N+ADV,
V+PRON+ADV

mals... The vet would not put the dog down.

NOTE **Destroy** means almost the same as **put down**.

15 When the driver of a vehicle **puts down** passengers, he or she stops in order to let them get out. ❑ *The bus was stopping to put someone down... The taxi put me down in the Unter den Eichen. ...the place where the girls had been put down.*

V+ADV+N,
V+N+ADV,
V+PRON+ADV

NOTE **Pick up** means the opposite of **put down**.

♦ A **put-down** point is a place where a bus or coach stops in order to let people get off. ❑ *The bus had used Smith's as its pick-up and put-down point. ...a put-down point in the village.*

ADJECTIVE

16 When an aeroplane **puts down** somewhere, it lands there for a short time. ❑ *We ought to put down at Aumont some time between five thirty and six... They will put down in Rome to refuel.*

V+ADV:
USUALLY+A

put down as If you **put** someone or something **down as** a particular type of person or thing, you decide, often wrongly, that they are of that type. ❑ *I'd have put you down as somebody reasonably successful in most things... He looked fat and respectful, and was put down by those above him as willing, but slow.*

V+N+ADV+PREP,
V+PRON+ADV+PREP,
V+ADV+N+PREP

put down to If you **put** one thing **down to** another thing, you believe that it is caused by the other thing. ❑ *Most bad shots can be put down to one of half a dozen basic faults... It seemed unsafe to put down anything to coincidence... He puts it down to a deep fear of change.*

V+N+ADV+PREP,
V+ADV+N+PREP,
V+PRON+ADV+PREP

put forth If you **put forth** an idea or theory, you state it or publish it so that people can consider it and discuss it. [FORMAL] ❑ *Psychologists have put forth several theoretical models to explain the bases of interpersonal attraction... English and Welsh bishops met, discussed the matter, and put forth their conclusions.*

V+ADV+N,
V+N+ADV

NOTE **Set forth** means almost the same as **put forth**.

★put forward

1 If you **put forward** an idea or proposal, you state it or publish it so that people can consider it and discuss it. ❑ *The TUC put forward a plan for national recovery... The idea was first put forward by J. Good... Lipset does not put the proposition forward as a universal truth.*

V+ADV+N,
V+N+ADV

NOTE **Set out** means almost the same as **put forward**.

2 If you **put forward** a person or their name, you officially suggest that they should be considered for a particular job or position. ❑ *The organization put forward eight candidates for the NUS executive. ...a woman who hesitates to put her own name forward... No one put me forward as a possible alternative to Jefferson. ...this consistent pattern of people putting themselves forward.*

V+ADV+N,
V+N+ADV,
V+PRON+ADV,
V+REFL+ADV:
ALSO+for

NOTE **Nominate** is a more formal word for **put forward**.

3 If you **put forward** an event, you cause it to take place earlier than planned. ❑ *It was decided to put forward the dancing display.*

V+ADV+N,
V+N+ADV,
V+PRON+ADV

NOTE **Bring forward** means almost the same as **put forward**.

4 If you **put** a clock or watch **forward**, you adjust it so that it shows a later time, for example when you travel from one time zone to another. ❑ *Don't forget to put your clocks forward tonight; it's the start of British Summer Time.*

V+N+ADV,
V+PRON+ADV,
V+ADV+N

NOTE **Put back** means the opposite of **put forward**.

★put in

1 If you **put** one thing **in** another, you place it inside the other thing. ❑ *If you pour hot water into a glass, put a spoon in first to absorb the heat... 'I don't know,' said Murdo, putting a spoonful of sugar in his tea... I folded my apron and put it in the drawer... He puts in the coins and dials the number in Toulouse.*

V+N+ADV/PREP,
V+PRON+ADV/PREP,
V+ADV+N

♦ An **input** is a quantity of something that is placed inside something else, or the act of placing it there. [AMERICAN] ❑ *...decline in soil fertility even without chemical inputs. ...a high fluid input.*

N-COUNT,
N-UNCOUNT

2 If you **put in** plants or crops, you plant them in the ground. ❑ *Brazilian farmers put in a few hundred more coffee bushes... I'll put the cabbages in... You can put them in after peas or beans or early potatoes.*

V+ADV+N,
V+N+ADV,
V+PRON+ADV

3 If you **put in** new equipment or new parts, you fix them in place in a building or a machine. ❑ *The designer could put in a more powerful engine... I had a new lock put in...*

V+ADV+N,
V+N+ADV/PREP,
V+PRON+ADV/PREP

Jim put that door in himself.

NOTE Install is a more formal word for **put in**.

4 If you **put** money **in** a bank or an account, you give the money to the bank, which will look after it for you. ❑ *His father put the money in for him... She took twenty-five rupees out of it and put it in a deposit account... With a Giro account you can put in and draw out cash during normal Post Office opening hours.*

V+N+ADV/PREP,
V+PRON+ADV/PREP,
V+ADV+N

NOTE Deposit is a more formal word for **put in**, and **pay in** means almost the same.

5 If you **put** money **in** a business, a project, or a country, you provide money that it needs, and receive a profit if it is successful. ❑ *I have put money in shows, including 'Evita'... They were putting in new investment.*

V+N+ADV/PREP,
V+PRON+ADV/PREP,
V+ADV+N

NOTE Invest is a more formal word for **put in**.

6 If you **put in** time or effort doing something, you spend time or work hard doing it. ❑ *Half of them were putting in forty-five hours a week or more... I was certainly pleased by the level of effort everyone put in today.*

V+ADV+N,
V+N+ADV

♦ The **input** in an activity is the time or effort spent on it. ❑ *...requiring the input of more labour... Input from the workers is vital.*

N-COUNT,
N-UNCOUNT

7 If you **put in** a remark or comment, you interrupt someone when they are speaking in order to add some information or to give your opinion. ❑ *'We're not talking about women now, dear,' Alison put in smartly... 'But didn't you hear what I said?' put in Sally Jones.*

V+ADV+QUOTE

NOTE Interject is a more formal word for **put in**, and **chip in** means almost the same.

8 If you **put** something **in** a piece of writing, speech, or a drawing, you include it or cause it to be included. ❑ *When she read my story, she suggested I put in a description of the girl. ...putting advertisements in the London papers... When we got to camp he put it in his report.*

V+ADV+N,
V+N+ADV/PREP,
V+PRON+ADV/PREP

♦ Someone's **input** to a conversation consists of all that they say. ❑ *...comparing the speech intention with the perceived speech input.*

N-COUNT,
N-UNCOUNT

9 If you **put in** an order, a bill, or a request, you officially ask someone to give you goods or money, or to do something for you. ❑ *You'll put in an immediate request for transfer to Singapore... Your printers put in a hefty wage claim. ...even if every bill you put in is absolutely genuine. ...if we put another order in perhaps.*

V+ADV+N,
V+N+ADV,
V+PRON+ADV

10 If you **put in** a phone call or a signal, you contact someone using a telephone or radio. ❑ *He put in the call and made himself another drink... I'll try to put a signal in to Control.*

V+ADV+N,
V+N+ADV,
V+PRON+ADV:
ALSO+to

11 To **put** someone or something **in** a particular state means to cause them to be in that state. ❑ *'I know,' said Meadows. 'It puts me in a rather difficult position.'... He has put me in charge of everything... Put yourself in a cool and patient frame of mind.*

V+PRON+PREP,
V+REFL+PREP,
V+N+PREP

12 If you **put** someone or something **in** a particular class or range, you estimate or judge them to belong in that class or range. ❑ *In America the microchip industry has been put in the 'top ten' industries for urgent attention... That would have put him in his eighties... Many people wouldn't put him in the same class as Verdi.*

V+N+PREP,
V+PRON+PREP

13 When people **put in** a person or group, they elect or appoint that person or group to do a particular job. ❑ *The French preferred the system of direct rule, putting in their own governors... They're putting me in as editor.*

V+ADV+N,
V+PRON+ADV,
V+N+ADV:
ALSO+as

NOTE Bring in means almost the same as **put in**.

14 If you **put** someone **in** an institution such as a jail, a hospital, or a special type of school, you cause them to go there or be there. ❑ *Should he put his elderly father-in-law in a nursing home?... They will declare me insane and put me in a psychiatric clinic... This was before John had been put in prison.*

V+N+PREP,
V+PRON+PREP

15 If you **put** someone **in** a particular room in a building, you ask them or allow them to be there or sleep there. ❑ *I was still in my room downstairs, and Sarah was put in the room above me... There's someone to see you, Sarah. I've put him in the study.*

V+N+PREP,
V+PRON+PREP

16 If you **put** someone **in** particular clothes, you cause them to be dressed in them. ❑ *You're not thinking of putting him in shorts and a shirt?... After this unfortunate event, the inspectors were put in uniform and given truncheons.*

V+PRON+PREP,
V+N+PREP

17 If you **put** faith, trust, or hope **in** someone or something, you feel confident or

V+N+PREP

The symbol ★ shows key phrasal verbs

hopeful that they will do or be what you want. ❑ *They betrayed the people who put faith in them... Abram put his trust in the Lord.*

18 When a ship **puts in** at a place, it stops in that place for a short time. ❑ *Sooner or later a ship will put in here... We were refused permission to put in at Corfu.* V+ADV; ALSO+*at*

19 The **input** of electricity or other form of energy into a machine or system is the act of supplying it, the amount that is supplied, or the place where it enters the machine or system. ❑ *The energy input rate is so vast. ...the input current. ...the industry's over-reliance on high fuel inputs.* N-COUNT, N-UNCOUNT

20 The **input** of data or information into a computer system is the act of supplying it, the amount that is supplied, or the place where it enters the machine or system. ❑ *He replaced the keyboard input... It had a set of input devices. ...the paper tape input.* N-COUNT, N-UNCOUNT

put in for If you **put in for** something, you formally apply to have it. ❑ *'I didn't even know he applied.'—'Oh, he puts in for everything.'... After the gamekeeper John Daniel died, father put in for his job... He put in for leave, just to go to the funeral.* V+ADV+PREP

★put into

1 If you **put** one thing **into** another, you place it inside the other thing. ❑ *He put both his hands into his trouser pockets... I folded it carefully and put it into my shirt pocket.* V+N+PREP, V+PRON+PREP

2 If you **put** money **into** a bank or an account, you give the money to the bank, which will look after it for you. ❑ *How do I put money into my account?... My wife told me she was putting her salary into a savings account.* V+N+PREP, V+PRON+PREP

NOTE **Pay in** means almost the same as **put in**, and **take out** means the opposite.

3 If you **put** money **into** a business or a project, you provide money that it needs, and receive a profit if it is successful. ❑ *I put a lot of money into it... State funding is not put into alternative research... He had insisted on putting it into jewellery and pictures.* V+N+PREP, V+PRON+PREP

4 If you **put** time, effort, or other resources **into** an activity, you use it for doing that activity. ❑ *She put all her energy into tidying the place up. ...a feeling that resources need not be put into health and safety... All her imagination is put into her garden.* V+N+PREP, V+PRON+PREP

5 If you **put** an item **into** a piece of writing, a speech, or a drawing, you include that item or cause it to be included. ❑ *He tried but failed to put amendments into Callaghan's speech. ...all the American place-names that had been put into the titles of songs: 'Missouri Waltz', 'My Old Kentucky Home'.* V+N+PREP, V+PRON+PREP

NOTE **Insert** means almost the same as **put into**.

6 To **put** a feeling or attitude **into** someone or something means to cause them to feel it or have it. ❑ *...a noise that put fear into Frank's pounding heart. ...the passion put into the performance. ...a band of commanders whose successes put heart into the British people.* V+N+PREP, V+PRON+PREP

7 To **put** someone or something **into** another form or state means to cause them to be in that new form or state. ❑ *She wanted desperately to put her insight into words... It is not always easy to put it into modern English... Other people feel obliged to compete and put themselves into debt to do so.* V+N+PREP, V+PRON+PREP, V+REFL+PREP

8 To **put** someone or something **into** a particular class or type means to judge that they belong to that class or type. ❑ *This would put her into the category of a participant... He has told me that he puts the 'Gang of Four' into the same category as Ramsay MacDonald.* V+PRON+PREP, V+N+PREP

9 To **put** someone **into** a job or position means to appoint or elect them. ❑ *It was part of the plan to put Eisenhower into the job of Supreme Commander.* V+N+PREP, V+PRON+PREP

10 If someone **is put into** an institution such as a prison or mental hospital, they are sent to stay there by someone in authority. ❑ *She was about to be put into prison for a year... Put a child into an institution and all he wants is to go home.* V+N+PREP, V+PRON+PREP

11 If someone **is put into** a particular room in a building, they are told or allowed to be there or stay there. ❑ *When Josie returned, she was put into a room on the ground floor... I was put into a cell opposite the one I had been in all those months.* V+N+PREP; V+PRON+PREP: USUALLY PASSIVE

12 If you **put** someone **into** particular clothes, you cause them to dress them in those clothes. ❑ *Even tiny children were put into black frocks. ...putting him into grubby overalls... They were put into uniform and flown from Washington to Frankfurt.* V+N+PREP, V+PRON+PREP

13 If a ship **puts into** a port, it stops there for a short time. ❑ *We might have to put into Hammerfest for shelter.* V+PREP

For a full explanation of all grammatical labels, see pages xiii-xx

put on

★put off

1 If you **put off** an event or appointment, you delay or postpone it. If you **put** a person **off**, you delay seeing them or doing what they want you to do by telling them that you are too busy. ❑ *He had intended to put off seeing Daisy until after he had seen Gertrude... Don't put it off till tomorrow... She'll be here soon, unless I can put her off somehow... That would have put the end off for a while... Sollozzo can't be put off any more. You'll have to see him this week.*

V+ADV+N, V+PRON+ADV, V+N+ADV

2 To **put** someone **off** doing something or having something means to cause them to change their mind so that they no longer want to do it or have it. ❑ *I would not put anybody off wine-making... Nothing would put her off once she had made up her mind... Don't be put off because something doesn't have instant results.*

V+N+ADV/PREP, V+PRON+ADV/PREP, V+ADV+N

3 If something or someone **puts** you **off** what you are doing, they cause you to stop concentrating by making a sudden noise or distracting you in some other way. ❑ *Play stopped for nearly a minute when McEnroe was put off by a low-flying plane.*

V+N+ADV/PREP, V+PRON+ADV

4 To **put** someone **off** another person means to cause them to dislike that person. ❑ *I thought it more likely to put Gertrude off you... A number of people were put off Mike and termed him arrogant. ...a young actress who puts one off at first with her American briskness.*

V+N+ADV/PREP, V+PRON+ADV/PREP, V+ADV+N

♦ A **put-off** is something that causes you to dislike someone. [AMERICAN] ❑ *They are always alert for the slight put-off, the well-timed provocation.*

N-COUNT

♦ Someone or something that is **off-putting** causes you to dislike them. ❑ *...her rather off-putting manner... Those glasses are most off-putting. ...an off-putting mixture of affectation and stupidity.*

ADJECTIVE

5 If you **put** a light **off**, you move a switch so that it no longer shines. ❑ *I put the light off again... Don't forget to put all the lights off before you go to bed.*

V+N+ADV, V+PRON+ADV, V+ADV+N

NOTE **Switch off** and **put out** mean almost the same as **put off**.

6 When a ship or vehicle **puts** someone **off**, it stops somewhere in order to let them get off. ❑ *He was put off at Singapore.*

V+N+ADV, V+PRON+ADV, V+ADV+N

7 If you **put off** clothes, especially a uniform of some kind, you take them off and never wear them again. ❑ *...unwilling to put off the lovely dress for the last time... When a boy came of age in ancient Rome he put off his short tunic and assumed the toga virilis.*

V+ADV+N: NO PASSIVE

★put on

✓ In meanings 3-11, 18 and 19, the stress is on **on**.

1 If you **put** something **on** a horizontal surface, you place it above the surface, which supports it. ❑ *He put a hand on my shoulder. ...how the Americans ever managed to put a man on the moon... When it was all ready, she put it on a tray.*

V+N+PREP, V+PRON+PREP

2 If you **put** one thing **on** another, you attach or fix it to the other thing. ❑ *We put a new lock on the bedroom door... He took the ring and put it on Joseph's finger.*

V+N+PREP, V+PRON+PREP

3 When you **put on** a piece of clothing, you place it over a part of your body and wear it. ❑ *I put on my jacket... She put her glasses on... She zipped up the dress with difficulty. She had only put it on twice before... They put a scarlet robe on him.*

V+ADV+N, V+N+ADV/PREP, V+PRON+ADV/PREP

NOTE **Take off** means the opposite of **put on**.

4 When you **put on** make-up or ointment, you spread it over a part of your body. ❑ *She put lipstick on before every class... They must have put ointment on my burns... She has put on too much perfume.*

V+N+ADV/PREP, V+PRON+ADV/PREP, V+ADV+N

5 When a person or group **puts on** a play, concert, or other entertainment, they organize it or perform it. ❑ *He put on a play that closed after only eight performances... A production of A Midsummer Night's Dream was being put on at the school... We took nearly a year to put it on because Pamela was not available.*

V+ADV+N, V+N+ADV, V+PRON+ADV

NOTE **Stage** is a more formal word for **put on**.

6 When a person or organization **puts on** a service, they provide it. ❑ *Courses in History are put on at the request of other departments... They're putting on a special train service.*

V+ADV+N, V+N+ADV, V+PRON+ADV

NOTE **Lay on** means almost the same as **put on**, and **take off** means the opposite.

7 If someone **puts on** weight, they become heavier. ❑ *She put on over a stone... I can quickly spot whether they are putting weight on or losing it.*

V+ADV+N, V+N+ADV, V+PRON+ADV: NO PASSIVE

NOTE **Gain** means almost the same as **put on**, and **lose** means the opposite.

8 If you **put on** an electrical or gas device, you cause it to work by pressing a switch or turning a knob. ❑ *He put on the light... Shall I put the fire on?... They put the*

V+ADV+N, V+N+ADV, V+PRON+ADV

kettle on to make a cup of tea.

NOTE Turn on and switch on mean almost the same as put on.

9 If you are driving a vehicle and **put on** the brake, you operate it. ❑ *She had to put on her brake rather suddenly... Put the brake on and leave the car in gear.*

V+ADV+N,
V+N+ADV,
V+PRON+ADV

NOTE Apply is a more formal word for put on.

10 If you **put on** a CD, tape, or video, you place it in the CD player or in the tape machine so that you can hear it or see it. ❑ *She put on the Brahms Second Piano Concerto... Morris fixed himself a stiff drink and put an Aretha Franklin LP on the hi-fi.*

V+ADV+N,
V+N+ADV/PREP,
V+PRON+ADV/PREP

11 If you **put on** food, you begin to cook it. ❑ *She forgets to put the dinner on... He went into the kitchen and put on some potatoes to boil.*

V+N+ADV/PREP,
V+ADV+N,
V+PRON+ADV/PREP

12 If you **put** money **on** a race, a competition, or one of the competitors, you make a bet about who will win. ❑ *The only time I ever put a pound on a horse I felt sick... Nobody actually put any money on at those odds... I put a pound on for you.*

V+N+ADV/PREP,
V+PRON+ADV/PREP

13 If you **put** money **on** something, you are confident or sure that it is true, will happen, or will be successful. ❑ *Who would have put money on atomic energy in 1940?... He would have put money on it.*

V+N+PREP

14 To **put** an amount **on** the cost or value of something means to add it to the cost or value. ❑ *That decision will put another 5p a gallon on petrol... They have been known to put a tax on salt.*

V+N+PREP

NOTE Knock off means the opposite of put on.

15 To **put** a restriction **on** something means to make laws which stop people from doing it. ❑ *MAFF could help things along by putting an embargo on all grant aid... The United States put an immediate ban on all television coverage.*

V+N+PREP

16 If you **put** emphasis or reliance **on** something, you emphasize it or rely on it. If you **put** the blame for something on someone, you blame them for it. ❑ *Too much reliance was put on human nature. ...a system which would put more emphasis on individual freedom.*

V+N+PREP

17 If you **put** extra work, responsibility, or pressure **on** someone, you cause them to do it, have it, or feel it. ❑ *It puts a tremendous responsibility on us... People felt free to put more demands on the system.*

V+N+PREP

18 If you **put on** a look or a way of speaking or behaving, you look, speak, or behave in a way that is not natural to you or does not show what you really feel or think. If you say that someone **is putting** it **on**, you mean that they are pretending to feel something or to be something, or that they are exaggerating how ill or upset they are. ❑ *I don't see why you put on a phoney English accent. ...the grin she had put on for the cameras... I wondered if Clive was putting it on to avoid starting work.*

V+ADV+N,
V+N+ADV,
V+PRON+ADV,
V+it+ADV

19 If someone **is putting** you **on**, they are teasing you by trying to make you believe something that is not true. [AMERICAN, INFORMAL] ❑ *'You're putting me on,' said Deirdre... I also like the way you put me on a while ago. About his half a million.*

V+PRON+ADV,
V+N+ADV:
NO PASSIVE

NOTE Have on and kid mean almost the same as put on.

♦ A **put-on** is an action that is intended to tease or deceive someone. [INFORMAL] ❑ *I bet the whole thing was a put-on for those TV guys.*

N-SING

20 If you **put** someone **on** a bus, plane, train, or ship, you take them to it and make sure they get onto it. ❑ *Mummy put me on the train at Victoria... We put him on a plane to California this morning.*

V+N+PREP,
V+PRON+PREP

21 If you **put** someone **on** a committee or a particular job, you officially decide that they should have that position or do that work. ❑ *...companies that put trade union representatives on their boards... They put me on security work again at the weekends... 'Put him on the night shift,' Mr Ballott said.*

V+N+PREP,
V+PRON+PREP

22 If you **put** someone **on** the phone, you pass the phone to them so that they can speak to someone. ❑ *I asked him to put Lloyd on the phone... 'Can you put her on the phone?'—'Oh, she's in the hospital.'... Just put on Nell for one moment more, will you?*

V+N+ADV/PREP,
V+PRON+ADV/PREP,
V+ADV+N

23 If someone **is put on** a particular type of food, medical treatment, or punishment, they are given that food, treatment, or punishment. ❑ *After a while Laura saw the doctor and was put on a diet... They had to put him on oxygen... When they first came in they'd be put on pills.*

V+N+PREP,
V+PRON+PREP:
USUALLY PASSIVE

★put on to, put onto

1 If you **put** one thing **onto** another, you place it on top of the other thing or at-

V+N+PREP,

tach it to the other thing. ❑ *So she put a cloth onto her head, went into the church, and prayed... I put her back onto the bed.* V+PRON+PREP

2 If you **put** someone **onto** a bus, plane, train, or plane, you take them to it and make sure they get on it. ❑ *...putting me onto a French inter-village bus the next morning.* V+PRON+PREP, V+N+PREP

3 If you **put** someone **on to** someone or something, you tell them about someone or something that could help them. ❑ *Directory Enquiries put him on to the International Exchange... An accident put me on to the work of Husserl... I can put you onto a good thing, Charlie.* V+PRON+PREP, V+N+PREP

★put out

1 If a statement or story **is put out**, it is officially told to people. ❑ *The World Wildlife Fund put out a press release... The story that the committee will put out has nothing to do with the truth... He put something out to the Press Association.* V+ADV+N, V+N+ADV, V+PRON+ADV

NOTE **Issue** means almost the same as **put out**.

2 If a message or programme **is put out** on radio or television, it is sent or broadcast. ❑ *The pilot put out a radio message giving the exact position... The Open University courses were actually putting some of them out on the television screen... It was put out by the non-commercial network OXYZ.* V+ADV+N, V+N+ADV, V+PRON+ADV: ALSO+on

NOTE **Broadcast** is a more formal word for **put out**.

3 If you **put out** something that is burning, you cause it to stop burning. ❑ *He put the fire out. ...putting out the candles... The fire could not be put out too easily... I lit another cigarette, but immediately put it out.* V+N+ADV, V+ADV+N, V+PRON+ADV

NOTE **Extinguish** is a more formal word for **put out**.

4 If you **put out** a light, you cause it to stop shining by pressing or turning a switch. ❑ *Castle undressed and put out the light... He put his torch out... 'Will you put the lights out or shall I?'—'You put them out, dear.'* V+ADV+N, V+N+ADV, V+PRON+ADV

NOTE **Switch off** and **turn off** mean almost the same as **put out**.

5 If you are at home and **put** something **out**, you take it out of the house and leave it there for someone to collect. ❑ *She still can't remember to put out the milk bottles... You must not put your dustbin out before 7.30 a.m.* V+ADV+N, V+N+ADV, V+PRON+ADV

NOTE **Bring in** means the opposite of **put out**.

6 If you **put out** babies, invalids, or animals, you take them from a building and leave them outside for a while. ❑ *She used to put the babies out in the pram... They put their horses out to graze... I do everything from washing up dishes to putting out the cat at night.* V+N+ADV, V+ADV+N, V+PRON+ADV

7 If you **put** things **out** for someone, you put them somewhere where they will be noticed and used. ❑ *I put clean clothes out for you on the bed... All equipment and materials are put out at the beginning... I went into his office, opened his post and put it out on his desk... Now he goes about, putting out ashtrays and dishes, cushions and chairs.* V+N+ADV, V+PRON+ADV, V+ADV+N

NOTE **Lay out** means almost the same as **put out**, and **collect up** means the opposite.

8 If you **put out** a hand, an arm, or a foot, you move it forward and away from your body. ❑ *I slipped and put out my arm to save myself... Judy put out her hands and held Lynn tight... Put your left foot out... Denise put her hand out to restrain him.* V+ADV+N, V+N+ADV, V+PRON+ADV: NO PASSIVE

NOTE **Hold out** means almost the same as **put out**.

9 If you **put** your tongue **out**, you poke it through your lips, usually as a rude gesture. ❑ *He put his tongue out at his daughter playfully... 'Put out your tongue,' she said, and I obeyed.* V+N+ADV, V+ADV+N, V+PRON+ADV: NO PASSIVE

NOTE **Stick out** means almost the same as **put out**.

10 If you **put** your back or a joint in your body **out**, you accidentally cause a bone to be moved from its normal position. ❑ *More backs have been put out cleaning baths than in any other activity... It becomes weak and puts the kneecap out.* V+N+ADV, V+PRON+ADV

NOTE **Dislocate** is a more formal word for **put out**.

11 If you **are put out**, someone or something has upset or annoyed you. ❑ *Lally looked a bit put out... He didn't appear at all put out by the news... 'So?' asked von Amsburg, obviously put out by the general's answer.* PASSIVE: V+ADV

NOTE **Be disconcerted** is a more formal expression for **be put out**.

♦ Someone's **put-out** expression indicates that they have been upset or annoyed. ❑ *'He'll be right back,' she said in a slightly put-out tone.* ADJECTIVE

12 If you **put** yourself **out**, you make an effort to do something or help someone, although it may be inconvenient for you. ❏ *He was putting himself out to please her... 'He would not put himself out to do a thing', Dot said.*

V+REFL+ADV

13 If you **put** someone **out**, you cause them trouble or inconvenience. ❏ *Don't think you're putting her out in any way. She likes nothing better.*

V+PRON+ADV, V+N+ADV

14 If you **put** someone **out** of a place, vehicle, or job, you make them leave it, sometimes by force. ❏ *I was put out of the school on the ground that I was useless... You can be put out on your ear at the end of the month... We put him out of the house... Irving stopped the cab and put his wife out of it.*

V+PRON+ADV, V+N+ADV, V+ADV+N: ALSO+of

15 In a sporting competition, to **put out** a player or team means to defeat them so that they are no longer in the competition. ❏ *Another Spaniard, Emilio Sanchez, put out Jens Woehrmann in three sets. ...the debatable goal that put Villa out of the UEFA Cup in Milan.*

V+ADV+N, V+N+ADV, V+PRON+ADV: ALSO+of

NOTE **Knock out** means almost the same as **put out**.

16 When a boat or ship **puts out**, it leaves its harbour and sails into the sea. ❏ *We could see the boats putting out for the first of the summer herring... Occasionally it is too rough for the launch to put out.*

V+ADV

17 If someone **puts out**, they agree to have sex. [INFORMAL]

V+ADV

18 To **put** someone **out** means to cause them to become unconscious. ❏ *The doctor agreed to put her out altogether during the birth.*

V+PRON+ADV, V+N+ADV

19 When a plant or tree **puts out** buds, leaves or flowers, the buds, leaves or flowers grow and become visible on it. ❏ *When it starts putting out leaves, you know that summer is near... The dead stakes rot and disappear, but the hedge puts out new growth... It put out an exquisite spring blossom.*

V+ADV+N, V+N+ADV, V+PRON+ADV

20 If a company **puts out** products, it manufactures them, publishes them, or sells them. ❏ *...a small publishing firm that put out expensively bound reprints... Behind the gramophone there were some records put out by an American company.*

V+ADV+N, V+N+ADV, V+PRON+ADV

NOTE **Produce** means almost the same as **put out**.

21 The **output** of someone or something is the amount of something that they produce, or the thing that they produce. ❏ *...a 3 per cent fall in industrial output... Her rapid output of novels and poetry encouraged him.*

N-UNCOUNT

22 Computer **output** is the information which a computer produces as the result of a particular program or operation. ❏ *...output data... There's something wrong with this output.*

N-UNCOUNT

★**put out of** To **put** someone or something **out of** a state or condition, means to stop them being in it. ❏ *All three tanks were very quickly put out of action... Always put poisons out of reach... Technological developments may put them completely out of business.*

V+N+ADV+PREP

★put over

1 If you **put** one thing **over** another, you place it so that it covers the other thing. ❏ *The postmistress put a rug over her knees... She put a hand over his... He took off his anorak and put it over the back of the chair.*

V+N+PREP, V+PRON+PREP

2 If you **put** one thing **over** another on a vertical surface or on a piece of paper, you place or write it above the other thing. ❏ *Alan put a sign over the entrance gate. ...put dots over each letter.*

V+N+PREP, V+PRON+PREP

3 When you **put** an idea **over**, you succeed in describing or explaining it to someone. ❏ *There are enough of them to put over their point of view... The university's prospectuses didn't put it over the way I wanted to... With the modern resources available, you can put an article over nationally or world-wide.*

V+ADV+N, V+PRON+ADV, V+N+ADV

NOTE **Put across** and **get across** mean almost the same as **put over**.

put past If you would not **put** something **past** someone, you think that they are likely to do it or are capable of doing it, even though you disapprove of it. ❏ *I wouldn't put anything past her in the company she's keeping now... I wouldn't put it past you to hop on a plane and go after Liebermann yourself.*

V+N+PREP, V+PRON+PREP: WITH NEGATIVE

★put round → See put around

★put through

1 If you **put** something **through** a solid object, you pass it from one side to the other either by pushing it through a hole, or by by making a hole through it by force. ❏ *She simply put her hand through the letter-box and opened the door from the in-*

V+N+ADV/PREP, V+PRON+ADV/PREP

side... Put an iron rod through at each end to hold the ladder together... Put them through the rings on each side of the box... He put his foot through the plaster.

2 If you **put** your arm **through** someone else's arm, you link arms with them to show affection or to control their movements. ❑ *The trainer caught him up and put his arm through the boy's... Gertrude put her arm through Tim's and led him away.*

V+N+PREP, V+PRON+PREP

3 If you **put** objects or substances **through** a machine or a mechanical, electrical, or chemical process, you cause it to be affected and changed by them. ❑ *Put cooked vegetables and fruit through the blender... In the factories, they were put through an elaborate process to produce syrup.*

V+N+PREP, V+PRON+PREP

♦ The **throughput** of a machine or factory is the amount of material that it deals with or the rate at which it does so. [TECHNICAL] ❑ *...machines that can handle a rapid throughput of raw materials.*

N-COUNT

4 If you **put** plans, proposals, or problems **through** an official system, organization, or person, you ask them for advice, approval or support. ❑ *...putting our case through the normal media channels... No need to put it through my department at all. I'll handle it personally.*

V+N+PREP, V+PRON+PREP

5 If people in authority **put through** a proposal or plan, they formally agree to it. ❑ *They put through the first nuclear arms agreements... He was planning to put through his arms deal, despite official US disapproval... They had at last succeeded in putting a meaningful reform through.*

V+ADV+N, V+N+ADV, V+PRON+ADV

6 If you **put** a message **through** to someone, you succeed in sending it to them. ❑ *I've put a teleprinter request through to Washington... It would do no harm to put through the enquiry without revealing why it was being made... Yes, that would save putting it through the post.*

V+N+ADV/PREP, V+PRON+ADV/PREP, V+ADV+N

7 If you **put through** a phone call or the person making the call, you connect them with the person they want to speak to. ❑ *Please don't put any calls through until this class is over... Who? Martha? Okay. Yes, put her through... Warlimont put through a call to Blumentritt at OB West... Townsend picked up the receiver and was put through to the Laboratory.*

V+N+ADV, V+PRON+ADV, V+ADV+N: ALSO+to

8 If you **put** someone **through** school or college, you pay their fees and expenses for them. ❑ *He only put his daughter through college by selling off his wife's jewellery... His grandparents offered to put him through dental school... While working as a civil servant in Natal, he put himself through several diploma courses.*

V+N+PREP, V+PRON+PREP, V+REFL+PREP

9 If you **put** someone or something **through** an event or experience, you make them do it or suffer it. ❑ *It's not right to put him through a lot of tests... I'm sorry to put you through this again... Hoffmann put the lorry through a series of rough manoeuvres.*

V+PRON+PREP, V+N+PREP

10 The **throughput** of people in an organization or system is the number of people that it deals with. ❑ *...Gatwick, with an annual throughput rising to 10 million passengers a year... The organization has a faster throughput of people as well... Total passenger throughput is expected to rise.*

N-COUNT

★put to

1 If you **put** one thing **to** another, you place or hold it next to the other thing and touching it. ❑ *He put a finger to his lips in a gesture of silence... Don did this by putting a pistol to the forehead of the band leader... He struck a match and put it to his pipe.*

V+N+PREP, V+PRON+PREP

2 If you **put** a name, figure, date, or face **to** something or someone, you are able to remember, calculate, or estimate who, what, or how much they are. ❑ *He recognised the face, but he couldn't put a name to it... They might even put a figure to the resources required... Most people, when asked to put a date to it, assume that it was designed during the last century.*

V+N+PREP

3 If you **put** an idea, question, or problem **to** someone, you ask them to consider it or react to it. ❑ *...the sort of questions that I'll be putting to the scientists... They formally put the demand to me. ...a motion to be put to the next party Conference... He put it to you that Griffiths was driving.*

V+N+PREP, V+PRON+PREP

4 If something **puts** you **to** a lot of trouble or expense, it makes you spend a lot of your time or money doing something that you would prefer not to have to do. ❑ *But if we refuse to confirm it, it'll put you to the trouble of proving it for the court record... I'm only sorry that I put you to so much trouble.*

V+PRON+PREP, V+N+PREP

★put together

1 If you **put together** an object or its parts, you join its parts to each other so that it can be used. ❑ *The shipyards possess years of expertise in putting together such big metal structures... Grease the valve thoroughly and put the parts together again... Anyone can put it together in a few hours.*

V+ADV+N,
V+N+ADV,
V+PRON+ADV

NOTE **Assemble** is a more formal word for **put together**, and **take apart** means the opposite.

2 If you **put together** similar things, objects, or substances, or a particular combination of them, you place them near each other, in the same container, or touching each other. ❑ *Three tables were put together for them... They put them together in a test-tube... She put together a fresh fruit salad.*

V+N+ADV,
V+PRON+ADV,
V+ADV+N

3 If you **put together** a group of people, you choose them and form them into a team or group for a particular purpose. ❑ *This time Crook had put together a mighty army... They put together a small baseball team... The lawyers had put together an impressive assembly of defense witnesses.*

V+ADV+N,
V+N+ADV,
V+PRON+ADV

4 If you **put together** a project or a piece of work, you organize it or arrange it. ❑ *The agency has put together the biggest ever campaign for a new car... The whole production was somewhat hastily put together.*

V+ADV+N,
V+N+ADV,
V+PRON+ADV

5 If you **put together** words, facts, figures, or ideas, you consider them carefully and use them to create a piece of writing, a speech, a plan, or a theory. ❑ *He found it difficult to put a dozen words together at a time... I was busy writing a new play and I had to put my thoughts together... Beverley Nichols put together a collection of interviews with famous people... I have a lot of talent, if only I can put it together.*

V+N+ADV,
V+ADV+N,
V+PRON+ADV

6 If you say that one person or thing is better, or greater in size, amount or importance than a group of other people or things **put together** you are emphasizing how much better or greater they are. ❑ *He is smarter than all your colonels put together... The schools spend as much as the rest of the city put together... She was wiser than the other two put together.*

ADVERB

put towards If you **put** money **towards** something that you want to buy, you save the money until you have enough to buy it. ❑ *If I do win, I'll put the money towards a new car.*

V+N+PREP,
V+PRON+PREP

★put up

1 If you **put** something **up**, or **put** it **up** somewhere, you move it to a higher position or place it farther away from the ground. ❑ *He put up the collar of his jacket... I put the window up to hear this speech... I got a box and put it up against the wall... He put his hands up over his face and cried.*

V+ADV+N,
V+N+ADV,
V+PRON+ADV

2 If you **put** one thing **up** another, you push it so that it is inside the other thing. ❑ *He put his hand up her coat and pulled out the pin.*

V+N+PREP,
V+PRON+PREP

3 If you **put up** a building, wall, shelf, or similar structure, you build it or fix it in place. ❑ *We shall have to put up a fence... They're going to put up a whole block of apartments... It was always collapsing on my toes because I hadn't put it up properly.*

V+ADV+N,
V+PRON+ADV,
V+N+ADV

NOTE **Erect** and **construct** are more formal words for **put up**, and **pull down** means the opposite.

4 If you **put up** something that is folded, such as an umbrella, tent, or hood, you open it or spread it out so that it can be used. ❑ *Put your umbrella up... Why doesn't she put the hood up?... Take the tent and put it up some distance away from the camp.*

V+N+ADV,
V+PRON+ADV,
V+ADV+N

5 If you **put up** a notice, sign, or poster, you stick or fasten it to a wall, post, or noticeboard so that people can see it. ❑ *She put up a large sign outside her house... We would put the signs up for his inspection, then take them down... I cut his notes out and put them up in the classroom... These posters were put up all over the area.*

V+ADV+N,
V+N+ADV,
V+PRON+ADV

NOTE **Stick up** and **post up** mean almost the same as **put up**, and **take down** means the opposite.

6 If you **put up** opposition, resistance, or a fight, you oppose, resist, or fight something. ❑ *America has put up so much resistance to Concord... We had put up a fierce struggle.*

V+ADV+N

7 If you **put up** an idea, argument, or proposal, you tell it or suggest it to people so that they can consider it and discuss it. ❑ *...the argument that the Vatican is putting up all the time... He wouldn't have put up such a good case for himself... Why not check and*

V+ADV+N,
V+N+ADV,
V+PRON+ADV

then we'll put it up to the others?

NOTE **Put forward** and **put forth** mean almost the same as **put up**.

8 If you **put up** money for something, you provide the money that is needed to pay for it. ❑ *The banks will not put up money without government backing... They put up their own cash... The National Endowment for the Arts put up half the cost.* V+ADV+N

9 To **put up** the price or rate of something means to cause it to increase. ❑ *In about 1920, he put the price up to 2 shillings per pound... They will not put it up a lot because of the old people... Their governments put up prices too far... The mortgage rate had been put up on the house.* V+N+ADV, V+PRON+ADV, V+ADV+N

NOTE **Raise** means almost the same as **put up**, and **bring down** means the opposite.

10 If someone **puts** you **up** or if you **put up** somewhere, you stay with them or stay there for one or more nights. ❑ *The Murrays had put him up for the night... We can't put him up here... She was put up at the Grand Hotel... We put up at Chestnut Court.* V+PRON+ADV, V+N+ADV, V+ADV+N, V+ADV

11 If you **put** something **up** for sale or auction, for example, you make it available to be sold or auctioned. ❑ *The company should put its claims up for review by an arbitrator... The old flower and fruit market has been put up for sale... She put up her daughter for adoption in 1967.* V+N+ADV, V+ADV+N, V+PRON+ADV: USUALLY+for

12 If you **put up** or **are put up** in an election or contest, you are chosen to be a candidate or competitor in it. ❑ *They put up several candidates in Cornwall... He put up as an independent candidate... Jack is effective enough in his way; but put him up against a real boxer like Brood and he wouldn't stand a chance.* V+ADV+N, V+ADV: ERGATIVE

13 A **put-up** job is something that has been arranged beforehand in order to cheat or deceive someone. [INFORMAL] ❑ *It was a put-up job, if ever there was one.* ADJECTIVE

put upon

1 If you **put** one object **upon** another, you place it on top of the other thing. [LITERARY, OLD-FASHIONED] ❑ *He put his hand gently upon it and felt the coolness... A red cloth had been put upon the table.* V+N+PREP, V+PRON+PREP

NOTE **Put on** means almost the same as **put upon**.

2 If you **put** a particular value or interpretation **upon** something, you think it has that value or meaning. [FORMAL] ❑ *What value would they put upon her? ...the unfortunate interpretation you put upon my laughter.* V+N+PREP, V+PRON+PREP

3 To **put** pressure, demands, or restrictions **upon** someone means to cause them to suffer by what you ask them to do or not to do. [FORMAL] ❑ *His parents put demands upon him that are not in his interest. ...the pressures put upon them to prescribe more drugs. ...restrictions put upon them by their culture and religion.* V+N+PREP, V+PRON+PREP

4 If you **are put upon**, someone unfairly asks or expects you to do more than you originally offered or agreed to do. [OLD-FASHIONED] ❑ *We are not prepared to be put upon... Thank you, Ibrahim. I really am sorry to put upon you.* V+PREP: HAS PASSIVE

NOTE **Impose on** means almost the same as **put upon**.

♦ A **put-upon** person has been unfairly asked or expected to do too much. Their **put-upon** expression shows this. [INFORMAL] ❑ *...Halliwell, Orton's put-upon friend. ...an expression as mild and put-upon as his father's. ...the poor, put-upon, innocent soul!* ADJECTIVE

put up to If you **put** someone **up to** something, you ask and encourage them to do something wrong or foolish. ❑ *He wondered if Benny hadn't put Fitzsimmons up to it... Someone put Sid up to this... Julie herself had probably put them up to it.* V+N+ADV+PREP, V+PRON+ADV+PREP

★**put up with** If you **put up with** something or someone, you tolerate or accept them, even though you find it difficult or unpleasant. ❑ *I'm prepared to put up with it for the time being... The visitors could put up with any amount of boredom... 'Why do the people put up with it?' demanded Hilary.* V+ADV+PREP

NOTE **Endure** is a more formal word for **put up with**.

putter /pʌtəʳ/ (putters, puttering, puttered)

putter around If you **putter around**, you pass the time in a gentle, unhurried way, doing small and unimportant tasks. [AMERICAN] ❑ *I started puttering around outside, not knowing what I was doing.* V+ADV, V+PREP

puzzle /pˈʌzəl/ (puzzles, puzzling, puzzled)

puzzle out If you **puzzle** a problem **out**, you think hard about it and usually find the answer. ❑ *If you have time to puzzle it out... I leave them to puzzle it out... They understand how a child puzzles things out... Children pause to puzzle out the nature of the task.*

V+PRON+ADV,
V+N+ADV,
V+ADV+N

NOTE **Solve** is a more formal word for **puzzle out**.

puzzle over If you **puzzle over** something, you think hard about it in order to try to understand it. ❑ *There was scarcely time to puzzle over these features... They puzzled over what could be inside the houses... She puzzled over it, then recalled the conversation they had... He frowned and puzzled the matter over.*

V+PREP:
HAS PASSIVE:
ALSO V+N+ADV

NOTE **Ponder** is a more formal word for **puzzle over**.

Qq

quarrel /kwɒrəl, AM kwɔːr-/ **(quarrels, quarrelling, quarrelled)**

☑ American English uses the spellings **quarreling** and **quarreled**.

quarrel with

1 If you **quarrel with** someone, you disagree with them strongly and argue or sometimes fight with them. ❑ *'I don't want to quarrel with her,' she said. 'She's my oldest friend.'... She quarrelled with Christopher over the lease.*

V+PREP:
ALSO+over/about

2 If you **quarrel with** an idea, statement, or opinion, you disagree with it. ❑ *One may quarrel with McHale's contention... I think Canetti would quarrel with the use of the word madness... Royalty is intimacy. Nobody could quarrel with that.*

V+PREP:
HAS PASSIVE,
USUALLY WITH MODAL

queen /kwiːn/ **(queens, queening, queened)**

queen over

If someone **queens** it **over** you, they act in a way that shows that they think they are better than you, for example by telling you what to do. ❑ *...a dozen cats queened over by the mother... All right, but don't you try to queen it over me.*

V+N+PREP
V+it+PREP

NOTE **Lord over** means almost the same as **queen over**.

queue /kjuː/ **(queues, queueing/queuing, queued)**

★queue up

If you **queue up**, you stand in a line of people and wait for something. [BRITISH] ❑ *Supaya had to queue up at the factory every morning to see if there was any work... People were queueing up for his autograph.*

V+ADV

quicken /kwɪkən/ **(quickens, quickening, quickened)**

quicken up

If you **quicken** something **up**, or if it **quickens up**, its speed increases. ❑ *Start these movements slowly and then quicken them up... Then the pace began to quicken up.*

V+PRON+ADV,
V+N+ADV,
V+ADV+N,
V+ADV:
ERGATIVE

NOTE **Speed up** means almost the same as **quicken up**.

quiet /kwaɪət/ **(quiets, quieting, quieted)**

quiet down

If someone or something **quiets down**, or if you **quiet** them **down**, they become less noisy or active, or more calm. [AMERICAN] ❑ *When he quieted down, I began to tell him the simple truth... Meanwhile, things quieted down in Los Angeles.*

V+ADV,
V+ADV+N,
V+N+ADV,
V+PRON+ADV:
ERGATIVE

NOTE **Calm down** means almost the same as **quiet down**.

quieten /kwaɪətən/ **(quietens, quietening, quietened)**

quieten down

If something or someone **quietens down**, or if you **quieten** them **down**, they become less noisy or active, or more calm. [BRITISH] ❑ *He had matured and quietened down considerably. ...a cunning stratagem to quieten down the rebellious peasants.*

V+ADV,
V+ADV+N,
V+N+ADV,
V+PRON+ADV:
ERGATIVE

NOTE **Calm down** means almost the same as **quieten down**.

Rr

rabbit /ˈræbɪt/ **(rabbits, rabbiting, rabbited)**

rabbit on If someone **rabbits on** about something, they talk about it for a long time in a rather boring way. [BRITISH, INFORMAL] ❑ ...liberals on both sides rabbiting on endlessly about underprivilege. ...TV commentators with the ability to keep rabbiting on about whatever is happening.

V+ADV: USUALLY+about

rack /ræk/ **(racks, racking, racked)**

rack up If a business **racks up** profits, losses, or sales, it makes a lot of them. If a sportsman, sportswoman, or team **racks up** wins, they win a lot of matches or races. ❑ Lower rates mean that firms are more likely to rack up profits in the coming months... India, while not racking up such an impressive score, beat Japan 3-0.

V+ADV+N, V+PRON+ADV

rage /reɪdʒ/ **(rages, raging, raged)**

rage against If you **rage against** a person or situation, you express your great anger about them. [LITERARY] ❑ Postmen rage against the handwriting of correspondents.

V+PREP

rail /reɪl/ **(rails, railing, railed)**

rail against If you **rail against** a person or situation, you express your great anger about them. [LITERARY] ❑ He railed against the doctors for forbidding it.

V+PREP

rain /reɪn/ **(rains, raining, rained)**

rain down If a lot of things **rain down** on a person or place, they fall rapidly on them. [LITERARY] ❑ Millions of tons of volcanic ash rained down over a huge area... Their sticks rained down even harder.

V+ADV

rain off If a sports match **is rained off**, it has to stop, or it is not able to start, because of rain. [BRITISH] ❑ Today's match between Yorkshire and Kent has been rained off.

PASSIVE: V+ADV

rain out If a sports game **is rained out**, it has to stop, or it is not able to start, because of rain. [AMERICAN] ❑ Saturday's game was rained out.

PASSIVE: V+ADV

NOTE **Rained off** means the same as **rained out** in British English.

rake /reɪk/ **(rakes, raking, raked)**

rake in If someone **is raking in** money, or **raking** it **in**, they are earning a lot of money fairly easily. [INFORMAL] ❑ Western countries raked in 78 per cent of the income... They've got so many shops, they must be raking it in!

V+ADV+N, V+N+ADV, V+it+ADV

rake over If someone **rakes over** an unpleasant event in the past, they keep talking about it even though it would be better to forget it. ❑ Why travel back into the past to rake over old worries?... It is too early to rake over the reputations of those so recently dead.

V+ADV+N

rake up

1 If someone **rakes up** something unpleasant or embarrassing that happened to you in the past, they find out about it and tell other people in order to cause trouble. [INFORMAL] ❑ ...if one political Party was allowed to rake up all the misdeeds or mistakes of another party... Don't go raking up that filth that happened thirteen years ago.

V+ADV+N, V+PRON+ADV, V+N+ADV

2 If you **rake up** people or things, you find them and bring them together for a particular purpose. [INFORMAL] ❑ I'll see if I can rake up a few people to help you.

V+ADV+N, V+PRON+ADV, V+N+ADV

rally /ˈræli/ **(rallies, rallying, rallied)**

✓ In American English, **around** is much more common than **round**.

rally around If people **rally around** or **rally round** you, they work together to support you at a difficult time. ❑ Yes, I'm very lucky. Everyone has rallied round... The girls have rallied round and coped magnificently... There's a natural tendency for people to rally around their country's flag.

V+ADV, V+PREP

rally round → See **rally around**

ram /ræm/ (**rams, ramming, rammed**)
ram down

1 If you **ram** an object **down**, you push it hard and suddenly towards the ground. ❑ *Ram the stick down and it lifts up the catch... Reload it with gunpowder and ram down the wad.*

V+N+ADV,
V+ADV+N,
V+PRON+ADV

2 If you **ram** a fact or idea **down** someone's throat, especially when they know it already or do not want to know it, you tell them about it forcefully and repeatedly. ❑ *...wanting to ram his world record down their throats... Weinberger takes a harder line. He wants to ram it down their throats.*

V+N+PREP,
V+PRON+PREP

ram in If you **ram** an object **in**, you push it very hard and suddenly into a container. ❑ *Why don't we lift the lot up in the sheet and ram it all in?... He took out his pipe, rammed in some tobacco and lit up... The old man rammed the key in with a trembling finger.*

V+PRON+ADV,
V+ADV+N,
V+N+ADV

ram into

1 If you **ram into** something, you hit it very hard while moving towards it very quickly. If you **ram** one object **into** another, you move it quickly so that it hits the other object very hard. ❑ *Drivers still drunkenly ram into trees... He rammed his fist into Hooper's throat.*

V+PREP,
V+N+PREP,
V+PRON+PREP:
ERGATIVE

2 If you **ram** ideas or facts **into** someone, you force that person to learn them or remember them. ❑ *He felt that he had rammed it into a few minds sufficiently hard.*

V+PRON+PREP,
V+N+PREP

ramble /ræmbəl/ (**rambles, rambling, rambled**)

ramble on If someone **rambles on**, they talk or write for a long time in a rather confused and disordered way. ❑ *...listening to Miriam as she rambled on... He needed to ramble on about his financial affairs... But there I go, rambling on. Please forgive me.*

V+ADV

ramp /ræmp/ (**ramps, ramping, ramped**)

ramp up To **ramp up** something means to increase it. ❑ *Producers were ramping up production to meet the tidal wave of demand... Mr Skate wasted no time in ramping up security.*

V+ADV+N,
V+N+ADV,
V+PRON+ADV

range /reɪndʒ/ (**ranges, ranging, ranged**)

range against If one person or thing **is ranged against** another, they are opposed to or in conflict with the other one. ❑ *The forces of reaction will be strongly ranged against the next Labour Government. ...his rage at finding the system ranged against him.*

PASSIVE:
V+PREP

rank /ræŋk/ (**ranks, ranking, ranked**)

rank among If a person or thing **ranks among** a particular type or group, they have the qualities of that type or group. ❑ *Academically, Tony never ranked among the scholars... This county ranks among the wealthiest in the country.*

V+PREP

rap /ræp/ (**raps, rapping, rapped**)

rap out If you **rap out** something, especially an order or a question, you say it quickly and sharply. ❑ *'Is that the truth?' he suddenly rapped out... She rapped out the orders urgently. ...and rapped out the announcement.*

V+ADV+QUOTE,
V+ADV+N,
V+PRON+ADV,
V+N+ADV

rat /ræt/ (**rats, ratting, ratted**)

rat on If someone **rats on** you, they give information to people in authority that causes you to be punished or to have problems. [INFORMAL] ❑ *So you ratted on Gertrude?... If they got caught, it wouldn't be because of Quiller ratting on them.*

V+PREP:
HAS PASSIVE

rat out If someone **rats** you **out**, they tell someone in authority about something wrong you have done. [AMERICAN, INFORMAL] ❑ *A lot of kids are afraid to go to the guidance counselors, because they think if they go in there people are going to rat them out.*

V+N+ADV,
V+PRON+ADV,
V+ADV+N

ratchet /rætʃɪt/ (**ratchets, ratcheting, ratcheted**)

ratchet down If something **ratchets down** or **is ratcheted down**, it decreases by a fixed amount or degree, and seems unlikely to increase again. [JOURNALISM] ❑ *We're trying to ratchet down the administrative costs... Defence budgets around the world have been ratcheted down for more than a decade.*

V+ADV+N,
V+N+ADV,
V+PRON+ADV,
V+ADV:
ERGATIVE

NOTE **Ratchet up** means the opposite of **ratchet down**.

ratchet up If something **ratchets up** or **is ratcheted up**, it increases by a fixed amount or degree, and seems unlikely to decrease again. [JOURNALISM] ❑ *...an*

V+ADV+N,
V+N+ADV,
V+PRON+ADV,

attempt to ratchet up the pressure on Israel... He fears inflation will ratchet up as the year ends... Audiences' expectations are ratcheted up as they are exposed to high-budget productions.

V+ADV:
ERGATIVE

NOTE **Escalate** is a more formal word for **ratchet up**, and **ratchet down** means the opposite.

ration /ræʃən/ (rations, rationing, rationed)

ration out If you **ration out** something that you have very little of, you distribute it in small amounts among a group of people. ❑ *I rationed out the last of the food... They will ration it out, and you will accept what you're given... The limited funds available have to be rationed out among local groups.*

V+ADV+N,
V+PRON+ADV,
V+N+ADV

rattle /rætəl/ (rattles, rattling, rattled)

rattle around If you say that someone **rattles around** in a room or other space, you mean that the space is too large for them. ❑ *We don't want to move, but we're rattling around in our large house.*

V+PREP,
V+ADV:
ALSO+in

rattle off To **rattle** something **off** means to say or do it quickly and without effort. ❑ *...a machine capable of rattling off thousands of calculations per second... Rhoda, surprisingly, rattled off the Mozart sonata with ease.*

V+ADV+N,
V+PRON+ADV,
V+N+ADV

NOTE **Reel off** means almost the same as **rattle off**.

rattle on If someone **rattles on** about something, they talk about it for a long time, speaking quickly and in a rather irritating way. ❑ *Some of the women would rattle on about sex... She rattled on excitedly about Mrs Moffat... Denise was rattling on: 'I looked and you weren't there.'*

V+ADV:
USUALLY+about

NOTE **Rabbit on** means almost the same as **rattle on**.

rattle through If you **rattle through** something, you deal with it very quickly in order to finish it. [BRITISH] ❑ *They rattled through the rest of the meeting... He rattled through his envelopes again.*

V+PREP

rave /reɪv/ (raves, raving, raved)

rave about If someone **raves about** something or if they **rave on about** it, they speak or write about it very enthusiastically. ❑ *He rang me from New York to rave about a new writer he had discovered... United fans may rave on about the talent in their own team but it is no different here in Munich.*

V+ADV+N,
V+ADV+PREP

rave on about → See **rave about**

rave up If you **rave** it **up**, you enjoy yourself by drinking and dancing and behaving in a noisy and uncontrolled way. [OLD-FASHIONED] ❑ *...a huge audience raving it up under the stars.*

V+it+ADV

♦ A **rave-up** is an event at which people drink, dance, and behave in a noisy and uncontrolled way. [OLD-FASHIONED] ❑ *I was looking forward to a real rave-up. ...a rave-up holiday.*

N-COUNT

reach /riːtʃ/ (reaches, reaching, reached)

reach down

1 If you **reach down**, you bend your body towards the ground and stretch your arms in order to touch or grasp something. ❑ *I remove a glove with my teeth, reach down and and feel the cover... Dick reached down and grabbed his wrists.*

V+ADV

2 If something **reaches down** to a particular level, it extends downwards as far as that level. ❑ *Only expensive tube-wells can reach down to the reserves of water. ...a long blue skirt reaching down to the ground.*

V+ADV:
ALSO+to

★**reach out** If you **reach out**, or **reach out** a hand, you stretch your arm, and sometimes your body, in order to do something slightly far away from you. ❑ *Otto reached out for the bottle of wine... Howard reaches out of the window and hands the ticket to him. ...reach out a hand and touch the man's arm.*

V+ADV,
V+ADV+N

reach out for If people **reach out for** better things, they make great efforts to get or achieve them. ❑ *They now reach out for further satisfactions. ...reaching out for new standards. ...a society reaching out for a better quality of life.*

V+ADV+PREP

reach out to If you **reach out to** people, you give them help, advice, or comfort, or ask them for it. ❑ *His phenomenal capacity to reach out to people... They may reach out to another person for reassurance.*

V+ADV+PREP

♦ **Outreach** workers are employed by local government to find people who need

ADJECTIVE

help and persuade them to apply for it, so that social problems can be dealt with before they become severe. ❏ *...vacancies for outreach workers.*

★reach up

1 If you **reach up**, you stretch your body and arms upwards in order to touch or grasp something. ❏ *He reached up and slid the top bolt. ...reaching up to pull the lavatory chain.*   V+ADV

2 If something **reaches up** to a particular level, it extends upwards as far as that level. ❏ *...ferns reaching up like twelve-feet high umbrellas.*   V+ADV

read /riːd/ (reads, reading)

> ✅ The form **read** is used in the present tense and is the past tense and past participle of the verb.

read back If you **read** a piece of writing **back**, you read it again after writing it, in order to check that it is correct or acceptable. ❏ *The sentence was easy to read back. ...reading back some of what you have just said.*   V+N+ADV, V+ADV+N, V+PRON+ADV

read for If you **read for** a university degree, you study for it. [OLD-FASHIONED] ❏ *Two students reading for the same degree may cover very different ground.*   V+PREP

read into If you **read** a meaning or importance **into** something, you think it has that meaning or importance, but it may not. ❏ *It would be a mistake to read too much significance into the local election result... The authors warn us about reading too much into the figures... Jeremy was reading into it something that I never intended... Any religious crank can read his own meanings into the Bible.*   V+N+PREP, V+PRON+PREP

read off If you **read off** a measurement on a machine or other device, you look carefully and note the exact measurement shown on it. ❏ *You read off, on that centre line, your mean viability... You read off the number at the top of the bar.*   V+ADV+N, V+PRON+ADV, V+N+ADV

★read out

1 If you **read out** a piece of writing, you say the words aloud as you read it. ❏ *John Tyme read out a statement on behalf of 600 objectors... Lecturers who read their scripts out can be terribly dull... One of them then writes a paper and reads it out to the rest of us.*   V+ADV+N, V+N+ADV, V+PRON+ADV: ALSO+to

2 The **read-out** from a computer or similar machine is the printed information that it produces. ❏ *...machines that give an extremely fast, efficient read-out and are low in cost... Check that computer read-out to see if you're on target this time.*   N-COUNT

read over If you **read over** a piece of writing, you read it in order to check it or comment on it before it is used or published. ❏ *When my director read over what I had written, he was puzzled... The typescript is taken back to them, read over, discussed.*   V+ADV+N, V+PRON+ADV, V+N+ADV

★read through

If you **read through** a piece of writing, you read it from beginning to end. ❏ *I've read through your letter very carefully... Ask the student to read it through first.*   V+PREP, V+PRON+ADV, V+N+ADV

read up If you **read up** on a subject, you read a lot about it because you want to know it thoroughly. ❏ *...having read up the answer to this question in Whitaker's Almanack... I got out the encyclopaedia and read up about uranium... Lucas had read up on Mother Shipton just in case he was asked.*   V+ADV+N, V+PRON+ADV, ALSO V+ADV+on

rear /rɪər/ (rears, rearing, reared)

rear up When an animal such as a horse **rears up**, it suddenly lifts its front legs in the air and stands on its hind legs. ❏ *...a deer, rearing up with her ears back. ...Boxer, rearing up on his hind legs and striking out.*   V+ADV

reason /riːzən/ (reasons, reasoning, reasoned)

reason out If you **reason out** a problem or puzzle, you solve it by thinking about it carefully. ❏ *She was able to reason out many of the passages and their meanings... She decided that she would reason out the whole matter... Leave it to me. I can reason it out later.*   V+ADV+N, V+PRON+ADV, V+N+ADV

[NOTE] **Work out** and **figure out** mean almost the same as **reason out**.

reason with If you **reason with** someone, you use sensible, logical arguments in order to persuade them to agree with you or to do something. ❏ *If he tries to leave, try to reason with him... Couldn't you reason with her?... I had to reason with myself like this to soothe my nervousness.*   V+PREP: HAS PASSIVE

rebound /rɪbaʊnd/ **(rebounds, rebounding, rebounded)**

rebound on If someone's action or attitude **rebounds on** or **rebounds upon** you, it affects you, although it was intended only to affect someone else. ❑ *I didn't dare tell you what I thought of you, because I knew it would only rebound on her... His resentment and ill temper rebounded upon Cal.*   V+PREP

rebound upon → See **rebound on**

reckon /rɛkən/ **(reckons, reckoning, reckoned)**

reckon in If you are calculating something and **reckon** an item **in**, you include it. ❑ *When everything is reckoned in, they are not so badly paid... Don't forget to reckon in the service charge... If you reckon them in, I'm sure we've got at least twenty.*   V+N+ADV, V+ADV+N, V+PRON+ADV

reckon on If you **reckon on** something, you feel certain that it will happen and include it in your plans. ❑ *This was far beyond the four figure sum she had reckoned on... I reckoned on his support... They could not reckon on our neutrality... They had not reckoned on such a fight.*   V+PREP: HAS PASSIVE

NOTE **Bank on** means almost the same as **reckon on**.

reckon up If you **reckon up** a set of figures, you add them together to find the total. ❑ *I'll have to reckon it up, I can't say off-hand... She couldn't face reckoning up the length of time.*   V+PRON+ADV, V+ADV+N, V+N+ADV

NOTE **Tot up** means almost the same as **reckon up**, and **calculate** is a more formal word.

reckon with

1 If you **had** not **reckoned with** an event, you had not expected it and so were not prepared for it. ❑ *She had not reckoned with a surprise of this sort.*   V+PREP: HAS PASSIVE

NOTE **Bargain for** means almost the same as **reckon with**.

2 If you say that someone or something is to **be reckoned with**, you mean that they are a difficulty or threat to you. ❑ *There was also Gertrude to be reckoned with... The union had become a force to be reckoned with.*   PASSIVE: V+with

reckon without If you **had reckoned without** something, you had not expected it and so were not prepared for it. ❑ *...but the bishops reckoned without Margaret's determination... They reckoned without the keen instincts of Terry.*   V+PREP

reduce /rɪdjuːs, AM -duːs/ **(reduces, reducing, reduced)**

★reduce to

1 If you **reduce** an amount **to** a lower amount, you decrease it to the lower amount. ❑ *My father's wages had been reduced to 10 shillings a week. ...reduces the number of cancer tumours to less than half.*   V+N+PREP, V+PRON+PREP: USUALLY PASSIVE

2 If something or someone **is reduced to** a bad state or condition, they are caused to be in it. ❑ *...every building being reduced to rubble... A tough reporter was reduced to tears at the sight. ...flattening everything in its path, reducing it to dust.*   V+N+PREP, V+PRON+PREP: USUALLY PASSIVE

reek /riːk/ **(reeks, reeking, reeked)**

reek of

1 If an object or place **reeks of** a substance, it smells very strongly of that substance. ❑ *His breath reeked of gin. ...warehouses reeking of rotten bananas.*   V+PREP

2 If a product or piece of work **reeks of** an unpleasant quality, that quality is strongly noticeable in it. ❑ *Their song titles reek of portentousness... The article reeked of deception and evasiveness.*   V+PREP

reel /riːl/ **(reels, reeling, reeled)**

reel back If you **reel back**, you move backwards suddenly and unsteadily. ❑ *Daisy reeled back against the wooden partition. ...pushing against her tormentors, who reeled back in surprise.*   V+ADV

reel in If you **reel in** a fish or a fishing line, you pull it towards you by turning the handle of the reel to shorten the line. ❑ *A small blue shark took the line: Brody reeled it in... He reeled in his line.*   V+PRON+ADV, V+ADV+N, V+N+ADV

reel off If you **reel off** a speech or some information, you repeat it from memory quickly and easily. ❑ *He could reel off the names of all the capitals of Europe... He gets up and reels off the same speech every time... I have to memorize all this so I can reel it off to*   V+ADV+N, V+PRON+ADV, V+N+ADV

people I meet.
NOTE **Rattle off** means almost the same as **reel off**.

refer /rɪfɜːr/ (**refers, referring, referred**)
★**refer to**

1 If you **refer to** a particular subject or person, you talk about them or mention them. ❏ *In his letters to Vita he rarely referred to political events... I am not allowed to describe the officers or refer to them by name.*
V+PREP:
HAS PASSIVE

2 If you **refer to** something or someone as a particular thing, this is the name or expression you use to describe them or talk about them. ❏ *...the decline of what I refer to as the industrial working class... This kind of art is often referred to as 'minimal art'.*
V+PREP:
USUALLY+as,
HAS PASSIVE

3 If a word or code **refers to** something, it relates to it or describes it in some way. ❏ *The serial number refers to the country of origin... Until the end of the 18th Century, 'antique' referred specifically to Greek and Roman antiquities.*
V+PREP:
HAS PASSIVE

4 If you **refer to** a source of information such as a reference book, you look at it in order to find something out. ❏ *She could make a new dish without referring to any cookery books. ...information which can be referred to on future occasions.*
V+PREP:
HAS PASSIVE

NOTE **Consult** means almost the same as **refer to**.

5 If you **refer** someone **to** a source of information, you suggest that they look there because it contains useful information. ❏ *I refer you to a paper by Sutherland... On two occasions at least Gray refers us to Chekhov.*
V+PRON+PREP,
V+N+PREP

6 If someone **refers** a person or problem **to** a specialist or an organization, they ask the specialist or organization to deal with the person or problem. ❏ *She referred the matter to the European Court of Justice... She was referred by her doctor to a consultant... The death has been referred to the coroner.*
V+N+PREP,
V+PRON+PREP

reflect /rɪflɛkt/ (**reflects, reflecting, reflected**)

reflect on If you **reflect on** or **reflect upon** something, you spend a lot of time thinking about it. ❏ *He reflected on how different things might have been. ...reflecting upon the coming of Western culture.*
V+PREP:
HAS PASSIVE

reflect upon → See **reflect on**

refrain /rɪfreɪn/ (**refrains, refraining, refrained**)

refrain from If you **refrain from** doing something, you do not do it, although you may want to. ❏ *This will cause France to refrain from hostile action... He had to refrain from speaking when adults were speaking... Mary could not refrain from a faint smile.*
V+PREP:
HAS PASSIVE

rein /reɪn/ (**reins, reining, reined**)

rein back To **rein back** something such as spending means to control it strictly. ❏ *He promised that between now and the end of the year the government would try to rein back inflation.*
V+ADV+N,
V+N+ADV,
V+PRON+ADV

NOTE **Check** means almost the same as **rein in**.

rein in

1 If you are riding and you **rein in** your horse, you make it stop or go more slowly by pulling its reins. ❏ *He reined in his horse to a walk... They proudly reined in their horses before the park gates.*
V+ADV+N,
V+N+ADV,
V+PRON+ADV

2 To **rein in** someone who is behaving in an extreme or unacceptable way means to control them and make them behave properly. [FORMAL] ❏ *The colonels were going too far and would have to be reined in... They wanted to rein in the excesses of private landowners... He was reined in so severely that he almost resigned.*
V+ADV+N,
V+N+ADV,
V+PRON+ADV

relate /rɪleɪt/ (**relates, relating, related**)
★**relate to**

1 If something **relates to** a particular subject, it concerns that subject or is connected with it. ❏ *I wanted to ask you a question that relates to electricity... The present negotiations do not relate to disarmament. ...the law relating to pet ownership.*
V+PREP

2 If you can **relate to** other people, you can understand how they feel and communicate with them or deal with them easily. ❏ *Children need to learn to relate to other children. ...the way we think, structure our feelings, and relate to one another.*
V+PREP

The symbol ★ shows key phrasal verbs

relieve /rɪlíːv/ (relieves, relieving, relieved)

relieve of If you **relieve** someone **of** something, you cause them not to have it
any longer. ❑ *He relieved her of the plates she was holding... He wished to relieve her of
financial anxiety... I was relieved of my position as director.*

V+PREP:
HAS PASSIVE

rely /rɪláɪ/ (relies, relying, relied)
⋆rely on

[1] To **rely on** or **rely upon** something or someone means to need them in order
to survive or be successful. ❑ *She is forced to rely on her mother's money... Hong Kong's
prosperity relies heavily on foreign businesses... There were no facilities for analysing food, so I
had to rely on sight, taste and smell.*

V+PREP:
HAS PASSIVE

[NOTE] **Depend on** means almost the same as **rely on**.

[2] If you **rely on** or **rely upon** someone or something to work or behave in a particular way, you trust them to do this. ❑ *One could always rely on him to be polite and
do the right thing... They cannot be relied upon to offer much support or advice.*

V+PREP:
HAS PASSIVE,
USUALLY+to-INF

[NOTE] **Count on** is a more informal expression for **rely on**.

rely upon → See rely on

remark /rɪmɑ́ːrk/ (remarks, remarking, remarked)

remark on If you **remark on** or **remark upon** something, you say or write
something that shows you have noticed it. ❑ *His friends remarked on his sudden failure
to appear... This is the most remarked upon aspect of overcrowding.*

V+PREP:
HAS PASSIVE

remark upon → See remark on

remember /rɪmémbər/ (remembers, remembering, remembered)

remember to If you ask someone to **remember** you **to** another person, you
are asking them to pass your greetings to that person. ❑ *Don't forget to remember me
to your father.*

V+PRON+PREP

remind /rɪmáɪnd/ (reminds, reminding, reminded)
⋆remind of

[1] If you **remind** someone **of** something, you tell them about it so that they remember it. ❑ *Howard comes to the door to remind him of their appointment... May I remind you of something you said earlier... The idea is to remind you of your proper role in life.*

V+PRON+PREP,
V+N+PREP

[2] If one person or thing **reminds** you **of** another, they make you think of the other person or thing, because they are both similar in some way. ❑ *You remind me of my
friend Baxter... His political writings remind me of those of Sartre... I am reminded of a story
about Captain Hardy.*

V+PRON+PREP,
V+N+PREP

render /réndər/ (renders, rendering, rendered)

render down If fat **is rendered down**, it is turned into liquid, usually by
heating it. ❑ *The whale fat is rendered down to make soap... Render the lard down for a
rich stock.*

PASSIVE:
V+ADV

rent /rént/ (rents, renting, rented)

⋆rent out If someone **rents out** something such as a room or a piece of land,
they allow it to be used for a period of time in return for payment. ❑ *They had to rent
out the upstairs room for years. ...land that the farmer had previously rented out to tenants...
Councils have sold a large proportion of new dwellings instead of renting them out.*

V+ADV+N,
V+N+ADV,
V+PRON+ADV:
ALSO+to

[NOTE] **Let out** means almost the same as **rent out**.

report /rɪpɔ́ːrt/ (reports, reporting, reported)

⋆report back If you **report back** to someone, you give them an account of
something that you were asked to find out about. ❑ *This scene would make him late reporting back to the Governor... Attend the meeting and report back on their activities... It will
be days before any leak can be reported back.*

V+ADV:
ALSO+to/on,
ALSO PASSIVE:
V+ADV

repose /rɪpóuz/ (reposes, reposing, reposed)
repose in

[1] If you say someone **reposes in** a place, you mean they are buried there.
[LITERARY] ❑ *All his uncles were now reposing in the local churchyard.*

V+PREP

[2] If you **repose** your trust **in** someone, you trust them. [FORMAL] ❑ *...the trust reposed in him by Crewe.*

V+N+PREP,
V+PRON+PREP

reside /rɪzaɪd/ **(resides, residing, resided)**

reside in If a quality **resides** in something, it exists or is present in that thing.   V+PREP
❑ *Strength resides in the gun... Real power resides in the workshop and the office... Memory has been shown to reside in many different organisms.*

resort /rɪzɔːrt/ **(resorts, resorting, resorted)**

★resort to If you **resort to** a course of action that you do not really think is right   V+PREP:
or acceptable, you adopt it because you cannot see any other way of achieving what   HAS PASSIVE
you want. ❑ *Eventually the police resorted to CS gas to quell the rioters... He had resorted to stealing to feed his habit.*

rest /rest/ **(rests, resting, rested)**

rest with If a duty or decision **rests with** a person, that person is responsible   V+PREP
for it. [FORMAL] ❑ *The responsibility rests with the Committee... The decision was not his, but rested with his boss.*

result /rɪzʌlt/ **(results, resulting, resulted)**

★result from If a situation **results from** an event or action, it is caused by that   V+PREP
event or action. ❑ *Most of the damage resulted from bombing... Inflation results from an excess of demand over supply.*

★result in If something **results in** a particular situation or event, it causes that   V+PREP
situation or event to happen. ❑ *A warming of the earth's surface might result in the melting of the polar ice caps. ...an accident which resulted in the death of a child... Such behaviour may result in the executive being asked to leave.*

return /rɪtɜːrn/ **(returns, returning, returned)**

★return to

[1] When you **return to** a place, you go back there after you have been away. ❑ *I re-*   V+PREP
turned to my hotel.

[2] If you **return** something **to** someone, you give it back to them after having it for   V+N+PREP,
a time. ❑ *Will you be so good as to return the drawing to me.*   V+PRON+PREP

[3] If you **return** something **to** a place, you put it back there after removing it for a   V+N+PREP,
time. ❑ *He returned the gun to its holster.*   V+PRON+PREP

[4] If you **return to** a previous topic when talking or writing, you mention it or dis-   V+PREP:
cuss it again. ❑ *Now let me return to the question of inflation... We shall return to this*   HAS PASSIVE
theme in Chapter 7.

[5] If you **return to** a previous activity or state, you start doing it again or being in   V+PREP
it again after a break. ❑ *After lunch, Edward returned to his gardening... The Labour Party seems poised to return to power.*

rev /rev/ **(revs, revving, revved)**

rev up If you **rev up** a vehicle, you increase the speed of the its engine by press-   V+ADV,
ing the accelerator. ❑ *Moses revved up and the car shot forward. ...revving up at the*   V+PRON+ADV,
lights... I told you not to rev it up like that... Victor revved up his motorbike.   V+N+ADV,
   V+ADV+N

revel /revəl/ **(revels, revelling, revelled)**

☑ American English uses the spellings **reveling** and **reveled**.

revel in If you **revel in** a situation or experience, it gives you a feeling of great   V+PREP:
joy and you really enjoy this feeling. ❑ *She seemed to revel in her success. ...school-*   HAS PASSIVE
children revelling in the bright sunshine.

[NOTE] **Glory in** means almost the same as **revel in**.

revert /rɪvɜːrt/ **(reverts, reverting, reverted)**

revert to

[1] If people or things **revert to** a previous state or condition, often a worse or less   V+PREP
developed one, they change and start being in it again. ❑ *Pastures which once yielded good grass are reverting to marsh and bracken... He was reverting rapidly to adolescence.*

[NOTE] **Return to** and **go back to** mean almost the same as **revert to**.

[2] If you **revert to** something that was mentioned earlier, you begin talking about   V+PREP:
it again. [FORMAL] ❑ *At this point in the discussion I reverted to money matters... Can I re-*   HAS PASSIVE
vert to one other point before you continue?

[3] When money or property **reverts to** someone, it becomes their property because   V+PREP
they owned it before or because they are a descendant of the previous owner. [LEGAL]

revolve /rɪvɒlv/ (revolves, revolving, revolved)

☑ In American English, **around** is much more common than **round**.

revolve around If a discussion **revolves around** or **revolves round** a particular subject, it mainly concerns that subject. ❑ *The discussion revolved round three topics... The argument would revolve around what was considered 'reasonable'.*
NOTE **Centre around** means almost the same as **revolve around**.

V+PREP

revolve round → See **revolve around**

rid /rɪd/ (rids, ridding)

☑ The form **rid** is used in the present tense and is the past tense and past participle of the verb.

rid of If you **rid** a place, thing, or person **of** something unpleasant or unwanted, you remove it completely. [FORMAL] ❑ *It is difficult to rid clothes of cooking smells... Occupiers must rid their premises of rats and mice... He promised to carry on the battle to rid the world of landmines... He had rid himself of his illusions.*

V+N+PREP,
V+PRON+PREP,
V+REFL+PREP

ride /raɪd/ (rides, riding, rode, ridden)

ride out If you **ride out** a period of difficulty or danger, you manage to survive it without suffering serious harm. ❑ *We knew that we would be able to ride out the storm... The company can ride out the recession and do well again.*
NOTE **Weather** means almost the same as **ride out**.

V+ADV+N,
V+PRON+ADV,
V+N+ADV

ride up If a skirt or dress **rides up**, it moves upwards, out of its proper position. ❑ *This new petticoat is awful – it keeps riding up.*

V+ADV

riffle /rɪfəl/ (riffles, riffling, riffled)
riffle through

1 If you **riffle through** sheets of paper or the pages of a book, you look at them briefly, turning the pages quickly. [AMERICAN] ❑ *I riffled through four or five newspapers, trying to find the article.*

V+PREP

2 If you **riffle through** someone's belongings, you examine them quickly because you are trying to find something. [AMERICAN] ❑ *Tom passed the handbag to me. I riffled quickly through it.*

V+PREP:
HAS PASSIVE

rifle /raɪfəl/ (rifles, rifling, rifled)
rifle through

1 If you **rifle through** sheets of paper or the pages of a book, you look at them briefly, turning the pages quickly. ❑ *She had picked up Amy's book and was rifling through it.*
NOTE **Leaf through** means almost the same as **rifle through**.

V+PREP

2 If you **rifle through** someone's belongings, you examine them quickly because you are trying to find something. ❑ *Jean rifled through her desk.*

V+PREP:
HAS PASSIVE

rig /rɪg/ (rigs, rigging, rigged)

rig out If you **rig** yourself **out** or **are rigged out** in special or unusual clothes, you are wearing that particular kind of clothing. [INFORMAL] ❑ *...a photo showing them rigged out in black hats and stiff white collars... He had rigged himself out as a Red Indian.*
NOTE **Get up** means almost the same as **rig out**.

V+REFL+ADV:
USUALLY+A,
ALSO PASSIVE:
V+ADV+A

♦ A **rig-out** is a set of clothes that someone is wearing, especially unusual or very fashionable clothes. [INFORMAL] ❑ *Of course, she'd got herself a whole new rig-out for the trip... What an amazing rig-out!*

N-COUNT

rig up If you **rig up** a device or piece of equipment, you make it and fix it in place using whatever you have available. ❑ *He had rigged up a listening device... Some of the men had rigged up tents with their ponchos... If you haven't got a press, you can rig one up with a car jack.*

V+ADV+N,
V+N+ADV,
V+PRON+ADV

ring /rɪŋ/ (rings, ringing, rang, rung)
ring around → See **ring round**

★ring back If you **ring back** or **ring** someone **back**, you telephone them for a second time or after they have telephoned you. [BRITISH] ❑ *Tell her to ring back later... He asked if you'd ring him back when you got in.*
NOTE **Call back** and **phone back** mean almost the same as **ring back**.

V+ADV,
V+PRON+ADV,
V+N+ADV:
NO PASSIVE

ring in If you **ring in**, you report to someone at your place of work by telephoning them. [BRITISH] ❑ *I rang in to say I was ill.*
<u>NOTE</u> **Phone in** means almost the same as **ring in**.

V+ADV

ring off When you **ring off** at the end of a telephone conversation, you put the telephone receiver back in its place to close the line. [BRITISH] ❑ *The girl laughed and rang off... With a last 'Fine', Hogan had rung off.*
<u>NOTE</u> **Hang up** means almost the same as **ring off**.

V+ADV

ring out If a sound **rings out**, it is heard loudly and clearly. ❑ *The celebrations were suddenly interrupted when the voice of an elder rang out, 'Hear me!'... The old stable clock rings out ten o'clock.*

V+ADV,
V+ADV+N:
NO PASSIVE

ring round If you **ring round** or **ring around**, you telephone several people to discuss or ask about a particular thing. [BRITISH] ❑ *I got out the telephone book and began ringing round to heating contractors for estimates... I'll ring around and see what I can get.*
<u>NOTE</u> **Phone round** means almost the same as **ring round**.

V+ADV,
V+PREP

★ring up

1 If you **ring** someone **up**, you telephone them. ❑ *I rang her up to thank her... She had rung up Emily and had told her all about it... He was rung up in the night and asked if he'd come down... It's advisable to ring up first to make an appointment.*
<u>NOTE</u> **Phone up** means almost the same as **ring up**.

V+PRON+ADV,
V+ADV+N,
V+N+ADV,
V+ADV

2 When a sales assistant in a shop **rings up** an amount on the till, he or she records the amount of money that is being paid into the till by pressing the buttons. ❑ *She rang up £10.47 and gave me the receipt... He rang up the sale on the register.*

V+ADV+N,
V+PRON+ADV,
V+N+ADV

3 If a company **rings up** an amount of money, usually a large amount of money, it makes that amount of money in sales or profits. ❑ *The advertising agency rang up 1.4 billion dollars in yearly sales.*

V+ADV+N,
V+N+ADV,
V+PRON+ADV

rinse /rɪns/ (rinses, rinsing, rinsed)
rinse out

1 When you **rinse out** something that you have washed in soap, you get rid of the soap by washing the thing in clean water. ❑ *She left them in detergent overnight, then rinsed them out the next morning.*
<u>NOTE</u> **Rinse** means almost the same as **rinse out**.

V+PRON+ADV,
V+N+ADV,
V+ADV+N

2 If you **rinse** something **out**, you wash it quickly, often without using soap. ❑ *She rinsed out the glass.*
<u>NOTE</u> **Wash out** means almost the same as **rinse out**.

V+ADV+N,
V+N+ADV,
V+PRON+ADV

3 If you **rinse** your mouth **out**, you wash it by holding a mouthful of liquid in it, for example to get rid of an unpleasant taste.
<u>NOTE</u> **Wash out** means almost the same as **rinse out**.

V+N+ADV,
V+PRON+ADV,
V+ADV+N

rip /rɪp/ (rips, ripping, ripped)
★rip apart

1 If something **rips** people **apart**, it causes them to quarrel or fight so seriously that they can no longer be friends. ❑ *He said that communal carnage was ripping the country apart... To have fought Paul on this would have risked ripping the family apart.*
<u>NOTE</u> **Tear apart** means almost the same as **rip apart**.

V+ADV+N,
V+N+ADV,
V+PRON+ADV

2 If you **rip** someone **apart** or **rip** their opinion **apart**, you criticize them and say publicly that they are wrong, often by laughing at what they have said or done. ❑ *The presenters and audience ripped her apart, enjoying a laugh at her expense... We are the only paper in Britain that has consistently ripped apart these shallow lies and half-truths.*
<u>NOTE</u> **Tear apart** means almost the same as **rip apart**.

V+ADV+N,
V+N+ADV,
V+PRON+ADV

rip into If someone **rips into** you, they criticize you strongly. [INFORMAL] ❑ *If they disputed his allegation, Paul would rip into them with every foul word you could imagine.*
<u>NOTE</u> **Lay into** means almost the same as **rip into**.

V+PREP:
HAS PASSIVE

★rip off

1 If someone **rips** you **off**, they cheat you by charging you too much money for something. [INFORMAL] ◆ ❑ *The local shopkeepers were all trying to rip off the tourists... The court wastes my time and the lawyers rip me off!*
<u>NOTE</u> **Fleece** means almost the same as **rip off**.

V+ADV+N,
V+PRON+ADV,
V+N+ADV

If you say that something that you bought was a **rip-off**, you mean that you were cheated into paying too much for it. [INFORMAL] ❑ *They knew it was a rip-off.*   N-COUNT

[2] To **rip** something **off** means to steal it. [INFORMAL]   V+ADV+N,
V+N/PRON+ADV,

NOTE **Nick** is an informal word for **rip off**.

rip through If an object or sound **rips through** a place, it moves through it   V+PREP
very quickly and violently. ❑ *A roaring explosion ripped through the house... His para-*
chute crumpled as the bullets ripped through the silk.

★**rip up** If you **rip up** a piece of paper or cloth, you tear it into small pieces. ❑ *I*   V+ADV+N,
wanted to rip up my schedule and fill out a new one.   V+N+ADV,
V+PRON+ADV

NOTE **Tear up** means almost the same as **rip up**.

rise /raɪz/ (**rises, rising, rose, risen**)

rise above If you **rise above** a difficulty or problem, you manage to deal with   V+PREP:
it without letting it affect you. ❑ *A woman who can rise above such disadvantages is*   HAS PASSIVE
clearly exceptional... She was the victim of continual pain, but magnificently she rose above it.

★**rise up**

[1] If something **rises up**, it moves upwards. ❑ *He could see the smoke from his bonfire*   V+ADV
rising up in a white column... A whole flock of blackbirds rose up suddenly when we went by.

NOTE **Rise** means almost the same as **rise up**.

[2] You can say that something **rises up** when it appears as a large, tall shape. ❑ *The*   V+ADV
hills rose up in the distance... Sheer mountainsides rise up on either shore.

[3] If a thought, image, or feeling **rises up**, you suddenly think about it or feel it.   V+ADV:
❑ *When she said these words, the image of the boy Tom rose up... All of a sudden, a differ-*   USUALLY+A
ent figure from Mary's rose up in his mind... Old humiliations and terrors rose up within him.

[4] If people **rise up**, they start to rebel or fight against people in authority. ❑ *They*   V+ADV
will rise up and overthrow your imperialist government... The non-whites are one of these
days going to rise up and demand their rights.

♦ An **uprising** is an occasion when many people start to rebel or fight against peo-   N-COUNT
ple in authority. ❑ *...an uprising of the German masses. ...an armed uprising.*

roll /roʊl/ (**rolls, rolling, rolled**)

☑ **About** is used mainly in British English.

roll about → See **roll around**

roll around If you **roll around** or **roll about**, you move in a lying position by   V+ADV
turning your body over and over in different directions. ❑ *Next moment they were roll-*
ing about the floor... Two smallish children were rolling around fighting.

roll back

[1] If you **roll back** something that has been increasing in amount or importance,   V+ADV+N,
you cause it to start decreasing. ❑ *You had to do it by rolling back the power of the trade*   V+PRON+ADV
unions... The gains of last year will be in danger of being rolled back.

[2] To **roll back** prices, taxes, or benefits means to reduce them. [AMERICAN] ❑ *One*   V+ADV+N,
provision of the law was to roll back taxes to the 1975 level.   V+N+ADV,
V+PRON+ADV

roll down If you **roll down** a piece of clothing or material that has been folded   V+ADV+N,
over and over, you unfold the edge of it, in order to make it longer. ❑ *He began roll-*   V+N+ADV,
ing down his sleeves.   V+PRON+ADV

roll in

☑ In meaning 2, the stress is on **roll**.

[1] If something such as money **is rolling in**, you receive it in large quantities.   V+ADV
[INFORMAL] ❑ *Orders roll in... Once we get there the money will just start rolling in.*

[2] If you say that someone **is rolling in** money, you mean that they are very rich.   V+PREP
❑ *They're all rolling in money. And we haven't any... Hearing him talk, you'd think he was*
rolling in dough.

[3] If tanks or troops **roll in**, they move into a place in order to take control. ❑ *When*   V+ADV
the tanks rolled in, nearly 100 civilians were killed.

[4] If someone **rolls in**, they arrive somewhere in a very casual way. [BRITISH,   V+ADV
INFORMAL] ❑ *Ultimately, audiences rolled in from York and Hull... He rolled in, smoking a fag.*

roll into

[1] If you **roll** a piece of a substance or material **into** a round shape, you fold it so   V+N+PREP,

For a full explanation of all grammatical labels, see pages xiii-xx

that it is in that shape. ❑ *She started to roll the socks into a ball... He found a piece of*   V+PRON+PREP
cheese, rolled it into a ball, and popped it in his mouth.

2 When you talk about tanks or troops **rolling into** a place, you mean that they   V+PREP
move into that place in order to take control. ❑ *More than 100 tanks rolled into eastern*
Croatia... A convoy of United Nations trucks rolled into Sarajevo today.

3 If you say that a person **rolls into** a place, you mean that they arrive there in a   V+PREP
casual way. [BRITISH, INFORMAL] ❑ *They rolled into the town at a quarter to seven.*

roll on

1 If an activity or process **rolls on**, it continues to happen in a rather unexciting   V+ADV
way. ❑ *So the jokes and laughter rolled on... Life was automatically rolling on with all its rou-*
tine pleasures.

2 If you say **roll on** something, you mean that you want it to happen soon.   IMPERATIVE,
[BRITISH, INFORMAL] ❑ *All I can say is roll on a government like the German government...*   V+ADV
Roll on four o' clock!

3 **Roll-on** deodorant is sold in a container with a round ball in the top. You use   ADJECTIVE
the deodorant by rubbing the ball onto your skin.

4 **Roll-on roll-off** ferries are designed with a ramp in the side so that vehicles can   ADJECTIVE
be driven onto them and off them.

roll out If a new vehicle **rolls out**, or a company **rolls** it **out**, it is produced and   V+ADV,
is shown or made available to the public. [AMERICAN] ❑ *The first of the C-SA's rolled out*   V+ADV+N,
of the shop exactly on schedule... It rolled out the X-car compacts – the Chevrolet Citation,   V+PRON+ADV:
Buick Skylark and so on.   ERGATIVE

★roll over If you are lying down and you **roll over**, you turn your body so that a   V+ADV
different part of you is facing upwards. ❑ *I rolled over on my stomach... He rolled over*
and peered into Jack's face.

NOTE **Turn over** means almost the same as **roll over**.

★roll up

1 If you **roll up** something such as a piece of paper or material, you wrap it several   V+ADV+N,
times around itself in the shape of a cylinder or a ball. ❑ *You sort out the tent while I*   V+PRON+ADV,
roll up the sleeping bags.   V+N+ADV

♦ A **rolled-up** piece of paper or material has been folded or wrapped into a cylinder   ADJECTIVE
or ball shape. ❑ *He lunged at the wasp with a rolled-up newspaper... Another man carries a*
rolled-up stretcher.

♦ **Roll-up** describes things which can be folded or rolled into a cylindrical shape.   ADJECTIVE
❑ *...a roll-up garage door. ...a roll-up map.*

♦ A **roll-up** is a cigarette that you make yourself with tobacco and paper with a   N-COUNT
gummed edge. ❑ *She gave me one of her roll-ups.*

2 If a person or animal **rolls up**, they curl their bodies into a round shape.   V+ADV,
❑ *...which enable the animal to roll itself up into a ball.*   V+REFL+ADV

3 If you **roll up** your sleeves or trouser legs, you fold the edges over several times   V+N+ADV,
to make them shorter. ❑ *Just roll your trousers up and have a paddle... His father had his*   V+ADV+N,
sleeves rolled up.   V+PRON+ADV

4 If people **roll up** somewhere, they arrive in large numbers. ❑ *I was desperate for a*   V+ADV:
quiet weekend, but all these visitors kept rolling up... Roll up! Roll up! Come and see the   ALSO IMPERATIVE
Elephant Man.

romp /rɒmp/ (romps, romping, romped)

romp through If you **romp through** something, you do it quickly and easily.   V+PREP:
❑ *This is easy stuff, you'll romp through this... The National Anthem was romped through.*   HAS PASSIVE

root /ruːt/ (roots, rooting, rooted)

> ✅ **About** is used mainly in British English.

root about → See root around

root around If you **root around** or **root about** among things, you look   V+ADV,
among them, moving them all around, usually because you are searching for some-   V+PREP:
thing. ❑ *My sister was rooting about in the tins and bits of old iron bedstead... The inhabit-*   USUALLY+A
ants were nervous of having the bears rooting around their dustbins.

r<u>oo</u>t for If you **are rooting for** someone, you are giving them your support while they are doing something difficult. [INFORMAL] ❑ *Editorial friends on the newspapers were rooting for us... Good luck in the interview – I'll be rooting for you.*

V+PREP

root <u>out</u> If you **root** someone or something **out**, you find them and remove them in a determined way from a place or organization. ❑ *He's in the library somewhere. Let's go and root him out... A special detachment of investigators was formed to root out the leadership... He was determined to root out corruption in his department.*

V+PRON+ADV,
V+ADV+N,
V+N+ADV

root <u>up</u> If you **root up** a plant, you dig it up from the ground. ❑ *I had to root up all the plants and burn them.*

V+ADV+N,
V+N+ADV,
V+PRON+ADV

NOTE **Uproot** means almost the same as **root up**.

rope /r<u>ou</u>p/ **(ropes, roping, roped)**

rope <u>in</u> If you **rope** someone **in** to do something, you persuade them to help you to do it. [BRITISH, INFORMAL] ❑ *Some amazing people were roped in to work on these books... So you're roping me in?*

V+N+ADV,
V+ADV+N,
V+PRON+ADV

rope <u>off</u> If an area **is roped off**, it is separated from another area by a rope tied between posts to keep people away from it. ❑ *The track was roped off from the rest of the field... Much of the shop is roped off because they are doing major alterations.*

V+ADV+N,
V+N+ADV,
V+PRON+ADV:
USUALLY PASSIVE

rot /r<u>o</u>t/ **(rots, rotting, rotted)**

rot <u>away</u> When something **rots away**, it gradually decays until it falls to pieces or disappears completely. ❑ *His body is rotting away. ...ships that would certainly have rotted away under normal atmospheric conditions... The shack rotted away.*

V+ADV

rough /r<u>ʌ</u>f/ **(roughs, roughing, roughed)**

rough <u>out</u> If you **rough out** a drawing or idea, you draw or list the main features of it before you do it in detail. ❑ *I've roughed out a scene for my new play... I had roughed out a lead topic for the following day's chat show... She roughed out a sketch of the harbour.*

V+ADV+N,
V+N+ADV,
V+PRON+ADV

rough <u>up</u> If someone **roughs** you **up**, they attack you by hitting or beating you. [INFORMAL] ❑ *Pushers moved in and roughed up the young junkies... They roughed me up a bit.*

V+ADV+N,
V+PRON+ADV,
V+N+ADV

round /r<u>au</u>nd/ **(rounds, rounding, rounded)**

round <u>down</u> If you **round down** a figure or total, you change it by lowering it to the nearest whole number, the nearest 10, or the nearest 100, and so on. ❑ *We make a delivery charge of 15p in the pound, rounded down to the nearest pound.*

V+ADV+N,
V+N+ADV,
V+PRON+ADV:
ALSO+*to*

★round <u>off</u>

1 If you **round** something **off**, you do something to complete it in a satisfactory way. ❑ *I think you ought to see London, Paris, Rome – round off your education a bit... We'll round it off with some observations on Indian history... At the end of a lunch, the managers round off with a brandy or a liqueur.*

V+ADV+N,
V+PRON+ADV,
V+N+ADV,
V+ADV:
ALSO+*with*

NOTE **Finish off** means almost the same as **round off**.

2 If a point or shape **is rounded off**, it has been made into a smooth, curved shape by shaving or rubbing part of it away.

PASSIVE:
V+ADV

round <u>on</u> If you **round on** someone who is criticizing you, attacking you, or causing you difficulties, you suddenly respond angrily by criticizing or attacking that person yourself. ❑ *In Denver, he rounded on his critics... The girl rounded on me furiously. 'Do you think I'm ashamed?'*

V+PREP:
HAS PASSIVE

★round <u>up</u>

1 If the police or army **round up** a number of people, they arrest or capture them. ❑ *The police rounded up a number of suspects... Fifteen thousand rebels were rounded up in prison camps... They rounded everybody up and herded us into police vans.*

V+ADV+N,
V+N+ADV,
V+PRON+ADV

◆ A **round-up** is an occasion when many people are arrested or captured. ❑ *In a massive round-up they arrested several hundred prominent leaders. ...the nightly round-ups of hostages.*

N-COUNT

2 If you **round up** animals or things, you gather them together. ❑ *A dog catcher's main job is to round up strays... He had sought work as a cowboy, rounding up cattle... We've rounded up a selection of products.*

V+ADV+N,
V+N+ADV,
V+PRON+ADV

3 If you **round up** a figure or total, you change it by increasing it to the nearest

V+ADV+N,

whole number, the nearest 10, or the nearest 100, and so on. ❑ *Round up any odd half* `V+N/PRON+ADV:`
unit to the next whole number... We round the monthly total up to the nearest ten pounds. `ALSO+to`

4 A **round-up** on radio or television, or in a newspaper, is a brief summary of the `N-COUNT`
news. ❑ *...the eleven o'clock news followed by the sports round-up. ...the round-up of world*
news on the front page. ...some television programmes, such as the news round-up.

rout /raʊt/ (routs, routing, routed)

rout out If you **rout** someone or something **out**, you make them come out from `V+ADV+N,`
where they are. ❑ *Sometimes, the boys would rout out little squirrels and chase them...* `V+PRON+ADV,`
Rafferty appeared to have been routed out of bed. `V+N+ADV`

row /roʊ/ (rows, rowing, rowed)

row back If someone **rows back**, they change their mind about a decision or `V+ADV:`
plan that they have made. [JOURNALISM] ❑ *The administration has been steadily rowing* `USUALLY+on`
back from its early opposition to the visit... The government was forced to row back on an
austerity plan that would have involved wage cuts.

rub /rʌb/ (rubs, rubbing, rubbed)

rub along If two people **rub along** together, they are able to live or work to- `V+ADV:`
gether in a reasonably friendly way. [BRITISH, INFORMAL] `ALSO+together`

NOTE **Get on** means almost the same as **rub along**.

rub down

1 If you **rub down** a surface, you prepare it by rubbing it with something such as `V+ADV+N,`
sandpaper. ❑ *The boards have been rubbed down several times to get that gleaming finish...* `V+N+ADV,`
Eliminate bad marks by rubbing down the area gently with wire wool. `V+PRON+ADV`

2 If you **rub** a person or animal **down**, you rub them hard with a towel or a cloth, `V+PRON+ADV,`
usually to dry them. ❑ *...rubbing him down and brushing and combing his mane and tail...* `V+REFL+ADV,`
She rubbed me down with a towel... He would jump out and rub himself down frantically. `V+N+ADV`

★rub in

1 If you **rub** a substance **in**, you press it into something by continuously moving it `V+ADV+N,`
over its surface. ❑ *When hair is dry, rub in a little oil to make it smooth and glossy... Sift to-* `V+N+ADV,`
gether the flour, salt and mustard, and rub in the margarine. `V+PRON+ADV`

2 If you feel upset, guilty, or embarrassed about something and someone **rubs it** `V+it+ADV`
in, they remind you about it, often deliberately in order to make you feel worse.
❑ *When the child fails, never rub it in... 'How old are you, Mr Sharpe?'—'All right, no need to*
rub it in.'

rub off

1 If you **rub** something **off** a surface, you remove it by rubbing the surface with `V+ADV+N,`
something. ❑ *She rubbed off the dirt with her hand... Use a soft pencil because you can, if* `V+N/PRON+ADV,`
necessary, rub it off... The dye in the ink stays on the paper and does not rub off. `V+ADV:`
`ERGATIVE`

2 If someone else's quality or mood **rubs off** on you, it affects you and you start to `V+ADV:`
have it or feel it. ❑ *A kind of aura of happiness was being generated. It rubbed off on peo-* `USUALLY+on`
ple... They hoped that some of his prowess might rub off on them.

rub out

1 If you **rub out** something that you have written in pencil or chalk, you remove `V+ADV+N,`
it by rubbing it with a rubber or a cloth. `V+N+ADV,`
`V+PRON+ADV`

NOTE **Erase** is a more formal word for **rub out**.

2 To **rub** someone **out** means to kill or destroy them. [INFORMAL] ❑ *He has decided* `V+ADV+N,`
to destroy the documents, and rub out anyone who knows about them... He would have `V+PRON+ADV,`
gladly rubbed him out as he saw him as a threat. `V+N+ADV`

ruck /rʌk/ (rucks, rucking, rucked)

ruck up If cloth or a person's clothing **rucks up**, it moves upwards, out of its `V+ADV:`
correct position. ❑ *...the shirt, rucked up under his braces... There she was, with her jump-* `USUALLY+A`
er rucking up at the back.

NOTE **Bunch up** means almost the same as **ruck up**.

rule /ruːl/ (rules, ruling, ruled)

rule in If you say that you are **not ruling** anything **in**, you mean that you have `V+N+ADV,`
not yet decided that you will definitely do something. [BRITISH] ❑ *As he has been do-* `V+PRON+ADV,`
ing for some time now, he was ruling nothing in or out... We must, as I said, take care not to `V+ADV+N`
rule in or rule out any one solution.

rule off If you **rule off** a section on a piece of paper, you draw a straight line below it on the paper to divide it from the next section.

V+ADV+N,
V+N+ADV,
V+PRON+ADV

★**rule out**

1 If you **rule out** an idea or a course of action, you decide that it is impossible or
unsuitable. ❑ *Washington need not rule out a selective military aid program... They can't
rule out the possibility that he was kidnapped... Do not rule these out as gimmicks.*

V+ADV+N,
V+PRON+ADV,
V+N+ADV

NOTE **Dismiss** means almost the same as **rule out**.

2 If one thing **rules out** another, it prevents it from happening or being possible.
❑ *A search had ruled out the possibility of further bombs... The radio was on, effectively ruling out conversation... These results rule out the claim that the Shroud is merely a painting.*

V+ADV+N,
V+PRON+ADV,
V+N+ADV

NOTE **Preclude** is a formal word for **rule out**.

rule out of If someone **rules** you **out of** a contest or activity, they say that you
cannot be involved in it. If something **rules** you **out of** a contest or activity, it prevents you from being involved in it. ❑ *He has ruled himself out of the world championships next year in Stuttgart... A damaged hamstring has ruled him out of contention for
Wednesday's international against Spain.*

V+N+ADV+PREP,
V+PRON+ADV+PREP

rumble /rʌmbəl/ **(rumbles, rumbling, rumbled)**

rumble on If a person, discussion, or process **rumbles on**, they continue speaking or happening in a boring way for a long time. [BRITISH] ❑ *He rumbled on in this
vein for some time... The argument rumbled on.*

V+ADV

run /rʌn/ **(runs, running, ran)**

☑ The form **run** is used in the present tense and is also the past participle of the
verb. **About** is used mainly in British English.

★**run about**

1 → See **run around**

2 A **runabout** is a small car that you use mainly for short journeys. In American
English, **runabout** is used of cars with open tops. [INFORMAL] ❑ *It makes an ideal
shopping runabout.*

N-COUNT

★**run across**

1 If you **run across** a place or area, you run from one side of it to the other.
❑ *Then they all run across the street to the church. ...used in toy cars to make them run
across the floor.*

V+PREP

2 If you **run across** someone, you meet them unexpectedly. ❑ *He had not seen him
for two days when he ran across him at the Palace... It is very unusual to run across Americans in this part of the world.*

V+PREP

NOTE **Come across**, **bump into**, and **run into** mean almost the same as **run
across**.

★**run after**

1 If you **run after** someone or something that is moving, you chase them in order
to catch them or stop them. ❑ *Thomas ran after him, yelling to him to stop.*

V+PREP

2 If you **run after** something you want, you keep trying very hard to obtain it or
to achieve it. ❑ *He's always running after something, hoping for something. ...running after
a goal which always eludes us.*

V+PREP

NOTE **Pursue** is a formal word for **run after**.

3 If you **run after** someone, you try hard to persuade them to have a romantic or
sexual relationship with you. [INFORMAL] ❑ *Maybe father drank or ran after other wom-
en... Beautiful women run after me and I can't resist them.*

V+PREP

run along If you tell a child to **run along**, you are telling him or her to go
away. ❑ *Run along and play... Run along up to bed now, Sam.*

V+ADV:
USUALLY IMPERATIVE

★**run around**

1 If you **run around** or **run about**, you run excitedly and in different directions
within a particular area. ❑ *We needed a large garden where the kids could run around
freely... A dog was running around in the yard... She let them run about the place just as
they pleased.*

V+ADV,
V+PREP

2 If you **run around** doing something, you visit several places or do many different things in order to achieve something. ❑ *I ran around looking for work. ...after all the
feverish running around to make sure we arrived on time.*

V+ADV

For a full explanation of all grammatical labels, see pages xiii-xx

♦ If you ask someone for help or information and they give you the **runaround**, they deliberately mislead you or cause you difficulties. ❑ *I have been trying to make a phone call, and everybody I ask gives me the runaround.*   N-SING

run around with If you **run around with** a person or group of people, you spend a lot of time with them socially. [INFORMAL] ❑ *In the 1960s he used to run around a lot with Prince Bernhardt... What's his name – that guy you run around with?*   V+ADV+PREP

NOTE **Go about** means almost the same as **run around**.

⋆**run away**

1 If you **run away**, you move quickly and farther from a place or person. ❑ *The children run away like frightened deer if you approach them... She ran away laughing up the road.*   V+ADV

2 If you **run away** from somewhere, you leave secretly because you are unhappy. ❑ *She ran away one night, leaving these pictures... Some ran away to Canada... He had run away from home... Why did you run away from me?*   V+ADV: ALSO+from

♦ A **runaway** is a person who leaves their home secretly. ❑ *They failed to find any trace of the runaways. ...runaway slaves.*   N-COUNT, ADJECTIVE

3 If you **run away** with someone, you secretly leave your home in order to live with them or marry them. ❑ *They ran away and got married... She had divorced him and run away with another man... He and Belinda were planning to run away together.*   V+ADV+with, V+ADV+together: RECIPROCAL

4 If you **run away** from something difficult or unpleasant, you try to avoid dealing with it. ❑ *We cannot run away from technology. ...the truth that I had been running away from.*   V+ADV: USUALLY+from

5 A **runaway** animal or vehicle is moving but is no longer under the control of its rider or driver. ❑ *...her attempt to stop a runaway horse. ...a runaway tractor.*   ADJECTIVE

6 A **runaway** situation happens very rapidly or forcefully and cannot be controlled. ❑ *...the runaway success of 'Nicholas Nickleby'. ...the runaway inflation after the war.*   ADJECTIVE

run away with

1 If you let your feelings **run away with** you, you fail to control them, and they affect you so strongly that you cannot think or behave sensibly. ❑ *They let their emotions run away with them... They did not allow youthful zeal to run away with them.*   V+ADV+PREP

2 If you **run away with** a prize or competition, you win it very easily. ❑ *Her sister ran away with every prize at school.*   V+ADV+PREP

NOTE **Walk off with** means almost the same as **run away with**.

run by If you **run** something **by** someone, you tell them about it or mention it, to see if they think it is a good idea, or can understand it. ❑ *I'm definitely interested, but I'll have to run it by Larry Estes... Run that by me again.*   V+N+PREP, V+PRON+PREP

NOTE **Run past** means almost the same as **run by**.

⋆**run down**

1 To **run down** somewhere means to move quickly to a lower level or away from a place. ❑ *Marion, run down to the post box with this letter... She runs down the steps... The old man stood up with tears running down his face.*   V+ADV, V+PREP

2 If you **run down** someone or something, you criticize them strongly. ❑ *She was not used to people running down their own families... She began to run down everything. 'This is all rubbish.'*   V+ADV+N, V+PRON+ADV

3 If an industry or organization **is run down**, its size, importance, or activity is deliberately reduced. [BRITISH] ❑ *Hospitals were being run down because of the spending cuts... Our forces are so run down they don't deter anybody any more... This Government will go on running down the railways.*   V+ADV+N, V+N+ADV, V+PRON+ADV

♦ The **run-down** of an industry or organization is the deliberate reduction of its size, importance or activity. [BRITISH] ❑ *Union leaders fought against the run-down of the coal industry.*   N-SING

4 If someone **runs down** their stock or supply of something, they reduce the amount. [BRITISH] ❑ *Start to run down any freezer supplies as soon as possible... People reacted to inflation by running down their savings and buying goods instead.*   V+ADV+N, V+N+ADV, V+PRON+ADV

5 If a machine or device **runs down**, it gradually loses power or works more slowly. ❑ *The batteries in your radio are running down... Hey, the clock's working now. Did it just run down yesterday, or what?*   V+ADV

6 If a vehicle or its driver **runs** someone **down**, the vehicle hits and injures that person. ❑ *A coach nearly ran us down in front of Trinity Church... A car with Frankfurt license plates had run down and killed a French border patrolman... Then in March he tried to run Kathleen down.*

> V+PRON+ADV, V+ADV+N, V+N+ADV

NOTE **Knock down** and **run over** mean almost the same as **run down**.

7 If you **run down** someone or something you have been searching for, you find them after a lot of effort. [INFORMAL] ❑ *'We haven't run down your man,' he began. ...taking a book out, running down a reference and walking out again.*

> V+ADV+N, V+N+ADV, V+PRON+ADV

NOTE **Track down** and **trace** mean almost the same as **run down**.

8 If you **run down** a list of items, you read or mention them briefly and quickly. ❑ *Bradlee listened attentively as Woodward ran down what details the reporters had given him.*

> V+PREP

NOTE **Run through** means almost the same as **run down**.

♦ If you give someone a **rundown** on a situation or subject, you give them a summary of the important facts. ❑ *We've had a rundown on everyone connected with Olympus... I can give you a quick run-down.*

> N-SING

9 If someone is **run down**, they are very tired and unwell after working too hard or not having enough sleep for a while. ❑ *'You're probably run down,' Clarissa said. 'You need a holiday.'*

> ADJECTIVE

10 A building or area that is **run-down** is in poor condition, because it has not been looked after. ❑ *...two small rooms in a run-down building. ...a run-down urban area.*

> ADJECTIVE

★run in

1 If someone **runs in** from outside a room or building, they enter it, moving fast. ❑ *He ran in through the open glass doors of the sitting-room... I'll run in and get them.*

> V+ADV

2 If someone is **run in** by the police, they are arrested. [INFORMAL] ❑ *Shortly afterwards Mascall was run in... It was the kind of behaviour that gets motorists run in at this time of year... I could run you in for that.*

> V+N+ADV, V+PRON+ADV, V+ADV+N: USUALLY PASSIVE

3 If you have a **run-in** with someone, you have an argument or quarrel with them. [INFORMAL] ❑ *He's probably had a run-in at work with Ted.*

> N-COUNT

4 The **run-in** to an event is the period of preparation just before it takes place. ❑ *We did it for two weeks in Birmingham as a run-in for the main season. ...the run-in to the next general election.*

> N-COUNT

★run into

1 To **run into** a place means to enter it, moving fast. ❑ *...running into the playroom in tears... They had run into the nearest flat and taken the people hostage.*

> V+PREP

2 If you **run into** problems or difficulties, you unexpectedly begin to experience them. ❑ *He ran into trouble with his economic policies... Once Beveridge revealed these proposals, he ran into considerable opposition.*

> V+PREP: HAS PASSIVE

3 If you **run into** someone, you meet them unexpectedly. ❑ *You might run into him one of these days... I first ran into him at the theatre.*

> V+PREP

NOTE **Bump into, run across**, and **come across** mean almost the same as **run into**.

4 If something **runs into** a large number or amount, it reaches that number or amount. ❑ *If you include dams used for power, it runs into the thousands. ...exports running into billions of dollars.*

> V+PREP

5 If a vehicle or its driver **runs into** something, the vehicle accidentally hits it. ❑ *The bus ran into a car... He ran into the back of a van at a zebra crossing.*

> V+PREP: HAS PASSIVE

6 If one thing **runs into** another, it becomes difficult to detect the division between them. ❑ *...a streak of red running into purple... The words run into each other.*

> V+PREP

NOTE **Merge into** means almost the same as **run into**.

★run off

✓ In meaning 8, the stress is on **run**.

1 If you **run off**, you move quickly away from a place or person. ❑ *She gave a brief wave and ran off across the lawn... He dumped the stones he was carrying and ran off to look for more.*

> V+ADV

2 If you **run off** from somewhere, you leave secretly. ❑ *She had run off from home as a child... All the servants have run off and they have taken our horses.*

> V+ADV

NOTE **Run away** means almost the same as **run off**.

3 If you **run off** with someone, you secretly go away with them to live with them or marry them. ❑ *His wife ran off with another man... She ran off to Paris with a chap ten years her junior.*
V+ADV,
V+ADV+with:
RECIPROCAL

4 If a path, track, or corridor **runs off** from a place, it starts at that place and goes away from it. ❑ *...a narrow track running off into the forest... Another tunnel ran off on one side; this was dry, dusty and obviously little used.*
V+ADV:
USUALLY+A

NOTE **Lead off** means almost the same as **run off**.

5 If you **run off** copies of a piece of writing, you produce them using a machine such as a photocopier or a printer. ❑ *Could you run off five copies of this article for me, please.*
V+ADV+N,
V+N+ADV,
V+PRON+ADV

6 If you tell a child to **run off**, you are telling him or her to go away. ❑ *Run off and play with the others.*
V+ADV:
USUALLY IMPERATIVE

7 If a liquid **runs off** the ground or a surface, or if it **runs off**, it flows over it. ❑ *The rainwater may run off in sudden sheets which can do tremendous damage. ...the water running off the mountains.*
V+ADV,
V+PREP

8 If a machine or system **runs off** a particular supply of power, it uses that power in order to make it work. ❑ *In Brazil, all new vehicles now run off fuel alcohol from the waste of sugar production... It was the size of a London bus, but you could run it off a mains plug.*
V+PREP,
V+N+PREP:
ERGATIVE

run off with If someone **runs off with** something, they steal it. ❑ *They aim to grab as much as possible and run off with it to somewhere safe.*
V+ADV+PREP

★run **on**

✔ In meaning 5, the stress is on **run**.

1 If you **run on**, you continue to run in the same direction. ❑ *She darted from tree to tree, stopping and waiting and listening and running on again... She said: 'Where are the others?'—'Just a few minutes behind. I ran on ahead.'*
V+ADV

2 If a road or track **runs on** to a particular place, it continues in that direction. ❑ *From here, the railway line runs on to Gloucester... The main dusty track ran on towards Lesotho.*
V+ADV:
WITH A

3 If someone **runs on**, they continue talking for a long time. ❑ *'How I run on, don't I?' Percival said... Sometimes she let him run on for what seemed hours.*
V+ADV:
USUALLY+A

4 If something **runs on**, it continues to exist or operate longer than expected. ❑ *The list of British troops in Palestine ran on and on... Do you think that he tends to let his jokes run on too long?*
V+ADV

5 If a machine or system **runs on** a particular type of power, it uses it in order to work. ❑ *Many cars can run on unleaded petrol... The heating system was extremely economical because it ran on half-price electricity... The refrigerator ran on gas.*
V+PREP,
V+N+PREP,
V+PRON+PREP:
ERGATIVE

★run **out**

1 If you **run out** of a room or building, you leave it as fast as you can. ❑ *I ran out and slammed the door... Mrs Todd came running out into the garden... He ran out of the room and down the stairs.*
V+ADV:
ALSO+of

2 If a substance **runs out** from somewhere, it flows from there. ❑ *It is passed through a disc with holes in it to let the milk run out but retain the cream.*
V+ADV

3 If you **run out** of something, you have no more of it left. ❑ *We were rapidly running out of money... Mankind is running out of time.*
V+ADV:
USUALLY+of

4 If something **runs out**, it becomes used up so that there is no more left. ❑ *Time is running out fast... My luck seemed to have run out... Their money ran out.*
V+ADV

5 If a legal document or contract **runs out**, it is no longer valid. ❑ *My passport's run out... The patent on APM runs out in 1987.*
V+ADV

NOTE **Expire** is a more formal word for **run out**.

6 If someone **runs out** on a person they have a relationship with, they suddenly leave that person. ❑ *You know me well enough to know I wouldn't run out on you... I'm seeing her tonight, if she doesn't run out on me.*
V+ADV:
USUALLY+on

7 In cricket, if you are batting and **are run out**, your innings is ended, because the other team manage to get the ball to the wicket before you reach it. ❑ *Howarth was unluckily run out... He ran himself out in the last Test against Pakistan.*
V+N+ADV,
V+REFL+ADV,
V+PRON+ADV,
V+ADV+N

8 If you **run out** a length of rope, you unwind some of it and let it pass away from you. ❑ *It was certainly magnificent climbing. I ran out 130 feet of rope to bring Rusty up... I*
V+ADV+N,
V+N+ADV,
V+PRON+ADV,

often run the line out behind the boat... The line is allowed to run out until it bumps the bottom.

V+ADV: ERGATIVE

★run out of If someone **runs** another person **out of** a place, they use force to make that person leave. ❏ My father will kill you and run your family out of town... He grabbed the shotgun, fired back, and ran them out of the house.

V+N+ADV+PREP, V+PRON+ADV+PREP

★run over

1 If you **run over** to someone or something, you move quickly to them. ❏ She ran over and clutched her mother's hand... She ran over to the cooker where the pan was boiling over... Ellen ran over to the bed and threw herself across it.

V+ADV: ALSO+to

2 If a vehicle or its driver **runs over** someone or something, the vehicle hits them or drives over them, causing injury or damage. ❏ We almost ran over a fox that was crossing the road... I'm sure he would have run us over... What would happen if I were to become ill or get run over by a bus?

V+PREP, V+PRON+ADV, V+N+ADV

NOTE **Run down** and **knock down** mean almost the same as **run over**.

3 If a container of liquid **runs over**, it is too full and the liquid flows down its sides. ❏ Turn the tap off – the sink's running over.

V+ADV

NOTE **Overflow** is a more formal word for **run over**.

4 If you **run over** something, you repeat it or read it quickly, in order to practise it or check it. ❏ He asked her to come into his dressing room to run over some lines... Now I would just like to run over the arrangements again with you... He ran over his plans.

V+PREP: HAS PASSIVE

NOTE **Go over** and **run through** mean almost the same as **run over**.

5 If a meeting or event **runs over**, it lasts longer than it should. ❏ The meeting ran over so that he was late for lunch... Each of you will be allocated fifteen minutes and you will be penalized if you run over time.

V+ADV, V+ADV+N

run past If you **run** something **past** someone, you tell them about it or mention it, to see if they think it is a good idea, or can understand it. ❏ Before agreeing, he ran the idea past Johnson.

V+N+PREP, V+PRON+PREP

NOTE **Run by** means almost the same as **run past**.

★run through

1 If an idea, piece of news, or emotion **runs through** a group of people, it spreads through the group quickly, so that they all know it or feel it. ❏ A kind of shock-wave ran through the room... A tremor of excitement ran through the ship as Bill announced that they had sighted land.

V+PREP

2 If a quality or feeling **runs through** something, it affects every part of it or is present everywhere within it. ❏ ...the deep-rooted prejudice that runs through our society... I was impressed with the concept of fairness that ran through the report.

V+PREP

NOTE **Pervade** is a formal word for **run through**.

3 If you **run through** something, you repeat it or read it quickly, in order to practise it or check it. ❏ You could hear the performers running through the whole programme in the background... Some of you won't know this so I'll just run through it rather briefly... Dawlish ran through the notes that he had prepared... I ran through the options with him

V+PREP: HAS PASSIVE

NOTE **Go through** and **run over** mean almost the same as **run through**.

♦ A **run-through** for an event or performance is a rehearsal or practice for it. ❏ He agreed to come to a run-through... Run-throughs are time-consuming and irrelevant.

N-COUNT

4 If you **run through** a large amount of money, you spend it quickly and in a wasteful way. ❏ How he managed to run through £100,000 so quickly I will never understand!

V+PREP: HAS PASSIVE

5 If someone **runs** a person **through** with a sharp weapon, they push it violently all the way through the person's body. [LITERARY] ❏ As he turned I ran him through with my sword.

V+PRON+ADV, V+N+ADV: USUALLY+with

★run to

1 If you **run** to someone, you go to them for help, advice or protection. ❏ I didn't think he'd run to you with the story... We must learn to trust our own intuition and judgment, and not always run to the experts.

V+PREP

2 If something **runs to** a particular amount or size, it is that amount or size. ❏ A housewife's work can run to ten or twelve hours a day if she has small children... The transcript runs to 1,200 pages.

V+PREP

3 If you cannot **run to** a particular item, you cannot afford to buy it or pay for it.

V+PREP

[BRITISH] ❏ *I began to develop a taste for expensive clothes, but my grant didn't exactly run to that sort of thing.*

4 If someone's taste **runs to** a particular kind of thing, that is what they like. ❏ *Unfortunately, O'Shea's tastes in TV ran to situation comedy and sentimental serials... His taste for the arts also ran to poetry.*

V+PREP

★**run up**

1 To **run up** means to move quickly from a lower position to a higher one. ❏ *These small tropical lizards can run up walls... I heard her running up the stairs. ...people from downstairs running up to see what was happening.*

V+PREP, V+ADV

2 If someone **runs up** to you, they come quickly to where you are. ❏ *They ran up and started to attack me... I ran up to him and asked, 'Did you see two ladies come by?'*

V+ADV: ALSO+to

♦ In sport, a **run-up** is the running approach by an athlete or player to gather speed before jumping, throwing something, or kicking a ball. ❏ *He had no rhythm or speed in his run-up. ...a sprinting run-up.*

N-SING

3 If a set of steps or a road **runs up** to a place, or **runs up** an area of land, it leads in that direction. ❏ *Wooden steps ran up to an open front door... At first the road ran up a wide flat valley.*

V+ADV+A, V+PREP

4 If someone **runs up** bills or debts, they start to owe a lot of money because they fail to pay their bills. ❏ *He ran up a thousand dollars worth of bills in her name... She ran up a telephone bill of two hundred pounds!*

V+ADV+N, V+PRON+ADV

5 If you **run up** a piece of clothing, you make it quickly. ❏ *'We could go to the party as clowns,' I replied, wondering if Mrs Moffat could run me up a costume. ...a dreadful fellow whose wife had a hideous blazer run up for him.*

V+PRON+ADV, V+ADV+N: ALSO+for: ALSO V+PRON+ADV+N

6 If a flag **is run up**, it is raised to the top of a flag pole or mast. ❏ *Soldiers on the quay stood speechless as the flag was run up on the mast... The flag was run up and the National Anthem was sung.*

V+ADV+N, V+N+ADV, V+PRON+ADV: USUALLY PASSIVE

7 The **run-up** to an event is the period of time and the things that happen just before it. ❏ *The run-up to the election has been a time of confrontation.*

N-SING

run up against If you **run up against** problems or difficulties, you suddenly and unexpectedly begin to experience them. ❏ *You never know what you're liable to run up against... Economic growth would sooner or later run up against major problems.*

V+ADV+PREP: HAS PASSIVE

NOTE Run into and come up against mean almost the same as **run up against**.

rush /rʌʃ/ (rushes, rushing, rushed)

rush in If you **rush in**, you do or decide something too quickly, without thinking about it carefully enough. ❏ *...the fool who rushes in.*

V+ADV

rush into If you **rush into** something, you do it or decide about it too quickly, without thinking about it carefully enough. ❏ *Don't rush into marriage... We should not rush into the armed struggle.*

V+PREP: HAS PASSIVE

rush out If a company **rushes out** a product, it produces the product quickly in a very short period of time. ❏ *Three books on the General Election were rushed out within a couple of weeks.*

V+N+ADV, V+ADV+N, V+PRON+ADV

rush through If you **rush** something **through**, you deal with it quickly so that it is ready in a shorter time than usual. ❏ *The government rushed the legislation through before the summer recess... Could you rush this application through?*

V+N+ADV, V+PRON+ADV, V+ADV+N

NOTE Push through means almost the same as **rush through**.

rust /rʌst/ (rusts, rusting, rusted)

rust away When a metal object **rusts away**, it is gradually destroyed by rust. ❏ *...an old car which had been rusting away for years.*

V+ADV

rustle /rʌsəl/ (rustles, rustling, rustled)

rustle up

1 If you **rustle** something **up**, you provide or obtain it quickly, with very little planning. [INFORMAL] ❏ *He managed to rustle up a couple of blankets... He has had no trouble rustling up 35 friends and colleagues to invite to his wedding.*

V+ADV+N, V+N+ADV, V+PRON+ADV

2 If you **rustle up** a meal, you cook it quickly, using whatever food you have available at the time. ❏ *I'll rustle something up... We could rustle up an omelette.*

V+N+ADV, V+ADV+N, V+PRON+ADV

Ss

saddle /ˈsædəl/ (saddles, saddling, saddled)

saddle up If you **saddle up**, you put a saddle on a horse or pony. ❑ *Tell him to catch the ponies and saddle up... I saddled up and rode off... Mopani must have saddled up horses numberless times.*

V+ADV,
V+ADV+N,
V+N+ADV,
V+PRON+ADV

saddle with If you **are saddled with** a problem or responsibility which you do not want, you have to deal with it. ❑ *They were in danger of being saddled with more responsibility than power... They were saddled with the task of finding the whereabouts of Calthrop... The last thing I want is to saddle myself with a second mortgage.*

V+N+PREP,
V+PRON+PREP,
V+REFL+PREP:
USUALLY PASSIVE

NOTE Land with and lumber with mean almost the same as **saddle with**.

sail /seɪl/ (sails, sailing, sailed)

sail through If you **sail through** a difficult experience or situation, you deal with it easily and successfully. ❑ *Some women just sail through their pregnancies... At the rehearsal, she had sailed through, knowing every line.*

V+PREP,
V+ADV

NOTE Romp through means almost the same as **sail through**.

sally /ˈsæli/ (sallies, sallying, sallied)

sally forth If someone **sallies forth**, they go to a place quickly or energetically. [LITERARY] ❑ *Boldly they sallied forth to meet them. ...the safe place from which the child sallies forth to explore the world.*

V+ADV

sally out If someone **sallies out**, they leave a place in order to go somewhere. [LITERARY] ❑ *He was able to sally out and return undetected.*

V+ADV

salt /sɔːlt/ (salts, salting, salted)

salt away If you **salt away** money, you do not spend it, but save it or keep it somewhere for the future. ❑ *He was said to have salted away £4 million... They salt their funds away in numbered Swiss bank accounts... People don't know how much he's got salted away.*

V+ADV+N,
V+N+ADV,
V+PRON+ADV

NOTE Stash away means almost the same as **salt away**.

sand /sænd/ (sands, sanding, sanded)

sand down If you **sand down** a wood or metal surface, you rub it with sandpaper until it is completely smooth. ❑ *Sand down that bit before you start painting it... It took us ages to sand the doors down.*

V+ADV+N,
V+N+ADV,
V+PRON+ADV

save /seɪv/ (saves, saving, saved)

★save up

[1] If you **save up**, or **save up** money, you collect money by not spending it, usually so that you can buy something you want. ❑ *The relatives will all save up to put a child through secondary school... The main purpose of his travel is to save up enough money for a bicycle... They're saving some money up for a holiday... At least he had something saved up.*

V+ADV,
V+ADV+N,
V+N+ADV,
V+PRON+ADV:
ALSO+for

[2] If you **save** something **up**, you keep it so that you can use it or deal with it later. ❑ *Do you read through the children's work every time it's produced, or do you tend to save it up? ...if you'd saved up your stamps instead of throwing them away... Mother had dozens of poems, saved up in a small black notebook.*

V+PRON+ADV,
V+ADV+N,
V+N+ADV

savour /ˈseɪvər/ (savours, savouring, savoured)

☑ **Savour** is also spelled **savor** in American English.

savour of If something **savours of** a particular quality or thing, it reminds you of it; often used showing disapproval. ❑ *To do a good deed a day savours of priggishness... She had an aversion to anything that savoured of the supernatural.*

V+PREP

NOTE Smack of means almost the same as **savour of**.

saw /sɔː/ (saws, sawing, sawed, sawn)

☑ The past participle is either **sawed** or **sawn**.

saw off To **saw** something **off** means to cut a piece from something, using a saw. ❑ *We sawed the legs off the table... Jack had sawn off the broken ash bough... The lock on the door had been sawed off... Her wedding ring had to be sawn off her finger.*

V+N+ADV/PREP, V+ADV+N, V+PRON+ADV/PREP

♦ Something that is **sawn-off** has been made shorter by being cut with a saw. [BRITISH] ❑ *...sawn-off shotguns. ...sawn-off lengths of scaffolding. ...a sawn-off shell case that served as an ashtray.*

ADJECTIVE

NOTE In American English, **sawed-off** means almost the same as **sawn-off**.

saw up To **saw** something **up** means to cut it into pieces, using a saw. ❑ *We had to saw the chairs up for firewood... He spent all day sawing up the dead wood.*

V+N+ADV, V+PRON+ADV, V+ADV+N

scale /skeɪl/ (scales, scaling, scaled)

scale back If you **scale back** something such as spending or production, you make it smaller in size, extent, or amount than it used to be. ❑ *Despite the current price advantage, UK manufacturers are still having to scale back production.*

V+ADV+N, V+N+ADV, V+PRON+ADV

NOTE **Decrease** means almost the same as **scale back**.

scale down If something **is scaled down**, it is made smaller in size, amount, or extent than it used to be. ❑ *The project has been scaled down by about half of the original estimate... Overall goals must be scaled down in importance.*

PASSIVE: V+ADV

scale up If you **scale up** something, you make it greater in size, amount, or extent than it used to be. ❑ *Simply scaling up a size 10 garment often leads to disaster... Since then, Wellcome has been scaling up production to prepare for clinical trials.*

V+ADV+N, V+N+ADV, V+PRON+ADV

NOTE **Increase** means almost the same as **scale up**.

scare /skeər/ (scares, scaring, scared)

scare away

1 To **scare** animals or people **away** means to frighten them so that they go away. ❑ *The least shadow or movement would scare the fish away. ...words and magic lights to scare away ghosts... The smaller predators would sometimes be scared away by shouts and screams.*

V+N+ADV, V+ADV+N, V+PRON+ADV

NOTE **Scare off** means almost the same as **scare away**.

2 If something **scares** people **away**, it makes them so nervous that they decide not to do something that they were planning to do. ❑ *The dispute has scared away potential investors... The economy would suffer if a threat to imports scared Europeans away.*

V+ADV+N, V+N+ADV, V+PRON+ADV

NOTE **Discourage** is a more formal word for **scare away**.

scare off

1 If you **scare** people or animals **off**, you frighten them so that they go away. ❑ *I thought of scaring them off with a few shotgun pellets... The boys made enough noise to scare off a forest of animals.*

V+PRON+ADV, V+ADV+N, V+N+ADV

NOTE **Scare away** means almost the same as **scare off**.

2 If something **scares** people **off**, it makes them so nervous that they change their minds about something they were planning to do or have. ❑ *The damage caused by the pills had scared women off... He named a price he thought would scare me off. ...intimidating bureaucracy that scares off many people who are entitled to benefits.*

V+N+ADV, V+PRON+ADV, V+ADV+N

NOTE **Deter** is a more formal word for **scare off**.

scare up If you **scare up** something, you provide, produce, or obtain it, often when it is difficult to do so or when you do not have many resources. [AMERICAN, INFORMAL] ❑ *An all-star game might scare up a bit of interest... Why don't you see if you can scare up a cup of coffee?*

V+ADV+N, V+N+ADV, V+PRON+ADV

scatter /skætər/ (scatters, scattering, scattered)

☑ **About** is used mainly in British English.

scatter about → See scatter around

scatter around

1 If you **scatter** things **around** or **scatter** them **about**, you throw or drop them over a large area in rather a careless way. ❑ *Parrots scatter their food about and make a mess. ...papers scattered around and the remains of a campfire... Food was scattered about the table.*

V+N+ADV, V+PRON+ADV, V+N+PREP, V+PRON+PREP

2 If things or people **are scattered around** or **scattered about** an area, they are spread over that area in rather a disorganized way. ❑ *She now has five shops scattered around the town... People are scattered about the countryside.*

PASSIVE:
V+PREP,
V+ADV

scoop /skuːp/ **(scoops, scooping, scooped)**

scoop out If you **scoop out** something that is solid, or if you **scoop** something **out** of it, you make it hollow by removing the inside part of it, using a special tool such as a scoop or a spoon. ❑ *He showed me a skull, which he'd scooped out and dried... Slice the tops off the tomatoes and scoop out the seeds... We found the cave and began to scoop the earth out.*

V+ADV+N,
V+N+ADV,
V+PRON+ADV

scoop up If you **scoop** something **up**, you put your hands under it and lift it in a quick movement. ❑ *Stephanie scooped one of the lizards up... I watched Patrick scoop up a handful of snow from the window ledge... I had to scoop it up with my fingers.*

V+N+ADV,
V+ADV+N,
V+PRON+ADV

score /skɔːr/ **(scores, scoring, scored)**

score off

1 If you **score off** someone, you make a clever or insulting reply to something they have said. ❑ *They spent the whole evening scoring off each other... Teachers could not refrain from scoring off me.*

V+PREP

2 If you **score off** something that is written down, you draw a line through it to indicate that it is not wanted or needed. ❑ *Score off each number as it is read out... You'll find it easier if you score them off when you've answered them... I asked him to score my name off the list of players next Saturday.*

V+ADV+N,
V+PRON+ADV/PREP,
V+N+ADV/PREP

NOTE **Cross off** means almost the same as **score off**.

score out If you **score out** something that is written down, you draw a line through it so that people cannot read it. ❑ *The rest of the sentence is heavily scored out... The article was too long, and I had to score a couple of paragraphs out.*

V+ADV+N,
V+N+ADV,
V+PRON+ADV

NOTE **Cross out** means almost the same as **score out**, and **delete** is a more formal word.

scour /skaʊər/ **(scours, scouring, scoured)**

scour away If water or wind **scours away** a piece of land, the force of the water or wind gradually removes it. ❑ *Rainwater had scoured away the hillsides... Rivers scoured the soft sandstone away.*

V+ADV+N,
V+N+ADV,
V+PRON+ADV

NOTE **Erode** means almost the same as **scour away**.

scout /skaʊt/ **(scouts, scouting, scouted)**

☑ In American English, **around** is much more common than **round**.

scout around If you **scout around** or **scout round** for something, you go to different places looking for it. ❑ *I spend most of my time scouting round for books... We'd scout around to see if anyone was in the rooms nearby.*

V+ADV:
USUALLY+for

scout out If you **scout** something **out**, you succeed in finding it after you have been through an area searching for it. ❑ *Their mission is simply to scout out places where helicopters can land.*

V+ADV+N,
V+N+ADV,
V+PRON+ADV

NOTE **Locate** means almost the same as **scout out**.

scout round → See **scout around**

scrabble /skræbəl/ **(scrabbles, scrabbling, scrabbled)**

☑ About is used mainly in British English.

scrabble about → See **scrabble around**

scrabble around If you **scrabble around** or **scrabble about**, you use your hands in order to try to find something on the ground that you cannot see. ❑ *We scrabbled about in the grass and leaves and found the packet... Kate scrabbled around, looking for stones.*

V+ADV:
USUALLY+A

scrape /skreɪp/ **(scrapes, scraping, scraped)**

scrape along If you **scrape along**, you just manage to survive and have a fairly comfortable life. ❑ *...content to scrape along in life.*

V+ADV

NOTE **Get by** means almost the same as **scrape along**.

scrape away If you **scrape away** a substance, you remove it completely by means of a knife or other sharp object. ❑ *I dug the knife-blade in and scraped away an*

V+ADV+N,
V+N+ADV,
V+PRON+ADV

inch of the lead... The paint had been scraped away.

NOTE **Scrape off** means almost the same as **scrape away**.

scrape by If you **scrape by** on a particular amount of money, you just manage to survive using that money. ❑ *No household can hope to scrape by on forty pounds a week... We scrape by, but we never have much fun.*

V+ADV:
ALSO+*on*

NOTE **Get by** means almost the same as **scrape by**.

scrape into If you **scrape into** a school, university, or profession, you only just manage to be accepted there as a student or employee. ❑ *He only just scraped into university because of poor A levels.*

V+PREP

scrape off If you **scrape** a substance **off**, you remove it from a surface by rubbing or scratching it with something sharp. ❑ *Scrape as much wax as possible off with your fingernails... They would scrape it all off... The stiff brush bristles scraped off some of the encrusted filth. ...scraping snow off railway tracks with shovels.*

V+N+ADV/PREP,
V+PRON+ADV/PREP,
V+ADV+N

scrape out When you **scrape out** a container such as a bowl or a jar, you remove all the contents that are left in it with a special tool such as a spoon or knife. ❑ *She scraped out her bowl greedily... He scraped the tub out until every last bit of ice-cream was gone.*

V+ADV+N,
V+N+ADV,
V+PRON+ADV

scrape through If you **scrape through** an examination or a course of some kind, you just succeed in passing it with a very low grade. ❑ *...scholars who scrape through college or university... He was lucky to scrape through because he never did any work.*

V+PREP,
V+ADV

scrape together If you **scrape together** an amount of money or a number of things that you need, you manage with difficulty to obtain them. ❑ *If we could scrape together a dozen people, we could hire a minibus. ...scraping the funds together from their hard-won budgets.*

V+ADV+N,
V+N+ADV,
V+PRON+ADV

NOTE **Scrape up** means almost the same as **scrape together**.

scrape up

1 If you **scrape up** an amount of money, you manage with difficulty to get the money you need. ❑ *He scraped up the money to start his Hollywood restaurant... I can give you a few shillings that I scraped up. ...scraping the fees up to send their boys to school.*

V+ADV+N,
V+N+ADV,
V+PRON+ADV

NOTE **Scrape together** and **get together** mean almost the same as **scrape up**.

2 If you **scrape** something **up**, you remove it from the ground using a tool with a sharp edge, such as a shovel. ❑ *She took a scoop from her pocket and scraped up as much of the scattered seed as she could... They scraped up the dust and put it into bags.*

V+ADV+N,
V+N+ADV,
V+PRON+ADV

scratch /skrætʃ/ (**scratches, scratching, scratched**)

✅ **About** is used mainly in British English.

scratch about → See **scratch around**

scratch around If you **scratch around** or **scratch about** a place, you look for something that you cannot see on the ground, using your hands or something sharp such as a stick. ❑ *Chickens will scratch about in the dung of other animals and will salvage any undigested grain... So far, only a dozen men have scratched around in a few kilometres of an area the size of Africa.*

V+ADV,
V+PREP

scratch out If you **scratch out** something that is written down, you draw a line through it with a pen or a sharp instrument so that it cannot be seen. ❑ *Mayhew took off his helmet and scratched out something written on the side... He scribbled down lines and then scratched them out again.*

V+ADV+N,
V+PRON+ADV,
V+N+ADV

NOTE **Cross out** means almost the same as **scratch out**.

screen /skriːn/ (**screens, screening, screened**)

screen off If a part of a room **is screened off**, it has been separated from the rest of the room by a screen or partition. ❑ *It was one long room that had a sleeping area screened off... He was in a little cabin screened off from the open space. ...torn curtains screening off the bunks from the rest of the cabin.*

V+N+ADV,
V+PRON+ADV,
V+ADV+N:
ALSO+*from*,
USUALLY PASSIVE

NOTE **Partition off** means almost the same as **screen off**.

screen out If an organization or country **screens out** certain people, it keeps them out because it thinks they may cause problems. ❑ *The company screened out applicants motivated only by money.*

V+ADV+N,
V+N+ADV,
V+PRON+ADV

screw /skru:/ (**screws, screwing, screwed**)

screw down If you **screw** something **down**, you close or fasten it firmly, using screws or using something which has a screw-top. ❑ *When the bottles are warm, screw the caps down tightly and place in the refrigerator... The lid had not been screwed down properly.*

V+N+ADV,
V+ADV+N,
V+PRON+ADV

screw out of If you **screw** something **out of** someone, you persuade them to give it to you using force or strong arguments. [BRITISH, INFORMAL] ❑ *I managed to screw a bit more money out of him... Don't worry, they'll never screw a confession out of my father.*

V+N+ADV+PREP,
V+PRON+ADV+PREP

⋆**screw up**

1 If you **screw up** your face or eyes, you move or twist them so that they no longer have their natural shape. ❑ *The man screwed up his face in disgust... She screwed up her eyes as she faced the sun.*

V+ADV+N,
V+N+ADV,
V+PRON+ADV

2 If you **screw up** something such as paper or material, you bend or twist it in your hands so that it is creased and crumpled. [BRITISH] ❑ *She laughed and, screwing up the piece of newspaper, tossed it into a corner... My clothes were screwed up in a white plastic bag.*

V+ADV+N,
V+N+ADV,
V+PRON+ADV

NOTE **Scrunch up** means almost the same as **screw up**.

3 If you **screw up** or if you **screw** something **up**, you cause a plan or arrangement to fail or go wrong. [INFORMAL] ❑ *She could screw things up for us... He can't do that; that screws up all my arrangements... In 1983, the cereal farmers screwed it up... What I do best is out there in the boxing ring, even if I've screwed up outside it.*

V+N+ADV,
V+ADV+N,
V+PRON+ADV,
V+ADV

4 Something that **screws** you **up** makes you nervous, worried, or confused. [INFORMAL] ❑ *Her mother's screwed her up and given her values she despises. ...a laborious series of investigations that might screw me up for weeks.*

V+PRON+ADV,
V+N+ADV

♦ Someone who is **screwed-up** is very confused, worried, or nervous, often over a long period of time. [INFORMAL] ❑ *I guess I'm just a screwed-up cop. ...a screwed-up, suffering man.*

ADJECTIVE

scribble /skrɪbᵊl/ (**scribbles, scribbling, scribbled**)

scribble down If you **scribble down** something, you write it quickly or roughly. ❑ *I attempted to scribble down the names... He took my name and address, scribbling it down in his notebook.*

V+ADV+N,
V+N+ADV,
V+PRON+ADV

scrounge /skraʊndʒ/ (**scrounges, scrounging, scrounged**)

scrounge up If you **scrounge up** something that you need, you get it with difficulty, usually by asking other people for it. [AMERICAN] ❑ *Golf and fishing can be arranged if you can scrounge up your own equipment.*

V+ADV+N,
V+PRON+ADV,
V+N+ADV

scrub /skrʌb/ (**scrubs, scrubbing, scrubbed**)

scrub off If you **scrub** dirt or stains **off** something, you remove them by rubbing hard. ❑ *Mrs Sturgill scrubbed the caked blood off her cheeks... He tried without success to scrub it off. ...sponges for scrubbing off the dirt.*

V+N+PREP/ADV,
V+PRON+PREP/ADV,
V+ADV+N

scrub out If you **scrub** a place **out**, you clean it very thoroughly. ❑ *Not much of a holiday for me, scrubbing this whole place out!... She agreed to scrub out the hall in return for lessons. ...the awful job in the laundry, scrubbing it out every day.*

V+N+ADV,
V+ADV+N,
V+PRON+ADV

NOTE **Clean out** means almost the same as **scrub out**.

scrunch /skrʌntʃ/ (**scrunches, scrunching, scrunched**)

scrunch up If you **scrunch** something **up** or if it **scrunches up**, it is bent or twisted so that it no longer has its natural shape. ❑ *She started to read it, then scrunched it up and threw it in the bin. ...looking for a ten-pound note, which would be all scrunched up... She turns her back and scrunches up into an awkward position... I'd lain scrunched up for hours in a flimsy bunker.*

V+PRON+ADV,
V+N+ADV,
V+ADV+N,
V+ADV:
ERGATIVE

seal /si:l/ (**seals, sealing, sealed**)

seal in If something **seals in** a smell or liquid, it prevents it from getting out of a food. ❑ *The coffee is freeze-dried to seal in all the flavour.*

V+ADV+N,
V+N+ADV,
V+PRON+ADV

⋆**seal off**

1 If you **seal off** a place, you prevent people from getting into it or out of it by blocking all the entrances. ❑ *Police had already sealed off one of the entrances... They*

V+N+ADV,
V+ADV+N,
V+PRON+ADV

sealed the main road off... The meeting was in a locked school building sealed off by hundreds of police.

NOTE **Cordon off** means almost the same as **seal off**.

2 If someone **is sealed off** from something that they would normally be involved in, or if they **seal** themselves **off**, they are separated from it. ❏ *...people sealed off from social influences... He is the proverbial recluse, sealed off from the rest of the world... They have sealed themselves off from further development.*

PASSIVE: V+ADV, ALSO V+REFL+ADV: USUALLY+*from*

NOTE **Cut off** means almost the same as **seal off**.

seal up If you **seal** something **up**, you close it so that nothing can get in or out. ❏ *They were already sealing up the exits... The windows on the west side were sealed up... The box had been examined but they had sealed it up again.*

V+ADV+N, V+N+ADV, V+PRON+ADV

NOTE **Close up** means almost the same as **seal up**.

search /sɜːtʃ/ (searches, searching, searched)

search out If you **search** something or someone **out**, you keep looking for them until you find them. ❏ *I have been searching out old sewing patterns... Paul McAlinden searched out the illustrations for these pages... He sent a company of soldiers to search them out and destroy them.*

V+ADV+N, V+PRON+ADV, V+N+ADV

NOTE **Hunt out** and **unearth** mean almost the same as **search out**.

section /sekʃ°n/ (sections, sectioning, sectioned)

section off If an area **is sectioned off**, it is separated by a wall, fence, or other barrier from the surrounding area. ❏ *The kitchen is galley shaped, sectioned off from the rest of the room by a half wall.*

V+ADV+N, V+N+ADV, V+PRON+ADV: USUALLY PASSIVE

see /siː/ (sees, seeing, saw, seen)

see about When you **see about** something, you arrange for it to be done or provided. ❏ *Rudolph went to the station to see about Thomas's ticket... The superintendent sent me to see about painting your apartment.*

V+PREP

★**see as** If you **see** someone or something **as** a particular thing, you regard them in a way which suggests that they are that thing. ❏ *He saw her as a holy woman, innocent, calm, untouchable... The committee saw higher education as an activity with its own values and aims... He no longer saw himself as a contender in the 1908 Presidential stakes.*

V+PRON+PREP, V+N+PREP, V+REFL+PREP

NOTE **Consider** is a more formal word for **see as**.

★**see in** If you **see** a particular quality or characteristic **in** someone or something, you believe that they have that quality or characteristic. ❏ *I saw a delicacy in him that I had never seen before... She saw something in me that she didn't like... No one had understood what she saw in Dave.*

V+N+PREP, V+PRON+PREP

see into If you **see** someone **into** a place, you go with them and make sure that they go in there. ❏ *He saw me into a taxi... I helped Kate undress and saw her into bed... Hattie left after seeing me safely into David's apartment.*

V+PRON+PREP, V+N+PREP

see off

1 When you **see** someone **off**, you go with them to the station, airport, or port that they are leaving from, and say goodbye to them there. ❏ *She saw him off at the station... I came to see you off at Heathrow... Also there to see us off was John Ryan... 'Are you seeing someone off too?'*

V+PRON+ADV, V+N+ADV, V+ADV+N

NOTE **Wave off** means almost the same as **see off**.

2 To **see** someone or something **off** means to force them to leave a place. ❏ *Up and at them! – We'll see them off yet!... I saw off those children who were hanging around the sheds... They were to see off the Germans and then resist the Russians.*

V+PRON+ADV, V+ADV+N, V+N+ADV

3 In a game or competition, if you **see off** your opponents, you succeed in improving your position so that you win it. [BRITISH] ❏ *Burgess relied on his change of pace to see off the opposition.*

V+ADV+N, V+PRON+ADV

see out

1 If you **see** someone **out** of a room or a building, you go with them to the door as they leave. ❏ *As I saw the cops out I was trembling... She saw him out of the kitchen.*

V+N+ADV, V+PRON+ADV

2 If you **see out** a period of time, you continue with what you are doing until that period of time is over. ❏ *The war was over. I was seeing out my time in the army... He has decided to see out one last term in his teaching job.*

V+ADV+N, V+N+ADV, V+PRON+ADV

NOTE **Stick out** means almost the same as **see out**.

3 If something **sees** a period of time **out**, it lasts until the end of that time. [INFORMAL] ❑ *I bought some food yesterday to see the week out... Somehow, I don't think these sandals are going to see out the holiday, do you?*

V+N+ADV,
V+ADV+N

NOTE **Last out** means almost the same as **see out**.

see over

1 If you **see over** a house, building, exhibition, and so on, you go there to look at the different parts of it. ❑ *We've seen over two houses today, but I didn't like either of them.*

V+PREP

NOTE **Look round** means almost the same as **see over**.

2 An **overseer** is someone who watches work being done to make sure that it is done properly.

N-COUNT

see round If you **see round** a building, town, exhibition, and so on, you visit it and look at the different parts of it. ❑ *We spent the best part of the morning seeing round the museum... I'm going to see round a house this afternoon... Would you like to see round?*

V+PREP,
V+ADV

NOTE **Look round** means almost the same as **see round**.

★see through

1 If you can **see through** something, you are able to look from one side of it to the other. ❑ *He couldn't see through the clouds of white dust... I managed to see four prisoners through a wire net... She saw him through the kitchen window.*

V+PREP,
V+N+PREP,
V+PRON+PREP

♦ **See-through** clothes are made of thin cloth, so that you can see a person's body or underclothes through them. ❑ *...a see-through blouse. ...a see-through bra of black net and lace.*

ADJECTIVE

2 If you **see through** a person or **see through** what they are doing, you realize what their intentions are, even though they are trying to hide them. ❑ *She had learned to see through him... The jailers saw through my scheme... Her excuses were lame but he did not see through them.*

V+PREP:
HAS PASSIVE

3 If someone or something **sees** you **through** a difficult time in your life, they support you during this time. ❑ *He was a great friend of mine and saw me through all the hard times... I must see Gertrude through this awful trial... I now have fifteen thousand dollars to see me through until my book is published.*

V+PRON+PREP,
V+N+PREP,
V+PRON+ADV,
V+N+ADV

NOTE **Get through** means almost the same as **see through**.

4 If you **see** a task, plan, or project **through**, you continue to do it until it is successfully completed. ❑ *...the joy that comes from seeing each job right through... He began his hunger strike on March 1 and he vowed to see it through.*

V+N+ADV,
V+PRON+ADV

NOTE **Stick out** means almost the same as **see through**.

★see to If you **see to** something or someone that needs attention, you deal with them. ❑ *Don't you worry about that. I'll see to that... A man was there to see to our luggage... Is this lady being seen to?*

V+PREP:
HAS PASSIVE

seek /siːk/ (seeks, seeking, sought)

seek out If you **seek out** someone or something, you try to find them. [FORMAL] ❑ *It was unusual for anyone to seek out her husband unnecessarily... Laura used to seek Gillian out when she had quarrelled with all her friends... I used to seek her out on her way home from school.*

V+ADV+N,
V+N+ADV,
V+PRON+ADV:
USUALLY+A

seize /siːz/ (seizes, seizing, seized)

seize on If you **seize on** or **seize upon** something, you show great interest in it, often because it is useful to you. ❑ *The Administration immediately seized on the idea of sending the forces back into the Gulf... This was one of the points that Vasiliou seized upon with some force.*

V+PREP:
HAS PASSIVE

seize up If a part of your body **seizes up**, it suddenly stops functioning properly, usually because you have used or exercised it too much. You can also say that something such as a machine, engine, or system **seizes up** when it stops working altogether. ❑ *Your back may seize up... I had done enough to prevent my heart and lungs seizing up... My minivan just seized up, and we couldn't get it started again.*

V+ADV

seize upon → See **seize on**

select /sɪlɛkt/ **(selects, selecting, selected)**

select out If you **select out** things from a group, you choose the things you want from that group. ❑ *Clough selected out the team members he wanted for the match on Tuesday... Try to select unbruised fruit out for jam-making.*

> V+ADV+N,
> V+N+N+ADV,
> V+PRON+ADV

sell /sɛl/ **(sells, selling, sold)**

★sell off If you **sell** something **off**, you get rid of it by selling it, usually because you need some money. ❑ *He had to sell his cattle off at derisory prices... She was forced to sell off her land... We'll have to sell it off bit by bit.*

> V+N+ADV+N,
> V+ADV+N,
> V+PRON+ADV

♦ A **sell-off** is the sale of something such as a business as a way of raising money. ❑ *The sell-off has to be approved by the European Commission. ...the sell-off of British coal. ...sell-offs to private interests.*

> N-COUNT

sell on

> ✓ In meaning 2, the stress is on **sell**.

1 If you buy something and then **sell** it **on**, you sell it to someone else soon after buying it, usually in order to make a profit. ❑ *Mr Farrier bought cars at auctions and sold them on... The arms had been sold to a businessman; he sold them on to paramilitary groups.*

> V+N+ADV,
> V+PRON+ADV:
> ALSO+to

2 If someone **is sold on** something, they are very enthusiastic about it. [INFORMAL] ❑ *I'm not really sold on Mahler... He was totally sold on the ethic of free enterprise... I've tried to sell this film on you before.*

> V+N+PREP,
> V+PRON+PREP:
> USUALLY PASSIVE

★sell out

1 If a shop **is sold out** of something, or **has sold out** of it, it has all been sold, and there is none of it left in the shop. ❑ *Shops almost immediately sold out of the advertised goods... Sold out of baguettes by 5.00 pm? That was unheard of. French bakers are never sold out of baguettes... I'm sorry, we've sold out of that particular brand.*

> V+ADV:
> OR PASSIVE:
> V+ADV:
> USUALLY+of

2 If a performance of a play, film, or other form of entertainment **is sold out**, all the tickets have been sold. ❑ *The first performance was sold out and the play became a tremendous hit... The show is already sold out at Hammersmith.*

> PASSIVE:
> V+ADV

♦ If you describe a play, concert, or other event as a **sell-out**, you mean that it is very successful because all the tickets for it have been sold. ❑ *The show was a sell-out... Tomorrow's race would be a sell-out. ...a sell-out crowd.*

> N-SING

3 If you **sell out**, you sell almost everything you have, usually because you need some money. [AMERICAN] ❑ *I hear she's going to sell out and move to the city. ...selling out our interests in the olive oil business... When I married I sold out my share of the shop.*

> V+ADV,
> V+ADV+N,
> V+PRON+ADV:
> ALSO+to

4 If you **sell** somebody **out**, you betray them in order to gain an advantage for yourself. ❑ *They would sell out their country rather than take a stand... So you sold him out for eighty-five cents... All but my landlady gradually sold out to the other side... They thought of him as one who had sold out and was no longer to be regarded as a friend.*

> V+ADV+N,
> V+PRON+ADV,
> V+N+ADV,
> V+ADV:
> ALSO+to

♦ If you describe someone's behaviour as a **sell-out**, you mean that they have betrayed you in order to gain an advantage. [INFORMAL] ❑ *This meeting was just another sell-out to the management. ...a sell-out that perverted the people's will. ...a sell-out of socialism.*

> N-COUNT

sell up If you **sell up**, you sell everything you have, such as your house or your business, because you need some money. [BRITISH] ❑ *Farmers sell up in order to survive... The owners have sold up and gone.*

> V+ADV

send /sɛnd/ **(sends, sending, sent)**

send ahead If you **send** something **ahead** when you are going on a journey, you arrange for it to be taken to your destination before you arrive there. ❑ *He had sent his baggage ahead. ...the small trunk that they had sent ahead with Billy's belongings.*

> V+N+ADV,
> V+PRON+ADV

> NOTE **Forward** is a more formal word for **send ahead**.

★send away

1 If you **send** someone **away**, you tell them to go away from you, or you arrange for them to go somewhere. ❑ *'What are you doing here?'—'Don't send me away again!'... They persuaded me to send her away to a convalescent home... Sending their children away meant an appreciable increase in fees.*

> V+PRON+ADV,
> V+N+ADV

2 If you **send away** for something, you write to a firm or organization and ask them to send it to you. ❑ *She was going to send away for the samples... I'm thinking of*

> V+ADV:
> USUALLY+for

sending away for one of those dolls.

NOTE **Send off** means almost the same as **send away**.

★**send back** If you **send** something **back**, you return it to the place that it came from, usually because there is something wrong with it, or because you do not want it. ❏ *My aunt had a wig, but she sent it back to be redressed... She sent back her breakfast tray untouched... He sent back the Booker prize money he won.*

V+PRON+ADV,
V+ADV+N,
V+N+ADV

send down

1 If a student **is sent down**, he or she is made to leave a university or college because of bad behaviour. [BRITISH] ❏ *He was sent down from Trinity College for sexual misdemeanors.*

PASSIVE:
V+ADV

2 If someone convicted of a crime **is sent down**, they are sent to prison. [BRITISH] ❏ *Clive's brother had been brought to court and sent down for larceny... His fingerprints were all over it – that would be enough to send him down for several more years.*

V+N+ADV,
V+PRON+ADV:
USUALLY PASSIVE

★**send for**

1 If you **send for** someone, you ask them to come and see you by sending a message. ❏ *'Shall I send for Doctor Rajendra, Lila?' he asked... I explained that I had been sent for.*

V+PREP:
HAS PASSIVE

2 If you **send for** something, you ask for it to be sent to you by sending a request. ❏ *You can send for a copy by writing to PO Box 28, Cheltenham... Mechanical resuscitation equipment was sent for, but no-one knew how to operate it.*

V+PREP:
HAS PASSIVE

send forth If you **send** someone **forth**, you arrange or tell them to go somewhere for you. [LITERARY] ❏ *I'm sending you forth on your voyage of discovery... A sudden fine morning would send us forth for a day's nutting or blackberrying.*

V+N+ADV,
V+PRON+ADV,
V+ADV+N

★**send in**

1 If you **send in** something such as a report or an application, you send it to a place where it can be dealt with officially. ❏ *I was expected to send in a written report every two months... Humboldt sent in his resignation... We're hoping that readers will send in their ideas for saving money.*

V+ADV+N,
V+N+ADV,
V+PRON+ADV

NOTE **Submit** means almost the same as **send in**.

2 If you **send in** for something, you ask for it to be posted to you by a firm, business, or other organization. ❏ *Don't forget to send in for your free information packs.*

V+ADV:
USUALLY+for

3 When a group of people, especially soldiers or police, **are sent in**, they are sent to a place in order to deal with a dangerous or difficult situation. ❏ *The army was going to be sent in to quell the rioting... The Government threatened to send in agents to collect the tax.*

V+ADV+N,
V+N+ADV,
V+PRON+ADV

4 When you **send** someone **in**, you tell them to go into a room where someone else is waiting to see them. ❏ *Send Clemenza in to me... Clare was sent in to tell me the news... The door opened, and the secretary sent in a tall thin man.*

V+N+ADV,
V+PRON+ADV,
V+ADV+N

★**send off**

1 If you **send off** a letter, telegram, or parcel, you post it somewhere. ❏ *He had sent off the rest of the family's belongings the day before... Write the stories and send the lot off to the office... I won't send it off just yet.*

V+ADV+N,
V+N+ADV,
V+PRON+ADV

2 If you **send off** for something, you write to someone and ask them to post it to you. ❏ *Send off for lists of jobs... Can we have time to note down where to send off for them?*

V+ADV:
USUALLY+for

NOTE **Send away** means almost the same as **send off**.

3 If you **send** someone **off**, you ask or tell them to go somewhere else. ❏ *I sent Georgie off with strict instructions not to come back till later... He told Virginia to send the girls off to the ranch... She sent him off to her sister's so we could talk in private.*

V+N+ADV,
V+PRON+ADV:
ALSO+to

NOTE **Send away** means almost the same as **send off**.

4 If a football player **is sent off**, the player is made to leave the field during a game as a punishment for seriously breaking the rules. ❏ *Henry was sent off after allegedly punching Garnham... Referee! Send him off!*

V+N+ADV,
V+PRON+ADV:
USUALLY PASSIVE

5 A **send-off** is an occasion when people come together to say goodbye to someone who is starting a journey or going away to live in another place. [INFORMAL] ❏ *They certainly gave us a fine send-off.*

N-COUNT

send on If you **send on** letters or parcels, you send them to someone else after you have received them. ❏ *Do you still want me to send on 'Let's Write a Novel'?... Send*

V+ADV+N,
V+N+ADV,
V+PRON+ADV:

the letter on to your accountant... If she sends it to me I'll send it on to you... His form had been sent on to us.

ALSO+to

NOTE Forward is a more formal word for **send on**.

★send out

1 If you **send out** something such as letters or leaflets, you send copies of them to a lot of people. ❏ ...sending out questionnaires to 34000 doctors... We sent out a leaflet to every household... I send letters out to all the landladies and landlords who have offered accommodation.

V+ADV+N,
V+PRON+ADV,
V+N+ADV:
ALSO+to

2 If a machine **sends out** a sound or a light, it causes sound or light to travel in a particular direction. ❏ ...a small but powerful searchlight that could send out a flashing beam... An automatic radio beacon capable of sending out a continuous signal was to be switched on.

V+ADV+N,
V+N+ADV,
V+PRON+ADV

NOTE **Give out** means almost the same as **send out**, and **emit** is a more formal word.

3 When a plant **sends out** roots or shoots, they grow. ❏ If you cut your rubber plant back, it should send out new side shoots.

V+ADV+N,
V+N+ADV,
V+PRON+ADV

NOTE **Produce** means almost the same as **send out**.

send out for If you **send out for** food, for example pizzas or sandwiches, you phone and ask for it to be delivered to you. ❏ Let's send out for a pizza and watch The Late Show.

V+ADV+PREP

send up

1 If you **send** someone **up**, you imitate them in a way that makes them appear foolish. [BRITISH, INFORMAL] ❏ He walked behind me so as to be able to send me up for the amusement of passers-by. ...the sort of person it is only too easy to send up.

V+PRON+ADV,
V+N+ADV

NOTE **Take off** means almost the same as **send up**.

♦ A **send-up** is a piece of writing or acting in which someone or something is imitated in order to make them appear foolish. [BRITISH, INFORMAL] ❏ ...his cheeky send-up of the scene. ...Victoria Wood's fly-on-the-wall send-ups.

N-COUNT

2 If someone who is on trial **is sent up**, they are found guilty and sent to prison. [AMERICAN] ❏ If I'm going to be sent up for killing one guy, then I might as well kill three more.

V+N+ADV,
V+PRON+ADV:
USUALLY PASSIVE

NOTE **Send down** means almost the same as **send up**.

separate /sepəreɪt/ (separates, separating, separated)

separate off If you **separate** something **off** from a large group of things, you remove it completely from that group. ❏ They have taken great care to separate off groups for slaughter from the main herd... The literacy campaign has been separated off from mainstream adult education.

V+ADV+N,
V+N+ADV,
V+PRON+ADV:
ALSO+from

separate out If you **separate out** a group of things or people, you divide them into smaller groups in order to make them easier to deal with. ❏ Most schools decide to separate out their pupils into different groups according to age. ...separating out bits of paper, some white, some orange... When they play with language, children separate it out for a special kind of attention.

V+ADV+N,
V+PRON+ADV,
V+N+ADV

serve /sɜːrv/ (serves, serving, served)

★serve as If one thing **serves as** or **serves for** another thing, it is used instead of that other thing, often because nothing more suitable is available. ❏ There was a long, grey building that served as a cafeteria... ...an old car tyre which evidently served as a children's swing. ...a sawn-off shell case that served for an ashtray.

V+PREP

NOTE **Do for** means almost the same as **serve as**.

serve for → See serve as

serve on

1 If you **serve on** a committee or other organized group, you are a member of it. ❏ He has not served on a council before... I have been pretty disillusioned with juries ever since I served on one.

V+PREP

2 If you **serve** a legal document **on** someone, or **serve** it **upon** them, you deliver it to them. The document usually orders them to appear in a court of law or to do something that they have previously refused to do. ❏ A House Committee tried to serve a subpoena on Harry Truman... This notice had been served on her six weeks before.

V+N+PREP,
V+PRON+PREP

serve out

1 When you **serve out** food, you give it to people at the beginning of a meal, or during it. ❑ *Miss Clare and I served out slices of cold meat... We spend about two hours a day serving out the children's dinners.*

NOTE **Serve up** and **dish up** mean almost the same as **serve out**.

V+ADV+N,
V+N+ADV,
V+PRON+ADV

2 If someone **serves out** their term of office, contract, or prison sentence, they do not leave before the end of the agreed period of time. ❑ *The governor has declared his innocence and says he plans to fight and serve out his term... I was resigned to serving out the sentence.*

V+ADV+N,
V+PRON+ADV

★serve up

1 When you **serve up** food, you give it to people at the beginning of a meal. ❑ *They serve up far more food than could possibly be eaten... When you want them to try something new, serve it up casually.*

NOTE **Dish up** means almost the same as **serve up**.

V+ADV+N,
V+PRON+ADV,
V+N+ADV

2 If a particular type of entertainment **is served up**, it is presented to people. ❑ *The amount of music served up at the Proms is truly staggering. ...turgid patriotic and religious programmes served up by the authorities... What I find hard to stomach is the rubbish served up on television and radio these days.*

V+ADV+N,
V+N+ADV,
V+PRON+ADV:
USUALLY PASSIVE

serve upon → See serve on

set /sɛt/ (sets, setting)

✔ The form **set** is used in the present tense and is the past tense and past participle of the verb.

★set about

If you **set about** doing something, you start to do it in an energetic or purposeful way. ❑ *The next morning they awoke and set about cleaning and sweeping the house... I set about finding a flat bit of ground on which to pitch my tent... Vespasian set about his small task very seriously.*

V+PREP:
ALSO+-ING

★set against

1 When one fact or argument **is set against** another, it is compared with the other one in order to be more easily understood. ❑ *This slight improvement has to be set against an enormous increase in crime... Set against that time-span, writing is very much a new invention.*

V+N+PREP,
V+PRON+PREP:
USUALLY PASSIVE

NOTE **Balance against** means almost the same as **set against**.

2 If you **set** an amount of money **against** tax or **against** another source of income or debt, you tell the tax authorities that that amount was spent in connection with your job or business in order to reduce the amount of tax you have to pay. ❑ *This allows them to set the net loss against taxable income earned elsewhere... The Green Paper laid down proposals for tax credits which could be set against tax liability.*

V+N+PREP,
V+PRON+PREP:
USUALLY PASSIVE

NOTE **Set off against** means almost the same as **set against**.

3 To **set** one person **against** another means to make them become enemies or rivals. ❑ *The last thing I wanted to do was to set her against me... As a result of this war, parent had been set against child and child against parent.*

V+PRON+PREP,
V+N+PREP

4 If you **are set against** something, you have firmly decided that you do not want to have it, or do not want it to happen. ❑ *He had wanted to go into the army, but his mother had been so set against it that he had given up the idea... He seemed set against the key people in the company except me... That's why my husband's so set against drink.*

PASSIVE:
V+PREP

5 If something **is set against** a particular background, it is placed there so that it is clearly visible and contrasts with what is behind it. ❑ *There, set against a huge ochre-coloured screen, was the Shroud. ...faces in black and dark brown carved wood set against white emulsion.*

V+N+PREP,
V+PRON+PREP:
USUALLY PASSIVE

6 If a play, film, or story **is set against** a particular background, the action of the story takes place in a particular setting which is always present and which is an important part of the whole work. ❑ *The career of one deadbeat rock group of the early '60s is set against a tapestry of teenage life in the provinces... Set against the background of the Russian Revolution, Reds is 'an historical romantic movie'.*

PASSIVE:
V+PREP

set apart

If something **is set apart** for a special use or purpose, it is kept for that use or purpose and not used for anything else. ❑ *One day of the week should be set apart for relaxation... There are no rooms specifically set apart for quiet study.*

V+PRON+ADV,
V+N+ADV:
USUALLY PASSIVE

set apart from If a feature or characteristic **sets** you **apart from** other people it makes you noticeably different from the others. ❑ *He had gained a lot of weight and it set him apart from the rest of the men... These attributes set humans apart from even the highest primates.*

V+PRON+ADV+PREP,
V+N+ADV+PREP

★set aside

1 If you **set aside** something such as time or money, you do not use it immediately but keep it for a special use or purpose. ❑ *With a separate budget account you set aside equal monthly sums to cover your total yearly expenditure... Try to set some money aside for this... Some time should be set aside for reading and writing and maths.*
NOTE **Put aside** means almost the same as **set aside**.

V+ADV+N,
V+N+ADV,
V+PRON+ADV:
ALSO+for

2 If you **set aside** a belief, principle, or feeling, you decide that you will not be influenced by it because there are other, more important considerations at the time. ❑ *...a coalition of patriots that would set aside party dogma and lead the nation towards recovery... It would be good for the morale of the entire village if we set our personal feelings aside.*
NOTE **Put aside** means almost the same as **set aside**.

V+ADV+N,
V+N+ADV,
V+PRON+ADV

3 If a judge or court **sets aside** a decision or judgement, they state that it is not legally valid or has no legal force. ❑ *Marshall believes that the courts have the right to set aside acts of Congress... He at last won a fresh hearing before the Court of Criminal Appeal, which declined to set aside his original conviction.*
NOTE **Overturn** means almost the same as **set aside**.

V+ADV+N,
V+N+ADV,
V+PRON+ADV

4 If you **set** something **aside**, you move it out of your way for a while with the intention of going back to it later. ❑ *The mixture concerned should be set aside in a cool place... Set it aside to dry... He gazed at the bottle longingly, then set it firmly aside.*
NOTE **Put aside** and **lay aside** mean almost the same as **set aside**.

V+PRON+ADV,
V+N+ADV,
V+ADV+N

★set back

1 If something **sets** you **back** or **sets back** your plans, it causes a delay and makes you wait before you can continue with what you want to do. ❑ *This has set back the whole programme of nuclear power in America... The unusual cold of the early spring had set them back with the painting.*
NOTE **Hold up** means almost the same as **set back**.

V+ADV+N,
V+PRON+ADV,
V+N+ADV

♦ A **setback** is an event that delays your progress or makes your position less favourable than it was before. ❑ *The by-election result is being interpreted as a serious setback for the government... She recovered from the initial setback... The Union suffered a serious setback.*

N-COUNT

2 If a building **is set back**, it is positioned at some distance from the road or from the edge of the area where it stands. ❑ *The farms were all set back a mile or so from the road... The new station will be set back five hundred metres from the present site.*

PASSIVE:
V+ADV:
USUALLY+A

3 If something **sets** you **back** a certain amount of money, it costs you that much. [INFORMAL] ❑ *The legal costs of the case set him back something in the order of £10,000... Even two nights at any reasonable hotel was going to set me back enough to hurt... It did set us back a bit.*

V+PRON+ADV+N,
V+N+ADV+N

★set down

1 If you **set down** something that you have been holding, you put it on a table or on the ground. ❑ *She set his dinner down and handed him a napkin... The colonel lifted his cup, glared at it, set it down again... Jeremy also noticed this as he set down the coffee pot.*
NOTE **Put down** means almost the same as **set down**.

V+N+ADV,
V+PRON+ADV,
V+ADV+N:
ALSO+on

2 If you **set down** your thoughts, feelings, or a series of events, you write them all down because you want to keep a record of them. ❑ *They were asked to set down a summary of their views... When he retired to Britain he set down the story of his career... There was a serious political conversation and Herr Ballin set it down with reasonable accuracy.*

V+ADV+N,
V+PRON+ADV,
V+N+ADV

3 When something **is** officially **set down**, it is recorded as being a law or regulation. ❑ *There would have to be a limit set down by statute... These Cheyennes expected to live on the reservation with the Sioux as set down in the treaty of 1868... There are laws which attempt to set down standards whereby the animal is properly protected.*
NOTE **Lay down** means almost the same as **set down**.

V+ADV+N,
V+PRON+ADV:
USUALLY PASSIVE

4 If a bus or train **sets** you **down**, it stops and lets you get out. ❑ *Can you set me*

V+PRON+ADV,

down here?... They set me down at the door... He soon made an excuse and asked to be set down. | V+N+ADV: USUALLY+A

NOTE **Put down** means almost the same as **set down**.

5 If a plane or helicopter **sets down**, it lands somewhere. ❑ *A Chinook, forty feet long with rotors front and back, set down on the airstrip... You can get a look at the terrain out the window and pick your place to set down.* | V+ADV

set down as If you **set** someone **down as** a particular kind of person, you decide that you know what they are like and firmly believe it, even though you might be wrong. ❑ *I had quite set her down as being of the other persuasion... People who told jokes, even very good jokes, were automatically set down as bores.* | V+PRON+ADV+PREP, V+N+ADV+PREP

set forth

1 If you **set forth** facts, ideas, or opinions, you explain them either in writing or in speech in a clear and organized way. [FORMAL] ❑ *She led them into a parlour and Bartolomeo set forth the purpose of their visit... The plan set forth long-term proposals... Our projections for these four groups of nations are set forth in Figure 5.* | V+ADV+N, V+PRON+ADV

NOTE **Expound** is a more formal word for **set forth**.

2 When you **set forth**, you start a journey. [LITERARY] ❑ *Four thousand set forth and three thousand did not return... He and Lamin set forth on the trail.* | V+ADV

NOTE **Set out** and **set off** mean almost the same as **set forth**.

★set in

1 If something unpleasant **sets in**, it begins and seems likely to continue or develop. ❑ *By the time he had got it back in place, panic had set in... A feeling of anti-climax set in... They had to find a roof to live under before the cold weather set in.* | V+ADV

2 If something **is set in** or **set into** a surface, it has been fixed into a hollow or hole in the surface so that it does not stick out. ❑ *He had virtually lived in the small office with his bunk set in an alcove to one side. ...nine large panels set in a rich framework... He dropped the keys down a large drain set into the pavement.* | PASSIVE: V+PREP

♦ If something is **inset** with a decoration or piece of material, the decoration or material has been fixed into its surface and can be seen but does not stick out. ❑ *...gold or silver inset with gems. ...little panels inset on the facade.* | ADJECTIVE

set into → See **set in**

★set off

1 When you **set off**, you start a journey. ❑ *She reversed off the grass and set off down the road... He set off on another of his European pleasure tours... We set off for Knebworth under grey skies... At exactly four minutes to three they set off.* | V+ADV: USUALLY+A

NOTE **Set out** means almost the same as **set off**.

2 If something **sets off** a process or series of events, it causes the process or events to start happening. ❑ *The broadcast was to set off a train of thoughts and actions... The biggest event of the previous winter had been an electrical storm that had set off all the alarms... Rioting in Brixton last month was set off by charges of police harassment.* | V+ADV+N, V+PRON+ADV

NOTE **Trigger off** means almost the same as **set off**.

3 If you **set off** a bomb or firework, you cause it to explode. ❑ *The mines blew three holes in the ship's sides but failed to set off the explosives as they had hoped... Two bombs were set off by someone in the crowd.* | V+ADV+N, V+PRON+ADV

4 If something **sets** someone **off**, it makes them start doing something such as laughing, complaining, or telling stories. ❑ *From then on any glimpse of the moon was enough to set Hank off on his singing... Marcus looked green, as though the mention of vertigo had set him off.* | V+N+ADV, V+PRON+ADV: ALSO+on

5 If one thing **sets** something else **off**, it provides a contrast that makes the other thing look more attractive or more noticeable than it would on its own. ❑ *The uniform set off his figure to advantage... It was very fine soft hair of a dusty brown shade that set off her darker eyebrows. ...the way the bands of design set each other off to advantage by contrast.* | V+ADV+N, V+N+ADV, V+PRON+ADV

NOTE **Show off** means almost the same as **set off**, and **enhance** is a more formal word.

set off against If you **set** an amount of money **off against** a source of income or debt, you tell the tax authorities that that amount was spent in connection with your job or business in order to reduce the amount of tax you have to pay. | V+N+ADV+PREP, V+PRON+ADV+PREP: USUALLY PASSIVE

❑ *The loss on one venture can be set off against the taxable profits on another... A non-producing plantation appears on the tax return as a loss to be set off against a wealthy investor's other taxable income.*

NOTE Set against means almost the same as **set off against**.

set on

1 If animals or people **set on** you or **set upon** you, or if you **are set on** or **set upon** by them, they make a sudden and unexpected physical attack on you. ❑ *Some rival gang set on them... He was set on by toughs, hunted by girls and warned several times by the police... I was being set upon by older boys and given a beating every morning.*

V+PREP:
HAS PASSIVE

2 If someone **sets** animals or people **on** you, or **sets** them **upon** you, they cause the animals or people to attack you. ❑ *He knew, as we did, the answer to that one: we set our dogs on the gypsies... This so angered her that she set his own hounds upon him.*

V+N+PREP,
V+PRON+PREP

3 The **onset** of an unpleasant situation or event is its beginning. ❑ *...the onset of war. ...his response to the onset of blindness.*

N-SING

★set out

1 When you **set out**, you start a journey. ❑ *We set out along the beach... Shortly after seven they set out on bicycles... She longed to set out for Europe, to see England, her father's country... Mr Dekker and his son set out to walk to Whitelake River.*

V+ADV

NOTE Set off means almost the same as **set out**.

♦ If you talk about the **outset** of an event, process, or period of time, you mean its beginning. ❑ *You should explain this to him at the outset... The police had participated from the outset.*

N-SING

2 If you **set out** to do something, you start taking action or making plans with the intention of achieving a particular result. ❑ *They had failed in what they had set out to do... There he had set out to establish his own business... This chapter sets out to explain some of the relevant terms and principles.*

V+ADV:
WITH *to*-INF

3 If you **set out** facts, ideas, or opinions, you explain them either in writing or in speech in a clear and organized way. ❑ *Darwin set out his theory in detail in 'The Origin of Species'... Keynes set it all out in a famous series of letters to The Times... His conclusions were set out in his booklet 'Greener Grass'.*

V+ADV+N,
V+PRON+ADV,
V+N+ADV

4 If you **set** things **out**, you put them somewhere in an organized way so that they can be used or so that they can be seen easily. ❑ *She had set out wine and a jug of water... I took off my boots and socks and set them out to dry on a rock... Tim had already cleared the plates away, and the chess board had been set out between the wine glasses.*

V+ADV+N,
V+PRON+ADV,
V+N+ADV

NOTE Lay out means almost the same as **set out**.

set to

1 If you **set to**, you start working or dealing with something busily and energetically. ❑ *I cleaned my room, then I set to to help my parents... I knew the nurses would set to, scrubbing my room.*

V+ADV

2 If two people **set to**, they begin arguing or fighting. [OLD-FASHIONED] ❑ *For a minute, it looked as if they'd set to, but things calmed down.*

V+ADV

♦ A **set-to** is a fight or violent argument. [INFORMAL] ❑ *On the following Tuesday we had a real set-to.*

N-COUNT

★set up

1 If you **set up** something such as a structure, monument, or piece of equipment, you place it or build it somewhere. ❑ *They occupied buildings and set up road blocks and machine-gun posts... A fund was launched to set up a monument in memory of the dead men... They took the tent down and set it up again at each new camping site... Set the tea table up, it will be more convenient.*

V+ADV+N,
V+PRON+ADV,
V+N+ADV

2 If you **set** something **up**, you make the arrangements and preparations that are necessary for it to start. ❑ *The newspaper correctly reported that the government had set up an investigation... The first thing to do in a crisis is to set up a committee... They had been trained in a special school set up by Brigadier James Gavin... Laboratory experiments on the transmission of infection have been set up.*

V+ADV+N,
V+N+ADV,
V+PRON+ADV

♦ A particular **set-up** is a particular system or way of organizing something. ❑ *I've only been here a couple of days and I don't quite know the set-up. ...the British political set-up.*

N-COUNT

3 If you **set up** a device or piece of machinery, you do the things that are neces-

V+ADV+N,

The symbol ★ shows key phrasal verbs

sary for it to be able to start working. ❑ *Setting up the camera can be tricky... I set up the computer so that they could work from home.*

4 If you **set up** somewhere or **set** yourself **up** doing something, you start a firm, business, or company. ❑ *The firm is run by a former IBM designer who set up on his own... Anyone with an old lorry can set up as a contractor... He's probably set himself up in business... I persuaded him to set me up in a photocopying shop.*

V+ADV,
V+REFL+ADV,
V+PRON+ADV,
V+N+ADV:
WITH A

5 If you **set up** home or **set up** shop, you buy a house or business of your own and start living or working there. ❑ *They married, and set up home in Ramsgate. ...20 businessmen hoping to set up shop in Japan.*

V+ADV+N

6 If something **sets** you **up**, it puts you in a satisfactory condition or position, for example by providing you with money or by making you feel healthy and energetic. ❑ *He insisted on a contract that would set him up for life... There was no porridge to set them up for the cold winter's day.*

V+PRON+ADV,
V+N+ADV

7 If something **sets up** a process or series of events, it causes the events to begin and continue. ❑ *It may become possible to set up a nuclear chain reaction... Unfortunately physical appearances automatically set up prejudices in our minds.*

V+ADV+N,
V+PRON+ADV

8 If someone **sets** you **up**, they make people think that you have done something wrong when you have not, or they deceive you into a situation in which you might be harmed. [INFORMAL] ❑ *He and Pearson have been working together from the very beginning trying to set you up... He was paid to set the Mayor up.*

V+PRON+ADV,
V+N+ADV

NOTE **Frame** means almost the same as **set up**.

♦ A **set-up** is a situation in which someone makes it seem as if an innocent person has committed a crime. [INFORMAL] ❑ *The whole thing was just a set-up, organised by Jim and his cronies.*

N-COUNT

set upon → See set on

settle /setəl/ (settles, settling, settled)

★settle down

1 If you **settle down** to something, you start doing it, with the intention of doing it seriously and for quite a while. ❑ *We settled down to wait... He had settled down to watch a sports programme... At eight o'clock he settles down for supper.*

V+ADV

2 When someone **settles down**, they start living a quiet life in one place, especially when they get married or buy a house. ❑ *Alan told her that after this, he would settle down and marry her... You have to get a job and settle down.*

V+ADV

3 If people **settle down** or if you **settle** them **down**, they stop talking or being worried and become calm, peaceful, or quiet. ❑ *It took her some time to settle down... The meeting settled down again... Eddie's presence settled me down.*

V+ADV,
V+PRON+ADV,
V+N+ADV:
ERGATIVE

NOTE **Calm down** means almost the same as **settle down**.

4 If something **settles down**, it becomes calmer and more stable. ❑ *His stomach had settled down enough to permit him a beer or two... Her life had settled down.*

V+ADV

5 If you **settle down** for the night, you get ready to lie down and sleep. ❑ *They put up their tents and settled down for the night.*

V+ADV

★settle for If you **settle for** something, you choose or accept it, even though it is not what you really want, because nothing else is available. ❑ *Don't settle for second best... When in doubt he settled for hamburgers.*

V+PREP

★settle in If you **settle in** or you **are settled in**, you become used to living in a new house or town or doing a new job. ❑ *Madame gave her three weeks to settle in... And how are you settling in, Mr Swallow?... There's plenty of time to get settled in.*

V+ADV:
ALSO PASSIVE:
V+ADV

settle into If you **settle into** a routine, activity, or a way of behaving, you start doing it in a way that suggests that it will continue for some time. ❑ *Some babies are slow to settle into a routine... The boat settled into a slow side-to-side roll. ...just as I was settling into normal conversation.*

V+PREP

settle on

1 If you **settle on** or **settle upon** something, you decide to have it or use it after thinking or talking about it. **Settle upon** is more formal. ❑ *A week ahead of the joint negotiations, exporters settled on a figure of 52.1 million... Have you settled on a name for him yet?*

V+PREP:
HAS PASSIVE

NOTE **Decide on** means almost the same as **settle on**.

2 If money **is settled on** someone, it is left to them in a will. [FORMAL] ❑ *Some money was settled on him when he was adopted.*

PASSIVE:
V+PREP

settle up When you **settle up** with someone, you pay them what you owe them. ❑ *As soon as the money arrived I was able to settle up with him... We settled up last week.*

V+ADV+with,
V+ADV:
RECIPROCAL

NOTE **Square up** means almost the same as **settle up**.

settle upon → See settle on

sew /sou/ (sews, sewing, sewed, sewn)

sew on If you **sew** something **on**, you attach it to something else by sewing it. ❑ *I had to sew on a couple of buttons that were coming loose... I'll sew the button on your coat.*

V+N+ADV/PREP,
V+ADV+N,
V+PRON+ADV/PREP

sew up

1 If you **sew up** something that has been torn, you join it back together by sewing it. ❑ *She could find no needle or thread to sew up the torn lacing... A doctor was sewing up the cut over his eye.*

V+ADV+N,
V+N+ADV,
V+PRON+ADV

2 If you **sew up** something such as a business deal or an election, you arrange it in such a way that you can be sure of favourable results. [INFORMAL] ❑ *We thought that everything was sewn up so we were surprised when they didn't sign the contract. ...the local organizations that sewed up this year's elections.*

V+ADV+N,
V+PRON+ADV

shack /ʃæk/ (shacks, shacking, shacked)

shack up When someone **shacks up** with someone else or when two people **shack up** together, they start living together as lovers. [INFORMAL] ❑ *He wants to shack up with me... If we'd been five years younger, we'd just have shacked up together.*

V+ADV,
V+ADV+with,
V+ADV+together:
RECIPROCAL

shade /ʃeɪd/ (shades, shading, shaded)

shade in If you **shade in** an area in a drawing or painting, you make it appear dark, for example by filling it in with pencil lines or with a dark colour. ❑ *He was shading in the straps on the ankles.*

V+ADV+N,
V+N+ADV,
V+PRON+ADV

NOTE **Colour in** means almost the same as **shade in**.

shade into When something **shades into** something else, there is no clear division between the two things, so that you cannot tell where one thing ends and the other begins. ❑ *...reds shading into pinks... Professor Wilson now sees instinct and culture as shading into one another.*

V+PREP

NOTE **Merge into** and **blend into** mean almost the same as **shade into**.

shake /ʃeɪk/ (shakes, shaking, shook, shaken)

shake down

1 If someone **shakes** you **down**, they use threats or search you physically in order to obtain something from you. [AMERICAN] ❑ *They vowed to root out officials who shake down villagers for illegal fees and taxes... Residents complain about being harassed, roughed up, sometimes even shaken down for their money.*

V+N+ADV,
V+PRON+ADV,
V+ADV+N

2 If something **shakes down**, it happens in a particular way. [INFORMAL] ❑ *We'll need to wait and see how it shakes down.*

V+ADV

NOTE **Work out** means almost the same as **shake down**.

3 If you **shake down**, you become used to a new situation, such as a job or course. [INFORMAL] ❑ *The third division had just arrived, but was at low strength and had not yet shaken down.*

V+ADV

★shake off

1 If you **shake off** something that you do not want, such as an illness or a bad habit, you manage to recover from it or get rid of it. ❑ *Businessmen are frantically trying to shake off the bad habits learned under six decades of a protected economy... Get your body moving to boost energy, stay supple and shake off winter lethargy... He had difficulty in breathing and was generally feeling bad. He just couldn't shake it off... Such habits cannot be shaken off in the course of a few decades.*

V+ADV+N,
V+N+ADV,
V+PRON+ADV

2 If you **shake off** someone who is following you, you manage to get away from them, for example by running faster than them. ❑ *It had taken Franklin several hours to shake off the police... I caught him a lap later, and although I could pass him, I could not shake him off... It seems that he was unaware that they had shaken off their pursuers.*

V+ADV+N,
V+N+ADV,
V+PRON+ADV

3 If you **shake off** someone who is touching you, you move your arm or body

V+ADV+N,

sharply so that they are no longer touching you. ❑ *He grabbed my arm. I shook him off... She shook off his restraining hand.*   V+N+ADV, V+PRON+ADV

shake <u>out</u>

1 If you **shake out** something such as a piece of cloth, you hold it by one of its edges and move it about vigorously, for example in order to open it out or to make it flat. ❑ *...a napkin which she shook out and spread on the table. ...shaking out her umbrella.*   V+N+ADV, V+ADV+N, V+PRON+ADV

2 To **shake out** something such as a business means to remove the things that are stopping it from being successful or profitable. ❑ *They pledged to shake out British industry, to make it more efficient... Mr Prodi pushed ahead with privatisation and tried to shake the fat out of the economy.*   V+ADV+N, V+N+ADV, V+PRON+ADV: ALSO+of

shake <u>up</u>

1 If something bad, unexpected, or frightening **shakes** you **up**, it makes you feel very shocked and upset. ❑ *Did that lightning shake you up?... I'm a little shaken up at the moment.*   V+N+ADV, V+PRON+ADV

2 If you **shake** things **up**, you mix them together by shaking the container that they are in. ❑ *Here are the raffle tickets; shake them up well before you pick one.*   V+PRON+ADV, V+N+ADV, V+ADV+N

NOTE **Mix up** means almost the same as **shake up**.

3 If you **shake up** something such as an organization, institution, or business, you make major changes in it, usually in order to improve it. ❑ *The management aims to shake up its newly acquired companies... A rival bid is always good for shaking up the board of directors.*   V+ADV+N, V+N+ADV, V+PRON+ADV

♦ A **shake-up** is a major change that affects the whole of something such as an organization. ❑ *Many were eager for a shake-up in the two-party system... I felt my life needed a shake-up.*   N-COUNT

shame /ʃeɪm/ (shames, shaming, shamed)

shame <u>into</u> If you **shame** someone **into** doing something, you force them to do it by making them feel ashamed. ❑ *Father was shamed into an admission.*   V+N+PREP, V+PRON+PREP: ALSO+-ING

shape /ʃeɪp/ (shapes, shaping, shaped)

★shape <u>up</u>

1 If someone or something **is shaping up** in a particular way, they are developing or progressing in that way. ❑ *The summer was shaping up as a mediocre one... The Campaign is shaping up as one of the most intensive sales campaigns ever... This event is shaping up to be a very special day for the whole of Brent's Community.*   V+ADV: WITH A

2 If you **shape up**, you become fit, healthy, or prepared for something. ❑ *We were shaping up for the attack on the Tories.*   V+ADV

3 If you ask how someone or something **is shaping up**, you want to know how well they are doing in a particular situation or activity. ❑ *I did have a few worries about how Hugh and I would shape up as parents... Girls are being recruited now. I heard they are shaping up very well.*   V+ADV: WITH A

4 If you tell someone to **shape up**, you are telling them to start behaving in a sensible and responsible way. ❑ *It is of no value simply to tell one's adolescent children to shape up and do something useful.*   V+ADV

share /ʃeəʳ/ (shares, sharing, shared)

share <u>in</u> If you **share in** something such as a success or a responsibility, you are one of a number of people who achieve or accept it. ❑ *The company is offering you the chance to share in its success... Everybody shares in the cooking chores.*   V+PREP

share <u>out</u> If you **share** something **out** between a group of people, you divide it into parts and give some to each person. ❑ *...sharing out the money and possessions. ...the way housework and childcare is shared out... Elizabeth cut the cake, then shared it out.*   V+ADV+N, V+N+ADV, V+PRON+ADV

♦ If there is a **share-out** of something, several people are given equal or fair parts of it. ❑ *...a share-out of the profits.*   N-SING

sharpen /ʃɑːʳpən/ (sharpens, sharpening, sharpened)

sharpen <u>up</u>

1 If you **sharpen up** a knife or other tool, you make it sharper. ❑ *I was practical enough to sharpen up my knives... My tools were blunt so I had to sharpen them up.*   V+ADV+N, V+PRON+ADV, V+N+ADV

2 If something **sharpens up** or if you **sharpen** it **up**, it becomes better or more   V+ADV,

active. ❏ *The struggle against the Bill was sharpening up... It sharpened up her hearing.*   V+ADV+N,
...three useful games for sharpening up your mental calculating ability.   V+N+ADV, V+PRON+ADV: ERGATIVE

shave /ʃeɪv/ **(shaves, shaving, shaved)**

shave off

1 If someone **shaves off** their hair or beard, they remove it by shaving. ❏ *He had*   V+ADV+N, V+N+ADV, V+PRON+ADV: *shaved off his beard... A small patch of his hair was shaved off... As the grey hairs appear,*   ALSO+from *shave them off.*

2 If you **shave off** a thin piece of wood from a larger piece, you cut it off. ❏ *Use a*   V+ADV+N, V+N+ADV, *plane to shave off a small amount from the bottom of the door.*   V+PRON+ADV

shear /ʃɪəʳ/ **(shears, shearing, sheared, shorn)**

✔ The past participle can be either **sheared** or **shorn**.

shear off If something such as a piece of metal **shears off**, it breaks off, for ex-   V+ADV ample because of pressure or old age. ❏ *The aeroplane's wing sheared off.*

shell /ʃel/ **(shells, shelling, shelled)**

shell out If you **shell out** for something, you spend an amount of money on it,   V+ADV+N: especially when you do not really want to. [INFORMAL] ❏ *He's going to have to shell out*   ALSO+on/for *another three hundred million dollars for public transport facilities. ...any time he shells out fifty bucks... I shelled out sixty quid on that carpet.*

NOTE **Fork out** means almost the same as **shell out**.

shin /ʃɪn/ **(shins, shinning, shinned)**

shin down If you **shin down** something such as a tree or pole, you climb   V+PREP down it quickly and easily by using both hands and legs to grip it. ❏ *She shinned down the drainpipe to the lawn.*

shin up If you **shin up** something such as a tree or a pole, you climb up it quick-   V+PREP ly and easily by using both hands and legs to grip it. ❏ *I shinned up a lamp post to get a better view of the procession.*

shine /ʃaɪn/ **(shines, shining, shone)**

shine out If something **shines out**, it shines brightly and so can be seen very   V+ADV easily. ❏ *The town shines out as though it were golden. ...which makes its jewel shine out more brightly.*

shine through If a quality **shines through** in a situation, it can be seen clear-   V+ADV, ly. ❏ *...so that goodness can shine through... Two steady rays of lucidity shone through the*   V+PREP *confusion.*

ship /ʃɪp/ **(ships, shipping, shipped)**

ship in If goods **are shipped in**, they are brought into a place by boat. ❏ *...com-*   V+N+ADV, *ponents shipped in from industrialized countries... Weapons are freely shipped in for commer-*   V+ADV+N, V+PRON+ADV: *cial gain.*   USUALLY PASSIVE

ship off If people or things **are shipped off** to a place, they are taken there, es-   V+N+ADV, pecially by boat. ❏ *These pigs are shipped off to another farmer and he fattens them up... A*   V+ADV+N, V+PRON+ADV: *giraffe was being shipped off to Dublin.*   USUALLY PASSIVE

ship out

1 If people or things **are shipped out** to a place, they are taken there. ❏ *Every-*   V+N/PRON+ADV, *thing will have to be shipped out from England... They were shipped out by rail.*   V+ADV+N: USUALLY PASSIVE

2 If people, especially members of the armed forces, **ship out**, they leave a place.   V+ADV: ❏ *He shipped out of Vietnam in 1971, the same year Li was born... They told everybody that*   ALSO+of *they had had enough, that they were shipping out.*

shock /ʃɒk/ **(shocks, shocking, shocked)**

shock into If you **are shocked into** doing something, you are so shocked or   V+N+PREP, surprised that you do it. ❏ *The assembly was shocked into silence... He was shocked into*   V+PRON+PREP: USUALLY PASSIVE, *withdrawing his request.*   ALSO+-ING

shoo /ʃuː/ **(shoos, shooing, shooed)**

shoo away If you **shoo away** a person or an animal, you wave your arms   V+ADV+N, or hands at them to make them go away. ❏ *We were not allowed to shoo away the*   V+N+ADV, V+PRON+ADV *pigs... The visitors were politely shooed away... They'd shooed her away as if she were a dog.*

shoot /ʃuːt/ (shoots, shooting, shot)

shoot away If a part of someone's body **is shot away**, a bullet or explosion destroys or seriously damages that part of their body. ❑ *Half his face had been shot away.*

> V+N+ADV,
> V+ADV+N,
> V+PRON+ADV

NOTE **Blow away** and **blow off** mean almost the same as **shoot away**.

shoot back If someone **shoots back** an answer or a comment, they reply quickly and often angrily to something someone has said. ❑ *'It did not succeed,' Kelly said. 'That's for sure,' Hamilton shot back.*

> V+ADV+QUOTE

shoot down

1 If someone **shoots** something or someone **down**, they make them fall to the ground by hitting them with a bullet or missile. ❑ *The enemy claimed to have shot down 22 of our planes... If he is intercepted, he shoots down one or two policemen... Their helicopter was shot down in flames... A firing squad will shoot him down.*

> V+ADV+N,
> V+N+ADV,
> V+PRON+ADV

NOTE **Bring down** means almost the same as **shoot down**.

2 If you **shoot** someone **down** or **shoot down** their ideas, you show that their ideas are wrong or foolish. ❑ *No doubt you could shoot me down by all kinds of quotations... My suggestion was immediately shot down by everyone else at the meeting.*

> V+N+ADV,
> V+ADV+N,
> V+PRON+ADV

shoot for If you **shoot for** something, you try to achieve it. ❑ *I shall be approaching the first race with a winning attitude. You have to shoot for the top.*

> V+PREP

NOTE **Aim for** means almost the same as **shoot for**.

shoot off

1 If someone or something **shoots off**, they leave very quickly. ❑ *We saw the bus shoot off at a terrific speed... Brooks has gone shooting off in the other direction.*

> V+ADV

2 If a part of someone's body **is shot off**, a bullet or explosion destroys or seriously damages that part of their body. ❑ *...poor devils getting their arms and legs shot off.*

> V+N+ADV,
> V+ADV+N,
> V+PRON+ADV

NOTE **Blow off** and **blow away** mean almost the same as **shoot off**.

shoot out

1 If someone **shoots out**, they leave a room very quickly. ❑ *He just shot out of the room before I could say anything.*

> V+ADV:
> ALSO+of

2 If something **shoots out**, it moves suddenly so that it is sticking out. ❑ *His arm shot out to point at her. ...its tongue shoots out.*

> V+ADV

3 A **shoot-out** is a fight in which people shoot at each other with guns. ❑ *He was wounded during a shoot-out with British troops.*

> N-COUNT

shoot through If something **shoots through** a barrier of some kind, it suddenly moves through it so that it is on the other side of it. ❑ *Later, witnesses said that they saw the truck shoot through the police cordon without stopping.*

> V+PREP

shoot up

1 If something **shoots up**, it grows or increases very quickly. ❑ *...when the rents shoot up in December... Nancy began to run a fever which eventually shot up to 43 degrees... Your children have really shot up since the last time I saw them.*

> V+ADV

2 If someone **shoots up** a place, they move around in it shooting a gun. ❑ *He has his own reasons to shoot up the place. ...coming out at night and shooting up the area.*

> V+ADV+N,
> V+N+ADV,
> V+PRON+ADV

3 If someone **shoots up**, they inject illegal drugs into themselves. [INFORMAL]

> V+ADV

shop /ʃɒp/ (shops, shopping, shopped)

shop around

1 If you **shop around**, you go to different shops in order to compare the prices and quality of something before you decide to buy it. ❑ *The prices are variable so shop around... There are plenty of savings if you're prepared to shop around.*

> V+ADV

2 If you **shop around** for a particular deal, contract, or arrangement, you try to get what you want by comparing the value and quality of several similar deals or contracts before deciding which one to accept. ❑ *She can shop around for the job where her chances of promotion are best... The would-be student is free to shop around... We'll shop around the building societies to find the best terms.*

> V+ADV,
> V+PREP

shore /ʃɔːr/ (shores, shoring, shored)

shore up

1 If you **shore up** something that is weak or about to fail, you do something in order to strengthen it. ❑ *Lewis and his men were already moving to shore up public confi-*

> V+ADV+N,
> V+N+ADV,
> V+PRON+ADV

dence in the system... The nine million pounds provided by the Government to shore the
group up was not enough.

2 If you **shore up** a wall or a building, you put a strong support next to it or under it in order to stop it from falling down. ❑ The villagers shored up sagging huts...
Perched on this cliff, shored up on girders, was the Marine Cafe.

NOTE **Prop up** means almost the same as **shore up**.

V+ADV+N,
V+N+ADV,
V+PRON+ADV

shout /ʃaʊt/ (shouts, shouting, shouted)

shout down If people **shout** a person **down**, they prevent the person from being heard by shouting at them. ❑ The crowd shouted the speaker down. ...the attempt to
shout down the Prime Minister. ...jeering and more or less shouting them down.

NOTE **Hoot down** and **howl down** mean almost the same as **shout down**.

V+N+ADV,
V+ADV+N,
V+PRON+ADV

shout out If you **shout** something **out**, you suddenly shout it. ❑ I just had time
to shout out and warn them not to cross the road... They began to dance and shout out
praises to God because they were cured... We began to shout out that we wanted our money
back... She shouted out that she was unjustly imprisoned... Kate applauded and shouted out,
'Bravo!'

NOTE **Call out** means almost the same as **shout out**.

V+ADV,
V+ADV+N,
V+ADV+REPORT,
V+ADV+QUOTE,
V+N+ADV,
V+PRON+ADV

shove /ʃʌv/ (shoves, shoving, shoved)

shove off If you tell someone to **shove off**, you are telling them angrily to go
away. [BRITISH, INFORMAL] ❑ You shove off. See?

NOTE **Buzz off** and **push off** mean almost the same as **shove off**.

IMPERATIVE,
V+ADV

shove up If you tell someone to **shove up**, you are telling them in rather a rude
way to move in order to make room for someone else. [BRITISH, INFORMAL] ❑ Shove
up, make room for him over here.

NOTE **Budge up** means almost the same as **shove up**.

IMPERATIVE,
V+ADV

show /ʃoʊ/ (shows, showing, showed, shown)

☑ In American English, **around** is much more common than **round**.

show around

1 If you **show** someone **around** or **show** them **round** a place, you go there with
them, pointing out all the interesting or important features. ❑ I was showing a group
of visitors around the school... It was Ivan's job to show him around the city... Karen showed
Kitty around with obvious pride... We'll eat now and then I'll show you round – OK?

NOTE **Take around** means almost the same as **show around**.

V+N+PREP,
V+PRON+PREP,
V+N+ADV,
V+PRON+ADV

2 If you **show** something **around**, you give it to several people to look at. ❑ I
showed my holiday snaps around when I got into work... His son found a hundred-pound
note and ecstatically showed it around to his family.

V+N+ADV,
V+PRON+ADV

show in When you **show** someone **in**, you lead them into a room or building.
❑ A servant came to the door and showed me in... Miss Livingstone showed in a guest.

NOTE **Show out** means the opposite of **show in**.

V+PRON+ADV,
V+ADV+N,
V+N+ADV

★show off

1 If you **show off**, you try to impress people by making your skills or good qualities very obvious; used showing disapproval. ❑ Don't show off... He was afraid of the others might think he was showing off or being superior. ...kids showing off on the diving board.

♦ If you say that someone is a **show-off**, you mean that they try to impress people
by behaving in a way that shows their skills or abilities very obviously; used showing
disapproval. [INFORMAL] ❑ Even in those days, I was a show-off.

V+ADV

N-COUNT

2 If you **show off** something that you own, you show it to a lot of people because
you are proud of it. ❑ He was eager to show off the new car. ...tossing their heads and
arms, showing off their jewellery... It had given me intense pleasure to show my trophies off
to her.

V+ADV+N,
V+N+ADV,
V+PRON+ADV:
NO PASSIVE

3 If something **shows off** another thing, it makes the other thing seem more attractive or effective because it emphasizes the good qualities of that other thing.
❑ ...a most becoming tan that showed off her white hair beautifully... Set up situations
which will show off these skills to the best advantage of the team.

NOTE **Set off** means almost the same as **show off**, and **enhance** is a more formal
word.

V+ADV+N,
V+N+ADV,
V+PRON+ADV:
NO PASSIVE

show out When you **show** someone **out**, you go with them to the door as they leave a room or building. ❏ *Will you show Miss Nester out please?... He was just being shown out as I arrived... After she had shown him out of the office, she sat down wearily.*

V+N+ADV,
V+ADV+N,
V+PRON+ADV:
ALSO+of

NOTE **Show in** means the opposite of **show out**.

show round → See **show around**

show through

1 If something **shows through** a barrier of some kind, it is noticeable behind that barrier. ❏ *A chink of light showed through the curtains... Few buildings showed through the trees... The light showed through into the next room.*

V+PREP,
V+ADV

2 If your feelings **show through**, you reveal them to other people, often without intending to. ❏ *I know that my sadness may show through... His eagerness and willingness to participate showed through right from the start.*

V+ADV

★show up

1 If you **show up**, you arrive at a place where people are expecting you. ❏ *Over a hundred people showed up at the meeting... How would his three new friends feel about it if he showed up with his little brother?*

V+ADV:
USUALLY+A

NOTE **Turn up** means almost the same as **show up**.

2 When something **shows up**, it can be seen clearly. ❏ *Dark colours will not show up against a similar background... Bloodstains show up as white on the negative... The redness of sunburn doesn't show up until several hours after the damage is done.*

V+ADV

3 If a particular result or observation **is shown up** in a test or experiment, it is made noticeable as part of the result of that experiment. ❏ *Small differences in temperament are bound to show up... This distortion of the patient's time sense shows up in a revealing experiment. ...the intensity of past infection shown up by blood tests... It isn't always easy to show up this trend.*

V+ADV,
V+N+ADV,
V+ADV+N,
V+PRON+ADV:
ERGATIVE

4 If someone is with you and they **show** you **up**, they make you feel embarrassed and ashamed of them. ❏ *Don't make a big thing of it – don't show him up.*

V+PRON+ADV,
V+N+ADV

show up as If something or someone **is shown up as** being bad, unpleasant, and so on, people start to realize that they are bad, unpleasant, and so on. ❏ *Their air combat skills were shown up as inferior to those of the NATO pilots... They have been shown up as being very undemocratic.*

V+N+ADV+PREP,
V+PRON+ADV+PREP

shrink /ʃrɪŋk/ **(shrinks, shrinking, shrank, shrunk)**

shrink away If you **shrink away**, you move away from something that has frightened or horrified you. ❏ *The circle of boys shrank away in horror... It would be impossible for him not to shrink away from any physical contact.*

V+ADV:
ALSO+from

shrink from If you **shrink from** doing something, you are reluctant to do it because you find it unpleasant. ❏ *I kept wanting to yawn, but shrank from lifting my grimy hands to my face... He shrank from giving Frank a direct answer.*

V+PREP:
USUALLY+-ING

NOTE **Shy away from** means almost the same as **shrink from**.

shrivel /ʃrɪvəl/ **(shrivels, shrivelling, shrivelled)**

✓ American English uses the spellings **shriveling** and **shriveled**.

shrivel up When something **shrivels up**, it becomes dry and wrinkled because it loses moisture. ❏ *The fish had shrivelled up a bit... I was late for tea, and mine would be shrivelled up in the oven. ...shrivelling up like old apples... The sun had shrivelled the tomatoes up.*

V+ADV,
V+N+ADV,
V+PRON+ADV,
V+ADV+N:
ERGATIVE

NOTE **Wither** means almost the same as **shrivel up**.

shrug /ʃrʌg/ **(shrugs, shrugging, shrugged)**

shrug off If you **shrug** something **off**, you ignore it or treat it as if it is not really important or serious. ❏ *Designers tend to shrug this problem off... The Chairman shrugs off any criticism that their operations are unscrupulous.*

V+N+ADV,
V+ADV+N,
V+PRON+ADV

NOTE **Brush off** means almost the same as **shrug off**.

shuffle /ʃʌfəl/ **(shuffles, shuffling, shuffled)**

shuffle off If you **shuffle** something **off**, you try to avoid talking about it or dealing with it because you find it difficult or embarrassing. ❏ *He shuffled the question off and changed the topic... The Government should not try to shuffle the responsibility off onto the public.*

V+N+ADV,
V+PRON+ADV,
V+ADV+N

shut /ʃʌt/ **(shuts, shutting)**

> ☑ The form **shut** is used in the present tense and is the past tense and past partici-
> ple of the verb.

shut away

1 If you **shut** someone or something **away**, you put them in a special place where   V+N+ADV,
people cannot see them or take them away. ❏ *The dog and cats were shut away in case*   V+PRON+ADV,
they ran off. ...shutting the elderly away in geriatric hospitals... I kept it shut away in a   V+ADV+N
spare, unfurnished room.

NOTE **Lock away** means almost the same as **shut away**.

2 If you **shut** yourself **away**, you stay in one building or room for a long time and   V+REFL+ADV
avoid meeting people. ❏ *He became an intensely private man, shutting himself away in his*
hotel room... I shut myself away in a library that night and wrote a letter.

★shut down

1 If someone **shuts down** a factory or business or if it **shuts down**, it closes   V+ADV+N,
and stops working. ❏ *Smaller towns shut down their water plants completely and told*   V+N+ADV,
residents to buy bottled water... If they walked out that would shut the whole factory   V+PRON+ADV,
down... More than 10 per cent of the country's 301 production plants have shut down this   V+ADV:
year.   ERGATIVE

NOTE **Close down** means almost the same as **shut down**.

♦ A **shutdown** is the closing of a factory, shop, or other business. ❏ *Irish bar propri-*   N-COUNT
etors called for a shutdown between 3 and 5 pm.

2 If a machine or an engine **shuts down** or if it **is shut down**, it stops working   V+ADV,
altogether for a short time. ❏ *Computers supplying the information had automatically shut*   V+ADV+N,
down... There was supposed to be a foolproof system for shutting down the system... One of   V+N+ADV,
the 747's four engines had been shut down after showing a fault.   V+PRON+ADV:
    ERGATIVE

NOTE **Shut off** means almost the same as **shut down**.

shut in

1 If someone **shuts** you **in** a room or other confined space, they close the door so   V+N+PREP,
that you cannot leave. ❏ *She just shut her husband in the garage by mistake... His brother*   V+PRON+PREP,
shut him in a wooden chest... We were shut in for the night.   V+N+ADV,
    V+PRON+ADV

NOTE **Shut up** means almost the same as **shut in**, and **imprison** and **confine** are
more formal words.

2 If you **shut** yourself **in** a room, you go in there and shut the door so that no-   V+REFL+PREP,
body else can get in. ❏ *She shut herself in the bathroom and wept... She slammed the door*   V+REFL+ADV
and shut herself in.

shut off

1 If you **shut off** an engine or the power supply to a machine, you turn it off to   V+ADV+N,
stop it working. ❏ *I stopped the car and shut off the engine... Foster shut off the heat in the*   V+N+ADV,
main cabin... When I shut the motor off I could hear the birds.   V+PRON+ADV

NOTE **Turn off** means almost the same as **shut off**.

2 If someone **shuts off** the supply of a particular commodity or type of goods,   V+ADV+N,
they stop sending the commodity or goods to the people who normally use them.   V+N+ADV,
❏ *Some nations had shut off oil or coffee as a means of blackmail... And that was when they*   V+PRON+ADV
shut off funds, saying they did not believe the programme could work.

NOTE **Cut off** means almost the same as **shut off**.

3 Something that **shuts off** a view prevents it from being seen by obscuring it. ❏ *A*   V+ADV+N,
row of trees shut off the scene... She closed the curtains to shut off the view of the valley...   V+N+ADV,
The sun's rays are shut off by soot.   V+PRON+ADV

NOTE **Block out** means almost the same as **shut off**.

4 If you **shut** yourself **off**, you avoid talking to other people or getting involved   V+REFL+ADV:
with them. ❏ *Why have you shut yourself off from your mother and me for two years?...*   USUALLY+*from*
They use a variety of devices to shut themselves off from the other patients.

★shut out

1 If you **shut** something or someone **out**, you prevent them from getting into a   V+N+ADV,
place, for example by closing the doors. ❏ *...owners who shut their dogs out all day...*   V+ADV+N,
They had covered the holes to shut out the water.   V+PRON+ADV

2 To **shut out** sound or light means to prevent it from reaching a place. ❏ *He put*   V+ADV+N, *his hands over his ears to shut out the noise... Walls rising on either side shut out the sunlight... All direct light is shut out from the forest floor.*

V+PRON+ADV,
V+N+ADV

3 If you **shut out** a thought or feeling, you try to stop yourself from thinking about it. ❑ *I did not even try to shut out the speculations about my future... She found it impossible to shut out the pain... He decided to shut it out of his mind.*

V+ADV+N,
V+PRON+ADV,
V+N+ADV

NOTE **Block out** and **blot out** mean almost the same as **shut out**.

4 If you **shut** someone **out** of something, you prevent them from having anything to do with it. ❑ *She is very reclusive, to the point of shutting me out of her life... They refused to allow Republicans to offer amendments, effectively shutting them out of the process... She had effectively shut him out by refusing to listen.*

V+N+ADV,
V+PRON+ADV:
USUALLY+of

★**shut up**

1 If you **shut up**, you stop talking. If you tell someone to **shut up**, you are telling them to stop talking in rather a rude, abrupt way. ❑ *Everybody shuts up as soon as you mention it... Oh, shut up about yourself!*

V+ADV:
ALSO IMPERATIVE

2 If someone **shuts** you **up**, they prevent you from talking. ❑ *Turn the television on. That usually shuts them up... I just said it to her one day to shut her up.*

V+PRON+ADV,
V+N+ADV

NOTE **Silence** is a more formal word for **shut up**.

3 If you **are shut up** in a building, room, or other confined space, you are kept in there and cannot get out. ❑ *They wanted to shut Sarah up in a mental hospital... He was shut up for life as a dangerous criminal... They shut her up in the remand centre for a whole year.*

V+N+ADV,
V+PRON+ADV:
USUALLY+A

NOTE **Shut in** means almost the same as **shut up**, and **imprison** and **confine** are more formal words.

shy /ʃaɪ/ (shies, shying, shied)

shy away from If you **shy away from** doing something, you avoid doing it, often because you are afraid or not confident enough. ❑ *Some mothers shy away from breast-feeding... A few have shied away from careers in big industry.*

V+ADV+PREP:
ALSO+-ING

NOTE **Shrink from** means almost the same as **shy away from**.

sick /sɪk/ (sicks, sicking, sicked)

sick up When you **sick** food **up**, you vomit. [INFORMAL] ❑ *She promptly sicked everything up all over poor Karen... Look out, the dog is sicking up his dinner.*

V+N+ADV,
V+PRON+ADV,
V+ADV+N

NOTE **Bring up** and **throw up** mean almost the same as **sick up**.

side /saɪd/ (sides, siding, sided)

side against If people **side against** you, they join together in order to defeat you in a quarrel or an argument. ❑ *Her supporters sided against me.*

V+PREP

NOTE **Gang up** means almost the same as **side against**, and **side with** means the opposite.

side with If you **side with** someone, you support them in a quarrel or argument. ❑ *The daughters sided with their mothers. ...siding with people who encouraged civil disobedience... He may have sided with them for personal gain.*

V+PREP

NOTE **Side against** means the opposite of **side with**.

sidle /saɪdəl/ (sidles, sidling, sidled)

sidle up If someone **sidles up** to you, they approach you in a cautious or uncertain way, as if they do not want anyone to notice. ❑ *Sylvia had managed to sidle up to Gertrude... I sidled up and touched her with a finger.*

V+ADV:
USUALLY+to

sift /sɪft/ (sifts, sifting, sifted)

sift through If you **sift through** a large collection of something, you examine it carefully and thoroughly, usually because you need to organize it or find something out. ❑ *Every day he sifted through the reports... A computer could sift through a huge number of records... There are archives and documents to be sifted through.*

V+PREP:
HAS PASSIVE

sign /saɪn/ (signs, signing, signed)

sign away If you **sign** something **away** or **sign** it **over**, you sign an official document stating that you no longer own it or have a right to it. ❑ *Chiefs were encouraged to sign away land that appeared to be unoccupied... That means that you sign away your right to claim more money if your illness gets worse... One way of avoiding death duties might be to sign the house over to your son now.*

V+ADV+N,
V+N+ADV,
V+PRON+ADV

sign for If you **sign for** something, you officially state that you have received it, by signing a form or book. ❏ *When the postal clerk delivers your order, check the carton before signing for it.*

V+PREP

★**sign in**

1 If you **sign in** or if someone **signs** you **in**, you sign your name in a book or on a special form in a hotel, club, or other institution when you arrive. ❏ *They sign in at the reception desk... Humboldt went to Mount Sinai Hospital and signed himself in... A smiling middle-aged lady was behind the desk, signing in the new students.*

V+ADV,
V+REFL+ADV,
V+ADV+N,
V+PRON+ADV:
ERGATIVE

NOTE **Book in** means almost the same as **sign in**, and **register** is a more formal word.

2 If you **sign** someone **in** at a club or other institution of which you are a member but they are not, you sign your name in a special book to say that they are there as your guest. ❏ *Just get someone to sign you in... I don't think you'll have to be signed in.*

V+PRON+ADV,
V+N+ADV,
V+ADV+N

sign off

1 If you **sign off** at the end of a letter or a radio conversation, you write or say your final message. ❏ *It's just about tea time so I'll sign off now. With love, take care. Dad.*

V+ADV

2 If you are ill and a doctor **signs** you **off**, he or she writes a note to your employer, saying that you are not able to go to work for a particular period of time. ❏ *Shall we sign her off for a week?*

V+PRON+ADV,
V+N+ADV

3 When someone who has been unemployed **signs off**, they officially inform the authorities that they have found a job, so that they no longer receive money from the government. [BRITISH] ❏ *If he sold his art he would be breaking the law, but if he signed off the dole he wouldn't.*

V+ADV,
V+PREP

4 If someone **signs off** a deal or a plan, they agree to it officially, usually by signing their names on a document. ❏ *...the 2.7 billion pound Channel Tunnel rail link, which ministers hope to sign off next month.*

V+ADV+N,
V+N+ADV,
V+PRON+ADV

sign on

1 If you **sign on** at a government unemployment office, you go there and sign your name on a form to confirm that you are unemployed, so that you can receive state unemployment benefit. [BRITISH] ❏ *...people arriving to sign on at the main Reading benefit office.*

V+ADV

2 If you **sign on** or if someone **signs** you **on** with a company or for an academic course, you sign a contract or form in which you agree to work for the company or to do the course. ❏ *You could sign on for a full-time course... The boys' ambitions were to sign on with the whaling fleet... Well, maybe I can sign you on for one run – to try out the new ship.*

V+ADV,
V+PRON+ADV,
V+ADV+N,
V+N+ADV:
ERGATIVE

NOTE **Sign up** means almost the same as **sign on**.

sign out

1 If you **sign out** of a hotel, club, or other institution, you sign your name in a book or on a special form when you leave. ❏ *That Friday I signed out for a weekend... Signing out of our dormitory, we indicated that we had permission from our parents to visit a family in New York.*

V+ADV:
ALSO+of

2 If you **sign** something **out**, you sign your name in a book or on a card to say that you have taken it or borrowed it from an organization or institution that you belong to. ❏ *Bernstein signed out a company car and drove to McLean.*

V+ADV+N,
V+N+ADV,
V+PRON+ADV

sign over → See sign away

★**sign up** If you **sign up**, or if someone **signs** you **up**, you sign an official document saying that you will do something, such as a job or a course of study. ❏ *He signed up as a painter on the Federal Art Project... Richard Boot was signed up to play the lead in Miroslav's new film... The picture editor of the Telegraph magazine had signed up Don Whillans... Who's that wonderful man? Sign him up immediately!*

V+ADV,
V+N+ADV,
V+ADV+N,
V+PRON+ADV:
ERGATIVE

silt /sɪlt/ (silts, silting, silted)

silt up If a river, lake, or other area of water **silts up** or **is silted up**, it becomes blocked with silt. ❏ *The lake silted up... The channels have been silted up. ...simply scoured away the hillsides, silting up the riverbeds and causing floods.*

V+ADV,
V+ADV+N:
ERGATIVE

The symbol ★ shows key phrasal verbs

simmer /ˈsɪmər/ **(simmers, simmering, simmered)**

simmer down If you **simmer down**, you stop being angry about something. [INFORMAL] ❑ *The others sat around, giving me time to simmer down; someone handed me a water-bottle... 'Simmer down,' I said. 'It's not our problem.'*

NOTE **Calm down** and **cool down** mean almost the same as **simmer down**.

V+ADV

sing /sɪŋ/ **(sings, singing, sang, sung)**

sing along If you **sing along** with a piece of music, you sing it while you are listening to someone else perform it. ❑ *We listen to children's shows on the radio, and Janey can sing along with all the tunes... Would-be Elvis Presleys can sing along to 'Jailhouse Rock' and 'Blue Suede Shoes'. ...fifteen hundred people all singing along and dancing.*

V+ADV:
ALSO+*to/with*

sing out

1 If you **sing out**, you sing loudly. ❑ *He sang full out as if he were singing in public... The strains of heavenly harmony sang out for the third time... You didn't have to sing out quite as loud as you did.*

V+ADV

2 If you **sing** something **out**, you say it suddenly and loudly, often from a distance. ❑ *'That's right,' Etta sang out cheerfully... Her old friends would, sooner or later, sing out 'Has he married you yet, then?'*

V+ADV:
WITH QUOTE

sing up If you **sing up**, you sing more loudly, so that people can hear you better. ❑ *You boys at the back! Can you sing up?*

V+ADV

single /ˈsɪŋɡəl/ **(singles, singling, singled)**

★single out If you **single out** someone or something from a group, you choose them for special attention or treatment. ❑ *Neither Belinda nor Mrs Harlowe made any move to single him out for attention. ...to single out the key problems for each continent... Why have badgers been singled out as culprits?... She singled this one out as being the only possible one.*

V+PRON+ADV,
V+N+ADV,
V+ADV+N:
ALSO+*for/as*

NOTE **Pick out** means almost the same as **single out**.

sink /sɪŋk/ **(sinks, sinking, sank, sunk)**

sink back

1 If you **sink back**, you lean backwards or lie down after being in a more upright or sitting position. ❑ *She sank back on her pillows... Sonny sank back in the leather armchair... I sank back and tried to think.*

V+ADV:
USUALLY+A

2 To **sink back** into a former state or habit means to return to being in that state or having that habit. ❑ *He would sink back again into bitterness... There is a continual battle against sinking back into the old ways... There'll be no field officers, so everything will sink back. But that happens everywhere; you take one step forward and two steps back.*

V+ADV:
USUALLY+*into*

sink down

1 If something **sinks down**, it moves downwards. ❑ *The jet turns in a wide circle, sinking down toward the hills below... The bird sank down, kicking and fluttering.*

V+ADV

2 If you **sink down**, you sit or let yourself fall gently from an upright position. ❑ *Hagen sank down on the grass and sighed... She sank down in the chair, with her legs wide apart... They lit cigarettes and sank down to lie on the grass.*

V+ADV:
USUALLY+A

★sink in

✓ In meanings 3, 4, and 5, the stress is on **sink**.

1 If something **sinks in**, it goes deeper into the ground, water, or other substance. ❑ *It sunk in up to the hilt... The rain sinks in and there is no mud.*

V+ADV

2 When a fact or idea, usually an unpleasant one, **sinks in**, it gradually becomes recognized or understood. ❑ *It took a moment or two to sink in... The implications of this did not at first sink in... The prisoners had nothing to do but let their situation sink in.*

V+ADV

3 If you **are sunk in** a state or mood, especially a dull or inactive one, you are completely in it. ❑ *She remained sunk in silent contemplation... The nation seemed sunk in lethargy.*

PASSIVE:
V+ADV

4 If you **sink** something sharp **in** something solid, you cause it to pierce the surface and go deep into the solid. ❑ *The cat suddenly leapt off a roof and sank her claws in his neck... The other hyena lunges at its belly, sinks in its teeth and holds on.*

V+N+PREP/ADV,
V+ADV+N,
V+PRON+PREP/ADV

5 If you **sink** money **in** a product or project, you provide money for it, hoping to get a profit later. ❑ *Enormous sums of capital had to be sunk in a modern building... Fired*

V+N+PREP,
V+PRON+PREP

by his enthusiasm, I sank all our savings in a second-hand camera.

NOTE **Sink into** means almost the same as **sink in**.

*sink into

☑ In meaning 4 the stress is on **sink**.

1 If something **sinks into** the ground, water, or other substance, it moves down- | V+PREP,
wards and deeper into it. ❑ *The weight will sink into the wax... Her chair, her cello, and* | V+N+PREP,
she herself were sinking into the sand... I prefer to sink the rod tip well into the water. | V+PRON+PREP: ERGATIVE

2 If you **sink into** a chair, a bed, or other soft furniture, you sit in it or lie on it | V+PREP,
and let your body relax so that you are completely supported by it. ❑ *Floyd sank into* | V+REFL+PREP
a comfortable leather chair... She sank herself, with evident relief, into a soft armchair.

3 If you **sink** something sharp **into** something solid, you cause it to pierce the sur- | V+N+PREP,
face and go into the solid. ❑ *She sank her teeth so deeply into his finger that he loosened* | V+PRON+PREP,
his grip... The cat's long claws sank into the shoulder of Hallam's suit. | V+PREP: ERGATIVE

4 If you **sink into** a state or mood, especially a dull or inactive one, you pass | V+PREP
gradually into it. ❑ *He sinks into a period of extreme depression... I sank into sleep with a*
sigh of satisfaction... The poor man sinks further into debt.

5 If you **sink** money **into** a business or project, you spend money on it in the | V+N+PREP,
hope of making more money. ❑ *He's going to sink a lot of money into that theatre* | V+PRON+PREP
group... No company is likely to sink large sums into such a poor investment.

NOTE **Plough into** and **sink in** mean almost the same as **sink into**.

sip /sɪp/ (sips, sipping, sipped)

sip at If you **sip at** a drink or a container, you drink a small amount at a time. | V+PREP
❑ *Sandra decides to sip at her drink and behave as if nothing were wrong... He sipped com-*
pulsively at a plastic mug of cheap machine coffee.

siphon /saɪfən/ (siphons, siphoning, siphoned)

☑ **Siphon** is also spelled **syphon**.

siphon off

1 If you **siphon off** a liquid, you get it out of a container through a tube using at- | V+N+ADV,
mospheric pressure. ❑ *Then you siphon the water off... Claude pushed it out of the garage,* | V+ADV+N,
after siphoning off a little gas from the family's second car... If you want a sweet cider, sy- | V+PRON+ADV
phon it off without disturbing the sediment.

2 If you **siphon off** money or other resources from a source or supply, you sepa- | V+N+ADV,
rate or remove them from the rest, often in order to use them for a purpose for | V+ADV+N,
which they were not intended. ❑ *Money being poured into scientific work should be sy-* | V+PRON+ADV
phoned off for this purpose. ...strategically placed to siphon off trade from both towns... Sub-
stantial numbers of students should be siphoned off to the Junior Colleges.

sit /sɪt/ (sits, sitting, sat)

☑ **About** is used mainly in British English. In American English, **around** is much
more common than **round**.

sit about → See sit around

*sit around If you **sit around**, **sit about**, or **sit round**, you stay in the same | V+ADV,
place and do very little except sit. ❑ *The rest of us sat around happily in the hotel dining* | V+PREP:
room... We sat about drinking wine... They sit round and discuss the results... All I ever did | USUALLY+A
was sit around the house reading.

*sit back

1 If you **sit back**, you lean backwards so that the back of your body is supported | V+ADV:
by something and you can sit more comfortably. ❑ *He sat back and took a deep* | USUALLY+A
breath... She sits back in her chair... The little Bushman was sitting back against a wall.

2 If you **sit back** while something is happening or while other people are doing | V+ADV:
something, you deliberately do not become involved in it. ❑ *We cannot afford just to* | USUALLY WITH *and*+VERB
sit back and wait for the next industrial crisis... Maureen was sitting back and letting Kate get
on with it... All they have to do is sit back and enjoy the fun.

sit by If you **sit by** while something is happening, especially something that you | V+ADV
think is wrong, you allow it to happen and do not do anything about it. ❑ *...those*
who sit idly by while you slave over a hot stove... The two remaining members of the com-
mittee sat by half dozing... I felt I couldn't sit by and see you deceived... You don't sit by and

watch a small child destroy something.

NOTE **Stand by** means almost the same as **sit by**.

★sit down

1 If you **sit down** or **sit** yourself **down**, you lower your body until you are sitting on something. ❑ *We were both looking for a place to sit down... He sat down on the edge of the bed... After a bit we all sat down to tea... She sat herself down beside me.* — V+ADV, V+REFL+ADV; ALSO+A/to-INF

NOTE **Stand up** means the opposite of **sit down**.

♦ If you have a **sit-down**, you sit down and rest for a short time. ❑ *When we got to Firle Beacon we had a bit of a sit-down.* — N-SING

♦ A **sit-down** meal is a large or formal meal eaten while sitting at a table. ❑ *...a snack bar where you go when there is not time for a sit-down meal before a theatre.* — ADJECTIVE

♦ A **sit-down** strike or a **sit-down** is a strike or protest in which people sit down in their workplace or in a public place and refuse to move until they get what they are asking for. ❑ *...staging sit-down strikes that paralysed the traffic. ...civil rights marches and demonstrations, sit-downs, rent and rate strikes.* — ADJECTIVE, N-COUNT

2 If you **sit** someone **down**, you make them sit down, by persuasion, force, or by placing them in a sitting position because they are unable to do it by themselves. ❑ *I helped him to the door and sat him down on a convenient seat... I sat Kate down and pointed the rifle at her head.* — V+PRON+ADV, V+N+ADV

3 If you **sit down** and do something, you spend a lot of time and effort doing it, in order to try to achieve something. ❑ *They are not willing to sit down and negotiate... I sat down and wrote my first book... The bright ones will sit down and tackle the work necessary.* — V+ADV; WITH *and*+VERB

sit for

1 If you **sit for** an artist, a photographer, a painting, or a photograph, you place yourself in a particular position so that the artist can paint your picture or the photographer can take your photograph. ❑ *She had sat for painters like Rossetti... I have sat for my portrait before.* — V+PREP

2 If you **sit for** an examination, you do the things that are required by the institution that organizes it, such as answering questions or doing practical tests. ❑ *Ash never sat for an examination again... Keynes sat for the Civil Service examinations and did badly.* — V+PREP

sit in

1 If you **sit in** on a meeting or similar event, you are allowed to be present but are not expected to take part. ❑ *I'd love to have sat in on the meeting... I was asked by Asian friends to sit in on a conference... At meetings of the Midland Employers' Federation, I used to sit in as an observer... We will arrange for you to sit in with an experienced worker during sessions.* — V+ADV; USUALLY+A/on

2 A **sit-in** is an event in which people protest against something by staying in a place until they get what they want. ❑ *Since his success in ending the sit-in, Morris had become well-known... There was a sit-in in the administration building.* — N-COUNT

sit on

1 If you **sit on** a committee, board, or panel, you are an official member of it. ❑ *She does a lot of welfare work and sits on various committees... Representatives of the workers should sit on the boards of directors... Women didn't sit on local juries.* — V+PREP

2 If you say that someone **is sitting on** a task or resource, you mean that they are not doing it quickly enough or using it enough. ❑ *He's been sitting on those applications for over a week. ...countries sitting on scarce and valuable commodities.* — V+PREP; HAS PASSIVE

sit out

1 If you **sit out** somewhere, you sit outside rather than inside a building. ❑ *Groups of people were sitting out on the grass during their lunch hour... We sat out at metal tables and drank white wine... They'd sit out there in the sun and watch.* — V+ADV; USUALLY+A

2 If you **sit out** an event or a period of time, you wait for it to finish, rather than continuing with what you were doing. ❑ *Don tried to persuade him to sit out the night there. ...spending two more days sitting out the bad weather.* — V+ADV+N, V+PRON+ADV; NO PASSIVE

3 If you are at a dance and **sit out**, you do not dance, but sit at the side of the room. [OLD-FASHIONED] ❑ *In the old days a girl could go to a dance and sit out... We'll be able to sit out together, then.* — V+ADV

sit over

☑ In meaning 2, the stress is on **over**.

1 If you **sit over** an object or activity, you spend a long time occupied with it or   V+PREP
doing it. ❏ *They were sitting over a long lunch... We sat over it for the rest of the evening.*

2 If you **sit over** someone, you watch them very carefully, for example because   V+PREP
they are ill or because you want to make sure that they do not do anything wrong.
❏ *Fanny tried to make him drink, sat over him.*

sit round → See sit around

sit through If you **sit through** an event or period of time, especially an un-   V+PREP
pleasant one, you stay until it is finished. ❏ *The professor sat through the entire monologue with growing impatience... I've sat through many weary hours as a delegate.*

★sit up

1 If you **sit up**, you move into an upright sitting position when you have been   V+ADV
leaning back or lying down. ❏ *I tried to sit up to take off my jacket... The baby was sitting
up unaided... Marie is awake now and sits up in the seat.*

♦ **Sit-ups** are an exercise in which you repeatedly move from lying down on the   N-COUNT
floor to a sitting position. ❏ *We did all the exercises with the class, push-ups, sit-ups, knee
bending... Sit-ups are an advanced exercise for athletic training.*

2 If you **sit** someone **up**, you move them into a sitting position when they have   V+N+ADV,
been leaning back or lying down. ❏ *She sat him up and made him comfortable.*   V+PRON+ADV

3 If you **sit up** at night, you do not go to bed although it is very late. ❏ *She had sat*   V+ADV
*up all night... Ellen would sit up working on his plans and drawings... Breaking the bedtime
rules by sitting up far too late.*

NOTE **Stay up** means almost the same as **sit up**.

4 If something makes you **sit up**, it makes you suddenly pay attention to what is   V+ADV
happening. ❏ *The whole audience began to sit up and take notice.*

size /saɪz/ (sizes, sizing, sized)

size up If you **size up** people or situations, you look at them or think about   V+N+ADV,
them, in order to judge them in some way. ❏ *We went over to size up our potential ri-*   V+ADV+N,
vals. ...a man who could size up a chaotic situation... He had sized me up wrongly.   V+PRON+ADV

NOTE **Weigh up** means almost the same as **size up**.

skate /skeɪt/ (skates, skating, skated)

☑ In American English, **around** is much more common than **round**.

skate around → See skate over

skate over If you **skate over**, **skate around**, or **skate round** a subject or   V+PREP:
problem, you avoid discussing it or dealing fully with it, because you find it too diffi-   HAS PASSIVE
cult or embarrassing. ❏ *Girls' books skate over the technicalities of adult life... He skated
warily round the subject once or twice... Women prefer to skate around the issue of sexual
preference.*

NOTE **Skirt around** means almost the same as **skate over**, and **evade** is a more
formal word.

skate round → See skate over

sketch /sketʃ/ (sketches, sketching, sketched)

sketch in

1 If someone who is drawing **sketches in** something, they add it quickly and   V+ADV+N,
roughly to the drawing, usually before deciding whether to keep it, rub it out, or   V+PRON+ADV,
change it. ❏ *...a huge sign, CALDERWOOD'S, that the architects had sketched in at the en-*   V+N+ADV
trance... Scylla rapidly sketched in England, adding Ireland off to the left.

2 If you **sketch in** an idea or fact, you add a few details about it, but do not deal   V+ADV+N,
with it fully. ❏ *Here it is only necessary to sketch in the broad outlines of the reform... I'm*   V+PRON+ADV,
going to sketch in a bit of the background by way of introduction.   V+N+ADV

NOTE **Sketch out** means almost the same as **sketch in**, and **outline** is a more formal word.

sketch out

1 If someone who is drawing **sketches out** something, they draw all the main fea-   V+ADV+N,
tures, but do not put in the details. ❏ *With a pencil and ruler he sketches out the route.*   V+PRON+ADV,
V+N+ADV

2 If you **sketch out** an idea, situation, or incident, you give a brief, general description of it, not including the details. ❑ *We will just sketch out the outline of the two systems... I'll just sketch out what happened... The background to this incident is sketched out by Oliver Goldsmith.*

V+ADV+N,
V+PRON+ADV,
V+N+ADV

NOTE **Sketch in** means almost the same as **sketch out**, and **outline** is a more formal word.

skill /skɪl/ (skills, skilling, skilled)

skill up If you **skill up**, you improve the skills that relate to your job. ❑ *Much has been muttered about 'skilling up', but so far little has been done about achieving change.*

V+ADV

skim /skɪm/ (skims, skimming, skimmed)

skim off

1 If you **skim off** a substance which is floating on the top of a liquid, you remove it. ❑ *Skim off the froth, and strain the beer into a wooden barrel... Skim the scum off from time to time.*

V+ADV+N,
V+N+ADV,
V+PRON+ADV

2 If someone **skims off** the best part of something, or money which belongs to other people, they take it for themselves. ❑ *He has been accused of skimming the cream off the economy... Rich Italian clubs such as AC Milan cannot simply skim off all of Europe's stars... If I read this right, he skimmed off about thirty million.*

V+N+ADV/PREP,
V+ADV+N,
V+PRON+ADV

skim through If you **skim through** a piece of writing, you read through it quickly without looking at the details. ❑ *I thought I would skim through a few of the letters.*

V+PREP

NOTE **Flick through** means almost the same as **skim through**.

skimp /skɪmp/ (skimps, skimping, skimped)

skimp on If you **skimp on** something, you use less time, money, or material for it than you really need, so that the result is unsatisfactory. ❑ *Never skimp on your warm-up exercises... She was skimping on food.*

V+PREP:
HAS PASSIVE

skirt /skɜːʳt/ (skirts, skirting, skirted)

☑ In American English, **around** is much more common than **round**.

skirt around

1 If you **skirt around** or **skirt round** something, you go around the edge or the outside of it. ❑ *They skirted round a bus... The path skirts around a large pond.*

V+PREP

2 If you **skirt around** or **skirt round** a subject or question, you avoid dealing with it, usually because it is difficult or controversial. ❑ *We spent a lot of time skirting around the main issues... Leading figures accused NATO of trying to skirt round the Treaty.*

V+PREP:
HAS PASSIVE

skirt round → See **skirt around**

skive /skaɪv/ (skives, skiving, skived)

skive off If you **skive off** your work or studies, you avoid doing your work by staying away from the place where you should be working. [BRITISH, INFORMAL] ❑ *He's skiving off again. ...skiving off school.*

V+ADV,
V+PREP

slack /slæk/ (slacks, slacking, slacked)

slack off

1 If something or someone **slacks off**, they become slower, less active, or less intense. [BRITISH] ❑ *The government says the nation's economic growth slacked off in the second-quarter of this year.*

V+ADV

NOTE **Slacken off** means almost the same as **slack off**.

2 If someone is **slacking off**, they are not working as hard as they should. ❑ *If someone slacks off, Bill comes down hard.*

V+ADV

slacken /slækən/ (slackens, slackening, slackened)

slacken off If something **slackens off**, it becomes slower, less active, or less intense. [BRITISH] ❑ *Business finally slackened off. ...when the tourist boom slackens off.*

V+ADV

NOTE **Slack off**, **slow down**, and **ease off** mean almost the same as **slacken off**.

slag /slæg/ (slags, slagging, slagged)

slag off If you **slag** someone **off**, you criticize them in an unpleasant way. [BRITISH, INFORMAL] ❑ *He's always slagging people off behind their backs... The only reason he won the Nobel prize was because he slagged off Russia.*

V+N+ADV,
V+ADV+N,
V+PRON+ADV

slam /slæm/ (slams, slamming, slammed)

slam down

1 If you **slam** something **down**, you put it down with a lot of force, often because you are angry. ❑ *She slammed the jug down onto the tray. ...slamming the lid down on my fingers.*

V+N+ADV,
V+ADV+N,
V+PRON+ADV

2 If you **slam down** the phone, you end a conversation suddenly by putting the receiver back down, often because you are angry. ❑ *She slammed down the phone. ...She was almost moved to slam down the receiver... That's one good reason to slam the phone down.*

V+ADV+N,
V+N+ADV

slap /slæp/ (slaps, slapping, slapped)

slap around If someone **slaps** you **around**, they hit you a few times. ❑ *I'll just slap him around a little.*

V+N+ADV,
V+PRON+ADV

NOTE **Rough up** means almost the same as **slap around**.

slap down

1 If you **slap** something **down**, you put it forcefully onto a surface, making a loud noise. ❑ *She shuffled the cards loudly and slapped them down... She slapped down a thick white cup and saucer.*

V+N+ADV,
V+ADV+N,
V+PRON+ADV

2 If you **slap** someone **down**, you speak to them unkindly or harshly, usually in order to prevent them from doing or saying something. ❑ *Men are afraid to be romantic because women slap them down... Rather than slapping down newcomers, we ought to be encouraging them.*

V+PRON+ADV,
V+ADV+N,
V+N+ADV

slap on If you **slap** a substance **on**, you put it carelessly onto something. ❑ *I smear the toast with butter, then slap on a spoonful of marmalade... You mix the paint and just slap it on the cleaned metal.*

V+ADV+N,
V+N+ADV/PREP,
V+PRON+ADV/PREP

slave /sleɪv/ (slaves, slaving, slaved)

slave away If you **slave away**, you work hard at something for a long time. ❑ *Here I am, slaving away, running a house and family... Joseph slaved away at cutting the grass.*

V+ADV:
ALSO+at

NOTE **Slog away** means almost the same as **slave away**.

sleep /sliːp/ (sleeps, sleeping, slept)

sleep around If someone **sleeps around**, they have sex with a lot of different people rather than having a sexual relationship with only one person; used showing disapproval. [INFORMAL] ❑ *I did everything I could to hurt her, including sleeping around... Young people today do not sleep around, drink alcohol, or smoke, according to a survey published today.*

V+ADV

sleep in If you **sleep in**, you stay asleep in the morning for longer than you usually do. [BRITISH] ❑ *...the guilt I felt if I slept in.*

V+ADV

NOTE **Lie in** means almost the same as **sleep in**.

sleep off If you **sleep off** the effects of eating or drinking too much, you recover from the effects by sleeping. ❑ *...sleeping off his drinks in one of the wicker chairs... We went back to our room to sleep it off... He claimed he was drunk and was looking for somewhere to sleep it off.*

V+ADV+N,
V+N+ADV,
V+PRON+ADV

sleep on If you **sleep on** an idea, you delay making a decision about it until the next day. ❑ *Are you sure you don't want to sleep on it? You may have changed your mind by tomorrow.*

V+PREP

sleep out If you **sleep out**, you sleep outdoors. ❑ *There were all kinds of reasons why they slept out... The inspector went round asking why the men sleep out in this bitter weather.*

V+ADV

sleep over If someone, especially a child, **sleeps over** in a place such as a friend's home, they stay there for one night. ❑ *She said his friends could sleep over in the big room downstairs.*

V+ADV

sleep through If you **sleep through** a noise or disturbance, you fail to wake up in spite of it. ❑ *The girl slept through everything.*

V+PREP

sleep together

1 If two people **sleep together**, they have a sexual relationship, especially when

V+ADV

they are not married to each other. ❑ *They were presumably sleeping together... She assumed that we should sleep together.*

  2 You can also say that two people **sleep together** when they sleep in the same   V+ADV
bed or room. ❑ *He and his mother slept together in her bed until he was nearly four..... The
children sleep together to keep warm.*

★sleep with

  1 If you **sleep with** someone, you have sex with them, especially when you are   V+PREP
not married to them. ❑ *I heard all the gossip about who was sleeping with whom... Do you
think I should sleep with David?*

  2 To **sleep with** someone also means to sleep in the same bed or room as them.   V+PREP
❑ *The baby sleeps with his mother.*

slice /slaɪs/ (slices, slicing, sliced)

  slice off If you **slice** something **off**, you remove it by cutting it. ❑ *She sliced off*   V+ADV+N,
another chunk... The bottom half of the main hull was sliced off and replaced with a new sec-   V+N+ADV,
tion.   V+PRON+ADV

  slice up If you **slice** something **up**, you cut it into smaller pieces. ❑ *Surely we*   V+ADV+N,
could feed ourselves without slicing up animals. ...slicing the bread up... This area was sliced   V+N+ADV,
up to suit the developers.   V+PRON+ADV

slick /slɪk/ (slicks, slicking, slicked)

  slick down If you **slick** your hair **down**, you make it smooth and shiny by put-   V+N+ADV,
ting water or hair oil on it. ❑ *Their hair was neatly combed and slicked down.*   V+ADV+N,
  V+PRON+ADV
  NOTE **Smooth down** means almost the same as **slick down**.

slim /slɪm/ (slims, slimming, slimmed)

slim down

  1 If a company or other organization **slims down** or is **slimmed down**, it em-   V+ADV,
ploys fewer people, in order to save money or become more efficient. ❑ *Many firms*   V+N/PRON+ADV,
have had little choice but to slim down. ...the plan to slim down the coal industry.   V+ADV+N:
  ERGATIVE

  2 If you **slim down**, you try to make yourself thinner and lighter by eating less   V+ADV,
food. ❑ *Doctors have told Benny to slim down. ...salon treatments that claim to slim down*   V+N/PRON+ADV,
thighs.   V+ADV+N:
  ERGATIVE

slip /slɪp/ (slips, slipping, slipped)

★slip away

  1 If you **slip away**, you leave a place quietly, often so that people do not notice   V+ADV
you. ❑ *I hope we can slip away before she notices... I slipped away down a side street.*
  NOTE **Slip off** means almost the same as **slip away**.

  2 If something **slips away**, it disappears gradually or without effort. ❑ *You can feel*   V+ADV
*the stresses and strains of the day slipping away as you run... I feel my life is slipping away to
no purpose.*

slip by

  1 If you say that time or an event **slips by**, you mean that it passes and so is gone.   V+ADV
❑ *We should not allow the time to slip by without making renewed efforts... The occasion
slipped by... The days slipped by without any sign of the promised spell of fine weather.*

  2 To **slip by** also means to go past someone or something quietly, so that peo-   V+ADV,
ple do not notice. ❑ *The canoe underneath slips by quite slowly... I managed to slip by*   V+PREP
him.

slip down

  1 To **slip down** means to fall down by sliding. ❑ *She slipped down... She pulled up*   V+ADV
her sock which had slipped down.

  2 If you say that a drink **slips down** easily, you mean that it is pleasant to drink   V+ADV
and you could drink a lot of it. [INFORMAL] ❑ *The beer slipped down very easily.*

★slip in

  1 If you **slip** something **in**, you put it somewhere or include it quietly, often with-   V+ADV+N,
out telling anyone. ❑ *We thought it was time to slip in the odd phoney headline... We pre-*   V+N+ADV,
vented the bartender from slipping in any vodka.   V+PRON+ADV

  2 If you **slip in**, you go into a place quietly, often so that people do not notice you.   V+ADV
❑ *You should be able to slip in unnoticed by him... They slip in and out of the office.*

★slip into

1 If you **slip into** a place, you go into it quietly, often so that people do not notice you. ❏ *He must have slipped into the house... Cordelia slipped into the kitchen.*   V+PREP

2 If you **slip** something **into** a place, you put it there quietly, often so that people do not notice. ❏ *The man in white picked the letter up and slipped it into his jacket pocket.*   V+PRON+PREP, V+N+PREP

3 If you **slip into** a piece of clothing, you put it on quickly. ❏ *I slipped into my pyjamas.*   V+PREP

4 If you **slip into** a particular situation or way of behaving, that situation gradually starts happening, or you begin behaving in that way. ❏ *He tries to slip into the parental role... The country was slipping into recession... We frequently slip into the habit of telling lies.*   V+PREP

slip off

1 If you **slip off**, you leave a place quietly, often so that people do not notice you. ❏ *Then slip off and ask for the manager... The ship slipped off to a Spanish port.*   V+ADV

NOTE **Slip away** means almost the same as **slip off**.

2 To **slip off** something means to fall off it by slipping. ❏ *The fruit knife slipped off the table... Soon the thatch begins to slip off.*   V+PREP, V+ADV

3 If you **slip off** a piece of clothing, you take it off quickly. ❏ *She slipped off her dress... I slipped off my coat, poured myself a drink, and tried to look relaxed.*   V+ADV+N, V+N+ADV, V+PRON+ADV

slip on If you **slip on** a piece of clothing, you put it on quickly. ❏ *He slipped on his shoes and went out... Just let me slip on my jacket and I'll come with you.*   V+ADV+N, V+N+ADV, V+PRON+ADV

★slip out

1 If you **slip out** of a place, you leave it for a short while, usually quietly. ❏ *I slipped out to phone the police... I just slipped out for a packet of fags... She had slipped out of her seat and escaped.*   V+ADV: USUALLY+A/of

2 If you say that a piece of information **slipped out**, you mean that you told it to someone without meaning to. ❏ *I'm sorry. It slipped out.*   V+ADV

3 If you **slip out** of a piece of clothing, you take it off quickly. ❏ *She slips out of her working clothes.*   V+ADV: USUALLY+of

slip through If something **slips through** a set of checks or rules, it is accepted when it should not have been. ❏ *...hardened trouble-makers who have slipped through the security checks... The slightest little bit of inattention can let something slip through.*   V+ADV, V+PREP

slip up If you **slip up**, you make a mistake. ❏ *We must have slipped up somewhere... She's slipped up in the calculations; I don't think it can be as much as that.*   V+ADV

♦ A **slip-up** is a mistake, especially one that is small or unimportant. [INFORMAL] ❏ *There must have been a slip-up... A similar slip-up occurred later in the week.*   N-COUNT

slog /slɒg/ (slogs, slogging, slogged)

slog away If you **slog away** at something, you continue to work hard at it for a long time. ❏ *The second group are slogging away at revision... Having got the job, he likes to really slog away at it.*   V+ADV: USUALLY+at

NOTE **Slave away** and **beaver away** mean almost the same as **slog away**.

slog through If you **slog through** something difficult, you continue moving through it or working at it with a lot of effort. ❏ *He preferred to slog through long lists of spelling. ...slogging through twenty feet of snow.*   V+PREP: HAS PASSIVE

NOTE **Plough through** means almost the same as **slog through**.

slop /slɒp/ (slops, slopping, slopped)

☑ **About** is used mainly in British English.

slop about → See slop around

slop around If you **slop around** or **slop about**, you spend time in a place being lazy and doing nothing. ❏ *...slopping around in the university for a year or two. ...inviting us to slop around all afternoon.*   V+ADV

NOTE **Slouch around** means almost the same as **slop around**.

slop out To **slop out** in a prison means to empty the buckets that the prisoners use as toilets. ❏ *...first thing in the morning, when they are slopping out... Slopping out at Reading prison continues to be disgusting, the Board says.*   V+ADV

slop over If a liquid **slops over**, it spills over the edge of the container it is in. ❏ *Some of the milk slopped over onto the grass. ...made the rain in the gutters slop over and stream down the glass... The stew slopped over the container.*

V+ADV,
V+PREP

slope /sləʊp/ **(slopes, sloping, sloped)**

slope off If you **slope off**, you go away quickly and quietly, as if you are trying to escape or avoid something. [INFORMAL] ❏ *I have a feeling that most of them have sloped off... He'll be sloping off home to his supper.*

V+ADV

slot /slɒt/ **(slots, slotting, slotted)**

slot into

1 If you **slot** someone or something **into** a schedule, scheme, or organization, you find a place for them within it. ❏ *The unions are slotted into the state apparatus... All the components of a full terrestrial ecosystem begin to slot into place.*

V+N+PREP,
V+PRON+PREP,
V+PREP:
ERGATIVE

2 If you **slot** something **into** a narrow opening, you put it carefully into the opening. ❏ *They slotted the papers neatly back into the file... The woman took the gun and showed how the cylinder slotted into the barrel.*

V+N+PREP,
V+PRON+PREP,
V+PREP:
ERGATIVE

slouch /slaʊtʃ/ **(slouches, slouching, slouched)**

☑ **About** is used mainly in British English.

slouch about → See slouch around

slouch around If you **slouch around** or **slouch about**, you spend time being lazy and not doing anything. ❏ *She slouched about in a dressing gown.*

V+ADV

NOTE **Slop around** means almost the same as **slouch around**.

slough /slʌf/ **(sloughs, sloughing, sloughed)**

slough off

1 If you **slough off** something that you no longer need, you get rid of it. [FORMAL] ❏ *Women are less willing than their husbands to slough off a friendship after a move.*

V+ADV+N,
V+PRON+ADV

2 If an animal such as a snake **sloughs off** its outer skin, it goes through a natural process which causes this skin to come off. ❏ *A new skin grows beneath the old which is then sloughed off... As the dead cells are sloughed off, the skin becomes red and irritated.*

V+ADV+N,
V+N+ADV,
V+PRON+ADV

NOTE **Shed** means almost the same as **slough off**.

slow /sləʊ/ **(slows, slowing, slowed)**

*slow down

1 If something **slows down** or if you **slow** it **down**, it starts to move or happen more slowly. ❏ *Economic growth has slowed down dramatically... The van slowed down... Governments have tried to slow down the inflationary spiral... Harold slowed the car down... We did not stop his southward advance but did much to slow it down.*

V+ADV,
V+ADV+N,
V+N+ADV,
V+PRON+ADV:
ERGATIVE

NOTE **Slow up** means almost the same as **slow down**, and **speed up** means the opposite.

♦ A **slowdown** is a reduction in speed or activity. ❏ *He projects a slowdown in the rate of expansion of world trade.*

N-COUNT

♦ A **slowdown** is also a protest by workers in which they deliberately work slowly and cause problems for their employers. [AMERICAN] ❏ *There were peace marches, rent strikes, and work slowdowns.*

N-COUNT

2 If someone **slows down**, they become less active, when they have been working very hard or have been very energetic. ❏ *He needs to slow down a little or he'll get an ulcer.*

V+ADV

NOTE **Relax** means almost the same as **slow down**.

slow up If something **slows up** or if you **slow** it **up**, it starts to move or happen more slowly. ❏ *Steep hills slow them up... Instability slows up a country's development... The resistor slows the current up... 'Car broken down?' bawled the driver as he slowed up.*

V+N+ADV,
V+ADV+N,
V+PRON+ADV,
V+ADV:
ERGATIVE

NOTE **Slow down** means almost the same as **slow up**, and **speed up** means the opposite.

smack /smæk/ **(smacks, smacking, smacked)**

smack of If something **smacks of** something unpleasant, it is similar to it and reminds you of it. ❏ *Any literature other than romantic novels smacked to her of school.*

V+PREP

...secret consultations which smacked of a cover-up.

NOTE Savour of means almost the same as **smack of**.

smarten /smɑ:rtⁿn/ (smartens, smartening, smartened)

smarten up To smarten up a person or place means to make them look neater and tidier. ❑ *We could smarten up a bit and then go... He resists every suggestion for smartening up his personal appearance... The New Electric Cinema has been smartened up.*

V+ADV,
V+ADV+N,
V+N+ADV,
V+PRON+ADV:
ERGATIVE

NOTE Spruce up means almost the same as **smarten up**.

smash /smæʃ/ (smashes, smashing, smashed)

smash down If you smash down something such as a door, you hit it and break it so that it falls onto the ground. ❑ *I'm going to smash this door down if you don't come out... King Kong lurched around smashing down skyscrapers.*

V+N+ADV,
V+ADV+N,
V+PRON+ADV

smash in To smash something in means to hit it very hard so that it breaks and often so that the pieces fall inwards. ❑ *We'll smash the window in... This was what had been used to smash in the back of Stryker's skull.*

V+N+ADV,
V+ADV+N,
V+PRON+ADV

smash up

1 If you smash something up, you hit it so that it breaks into many pieces and is completely destroyed. ❑ *He started smashing up all the furniture... They smashed the place up.*

V+ADV+N,
V+N+ADV,
V+PRON+ADV

2 If you smash up your car, you damage it by crashing it into something. ❑ *All you told me was that he'd smashed up yet another car... Six students smashed up a car.*

V+N+ADV,
V+ADV+N,
V+PRON+ADV

NOTE Wreck means almost the same as **smash up**.

♦ A **smash-up** is a bad car crash. [INFORMAL] ❑ *We saw a terrible smash-up on the way home.*

N-COUNT

smell /smɛl/ (smells, smelling, smelled/smelt)

★smell of

1 If something smells of a particular thing, it has a smell like that thing. ❑ *The room was hot and smelled of hospitals... She smelled of soap and talcum powder.*

V+PREP

2 You can say that something smells of an unpleasant quality when it seems to have that quality. ❑ *Such an action would have smelt, to her, of defeat.*

V+PREP

NOTE Smack of and savour of mean almost the same as **smell of**.

smell out

1 If you smell someone out, you discover where they are even though they may be hiding or doing something in secret. ❑ *Maggie could smell out evildoers and cast spells on them.*

V+ADV+N,
V+N+ADV,
V+PRON+ADV

NOTE Root out means almost the same as **smell out**.

2 If an animal smells something out, it finds where it is by following its smell. ❑ *We'll take the dog – she'll smell those rabbits out.*

V+N+ADV,
V+ADV+N,
V+PRON+ADV

smoke /smoʊk/ (smokes, smoking, smoked)

smoke out

1 If you smoke out a person or animal, you force them to come out of a place by filling it with smoke. ❑ *...smoking out a bees' nest.*

V+ADV+N,
V+N+ADV,
V+PRON+ADV

2 If you smoke someone out, you manage to find them or force them to reveal themselves. ❑ *...using modern technology to smoke out tax evaders... You've got to smoke him out like a rat or a snake.*

V+ADV+N,
V+PRON+ADV,
V+N+ADV

smooth /smuːð/ (smooths, smoothing, smoothed)

smooth down If you smooth down your hair or your clothes, you press them with your hands to make them flat. ❑ *Gertrude smoothed down her dress... She smoothed down her short blonde hair.*

V+ADV+N,
V+PRON+ADV,
V+N+ADV

NOTE Flatten means almost the same as **smooth down**.

smooth out

1 If you smooth out a surface, you press it down with something in order to make it flat. ❑ *Martha smoothed out the newspaper on the table... Using the flat side, smooth out any rough surfaces.*

V+ADV+N,
V+PRON+ADV

NOTE Flatten means almost the same as **smooth out**.

2 If you smooth out a problem or difficulty, you solve it, especially by talking to the people concerned. ❑ *Baker was smoothing out differences with European allies... It's*

V+N+ADV,
V+ADV+N,
V+PRON+ADV

O.K. I smoothed things out.

NOTE **Sort out** means almost the same as **smooth out**.

3 If you **smooth out** a process or situation, you make it more even and regular. ❑ *Daily fluctuations in power output could be smoothed out... We need more cash to smooth out the monthly outgoings.*   V+ADV+N,
V+PRON+ADV

NOTE **Even out** means almost the same as **smooth out**.

smooth over If you **smooth over** a problem or difficulty, you talk about it in   V+ADV+N,
a way that makes it seem less serious and easier to deal with. ❑ *I tried to smooth over*   V+PRON+ADV
the awkwardness of this first meeting... He was grateful for her help in smoothing over what could have become an embarrassing scene.

NOTE **Gloss over** means almost the same as **smooth over**.

snap /snæp/ (snaps, snapping, snapped)

snap out If speech or a sound **snaps out**, it is heard suddenly and loudly. ❑ *The*   V+ADV
sound snapped out in the night like a pistol shot... 'Halt!' her voice snapped out.

snap out of If you **snap out of** a sad mood or a moment of concentration,   V+ADV+PREP,
you quickly change by forcing yourself to act more cheerfully or sociably. If you tell   V+ADV+PREP+*it*
someone to **snap out of** it, you want them to stop being being sad or depressed.
❑ *I snapped out of this melancholy the moment a friend called... 'Do you mind if I ask what you live on?' Abruptly I snapped out of my calculations. 'Yes, I do.'... She's had this before and has snapped right out of it.*

★snap up

1 If you **snap** something **up**, you buy it quickly while it is cheap before anyone   V+ADV+N,
else can buy it. ❑ *U.S. and European pension funds have been snapping up shares of steel*   V+PRON+ADV,
companies... He snapped it up for £2,000 after the British Museum had felt it beyond their re-   V+N+ADV
sources... All these houses were snapped up as soon as they were offered for sale.

2 If you **snap up** a chance or opportunity, you take advantage of it quickly before   V+ADV+N,
it becomes too late. ❑ *There was a time when Morris would have snapped up a chance like*   V+PRON+ADV,
this.   V+N+ADV

snarl /snɑːʳl/ (snarls, snarling, snarled)

snarl up When traffic **is snarled up**, the road is blocked so that the traffic can-   V+N+ADV:
not move freely. When a process **is snarled up**, it becomes blocked or overworked   USUALLY PASSIVE
so that it cannot continue smoothly. ❑ *The traffic was snarled up due to riots on the campus... He had eaten a bowl of cereals, drunk half a cup of coffee and was snarled up in a traffic jam at the roundabout... The distributors are snarled up.*

snatch /snætʃ/ (snatches, snatching, snatched)

snatch away If you **snatch** something **away** from someone, you take it from   V+PRON+ADV,
them forcefully with a sudden movement. ❑ *Then he snatched away his coat, which I*   V+ADV+N,
was still holding for him... He suddenly reached over and snatched it away from me... I don't   V+N+ADV:
mean that you have to snatch the bottle away.   ALSO+*from*

NOTE **Grab** means almost the same as **snatch away**.

snatch up If you **snatch** something **up**, you pick it up very quickly and with a   V+ADV+N,
violent movement. ❑ *I snatched up Otto's glass just as it began to topple off the table...*   V+PRON+ADV
She snatched up an oil-can and threw it all on the fire... He snatched her up as if she were made of straw.

NOTE **Grab** means almost the same as **snatch up**.

sneak /sniːk/ (sneaks, sneaking, sneaked)

☑ The form **snuck** is also used in American English for the past tense and past participle.

sneak up on

1 If someone **sneaks up on** you, they try and approach you without being seen or   V+ADV+PREP
heard, perhaps to surprise you or do you harm. ❑ *I managed to sneak up on him when you knocked on the door.*

NOTE **Creep up on** means almost the same as **sneak up on**.

2 If something **sneaks up on** you, it happens or occurs when you are not expect-   V+ADV+PREP
ing it. ❑ *Sometimes our expectations sneak up on us unawares.*

NOTE **Creep up on** means almost the same as **sneak up on**.

sneeze /sniːz/ (sneezes, sneezing, sneezed)

sneeze at If something is **not to be sneezed at**, it is worth having. ❑ *It was*   V+PREP
an invitation not to be sneezed at.

NOTE **Not to be sniffed at** means almost the same as **not to be sneezed at**.

sniff /snɪf/ (sniffs, sniffing, sniffed)

☑ About is used mainly in British English. In American English, **around** is much
more common than **round**.

sniff about → See sniff around
sniff around

[1] If someone **is sniffing around**, **sniffing about**, or **sniffing round**, they are   V+ADV,
trying to find out information about something, especially information that some-   V+PREP
one else does not want known. [INFORMAL] ❑ *But really, what harm could it possibly do*
to pop down there and just sniff around?... They might have sent a couple of plain-clothes
men to sniff round his apartment while the doctors patched him up.

NOTE **Nose around** means almost the same as **sniff around**.

[2] If a person or organization **is sniffing around**, **sniffing about**, or **sniffing**   V+ADV,
round someone, they are trying to get them, for example as a lover, employee, or   V+PREP:
client. [INFORMAL] ❑ *When I had to go away to university, I was convinced that other men*   NO PASSIVE
would be sniffing round her... Rioch knows the big clubs have been sniffing around Andy
Walker.

sniff at

[1] If you **sniff at** something, you say or suggest that it is not very good. ❑ *There's*   V+PREP
only one true way to get respect from those who sniff at our cultural efforts – and that is to be
the best.

[2] If something is **not to be sniffed at**, it is worth having. ❑ *Victory in international*   V+PREP
football can never be sniffed at.

NOTE **Not to be sneezed at** means almost the same as **not to be sniffed at**.

sniff out

[1] If you **sniff** something **out**, you discover it by looking for it, often by guessing   V+ADV+N,
where it might be. [INFORMAL] ❑ *Gordon and his two friends sniffed out some lovely little*   V+PRON+ADV
quiet beaches... He'd told me that he was sniffing out more books.

NOTE **Nose out** means almost the same as **sniff out**.

[2] When a dog used by a group such as the police **sniffs out** hidden explosives or   V+N+ADV,
drugs, it finds them using its sense of smell. ❑ *A police dog, trained to sniff out explo-*   V+ADV+N,
sives, found evidence of a bomb in the apartment.   V+PRON+ADV

sniff round → See sniff around

snow /snoʊ/ (snows, snowing, snowed)

snow in If you **are snowed in**, you are prevented from leaving your house or   PASSIVE:
travelling anywhere because there is so much snow on the ground. ❑ *'Perhaps we'll be*   V+ADV
snowed in for a week!' cried Liz gleefully.

NOTE **Snow up** means almost the same as **snow in**.

snow under If you **are snowed under**, you have more work to deal with   V+PRON+ADV,
than you can manage, especially paperwork. ❑ *I've been snowed under by reports from*   V+N+ADV:
over 200 organisations... At present we're snowed under with an irrational expansion of blind   USUALLY PASSIVE
data-gathering.

snow up If you **are snowed up**, you are prevented from leaving your house or   PASSIVE:
travelling anywhere because there is so much snow on the ground. ❑ *Were you*   V+ADV
snowed up in Dawlish at all?... We were snowed up for a week.

NOTE **Snow in** means almost the same as **snow up**.

snuff /snʌf/ (snuffs, snuffing, snuffed)

snuff out

[1] If someone **snuffs out** something such as a rebellion or disagreement, they put   V+ADV+N:
an end to it by using violence or other oppressive means. ❑ *In the past the voice of dis-*   USUALLY PASSIVE
sension has been quickly snuffed out.

NOTE **Crush** means almost the same as **snuff out**.

[2] If you **snuff out** a candle or a flame, you put it out by pinching it with your fin-   V+ADV+N,

gers or by putting a cover over it for a few seconds. ❏ *She snuffed out the candle and closed her eyes.*

NOTE **Extinguish** is a formal word for **snuff out**.

3 If someone **snuffs out** someone else, they kill them. [AMERICAN, INFORMAL] ❏ *A bullet meant for Riley snuffed out a passing gangster... You've got the power. You can do anything you want. You can snuff him out or not.*

NOTE **Rub out** means almost the same as **snuff out**.

snuggle /snˈʌgəl/ **(snuggles, snuggling, snuggled)**

snuggle down If you **snuggle down**, you move deeper into your bedclothes in order to get warm and comfortable. ❏ *We got sleeping bags out and snuggled down... Just as I was snuggling down I heard a scratching sound on the tent door.*

snuggle up If you **snuggle up** to someone, you settle yourself into a warm, comfortable position by sitting or lying so that your body is against theirs. ❏ *Sally snuggled up to him... Geraldine snuggled up against him on the front seat.*

NOTE **Cuddle up** means almost the same as **snuggle up**.

soak /soʊk/ **(soaks, soaking, soaked)**

soak in If you **soak** yourself **in** a particular subject, you study it very intensely in order to learn as much about it as possible. ❏ *I soaked myself in the works of Dickens and George Eliot.*

soak off If you **soak** something **off** a surface, you remove it by using water to loosen it. ❏ *He's going to soak all the paint off it... They can soak them off with pieces of wet cotton wool... None of the paint had soaked off.*

soak through If someone or something **is soaked through**, they are completely wet, usually because they have been outside in the pouring rain. ❏ *By morning, their gear was soaked through.*

★soak up

1 If something **soaks up** a liquid, it gradually absorbs the liquid. ❏ *The parched soil soaked up what seemed like a huge volume of water... Leave it for about 5 minutes during which time the granules will soak up the water.*

NOTE **Absorb** means almost the same as **soak up**.

2 If you **soak up** sunshine, you sit or lie for a long time in the sun because you enjoy it. [INFORMAL] ❏ *She sat on the edge of her seat, leaning back to soak up the sun... She liked to soak up the Mediterranean sunshine.*

3 If you **soak up** the atmosphere in a place that you are visiting, you observe or get involved in the way of life there, because you enjoy it or are interested in it. [INFORMAL] ❏ *Keaton comes here once or twice a year to soak up the atmosphere.*

NOTE **Absorb** is a more formal word for **soak up**.

4 If something **soaks up** money or resources, it uses more than you consider reasonable or practical. ❏ *Population growth soaked up 70 per cent of the increase in national incomes... Expanded production is soaked up by worsening terms of trade.*

sob /sɒb/ **(sobs, sobbing, sobbed)**

sob out If someone **sobs out** something, they try to say it while they are crying. ❏ *They were scarcely speaking to each other except to sob out some extra insult... He sobbed out the story of what had happened... She sobbed out some of her anxieties and troubles.*

sober /soʊbər/ **(sobers, sobering, sobered)**

sober up When someone who is drunk **sobers up**, the effect of the alcohol disappears and they become sober again. ❏ *When you sober up you may be ashamed of what you've done... I caught Mrs Mawne's eye and sobered up almost immediately... He'll have to be sobered up, and quickly.*

sod /sɒd/ **(sods, sodding, sodded)**

sod off **Sod off** is an insulting and offensive way of telling someone to go away. [BRITISH, INFORMAL, RUDE] ❏ *Just shut up and sod off... You could tell him to sod off.*

soften /sɒfən, AM sɔːf-/ **(softens, softening, softened)**

soften up

1 If you **soften** someone **up**, you praise them or try to please them because you want to ask them to do something for you which they do not really want to do. ❏ *I*

V+PRON+ADV,
V+N+ADV

V+ADV+N,
V+N+ADV,
V+PRON+ADV

V+ADV

V+ADV:
USUALLY+A

V+REFL+PREP

V+N+ADV/PREP,
V+PRON+ADV/PREP,
V+ADV

PASSIVE:
V+ADV

V+ADV+N,
V+PRON+ADV,
V+N+ADV

V+ADV+N:
NO PASSIVE

V+N+ADV,
V+ADV+N,
V+PRON+ADV

V+ADV+N,
V+PRON+ADV

V+ADV+N:
NO PASSIVE

V+ADV,
V+PRON+ADV:
ERGATIVE

IMPERATIVE,
V+ADV

V+PRON+ADV,
V+ADV+N,
V+N+ADV

wondered if there was any hope of softening him up... The Government softened up the electorate by releasing its tax package.

NOTE **Butter up** means almost the same as **soften up**.

2 When soldiers or sailors **soften up** a target, they make a preliminary attack to weaken the target before the main attack is launched. ❑ *I watched two helicopters soften up a mountainside with their machine guns and bombs.*   V+ADV+N, V+N+ADV, V+PRON+ADV

soldier /ˈsəʊldʒəʳ/ (soldiers, soldiering, soldiered)

soldier on If you **soldier on**, you continue doing something and working hard at it, even though it is difficult and unpleasant. ❑ *You have to admire them as they soldier on smiling in the face of adversity... One simply soldiered on becoming older and balder.*   V+ADV

sop /sɒp/ (sops, sopping, sopped)

sop up To **sop up** a liquid means to force it off a surface by using an absorbent cloth or material. ❑ *My bandage would sop it up all right.*   V+PRON+ADV, V+ADV+N

sort /sɔːʳt/ (sorts, sorting, sorted)

★sort out

1 If you **sort out** a group of things that are in a mess or are not ready, you arrange them so that they become organized or ready. ❑ *It took quite a while to sort out all our luggage... Sort them out alphabetically... Couldn't you have washed up and sorted the place out before coming down?... With Mum and Dad in one bedroom, the six of them had to sort themselves out in the remaining rooms for sleeping.... Mrs Kirk and I got everything sorted out.*   V+ADV+N, V+PRON+ADV, V+N+ADV, V+REFL+ADV

NOTE **Arrange** means almost the same as **sort out**.

2 If you **sort out** a group of things, you consider them carefully and divide them into categories that are clearly different from each other. ❑ *It was an intelligence test, intended to sort out the children capable of attempting the papers... Some secondary schools begin at once to sort out children who read with less confidence or skill... It is difficult to sort out fact from fiction.*   V+ADV+N, V+N+ADV, V+PRON+ADV: ALSO+from

3 If you **sort out** a problem or misunderstanding, you deal with it and find a solution to it. ❑ *We'd just have to sort it out for ourselves... We have to sort things out between us. ...a network of affection and support within which we were able to sort out our personal problems... I've seen problems like this sort themselves out again and again.*   V+PRON+ADV, V+N+ADV, V+ADV+N, V+REFL+ADV

NOTE **Resolve** is a more formal word for **sort out**.

4 If you **sort yourself out**, you organize yourself or calm yourself so that you can act effectively and reasonably. ❑ *We're in a state of complete chaos here and I need a little time to sort myself out.*   V+REFL+ADV

NOTE **Get yourself together** means almost the same as **sort yourself out**.

5 If you **sort someone out**, you punish them very forcefully or violently. [BRITISH] ❑ *He was bigger and stronger than I was, and no doubt would have sorted me out very quickly had we actually come to blows.*   V+PRON+ADV, V+N+ADV

sound /saʊnd/ (sounds, sounding, sounded)

sound off If you **sound off**, you express your opinions strongly and loudly without being asked. [INFORMAL] ❑ *On most matters she's quite prepared to sound off without inhibition... He found himself sounding off about the cost of living.*   V+ADV

sound out

1 If you **sound** someone **out**, you ask them questions in order to find out their views, especially about what should or will happen in a particular situation. ❑ *Joining in gave me a chance to sound out their attitudes... Kids at school were always sounding her out about their chances of being moved to the top of the list... All the members of the English Department who have been sounded out on the subject suggested your name.*   V+ADV+N, V+PRON+ADV, V+N+ADV

2 When a noise **sounds out**, it can be heard clearly above all the other sounds that are present. ❑ *The hooter sounded out like a lighthouse foghorn... The ambulance klaxon sounds out as it drives off.*   V+ADV

soup /suːp/ (soups, souping, souped)

soup up If you **soup up** a car, you make it more powerful by adjusting the engine or adding special parts. [INFORMAL] ❑ *The boy who is lazy in class will spend hours souping up motor engines.*   V+ADV+N, V+PRON+ADV

♦ A **souped-up** car has had its engine adjusted so that it is more powerful. [INFORMAL] ❑ *On weekends he drove a souped-up MG in the California races.*   ADJECTIVE

space /speɪs/ (spaces, spacing, spaced)
space out
1 If you **space** things **out**, you arrange them so that they are not all grouped together, but have gaps or intervals of time between them. ❑ *We began to space out our meetings... This is a rough copy which will give you the chance to space it out well... These books should have large print well spaced out on the page.*   V+ADV+N, V+PRON+ADV, V+N+ADV

2 Someone who is **spaced out** cannot think clearly because they are under the influence of drugs. [INFORMAL] ❑ *I gathered up my belongings and said good-bye to the women, even though most were totally spaced out.*   ADJECTIVE

spark /spɑːrk/ (sparks, sparking, sparked)
spark off
If one thing **sparks off** a state or event, it causes the state or event to exist or happen, often by accident rather than deliberately. ❑ *There was a risk that the decision would spark off a conflict... His letter of praise and support had sparked off a friendship between the two men... Can they meet the demand sparked off by the boom in TV video?*   V+ADV+N, V+PRON+ADV, V+N+ADV

speak /spiːk/ (speaks, speaking, spoke, spoken)
★speak for
1 If you **speak for** a group of people, you represent them and explain their views. ❑ *We believe that, in putting forward our policies, we are speaking for the majority of the British people.*   V+PREP

2 If you **speak for** an idea, a proposal, or a set of beliefs, you support it by explaining it and saying what is good about it. ❑ *I spoke for going south.*   V+PREP

NOTE **Stand up for** means almost the same as **speak for**.

3 If you **speak for** yourself, you say what you think, even though you know that it is not what other people think. ❑ *Speak for yourself, Chas. I drive just to get from place to place... I'm only speaking for myself, not for my colleagues.*   V+PREP+REFL: ALSO IMPERATIVE

4 If something **speaks for** itself, it has qualities which are so apparent that you can easily see what they are. ❑ *The facts in Samsonov's case speak for themselves.*   V+PREP

5 If you say that someone is **spoken for**, you mean that they are married or already have a boyfriend or girlfriend. ❑ *Sorry Jan. He's spoken for.*   ADJECTIVE

speak out
If you **speak out**, you express your views forcefully and publicly, especially in order to criticize or oppose something. ❑ *She spoke out against her husband at the hearing... As citizens we must speak out against the causes of injustice... He spoke out strongly against subsidies.*   V+ADV: ALSO+*against*

♦ If you are **outspoken**, you give your opinions about things openly and honestly, even if they are likely to shock or offend people. ❑ *...an outspoken critic of extremists.*   ADJECTIVE

★speak up
1 If you **speak up** about something, you say publicly what you believe, especially in support of a person or an idea. ❑ *Never be frightened of speaking up for your beliefs... The cricketers themselves should speak up in favour of non-racial cricket... Why do they not speak up for themselves?*   V+ADV: USUALLY+*for*

2 If you **speak up**, you begin to speak more loudly. ❑ *Could you please speak up. We can't hear you at the back.*   V+ADV

speed /spiːd/ (speeds, speeding, speeded)
★speed up
1 When something **speeds up** or when you **speed** it **up**, it moves or travels faster. ❑ *You notice that your breathing has speeded up a bit... He pushed a lever that speeded up the car... You can do some slower movements, then speed them up a bit.*   V+ADV+N, V+PRON+ADV, V+N+ADV, V+ADV: ERGATIVE

NOTE **Accelerate** is a more formal word for **speed up**.

2 When a process or activity **speeds up** or when something **speeds** it **up**, it happens at a faster rate. ❑ *Bad housing and poverty speed up the breakdown of family life... Job losses are speeding up... I had already taken steps to speed up a solution to the problem.*   V+ADV+N, V+PRON+ADV, V+N+ADV, V+ADV: ERGATIVE

NOTE **Accelerate** is a more formal word for **speed up**.

spell /spel/ (spells, spelling, spelled/spelt)
spell out
1 If you **spell** something **out**, you explain it in detail or in a very clear way. ❑ *Let*   V+ADV+N,

me try and spell out what I mean by that... But the doctor had merely been spelling it all out
for us... The first person to spell this out was Alvin Toffler in his book Future Shock.

NOTE **Explicate** is a more formal word for **spell out**.

2 If you **spell out** a word, you write or speak each letter in the word one after the
other. ❑ *We had to spell out the words we heard... His Christian names even spell out
RAF – Ronald, Andrew, Fellowes... To communicate with her you have to spell words out on
her hand.*

V+PRON+ADV,
V+N+ADV

V+ADV+N,
V+N+ADV

spew /spjuː/ (spews, spewing, spewed)

spew out When a machine **spews** something **out**, it produces it very quickly.
❑ *More and more, airline weather forecasts and flight plans were being spewed out by computers.*

V+ADV+N

spew up If someone **spews up**, they vomit. [INFORMAL] ❑ *He spewed up as soon
as he got outside.*

V+ADV

NOTE **Throw up** means almost the same as **spew up**.

spice /spaɪs/ (spices, spicing, spiced)

spice up If you **spice up** something that you do or say, you make it more exciting or lively. ❑ *John, not content with dragging up a story more dead than dated, has
spiced it up with all kinds of innuendoes.*

V+N+ADV,
V+PRON+ADV,
V+ADV+N:
ALSO+with

spill /spɪl/ (spills, spilling, spilled/spilt)

spill out

1 When liquids or objects **spill out** of a container, they splash, pour, or fall out of
it. ❑ *Water spilled out of the vase... Be careful, so that the contents don't spill out or break
the fragile box.*

V+ADV:
USUALLY+ofA

2 You talk about people or things **spilling out** of a place when large numbers of
them come from it in a hurried, disorganized, or untidy way. ❑ *...thousands of visitors
who spilled out of the hotels and lined the processional route... Chairs from the tavernas on
either side of the street spill out until there is only a narrow pathway left.*

V+ADV:
ALSO+of

NOTE **Pour out** means almost the same as **spill out**.

3 If you **spill out** information or a secret, you tell it to someone in a hurried way.
❑ *He will talk to anyone and spill out his life story to a total stranger... He was tempted to
spill out everything he had been thinking. ...the overwhelming urge to spill it all out and be
done with it... The words just spill out.*

V+ADV+N,
V+PRON+ADV,
V+ADV:
ERGATIVE

spill over

1 If the liquid in a container **spills over**, it flows or is accidentally poured over its
edge. ❑ *...like a bucket full of water, almost spilling over. ...so startled that his steady hand
trembled and some coffee spilt over the edge of his cup.*

V+ADV,
V+PREP

2 If people or things **spill over** from one place to another, there are too many of
them to fit or stay in the first place. ❑ *These dark-suited figures were filling the pavements
and spilling over into the roadways... Most of them live outside China but some spill over the
northern and southern borders.*

V+ADV+A,
V+PREP

♦ The **overspill** from an overcrowded city or place consists of the people or parts of
it which do not fit in and so have to go somewhere else. ❑ *The overspill from Heathrow
became concentrated on Gatwick... These flats are an overspill development..*

N-SING,
ADJECTIVE

3 If something in one situation **spills over** into another, it has an accidental or
negative effect on it. ❑ *Any troubles at work could also spill over into your private life. ...ha-
tred for Daniel's father, some of which always spilled over onto Daniel.*

V+ADV:
WITH+into/onto

spin /spɪn/ (spins, spinning, spun)

☑ The form **span** is sometimes used in old-fashioned English as the past tense. In
American English, **around** is much more common than **round**.

spin around If something or someone **spins around** or **spins round**, they
turn quickly around a central point, and face in another direction, or continue turning. ❑ *'Right, that's it, then,' he said firmly, spinning round from the window. ...the part of
the engine that was spinning around... She started spinning round and round.*

V+ADV

spin off If a part of something **is spun off**, it is separated from the whole, because it is not relevant or important, or because it would be more useful in another

PASSIVE:
V+ADV

place. ❏ ...*a minor Conoco chemical division that could easily be spun off.* ...*autonomous, semi-attached units which can be spun off, and destroyed.*

♦A **spin-off** is something useful that develops unexpectedly as a result of activities which were intended to achieve something else. ❏ *The search for knowledge frequently has beneficial spin-offs for mankind... They come into commercial or domestic use as a result of spin-off from the space program.*   N-COUNT, N-UNCOUNT

♦ A **spin-off** is also a book, film, or television series that is derived from a similar book, film, or television series which has been very successful.   N-COUNT

spin out If you **spin** something **out**, you make it last as long as possible. ❏ *We found it exhausting spinning out the conversation... The Mudpore thing carried extra pay, so I spun it out as long as I could.*   V+ADV+N, V+PRON+ADV, V+N+ADV

spin round → See spin around

spirit /spɪrɪt/ **(spirits, spiriting, spirited)**

spirit away If you **spirit** someone **away** or **spirit** them **off**, you quickly and secretly take them from the place where they were. ❏ *Heissman was spirited away because Otto had arranged it... They simply spirited him away at the end of the war for his own safety.*   V+ADV+N, V+PRON+ADV, V+N+ADV

spirit off → See spirit away

spit /spɪt/ **(spits, spitting, spat)**

spit out

1 If you **spit** something **out**, you get rid of it from your mouth by blowing hard. ❏ *He sipped at it cautiously. He spat out the first few drops at once; the taste was terrible... They insisted that it was drinkable, even after spitting it out time and time again.*   V+ADV+N, V+PRON+ADV, V+N+ADV

2 If you **spit out** words, you say them in an angry way, so that you seem to be forcing them out of your mouth. ❏ *He spat out his answer... 'Economy!' Mr Willet spat out, with disgust. 'I don't call that economy!'... 'Don't tell me anything Vulkan said.' He spat the words out like bloody teeth.*   V+ADV+N, V+ADV+QUOTE, V+N+ADV

3 You say **'spit** it **out'** to someone as a way of encouraging them to say something which they seem reluctant to say. [INFORMAL] ❏ *'But just to find out, I mean...'—'Spit it out.'*   IMPERATIVE, V+*it*+ADV

splash /splæʃ/ **(splashes, splashing, splashed)**

splash down When a space vehicle **splashes down**, it lands in the sea at the end of a space flight. ❏ *The three astronauts splashed down safely at nine o'clock this morning.*   V+ADV

♦ A **splashdown** is the landing of a space vehicle in the sea after a flight.   N-COUNT

splash out If you **splash out** on something, especially on a luxury, you spend a lot of money on it. [BRITISH] ❏ *We splashed out on a colour television... Once in Pankot she would splash out by using the whole of her allowance.*   V+ADV: ALSO+on

split /splɪt/ **(splits, splitting)**

☑ The form **split** is used in the present tense and is the past tense and past participle of the verb.

split off

1 If you **split off** a part of something, or if it **splits off**, it becomes separated from the rest, for example by being cut or divided, or by breaking. ❏ *If you are splitting off a big piece you can use an axe... Such policies divide families. They split the suburbs off from the city. ...the failure of the attempt to split them off... A chain reaction comes about when a particle splits off from one atom nucleus.*   V+ADV+N, V+N+ADV, V+PRON+ADV, V+ADV: ERGATIVE

NOTE **Break off** means almost the same as **split off**.

2 When people **split off** from a group, they stop being members of that group, and form a separate one. ❏ *The hard left will split off and form a new party... They united with the Socialists in the 1960s and split off again at the end of the decade*   V+ADV: ALSO+from

NOTE **Break away** means almost the same as **split off**.

split on If you **split on** someone, you betray them by revealing a secret about them to other people. [BRITISH, INFORMAL]   V+PREP

NOTE **Tell on** means almost the same as **split on**.

★split up

1 If you **split** something **up** or if it **splits up**, it is divided into several smaller sections or parts. ❑ *You might achieve more by splitting them up into small groups... I was splitting the cycle up into finer and finer pieces... One idea is to split up the session into a series of sets... I think it will be appropriate if we split up into working groups.*
NOTE **Separate** means almost the same as **split up.**

V+PRON+ADV,
V+N+ADV,
V+ADV+N,
V+ADV:
ERGATIVE,
USUALLY+*into*

2 If a group of people **split up** or if they get **split up**, they go away in different directions. ❑ *In Hamburg the girls split up... They drove to London, where the party split up... A large group of us went from the village but we soon got split up. I never saw them again.*

V+ADV:
ALSO PASSIVE:
V+ADV

3 If two people **split up**, they end their relationship or marriage. ❑ *I went out with him for a year and then we split up for three months... After he split up with his wife, he went to Arizona.*

V+ADV,
V+ADV+*with*:
RECIPROCAL

spoil /spɔɪl/ (spoils, spoiling, spoiled/spoilt)

spoil for If you **are spoiling for** trouble or a fight, you are ready or eager for it. ❑ *The unions are spoiling for a fight about pay and conditions once again.*

V+PREP

sponge /spʌndʒ/ (sponges, sponging, sponged)

sponge down If you **sponge** someone or something **down**, you clean them by wiping or rubbing them gently with a wet sponge or cloth. ❑ *Sponge down the work surface with a wet cloth... She bathed the wound and laid a bandage over it. Then she sponged Ari down.*

V+ADV+N,
V+N+ADV,
V+PRON+ADV

sponge off → See **sponge on**

sponge on Someone who **sponges on** other people or **sponges off** them takes advantage of them by getting money and other things from them without giving back anything in return; used showing disapproval. [INFORMAL] ❑ *She found it distasteful the way Clarissa sponged on them... The young unemployed are not simply layabouts who sponge off the Welfare State.*

V+PREP

spoon /spuːn/ (spoons, spooning, spooned)

spoon out If you **spoon out** food, you give someone a portion of it, using a spoon. ❑ *Rey spooned out a small portion of the pudding for himself. ...spooning it out of paper cups.*
NOTE **Serve out** means almost the same as **spoon out.**

V+ADV+N,
V+PRON+ADV,
V+N+ADV:
ALSO+*of*

spoon up If you **spoon up** food, you eat it or pick it up, using a spoon. ❑ *...spooning up milk puddings.*

V+ADV+N,
V+PRON+ADV

spout /spaʊt/ (spouts, spouting, spouted)

spout out If someone **spouts out** words, they say something as if they are not thinking about what they are saying. ❑ *The answer was mechanically spouted out to us: 'obstructing pedestrian traffic'. ...spouting out rubbish about love and loyalty.*

V+ADV+N

sprawl /sprɔːl/ (sprawls, sprawling, sprawled)

sprawl out If you **sprawl out** somewhere or if you **are sprawled out**, you sit or lie down, spreading your legs and arms in a relaxed or careless manner. ❑ *Segal sprawled out on the couch... Thomas was sitting on a bench under a tree, his legs sprawled out in a V.*
NOTE **Stretch out** means almost the same as **sprawl out.**

V+ADV:
USUALLY+A,
ALSO PASSIVE:
V+ADV

spread /spred/ (spreads, spreading)

✓ The form **spread** is used in the present tense and is the past tense and past participle of the verb.

★spread out

1 If something **spreads out** or **is spread out**, it grows wider or covers a wider area than before. ❑ *Sunlight can be spread out by an instrument called a spectroscope... If the temperature goes above 68°F (20°C) spread it out more thinly and turn it often... The damage is scarcely apparent because it is spread out over such a long period of time.*

V+N+ADV,
V+PRON+ADV,
V+ADV+N,
V+ADV:
ERGATIVE

2 If people **spread out**, they move away from each other so that they are far apart. ❑ *They followed him and spread out, nervously, in the forest... When they saw him coming, the gang spread out across the pavement, completely blocking it.*

V+ADV

3 If people or things **are spread out**, they are scattered or far apart, and cover a

PASSIVE:

large area. ❑ *There in the harbour was a line of dark battleships spread out under the night sky... These American villages are far more spread out than the German ones ever were.* `V+ADV`

4 If a city, building, or land **is spread out** or **spreads out**, it covers a large area; often used when you are looking down on it from a higher point, or when the place seems very spacious. ❑ *I turned around at the top of the hill. The farmland spread out below me... Out through the window, you can see the town spread out below... The embassy itself is more palatial, spread out over the second floor of Eagle House.* `V+ADV: ALSO PASSIVE: V+ADV`

5 If you **spread** something **out** over a surface, you open or arrange it there, so that you can use it or see it easily. ❑ *They took seats directly opposite me and spread out their newspapers... She took the folded blanket from its corner and spread it out... He sipped at the drink as he spread the sheets of stiff paper out on the desk.* `V+ADV+N, V+PRON+ADV, V+N+ADV`

NOTE **Lay out** means almost the same as **spread out**.

6 If you **spread out** your fingers, arms, legs, and so on, you stretch them and move them so that they are far apart. If you **are spread out**, you lie or stand somewhere with your arms and legs apart. ❑ *Then he spread his hand out... She threw herself on the bed and spread out her limbs... She lifted up a hand and held it there, the fingers spread out... We caught sight of a figure spread out against a wall, being searched by a policeman.* `V+N+ADV, V+ADV+N, V+PRON+ADV`

spread over If something **is spread over** a period of time, it happens throughout that period, rather than at a single point. ❑ *The job losses may not seem catastrophic when spread over a period... You can spread repayments over 6, 12, 18, 24 or 30 months... We had to space the stuff out bit by bit; spread it over a few weeks... They had experience spreading over twenty years.* `V+N+PREP, V+PRON+PREP, V+PREP: ERGATIVE`

spring /sprɪŋ/ (springs, springing, sprang, sprung)

spring back If something **springs back** after being stretched or pushed, it quickly returns to its original position or shape. ❑ *The more you stretch a muscle, the more it will spring back into place.* `V+ADV`

spring from

1 If one thing **springs from** another, or **springs out of** it, it is the result of that other thing or it originated there. ❑ *Almost all the psychological ills that a man can suffer spring from self-doubt... Her hostility to him sprang out of sheer envy.* `V+PREP`

2 You ask where someone or something **has sprung from** when you are surprised at their unexpected appearance. ❑ *Well, well, Niccolo, where have you sprung from?... So where had all these other towns suddenly sprung from?* `V+PREP`

spring on

1 If you **spring** a remark or action **on** someone, or **spring** it **upon** them, you suddenly say or do something which surprises them. **Spring upon** is more formal. ❑ *I wondered what he was going to spring on me next... At what point are you going to spring the news on him?* `V+N+PREP, V+PRON+PREP`

2 If a person or animal **springs on** you, they suddenly attack you. [OLD-FASHIONED] ❑ *They had opened the door of a tiger's cage, and the beast had sprung on me.* `V+PREP`

NOTE **Leap on** means almost the same as **spring on**.

spring out of → See spring from

★spring up

1 If something **springs up**, it suddenly appears or comes into existence. ❑ *Here where it only rains once every five or ten years, grass will spring up within days of a rainstorm... A fresh wind had sprung up... These friendships spring up and very often don't last.* `V+ADV`

2 If someone **springs up**, they stand up very quickly with a jumping movement. ❑ *He kept having thoughts of springing up and running away... Feet together, spring up and touch the wall as high as you can.* `V+ADV`

NOTE **Jump up** means almost the same as **spring up**.

spring upon → See spring on

sprout /spraʊt/ (sprouts, sprouting, sprouted)

sprout up If things **sprout up**, large numbers of them suddenly appear. ❑ *Caravans had suddenly sprouted up in the fields. ...the magazines that sprouted up as part of the youth culture of the sixties.* `V+ADV`

NOTE **Spring up** means almost the same as **sprout up**.

spruce /spruːs/ **(spruces, sprucing, spruced)**

spruce up If you **spruce** yourself **up** or if you get **spruced up**, you make your-self look neat and smart. If you **spruce up** an object or place, you improve its ap-pearance. ❑ *Spruce yourself up a bit – you look a mess!... If you spruce the bodywork up and the interior, you'll have no trouble selling it.*

V+REFL+ADV,
V+N+ADV,
V+PRON+ADV,
V+ADV+N

spur /spɜːr/ **(spurs, spurring, spurred)**

spur on If something **spurs** you **on**, it encourages you to act in a particular way. ❑ *It was personal ambition that spurred him on... The development of British industry, in its turn, was spurred on by the existence of vast captive markets. ...spurred on by success.*

V+PRON+ADV,
V+N+ADV,
V+ADV+N

spurt /spɜːrt/ **(spurts, spurting, spurted)**

spurt out If liquid **spurts out**, it comes out quickly and suddenly in a series of pulsing movements. ❑ *More tears spurted out... I cut my wrist and the blood spurted out.*

V+ADV

sputter /spʌtər/ **(sputters, sputtering, sputtered)**

sputter out If something **sputters out**, it stops functioning, happening, or ex-isting, often in a rather feeble way. ❑ *Hughes rose to begin his talk just as the engine sputtered out and the hall was plunged into darkness.*

V+ADV

NOTE **Die** means almost the same as **sputter out**.

spy /spaɪ/ **(spies, spying, spied)**

spy on If you **spy on** someone, or **spy upon** them, you watch them secretly. **Spy upon** is more formal. ❑ *They spied on us to see how many turned up to the meet-ings... She hid behind a bush to spy upon him.*

V+PREP

spy out If you **spy** something **out**, you get information about it secretly or while pretending to do something else. ❑ *You've probably been sent here to spy out my latest designs... Shaw was one of the first to spy out her talent at this performance.*

V+ADV+N,
V+PRON+ADV

spy upon → See **spy on**

square /skweər/ **(squares, squaring, squared)**

square away If you **square** something or someone **away**, you deal with them so that the situation is satisfactory. [AMERICAN] ❑ *Negotiators have already squared away a lot of the agreements that will be signed at the Earth Summit.*

V+ADV+N,
V+N+ADV,
V+PRON+ADV

square off

1 If you **square** something **off**, you change it so that it has the shape of a square. ❑ *Peel a thick-skinned orange and square off the ends with a knife. ...white modern buildings that look like squared-off wedding cake.*

V+ADV+N,
V+N+ADV,
V+PRON+ADV

2 If one group or person **squares off** against or with another, they prepare to fight them. [AMERICAN] ❑ *In Florida, farmers are squaring off against cities for rights to groundwater... French soldiers squared off with a gunman at a road checkpoint... The Los An-geles Lakers and the Chicago Bulls square off for the first game of the season.*

V+ADV:
ALSO+against/with

square up

1 If you **square up** to a person, you stand facing them in a threatening way. ❑ *...two girls squaring up to one another. ...squaring up for a fight.*

V+ADV:
USUALLY+to

NOTE **Confront** is a more formal word for **square up**.

2 If you **square up** to a problem or difficult situation, you accept that you have to deal with it. ❑ *You've got to square up to failure and try to carry on.*

V+ADV:
USUALLY+to

3 If you **square up** with someone, you pay the bills or money that you owe them. [INFORMAL] ❑ *Do you want to square up now or later?... I've got to square up with the bank before I can pay you.*

V+ADV,
V+ADV+with:
RECIPROCAL

NOTE **Settle up** means almost the same as **square up**.

squash /skwɒʃ/ **(squashes, squashing, squashed)**

squash in If you **squash in**, you manage to get into a place where there is not much room for you. ❑ *The crowd rushed under the trees, squashing in under the shelter.*

V+ADV:
USUALLY+A

NOTE **Squeeze in** means almost the same as **squash in**.

squash into If you **squash into** a place, you manage to get inside it, even though there is not much room. ❑ *We all squashed into the room to hear him give his talk.*

V+PREP

NOTE **Squeeze into** means almost the same as **squash into**.

The symbol ★ shows key phrasal verbs

squash up If something or someone **is squashed up**, they are forced into a very small space. ❑ *Lally and the others sat squashed up inside the car... Her dress was squashed up in her case.*

V+N+ADV,
V+PRON+ADV,
V+ADV+N:
USUALLY PASSIVE

squeal /skwiːl/ **(squeals, squealing, squealed)**

squeal on If someone **squeals on** a person who has committed a crime, they inform the police about it. [INFORMAL] ❑ *Nobody's squealed on us, so just calm down.*

V+PREP

squeeze /skwiːz/ **(squeezes, squeezing, squeezed)**

★squeeze in

1 If you **squeeze in**, you manage to sit or stand in a place where there is not much room for you. ❑ *She squeezed in beside me... Can I just squeeze in there?... Two could squeeze in if they weren't too large.*

V+ADV

2 If you **squeeze** something **in**, you manage to find time to do it, even though you are busy doing other things. ❑ *You can squeeze in your hobbies and reading... The programme had been his idea, and would be squeezed in amongst his other work.*

V+ADV+N,
V+N+ADV,
V+PRON+ADV

NOTE **Fit in** means almost the same as **squeeze in**.

squeeze into If you **squeeze into** a place, you manage to get inside it, even though there is not much room. ❑ *There were so many children you could hardly squeeze into the room... Jill squeezes into the seat beside you.*

V+PREP

NOTE **Squash into** means almost the same as **squeeze into**.

squeeze off If you **squeeze off** a shot, you fire a bullet from a gun. ❑ *He aimed for the center of the man's head and squeezed off a single round.*

V+N+ADV,
V+ADV+N,
V+PRON+ADV

squeeze out

1 If you **squeeze** liquid or air **out** of something, you remove it by pressing it very hard. ❑ *Squeeze the surplus water out... The breath was being squeezed out of his lungs. ...squeezing out the final few drops.*

V+N+ADV,
V+ADV+N,
V+PRON+ADV:
ALSO+of

2 If you **squeeze** money **out** of someone, you manage to persuade them to give it to you. ❑ *Has he been able to squeeze extra cash out of his tight-fisted employer?... I bet they squeeze more out of the Welfare State than we do. ...an effort to squeeze out a little more money for wages.*

V+N+ADV,
V+ADV+N,
V+PRON+ADV:
USUALLY+of

3 If you **squeeze** someone **out** of a particular activity, you prevent them from taking part in it. ❑ *New settlement is beginning to squeeze the farmers out... Large scale bureaucracies have undoubtedly squeezed out the individual entrepreneur.*

V+N+ADV,
V+ADV+N,
V+PRON+ADV

NOTE **Exclude** is a more formal word for **squeeze out**.

squeeze through If you **squeeze through**, you manage to get through a small space. ❑ *The doorway was merely a gap, barely enough to squeeze through... She opened the gate and squeezed through... They can't squeeze through the window.*

V+ADV,
V+PREP

squirrel /skwɪrəl, AM skwɜːrəl/ **(squirrels, squirrelling, squirrelled)**

✓ American English uses the spellings **squirreling** and **squirreled**.

squirrel away If you **squirrel away** something, especially money, you put it somewhere secret or safe, so that you can use it in the future. ❑ *...funds that the chairman of the board of my company had managed to squirrel away in Switzerland.*

V+ADV+N,
V+N+ADV,
V+PRON+ADV

NOTE **Stash away** and **hoard** mean almost the same as **squirrel away**.

stack /stæk/ **(stacks, stacking, stacked)**

stack up

1 If you **stack up** a number of things, you arrange them in a tall pile. ❑ *Melanie stacked up the plates and carried them to the sink... He stacked up a few rows of stones.*

V+ADV+N,
V+N+ADV,
V+PRON+ADV

NOTE **Pile up** means almost the same as **stack up**.

2 If you ask how one person or thing **stacks up** against other people or things, you are asking how they compare with the others. [INFORMAL] ❑ *The British will be out to see how they stack up to the competition... How does this drug stack up when used on children?*

V+ADV:
ALSO+to/against,
NO PASSIVE

NOTE **Compare** is a more formal word for **stack up**.

3 If facts or figures do not **stack up**, they do not make sense or give the results you expect. ❑ *There have been a number of explanations, but none of them stack up.*

V+ADV

staff /stɑːf, stæf/ **(staffs, staffing, staffed)**

staff up When a firm **staffs up**, it increases the number of people it employs until it has the right number. ❑ *It's vital that we finish staffing up by the end of the year.*

V+ADV

stake /steɪk/ **(stakes, staking, staked)**

stake on If you **stake** money, your reputation, or something valuable **on** or **upon** the result of something, you risk losing your money or your reputation if it does not work as you thought it would. ❑ *He has staked his reputation as a prophet on this assertion... She has staked everything on what will happen when she gets there... I wouldn't like to stake my life on that.*

V+N+PREP,
V+PRON+PREP

stake out

1 If you **stake out** a particular area of land, or if you **stake out** a claim to it, you make it clear that you have a special interest in that piece of land, although you may not actually own it. ❑ *The settlers were staking out ranches and land claims on territory in the South. ...the geographical area they staked out for themselves.*

V+ADV+N,
V+N+ADV,
V+PRON+ADV

2 If you **stake out** your attitude or position on a particular issue, you define the limits or boundaries of that attitude or position. ❑ *The committee's report stakes out the new frontiers of acceptable advance... We need to challenge the position they have staked out for themselves.*

V+ADV+N,
V+N+ADV,
V+PRON+ADV

3 If someone **stakes out** a building, they stay hidden near the building in order to watch anyone who enters or leaves it. [INFORMAL] ❑ *You staked out the house to watch me walk into your trap... The police staked the flat out for twelve hours before moving in to make arrests.*

V+ADV+N,
V+N+ADV,
V+PRON+ADV

♦ A **stake-out** is a situation in which someone stays hidden near a building in order to watch anyone who enters or leaves it. [INFORMAL] ❑ *...a police stake-out.*

N-COUNT

stake upon → See stake on

stammer /stæmər/ **(stammers, stammering, stammered)**

stammer out If you **stammer** something **out**, you say it with difficulty, hesitating and repeating words or sounds because you are nervous. ❑ *Before he could stammer out his thanks, she walked away... I stammer out some sort of explanation... 'I think she's lovely,' Marsha stammered out... The father was just able to stammer out that perhaps the son should leave the room.*

V+ADV+N,
V+ADV+QUOTE,
V+ADV+REPORT,
V+N+ADV,
V+PRON+ADV

stamp /stæmp/ **(stamps, stamping, stamped)**

stamp down If you **stamp** something **down**, you lift your feet one after the other and put them down very hard on it in order to make it flatter or firmer. ❑ *She buried the money, stamping down the earth over it... He put dirt around the base of the cross, and stamped it down hard with his feet... He put the cardboard boxes in a heap and stamped them down.*

V+ADV+N,
V+PRON+ADV,
V+N+ADV

stamp on

1 If you **stamp on** something, you put your foot down on it very hard, usually in order to damage it or hurt it. ❑ *...boys who stamped on beetles when they found them... I stamped heavily on her foot and muttered, 'Shut up.'... I was kicked, struck and stamped on.*

V+PREP:
HAS PASSIVE

2 If someone **stamps on** a dishonest or undesirable activity, they act immediately to stop it happening or spreading. ❑ *The tone of her voice was designed to stamp on this topic of conversation once and for all... Mrs Amaury's story had to be stamped on before it got any further... The government's first duty is to defend the currency by stamping on inflation.*

V+PREP:
HAS PASSIVE

3 If someone or something **stamps** themselves **on** or **stamps** themselves **upon** another thing, they have a strong effect on it. **Stamp upon** is more formal. ❑ *Britain was to stamp itself upon India in a way that was to shape history for many years... He had already stamped his presence on the face of science... His class background and schooling were indelibly stamped upon his work.*

V+REFL+PREP,
V+N+PREP,
V+PRON+PREP

stamp out

1 If you **stamp** something **out**, you put an end to it or destroy it completely. ❑ *They are determined to stamp out political extremism... The rail strike was stamped out with particular brutality... The language was stamped out.*

V+ADV+N,
V+N+ADV,
V+PRON+ADV

[NOTE] **Eliminate** and **eradicate** are more formal words for **stamp out**.

2 If you **stamp out** something that is burning, you keep treading on it with your feet in order to stop it burning. ❑ *I stamped out the flaming paper with my foot... A small*

V+ADV+N,
V+PRON+ADV,
V+N+ADV

fire was going and he stamped it out... The hardly touched cigarette had been stamped out.

NOTE **Extinguish** is a more formal word for **stamp out**.

3 If something **is stamped out** by a machine or tool, it is cut out from a substance such as wood, metal, or paper. ❑ *It had been stamped out by a machine.*

V+N+ADV,
V+ADV+N,
V+PRON+ADV:
USUALLY PASSIVE

NOTE **Punch out** means almost the same as **stamp out**.

stamp upon → See stamp on

stand /stænd/ **(stands, standing, stood)**

☑ **About** is used mainly in British English. In American English, **around** is much more common than **round**.

stand about → See stand around

stand around If you **stand around**, **stand about**, or **stand round**, you stand rather aimlessly in a place because you have nothing to do. ❑ *They seemed content to stand around for a time chatting... He stood about for a little, then he went to his room. ...disconsolate passengers standing around the ticket counters.*

V+ADV,
V+PREP

stand aside

1 If you **stand aside**, you move to a position where you will not block other people. ❑ *Gareth stood aside to let him pass... I told the girls to stand aside to make way... She made them stand aside while the more important guests were served.*

V+ADV

2 If someone **stands aside**, they resign from an important job or position, often in order to let someone else take their place. [BRITISH] ❑ *The President said he was willing to stand aside if that would stop the killing.*

V+ADV

NOTE **Stand down** means almost the same as **stand aside**.

3 If you **stand aside** from a disagreement or difficult situation, you separate yourself from it and refuse to become involved in it. ❑ *We wish to stand aside from these quarrels... He had, in the past, stood aside quite passively during any arguments.*

V+ADV:
ALSO+from

★stand back

1 If you **stand back**, you move away from something or someone. ❑ *'Will you ladies kindly stand back a minute, please,' Ned said... Karin stood back a little and paused... He stood back from the doorway, allowing her to enter.*

V+ADV:
ALSO+from

2 If you **stand back** from a situation, you put yourself in a position in which you are not too closely involved in it. ❑ *I think someone ought to stand back and look critically at this issue... It can be difficult to stand back from your problems in an objective way.*

V+ADV:
ALSO+from

3 If a building **stands back** from a road or other area, it is some distance away from it. ❑ *...the Royal Hospital, standing back behind the trees... The village was hidden away, standing back from the bigger hills.*

V+ADV:
ALSO+from

NOTE **Be set back** means almost the same as **stand back**.

stand between If something or someone **stands between** you and a likely situation, it prevents that situation from arising. ❑ *...the men who stand between you and the top jobs. ...the barriers which stand between the average person and this knowledge... Damages awarded by the courts were all that stood between the family and destitution.*

V+PREP

★stand by

☑ In meaning 4, the stress is on **stand**.

1 If you **stand by** and let something unpleasant happen, you do not try to do anything to stop it. ❑ *We cannot stand by and watch while our allies are attacked... We watched the troops standing by while strikers wrecked a bus... The police were just standing by and looking on.*

V+ADV:
USUALLY+A

NOTE **Sit by** means almost the same as **stand by**.

♦ A **bystander** is a person who is present when something happens, and who sees it but does not take part in it. ❑ *Innocent bystanders can get hurt, but that is the price one has to pay in a free society.*

N-COUNT

NOTE **Onlooker** means almost the same as **bystander**.

2 If you **stand by**, you are ready to provide help or take action if it becomes necessary. ❑ *Government engineers were standing by to provide emergency repairs... Stand by with lots of water in case a fire breaks out.*

V+ADV

♦ A **stand-by** is something that is always ready to be used instead of another thing if the other thing is not available. ❑ *There's always that old stand-by, cheese on toast.*

N-SING,
N-UNCOUNT

...emergency stand-by services... It was one of three Boeings put on standby for the trip.

♦A **standby** ticket for something such as the theatre or a plane journey is a cheap ticket that you buy just before the performance starts or the plane takes off, if there are any seats left. ❑ *I've got a standby booking on a Caravelle to Brussels.* ADJECTIVE

3 If you **stand by** someone, you continue to give them help or support, especially when they are in trouble. ❑ *If they try to make you resign, we'll stand by you... He considered it his duty to stand by her.* V+PREP

NOTE **Stick by** means almost the same as **stand by**.

4 If you **stand by** an earlier decision, promise, or agreement, you continue to support it or keep it. ❑ *I said I would do it and I stand by my promise... He confirmed that his Government would stand by the NATO decision.* V+PREP

NOTE **Abide by** and **adhere to** are more formal expressions for **stand by**, and **go back on** means the opposite.

★stand down

1 If someone **stands down**, they resign from an important position, often in order to let someone else take their place. ❑ *She was asked if she was prepared to stand down in favour of a younger candidate... She has made it clear she will never stand down as monarch.* V+ADV

NOTE **Step down** means almost the same as **stand down**.

2 In a courtroom, if a witness is asked to **stand down**, they are asked to leave the witness box. ❑ *The defendant may now stand down.* V+ADV

★stand for

1 If you say that a letter or initial **stands for** a particular word or name, you mean that it is an abbreviation for that word or name. ❑ *What does GCSE stand for?... T.E.C. stands for Technical Education Certificate.* V+PREP

2 The ideas or attitudes that someone **stands for** are the ones that they support or represent. ❑ *I disagreed so fundamentally with what the party stood for... Everything you'd stood for had been condemned and ridiculed.* V+PREP

3 If someone **stands for** election or **stands for** a post that is decided by an election, they are a candidate for that post. ❑ *No-one would stand for election... He stood for Governor of New York... It is very difficult to stand for local government as an independent.* V+PREP

4 If you will not **stand for** something, you will not allow it to happen or continue. ❑ *He warned that the Army would not stand for it much longer... They would not stand for their obstruction by secretive bureaucratic means.* V+PREP: WITH NEGATIVE

NOTE **Put up with** means almost the same as **stand for**, and **tolerate** is a more formal word.

stand in If you **stand in** for someone, you take their place or do their job, because they are ill or not there. ❑ *You will stand in for me at the meeting?... Goin had volunteered to stand in for the now absent Heyter... She stood in for me several times.* V+ADV: USUALLY+for

♦ A **stand-in** is a person who takes someone else's place or does someone else's job because the other person is ill or not there. ❑ *If you employ a home help, make sure your stand-in is liked by the children.* N-COUNT

stand off If you **stand** someone **off**, you stop them from coming close to you or interfering with what you are doing. ❑ *She stood off curious intruders by day and by night... You were the only one who could stand off the old man.* V+ADV+N, V+N+ADV, V+PRON+ADV: NO PASSIVE

★stand out

1 If something **stands out**, it can be seen very clearly. ❑ *The name on the van stood out clearly... The bones of his face stood out like a skeleton's.* V+ADV

2 If something **stands out** from other things of the same kind, it is much better or much more important than those other things. ❑ *Two findings stand out as particularly significant... The Australian tour stands out as the most satisfying and enjoyable of them all... There was one episode which stood out from the rest.* V+ADV: ALSO+from

♦ A **stand-out** is something which is much better or more important than other things of the same kind. ❑ *'Winona' is a stand-out, a great pop song.* N-COUNT

♦ A **stand-out** person or object is one which is much better or more important than others of the same kind. ❑ *Paul was a stand-out performer in that match.* ADJECTIVE

♦ Something or someone that is **outstanding** is much better or more important ADJECTIVE than other things of the same kind. ❏ *She would never be an outstanding actress... There are significant exceptions, of which oil is the outstanding example.*

3 If a debt or a problem is still **outstanding**, it has not yet been paid or solved. ❏ *There is fifty pounds outstanding, I believe. ...an outstanding problem that needs working on.* ADJECTIVE

stand out against If you **stand out against** something, you remain opposed to it, even though a lot of other people do not agree with you. ❏ *It's no easy thing for a politician to stand out against the tide of materialism... He alone had stood out against the hunting of whales.* V+ADV+PREP

stand out for If you **stand out for** something, you want it and refuse to accept anything else. ❏ *The union decided to stand out for its original claim.* V+ADV+PREP

NOTE **Hold out for** and **stick out for** mean almost the same as **stand out for**.

stand over If you **stand over** someone, you stand very close to them, usually because you want to watch what they are doing. ❏ *He wasn't hungry, but she stood over him and made him eat his lunch... The wardens had to stand over them while they scrubbed it.* V+PREP

stand round → See stand around

★stand up

1 If you **stand up**, you change your position so that you are standing rather than sitting or lying. ❏ *Lewis Jones refused to stand up when he came into the room... Can you imagine standing up in the middle of a hall and saying what you think?... I put down my glass and stood up.* V+ADV

NOTE **Get up** means almost the same as **stand up**.

♦ **Stand-up** comedy is comedy in which a comedian stands alone in front of an audience and tells jokes. ❏ *...a stand-up comedian.* ADJECTIVE

♦ A **stand-up** fight or argument is one in which people hit or shout at each other in an unrestrained way. ❏ *It started as a quarrel but turned into a stand-up fight.* ADJECTIVE

2 If something such as a claim or piece of evidence **stands up**, it is accepted as true. ❏ *The prosecution had no evidence which would stand up in a court of law... These claims just don't stand up.* V+ADV

3 If you **stand** someone **up**, especially someone you are just beginning a romantic relationship with, you fail to keep an arrangement to meet them. [INFORMAL] ❏ *I feel really bad about standing you up that day... I think I've been stood up.* V+PRON+ADV, V+N+ADV

stand up for If you **stand up for** a person or principle that is being attacked or criticized, you take forceful action in order to defend that person or principle. ❏ *I'm glad to see that he's standing up for himself... Only one man stood up for me and he was jeered. ...people who stood up for human rights... Don't be afraid to stand up for your rights.* V+ADV+PREP

NOTE **Defend** means almost the same as **stand up for**.

stand up to

1 If something or someone **stands up to** rough treatment, they survive it and remain unharmed. ❏ *This carpet stands up to the wear and tear of continual use... The economy would not stand up to wartime pressures... My mother stood up to the whole ordeal.* V+ADV+PREP

2 If you **stand up to** someone, especially someone more powerful than you are, you defend yourself against their attacks or demands. ❏ *He's too weak to stand up to her... Why didn't you stand up to Phillip more if you dislike him so much?* V+ADV+PREP

stare /steə^r/ (stares, staring, stared)

stare down → See stare out

stare out If you **stare** someone **out** or **stare** them **down**, you stare into their eyes intensely until you make them look away, thus showing that they accept your authority or superiority. ❏ *Wasps should be either stared out or engaged in mortal combat... Her mother tried to stare Hagen down.* V+N+ADV, V+PRON+ADV

start /stɑː^rt/ (starts, starting, started)

start back

1 If you **start back** somewhere, you begin returning to or towards the place where V+ADV:

you have come from. ❑ *She started slowly back to the bedroom... We started back on the long journey home... Some were fearful of starting back north.* `USUALLY+A`

2 If you **start back**, you move suddenly backwards because something has shocked or startled you. ❑ *I might cause her to start back in revulsion and terror... The next moment she started back and I heard her catch her breath sharply.* `V+ADV`

start in If you **start in** on a task or subject, you begin to do it or to deal with it. ❑ *It proves if you start in early enough, you can do it... We went back into the living-room and started in on breakfast.* `V+ADV: ALSO+on`

⋆start off

1 When people or vehicles **start off**, they begin to move and go somewhere. ❑ *When they started off again he was unconscious... It started off down Cresta Ridge Drive, negotiating each hairpin... We were due to start off for Branscombe Castle at eleven sharp.* `V+ADV: USUALLY+A`

NOTE **Move off** and **set off** mean almost the same as **start off**.

2 To **start off** in a particular state, position, or manner means to be in that state or position or to act in that manner at the beginning of a process, existence, or career. ❑ *...those who start off at the very bottom of the social scale... All rice starts off brown... I started off as a bookseller in Bristol... Let's start off by sorting out who is involved.* `V+ADV: USUALLY+A`

3 To **start** someone **off** means to cause them to begin doing something. ❑ *I shall start them off and let them finish four or five tasks... The mention of their names could start her off again.* `V+PRON+ADV, V+N+ADV`

4 To **start** a process **off** means to cause it to begin. ❑ *...the event which starts off the growth of a cancer tumour... I asked a simple little question to start the interview off... I suspect she started it off – picked the poor beast up wrongly.* `V+ADV+N, V+N+ADV, V+PRON+ADV`

♦ The **starting-off** point of a process or project is the time or the stage of development when it begins. ❑ *...the starting-off point for a fairer housing policy.* `ADJECTIVE`

⋆start on

1 If you **start on** something that needs to be done, you begin doing it or dealing with it. ❑ *She put the forks in a neat pile and started on the knives... We want to start her on music lessons soon. ...a bad day on which to start on anything of importance.* `V+PREP, V+N+PREP, V+PRON+PREP: HAS PASSIVE`

2 If you **start on** someone, you treat them severely or unfairly, for example by criticizing them, teasing them, or hitting them. [INFORMAL] ❑ *I warn you, don't start on my father!... They started on Jim over the Welsh business... They start on him and he gets so embarrassed.* `V+PREP`

⋆start out

1 If you **start out**, you begin to move and go somewhere. ❑ *They started out to church. ...longing to start out for Hayport.* `V+ADV: USUALLY+A`

NOTE **Set off**, **set out**, and **start off** mean almost the same as **start out**.

2 To **start out** doing something or being something means to do it or be it at the beginning of a situation, process, career, or existence. ❑ *What started out as fun for the parents becomes an endless chore... We have to start out by understanding managers... A bruise would start out black and blue, then become purple.* `V+ADV: USUALLY+A`

NOTE **Start off** means almost the same as **start out**, and **end up** means the opposite.

3 If you **start out** to do something, you intend to do it. ❑ *You've done what you started out to do... She doesn't have anything to do with what I originally started out to say.* `V+ADV: WITH to-INF`

NOTE **Set out** means almost the same as **start out**.

start over If you **start over**, you begin doing something right from the beginning again, for example because you did it wrong last time or you have decided to do something different. ❑ *You must go back to the beginning and start over again... How will you earn your living then, starting over at thirty, thirty-five, even?* `V+ADV`

⋆start up

1 If you **start up** a new business or organization, or if it **starts up**, you organize or arrange it and it begins to operate. ❑ *She wanted to start up a little country pub... They've just started up a discussion group in Plotinus... Every year many people decide to start up in business.* `V+ADV+N, V+N+ADV, V+PRON+ADV, V+ADV: ERGATIVE`

NOTE **Set up** means almost the same as **start up**.

♦ **Start-up** money is used to organize or arrange a new business, organization, or activity. ❑ ...start-up costs.   ADJECTIVE

2 If you **start up** an engine or a motor vehicle, or if it **starts up**, you make it begin to operate. ❑ The officer got in and started up the motor... He limped back to the cycle, leapt on and started it up... There was a car starting up in the background.   V+ADV+N, V+N/PRON+ADV, V+ADV: ERGATIVE

3 If you are sitting quietly or sleeping and **start up**, you move suddenly into a sitting or standing position because you are startled or surprised by something. ❑ 'Oh no!' she cried, starting up suddenly from the pillow... They dozed off until Michael suddenly started up anxiously and looked at his watch.   V+ADV: USUALLY+A

4 If a sound, activity, or event **starts up** or if you **start** it **up**, it begins to be heard or to take place. ❑ The music started up in the Ballroom. ...months of waiting for trade to start up again... The rain has started up again... The book, when published, would start up a literary controversy.   V+ADV, V+ADV+N, V+PRON+ADV: ERGATIVE

5 You refer to someone as an **upstart** when they behave as if they are important, but you think that they are too new in a place or job to be treated as important; used showing disapproval. ❑ We have to put this upstart in his place.   N-COUNT

starve /stɑːrv/ (starves, starving, starved)

starve for If you **are starved for** something, you have not had much of it for some time and you want some. ❑ I was so starved for a bit of natural light... I'm starved for the taste of rare midwestern beef... They were starved for some kind of affection which he never gave.   PASSIVE: V+PREP

starve into If someone **is starved into** a state or action, they are given no food and so are forced to enter that state or do that action. ❑ They can be starved into retreat, but not into submission. ...damage their health by starving themselves into a state of emaciation.   V+N+PREP, V+PRON+PREP, V+REFL+PREP: USUALLY PASSIVE

starve of If someone or something **is starved of** something they need, they do not get enough of it and therefore suffer. ❑ He was obviously starved of decent home cooking... By neglecting black talent, the British theatre could be starving itself of a vital new force.   V+N+PREP, V+PRON+PREP, V+REFL+PREP: USUALLY PASSIVE

starve out To **starve out** a group of people means to force them to surrender or leave a place by not giving them any food. ❑ In a short time the soldiers starved us out. ...the inhumanity of starving out a civilian population.   V+PRON+ADV, V+ADV+N, V+N+ADV

stash /stæʃ/ (stashes, stashing, stashed)

stash away

1 If you **stash away** money or valuable things, you hide them or put them somewhere because you are saving the money or collecting the things. ❑ ...those who stash away their funds in Swiss bank accounts... She rose early and hurried to stash the bills away in safety... I stashed it away with all the others.   V+ADV+N, V+N+ADV, V+PRON+ADV

2 If you **stash** someone **away**, you hide them somewhere, for example because they are in danger. ❑ The kid was stashed away with her sister in the Bronx... Mel suspected she had a lover somewhere, stashed away.   V+ADV+N, V+PRON+ADV, V+N+ADV: USUALLY PASSIVE

stave /steɪv/ (staves, staving, staved)

stave off To **stave off** an unpleasant event means to prevent it happening. ❑ There wasn't much that Abel could have done to stave off disaster... Batik cannot stave off the challenge from cheaper machine-made prints... Chrysler staved off bankruptcy earlier this year.   V+ADV+N, V+PRON+ADV, V+N+ADV

NOTE **Avert** is a more formal word for **stave off**.

stay /steɪ/ (stays, staying, stayed)

stay ahead If you **stay ahead** of someone or something, you manage to remain in a better position than them. ❑ That way you'll only just stay ahead of inflation... To stay ahead of them would cost money... Successful firms must stay ahead in the technology race.   V+ADV: USUALLY+of

★**stay away** If you **stay away** from a place, you do not go there. ❑ As yet he had never stayed away for a night... This town is unsafe: stay away from here... You get fed up being picked on, so you stay away from school.   V+ADV: ALSO+from

★stay away from

1 If you **stay away from** a person, you try to avoid meeting them or talking to them. ❑ *My instructions are to stay away from him.*   V+ADV+PREP

2 If you **stay away from** an activity or subject, you avoid doing the activity or talking about the subject. ❑ *Underdeveloped countries will focus on economic issues and stay away from politics... I had stayed away from problems of definition.*   V+ADV+PREP

stay back If you **stay back** in a place, you remain there and do not move forward or leave, even if other people do. ❑ *Stay back here a moment with me until you get used to it... I stayed back home, studying half-heartedly... Stay back behind the barrier.*   V+ADV: USUALLY+A

stay behind If you **stay behind**, you remain in a place after most of the other people have gone. ❑ *You can just stay behind and do it over again... Why had she not stayed behind to talk to them? ...the people who had stayed behind after independence.*   V+ADV
NOTE **Remain** is a more formal word for **stay behind**.

stay down

1 If a swimmer or diver **stays down**, they remain underwater. ❑ *If he controlled his breathing, he could stay down for at least half an hour more... I was eventually able to stay down for over three and a half minutes.*   V+ADV

2 If food that you have eaten **stays down**, you do not vomit. ❑ *Meals stay down better when they consist entirely of solids... If this stays down and she begs for more, let her have it.*   V+ADV

★stay in

If you **stay in**, you remain at home rather than going out and enjoying yourself. ❑ *She had to stay in and do the dishes... We stayed in the whole evening, didn't go to the disco at all.*   V+ADV
NOTE **Stop in** means almost the same as **stay in**, and **go out** means the opposite.

stay off If you **stay off**, you do not go to work or school, for example because you are ill. ❑ *If I'm not better, I think I shall stay off tomorrow.*   V+ADV

★stay on

If you **stay on** somewhere, you remain there longer than other people, longer than in the past, or longer than you planned. ❑ *Pupils have to stay on at school till they are 16... He can stay on for three months... He had stayed on to have a drink.*   V+ADV
NOTE **Leave** means the opposite of **stay on**.

★stay out

1 If you **stay out**, you remain away from home, especially when you are expected to be there. ❑ *We stayed out all night... Her mother didn't like her to stay out late.*   V+ADV
NOTE **Stop out** means almost the same as **stay out**.

2 If workers who are on strike **stay out**, they remain on strike. [BRITISH] ❑ *The men stayed out for the best part of a year... The 400 women at the factory stayed out on strike for eleven weeks.*   V+ADV

★stay out of

1 If you **stay out of** a place, you do not enter it. ❑ *His family paid him to stay out of Britain... Tell everybody to stay out of the bathroom for the next half an hour.*   V+ADV+PREP

2 If you **stay out of** a situation or activity, you do not get involved or take part in it. ❑ *We've begged them a thousand times to stay out of this fight... I stayed out of the social life of the school... You made a wise choice by staying out of this thing.*   V+ADV+PREP
NOTE **Keep out of** means almost the same as **stay out of**.

stay over If you visit someone and decide to **stay over**, you spend the night there instead of leaving. ❑ *Better yet, come Monday, stay over, and go on from here Tuesday.*   V+ADV

★stay up

If you **stay up**, you go to bed much later than usual. ❑ *Nobody would stay up to give us any supper when we got back... They seem to stay up until the parents themselves go to bed... He must have stayed up working all night.*   V+ADV
NOTE **Stop up** means almost the same as **stay up**.

stay with If you **stay with** a fact, a task, an attitude, or a situation, you continue using it, doing it, having it, or being involved with it, rather than changing it or doing something else. ❑ *Let us stay with the official figure for the Flanders campaign. ...the discipline to keep persevering, to stay with the battle... We cannot stay with that questioning mood for long.*   V+PREP

steal /stiːl/ (steals, stealing, stole, stolen)

steal away If you **steal away** from a place or a task, you leave it quietly or secretly. [LITERARY] ❏ *Ralph stole away through the branches. ...whenever he could steal away from his duties.*

V+ADV:
USUALLY+A

steal over If light **steals over** a place, it gradually shines more brightly on it. [LITERARY] ❏ *We'll have dinner and talk until the dawn steals over the Blue Mountains... The sun rose and a broad streak of light stole over the ship.*

V+PREP

steal up If you **steal up** on someone, you move quietly until you are next to them, and surprise them or attack them. [LITERARY] ❏ *We could steal up on one – paint our faces so they wouldn't see... 'Nice view,' said the youth, who had stolen up silently behind him.*

V+ADV:
ALSO+on

NOTE **Sneak up** and **creep up** mean almost the same as **steal up**.

steam /stiːm/ (steams, steaming, steamed)

steam away If a kettle or saucepan **is steaming away**, it is producing steam continually, often because someone has forgotten to switch it off or reduce the heat. ❏ *The kettle was steaming away on the Primus stove.*

V+ADV

steam off If one thing is stuck to another and you **steam** it **off**, you remove it from the other thing by using steam to melt the glue. ❏ *You can steam the stamps off the envelopes.*

V+N+ADV/PREP,
V+PRON+ADV/PREP

steam up

1 If something made of glass such as a window or mirror **steams up**, it becomes covered with steam or mist. ❏ *My glasses steamed up as soon as I walked into the room... The windows always get steamed up when I'm cooking... 'You saved?' he bellowed suspiciously to the newcomer, steaming up the glass as he spoke.*

V+ADV,
V+ADV+N:
ERGATIVE

NOTE **Mist up** means almost the same as **steam up**.

2 If someone is **steamed up**, they are very annoyed, angry, or excited about something. ❏ *My friend was very steamed up about this project... What was she getting so steamed up about?*

ADJECTIVE

NOTE **Het up** means almost the same as **steamed up**.

steer /stɪəʳ/ (steers, steering, steered)

steer away from If you **steer away from** a subject or action, you avoid talking about it or doing it. ❏ *I like to steer away from serious topics... Kitty was steering all the conversation away from any talk of herself... The reporters had some information that he had to steer them away from.*

V+ADV+PREP,
V+N+ADV+PREP,
V+PRON+ADV+PREP

stem /stɛm/ (stems, stemming, stemmed)

★stem from If a situation or problem **stems from** something, it was caused by that thing. ❏ *Attitudes like these stem from ignorance. ...the obvious risks which stem from regular alcohol drinking.*

V+PREP

step /stɛp/ (steps, stepping, stepped)

step aside → See step down

step back

1 If you **step back** from a problem or situation, you try to think about it again in a fresh way, ignoring previous ideas or personal feelings. ❏ *Step back and look at how little a young adult often has to spend... It is tempting to step back and ask whether it is worth introducing such a complicated scheme.*

V+ADV

NOTE **Stand back** means almost the same as **step back**.

2 If you **step back** into a previous situation, you return to being in it or feel as if you have returned to it. ❏ *Many women would willingly step back into the manual or service work in which they started... You feel, as you land, that you have stepped back two hundred million years.*

V+ADV

★step down If you **step down** or **step aside** from an important job or position, you resign from it, often in order to let someone else take your place. ❏ *Robert offered to step down if that would promote negotiations. ...before stepping down last month because of illness. ...if I stepped aside as vice-presidential candidate.*

V+ADV

NOTE **Stand down** means almost the same as **step down**.

step forward In a difficult situation, if someone **steps forward**, they offer to help. ❏ *The Russians stepped forward and offered to pay the entire cost... Close relatives im-*

V+ADV

mediately stepped forward to take their place.

★step in In a difficult situation, if you **step in**, you get involved in it and try to   V+ADV
help. ❑ *She really appreciates the way you stepped in and saw to things... The government
has often had to step in to protect employees from employers... David stepped in quickly. 'I
think you had better apologize.'*
NOTE **Intervene** is a more formal word for **step in**.

step on If you tell the driver of a car to **step on** it, you are telling him or her to   IMPERATIVE,
drive fast, because you are in a hurry. ❑ *We'll have to step on it to get to Winchester by*   V+PREP+*it*
eight.

step out
1 If someone **steps out** of a role or situation, they leave it. ❑ *I don't regret stepping*   V+ADV:
out of the security of marriage.   USUALLY+*of*

2 If someone **steps out**, they appear in public, especially wearing particular clothes   V+ADV:
or with a particular boyfriend or girlfriend. [INFORMAL] ❑ *Raise a few eyebrows by step-*   ALSO+*with*,
ping out in these tiny shorts this summer... She is said to be stepping out with actor Matt   RECIPROCAL
Dillon.

★step up
1 If you **step up** something, you increase the speed, amount, or extent of it.   V+ADV+N,
❑ *...when a nation decides to step up arms production... Now if you want to step your volt-*   V+N+ADV,
age up it's quite simple... Congress have been stepping up their preparations for the final   V+PRON+ADV
showdown.
♦ A **step-up** in something is an increase in its speed, amount, or extent. ❑ *...a step-*   N-SING
up in the pace of life... There has been a marked step-up in police activity.
2 If you **step up**, you take responsibility for something or agree to do something.   V+ADV:
❑ *We hope people will step up and say, I'll be a leader in my community.*   ALSO+*to*

stick /stɪk/ (sticks, sticking, stuck)

stick around If you **stick around**, you stay where you are, often because you   V+ADV,
are waiting for something. [INFORMAL] ❑ *Mike wanted me to stick around for a couple of*   V+PREP
days... Maybe I'll just stick around here a while... There's nothing else to stick around for.
NOTE **Hang around** means almost the same as **stick around**.

stick at
1 To **stick at** a particular amount, stage, or point in a process means to stop and   V+PREP:
not increase, decrease, change, or progress. ❑ *These will probably stick at roughly the*   ALSO PASSIVE:
same levels as in 1975... If he sticks at a word or stumbles over a phrase, don't rush in... We   V+PREP
all seemed to be stuck at this level of development.

2 If you **stick at** a task or job, you continue working at it or trying as hard as you   V+PREP,
can, even if it is very difficult or unpleasant. ❑ *It's been very tricky and I've had to stick*   V+PREP+*it*
*at it... If she stuck at it she would have her degree in two years... Their grandfather never
stuck at one job for more than a week.*
NOTE **Persevere** is a more formal word for **stick at**, and **keep at** and **stick to**
mean almost the same.

stick back If you **stick** something **back** somewhere, you put it there or attach   V+N+ADV,
it there again, after it has fallen off, broken off, or been taken away for a while.   V+PRON+ADV:
[INFORMAL] ❑ *He stuck the knife back in his belt... She closed up the big atlas and stuck it*   USUALLY+A
back on the shelf... They mixed some glue and stuck it back on the handle.

stick by
1 If you **stick by** someone, you continue to give them help or support, especially   V+PREP
when they are in difficulty. ❑ *It was her duty to stick by dear James through thick and
thin... Despite her husband's appalling life of crime, she had stuck faithfully by him... He was
a good officer who stuck by his men when they got into trouble.*
NOTE **Stand by** means almost the same as **stick by**, and **abandon** and **desert**
mean the opposite.
2 If you **stick by** something, you continue to use it or believe in it and do not   V+PREP
change your mind. ❑ *We stick by what we have argued all through this book... I stick by
the traditional club which has stood the test of time.*
NOTE **Adhere to** is a more formal expression for **stick by**, and **abandon** means
the opposite.

stick down

1 If you **stick** something **down** somewhere, you put it there. [INFORMAL] ❑ *I saw him stick two fingers down into it and withdrew a white peppermint... I just stuck this thing down here as I left... Tell me precisely why you stuck that doll down that hole.*

V+N+ADV/PREP,
V+PRON+ADV/PREP

2 If you **stick** something **down**, you seal it or attach it firmly to something else, usually by using glue or tape and then pressing it. ❑ *Fill out the coupons, copy the address, add the five pounds, and stick down the envelope... Pictures could be stuck down at odd angles, and the page could be assembled.*

V+ADV+N,
V+N+ADV,
V+PRON+ADV

3 If you **stick** something **down** on paper, you write or draw it quickly or roughly. [INFORMAL] ❑ *Just stick it down and we'll look at it properly later... He'd stuck my name down on the list.*

V+PRON+ADV,
V+N+ADV,
V+ADV+N

★stick in

> ✓ In meaning 4, the stress is on **stick**.

1 If you **stick** someone or something **in** a place or container, you cause them to go in there or put them in there. [INFORMAL] ❑ *No, don't just stick it in your pocket... I do sometimes stick papers and books in there... We didn't stick them in hospital... Her thumb was stuck firmly in her mouth and she was fast asleep.*

V+PRON+PREP,
V+N+PREP

2 If you **stick** something sharp **in** something solid, you cause it to pierce the surface and stay there. ❑ *These darts are rigged. Some of them don't stick in the board... A garden fork had been left sticking in the newly-dug ground... I hit him! The spear stuck in... One of them stuck a needle in its spine.*

V+ADV,
V+PREP,
V+N+ADV/PREP,
V+PRON+ADV/PREP:
ERGATIVE

3 If you **stick** something **in** something, you attach it there firmly using glue or tape. ❑ *I soon tired of sticking in stamps... He stuck a Labour poster in his window.*

V+ADV+N,
V+N+PREP/ADV,
V+PRON+PREP/ADV

4 If something **sticks in** your mind or memory, you continue to remember it very clearly. ❑ *This strange conversation was to stick in Meehan's mind. ...behaviour which sticks in the popular consciousness... They stuck in your memory... They haunted my eyes and stuck in my dreams.*

V+PREP

5 If you are writing or drawing and **stick** something **in**, you write it or draw it roughly or quickly. [INFORMAL] ❑ *Better stick in there: 'possibility of Birmingham'... I've endeavoured to avoid boring legal jargon in this book; I stick it in only when it is vital.*

V+N+ADV/PREP,
V+PRON+ADV/PREP

NOTE **Take out** and **remove** mean the opposite of **stick in**.

6 If you have a difficult task or a lot of work to do and get **stuck in**, you start doing it, usually with a lot of energy or enthusiasm. [INFORMAL] ❑ *We rolled up our sleeves, got stuck in and made a start... They have to get stuck in for once. It is no good waiting.*

ADJECTIVE

★stick on

1 If you **stick** something **on** a surface, you attach it to the surface using glue, tape, or drawing pins. ❑ *Stick a numbered label on each case... Cut out interesting items from newspapers and stick them on noticeboards... He saw a picture of Stanley Baldwin stuck on the wall... The hat seems to be stuck on with glue... Bandages won't stick on the palm.*

V+N+PREP/ADV,
V+PRON+PREP/ADV,
V+ADV+N,
V+ADV:
ERGATIVE

♦ **Stick-on** things have a layer of glue on one side so that they can be attached to surfaces easily. ❑ *Label fuses with stick-on labels.*

ADJECTIVE

♦ **Stuck-on** things have been attached to a surface with glue or adhesive. ❑ *...the first page covered by a stuck-on tab of paper.*

ADJECTIVE

2 If you **stick** one thing **on** another, you place it on there casually or carelessly. [INFORMAL] ❑ *She poked away at the fire, stuck on another lump of coal. ...the bottles going clink clink as Pa stuck them on the stack. ...an orange hat stuck on her dark red curls.*

V+ADV+N,
V+PRON+ADV/PREP,
V+N+ADV/PREP

3 If you **are stuck on** an object or idea, you like it very much. [INFORMAL] ❑ *...after it was all arranged, and they were absolutely stuck on it... The government isn't going to get stuck on any set of fancy doctrinaire ideas.*

PASSIVE:
V+PREP

★stick out

1 If you **stick** something **out**, you push it so that it appears from inside or behind something else. ❑ *Lally stuck her head out of a window... Lynn stuck out her tongue... Is that tummy really all fat or do you stick it out when you are standing?*

V+N+ADV,
V+ADV+N,
V+PRON+ADV

2 If something **sticks out**, it extends beyond something else, because of its length or because of the direction in which it is pointing. ❑ *...if the arm is sticking out... There was a little chimney sticking out of the roof... She sat on the beach, her bony legs sticking straight out in front of her... He looked at the crumpled bills sticking out between his fingers.*

V+ADV:
USUALLY+A

NOTE **Protrude** is a more formal word for **stick out**.

3 If a quality or feature of someone or something **sticks out**, it is very obvious or noticeable. ❏ ...*a home that would not stick out on a European or North American estate... She was going out with someone else tonight: that had stuck out a mile.* V+ADV

NOTE **Stand out** means almost the same as **stick out**.

4 If you **stick out** a difficult or unpleasant situation, you continue being involved in it, rather than leaving it. ❏ *Sometimes I wonder if I can stick this job out much longer... I stuck it out until the situation became ugly... The women have stuck it out and won what they were fighting for.* V+N+ADV, V+PRON+ADV

NOTE **Endure** is a more formal word for **stick out**.

stick out for If you **stick out for** something, you keep demanding it until you get it, and do not accept anything different or less than you have asked for. ❏ *He stuck out for twice the usual salary, and got it.* V+ADV+PREP

NOTE **Hold out for** means almost the same as **stick out for**.

★stick to

1 If a substance or object **sticks to** a surface, it becomes accidentally attached to it and is difficult to remove. ❏ ...*powdered sand that sticks to your hair and skin. ...the invalid, whose clothes were sticking to him... The eggs scorched and stuck to the pan.* V+PREP

NOTE **Adhere to** is a more formal word for **stick to**.

2 If you **stick to** what you have decided to do or what you are expected to do, you continue doing it in the same way, even if you would prefer not to or if people try to make you change. ❏ *I was pleased to see the lads were sticking to their task... 'Of course we'll stick to our policy,' said McPherson. ...unless they stick to their promise... Stick strictly to the diet to gain full relief... I have my own likes and dislikes and choose to stick to them... I didn't have to stick to any set route.* V+PREP

NOTE **Keep to** means almost the same as **stick to**.

3 If you **stick to** something or someone when you are travelling, you stay close to them. ❏ *There are interesting hikes inland, but most ramblers stick to the clifftops... Stick to well-lit roads.* V+PREP

4 If you are talking and **stick to** a subject, you talk only about that subject, and not about anything else. ❏ *Let me stick to painting for a moment... I think we should stick to the point... Stick to the facts.* V+PREP

NOTE **Keep to** means almost the same as **stick to**.

5 If you **stick to** rules, you do what they say you must do. ❏ *Obviously we are disappointed but the committee could do nothing less than stick to the rules... Police must stick to the highest standards if they are to win back public confidence.* V+PREP

6 If you **stick to** someone, you keep supporting and trusting them, especially when they are in a difficult situation. ❏ *She is sticking to her husband through thick and thin. ...under the circumstances Dolores had better stick to her old man.* V+PREP

NOTE **Stand by** and **stick by** mean almost the same as **stick to**.

★stick together

1 If you **stick** things or parts **together**, you attach or fix them to each other. ❏ *When I come back, we'll stick them together again... Once they'd made all the bits it would be cheaper to stick them together in the factory... I have struggled like that to stick together different materials with unsuitable glue.* V+PRON+ADV, V+ADV+N, V+N+ADV

2 If things **stick together**, they become attached to each other and are difficult to separate. ❏ *Their feathers stick together if they don't keep them warm... I don't want to move in case my nails stick together. ...shaking the chips to loosen the few which had stuck together.* V+ADV

3 If people **stick together**, they stay with each other and support each other, especially when they are in a difficult situation. ❏ *We have to stick together to guard against outside meddlers... Life was none too easy in the colony, but the boys learnt to stick together... Only by sticking together will they improve conditions.* V+ADV

★stick up

1 If you **stick up** a picture, notice, or object, you attach it to a wall or noticeboard so that it can be seen. ❏ *They stick up pictures of women all round the rooms... She suggests that women stick up a notice in their Welfare Clinic... 'You don't mind if I stick this up?' Donald held up a crucifix.* V+ADV+N, V+PRON+ADV, V+N+ADV

2 If something long **sticks up**, it points upwards in an upright position. ❏ ...*a nail* V+ADV:

sticking up from a board. ...his long legs bent, his knees sticking up towards his chin... Above the forehead the tufts of grey hair stuck up at all angles.   USUALLY+A

NOTE **Protrude** and **project** are more formal words for **stick up**.

3 If you **stick** something **up** somewhere, you push it inside there with some force. [INFORMAL] ❏ They're always sticking up potatoes up my exhaust pipe.   V+N+PREP, V+PRON+PREP

4 If someone **sticks up** a bank, a shop, or a person, they rob them, using a gun as a threat. [AMERICAN] ❏ If I wanted to stick up a bank, I'd do it just before a long weekend... Did they ever catch the robbers that stuck up your friend?... I didn't think the bank was going to get stuck up today.   V+ADV+N, V+N+ADV

NOTE **Hold up** means almost the same as **stick up**.

♦ A **stick-up** is a robbery in which the thieves use guns. [AMERICAN, OLD-FASHIONED] ❏ Poor guy. Was it a stick-up?   N-COUNT

5 If you describe someone as **stuck-up**, you mean that they think they are very important or high class and are not friendly; used showing disapproval. [INFORMAL] ❏ ...a small company where no one is stuck-up.   ADJECTIVE

stick up for If you **stick up for** a person, a principle, or a belief, you support or defend them, using force if necessary. ❏ I'll stick up for you... I was too small to stick up for my rights. ...at a public school you have to be able to stick up for yourself.   V+ADV+PREP

NOTE **Stand up for** means almost the same as **stick up for**.

⋆stick with

1 If you **stick with** something, you continue to use it or do it, and do not change to something else. ❏ I stuck with what was to be my staple diet: brown rice... Will they stick with the business or run off to start something else?... Jim and Ginny had such difficulty ever sticking with anything.   V+PREP

NOTE **Stick at** and **stick to** mean almost the same as **stick with**.

2 If you **stick with** someone, you stay close to them. ❏ Stick with me and you'll be okay, don't you worry... Ducret shouted to the driver to stick with the President... I'll stick with him, step by step.   V+PREP

3 If you **are stuck with** someone or something, you feel that you did not choose them and do not like them or want them, but you do not have the power to change the situation. ❏ ...some useless secretary he was stuck with... They sell everything they have got for fear of being stuck with a load of cheap goods.   PASSIVE: V+PREP

4 If an idea or memory **sticks with** you, you continue to remember it for a long time. ❏ One note of memory stuck with him: singing with Nino Valenti... That idea stuck with me. It's simple, but it is dynamic... It's funny how some things stick with you.   V+PREP

stiffen /stɪfən/ (stiffens, stiffening, stiffened)

stiffen up If your muscles or joints **stiffen up**, or if something **stiffens** them **up**, they become difficult to bend or move.. ❏ These clothes restrict your freedom of movement and stiffen up the whole body... I just stiffened up, and the more they told me to 'be natural', the more I felt not at all relaxed.   V+N+ADV, V+ADV+N, V+PRON+ADV, V+ADV: ERGATIVE

stir /stɜːr/ (stirs, stirring, stirred)

⋆stir in If you **stir** a substance **in**, you mix it with another substance, using a tool such as a spoon. ❏ When the yeast is dissolved, stir the flour in gradually... She had stirred in the sugar.   V+N+ADV, V+ADV+N, V+PRON+ADV

NOTE **Mix in** means almost the same as **stir in**.

stir into If you **stir** one substance **into** another, you mix it with the other substance so that the two substances are blended together. ❏ He stirred some cream into his coffee... Strain the liquid and stir this into the margarine and flour... The gelatine can be stirred into a hot liquid or custard until dissolved.   V+N+PREP, V+PRON+PREP

NOTE **Mix into** means almost the same as **stir into**.

⋆stir up

1 If something **stirs up** dust or mud, it causes it to rise and move around. ❏ Some gentle winds stirred up the dust.   V+ADV+N, V+N+ADV, V+PRON+ADV

NOTE **Disturb** is a more formal word for **stir up**.

2 To **stir up** trouble or **stir up** a feeling means to cause trouble or to cause people to have the feeling. ❏ He was prevented from speaking on the grounds that it would 'stir up trouble'. ...a rally called to stir up popular support for nuclear disarmament... Being back   V+ADV+N, V+N+ADV, V+PRON+ADV in the hospital stirred up unpleasant memories... *She was one of those people who likes stirring things up.*

NOTE Provoke and **incite** are more formal words for **stir up**.

stitch /stɪtʃ/ (stitches, stitching, stitched)
stitch up
1 When doctors **stitch up** an open wound, they use a special needle and thread to join the edges of it together so that it is completely closed. ❑ *My mother took a needle in her hand to stitch up terrible wounds... She scraped the dirt out of my wounds and stitched up one finger.*

V+ADV+N,
V+N+ADV,
V+PRON+ADV

NOTE Sew up means almost the same as **stitch up**, and **suture** is a more technical word.

2 To **stitch** someone **up** means to trick them so that they are put in a difficult or unpleasant situation, especially one where they are blamed for something they have not done. [BRITISH, INFORMAL] ❑ *He claimed that a police officer had threatened to stitch him up and send him to prison.*

V+N+ADV,
V+ADV+N,
V+PRON+ADV

NOTE Frame is a more formal word for **stitch up**.

3 To **stitch up** an agreement, especially a complicated agreement between several people, means to arrange it. [BRITISH, INFORMAL] ❑ *Shiraz has stitched up major deals all over the world to boost sales.*

V+N+ADV,
V+ADV+N,
V+PRON+ADV

NOTE Secure is a more formal word for **stitch up**.

stock /stɒk/ (stocks, stocking, stocked)
stock up
1 If you **stock up** with things, you buy a lot of them in case you cannot get them later. ❑ *Stock up with groceries and canned foods once a fortnight... I stocked up on some gourmet frozen dishes... All the lads were keen to stock up in case of shortages.*

V+ADV:
USUALLY+with,
ALSO+on

2 If you **stock up** something such as a cupboard, shelf, or room, you fill it with food or other things. ❑ *I had to stock the boat up with food... Customers travel from hundreds of miles away to stock up their deep freezes... Start planning for Christmas now by stocking up the freezer with some festive dishes.*

V+N+ADV,
V+ADV+N,
V+PRON+ADV:
ALSO+with

stoke /stəʊk/ (stokes, stoking, stoked)
stoke up
1 If you **stoke up** a fire, you make it burn faster by adding more fuel and poking it with a stick or a poker. ❑ *He crouched to stoke up the flames... The servants were there to stoke up coal fires... Miss Jackson and I stoked the fire up.*

V+ADV+N,
V+N+ADV,
V+PRON+ADV

2 If you **stoke up** a particular feeling or idea, you encourage people to feel more excited, angry, or enthusiastic about something. ❑ *...stoking up popular prejudice... He stoked up their anger with his insensitive remarks.*

V+ADV+N,
V+N+ADV,
V+PRON+ADV

NOTE Stir up means almost the same as **stoke up**.

stop /stɒp/ (stops, stopping, stopped)
stop away If you **stop away**, you deliberately do not go to a place. ❑ *The roads have been clear so people are stopping away or they're coming in some other way... She's been stopping away from school.*

V+ADV:
ALSO+from

NOTE Stay away means almost the same as **stop away**.

stop behind If you **stop behind**, you stay in a place after other people have left. ❑ *Mr. Piggott made the whole class stop behind.*

V+ADV

NOTE Stay behind means almost the same as **stop behind**.

stop by If you **stop by**, you visit a place for a short time. [INFORMAL] ❑ *I thought I might stop by and say hello... They invited us to stop by the house for coffee... Stop by the Baylands Nature Center for a cup of coffee and conversation with a park ranger.*

V+ADV,
V+PREP

NOTE Drop by means almost the same as **stop by**.

stop in
1 If you **stop in**, you stay at home rather than going out. ❑ *I stop in each morning to read... I'd rather stop in, thanks.*

V+ADV

NOTE Stay in is means almost the same as **stop in**.

2 If you **stop in** at a place, you visit it for a short time. ❑ *Yesterday, I stopped in to visit a friend of mine... I stopped in at the restaurant... We stopped in at Wingelinna to say*

V+ADV:
USUALLY+at

goodbye.

NOTE Stop by and stop off mean almost the same as stop in.

★stop off If you **stop off** somewhere, you stay there for a short time in the middle of a journey. ❑ *On the way home I stopped off in London to attend a conference... Do you mind if I stop off for some groceries?... I'll stop off at headquarters and give his wife a call.*
V+ADV:
USUALLY+A

stop out If you say that someone **stopped out**, you mean that they stayed out late at night when you thought they ought to have come home. ❑ *Billie stopped out all night last Saturday.*
V+ADV

NOTE Stay out means almost the same as stop out.

♦ If you say that someone is a **stop-out**, you mean that they are the sort of person who likes to stay out late; used showing disapproval. [INFORMAL] ❑ *...dirty little stop-out.*
N-COUNT

stop over

[1] If you **stop over** somewhere, you stay there for one or more nights in between two parts of a journey, especially a plane journey. ❑ *I stopped over in Paris on my way here.*
V+ADV

NOTE Stop off means almost the same as stop over.

♦ A **stopover** is a short stay in a particular place between parts of a long journey. ❑ *...a five-week tour abroad with a three-day stopover in the United States.*
N-COUNT

[2] If you **stop over**, you visit a place for a short time. ❑ *Stop over for coffee in the morning... Why don't you stop over sometime? Doreen would love to see you.*
V+ADV

NOTE Stop by and come over mean almost the same as stop over.

stop up

[1] If you **stop up** something, you cover or fill a hole or gap in it so that nothing can get through it. ❑ *Stop up each crack as it occurs... They shut every door and window in the house, and stopped up every chimney.*
V+ADV+N,
V+N+ADV,
V+PRON+ADV

NOTE Block up means almost the same as stop up.

[2] If you **stop up**, you go to bed much later than usual. ❑ *I stopped up to watch the match.*
V+ADV

NOTE Stay up means almost the same as stop up.

store /stɔːʳ/ (stores, storing, stored)

store away To **store** things **away** means to put them in a safe place and keep them until they are needed. ❑ *They stored their tackle away during the winter... The body takes the energy-value it needs and stores away the rest... The goods were stored away at the back of the warehouse.*
V+N+ADV,
V+ADV+N,
V+PRON+ADV

NOTE Stow away means almost the same as store away.

store up To **store** something **up** means to keep it until the time is right to use it. ❑ *She had some sausage carefully stored up for the occasion... Jane had noticed what he said, and stored it up as a weapon... Plants store up energy in the summer.*
V+N+ADV,
V+PRON+ADV,
V+ADV+N

NOTE Save up means almost the same as store up.

storm /stɔːʳm/ (storms, storming, stormed)

storm in If you **storm in**, you rush into a place suddenly and noisily, often because you are very angry. ❑ *Geoffrey looked up as Peter stormed in, more excited than anyone had seen him before.*
V+ADV

storm into If you **storm into** a place, you rush into it suddenly and noisily, often because you are very angry. ❑ *John stormed into his room... Ira came storming into the clinic.*
V+PREP

storm off If you **storm off**, you go away suddenly because you are very angry. ❑ *Within minutes, he'd stormed off angrily... In a rage I stormed off to the police station.*
V+ADV

storm out If you **storm out**, you leave a place very suddenly because you are very angry. ❑ *He said a few strong words to the owner and stormed out... It was all too much for Alec, who stormed out of the room.*
V+ADV:
ALSO+of

stow /stəʊ/ (stows, stowing, stowed)

stow away

[1] If you **stow** something **away**, you put it carefully in a place until it is needed. ❑ *She had stowed her canvasses away... He accepted the money gratefully and stowed it*
V+N+ADV,
V+PRON+ADV,
V+ADV+N

away in his suitcase... His baggage was safely stowed away in the plane... Bill instructed the driver to stow away the white ribbons.

NOTE **Store away** means almost the same as **stow away**.

2 If someone **stows away**, they hide in a ship, aeroplane, or other vehicle in order   V+ADV
to make the journey secretly and without paying the fare. ❑ *She had not forgotten her original objective – to stow away on a flight to New York... He made his escape and stowed away to America.*

♦ A **stowaway** is a person who hides in a ship, aeroplane, or other vehicle in order   N-COUNT
to make the journey secretly without paying the fare. ❑ *There's a stowaway on Flight 80.*

straighten /ˈstreɪtᵊn/ (straightens, straightening, straightened)

straighten out

1 If you **straighten out** something that is twisted, bent, or crumpled, or if it   V+ADV+N,
straightens out, it becomes completely straight. ❑ *Sylvia sits down on the wooden*   V+N+ADV,
picnic bench and straightens out her legs... He straightened out the paper... The road through   V+ADV:
the canyon doesn't straighten out.   ERGATIVE

2 If you **straighten out** a confused situation, you succeed in organizing it and   V+ADV+N,
putting it in order. ❑ *A legal contract does help to straighten out the mess when things go*   V+N+ADV,
wrong... The baby sitter had straightened out the room... It'll take six weeks to get things   V+PRON+ADV
straightened out... Everything will be straightened out before we leave.

NOTE **Sort out** and **straighten up** mean almost the same as **straighten out**.

3 If you **straighten** someone **out**, you help them with their problems and stop   V+PRON+ADV,
them from being worried or confused. ❑ *Geoff had his problems, but I straightened him*   V+N+ADV
out and we got married... You straightened the kid out, stopped him going bad.

straighten up

1 When you **straighten up**, you make your back or body completely straight and   V+ADV
you stand upright. ❑ *He straightens up, combs his hair, and walks into the meeting... He released his grip and let Breslow straighten up.*

2 If you **straighten up** a confused situation, you succeed in organizing it and put-   V+ADV+N,
ting it in order. ❑ *We must get it all straightened up soon... As soon as we can straighten*   V+N+ADV,
up matters here we will book a passage to America.   V+PRON+ADV

NOTE **Sort out** and **straighten out** mean almost the same as **straighten up**.

strain /streɪn/ (strains, straining, strained)

strain at If you **strain at** a rope or cord of some kind, you pull very hard on it.   V+PREP
❑ *They strained at the ropes. ...vicious dogs straining at their leashes.*

strain off If you **strain** a liquid **off**, you separate it from something solid using   V+PRON+ADV,
something such as a sieve or a funnel. ❑ *When the mixture is boiling, strain it off into*   V+ADV+N,
jars... Strain off the water and dry the sediment.   V+N+ADV

strap /stræp/ (straps, strapping, strapped)

strap in If you **strap** someone **in**, you fasten them firmly into a seat, using a belt   V+REFL+ADV,
or strap. ❑ *Gwen pulled down a folding seat and strapped herself in... Check to see that the*   V+N+ADV,
children are strapped in securely.   V+PRON+ADV

NOTE **Buckle in** means almost the same as **strap in**.

strap into If you **strap** someone **into** a seat, you fasten them firmly there,   V+REFL+PREP,
using a belt or strap. ❑ *Quite a few of them knew how to strap themselves into the helicop-*   V+N+PREP,
ter... The twins were strapped into their seats. ...a seat into which the baby can be strapped.   V+PRON+PREP

NOTE **Buckle into** means almost the same as **strap into**.

strap on If you **strap** something **on**, you fasten it in position, using a belt or   V+ADV+N,
strap. ❑ *Mona hastily strapped on her skis... He strapped on his new watch.*   V+N+ADV,
   V+PRON+ADV

strap up If someone **straps up** a part of their body, they put a bandage or sup-   V+N+ADV,
port around it in order to avoid using it. ❑ *They strapped it up for me at hospital. ...the*   V+PRON+ADV,
harness that kept his right leg strapped up.   V+ADV+N

stress /stres/ (stresses, stressing, stressed)

stress out If something **stresses** you **out**, it makes you feel tense and anxious.   V+N+ADV,
[INFORMAL] ❑ *This business is really stressing me out.*   V+PRON+ADV

stretch /stretʃ/ (stretches, stretching, stretched)

stretch away If a flat area of land **stretches away**, it extends for some dis-   V+ADV:

tance. ❑ *The beach stretched away before them in a gentle curve... The coast stretching away straight and black... He observes sunny lawns stretching away to mountains.*   USUALLY+A

★**stretch out**

1 If you **stretch out** or **stretch** yourself **out** somewhere, you lie there with your legs and body in a straight line. ❑ *I just want to stretch out in my own bed... Stretch out in comfort... She groaned and stretched herself out flat on the sofa.*   V+ADV, V+REFL+ADV

2 If you **stretch out** your arm or leg, you hold it out straight. ❑ *He stretched out a thin arm and took our hands... She stretched out her hand for the money. ...stretching one leg out sideways.*   V+ADV+N, V+N+ADV, V+PRON+ADV

strike /straɪk/ (strikes, striking, struck)

strike at If you **strike at** someone or something, you do or say something which attacks them. ❑ *The opposition had struck at the root of Labour's strategy... They are using this alliance to strike at the Palestinians... McPherson saw a chance to strike at Barber.*   V+PREP

strike back If you **strike back**, you attempt to harm someone because they have harmed you. ❑ *As he grows older he begins to strike back. ...striking back against the contempt of their enemies.*   V+ADV

NOTE **Hit back** means almost the same as **strike back**.

strike down

1 If someone **is struck down**, they are badly injured or killed. ❑ *President Kennedy was struck down by an assassin's bullet... It would be so awful to be struck down before one's time... Polio struck him down.*   V+N+ADV, V+PRON+ADV, V+ADV+N: USUALLY PASSIVE

2 If a judge or court **strikes down** a law or regulation, they say that it is illegal and end it. [AMERICAN] ❑ *The Supreme Court today struck down a law that prevents criminals from profiting from books or movies about their crimes.*   V+N+ADV, V+ADV+N, V+PRON+ADV

strike off

1 If someone such as a doctor or lawyer **is struck off**, their name is taken off the official register and they are not allowed to do medical or legal work any more. [BRITISH] ❑ *'You should be struck off!' Dr Leon shouted... You can be struck off the roll for that.*   PASSIVE, V+ADV, V+PREP

2 → See **strike out**

strike on If you **strike on** or **strike upon** a solution, answer, or idea, you think of it unexpectedly and suddenly. ❑ *He had for once struck on a quite shrewd judgement... Then they struck upon the idea of making their own yoghurt.*   V+PREP

NOTE **Hit on** means almost the same as **strike on**.

strike out

1 If you **strike out**, you begin to do something different, often because you want to become more independent. ❑ *He decided to strike out on his own... The company was striking out in new directions in the field of drama.*   V+ADV: USUALLY+A

2 If you **strike out** or **strike off** somewhere, you start to move in a determined way in a particular direction. [LITERARY] ❑ *He decided to leave the path and strike out across the grass... We struck off northward through the woods... He covered another twenty yards beside the rail and then struck off left into the mangroves.*   V+ADV: USUALLY+A

3 If you **strike out** at someone, you aim a blow or punch at them. ❑ *He strikes out blindly, trying to get away.*   V+ADV: USUALLY+A

NOTE **Hit out** means almost the same as **strike out**.

4 If you **strike out** something that is written down, you put a line through it because it is wrong or because you do not want it to be seen. ❑ *Strike out the questions which do not apply to you... She read through her essay and struck a few words out here and there.*   V+ADV+N, V+N+ADV, V+PRON+ADV

NOTE **Cross out** means almost the same as **strike out**, and **delete** is a more formal word.

5 In baseball, if a pitcher **strikes out** a batter, or if a batter **strikes out**, the batter fails to hit three balls thrown properly by the pitcher, and is out. ❑ *He struck out ten batters, and allowed only two runs... Canseco, nursing a back injury, struck out.*   V+ADV+N, V+N/PRON+ADV, V+ADV: ERGATIVE

6 If someone **strikes out**, they fail. [AMERICAN, INFORMAL] ❑ *The lawyer admitted that he was the firm's second lawyer. The first one had struck out completely.*   V+ADV

For a full explanation of all grammatical labels, see pages xiii-xx

strike up

1 When you **strike up** a conversation or friendship with someone, you begin it. ❏ *Alice and I struck up a friendship immediately... They began to try and strike up contacts with sympathizers... As soon as she struck up any kind of acquaintance he felt jealous.*   V+ADV+N

2 When musicians **strike up**, they begin to play music. ❏ *The band strikes up at noon... The orchestra struck up the national anthem... The band had just struck up Duke Ellington's 'Satin Doll'.*   V+ADV, V+ADV+N

strike upon → See strike on

string /strɪŋ/ (strings, stringing, strung)

string along

1 If you **string** someone **along**, you deceive them by encouraging them to believe that you both have the same desires, beliefs, or hopes; used showing disapproval. [INFORMAL] ❏ *He dreamed of being Vice-President, and Roosevelt had strung him along... Gareth's just strung you along; he won't marry you.*   V+PRON+ADV, V+N+ADV

2 If you **string along** with someone, you go somewhere with them rather casually for a short time. [INFORMAL] ❏ *I'll string along with you... He'll string along if he gets bored.*   V+ADV: ALSO+with

NOTE **Tag along** means almost the same as **string along**.

string out If things **are strung out**, they are spread out in a long line. ❏ *...boom towns which are strung out along dirt roads... The genes are strung out along the chromosomes... The soldiers were hammering in concrete posts and stringing out the wire... The Indians strung them out in a fifteen mile line.*   V+N+ADV, V+ADV+N, V+PRON+ADV: USUALLY PASSIVE

string together If you **string** things **together**, you make them into one thing by adding them to each other, one at a time. ❏ *...a knack for stringing sentences together... I sang her a wistful ballad and strung together some rhymes to amuse her... No sooner are two thoughts strung together than there is an interruption.*   V+N+ADV, V+ADV+N, V+PRON+ADV

string up

1 If you **string** something **up**, you hang or tie it high in the air between two or more objects. ❏ *They had strung the straw man up between two poles... He took down the red lights and strung up the blue ones... Core the apples and string up the slices.*   V+N+ADV, V+ADV+N, V+PRON+ADV

NOTE **Put up** means almost the same as **string up**.

2 To **string** someone **up** means to kill them by hanging them. [INFORMAL] ❏ *...stringing you up from the nearest lamp post. ...a little corpse, strung up as a warning... She found a dead cat strung up on her porch.*   V+PRON+ADV, V+N+ADV, V+ADV+N

3 If you **are strung up**, you feel tense and nervous. [INFORMAL] ❏ *I was too strung up to eat anything... I began to get strung up.*   PASSIVE: V+ADV

strip /strɪp/ (strips, stripping, stripped)

strip away

1 If you **strip away** something that is attached to a surface, you remove it completely. ❏ *Someone got on the roof and stripped away the lead... The pale grey wallpaper had been stripped away.*   V+ADV+N, V+N+ADV, V+PRON+ADV

NOTE **Strip off** means almost the same as **strip away**.

2 To **strip away** people's rights, beliefs, or attitudes means to get rid of them completely. ❏ *...stripping away the symbols of individuality. ...stripping away their remaining civil rights... This pretence is to be stripped away on the Day of Judgement.*   V+ADV+N, V+N+ADV, V+PRON+ADV

strip down If you **strip down** an engine or a piece of equipment, you take it to pieces, usually in order to clean it or repair it. ❏ *She offered to help them in dismantling and stripping down the bike... Can you lubricate the engine without stripping it down?*   V+ADV+N, V+PRON+ADV, V+N+ADV

strip of If someone **is stripped of** something such as their property, rights, or title, those things are taken away from them. ❏ *She was rejected by her husband and automatically stripped of all her property and possessions. ...a group stripped of its civil rights... They stripped the bodies of their gear.*   V+N+PREP, V+PRON+PREP: USUALLY PASSIVE

strip off

1 When you **strip off** your clothes, or **strip off**, you undress. ❏ *Casson stripped off his raincoat... Gertrude was unlacing her plimsolls and stripping off her socks... They stripped off and dived in.*   V+ADV+N, V+PRON+ADV, V+N+ADV, V+ADV

2 If you **strip off** something that is attached to a surface, you remove it complete-   V+ADV+N, ly. ❑ *They spent two weeks stripping off all the brown paint. ...stripping off the tarpaulins... The bark could easily be stripped off.*

V+N+ADV,
V+PRON+ADV

NOTE **Strip away** means almost the same as **strip off**.

strip <u>out</u>

1 If you **strip** a place **out**, you take out everything that is inside it so that you can decorate it or rebuild it. ❑ *The nursery was stripped out and painted white.*

V+N+ADV,
V+PRON+ADV,
V+ADV+N

2 If you **strip out** information from a financial or statistical calculation, you ignore it because it is not relevant to what you are trying to discover. ❑ *Look at your budget today and strip out the costs that you won't have in the future.*

V+ADV+N,
V+N+ADV,
V+PRON+ADV

struggle /strʌgəl/ (struggles, struggling, struggled)

struggle <u>on</u> If you **struggle on**, you manage with great difficulty to continue doing something. ❑ *Some struggled on, but those who couldn't were left for dead... Fifteen years older than Gladys, he struggled on manfully only for a few years longer.*

V+ADV

NOTE **Soldier on** means almost the same as **struggle on**.

stub /stʌb/ (stubs, stubbing, stubbed)

stub <u>out</u> When someone **stubs out** a cigarette or cigar, they stop it burning by pressing the end against something hard. ❑ *Phillip stubs out his cigarette and lights another. ...stubbing her half-smoked cigarette out in one of the tin lids. ...rolling their own cigarettes and stubbing them out on the furniture.*

V+ADV+N,
V+N+ADV,
V+PRON+ADV

NOTE **Extinguish** is a more formal word for **stub out**.

stumble /stʌmbəl/ (stumbles, stumbling, stumbled)

stumble across If you **stumble across** something or someone, you discover or meet them unexpectedly. ❑ *In the course of their search they may stumble across something quite different... Had I stumbled across another human being, I would have hidden.*

V+PREP

NOTE **Come across** means almost the same as **stumble across**.

stumble on If you **stumble on** or **stumble upon** something or someone, you discover or meet them unexpectedly. ❑ *Sir Alexander Fleming stumbled on his great discovery of penicillin quite by accident... Kairi stumbled upon something that was to alter their lives... If a solution ever happens it will be stumbled upon.*

V+PREP:
HAS PASSIVE

NOTE **Come across** means almost the same as **stumble on**.

stumble upon → See stumble on

stump /stʌmp/ (stumps, stumping, stumped)

stump <u>up</u> If you **stump up** a sum of money, you pay the money that is required for something, often reluctantly. [BRITISH] ❑ *The government is being asked to stump up the rest of the cash. ...asking investors to stump up £50m to help finance the films.*

V+ADV+N

NOTE **Cough up** means almost the same as **stump up**.

subject /səbdʒekt/ (subjects, subjecting, subjected)

subject to If you **subject** someone **to** something unpleasant, you make them experience it. ❑ *A court order was obtained, permitting the police to subject Arthur to a lie detector test... They stayed at home rather than subject themselves to bureaucratic checks at the border... The air bases were subjected to intense air attack.*

V+N+PREP,
V+PRON+PREP,
V+REFL+PREP

subscribe /səbskraɪb/ (subscribes, subscribing, subscribed)

subscr<u>i</u>be to

1 If you **subscribe to** an opinion or belief, you have this opinion or belief and share it with a number of other people. ❑ *A large number of them now subscribe to the Mohammedan faith... They find they cannot subscribe to the values of an older generation... The rest of us do not subscribe to this theory.*

V+PREP:
HAS PASSIVE

2 If you **subscribe to** a magazine or a newspaper, you pay to receive copies of it regularly. ❑ *She subscribed to Reader's Digest and TV Guide... I started subscribing to a morning newspaper.*

V+PREP

suck /sʌk/ (sucks, sucking, sucked)

suck <u>off</u> If someone having sex **sucks** their partner **off**, they lick or suck their partner's genitals until their partner has an orgasm. [INFORMAL]

V+N+ADV,
V+PRON+ADV,
V+ADV+N

suck <u>up</u> to If you **suck up to** someone in a position of authority, you try to please them by flattering them or by doing things for them, especially in order to

V+ADV+PREP

gain some advantage for yourself; used showing disapproval. [INFORMAL] ❑ *There was no need for them to suck up to Mrs Norberg so much... 'They were trying to be amiable and agreeable.'—'Sucking up to me, you mean?'*

sucker /sʌkər/ (suckers, suckering, suckered)

sucker into If you **sucker** someone **into** doing something, you deceive them, usually so that they do something that is against their own interests. [AMERICAN] ❑ *It is becoming harder for the authorities to sucker healthy banks into taking over smaller ones.*

V+N+PREP,
V+PRON+PREP:
ALSO+-ING

NOTE **Trick into** means almost the same as **sucker into**.

sum /sʌm/ (sums, summing, summed)

★sum up

1 If you **sum up** a situation, you state or describe briefly its most important aspects or characteristics. ❑ *I can't sum up his whole philosophy in one sentence... To sum all this up, what we need is a reform of the grant-aid system... She was searching for the words that would sum it up.*

V+ADV+N,
V+N+ADV,
V+PRON+ADV

NOTE **Summarize** means almost the same as **sum up**, and **encapsulate** is a more formal word.

2 When someone **sums up** at the end of a speech, argument, or debate, they state briefly and clearly its main points as a conclusion. When a judge **sums up** at the end of a trial, he or she makes a speech to the jury reminding them of the evidence and the main arguments of the case. ❑ *At the end of the discussion, he summed up, and added a few points... To sum up: within our society there still exist rampant inequalities.*

V+ADV

NOTE **Summarize** means almost the same as **sum up**.

♦ The **summing-up** at the end of a trial is a speech in which the judge reminds the jury of the evidence and the main arguments of the case. ❑ *In his summing-up, the judge again returned to the motive.*

N-COUNT

3 If something **sums up** a situation, it represents or suggests to you the most important and typical features of that situation. ❑ *...a crusade which summed up one aspect of the Sixties... His attitude was summed up by another incident a little later last winter.*

V+ADV+N,
V+N+ADV,
V+PRON+ADV

NOTE **Epitomize** is a more formal word for **sum up**.

4 If you **sum up** someone or something, you pass an opinion on them or make an accurate judgement of them. ❑ *He was able to sum us up in a very short time... She asked him to sum himself up, and he allowed that he had an easy temperament... It was as though she was summing up the differences between her world and ours.*

V+PRON+ADV,
V+ADV+N,
V+N+ADV

NOTE **Size up** means almost the same as **sum up**.

♦ A **summing up** is an opinion or judgement about something or someone. ❑ *It seemed a pretty fair summing up of two thousand years of Western civilization... 'She was all right,' was Lester's summing up.*

N-SING

summon /sʌmən/ (summons, summoning, summoned)

summon up

1 If you **summon up** your strength, energy, courage, and so on, you make a great effort in order to do something. ❑ *...if you can't summon up enough energy to get up early... She did not seem able to summon up the effort to return to London... He eventually summoned up the courage to ask them if Melanie was all right.*

V+ADV+N:
USUALLY+to-INF

NOTE **Muster up** means almost the same as **summon up**.

2 If you **summon up** support, help, or resources, you persuade people to give you support or help. ❑ *He was hoping to summon up support for his measures... Almost overnight Wren seems to have summoned up a team of craftsmen of the necessary talent.*

V+ADV+N,
V+N+ADV,
V+PRON+ADV

NOTE **Drum up** means almost the same as **summon up**.

3 If you **summon** someone **up**, you order them to come to you. [FORMAL] ❑ *She summoned up the remainder of the family... A short time later we were summoned up.*

V+ADV+N,
V+PRON+ADV

NOTE **Call up** means almost the same as **summon up**.

4 If something **summons up** a memory or thought, it causes you to remember, feel, or think a particular thing. ❑ *The odour summoned up memories of my childhood. ...all the emotions to be summoned up during their work.*

V+ADV+N,
V+PRON+ADV

NOTE **Conjure up** and **evoke** mean almost the same as **summon up**.

surge /sɜːʳdʒ/ (surges, surging, surged)

surge up

1 If an emotion or sensation **surges up** in you, you suddenly feel it very intensely. [LITERARY] ❏ *His true feelings keep surging up inside him... The impulses of anarchy and madness surge up to challenge the rule of reason and convention.*

V+ADV:
USUALLY+A

NOTE **Well up** means almost the same as **surge up**.

2 If a sound **surges up**, you suddenly hear it very loudly and powerfully. [LITERARY] ❏ *A huge roar of applause and cheers surged up from the crowd... Chords of smooth music surged up in my head.*

V+ADV:
USUALLY+A

NOTE **Rise up** means almost the same as **surge up**.

3 An **upsurge** in something is a sudden and serious increase in it. ❏ *...a massive upsurge of social unrest. ...an upsurge in industrial production. ...the inflationary upsurge.*

N-SING

suss /sʌs/ (susses, sussing, sussed)

suss out

1 If you **suss out** someone or something, you discover what they are really like. [BRITISH, INFORMAL] ❏ *She had me sussed out in ten minutes... How long it took to suss out the true nature of that lovely stuff!*

V+PRON+ADV,
V+ADV+N,
V+N+ADV

NOTE **Work out** means almost the same as **suss out**.

2 If you **suss out** a problem, you discover how to do it or solve it. [BRITISH, INFORMAL] ❏ *At last she sussed out the reason for this.*

V+ADV+N,
V+PRON+ADV,
V+N+ADV

NOTE **Sort out** means almost the same as **suss out**.

swab /swɒb/ (swabs, swabbing, swabbed)

☑ Swab is also spelled **swob** in American English.

swab down If you **swab down** a floor or wall, you clean it thoroughly with a wet mop or brush and water. ❏ *A relatively easy way to swab it down is with a softish brush.*

V+PRON+ADV,
V+ADV+N,
V+N+ADV

NOTE **Wash down** means almost the same as **swab down**.

swab out If you **swab out** a room or container, you clean it thoroughly with a wet mop or brush and water. ❏ *Swab it out with hot water and a little disinfectant.*

V+PRON+ADV,
V+ADV+N,
V+N+ADV

NOTE **Wash out** means almost the same as **swab out**.

swallow /swɒloʊ/ (swallows, swallowing, swallowed)

swallow down If you **swallow down** something that is in your mouth, you cause it to pass from your mouth into your stomach. ❏ *'Go on and drink,' he said. She swallowed it down... He swallowed down the last lump of bread... The fish may have swallowed the bait down.*

V+PRON+ADV,
V+ADV+N,
V+N+ADV

NOTE **Gulp down** means almost the same as **swallow down**.

swallow up

1 If you **swallow** something **up**, you take it into your mouth and cause it to pass into your stomach. ❏ *...opening her eyes wider and wider, as if to swallow him up... They believed at that time that sinners in general were literally swallowed up by hell, which they entered through the mouth of the Devil.*

V+PRON+ADV,
V+ADV+N,
V+N+ADV

2 If something **is swallowed up** by something else, it becomes part of it and no longer has a separate identity of its own. ❏ *As rural smallholdings are swallowed up by larger farms, people are flooding to the city... The residents in the square feared the Museum was going to swallow it all up.*

V+ADV+N,
V+N+ADV,
V+PRON+ADV:
USUALLY PASSIVE

NOTE **Be absorbed** means almost the same as **be swallowed up**.

3 If someone or something **is swallowed up**, for example by a crowd or cloud, they are hidden by it or disappear into it, and you cannot see them any more. ❏ *And then the mist came down. In no time at all, every object in sight had been swallowed up–bushes, rocks, trees, fences... A moment later she moved away, and was instantly swallowed up in the crowd of passengers around the Trans America counters.*

V+ADV+N,
V+PRON+ADV,
V+N+ADV:
USUALLY PASSIVE

NOTE **Be engulfed** means almost the same as **be swallowed up**.

4 If something **swallows up** money or resources, it uses them entirely, and they have hardly any effect on it. ❏ *These livestock units swallowed up 22.4% of the money... It is very expensive, and is inclined to swallow up all available resources.*

V+ADV+N,
V+PRON+ADV

NOTE **Use up** means almost the same as **swallow up**.

For a full explanation of all grammatical labels, see pages xiii-xx

swap /swɒp/ **(swaps, swapping, swapped)**

☑ Swap is also spelled **swop**. In American English, **around** is much more common than **round**.

swap around If you **swap** things **around** or **swap** them **round**, you move them so that each one is in a place where one of the others was before. ❑ *I swapped them round when he wasn't looking. ...swapping around the beds for the night at 5.30.*
V+PRON+ADV,
V+N+ADV,
V+ADV+N

swap over If you **swap** two things **over**, you take them and put each one in the place where the other one was before. ❑ *You can always swap it over at a later stage... See if you can swap them over.*
V+PRON+ADV,
V+N+ADV,
V+ADV+N

swap round → See swap around

swear /sweər/ **(swears, swearing, swore, sworn)**

swear by If you **swear by** something, you believe that it is especially effective, reliable, or useful for a particular purpose. ❑ *Gas is better than electricity for cooking, I always swear by it... Some swear by vitamin tablets, and others put their trust in milk.*
V+PREP

swear in When someone **is sworn in**, they make a solemn promise or promises, either at the beginning of a trial in a court of law or when they are starting a new official appointment. ❑ *The jury was sworn in on March 14... General Figueiredo will be sworn in on Wednesday.*
V+ADV+N,
V+PRON+ADV:
USUALLY PASSIVE

♦ The **swearing-in** at the beginning of a trial or official appointment is the act of making a solemn promise or promises. ❑ *I took the bus to Baltimore for the medical examination and swearing in.*
N-SING

swear off If you **swear off** something such as alcohol or smoking, you decide not to drink alcohol or to smoke any more. [INFORMAL] ❑ *I've sworn off alcohol for the time being.*
V+PREP

NOTE **Give up** means almost the same as **swear off**, and **renounce** is a more formal word.

sweat /swet/ **(sweats, sweating, sweated)**

sweat off

1 If you **sweat off** weight, you lose weight by causing yourself to sweat heavily, for example through vigorous exercise or steam baths. ❑ *He managed to sweat off five pounds before the weigh-in.*
V+ADV+N,
V+PRON+ADV

2 If you **sweat off** a fever or other illness, you get rid of it by keeping yourself very warm and causing yourself to sweat heavily. ❑ *Just go to bed and try to sweat it off.*
V+PRON+ADV,
V+ADV+N

sweat out

1 If you **sweat out** a period of time or **sweat** it **out**, you endure a difficult situation, waiting patiently for it to end. ❑ *Cut off from the remainder of the country, the invasion force sweated it out... He sweated it out to the end... The problem was how to sweat out the next six weeks.*
V+it+ADV,
V+ADV+N,
V+N+ADV

2 If you **sweat out** something, you get rid of it from your body or system by causing yourself to sweat heavily. ❑ *You could always go running. That way, you could sweat out the gin.*
V+ADV+N,
V+PRON+ADV

sweat over If you **sweat over** something, you work very hard at it. ❑ *They sweated over every move... I really sweated over it.*
V+PREP

sweep /swiːp/ **(sweeps, sweeping, swept)**

sweep aside To **sweep** something **aside** means to make it seem unimportant and irrelevant, or to treat it as if it does not matter at all. ❑ *The realities of the war swept those doubts aside... His Parliamentary genius swept aside many obstacles... He himself dismissed his work, you know. Swept it aside... My suggestion was swept aside.*
V+N+ADV,
V+ADV+N,
V+PRON+ADV

★sweep away

1 To **sweep** something **away** means to destroy or remove it entirely, usually because it is considered outdated or wrong. ❑ *...to eliminate traditional landscapes entirely, sweeping away the hedges, meadows, old woods, and footpaths. ...the rush to sweep the old away and bring in the new... Almost the entire manufacturing base has been swept away.*
V+ADV+N,
V+N+ADV,
V+PRON+ADV

NOTE **Eradicate** is a more formal word for **sweep away**.

2 When someone or something **is swept away** by a river or the sea, the current is
V+N+ADV,

so strong that it pulls them from the place where they were and carries them off or destroys them. ❑ *...a memorial tablet to the Paget family, swept away by a huge wave... We were finally brought to a halt: the entire road had been swept away.*

V+ADV+N,
V+PRON+ADV:
USUALLY PASSIVE

3 If someone **is swept away**, their emotions are so strong that they cannot behave calmly and sensibly. ❑ *His life was too well regulated to be affected by affairs of the heart, while she always allowed herself to be swept away... He was suddenly swept away by the full force of her wild irresponsible seduction.*

PASSIVE:
V+ADV

NOTE **Be carried away** means almost the same as **be swept away**.

sweep out If you **sweep out** a room, you clean it thoroughly with a broom, getting rid of all the dust and so on. ❑ *...clearing the tables after each meal and sweeping out the dining rooms... They're in Grandfather's old room. I've swept it out and put some sheets on the beds... Mrs Pringle appeared, on her way to sweep the school out.*

V+ADV+N,
V+PRON+ADV,
V+N+ADV

★sweep up

1 If you **sweep up** things from a place, you collect them with a broom in order to get rid of them. ❑ *Kathy was in the middle of the crossing, sweeping up the glass from my broken headlights... The gardening girls were sweeping up leaves and cutting the grass... They can sweep up afterwards.*

V+ADV+N,
V+N+ADV,
V+PRON+ADV,
V+ADV

2 If you **are swept up** in something, you become very involved in it, and perhaps cannot think about anything else. ❑ *After Karen learned her father was alive she, too, became swept up in the desire to return home... I had not yet been swept up into the Civil Rights Movement... She was swept up by a passion of creativity.*

PASSIVE:
V+ADV:
USUALLY+A

NOTE **Be caught up** means almost the same as **be swept up**.

sweeten /swiːtən/ (**sweetens, sweetening, sweetened**)

sweeten up If you **sweeten** someone **up**, you do something nice for them or give them something, in order to prepare them for something unpleasant or to persuade them to do something. ❑ *They sweetened him up by offering him another £1000 a year.*

V+PRON+ADV,
V+ADV+N,
V+N+ADV

NOTE **Butter up** and **soften up** mean almost the same as **sweeten up**.

swell /swel/ (**swells, swelling, swelled, swollen**)

☑ The past participle can be either **swelled** or **swollen**.

swell up

1 If a part of your body **swells up**, it becomes larger and rounder than normal, usually as a result of an injury or illness. ❑ *A mosquito had bitten her and her whole arm had swollen up... After a few minutes my throat started to swell up.*

V+ADV

NOTE **Puff up** means almost the same as **swell up**, and **go down** means the opposite.

2 If something such as reaction, feeling, or sound **swells up**, it suddenly becomes much stronger or more noticeable. ❑ *...the protests that swelled up in the 1950s against Britain's possession of nuclear weapons... And why shouldn't he? Resentment swelled up inside his breast. ...standing there as the chorus swelled up.*

V+ADV

3 If the sea **swells up**, the waves become larger and stronger. [LITERARY] ❑ *We stood together on the brink. The sea was not far below us; it swelled up towards us like a beckoning arm.*

V+ADV

swill /swɪl/ (**swills, swilling, swilled**)

swill down If you **swill down** a drink, you drink it quite fast. If you **swill down** food, you drink something at the same time as you are eating. ❑ *Everyone laughed and swilled down another drink. ...the choicest of meats to eat and swill down with claret.*

V+ADV+N,
V+PRON+ADV

swing /swɪŋ/ (**swings, swinging, swung**)

☑ In American English, **around** is much more common than **round**.

swing around If you **swing around** or **swing round**, you suddenly turn and face in the opposite direction. ❑ *There was a knock on his door. He swung round startled... Marianne touched Gareth on the arm and he swung around fiercely, ready to attack.*

V+ADV

NOTE **Turn around** means almost the same as **swing around**.

swing round → See **swing around**

swing round to If a conversation **swings round to** a particular topic, you start talking about something different, often without appearing to change topic completely. ❑ *These remarks were apparently about David's character, but subtly they swung round to being about our relationship... After a time he swung the conversation round to discussing the police.*

NOTE **Turn to** means almost the same as **swing round to**.

V+ADV+PREP,
V+N+ADV+PREP,
V+PRON+ADV+PREP:
ERGATIVE

switch /swɪtʃ/ **(switches, switching, switched)**

☑ In American English, **around** is much more common than **round**.

switch around If you **switch** things **around** or **switch** them **round**, you move them or change them so that each one is in a place where one of the others was before. ❑ *You might have warned me that you switched the men's and women's toilets around last night in your building.*

V+N+ADV,
V+PRON+ADV,
V+ADV+N

★switch off

1 If you **switch off** an electrical device, engine, and so on, you stop it working by pressing a switch. ❑ *He switched the radio off... He drew his car into the side of the lane, and switched off the engine... Let's switch it off now, we've finished... A man banged on his door to tell him to switch off.*

V+N+ADV,
V+ADV+N,
V+PRON+ADV,
V+ADV

NOTE **Turn off** means almost the same as **switch off**, and **switch on** means the opposite.

2 If you **switch off** a television or radio programme, you stop watching or listening to it by pressing a switch on your set. ❑ *I could not even summon the energy to switch off the ballet... It was a programme about minorities in a late stage of industrial capitalism. Philip switched off.*

V+ADV+N,
V+N+ADV,
V+PRON+ADV,
V+ADV

NOTE **Switch on** means the opposite of **switch off**.

3 If you **switch off** a particular kind of behaviour, you suddenly stop behaving in that way. ❑ *...attempts simply to switch off an unwanted mood... She had suddenly switched off the emotional and physical warmth with which I associated her.*

V+ADV+N,
V+PRON+ADV

NOTE **Switch on** means the opposite of **switch off**.

4 If you **switch off** when you are listening to something, you stop paying attention to it, because you are no longer interested. [INFORMAL] ❑ *The lecture was so boring I just switched off... I listened to him for perhaps a couple of minutes and then switched off.*

V+ADV

★switch on

1 If you **switch on** an electrical device, engine, and so on, you start it working by pressing a switch. ❑ *He ran up the stairs and switched on the light on the landing... She had switched a fire on because she felt rather cold... 'Here's the electric light.'—'All right. Don't switch it on.'... When the child switches on he listens to the story and then answers a series of questions.*

V+ADV+N,
V+N+ADV,
V+PRON+ADV,
V+ADV

NOTE **Turn on** means almost the same as **switch on**, and **switch off** means the opposite.

2 If you **switch on** a television or radio programme, you start watching or listening to it by pressing a switch on your set. ❑ *I switched on the news. ...people who switch on five minutes after the beginning of the programme.*

V+ADV+N,
V+N+ADV,
V+PRON+ADV,
V+ADV

NOTE **Switch off** means the opposite of **switch on**.

3 If you **switch on** a particular kind of behaviour, you suddenly start behaving in that way; used showing disapproval. ❑ *He had the ability to switch on the concentration when necessary... The girl behind the counter switched on an automatic smile as he approached.*

V+ADV+N,
V+PRON+ADV

NOTE **Switch off** means the opposite of **switch on**.

switch over

1 If you **switch over** from one thing to another, you change from using or doing the first to the second. ❑ *Airline and chain-hotel bookings switched over to computers... They will switch over completely in a few weeks.*

V+ADV

2 When you are watching television, if you **switch over**, you change the setting on the television set in order to see something on a different channel. ❑ *My father always switches over during the adverts.*

V+ADV

switch round → See **switch around**

The symbol ★ shows key phrasal verbs

swivel /swɪvəl/ **(swivels, swivelling, swivelled)**

☑ American English uses the spellings **swiveling** and **swiveled**. In American English, **around** is much more common than **round**.

swivel around If you **swivel around** or **swivel round**, especially when you are sitting, you turn quickly and face in another direction, or continue turning. If you **swivel** something **around** or **swivel** it **round**, you turn it quickly. ❑ *I swivelled right round in my chair... He swivelled around to greet her as she came in... Michael slowly swivelled his chair round.*

V+ADV,
V+N+ADV,
V+PRON+ADV:
ERGATIVE

NOTE **Turn around** means almost the same as **swivel around**.

swivel round → See **swivel around**

swob /swɒb/ **(swobs, swobbing, swobbed)** → See **swab**

swoop /swuːp/ **(swoops, swooping, swooped)**

swoop down

1 When a bird **swoops down**, it suddenly moves downwards through the air towards the ground. ❑ *An adult swift swooped down and glided across the roof.*

V+ADV

2 If a group of soldiers, policemen, or other people **swoops down** on you, they suddenly move towards you and attack you. ❑ *British troops swooped down twice in pre-dawn raids on their headquarters... Whenever a rancher or miner got careless a band of raiders would swoop down to capture horses or cattle.*

V+ADV

swop /swɒp/ **(swops, swopping, swopped)** → See **swap**

swot /swɒt/ **(swots, swotting, swotted)**

swot up If you **swot up** a subject or **swot up** on it, you read as much as you can about it, usually because you are going to be asked questions about it or take an examination. [BRITISH, INFORMAL] ❑ *He attended sessions in Congress, swotted up American history, and met some politicians... They have to swot it all up... I was swotting up on my transformational grammar.*

V+ADV+N,
V+PRON+ADV,
V+ADV+on

NOTE **Mug up** means almost the same as **swot up**, and **revise** is a more formal word.

syphon /saɪfən/ **(syphons, syphoning, syphoned)** → See **siphon**

Tt

tack /tæk/ (tacks, tacking, tacked)

tack down If you **tack** something **down**, you fix it to a floor or surface by using tacks. ❑ *...tacking floorboards down... Carpets should always be tacked down securely.*

V+N+ADV,
V+ADV+N,
V+PRON+ADV

tack on If something **is tacked on**, it is added to something else that is already complete, often in a way that seems unsatisfactory. ❑ *The second legal point is tacked on to the end of Regulation 4(i)i... Bank End Cottage was on a lane through two gates, tacked on to the end of a farm.*

V+N+ADV,
V+PRON+ADV,
V+ADV+N:
USUALLY PASSIVE

NOTE Tag on means almost the same as **tack on**.

tack up If you **tack** something **up**, you fasten it to a vertical surface by using tacks. ❑ *Perhaps fifty men and women were at work, tacking up curtains and hoovering carpets... I'd seen advertisements for them tacked up in many rural areas.*

V+ADV+N,
V+N+ADV,
V+PRON+ADV

tag /tæg/ (tags, tagging, tagged)

tag along If you **tag along** with someone, you go with them, especially when they have not asked you to. ❑ *Our younger sisters always wanted to tag along when we went somewhere with our friends... Do you mind if I tag along?*

V+ADV

tag on If a remark **is tagged on**, it is added to the end of something that you have said or written. ❑ *This information was revealed in a casual phrase, tagged on to the end of the conversation.*

V+ADV+N,
V+N+ADV,
V+PRON+ADV:
USUALLY PASSIVE

NOTE Tack on means almost the same as **tag on**.

tail /teɪl/ (tails, tailing, tailed)

tail away When a person's voice or what they are saying **tails away** or **tails off**, it gradually becomes quieter and then silent. ❑ *As I walked in her voice tailed away... Conversation tended to tail off when he approached.*

V+ADV

tail back When traffic **tails back**, a long queue of it forms along a road, moving very slowly or not at all, for example because of road works or an accident. [BRITISH] ❑ *Traffic tailed back from the roundabout to the M4 junction.*

V+ADV

♦ A **tailback** is a long queue of stationary or slowly-moving traffic that forms, for example, because of road works or an accident. [BRITISH] ❑ *Almost at once they hit a tailback of rush hour traffic in the Midland Road.*

N-COUNT

tail off

1 When something **tails off**, it gradually becomes less in amount or value, often before coming to an end completely. ❑ *The rains tail off in September... The average figure has tailed off in the last few years... For many manual workers, income tails off as retirement approaches.*

V+ADV

2 → See **tail away**

take /teɪk/ (takes, taking, took, taken)

☑ In American English, **around** is much more common than **round**.

take aback If you **are taken aback** by something, you are so surprised or shocked by it that you stop what you are doing and cannot think or behave normally. ❑ *I was a bit taken aback by this sudden reversal... He caught sight of my appearance for the first time and was taken aback at how different I looked... The sound of her voice took him aback.*

V+PRON+ADV,
V+N+ADV:
USUALLY PASSIVE

take after If you **take after** a member of your family, you resemble them in your appearance, behaviour, or character. ❑ *You don't take after your sister... He took after his grandfather where character was concerned... If Cathy took after him she'd be a real good looking girl.*

V+PREP

take against If you **take against** someone or something, you start to dislike them, often for no good reason. [BRITISH] ❑ *The Producer started taking against Dan and the whole script. ...a person whom it was indeed easy to take against.* V+PREP

NOTE **Take to** means the opposite of **take against**.

★**take along** If you **take** someone or something **along** when you are going somewhere, they accompany you there or you have them with you. ❑ *I asked Mr Sutton to take me along to the club... She always took her children along... I also take along a small black bag.* V+PRON+ADV, V+N+ADV, V+ADV+N

★**take apart**

1 If you **take** something **apart**, you separate it into the different parts that it is made from. ❑ *They were the hands of a man who liked to take engines apart... Most of these machines have to be taken apart to be cleaned... Their tasks include taking apart and reassembling large bits of furniture.* V+N+ADV, V+N+ADV, V+PRON+ADV

NOTE **Dismantle** is a more formal word for **take apart**, and **put together** means the opposite.

2 If you **take apart** something such as an argument or an essay, you analyse it carefully in order to show what its weaknesses are. ❑ *He had read the material and was prepared to take apart the statement that rhetoric is an art... The essay had not been a particularly great success and I'd taken it apart somewhat.* V+ADV+N, V+PRON+ADV, V+N+ADV

take around If you **take** someone **around** a place, or **take** them **round** it, you go there with them and show them all the interesting or important features. ❑ *I took my godson around my laboratory... Parties of visitors are taken round on Saturday afternoons... Why don't you just take me round now and tell me what's been happening.* V+N+ADV/PREP, V+PRON+ADV/PREP

NOTE **Show around** means almost the same as **take around**.

take aside If you **take** someone **aside**, you separate them from the rest of a group in order to talk to them privately. ❑ *He made a point of taking Daniel aside and telling him not to worry... He took me aside and began to talk to me about his boyhood in London. ...taking aside the boy or girl who is causing trouble.* V+N+ADV, V+PRON+ADV, V+ADV+N

★**take away**

1 If you **take** something **away** from a place or position, you remove it and put it somewhere else. ❑ *Do you want to take any of this away with you, Ian?... Take your hands away... A maid came to take away the tray... I took the camera away from my eye and gazed unbelievingly. ...but the rug had been taken away for cleaning.* V+N+ADV, V+ADV+N, V+PRON+ADV; ALSO+from

NOTE **Put back** means the opposite of **take away**.

♦ A **takeaway** is a shop or restaurant which sells cooked food that you eat somewhere else, for example at home. [BRITISH] ❑ *...the man behind the counter at the Chinese takeaway.* N-COUNT

♦ **Takeaway** food or a **takeaway** is hot cooked food that is sold to be eaten somewhere else. [BRITISH] ❑ *I really fancy an Indian takeaway. ...takeaway pizzas.* ADJECTIVE, N-COUNT

NOTE In American English, **take-out** means almost the same as **takeaway**.

2 If you **take** something **away** from a person, you remove it and prevent them from having it any more. ❑ *They took my name and address, took away all my possessions, and sent me down to the cells... I took the knife away from him. I don't know how... These men wanted to help them keep their land, not take it away from them... Even his rights as a citizen had been taken away from him. ...people from whom everything has been taken away.* V+ADV+N, V+N+ADV, V+PRON+ADV; ALSO+from

3 If someone **takes** you **away**, you go with them to stay in another place. ❑ *She had taken the children away with her to her parents' house... I want to take Billy away with me... It seemed a pity to take her away from it all... My parents took me away to Vermont.* V+N+ADV, V+PRON+ADV; ALSO+with/A

4 If someone **takes** you **away**, they force you to go with them, for example to prison or a mental hospital. ❑ *His parents were taken away in a dark van... She was taken away by a doctor... Two officers took him away to Glasgow Central Police Station... They had taken her away. They had kidnapped her.* V+N+ADV, V+ADV+N, V+PRON+ADV

5 If something **takes** you **away** from a person, place, or activity, it prevents you from being with that person, being in that place, or continuing that activity. ❑ *My husband's job took him away a lot... She enjoys her work but it takes her away from her family... Do you have to take a working man away from his Sunday dinner?* V+PRON+ADV, V+N+ADV; USUALLY+from

6 To **take away** something such as a quality or idea means to destroy it, spoil it, V+ADV+N:

or get rid of it in some way. ❑ *This would take away the justification for it... Nothing seems to take away your appetite... His teasing remark did take away some of the terror from the operation.*

ALSO+*from*

7 If something **takes** your breath **away**, it is so beautiful, exciting, or surprising that you are unable to speak or breathe normally for a moment. ❑ *It was so beautiful it took her breath away... Aurelia's beauty had taken his breath away... The idea fairly took my breath away.*

V+N+ADV

8 If you **take** something **away** from an experience or situation, it has a lasting effect or influence on you in that respect. ❑ *But, as with the lecture, it is not clear what they take away from it... It's the one thing you really took away from that gloomy convent.*

V+N+ADV: USUALLY+*from*

9 If you **take** one number or amount **away** from another, you subtract the first from the second. ❑ *He could add up numbers up to ten and take them away too, though this was hard sometimes... This last amount is then taken away from each annual figure of earnings.*

V+PRON+ADV, V+ADV+N, V+N+ADV: ALSO+*from*

★take away from

1 If someone **takes** you **away from** your husband, wife, or lover, they cause you to leave your husband, wife, or lover, and have a relationship with them instead. ❑ *He would kill anyone who tried to take her away from him... I always knew she'd take you away from me. ...though you took Bruno away from me.*

V+PRON+ADV, V+N+ADV

2 To **take away from** something means to make it lower in value, standard, or amount than it should be or than it was. ❑ *Whatever he may have been like as a person, nothing can take away from his achievements as a scientist. ...joking about alcohol increasing the desire but taking away from the performance.*

V+ADV+PREP

NOTE **Detract from** is a more formal expression for **take away from**.

★take back

1 When you **take** something **back** to the place where you were or where it was before, you go to that place with it. ❑ *'More hot coffee?' She shook her head so he took the tray back. ...spending an hour shopping for gifts to take back with me. ...trying to store up impressions to take back to her stepdaughters... The courier was to take it back to Florence the next day.*

V+N+ADV, V+ADV+N, V+PRON+ADV: ALSO+*to*

2 If you **take back** something which you borrowed or bought, you return it to the place or person that you got it from, for example because you have finished using it or because it is damaged. ❑ *We're going to take the typewriter back to the shop... You will take this book back to Father Huismans... They were totally useless, but he wouldn't take them back to the shop.*

V+N+ADV, V+PRON+ADV, V+ADV+N: ALSO+*to*

3 If you **take back** something which you gave to someone, you agree to accept it from them. If a shop or person **takes back** something which they sold you, they agree to accept it again and to return your money, for example because it is unsuitable or does not work. ❑ *Belinda would not promise anything. Nor would she take back the ring... Shops are often reluctant to take back unsatisfactory goods.*

V+ADV+N, V+PRON+ADV, V+N+ADV

4 If you **take back** something which you had before, you act forcefully so that you have it again. ❑ *You should just have taken your money back and then let me go... We should take back our lost territories in Staten Island... They had taken that amount from his father and he was taking it back from them.*

V+N+ADV, V+ADV+N, V+PRON+ADV

5 If you **take** someone **back** to the place where they were or to your home, you go with them there, usually after arranging to do so. ❑ *How could I take Billy back to York and then arrive in Whitby on time?... I may be taking a friend back with me... They offered to take her back to the hotel.*

V+N+ADV, V+PRON+ADV

6 If you **take** someone **back** after a quarrel or separation, you agree to let them live with you or work with you again. ❑ *Her father would never take her back... She is grateful that he takes her back after her affair... The bank was persuaded to take me back... She wrote to Mrs Cox saying she would be willing to take back the child.*

V+PRON+ADV, V+N+ADV, V+ADV+N

7 If you **take back** something that you have said or thought, you admit that you were wrong. ❑ *I'm going to have to take back all those things I thought about you... Shirley said, 'Take that back or I'll slap your face.'*

V+ADV+N, V+PRON+ADV, V+N+ADV

NOTE **Retract** is a more formal word for **take back**.

8 If you **take** someone or something **back** to the past, you start discussing or con-

V+PRON+ADV,

sidering what happened then. ❏ *Helen then takes us back to her childhood... We can use these studies to take us further back in time. ...to take the historical record further back.*   V+N+ADV

9 If you say that something **takes** you **back**, you mean that it reminds you of a period in your past, and makes you think about it again. ❏ *There was a smell of hot jam that took Tom back to his childhood... Then they sang some sort of Revolutionary ballad. It took us back thirty years to another time.*   V+N+ADV, V+PRON+ADV

★take down

1 If you **take** someone or something **down**, you go with them, or make them go with you, to a lower level, position, or place. You also use **take down** when you are going with them to a different part of a building, town, or country. ❏ *The judge sent the jury away to consider their verdict, and I was taken down to the cells again... She had taken her washing down to the laundry... I thought I'd take a sleeping-bag down to the beach and spend the night there... Their parents took them down to New York City... Hold his hand and take him down the steps carefully.*   V+ADV+N, V+N+ADV/PREP, V+PRON+ADV/PREP

NOTE **Take up** means the opposite of **take down**.

2 If you **take** something **down** from a high place such as a shelf, you reach up and get it, so that you can use it. ❏ *I went over to a shelf and took down a can... He took down a volume of verse... She took down a suitcase from the top of the wardrobe, and opened it.*   V+ADV+N, V+PRON+ADV, V+N+ADV

NOTE **Put back** means the opposite of **take down**.

3 If you **take down** something that is attached to a wall, post, or other object, you unfasten or disconnect it, and remove it. ❏ *The removal men won't take down electrical fittings if wired up to the mains... The saddest moment of course is when on Twelfth Night one has to take down all the Christmas decorations... He was prosecuted for refusing to take the sign down.*   V+ADV+N, V+N+ADV, V+PRON+ADV

NOTE **Put up** means the opposite of **take down**.

4 If you **take down** a barrier, tent, or other structure, you undo or unfasten it, and remove it or put it away. ❏ *Wendy and I took the tent down, packed the van and set out for home... They've taken all the swings down... The scaffolding won't be taken down until next year.*   V+N+ADV, V+ADV+N, V+PRON+ADV

NOTE **Dismantle** is a more formal word for **take down**, and **put up** means the opposite.

5 If you **take down** what someone is saying, you listen to them and write it down or record it. ❏ *The postmistress began to take down the message... He set up a tape recorder at Peter's bed to take down anything he might say. ...as if he was about to take the story down for his newspaper... Is this true? I don't know. I am simply taking it all down.*   V+ADV+N, V+N+ADV, V+PRON+ADV

6 If someone or something **takes** you **down**, they make you feel less confident or less happy with yourself. [INFORMAL] ❏ *Did some rotten cow take you down?... She was almost taken down, but not quite, by an English accent.*   V+PRON+ADV, V+N+ADV

NOTE **Demoralize** is a more formal word for **take down**.

★take in

☑ In meaning 2, the stress is on **take**.

1 If you **take** someone or something **in**, you go with them into a room, building, or other place, such as the centre of a town. ❏ *She said that she would take her drink in with her to dinner... I drove him to the centre of the town – he said he didn't want to take his car in... I took him in to meet Miss Gray... I took in the coffee.*   V+N+ADV, V+PRON+ADV, V+ADV+N

2 If you **take** someone **in** your arms, you put your arms around them. If you **take** something **in** your hand, you hold it. ❏ *I took her in my arms, and kissed her... Jenny came, then, and took the child in her arms... He takes the glass in his left hand still holding the gun in his right.*   V+PRON+PREP, V+N+PREP

3 If you **take** someone **in** to your house, you allow them to live there, either as a favour or in return for payment. ❏ *It was kind of her to take me in. ...houses in which the owner regularly takes in several lodgers... I do you a favour and take Freddie in when you're having a bad time, don't I?*   V+PRON+ADV, V+ADV+N, V+N+ADV

4 If an organization, school, or hospital **takes** you **in**, they accept you or have you as a member, student, patient, and so on. ❏ *He told me that unfortunately they couldn't take me in... The Department take in between 80 and 90 undergraduates a year... We ought to be expanding in order to take in new people.*   V+PRON+ADV, V+ADV+N, V+N+ADV

♦The **intake** of an institution or organization is the number of people who come into it at a particular time. ❑ *...huge intakes of new recruits.*   N-COUNT

5 If the police **take** you **in**, they make you go with them to a police station in order to answer questions or to arrest you. ❑ *First we take him in for questioning... 'Just a moment, you,' they said. 'We are taking you in.'*   V+PRON+ADV, V+N+ADV

6 If you **are taken in** by someone, they deceive or trick you in some way. ❑ *I had given him the money before I was conscious of having been taken in... I wasn't going to be taken in by this kind of sentimentality... Even after years of close acquaintance he could take you in.*   V+PRON+ADV, V+N+ADV, V+ADV+N: USUALLY PASSIVE

7 If you **take in** something that you see, hear, or read, you pay attention to it and are able to understand it, remember it, or evaluate it. ❑ *I didn't take in all that he was saying... Mrs Stannard shook hands, her eyes taking in Karin from head to foot... 'Anticlimax, old boy,' he said, taking in the situation at a glance... Alex had been the perfect pupil, listening and watching and taking it in.*   V+ADV+N, V+PRON+ADV, V+N+ADV

8 To **take** something **in** means to include it. ❑ *The truth takes in both extremes... His talk took in Freud, Wagner, and Goethe.*   V+ADV+N, V+PRON+ADV, V+N+ADV

NOTE **Embrace** is a more formal word for **take in**.

9 If one thing **takes in** another, it is big enough to include the other thing within it. ❑ *Ethiopia's large territorial area takes in a population of more than 40 million people.*   V+ADV+N, V+N/PRON+ADV: NO PASSIVE

10 If you **take in** something such as a film, a museum, or a place, while you are on holiday or travelling somewhere, you go to see it or visit it. ❑ *He told them of weekends in London where one could always take in a show... We had taken in all the movies... I flew on to California, deciding to take in Florida on the way home.*   V+ADV+N, V+N+ADV, V+PRON+ADV

11 If you **take in** the milk, the washing, the newspaper, and so on, you bring it into your house from outside. ❑ *...fifteen minutes later, when she took in the milk... She got up to take in the washing.*   V+ADV+N, V+N+ADV, V+PRON+ADV

12 If you **take in** washing, sewing, typing, and so on, you earn money at home by washing, sewing, or typing for other people. ❑ *All this while she continued taking in washing for the well-off people in neighbouring streets... I thought I'd take in dressmaking in a small way... Jane took in clerical work at home.*   V+ADV+N, V+N+ADV

13 If you **take in** your car, a machine, and so on, you go with it to a place where it can be serviced or repaired. ❑ *I had to take the car in this morning... We took in the sewing machine to be repaired.*   V+N+ADV, V+ADV+N, V+PRON+ADV

14 When people or animals **take in** air, drink, food, and so on, it enters their bodies, for example because they breathe it or swallow it. ❑ *Sharks take in water through the mouth... She sat taking in breaths of fresh air.*   V+ADV+N, V+N+ADV, V+PRON+ADV

♦ Someone's **intake** of food, drink, or air is the amount that enters their body, or the process of it entering their body. ❑ *...the average daily intake of iron in a normal diet. ...oxygen intake.*   N-UNCOUNT

♦ You talk about an **intake** of breath when someone breathes in quickly and deeply, perhaps because they are shocked at something. ❑ *There is an intake of breath and some of us look at each other.*   N-COUNT

15 If you **take in** a dress, jacket, or other item of clothing, you make it smaller and tighter by altering its seams. ❑ *He lost so much weight that he had to take in all his trousers.*   V+ADV+N, V+N+ADV, V+PRON+ADV

NOTE **Let out** means the opposite of **take in**.

16 If a store, restaurant, theatre, or other business **takes in** a certain amount of money, they get that amount from people buying goods or services. [AMERICAN] ❑ *They plan to take in $1.6 billion.*   V+ADV+N, V+N+ADV, V+PRON+ADV

★take into

1 If you **take** someone or something **into** a place, you go with them there. ❑ *I took my cup of tea into the sitting room and sat there wondering... I took him into the nearest pub... We must get a message to her mother, before I take her into Caxley.*   V+N+PREP, V+PRON+PREP

2 If you **take** someone **into** an organization, school, or hospital, you accept them as a member, student, patient, and so on. ❑ *Mr Phillips would have taken Simon into the business, had he so wanted... If I had been taken into the local psychiatric hospital they could only have prescribed further drugs... Then my boss offered to take me into the firm as a full time member of her staff.*   V+N+PREP, V+PRON+PREP

The symbol ★ shows key phrasal verbs

3 When people or animals **take** something **into** their bodies, it enters their bodies, for example because they breathe it or swallow it. ❏ *...feeling as if I'd rather not breathe than take the dust into my lungs... The fish will hit the bait hard, as it takes it into its mouth.* V+N+PREP, V+PRON+PREP

4 If something **takes** you **into** a particular subject or activity, it causes you to consider it or become involved in it. ❏ *These thoughts could take me into places I didn't want to be... To do this, I have to take you into the relations existing between ideology and politics... What had taken him into politics in the first place?* V+N+PREP, V+PRON+PREP, V+N+PREP

5 To **take** something **into** a new state or situation means to cause it to be in that state or situation. ❏ *Successive administrations had been forced to take firms into public ownership... Years of low investment had re-enforced low profits, taking Britain into a spiral of decline... Women have succeeded in taking women's studies into the university curriculum.* V+N+PREP, V+PRON+PREP

6 If you say that something will **take** you **into** a future period of time, you mean that it will last or continue to be effective until that time. ❏ *...a package of policies which will take farming into the next century in a prosperous state... Coal will take us into the next century and may go on for another hundred years or so. ...a preliminary season of ten weeks which would take him into May.* V+N+PREP, V+PRON+PREP

★take off

1 If you **take** something **off**, you remove it or separate it from the place where it was. ❏ *Without moving the packing case from its position he took off the top. ...as soon as you take off the pressure... How do you measure the social costs of taking traffic off London roads?... Bring the water to the boil, then take it off the heat and leave it to cool down.* V+ADV+N, V+N+ADV/PREP, V+PRON+ADV/PREP

NOTE **Put on** means the opposite of **take off**.

2 If you **take off** your clothes or something that you are wearing, you undress or remove it. ❏ *She took off the amber necklace and put it on the dressing-table... I had taken my clothes off because of the heat... She stood up, undid her skirt and took it off.* V+ADV+N, V+N+ADV, V+PRON+ADV

NOTE **Put on** means the opposite of **take off**.

3 If you **take** something **off** someone, you use force or your authority to get it from them. ❏ *We were defending the principle that you cannot take things off other people by force... They were going to take some money off you... If I had a gun I'd go and take it off them.* V+N+PREP, V+PRON+PREP

4 When an aeroplane or bird **takes off**, it leaves the ground and starts flying. ❏ *A steady stream of aircraft was taking off and landing... After refuelling we took off... The swans took off from the lake.* V+ADV

NOTE **Land** means the opposite of **take off**.

♦ **Takeoff** is the beginning of a flight, when an aircraft leaves the ground. ❏ *Ninety per cent of all aircraft accidents occur at either take-off or landing. ...the overwhelming din of takeoffs.* N-UNCOUNT, N-COUNT

5 If something such as a product or activity **takes off**, it suddenly becomes very successful and popular. ❏ *When the micro market really takes off, the Japanese will once again be its principal competitors... It will be interesting to see how the campaign takes off.* V+ADV

♦ **Takeoff** is the stage in the development of a product or activity when it begins to be successful. ❏ *The government had already provided the groundwork for economic take-off by creating almost full employment.* N-UNCOUNT

6 If you **take off** or **take** yourself **off**, you go away, often suddenly and unexpectedly. ❏ *They took off for a weekend in the country... He lived with her for a bit, but then took off again, to the Far East this time... I thought I would take myself off on a little trip.* V+ADV, V+REFL+ADV: USUALLY+A

7 If you **take** someone **off** to a particular place or institution, you make them go there with you. ❏ *She came down with pneumonia and was taken off to hospital... Then they took him off to prison.* V+N+ADV, V+PRON+ADV

8 If you **take** someone **off** a task or list, you stop them doing that task or being on that list. ❏ *The Police will take every one of its detectives off whatever he is on... He was taken off the case on orders from headquarters... The next day, I found Laura had taken me off the list.* V+N+PREP, V+PRON+PREP

9 If you **take** time **off**, you spend it doing something different from your normal routine or job. ❏ *Bill and I took time off from work and flew to France... You have to take off Christmas Day as a holiday... They could not afford to take a day off work.* V+N+ADV, V+ADV+N, V+N+PREP

10 If you **take off** something such as an amount of money or a mark, you subtract V+ADV+N, it from a total. ❏ *Your employer will take off some of your wages to pay your national insurance contribution... Half a point would be taken off for a mistake in spelling.*

V+N+ADV,
V+PRON+ADV

NOTE **Add on** means the opposite of **take off**.

11 If you **take** someone **off**, you imitate their appearance or behaviour, usually in order to make other people laugh. [BRITISH] ❏ *Mike can take off his father to perfection.*

V+ADV+N,
V+N+ADV,
V+PRON+ADV

NOTE **Mimic** means almost the same as **take off**.

◆ A **takeoff** of someone is an imitation of their appearance or behaviour that is done in order to make people laugh. ❏ *He did a very amusing take-off of the headmaster.*

N-COUNT

12 If someone in authority **takes** you **off** a particular type of food, medical treatment, or punishment, they stop it from being given to you. ❏ *The doctor took her off insulin. ...people being forcibly taken off drugs.*

V+N+PREP,
V+N+PREP

NOTE **Put on** means the opposite of **take off**.

13 If a bus, train, or plane service **is taken off**, it stops operating and is no longer available for people to use. ❏ *The 7.18 London train was taken off for the winter.*

V+ADV+N,
V+N+ADV,
V+PRON+ADV:
USUALLY PASSIVE

NOTE **Be withdrawn** is a more formal expression for **be taken off**.

14 If a play **is taken off** at a particular theatre, its performances there end. ❏ *'My Fair Lady' was taken off when it was at the peak of its success... I've no idea why it was taken off.*

V+N+ADV,
V+PRON+ADV,
V+ADV+N:
USUALLY PASSIVE

★take on

✓ In meaning 6, the stress is on t**a**ke.

1 If you **take on** a job, task, or responsibility, you accept it and try to do what is required. ❏ *She takes on more work than is good for her... He should have had it attended to before he took the job on... I must say I think it's very nice of him to take it on.*

V+ADV+N,
V+N+ADV,
V+PRON+ADV

2 If something **takes on** a new quality or appearance, it develops that quality or appearance. ❏ *His voice took on a new note of uncertainty... From this point on, the whole scheme began to take on a more practical aspect... The word 'profession' is taking on a new meaning.*

V+ADV+N

NOTE **Assume** is a more formal word for **take on**.

3 If someone **takes** you **on** at a place of work, they employ you. ❏ *They took me on because I was a good mathematician... I was keen to take him on to my editorial staff... Employers take on fewer young people.*

V+PRON+ADV,
V+ADV+N,
V+N+ADV

4 If you **take on** a rival or opponent, especially one who is bigger or more powerful than you, you fight or compete against them. ❏ *Industry, he said, was better equipped than ever before to take on the competition and win. ...the Government's decision to take on the unions... They wouldn't let him take me on.*

V+ADV+N,
V+PRON+ADV,
V+N+ADV

NOTE **Tackle** means almost the same as **take on**.

5 If a bus, train, ship, or plane **takes on** passengers, goods, or fuel, it stops in order to allow the passengers to get on or the goods or fuel to be loaded. ❏ *Buses stopped by request to take on more passengers... We sailed to Ajaccio in order to take on fresh lobster... We're only stopping briefly to take on fuel.*

V+ADV+N,
V+PRON+ADV,
V+N+ADV

6 If you **take** something **on** yourself or **take** it **upon** yourself, or if you **take** it **upon** yourself to do something, you decide to do it without asking anyone for permission or approval. **Take upon** is slightly more formal. ❏ *Mrs Cook took matters upon herself... Mrs Kaul took it upon herself to turn round and say 'Be quiet!'... I couldn't take it on myself to provide you with that information.*

V+N+PREP+REFL,
ALSO V+it+PREP+REFL:
WITH to-INF

7 If you say **'Don't take on'** to someone, you mean that they should not get angry or upset about a situation, or make a fuss about it. [INFORMAL] ❏ *Now don't take on, darling! Honestly, I won't be any time at all... No need to take on so, ma!*

V+ADV:
USUALLY WITH NEGATIVE

★take out

1 When you **take** something **out**, you remove it from a container or from the place where it was. ❏ *Emma opened her bag and took out her comb... Davis was taking a report out of the office... I felt in my jacket for my address book, and took it out.*

V+ADV+N,
V+N+ADV,
V+PRON+ADV:
ALSO+of/from

NOTE **Put back** means the opposite of **take out**.

◆ A **take-out** or **take-out** food is hot cooked food that is sold to be eaten somewhere else. [AMERICAN] ❏ *...the Chinese takeout dinner. ...a take-out of spaghetti sauce.*

ADJECTIVE,
N-COUNT

NOTE In British English, **takeaway** means almost the same as **take-out**.

2 To **take** something **out** means to remove it for ever from the place where it was, for example because it is unwanted or damaged. ❏ *They could edit that film, take bits out. ...to take the sulphur out of natural gas... If you don't like the fireplace you can take it*

V+N+ADV,
V+PRON+ADV,
V+ADV+N:
ALSO+of

out... The only way to get the sculptures into the museum would be to take out the ground floor windows on Fifth Avenue.

3 If you **take** someone **out**, for example to a restaurant or a film, they go there with you, and you pay for everything. ❏ *I took Andrea out to dinner one evening... Why don't you take the children out?... He offered to take us out for a drink or something.*

V+N+ADV,
V+PRON+ADV,
V+ADV+N

4 If you **take** someone **out**, you kill them. If you **take** something **out**, you destroy it or damage it so that it can no longer be used. [INFORMAL] ❏ *He and his brother have taken out 58 enemy soldiers between them... 'You see that gun?' he said. 'Now, that'll take out a police station for you.'... Several miles of railway line were taken out by bombs that went off at six hundred yard intervals.*

V+ADV+N,
V+N+ADV,
V+PRON+ADV

NOTE **Wipe out** means almost the same as **take out**.

5 If you **take out** something such as a licence, an insurance policy, or a bank loan, you arrange to get it from a court of law, an insurance company, or a bank. ❏ *I want to take out a mortgage... He had lived seventeen years in Chicago, but he had never taken out naturalisation papers... The policy gives life cover, so if you took it out on your husband's life, you'd get a lump sum if he died.*

V+ADV+N,
V+PRON+ADV

6 If you **take out** money from a bank or a bank account, you obtain it by writing a cheque or filling in a form. ❏ *Where can I take cash out and how much can I withdraw at any one time?... You can also take out money at any other branch of your own bank... You get interest even on the amount withdrawn right up to the time you take it out.*

V+N+ADV,
V+ADV+N,
V+PRON+ADV

NOTE **Withdraw** is a more formal word for **take out**.

7 If you **take out** a book from a library, you borrow it for a time. ❏ *Can I take a book out right away?... She would recommend titles that he could ask his mother to take out for him from the adult section of the library... The book had been on the shelves for several months, but so far no one had taken it out.*

V+N+ADV,
V+ADV+N,
V+PRON+ADV

8 If you **take** time **out**, you spend time doing something different from what you are supposed to be doing, or from what you normally do. [INFORMAL] ❏ *In the middle of the campaign, he took time out to attend a meeting of local officials... The plumber was taking time out for a cigarette... She would have to take a day out from her bread baking.*

V+N+ADV

NOTE **Take off** means almost the same as **take out**.

take out of

1 If something **takes** a lot **out of** you, or **takes** it **out of** you, it makes you feel exhausted. [INFORMAL] ❏ *I find that people take so much out of me... The work an artist does takes so much out of him, in the way of feeling and emotion... A five-block walk in that heat could take it out of you.*

V+N+ADV+PREP,
V+it+ADV+PREP

2 If something **takes** you **out of** yourself, it makes you stop thinking about your problems or the situation you are in. ❏ *People will adore this film: it takes you right out of yourself... That cheered me up, took me out of myself, cured my depression... The glory of the play and its magnificent poetry took you out of yourself.*

V+PRON+PREP,
V+N+PREP:
WITH REFL

take out on If you **take** something **out on** someone, you behave in an unpleasant way towards them because you feel angry or upset, even though it is not their fault. ❏ *I was in a depressed and hostile mood, needing to take my bad feelings out on someone... When Kurt was in one of his moods, he took it out on everyone... She took out most of her unhappiness on her husband.*

V+N+ADV+PREP,
V+it+ADV+PREP,
V+ADV+N+PREP

★take over

1 To **take over** a company or business means to gain control of it by buying it or buying a majority of its shares. ❏ *Some people wanted to take over my father's oil importing business... The I.P.C. was taken over by the huge Reed Paper Group... No tycoon has ever been able to take it over.*

V+ADV+N,
V+N+ADV,
V+PRON+ADV

NOTE **Buy out** means almost the same as **take over**.

♦ A **takeover** is the act of gaining control of a company by buying it or buying a majority of its shares. ❏ *The trend towards takeovers has intensified... All middle-size oil companies are likely candidates for takeover... His firm might be vulnerable to a takeover bid.*

N-COUNT,
N-UNCOUNT,
ADJECTIVE

2 If people **take over** a country, region, or city, they gain control of it, usually with the help of an army. ❏ *Once again the military had taken over... Well-trained and equipped troops could probably take over the country... They had preferred to destroy the town rather than take it over. ...wanting to send in the National Guard and take the city over.*

V+ADV,
V+ADV+N,
V+PRON+ADV,
V+N+ADV

♦ A **takeover** is the act of gaining control of a country, region, or city, usually with the help of an army. ❑ *...the danger of a military takeover.*   N-COUNT

3 If people who are protesting about something **take over** a factory or other building, they enter it and stay there, preventing it from being used normally, as part of their protest. ❑ *The television station was taken over and held for some hours by technicians... Feminists in Italy took over hospital clinics... They took over the university for a week in protest.*   V+ADV+N, V+PRON+ADV, V+N+ADV

NOTE **Occupy** is a more formal word for **take over.**

♦ A **takeover** is the act of occupying a factory or other building as a form of protest. ❑ *The student takeover was just the beginning.*   N-COUNT

4 If you **take over** a house, flat, or room, you start living in it or using it. ❑ *She had taken the house over some months before... She wanted a flat of her own, but I suggested she take over mine while I was in California... Doctor Ford had taken it over, possibly the only place available in the house.*   V+N+ADV, V+ADV+N, V+PRON+ADV

5 If you **take over** a job or a responsibility, you start doing it or being responsible for it after someone else has finished. ❑ *Thornaby took over as secretary in 1976... I took over from a man who was brilliant at recruiting agents... Heever returned to take over the questioning... Relatives took their debts over.*   V+ADV: ALSO+as/from; ALSO V+ADV+N, V+N+ADV, V+PRON+ADV

6 If you **take** trouble, care, or time **over** something, you do it slowly, carefully, and thoroughly. ❑ *He had taken particular pains over the report... This is a purchase which it is worth taking a lot of trouble over... She washed herself most carefully and took a long time over it.*   V+N+PREP

7 If you **take** something or someone **over** to a place or person, you carry them or lead them to that place or person. ❑ *Leave the door open while I take him over to the house... The woman took two full bottles over to the group round the big table... Then he takes a chair over and sits down to look at her.*   V+PRON+ADV, V+N+ADV, V+ADV+N: ALSO+to

8 If a feeling, thought, or activity **takes** you **over**, it affects you so strongly or takes so much of your time that you find it difficult to do anything else. ❑ *If the woman feels there are forces which took her over, she is confirmed in her role of dependency... I let the thought take me over... So often his busy life took him over for weeks on end and he lost all contact with us.*   V+PRON+ADV, V+N+ADV

9 If one thing **takes over** from another, it becomes more important, successful, or powerful than the other thing, and eventually replaces it. ❑ *Microfilms might even take over from libraries... Reading to learn now seems to take over from learning to read... The science of medicine took over from the art of healing.*   V+ADV: USUALLY+from

take round → See **take around**

take through If you **take** someone **through** a procedure or task, you discuss it or do it with them, so that they know what to do. ❑ *Helen, would you be kind enough to take Elaine through the schedule... Lodge took the actors through the scene again... If you wish, someone will take you through the sums.*   V+N+PREP, V+PRON+PREP

take to

1 If you **take to** someone or something, you begin to like them. ❑ *It was impossible to tell whether he had taken to Rose or not... I didn't think at first I'd take to him – but I did... I was taught Geography at school but never took to it.*   V+PREP

NOTE **Take against** means the opposite of **take to.**

2 If you **take to** doing something, you begin to do it as a regular habit. ❑ *He took to wearing black leather jackets... As they grow larger, they take to eating fish... This he had achieved by taking to a life of crime.*   V+PREP+-ING, V+PREP

3 If you **take to** a place, you go there, usually as a result of a difficult or dangerous situation. ❑ *Their leaders took to hideouts in the Pondoland hills... I took to my bed with a fever that lasted two weeks... The local inhabitants took to the streets to defend themselves and their property.*   V+PREP

★take up

1 If you **take** someone or something **up**, you go with them, or make them go with you, to a higher level, position, or place. You also use **take up** when you are going with them to a different part of a building, town, or country. ❑ *If you'll excuse me, I'll take her tea up... I will take Fanny up to my room now... A guard took them up the hill... I*   V+N+ADV/PREP, V+PRON+ADV/PREP, V+ADV+N *went downstairs again, and Aunt Bertha took up the beer.*

NOTE **Take down** means the opposite of **take up**.

2 If something **takes up** a particular amount of time, space, or effort, it uses that amount. ❑ *Dresses don't take up much space... The baby took up all her energy and attention... At the moment 'Oliver' is taking a lot of my time up.*

V+ADV+N,
V+N+ADV,
V+PRON+ADV

NOTE **Occupy** is a more formal word for **take up**.

3 If you **take up** an activity or job, you start doing it. ❑ *I thought I'd take up fishing... She decided to take up medicine as a career... I might take it up professionally.*

V+ADV+N,
V+PRON+ADV,
V+N+ADV

NOTE **Go in for** means almost the same as **take up**.

4 If you **take up** a point, idea, or issue that you think is important, you draw attention to it and cause it to be discussed or dealt with. ❑ *The committee is expected to take up the question of the government's role in the arts... Mr Biffen took this point up by harking back to his own career... He declined the offer and took the matter up with his shop steward... We took this up with the social worker.*

V+ADV+N,
V+N+ADV,
V+PRON+ADV,
ALSO+with

NOTE **Pick up** means almost the same as **take up**, and **pursue** is a more formal word.

♦ If you are quick on the **uptake**, you understand an idea or situation quickly. ❑ *She was not very quick on the uptake and needed time to register and take everything in.*

N-SING

5 If you **take up** an offer, challenge, or opportunity, you accept it. ❑ *She wished Jane would take up Derek's offer to decorate the house... Harlech television took up the challenge and made a splendid documentary about it... Lionel allowed a pause for elaboration but she did not take it up.*

V+ADV+N,
V+PRON+ADV,
V+N+ADV

NOTE **Decline** means the opposite of **take up**.

♦ **Take-up** is the rate at which people apply for or buy something which is being offered to them. ❑ *Initially, there wasn't much take-up of the home improvement offers.*

N-UNCOUNT

6 If you **take up** a particular attitude, belief, or way of doing something, you start to have it. ❑ *He hated to see her taking up this hard, uncompromising attitude... They had abandoned Californian living patterns and had taken up European ones... Such styles may later be taken up by the media.*

V+ADV+N

NOTE **Adopt** is a more formal word for **take up**.

7 If you **take up** an activity that was interrupted, you continue doing it from the point where it had stopped. ❑ *Sam took up the story... Nicola was taking up where she had left off. ...the plan to kill him, which she had abandoned, or had she taken it up again?*

V+ADV+N,
V+PRON+ADV,
V+N+ADV

NOTE **Pick up** means almost the same as **take up**.

8 If you **take up** a song or chant that other people are singing or shouting, you start singing it or shouting it with them. ❑ *The other boys took up the cry till the mountain rang... She intoned a song and the other women took it up.*

V+ADV+N,
V+PRON+ADV,
V+N+ADV

9 If you **take up** an object, you begin to hold it or carry it. [OLD-FASHIONED] ❑ *She took up the box and tapped the lid... When they had finished eating, the men took up their tools again... She took it up, and threw it.*

V+ADV+N,
V+PRON+ADV

NOTE **Pick up** means almost the same as **take up**.

10 If you **take up** a particular position, you move to it, because you have been told to or because it is the best position for what you want to do. ❑ *The fire engines had taken up position by the runway... As the herd gallops away, he takes up the rear... Machine-gunners were to take up positions to cover the main charge.*

V+ADV+N,
V+N+ADV,
V+PRON+ADV

11 If something that is fixed to a surface **is taken up**, it is removed from that surface. ❑ *The rails were taken up and used to make weapons... Then she takes the lino up, and scrubs the boards underneath.*

V+N+ADV,
V+PRON+ADV,
V+ADV+N

NOTE **Pull up** means almost the same as **take up**.

12 If you **take up** something such as a dress or a pair of trousers, you shorten it by folding up the bottom edge and stitching it in place. ❑ *You can always take that skirt up if you don't like it that long... I've taken it up twice, and it still looks wrong.*

V+ADV+N,
V+N+ADV,
V+PRON+ADV

NOTE **Let down** means the opposite of **take up**.

13 If someone **takes** you **up** when you are starting a career, they help, support, and encourage you to succeed. ❑ *He was my agent – a dealer who took me up, and stuck to me... Stanley and Guy had taken up young Balintoy... You're lucky to have been taken up by a clergyman.*

V+N+ADV,
V+PRON+ADV,
V+ADV+N

NOTE **Patronize** is a more formal word for **take up**.

14 To **take up** moisture, gas, or other substance means to absorb it. ❏ *Red blood cells take up oxygen... A growing crop will take up and store the nitrogen and other elements in the soil.*

♦ A person's or machine's **uptake** of something is the amount of it that they use. [TECHNICAL] ❏ *An athlete has a maximum oxygen uptake of four litres per minute... She increased the water uptake.*

[NOTE] **Intake** means almost the same as **uptake**.

15 If you **take up** a collection of money, you collect it from people. ❏ *He took up a collection and sent the money to Jerusalem.*

V+ADV+N, V+N+ADV, V+PRON+ADV

N-SING

V+ADV+N

take upon → See **take on**

take up on

1 If you **take** someone **up on** an offer they have made, you accept their offer. ❏ *She paused a while, in case he might care to take her up on her offer... But this suggestion is absurd, and no one takes him up on it... That's very kind of you, Mr Zapp, I'll take you up on that generous invitation.*

V+PRON+ADV+PREP, V+N+ADV+PREP

2 If you **take** someone **up on** something they have said or done, you ask them to explain or justify what they have said or done, because you think that they are wrong. ❏ *I think I would like to take Tony up on something that he said... I'm going to be very unkind and very rude and take you up on this.*

V+N+ADV+PREP, V+PRON+ADV+PREP

[NOTE] **Pick up on** means almost the same as **take up on**.

take up with

1 If you **take up with** someone, you begin to be friendly with them and spend a lot of time with them. ❏ *For a little time after she took up with Mr Marvin she went on singing in public. ...Doreen being the first girl he'd taken up with after Ginny.*

V+ADV+PREP

2 If you **are taken up with** something, it keeps you busy or fully occupied. ❏ *She was too taken up with her own feelings to pay much attention to his... The meeting I attended was taken up with discussion of the group's failure to attract new members.*

PASSIVE: V+ADV+PREP

talk /tɔːk/ (talks, talking, talked)

> ☑ In American English, **around** is much more common than **round**.

talk around If people **talk around** or **talk round** a subject or problem, they discuss it in a general way, often failing to deal with the main points. ❏ *I just have a feeling that I've somehow talked around the point.*

V+PREP

talk at If you **talk at** someone, you talk to them without letting them speak or without listening to their opinions. ❏ *Charles had been talking at him for hours, permitting few interruptions... I've kept you too long, I've talked at you too much.*

V+PREP: HAS PASSIVE

talk away If you **talk away**, you talk continuously for a period of time. ❏ *You were talking away like a nine-year-old kid... Along she came, wagging her stick and talking away to herself.*

V+ADV

talk back If you **talk back** to someone in authority such as a parent or teacher, you answer them in a bold or rude way. ❏ *Don't talk back to me like that!... He, however, talked back firmly to his generals... She was shocked to hear me talking back so forcefully.*

V+ADV: USUALLY+to

[NOTE] **Answer back** means almost the same as **talk back**.

talk down

1 If someone **talks** you **down**, they talk longer or louder than you do and so make you stop talking. ❏ *I objected to the proposal, but they talked me down... He made another weak protest and was talked down by Jenny.*

V+PRON+ADV, V+N+ADV

2 To **talk down** the pilot of an aircraft means to give them instructions over the radio so that they can land the aircraft, for example in bad weather or in an emergency.

V+N+ADV, V+PRON+ADV, V+ADV+N

3 If someone **talks down** a particular thing, they make it less interesting, valuable, or likely than it originally seemed. ❏ *They even blame the government for talking down the nation's fourth biggest industry... Businessmen are tired of politicians talking the economy down.*

V+ADV+N, V+N+ADV, V+PRON+ADV

[NOTE] **Talk up** means the opposite of **talk down**.

4 To **talk** someone **down** in negotiations means to persuade them to accept less money than they originally asked for. [BRITISH] ❏ *We talked them down and struck a*

V+ADV+N, V+N+ADV, V+PRON+ADV:

deal... When he makes you an offer, you send me in and I'll talk him down another thou- ALSO WITH NUMBER
sand... This leaves the Prime Minister, like his predecessors, earnestly trying to talk down
wages.

talk down to If someone **talks down to** you, they talk to you in a way that V+ADV+PREP:
shows that they think that they are more important or more clever than you. ❏ *Par-* HAS PASSIVE
ents can't dictate to their adolescent children or talk down to them... I think some of the
teachers felt they were being talked down to.
NOTE **Patronize** is a more formal word for **talk down to**.

★talk into

1 If you **talk** someone **into** doing something, you persuade them to do it. ❏ *She* V+PRON+PREP,
talked me into taking a week's holiday... He talked the Pondo leaders into ending the V+N+PREP
uprising.
NOTE **Talk out of** means the opposite of **talk into**.

2 If you **talk** yourself **into** a particular situation or state, you get yourself into it by V+REFL+PREP
talking. ❏ *He has talked himself into a position where he will have no option but to go... We*
can talk ourselves into anything.

talk out

1 If people **talk out** a problem, plan, or idea, they discuss it thoroughly. V+ADV+N,
❏ *Marianne had come to talk out her plan of campaign. ...listening to other people talk out* V+N+ADV,
their problems... They began talking things out between themselves... They helped me by let- V+PRON+ADV
ting me talk it out over several days.

2 If you **talk** yourself **out**, you talk so much that you feel that you have nothing V+REFL+ADV
more to say. ❏ *He said little, simply letting me talk myself out each time... We were enjoying*
the kind of relationship we had, talking ourselves out and not feeling bored.

★talk out of

1 If you **talk** someone **out of** doing something, you persuade them not to do it. V+PRON+ADV+PREP,
❏ *He tried to talk me out of buying such a big car... Fortunately, Faye Seidel talked her hus-* V+N+ADV+PREP
band out of his plan.
NOTE **Talk into** means the opposite of **talk out of**.

2 If you **talk** yourself **out of** a particular situation or state, you get yourself out of V+REFL+ADV+PREP
it by talking. ❏ *I tried to talk myself out of a fight... She managed to talk herself out of go-*
ing.

★talk over
If you **talk** something **over**, you discuss it with someone. ❏ *I'll talk it* V+PRON+ADV,
over with Len tonight and let you know tomorrow... There's plenty of opportunity for you to V+N+ADV,
talk your problems over... We all met in Pat's room, to talk over what we had seen. V+ADV+N:
USUALLY+with

talk round

1 If you **talk** someone **round**, you persuade them to agree with you or to do what V+N+ADV,
you want them to do. ❏ *I must talk Daddy round. He won't like it... He didn't really want* V+PRON+ADV
to go to France, but I managed to talk him round.

2 → See **talk around**

★talk through

1 If people **talk through** a problem, plan, or idea, they discuss it thoroughly until V+ADV+N,
some sort of agreement is made. ❏ *We had already talked through many problematic* V+PRON+ADV,
areas and wanted to move on... At breakfast, I talked through the options with Jennifer... We V+N+ADV:
often find that people like to talk it through with someone. USUALLY+with
NOTE **Talk over** means almost the same as **talk through**.

2 If you **talk** someone **through** a difficult situation, you help or support them by V+N+PREP,
talking to them and reassuring them. ❏ *Boon had talked a pregnant mother through her* V+PRON+PREP
first labour pains... You may find your coach talking you through certain phases of the train-
ing session.

★talk to

1 If you **talk to** someone, you have a conversation with them. ❏ *I just wanted to* V+PREP:
talk to you... I was talking to Mike about this... I find her so easy to talk to... You were talk- HAS PASSIVE
ing to her at the party... The child wants to be talked to and reassured.

2 If you give someone a **talking-to**, you speak to them seriously or forcefully, espe- N-SING
cially about something they have failed to do or have done wrong. ❏ *Grab them, hold*
them face to face, and give them a talking-to.

talk up

1 If someone **talks up** a particular thing, they make it sound more interesting, valuable, or likely than it originally seemed. ❑ *Politicians accuse the media of talking up the possibility of a riot... He'll be talking up his plans for the economy.*

NOTE **Talk down** means the opposite of **talk up**.

V+ADV+N,
V+N+ADV,
V+PRON+ADV

2 To **talk** someone or something **up** in negotiations means to persuade someone to pay more money than they originally offered or wanted to. [BRITISH] ❑ *Allan Clarke kept talking the price up, while Wilkinson kept knocking it down.*

NOTE **Talk down** means the opposite of **talk up**.

V+ADV+N,
V+N+ADV,
V+PRON+ADV:
ALSO WITH NUMBER

★talk with If you **talk with** someone, you have a conversation with them. [AMERICAN] ❑ *I'd like to talk with you about your husband... I'd spent an hour talking with a new student called Kathleen. ...every time we meet and talk with a companion... Grout had often talked with the farmers.*

V+PREP

tamp /tæmp/ (tamps, tamping, tamped)

tamp down If you **tamp** something **down**, you press it down several times so that it becomes more solid and compact. ❑ *It will probably be necessary to tamp the clay down... One man shovelled tarmac into the hole, the other tamped it down.*

V+N+ADV,
V+PRON+ADV,
V+ADV+N

tamper /tæmpər/ (tampers, tampering, tampered)

tamper with If you **tamper with** something, you try to change it in some way when you have no right to do so. ❑ *Someone had tampered with the register of the church and changed the christening records... I'm against tampering with nature in such a vital matter... He claimed that his briefcase had been tampered with on the flight.*

V+PREP:
HAS PASSIVE

NOTE **Interfere with** means almost the same as **tamper with**.

tangle /tæŋgəl/ (tangles, tangling, tangled)

tangle up

1 If something such as string or wire **is tangled up**, it is twisted into an untidy mass which is difficult to separate or sort out. ❑ *Use a light cord rather than a string which gets tangled up... Don't do that; you're tangling them up!... It ripped the hinges and tangled up the barbed wire.*

V+N+ADV,
V+PRON+ADV,
V+ADV+N

2 If someone or something **is tangled up** in wires or ropes, they are caught or trapped in them so that it is difficult to free them. ❑ *He's out there tangled up in the wire... He was tangled up in a mess of chains.*

PASSIVE:
V+ADV:
USUALLY+in

3 If you get **tangled up** in a complicated or unpleasant situation, you become involved in it and cannot get free of it. ❑ *Politicians normally avoid getting tangled up in anything to do with their electorate's savings.*

PASSIVE:
V+ADV:
USUALLY+in

♦ If you are **tangled up** in a complicated or unpleasant situation, you are involved in it. ❑ *For many days now Buddy and Joe had appeared to be more and more tangled up in secrets.*

ADJECTIVE

tangle with If you **tangle with** someone, you get involved in a fight or quarrel with them. [INFORMAL] ❑ *I wouldn't tangle with him if I were you... I'm tangling with some tough guys, Jerry.*

V+PREP:
HAS PASSIVE

NOTE **Mess with** means almost the same as **tangle with**.

tap /tæp/ (taps, tapping, tapped)

tap for If you **tap** someone **for** something, you persuade them to give you something you want, especially money or information. [INFORMAL] ❑ *I'll tap my Dad for a couple of hundred... Get to know the neighbours fast so that you can tap them for sugar, milk and teabags.*

V+N+PREP,
V+PRON+PREP

tap in

1 If you **tap in** something sharp such as a nail, you force it into a surface by hitting it with quick, light blows. ❑ *I found a spot close to the tepee, and started to tap in the pegs... He tapped the drawing pins in gently with a book.*

V+ADV+N,
V+N+ADV,
V+PRON+ADV

2 If you **tap** numbers or letters **in**, you type them into a machine by pressing the keys or buttons with your fingers. ❑ *Simply put your card into the machine, tap in your personal number and you can withdraw up to £100 a day... Presumably there are codes that you have to tap in before you can get access to the information.*

V+N+ADV,
V+PRON+ADV,
V+ADV+N

NOTE **Key in** means almost the same as **tap in**.

tap into If someone or something **taps into** a source of something such as energy, information, or money, they manage to obtain energy, information, or money from it, sometimes illegally. ❑ *You have to find the right places to tap into the heat sources.* ...*tapping into the body's reserve energy.* ...*tapped into the university's private funds.* `V+PREP`

tap out To **tap out** a sound means to produce it by hitting a surface lightly and repeatedly. ❑ *I could hear the telegraph instrument tapping out morse.* ...*tapping out the rhythm.* `V+ADV+N, V+N+ADV, V+PRON+ADV`

tape /teɪp/ **(tapes, taping, taped)**

tape up If you **tape** something **up**, you fasten tape around it firmly, in order to protect it or to hold it in a certain position. ❑ *I cleaned and disinfected the scratches and taped them up carefully... Tape the windows up and leave the room.* `V+PRON+ADV, V+N+ADV, V+ADV+N`

taper /teɪpər/ **(tapers, tapering, tapered)**

taper off If something **tapers off** or if you **taper** it **off**, it gradually becomes greatly reduced in size, quantity, or amount. ❑ ...*in the 1970s, as the economic boom tapered off... Patterson's voice kind of tapered off... Keep this diet up for several days, then taper it off... The plan was to inject the drugs, then taper off the dosage.* `V+ADV, V+PRON+ADV, V+ADV+N, V+N+ADV: ERGATIVE`

tart /tɑːrt/ **(tarts, tarting, tarted)**

tart up

1 If a woman **tarts** herself **up**, she tries to make herself look especially smart and attractive. [BRITISH, INFORMAL] ❑ *I didn't know whether to tart myself up or just go in my normal clothes.* `V+REFL+ADV`

NOTE **Doll up** means almost the same as **tart up**.

2 If someone **tarts up** a room or building, they try to improve its appearance, often in a way that you consider vulgar. [BRITISH, INFORMAL] ❑ *They put in furniture, antiques, fabrics, anything to tart up the place.* ...*a monstrosity of a house he tarted up with a tennis court and swimming pool... It was a nice old pub till they decided to tart it up.* `V+ADV+N, V+N+ADV, V+PRON+ADV`

tax /tæks/ **(taxes, taxing, taxed)**

tax with If you **tax** someone **with** something wrong that you think they have done, you show them the evidence and ask them for an explanation. [FORMAL] ❑ *An old friend advised him not to tax Mr Profumo with the information... Mr Wigg contemplated for a moment taxing the Minister with it.* `V+N+PREP, V+PRON+PREP`

team /tiːm/ **(teams, teaming, teamed)**

★team up If you **team up** with someone, you join them so that you can do something together. ❑ *Tom and Joe were now due to go home, and so I teamed up with two Americans... Conservatives teamed up with Opposition Peers... It's strange that such a good producer and a great artist have not really teamed up well.* `V+ADV+with, V+ADV: RECIPROCAL`

tear /teər/ **(tears, tearing, tore, torn)**

tear apart

1 To **tear** something **apart** means to pull it into pieces violently. ❑ ...*lions and panthers which could tear a goat apart in seconds... I saw a jacket so torn apart that no one would ever want it again.* `V+N+ADV, V+PRON+ADV`

2 If something **tears** an organization or a country **apart**, it causes them to experience great conflicts or disturbances. ❑ *He was fighting against the 'anarchy' which he insisted was tearing the Church apart.* `V+N+ADV, V+PRON+ADV`

3 If something **tears** you **apart**, it makes you feel very upset, worried, and unhappy. ❑ *Don't think it hasn't torn me apart to be away from you... She is torn apart by conflicting pressures.* ...*agonies which tear him apart.* `V+N+ADV, V+PRON+ADV`

4 If someone **tears** an idea or a theory **apart**, they criticize it severely. ❑ *I can imagine a Marxist tearing the theory apart as elitist and sentimental.* `V+N+ADV, V+PRON+ADV`

NOTE **Pull apart** and **take apart** mean almost the same as **tear apart**.

tear at To **tear at** something means to try violently to pull it into pieces. ❑ *He took the meat that Sam had given him and began to tear at it... Without any warning, the two animals were tearing at each other's throats.* `V+PREP`

tear away

1 If you **tear** someone **away** from a place or activity, you force them to leave the place or stop doing the activity. ❑ *What a shame it was to tear Dolly away from the* `V+N+ADV, V+REFL+ADV, V+PRON+ADV:`

play... I tore myself away and came to Paris... I would like to tear you away from Italy and take you on a trip. `USUALLY+from`

2 To **tear** something **away** means to pull it violently from the thing that it is attached to. ❑ The road was covered in leaves which had been torn away by the strong winds... Grasp the flesh and tear it away from the shell... I could always tear away a piece of the wall. `V+N+ADV, V+PRON+ADV, V+ADV+N; ALSO+from`

3 A **tearaway** is a young person who behaves in a wild and uncontrolled way. [BRITISH] ❑ Colin was a bit of a tearaway in his youth. `N-COUNT`

tear down If you **tear down** something such as a building, tree, or statue, you destroy it completely. ❑ It is often cheaper to tear down the buildings than to repair them. ...tearing down woodlands... We have a theatre in town, but they're tearing it down next year. `V+N+ADV, V+PRON+ADV, V+ADV+N`

NOTE **Pull down** means almost the same as **tear down**, and **demolish** is a more formal word.

tear into If you **tear into** someone, their work, or their behaviour, you criticize them very strongly. [INFORMAL] ❑ In a rage I tore into the demonstrators, asking why they were there... I didn't like the way you tore into Dempsey's paper at the seminar. `V+PREP`

NOTE **Lay into** means almost the same as **tear into**.

tear off

1 If you **tear off** your clothes, you take them off quickly and violently. ❑ I opened the window and tore off my shirt... They raced round the reservation tearing off their clothes... She tore her sandals off and jumped in. `V+ADV+N, V+N+ADV, V+PRON+ADV`

2 If you **tear** something **off**, you remove it from the thing it is attached to by pulling it violently. ❑ I like to get a new loaf and tear the crust off and eat it... He tore the metal tab off his beer can... He leans back on an elbow, tears off a grass-stalk, and bites its end. `V+N+ADV/PREP, V+ADV+N, V+PRON+ADV/PREP`

3 If you **tear off** somewhere, you go there very quickly. [INFORMAL] ❑ He tore off home... I watched them tearing off into the distance... He jumps into the car and tears off like a race driver. `V+ADV: USUALLY+A`

tear out If you **tear out** something that is attached to another thing, you separate it with your hands, using force. ❑ I write the list in my book, tear out the top copy, and send it with the laundry... She tore several sheets of paper out of the back of the book. `V+ADV+N, V+N+ADV, V+PRON+ADV; ALSO+of`

★**tear up**

1 If you **tear up** paper or material, you pull it into a lot of small pieces with your hands. ❑ He hadn't torn up Caldicott's cheque... We bought bandages rather than tearing up a large sheet for this purpose... She smiled and folded the letter, intending to tear it up and throw it out of the window. `V+ADV+N, V+PRON+ADV, V+N+ADV`

NOTE **Rip up** means almost the same as **tear up**.

2 If something **is torn up**, it is damaged or destroyed. ❑ Thousands of trees have been torn up in recent years... Parks, once bursting with flowers, were now being torn up in favour of factories... We do not yet have baseball crowds tearing up the grounds or breaking up trains. `V+N+ADV, V+ADV+N, V+PRON+ADV`

tease /tiːz/ **(teases, teasing, teased)**

tease out

1 If you **tease** something **out**, you separate it very carefully from the thing that contains it. ❑ Jimmy leant across and tried to tease it out of the packet... Break up the food or tease out the hard bits. `V+PRON+ADV, V+ADV+N, V+N+ADV`

NOTE **Extract** is a more formal word for **tease out**.

2 If you **tease out** information or a solution, you succeed in obtaining it even though this is difficult. ❑ They try to tease out the answers without appearing to ask... There had to be an answer – he was sure he could tease it out if only he had time... I tried to tease some criticism out of him about the car. `V+N+ADV, V+ADV+N, V+PRON+ADV: ALSO+of`

tee /tiː/ **(tees, teeing, teed)**

tee off

1 When a golfer **tees off**, he or she hits the first shot at the start of a round of golf. ❑ Hit a few practice shots before you tee off just to warm off. `V+ADV`

2 If someone or something **tees** you **off**, they make you angry or annoyed. `V+N+ADV,`

[AMERICAN, INFORMAL] ❑ *Something the boy said to him teed him off... That really teed off the old boy.*

NOTE **Annoy** is a more formal word for **tee off**.

tee up To **tee up** means to place a golf ball on a tee so that it is ready for you to hit it at the start of a hole. ❑ *I asked Ben to tee up a ball and hit it onto the green.*

V+ADV,
V+ADV+N,
V+N+ADV

teem /tiːm/ **(teems, teeming, teemed)**

teem down If it **is teeming down**, it is raining very heavily. ❑ *It was teeming down and we all got soaked.*

V+ADV

NOTE **Pour** means almost the same as **teem down**.

tell /tel/ **(tells, telling, told)**

tell against If facts or opinions **tell against** a person or plan, they indicate that the person or plan is unlikely to succeed. ❑ *The figures, therefore, told against Concorde... These facts, if put in the report, would tell against the woman.*

V+PREP

NOTE **Count against** means almost the same as **tell against**.

tell apart If you can **tell** similar people or things **apart**, you can identify them individually because you can recognize the differences between them. ❑ *It is impossible to tell the packing cases apart... His relatives were starting to drift in. I couldn't tell them apart.*

V+N+ADV,
V+PRON+ADV

★**tell off** If you **tell** someone **off**, you speak to them angrily because they have done something wrong. ❑ *All the senior mistress does is to tell the girls off for wearing the wrong colour blouse... He had a reputation for telling off generals... If I was told off by my parents, I could come along to the kitchen.*

V+PRON+ADV,
V+N+ADV,
V+ADV+N

NOTE **Reprimand** is a formal word for **tell off**.

♦ If you give someone a **telling-off**, you speak to them angrily because they have done something wrong. ❑ *When she got back she would give him such a telling-off about that doll.*

N-COUNT

NOTE **Ticking-off** means almost the same as **telling-off**.

tell on

1 If you **tell on** someone who has done something wrong, you inform someone in authority about it. [INFORMAL] ❑ *Do you think it's right to make a man tell on his friends to save himself?... But honour was satisfied, I hadn't told on them.*

V+PREP

NOTE **Grass on** means almost the same as **tell on**.

2 If pressure or strain **tells on** you, people begin to realize that you cannot cope with it. ❑ *But the pressure was beginning to tell on him too... He had been there for a long time now, and it was beginning to tell on his face... The strain of year-round cricket is telling on many of the world's top players.*

V+PREP

tend /tend/ **(tends, tending, tended)**

tend to If you **tend to** someone or something, you pay attention to them and deal with their problems and needs. ❑ *Excuse me, I have to tend to the other guests... In his spare time he tends to the family business.*

V+PREP

NOTE **Attend to** means almost the same as **tend to**.

tend towards If something **tends towards** a quality, it shows more of that quality than others. ❑ *It is no doubt inevitable that the 'neutral' society should tend towards uniformity... In some countries, the military hierarchy tends towards the right.*

V+PREP

tense /tens/ **(tenses, tensing, tensed)**

tense up If you or the muscles in your body **tense up**, your muscles stiffen and stretch tight, usually because you are afraid or are preparing yourself to make a movement. ❑ *Try to relax while you're saying it. Don't tense up... 'What are you talking about?' I asked, the skin of my cheekbones tensing up.*

V+ADV

NOTE **Tighten up** means almost the same as **tense up**.

♦ If you are **tensed up**, you feel nervous and worried and cannot relax properly. ❑ *Relax. You're all tensed up... When night came I was all tensed up for another argument.*

ADJECTIVE

NOTE **Worked up** means almost the same as **tensed up**.

thaw /θɔː/ **(thaws, thawing, thawed)**

thaw out

1 When you **thaw out** frozen food, or when it **thaws out**, you take it out of the

V+N+ADV,

freezer for some time so that it it is no longer frozen. ❑ *Pre-cooked food can be thawed out quicker than a joint or poultry... There was a joint thawing out on the kitchen table.*

NOTE **Defrost** means almost the same as **thaw out**.

2 If you **thaw out**, you get warm by a fire after you have got very cold outside. [INFORMAL] ❑ *What joy to take refuge in a stove-heated cabin and thaw out with a mug of steaming tea.*

V+ADV+N,
V+PRON+ADV,
V+ADV:
ERGATIVE

V+ADV

thin /θɪn/ (thins, thinning, thinned)

thin down When you **thin down** a liquid, you add water or another liquid to make it weaker and less thick. ❑ *Meanwhile, thin down the mayonnaise with the cream... The paint has been thinned down too much... To whip it, first thin it down with a little milk.*

V+ADV+N,
V+PRON+ADV

thin out If someone **thins out** an area or the people or things in it, the area becomes less crowded as some of the things or people move away or are removed. ❑ *The wood had been neglected and a programme has begun to thin out the mature trees... The trees thin out to a bare spot at the summit... Western cities are thinning out as people move to the suburbs.*

V+ADV+N,
V+PRON+ADV,
V+ADV:
ERGATIVE

think /θɪŋk/ (thinks, thinking, thought)

think ahead If you **think ahead**, you make plans or arrangements for the things you want to do in the future. ❑ *We need to analyse the situation and think ahead... Holland is one of those countries which think ahead.*

V+ADV

NOTE **Plan ahead** means almost the same as **think ahead**.

★**think back** If you **think back**, you make an effort to remember things that happened to you in the past. ❑ *Think back to some of your history lessons... It gives you an opportunity to think back over the year... Thinking back later I often regretted not staying to talk with him.*

V+ADV:
ALSO+to/over

NOTE **Look back** means almost the same as **think back**.

★**think of**

1 If you can **think of** something that exists or is a fact, you know it and can therefore suggest it to other people. ❑ *I can think of at least two examples of this Government's stupidity... He can think of no reason for going on living... He had examined every argument he could think of.*

V+PREP:
WITH MODAL

2 If you **think of** an idea, you use your imagination and intelligence to create it or develop it. ❑ *...a scheme which, so far as he knew, had never even been thought of before... So I began to think of new methods.*

V+PREP:
HAS PASSIVE

3 If you **think of** doing something, you consider the possibility of doing it. ❑ *We began to think of moving... I'm also thinking of buying you a fur coat... His family have discovered that he is thinking of adopting his two nephews.*

V+PREP:
USUALLY+-ING

think out If you **think out** a plan or a piece of writing, you prepare it fully and in detail before doing anything. ❑ *She needed time to think out a strategy to deal with Gareth... I'm too tired to try to think it out... He's a great believer in thinking things out.*

V+ADV+N,
V+PRON+ADV,
V+N+ADV

NOTE **Work out** means almost the same as **think out**.

★**think over** If you **think** something **over**, you consider it carefully before making a decision. ❑ *I wanted to think over one or two business problems... He said he would leave me alone to think things over for five minutes.*

V+ADV+N,
V+N+ADV,
V+PRON+ADV

★**think through** If you **think** a situation **through**, you consider it thoroughly, together with all its possible effects or consequences. ❑ *I haven't really thought the whole business through in my own mind... I've been thinking it all through and I do just want to see for myself. ...the desire to think through a difficulty.*

V+N+ADV,
V+PRON+ADV,
V+ADV+N

★**think up** If you **think up** a clever idea, you use your imagination or intelligence to create it. ❑ *I kept thinking up ways I could murder him without getting caught... He informed me of a new financial agreement he had thought up... 'Some suggestion.' Calderwood snorted. 'Did you think this up all by yourself?'*

V+ADV+N,
V+N+ADV,
V+PRON+ADV

NOTE **Devise** means almost the same as **think up**.

thirst /θɜːʳst/ (thirsts, thirsting, thirsted)

thirst for If you **thirst for** something, you want it very much. [LITERARY] ❑ *The story is so exciting it makes you thirst for the next episode... He appealed successfully to a nation thirsting for a new start.*

V+PREP:
HAS PASSIVE

thrash /θræʃ/ (thrashes, thrashing, thrashed)

thrash out

[1] If people **thrash out** something such as a plan or an agreement, they decide on it after a great deal of discussion. ❑ *The foreign ministers have thrashed out a suitable compromise formula... How foreign fund-managers will be compensated has yet to be thrashed out.*

V+N+ADV,
V+ADV+N,
V+PRON+ADV

NOTE **Hammer out** means almost the same as **thrash out**.

[2] If you **thrash out** a difficult problem or idea, you discuss it in detail until you reach an agreement or arrive at a solution. ❑ *Try and see how many of these questions you can thrash out between the three of you... We'll thrash this out after dinner... A new economic strategy is being thrashed out.*

V+ADV+N,
V+PRON+ADV,
V+N+ADV

throttle /ˈθrɒtəl/ (throttles, throttling, throttled)

throttle back If you **throttle back** or **throttle down** when you are driving a motor vehicle or aircraft, you make it go slower by reducing the pressure on the accelerator. ❑ *I throttled the motor right back... Hendricks throttled down, and the boat settled into a slow drift.*

V+N+ADV,
V+PRON+ADV,
V+ADV

throttle down → See throttle back

throw /θroʊ/ (throws, throwing, threw, thrown)

☑ **About** is used mainly in British English. In American English, **around** is much more common than **round**.

throw about

[1] → See throw around

[2] If you **throw** yourself **about**, you move your body suddenly and in different directions, usually because you are ill or angry. ❑ *David had thrown himself about wildly... The animal is throwing its head about.*

V+REFL+ADV,
V+N+ADV

throw around

[1] If you **throw** your arm or arms **around**, **about** or **round** someone, you embrace them or hug them to show your affection for them. ❑ *I wanted to throw my arms about him... She threw her arms around his neck... He threw his arms round his brother and began to cry.*

V+N+PREP

[2] If you **throw** things **around** or **throw** them **about**, you throw them in different directions in an angry way. ❑ *He began to throw bread about the room... He had terrorized everyone by throwing things about. ...throwing bits of stuff around in a blind fury.*

V+N+ADV/PREP,
V+PRON+ADV/PREP

[3] If people **throw** something **around** or **throw** it **about**, they throw it from one person to the other, usually as part of a game. ❑ *I saw him throwing a cricket ball about with some other boys... He doesn't join any of the games. He doesn't even throw a football around.*

V+N+ADV

[4] If you **throw** money **around** or **throw** it **about**, you spend it freely and in large amounts, especially on things that are not necessary, useful or sensible. ❑ *Ford, however, does not have money to throw about... If you throw enough money around you don't have enemies.*

V+N+ADV,
V+PRON+ADV

[5] If you **throw** one thing **around** or **throw** it **round** another, you place it so that it surrounds or encircles the other thing. ❑ *...with a rope thrown around his waist... 'Coming!' said she, throwing a scarf round her neck.*

V+N+PREP,
V+PRON+PREP

[6] If you say that someone **throws around** a word or name, you disapprove of the fact that they mention it frequently, often in an inappropriate way in order to impress someone. [INFORMAL] ❑ *Occasionally, he throws fancy words around... The name that I've heard thrown around a lot is Jim Morrison.*

V+N+ADV,
V+ADV+N,
V+PRON+ADV

throw aside

[1] If you **throw** a covering or curtain **aside**, you move it quickly to one side so that it is no longer in your way. ❑ *She threw the bedclothes aside and jumped out of bed. ...throwing aside the mosquito netting.*

V+N+ADV,
V+PRON+ADV,
V+ADV+N

[2] If you **throw aside** an attitude, principle, or idea, you suddenly abandon it, reject it, or change it. ❑ *The time came to throw aside all indecisiveness. ...a lesson eagerly learned but then carelessly thrown aside.*

V+ADV+N,
V+N+ADV,
V+PRON+ADV

★throw at

[1] If you **throw** an object **at** someone or something, you try to make the object hit

V+N+PREP,

them, by moving your hand forward very fast and letting go of the object. ❑ *He* — V+PRON+PREP
threw a dart, hard, at the board... Roger stooped, picked up a stone, aimed, and threw it at
Henry... Rioters threw stones at policemen and passing cars.

2 If you **throw** a look, remark, or question **at** someone, you look at them, or say — V+N+PREP,
something to them, suddenly and often aggressively. ❑ *She threw nervous glances at* — V+PRON+PREP
him every now and again... He sang, whistled, threw remarks at the silent Ralph... 'It's where
your father works.' She threw this at him just a little too casually.

3 To **throw** something **at** an enemy or opponent means to attack or challenge — V+N+PREP,
them with it. ❑ *The silliest soldier would not throw his whole strength at a break-through* — V+PRON+PREP
without tanks. ...other laws they could throw at me if they chose.

4 If you **throw** money **at** a difficult situation or problem, you try to solve it by — V+N+PREP,
spending more money rather than by thinking of new ways that might work better; — V+PRON+PREP
used showing disapproval. ❑ *The Prime Minister is against throwing money at the inner*
cities... The response of the West at present is simply to throw pound notes at them.

5 If you **throw** yourself **at** someone or something, you run or jump quickly and — V+REFL+PREP
desperately towards them. ❑ *Kairi threw herself at him, wailing with terror... He abruptly*
throws himself at Gaspar and seizes the barrel of the gun.

6 If you **throw** yourself **at** someone you are attracted to, you behave in a way that — V+REFL+PREP
makes it obvious that you want to have a relationship with them, and do not care
that other people find your behaviour unacceptable or embarrassing. ❑ *...hundreds of*
girls who would be more than honoured to throw themselves at his head... Connie had
thrown herself at his feet and he had rejected her.

★**throw awa̱y**

1 If you **throw away** from you an object you were holding, you move your hand — V+ADV+N,
suddenly and let go of it, so that it moves rapidly away. ❑ *He threw away his brush,* — V+PRON+ADV,
but stopped to pick it up... He threw her away from him... He read one page and then threw — V+N+ADV:
the paper away from him. — ALSO+from

2 When you **throw away** something that you no longer want or need, you get rid — V+PRON+ADV,
of it, for example by putting it in a dustbin. ❑ *You should throw those away and get a* — V+ADV+N,
pair of these... Throw away medicine after an illness is over... 30 million tonnes of refuse are — V+N+ADV
thrown away in the UK.

NOTE **Discard** is a more formal word for **throw away**, and **keep** means the opposite.

♦ A **throw-away** product is intended to be used only once, or only for a short — ADJECTIVE
time, before being got rid of. ❑ *...a throw-away toothbrush. ...throw-away chopsticks.*
NOTE **Disposable** means almost the same as **throw-away**.

3 If someone **throws away** something valuable that they have, they waste it ra- — V+N+ADV,
ther than using it sensibly. ❑ *He is evidently prepared to throw his money away... To* — V+PRON+ADV,
throw it all away when we're so near!... They threw away their advantage... Throw away his — V+ADV+N
career for a girl?

4 A **throwaway** remark is spoken casually and quietly, although it is important, — ADJECTIVE
and therefore only people who are listening carefully will hear it or realize its importance. ❑ *...making your point in a throwaway line.*

★**throw ba̱ck**

1 If you **throw** something or someone **back** somewhere, you put them carelessly — V+N+ADV,
in the place where they were before or force them to return there. ❑ *Hagen threw his* — V+PRON+ADV,
papers back into the basket. ...catching fish, weighing them and throwing them back... I was — V+REFL+ADV:
collared by the police and thrown back onto Schenk Street... I would have thrown myself back — USUALLY+A
under the covers in a blind panic.

2 If you **throw back** a covering such as a piece of cloth, you pull it or fold it, so — V+ADV+N,
that the thing that was covered becomes visible. ❑ *She threw back the covers on the* — V+N+ADV,
bed... He threw back the curtains. ...a veil, which she threw back over her hat. — V+PRON+ADV

3 If you **throw back** your head or arms, you move them backwards suddenly. ❑ *I* — V+ADV+N,
threw back my head and yelled 'Help!'... He sleeps still with his arms thrown back... Valentino — V+N+ADV,
threw himself back in his chair and roared with laughter. — V+REFL+ADV,
— V+PRON+ADV

4 If you **throw back** a drink, you drink it quickly, often in one gulp. ❑ *Stock threw* — V+ADV+N,
back two vodkas in quick succession. — V+N+ADV,
— V+PRON+ADV

NOTE **Knock back** and **put back** mean almost the same as **throw back**.

5 If something **throws back** light or sound, it reflects the light or causes the sound to echo. ❑ *...a shirt so white it threw the sun's light back. ...drifting fog that would suddenly throw the headlight beam back through the windscreen... Mirage fighters take off from the airport, throwing back a sound like a crack of thunder.*

V+N+ADV,
V+ADV+N,
V+PRON+ADV

6 To **throw** someone **back** to an earlier time means to cause them to remember it. ❑ *The scene threatened to throw me back eight years, to the time I had been beaten up... That headline threw our little group back on memories of the Thirties. ...throwing ourselves back to a simpler time.*

V+PRON+ADV,
V+N+ADV,
V+REFL+ADV

7 If you say that something is a **throwback** to something that existed or was common a long time ago, you mean that it is very similar to it. ❑ *His pro-British sentiments were a throwback to the old colonial days.*

N-SING

8 If you **are thrown back** on someone or something, you have to rely on them once more, after a period of not needing them. ❑ *Ethnic groups were thrown back on their own resources... We are thrown back onto mother... I feel very strongly that this throws him back upon himself.*

V+N+ADV,
V+PRON+ADV:
WITH PREP,
USUALLY PASSIVE

throw back at If you **throw** a mistake or weakness **back at** someone, you remind them of it, usually in order to hurt them. ❑ *Satisfying, isn't it, to throw everything back at him? ...throwing their childless marriage right back at her.*

V+N+ADV+PREP,
V+PRON+ADV+PREP

★throw down

1 If you **throw down** something you are holding, you move your hand downwards and let go of it so that it falls rapidly downwards. ❑ *He threw down his napkin and went out of the room... He threw the gun down on the floor... She went to throw garbage down the incinerator... Take this stick and throw it down in front of the king.*

V+ADV+N,
V+N+ADV/PREP,
V+PRON+ADV/PREP

2 If you **throw** yourself **down**, you deliberately fall or move rapidly towards the ground. ❑ *She threw herself down on her knees and prayed... He threw himself down beside me and closed his eyes.*

V+REFL+ADV

3 If soldiers **throw down** their arms, they surrender or stop fighting. ❑ *The soldiers often looked as if they would like to throw down their arms and join the protesting students.*

V+ADV+N,
V+N+ADV,
V+PRON+ADV

4 If you **throw down** something you are eating or drinking, you eat or drink it very quickly, often in one gulp. ❑ *He threw down the rest of his coffee and stood up... The whole thing was a ghastly mistake. I thought I'd throw down a few pills and – zap! – instant answers.*

V+ADV+N,
V+N+ADV,
V+PRON+ADV

5 If you **throw down** a challenge to someone, you do something new or unexpected in a bold or forceful manner that will probably cause them to reply or react equally strongly. ❑ *The regional parliament threw down a new challenge to the central authorities by passing a law allowing private ownership of businesses... Government ministers have been responding to the challenge thrown down by their former colleague.*

V+N+ADV,
V+ADV+N,
V+PRON+ADV

★throw in

☑ In meaning 2, the stress is on **thr<u>o</u>w**.

1 If you **throw** an object **in** a container or other place, you put it there casually, sometimes with force. ❑ *She threw both letters in the bin... Add a teaspoonful of salt, and throw in the rice... They threw it in the river, and went home.*

V+N+ADV/PREP,
V+ADV+N,
V+PRON+ADV/PREP

2 If someone **throws** a person **in** jail, prison, or a cell, they force them to enter it and stay there. ❑ *The cop threatened to throw all of us in jail.*

V+N+PREP,
V+PRON+PREP

3 If you **throw in** a word or comment when talking or writing, you add it in a casual or unexpected way. ❑ *...Mr Edgar H. Humbert (I threw in the 'Edgar' just for fun)... 'It's simply disgraceful of you, Philip,' threw in Ann.*

V+ADV+N,
V+ADV+QUOTE,
V+N+ADV,
V+PRON+ADV

NOTE **Toss in** means almost the same as **throw in**.

4 If you **throw in** an extra item when you are selling something or arranging something, you add it or include it in order to persuade people to buy the thing or accept the arrangement. ❑ *They threw in the matching handbag for another hundred. ...a few minor reforms thrown in to sweeten the temper of the local people.*

V+ADV+N,
V+N+ADV,
V+PRON+ADV

5 If someone in authority **throws in** soldiers or workers, they order them to go somewhere and start fighting or working. ❑ *He could not throw in his final reserves on the Central Front. ...throwing in different shifts of carpenters and masons.*

V+ADV+N,
V+N+ADV,
V+PRON+ADV

6 If your team in a football match has a **throw-in** because the other team has kicked the ball off the pitch, one of your players stands at the edge of the pitch and throws the ball to one of your team. ❑ *A quick throw-in gave the player a chance to score.*

N-COUNT

★throw into

1 If you **throw** an object **into** a container or place, you put it there casually, sometimes with force. ❏ *He threw his papers into the basket... She threw it into a cupboard.*
V+N+PREP, V+PRON+PREP

2 If someone **throws** a person **into** jail, prison or a cell, they force them to enter it and stay there. ❏ *They arrested several leaders and threw them into prison.*
V+N+PREP, V+PRON+PREP

3 If you **throw** yourself **into** a place, you move there quickly and forcefully. ❏ *She threw herself into Rudolph's arms... Peggy threw herself into a chair.*
V+REFL+PREP

4 To **throw** someone or something **into** a particular state means to cause them suddenly to be in that state. ❏ *The driver threw the car into reverse... He turned out the light, throwing the room into blackness... Her voice threw me into a rage.*
V+N+PREP, V+PRON+PREP

5 If you **throw** yourself **into** a task, activity, or situation, you begin to do it with a lot of effort and energy. ❏ *Mrs Kaul threw herself into her work... He threw himself into the battle against Chamberlain... Everyone threw themselves energetically into clearing it away.*
V+REFL+PREP

6 If you **throw** energy or resources **into** an activity or enterprise, you use a lot of energy or resources to try and make it succeed. ❏ *Many women throw all of their energies into a career. ...throwing an estimated 100,000 troops into the manoeuvres.*
V+N+PREP, V+PRON+PREP

throw off

1 If you **throw off** your clothes or something covering you, you remove them from your body quickly and carelessly. ❏ *Laverne threw off her T-shirt. ...throwing it off and handing it to him... He threw off his blanket and lay still.*
V+ADV+N, V+N+ADV, V+PRON+ADV

2 If you **throw off** someone or something that is restricting you, you free yourself from them. ❏ *Throw off the chains of the slavemaster... Britain threw off some of the illusions... Some children throw off their ailments quickly.*
V+ADV+N, V+N+ADV, V+PRON+ADV

3 If something **throws off** heat, light, or other form of energy, it releases it. ❏ *...a little furnace, throwing off a haze of visible heat... The thinking brain throws off electrical and chemical discharges... Other particles will be thrown off in all directions.*
V+ADV+N, V+N+ADV, V+PRON+ADV

NOTE **Emit** is a formal word for **throw off**.

4 To **throw** someone or something **off** means to cause them to make a mistake or to fail. ❏ *He had been thrown off by an ambiguity in the term 'quality'... A faulty gauge can throw your calculations way off. ...throwing the building programme off schedule.*
V+N+ADV/PREP, V+PRON+ADV/PREP, V+ADV+N

5 To **throw** someone **off** the scent, track, or trail means to deliberately deceive, confuse, or mislead them. ❏ *I will change transportation to throw them off, and use back roads... That should throw him off the track or at least leave him uncertain... The story threw the police off the right scent.*
V+PRON+ADV/PREP, V+N+ADV/PREP, V+ADV+N

throw on

☑ In meanings 2-5, the stress is on **thr<u>o</u>w**.

1 If you **throw on** your clothes, you put them on quickly and carelessly. ❏ *He threw on his clothes and went downstairs... I threw Clem's red jacket on over my dress.*
V+ADV+N, V+N+ADV, V+PRON+ADV

2 If you **throw** yourself **on** or **upon** someone or something, you rush at them, deliberately fall on top of them, or attack them. ❏ *She threw herself on the bed... Joseph threw himself on his father, crying and kissing his face.*
V+REFL+PREP

3 If something **throws** light or shadow **on** or **upon** someone or something, it causes them to be covered in light or shadow. [LITERARY] ❏ *Its light threw a faint radiance on the sleeping girl... A large beech tree threw its shadow upon the grass.*
V+N+PREP

4 To **throw** light **on** or **upon** a problem means to help people to understand it or solve it. ❏ *...an attempt to throw light on this perplexing situation... Can't Mrs. Welch throw any light on the matter?... The diaries throw a new light upon certain incidents.*
V+N+PREP

5 To **throw** doubt or suspicion **on** or **upon** someone or something means to cause people to doubt them or suspect them. ❏ *A re-examination of the evidence has thrown doubts on this view... Meehan tried to throw suspicion on the two youths... Recent research has tended to throw doubt upon this concept.*
V+N+PREP

throw onto, throw on to

If you **throw** one thing **onto** or **on to** another, you cause it to fall with force on top of the other thing. ❏ *She threw her books violently onto the floor... She threw it on to the porcelain tiles and smashed it... Kitty threw herself onto the bed.*
V+N+PREP, V+PRON+PREP, V+REFL+PREP

★throw out

1 If you **throw out** an object you are holding, you cause it to move away from
V+N+ADV,

you by moving your hand forward and letting go of it. ❑ *They threw the net out and could not pull it back in... He threw it out into the sunlight... He looked again at the papers and threw them out of the window... She threw out handfuls of wheat.*

  V+PRON+ADV,
  V+ADV+N:
  ALSO:+of

2 If you **throw out** an object you no longer want, you get rid of it, for example by putting it in a dustbin. ❑ *...throwing out their rubbish on to the courtyards... I can remember my parents throwing out their old furniture... What's this? Should I throw it out and wash the pot?*

  V+ADV+N,
  V+PRON+ADV,
  V+N+ADV

NOTE **Throw away** means almost the same as **throw out**.

3 If you **throw out** someone's ideas, proposals, or work, you reject them because you find them unacceptable. ❑ *At first he threw out almost every headline I wrote... New societies may be tempted to throw out the principles of democracy... The Grand Jury threw out the Bill.*

  V+ADV+N,
  V+N+ADV,
  V+PRON+ADV

4 If a judge **throws out** a case, he or she rejects it and the accused person does not have to stand trial. ❑ *The defense wants the district Judge to throw out the case.*

  V+N+ADV,
  V+ADV+N,
  V+PRON+ADV

5 If you **throw** someone **out** of a place, job, or institution, you force them to leave it. ❑ *They'll throw out their councillor if he doesn't vote for it... Axel threw his brother out of the house... He was nearly thrown out of college... They'll throw me out of Britain.*

  V+ADV+N,
  V+N+ADV,
  V+PRON+ADV:
  ALSO:+of

6 If you are speaking and **throw out** ideas or suggestions, you mention them for people to consider. ❑ *Bernstein threw out a name he had never heard before... Whiting would only throw out hints... Actors worked from suggestions thrown out to them from the floor.*

  V+ADV+N,
  V+N+ADV,
  V+PRON+ADV

7 If something **throws out** smoke, light, heat, or a smell, it produces it and releases it, usually in large quantities. ❑ *...chimneys throwing out huge plumes of black smoke. ...throwing out beams and rays... It throws out an intense smell of tea-leaves.*

  V+ADV+N,
  V+N+ADV,
  V+PRON+ADV

NOTE **Emit** is a formal word for **throw out**.

8 If you **throw out** a hand, arm, or leg, you move it suddenly away from your body. ❑ *Bond stumbled and threw out his right hand for support... She threw out her hands, laughing.*

  V+ADV+N,
  V+N+ADV,
  V+PRON+ADV

throw over

1 If you **throw** one thing **over** another, you cause it to move above and past the other thing until it is on the other side of it. ❑ *I threw my brief-case over the wall... She ran to the low fence and threw herself over it... He was frightened he might throw himself over.*

  V+N+ADV/PREP,
  V+PRON+ADV/PREP,
  V+REFL+ADV/PREP

2 If you **throw** one thing **over** another, you place it so that it covers the other thing or is supported by it. ❑ *Covers were hastily thrown over the stalls... He threw his sweater over the chair... Thomas picked Claude up and threw him over his shoulder.*

  V+N+PREP,
  V+PRON+PREP

3 If you **throw** something **over** to someone, you pass it to them casually or carelessly. ❑ *He threw over a newspaper... They're in the chest there. And throw those beers over, too.*

  V+ADV+N,
  V+N+ADV,
  V+PRON+ADV

4 If you **throw over** a boyfriend or girlfriend, you end your relationship with them. [OLD-FASHIONED] ❑ *Eventually the girl threw him over for a young minister. ...just after he'd been thrown over by Claudia.*

  V+PRON+ADV,
  V+N+ADV,
  V+ADV+N

NOTE **Chuck** means almost the same as **throw over**.

throw overboard

1 If you are on a ship and **throw** something **overboard**, you throw it over the side of the ship into the water. ❑ *Throw them overboard to lighten the ship... They threatened to throw themselves overboard.*

  V+PRON+ADV,
  V+REFL+ADV,
  V+N+ADV,
  V+ADV+N

2 If you **throw** an idea or plan **overboard**, you reject it completely. ❑ *The country threw Baldwin's policy overboard... You had to throw overboard everything known, good, loving, and trusted.*

  V+N+ADV,
  V+ADV+N,
  V+PRON+ADV

throw round → See throw around

throw together

1 If you **throw** something **together**, you make it or arrange it quickly and not very carefully. ❑ *...throwing together an alcoholic mixture which left them breathless... This is no crisis measure hastily thrown together. ...a small building, recently thrown together.*

  V+ADV+N,
  V+N+ADV,
  V+PRON+ADV

2 If people **are thrown together** by a situation or event, it causes them to meet each other and get to know each other. ❑ *They were thrown together in Paris in the Thirties. ...manage things so that he and the woman are thrown together.*

  PASSIVE:
  V+ADV

★throw **up**

1 If something **throws up** small particles such as dust, stones, or water, it causes them to rise upwards into the air. ❑ *A passing car threw up a cloud of white dust.* *...throwing up a shower of wood chips...* *The wheels would throw sparks up into our faces.*

V+ADV+N,
V+N+ADV,
V+PRON+ADV

2 If you **throw up** something you are holding, you cause it to move upwards into the air by moving your hand quickly and letting go of it. ❑ *Adam threw the ball up and they started to play...* *Howarth threw up his lucky 20-cent piece.*

V+N+ADV,
V+PRON+ADV,
V+ADV+N

3 If you **throw up** your arms or hands, you lift them quickly from your sides and move them upwards. If you **throw up** your head, you move it upwards and tilt it backwards. ❑ *Mrs Pringle threw her hands up in astonishment...* *Bond threw up an arm to protect himself...* *She threw up her head with a little laugh.*

V+ADV+N,
V+ADV+N,
V+PRON+ADV

4 If people **throw up** a building or structure, they build or make it very quickly. ❑ *...travelling actors throw up a canvas-and-wood stage.* *...throw up a ranch house.*

V+ADV+N,
V+PRON+ADV

5 If a situation, country, or activity **throws up** particular types of things or people, it produces them or causes them to become well-known. [BRITISH] ❑ *The new equipment threw up major problems over safety...* *Neither country has thrown up class-based parties...* *Your research has thrown up some very fascinating facts, hasn't it?*

V+ADV+N,
V+N+ADV,
V+PRON+ADV

6 If you **throw up** a job, position, or activity you leave it or stop doing it suddenly and unexpectedly. ❑ *Even if I'd thrown up my job, it wouldn't have worried me...* *He considered throwing it up for something easier.*

V+ADV+N,
V+PRON+ADV,
V+N+ADV

NOTE **Chuck in** means almost the same as **throw up**.

7 If someone **throws up**, they vomit. [INFORMAL] ❑ *Halfway through the meal, I collapsed and crawled outside to throw up.*

V+ADV

thr<u>o</u>w upon → See **throw on**

thrust /θr<u>ʌ</u>st/ (thrusts, thrusting)

✓ The form **thrust** is used in the present tense and is the past tense and past participle of the verb.

thrust up If something tall or pointed **thrusts up** somewhere, it is higher than the surrounding things and can be clearly seen. [LITERARY] ❑ *...the bell-tower thrusting bravely up beside it.* *...an imposing rock needle thrusting up at least 250 feet.*

V+ADV:
USUALLY+A

thrust upon To **thrust** something **upon** someone means to force them to have it, deal with it, or experience it. ❑ *An enormous political responsibility had been thrust upon me...* *She had thrust herself upon him.*

V+N+PREP,
V+REFL+PREP,
V+PRON+PREP

thumb /θ<u>ʌ</u>m/ (thumbs, thumbing, thumbed)

thumb through If you **thumb through** a book or other written material, you glance at the pages briefly and turn them over, rather than reading each page carefully. ❑ *Bernstein thumbed through a local afternoon paper...* *She picks it up and thumbs through its pages.*

V+PREP:
HAS PASSIVE

thump /θ<u>ʌ</u>mp/ (thumps, thumping, thumped)

thump **out**

1 If you **thump out** a tune on a piano, you play it by hitting the keys very hard. ❑ *The Stereophonics thumped out a rousing number.*

V+ADV+N,
V+PRON+ADV

2 If a message **is thumped out**, it is expressed very forcefully. ❑ *The message was thumped out in his newspapers' editorials week after week.*

V+ADV+N,
V+N+ADV,
V+PRON+ADV

tick /t<u>ɪ</u>k/ (ticks, ticking, ticked)

tick aw<u>a</u>y If a clock or other mechanical device **ticks away** or **ticks on**, it makes a continual ticking noise. ❑ *I could hear my wrist-watch ticking away.* *...a time-bomb ticking away in a safe...* *The metronome ticked on slowly.*

V+ADV

tick by If you say that time, especially seconds or minutes, **ticked by**, you are emphasizing the fact that time was passing, usually just before something important or exciting was expected to happen. ❑ *The minutes ticked by. Then Eisenhower announced his decision.*

V+ADV

tick down If you say that time or a clock **is ticking down**, you are emphasizing that time is passing, usually just before something important or exciting is expected to happen. ❑ *As the clock ticks down to midnight, we feel the obligation to remind everyone that this is a truly very dangerous situation.*

V+ADV:
ALSO+to

tick off

398

tick off

1 If you **tick off** items on a list, you write a tick or other mark next to them, in order to show that they have been dealt with. [BRITISH] ❑ *I tick off the items in my book... Tick them off as each job is finished. ...ticking the names off the Electoral Roll.*

V+ADV+N,
V+PRON+ADV/PREP,
V+N+ADV/PREP

2 If you **tick off** items on your fingers, you say them one by one and touch your fingers with another finger at the same time, usually to make sure you have not forgotten an item. [BRITISH] ❑ *'I want three things out of this.' He ticked them off on his fingers... I have ticked off the months on my fingers... She ticked the items off on her fingers.*

V+PRON+ADV,
V+ADV+N,
V+N+ADV

3 If you **tick** someone **off**, you speak angrily to them because they have done something wrong. [BRITISH, INFORMAL] ❑ *David had ticked her off for not getting some work right... 'Not much good ticking off the children,' she remarked, 'when the parents are just as rude.*

V+PRON+ADV,
V+ADV+N,
V+N+ADV:
ALSO+for

NOTE **Scold** is a more formal word for **tick off**, and **tell off** means almost the same.

♦ If you give someone a **ticking-off**, you speak angrily to them because they have done something wrong. [BRITISH, INFORMAL] ❑ *Then Lally confessed and got a ticking-off.*

N-COUNT

NOTE **Telling-off** means almost the same as **ticking-off**.

4 If you say that something **ticks** you **off**, you mean that it annoys you. [AMERICAN, INFORMAL] ❑ *I just think it's rude and it's ticking me off... She's still ticked off at him for brushing her off and going out with you instead.*

V+N+ADV,
V+PRON+ADV

5 If you say that a clock **ticks off** time, or that the time **ticks off**, you are emphasizing that the time is passing, especially before something important is expected to happen. ❑ *The clock ticked off the seconds to the meeting. ...the seconds ticking off inside his head.*

V+ADV+N,
V+ADV:
ERGATIVE

tick on

1 → See **tick away**

2 If you say that an idea or system **ticks on**, you mean that it continues to exist or to be accepted and does not stop or get changed. ❑ *Thoughts of this sort did go ticking on, useless or not... The universe of Newton ticked on without a hitch for about two hundred years.*

V+ADV

tick over

1 If an engine or similar device **is ticking over**, it is operating steadily or slowly, because it is not being used much. [BRITISH] ❑ *Now the reactor was merely ticking over as it generated electrical power for the ship... With transistors, the computer had shrunk and a ten-kilowatt generator would have kept it ticking over.*

V+ADV

NOTE **Idle** is a more technical word for **tick over**.

2 If a person, a system, or a business **is ticking over**, they are working, but not producing very much or making much progress. [BRITISH] ❑ *The company can generate enough money to keep it ticking over... Keep all the essential processes ticking over... Putting your money in a building society is just ticking over, playing safe.*

V+ADV

tick up If the price, value, or level of something **ticks up**, it rises by a small amount. ❑ *Hepworth shares ticked up 3p to 200p yesterday... Plans to buy cars ticked up a bit in July after a sharp drop the month before.*

V+ADV

tide /taɪd/ (tides, tiding, tided)

tide over If you give someone money or help in order to **tide** them **over**, you do it so that they can get through a period of time when they are having problems. ❑ *I only want to borrow enough to tide me over till Monday. ...if you need a few dollars to tide you over. ...the grain surpluses that helped tide the world over the 1972-74 shortages.*

V+PRON+ADV/PREP,
V+N+ADV/PREP:
NO PASSIVE

tidy /taɪdi/ (tidies, tidying, tidied)

tidy away When you **tidy** things **away**, you put them somewhere neatly after using them or dealing with them. [BRITISH] ❑ *She tidied the box away in her dressing-table... I suggested we tidied them away, but she's got more than a hundred. ...to tidy away letters before locking up.*

V+N+ADV,
V+PRON+ADV,
V+ADV+N

tidy out When you **tidy out** a cupboard or a room, you take everything out of it, get rid of the things you do not want, and put the rest back neatly.

V+ADV+N,
V+N+ADV,
V+PRON+ADV

★tidy up

1 When you **tidy up** a place, a container, or the things in them, you put all the

V+ADV+N,

For a full explanation of all grammatical labels, see pages xiii-xx

things back in their proper places so that the place or container is neat again. ❏ *I started to tidy up the drawers... He went back to the studio and tidied it up... Tidy everything up and put it away in my locker... Eva was tidying up after lunch.*

V+PRON+ADV,
V+N+ADV,
V+ADV

2 If you **tidy up** a person, you quickly make them look cleaner or smarter, for example by washing their hands and face, brushing their hair, or straightening their clothes. ❏ *I tidied myself up before we landed. ...when Deanna had tidied him up... Leggett tidied up his friend and asked what the quarrel was about.*

V+REFL+ADV,
V+PRON+ADV,
V+ADV+N

3 If you **tidy up** a piece of work, a project, or a situation, you deal with the small unfinished or unsatisfactory parts of it, so that it is completely ready or finished. ❏ *I had a week to tidy up all last-minute details... You haven't made any serious errors, it's just a question of tidying it up.*

V+ADV+N,
V+PRON+ADV,
V+N+ADV

tie /taɪ/ (ties, tying, tied)

tie back If you **tie** something **back**, you fasten it into a position so that it cannot move and is not in the way. ❏ *Her hair was long and tied back. ...brushing her hair and tying it back.*

V+N+ADV,
V+ADV+N,
V+PRON+ADV

tie down

1 If you **tie** someone or something **down**, you tie them to the ground or in a low position. ❏ *I wasn't sure whether I should tie the camels down or not... One of the prison guards was confining him and tying him down.*

V+N+ADV,
V+ADV+N,
V+PRON+ADV

2 A person or thing that **ties** someone **down** restricts their freedom. ❏ *You're not tied down to a date... He doesn't like to tie himself down... She doesn't want children because she says they tie you down.*

V+N+ADV,
V+PRON+ADV,
V+REFL+ADV

3 To **tie down** enemy troops means to force them to stay in one place for a while so that they cannot take action against you. [TECHNICAL] ❏ *In New Zealand the Maori Wars tied down 10,000 troops in the mid-1860s.*

V+ADV+N,
V+N+ADV,
V+PRON+ADV

tie in with If one thing **ties in with** another, it is closely connected to it, fits in with it, or agrees with it. ❏ *His beliefs didn't seem to tie in at all with reality... Estimates from the World Bank tie in well with these figures... The first letter seemed to tie in with the other... Does this tie in with what you were doing on 'Quality'?*

V+ADV+PREP

★tie up

1 If you **tie** something **up**, you put string or rope round it so that it is firm or secure. ❏ *Clarissa came in, carrying some canvases tied up in brown paper. ...with their lunch tied up in white paper.*

V+N+ADV,
V+ADV+N,
V+PRON+ADV

2 If you **tie up** a person or an animal, you fasten ropes or chains around them so that they cannot move or escape. ❏ *I tied my goat up during the day... I tied him up to a fence.*

V+N+ADV,
V+ADV+N,
V+PRON+ADV

3 When you **tie up** laces, you fasten them in a bow. ❏ *He saw the man bending down and tying up his shoelace.*

V+ADV+N,
V+N+ADV,
V+PRON+ADV

NOTE **Do up** means almost the same as **tie up**.

4 When a boat **ties up** or **is tied up**, it is attached to something with a rope or chain, for example in a harbour. ❏ *The ships made for port and tied up... The Morning Rose was tied up alongside the harbour wall.*

V+ADV:
ALSO PASSIVE:
V+ADV:
ERGATIVE

NOTE **Moor** is a more formal word for **tie up**.

5 To **tie** something **up** also means to use it in some way, with the result that it is not available for other people or other purposes. ❏ *The big companies were tying up supplies of minerals in long-term contracts... People don't want to tie their money up for long periods... They marched on the expressway, tied up two tunnels and blocked a bridge.*

V+ADV+N,
V+N+ADV,
V+PRON+ADV

6 If you are **tied up**, you are busy, with the result that you are not free to do anything else. ❏ *I'm tied up right now, can you call me back later?*

PASSIVE:
V+ADV

7 If you **tie up** an issue or problem, you deal with it in a way that gives definite conclusions or answers. ❏ *Cobb ties it up in 100 pages of the book.*

V+N+ADV,
V+ADV+N,
V+PRON+ADV

8 Something that **ties up** with something else or **is tied up** with it is closely linked with it. ❏ *The vulnerability of the professions is tied up with their special strength... It supposedly tied up with her interest in dance.*

V+ADV:
OR PASSIVE:
V+ADV:
ALSO+with,
RECIPROCAL

tighten /taɪtᵊn/ (tightens, tightening, tightened)

tighten up

1 When you **tighten up** a fastening, you move it so that it is more firmly in place or holds something more firmly. ❏ *The steward would get out on the wing to tighten up*

V+ADV+N,
V+N+ADV,
V+PRON+ADV

some loose wire... You'd better tighten those screws up... Tighten it up with a spanner.

NOTE **Loosen** means the opposite of **tighten up**.

2 If a muscle in your body **tightens up** or if you **tighten** it **up**, it becomes tense and stiff rather than being relaxed. ❑ *These exercises are to tighten up the abdominal muscles... No woman wants to make these muscles more relaxed, instead she wants to tighten them up and get rid of the surrounding fat... As your arm straightens back, the back of the arm tightens up.*

V+ADV+N,
V+N+ADV,
V+PRON+ADV,
V+ADV:
ERGATIVE

3 If someone **tightens up** a rule or system, they make it stricter or more efficient. ❑ *...as regulations on the testing of drugs are tightened up in the rich countries... He said he would take steps to tighten up the administration... There has been a demand to tighten up the law.*

V+ADV+N,
V+N+ADV,
V+PRON+ADV

4 If a group, team, or organization **tightens up**, they make an effort to control what they are doing more closely, in order to become more efficient and successful. ❑ *I want us to be a bit more sensible this time and tighten up.*

V+ADV

NOTE **Loosen up** means the opposite of **tighten up**.

tinker /tɪŋkəʳ/ (tinkers, tinkering, tinkered)

☑ **About** is used mainly in British English.

tinker about → See tinker around

tinker around If you **tinker around** with something, or **tinker about** with it, you play with it and make small alterations and adjustments to it. ❑ *Some of the kids tinker about in the workshop. ...tinkering around with machines.*

V+ADV:
ALSO+with

tinker with If you **tinker with** something, you try to mend it or improve it in some way by making a lot of small alterations and adjustments to it. ❑ *They have no desire to tinker with engines... I like tinkering with figures.*

V+PREP:
HAS PASSIVE

tip /tɪp/ (tips, tipping, tipped)

tip off If you **tip** someone **off**, you tell them that something has happened or that it is going to happen when other people were trying to keep it secret. ❑ *The burglars were tipped off by a lookout and escaped... They tipped the police off.*

V+N+ADV,
V+PRON+ADV

♦ A **tip-off** is a piece of information that you give to someone, usually as a warning that something is going to happen. ❑ *The building was evacuated as the result of a tip-off.*

N-COUNT

tip over When you **tip** an object **over** or when it **tips over**, it falls or turns onto its side or upside down. ❑ *The last of the glasses broke when Sean tipped over the sideboard... She tipped the pan over and a dozen fish fell out... The boat transporting them had somehow tipped over.*

V+ADV+N,
V+N+ADV,
V+PRON+ADV,
V+ADV:
ERGATIVE

NOTE **Overturn** means almost the same as **tip over**.

tip up If you **tip up** a container such as a bucket or glass, you make it lean to one side so that its contents begin to pour out of it. ❑ *She tipped up the sherry glass... I had to hold the can to his mouth and tip it up as his head went back.*

V+ADV+N,
V+N+ADV,
V+PRON+ADV

NOTE **Tilt** means almost the same as **tip up**.

tire /taɪəʳ/ (tires, tiring, tired)

★**tire of** If you **tire of** something, you become bored with it and are no longer interested in it. ❑ *They will tire of the sport soon enough... Father would simply stop talking when he tired of my questions.*

V+PREP

tire out If something **tires** you **out**, it makes you exhausted. ❑ *Even climbing up the stairs would tire him out... He would walk back in the evening, and so tire himself out and be able to sleep... It is necessary to keep the cough from being so frequent that it tires the person out or interferes with sleep.*

V+PRON+ADV,
V+REFL+ADV,
V+N+ADV

NOTE **Wear out** means almost the same as **tire out**.

♦ If you are **tired out**, you are exhausted. ❑ *By the time he got round to them he was tired out. ...tired-out parents.*

ADJECTIVE

tog /tɒg/ (togs, togging, togged)

tog out If you **tog** yourself **out** or **are togged out**, you are dressed in special or unusual clothes. ❑ *The kids had togged themselves out in their best clothes... Every year they arrive, togged out for the party.*

V+REFL+ADV:
USUALLY+A

NOTE **Rig out** means almost the same as **tog out**.

tog up If you **are togged up**, you are dressed in the right clothing for a particular activity. [INFORMAL] ❑ *Sheila was all togged up like a camper.*

PASSIVE:
V+ADV

toil /tɔɪl/ **(toils, toiling, toiled)**

toil away If you **toil away**, you work hard at something continuously over a long period of time, especially something that is unpleasant and physically very tiring. ❑ *...the coalminer toiling away in the black deeps... Our mothers toiled away in the kitchen most of their lives.*

V+ADV

NOTE **Slave away** means almost the same as **toil away**.

tone /toʊn/ **(tones, toning, toned)**

tone down

1 If you **tone** something **down**, you make it less strong, severe, or offensive. ❑ *He advised me to tone down my article... Tone down that language!... The accent seemed to have been toned down.*

V+ADV+N,
V+N+ADV,
V+PRON+ADV

NOTE **Moderate** means almost the same as **tone down**.

2 If you **tone down** a colour or a flavour, you make it less bright or strong. ❑ *When Ken Hom wrote his first book for the BBC he was asked to tone down the spices and garlic in his recipes.*

V+N+ADV,
V+ADV+N,
V+PRON+ADV

tone in If something **tones in** with something else, it looks nice with it because their colours are similar. ❑ *The hat toned in with the dress Nance was wearing... That carpet doesn't really tone in with the curtains.*

V+ADV:
ALSO+with

NOTE **Match** means almost the same as **tone in**.

tone up If something **tones up** your muscles, it makes them firm and strong. ❑ *This exercise should help to tone up the stomach muscles.*

V+ADV+N,
V+N+ADV,
V+PRON+ADV

tool /tuːl/ **(tools, tooling, tooled)**

tool up When a factory **tools up** or **is tooled up**, it gets its machinery ready to produce things. ❑ *The costs of tooling up for this new model were $50 million... We are tooled up to produce now.*

V+ADV:
OR PASSIVE:
V+ADV

top /tɒp/ **(tops, topping, topped)**

top off If you **top** something **off**, you do something to complete it in a satisfactory way. ❑ *The discovery of the volcanoes topped off an exciting week... We topped the evening off with a few drinks... He ate a plate of steak and eggs and then topped it off with ice cream and loganberries.*

V+ADV+N,
V+N+ADV,
V+PRON+ADV:
ALSO+with

NOTE **Round off** means almost the same as **top off**.

★**top up** If you **top up** something such as a container or a drink, you fill it up again when it has been partly emptied. [BRITISH] ❑ *Philip topped up his gin and tonic... Shall I top your glass up?... The radiator will have to be topped up because of evaporation.*

V+ADV+N,
V+N+ADV,
V+PRON+ADV

◆ A **top-up** is another serving of a drink in the same glass that you have just used. [BRITISH] ❑ *Anyone ready for another top-up?*

N-COUNT

topple /tɒpəl/ **(topples, toppling, toppled)**

topple over If something **topples over**, it becomes unsteady and falls. ❑ *She looked at the young tree nervously, as if expecting it to topple over.*

V+ADV

NOTE **Keel over** means almost the same as **topple over**.

toss /tɒs, AM tɔːs/ **(tosses, tossing, tossed)**

☑ **About** is used mainly in British English.

toss about → See toss around

toss around

1 To **toss** something **around** or **toss** it **about** means to move or shake it roughly. ❑ *She started to toss her head about. ...tossing her hair around a lot... The plane was tossed about like a small boat in a storm... They were too old now for pillow fights or to be tossed around.*

V+N+ADV,
V+PRON+ADV

2 If you **toss** an idea or phrase **around** or **toss** it **about**, you mention or suggest it, but not in a very serious way. ❑ *London newspapers started tossing around phrases like 'The big three'... We tossed a few ideas around.*

V+ADV+N,
V+N+ADV,
V+PRON+ADV

toss away If you **toss** something **away**, you get rid of it in a casual or careless way. ❑ *She tossed away her cigarette... He made a gesture of tossing something away.*

V+ADV+N,
V+PRON+ADV,
V+N+ADV

toss back

toss back

1 If you **toss back** your head, you move it back sharply. If you **toss back** your hair, you move your head back sharply so that your hair is no longer over your face. ❑ *He tosses his head back. ...rubbing his hand on his chest and tossing back his head... He removed his hand from the table and tossed back his blond hair.*

V+N+ADV,
V+ADV+N,
V+PRON+ADV

2 If you **toss back**, **toss down**, or **toss off** a drink, you drink it quickly. ❑ *He tossed back another glass of wine... When the drink came, he tossed it down in one gulp... She tossed her second sherry off even quicker than the first.*

V+ADV+N,
V+PRON+ADV,
V+N+ADV

toss down → See **toss back**

toss in If you **toss in** a comment or a piece of information, you give it casually in the middle of a conversation. ❑ *...tossing in the odd juicy titbit... I tossed a few comments in.*

V+ADV+N,
V+N+ADV,
V+PRON+ADV

NOTE **Toss out** means almost the same as **toss in**.

toss off

1 → See **toss back**

2 If you **toss off** something such as a letter or an article, you write it very quickly. ❑ *I tossed off a letter to my parents.*

V+ADV+N,
V+N+ADV,
V+PRON+ADV

NOTE **Dash off** means almost the same as **toss off**.

3 If someone **tosses off**, they masturbate. [INFORMAL, RUDE]

V+ADV

NOTE **Jack off** and **jerk off** mean almost the same as **toss off**.

toss out If you **toss out** an idea or a comment, you give it casually or without being asked. ❑ *She would toss out an idea that they'd never expected from her... I tossed a few suggestions out to see how they'd react.*

V+ADV+N,
V+N+ADV,
V+PRON+ADV

NOTE **Toss in** means almost the same as **toss out**.

toss up If you **toss up**, you make a decision about something by throwing a coin into the air and guessing which side of the coin will be on top when it falls. ❑ *We tossed up to decide who should pay the bill.*

V+ADV

♦ A **toss-up** is a situation in which either of two results seems equally likely. ❑ *It was a toss-up who would get there first.*

N-SING

tot /tɒt/ (tots, totting, totted)

tot up To **tot up** numbers means to add them together in order to get the total number or amount of something. [BRITISH] ❑ *I'll just tot up what you owe me... We totted all the figures up.*

V+ADV+N,
V+N+ADV,
V+PRON+ADV

touch /tʌtʃ/ (touches, touching, touched)

touch down When an aircraft **touches down**, it lands. ❑ *He watched the plane as it touched down... We touched down at Heathrow.*

V+ADV

NOTE **Take off** means the opposite of **touch down**.

♦ **Touchdown** is the landing of an aircraft. ❑ *Failure of any mechanical system to function after touchdown could destroy human lives.*

N-UNCOUNT,
N-COUNT

touch off If something **touches off** a situation or series of events, it causes it to start happening. ❑ *The police action touched off another night of rioting... Recent heavy rains could touch off mudslides.*

V+ADV+N

NOTE **Spark off** means almost the same as **touch off**.

★touch on If you **touch on** or **touch upon** a subject, you mention it or write briefly about it. **Touch upon** is more formal. ❑ *I've touched on a couple of topics already... They had touched on the possibility of an atomic bomb. ...the themes which have been touched upon in this chapter.*

V+PREP:
HAS PASSIVE

touch up

1 If you **touch** something **up**, you improve its appearance by covering up small marks with paint or another substance. ❑ *He touched the car up a bit and sold it... For dark scratches try touching up woodwork with shoe polish... She touches up her hair.*

V+N+ADV,
V+ADV+N,
V+PRON+ADV

♦ **Touched-up** means improved by having small marks painted over. ❑ *...a touched-up photo of President Nixon.*

ADJECTIVE

2 To **touch up** someone means to touch their body in order to gain sexual excitement. [INFORMAL] ❑ *You've been touching her up, haven't you? ...touching up girls on country buses.*

V+PRON+ADV,
V+N+ADV,
V+ADV+N

NOTE **Feel up** means almost the same as **touch up**.

tou̱ch upon → See touch on

tough /tʌf/ (toughs, toughing, toughed)

tough out If you **tough out** a difficult situation, you do not give in or show any weakness in that situation. ❑ *I think it was very brave of him to tough it out... Cabinet ministers signalled their determination to tough out the controversy.*

V+N+ADV,
V+ADV+N,
V+PRON+ADV

toughen /tʌfən/ (toughens, toughening, toughened)

toughen up If you **toughen up**, or if you **are toughened up**, you become stronger and harder, and less gentle or sensitive. ❑ *I would have to toughen up... It was time to toughen ourselves up... He was toughened up by all his physical labour.*

V+ADV,
V+REFL+ADV,
V+N+ADV,
V+PRON+ADV

tout /ta̱ʊt/ (touts, touting, touted)

☑ In American English, **around** is much more common than **round**.

tout around If you **tout around** or **tout round** for something, you try to obtain it by asking a lot of different people. ❑ *...touting round for books.*

V+ADV:
ALSO+for

tout round → See tout around

tow /to̱ʊ/ (tows, towing, towed)

tow away If a vehicle **is towed away**, it is removed from a place by being attached to another vehicle and pulled along. ❑ *If your car breaks down on the motorway, you can have it towed away... He found his van had been towed away by the police.*

V+N+ADV,
V+ADV+N,
V+PRON+ADV

tower /ta̱ʊər/ (towers, towering, towered)

tower above If someone or something **towers above** you or **towers over** you, they are a lot taller than you and make you seem small. ❑ *The old chief towered above everybody... The trees towered above me... The sides of the great ship towered over them.*

V+PREP

tower over → See tower above

tower up If something **towers up**, it is very tall and impressive. ❑ *The Catholic church was towering up behind her... She towered up immense and strong.*

V+ADV

toy /tɔ̱ɪ/ (toys, toying, toyed)

★**toy with**

1 If you **toy with** an idea or suggestion, you consider it casually, without making any decisions about it. ❑ *I've been toying with the idea for some time... The United States is still toying with military solutions. ...toying with the possibility of leaving.*

V+PREP:
HAS PASSIVE

2 If you **toy with** an object, you keep moving it about with your fingers, usually while you are thinking about something else. ❑ *He picked up a pencil and toyed with it idly... He reached for his spectacles and toyed with them.*

V+PREP

NOTE **Play with** means almost the same as **toy with**.

3 If you **toy with** food or drink, you do not eat it or drink it with any enthusiasm, but only take a bite or a little drink from time to time. ❑ *She toyed with the one shrimp remaining on her plate... She had no appetite, and merely toyed with the bread and cheese.*

V+PREP

trace /tre̱ɪs/ (traces, tracing, traced)

trace out If you **trace** something **out**, you write it or mark it clearly and carefully. ❑ *The names were traced out in stark black print... She traced out a bow on the envelope... She traced out A, B, C, and D in the dust with a stick.*

V+N+ADV,
V+ADV+N,
V+PRON+ADV

track /træ̱k/ (tracks, tracking, tracked)

★**track down** If you **track down** someone or something, you find them after searching for them with effort. ❑ *You have to cover a wide area to have any hope of tracking down the submarine. ...driving miles to track down parts for his tractor... One journalist succeeded in tracking the victims down and finding out what had happened to them... He eventually tracked the book down in the university library... If he refused, they would not hesitate to track him down.*

V+ADV+N,
V+N+ADV,
V+PRON+ADV

NOTE **Hunt down** means almost the same as **track down**.

trade /tre̱ɪd/ (trades, trading, traded)

trade in If you **trade in** an old car, machine, or piece of equipment, you give it to a dealer when you buy a new one so that you get a reduction on the price. ❑ *We wanted to trade in the piano for one with a better tone... You might trade the car in for a smaller one... It will cost £21 to repair. Is it worth it, or shall I trade it in for a new one?*

V+ADV+N,
V+N+ADV,
V+PRON+ADV:
USUALLY+for

♦A **trade-in** is a business deal in which someone exchanges an old car, machine, or piece of equipment for a new one at a reduced price.   N-COUNT

trade off

✓ In meaning 2, the stress is on **tr<u>a</u>de**.

1 If you **trade off** one thing against another, you exchange all or part of one thing for another, as part of a negotiation or compromise. ❑ *They cynically tried to trade off a reduction in the slaughter of dolphins against a resumption of commercial whaling... There is a possibility of being able to trade off information for a reduced sentence.*   V+N+ADV, V+ADV+N, V+PRON+ADV: USUALLY+*for/against*

♦ A **trade-off** is a situation where you make a compromise between two things, or where you exchange all or part of one thing for another. [JOURNALISM] ❑ *The newspaper's headline indicates that there was a trade-off at the summit. ...the trade-off between inflation and unemployment. ...the trade-off of territory or land for peace.*   N-UNCOUNT

2 If someone **trades off** something, they make use of it for their own advantage, often in an unfair way. [BRITISH] ❑ *They would be able to trade off their looks and manage on that alone.*   V+PREP

trade on If someone **trades on** something such as another person's weakness, they make use of it in an unfair way to gain an advantage for themselves. ❑ *...people who trade on the hopes of the desperately ill... The Democrats traded on the unpopularity of the two main parties.*   V+PREP: HAS PASSIVE

NOTE **Exploit** means almost the same as **trade on**.

trade up If someone **trades up**, they sell something such as their car or their house and buy a more expensive one. ❑ *Mini-car owners are trading up to 'real' cars... Homeowners will feel more comfortable and they may feel ready to trade up.*   V+ADV: ALSO+*to*

trail /treɪl/ (trails, trailing, trailed)

trail away If a speaker's voice **trails away**, it gradually becomes quieter or more hesitant until it stops completely. ❑ *He didn't finish what he'd intended saying. His voice trailed away.*   V+ADV

trail off If someone who is speaking **trails off** or if their voice **trails off**, they gradually speak more quietly and hesitantly until they stop completely. ❑ *'You see, there are circumstances,' he trailed off... His voice trailed off as he reached the landing.*   V+ADV

train /treɪn/ (trains, training, trained)

train on If you **train** something such as a gun, light, or camera **on** or **upon** someone or something, you aim it at them and keep it pointing steadily towards them. **Train upon** is more formal. ❑ *She trained her binoculars on the car speeding towards them... One gun was trained on Jo... All the searchlights were trained upon a single aircraft.*   V+N+PREP, V+PRON+PREP

train up If you **train up** a person, you teach them how to do something so that they reach a particular standard. [BRITISH] ❑ *They need to train up large numbers of local people as clerks and accountants... They rented a shop, hired some lads, and trained them up. ...beginners who were going to be trained up for the National Dancing Championships.*   V+ADV+N, V+PRON+ADV, V+N+ADV

train upon → See train on

trample /træmpəl/ (tramples, trampling, trampled)

trample on

1 If you **trample on** or **trample upon** something, you tread on it heavily so that it is damaged. **Trample upon** is more formal. ❑ *He knocked the statue over and trampled on it... They were kicked, bitten, and trampled on... He found his plants trampled upon.*   V+PREP: HAS PASSIVE

2 If you **trample on** or **trample upon** a person, their rights, or their feelings, you behave towards them in an unfair, insensitive, or cruel way. **Trample upon** is more formal. ❑ *Half the population trample on the rights of the other half... Neither will we allow ourselves to be trampled on... National distinctions cannot be trampled upon.*   V+PREP: HAS PASSIVE

trample upon → See trample on

trap /træp/ (traps, trapping, trapped)

trap into If you **trap** someone **into** saying or doing something, you make them say or do it by tricking them or misleading them. ❑ *...trying to trap Vita into an admission about her past... The student was finally trapped into making a mistake.*   V+N+PREP, V+PRON+PREP: ALSO+-*ING*

NOTE **Trick into** means almost the same as **trap into**.

For a full explanation of all grammatical labels, see pages xiii-xx

trip up

trespass /trɛspəs/ **(trespasses, trespassing, trespassed)**

    trespass upon If you **trespass upon** someone's generosity or friendship, you take advantage of them by asking too much from them. [FORMAL, OLD-FASHIONED] ❑ *May I trespass upon your sense of justice?*

V+PREP:
HAS PASSIVE

trick /trɪk/ **(tricks, tricking, tricked)**

    trick into If you **trick** someone **into** doing something, you manage to get them to do it by misleading them or not telling them the truth. ❑ *She has been tricked into marriage. ...girls tricked by promises of work into leaving home... She tricked me into thinking it was gold.*

V+N+PREP,
V+PRON+PREP:
ALSO+-ING

    trick out If someone or something **is tricked out** in a particular way, they are made to look that way. ❑ *...cupboards with sliding doors tricked out to look like Georgian cocktail cabinets... She'd be a funny kind of tailor not to have tricked me out better.*

V+N+ADV,
V+PRON+ADV:
USUALLY PASSIVE

trickle /trɪkəl/ **(trickles, trickling, trickled)**

    trickle down If money, benefits, or other things **trickle down**, they are passed on gradually from the people at the top of a system to people lower down the system. ❑ *The growing discrepancy is starting to make the villagers despair that any of the city's wealth will trickle down to them.*

V+ADV:
ALSO+to

    ♦ A **trickle-down** effect or policy is passed on gradually from the people at the top of a system to people lower down the system. ❑ *Investment has not only created new jobs in areas of high unemployment, but has had a trickle-down effect on supplier firms.*

ADJECTIVE

trifle /traɪfəl/ **(trifles, trifling, trifled)**

    trifle with If you **trifle with** someone or something, you treat them in a frivolous or disrespectful way. ❑ *Mitchell was not someone to be trifled with... He was in no mood to be trifled with... One does not trifle with history.*

V+PREP:
HAS PASSIVE

trigger /trɪgər/ **(triggers, triggering, triggered)**

    trigger off If something **triggers off** an event or particular reaction, it causes it to happen. ❑ *The report triggered off a parliamentary debate... Radiation can damage DNA and trigger off cancer... Many of the ideas were triggered off by things which were not actively looked for.*

V+ADV+N,
V+PRON+ADV,
V+N+ADV

    NOTE **Spark off** and **set off** mean almost the same as **trigger off**.

trim /trɪm/ **(trims, trimming, trimmed)**

    trim away If you **trim away** a part of something, you cut it off, because it is not needed. ❑ *Kellner was trimming away the excess carpet... You can trim the flesh away a little so that you can see the ribs.*

V+ADV+N,
V+N+ADV,
V+PRON+ADV

    trim off If you **trim off** parts of something, you cut them off, because they are not needed. ❑ *Remove as many bones as possible, and trim off the fins... Thread them through the hole, then trim the ends off. ...a book with all its margins trimmed off to save weight.*

V+ADV+N,
V+N+ADV,
V+PRON+ADV

trip /trɪp/ **(trips, tripping, tripped)**

★**trip over**

    1 If you **trip over** something, you knock your leg against it and fall over or nearly fall over. ❑ *He stuck out his foot, and I tripped over it, but recovered... He tripped over and came down with a crash.*

V+PREP,
V+ADV

    2 If you **trip over** something you are saying, you say it hesitantly or make mistakes because you are nervous. ❑ *Children understand the meaning even when they trip over unexpected words... Frederica spoke a few lines, tripping over words and recovering her dignity.*

V+PREP

trip up

    1 If someone or something **trips** you **up**, they cause you to fall over or nearly fall over by obstructing your feet when you are walking. ❑ *When people run after you, your friends trip them up or threaten them... The road was full of holes and rocks which could trip you up. ...walking cautiously to avoid tripping up.*

V+PRON+ADV,
V+N+ADV,
V+ADV:
ERGATIVE

    2 To **trip** someone **up** also means to make them confused so that they say something that they did not intend to say. ❑ *The judges' questions tripped him up completely... Even the cleverest of us can be tripped up from time to time.*

V+PRON+ADV,
V+N+ADV

    NOTE **Catch out** means almost the same as **trip up**.

The symbol ★ shows key phrasal verbs

trot /trɒt/ (trots, trotting, trotted)

trot off If you **trot off** somewhere, you go there fairly quickly and in a purposeful way. ❑ *He described his little girl trotting off to school in her new blazer... He trotted off to tell his grandmother all about it.*

V+ADV: USUALLY+A

trot out If you **trot out** old ideas, excuses, or pieces of information, you repeat or produce them in a boring way that shows that you have not really thought about them seriously; used showing disapproval. ❑ *...politicians who could be guaranteed to trot out the party line... Alison can hear it when I do, and you're not trotting it all out twice... We heard the usual excuses trotted out by the man in charge.*

V+ADV+N, V+PRON+ADV, V+N+ADV

truckle /trʌkəl/ (truckles, truckling, truckled)

truckle to If you **truckle to** someone, you behave in a humble way towards them and do whatever they tell you to do. [FORMAL, OLD-FASHIONED] ❑ *I am sick of having to truckle to the professors... Only a weak and spineless man would truckle to the powerful and ruthless.*

V+PREP: HAS PASSIVE

truss /trʌs/ (trusses, trussing, trussed)

truss up If you **truss** someone **up**, you tie them with ropes very tightly so that they cannot move. [FORMAL] ❑ *Finally I had to truss him up like a turkey to get at his foot... The bulls were trussed up with ropes... Madame Berte was trussed up hand and foot with the clothes line.*

V+PRON+ADV, V+N+ADV

trust /trʌst/ (trusts, trusting, trusted)

trust to If you **trust to** someone or something, you rely on them to do something for you or to take care of you. ❑ *The people of England are discovering that it is no good trusting to the old politicians... He would just have to trust to luck.*

V+PREP

try /traɪ/ (tries, trying, tried)

★try for If you **try for** something, you make an effort to get it or achieve it. ❑ *The Government tried for this two-thirds majority and failed... The school advised Mr Denby to let his son try for university.*

V+PREP

★try on

1 If you **try on** a piece of clothing, you put it on to see if it fits you or if it looks nice. ❑ *Poppy Green came to the house to try on her party dress... She tried it on for size... Always try shorts on in the shop.*

V+ADV+N, V+PRON+ADV, V+N+ADV

2 If someone is **trying** it **on**, they are attempting to trick you or make you angry. [BRITISH, INFORMAL] ❑ *So don't try it on, my poor misguided boy, or else... She is probably trying it on to see how far she can go with you... I was only trying it on, Mary. All right, let's start again.*

V+it+ADV

★try out

1 If you **try** something **out**, you test it in order to find out how useful or effective it is. ❑ *Oxford is trying out another idea to help working parents... First they tried it out on a small group of children.*

V+N+ADV, V+PRON+ADV: ALSO+on

♦ If you give something a **try-out**, you test it so that you can find out how useful or effective it is. ❑ *A neighbour had given the machine a good try-out.*

N-COUNT

2 If you **try** someone **out**, you ask them to do a small task, so that you can see how good or useful they are before you ask them to do a particular job. ❑ *Just try me out for a week, you'll see... You can try your horse out in a local competition first.*

V+PRON+ADV, V+N+ADV

try out for If you **try out for** a sports team or an acting role, you compete or you perform a test in an attempt to be chosen. ❑ *He should have tried out for the Olympic 100 metres squad.*

V+ADV+PREP

tuck /tʌk/ (tucks, tucking, tucked)

tuck away

1 If you **tuck away** something that is valuable, you store it in a safe place. ❑ *She had a bit of money tucked away... The bike can be folded and tucked away in a suitcase. ...rolling up the bill and tucking it away for safety.*

V+ADV+N, V+PRON+ADV, V+N+ADV

NOTE **Stash away** means almost the same as **tuck away**.

2 If something **is tucked away**, it is in a quiet place where very few people go. ❑ *The parish church is tucked away behind the cathedral... He is tucked away in a tiny office.*

PASSIVE: V+ADV

NOTE **Be hidden away** means almost the same as **be tucked away**.

★tuck in

1 If you **tuck** someone **in** or **tuck** them **up**, especially a child, you make them comfortable in bed by straightening their sheets and blankets and pushing the loose ends firmly under the mattress. ❏ *He was asleep before I tucked him in... Get her to tuck you up in bed... She bent over, pretending to be tucking in the child.*   V+PRON+ADV, V+ADV+N, V+N+ADV

2 If you **tuck in** material such as a sheet, or the clothes you are wearing, you push the loose ends into a narrow space, in order to hold them in position. ❏ *I tucked my blouse in at the waist... She began buttoning up her shirt and stood up to tuck it in... He tucked in his shirt tails.*   V+N+ADV, V+PRON+ADV, V+ADV+N

3 If you **tuck in**, you eat something with a lot of pleasure. [BRITISH, INFORMAL] ❏ *Well, there we are, tuck in... Mary put a plate of scrambled eggs and bacon in front of Morris and he tucked in appreciatively.*   V+ADV: ALSO IMPERATIVE

NOTE **Dig in** means almost the same as **tuck in**.

4 If you **tuck** a part of your body **in**, you use your muscles and move it inwards rather stiffly. ❏ *Tuck your elbows in and sit up straight... He hunched his shoulders and tucked in his stomach.*   V+N+ADV, V+ADV+N, V+PRON+ADV

tuck into

1 If you **tuck** something **into** a narrow space, you press or push it into that space. ❏ *'Oh, do stand still!' she said, tucking Paul's shirt into his shorts... Madeline crumpled the note and tucked it into her glove... He wore hiking boots into which he tucked the bottom of his jeans.*   V+N+PREP, V+PRON+PREP

2 If you **tuck into** food, you eat it with a lot of pleasure. [BRITISH, INFORMAL] ❏ *'Was that a helicopter?' she asked, tucking into her breakfast. ...tucking into mountains of greasy chips and sticky buns.*   V+PREP

tuck up

1 → See **tuck in**

2 If you **tuck** your legs or your feet **up** when you are sitting down, you move them underneath your body so that you are sitting on them. ❏ *'That's where you're wrong,' said Ellen, tucking her feet up under her black skirt... She tucked up her feet and gazed at him... Her restless, elegant legs were tucked up onto the sofa.*   V+N+ADV, V+ADV+N, V+PRON+ADV

tug /tʌg/ (tugs, tugging, tugged)

tug at If you **tug at** something, you give it a quick and usually strong pull. ❏ *He tugged at the metal handle, and it came off in his hand... I had to tug at his hand to loosen it... He began to tug at the grass.*   V+PREP

NOTE **Yank** means almost the same as **tug at**.

tumble /tʌmbəl/ (tumbles, tumbling, tumbled)

tumble down If someone or something **tumbles down**, they fall down. ❏ *It only needed a push and the whole building would come tumbling down... Did the walls really come tumbling down?*   V+ADV

♦ A **tumbledown** building is in such a bad condition that it is partly falling down or has holes in it. ❏ *...a deserted, tumbledown building.*   ADJECTIVE

tumble over If someone or something **tumbles over**, they fall down. ❏ *She tumbled over and hit her head on the concrete. ...a barrier designed to stop cars tumbling over a steep drop.*   V+ADV, V+PREP

tumble to If you **tumble to** something, you suddenly understand it or realize what is happening. [INFORMAL] ❏ *I soon tumbled to the fact that I was wasting my time... At least nobody tumbled to what these pipes were for a long time... I can't guarantee to get you out of trouble if he tumbles to what's going on.*   V+PREP: HAS PASSIVE

tune /tjuːn, AM tuːn/ (tunes, tuning, tuned)

★tune in If you **tune in**, you set the controls of your radio or television so that you can listen to or watch a particular programme. ❏ *Tune in next week to hear how English is taught in China... There must be millions of people tuning in to see the World Snooker Championships.*   V+ADV

tune into

1 If you **tune into** a particular channel or station, you set the controls on your radio or television so that you can listen to or watch that channel or station. ❏ *Film en-*   V+PREP

The symbol ★ shows key phrasal verbs

thusiasts can tune into their own channels... I've been listening to the early morning radio, tuned into Delhi.

2 If you **are tuned into** someone or something, you understand them very well and are sympathetic towards them. ❑ *She was so tuned into you that she could 'read' your mind... People are becoming more tuned into what computers can actually do.*

PASSIVE: V+PREP

tune out If you **tune out**, you stop listening or paying attention to what is being said. ❑ *Whatever you're talking about, children rapidly tune out if you go beyond them... Rose heard the familiar voice, but tuned out the words.*

V+N+ADV, V+ADV+N, V+PRON+ADV, V+ADV

tune up

1 When a group of musicians **tune up**, they adjust their instruments so that they produce the right notes. ❑ *The orchestra was tuning up for its regular Sunday afternoon broadcast... The sound suggests they are tuning up.*

V+ADV

2 If you **tune up** a car, you adjust its engine so that it goes faster or more efficiently.

V+ADV+N, V+N+ADV, V+PRON+ADV

turf /tɜːʳf/ (turfs, turfing, turfed)

turf out

1 If you **turf** someone **out**, you force them to leave a particular place. [BRITISH, INFORMAL] ❑ *Settlers are aware that the chief can turf them out if he takes a dislike to them... When I turfed him out, he told me he was going straight to your place.*

V+PRON+ADV, V+N+ADV

NOTE **Kick out** and **chuck out** mean almost the same as **turf out**.

2 If you **turf out** unwanted things, you get rid of them. [BRITISH, INFORMAL] ❑ *I turfed out a lot of stuff last week.*

V+ADV+N

turn /tɜːʳn/ (turns, turning, turned)

✅ **About** is used mainly in British English. In American English, **around** is much more common than **round**.

turn about

1 If something or someone **turns about** or if you **turn** them **about**, they move so that they are facing in a different direction. ❑ *He turned about and tiptoed away... The old method of harvesting barley is to turn it about until it is quite dry.*

V+ADV, V+PRON+ADV, V+N+ADV: ERGATIVE

NOTE **Turn around** means almost the same as **turn about**.

♦ **About-turn** is a command which is used to tell a group of people who are marching in a particular direction to turn round and march in the opposite direction. ❑ *Right about-turn! Quick march!*

IMPERATIVE

2 A **turnabout** is a complete change in opinion or attitude. ❑ *I was eager to know what had caused the turnabout.*

N-COUNT

3 An **about-turn** is an unexpected and complete change in opinion or attitude. ❑ *Sandy Lyle yesterday did an about-turn and agreed to play... One of the reasons prompting the about-turn was the increasing expense.*

N-COUNT

turn against If someone **turns against** or **is turned against** you, they start to dislike you or disapprove of you. ❑ *They might at any time turn against their masters... Public opinion turned against Hearst... You turn everyone against me... My daughter, who I was very close to, has been turned against me by her father.*

V+PREP, V+N+PREP, V+PRON+PREP: ERGATIVE

★turn around

1 If someone or something **turns around** or **turns round**, or you **turn** them **around** or **turn** them **round**, they move so that they are facing in the opposite direction. ❑ *After much effort, he manages to turn the car around... She'd turn her hat around so that the ribbons hung over her face... She would turn round and whisper jokes with the others... Toby turned her round to face me.*

V+ADV, V+PRON+ADV, V+N+ADV: ERGATIVE

2 If something such as a plan, project, or business that is failing **turns around** or if you **turn** it **around**, it becomes successful and profitable. ❑ *...if the economy turns around and the prices go up. ...an attempt to turn around last year's losses of £20 million... The company were in such bad shape that nobody could have turned things around in four years.*

V+ADV, V+ADV+N, V+N+ADV, V+PRON+ADV: ERGATIVE

♦ A **turnaround** is a sudden improvement, especially in the success of a business or country's economy. ❑ *There is little prospect of a sudden turnaround.*

N-COUNT

NOTE **Turnround** means almost the same as **turnaround**.

3 If something **turns** your life **around**, it completely changes the way you live,

V+N+ADV,

usually for the better. If you **turn** your life **around**, you do something that im-
proves your life a lot. ❑ *Susan Powter was a miserable, overweight single mother who*
turned her life around.

V+ADV+N,
V+PRON+ADV

4 If you **turn** a question, sentence, or idea **around**, or if you **turn** it **round**, you
change the way in which it is expressed or considered. ❑ *It's an example of how you*
can turn around the sentence and create a whole new meaning... When you first asked me
about this I turned the whole question round... So by putting it in the third person I can turn
it round a bit and make it funny.

V+ADV+N,
V+N+ADV,
V+PRON+ADV

5 If someone **turns around** or **turns round** and does something, they do some-
thing unexpectedly or unfairly. [INFORMAL] ❑ *He left her, then turned around and went*
out with her best friend!... Won't the child turn round and blame the school?

V+ADV:
WITH *and*+VERB

turn aside If you **turn aside** from someone or something, you move away from
them or avoid them. ❑ *He turned discreetly aside to wipe his nose... The Government has*
turned aside from its collision course with the unions.

V+PREP:
ALSO+*from*

★**turn away**

1 If you **turn away** from someone or something, you move away from them so
that you are no longer facing them. ❑ *I had to turn away to avoid letting him see my*
smile... Kunta turned away from the water's edge.

V+ADV:
ALSO+*from*

2 If you **turn** something **away** from someone or something, you move it to a dif-
ferent position so that it is no longer facing them. ❑ *She turned his chair away from the*
window... Karen turned her eyes away from Kitty.

V+N+ADV,
V+PRON+ADV:
ALSO+*from*

3 If you **turn** someone **away**, you refuse to allow them to enter a place, or refuse
to help them. ❑ *We don't turn anybody away because the old business was built up on*
friendship... The college has been forced to turn away 300 prospective students... Clerical
workers and secretaries were turned away by gangs of men when they arrived at work.

V+N+ADV,
V+ADV+N,
V+PRON+ADV

turn away from If you **turn away from** something, or **are turned away**
from it, you reject it or lose interest in it. ❑ *Women are turning away from hand-made*
clothes to machine printed dresses. ...stores which had done so much to turn people away
from processed food... Mrs Norberg threw out a challenge that Daniel did not turn away
from.

V+ADV+PREP,
V+N+ADV+PREP,
V+PRON+ADV+PREP:
ERGATIVE

★**turn back**

1 If you **turn back** or **are turned back** when you are travelling somewhere, you
stop and return to the place you started from. ❑ *The snow started to fall, so we turned*
back... The police were turning back thousands of mourners... A lot of the cars had been
turned back at the border... We were turned back by machine-gun fire.

V+ADV,
V+ADV+N,
V+N+ADV,
V+PRON+ADV:
ERGATIVE

2 If you say that you cannot **turn back**, you mean that you cannot change your
plans and decide not to do something, because of the action that you have already
taken. ❑ *She had made her decision and from that point there could be no turning back.*

V+ADV:
WITH NEGATIVE

3 If you **turn back** material or paper, you fold one part of it over so that it is cov-
ering the other part. ❑ *He leaped out of the bed and turned back the blankets... She was*
holding two papers but they were turned back so I couldn't see.

V+ADV+N,
V+N+ADV,
V+PRON+ADV

★**turn down**

1 If you **turn down** a person, their request, or their offer, you refuse their request
or offer. ❑ *I turned down an invitation for Saturday... I couldn't very well turn him down...*
She applied for a job in a restaurant, but was turned down... Their claim has been turned
down.

V+ADV+N,
V+PRON+ADV,
V+N+ADV

[NOTE] **Reject** means almost the same as **turn down**.

2 When you **turn down** something such as a radio or a heater, you adjust the
controls and reduce the amount of sound or heat being produced. ❑ *Turn the sound*
down... It's a bit hot in here – turn it down... She turned down the gas fire.

V+N+ADV,
V+PRON+ADV,
V+ADV+N

[NOTE] **Turn up** means the opposite of **turn down**.

3 If the rate or level of something **turns down**, it decreases. [BRITISH, JOURNALISM]
❑ *The divorce rate turned down in the 1950s.*

V+ADV

♦ If there is a **downturn** in the rate, level, or success of something, it decreases or
becomes less successful. ❑ *The downturn in inflation has only taken place in the last three*
months... The company blamed its downturn on interest rates.

N-COUNT

[NOTE] **Upturn** means the opposite of **downturn**.

4 If you **turn down** material or paper, you fold it so that one part of it is covering

V+ADV+N,

the other part. ❑ *The room bearer had turned down their bedcovers... Some of the cards were turned down at the edges... She won't turn down the collar of her coat.*
V+N+ADV,
V+PRON+ADV

turn in

1 When you **turn in**, you go to bed. [INFORMAL] ❑ *Before turning in for the night he asked for an early morning call... I'd like to wait until they've all turned in for a good night's sleep, then I'd stage a riot.*
V+ADV

NOTE **Retire** is a more formal word for **turn in**.

2 If you **turn in** someone who is suspected of a crime, you take them to the police. ❑ *Can you trust him? Do you think he might turn you in?... They had been turned in by one of their own sons. ...escapees who turned themselves in.*
V+PRON+ADV,
V+N+ADV,
V+REFL+ADV,
V+ADV+N

3 If you **turn** something **in**, you give it to someone in authority because it is their responsibility to deal with it. ❑ *They agreed to turn in their guns... He was sure he had turned his uniform in when he left the force... Meehan bought a car and then had to turn it in because it had been stolen.*
V+ADV+N,
V+N+ADV,
V+PRON+ADV

4 When you **turn in** a completed piece of work, especially written work, you give it to the person who asked you to do it. ❑ *Some of the students began to turn in superb work... David and Chris turned in the type of workmanlike results I had expected of them.*
V+ADV+N,
V+PRON+ADV

NOTE **Hand in** and **give in** mean almost the same as **turn in**.

5 If you **turn** something **in**, you return it to the place or person you borrowed it from. [AMERICAN] ❑ *The official showed up to tell her to turn in her library books.*
V+N+ADV,
V+PRON+ADV,
V+ADV+N

NOTE **Return** means almost the same as **turn in**.

★turn into

If someone or something **turns into** another thing or if you **turn** them **into** it, they change and become that other thing. ❑ *Maggots turn into flies, and caterpillars into butterflies... Having a gun can turn a coward into a dangerous criminal... The novel had been turned into a television series.*
V+PREP,
V+N+PREP,
V+PRON+PREP:
ERGATIVE

★turn off

1 When you **turn off** a device, machine, or appliance, you adjust the controls in order to stop it working. ❑ *Turn the gas fire off when you leave the room... How do you turn it off?... He must have turned off the radio.*
V+N+ADV,
V+PRON+ADV,
V+ADV+N

NOTE **Switch off** means almost the same as **turn off**, and **turn on** means the opposite.

2 If you **turn off** the road or path you are going along, you start going along a different road or path which leads away from it. ❑ *They turned off the main road... Small groups occasionally would turn off the trail to hunt... This is where I turn off.*
V+PREP,
V+ADV

◆ A **turn-off** is a road which leads away from the side of another road. [BRITISH] ❑ *Be careful, or you'll miss the turn-off.*
N-COUNT

3 If something **turns** you **off** or if you **turn off**, you stop being excited or interested. [INFORMAL] ❑ *Had I turned her off by not being daring enough? ...customers turned off by poor advertising techniques... The lecture was so boring that I just turned off.*
V+PRON+ADV,
V+N+ADV,
V+ADV

◆ Something that is a **turn-off** causes you to lose interest or enthusiasm. [INFORMAL] ❑ *All this legal stuff is a total turn-off for us.*
N-COUNT

4 If something or someone **turns** you **off**, you do not find them sexually attractive or they stop you feeling sexually excited. [INFORMAL] ❑ *Aggressive men turn me off.*
V+N+ADV,
V+PRON+ADV

NOTE **Turn on** means the opposite of **turn off**.

◆ Something that is a **turn-off** stops you feeling sexual excitement. [INFORMAL] ❑ *When you see something like that, you realise what a turn-off fame can be.*
N-COUNT

NOTE **Turn-on** means the opposite of **turn-off**.

★turn on

☑ In meanings 4-7, the stress is on **turn**.

1 When you **turn on** a device, machine, or appliance, you adjust the controls so that it starts working. ❑ *Shall I turn the fire on?... I have a radio too, but I seldom turn it on except for concerts... She turned on the shower.*
V+N+ADV,
V+PRON+ADV,
V+ADV+N

NOTE **Switch on** means almost the same as **turn on**, and **turn off** means the opposite.

2 If someone or something **turns** you **on**, they make you interested or excited, especially sexually. [INFORMAL] ❑ *I don't really turn you on, do I?... It says some women are turned on by the smell and feel of leather.*
V+PRON+ADV,
V+N+ADV

◆ Something or someone that is a **turn-on** makes you interested or excited, espe-
N-COUNT

cially sexually. [INFORMAL] ❑ *I find long hair a real turn-on.*

NOTE **Turn-off** means the opposite of **turn-on**.

3 If you **turn on** a particular way of behaving, you suddenly start behaving in that way. ❑ *...a kid who knew how to turn on the charm... Maternal behaviour couldn't be turned on and off at will.*

V+ADV+N,
V+PRON+ADV

NOTE **Switch on** means almost the same as **turn on**.

4 If a person or animal **turns on** or **turns upon** you, they suddenly attack you or speak angrily to you. **Turn upon** is more formal. ❑ *She turned on the men. 'How can you treat your daughters like this!'... Amir's dogs turned upon their master and tore him to pieces.*

V+PREP

NOTE **Round on** means almost the same as **turn on**.

5 If something **turns on** or **turns upon** a particular thing, its success or truth depends on that thing. **Turn upon** is more formal. ❑ *His own future will turn on whether or not he can convince enough voters... The whole issue turns on the question of finances.*

V+PREP

NOTE **Hinge on** means almost the same as **turn on**.

6 If your thoughts or a conversation **turn on** or **turn upon** a particular subject, they are concerned with that subject. **Turn upon** is more formal. ❑ *For a moment my thoughts turned on that gross and stupid man... Her mind turned upon the horrors depicted in the film... The conversation turned on the question of athleticism.*

V+PREP

7 If you **turn** something such as a gun, a light, or a type of look **on** someone or something, or **turn** it **upon** them, you aim it at them or keep it pointing steadily at them. **Turn upon** is more formal. ❑ *She turned a flashlight on Karen... Firefighters turned their hoses on the flames... Mrs Mawne turned a frosty glance upon Mr Willet.*

V+N+PREP,
V+PRON+PREP

NOTE **Train on** means almost the same as **turn on**.

turn on to To **turn** someone **on to** something means to make them become interested in it or excited by it. ❑ *It was watching Jack Nicklaus win the 1986 Masters on television that turned him on to golf... His parents were so keen to turn him on to literature that they locked him in his bedroom for half an hour every evening with a copy of Treasure Island.*

V+N+ADV+PREP,
V+PRON+ADV+PREP

★turn out

1 If something **turns out** a particular way, it happens in that way. ❑ *Nothing ever turned out right... It turned out to be a fairly sensational evening... That's the way things turn out.*

V+ADV:
WITH+A/to-INF

NOTE **Work out** means almost the same as **turn out**.

2 When you are commenting on pleasant weather, you can say that it has **turned out** nice or fine, especially if this is unexpected. [BRITISH] ❑ *It's turned out nice again.*

it+V+ADV:
WITH ADJ

3 If something or someone **turns out** to be a particular thing, they are discovered to be that thing. ❑ *The Marvins' house turned out to be an old converted barn... Mrs Moffat had turned out to be the perfect landlady... It turned out that the message sent to him had been intercepted.*

V+ADV:
WITH to-INF OR REPORT

4 When you **turn out** a light or a gas fire, you adjust the controls so that it stops giving out light or heat. ❑ *She didn't bother to turn the light out when she went out of the room... Pa had turned out the gas in the kitchen... His hand was on the light to turn it out again.*

V+N+ADV,
V+ADV+N,
V+PRON+ADV

NOTE **Turn off** means almost the same as **turn out**, and **turn on** means the opposite.

5 If you **turn** someone **out** of a place, you force them to leave it. ❑ *I wouldn't want to turn you out of the house with the child ill... There's rumours going that she'll be turned out of the school-house... There are plenty of others likely to find themselves turned out on the streets after closing-time.*

V+PRON+ADV,
V+N+ADV:
USUALLY+of

NOTE **Turf out, kick out** and **chuck out** mean almost the same as **turn out**.

6 If you **turn out** a container or **turn** its contents **out**, you empty it completely. ❑ *I have turned out the cupboard under the stairs... She opened her purse and turned out the contents onto the table... Come on, turn your pockets out!*

V+ADV+N,
V+N+ADV,
V+PRON+ADV

◆ If you have a **turnout**, you sort through the things in a room or other place and throw away the unwanted things. ❑ *On Saturday I began my usual turnout.*

N-COUNT

7 If a business or other organization **turns out** something, it produces it, usually in large quantities. ❑ *Salford was turning out the type of graduate they wanted... Better-*

V+ADV+N,
V+PRON+ADV

quality goods were being turned out at lower prices.

NOTE **Churn out** means almost the same as **turn out**.

8 If people **turn out** for a particular event or activity, they go and take part in it or watch it. ❑ *Voters turned out in extraordinary numbers for the election... 50,000 people turned out during the bank holiday weekend to watch the airshow.*

V+ADV:
USUALLY+A

NOTE **Turn up** means almost the same as **turn out**.

♦ The **turnout** at an event is the number of people who go to it or take part in it. ❑ *It was such a small turnout!*

N-COUNT

9 If you say that someone **is turned out** smartly, nicely, neatly, and so on, you mean that they are dressed in that way. ❑ *...attractive-looking girls, well turned out and smart. ...Soviet officers, elegantly turned out in black hats.*

PASSIVE:
V+ADV

♦ Someone's **turnout** is the way they are dressed and how neat they are. ❑ *Claude approved of Daniel's turnout, with the exception of his tie.*

N-COUNT

★turn over

1 If something or someone **turns over** or if you **turn** them **over**, they move so that they are facing in a different direction. ❑ *She turned over and went to sleep... He turned the novel over to see the title... When the pancake is set, turn it over and cook the other side... The students were asked to turn over their papers and begin the exam.*

V+ADV,
V+N+ADV,
V+PRON+ADV,
V+ADV+N:
ERGATIVE

2 If you **turn over** someone suspected of a crime to the police or the authorities, you take them to the police or authorities. ❑ *If he'd suspected him, he'd have turned the man over right away... If you turn me over to the police I'll tell them nothing... They were caught by security patrols and turned over to the police.*

V+N+ADV,
V+PRON+ADV,
V+ADV+N:
USUALLY+to

NOTE **Turn in** means almost the same as **turn over**.

3 If you **turn** something **over** to someone, you give it to them or make them responsible for it. ❑ *He had refused to turn over funds that belonged to Potter. ...turning over control of the schools to local authorities... I turned the cheque over to the Treasurer.*

V+ADV+N,
V+N+ADV,
V+PRON+ADV:
USUALLY+to

NOTE **Hand over** means almost the same as **turn over**.

4 If you **turn** something **over** to a different function or use, you change its function or use. ❑ *The automobile industry had to turn their production facilities over to the creation of weapons... Soon afterwards I turned over part of the shop to antiques.*

V+N+ADV,
V+PRON+ADV,
V+ADV+N:
USUALLY+to

5 If you **turn over** when you are watching television, you change the programme you are watching and watch another one instead. ❑ *We turned over to see if we could find anything more interesting on... Turn over, I can't stand this programme.*

V+ADV

NOTE **Switch over** means almost the same as **turn over**.

6 When you talk about the rate that people or things **turn over** in a particular place, you are talking about how long they stay there before moving or being sent somewhere else. ❑ *In a grocery store, milk turns over more rapidly than, say, canned asparagus.*

V+ADV

♦ The **turnover** of people in an organization is the rate at which people leave and are replaced by others. ❑ *The group has an extremely high turnover of members.*

N-UNCOUNT

♦ The **turnover** of a company is the value of the goods or services that it has sold during a particular period of time. ❑ *Annual turnover is about £9,000 million.*

N-UNCOUNT

7 If you **turn** something **over** in your mind, you think carefully about it. ❑ *I had thought about the problem all day, turning it over in my mind... Going home that night, Dr Renshaw turned over the facts of the case... We ate in silence, turning over this uncomfortable rumour in our minds.*

V+N+ADV,
V+PRON+ADV,
V+ADV+N

NOTE **Chew over** and **mull over** mean almost the same as **turn over**, and **consider** is a more general word.

8 When an engine **turns over**, it continues running steadily at a low speed. ❑ *The car engines turn over, ready for the race.*

V+ADV

NOTE **Tick over** means almost the same as **turn over**.

9 If someone **turns over** a place, they search it thoroughly or steal things from it in an organized way, usually causing a lot of damage. [INFORMAL] ❑ *Half the school is on probation for turning over a supermarket... They turned room 37 over – it looked as if a tornado had hit it.*

V+ADV+N,
V+N+ADV,
V+PRON+ADV

NOTE **Do over** means almost the same as **turn over**.

10 A **turnover** is a small piece of pastry that has been filled with fruit or jam, folded over, and baked. ❑ *...an apple turnover.*

N-COUNT

For a full explanation of all grammatical labels, see pages xiii-xx

★turn round

1 → See **turn around**

2 If you **turn round** a plan, project, or business that is failing, you change it so that it becomes successful and profitable. ❑ *It's a cruel deception to pretend that you could turn round the economy in a week... The engineering group is at last fighting to turn round its business.*

V+ADV+N,
V+N+ADV,
V+PRON+ADV

♦ A **turnround** is a sudden improvement, especially in the success of a business or country's economy. ❑ *With so little room to move, the turnround will be gradual.*

N-COUNT

NOTE **Turnaround** means almost the same as **turnround**.

★turn to

1 If you **turn to** someone, you ask them for something such as help, advice, or information. ❑ *If they feel they've been wronged, they'll turn to a solicitor... Thank you, Geoff. Now we turn to John Venables to see what he thinks... Children can get along well without having to turn to an adult for support... I have no other friend to turn to.*

V+PREP:
HAS PASSIVE

2 If you **turn to** a particular topic when you are talking or writing, you start to talk or write about it. ❑ *Let us turn to a completely different country, Japan... Now I can turn to what prison did to you.*

V+PREP

★turn up

1 If someone **turns up**, they arrive somewhere. ❑ *He turned up at rehearsal the next day looking awful... If it's a boring game the crowds won't turn up next time... When you didn't turn up on Friday we tried to get in touch with you.*

V+ADV

NOTE **Show up** means almost the same as **turn up**.

2 If something **turns up** or **is turned up**, it is found, discovered, or noticed. ❑ *You must be willing to take a job as soon as one turns up... Protein turns up in almost every food... Scientists have turned up no useful information on how best to treat it... If I turn anything up, I'll let you know.*

V+ADV,
V+ADV+N,
V+N+ADV,
V+PRON+ADV:
ERGATIVE

3 When you **turn up** something such as a radio or heater, you increase the amount of sound or heat being produced, by adjusting the controls. ❑ *Turn the volume control up... Turn up the heat and stir in the soy sauce... The TV was turned up loudly so that no-one would hear them talking.*

V+N+ADV,
V+ADV+N,
V+PRON+ADV

NOTE **Turn down** means the opposite of **turn up**.

4 When someone **turns up** something such as a dress, skirt, or pair of trousers, they shorten it by folding up the bottom edge, sometimes stitching it in place. ❑ *Will you turn my jeans up for me, mum?... I turned it up but the hem is all crooked now.*

V+N+ADV,
V+PRON+ADV,
V+ADV+N

NOTE **Let down** means the opposite of **turn up**.

♦ The **turn-ups** of someone's trousers are the ends of the trouser legs, which are folded upwards so that they show on the outside. ❑ *He was wearing a pair of grey flannel trousers, with turn-ups.*

N-PLURAL

5 If you **turn** something **up**, you move it so that it is pointing in an upward direction. ❑ *She turned up her collar before facing the bad weather... She turned up the palm of one hand in a gesture of resignation... Her blonde plaits were turned up and tied with a neat black velvet bow.*

V+ADV+N,
V+N+ADV,
V+PRON+ADV

6 If there is an **upturn** in something such as a country's economy, it starts to improve. ❑ *When the upturn comes in world trade. ...an upturn in demand.*

N-COUNT

NOTE **Downturn** means the opposite of **upturn**.

turn upon → See **turn on**

type /taɪp/ (types, typing, typed)

type away If you **type away**, you type busily and for a long time. ❑ *Gerald was typing away in his office.*

V+ADV

type in If you **type in** a name, word, letter, and so on, you use a computer or word processor to record it. ❑ *If you want the dictionary, you type in the letter D... She's typed the wrong name in... Fresh details will be typed in by the doctor on the spot.*

V+ADV+N,
V+N+ADV,
V+PRON+ADV

NOTE **Key in** means almost the same as **type in**.

type into If you **type** something **into** a computer or word processor, you put information or text into it by pressing the keys on the keyboard. ❑ *You can throw a program by typing nonsense into the computer... Your responses will be typed into the system.*

V+N+PREP,
V+PRON+PREP

type out If you **type** something **out**, you write it in full using a typewriter or word processor. ❑ *The two of us stood by while two typists typed out the whole document again... I read it down the phone to a man called Dave, who typed it out... I'll get this play typed out in the next few days.*

V+ADV+N,
V+PRON+ADV,
V+N+ADV

type up If you **type up** your ideas, notes, or handwritten text, you produce a completed version of them on a typewriter. ❑ *I'll go and type up these notes... After thinking about it, she typed it up, then we both read it... The report was typed up by the sec-retary.*

V+ADV+N,
V+PRON+ADV,
V+N+ADV

Uu

urge /ɜːʳdʒ/ (urges, urging, urged)

urge on

☑ In meaning 2, the stress is on **urge**.

1 If you **urge** someone **on**, you encourage them to do something. ❑ *Both decisions urged the Tartars on to new forms of protest... I am trying to urge him on to 'try things out for himself'... The President, reportedly urged on by his vice-president, has decided to attend the talks.*

NOTE **Egg on** means almost the same as **urge on**, and **encourage** is a more formal word.

2 If you **urge** something **on** someone, or **urge** it **upon** them, you try to persuade them to accept it, even though they do not really want to. **Urge upon** is slightly more formal. ❑ *Frank had another reason for urging caution on them both at this moment... That's a wise thought and I urge it on them... Mr Profumo accepted the wording urged upon him by his colleagues.*

V+N+ADV,
V+PRON+ADV,
V+ADV+N

V+N+PREP,
V+PRON+PREP

urge upon → See urge on

use /juːz/ (uses, using, used)

★**use up** If you **use up** a supply of something, you finish it so that none of it is left. ❑ *She did use up a tremendous amount of energy... He used up all the coins he had... Put the leftovers in a tub and use it all up the next day.*

V+ADV+N,
V+PRON+ADV,
V+N+ADV

usher /ʌʃəʳ/ (ushers, ushering, ushered)

usher in If one thing **ushers in** another thing, it indicates that the other thing is about to begin. [FORMAL] ❑ *The French Revolution ushered in a new age... He entered the Polytechnic, ushering in an illustrious career in military science.*

V+ADV+N,
V+PRON+ADV

Vv

vamp /væmp/ (vamps, vamping, vamped)

    vamp up If you **vamp** something **up**, you make it seem as if it is new and excit-   V+N+ADV,
ing by adding things to it. ❏ *...a musical comedy vamped up for the audience... We can*   V+PRON+ADV,
always vamp it up a bit, then we'd sell it all right.   V+ADV+N

varnish /vɑːrnɪʃ/ (varnishes, varnishing, varnished)

    varnish over If you **varnish over** a situation or an event, you hide unpleasant   V+PREP:
aspects of it or pretend that they do not exist. ❏ *Conflict is varnished over with polite*   HAS PASSIVE
words.

    NOTE **Gloss over** and **paper over** mean almost the same as **varnish over**.

veer /vɪər/ (veers, veering, veered)

    veer off If something that is moving in a particular direction **veers off**, it sud-   V+ADV
denly changes direction. ❏ *The general direction of the gulls is southwards, but they will*
always veer off to follow a shoal of herring or mackerel.

venture /vɛntʃər/ (ventures, venturing, ventured)

    venture forth If you **venture forth**, you go somewhere, especially somewhere   V+ADV
that might be dangerous. [LITERARY] ❏ *I did indeed venture forth again that night.*

    NOTE **Sally forth** means almost the same as **venture forth**.

verge /vɜːrdʒ/ (verges, verging, verged)

    verge on If a particular quality **verges on** another, it begins to be very similar   V+PREP
to it. ❏ *I had a feeling of distrust verging on panic... It was the kind of smile that verged on*
laughter. ...games which verge on criminality.

    NOTE **Border on** means almost the same as **verge on**.

vie /vaɪ/ (vies, vying, vied)

    vie with If you **vie with** someone, you try hard to get something before they do,   V+PREP
or to do something better than they do. ❏ *Pressure is mounting as a number of compa-*
nies and entrepreneurs vie with each other for the coveted trophies... To attract customers
they vied with each other to offer higher savings interest rates.

visit /vɪzɪt/ (visits, visiting, visited)

    visit with If you **visit with** someone, you go and see them and spend time with   V+PREP
them. [AMERICAN] ❏ *He had not visited with the rascal since 1946.*

vote /voʊt/ (votes, voting, voted)

    vote down If something or someone **is voted down**, they are rejected, espe-   V+N+ADV,
cially as a result of a formal vote. ❏ *My proposal was voted down... This particular group*   V+ADV+N,
got voted down... The committee decided to advise Parliament to vote down the measure.   V+PRON+ADV

    vote in When people **vote in** a person or group of people, they give them   V+N+ADV,
enough votes in an election for them to hold a position of power. ❏ *There are already*   V+PRON+ADV,
enough pensioners to vote a government in or out... So they voted him in, did they?... All the   V+ADV+N
directors were voted in by proxies.

    NOTE **Elect** means almost the same as **vote in**.

    vote out When people **vote out** a person or group of people, they do not give   V+N+ADV,
them enough votes in an election to allow them to continue holding a position of   V+PRON+ADV,
power. ❏ *They voted Councillor Hitchcock out of her seat... No-one ever wanted to vote you*   V+ADV+N:
out of office... He was voted out in 1983.   ALSO+of

    vote through If a law or proposal **is voted through**, a majority of people ac-   V+N+ADV/PREP,
cept it in a formal election. ❏ *...the land reform programme was voted through the*   V+PRON+ADV/PREP,
Phillipine Congress... The new measures were voted through, but only by a small margin...   V+ADV+N:
The committee voted the motion through by an overwhelming majority.   USUALLY PASSIVE

vouch /vaʊtʃ/ (vouches, vouching, vouched)
vouch for

1 If you say that you can or will **vouch for** someone, you mean that you are sure that they will behave correctly, and that you take responsibility for their good behaviour. ❑ *Don Tomassino vouched for you personally... He said you'd vouch for him.*   V+PREP

2 If you say that you can **vouch for** something, you mean that you know from your own personal experience or knowledge that it is true or correct. ❑ *I can vouch for the accuracy of my information... She was down there all right. I'll vouch for that.*   V+PREP: HAS PASSIVE

Ww

wade /weɪd/ **(wades, wading, waded)**

wade in If you are faced with a difficult situation or a lot of work and **wade in**, you start dealing with it in a determined and energetic way. ❑ *Bill itched to wade in and 'sort them out'... Get to San Francisco at once and watch him wade in.*

V+ADV

wade into If you **wade into** someone or something that is causing problems, you start dealing with them in a determined and energetic way. ❑ *Only he had sufficient vitality to wade into the three-hundred page report.*

V+PREP

wade through If you **wade through** a lot of written material, you spend a lot of time and effort reading it. ❑ *A lawyer was wading through the three-hundred-page file. ...to start wading through the mass of paper-work.*

V+PREP

NOTE **Plough through** means almost the same as **wade through**.

wait /weɪt/ **(waits, waiting, waited)**

☑ **About** is used mainly in British English.

wait about → See **wait around**

wait around If you **wait around** or **wait about**, you spend a long period of time doing very little before something happens or before you can do something or see someone. ❑ *Julie had waited around for nearly a whole year... Two detectives were waiting around to question the old man. ...waiting about while Mr Wilde checked off the things on the list.*

V+ADV:
USUALLY+A

wait behind If you **wait behind**, you deliberately stay in a place after everyone else has left, for example because you want to talk to someone alone. ❑ *She walked out, leaving Doctor Percival to wait behind for the bill.*

V+ADV

wait in If you **wait in**, you deliberately stay at home and do not go out, for example because someone is coming to see you. [BRITISH] ❑ *I waited in all the afternoon... 'I'll wait in for it.'—'No need for that.'*

V+ADV

NOTE **Stay in** means almost the same as **wait in**.

wait on

1 If someone **waits on** you in a restaurant or at a formal party, they serve you food and drink. ❑ *...sitting around a dinner table, being waited on by uniformed waitresses... 'Help yourself,' I say. 'I'm not waiting on you.'*

V+PREP:
HAS PASSIVE

2 If you **wait on** or **wait upon** someone, you take care of all their needs and do anything that they ask you to do. **Wait upon** is more formal. ❑ *Ever since the world started, men have been waited on by women... I found it a remarkable experience to be waited upon by eight servants.*

V+PREP:
HAS PASSIVE

3 If you **wait on** someone, you wait somewhere until they have finished what they are doing and can talk to you or go with you. [AMERICAN] ❑ *I've got some good news. That's why I waited on you out here... Get your chores done, Miss Jordache. We'll be waiting on you... 'Wait on, Mr South!' a child called.*

V+PREP,
V+ADV

4 If you **wait on** or **wait upon** an event, you wait until it happens before doing or deciding something. **Wait upon** is more formal. ❑ *The company is prepared to delay the deal and wait on events... She laughed—but waited on his response none the less. ...the future of a world waiting upon their decision.*

V+PREP

wait out If you **wait out** a period of time or an event, especially a difficult one, you wait for it to pass or to happen. ❑ *So we chatted as we waited out the ten minutes... They erected a small stockade, dug in, and waited out the night... A large assembly had gathered to wait out the hearing... Anne calmed her and persuaded her to sit and wait it out.*

V+ADV+N,
V+PRON+ADV:
NO PASSIVE

NOTE **Sit out** means almost the same as **wait out**.

wait <u>u</u>p

1 If you **wait up**, you deliberately do not go to bed, because you know that some-one who lives in the same place as you will be returning home late at night. ❏ *I can't make it home until late. Tell her not to wait up... He was waiting up for me when I got in.*

V+ADV:
ALSO+for

2 If you say **'Wait up'** to someone, you want them to wait until you reach them or finish what you are doing. [AMERICAN, INFORMAL] ❏ *Wait up – I'm coming.*

IMPERATIVE,
V+ADV

NOTE In British English, **hang on** means almost the same as **wait up**.

wait upon → See wait on

wake /we<u>ɪ</u>k/ (wakes, waking, woke, woken)

✓ American English also uses the form **waked** for the past tense and past partici-ple of the verb.

★wake <u>u</u>p

1 When you **wake up**, or when someone or something **wakes** you **up**, you be-come conscious again after being asleep. ❏ *Ralph, wake up! ...young babies waking up at night and crying... I'll wake Buller up... I won't wake him up yet. ...enough racket to wake up half the occupants of the cabin.*

V+ADV,
V+N+ADV,
V+PRON+ADV,
V+ADV+N:
ERGATIVE,
ALSO IMPERATIVE

◆ A **wake-up** call is a telephone call that you ask someone to make to you so that it wakes you up, for example because you do not have an alarm clock. ❏ *...New York's most prestigious wake-up service.*

ADJECTIVE

2 If an activity or event **wakes** you **up** after you have been inactive or bored, it makes you more active or interested. ❏ *Some of the students challenge him a little to wake him up... Those exercises woke Donald up, I can tell you... I once waked up a dull meeting by proposing that... The other two students wake up briefly, exchange glances and snigger.*

V+PRON+ADV,
V+N+ADV,
V+ADV+N,
V+ADV:
ERGATIVE

◆ If you say that something is a **wake-up** call to a person or group of people, you mean that it will make them notice something and start to take action. ❏ *The Ambas-sador said he hoped the statement would serve as a wake-up call to the government.*

ADJECTIVE

wake <u>u</u>p to If you **wake up to** a problem or a dangerous situation, you be-come aware of it. ❏ *The West began to wake up to the danger it faced... The Church must wake up to the financial problems of the clergy. ...by the time they woke up to the fact that they needed our technology.*

V+ADV+PREP

NOTE **Realize** is a more formal word for **wake up to**.

walk /wɔ:k/ (walks, walking, walked)

★walk aw<u>a</u>y from If someone **walks away from** a difficult or unpleasant situation, they leave it rather than trying to deal with it; used showing disapproval. ❏ *'You can't walk away from this, Frank,' Patterson said... So many customers have walked away from its $40-per-barrel contracts.*

V+ADV+PREP

walk aw<u>a</u>y with → See walk off with

walk <u>i</u>n on If you **walk in on** someone when they are doing something private or secret, you enter the place where they are and interrupt them, and embarrass them or yourself, usually unintentionally because you did not know they were there. ❏ *...as adolescents, they had walked in on their parents' embraces and caresses... I imagine their embarrassment at walking in on me.*

V+ADV+PREP

walk <u>i</u>nto

1 If you **walk into** an unpleasant or dangerous situation, you become involved in it unexpectedly, sometimes because you are careless. ❏ *He had walked into a trap... You might be walking into an ambush... How come you can walk into a situation like this?*

V+PREP

2 If you **walk into** a job, you manage to get it very easily. ❏ *He just walked into the job without even an interview. ...how Cockburn came to walk straight out of The Times and into the Daily Worker.*

V+PREP

walk <u>o</u>ff If you **walk off** an unpleasant feeling, you go for a walk in order to stop having the feeling. ❏ *He went out to walk off his disquiet in the night air... She man-aged to walk off her headache... It is better for you to walk it off.*

V+ADV+N,
V+PRON+ADV:
NO PASSIVE

walk <u>o</u>ff with

1 If someone **walks off with** something, they take it without asking the person to whom it belongs. ❏ *Not realizing what she was doing, she had walked off with it... She*

V+ADV+PREP

wants to know what to do about the man who has walked off with her pruning hook.

NOTE **Go off with** means almost the same as **walk off with**.

2 If you **walk off with** something such as a prize, or **walk away with** it, you win it or achieve it very easily. [INFORMAL] ❏ *One reader will walk off with the £35,000 first prize... She will walk away with the title.* — V+ADV+PREP

walk on If you **walk on** in a play, you have a very minor part in it, often one that does not require you to speak. ❏ *Why don't you come and walk on in 'The High Bid', at Her Majesty's Theatre?... She desperately wants a part in the play, whether she has a leading role or is only walking on.* — V+ADV

♦ A **walk-on** part is a very minor part in a play. ❏ *My sister had a walk-on part.* — ADJECTIVE

★**walk out**

1 If you **walk out** of a meeting, a performance, or an unpleasant situation, you leave it suddenly, as a way of showing that you dislike it or that you are angry. ❏ *Haig walked out of the conference... Many of the audience walked out through sheer boredom... 'You did not,' I said sourly, standing up and walking out.* — V+ADV: ALSO+of

♦ A **walk-out** is a protest in which you leave a meeting or performance to show your dislike or anger. ❏ *The students had called for a walk-out.* — N-COUNT

2 If workers **walk out**, they suddenly go on strike. ❏ *The firemen voted to walk out in support... When 160 men walked out in August, union officials were taken aback.* — V+ADV

♦ A **walk-out** by workers is a sudden strike. ❏ *...ending the 43-day walk-out.* — N-COUNT

walk out on If you **walk out on** someone with whom you have a close relationship, you leave them suddenly and often end the relationship. ❏ *His girlfriend walked out on him... They had walked out on me after the scene at Inge's flat... If I try to discipline him, he just walks out on me without listening.* — V+ADV+PREP

walk over

1 If someone **walks over** you, they treat you very badly, especially by telling you what to do all the time. [INFORMAL] ❏ *...allow officials to walk all over them... Father is much less inclined to lie back and allow himself to be walked over.* — V+PREP: HAS PASSIVE

NOTE **Trample on** means almost the same as **walk over**.

2 A **walkover** is a success or victory that is achieved without much effort. ❏ *By yielding to a forceful Government, those victims allow injustice a walkover.* — N-SING

wall /wɔːl/ **(walls, walling, walled)**

wall in If someone or something **is walled in**, they are surrounded or enclosed by a wall or barrier. ❏ *They walled in the front of their cave and built steps from it... Once in it you are enclosed, walled in by tombs of kings.* — V+ADV+N, V+PRON+ADV: USUALLY PASSIVE

wall off If part of a place **is walled off**, it is separated from the rest of the place by a wall. ❏ *The area was walled off... It had an end walled off to form a gas chamber.* — PASSIVE: V+ADV

wall up If someone **is walled up**, they are put in a place and prevented from leaving it by blocking every exit with a wall. ❏ *...a peasant-girl, who's had herself walled up in a specially prepared cell in her local church... Creon punishes Antigone by walling her up alive in a tomb. ...get the horse in and wall him up in one corner with planks so he can't slip down.* — V+N+ADV, V+PRON+ADV, V+ADV+N

wallow /wɒloʊ/ **(wallows, wallowing, wallowed)**

wallow in If you **wallow in** a situation or emotion, you think about it or remain in it for a long time, because you are enjoying it. ❏ *...wallowing in self-pity.* — V+PREP

waltz /wɔːlts/ **(waltzes, waltzing, waltzed)**

waltz off with If you **waltz off with** something such as a prize or award, you win it. [INFORMAL] ❏ *She swept the board, waltzing off with three gold medals.* — V+ADV+PREP

want /wɒnt/ **(wants, wanting, wanted)**

want for If you do not **want for** something, you have or get as much of it as you need. [FORMAL] ❏ *Now the responsibility was ours to see that she did not want for understanding and sympathy... As long as Alan was here, he would not want for hot food.* — V+PREP: WITH NEGATIVE

want in If someone is arranging a plan, project, or business deal and you **want in**, you want to be involved or have a share in it. [INFORMAL] ❏ *They all want in... The Swiss wanted in on whatever deal Patterson was trying to put together.* — V+ADV: ALSO+on

NOTE **Want out** means the opposite of **want in**.

want out

1 If you **want out**, you no longer want to be involved in a plan, project, or business deal that you are part of. [INFORMAL] ❑ *I want out. I want to sell up... If you want out, right now, just say so, and I'll understand... The main flaw in this package, I now see, is the fact that City Bank wants out.*

NOTE **Want in** means the opposite of **want out**.

V+ADV

2 If you **want out** of a place, you want to leave it. [INFORMAL] ❑ *He knew he was in the hospital and really wanted out... The cat ran in; he patted it and it wanted out again... I want out of here right now.*

V+ADV:
ALSO+of

ward /wɔːʳd/ (wards, warding, warded)
ward off

1 To **ward off** something unpleasant or dangerous means to prevent it from affecting you or harming you. ❑ *...sufficient food and clothing to ward off starvation and ill-health. ...the ornaments at the head of the bed, placed there to ward off evil spirits. ...before anti-aircraft equipment arrived to ward off further attacks.*

V+ADV+N,
V+PRON+ADV

2 If you **ward** someone **off**, you prevent them going somewhere or doing something. ❑ *'I'm sorry the room's such a mess,' Elaine said, warding him off... I turned to him in amazement, but he warded me off. 'No, no, enough revelations for one evening.'*

V+PRON+ADV,
V+N+ADV

warm /wɔːʳm/ (warms, warming, warmed)

warm down If you **warm down** after doing exercise, you do some gentle movements before stopping the exercise completely. ❑ *Remember to warm up beforehand and warm down afterwards to avoid stiffness.*

V+ADV

warm to If you **warm to** or **warm towards** a person, you become fonder of them. If you **warm to** or **warm towards** an idea or task, you become more interested in the idea, or more keen to do the task. ❑ *I warmed to him in the bar... Tom found himself warming towards Vic... Bricklayers warmed to the work – it was at last an opportunity to use their skills.*

V+PREP

warm towards → See **warm to**

★warm up

1 If you **warm up** cold food, you put it on a cooker and heat it until it is ready to be eaten. ❑ *Start warming up the soup now. ...scooped one of the cold slices into the oven to warm it up... I keep lots of food that's quickly thawed and easily warmed up.*

V+ADV+N,
V+PRON+ADV,
V+N+ADV

NOTE **Heat up** means almost the same as **warm up**.

2 If the weather, the day, or part of the earth **warms up**, the temperature rises and it gradually gets hotter. ❑ *The weather was warming up... Nobody is sure how far and how fast the earth will warm up as carbon dioxide and other gases build up in the atmosphere.*

V+ADV

3 If you **warm up** or if something **warms** you **up**, you start to feel warm again after you have been cold. ❑ *She began to warm up... Come in and warm up by the stove... You're a whisky man, Doc. That's the stuff to warm you up.*

V+ADV,
V+PRON+ADV,
V+N+ADV:
ERGATIVE

NOTE **Thaw out** means almost the same as **warm up**.

4 If you **warm up** just before a physical activity or event such as a race, you prepare yourself for it, usually by practising or doing some exercises. ❑ *They jogged around the track twice, warming up. ...while the singers were warming up.*

V+ADV

NOTE **Limber up** means almost the same as **warm up**.

◆ A **warm-up** is preparation which you do just before a physical activity or event. ❑ *During the warm-up exercises, I was still shaking.*

N-SING,
ADJECTIVE

5 If a situation, event, or activity **warms up**, or if you **warm** it **up**, it becomes more intense or exciting. ❑ *The campaign against the brothers began to warm up... Business'll be warming up soon... The studio has been warming up America to go film-mad for most of this year.*

V+ADV,
V+ADV+N,
V+N+ADV,
V+PRON+ADV:
ERGATIVE

NOTE **Hot up** means almost the same as **warm up**.

6 When a machine, engine, or electrical device **warms up**, or when you **warm** it **up**, it starts working and becomes ready for use. ❑ *...a muffled roaring sound, like the engines of jet planes warming up on a distant runway... Mr McElrea then gave final instructions to Richie as he warmed up the engines... I went across and switched on the TV and waited for it to warm up.*

V+ADV,
V+ADV+N,
V+PRON+ADV:
ERGATIVE

7 If a comedian or speaker **warms up** an audience, or if the audience **warms up**, the audience is prepared for the main show or speaker by being told jokes, so that

V+N+ADV,
V+ADV+N,
V+PRON+ADV,

they are in a good mood. ❑ *They would always come out and warm up the audience... The crowd began to warm up.*

V+ADV:
ERGATIVE

warn /wɔːrn/ (warns, warning, warned)

warn away

warn away If you **warn** someone **away**, you tell them to leave a place because it is dangerous for them to be there. ❑ *F-14s circled the exercise area to warn aircraft away from the firing zone... They were warning us away, waving frantically and shouting... They were warned away from the firing range by one of the soldiers.*

V+N+ADV,
V+PRON+ADV,
V+ADV+N:
ALSO+from

warn off If you **warn** someone **off**, you tell them to go away or to stop doing something because of possible danger or punishment. ❑ *She makes agitated signs to warn him off, whispering that 'Mr Shaw is at work.'... I thought you were warning me off the drink... Lansing may discover that fact and warn off our friends.*

V+PRON+ADV/PREP,
V+ADV+N,
V+N+ADV/PREP:
ALSO+from

wash /wɒʃ/ (washes, washing, washed)

wash away

1 If rains, floods, or waves **wash away** something, they carry it away by force, usually causing a lot of damage or destruction. ❑ *The dam collapsed, washing away twenty-five villages... The big flood washed it away and then they put the swing bridge up... The tidal wave washed everything away.*

V+ADV+N,
V+PRON+ADV,
V+N+ADV

NOTE Sweep away means almost the same as **wash away**.

♦ A **washaway** is a hollow area caused by the earth being washed away by rain or floods; used mainly in Australian English. ❑ *I camped in a washaway near the ruin of a cottage.*

N-COUNT

2 To **wash away** smells, tastes, or other qualities of an object or substance means to remove them, usually using water. ❑ *Soaps wash away the natural odors of the human body... He drank the scotch, then washed the taste away with water.*

V+ADV+N,
V+N+ADV,
V+PRON+ADV

3 To **wash away** a problem, feeling, or situation means to cause it to end or to be forgotten. ❑ *All that had happened in the past was washed away... We will never be able to wash away the taint. ...trying to wash your troubles away. ...and then it just seemed to wash away.*

V+ADV+N,
V+N+ADV,
V+ADV:
ERGATIVE

wash down

1 If you **wash down** food, you drink something after eating it or while eating it. ❑ *...washing each mouthful down with coffee... He washed it down with whisky. ...if you wash down your meal with cola. ...chips, washed down with milk shakes.*

V+N+ADV,
V+PRON+ADV,
V+ADV+N:
USUALLY+with

2 If you **wash down** an object or surface, you wash all of it. ❑ *I mopped up the kitchen, washed down the walls. ...washed him down and dried him... He washed the windshield down.*

V+ADV+N,
V+PRON+ADV,
V+N+ADV

3 If rocks or soil **are washed down** by rains or floods, they are carried by the water to another place. ❑ *A row of stone kept the soil from being washed down the steep hills in heavy rain... Boulders and scree were washed down by the floods... Soil from the mountains washes down in the rivers.*

V+ADV+N,
V+PRON+ADV:
USUALLY PASSIVE:
ALSO V+ADV:
ERGATIVE

wash off

1 If you **wash** dirt or other unwanted things **off**, you remove them from the surface of something using water. ❑ *Take them home and wash off the mud and sand... She washed the blood off... Wash all the bleach off the sides... She was told not to wash it off... It does not rub off or, if allowed to dry, wash off either.*

V+ADV+N,
V+N+ADV/PREP,
V+PRON+ADV/PREP,
V+ADV:
ERGATIVE

2 If you **wash** someone **off**, you remove the dirt or blood from their body, using water. ❑ *Let Sally wash you off... Wash yourself off and put these clothes on... He washed himself off.*

V+PRON+ADV,
V+REFL+ADV,
V+N+ADV

★wash out

1 If you **wash out** clothes, you clean them using water. ❑ *...a mother washing out her baby's nappies... Go down to the stream and wash your underwear out.... She let me wear it for a few days before she made me wash it out.*

V+ADV+N,
V+N+ADV,
V+PRON+ADV

2 If you **wash out** a container, you clean the inside of it with water. ❑ *I washed out the coffee things... Wash it out well and fill it with clear water... A milky bottle is easily washed out with cold water.*

V+ADV+N,
V+N+ADV,
V+PRON+ADV

NOTE Rinse out means almost the same as **wash out**.

3 If you **wash out** dirt, stains, or other unwanted things, or if they **wash out**, they are removed, using water. ❑ *Wash the sand out of them in shallow water... This is*

V+N+ADV,
V+ADV+N,
V+PRON+ADV,

good because it washes out some of the germs... Dominic had tried to wash it all out... The grey dye was washed out with the aid of a solvent... The ink, surprisingly, washed out easily.

V+ADV:
ERGATIVE,
ALSO+of

4 If you **wash out** a feeling or thought, you cause it to end or to be forgotten. □ *...preparing his breakfast with her own hands to wash out the guilt she felt... I ought to try to forget it, wash it out of my mind. ...an unclean feeling that you can't wash out of your head.*

V+ADV+N,
V+PRON+ADV,
V+N+ADV:
ALSO+of

5 If something **washes** you **out**, it causes you to feel exhausted or to fail to do what you were trying to do. [INFORMAL] □ *Only an utter catastrophe can wash me out... The trip just washed all of them out.*

V+PRON+ADV,
V+N+ADV,
V+ADV+N

♦ If someone is or looks **washed-out**, they are or look very tired and lacking in energy. □ *I returned to Chamonix, washed-out and depressed.*

ADJECTIVE

NOTE **Run down** means almost the same as **washed-out**.

6 A **washed-out** colour is pale and dull. □ *...eyes of washed-out grey. ...a canopy of washed-out blue.*

ADJECTIVE

7 If a game, event, or activity **is washed out**, it is prevented from taking place, usually because it rains. □ *The first day of play was washed out after only 90 minutes.*

PASSIVE:
V+ADV

♦ If an attempt, event, or project is a **washout**, it is a total failure. [INFORMAL] □ *The whole thing will be a washout if we don't arrive before sunset.*

N-COUNT

8 If someone or something **is washed out** from a place by rain or floods, they are carried away by force. □ *...prevent the seed from being washed out... Her home collapsed and she was washed out on the tide... The next tides will wash the hatched fish out to sea again... Another 40,000 tons of oil washed out of the damaged tanker.*

V+N+ADV,
V+PRON+ADV,
V+ADV+N:
USUALLY PASSIVE:
ALSO V+ADV:
ERGATIVE

wash over If something that someone does or says **washes over** you, you do not notice it or it does not affect you in any way. □ *The television headlines seemed to wash over her without meaning anything.*

V+PREP

★wash up

1 If you **wash up** the things such as pans, plates, and knives that have been used to cook and eat a meal, you clean them using water and detergent. [BRITISH] □ *He insisted on helping me wash up... We cleared the table and washed up the dishes... Tim carried the plates to the kitchen and washed them up.*

V+ADV,
V+ADV+N,
V+PRON+ADV,
V+N+ADV

♦ If you do the **washing-up**, you clean the things that have been used to cook and eat a meal, using water and detergent. [BRITISH] □ *There was enough water to do all the washing-up... Clean the sink with hot water and washing-up liquid.*

N-SING

2 If you are dirty and **wash up**, you clean yourself, especially your hands and face. [AMERICAN] □ *I washed up as best I could in the adjacent bathroom... He went to the bathroom to wash up and comb his hair.*

V+ADV

3 If someone or something **is washed up** on a piece of land, or **washes up** there, they are carried by the water of a river or the sea and left there. □ *Their boat was washed up ten miles to the south. ...pieces of wood have been washed up on the shores... Pyle's body washed up under the bridge at Dakao.*

V+N+ADV,
V+PRON+ADV:
USUALLY PASSIVE:
ALSO V+ADV:
ERGATIVE

4 If you say that someone is **washed up**, you mean that they are at the end of their career and no longer of any use. [INFORMAL] □ *I was not going to be all washed up, an ex-sportsman with nothing to do at 35.*

ADJECTIVE

waste /weɪst/ (wastes, wasting, wasted)

waste away

1 If someone **wastes away** or **is wasted away**, they become extremely thin or weak because they are ill or worried and they are not eating properly. □ *I don't want you to waste away... I hope your flesh will waste away... He was wasted away to no more than a skeleton.*

V+ADV:
ALSO PASSIVE:
V+ADV

2 If something **wastes away**, it becomes smaller or weaker until it eventually disappears because it is not being properly looked after. □ *Whenever muscles are rested they start to waste away and rapidly lose strength... Our planners have allowed rural communities to waste away.*

V+ADV

watch /wɒtʃ/ (watches, watching, watched)

★**watch for** If you **watch for** something which is likely to happen in the future, you wait carefully for it because it might be important or unpleasant. □ *You have to watch for the union problem... Watch carefully for signs of growth... Watch our travel pages for final details.*

V+PREP:
HAS PASSIVE

★**watch out** If you tell someone to **watch out**, you are warning them to be careful because something unpleasant might happen to them. ❑ *If you don't watch out, he might stick a knife into you... You behave yourself or you'd better watch out... The mood was gentle, and yet, I had been told to watch out.*

NOTE **Look out** means almost the same as **watch out**.

V+ADV:
ALSO IMPERATIVE

★**watch out for** If you **watch out for** something, you stay alert so that you will notice it when it appears or happens because it is likely to be important. ❑ *Watch out for the warning signs of depression like insomnia... This is a good place to watch out for wild animals.*

NOTE **Look out for** means almost the same as **watch out for**.

V+ADV+PREP

watch over If you **watch over** someone or something, you take care of them because you are responsible for them. ❑ *The wives took turns to watch over the children... From this point on the two tribes would be watched over and controlled by the Army.*

NOTE **Guard** means almost the same as **watch over**.

V+PREP:
HAS PASSIVE

water /wɔ:tər/ **(waters, watering, watered)**

water down

1 If a speech or written statement **is watered down**, it is made much weaker and less forceful or controversial. ❑ *The paragraph had in any case been watered down, and the final draft was a compromise... He watered down the article guaranteeing the right to strike.*

V+ADV+N,
V+PRON+ADV:
USUALLY PASSIVE

2 If you **water down** food or drink, you add water to it to make it weaker. ❑ *No, it's not watered down. It's quite potent stuff for beer.*

NOTE **Dilute** is a more formal word for **water down**.

V+ADV+N,
V+N+ADV,
V+PRON+ADV

wave /weɪv/ **(waves, waving, waved)**

wave aside If you **wave aside** an idea, reason, or objection, you show that you do not want to consider it because you do not think it is important enough. ❑ *The Chief waved his objection aside... Miss Jackson waved aside these little difficulties.*

NOTE **Brush aside** means almost the same as **wave aside**, and **dismiss** is a more formal word.

V+N+ADV,
V+ADV+N,
V+PRON+ADV

wave away If you **wave** someone or something **away**, you signal with your hand that you do not want them near you at the moment. ❑ *She waved him away when he ventured near her desk... Another mistake many businessmen make at lunch is to wave away the sweets trolley but indulge in cheese and biscuits.*

V+PRON+ADV,
V+ADV+N,
V+N+ADV

wave down

1 If you **wave down** a vehicle, you stand by the road or in the road and signal with your hands for the driver to stop. ❑ *At Napoleon's Hill, a policeman waved them down and told them to get off the main road.*

NOTE **Flag down** means almost the same as **wave down**.

V+PRON+ADV,
V+N+ADV,
V+ADV+N

2 If you **wave down** people's reactions to you, you signal to them that you do not want to be interrupted and that you wish to continue what you are saying. ❑ *The Prime Minister waved down the applause and seemed to forget all about the cameras as he leaned forward... He waved down my protest with a limp palm.*

V+ADV+N,
V+PRON+ADV

wave off

1 If you **wave** someone **off**, you wave to them as they leave somewhere. ❑ *They go to wave their boys off on the troop trains... At ten o'clock Mr Bhoolabhoy said goodnight, they waved him off and then told Ibrahim he could lock up.*

NOTE **See off** means almost the same as **wave off**.

V+N+ADV,
V+PRON+ADV,
V+ADV+N

2 If you **wave** someone or something **off**, you wave your arms as a signal that you do not want them to come any closer. ❑ *...a man waving off the flies.*

NOTE **Ward off** and **fend off** mean almost the same as **wave off**.

V+ADV+N,
V+PRON+ADV,
V+N+ADV

wave on If someone in authority **waves** traffic **on**, they signal with their hands for the traffic to continue going forwards. ❑ *A soldier asked the driver in front of us to open the boot of her car, but he waved us on... Policemen were everywhere, waving drivers on and sometimes flagging them down.*

V+PRON+ADV,
V+N+ADV,
V+ADV+N

wave through If someone in authority **waves** you **through**, they allow you to enter a place. ❑ *...a lone official waving vehicles through... They waved us through the*

V+N+ADV/PREP,
V+PRON+ADV/PREP

gate, and there was already no room there. ...arriving at an airport and being waved through immigration control by mistake.

wear /weə^r/ (wears, wearing, wore, worn)

wear away

1 If you **wear** something **away** or if it **wears away**, it becomes thin and eventually disappears because it is used a lot or rubbed a lot. ❑ Like fingernails, they are made of a dead horny material and gradually wear away. ...the smell and sound of the chalk wearing itself away to nothing... The grass was still worn away where the children used to play.

V+ADV,
V+N+ADV,
V+PRON+ADV,
V+ADV+N,
V+REFL+ADV:
ERGATIVE

NOTE **Wear down** means almost the same as **wear away**.

2 If something **wears away** emotions or characteristics, it gradually weakens them until they are no longer noticeable. ❑ Time and absence wear away pain and grief... Hard work and bad food appeared to have worn away her feminine characteristics.

V+ADV+N,
V+PRON+ADV

3 If a period of time **wears away**, it passes slowly. ❑ The shadows slowly lengthened again as the afternoon wore away and the sun moved down towards the far horizon.

V+ADV

NOTE **Wear on** means almost the same as **wear away**.

wear down

1 If you **wear** people **down**, you weaken them or their position by being more persistent than they are. ❑ It was one of the recognised nuisance-tactics designed to wear down the patience of the court... These night calls are wearing me down... He fought with a kind of hideous, heedless, mechanical energy, slowly wearing his man down... Let him wear himself down.

V+ADV+N,
V+PRON+ADV,
V+N+ADV,
V+REFL+ADV

2 If you **wear** something **down** or if it **wears down**, the top gradually disappears because its surface is constantly rubbed. ❑ As the teeth wear down, new ones start growing... All the green crayons were wearing down fast... No one could deny that large numbers of visitors had worn down the top of Helvellyn in the Lake District... The stairs were worn down like the doorstep.

V+ADV,
V+ADV+N,
V+N+ADV,
V+PRON+ADV:
ERGATIVE

★wear off

When a feeling **wears off**, it disappears slowly until it no longer exists or has any effect. ❑ By the next afternoon the shock had worn off... The effect of the aspirin had worn off and her toothache had come back... The pain soon wears off.

V+ADV

wear on

If time **wears on**, it seems to pass very slowly. ❑ So the day wore on and still they sat, drinking, smoking, talking... As the night wore on the absence of electricity made matters worse... As Monday wore on they discussed Helen's absence.

V+ADV

★wear out

1 When something **wears out** or when you **wear** it **out**, it is used so much that it becomes thin or weak and unable to be used any more. ❑ Sooner or later the soles of your favourite shoes are going to wear out... The wardrobe contained only clothes she had worn out or rejected... I just played the record it until it was worn out.

V+ADV,
V+N+ADV,
V+PRON+ADV,
V+ADV+N:
ERGATIVE

♦ Something that is **worn-out** has become so old, damaged, or thin that it cannot be used any more. ❑ ...a worn-out sofa.

ADJECTIVE

2 If something **wears** you **out**, it makes you become so tired that you cannot continue what you were doing. ❑ Visitors wear us out more than the children do... There is no point in wearing yourself out... That isn't show jumping. It's a marathon designed to wear the horse out.

V+PRON+ADV,
V+REFL+ADV,
V+N+ADV

NOTE **Exhaust** means almost the same as **wear out**.

♦ Someone who is **worn-out** is extremely tired. ❑ She certainly had looked worn out when he came home.

ADJECTIVE

3 If someone **wears out** their welcome with you, or if it **wears out**, they spend a lot of time with you and you are no longer happy about it. You can also say that a feeling **wears out** or is **worn out**. ❑ 'Could you not stay with us while you are solving your mystery?'—'Oh, we don't want to wear out our welcome.'... His stubborn resistance to anything new eventually wore out the patience of his superiors... No matter how often they turn up, their welcome never wears out.

V+N+ADV,
V+ADV+N,
V+PRON+ADV,
V+ADV:
ERGATIVE

wear through

If something such as a piece of clothing **wears through** or is **worn through**, it develops a hole where the material has become weak and thin. ❑ When holes began to wear through the soles of my shoes we went downtown to select a new pair... The carpeting through the hall and up the spiral staircase was almost worn through in spots.

V+ADV,
ALSO V+PREP:
HAS PASSIVE

The symbol ★ shows key phrasal verbs

weary /wɪəri/ (wearies, wearying, wearied)

weary of If you **weary of** something, you become very bored with it and lose
interest in it. [FORMAL] ❑ *He is beginning to weary of sitting still... I never weary of books
that I like... Life may be hated or wearied of, but never despised.*

NOTE **Tire of** means almost the same as **weary of**.

*V+PREP:
HAS PASSIVE*

weed /wiːd/ (weeds, weeding, weeded)

weed out If you **weed out** things that are useless or unwanted in a group, you
get rid of them. ❑ *Natural selection has weeded out the weakest... Teachers should report
on their own incompetent colleagues if they want to weed them out of the profession... I
sometimes think it's their way of weeding the rest of us out.*

*V+ADV+N,
V+PRON+ADV,
V+N+ADV*

weigh /weɪ/ (weighs, weighing, weighed)

weigh against

1 If you **weigh** one thing **against** another, you consider the relative importance
of each of them in order to decide what you should do. ❑ *However, you must weigh
the benefits against the potential hazards... Nevertheless, there will be real difficulties in
weighing local priorities against national ones... These factors have to be weighed against the
dangers and anxiety of pregnancy.*

*V+N+PREP,
V+PRON+PREP*

NOTE **Balance against** and **set against** mean almost the same as **weigh
against**.

2 If something **weighs against** a situation, it makes the situation seem more dangerous or difficult. ❑ *Political events weighed heavily against having children... But weighing against this comforting thought is the fact that he is travelling on a charter flight.*

V+PREP

weigh down

1 If you **are weighed down** by something heavy, you cannot move easily because it is so heavy. ❑ *...a leaking boat which was weighed down by five men... The pearls
weighing down her ears were hitting her savagely on the cheek... The sand in his shoes
weighed him down.*

*V+N+ADV,
V+ADV+N,
V+PRON+ADV:
USUALLY PASSIVE*

2 If you **are weighed down** by a difficulty or problem, it causes you to worry a
great deal. ❑ *So you're weighed down with problems... Maybe he was weighed down by the
burden of state secrets... The stress of maternal responsibility was beginning to weigh her
down.*

*V+N+ADV,
V+PRON+ADV:
USUALLY PASSIVE*

weigh in

1 If you **weigh in** on a discussion or a task, you begin to take part in it rather
forcefully. ❑ *The Queen Mother weighed in with some advice... When the time came to lay
the concrete, we all weighed in... The Treasury Secretary weighed in with an opinion.*

*V+ADV:
USUALLY+A*

NOTE **Come in** means almost the same as **weigh in**.

2 When the competitors at an event **weigh in**, they are weighed to check their
weight shortly before or after the event. ❑ *Weighing in at 200 pounds, he's a little overweight.*

*V+ADV:
ALSO+at*

♦ When there is a **weigh-in** at an event, each competitor is weighed to check their
weight shortly before or after the event. ❑ *Angry words were exchanged at the weigh-in
this morning.*

N-COUNT

weigh on If a problem **weighs on** or **weighs upon** you, it makes you worry.
Weigh upon is more formal. ❑ *I could still sleep at night, however serious the problems
weighing on me were... To keep silent about such a situation would weigh heavily upon our
consciences.*

V+PREP

weigh out If you **weigh** something **out**, you measure a certain weight of it in
order to make sure that you have the correct amount. ❑ *He weighed out a pound of tomatoes... Collect and weigh out all the ingredients to be used before starting.*

*V+ADV+N,
V+PRON+ADV,
V+N+ADV*

★weigh up

1 If you **weigh** things **up**, you consider their importance in relation to each other
in order to help you make a decision. ❑ *I weighed up the pros and cons... Having
weighed everything up, he must have decided it was the right thing to do... Next time
they thought of committing a crime they would weigh it up and think, 'Well it just isn't worth
it.'*

*V+ADV+N,
V+N+ADV,
V+PRON+ADV*

2 If you **weigh** someone **up**, you try and find out what they are like and form an

V+N+ADV,

opinion of them by talking to them, watching them, and listening to them. [BRITISH] ❑ *We argued like this for a while, weighing each other up.*

V+PRON+ADV,
V+ADV+N

NOTE **Size up** means almost the same as **weigh up**.

weigh upon → See weigh on

weight /weɪt/ **(weights, weighting, weighted)**

weight down If you **weight** something **down**, you add something heavy to it to prevent it moving easily. ❑ *Put the stuff in a bag and weight that down with old motor tyres. ...a plastic sheet weighted down with straw bales.*

V+N+ADV,
V+PRON+ADV,
V+ADV+N

well /wel/ **(wells, welling, welled)**

well up

1 If a quantity of liquid **wells up**, it comes to the surface in a sudden rush. ❑ *Tears welled up in his eyes and he brushed them aside. ...where water has welled up from the ocean beneath.*

V+ADV

2 If an emotion **wells up** inside you, it suddenly affects you quite strongly. ❑ *Happiness welled up inside me... All his fury against Zoe welled up in him.*

V+ADV:
USUALLY+A

NOTE **Rise up** means almost the same as **well up**.

wheel /ʰwiːl/ **(wheels, wheeling, wheeled)**

☑ In American English, **around** is much more common than **round**.

wheel around If you **wheel around** or **wheel round**, you turn round suddenly. ❑ *I wheeled around and shook off the hand she had placed on my shoulder... He wheeled round with delight.*

V+ADV

wheel round → See wheel around

while /ʰwaɪl/ **(whiles, whiling, whiled)**

while away If you **while away** the time in a particular way, you spend time in that way because you are waiting for something or because you have nothing else to do. ❑ *How about whiling away the time by telling me a story?... They served food to help the passengers while away the hours.*

V+ADV+N,
V+N+ADV:
NO PASSIVE

whip /ʰwɪp/ **(whips, whipping, whipped)**

whip out If you **whip** something **out**, you produce it from a place very quickly and suddenly. [INFORMAL] ❑ *He stopped long enough to whip out a pencil and write on the wall... Quickly, she whipped a knife out and cut herself free.*

V+ADV+N,
V+N+ADV,
V+PRON+ADV

whip up

1 If you **whip up** an emotion in people, you deliberately encourage them to feel that emotion. You can also say that you **whip** people **up** when you deliberately cause or encourage them to feel a particular emotion. ❑ *The television interview whipped up half the American people into a frenzy of rage... The reporters whipped up sympathy with stories of pensioners dying from the cold... The hatred is whipped up by the continual flow of rumors.*

V+ADV+N,
V+N+ADV,
V+PRON+ADV

NOTE **Stir up** means almost the same as **whip up**.

2 If the wind **whips up** dust or waves, it makes dust or waves rise up in a sudden swirling movement. ❑ *The wind whips up the sea forming waves which spread out across the bay... A gale can whip up waves measuring 20 to 25m from trough to crest... A cool breeze whipped up a swirl of dust.*

V+ADV+N,
V+N+ADV,
V+PRON+ADV

3 If you **whip up** a substance such as cream or egg, you stir it very fast until it becomes frothy, thick, or stiff. ❑ *I got him to grate the cheese whilst I whipped up eggs for three omelettes... To make an instant sauce from it, whip it up with a little sugar.*

V+ADV+N,
V+PRON+ADV,
V+N+ADV

4 If you **whip up** something that takes time to prepare, you make or do it quickly. [INFORMAL] ❑ *I could whip up a salad, if you like... You've got a day left, Audrey, you could whip up two thousand words.*

V+ADV+N,
V+PRON+ADV:
NO PASSIVE

5 If someone **whips up** a horse or other animal, they encourage it to move faster. ❑ *At this moment the man on the box whipped up his horses and the van moved out of the yard... He had to guide the plough and whip up the oxen.*

V+ADV+N,
V+PRON+ADV

whisk /ʰwɪsk/ **(whisks, whisking, whisked)**

whisk away If you **whisk** someone or something **away**, you remove them from a place very quickly. ❑ *'It'll get burnt!' said Louisa, whisking it away and putting it clear of the flames... The royal couple were whisked away from a brief welcome at the air-*

V+PRON+ADV,
V+N+ADV,
V+ADV+N

port... 'You mustn't let us keep you,' she said, whisking away my plate as soon as I'd finished.

whittle /ˈhwɪtəl/ (whittles, whittling, whittled)

whittle away To **whittle** something **away** means to gradually make it smaller or less effective over a period of time. ❑ *This may whittle away our liberties... Traditionalists would see the changes as whittling away the virtues of a well-established institution... Their 9-12 lead was gradually whittled away in the final quarter of the game.*

V+ADV+N,
V+N+ADV,
V+PRON+ADV

whittle away at To **whittle away at** something means to gradually make it smaller or less effective over a period of time. ❑ *This constant hunting whittles away at the numbers of fish... They whittle away at your self-respect until there is nothing left.*

V+ADV+PREP

whittle down To **whittle** something **down** means to gradually make it smaller or less effective over a period of time. ❑ *They were slyly whittling down the power of the Corleone Family... Profits are whittled down by the ever-rising cost of energy... Roskill began with 78 possible sites, whittled it down to 29, and finally to four.*

V+ADV+N,
V+N+ADV,
V+PRON+ADV

whoop /ˈhwuːp, AM huːp/ (whoops, whooping, whooped)

whoop up If you **whoop it up**, you have an enjoyable and exciting time, for example by going to parties or doing all the things you like doing. [INFORMAL] ❑ *...while he and Janet were whooping it up in France.*

V+it+ADV

NOTE **Live it up** means almost the same as **whoop it up**.

wig /wɪg/ (wigs, wigging, wigged)

wig out If someone **wigs out**, they behave in a crazy or very excited way. [BRITISH, INFORMAL] ❑ *He didn't wig out. He was visibly shaking but he didn't go crazy... Masses of people wigged out to the sound systems at a dozen groovy locations.*

V+ADV:
ALSO+to

NOTE **Freak out** means almost the same as **wig out**.

♦ A **wig-out** is an occasion when people behave in a crazy or very excited way. [BRITISH, INFORMAL] ❑ *Most of the audience seemed determined to use the slightest excuse to have a rare old wig-out.*

N-COUNT

♦ Someone who is **wigged-out** is behaving in a crazy way. [BRITISH, INFORMAL] ❑ *Toward the end of that time he got pretty depressed and wigged-out.*

ADJECTIVE

wimp /wɪmp/ (wimps, wimping, wimped)

wimp out If you **wimp out**, you decide not to do something because you are afraid. [INFORMAL] ❑ *They wimped out of doing anything that might be even slightly risky.*

V+ADV

NOTE **Chicken out** means almost the same as **wimp out**.

win /wɪn/ (wins, winning, won)

★win back If you **win back** something that you have lost, you get it back through your own efforts. ❑ *The party badly needs to find a way to win back straying voters... Management have won back decision-making power from the shop floor militants... How are you going to use the horse to win the automobile back?*

V+ADV+N,
V+N+ADV,
V+PRON+ADV

NOTE **Regain** is a more formal word for **win back**.

win out If something or someone **wins out**, they succeed or defeat others after a struggle. ❑ *They had fought a civil war and had won out over fantastic odds... In the battle between reformists and radicals, the reformists won out, because they had the weight of European support behind them.*

V+ADV:
ALSO+over

★win over If you **win** someone **over** or **win** them **round**, you persuade them to support you or agree with you. ❑ *Local radio stations have done their best to win over new audiences... Benn had succeeded in winning over those in authority to the workers' cause... I was completely won over by the courtesy and direct simplicity of the people... Gentle persuasion soon won him round.*

V+ADV+N,
V+N+ADV,
V+PRON+ADV:
ALSO+to

win round → See **win over**

win through If you **win through** a difficult situation or experience, you succeed in overcoming it. ❑ *I know that we will win through this terrible struggle one day... Two Birmingham companies have won through the first two rounds of the Reed National Management Game... Liverpool won through with a performance that was at times dazzling.*

V+PREP,
V+ADV

win through to If you **win through to** a particular position or stage of a competition, you achieve it after a great effort or by defeating opponents.

V+ADV+PREP

❏ *...Sabatini, who won through to the final after defeating the world number one.*

NOTE **Get through to** means almost the same as **win through to**.

wind /waɪnd/ (winds, winding, winded, wound)

wind back When you **wind back** the tape in a cassette player or the film in a camera, you make it move back towards its starting position. ❏ *Wind it back till the counter's at 157... It'll have to be wound back.*

NOTE **Rewind** is a more formal word for **wind back**.

V+PRON+ADV,
V+ADV+N,
V+N+ADV

★wind down

1 When you **wind down** the window of a car, you open it by moving it downwards, using a handle or control switch. ❏ *Philip stopped at a red light and wound down his window.*

NOTE **Wind up** means the opposite of **wind down**.

V+ADV+N,
V+N+ADV,
V+PRON+ADV

2 If a mechanical device such as a clock **winds down**, it gradually works more slowly and eventually stops completely.

NOTE **Run down** means almost the same as **wind down**.

V+ADV

3 When you **wind down** after doing something that has made you feel tired or tense, you gradually relax. [INFORMAL] ❏ *We went to the local pub to wind down.*

NOTE **Unwind** means almost the same as **wind down**.

V+ADV

4 If something such as a business or institution **winds down** or if someone **winds** it **down**, the amount of work that it does or the number of people employed is gradually reduced before it is closed down completely. ❏ *Unfortunately, we had to wind down the Liverpool office... The government is winding down the National Health Service. ...images of a nation winding down economically.*

NOTE **Wind up** means almost the same as **wind down**.

V+ADV+N,
V+N+ADV,
V+PRON+ADV,
V+ADV:
ERGATIVE

wind forward If you **wind forward** or **wind on** the tape in a cassette player or the film in a camera, you make it move forward to a new position. ❏ *Just wind it forward until you can see the number 'one' in the little window.*

V+PRON+ADV,
V+ADV+N,
V+N+ADV

wind on → See **wind forward**

★wind up

1 If you **wind up** a length of something, you wrap it round itself to reduce its length and form it into a ball or roll. ❏ *Lift the rod, lower it and wind up the line... Wind the string up into a ball... Her long, uncut hair was wound up into a bun.*

V+ADV+N,
V+N+ADV,
V+PRON+ADV

2 When you **wind up** a mechanical device such as a watch, you turn a knob, key, or handle on it round and round in order to make it operate. ❏ *Frank wound up the old gramophone... It was as though two machines, wound up and synchronized, had run down at exactly the same time.*

V+ADV+N,
V+N+ADV,
V+PRON+ADV

♦ A **wind-up** device or mechanism is one that is operated by clockwork. ❏ *...a wind-up racing car.*

ADJECTIVE

3 When you **wind up** the window of a car, you close it by making it move upwards, using a handle or a control switch. ❏ *Wind up that window, I'm getting a draught here.*

V+ADV+N,
V+N+ADV,
V+PRON+ADV

NOTE **Wind down** means the opposite of **wind up**.

4 When you **wind up** an activity, you finish it or stop doing it. ❏ *It was time to wind up the game... By the time we wound up the conversation, I knew that I would not be going... When my turn came to wind up the debate, I felt very nervous... The proceedings wind up at midnight, with a conga all round the hall.*

V+ADV+N,
V+N+ADV,
V+PRON+ADV,
V+ADV:
ERGATIVE

5 When someone **winds up** a business or other organization, they close it down completely. ❏ *The company was wound up in 1971... A Bill was introduced to wind up the Shipbuilding Industry Board.*

V+ADV+N,
V+PRON+ADV

♦ The **winding-up** of a business or other organization is its official closure. ❏ *...provisions only applicable in a winding-up. ...compulsory winding-up.*

N-SING

6 If you **wind up** in a particular place or situation, you are in it as the end result of a series of events or processes. ❏ *We wound up at the Szanghi restaurant... If I stay here long enough, I'll wind up marrying him... He usually wound up voting for Democrats... He knew it was going to wind up in a fight.*

V+ADV:
WITH A/-ING

NOTE **Finish up** and **end up** mean almost the same as **wind up**.

7 If you **wind** someone **up**, you deliberately say or do things to annoy them or get

V+N+ADV,

them excited. [BRITISH, INFORMAL] ❑ *He's always winding his teachers up... Gareth's remarks had wound him up to full pitch.*

8 If you **wind** someone **up**, you say untrue things in order to trick them. [BRITISH, INFORMAL] ❑ *You're joking. Come on, you're winding me up.*

♦ A **wind-up** is a trick that is played on someone to make them believe something that is not true. [BRITISH, INFORMAL] ❑ *Is this a wind-up, or what?*

winkle /wɪŋkəl/ (winkles, winkling, winkled)

winkle out

1 If you **winkle** information **out** of someone, you get it from them when they do not want to give it to you, often by tricking them. [BRITISH, INFORMAL] ❑ *The security services will pretty well go to any lengths to winkle out information... The detective was trying to winkle information out of her.*

NOTE **Worm out** means almost the same as **winkle out**.

2 If you **winkle** someone **out** of a place where they are hiding or which they do not want to leave, you make them leave it. [BRITISH, INFORMAL] ❑ *He somehow managed to winkle Picard out of his room... Political pressure finally winkled him out and on to a plane bound for Berlin... It will not be easy to winkle out the old guard and train younger replacements.*

NOTE **Flush out** means almost the same as **winkle out**.

winnow /wɪnoʊ/ (winnows, winnowing, winnowed)

winnow out

If you **winnow out** part of a group of things or people, you identify the part that is not useful or relevant and the part that is. ❑ *The committee will need to winnow out the nonsense and produce more practical proposals if it is to achieve results... Time has winnowed out certain of the essays as superior.*

wipe /waɪp/ (wipes, wiping, wiped)

wipe away

If you **wipe away** dirt or liquid from something, or if you **wipe** it **off**, you remove it using a cloth or your hand. ❑ *She wiped away their childish tears. ...wiping away the chalk marks... I need a handkerchief to wipe off the sand.*

wipe down

If you **wipe** something **down**, you rub it with a damp cloth to clean or dry its surface. ❑ *The walls will have to be wiped down... Make sure you wipe down all the work surfaces.*

wipe off

1 → See **wipe away**

2 If you **wipe off** a debt or money that is owed to you, you accept that the money will not be repaid. ❑ *Twelve million pounds was simply wiped off by the Government. ...wiping off the threatened deficit.*

NOTE **Write off** means almost the same as **wipe off**.

★wipe out

1 If you **wipe out** something that has contained liquid or food, you rub the inside of it with a cloth or piece of paper to clean it. ❑ *I carefully wipe out the wash basin with a tissue... Wipe out the frying pan with kitchen paper... Wipe the bucket out when you've finished.*

2 To **wipe** someone or something **out** means to destroy or get rid of them completely. ❑ *They planned one big assault to wipe out the remains of the ghetto... Epidemics wiped out the local population... Uncle Aaron was determined to wipe out the memory of his years in Auschwitz... You can wipe clover out of a pasture by applying artificial nitrogen.*

NOTE **Eradicate** is a more formal word for **wipe out**.

wipe up

If you **wipe up** dirt or liquid from something, you remove it using a cloth. ❑ *He begins to wipe up the mess. ...throwing mud then wiping it up.*

wire /waɪər/ (wires, wiring, wired)

wire up

If you **wire** something **up**, you connect it to something else with electrical wires so that electricity or electrical signals can pass between them. ❑ *...electrical fittings wired up to the mains... Make sure the plug is wired up properly.*

wise /waɪz/ (wises, wising, wised)

wise up

If someone **wises up** to a situation or state of affairs, or if they **are wised up** to it, they realize or become aware of it. [INFORMAL] ❑ *Christopher wised up*

V+PRON+ADV

V+N+ADV,
V+PRON+ADV

N-COUNT

V+ADV+N,
V+N+ADV,
V+PRON+ADV:
ALSO+of

V+ADV+N,
V+N+ADV,
V+PRON+ADV:
ALSO+of

V+ADV+N,
V+N+ADV,
V+PRON+ADV

V+ADV+N,
V+N+ADV,
V+PRON+ADV

V+N+ADV,
V+ADV+N,
V+PRON+ADV

V+N+ADV,
V+ADV+N,
V+PRON+ADV

V+ADV+N,
V+N+ADV,
V+PRON+ADV

V+ADV+N,
V+N+ADV,
V+PRON+ADV

V+ADV+N,
V+PRON+ADV,
V+N+ADV

V+ADV+N,
V+N+ADV,
V+PRON+ADV:
ALSO+to

V+ADV:
USUALLY+to,
ALSO IMPERATIVE

to the fact that the whole district was being bought up by property developers... Of course they will wise up and get out sooner or later... Wise up, Barrett!

wish /wɪʃ/ (wishes, wishing, wished)

wish away If you **wish** something **away**, you hope to get rid of it although you do not do anything practical to remove it. ❑ *It seems unlikely that the statistical errors can be wished away... Wishing them away won't get rid of your problems.*

V+ADV+N,
V+PRON+ADV,
V+N+ADV

wish on If you **wish** something **on** someone else, or **wish** it **upon** them, you hope very much that it will happen to them or that they will be influenced by it. **Wish upon** is slightly more formal. ❑ *The one thing I would not wish on my worst enemy is eternal life. ...a very convenient tradition which has been wished upon the nurses.*

V+N+PREP,
V+PRON+PREP

wish upon → See wish on

wither /wɪðər/ (withers, withering, withered)

wither away If something **withers away**, it gradually becomes weaker until eventually it no longer exists. ❑ *Links with the outside community withered away... His eagerness to fight back could not be permitted to wither away.*

V+ADV

wolf /wʊlf/ (wolfs, wolfing, wolfed)

wolf down If you **wolf** food **down**, you eat it all very quickly and greedily. ❑ *I wolfed down an enormous meal... He wolfed the food down, bones and all.*

V+ADV+N,
V+N+ADV,
V+PRON+ADV

NOTE **Gobble down** means almost the same as **wolf down**.

wonder /wʌndər/ (wonders, wondering, wondered)

wonder at If you **wonder at** something, you are surprised or puzzled by it. ❑ *One can only wonder at children's reserves of strength when this kind of thing happens... This prosperity is more wondered at than envied.*

V+PREP:
HAS PASSIVE

NOTE **Marvel at** means almost the same as **wonder at**.

work /wɜːrk/ (works, working, worked)

★**work at** → See work on

work away If you **work away**, you continue working hard for a long time. ❑ *...scientists working away at perfecting the weapons... I was able to keep warm as I worked away in the snow.*

V+ADV:
ALSO+at

work in

1 When you are preparing a mixture or a surface, if you **work** a substance **in**, you rub or mix it gradually and carefully into the mixture or surface. ❑ *We worked the fat in with our fingers... Sprinkle dry salt on the butter and work it in thoroughly.*

V+N+ADV,
V+PRON+ADV,
V+ADV+N

2 If you are doing or saying something and you **work** something else **in**, you manage to include it. ❑ *During his speech, he managed to work in several sly remarks about the Prime Minister... I'll try and work it in some time during the day.*

V+ADV+N,
V+PRON+ADV,
V+N+ADV

NOTE **Squeeze in** means almost the same as **work in**.

3 A **work-in** is a form of industrial action in which workers occupy buildings and take over the running of a factory or business to protest about plans to close it.

N-COUNT

work into If you **work** a substance **into** a mixture or surface, you rub it in or mix it in gradually and carefully. ❑ *To get the necessary lightness it should be worked into the soil with sand or ashes.*

V+N+PREP,
V+PRON+PREP

work off

☑ In meaning 3, the stress is on **work**.

1 If you **work** something **off**, you gradually overcome the effects of it by doing something energetic or something different. ❑ *We should all be able to work off our stress physically... He worked off his embarrassment by harassing us with questions... He had given us as much food as we could eat, and wouldn't hear of letting us work off our meal... If parents feel irritated at their children, they may try to work it off as teasing.*

V+ADV+N,
V+PRON+ADV,
V+N+ADV

2 If someone **works off** a debt, they repay it by working without pay for the person who lent them the money. ❑ *They had to sell their possessions or work off the amount as the lender's slave... He agreed to go without pay until he had worked off the family debt.*

V+ADV+N,
V+PRON+ADV

3 If a piece of equipment **works off** a particular source of power, this is the source of power that it uses to make it function. ❑ *There is a special wire cutter which works off a battery... You can buy quite cheap and simple welding sets that work off the mains.*

V+PREP

★work on

1 If you **work on** something or **work at** it, you spend time and effort trying to improve it. ❑ *He has been working all season on his game... She works hard at keeping herself fit.*

V+PREP:
HAS PASSIVE

2 If you **work on** an assumption or idea, you rely on it being true or correct when you develop your own ideas or plans. ❑ *British officials are working on the assumption that the captives are alive... Evolution theory works on the idea that the fittest survive and produce fit offspring.*

V+PREP

3 If you **work on** someone, you spend time trying to influence them or persuade them to do something. ❑ *The good priest worked on me with the finest tenderness and understanding... I think he could be worked on.*

V+PREP:
HAS PASSIVE

★work out

1 If you **work out** the answer to a mathematical problem, you calculate it. ❑ *I've worked it out, it's 3,171.875 tons... The weekly rate is worked out by dividing by 52... Calculate how much you owe each person, then work out how much you can afford to pay each of them... He worked the sum out twenty times on the adding machine.*

V+ADV+N,
V+N+ADV,
V+PRON+ADV

2 If something **works out** at a particular amount, it is found to be that amount after all the calculations have been made. ❑ *It worked out about a hundred pounds in the end... At the moment her fuel bills work out at £20 a week.*

V+ADV:
WITH A

3 If you **work out** a solution or a plan, you think about it carefully and find a solution or decide what to do. ❑ *We are always hopeful that a more peaceful solution can be worked out... We could begin to work out the best ways to help these youngsters... I stopped and sat down to work out where I would go next.*

V+ADV+N,
V+N+ADV,
V+PRON+ADV

4 If you manage to **work out** something that seems strange, you think about it and manage to understand it. ❑ *He couldn't at first work out why the room was at once so strange and so familiar... I'm trying to work out what's wrong... I'm not sure what's missing. We'll work it out when we see yours.*

V+ADV+N,
V+N+ADV,
V+PRON+ADV

NOTE **Figure out** means almost the same as **work out**.

5 If you say that you cannot **work** someone **out**, you mean that you cannot understand them. [INFORMAL] ❑ *I just can't work you out, you never seem to enjoy anything.*

V+N+ADV,
V+PRON+ADV:
USUALLY NEGATIVE

NOTE **Suss out** is a more informal expression for **work out**.

6 If a situation **works out** in a particular way, it happens or progresses in that way. ❑ *I asked him how he was, and how his job was working out... It's funny how life worked out.*

V+ADV:
WITH A

NOTE **Turn out** means almost the same as **work out**.

7 If a situation, arrangement, or plan **works out**, it is successful. ❑ *...so it really didn't have any chance to work out at all... He's moody because things aren't working out at home.*

V+ADV

8 If you **work out**, you do physical exercises in order to make your body fit and strong. ❑ *She worked out in a ballet class three hours a week.*

V+ADV

♦ A **workout** is a period of physical exercise or training. ❑ *He felt relaxed because of the light workout he had just done... They go to the gym for a workout every Wednesday evening.*

N-COUNT

9 If a process **works** itself **out**, it reaches a conclusion or satisfactory end. ❑ *Popular theories depend on the great historical purpose working itself out... What she was engaged in was the dream, which worked itself out in her.*

V+REFL+ADV

NOTE **Resolve** means almost the same as **work out**.

10 If you **work out** your service or your notice, you continue to work at your job until you have completed a specified period of time. ❑ *...including 30,000 conscripts still working out their reserve service... She was given a month's pay and asked to leave immediately, rather than working out her notice.*

V+ADV+N,
V+N+ADV,
V+PRON+ADV

11 If a mine **is worked out**, all the coal or metal has been removed from it. ❑ *As more and more seams were worked out, the danger of pit closures increased.*

PASSIVE:
V+ADV

NOTE **Be exhausted** means almost the same as **be worked out**.

work over If someone **works** you **over**, they attack you, either physically or by shouting at you and criticizing you. [INFORMAL] ❑ *Morris and Richards worked Robinson over to get the truth out of him... I kept on reading as she worked me over.*

V+N+ADV,
V+PRON+ADV,
V+ADV+N

For a full explanation of all grammatical labels, see pages xiii-xx

work through If you **work through** a problem or difficulty, you deal with it carefully and thoroughly until you find a satisfactory solution. ❑ *They work through a series of issues and problems with key employees... While Diana disentangles that question I was able to work through the next... The teacher sets the experiment or project and the students work it through.* · V+ADV+N, V+PRON+ADV

work towards If you **work towards** something, you try very hard to achieve it or make it happen. ❑ *My mother was working towards her master's degree in education... It called for the trade union movement to work towards greater industrial democracy.* · V+PREP: HAS PASSIVE

★**work up**

1 If you **work** yourself **up**, you gradually make yourself very upset or angry about something. ❑ *I don't want you to resign. Now tell me why you are so worked up over that editorial... Of course it's yours, my dear. There's no need to get so worked up about it.* · V+REFL+ADV: USUALLY+A

2 If someone **works up** something such as a feeling, the energy to do something, or an appetite, they gradually develop it and increase it until they have what they need. ❑ *It had taken months to work up the courage to participate... She went for a run to work up an appetite... I can hardly work up enough energy.* · V+ADV+N

3 If you **work** yourself **up** to do something, you get ready to do it because you are enthusiastic or excited about it. ❑ *A group of girls excitedly work themselves up to going on some wild diet.* · V+REFL+ADV: WITH to/to-INF

4 When you are doing something regularly, if you **work up** to a particular amount or level, you gradually increase or improve what you are doing until you reach that amount or level. ❑ *She recommends starting with a teaspoonful or less and working up gradually to 2 or 3 tablespoonfuls... Repeat movements l, 2 and 3 four times at first and gradually work up to about six repetitions.* · V+ADV: USUALLY+to

NOTE **Build up** means almost the same as **work up**.

5 If you **work up** something, you spend time and effort on it to make it complete or successful. ❑ *One day I may work this idea up into a story. ...as though he were working up a character in a book... He would be able to work up a sound business.* · V+N+ADV, V+ADV+N, V+PRON+ADV

worm /wɜːrm/ (worms, worming, wormed)

worm out If you **worm** information **out** of someone, you gradually find it out from them by constantly asking them about it. ❑ *He might worm the story out of her by emotional pressure... The truth had been wormed out of him by his lawyers.* · V+N+ADV, V+PRON+ADV: USUALLY+of

worry /wʌri, AM wɜːri/ (worries, worrying, worried)

worry at

1 If you **worry at** a problem, you think about it continually and anxiously in order to find a way of solving it. ❑ *God knows the truth of the matter, there is little point in worrying at it.... But I can't just let it happen. I worry at it: I keep digging it up to find an answer.* · V+PREP

2 When a dog or other animal **worries at** something, it holds it in its teeth, continually shaking it and moving it about. ❑ *Bunching the towel up beneath her she would worry at it until she found a suitable part to suck.* · V+PREP

wrap /ræp/ (wraps, wrapping, wrapped)

★**wrap up**

1 When you **wrap** something **up**, you fold a piece of paper, cloth, or other material round it so that it is completely covered. ❑ *He had bought a teapot and was waiting for them to wrap it up... He had wrapped up a parcel of his manuscripts and a few books... My hair is wrapped up in a towel because I've just washed it.* · V+PRON+ADV, V+ADV+N, V+N+ADV

NOTE **Do up** means almost the same as **wrap up**.

2 If you **wrap up** or **wrap** yourself **up**, you put warm clothes on. ❑ *Wrap up well. It's cold outside... Wrap up warm and relax by going to bed or resting in your chair... I read somewhere that if you wrap up well in summer it insulates you against the heat... The children came to school wrapped up in coats and scarves.* · V+ADV, V+REFL+ADV: ALSO PASSIVE: V+ADV: USUALLY+A

3 If you **wrap up** something such as a job, agreement, or activity, you complete or end it in a satisfactory way. ❑ *The whole deal was wrapped up within a few days... That about wraps it up for this week... He was wrapping up a five-week tour abroad with a three-day stopover in Paris.* · V+N+ADV, V+PRON+ADV, V+ADV+N

NOTE **Wind up** means almost the same as **wrap up**.

The symbol ★ shows key phrasal verbs

4 If you tell someone to **wrap up**, you are telling them in a rude way to stop talking. [BRITISH, INFORMAL]

IMPERATIVE,
V+ADV

wrap up in If someone **is wrapped up in** a particular person or thing, they spend nearly all their time thinking about that person or thing and so have little time for anything else. ❑ *They are completely wrapped up in the baby... He will be wrapped up in his work, leaving little time for you. ...adolescents who are wrapped up in themselves.*

PASSIVE:
V+ADV+PREP

wrestle /resəl/ (wrestles, wrestling, wrestled)
wrestle with

1 If you **wrestle with** a problem or a difficult situation, you try to deal with it or find a solution to it. ❑ *For decades, mathematicians have wrestled with this problem... Viktor was wrestling with the intricacies of international telephone calls.*

V+PREP:
HAS PASSIVE

2 If someone **is wrestling with** something large or heavy, they are having difficulty holding it or controlling it. ❑ *She wondered if she should go and help the man wrestling with the map.*

V+PREP

wriggle /rɪɡəl/ (wriggles, wriggling, wriggled)
wriggle out of

If you **wriggle out of** doing something that you are expected to do but that you do not want to do, you manage to avoid doing it. ❑ *I can't manage to wriggle out of accompanying my parents to Europe... They use classy lawyers and accountants to wriggle out of paying taxes.*

V+ADV+PREP:
USUALLY+-ING

NOTE **Get out of** means almost the same as **wriggle out of**.

wring /rɪŋ/ (wrings, wringing, wrung)
wring out

1 If you **wring out** a wet cloth or a wet piece of clothing, you squeeze the water out of it by twisting it strongly. ❑ *Don't wring it out, pat it dry with a towel.*

V+PRON+ADV,
V+ADV+N,
V+N+ADV

2 If you **wring** something **out** of someone, you force them to give it to you, although they do not want to. ❑ *I spend a great deal of my time trying to wring the costs for this litigation out of the Legal Aid fund... His captors were obviously trying to wring out information from him.*

V+ADV+N,
V+N+ADV,
V+PRON+ADV:
USUALLY+of

write /raɪt/ (writes, writing, wrote, written)
write away

If you **write away** or **write off** to a company or organization, you send them a letter, asking them to send you a product or some information. ❑ *You just write away giving your name, address and enclosing three tokens... Why don't you write off to Sussex University and ask for their prospectus?*

V+ADV:
USUALLY+A

NOTE **Send off** and **send away** mean almost the same as **write away**.

★write back
If you **write back** to someone, you reply to a letter that they sent you. ❑ *I wrote, explaining our difficulty and asking for suggestions. Samarkand wrote back at once... First of all Christopher wrote to my father, and my father wrote back saying you must be joking... You could write a letter back saying that you don't want to go.*

V+ADV,
V+N+ADV

★write down
When you **write** something **down**, you record it on a piece of paper using a pen or pencil. ❑ *The magistrate had to write all the evidence down... Write down any four digit number... They ask me the date and the flight number: I always write it down so I'll remember.*

V+N+ADV,
V+ADV+N,
V+PRON+ADV

NOTE **Put down** means almost the same as **write down**.

★write in

1 If you **write in** to an organization, you send them a letter. ❑ *We are offering a half-price holiday to the first person to write in with the correct explanation... The majority of those who had already written in to give their views had backed the idea.*

V+ADV:
USUALLY+A

2 If you **write in** a piece of information on a form or document, you add the information by writing it in the appropriate place. ❑ *I'll give you my diploma and write in your name so you can pretend you got through... He arranged the meeting for Tuesday and wrote it in on the kitchen calendar in red pencil.*

V+ADV+N,
V+PRON+ADV,
V+N+ADV:
USUALLY+A

3 If a part **is written in** to a play, or if a clause **is written in** to a contract, the part or clause is added after the play or document has been created. ❑ *The Prince had assumed that a special part was being written in for him... The new contract has the same clause written in.*

PASSIVE:
V+ADV:
USUALLY+A

4 In the United States, if someone who is voting in an election **writes in** a person

V+ADV+N,

whose name is not on the list of candidates, they write that person's name on the voting paper and vote for him or her. [AMERICAN] ❑ *I think I'll write in Pat Wilson... I'm going to write him in on my ballot next year.*

V+N+ADV, V+PRON+ADV

write into If a particular rule or detail **is written into** a contract or agreement, it is included in it. ❑ *The new arrangements have been written into the agreement.*

PASSIVE: V+PREP

★write off

☐1☐ → See write away

☐2☐ If you **write** someone or something **off**, you decide that they are unimportant, useless or unlikely to be successful and that they are not worth further consideration. ❑ *Do not sound harassed, or you will be written off as a hysterical woman... 'Whatever you do,' she pleaded, 'don't write off philosophy without even trying it'. ...injuries that threatened to write him off in his late twenties.*

V+N+ADV, V+ADV+N, V+PRON+ADV: ALSO+as

NOTE **Dismiss** is a more formal word for **write off**.

☐3☐ If someone **writes off** a vehicle, they have a crash in it and it is so badly damaged that it is not worth repairing. [BRITISH] ❑ *She had crashed the car twice, writing it off completely on the second occasion... Should an insured car be written off in an accident, the insurers will usually pay the current value of the vehicle.*

V+PRON+ADV, V+ADV+N, V+N+ADV

♦ If a vehicle is a **write-off** after an accident, it is so badly damaged that it is not worth spending money on it to repair it. [BRITISH] ❑ *The Boylans' car was a write-off so they decided to abandon the trip.*

N-COUNT

☐4☐ If someone **writes off** a debt or an amount of money that has been spent on a project, they accept that they are never going to get the money back. ❑ *Should we not write off many of the debts that are crippling Third World countries?... Normal accounting practice is to write off the loss immediately in the year in which it is incurred... 'Last year I wrote off six thousand dollars' worth of bad debts,' he said.*

V+ADV+N, V+PRON+ADV, V+N+ADV

♦ A **write-off** is an official declaration that a debt is not going to be repaid. ❑ *The only state assistance was a write-off of 64 million pounds.*

N-COUNT

☐5☐ If you **write off** a plan or project, you accept that it is not going to be successful and do not continue with it. ❑ *We decided to write off the rest of the day and go shopping... The prices were much higher. So we decided to write that off... It's too soon to write off the whole consultation process as a failure... They've stopped the project and will write this off as part of the growing pains of a new organization.*

V+ADV+N, V+N+ADV, V+PRON+ADV: ALSO+as

★write out

☐1☐ When you **write out** something such as a report, a list, or a word, you write it on paper. ❑ *When you have done your reports type them or write them out very clearly... I wondered whether he wrote his material out first or just composed it in his head... The editor wrote me out a list of places I must visit... His name was Mayhew, it was written out in enormous red letters.*

V+PRON+ADV, V+ADV+N, V+PRON+ADV+N, V+ADV+N

☐2☐ When someone **writes out** something such as a cheque, receipt, or prescription, they write all the necessary information on it. ❑ *I went directly to my cabin to write out the death certificate... If you are at your own branch you simply write out a cheque and give it to the cashier... I could write you a cheque out now, or give you the cash tomorrow morning.*

V+ADV+N, V+PRON+ADV+N, V+PRON+ADV, V+N+ADV

NOTE In American English, **write up** means almost the same as **write out**.

☐3☐ If a character in a drama series on television or radio **is written out**, the story is changed so that the character leaves or dies and is no longer part of the series. ❑ *Shannon kept searching for fame, but was quickly written out of the script... She is written out of the narrative early.*

PASSIVE: V+ADV

★write up

☐1☐ When you **write up** something that has been done or said, you record it on paper in a neat and complete form, usually using notes that you have made. ❑ *He usually spent solitary evenings writing up his work... Anything I was told, I had to write up in my reports... I'm going to enjoy writing it up for the journals.*

V+ADV+N, V+N+ADV, V+PRON+ADV

♦ A **write-up** is an article in a newspaper or magazine, in which someone describes and gives their opinion of something such as a play, a new product, or a place they have visited. ❑ *Somebody told me you got a terrific write-up in the 'Guardian'.*

N-COUNT

☐2☐ If you **write** something **up** somewhere, you write it on a wall, board or notice.

V+N+ADV, V+PRON+ADV,

❑ *...the desire which so many people obviously have to write their names up everywhere... Yes, write it up on the board... His name was written up everywhere I looked.*

V+ADV+N:
USUALLY+A

3 When someone **writes up** something such as a cheque, receipt, or prescription, they write all the necessary information on it. [AMERICAN] ❑ *I don't want you to have to write up a slip just for eighty cents... She wrote up the ticket, tore out the coupon, and stuck it in the book... Write me up a cheque if you don't have the right change.*

V+ADV+N,
V+PRON+ADV+N,
V+PRON+ADV,
V+N+ADV

NOTE **Write out** means almost the same as **write up**.

Xx Yy Zz

x /eks/ (x's, x'ing, x'd)

x out If you **x out** someone or something, you stop thinking about them. [INFORMAL] ❏ *When I thought of Morgan, I simply x'd her out.*
NOTE **Blot out** means almost the same as **x out**.

V+PRON+ADV,
V+N+ADV,
V+ADV+N

yearn /jɜːʳn/ (yearns, yearning, yearned)

yearn for If you **yearn for** something, you have a strong desire for it. [FORMAL] ❏ *Most people yearn for some truth in a relationship... He yearned for academic recognition.*
NOTE **Long for** means almost the same as **yearn for**.

V+PREP

yell /jel/ (yells, yelling, yelled)

yell out If you **yell out** or if you **yell** something **out**, you shout loudly, for example because you are excited, angry, or in pain. ❏ *The nurse hastened to her aid when she yelled out and collapsed... I yelled out, 'Come down!'... He yelled out to his leader that the job was impossible... The older boys yelled out insults. ...a voice in the office yelling my name out.*
NOTE **Shout out** means almost the same as **yell out**.

V+ADV,
V+ADV+QUOTE,
V+ADV+REPORT,
V+ADV+N,
V+N+ADV,
V+PRON+ADV

yield /jiːld/ (yields, yielding, yielded)

yield to

1 If you **yield to** someone or something, you stop resisting them. [FORMAL] ❏ *The Chancellor yielded to the critics and halved the March Budget... She was yielding to public pressure... He was progressively yielding to American demands.*

V+PREP

2 If one thing **yields to** another thing, it is replaced by this other thing. [FORMAL] ❏ *The wilderness of ugly warehouses is to yield to complete redevelopment... Radio has long been under pressure to yield to television... The swamp would yield to drier land.*

V+PREP

yield up If you **yield up** a secret, you reveal it. [FORMAL] ❏ *...methods of making the brain yield up its secrets... He must be allowed to save face by yielding them up voluntarily.*
NOTE **Disclose** means almost the same as **yield up**.

V+ADV+N,
V+PRON+ADV,
V+N+ADV

zero /zɪəroʊ/ (zeros/zeroes, zeroing, zeroed)

zero in on

1 To **zero in on** a target means to aim at it very accurately or move towards it. ❏ *The missile then zeros in on the target. ...guns so powerful they could zero in on Omaha Beach.*

V+ADV+PREP

2 If you **zero in on** a problem or subject, you concentrate all your attention on it. ❏ *I want to talk generally before I zero in on any one speciality... By zeroing in on a particular lifestyle, we exclude a vast number of alternatives.*

V+ADV+PREP

zip /zɪp/ (zips, zipping, zipped)

★zip up

1 When you **zip up** something such as a piece of clothing, you fasten it using a zip. ❏ *She zipped up the dress with difficulty... He zipped his jeans up... I had to struggle out of the dress and half zip it up and then struggle back into it.*
NOTE **Do up** means almost the same as **zip up**.

V+ADV+N,
V+N+ADV,
V+PRON+ADV

♦ A **zip-up** piece of clothing is one which fastens with a zip. ❏ *...zip-up boiler-suits.*

ADJECTIVE

2 If you **zip** someone **up**, you fasten the zip on their clothes for them. ❏ *Zip me up at the back, please.*

V+PRON+ADV,
V+N+ADV

The symbol ★ shows key phrasal verbs

zoom /zuːm/ (zooms, zooming, zoomed)

zoom in If a photographer or camera **zooms in** on the person or thing being photographed, they make the image larger by changing the focus. ❑ *I should have zoomed in closer on the driver's face.*

V+ADV: ALSO+*on*

zoom off If you **zoom off** somewhere, you go there in a hurry. [INFORMAL] ❑ *In the summer, we all zoom off to Felixstowe on our bikes... He zoomed off to the USA.*

V+ADV: USUALLY+A

zoom out If a photographer or camera **zooms out**, they draw back from what is being photographed and show the things that surround it. ❑ *Zoom out now, and get the overall effect.*

V+ADV

Particles Index

The Particles Index is an extensive guide to the way in which particles are used in English phrasal verbs. It acts as an index to the dictionary, listing phrasal verb headwords alphabetically within given categories of meaning. It also gives the actual number of occurrences of each particle, which will be of interest to teachers, who may use this information to determine which phrasal verbs to focus on. There is an entry for each of the forty-eight particles which are found in the phrasal verb headwords. Some of the headwords contain more than one particle. In most cases, the first particle is an adverb and the second one a preposition. The index deals with two-particle combinations under the first of the particles.

Some particles occur in a large number of different phrasal verbs. Eighteen of them occur in fifty or more combinations. The commonest particles are **up**, **out**, **off**, **in**, **on**, and **down**, in descending order of frequency. **Up** and **out**, in particular, are extremely common: 28% of the phrasal verbs listed here include either **up** or **out**. In contrast, some of the particles such as **aback** and **across** occur in very few phrasal verbs: fifteen of them occur in fewer than ten combinations. The index lists groups of phrasal verbs which share particular meanings, and thus the patterns of meaning of the particles themselves can be seen. Some of these meanings are 'literal': that is, they are the main meanings of the particle in question. These literal meanings are usually to do with physical position or direction of movement. We do not give lists of combinations which have these purely literal meanings.

The lists contain all the central and typical examples of phrasal verbs which include a particular particle. Sometimes a phrasal verb fits into more than one category of particle meaning, as the meanings may overlap, or one may be a metaphorical extension of another, and sometimes it is difficult to say exactly what meaning is contributed by the particle to the phrasal verb. Only the clearest-cut cases therefore appear in the lists. In addition, many phrasal verbs have more than one sense. Often the particle has the same meaning in all these senses, but sometimes it has different meanings. In these cases, we include the phrasal verb in more than one list, but we add a sense number where this avoids confusion. The meanings of English phrasal verbs are not always obvious. Yet the Particles Index shows very clearly how phrasal verbs are not just arbitrary combinations of verbs and particles. Instead, they fit into the broad patterns of choice and selection in English. When a new combination occurs, it too fits into these patterns. The Particles Index will help you to deal with these new combinations, and phrasal verbs as a whole will become a more manageable part of the vocabulary of English.

aback is an adverb. In modern English, it only occurs in the phrasal verb **take aback**.

about is an adverb and a preposition. It occurs in 95 phrasal verbs in this dictionary.

1 Movement
About is used in literal combinations to indicate movement in many different directions over a period of time, often without any specific aim or purpose. For example, if you **drift about**, you travel to a lot of different places; if someone **lays about** with a weapon, they move it randomly in many directions; and if you **hurl** things **about**, you throw them violently in several directions. Some combinations have the meaning of looking in many different places. These phrasal verbs are often followed by the preposition *for*. For example, if you **cast about** for something, you search for it in many places. **About** is used in a similar way in combinations which have the meaning of distributing or spreading something to many different places or people. For example, if you **scatter** things **about**, you distribute them over a wide area. If news **gets about**, it reaches many people. When **about** is used as a preposition, it has the additional meaning of 'within a particular place': you mention the place in the noun group after **about**. For example, if you **crash about** the kitchen, you move in many different directions in the kitchen, making a lot of noise. **Around** and **round** have similar meanings: see **around** 1 and **round** 1. **About** is used mainly in British English, and in American English, **around** is much more common than **round**.

2 Inactivity and aimlessness
About is also used to indicate lack of activity, lack of purpose, or lack of achievement over a period of time. For example, if you **lounge about**, you spend your time being lazy and doing nothing. When **about** is used as a preposition, it has the additional meaning of 'in a particular place': you mention the place in the noun group after **about**. For example, if you **mope about** the house, you spend time in the house rather aimlessly and feeling unhappy. **About** also occurs in a few combinations indicating that something is present in a place, although you are not sure where. For example, if something **is kicking about** in a place, it is somewhere in that place, but you do not know exactly where. These phrasal verbs are usually used in continuous tenses. **About** is also used as an adverb in some informal or rude combinations to indicate wasting time or behaving foolishly. For example, if you **lark about**, you behave in a foolish or silly way. **Around** and **round** have similar meanings: see **around** 2 and **round** 7. **About** is used mainly in British English, and in American English, **around** is much more common than **round**.

faff about	fiddle about	fool about	hang about	kick about
lark about	laze about	lie about	loaf about	loll about
lounge about	mess about	mope about	muck about	play about
sit about	slop about	stand about	tinker about	wait about

3 Encirclement
You use **about** as a preposition in combinations which have the literal meaning of putting one thing round another so that it forms a circle round it. You mention the second thing in the noun group after **about**. For example, if you **throw** your arms **about** someone, you throw them round the person. **Around** and **round** have similar meanings, and are less formal: see **around** 4 and **round** 4. **About** is used mainly in British English, and in American English, **around** is much more common than **round**.

4 Turning
You use **about** as an adverb in literal combinations such as **face about** and **turn about** in order to say that someone or something turns until they are facing in the opposite direction. This is a formal use. **Around** and **round** have similar meanings, and are less formal: see **around** 3 and **round** 2. **About** is used mainly in British English, and in American English, **around** is much more common than **round**.

5 **Action**
About is used as an adverb in a few combinations which have the idea of an event happening or someone doing something. For example, to **bring** something **about** means to make it happen.

bring about	come about	go about	set about

6 **Introduction of subject**
About is used as a preposition in many combinations with the literal meaning 'concerning a particular subject'. You mention the subject in the noun group after **about**. For example, to **know about** a subject means to know things concerning that subject, and if you **hear about** something, you get information concerning it.

above is both a preposition and an adverb, although it is used mainly as a preposition in phrasal verbs. It occurs in 5 phrasal verbs in this dictionary. Its literal meaning is to do with position, to say that one thing is at a higher level than another. **Tower above** has the added sense of making other people or things seem smaller than they are, and **rise above** has the meaning of overcoming difficulties. The other three combinations refer to the extended meaning of **above**, implying greater importance or higher rank. For example, if you **put** one thing **above** another, you consider that the first thing is more important than the second.

get above	marry above	put above	rise above	tower above

across is both a preposition and an adverb. It occurs in 6 phrasal verbs in this dictionary. Its basic meaning is to do with movement from one side of an area to the other, and it occurs with this meaning in a few literal combinations with very common verbs, such as **come across 1** and **run across 1**.

1 **Finding**
Across is used in a few combinations which have 'find' as part of their meaning. For example if you **stumble across** something, you find it unexpectedly.

come across 2	run across 2	stumble across

2 **Communicating**
Across is also used in a few combinations which refer to communication and understanding. For example, if an idea **gets across**, people understand it. **Over** has a similar meaning: see **over** 11.

come across 4	get across	put across 1

after is a preposition. It occurs in 15 phrasal verbs in this dictionary. The basic meaning of **after** is to do with the sequence of events in time, indicating that one event happens later than another. Some of the meanings of **after** occur in only one combination. For example, the meaning of **after** in **look after** is different from any of its other meanings. There are three main meanings for **after** which occur in several combinations.

1 **Following and hunting**
After occurs with intransitive verbs in combinations which have 'follow', 'chase', or 'hunt' as part of their meaning. You mention the person or animal being chased in the noun group following **after**.

chase after	come after	get after
go after 1	make after	run after 1

2 Wanting

After also occurs with intransitive verbs in combinations which express ideas of wanting to obtain something or trying hard to obtain it. This may be regarded as a metaphorical use of the previous category. You mention the thing that you want in the noun group following **after**. Some of these verbs can be used in combination with **for** instead of **after**.

ask after	go after 2	hanker after	hunger after	inquire after
lust after	run after 2			

3 Similarity and imitation

Some combinations with **after** express the idea that one thing is similar to another in some way. For example, if you **take after** someone, you resemble them, and if you **call** something **after** another thing, you give it the same name as the other thing.

call after	name after	take after

against is a preposition. It occurs in 30 phrasal verbs in this dictionary. One meaning of **against** is to do with position, indicating that one thing is next to another and touching it, or with movement into that position, but it is also used very commonly to express ideas of opposition. **Against** occurs with two main meanings in phrasal verbs.

1 Opposition and prevention

You use **against** in combinations which have 'attack' or 'oppose' as part of their meaning. For example, if two people **side against** you, they join together in order to defeat you, and if you **kick against** something, you protest about it. You mention the person or thing being attacked or opposed in the noun group after **against**. Some combinations have 'prevent' or 'protect' as part of their meaning. The noun group after **against** refers to something potentially harmful, which you want to avoid. For example, to **guard against** something means to take action to prevent it happening or harming you.

go against 5	guard against	hedge against	insure against	inveigh against
kick against	offend against	plot against	proceed against	protect against
provide against	rage against	rail against	range against	set against 3
side against	take against	turn against		

2 Comparison and detraction

Against occurs in combinations with transitive verbs where you are comparing two things. You mention the second thing in the comparison in the noun group after **against**. For example, if you **balance** one thing **against** another, you assess their relative importance. **Against** occurs in combinations with intransitive verbs where you are saying that something is making a situation likely, less favourable, or less successful. You mention the situation or person that is affected in the noun group after **against**. For example, if something **counts against** you, it is a disadvantage to you and may lead to your defeat, and if one thing **militates against** another, it makes it less likely to happen or succeed.

balance against	count against	find against	go against 4	match against
measure against	militate against	set against 1	tell against	weigh against

ahead is an adverb. It occurs in 14 phrasal verbs in this dictionary.

1 Progress

Ahead is most frequently used in combinations with intransitive verbs of movement to refer to progress of some kind, usually in a non-literal sense, rather than referring to actual movement. For example, if you **forge ahead**, you make rapid progress in what you are doing, but you do not have to be moving physically. You can mention the activity you are involved in after the preposition *with*. When you are saying that one person is making more progress than another, the second person is mentioned after the preposition *of*.

forge ahead	get ahead	go ahead	plough ahead
press ahead	pull ahead	push ahead	

2 Futurity
If you use **ahead** with verbs of thinking and looking, it often means that you are doing something in advance. For example, if you **plan ahead**, you make plans about what you may do in the future. Some combinations have the meaning of something being likely to happen in the future. For example, if something **looms ahead**, it is likely to happen soon.

lie ahead	look ahead	loom ahead
plan ahead	send ahead	think ahead

along is an adverb and a preposition. It occurs in 24 phrasal verbs in this dictionary.

1 Travel
Along occurs most frequently in literal combinations with verbs of motion to indicate movement in a certain direction, as in **go along** or **move along**, and it is often used, usually as an adverb, to imply departure, for example in **get along** and **push along**.

bomb along	pass along	run along

2 Progress
You can use **along** as an adverb in a non-literal way with verbs of motion to indicate progress. For example, if a project **is coming along**, it is making progress. Some combinations emphasize that something is not progressing very well, so if you say that a job **is dragging along**, you think it is taking you a long time to do it.

come along 4	drag along	drift along	get along 2	go along 4
help along	jog along	move along 3		

3 Accompanying
You use **along** as an adverb in some combinations with transitive verbs to indicate that you are taking someone or something with you, so if you **bring along** a friend to a party, you take them with you. **Along** can also be used in intransitive combinations to show that someone is accompanying someone else, so if you **tag along** with someone, you accompany them.

bring along	come along 2	sing along	tag along	take along

4 Acceptance
Along is sometimes used as an adverb to indicate acceptance of someone or something, especially when it is followed by *with*. If you **go along with** a plan, you agree with it and accept it, and if you **get along** with someone, you are friendly with them and accept them.

get along 1	go along with	play along	rub along

among is a preposition. It occurs in 4 phrasal verbs in this dictionary. The basic meaning of **among** is to do with physically being in the middle of a group or surrounded by them. The combinations in this dictionary use **among** in the extended sense of being included or considered as part of a particular class. For example, if someone **ranks among** the members of a particular group, they are one of those members. You mention the group in the noun group after **among**.

| class among | count among | number among | rank among |

apart is an adverb. It occurs in 11 phrasal verbs in this dictionary. The basic meaning of **apart** is to do with position, indicating that one thing is at a distance from another. **Together** often has opposite meanings to **apart**.

1 Undoing and collapse

Apart occurs with transitive verbs in combinations which describe the process of undoing or dismantling something which was originally one piece or unit. For example, to **take** something **apart** means to undo it so that it is in separate parts. **Pull apart**, **take apart**, and **tear apart** also have meanings to do with analysing something and considering its individual parts. This is a metaphorical use of the 'undoing' meaning. **Apart** occurs with intransitive verbs in combinations which mean 'collapse', and refer to either the physical collapse of an object or the mental collapse of a person. For example, **fall apart** can refer either to a physical collapse or a mental breakdown.

| come apart | fall apart | pull apart 1 | rip apart |
| take apart | tear apart | | |

2 Separation

Apart is used in combinations which describe a process of separation between two or more things. The separation may involve physical movement away from each other. For example, if you **pull apart** two people or animals who are fighting, you physically separate them. But the combinations often have an extended meaning involving relationships or the act of distinguishing. If two people **grow apart**, their relationship becomes less close as they develop separate interests. **Apart** occurs in **set apart** and **tell apart** to indicate that one thing or person is distinguished from another.

| drift apart | grow apart | pull apart 2 | set apart | tell apart |

around is an adverb and a preposition. It occurs in 119 phrasal verbs in this dictionary.

1 Movement

Around is used in literal combinations to indicate movement in many different directions over a period of time, often without any specific aim or purpose. For example, if you **run around** you run in a lot of different directions; if you **shop around**, you go to several different shops in order to compare the price and quality of the goods; and if you **push** something **around**, you move it in several different directions. Some combinations have the meaning of looking in a lot of different places or asking several people in order to find something. These phrasal verbs are often followed by the preposition *for*. For example, if you **ask around** for something, you ask several people for it. **Around** is used in a similar way in combinations which have the meaning of distributing or spreading something to many different places or people. For example, if you **pass** things **around**, you pass them from one person to another in a group, and if you **scatter** things **around**, you spread them over a wide area. When **around** is used as a preposition, it has the additional meaning of 'within a particular place'. You mention the place in the noun group after **around**. For example, if you

run around the room, you run in many different directions in the room; and if you **nose around** a place, you look in several different places for things in it. **About** and **round** have similar meanings: see **about** [1] and **round** [1]. **About** is used mainly in British English, and in American English, **around** is much more common than **round**.

[2] **Inactivity and aimlessness**
Around is used to indicate lack of activity, lack of purpose, or lack of achievement over a period of time. For example, if you **loll around**, you spend time being lazy and doing nothing. When **around** is used as a preposition, it has the additional meaning of 'in a particular place'. You mention the place in the noun group after **around**. For example, if you **hang around** a place, you spend time there doing very little. **Around** also occurs in a few combinations indicating that something is present in a place, although you are not sure where. For example, if something **is kicking around** in a place, it is somewhere in that place, but you do not know exactly where. These phrasal verbs are usually used in continuous tenses. **Around** is also used as an adverb in some informal or rude combinations to indicate wasting time or behaving in a silly way. For example, if you **mess around**, you behave in a foolish or irritating way. **About** and **round** have similar meanings: see **about** [2] and **round** [7]. **About** is used mainly in British English, and in American English, **around** is much more common than **round**.

bumble around	fiddle around	fool around	hang around	kick around
lie around	loaf around	loll around	lounge around	mess around
mope around	muck around	play around	putter around	sit around
stand around	stick around	tinker around	wait around	

[3] **Turning**
You use **around** as an adverb in combinations which have the meaning of turning so as to be facing in the opposite direction, or turning in a complete circle or series of circles. For example, to **spin around** means to turn quickly and face in the opposite direction, or to turn round in a circle. **Round** has a similar meanings: see **round** [2]. In American English, **around** is much more common than **round**.

look around	pull around	spin around	swing around	swivel around
turn around 1	wheel around			

[4] **Surrounding**
Around is used in many combinations with the literal meaning of surrounding or encircling someone or something. For example, when people **gather around**, they come together and surround someone or something, and when you **throw** your arms **around** someone, you put them so that they form a circle round them. **Round** and **about** have similar meanings: see **round** [4] and **about** [3]. **About** is used mainly in British English, and in American English, **around** is much more common than **round**.

[5] **Avoidance**
You use **around** in a few combinations which have meanings to do with avoiding something, either a physical object or a problem. For example, if you **talk around** a subject, you avoid talking about it directly. **Round** has a similar meaning: see **round** [8]. In American English, **around** is much more common than **round**.

get around 3,4	go around	skirt around	talk around

6　Focusing

You use **around** as a preposition in **centre around** and **revolve around** where the meaning is to focus on something or concentrate on it. For example, if a discussion **revolves around** a subject, it concentrates on that subject. **Round** has a similar meaning: see **round** 9. In American English, **around** is much more common than **round**.

as is a preposition. It occurs in 8 phrasal verbs in this dictionary. **As** is one of the commonest words in English, and it is especially used in comparisons. It is used in phrasal verbs in order to indicate that someone or something is considered to have a particular role or function. For example, if you **masquerade as** a particular kind of person, you pretend to be that kind of person, and if you say that one thing **serves as** another, you mean that it is used instead of it. **As** also occurs as the second particle in combinations which include two particles, for example **go down as** and **pass off as**.

do as	hail as	know as	mark as
masquerade as	pass as	see as	serve as

aside is an adverb. It occurs in 15 phrasal verbs in this dictionary. Its basic meaning is to do with movement from a position in front of something towards the side of it.

1　Rejection

Aside is frequently used with transitive verbs of movement in combinations which mean that something is being rejected. For example, if you **brush aside** someone's comments, you reject or ignore what they say.

brush aside	cast aside	lay aside 2	push aside 2
set aside 3	sweep aside	throw aside 2	wave aside

2　Postponing

You can use **aside** in literal combinations to show that you are moving something away from you, usually not far away and temporarily. For example, if you **lay aside** a book, you place it somewhere near you until you are ready to read it again. These combinations can also be used in a non-literal sense in relation to ideas, tasks, or emotions. For example, if you **leave aside** a suggestion, you do not deal with it immediately because you intend to consider it or discuss it later.

lay aside 1	leave aside	put aside	set aside 4

3　Yielding or vacating

Aside means 'sideways', so if you **step aside** you move sideways to get out of someone's way. You can also use this in a non-literal way, for example if you **step aside** from a job, you resign so that someone else can have your job.

stand aside	step aside	turn aside

4　Isolation and privacy

Aside sometimes gives an idea of moving somewhere in order to have a private conversation with somebody, so if you **pull** someone **aside**, you take them somewhere where other people cannot hear what you are saying.

pull aside	take aside

at is a preposition. It occurs in 47 phrasal verbs in this dictionary. The most common use of **at** is to do with indicating points in space and time, to say where something is, or where or when something happens. There are two basic meanings of phrasal verbs with **at** in this dictionary, and they have the meaning of directing or focusing an action on someone or something.

1 Direction

At is used in combinations which indicate that an action is carried out in a particular direction. For example, if you **aim at** a target, you try to achieve that target, and if you **talk at** somebody, you are talking in their direction, regardless of whether they are listening to you.

aim at	drive at	get at 1	go at	laugh at
level at	look at	marvel at	talk at	throw at 1
work at				

2 Attempting, attacking, seizing, and holding

At occurs in combinations with verbs which express ideas of attacking, hitting, seizing, holding, and so on. These verbs are mainly intransitive, although they can often be used transitively too, without **at**. By using them in combinations with **at**, instead of as transitive verbs, you imply that someone is trying to attack or seize or hold something, perhaps unsuccessfully, rather than actually doing so. For example, if you **jab at** something, you try to hit it but do not succeed, or if you **get at** someone, you attack them verbally by shouting at them or criticizing them. **At** is also used in a similar way in combinations with the meaning of breaking off or removing small pieces from something, especially in small, repeated movements. For example, if you **pick at** your food, you only eat small amounts of it, and to **tear at** something means to try and pull it into small pieces. Other combinations indicate that a person or animal suddenly seizes something, or attempts to do so. For example, if a wild animal **claws at** you, it tries to catch you in its claws. You can also use **at** in a non-literal sense of 'seizing'. For example if you **grab at** or **leap at** an opportunity or offer, you try to take advantage of it, and if you **guess at** a question or problem, you try to understand it and provide an answer, although you do not really have enough information.

claw at	come at	fly at	get at 4	grab at
grasp at	guess at	hack at	hit at	jab at
jump at	leap at	nibble at	paw at	peck at
pick at	play at	pluck at	poke at	prod at
pull at 1	sip at	strike at	tear at	throw at 3
tug at	worry at			

away is an adverb. It occurs in 140 phrasal verbs in this dictionary.

1 Movement

Away is used in literal combinations to indicate movement in a direction farther from you, or movement from the place where you are or were. You use **away** with verbs which describe movement. For example, **run away** means to run from someone or something in the opposite direction, and **pull** something **away** means to pull someone or something from the place where they were. These combinations are often followed by an adjunct referring to direction or place, usually beginning with the prepositions *from* or *to*.

break away 2	come away 1	chase away	fall away 2	get away 1,2
go away 1	look away	move away 1	pull away 1,2	run away 1
send away 1	stretch away			

2   Withdrawing and non-involvement

Away occurs in combinations which have meanings to do with someone avoiding or withdrawing from an activity, or ceasing to be involved in an activity. They can be regarded as metaphorical uses of the previous group. For example, **shy away from** means to avoid doing something because you are afraid or have no confidence. Some combinations have meanings to do with avoiding a place. These combinations are often followed by the preposition *from*.

back away	break away 1,4	frighten away 2	get away from
grow away from	keep away 1,2,3	move away from	pull away 5
run away 2,3,4	scare away 2	shrink away	shy away from
slip away 1	stay away	stay away from 1,2	steal away
steer away from	stop away	turn away from	walk away from
warn away	wave away	whisk away	

3   Removing, transferring, and separating

Away is used in combination with transitive verbs to indicate that something is taken from the place where it was or taken from the person who had it before. For example, to **snatch** something **away** from someone means to take it from them forcefully. Some combinations have meanings to do with taking a person from one place to another. Combinations such as **give away** have meanings to do with transferring something from one person to another. These combinations are often followed by the prepositions *from* or *to*. **Away** occurs with intransitive verbs in combinations such as **break away** and **come away** to indicate that something becomes separated from the thing that it was attached to. Such combinations are often followed by the preposition *from*.

break away 3	call away	come away 2	fall away 1
get away 3	give away 1,2,5	kiss away	move away 2
pull away 3,4	sign away	snatch away	spirit away
take away 1,2,3,4,8	take away from 1	tear away 2	throw away 1
tow away	turn away 1,2		

4   Storing, hiding, and isolating

You use **away** in phrasal verbs which have meanings to do with putting things in a safe place, or storing or hiding them. For example, **pack** something **away** means to put something in a bag or other container. You also use **away** in combinations which have isolation as part of their meaning. For example, something which **is buried away** is difficult to find, and someone who has **locked** himself or herself **away** has gone somewhere where they will not be disturbed. These combinations are often followed by an adjunct in which you mention the place where the person or thing is put or hidden.

bury away	clear away	file away	give away 4
hide away 1,2,3	hoard away	lock away 1,2,3,4	pack away
put away 1,3,4	salt away	shut away 1,2	squirrel away
stash away 1,2	store away	stow away 1,2	tidy away
tuck away 1,2			

5   Getting rid of things and destroying things

Away is used in combinations, mainly with transitive verbs, where you are saying that something is removed entirely. You add **away** to the verb to show that nothing is left. Many of the combinations mean 'destroy' or 'get rid of'. For example, **strip** something **away** means to remove it completely. A few combinations mean 'use something completely', and they often also suggest ideas of wasting it.

blow away 1,2,3,5	brush away	burn away	cast away
chuck away	cut away	do away with 1,2	drive away
explain away	frighten away 1	gamble away	idle away
magic away	make away with	pass away 2	pour away
pump away 2	scare away	scrape away	shoot away
strip away 1,2	sweep away 1,2	take away 5	tear away 1
throw away 2,3	toss away	trim away	turn away 3
wash away 1,2,3	while away	wipe away	wish away

6 Disappearing

You use **away** in combinations to indicate that something gradually disappears or is gradually destroyed until it does not exist at all. For example, **fade away** means to fade entirely. The verbs in these combinations are mostly intransitive.

boil away	chip away at	crumble away	die away
drop away	eat away 1,2,3	eat away at 1,2	ebb away
erode away	fade away 1,2,3	fall away 3,4,5	fritter away
go away 2	melt away 1,2,3	moulder away	pass away 1
pine away	rot away	rust away	scour away
slip away 2	tail away	trail away	waste away 1,2
wear away 1,2,5	whittle away	whittle away at	wither away

7 Continuous activity

You use **away** with intransitive verbs describing processes or activities in order to indicate that the process or activity continues throughout a period of time. For example, **work away** means to work hard for a long time, and **bang away** means to continue hitting something for a long time. These verbs are often used in a continuous tense, or with words which indicate continuousness, such as *would*, *continue*, or *keep*. Many of the phrasal verbs have the meaning 'work', and you can mention the thing being done in an adjunct, after the preposition *at*.

bang away	beaver away	blast away	blaze away	chip away at
grind away	hack away at	hammer away at	jabber away	peg away
plod away	plug away	puff away	pump away 1	slave away
slog away	steam away	talk away	tick away	toil away
type away	work away			

back is an adverb. It occurs in 89 phrasal verbs in this dictionary.

1 Returning and movement backwards

Back is used in literal combinations with verbs of movement to say that someone or something returns to a place that they were in before. For example, when you **start back**, you start travelling in the direction that you came from, and if something **blows back**, the wind moves it in the direction that it was coming from.

blow back	come back 1	double back 1	get back 1,2	go back 1
head back	lie back	look back 1	pull back 2	push back 2
put back 2	row back	sink back 1	sit back 1	spring back
stand back 1	start back 1	toss back 1	turn back 1,3	

2   Position

You use **back** in combinations indicating a position at a distance from a central point or from a place where something is happening. For example, if an army **falls back**, it retreats, and if you **tie back** your hair, you tie it so that it is away from your face. You can extend this use of **back** to say that you separate yourself from something that is happening when you are unwilling to get involved. For example, if you **stand back** while something is happening, you do not become involved in it.

beat back	call back 3	draw back	drop back
fall back 1,2	get back 5	hang back	hold back 4
pull back 1,3,4	reel back	set back 2	sit back 2
stand back 2,3	start back 2	stay back	step back 1
tail back	throw back 3	tie back	

3   Time

You use **back** in combinations which have the meaning of belonging to the past or thinking about the past. For example, if something **carries** you **back**, it makes you think about something in the past.

bring back 1,2	carry back	cast back	come back 5
date back	flash back	go back 2,3,4	hark back to 1,2
look back 2	take back 8,9	think back	throw back 6,7

4   Returning or retrieving something

You use **back** in combinations with meanings to do with returning something to a place where it was before, or to a person who had it before. For example, if you **give** something **back**, you give it to the person who had lent it to you, and if you **get** something **back**, someone gives it to you after you had lent it to them. This use of **back** is very productive.

claw back	die back	get back 3,4	give back 1,2
go back 8,9	hand back	kick back 1	pay back 1
plough back	put back 1,3,6	put back into	send back
shoot back	stick back	take back 1–5,7	throw back 1,2,5,8
win back	wind back		

5   Repeating or returning to an action

You can extend the above use of **back** in combinations with the meaning of returning to or repeating an act. For example, if you **get back into** an activity, you start doing it again. Several of these combinations have the meaning of repeating the action that someone else has done. For example, if you **hit** someone **back**, you hit them after they have hit you. This use of **back** is very productive.

answer back	bite back 2	bounce back	call back 1,2
come back 2,3,4	come back to	fall back on	fight back 1
get back 6	get back at	get back into	get back to
go back 5,6,7	go back on	go back over	go back to 1,2,3
hit back 1,2	pay back 2	phone back	play back
put back on	read back	report back	ring back
shoot back	sink back 2	step back 2	strike back
take back 6	talk back	throw back at	write back

6 Controlling or suppressing

You use **back** in combinations with meanings to do with controlling or suppressing something, especially an emotion, or preventing something from progressing. For example, if you **choke back** tears, you suppress them and stop them from coming.

bite back 1	choke back 1,2	cut back	cut back on
fight back 2	force back	hold back 1–7	keep back 1,2,3
knock back 4	push back 1	put back 4,5	rein back
roll back	scale back	set back 1	

7 Drinking

You use **back** in a few combinations meaning to drink something quickly, often in one gulp.

knock back 1	put back 7	throw back 4	toss back 2

before is both a preposition and an adverb. It is often used to indicate that something is in front of something else. **Before** only occurs in 5 phrasal verbs in this dictionary, and in them this meaning is extended to talk about presenting ideas or matters to someone, especially someone in authority. For example, if a case **goes before** a judge, the judge considers it.

come before	go before	lay before	lie before	put before

behind is an adverb and a preposition. It occurs in 10 phrasal verbs in this dictionary. Its basic meaning is to do with relative position in space or time.

1 Relative position

Behind occurs in literal combinations which refer to the position of one person or thing in relation to another. For example, if someone **stops behind**, they stay in a place after other people have left, and if you **leave** something **behind**, you do not take it with you when you go somewhere.

leave behind 1	stay behind	stop behind	wait behind

2 Progress

Behind is also used to indicate relative progress, and to say that one person or thing is less advanced than another. For example, if you **get behind** with your work, you do not make as much progress as you should.

fall behind	get behind	lag behind	leave behind 4

3 Concealment and support

Behind is used literally to indicate that something is on the other side or at the back of another thing so that it supports or hides it. However, it is used metaphorically in phrasal verbs. For example, if you **hide behind** something, you use it as an excuse so that you can conceal your feelings, and if you **get behind** someone, you help or support them.

get behind 2	hide behind	lie behind	put behind

below is both a preposition and an adverb. Its basic meaning is to do with position, to say that one thing is at a lower level than something else. It only occurs in 1 phrasal verb in this dictionary, **go below**, and this refers to movement from a higher level on a boat to a lower level.

beneath is both a preposition and an adverb. Its basic meaning is to do with position, to say that one thing is under or at a lower level than another. It only occurs in 1 phrasal verb in this dictionary, **marry beneath**, and this refers to relative position or rank in society.

between is mainly used as a preposition. Its basic meaning is to do with movement from one point to another, or position in the middle of two things. It only occurs in 3 phrasal verbs in this dictionary. It is used to indicate movement in **pass between**. It also occurs in **come between** and **stand between**, where it is used non-literally to refer to something that prevents you from doing or having something you want by appearing to interfere with it.

beyond is both a preposition and an adverb. Its basic meaning is to do with position, to indicate that one thing is farther away from something else. It only occurs in 2 phrasal verbs in this dictionary, **get beyond** and **go beyond**, where it is used metaphorically to express ideas of doing something more advanced or more extreme than before.

by is an adverb and a preposition. It occurs in 23 phrasal verbs in this dictionary. Some meanings of **by** occur in a very few combinations. For example, **get by** and **scrape by** have the meaning of managing to survive with difficulty because of limited resources. **Come by** has the meaning of acquiring or gaining. There are four main uses of **by** in phrasal verbs.

1   Movement past a person or thing
Some phrasal verbs use **by** as an adverb or a preposition with the meaning of moving past a person or thing, often passing very close to them. **Brush by** and **push by** are examples of this meaning. Some combinations do not refer to physical objects, but to situations or experiences. **By** is usually an adverb in these combinations. For example, if you let someone's remarks or actions **go by**, you let them take place without allowing them to affect you. Some similar combinations relate to the passage of time. For example if you say that time or an event **slips by**, you mean that it passes and is gone.

brush by	get by	go by	pass by	push by
run by	sit by	slip by	stand by 1	tick by

2   Visiting
In some phrasal verbs with **by**, the meaning is of visiting someone casually and often only for a short time. **By** is usually an adverb but can be a preposition. For example, if you **stop by**, you visit a place for a short time, and if you **go by** a place, you go there for a short time in order to do or get something.

call by	come by	drop by	go by 3	run by
sit by	slip by	stand by 1	stop by	tick by

3   Consistency and loyalty
You use **by** as a preposition in some phrasal verbs to indicate that someone always obeys a rule or principle, or always supports or helps someone, however difficult this may be. For example, if you **abide by** a law, agreement, or decision, you do what it says you should do. If you **stick by** someone, you help or support them when they are in difficulty.

abide by	go by 4	live by
stand by 3	stick by	swear by

4 Preparation and readiness

In a few combinations with **by** as an adverb, the meaning is that people or things are kept in preparation for something that might happen. For example, if you **lay** a store of something **by**, you save it for future use, and if you **stand by**, you are ready to provide help or take action if it becomes necessary.

lay by	put by	stand by 2

down is an adverb and a preposition. It occurs in 204 phrasal verbs in this dictionary. The basic meaning of **down** is to do with movement from a higher position or level to a lower one.

1 Movement and position

You use **down** in literal combinations to indicate movement from a higher position or place to a lower one. For example, if you **shin down** a tree or pole, you climb very rapidly from a higher point on it towards the ground. If a plane **comes down**, it moves towards the ground and lands, and if you say it **is pouring down**, you mean that rain is falling very heavily. **Up** can often be used instead of **down** to indicate movement in the opposite direction.

beat down 1,2	bucket down	cast down 3	come down 1,2,3,8,11
flutter down	get down 1,2,3	go down 1,3,6	lash down 2
move down 1	pass down	pelt down	phone down
piss down	pour down	pull down 1	put down 15,16
rain down	ram down 1	reach down 2	roll down
run down 1	set down 4,5	shin down	sink down 1
snuggle down	splash down	swoop down 1	take down 1,2,3
talk down 2	teem down	touch down	trickle down
turn down 4	wash down 3	wind down 1	

Down occurs as an adverb in combinations where you are describing movement from an upright or standing position to a lying, sitting, or crouching position, and so on. For example, if you **lie down**, you move into a horizontal position, and if you **kneel down**, you sit with your legs bent underneath your body.

bed down 1,2	bend down	bow down 1	crouch down	doss down
flop down	get down 4	go down 7,23	huddle down	hunker down 1
keep down 2	kip down	kneel down	lie down	plonk down 2
plump down 1	put down 5,11	reach down 1	sink down 2	sit down 1,2
stay down 1	throw down 2			

You also use **down** as an adverb in combinations which refer to someone putting something onto a surface. For example, if you **slap** something **down** on a table, you put it on the table with a lot of force.

bang down	lay down 1,3	plonk down 1	plop down	plump down 2
put down 1,2	set down 1	slam down 1,2	slap down 1	stick down 1
throw down 1				

A few combinations with **down** refer to movement towards you either horizontally or in time, rather than from a higher position to a lower one. For example, if something **bears down on** you, it approaches you, and if traditions or stories **are passed down** to you, they are taught or told to you by an older generation.

bear down on 1	come down 9,10	get down 5	go down 4,5
hand down 1	move down 2	pass down 1,3	

2 Decreasing, lowering, and reducing

Down occurs as an adverb in combinations which refer to a decrease in size, degree, standard, intensity, and so on. For example, if the cost of something **goes down**, it becomes less expensive; if you **turn down** a television, radio, or record player, you make it quieter; and if you **water down** food or drink, you make it weaker.

Some of the combinations describe processes of reducing the physical size of something, perhaps by cutting or removing part of it. For example, if you **grind** something **down**, you make it smoother and smaller by rubbing it against a hard surface or on a machine. A few combinations refer to complete changes in state or shape. For example, if you **melt** something **down**, you melt it until it melts completely, and if a substance **breaks down**, it separates into the parts from which it is made.

Other combinations include verbs which are also adjectives, in particular adjectives describing qualities which are low in intensity or amount, such as *cool*, *narrow*, and *quiet*. These combinations express ideas of something becoming even lower in intensity or amount. For example, if something **cools down**, it becomes cooler, and if you **narrow down** a choice or subject, you make it narrower or more selective.

beat down 3	boil down 1,2	boil down to	break down 3,4
bring down 2	calm down 1,2	change down	come down 6,7,14
come down to	cool down 1,2	count down	cut down 1
cut down on	damp down 1,2	dampen down 1	die down
dress down 1	drive down	dumb down	go down 8,9,10,12
grind down 2	knock down 5	let down 3,4	mark down 2,3
melt down	move down 3,4	narrow down	pare down
pipe down	plane down	play down	quiet down
quieten down	ratchet down	render down	round down
run down 3,4,5	scale down	settle down 3,4	simmer down
slim down	slow down 1,2	thin down	throttle down
tone down	turn down 2,3	warm down	water down 1,2
whittle down	wind down 2,3		

3 Fastening and fixing

You use **down** as an adverb in combinations where you are describing processes of fastening or fixing something to the ground, or making it secure. For example, if you **nail** something **down**, you use nails to fasten it to a lower surface, and when something **beds down**, it settles firmly into position so that it cannot be shaken loose. Some of these combinations have metaphorical meanings. For example, you talk about **nailing** people **down** when you mean that you are forcing them to state clearly their opinions or intentions.

batten down	bed down 3	lash down 1	lay down 5,6
nail down 1,2,3	pin down 1,2	put down 3	screw down
stamp down	stick down 2	tack down	tamp down
tie down 1,2	weight down		

4 Collapsing, attacking, and destroying

You use **down** as an adverb in combinations which contain ideas of collapsing, cutting, and destruction. **Down** helps to give the idea that something falls to the ground or is forced to the ground during the process. For example, if you **chop down** a tree, you cut through its trunk until it falls, and if a building **burns down**, it is completely destroyed by fire and collapses onto the ground.

Other combinations contain ideas of attacking, destroying, and killing. For example, when people are **mown down**, they are killed in a violent way, and when someone or something is **brought down**, they are attacked and killed, and fall to the ground.

batter down	blow down	break down 6,7	bring down 3,4
burn down	call down on	chop down	come down 4,5
cut down 2	dress down 2	fall down 1,2,3	go down 2,16
gun down	hack down	hew down	kick down
knock down 1,2,3	mow down	pull down 2	put down 4,14
run down 6,10	shake down 1	shoot down 1	slip down 1
smash down	strike down 1	swoop down 2	take down 4
tear down	tumble down		

5 Defeating and suppressing

Down occurs as an adverb in combinations which have 'defeat' as part of their meaning. For example, if you **argue** someone **down**, you succeed in forcing them to accept your point of view during an argument, and if you **back down**, you accept someone else's point of view. **Down** also occurs in combinations which mean 'suppress'. For example, if someone **clamps down** on you, they take action to control you or stop you doing something, and if people **are kept down**, they are kept in a state of powerlessness.

argue down	back down	bow down 3	break down 5
bring down 1,5	cast down 1,2	clamp down	climb down
come down on	come down with	crack down	do down
drag down 1,2	draw down	drive down	face down
fight down	get down 8	go down 17,18,19	go down with
grind down 1	hold down 1–5	hoot down	howl down
keep down 1,3	knock down 4	pin down 3	pull down 3
put down 9,10	shoot down 2	shout down	slap down 2
stare down	take down 6	talk down 1,4	tie down 3
vote down	wave down 2	wear down 1	

6 Completing or failing

Down is used in combinations to give an idea of thoroughness or completeness, and usually of ending or failing. It is always adverbial in these combinations. For example, if you **shut** a business **down**, it stops trading altogether, and if you **hunt** someone **down**, you hunt them and succeed in finding them. Some of the combinations mean 'stop functioning'. For example, if a machine **breaks down**, it stops operating.

break down 1,2	chase down	close down 1,2	come down 12
fall down 4,5	flag down	go down 21,22	hunt down
lay down 7,8,9	let down 1,2	load down 1,2	ram down 2
run down 7	send down 1,2	settle down 2	shut down 1,2
stand down 1,2	step down	strip down	throw down 3
track down	turn down 1	wave down 1	weigh down 1,2
wind down 4			

7 Eating and drinking

Down occurs as an adverb in combinations which refer to eating and drinking, and the action of food or drink passing from your mouth into your stomach. For example, if you **bolt down** your food, you eat it very quickly. **Down** also occurs in combinations such as **hold down** and

keep down, where you are talking about food remaining in a person's stomach, for example if you are talking about someone who is ill and therefore likely to vomit.

bolt down	chow down	drink down	get down 6	go down 14
gobble down	gulp down	hold down 6	keep down 4	slip down 2
stay down 2	swallow down	swill down	throw down 4	toss down
wash down 1	wolf down			

8 Writing and recording

You use **down** as an adverb in combinations which mean 'write' or 'record'. For example, if you **note** something **down**, you write it somewhere. It also occurs in a few combinations such as **go down as** and **put down to** which express ideas of deciding that something is a particular kind of thing, or that something is caused by a particular kind of thing.

copy down	get down 7	go down 20	go down as
hand down 2	jot down	lay down 2	mark down 1
mark down as	note down	put down 7,8,12,13	put down as
put down to	run down 8	scribble down	set down 2,3
set down as	stick down 3	take down 5	write down

9 Cleaning and flattening

You use **down** as an adverb in combinations which describe processes of cleaning, smoothing, or brushing surfaces, such as walls or the outside of objects. For example, if you **wash down** a wall, you clean it thoroughly with water, and if you **smooth down** the clothes that you are wearing, you press them until they lie flat.

brush down	clean down	damp down 3	dampen down 2
dust down 1	hose down	rub down 1,2	sand down
slick down	smooth down	sponge down	swab down
wash down 2	wear down 2	wipe down	

10 Work and activities

A few combinations which contain **down** as an adverb express ideas of starting to work at something. For example, if you **settle down** to work, you begin to work seriously.

buckle down	get down to	knuckle down	settle down 1	sit down 3

for is a preposition. It occurs in 68 phrasal verbs in this dictionary. **For** is one of the commonest words of English, and it is especially used when stating reasons, causes, purposes, aims, and so on. It often has no special use or meaning in combinations with verbs, apart from introducing a noun group in which you mention a reason, purpose, aim, and so on. For example, if you **make for** a place, you move in that direction; if you **angle for** something, you try to obtain it by indirect means; and if you **live for** something, that is the most important thing in your life.

For is also used to introduce the noun group which indicates the thing or person that you are dealing with or considering. For example, if you **allow for** something in your planning, you make sure that you will be able to deal with it; if you **root for** someone, you encourage them while they are doing something difficult; and if you **fall for** someone, you become very attracted to them or fond of them. **For** also occurs as the second particle in combinations which include two particles, for example **cry out for** and **stand up for**.

Some meanings of **for** are used in only a few combinations. For example, if an animal **goes for** you, it attacks you, and if someone **is gunning for** you, they are trying in a determined way to harm you.

forth is an adverb. It occurs in 11 phrasal verbs in this dictionary. It is a rather formal, literary, or old-fashioned word

1 Departure
Forth occurs in literal combinations with intransitive verbs which express ideas of departing from one place and going somewhere else. For example, if someone **sallies forth**, they go somewhere quickly and energetically, and if they **venture forth**, they go somewhere that might be dangerous.

go forth	send forth

2 Production
Forth also occurs in combinations which express ideas of something being produced or stated. They can be regarded as metaphorical or extended uses of the previous category. For example, if things **pour forth**, they appear suddenly in large quantities; and if you **set forth** an opinion, you present it to people by stating it clearly.

bring forth	call forth	come forth	hold forth	pour forth
put forth	set forth			

forward is an adverb. It occurs in 10 phrasal verbs in this dictionary. Its basic meaning is to do with movement in a direction in front of you.

1 Advancement in time and position
Forward occurs in a few combinations which refer to time. For example, if you **bring** something **forward**, it happens at an earlier time than planned, and if you **look forward to** something in the future, you want it to happen and expect to enjoy it. **Forward** also occurs in a few combinations which refer to position, for example if you **carry forward** an amount when you are doing accounts, you write it at the top of the next page or column.

bring forward 1	carry forward	go forward 1	look forward to
put forward 3	wind forward		

2 Presenting and appearing
Forward also occurs in combinations which contain ideas of something being presented or produced. These combinations sometimes refer to suggestions and offers. For example, if you **bring forward** an argument, you state it so that it can be discussed, and if you **step forward** in a difficult situation, you offer to help.

bring forward 2	come forward	come forward with	go forward 2
push forward	put forward 1	step forward	

from is a preposition. It occurs in 24 phrasal verbs in this dictionary. **From** is one of the commonest words of English, and it is especially used when mentioning sources or origins, or when indicating ideas of separation and exclusion. It is mostly used in the same ways in phrasal verb combinations.

1 Sources and origins

From is used in literal combinations with verbs which express ideas of developing, appearing, or originating. The noun group after **from** refers to the source or origins of whatever has developed, appeared, or originated. For example, if one word **derives from** another, the second word is the origin of the first; if something **emanates from** a particular person or thing, they started it; and if someone **hails from** a particular place, they were born there or live there.

2 Separation and prevention

From is used in literal combinations which express ideas of separation, prevention, difference, and exclusion. The noun group after **from** refers to the thing which is now separated, prevented, different, or excluded. For example, if you **depart from** an accepted belief or practice, you believe or do something different; if you **keep** someone **from** doing something, you stop them doing it; and if you **hide from** someone or something, you go somewhere where they cannot see you. **From** also occurs with this meaning as the second particle in combinations which include two particles, for example **get away from** and **set apart from**.

in is an adverb and a preposition. It occurs in 214 phrasal verbs in this dictionary. The basic meaning of **in** is to do with movement from the outside of an enclosed space or container to the inside of it. **Out** often has opposite meanings. **Into** is often used instead of **in** as a preposition when referring to movement, and phrasal verbs containing **into** are treated as separate entries.

1 Movement, entering, and arriving

In is used most frequently in literal combinations which express ideas of entering a place or arriving there. For example, if someone **breezes in**, they enter a place in a carefree manner, and if you **let** someone **in**, you open a door so that they can enter. When people or things **pour in**, large numbers of them arrive somewhere; if you **fly in**, you arrive at a place by aeroplane; and if a train **pulls in**, it enters the station as it arrives. A few combinations have an additional meaning of registering your arrival officially. For example, if you **book in** at a hotel, you arrive there and tell the hotel staff that you have arrived; if a competitor at an event **weighs in**, they are weighed to check their weight shortly before or after the event; and if a person in authority **swears** someone **in**, they register them officially. **In** is also used in combinations where it has the meaning 'approach'. These combinations are sometimes followed by the preposition *on*. For example, if something **zeroes in on** another thing, it moves towards it.

ask in	book in 1,2	breeze in	call in 2
check in 1,2	clock in 2	close in 3	come in 1–5,7,11,16,19
crowd in	draw in 1,2	drop in	flood in
fly in	get in 1,2,3,7	go in 1,2,3,4,6,7	home in 1,2
invite in	let in 1	look in 1	move in 1,2,3
pile in	pop in	pour in	pull in 1,2
put in 14,15,18	roll in 3,4	run in 1	ship in
show in	sign in 1,2	slip in 2	squash in
squeeze in	stop in 2	storm in	swear in
take in 1,2,13	weigh in 2	zero in on 1,2	zoom in

2 Inserting, penetrating, and absorbing

In is used in combinations which refer to the insertion of one thing inside another, sometimes going through a barrier of some kind, or to one thing absorbing another. For example, if water or air **comes in**, it penetrates a barrier and enters a place; if you **breathe in**, air moves into your lungs as you take a breath; and if you **stick** something **in**, you insert it somewhere. A few combinations with **in** are used to talk about gaining access to information, especially electronic information, after first passing through an entry system. For example, when you **log in** on a computer, you gain access to the system by keying a special word. Some of these combinations are used in an extended way. For example, you talk about information **going in** when you mean that you have understood it, and you say that you **soak** yourself **in** a subject when you study it intensely. It can also be used to say that you absorb something such as an atmosphere, so if you **drink in** your surroundings, you behave or feel as if you were able to take them into your body.

breathe in	bury in	clock in	come in 6
delve in	draw in 3	drink in	go in 5,8
hammer in	key in	let in 2	log in
pay in	plough in	plug in	plumb in
pump in	punch in	put in 1–4,6,19,20	ram in
set in 2	sink in 1,2,3,4	slip in 1	soak in
stick in 1–5	take in 7,14	tap in	throw in 1,2,3
tuck in 1,2	tune in	type in	

3 Collapsing, damaging, surrendering, and ending

In occurs in combinations which have meanings to do with damage or destruction. For example, if a roof or building **caves in**, it collapses inwards, and if you **kick in** a door, you break it down by kicking it from the outside. **In** also occurs in combinations which express ideas of surrender or defeat. For example, if you **give in**, you accept that you have to do something that you did not want to do. A few combinations with **in** are used to indicate that an activity ends. For example, if you **jack in** your job, you stop doing it.

bash in 1,2	break in 1	cave in 1,2	chuck in
do in 1,2	fall in 1	give in 1	jack in
kick in 1	pack in 2,3	smash in	

4 Mixing and including

In occurs in phrasal verbs which express ideas of two things being combined, so that they form a single substance. For example, if you **stir** a substance **in**, you add it to another substance and mix them together. **In** also occurs in combinations which refer to things being included in a larger group. For example, if someone who is selling several things **throws** an item **in**, they agree to include it in the price of the other things, and if you **reckon** an item **in** when you are calculating something, you include it in your calculations.

Some combinations with **in** are used to say that two or more things seem to belong together. These combinations are sometimes followed by the preposition *with*. For example, if one thing **chimes in with** another, they are consistent with each other.

add in	blend in	build in 1,2	chime in with
chip in 1	copy in	dig in 1	dub in
factor in	fit in 1,2,3	fit in with	fold in
get in 8	include in 1,2	ink in 2	merge in
mix in 1	put in 8	reckon in	rub in 1
rule in	sketch in 1	squeeze in 2	stand in
stir in	take in 8	throw in 4	tie in with
tone in	trade in	work in 1,2,3	write in 2,3

5   Gathering, collecting, and fetching

In is used as an adverb in combinations which have meanings associated with gathering or collecting something, and fetching or taking it somewhere. For example, if you **get in** the washing, you collect it and bring it indoors, and if someone **calls** something **in**, they ask for it to be collected and returned to them. If you collect a lot of things over a period of time, you can also use **in** to talk about accumulating those things, especially money. For example, if you talk about **raking in** money, you are talking in an informal way about earning a lot of money, and if you **lay in** food, you buy it and store it to use later. In also occurs in combinations where you are talking about fetching people and taking them somewhere. For example, if the police **haul** you **in**, they arrest you and take you to the police station. **In** is sometimes used to talk about giving something to a person who has authority for collecting it and dealing with it. For example, if you **hand in** a piece of work, someone collects it from you, and if you **cash** something **in**, you give it to someone in exchange for money.

bring in 2	buy in	call in 3	cash in 1
come in 8,18	gather in	get in 4,5	give in 2
hand in 1,2,3	haul in	lay in	pack in 1,4
pull in 3,4,5	put in 9	rake in	reel in
roll in 1,2	run in 2	send in 1,2	take in 5,11,12
trade in	turn in 2,3,4,5	write in 1	

6   Filling

In is used in a small number of combinations to say that you complete a shape or hole by filling it with something. For example, if you **colour** a shape or outline **in**, you fill the space with a colour, and if you **fill in** a gap in something such as a wall, you put a substance inside it to cover the gap.

block in 2	brick in	colour in	fill in 1,2,3	ink in 1
pencil in	shade in			

7   Remaining somewhere

Some phrasal verbs with **in** mean that someone stays in a particular place, or stays at home, instead of going somewhere else. For example, if you **eat in**, you have your meal at home rather than going to a restaurant for it, and if you **stop in**, you stay at home rather than going out. Some of the combinations in this category are to do with more long-term arrangements. For example, if a servant or student **lives in**, they stay in the same place to work, study, and sleep, rather than going elsewhere for some of these activities. **Out** is sometimes used with the opposite meaning, to indicate that someone goes somewhere to a different place, instead of staying at home.

dig in 2	eat in	keep in 2	lie in	live in 1
repose in 1	sleep in	stay in	stop in 1	take in 3
wait in				

8   Restricting and preventing

In occurs with a number of verbs to say that you keep someone somewhere and do not allow them to get out. For example, if you **lock** someone **in**, you put them somewhere and lock the door so that they cannot escape. Some of these combinations are usually used in the passive. For example, you talk about people being **hemmed in**, **snowed in**, or **walled in**, when they cannot move from a place. **In** is always an adverb with verbs like these. Some of these combinations are used metaphorically to express ideas of repressing or preventing something.

For example, you can say that someone **holds in** a feeling when they do not allow themselves to show it, or that something is **hedged in** by problems when those problems put restrictions on the things that it is possible to do.

block in 1	box in	brick in	buckle in	close in 1,2
crowd in on	fence in	hedge in	hem in 1,2	hold in
keep in 1	lock in	pen in 1,2	rein in	seal in
shut in	snow in	strap in	wall in	

9   Being involved and active

A large number of combinations with **in** express ideas of involvement with activities. For example, if you **count** someone **in**, you include them in an activity or task, and if you say that you **want in**, you mean that you would like to be involved. When **in** is prepositional, the noun group after **in** refers to the activity that people are involved with. For example, if you **dabble in** an activity, you do it occasionally and not seriously. Some of these combinations are followed by the preposition *on*: the noun group after *on* refers to the activity that you are talking about. For example, if you **muscle in** on an activity, you get involved in a situation where you are not wanted. You can also use some combinations in this category to talk about relationships with other people. They are usually used with the preposition *with* in this case. For example, if you **keep in with** someone, you try to become involved with them and the things they are interested in, and if you **fall in with** someone, you start to become friends with them. You can use **in** in a similar way to say that you become accustomed to an activity or situation. For example, if you **break** someone **in**, you help them get used to a new job, and if you **settle in**, you get used to living or working somewhere.

Some combinations with **in** refer to the interruption of an activity. For example, if you **butt in** when someone is talking, you enter the conversation by speaking at the same time as they do. **In** is always adverbial in these combinations. Some of them can be used with the preposition *on*: you mention the person or thing in the noun group after *on*.

barge in	break in 2,3,4,5	break in on	break in upon
bring in 3,4	burst in on	butt in	call in 1
cash in 2	chime in	chip in 2	come in 12,13,15
contract in	count in	cut in 1,2	dabble in
deal in 1,2	dip in	dive in	dob in 2
drag in	draw in 4	engage in	fall in with
fill in 5	get in 6,9	get in on	get in with
go in for 1,2,3	go in with	have in	horn in
interfere in	join in	jump in	keep in with
land in	let in for	let in on	listen in
look in 2	meddle in	mix in	move in 4
muck in	muscle in	opt in	partake in
phone in 1,2,3,4	pitch in	plunge in	push in 1,2
put in 5,7,10,11,13	put in for	ring in	rope in
run in 3	rush in	send in 3,4	settle in
share in	sink in 5	sit in 1,2	start in
step in	stick in 6	take in 4,10	throw in 5
toss in	wade in	walk in on	want in
weigh in 1			

10 Beginning

A few combinations with **in** are used to indicate that an activity begins. For example, if you **lead in**, you begin a discussion by making a short speech, and if a situation **sets in**, it begins to take place.

bring in 1	come in 9,10,14,17,20	creep in	dig in 4
fade in	kick in 2	lead in	phase in
set in 1	tuck in 3	usher in	

11 Focusing: actions, attitudes, and qualities

In also occurs as a preposition in a few combinations where you are talking about actions and attitudes. The noun group after **in** refers to the focus of the action or attitude. For example, if you **glory in** something, you take great pleasure in it, and if you **put** trust or confidence **in** someone, you feel confident or hopeful about something that they are going to do. **In** can be used to indicate that someone or something has a certain quality. For example, if you say that a quality or characteristic **resides in** someone or something, you mean they have it.

believe in 1,2,3	confide in	couch in	delight in	glory in
indulge in	luxuriate in	repose in	reside in	result in
revel in	see in	wallow in		

into is a preposition. It occurs in 118 phrasal verbs in this dictionary. Its basic meanings are to do firstly with movement from the outside of something to the inside, and secondly with change. **Out of** often has opposite meanings.

1 Movement, entering, and arrival

Into is used in literal combinations which express ideas of entering a place. You mention the place in the noun group after **into**. For example, if people **crowd into** a place, they all squeeze in there; if you say that someone **rolls into** a place, you mean that they arrive there very casually; and if you **see** someone **into** a place, you enter it with them.

2 Inserting, penetrating, and placing

Into occurs in combinations which refer to the insertion of one thing inside another, sometimes going through a barrier of some kind. The noun group after **into** refers to the place where it is inserted. For example, if you **plug** an electrical appliance **into** a socket, you insert the plug in the socket, and if you **delve into** a container, you put your hand inside it. Some combinations refer to someone or something being put in a particular place, position, institution, and so on. For example, if you **buckle** someone **into** a seat, you fasten them there, for example with a safety belt, and if you **pay** money **into** a bank account, you transfer it there. Some combinations are used with metaphorical meanings. For example, if you say that someone's eyes **bored into** you, you mean that they stared at you intensely, and if you **drill** something **into** someone, you make them understand or remember it by continually repeating it. A few combinations with **into** are used to talk about gaining access to information, especially electronic information, after first passing through an entry system. For example, if you **log into** a computer, you gain access to the system by typing a special word.

bore into	buckle into	build into 1	delve into	dig into
din into	dip into	dive into 1	drill into	drum into
go into 11	let into 3	log into	pay into	plug into
plumb into	pour into 2	punch into	put into	ram into 2
sink into 3	slip into 2	slot into 2	strap into	take into 3
tap into	throw into	tuck into 1	tune into	

3 Mixing and inclusion

Into occurs in combinations which express ideas of one thing being included as part of another: you mention the second thing in the noun group after **into**. For example, if you **build** something **into** a statement or plan, you include it in your statement or plan, and if you **marry into** a family, you marry a member of that family, and so become a part of it. **Into** is also used to suggest that one thing combines with another thing, often in a way which makes it hard to tell them apart. For example, if one colour **shades into** another, it is so similar to that other colour that it is hard to tell which is which, and if you **mix** one substance **into** another, you put it with the other substance and stir them so that they are blended together. A few combinations with **into** refer to the spending of money or other resources such as time on a particular plan or project. These combinations often imply that large amounts of money or resources are involved, so if you **pump** money **into** a business or organization, you invest large sums of money in it. **Into** is also used in a few combinations which refer to things fitting or belonging to particular categories. For example, if something **fits into** a particular group, it logically belongs to that group.

blend into	bring into 2	build into 2	dissolve into	factor into
fall into 3	fit into	fold into	marry into	melt into 2
merge into	mix into	phase into	plough into	pump into
put into	run into 6	shade into	sink into 5	slot into 1
stir into	work into	write into		

4 Changing

Into occurs in several combinations, which describe processes of change from one form or situation to another. The noun group after **into** refers to the new form or situation. For example, if one thing **turns into** another thing, it becomes that other thing; if something **burst into** flames, it suddenly begins to burn; and if an experience **makes** you **into** a particular type of person, you become that type of person because of that experience. A few of these combinations are used to say that someone starts behaving in a particular way. For example, if someone **bursts into** tears, they suddenly begin crying, and if they **lapse into** silence, they stop talking or making a noise.

break into	burst into	divide into	dub into	fall into
fly into	get into 4	go into 7	grow into	lapse into
launch into	make into	melt into 1	put into 7	roll into 1
settle into	sink into 4	slip into 4	take into 5	throw into 4
turn into				

5 Involvement and activities

Into occurs in combinations which express ideas of starting to be involved with an activity. You mention the activity in the noun group after **into**. For example, if you **enter into** a discussion with someone, you start to have a discussion with them, and if you **head into** a situation, you start to experience it. Some of these combinations express the idea of getting interested in a particular subject, especially in a hurried or enthusiastic way. For example, if you **pitch into** a particular task, you start to do it with a lot of energy; if you **dive into** an activity, you start to be involved without any preparation; and if you **fling** yourself **into** something, you begin to do it energetically and enthusiastically. A few combinations with **into** refer to the interruption of an activity. For example, if you **barge into** a conversation, you enter it by interrupting someone. **Into** also occurs in combinations which refer to the thorough investigation of something. For example, if you **delve into** a matter, you try to discover more information about it.

break into 3	buy into	delve into 2	dive into 2	enter into
fling into	get into	go into 6	head into	inquire into
look into	move into 3	pitch into 1	plunge into	push into 2
rush into	take into 5	throw into 5	wade into	walk into 1

6   Persuasion and forcing

Into occurs in combinations with transitive verbs which have the meaning of persuading or forcing someone to become involved in an activity. You mention the activity in the noun group after **into**. For example, if you **frighten** someone **into** doing something, you frighten them in order to force them to do that thing, and if you **trick** them **into** it, you get them to do it by fooling or misleading them.

bluff into	coax into	drag into	draw into	force into
frighten into	goad into	press into	pull into 2	push into 1
shame into	shock into	starve into	sucker into	talk into
trap into	trick into			

7   Contact, colliding, meeting, and attacking

Into occurs in combinations which refer to contact, and mean 'collide', 'meet', or 'attack'. The noun group after **into** refers to the person or thing that you collide with, meet, or attack. Some of these combinations suggest that the collision is fairly violent, so that if one vehicle **ploughs into** another one, it hits it forcefully, and if you **ram** one object **into** another, you move it so that it hits the other thing very hard. Some of the combinations simply mean that you meet something or someone, perhaps by chance. For example, if you **bump into** someone, you meet them unexpectedly. A few combinations are used to say that one person is attacking another person, either physically or by shouting at them and criticizing them. For example, if someone **tears into** you, they criticize you very severely, and if someone **lays into** you, they start to hit or kick you.

bang into	barge into 3	bump into	go into 13	lam into
lash into	lay into	pitch into 2	plough into 1	ram into
rip into	run into	tear into		

8   Consumption and using

Into occurs in combinations which mean 'consume' or 'use'. The noun group after **into** refers to the thing which is consumed or used. Some of these combinations suggest that you are doing so for the first time. For example, if you **break into** a sum of money that you have saved, you start to spend it, and if you **tuck into** food, you start to eat it. Other combinations refer to processes of destruction and damaging. For example, if one thing **bites into** another, it presses its surface and damages it, and if clothing **eats into** your body, it is too tight and causes you pain.

bite into	break into 5	cut into	dip into	eat into
lay into 3	tuck into 2			

of is a prepositional particle. **Of** is one of the commonest words of English, and it is mainly used with nouns in order to introduce and specify relationships of belonging, possession, or connection. It also has many general uses such as stating what something is, what it contains, what it is made from, or how much of it there is.

Of occurs in 30 phrasal verbs in this dictionary. Some of its meanings occur in very few combinations, most of which are old-fashioned or formal. For example, **admit of** and **permit of** can be used when talking about the range of possibilities in a situation; and **become of** and **come of** can be used when referring to the final result of a situation. **Of** has four main uses in phrasal verbs.

1 Knowledge and its communication

Of is used in some phrasal verbs to introduce the fact, knowledge, or piece of information that is being received or given. For example, if you **hear of** someone or something, you get news about them for the first time. If you **apprise** someone **of** something, you inform them about it, and if you **remind** them **of** it, you tell them about it so that they remember it.

apprise of	deliver of 1	hear of	know of	make of
remind of 1	think of			

2 Attributing qualities

Some phrasal verbs with **of** are used to state or claim that people or things have a particular quality or characteristic. For example, if something **partakes of** a particular quality, it has that quality, and if someone or something **reminds** you **of** another, they make you think of the other person or thing, because they are similar in some way.

partake of 2	reek of	remind of 2	savour of	smack of
smell of				

3 Evaluation, approval, and disapproval

In some phrasal verbs with **of**, the meaning involves making a judgement about something and expressing an attitude based on that judgement. For example, if you **approve of** someone or something, you like and admire them, and if you **tire of** something, you lose interest in it.

approve of	despair of	disapprove of	dream of 1	tire of
weary of				

4 Removal and elimination

You use **of** in a number of phrasal verbs with the meaning that something is removed from a person or situation, or is dealt with so that it does not remain or continue to have an effect. For example, if you **deprive** someone **of** something, you take it away from them or prevent them from having it.

deprive of	disabuse of	dispose of	divest of	partake of 1
relieve of	rid of	starve of	strip of	

off is an adverb and a preposition. It occurs in 240 phrasal verbs in this dictionary. The basic meaning of **off** is to do with movement away from something or separation from it. **On** sometimes has opposite meanings to **off**.

1 Departure

Literal verb combinations with **off** as an adverb or preposition often give an idea of departure. For example, when a rocket **blasts off**, it leaves the ground and starts its journey into space, and if you **get off** a bus, you leave it. When **off** is an adverb, **away** often has a similar meaning. With transitive verbs, **off** indicates that someone or something is being sent to another place. For example, if you **pack** someone **off** somewhere, you send them there.

Some combinations emphasize the manner of departure, for example casualness or even secrecy is implied in **slip off** and **slope off**. Several combinations are used as imperatives to tell someone in a rude way to go away, for example **clear off** and **bog off**. A few verbs in combination with **off** indicate that something such as heat or a smell is being released. For example, something might **give off** light or smoke, or **let off** a sound or energy. **Out** often has a similar meaning.

back off 1	blast off	bog off	bug off
bugger off 1,2	bundle off	bunk off	buzz off
cart off	clear off	come off 1,6	dash off 1
drop off 2	fire off 1	fuck off	get off 1–6
give off 1	go off 1	go off with 1,2	hare off
haul off	head off 3	lead off 1	let off 4,5,6
lift off	make off	move off	naff off
pack off	peel off 4	piss off 1	pop off 1,2
push off 1,2,3	put off 6	run off 1,2,3,4,6	see off 1,2
send off 1–5	set off 1	shoot off 1	shove off
slip off 1	slope off	sod off	spirit off
start off 1	storm off	strike off 2	take off 4,5,6,7
tear off 3	throw off 3	trot off	turn off 2
veer off	wave off 1,2	write off 1	zoom off

2 Removing and disposing

Off as an adverb or preposition in literal combinations often implies removing or disposing of something that you no longer need or want. For example, if you **take** your shoes **off**, you remove them, and if you **score off** an item from a list, you remove it from the list. **Off** can also be used in combinations such as **make off with** which implies stealing. In relation to people, **off** can imply removing them from your area of responsibility, so that if you **marry** your daughter or son **off**, you find a suitable person for them to marry, and if someone **is pensioned off**, their employers or the government make them retire from work. In a few combinations referring to people, **off** can mean 'kill', so if a person **knocks** somebody **off**, they kill them.

auction off	blow off 1,2	break off 1	bump off	burn off
cast off 1,2,3	check off	chip off	chop off	come off 2
cream off	cross off	cut off 1	draw off	dust off 1
ease off 2	fall off 1	finish off 5	fling off	get off 9
hack off 1	help off with	hive off	kick off 1,4	kill off
kiss off 2	knock off 1,4,5,7	leave off 1,2	lop off 1	make off with
mark off 3	marry off	pare off	pay off 3	peel off 1,2,3
pension off 1	pick off 1,2	pour off	put off 7	round off 2
rub off 1	run off 7	run off with	saw off	score off 2
scrape off	scrub off	sell off	shave off 1,2	shear off
shoot off 2	siphon off 1,2	skim off	slip off 2,3	slough off 1,2
soak off	steam off	strain off	strike off 1	strip off 1,2
sweat off 1,2	take off 1,2,3,8	tear off 1,2	throw off 1,2	tick off 1,2
trim off	walk off with 1	wash off 1,2	wipe off 1	

3 Obstructing and separating

In several phrasal verbs with **off**, the verb indicates a type of barrier, and the combination has the meaning of obstructing, blocking, or separating. For example, if the police **cone off** a lane of a motorway, they place plastic cones on the road so that people cannot drive on that lane, and if you **partition off** part of a room, you build a partition wall to separate that part of the room. Sometimes, the verb itself conveys the sense of obstruction or separation, as in **close off** and **split off**.

block off	box off	branch off 1	brick off	close off
cone off	cordon off	curtain off	cut off 2	divide off
fence off	go off 6	head off 1	mark off 1	partition off
rope off	rule off	screen off	seal off 1,2	section off
separate off	shut off 3	spin off	split off 1,2	wall off

4 **Rejecting**

Some combinations with **off** have the meaning of rejection. Sometimes they refer to abandoning a particular habit or thing, so if you **swear off** alcohol, you decide to stop drinking it completely. Other combinations imply that you are ignoring something. For example, if you **shrug off** or **brush off** what somebody says, you ignore it.

brush off 1,2,3	fend off 2	keep off 3,4	laugh off	lay off 1,3
pass off 2	put off 1	shake off	shrug off	shuffle off
shut off 4	swear off	wipe off 2	write off 2,3	

5 **Preventing and protecting**

Verb combinations with **off** often indicate that you are doing something to protect yourself or to prevent something from happening. For example, if you **ward off** something unpleasant or dangerous, you prevent it from affecting you or harming you, and if you **pay** someone **off**, you give them money in order to stop them threatening you or causing you trouble.

beat off	buy off	chase off	drive off	fend off 1
fight off	get off 8	head off 2	hold off 1,2	keep off 1,2
pay off 2	put off 2,3,4	scare off 1,2	stand off	stave off
throw off 4	ward off 1,2	warn off		

6 **Beginning**

You can use **off** to imply starting to do something, so if a discussion **kicks off**, it starts. Combinations with transitive verbs convey a sense of causing something to begin. For example, if something **sparks off** an argument, it causes the argument to start.

cop off with	get off with	kick off 2,3	lead off 2,3	set off 2,4
spark off	start off 2,3,4	tee off 1	touch off	trigger off

7 **Stopping and cancelling**

By contrast, phrasal verbs with **off** can also imply the ending of something, for example if you **knock off** work, you stop working and if someone's voice **trails off**, it gradually stops. Sometimes the verb conveys the reason why something has stopped, so if an event **is rained off**, it stops or is cancelled because of the rain.

back off 2	beg off	blow off 3,5	break off 2,3,4
call off 1,2	clock off	come off 5,7	cry off
cut off 3,4,5	get off 7,11	give off 3	go off 4,8,9
hoot off	knock off 3,10	lay off 2	leave off 3,4,5
let off 1	log off	pension off 2	put off 5
rain off	ring off	shut off 1,2	sign off 1,2,3
stay off	stop off	switch off 1,2,3,4	take off 9,12,13,14
trail off	turn off 1,3,4	write off 5	

8   Decreasing

Off is frequently used to show that something decreases. For example, if a feeling **passes off** or **eases off**, it decreases. **Off** sometimes combines with verbs formed from adjectives to indicate that something gradually has less of a quality. So if a hot object **cools off**, it loses heat and becomes cooler, and if a wet object **dries off**, it loses some of its moisture and becomes drier. Some combinations, such as **sleep off** and **work off**, refer to an activity which you do in order to reduce the effect of something unpleasant.

cool off 1,2	die off	drop off 3	dry off	ease off 1
fall off 2	get off 12	knock off 2	let off 2	level off 1,3
lop off 2	pass off 3	set off against	slack off 1	slacken off
sleep off	tail off 1,2	take off 10	taper off	walk off
wear off	work off 1			

9   Finishing and completing

People often use **off** to indicate that an activity or process is completed. For example, if you **polish off** a piece of work, you finish it, and if an event **passes off** in a particular way, it happens and ends that way.

bring off	carry off 1,2	come off 3,4	dash off 2	finish off 1,2,3
go off 5	knock off 6	pass off 1	pay off 1	play off
polish off	print off	rattle off	reel off	round off 1
run off 5	see off 3	sign off 4	top off	toss off 2
work off 2	write off 4			

10   Consuming

Phrasal verbs with **off** as a preposition sometimes indicate that something is being consumed or used. For example, if someone **lives off** a particular kind of food, they eat only that kind of food, and if a machine **runs off** a particular supply of power, it uses that power in order to make it work. You can also use some of these verbs in a pejorative way. For example, if you say that a person is **sponging off** someone, it means that the person is taking advantage of their generosity. **On** can often be used with a similar meaning.

dine off	feed off	live off 2	run off 8
sponge off	toss off 1	work off 3	

11   Falling asleep

There are a few phrasal verbs with **off** which refer to falling asleep. For example, if you **doze off** or **nod off**, you fall asleep.

doze off	drift off	drop off 1
get off 14	go off 10	nod off

12   Displaying

Verb combinations with **off** occasionally have a sense of putting on some sort of display, so if an object is **set off** by its background, the object is displayed more favourably because of its background, and if someone is **showing off** they are generally putting on some sort of display to try to impress people.

finish off	mouth off	set off 5	show off 1,2,3 sound off

13 Deceiving

Off sometimes occurs in phrasal verbs relating to deceiving or tricking. For example, if someone **fobs** something **off** on you, they deceive you into thinking it is worth having.

fob off	goof off	palm off	pass off as	play off against
rip off	skive off	throw off 5		

14 Exploding and firing

There is a small set of combinations with **off** which indicate that a weapon or an explosive device or material is fired or explodes. For example, if you **let off** a gun, a bomb, or a firework, you fire it or cause it to explode.

fire off 1	go off 2	let off 3	loose off	set off 3

on is an adverb and a preposition. It occurs in 208 phrasal verbs in this dictionary. The basic meaning of **on** is to do with position, indicating that one thing is above another, touching it and supported by it, or with movement into that position. **Onto** or **on to** is sometimes used instead of **on** as a preposition, and **upon** is a more formal alternative in some combinations. **Off** sometimes has opposite meanings to **on**.

1 Movement and position

On occurs in some literal combinations which refer to movement and position. For example, if you **get on** a bus, you get into it. Many of these combinations have extended meanings. For example, if an actor **walks on** in a play, he or she has a very unimportant part in it, and if someone is **sitting on** a task, they are not doing it quickly enough. To **look on** means to watch something, but with the added sense of not taking part in it. **Off** sometimes has opposite meanings.

call on 1	come on 2,3	come on to 1	descend on	fall on 5
get on 1,2	go on 16	look on 1	pile on 1	put on 1
put on to 2	sit on 2	stamp on 1	take on 5	throw on 2
trample on 1	wait on 3	walk on		

2 Holding, attaching, and adding

On is used in literal combinations which have 'hold', 'attach', or 'add' as part of their meaning. For example, if you **hang on**, you hold very tightly to something; if you **buckle** something **on**, you attach it by means of buckles, and if you **slap** paint **on**, you paint a surface carelessly. **On** also occurs in combinations which refer to dressing. For example, when you **put on** your clothes, you get dressed in them.

Off sometimes has opposite meanings, although often in combination with different verbs. For example, **put on** and **take off** have opposite meanings.

add on	buckle on	dab on	fall on 3
get on 4	go on 14	hang on 1,3	have on 1
help on with	hold on 1,3	hold on to 1,2,3,5	latch on to 1,3
move on 4	pile on 2	pop on	pull on 1,2
put on 2,3,4,7,14,20,22	put on to 1	sew on	slap on
slip on	stick on 1,2	strap on	tack on
tag on	throw on 1	throw on to	try on 1

3 Continuing

On is used in combinations which describe activities in order to say that an activity is continued or that it lasts for a long time. For example, if you **carry on** with an activity, you continue doing it, and if you **struggle on** with it, you manage to continue doing it with great difficulty. Some combinations imply that the activity continues for an unacceptably long time. For example, if you say that someone **drones on**, you mean that they talk in a boring way for a long time, and if a process **drags on**, it continues for longer than necessary.

On is also used with verbs of movement, to indicate that a journey or movement continues. For example, if you **push on**, you continue travelling somewhere. **On** is used with transitive verbs in combinations such as **hand on** and **pass on** to indicate that something is given from one person to another, and so refers to a continuity of ownership.

bang on	bash on	carry on 1–5	drag on
dream on	drone on	get on 5,8	get on at
go on 1–9	grind on	hand on	hang on 5
harp on	hold on 2	hold on to 4,6	hurry on 1,2
keep on 1,2,3	keep on at	linger on	live on 3
move on 1,6	pass on 1,2,3,5,7	play on 3,4	plod on
plough on	press on 1,2	push on 1,2,3	rabbit on
ramble on	rattle on	roll on 1	rumble on
run on 1,2,3,4	sell on 1	send on	soldier on
stay on	struggle on	tick on 1,2	wave on
wear on			

4 Progressing and encouraging

On is used in combinations which have progress as part of their meaning. For example, if something is **coming on**, it is making progress or developing, and if people's ideas **move on**, they change and become more modern. A few combinations are used to indicate progress in time. For example, when winter or night **draws on**, it approaches. **On** also occurs in combinations which mean 'encourage'. For example, if you **egg** someone **on**, you encourage them to do something foolish.

bring on 2	cheer on	come on 1,10	crack on	draw on 1
egg on	get on 6,7,12	get on for	go on 10,18	goad on
lead on	lead on to 1	move on 3,5	spur on	step on
urge on 1	wind on			

5 Beginning and operating

On is used in combinations which express ideas of beginning or starting. For example, if something **brings on** an illness, it causes it to occur. Some combinations such as **move on to** and **get on to** indicate a change of topic in a conversation. **On** also occurs in combinations which refer to the operating of a machine or device. For example, when you **switch on** an electric light, you cause it to start shining, and if you **jam on** your brakes, you use them suddenly. **Off** is sometimes used with the opposite meaning, to indicate that something ceases to function.

bring on 1	cast on	catch on 1,2	clock on
come on 4,6,7,8,9	come on to 2,3	cotton on	embark on 1
enter on	get on 5	get on to 1	go on 13,17
grow on	have on 2	jam on	latch on to 2
log on	move on 2	move on to	pass on 6
put on 8,9,10,11	set on 3	sign on 1,2	start on 1
switch on 1,2,3	turn on 1,2,3		

6   Focusing: effects, actions, and feelings

On is used as a preposition in combinations which describe effects, actions, and feelings. **On** has a very general meaning or use in these combinations. Sometimes it appears to be a metaphorical use of the literal meanings of **on** to do with movement, position, or attachment, but in many cases, it has very little special meaning at all, and simply introduces a noun group which refers to the focus of the action described by the verb. This category of **on** includes a large number of combinations, and some of them are quite closely related to each other. Categories 7 to 10 of **on** are more specialized, and deal with particular groups of combinations, although **on** still has the same general meaning.

The noun group following **on** refers to the person or thing that is affected, or that the action or feeling is directed towards. For example, if you **prevail on** someone to do something, you persuade them to do it; if you **cheat on** someone, you behave dishonestly towards them; and if you **dote on** someone, you love them very much. A number of the combinations refer to actions such as giving, transferring, or aiming: after **on** you mention the person that something is given or transferred to, or the target that something is aimed at. For example, if you **lavish** money **on** someone, you spend a lot of money on them, and if someone **trains** a weapon **on** you, they aim it at you. **Upon** can be substituted for **on** in many of these combinations.

bring on 3	cheat on	dawn on	devolve on
dote on	engage on	fall on 1	fasten on 1
foist on	force on	frown on	gain on
get on 10	grass on	heap on	impress on 1,3
improve on	inform on	lavish on	lean on 1
look on 2	operate on	pin on 1	play on 1,2
pounce on 2	pour on	press on 3	prevail on
pull on 3	put on 15,17,18,21,23	put on to 3	rat on
rebound on	seize on	sell on 2	serve on 1,2
sit on 1	skimp on	split on	spring on 1
spy on	squeal on	stamp on 3	stick on 3
tell on 1,2	throw on 3,5	train on	turn on 7
urge on 2	wait on 1,2	weigh on	wish on
work on 3			

7   Attacking

On is used as a preposition in combinations which express ideas of attacking, either physically or, more often, by means of words. The verb is usually intransitive, and the noun group after **on** refers to the person or thing being attacked. For example, if an animal **turns on** you, it suddenly attacks you, and if you **round on** someone who has been criticizing you, you suddenly respond angrily. **Upon** can be substituted for **on** in some of these combinations.

beat on	dump on	fall on 4	jump on	lay on
pick on 1	pounce on 1	prey on 1,2	round on	set on 1,2
spring on 2	start on 2	trample on 2	turn on 4	

8   Closeness, interference, and connections

On is used as a preposition in combinations with intransitive verbs which express ideas of closeness and connection between two things. The noun group after **on** refers to one of the things, and the other is mentioned as the subject of the verb. Sometimes the two things are physically close. For example, if one country **borders on** another, the two countries are next to each other. In other cases, the connection is non-physical, and the combination implies interference or relevance. For example, if something **intrudes on** your way of life, it affects it in an unpleasant way, and if something such as a fact **bears on** a situation or matter, it is relevant to it. **Upon** can be substituted for **on** in some of these combinations.

bear on	border on 1,2	close on	encroach on 1,2
fasten on 2	impinge on	impose on	impress on 2
infringe on	intrude on	prey on 3	verge on

9 Discovering

On is used as a preposition in a few combinations which have 'find' as part of their meaning. The noun group after **on** refers to the thing which you find. For example if you **stumble on** something, you find it unexpectedly, and if you **hit on** the solution to a problem, you find or think of the solution. **Upon** can be substituted for **on** in some of these combinations, and **across** has a similar meaning.

chance on	come on 5	happen on	hit on 1	light on
strike on	stumble on			

10 Subjects and topics

On occurs as a preposition in combinations which refer to processes of mentioning, stating, deciding, thinking, and so on. The noun group after **on** refers to the subject or topic about which you are talking, deciding, or thinking. For example, if you **pronounce on** something, you give an expert opinion or judgement about it; if you **touch on** a subject, you mention it briefly; and if you **chew on** a problem, you think about it carefully for a long time. **Upon** can be substituted for **on** in some of these combinations.

bleat on about	brood on	centre on	chew on	decide on
discourse on	dwell on	elaborate on	embroider on	enlarge on
expand on	fix on	insist on	pronounce on	reflect on
remark on	settle on 1	sleep on	throw on 4	touch on
turn on 6				

11 Depending and expecting

On is used as a preposition in combination with verbs which express ideas of depending and expecting. The noun group which follows **on** refers to the thing which you expect or need. For example, if you **count on** something happening, you expect it to happen and include this in your plans, and if one thing **hinges on** another, the existence of the first depends entirely on the second. **Upon** can be substituted for **on** in some of these combinations.

bank on	bargain on	bet on 1,2	call on 2,3
count on 1,2	depend on 1,2,3	figure on	gamble on
hang on 2	hinge on	lean on 2	pin on 2
pivot on	plan on 1,2	put on 12,13,16	reckon on
rely on 1,2	stake on	turn on 5	wait on 4
work on 2			

12 Using

On is used as a preposition in combination with verbs which express ideas of use or basis. The noun group which follows **on** refers to the thing which you make use of or which forms the basis for something else. For example, if you **draw on** a particular thing, you make use of it in order to do something, and if something is **based on** a particular thing, it takes its general form or nature from that thing. **Upon** can be substituted for **on** in some of these combinations.

act on	base on	build on 1,2	draw on 2,3	model on
pattern on	trade on			

13 Consuming

On occurs as a preposition in combinations where you are saying that someone eats a particular thing, or that they make use of a particular thing or person. You mention the food or source in the noun group after **on**. For example, if you **dine on** a particular food, you eat it, and if you **batten on** someone, you make use of them in order to become successful or live comfortably, and so on. Similarly, if a machine or device **runs on** a particular fuel or type of power, it uses that fuel or power in order to function. Some of these verbs can be used with **off** instead of **on**, with almost the same meaning.

batten on	dine on	feed on
live on 2	run on 5	sponge on

onto is a preposition. It can also be written as **on to**. It occurs in 12 phrasal verbs in this dictionary. In addition, it is often used instead of the preposition **on**, when on refers to movement and position, or to actions such as holding and attaching. For example, you can say that someone **put** something **on** a surface or **onto** a surface. By choosing **onto** instead of **on**, you make the action seem more deliberate or precise. These uses of **onto** in phrasal verbs are mostly dealt with in the entries for phrasal verbs with **on**, and the Extra Column indicates it by showing patterns such as ALSO + *to* or USUALLY + *to*. **Onto** has the following meanings when it occurs in phrasal verb headwords.

1 Movement and holding

Onto or **on to** occurs in combinations which mean 'move' or 'hold': these combinations are both literal and non-literal. For example, **come onto** can refer to physical movement, or you can talk about **coming onto** a new topic in a conversation. Similarly, **hang onto** can mean 'hold something tightly in your hand' or 'keep and not lose or give away'. **Get onto** and **put onto** are also used to express ideas of contacting someone. For example, if you **get onto** someone, you contact them.

come onto	get onto	hang onto
hold onto	latch onto	move onto
push onto	put onto	throw onto

2 Direction

Onto occurs in a few combinations which indicate the direction in which a building, room, or other place faces or leads. For example, if one room **opens onto** another, you can go straight from one to the other.

back onto	give onto	open onto

out is an adverb. It occurs in 446 phrasal verbs in this dictionary. The basic meaning of **out** is to do with movement from the inside of an enclosed space or container to the outside of it. **In** often has opposite meanings.

In some varieties of English such as American English, and also in non-standard British English, **out** can also be used as a preposition with verbs of movement. So in American English you can say 'He went out the room', but in standard British English you need to add the preposition *of* and say 'He went out of the room'.

1 Leaving

You use **out** in literal combinations to indicate movement from the inside of somewhere to the outside. For example, if you are inside a house or room and **come out**, you move so that you are outside it; if you **bail out** of an aeroplane, you jump from it into the air with a parachute; if you say that people **spill out** of a place, you mean that large numbers of them come from it in a hurried or disorganized way; and if you **break out** of prison, you escape from it. Some combinations emphasize the sense of leaving a place and going somewhere else. This may involve travelling. For example, if you **set out**, you start a journey. Other combinations express the idea of leaving a place of work or a work activity. For example, when workers **punch out**, they record the time that they leave a factory or office, and if you **log out**, you finish using a computer by keying a special word. **In** and **into** often have opposite meanings.

back out 2	bail out 3	break out 1,3	breeze out	bug out 2
bust out of	buy out 2	check out 1,5	clear out 1	clock out
come out 1,4	draw out 1	fall out 4	fly out	get out 1,10
go out 1,7,14	let out 1	light out	log out	move out 2,3
pile out	pop out 2	pour out 3	pull out 1,2	punch out 2
put out 16	run out 1,6	sally out	see out 1	set out 1
ship out	shoot out 1	show out	sign out 1	slip out 1
spill out 2	start out 1,2	step out 1	storm out	strike out 2
want out 2				

2 **Removing, excluding, and preventing**

Out occurs in a large number of combinations which mean 'remove', 'get rid of', or 'force to leave a place'. The verbs in these combinations are mainly transitive. For example, if you **squeeze out** liquid or air from a container, you remove it by squeezing the container; when you **throw** things **out**, you get rid of things that you no longer need or want; and if you **root out** someone from an organization, you force them to leave the organization. Other combinations express ideas of preventing something from being seen or heard. For example, if an object **cuts out** the light, it prevents light from reaching a place, and if a part of a photograph is **masked out**, it is covered so that it is not printed. Some combinations express ideas of avoiding becoming involved or of preventing people from becoming involved in a situation. For example, if you **get out of** doing something, you avoid doing it; if you **freeze** someone **out** of an activity or situation, you prevent them from being involved; and if the management of a factory **locks out** the workers, they close the factory and prevent the workers from entering and working during an industrial dispute. Some other combinations indicate that someone or something is considered and perhaps accepted or admitted for a while, but is then rejected. For example, if you **rule out** an idea, solution, or course of action, you decide that it is impossible or unsuitable.

argue out of	bail out 4	black out 3,4,5	block out 1,2,3,4
blot out 1,2,3	boot out	breathe out	buy out 1
call out 3	cancel out	cast out	chuck out 1,2
close out	come out 6,8,15	contract out 1,2	count out 2,3
cross out	crowd out	cut out 1,2,4,5,6	do out of
drive out	drown out	drum out	edit out
empty out	fall out 1,2	filter out	flood out
flush out	freeze out	frighten out of	get out 2,5,6
get out of 2	go out 13	gut out	have out 1
hound out	include out	keep out 1,2	keep out of 1,2
kick out	knock out 2,7	leave out 1	let out 2,7
lock out 1,2,3	mask out	miss out 1,2	miss out on
muscle out	nose out 2	opt out	paint out
pull out 5	pump out 1,2	push out 1,2	put out 14
root out	rout out	rub out 1,2	rule out 1,2
run out 2	run out of	score out	scrape out
scratch out	shut out	slip out 3	smoke out 1
spit out 1	squeeze out 1,3	starve out	stay out of 1,2
strike out 4	strip out 1	sweat out 2	take out 1,2
talk out of	tear out	thin out	throw out 1–5
turf out 1,2	turn out 5,6	vote out	walk out 1,2
want out 1	wash out 3	weed out	wriggle out of
write out 3	x out		

3 **Searching, finding, and obtaining**

Out occurs in combinations which mean 'search', 'find', or 'obtain'. Some combinations contain an idea of removal. For example, if you **dig** something **out**, you find it and get it out of a place where it is hidden or stored, and if you **fish** something **out**, you pull it out of a liquid or a container. Other combinations are metaphorical, and refer to the obtaining of information. For example, if you **ferret out** information, you discover it after a thorough search, and if you **worm** information **out** of someone, you find it out by constantly asking them about it.

check out 2,3,4	dig out	drag out 2	draw out 4	eke out 2
fathom out	feel out	ferret out	figure out	find out 1,2
fish out 1	get out of 3	hunt out	iron out	look out 2
make out 1,2	nose out 1	pick out 1	piece out	prise out
pry out	pump out of	puzzle out	scout out	screw out of
search out	seek out	smell out 1,2	smoke out 2	sniff out
sort out 3	sound out 1	spit out 3	spy out	squeeze out 2
stake out 3	suss out 1,2	take out 5,6	try out	try out for
turn out 3	winkle out	winnow out	work out 1,3,4,5	worm out
wring out 2				

4 **Appearing**

Out also occurs in combinations which refer to the way something suddenly happens or appears. Many of these combinations contain an idea of something having been hidden or unseen, and then being revealed. For example, if something that you could not see **pops out**, it suddenly appears; if you **come out** in spots or rashes, they appear all over your body; and when a baby bird **hatches out**, it comes out of an egg by breaking the shell. Some of these combinations simply refer to how clearly something is seen. For example, if something **sticks out** or **stands out**, you can see it clearly.

break out 5	bring out 2,3	burst out 3	come out 9,10,16,19
come out in	get out 9	hatch out	jump out at
jut out 1,2	lean out	leap out	leap out at
let out 4	mark out 2	pick out 3,4	poke out 1,2
pop out 1	slip out 2	stand out 1,2	stick out 3
whip out			

5 **Locations outside and away from home**

Some phrasal verbs with **out** mean that someone does not remain in a place or remain at home, but goes somewhere else. For example, if you **eat out**, you have a meal at a restaurant rather than at home. Some of the combinations indicate that the activity takes place out of doors, as in **sleep out** and **camp out**. Metaphorical uses indicate that the activity itself is unusual, different, or new for the person or group involved. For example, if you **branch out**, you do something different from your normal activities or work, and if someone **marries out**, they marry someone of a different religion to them.

ask out	bed out	board out	branch out
break out	camp out	come out 2,3	dine out
eat out 1	get out 4	go out 2,3,4	hang out 2
hide out	invite out	marry out	move out 1
put out 6,10	sit out 1	sleep out	stay out 1,2
step out 2	stop out	strike out 1	take out 3,8
turn out 8			

6 Producing and creating

A number of phrasal verbs with **out** have the meaning of producing or emitting sounds, smells, light, heat, and so on. For example, when a radio or CD-player **blares out** noise or music, it produces loud noise or music, and if a machine **sends out** sound or light, it causes them to travel in a particular direction. Other combinations such as **ooze out** and **leak out** refer to liquids, gases, and so on being produced, leaked, or appearing. Some combinations relate specifically to the production of sounds or speech by a human voice. For example, if you **yell out**, you shout loudly, and if you **blurt** something **out**, you say it suddenly without thinking about it. You can also use **out** in combinations such as **churn out** and **turn out** that refer to producing things quickly and in large quantities.

act out 1,2	bang out 1,2	bark out	bash out
bawl out 1,2	beat out 1	belt out	blare out
blast out	blow out 5,8	blurt out	boom out
break out 2	bring out 1,5	burst out 1,2	call out 1
churn out	clap out 1	come out 5,12,14	come out with
crank out	crash out 1	cry out	fling out
get out 7,8	give out 4,5,6	go out 6,8	grind out 1
jerk out	knock out 4	lay out 2	leak out
let out 3	ooze out	peal out	pick out 5
play out 1,2,3	pour out 2	pump out 3,4	punch out 1
push out 3	put out 1,2,19–22	rap out	read out 1
ring out	roll out	rough out	rush out
send out 2,3	set out 3	shine out	shout out
sing out 1,2	sketch out 1,2	snap out	sob out
sound out 2	speak out	spell out 1,2	spew out
spill out 1,3	spit out 2	spout out	spurt out
stammer out	stamp out 3	tap out	throw out 6,7
thump out 1,2	toss out	trot out	turn out 7
yell out			

7 Increasing size, shape, or extent

You use **out** in phrasal verbs which indicate that something increases in physical size or extent. For example, if a thin person **fills out**, they become fatter, and if you **pad out** writing, you include unnecessary words or information in it. Often, **out** just emphasizes the action described by the verb, rather than changing its meaning, so that if something **spreads out**, it spreads and covers a wider area than before. Some combinations suggest that something is or becomes longer or more stretched, such as **stringing out** things. The increase is sometimes in terms of time rather than space. For example, if you **drag** something **out**, you make it last for longer than is necessary. Some combinations have the sense of changing the shape of something by cutting or scraping part of it away from the rest, in order to create a hole or a new shape, as in **carve out** and **hollow out**. **Out** also occurs in combinations which refer to something protruding or being held towards you, or to something being extended in a straight line. For example, if you **hold out** your hand, you stretch it in a straight line in front of you.

belly out	broaden out 1,2	bulk out	carve out 1,2
drag out 1	draw out 2,3,6	eke out 1	fan out 1,2
fill out 2	flare out	flesh out	fluff out
gouge out	grow out of 2	hew out	hold out 1,2
hollow out	let out 6	open out 1–5	pad out
pay out 3	plump out	puff out 1	put out 8,9
reach out	run out 8	scoop out	shake out
shoot out 2	spin out	sprawl out	spread out 1–4,6
stick out 1,2	straighten out 1	stretch out 1,2	string out
throw out 8	zoom out		

8 **Thoroughness and completeness**

You use **out** in combinations with verbs which describe activities in order to indicate that the activity is done thoroughly or completely. For example, when you **argue out** an idea or plan, you discuss in detail all its aspects; if you **type out** a piece of work, you produce a complete copy of it on a typewriter; and if you **scrub out** a place, you clean it very thoroughly. Some of the combinations involve verbs that are also adjectives, such as **clean out**, **dry out**, and **thin out**, which mean to become or make very clean, dry, or thin. Some phrasal verbs with **out** refer to the situation at the end of an activity. For example, if things **balance out**, they are equal in amount or value, after a period of time or when they have been added up, and if a situation, arrangement, or plan **works out**, it is successful.

argue out	average out	average out at	balance out
bliss out	bottom out	brush out	carry out 1,2
clean out 1,2	clear out 2	comb out	come out 11,18
come out of	copy out	deck out	do out
dry out 1,2	even out	fill out 1	fit out
flatten out 1,2	follow out	go out 5	hammer out
have out 2	hear out	hose out	kit out
lay out 4	level out	live out 2	make out 7
make out with	map out	muck out	multiply out
pack out	pan out	plan out	plot out
print out	reach out for	read out 2	rig out
rinse out 1,2,3	scrub out	set out 2	slop out
smooth out 1,3	stake out 2	start out	swab out
sweep out	talk out 1	thaw out 1,2	think out
thrash out	tidy out	tog out	trace out
trick out	turn out 1,9	type out	wash out 1,2
wipe out 1	work out 2,6,7,11	wring out 1	write out 1,2

9 **Duration and resisting**

Out is used in phrasal verbs to indicate that people or things do an activity or continue to exist until the activity is completed, until a period of time is over, or until an aim is achieved, even though this may be difficult. For example, if you **hold out**, you manage to resist an enemy, opponent, or attack, and if a supply of something **lasts out**, there is enough of it for as long as it is needed or for a particular period of time.

brave out	brazen out	face out	hold out 3,4,5
hold out for	hold out on	last out 1,2	live out 1
make out 8	mark out 3	ride out	see out 2,3
sit out 2,3	stand out against	stand out for	stare out
stick out 4	stick out for	sweat out 1	tough out
wait out	win out	work out 8,9	

10 **Ending or disappearing**

Out occurs in combinations with verbs which refer to activities in order to indicate that the activity ends completely. Some combinations indicate that an activity cannot continue any longer, because all the things or people involved have been used up or destroyed. For example, if a shop **is sold out** of something, it has all been sold, and if a fire **burns out**, it stops burning because there is nothing left to burn. Other combinations indicate that an activity ceases gradually, as in **peter out**, or is stopped abruptly or violently, as in **stamp out**. Some combinations indicate that the activity ceases prematurely because the person involved withdraws or refuses to continue, as in **back out** and **chicken out**. Other combinations indicate that the activity ceases because the person doing it is too tired to continue. These combinations are often passive. For example, if you **are played out**, you are exhausted and feel unable to do anything. A few combinations with **out** refer to falling asleep or losing consciousness, as in **pass out** and **black out**.

back out 1	beat out 2	black out 1	blow out 1,2,4,6
bomb out	bottle out	bow out	bowl out
burn out 1,2,3	butt out	chicken out	clap out 2
come out 13,17	conk out	cop out	crash out 2
cut out 3,7	die out	drop out	duck out
eat out 2	fade out 1,2,3	fag out	fish out 2
fizzle out	flake out	flunk out	get out 11
get out of 4	give out 2,3	go out 9,10,12,16	go out of
grind out 2	grow out of 1	hole out	knock out 1
lay out 5	lose out	lose out to	luck out
pass out 1,3	peg out 1,2	peter out	phase out
play out 4	psych out	puff out 2	pull out 3,4
pull out of	put out 3,4,18	put out of	rain out
run out 3,4,5,7	sell out 1,2,3	smooth out 2	snap out of
snuff out	sputter out	stamp out 1,2	stub out
take out 4	take out of 1	talk out 2	tire out
turn out 4	walk out on	wash out 4,5	wear out
wimp out	wipe out 2	work out 10	

⑪ **Arranging, dividing, selecting, and distributing**

Out occurs in some phrasal verbs with the meaning of arranging things in particular groups, as in **sort out**. Some combinations have the sense of dividing areas, amounts, or groups into smaller ones, for example **mark out** and **weigh out**. Others indicate that one or more items are selected from a group. For example, if you **single out** someone or something, you choose them for special attention or treatment. Other combinations refer to the distribution or sharing of things among different people, as in **give out** and **ration out**, or to the allocation of money for a specific purpose, for example **lash out** and **fork out**.

blow out 3	contract out 3	count out 1	deal out 2
dish out 1,3	dole out	farm out	fork out
give out 1	hand out 1	hang out 1	hire out
ladle out 1,2	lash out 3	lay out 1,3,6	lend out
let out 5,8	loan out	mail out	mark out 1
measure out	pace out	parcel out	pass out 2
pay out 1,2	peg out 3,4	pick out 2	plant out
portion out	pour out 1	prick out	pull out 6
put out 7	ration out	rent out	screen out
select out	send out 1	separate out	serve out 1
set out 4	share out	shell out	sign out 2
single out	sort out 1,2	space out 1	splash out
spoon out	spread out 5	stake out 1	straighten out 2
strip out 2	take out 7	tease out	weigh out

12　Paying attention and awareness

In a few phrasal verbs, **out** has the sense of paying attention to something, often because of the possibility of danger, for example **mind out**. If something is expected to happen, it is usually introduced by the preposition *for* as in **listen out for**.

listen out for	look out	look out for 1,2	mind out
point out 1,2	watch out	watch out for	

13　Supporting and helping

Out occurs in some phrasal verbs with the meaning of giving support to someone or helping them in some way. For example, if you **bail** someone **out**, you help them out of a difficult situation; if you **draw** someone **out**, you make them feel less nervous and more willing to talk.

bail out 1,2	bear out	bring out 4	call out 2	draw out 5
get out 3	hand out 2	help out	put out 12	reach out to
straighten out 3	take out of 2			

14　Attacking, criticizing, and protesting

In some phrasal verbs, **out** has the sense of criticizing or protesting against something or someone, either verbally or physically. For example, if you **lash out**, you criticize them very angrily or severely, or you scold them; if you **sort** someone **out**, you punish them, often using force or violence.

chew out	cry out against	deal out 1	dish out 2,4	fight out
hit out 1,2	kick out against	knock out 3	lash out 1,2	mete out
punch out 3,4	sort out 5	shoot out 3	take out on	

over is an adverb and a preposition. It is used in 114 phrasal verbs in this dictionary.

1　Movement and position

You use **over** in literal combinations with meanings to do with moving across a surface or being in a position above something. For example, if you **cross over** a road, you move across it from one side to the other, and if something **passes over**, it moves overhead. **Over** is extended in meaning in a few combinations with the meaning of supervising someone or being in a position of authority over them. For example, if you **stand over** someone, you stand beside them and watch them working. **Over** is also used metaphorically to indicate that someone or something threatens or worries you. For example if a problem **hangs over** you, it worries you a lot, and if you **hold** something **over** someone, you use it as a threat against them. You also use **over** in combinations with the meaning of moving or going towards a place, especially the place where someone is standing or going to their house to visit them. For example, if you **run over** to someone, you run to the place where they are, and if you **call over** to see someone, you go to their house to see them. **Over** is also used in some combinations with the meaning of moving something so that it faces in another direction. For example, if you **turn** something **over**, you turn it so that it is facing in the opposite direction.

ask over	bend over	bring over	call over 1,2
come over 1,2,3	cross over 1	double over	flick over
get over 5	go over 1,2,3	hang over 1	hold over 1
invite over	lean over	lord over	move over 2,4
pass over 3	preside over 1,2	pull over 1,2,3	put over 2
queen over	roll over	run over 1	see over 2
sit over 2	stand over	stay over 2	steal over
stop over 1,2	take over 7	throw over 1,3	tower over
turn over 1,2,10	watch over		

2 Overflowing and overwhelming feelings

You use **over** in combinations which describe a liquid spilling out of a container because it is too full. For example, if a liquid **slops over** the edge of a container, a small amount of it spills out. You also use **over** in combinations with the meaning of having a strong feeling or reaction towards someone or something. For example, if you **enthuse over** something, you feel very enthusiastic about it; and if feelings of anger **boil over**, they become so strong that you cannot stop yourself from showing them.

boil over 1,2	bowl over 2	brim over 1,2	bubble over with
come over 6,7	drool over	enthuse over	fall over 2
flow over	fuss over	get over 3	moon over
run over 3	slop over	spill over 1,2,3	take over 8

3 Falling and attacking

You use **over** in combinations which have the meaning of something falling or being pushed to the ground. In these combinations, **over** has the meaning of completing the action described by the verb. For example, if something **blows over**, the wind blows it and it falls to the ground; and if you **kick** something **over**, you kick it so that it falls on the ground. If someone **does** you **over**, they attack you by hitting or kicking you.

blow over 3	bowl over 1	do over 4	fall over 1	fuck over
go over 5	heel over	keel over	kick over	knock over
push over 1	run over 2	tip over	topple over	trip over 1
tumble over	work over			

4 Covering and hiding

You use **over** in combinations with meanings to do with something becoming covered with a layer of something. For example, if the sky **clouds over**, it becomes covered with a layer of cloud, and if you **put** one thing **over** another, you put it on it so that it covers it. Some combinations are used metaphorically with the meaning of avoiding or hiding from something. For example, if you **varnish over** an unpleasant situation, you hide the unpleasant aspects of it; and if you **skate over** a problem, you pretend that it does not exist.

cloud over 1,2,3	cover over	dub over	film over
freeze over	frost over	glaze over	gloss over
grass over	heal over	ice over	mist over 1,2
paint over	paper over	pass over 2	pave over
put over 1	skate over	smooth over	throw over 2
varnish over	wash over		

5 Considering and communicating

You use **over** in combinations which have the meaning of thinking about or looking at something in a thorough and detailed way. For example, if you **mull** something **over**, you think about it carefully for a long time, and if you **pore over** something, you look at it very carefully. **Over** is also used in a few combinations to do with managing to communicate with someone and make them understand what you are saying. For example, if you **get** something **over** to someone, you manage to explain it to them so that they understand it.

brood over	chew over	come over 5,8,9	get over 4
go over 4,6	hash over	look over	mull over
pick over	pore over	put over 3	puzzle over
rake over	read over	run over 4	see over 1
sweat over	take over 6	talk over	think over
turn over 7			

6 Changing and transferring

You use **over** as an adverb in combinations which have meanings to do with changing or transferring something. For example, if you **swap** two things **over**, you exchange their positions so that each is in the position that the other was in before. Some combinations have the meaning of giving something to someone in a formal way, so that the ownership of the thing is transferred to the other person. For example, if you **sign** something **over** to someone, you sign a document which says that they now own it. A few combinations have the meaning of changing your mind or changing the group that you support. For example, if you **win** someone **over**, you persuade them to change their mind and agree with you or support you.

buy over	carry over 1,2	change over 1,2	come over 4
cross over 2	do over 2	go over to 1,2	hand over 1,2,3
hand over to	make over	move over 1,3	sign over
swap over	switch over 1,2	take over 1–5,9	turn over 3,4,5,6
win over			

7 Ending and recovering

You use **over** in combinations which have meanings to do with something unpleasant being finished, usually in a satisfactory way. For example, if an argument **blows over**, it ends and is forgotten about, and if you **get over** an unpleasant experience, you recover from it.

blow over 1,2	get over 1,2	get over with	give over 1,2
throw over 4	tide over		

overboard is an adverb. Its basic meaning is to do with falling from a ship into the water. It only occurs in 2 phrasal verbs in this dictionary, **go overboard** and **throw overboard**, in which it is also used non-literally to indicate extreme actions.

past is a preposition and an adverb. Its basic meanings are to do with time that has passed or is over, and movement from one side of an object to another. It only occurs in 4 phrasal verbs in this dictionary. **Brush past** and **push past** are literal combinations which refer to movement, **run past** is also used metaphorically to mean that you mention something to someone, and **put past** occurs in a semi-fixed expression. If you say 'I wouldn't put anything past her', you mean that you think she is likely to do things which you disapprove of.

round is an adverb and a preposition. It occurs in 60 phrasal verbs in this dictionary.

1 Movement

You use **round** in literal combinations which have meanings to do with going to different places or different parts of a place. For example, if you **look round** a building, you look at all the different parts of it. Some combinations have meanings to do with looking for something in a lot of different places, or talking to a lot of different people, often in order to obtain information. For example, if you **phone round**, you phone several different people; and if you **hawk** something **round**, you offer it for sale to many different people. **Round** is used in a similar way in combinations which have the meaning of distributing something to a lot of people. For example, if you **hand** things **round**, you give them to people in a group. If a story or information is **put round**, it is told to several people. **About** and **around** have similar meanings: see **about** **1** and **around** **1**. **About** is used mainly in British English, and in American English, **around** is much more common than **round**.

2 Turning

You use **round** in combinations with the meaning of turning so as to be facing in the opposite direction, or turning in a complete circle or series of circles. For example, **spin round** means to spin so as to be facing in the opposite direction, or continue spinning in a circle. With this meaning, round is often repeated. For example, you might say that something **spins round and round**. **Around** has a similar meaning: see **around** $\boxed{3}$. In American English, **around** is much more common than **round**.

go round 5	look round	pull round 2	spin round	swing round
swivel round	turn round	wheel round		

$\boxed{3}$ **Visiting**

You use **round** as an adverb in combinations with the meaning of visiting someone, often informally. For example, if you **drop round**, you go and visit someone informally or casually.

ask round	call round	come round 1	drop round	go round 1

$\boxed{4}$ **Surrounding**

Round is used in combinations with the literal meaning of surrounding or encircling someone or something. For example, when people **gather round**, they come together and surround someone or something, and if you **put** something **round** something else, you place it so that it forms a circle around it. **Around** and **about** have a similar meaning: see **around** $\boxed{4}$ and **about** $\boxed{3}$. **About** is used mainly in British English, and in American English, **around** is much more common than **round**.

$\boxed{5}$ **Change of opinion**

You use **round** as an adverb in a few combinations which have the meaning of changing your mind about something or being persuaded about it. For example, if you **talk** someone **round**, you persuade them about something.

bring round 2	come round 3	talk round 1	win round

$\boxed{6}$ **Revival of consciousness**

You use **round** as an adverb in a few combinations with the meaning of becoming conscious or well again after a period of unconsciousness or illness. For example, to **bring** someone **round** means to make them conscious again.

bring round 1	come round 5	pull round 1

$\boxed{7}$ **Inactivity and aimlessness**

You use **round** in a few combinations which have the meaning of spending time in a place doing nothing. For example, if you **sit round**, you sit in a place and do nothing. **Around** and **about** have similar meanings, and are both more common: see **about** $\boxed{2}$ and **around** $\boxed{2}$. **About** is used mainly in British English, and in American English, **around** is much more common than **round**.

hang round	sit round	stand round

$\boxed{8}$ **Avoidance**

You use **round** in a few combinations with meanings to do with avoiding something, either a physical object or a problem. For example, if you **get round** a problem, you manage to avoid it. **Around** has a similar meaning: see **around** $\boxed{5}$. In American English, **around** is much more common than **round**.

get round 1	go round 6	move round	skirt round	talk round 2

9 **Focus**
You use **round** as a preposition in two combinations, **centre round** and **revolve round**, where the meaning is to focus on or concentrate on something. For example, if a discussion **centres round** a subject, it concentrates on that subject. **Around** has a similar meaning: see **around** **6**. In American English, **around** is much more common than **round**.

through is an adverb and a preposition. It occurs in 61 phrasal verbs in this dictionary.

1 **Movement**
You use **through** in literal combinations with the meaning of passing from one side of something to the other, for example passing from one side of a solid object to the other, often making a hole, or passing from one side of a room or other place to the other. For example, if something **pokes through** an object, it is visible because it has pierced the object; if you can **see through** something, you can look from one side of it to the other; and if you **go through** a place, you go from one side of it to the other.

2 **Completion and thoroughness**
You use **through** in combinations with meanings to do with completing something, for example a period of time, a piece of work, or an experience. For example, if you **pull through** after an illness, you survive and recover, and if you **rattle through** a piece of work, you complete it very quickly. Some combinations have the meaning of doing something very thoroughly, or continuing to do it until it is completely finished. For example, if you **think** something **through**, you think about it in great detail until you have understood it completely, and if you **see** something **through**, you continue to do it until it is completely finished. A few combinations have the meaning of completing a process. For example, if something **goes through** an official procedure, especially a long and complicated one, all the necessary parts of that procedure are done; and if you **push** something **through**, you succeed in getting it accepted.

blunder through	carry through 1	come through 4	follow through 2
get through 1	go through 9	live through	muddle through
pass through	play through	plough through 1	pull through 2
push through 3	put through 5	rattle through	romp through
run through 3	rush through	sail through	scrape through
see through 4	sit through	sleep through	slog through soak
through	take through	talk through 1	think through
vote through	win through		

3 **Reading or looking**
Through is used as a preposition in combinations with meanings to do with turning the pages of a book and reading it, especially quickly, or picking up a series of things and looking at them or turning them over because you are looking for something. For example, if you **flick through** a book, you turn all its pages quickly, not reading it very carefully, and if you **rifle through** things, you pick them up and examine them because you are looking for something.

flick through	go through 7	leaf through	look through 2
pick through	read through	riffle through	rifle through
sift through	skim through	thumb through	wade through

4 **Communication**
You use **through** as an adverb in combinations with the meaning of managing to communicate with someone, especially by telephone. For example, if you **put** someone

through, you connect them on the telephone with the person they want to speak to; and if you **get through** to someone, you succeed in speaking to them on the telephone, or you succeed in making them understand you.

come through 3	get through 3	phone through
put through 7	win through	

5 Obviousness and visibility
You use **through** in a few combinations with meanings to do with something being obvious, so that people can see it. For example, if a quality **shines through**, it can be seen clearly, and if you **see through** someone, you realize clearly what their real feelings or intentions are.

break through 3	come through 7	see through 2
shine through	show through 2	

to occurs in 66 phrasal verbs in this dictionary.

To is one of the commonest words in English, and its basic uses as a preposition are to do with directions, destinations, targets, and relationships. Often, it has no special meaning when used in combination with verbs, apart from introducing the noun group which refers to the thing or person that an action or attitude is directed towards. For example, if you **get to** a place, you arrive there; if you **aspire to** something, you try very hard to achieve it; and if you **warm to** someone, you start to like them.

To is also used to introduce the noun group which indicates the thing or person that is involved or connected in a relationship. For example, if something **belongs to** you, it is yours; if something **runs to** a particular amount, it is that amount; and if you **see to** someone or something that needs attention, you deal with them.

To is used as an adverb in a few combinations. For example, if you **pull** a door **to**, you close it quietly; if someone **comes to**, they regain consciousness; and if you **set to** when doing something, you start doing it.

bring to	come to	heave to
pull to	push to	set to

together is an adverb. It occurs in 25 phrasal verbs in this dictionary. Its meanings all include an idea of closeness, connection, or combination. **Apart** sometimes has opposite meanings. **Together** is sometimes used after other phrasal verbs, for example **go out** or **shack up**, in order to indicate that two people or groups are doing something with each other. You mention both people or groups as the subject of the verb. These phrasal verbs can also be used with *with* if you mention one of the people or groups as the subject of the verb, and the other in the noun group after *with*. Such phrasal verbs are marked RECIPROCAL in the Extra Column.

1 Nearness, position, and linking
You use **together** in literal combinations to indicate that people or things are near each other, or move near each other. For example, if people **huddle together**, they stand very close to each other; and if people **live together**, they live in the same house. Some combinations have the meaning of linking things or putting them in a group. The verb is usually transitive, and its object refers to the things which are combined. For example, if you **string** things **together**, you add them to each other, one at a time; if you **herd** animals or people **together**, you gather them in a group; and if you **add together** several numbers, you calculate their total.

2 Producing and organizing things

Together occurs in combinations which describe a process of making, collecting, or organizing something, often from a number of different parts. The verb is transitive, and its object refers to the result of the process. For example, if you **cobble** something **together**, you make it quickly and roughly.

cobble together	get together 3	knock together
patch together	scrape together	throw together

3 Groups and unity

Together occurs in combinations which describe how people work or act as a unit. For example, if people **band together**, they act as a group in order to achieve a particular purpose. These combinations mostly include an intransitive verb. **Together** also occurs in combinations which refer to the unity of a group, or the way in which different things combine successfully to form a whole. For example, if ideas **hang together**, they are consistent and do not contradict each other.

band together	bunch together	club together	get together 1
go together	hang together	hold together	knit together
pull together	stick together 3		

towards is a preposition. It occurs in 12 phrasal verbs in this dictionary. Its basic meaning is to do with movement in the direction of a particular thing, though not reaching it. **Towards** is used non-literally in phrasal verbs which express ideas of aims, tendencies, and actions in a particular direction. The noun group after **towards** refers to the goal which is aimed at, the result or situation which is likely to happen, and so on. For example, if you **work towards** something, you try to achieve it, and if you **are heading towards** a situation, it is becoming more likely. **Towards** also occurs in combinations which contain an idea of partly filling or contributing. For example, if an amount of money **goes towards** something, it is used as part of its cost.

count towards	gear towards	go towards	head towards
lean towards	move towards	predispose towards	push towards
put towards	tend towards	warm towards	work towards

under is both a preposition and an adverb. It occurs in 10 phrasal verbs in this dictionary. Its basic meaning is to do with position, to say that one thing is below something else. In **go under** and **pull under**, the combination refers to someone being below the surface of the water. **Under** is also used in phrasal verbs to indicate that someone is below someone else in rank or is controlled by them. For example, if something **comes under** a particular authority, · it is managed or controlled by it; and if you **buckle under** to someone, you do what they tell you to do. **Under** is used in a few other combinations with metaphorical meanings. For example, if you **are snowed under**, you have more work to do than you can manage.

up is an adverb and a preposition. It occurs in 526 phrasal verbs in this dictionary and is the commonest of the particles used in combinations. The basic meaning of **up** is to do with movement from a lower position or level to a higher one.

1 Movement and position

You use **up** in literal combinations to indicate movement from a lower position or place to a higher one. For example, if someone **jumps up**, they raise themselves to their feet, and if you **run up** a hill, you run from the bottom of the hill towards the top. **Down** can often be used instead of **up** to indicate movement in the opposite direction.

You can also use **up** with verbs which mean 'lift' to show that you are raising something to a higher position, so if you **pick up** something from the floor, you raise it from the floor to a higher level. In these combinations, the particle **up** implies movement upwards, while the verb gives an impression of how the movement is achieved. For example, if you **dig up** an object, you remove the soil or earth from above it in order to lift it out of the ground.

back up 4,5	bob up 1,2	break up 5,6	bubble up
budge up	buoy up 2	come up 1,2,4,5,13	dig up 1
double up 2	draw up 2,4	get up 1,2,3,4	go up 1,2,4,5,9
grub up	help up	hike up 1	hitch up
hold up 1,2	jack up 1	jump up 1	kick up 2
lick up	lift up 1,2	look up 1	mark up 3
move up 1,3	pick up 1,2	poke up 1	pop up 2
pull up 3,4	pump up 2	push up 2	put up 1,2,4
reach up 1,2	rear up	ride up	rise up 1,2
roll up 4	ruck up	run up 1,3,6	scoop up
scrape up 2	screw up 1	shin up	shove up
show up 1	sit up 1,2	snatch up	spoon up
spring up 2	stand up 1	start up 3	stick up 2,3
stir up 1	straighten up 1	take up 1,2,10,11	throw up 1,2,3
thrust up	tip up	tower up	turn up 1,5
well up 1	whip up 2	wind up 3	write up 2

2   Increasing and improving

As well as signifying movement upwards, **up** can also be used to indicate an increase in quantity or intensity. For example, if something **speeds up**, it begins to move or work more quickly. The verb often gives an indication of the cause or quality of the increase. For example, if a fire **blazes up**, it starts to burn more fiercely, and if someone **speaks up**, they begin to speak more loudly.

add up 3	back up 1,2,3	bank up 1,2	beef up
bid up	blaze up	blow up 3,5,6	boil up 1,2
bolster up	bone up on	brighten up 1,2,3,4	bring up 1
brush up	brush up on	buck up	buoy up 1,3
build up 1,2,3,4,5	bump up	camp up	change up
charge up	cheer up	churn up 1	colour up
come up 14,15,17	crank up 1,3,4	do up 3	doll up
dose up	dress up 1,3	fatten up	feed up 2
firm up 1	fix up 4	flare up 1,2,3	fluff up
freshen up 1,2	gen up	get up 7	ginger up
go up 6,7,13	grow up 1,2,3	grow up on	ham up
heap up	heat up 1,3	hike up 2	hoke up
hot up	hurry up 1,2,3	hype up 1,2	jack up 2
jazz up	key up	lift up 3,4	light up 1,2,3
line up 5	live up	liven up 1,2	look up 4
loosen up 1,2	mark up 1,2	mount up	move up 2,5
mug up	open up 8,10	paint up	patch up 1,2
pep up 1,2	perk up 1,2,3	pick up 8,17,18,19	pile up
play up 1	plump up	point up	poke up 2
polish up 1	pretty up	prop up 2	puff up 1,2
push up 1	put up 9	quicken up	ramp up
ratchet up	rave up	read up	rev up
save up 1	scale up	shape up 4	sharpen up 1,2
shoot up 1	sing up	sit up 4	skill up
smarten up	soup up	speak up 1,2	speed up

cont.

spice up	staff up	stand up for	steam up
step up 1	stick up for	stoke up 1,2	surge up 1,2,3
swell up 1,2,3	swot up	take up 13	talk up
tart up 1,2	tick up	tidy up 2	tighten up 2,3,4
tone up	touch up 1	toughen up	tune up 2
turn up 3,6	vamp up	wake up 2	wake up to
warm up 2,3,5	well up 2	whip up 1,5	whoop up
work up 1,2,4,5			

3   Preparing and beginning

You can use **up** with a number of verbs to indicate that something is being prepared or is starting. For example, if athletes **train up**, they take exercise in order to be in better condition in readiness for an event. If a new shop **opens up**, it starts to trade.

book up 1	boot up	brew up 1,2	build up to
butter up	cook up 3	crank up 2	cue up
dish up	draw up 1	feel up to	firm up 2
fit up 1	fix up 1,2,3	fry up	gear up
get up 5	go up 12	heat up 2	kit up
knock up 1,4	light up 4	limber up	line up 4
make up 6,7,8	move up 4	open up 4,5,7	perk up 4
pick up 16	pipe up	plan up	power up
psych up	pump up 3	put up 12	rig up
rise up 4	run up 5,7	rustle up	saddle up
set up 2,3,4,5,7	shape up 1,2	soften up 1,2	start up 1,2,4
strike up 1,2	suck up to	sweeten up	take up 3,6,7,8
tee up	tense up	tog up	tool up
throw up 5	tidy up 3	train up	tune up 1
warm up 1,4,6,7	whip up 3,4	wind up 2	work up 3

4   Fastening and restricting

Up is used in combinations to indicate that something is being fastened or restricted in some way. The verb frequently indicates what the fastening is, so if you **bandage up** a wound, you fasten a bandage over it, and if you **brick up** a hole in a wall, you fill it with bricks to stop people going through it. Some verbs with **up** are used to show that someone's movement is being restricted. For example, if you **belt up** when you get in a car or on a plane, you fasten yourself in using the safety belt.

bandage up	bang up	belt up 2	bind up	block up 1,2
board up	bottle up 1	brick up	buckle up	bundle up 1,2
bung up	button up	catch up in 1,2	chain up	clog up
close up 1	coop up	cork up	crumple up	dam up 1,2
do up 1,2,4	earth up	ease up	fasten up	fog up
freeze up	fur up	gum up 1	hang up 1,2	hook up 2
ice up	jam up	lace up	lay up 1,2	let up
lock up 1,3	mist up	muffle up	nail up 1,2	paste up
pen up	pin up 1,2,3	plug up	post up	prop up 1
pull up 6,7	put up 3,5	roll up 1,2,3	screw up 2	scrunch up
seal up	sew up 1	shore up 1,2	shut up 3	silt up
slow up	snarl up	snow up	squash up	steam up 1
stick up 1	stitch up 1	stop up 1	strap up	string up 1
sweep up 2	tack up	take up 12	tangle up 1,2	tape up
tense up	tie up 1–6	tighten up 1	truss up	tuck up 1
turn up 4	wait up 2	wall up	wind up 1	wrap up 1,2
zip up				

5 Approaching

Up can be used in combinations to indicate that two people are moving closer together or staying close together. For example if someone **catches up with** you they get closer to you; and if someone **creeps up on** you, they approach you quietly and secretly; and if you **keep up with** someone else, you stay close to them by moving at the same speed as them.

In combinations with transitive verbs, **up** indicates that things are being brought closer together, so if you **line up** some objects, you place them together in a line.

Some combinations give the idea that the quality of something is close to the quality of another thing, so if something **measures up to** what was expected, its quality is as good as it was expected to be.

balance up	bump up against	catch up 1,2	catch up on
catch up with 1,2	chat up	close up 3	come up 3,12
come up against	come up to 1,2	creep up on 1,2	cuddle up
draw up 3	even up	face up to	form up
go up 3	keep up 1–9,11	keep up with	lead up to 1,2
level up	line up 1,2	live up to	loom up
make up 4,9	make up to	marry up	match up
match up to	measure up 2	measure up to	nestle up
patch up 3	pick up 11	play up to	pull up 2,8
queue up	round up 2	run up 2	run up against
sidle up	sneak up on	snuggle up	square up 1,2
steal up			

6 Disrupting and damaging

Up is used in combinations to give the idea that something is not in its normal state, and has perhaps been spoilt or damaged in some way. For example, if you **mess up** a tidy room, you make it untidy, and if a machine **plays up**, it does not work properly. Several of these verbs can be used to refer to somebody doing a job badly, so if someone **botches up** a job, they do not do it very well.

act up 1,2	balls up	bash up	beat up
beat up on 1	bitch up	blow up 1,2	botch up
break up 4,8	bugger up	burn up 1,3	bust up 1,2
carve up 2	chew up 2	churn up 2	cock up
crack up 1	curl up 2	cut up 2	dope up
dry up 5,7	duff up	eat up 3,4	feed up 1
fit up 2	foul up	fuck up	go up 10
gum up 2	hang up 5	hold up 3	jack up 3
jumble up	keep up 10	kick up 1	knock up 3
louse up	mess up	mix up 1,2	muck up 1,2
muddle up 1,2	muss up	pack up 3	play up 2,3
punch up 2	rough up	screw up 3,4	seize up
set up 8	shake up 1,3	shoot up 2,3	slip up
smash up	stand up 3	stir up 2	string up 2,3
tear up 2	trip up 1,2	wash up 4	wind up 7

[7] **Completing and finishing**

Up is used in combinations to indicate that something has ended or been finished, so if you **hang up** when you are using the telephone, you end the conversation, and if someone **winds up** what they are doing, they finish doing it. Often, **up** indicates that something has been done thoroughly or completely. For example, if you **tear up** a piece of paper, you tear it into smaller pieces, you do not just tear the edge.

As an extension of this, you can use **up** to indicate that something has been totally consumed or **used up**. The verb often indicates how this happens, so if someone **drinks up**, they finish what they are drinking so that there is none left.

add up 1,2	add up to 1,2	belt up 1	blow up 4
book up 2	break up 7	burn up 2	buy up
chalk up	check up	chew up 1	chuck up 1
clam up	clean up 1,2,3,4	clear up 1,2,3,4	clock up
close up 2	come up 18	count up	cover up 1,2
crack up 2	crease up	drink up	dry up 1,2,3,4,6
dummy up	eat up 1,2,5	end up 1,2	fetch up
figure up	fill up	finish up 1,2,3	finish up with
fold up 2,3	follow up 1,2	give up 1,2,8	gobble up 2
grind up	hang up 3	hang up on	heal up
hoover up	hush up 1,2	knit up	knock up 2
land up	lap up	load up	lock up 2
make up 3,5	mash up	measure up 1	mop up 1,2,3
notch up	pack up 2	patch up 4	plough up
polish up 2	pull up 1	pump up 1	punch up 1
reckon up	ring up 2,3	rip up	run up 4
sew up 2	shrivel up	shut up 1,2	snap up 1,2
soak up 1,4	sober up	sop up	stitch up 3
straighten up 2	sum up 1,2	swallow up 1,4	tear up 1
throw up 6	tidy up 1,3	tie up 7	top up
toss up	tot up	type up	use up
wake up 1	wash up 1,2,4	weigh up 1	wind up 4,5,6
wrap up 3,4	write up 1,3		

[8] **Rejecting and surrendering**

There are several phrasal verbs where **up** indicates that something is being given away or rejected. For example, if you **pass up** an offer, you reject it, and if someone **pays up** or **coughs up** the money they owe you, they give it to you.

bear up 2	bring up 3	cast up	chuck up 2
cough up 1,2	deliver up	give up 3,4,5	give up on
give up to	hang up 4	heave up	hold up 7
pass up	pay up	put up with	sell up
settle up	sick up	spew up	square up 2
stand up 2	stump up	throw up 7	wash up

9   Happening and creating

There are a number of phrasal verbs with **up** which give the idea of something happening or being created. For example, if something **crops up**, it happens or appears, and if you **think up** a clever idea, you use your imagination or intelligence to create it, and if something **comes up** in a conversation or meeting, it is mentioned or discussed.

bring up 2	call up 4	come up 6–11,16	come up with 1
conjure up	cook up 1,2	crop up	drag up
dream up	free up	go up 8,11	make up 2
open up 2,9	pick up 5,6,7,15	pop up 1	rise up 3
show up 3	spring up 1	sprout up	summon up 4
take up 4	think up	throw up 5	turn up 2

10   Collecting and togetherness

Some combinations with **up** give the idea that something is being gathered together, and that it sometimes becomes smaller in the process. There is a set of such verbs where the verb tells you what sort of container is being used to collect things, so if you **bag up** some objects, you put them together in a bag, and if you **crate up** some bottles, you put them together in a crate.

When this sort of verb is used to refer to people, it tends to convey an idea of involvement, so if you **sign up** with an organization, you become a member of it or you become involved with it.

bag up	bind up with	bottle up 2	box up
bunch up	call up 1,2,3	chase up 1	clutter up
coil up	collect up	crate up	curl up 1
double up 1	drum up	fold up 1	gang up
gather up	heap up	herd up	hoard up
hook up 1,3	huddle up	join up 1,2,3	lay up 3
link up 1,2	look up 3	make up 1	meet up 1,2
mix up 3	mix up with	muster up	pack up 1
pair up	phone up	pick up 3,4	pick up with
pile up 1,2,3	put up 10	rake up 2	ring up 1
roll up 2	round up 1	save up 2	scrape up 1
shack up	shake up 2	sign up	stack up 1
stock up	store up	swallow up 2	sweep up 1
take up 15	take up on	take up with 1	team up
tie up 8	tuck up 2	wire up	wrap up in

11   Revealing and discovering

Up is used in some combinations to give the idea of information being revealed or discovered. For example, if someone **digs up** a secret, they discover it, and if they **own up** to something, they reveal the fact that they did it.

call up 5	catch up 3	chase up 2	come up with 2
dig up 3,4	dredge up	fess up	hunt up
look up 2	open up 3	own up	pick up 12,13,14
rake up 1	scrape up 1	show up 2,4	show up as
size up	throw up	weigh up 2	yield up

12   Separating

Up often indicates that a person or thing is moving away from someone or something else or is being separated from it. For example, if you **divide up** a quantity of something, you split it into smaller portions, and if a group of people splits up, the people go away in different directions. Some combinations indicate that a person is hiding or separating themselves from other people. For example, if you **lie up** somewhere, you go there to hide or rest.

break up 1,2,3	bust up 3	carve up 1	chop up	cut up 1
divide up 1,2	divvy up	give up 6	hide up	hole up
lay up 4	lie up	parcel up 2	saw up	slice up
split up 1,2,3				

upon is a preposition. It occurs in 86 phrasal verbs in this dictionary. **Upon** is a more formal alternative for the preposition **on**, and in most cases it is a simple variation of it. That is, most of the phrasal verbs which it occurs in also have variations with **on**, and these variations are nearly always more common and less formal. Phrasal verbs with **upon** are mostly treated together with the variations with **on** in this dictionary, unless the variation with **upon** is more common. You cannot substitute **upon** for **on** in all phrasal verbs with **on**: phrasal verbs which are informal are almost never used with **upon**.

Upon is used with the meanings which are explained in categories ⑥ to ⑫ of **on**. The following phrasal verbs do not have variations with **on** given in this dictionary, or have meanings where **on** cannot be substituted for **upon**.

call upon	come upon	loose upon
put upon	thrust upon	trespass upon

with is a preposition. It occurs in 58 phrasal verbs in this dictionary. **With** is one of the commonest words in English, and it is especially used when referring to relationships and connections, when mentioning the instrument or means by which an action is carried out, and when describing attributes. It is mostly used in the same ways in phrasal verb combinations.

① Activities and connections between people

With occurs in combinations which describe activities, relationships, and connections between people or groups of people. One person or group is mentioned as the subject of the verb, and the other is mentioned in the noun group which follows **with**. For example, if you **meet with** someone, there is a meeting between you and them, and if you **plead with** someone, you ask them for something. **With** also occurs as the second particle in similar combinations which include two particles, for example **get in with** and **run around with**.

acquaint with 2	break with 1	deal with 3	finish with
flirt with 1	go with 3	hang with	identify with 2
interfere with 3	level with	lie with 2	live with 1
meet with 3	mess with	play with 5	plead with
reason with	sleep with 2	stick with 2	tangle with
trifle with	visit with		

② Connections and associations between things

With occurs in combinations which express ideas of connections, associations, and correspondences between things. You mention one of the things as the subject or object of the verb, and you mention the other in the noun group which follows **with**. For example, if a book **deals with** a particular topic, it is about that topic, and if one thing **goes with** another, the two things are associated in some way. **Break with** and **part with** refer to the ending of a connection. **With** also occurs as the second particle in similar combinations which include two particles, for example **chime in with** and **tie in with**.

agree with	break with 2	deal with 2	disagree with 1
do with 1	finish with	go with 1	identify with 1
lie with 1	part with		

3 Dealing and involvement

With occurs in combinations which describe processes of taking action about something or getting involved in it. The noun group after **with** refers to the thing that you are taking action about or getting involved in. For example, if you **deal with** something, you do what is necessary to achieve the result that you want; if you **toy with** an idea or suggestion, you consider it; and if you **meddle with** something, you get involved in a way that other people do not approve of. **With** also occurs as the second particle in similar combinations which include two particles, for example **go through with** and **do away with**.

dally with	deal with 1,4	flirt with 2	grapple with
interfere with 1	juggle with 1	make with	meddle with
mess with	part with	play with 2	reckon with 1
tamper with	tinker with	toy with 2	wrestle with

4 Supporting

You use **with** in a few literal combinations which have support as part of their meaning. You mention the person or idea that is being supported in the noun group after **with**. For example, if you do not **hold with** something, you believe that it is wrong, and if you **stick with** something, you continue to support or use it. **With** also occurs as the second particle in combinations which include two particles, for example **go along with**.

agree with	disagree with 1	hold with	identify with 1
side with	stay with	stick with 1	

5 Attributes and provision

With occurs in a large number of combinations where you are simply referring to the presence or provision of things. You mention what is present, provided, or given in the noun group after **with**. For example, if something **bristles with** things, it has a large number of them, and if you **ply** someone **with** something, you give it to them. A few of the combinations have 'say', 'believe', or 'know' as part of their meanings. You mention what is said or learned after **with**. For example, if you **tax** someone **with** something, you accuse them of it. **With** also occurs as the second particle in similar combinations which include two particles, for example **help off with** and **finish up with**.

acquaint with 2	begin with 1	bristle with	dispense with	do with 2
endow with	land with	lumber with	meet with 2	pepper with 1
ply with	provide with	saddle with	stick with 3	tax with

without is usually a preposition. It occurs in 3 phrasal verbs in this dictionary: **do without**, **go without**, and **reckon without**. In each case, **without** refers to an absence of something, and you mention the thing which is not present in the noun group after **without**. For example, if you **go without** something, you do not have it. In the phrasal verbs **do without** and **go without**, you can use **without** as an adverb as well as a preposition.